Thought &
Language
Language
& Reading

Thought &
Language
Language
& Reading

REPRINT SERIES NO. 14

HARVARD EDUCATIONAL REVIEW

The first part of the title of this volume — *Thought and Language* — originally comes from Lev Semenovich Vygotsky's book of the same name. We thank MIT Press for their permission to use this title.

Library of Congress Number 79-89713. ISBN 0-916690-15-6.
Printed by Capital City Press, Montpelier, Vermont 05602. Cover design by Cynthia Brady.

Harvard Educational Review
Longfellow Hall, 13 Appian Way
Cambridge, Massachusetts 02138

This book is dedicated to the
memory of our friend and colleague
JEFFREY PAUL MOELLER
who died in August, 1977,
while climbing a mountain.

Thought & Language / Language & Reading

PART I

CHAPTER 1

Thought & Language

Theoretical Perspectives on Language & Reading

PART THREE

Selected Book Reviews on Language, Reading & Learning

Preface

JEANNE S. CHALL
Harvard University

Those who came of age professionally in the 1960s and early 1970s will find in this book of readings from HER a reunion and a homecoming. How exciting to meet again Brown and Bellugi in "Three Processes in Acquisition of Syntax," Read in "Pre-School Children's Knowledge of English Phonology," Moffett in "A Structural Curriculum in English," Freire in "The Adult Literacy Process as Cultural Action for Freedom." How comfortable these authors seem now, for so many of their ideas have been taken up by others in research and in practice. When originally published, their ideas were at the forefront of the linguistic revolution of our time, one which changed our perceptions of language and language development, and of the teaching of English and reading in schools.

Some of the early articles are more than historically evocative. John Carroll's "Words, Meanings, and Concepts" and Carol Chomsky's "Stages in Language Development and Reading Exposure," for example, are very current. In fact, these pieces in particular will probably gain more readers with the federal government's present support of basic studies on reading comprehension as well as its current interest in family and community influence on literacy.

The more recent articles offer their own excitement as they focus on issues with which we now grapple. At the risk of showing my own partiality, I mention a few that I think have received and will continue to receive much interest, including Olson's and Scribner and Cole's contrasting accounts of literacy's impact, the Resnicks' article on the historical nature of literacy, and Albert and Geschwind's piece on acquired disorders of literacy.

The book reviews are, in a sense, even more provocative. Eminent reviewers from a variety of disciplines inform our understanding of such books as Vygotsky's *Thought and Language*—already landmarks when reviewed—along with such books as Gibson and Levin's *Psychology of Reading*, that have since become landmarks. The new and older classics have so well endured that at this point it is hard to tell the difference between them. I must also note a personal treat among the reviews. Rereading the late I. A. Richards' review of my *Learning to Read: The Great Debate* brought back some of the excitement, tension, and awe that comes when a great scholar, writer, and poet reviews one's book. It proves, even now, to be wonderfully constructive.

In general, if one notes dates of publication, one becomes aware of what seems to be a trend. The articles of the 1960s tend to be concerned about aspects of language structure and language acquisition. In the early 1970s there seems to be a growing interest in meaning, in social uses of language, and in reading and writing. By the mid- and late 1970s there seems to be a greater concern for those who have problems in mastering language functions—adult illiterates, children and adults with reading and learning disabilities, and children and young people from low income and non-English language homes.

Overall this volume is a gift for educators and scholars who are over thirty-five as well as for the younger ones—in fact for all concerned with theoretical and practical matters of language, thought, and reading. Both those long immersed in these issues and those now charting the waters will enjoy this book as a reminder of our recent roots.

Introduction

The relation between thought and word is a living process. . . .
Lev Semenovich Vygotsky

A child utters his first sentence; a four-year old regales a peer with a bad joke; a first-grader struggles to read; a Japanese student learns a new language; an English teacher helps an adolescent compose her thoughts in writing; a political activist launches a campaign to eliminate illiteracy; an historian studies woodcuts by Dürer; a philosopher ponders an essay by Locke. What links each of these disparate activities is its place on an evolving continuum of communication—a continuum that connects human development with spoken and written language. This continuum is at once the subject and scope of this book.

Two decades ago, only a few of the above activities would have concerned a language researcher. However, prompted in part by Noam Chomsky's work on the structure of language and in part by advances in developmental psychology, the study of all aspects of language has flourished in the interim. During this time, we have developed technology capable of analyzing the smallest speech sounds. We have discovered commonalities in the acquisition of such diverse languages as Samoan and American sign language. We have demonstrated the rule-governed nature of nonstandard dialects. We have increased our understanding of language disorders such as aphasia, and, through neurolinguistic research, we have discovered knowledge to support, refute, and build theories of normal language. Finally, we have taken the first steps toward assessing what human language shares with the communication systems of other primates.

This period has also been marked by numerous developments in the field of reading. Technological advances have led to new approaches to the teaching of reading (e.g., computer-assisted instruction), to new insights into the process of reading (through, for example, eye-monitoring devices and the print-to-speech machines now being developed for the blind), and to more refined diagnoses and explanations of the major disorders of reading, alexia, and dyslexia (through the use of C.A.T. scans and experimental techniques—such as B.E.A.M. studies—for monitoring electrical activity in the brain). And, accompanying these technological advances has been an increasing emphasis on the social dimensions of reading instruction—as embodied in Paulo Freire's literacy campaigns and in ethnographic studies of classrooms, where the goal is to uncover the behavior and interaction patterns that promote or inhibit learning.

To date, however, the most fruitful developments in reading research have emerged from its convergence with other disciplines, particularly linguistics, psycholinguistics, cognitive psychology, and neurology. Earlier theories about what was involved in reading emphasized the perceptual aspects of the process, as is evident in the original term for reading failure, "word blindness." But during the 1960s, teachers, clinicians, and medical researchers increasingly observed that language disturbances frequently accompanied reading disorders. These reports and the growing interest in psycholinguistic experimentation prompted reading researchers to study the syntactic and phonological origins of certain reading disorders.

The results of these efforts have depended heavily on the assumptions experimenters have about language and the ways reading and language intersect. From one perspective, reading is a second-order process that builds on other language competencies. Researchers who share this view study the relationship between graphic information, or letter configurations, and phonological, or sound processes; their approach to beginning reading instruction emphasizes the internal or phonological structure of words. Words must first be decoded from print to the underlying sound structures. Decoding skills, in turn, must become automatic before mature reading occurs.

Another school of thought considers reading and language to be parallel processes. Here, the assumption is that the understanding of written language does not require translating visual symbols into some level of sound—that is, a phonological representation. Instead, readers can gain the meaning of print directly from the visual symbols. Within this view, initial reading instruction stresses comprehension skills rather than decoding ones, and it also emphasizes exposing children to interesting and varied reading material so they will develop their own strategies for making print meaningful.

These various views, and the controversies that have resulted from them, have a long history in the study of reading. Research that may resolve these issues is emerging from the investigation of brain pathology and from the developmental nature of learning. Marshall and Newcombe (1973), for example, from examining the speech errors in adult alexics, have developed a dual-encoding model of reading in which the reader can understand print—that is, enter the semantic system—either directly from the visual information or through phonologically mediated pathways. Other researchers, like Vernon in this volume and Chall (1979) elsewhere, emphasize the developmental nature of the reading process. According to these researchers, the strategies readers use will vary according to their cognitive development and the demands of the reading task.

The work of these researchers is indicative of the advantages that could result from a better integration of the varied perspectives on reading and language. This synthesis, however, is far from being achieved. The major purpose of this present volume is to encourage such an integration by bringing together essays—first published in the *Harvard Educational Review*—that identify and explicate critical issues and positions on language and reading; that examine many of the educational and political problems arising from these; and that illuminate, for researchers, practitioners, and students alike, the historical and philosophical developments that have made literacy and language such prominent concerns in education in the United States for the past twenty years.

Toward this end, the essays in this book have been organized into three parts. In Part I, *Thought and Language*, the authors tackle the issues of developing, testing, and refining theories to explain the psychology of reading and language. Philosophical in outlook, the articles here are centrally concerned with the source of meaning in human language and the importance of meaning for applied work. In Part II, *Language and Reading*, the focus shifts to a consideration of pedagogic and learning issues, often setting these within political and social contexts. Finally, in Part III, the themes and topics of the preceding sections are recapitulated in selected reviews of books that have contributed significantly to our understanding of language and literacy. These reviews are organized so as to mirror the historical and conceptual organizations of the rest of the volume.

The first chapter of Part I highlights some of the major theoretical and philosophical issues arising from the Chomskyan revolution in linguistics. As the articles attest, the unique perspective Noam Chomsky brings to the study of language has provoked controversy—both within and outside the field—about such issues as the validity of nativist assumptions about language learning and the empirical status of behaviorism. For these reasons, perhaps readers would do well to compare the arguments in the first four essays with the remaining two.

Serving as an introduction to the rest of the section, the articles by Paul Postal and Carol Chomsky outline some of the central tenets of transformational grammar and demonstrate how the syntactical and phonological systems of English are thought to operate within the conceptual framework developed in *Aspects of the Theory of Syntax* (Chomsky, 1965) and *The Sound Pattern of English* (Chomsky & Halle, 1968). Both articles provide clear descriptions of the goals of modern linguistic theory, and for students of reading theory, Chomsky's essay offers an especially useful account of how both young and mature readers can utilize different processing strategies to extract meaning from print. The article is rich in suggestions for both improving spelling instruction and hastening the acquisition of skilled reading.

John Carroll's essay on concept formation and semantic development provides a useful contrast to Postal's and Chomsky's articles. Written in 1964, and still indebted to empiricist psychology (see Skinner, 1957), the essay shows how the logic of behaviorism and information processing can be extended to the problem of concept learning in schools. While much of Carroll's argument needs to be revised in light of recent developments in linguistics and developmental psychology (Anglin, 1977; Brown, 1973; Carey, 1979; Nelson, 1973; Rosch, 1974), his article is exemplary in uniting the practical considerations of the teacher with the theoretical and empirical concerns of the psychologist.

The remaining articles in this group document the movement away from the structural, or purely syntactic, accounts of language and language comprehension that prevailed in the middle and late 1960s. For many of the same reasons that prompted Carroll to claim that linguists have yet to develop a comprehensive view of semantics, Carol Feldman questions the assumptions of semanticists who will only explain language by means of closed, formal systems of representation. She argues that any theory of meaning must account for the communicative intentions of language users—an argument David Olson extends by revealing the assumptions behind the debates on the locus of meaning that have raged among specialists of reading comprehension, language acquisition, and linguistic theory. From an examination of the influence of the alphabet on the evolution of language, Olson proposes a dualistic view of language meaning in which structural, context-free accounts satisfactorily explain one dimension and in which context-dependent accounts explain the other dimension.

He also argues that one function of schools must be to equip children with the skills needed to make the transition from context-dependent knowledge to knowledge more universally defined.

Moving well beyond the structural concerns of the preceding articles, Thomas Wolf traces the influence of different schools of psychology that has led to the definition of reading as an active, constructive process with ties to other complex cognitive activities. He explains how this new but, in an etymological sense, very old definition allows one to view reading as an act applicable not only to text materials but equally to art and literature. By demonstrating the relationship of reading to other modes of symbolic processing, he provides still another perspective on theories of reading and language.

The experimentally-oriented articles in Chapter 2 fan out in several directions, reflecting the perspectives of reading researchers and cognitive developmental psychologists. While many of the authors show the strong influence of linguistic theory, and some, notably Charles Read and C. Chomsky, demonstrate the value of working within the framework of transformational grammar, as a whole they reflect the exploratory nature of early psycholinguistic research. The primary concern here is with how language is acquired, how language processes actually work—in both speaking and reading—and, as part of this research, what developmental milestones characterize children's knowledge of syntax, phonology, and semantics.

Roger Brown and Ursula Bellugi provide an excellent introduction to psycholinguistic experiments with young children. Their article details processes underlying children's acquisition of syntax, and it establishes many of the theoretical and methodological assumptions that have guided research in the field now called developmental psycholinguistics. Some of these assumptions, which range from the disavowal of classic learning theory to the belief that only naturalistic, longitudinal studies will divulge the influence of language on thought, can be seen in Marilyn Edmonds's article and in Kenji Hakuta and Herlinda Cancino's review of research in second-language acquisition. These articles also demonstrate the growing trend toward discourse analysis, as emphasized in sociolinguistics and research into "pragmatics" or the functional uses of language. Readers interested in nativist accounts of language will find the Piagetian perspective offered in Edmonds's semantic account of the evolution of syntax to be an interesting, if controversial, rebuttal to Chomsky's innateness hypothesis.

The articles by Read and C. Chomsky exemplify the cross-fertilization possible between the language and reading fields. In Read's paper, the data gathered from preschool children's invented spellings—that is, their uncorrected attempts to represent words in print—discloses the development of their phonological knowledge of English. He demonstrates how invented spellings are not random productions but reflect children's organization of the sound system and of sound-letter correspondences—systems of organization very different from the adult's.

Another aspect of the child's language system is emphasized in Carol Chomsky's study of syntactic development. Drawing upon her research on children's comprehension of nine complex snytactic structures, she suggests that children's linguistic development continues into their elementary school years. She also suggests that extensive sustained exposure to written language may contribute to general language development independently of IQ or socioeconomic variables. Her views about the effects of literacy and literacy training may be usefully compared with the articles by Olson and by the Goodmans.

Well known to many language arts teachers, the work of Yetta and Kenneth Goodman stresses the importance of the communicative skills children bring to the earliest stages of reading. In their article here, the Goodmans employ protocols from their own research to demonstrate how linguistic concepts can help make sense of children's oral reading errors, and, in turn, how these reading errors can provide insights into psychological and linguistic processes. The Goodmans' approach is apt to be viewed particularly favorably by those who think that reading and language are parallel processes and that the perception of written language requires no phonological mediation — the decoding of symbols to sound — but can directly access the semantic system.

As its title indicates, Chapter 3 offers a brief overview of critical issues in language arts instruction that emerged in the last decade. Taken as a whole, these articles highlight the need for unifying concepts in the language arts — a field often criticized for its lack of sound theoretical principles. Accordingly, the authors advance several suggestions for how English teachers, linguists, and rhetoricians might conceptualize a theory of language instruction in a manner compatible and consistent with the humanistic aims of a liberal education.

In the first essay, Raven McDavid, Jr. invokes the concept of a point integrator — a construct drawn from personality theory to characterize intellectuals such as Einstein — to discuss the value of H. L. Mencken's interdisciplinary approach to the study of language, literature, and American culture. Using a different conceptual vehicle, Richard Young and Alton Becker draw heavily upon a theory of linguistics known as tagmemics to develop a model of language use that considers larger units of discourse (e.g., paragraphs, poems, essays, short stories) as vehicles for teaching composition and analyzing literary style. In both essays, the reader can discern the promise and difficulty of fusing the goals of humanism with the structural objectives of modern linguistics.

Peter Rosenbaum's article explains why transformational grammar represents a conceptual advance over all previous methods of analyzing language (such as tagmemics) and why the paradigm is especially important for English instruction. In Rosenbaum's view, knowledge gained from the study of linguistic competence — a central concept in Chomsky's theory — offers the clearest means yet developed for tackling problems in teaching composition and in evaluating students' oral language skills. Behavioristic accounts of learning, he contends, are seldom profitable.

The differences in opinion separating McDavid, Young and Becker, and Rosenbaum are, in one sense, mediated in the fourth essay by James Moffett. In his article, Moffett analyzes the "structures" of English and the language arts. He argues that efforts to separate English instruction into literature, composition, and language have fragmented learning and obscured the goals of the profession. To his way of thinking, teachers must view the language arts as a symbol system and must regularly call upon their students to write and speak for audiences of all types. In this manner, students will begin to grasp the speaker-listener-subject relationships that underlie all forms of spoken and written discourse, which is the true goal of a structural curriculum.

In contrast to a hopeful and authoritative outlook in Moffett's essay, this chapter concludes somewhat discordantly as Wayne O'Neil and John Dixon offer two very different views about the goals of language instruction. As their divergent reports of the Dartmouth Conference on language instruction make clear, the conference never fully resolved many of the central problems in English instruction, including what language is, how it should be studied, and what role it should be given in the curriculum. Qualitative differences in the priorities expressed at this conference and those evidenced in our present concern for "basics" are readily apparent.

The articles which begin Part II provide broad, societal contexts from which to understand language and reading. In Chapter 4, the consideration of language and literacy shifts from theories of how children learn to speak, read, and write, to the ways people of all ages use, and to some extent are used by, the written language. The cognitive skills involved in literacy are examined together with the many functions literacy can serve, raising questions about the impact of literacy on both cognitive processes and social organization.

Neil Postman's essay, the conclusions of which he has since repudiated, reflects the turmoil of the late 1960s, when he believed that reading was being used as a tool of oppression. Maintaining that reading instruction was being used to make children into obedient citizens, Postman proposes, as an alternative, the use of electronic media to equip children with a more liberating, "multi-media" literacy.

Paulo Freire's essay, like Postman's, begins with the premise that "every educational practice implies a concept of man and the world." For Freire, however, that concept can be liberating as well as repressive. Drawing on his experience with illiterate peasants in Brazil and Chile, Freire holds that literacy is not merely a technical skill but a process whereby people gain the power to abstract, codify, and analyze their experience objectively. In this manner, literacy becomes a means to promote freedom and end oppression.

Central to Freire's theory is the assumption that literacy helps shape thought. Similarly, Olson presented psychological and historical evidence to suggest that the characteristics of alphabetic literacy have shaped Western thought and culture. Such views are directly challenged by Sylvia Scribner and Michael Cole in their study of the Vai people in Liberia — one of the few African cultures with an indigenous writing system. The researchers found no evidence that literacy produces generalized cognitive skills; literate Vai are no more analytical than illiterate Vai. But in non-literacy tasks which elicited skills also employed in reading and writing (like the ability to take another's perspective), the literate subjects generally were more adept than nonliterate ones. While Scribner and Cole are careful not to draw sweeping conclusions from what is admittedly limited evidence, they provide provocative findings about the nexus between literacy and thought.

The effect that society can have on literacy is the subject of the final essay in this chapter by Daniel and Lauren Resnick. Rather than emphasizing the effects literacy can have on the individual or the community, these authors present a series of case studies to show how varying political and economic circumstances have shifted the meaning, criteria, and goals of literacy instruction. In so doing, they consider whether current instructional methods are compatible with prevailing literacy standards.

As the Resnicks' article suggests, many methods have been tried over the years to ensure that literacy skills are transmitted from one generation to the next. In the United States, in particular, the quest for the "best" method has been a source of controversy since at least the early 1900s when Edmund Burke Huey advocated a "sight" approach to beginning reading instruction. Since that time, the concern for methods has branched in several directions, leading researchers to consider such issues as whether "linguistic" approaches to reading are superior to "phonics" ones; whether children are conceptually ready to begin reading instruction by the first grade; and whether adult illiterates can or should be taught to read in the same manner as developing children. The next group of articles in Chapter 5 offers some recent, and often divergent, views about appropriate instructional methods.

Like the Goodmans, Frank Smith contends that learning to read is not a process of matching sounds to letters; he is especially critical of methods that directly or indirectly seek to teach it as if it were. Using principles from the study of information processing, he argues that mastery of reading involves a recognition by children that printed language is meaningful and has its own conventions. With these insights, Smith claims, children can teach themselves to read by drawing on their knowledge of the world, their expectations, and their guesses about the nature of written language.

A diametrically opposed view of reading instruction, one grounded in learning-theory psychology (see Bereiter & Engelmann, 1966) is presented by Wesley Becker. Employing the evaluation results of the national Follow Through program, Becker argues that systematic, carefully sequenced instruction in sound-symbol correspondences is superior to other methods for teaching the basics of reading. He notes, however, that neither this approach nor the other Follow Through approaches were successful in improving vocabulary and comprehension skills. His conclusions offer an analysis of how systematic programmed instruction might be developed in each of these areas.

Nan Elsasser and Vera John-Steiner's article shifts the focus of concern from children to college students and from reading to writing instruction, an issue that has gained national prominence as a result of declining SAT scores and the minimum competency movement. In essence, Elsasser and John-Steiner hold that learning to write is not a matter of systematically mastering technical skills; rather, it involves an appreciation of one's participation and power in society and an ability to objectify and analyze communicative intent. They describe the operation of their small pilot writing program for Chicano and Native-American students that is based on theoretical ideas drawn from Vygotsky and Freire.

A program much grander in scale but based, in part, on similar ideas is presented in Jonathan Kozol's narrative on the Cuban Literacy Crusade of the early 1960s. Kozol explains how this program enlisted thousands of young men and women to work to bring all Cubans to a minimal level of literacy in less than twelve months. These youngsters were inspired by the continuing fervor of the Cuban revolution, and by the end of one year, they nearly eradicated illiteracy among the Cuban people. In view of this success, Kozol is currently advocating a similar crusade to eliminate illiteracy and functional illiteracy in the United States.

R. P. McDermott's approach to reading instruction concludes this section and offers yet another perspective on the elements of successful teaching. Unlike the previous authors, McDermott deemphasizes the importance of the methodology and psychological underpinnings of instruction. Instead, he shows how very different teaching approaches can work in some contexts but not in others. The issue in reading and literacy,

McDermott argues, is not a matter of phonics versus look-say instruction, nor is it directive versus nondirective instruction. Rather it is one of trust from which builds a sense of mutually sought, clearly defined goals for teachers and their students. This trust, McDermott contends, must be continuously negotiated if purposeful learning is to occur.

The final chapter presents an overview of disorders in language and reading, drawing on several disciplines and paradigms. Each of the fields represented in these articles — neurology, education, experimental and cognitive psychology, and neuropsychology — focuses on a different unit of investigation. Nonetheless, all share the underlying assumption that the study of language and reading dysfunctioning will add much to our understanding of the process itself.

This assumption is perhaps best exemplified in Eric Lenneberg's article on childhood language disorders. He attempts to explain language by examining the major categories neurologists use to diagnose and remediate speech and language problems in children. In addition to suggesting a method for looking at each of the disorders, Lenneberg implies that we can overcome certain disorders by encouraging children's innate abilities to develop language naturally in linguistically rich environments. This biological orientation, which can be partially credited with laying the foundations for recent neurolinguistic research (see, for example, Goodglass, 1978), shares much in common with the thinking of A. R. Luria (1966, 1970), who pioneered the integration of neurology, psychology, and linguistics in the study of aphasia.

In Lenneberg's piece, and others, specific reading and language disorders are viewed as complex problems that should be examined within a language-based, multisyndrome framework. In contrast to earlier approaches that viewed all reading failure as a unitary phenomenon best explained in terms of perception, recent analyses emphasize reading as an integrated, multidimensional task. For example, Morton Wiener and Ward Cromer, in their piece, argue that reading problems must be categorized according to where they fit within the reading process — from initial decoding or word identification through comprehension. By making this appeal, these educators demonstrate the differences between past and present practices in diagnosing reading failure. Magdalen Vernon's article also points out how research has veered away from one-dimensional explanations of reading failure in the last decade. She organizes reading failures in terms of children's inabilities to master specific steps in a sequence that leads to the development of mature reading skill. The child's inabilities are seen as a result of the absence of some linguistic or conceptual prerequisite. Together with Chall's recent model of the stages of reading (1979), which is discussed in the Resnicks' article, this essay indicates new ways to consider the developmental aspects of reading failure.

Unlike Vernon's emphasis on cognitive development, Frank Vellutino stresses solely the linguistic components of reading and demonstrates the inadequacies of purely perception-based theories of reading disability. Taking the position that reading failure can be explained completely on linguistic grounds, Vellutino departs from researchers whose classifications include a small group of perception-based disorders (Denckla, 1978; Mattis, French, & Rapin, 1975).

With their review of neurological, neuropsychological, and psycholinguisitc findings on acquired disorders of reading, Martin Albert and Norman Geschwind, whose article was prepared especially for this volume, summarize much of what we know about the neurophysiological mechanisms underlying severe reading loss in adults. They emphasize the need to study the preserved capacities of patients who have lost their ability to read, and they draw cautious parallels between acquired and congenital disorders of reading. Representative of an important direction in current neurolinguistic research, their article illustrates the need for a better understanding of the physiological basis of reading breakdown.

The book reviews, which comprise Part III, offer a conclusion to this volume. The first three present varying perspectives on the nature of language and its implications for psychology and epistemology. Jack Reitzes offers a description of J. L. Austin's theory of language—a theory which emphasizes performance as opposed to a structural account of the foundation of meaning. Reviews by John Carroll and John MacDonald respectively examine the source of language and the best means of characterizing the sound system in the structure of language. In all three, the distinction between competence and performance made by Chomsky hovers over the question of how language and thinking are related.

I. A. Richards and Robert Ruddell elaborate the themes of how reading builds upon linguistic development and how the differences between reading and listening may ultimately favor a decoding approach to beginning reading instruction. Ellen Ryan's review, for the most part devoted to language development at preliterate stages, explores the implication of semantic development for early childhood education and reading. Her argument underlines the essential role of general cognitive capacities in all communicative development, a view with implications comparable to those developed by the Goodmans, Smith, and Wolf.

The next several reviews examine topics of importance to English and language arts instruction. Accordingly, Courtney Cazden and Gordon Pradl discuss the value of social intercourse in language learning and the importance of play as a tool for developing imaginative and critical thinking. This theme is further explored by Maxine Greene in her appraisal of Louise Rosenblatt's language-experience approach to the teaching of literature and by Ralph Miller in his historical analysis of the role of literature in the English curriculum since the turn of the century.

The next six reviews contemplate the function of literacy, the effects of social class on learning to read, and the reasons why children fail to learn in school. In Joanna Williams's and David Harman's essays, the importance of reading for all segments of our population—including the often-forgotten illiterate adult—is emphasized. The reviews by Joseph and Alexandra Grannis, Paul Nash, Sandra Stotsky, and Jeanne Chall all advocate greater efforts to deal with the learning problems of every child in school. Reminding us of the powerful effects of social class upon the children's learning difficulties, these authors assert the need for teaching methods that will compensate for differences among children of various racial and socioeconomic backgrounds.

The last three reviews consider the biological sources of reading and language disorders. Jean Berko Gleason discusses classifications for isolating and defining language disorders along a developmental continuum in relation to the many standard instruments used to describe language. Together with Martha Denckla, she feels that the potential for mismatch between the assessment tools and the disorders themselves often makes it difficult to isolate individual learning disabilities. Denckla suggests, nevertheless, that as instruments and theories grow more refined, so will our understanding of what causes breakdowns in children's learning. In her view we have gone well beyond earlier achievements in reading and language research. Finally, Arthur Blumenthal's review ends the book with a cautionary reminder that despite gains made, much work remains before us.

The editors hope that this volume will both suggest to the reader specific areas where such work is indicated and provide a context for that research. By drawing this breadth of material into one volume, we hope to have presented a view of language and literacy that stretches from the child's first utterance through the adult's increasingly abstract representations of reality. Such a framework, it is our belief, best illuminates the continuum of human development that binds thought and language — and language and reading.

MARYANNE WOLF
MARK K. McQUILLAN
EUGENE RADWIN
Editors

References

Anglin, J. *Word, object, and conceptual development.* New York: Norton, 1977.

Bereiter, C., & Engelmann, S. *Teaching disadvantaged children in the preschool.* Englewood Cliffs, N. J.: Prentice-Hall, 1966.

Brown, R. *A first language: The early stages.* Cambridge, Mass.: Harvard University Press, 1973.

Carey, S. The child as word-learner. In M. Halle, J. Bresnan, & G. A. Miller (Eds.), *Linguistic theory and psychological reality.* Boston: MIT Press, 1978.

Chall, J. The great debate: Ten years later, with a modest proposal for reading stages. In L. P. Resnick & P. A. Weaver (Eds.), *Theory and practice of early reading,* Vol. 1. Hillsdale, N. J.: Erlbaum, 1979.

Chomsky, N. *Aspects of the theory of syntax.* Cambridge, Mass.: MIT Press, 1965.

Chomsky, N., & Halle, M. *The sound pattern of English.* New York: Harper & Row, 1968.

Denckla, M. Minimal brain dysfunction and dyslexia: Beyond diagnosis by exclusion. In J. S. Chall & A. Mirsky (Eds.), *Education and the brain,* 77th Yearbook of the National Society for the Study of Education. Chicago: University of Chicago Press, 1978.

Goodglass, H. *Selected papers in neurolinguistics.* München, Germany: Wilhelm Fink Verlag, 1978.

Luria, A. R. *Higher cortical functions in man.* New York: Basic Books, 1966.

Luria, A. R. *Traumatic aphasia.* The Netherlands: Mouton, 1970.

Marshall, J., & Newcombe, F. Patterns of paralexia: A psycholinguistic approach. *Journal of Psycholinguistic Research,* 1973, **2,** 175-199.

Mattis, S., French, J., & Rapin, I. Dyslexia in children and young adults: Three independent neurological syndromes. *Developmental Medicine and Child Neurology,* 1975, **17,** 150-163.

Nelson, R. Structure and strategy in learning to talk. *Monographs of the Society for Research in Child Development,* 1973, **38,** No. 149.

Rosch, E. H. On the internal structure of perceptual and semantic categories. In T. E. Moore (Ed.), *Cognition and the acquisition of language.* New York: Academic Press, 1973.

Skinner, B. F. *Verbal behavior.* New York: Appleton-Century-Crofts, 1957.

PART I

Thought & Language

CHAPTER 1

Theoretical Perspectives
on Language
& Reading

Underlying and Superficial Linguistic Structure

PAUL M. POSTAL
Massachusetts Institute of Technology

Few of the developments in modern linguistics have been the source of greater controversy and excitement than transformational generative grammar. In this essay Paul Postal offers a succinct description of the goals and assumptions that guide research in this relatively new paradigm. Arguing that an adequate description of linguistic competence is logically prior to a psychology of language, the author contends that the first goal of language study is to explicate the rules governing the generation of syntactic, semantic, and phonological knowledge.

A linguistic description of some natural language is designed to provide a specification of the knowledge which speakers of that language have which differentiates them from non-speakers.[1] This knowledge is evidently enormous in extent and varied in nature. It includes, among other things, the ability to distinguish those noises which are sentences of the language (*well-formed* or *grammatical*) from those which are not; to recognize similarities between utterances and their parts; to recognize identities of various sorts from full rhyme on the phonological level to identity of meaning or paraphrase on the semantic level, etc. Since each speaker is a finite organism, this knowledge must be finite in character, i.e. learnable. Yet a moment's thought is sufficient to show that someone who has learned a natural language is in fact in possession of full information about an infinite set of linguistic objects, namely the sentences. This follows because there is no longest sentence. Given any sentence we can always find a longer one by replacing some noun with a noun and following modifier, or by replacing some verbal phrase with a conjunc-

The present work was supported in part by the U.S. Army Signal Corps, the U.S. Air Force Office of Scientific Research, the U.S. Office of Naval Research; and in part by the National Science Foundation. I am indebted to Morris Halle for helpful comments and criticisms.

[1] The following abbreviations are used throughout the article:
NP-Noun Phrase; S-Sentence; VP-Verb Phrase; *-non-sentence.

Harvard Educational Review Vol. 34 No. 2 Spring 1964, 246–266

tion of two verbal phrases, etc. Of course, the finite and in fact rather small bound on human memory will prevent actual speech behavior from making use of more than a small finite subclass of all possible sentences. But this in no way affects the psychologically and linguistically fundamental fact that knowledge of a natural language provides a speaker in principle with knowledge of an infinite set of linguistic objects. Only this assumption, for example, makes it possible to explain why, as the limits on memory are weakened, as with the use of pencil and paper, speaker's abilities to use and understand sentences are extended to those of greater length. It is no accident that traditionally, for example, written German involves lengthy and complex constructions not normally found in the spoken language. The analogy with arithmetic is appropriate here. One who has learned the rules of arithmetic is clearly capable in principle of determining the result of multiplying any two of the infinite set of whole numbers. Yet obviously no one ever has or ever could compute more than a small finite number of such multiples.

In principle knowledge by a finite organism of an infinite set of linguistic facts is neither paradox nor contradiction, but results from the fact that there are kinds of finite entities which specify infinite sets of objects. In mathematics these are often referred to by the term 'recursive.' For example, consider the set of rules:

(1) $A \rightarrow X$

(2) $X \rightarrow X+X$

where the arrow is to be interpreted as the instruction to rewrite the left symbol as the righthand string of symbols. It is evident that continued application of these rules will specify an endless, unbounded, i.e. strictly infinite set of strings of the form X, XX, XXX, XXXX, etc. And a person who learned these two rules plus the finite set of instructions for applying them would, in a precise sense, have learned the infinite set of possible outputs.

It is in exactly this sense that we must postulate that a speaker has learned the infinite set of sentences of his language, by learning some finite set of rules which can enumerate, list, specify, or, as it is usually said, *generate* these sentences. Such a set of rules can be called a *grammar* or *syntax*.

A *language* in these terms is then just the set of strings of symbols (the 'X's in the above trivial example) enumerated by the grammar. We shall see below that this conception of language must be greatly enriched. When we have come to the point of seeing each sentence as a string of symbols of some type, it is natural to ask about the nature of these symbols in actual natural languages like English, Chinese, etc. It is traditional to think of these as *words*, i.e. roughly as minimum units of pronunciation, those elements which may be uttered independently. Modern linguistics has greatly emphasized, however, that words are themselves in fact composed of or are analyzable into syntactically significant parts, usually referred to as *morphemes*. For example, it would be pointed out that the word:

(3) uninterrupted

is composed of at least three morphemes *un+interrupt+ed*, the first of which is also found in (4), the second of which is also found in (5), and the third which is also found in (6):

(4) unhappy

(5) interruptable

(6) destroyed

It thus follows that the syntactic structure of each sentence must be represented as a string of words with morpheme boundaries also indicated.

However, all linguists are in effect agreed that sentence structure is not exhausted by division into words and morphemes. Most crucially, the words and morphemes must be considered as grouped into significant sequences, in other words to be *parsed*, or *hierarchically bracketed*. Thus in the sentence:

(7) Harry liked the nice girl

most linguists would probably agree that the elements must be bracketed something like:

Harry	liked	the	nice	girl
	liked	the	nice	girl
	like	ed	the	nice	girl
			nice	girl

Such a bracketing indicates that the sentence is first made up of two basic parts, *Harry* and everything else; that everything else is made up of two primary parts *liked* and the remainder, etc. However, it would further be agreed that such bracketing representations are inadequate if not accompanied by an associated *labelling* of the segments obtained by the bracketing. It has become common to represent such labelled bracketings in the form of rooted trees like Diagram 1 but such are perfectly equivalent to (labelled) box diagrams like that above or labelled parenthesizations, or any other suitable diagrammatic equivalent.

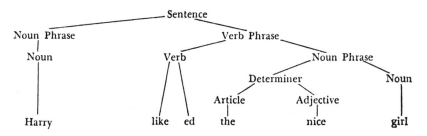

7

Such a labelled bracketing provides far more explanatory insight into the structure of a sentence than the mere bracketing alone. It accounts for similarities between various sequences, i.e. for example our knowledge that *Harry* and *the nice girl* are in some sense similar kinds of elements as against *liked,* or *the*. I shall refer to the kind of linguistic structure represented by labelled bracketings in any of their various forms as *phrase markers*. Such structures describe for each sentence (string of minimal syntactic symbols) what parts make it up, how these are grouped together into significant sequences, and what type of grouping each is.

Linguists are rather well agreed on the fact that each sentence of a natural language is correctly represented by at least one phrase marker of some kind. This agreement is, of course, accompanied by many disagreements of various types, both substantive and terminological, which need not concern us here. Since each speaker knows an unbounded set of sentences, and since it is agreed that each sentence has one phrase marker, it follows that each speaker must learn a finite set of rules which can enumerate not only strings of symbols (words or morphemes) but rather an infinite set of correct phrase markers. It follows then that a linguistic description of a language must contain just this finite set of rules. A crucial problem for linguistic theory is then the specification of the character or form of such rules, the way they associate phrase markers with an infinite output of strings of symbols, etc.[2]

UNDERLYING GRAMMATICAL STRUCTURE

However, in stopping at the point, in effect widely agreed upon, that the syntactic structure of a sentence is given by a *single* phrase marker, we will have seemed to embrace a position which we cannot in fact accept. There is overwhelming evidence showing that the syntactic structure of the sentences of natural languages is by no means adequately representable by single phrase markers, regardless of how elaborated. Although each sentence certainly has one phrase marker which provides a labelled bracketing of the actual string of morphemes and words which are directly related to its phonetic manifestation, this is only the most superficial aspect of syntactic structure. There is

---

[2] For a discussion of phrase markers, phrase marker assignment, rules which generate phrase markers, relation of phrase markers to generally held linguistic views cf. Noam Chomsky, "On the Notion 'Rule of Grammar'," *Structure of Language and its Mathematical Aspects*, ed. Roman Jakobson (Providence, R. I.: American Mathematical Society, 1961); Noam Chomsky, "A Transformational Approach to Syntax," *Third Texas Conference on Problems of Linguistic Analysis in English*, ed. A. A. Hill (Austin, Tex.: U. of Texas Press, 1962); Noam Chomsky, "The Logical Basis of Linguistic Theory," *Proceedings of IXth International Congress of Linguistics*, ed. H. Lunt (The Hague: Mouton, 1964); and Paul Postal, *Constituent Structure*, a Supplement to International Journal of American Linguistics (1964).

a whole other domain of required structure which is crucial for describing both the formal syntactic properties of sentences and the way they are understood, i.e. their semantic properties.[3] The superficial phrase marker of each sentence is chiefly relevant only to the way sentences are pronounced. To determine what sentences mean, one must attend to the far more abstract underlying structure.

Consider the following English sentences:

(8) drink the milk

(9) go home

(10) don't bother me

These are normally referred to as *imperative sentences*. And in terms of their superficial phrase markers it is evident that they consist of an uninflected verb plus other elements of the Verb Phrase but no preceding 'subject' Noun Phrase of the kind found in declaratives like:

(11) he drank the milk

(12) I went home

(13) John didn't bother me

English also contains so called *reflexive pronouns* like the underlined 'objects' in such sentences as:

(14) the man cut *himself*

(15) John admired *himself* in the mirror

(16) you overestimate *yourself*

If one now inquires into the rules which govern the occurrence of this kind of reflexive form in English, one finds, among other things, that there are sentences of the form $NP_1 + Verb + reflexive\ pronoun + Y$ just in case one can also find sentences of the form $NP_2 + Verb + NP_1 + Y$. That is, those verbs which take reflexive pronoun 'objects' are just those which can elsewhere occur with 'objects' identical to the 'subjects' of the reflexive sentences.[4] Hence one finds:

(14)–(16) and:

(17) John cut the man

(18) I admired John in the mirror

(19) she overestimates you

but we do not find:

(20) *Harry demands himself

(21) *you concede yourself

(22) *Mary completes herself

---

[3] This conclusion is in effect implied by the whole literature which argues that adequate grammatical description involves transformational rules.

[4] The grammatical descriptions in this paper are highly oversimplified in a number of ways irrelevant to the points they are designed to illustrate. For more detailed and extensive description of reflexives cf. Robert B. Lees and E. Klima, "Rules for English Pronominalization," *Language*, XXXIX (1963), 17-28.

and accordingly there are also no English sentences:

(23) *I demand Harry

(24) *John concedes you

(25) *you complete Mary

although one can find:

(26) I demand the answer

(27) John concedes the game

(28) you complete the task

   These facts show that the rule for forming reflexives of the type being considered is in effect based on *a possible equivalence* of 'subject' and 'object' Noun Phrase and suggests that reflexive sentences be described by rules which in some sense 'derive' reflexive sentences from structures in which there are equivalent 'subjects' and 'objects'. Hence (14)–(15) would be derived from abstract structures something like the following schematically indicated *phrase markers:*

(29)

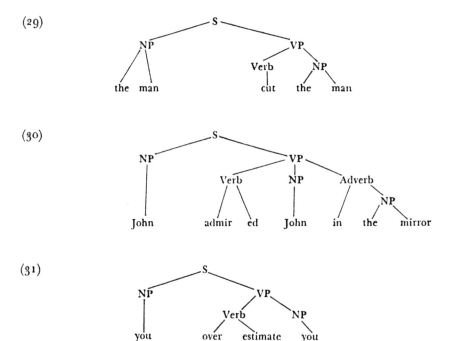

(30)

(31)

Notice that the rules which associate 'subjects' and 'objects' with verbs, these rules being part of the set which enumerate phrase markers like (29)–(31), will be *simpler* if they are allowed to produce such structures as (29)–(31) than if not, since, as we have seen, all the possible 'subjects' and 'objects' of (29)–(31) must be allowed with their respective verbs in any event. Hence to pre-

10

vent derivation of structures like (29)–(31) and their analogues would require *adding* special restrictions to the grammar prohibiting identical 'subjects' and 'objects' with a single verb.

But now if structures like (29)–(31) are enumerated they provide a simple means for describing correctly reflexive sentences if one simply adds the rule that the second Noun Phrase in a structure $NP_1+Verb+NP_2+X$ is replaced by the appropriate reflexive pronoun when $NP_1=NP_2$. This correctly derives just those reflexive strings which meet the equivalence condition stated before and permits retention of the non-complicated verb-'object' and 'subject'-verb selection rules by eliminating the need for special restrictions to prevent the enumeration of the analogues of (29)–(31). This follows because this new reflexive rule converts (29)–(31) and all similar phrase markers into the superficial phrase markers which must represent the occurring reflexive sentences like (14)–(16) and these must be described anyway.

But this analysis of reflexives provides an immediate explanation of why an English speaker *understands* reflexive sentences to refer to 'objects' identical to their 'subjects,' *if* we insist that the understanding of a sentence refers to abstract structures like (29)–(31) rather than to the superficial phrase markers of actual sentences like (14)–(16) in which the 'subject'-'object' equivalences cannot possibly be marked.[5]

This very natural and explanatorily powerful description of reflexive sentences requires, however, a radical shift in one's notion of grammatical structure. It requires that the grammatical structure of a sentence be taken to consist, not of a *single phrase marker*, but at least of a *set of phrase markers*, these being related by the kind of rules illustrated by our description of the reflexive. This leads to a picture of syntax in which there is a basic division into two components, one containing rules which derive very abstract *underlying phrase markers* like those represented by (29)–(31); the other containing rules like the reflexive above. These latter rules apply to whole phrase markers and derive new phrase markers. The last such phrase marker derived by the final rule of this second component is called a *final derived phrase marker* and represents the superficial labelled bracketing of the actual string of words of the sentence. Rules which derive phrase markers from phrase markers have been called *transformations*. The rules which enumerate underlying phrase markers are simpler in character. It was assumed at first that these were roughly variants of rules like (1) and (2) above, i.e. rules which operated exclusively on strings of symbols by replacing single symbols by certain distinct strings of

---

[5] The claim that the semantic interpretation or meaning of a sentence is determined by the *underlying* structure assigned it by the syntax is argued extensively in Jerrold Katz and P. M. Postal, *An Integrated Theory of Linguistic Descriptions* (Cambridge, Mass.: M.I.T. Press, 1964).

other symbols. These were called *phrase structure* or *constituent structure* rules. Such phrase structure rules as the following have been proposed:

(32)   Sentence → NP+VP

(33)   NP → Determiner+Noun

It has become increasingly apparent, however, that underlying phrase markers cannot in fact be correctly described exclusively with rules of this type. It appears that such rules must be supplemented by more powerful devices to help account for so-called 'selectional restrictions' such as the fact that certain verbs occur only with animate 'subjects' and inanimate 'objects,' others with inanimate 'subjects' and animate 'objects,' others with animate 'subjects' and animate 'objects,' etc. It appears that the sub-component of syntactic rules which enumerates underlying phrase markers is itself divided into two elements, one containing phrase structure rules and the other containing a *lexicon* or *dictionary* of highly structured morpheme entries which are inserted into the structures enumerated by the phrase structure rules. Although quite new and too complicated to say more about here, research into this area of syntactic structure promises to yield great insights into many areas of traditional interest, including characterizations of such notions as *word, inflection, derivation, Noun,* and *Verb,* as well as resolving the original difficulties with selectional restrictions.[6]

We can provide more motivation for an extension of the notion of grammatical structure to include a whole set of phrase markers for each sentence, including most crucially abstract underlying phrase markers, by returning to imperative sentences which superficially have no 'subjects.' These may also contain reflexives:

(34)   wash yourself

(35)   don't kill yourself

However, there is a crucial restriction on the reflexive pronouns which can occur in imperative sentences, namely only *yourself* is permitted. Hence there are no sentences like:

(36)   *wash himself

(37)   *wash themselves

(38)   *don't kill myself

(39)   *don't kill herself

But we recall the fact that reflexives are based on an equivalence of 'subject' and 'object.' This means that if we are to embed imperative reflexives into the simple description of reflexives given earlier, imperatives must be derived from underlying phrase markers which contain *you* 'subjects.'

As support for this, consider so called 'tag' questions like:

---

[6] For a discussion of the topics of this paragraph cf. Noam Chomsky, *Aspects of the Theory of Syntax* (Cambridge, Mass.: M.I.T. Press, 1965).

(40) Mary will come, won't she

(41) John can run, can't he

(42) I have won, haven't I

It is evident that the part of such questions which follows the intonation break (represented by the comma) involves a repetition of the Auxiliary[7] and 'subject' of the first pre-comma part, with the proviso that the order must be changed, the negative added, and the 'subject' pronominalized.[8] But there are tag sentences in which the first part is *imperative* in form:

(43) eat the meat, will you

(44) go home, won't you

And there is a constraint here that the pronoun form after the commas can only be *you*. Hence we find no English sentences like:

(45) *eat the meat, will $\left\{ \begin{array}{l} \text{she} \\ \text{he} \\ \text{they} \end{array} \right\}$

(46) *go home, will $\left\{ \begin{array}{l} \text{I} \\ \text{we} \end{array} \right\}$

But this can be readily explained in terms of the fact that the second Noun Phrase is a repeated pronominalized form of the 'subject' Noun Phrase before the comma, if it is assumed that imperatives have in their underlying phrase markers a *you* 'subject' Noun Phrase in front of the verb. We see then that the evidence of reflexives and tag sentences converges on the conclusion that the underlying structure of imperatives contains a second person 'subject.' But now this can immediately provide an explanation of the fact that every English speaker understands an imperative to refer to the second person if, as before, we assume that the structures relevant to understanding are the underlying phrase markers.

Here as before we must posit a transformational rule which will derive the superficial structure of imperatives from the underlying phrase markers. Notice that the Auxiliary repetition of tag questions shows that the underlying phrase markers of imperatives must contain the modal *will* (*will* + *contracted not* = *won't*) since this is the form found in imperative tags and in fact is the only permitted Auxiliary form:

(47) *eat the meat, did he

(48) *eat the meat, can he

But this provides an explanation of why we understand that imperative sentences refer to the future. The transformational rule which derives the super-

---

[7] That is, the constituent which in underlying phrase markers represents such elements as the Tense morphemes, as well as *will, may, be, can, have,* etc.

[8] When the initial element is itself negative, then the part after the comma must be non-negative.

ficial forms of imperative sentences will delete the *will* (and preceding tense morpheme) and optionally delete the 'subject'. Optionally only because we find imperatives with explicit *you*:

(49)   you eat your meat

(50)   you go home (or I'll tell your mother)

These also have a *non* imperative declarative semantic interpretation but this need not concern us here.

We have suggested that in order to provide an account of both the formal properties of sentences and the way in which they are understood it is necessary to extend the notion of grammatical structure in such a way that each sentence is represented by a whole set of phrase markers, including crucially quite abstract underlying ones. This conclusion is greatly strengthened if we consider so-called grammatical relations like *subject-verb*, or *verb-object*.[9] To understand a sentence it is obviously quite crucial to know which parts bear which relations to which other parts. For example, despite the fact that the following sentences contain identical elements we understand them differently:

(51)   Mary loves John

(52)   John loves Mary

In (51) we understand that it is Mary who does the loving and John who receives the affection; in (52) conversely. The fact that these differences are associated with a distinct order of elements might suggest that the various relations involved can be precisely characterized in terms of *order*. We can say that in a phrase marker the first Noun Phrase bears the *subject* relation to the Verb, the Noun Phrase following the Verb bears the *object* relation to this element, etc. However, attractive as this proposal is, it obviously fails for *superficial* phrase markers because of the enormous number of cases like:

(53)   John was loved by Mary

(54)   Mary was loved by John

(55)   John is anxious to please Mary

(56)   John is easy for Mary to please

In (53) the relations between *John* and *Mary* and the Verb are the same as in (51), while in (54) they are the same as in (52). Yet the order of constituents in (53) is like that in (52) and the order in (54) is like that in (51). Similarly in (55) we recognize that *John* is the 'subject' of *please* while in (56) it is the 'object' of this Verb. Yet its relative order is the same. In short we see that in the actual superficial forms of sentences the crucial grammatical relations are not associated with any unique configurations of constituents.

[9] For a fuller discussion of grammatical relations and their characterization in precise linguistic terms cf. Chomsky, "Logical Basis of Linguistic Theory," and *Aspects of the Theory of Syntax,* and Katz and Postal, *loc. cit.*

It seems, however, that in underlying phrase markers this is the case. That is, in underlying phrase markers grammatical relations are uniquely and uniformly definable in terms of constituents and their order. Hence the underlying structures of (52) and (54) are quite similar to those of (51) and (52) respectively and the actual order to elements in (53) and (54) is derived by the so-called *passive transformation*[10] which, among other things, inverts 'subject', and 'object' Noun Phrases. This solution is formally motivated *inter alia* by the fact that for a fixed Verb type those Noun Phrase elements which can occur in the initial position of passive sentences are just those which can occur in the 'object' position of declaratives. Hence one finds:

(57) John admires Harry

(58) John admires truth

but not:

(59) *truth admires John

and similarly:

(60) Harry is admired by John

(61) truth is admired by John

but not:

(62) *John is admired by truth

and:

(63) John demands a raise

(64) John believes Harry

but not:

(65) *John demands Harry

(66) *John believes love

and similarly:

(67) a raise is demanded by John

(68) Harry is believed by John

but not:

(69) *Harry is demanded by John

(70) *love is believed by John

If passive sentences are not derived from underlying structures in which the 'subject' and 'object' elements are in the same order as in active sentences, all these selectional facts must be stated twice. Thus again we find formal motivation for abstract underlying phrase markers which contain structures of just the type needed to explain the way the occurring sentences are understood.

[10] For a description of this rule cf. Noam Chomsky, *Syntactic Structures* (The Hague: Mouton and Co., 1957) and Chomsky, "Transformational Approach to Syntax." For a slightly revised and more up to date description cf. Katz and Postal, *op. cit.* and Chomsky, *Aspects of the Theory of Syntax.*

Consider finally (55) and (56). These sentences are in a sense fundamentally different from any considered before because their underlying structure must be taken to include a *pair* of underlying phrase markers which are combined to produce the occurring sentences. The transformations which perform such combining operations have been called *generalized transformations*.[11] Sentences like (55) in which the initial Noun Phrase (NP) is understood as the 'subject' of the verb in the infinitive phrase must be derived from a pair of structures of roughly the form $NP_1+is+Adjective+Complement, NP_1+Verb+NP_2$. That is, the two phrase markers which are combined must have identical 'subject' Noun Phrases. This restriction is necessary to account for the fact that those verbs which can occur in the infinitives of sentences like (55) are just those which can take as 'subject' the initial Noun Phrase. Hence one does not find:

(71)   *truth is anxious to see Mary

(72)   *love is anxious to marry Mary

because there is no:

(73)   *truth sees Mary

(74)   *love marries Mary

etc. But these formal reasons force us to derive sentences like (55) from underlying structures in which *John* is the 'subject' of the verb *please* in terms of the uniform configurational account of grammatical relations roughly sketched earlier.

In (56) the situation is analogous although reversed. Here the sentences must be derived from a pair of underlying structures with the forms:

$NP_1+is+Adjective+Complement, NP_2+Verb+NP_1$

In this case the equivalence of Noun Phrases is between the 'object' Noun Phrase of the second underlying phrase marker and the 'subject' of the predicative type phrase marker. This is necessary because those verbs which can occur in the *for* phrases of sentences like (56) are just those which can occur with the sentence initial Noun Phrase as 'object.' Hence one does not find:

(75)   *truth is easy for Mary to please

(76)   *meat is easy for Mary to prove

because one cannot find:

(77)   *Mary pleases truth

(78)   *Mary proves meat

But this means that one is forced by these formal facts to derive sentences like

---

[11] It now seems likely that combinations of phrase markers are in fact performed by a single generalized transformation which is part of the component which generates underlying phrase markers rather than the component which contains simple transformations like the reflexive, passive, etc. Cf. Katz and Postal, *op. cit.* and Chomsky, *Aspects of the Theory of Syntax*.

(56) from underlying structures in which *John* is indeed the 'object' (by the uniform characterization given above) of *please*. So that again the independently motivated underlying structures provide a correct account of the way sentences are understood with respect to grammatical relations.

LINGUISTIC SUMMARY

We have briefly considered a few of the enormous number of cases which support the view that the grammatical structure of sentences can only be adequately represented by structural descriptions which include highly abstract underlying phrase markers. We see then that a linguistic description must minimally include rules to generate the correct set of underlying phrase markers, rules to combine underlying phrase markers in the case of sentences which are complex [like (55) and (56)], and finally rules to derive the correct superficial phrase markers of sentences from their abstract structures. A full account of the nature of all such rules has yet to be given, although tremendous progress has been made in recent years and the outlines of correct solutions appear to be relatively clear. The crucial point is that any adequate theory of grammar must provide an account of such rules for only in this way can such a theory provide the theoretical apparatus which individual linguistic descriptions must draw on in order to explain the finite mechanism a speaker has learned which yields his knowledge of the underlying and superficial structures of the endless class of well formed utterances.

We have been speaking essentially only of syntactic structure. It is obvious that a full linguistic description must contain other aspects. First, it must contain a *phonological component* whose rules specify the phonetic character of each structure generated by the syntactic rules. It appears that the phonological component operates exclusively on the *final derived phrase markers* of the syntax and associates a phonetic representation with each. The phonetic rules must also, quite crucially, characterize the notion of 'phonetically possible morpheme.' That is, it is these rules which will state that in English, although neither *ftorts* or *geyk* is an actual morpheme, the latter but not the former is a possible morpheme, and might be introduced tomorrow as the name of a new soap, or a new concept. Much progress has also been made recently in our knowledge of the form and character of phonological rules but this will not concern us further.[12]

[12] For descriptions of the phonological component cf. Morris Halle, *The Sound Pattern of Russian* (The Hague: Mouton and Co., 1954); Morris Halle, "Phonology in a Generative Grammar," *Word*, XVIII (1962) 54-73; Noam Chomsky, "Explanatory Models in Linguistics," *Logic, Methodology, and the Philosophy of Science*, ed. E. Nagel, P. Suppes, A. Tarski (Stanford, Calif.: Stanford Univ. Press, 1961); Chomsky, "Logical Basis of Linguistic Theory;" and Noam Chomsky and G. A. Miller, "Introduction to the Formal Analysis of Natural Lan-

Most important, however, is the fact that a full linguistic description must contain a *semantic component* whose task is to assign each sentence a *meaning*. We have shown that the syntactic structure relevant to this task is present in underlying but not superficial grammatical structure. But nothing has been said precisely about how semantic interpretations are assigned to the structures which the syntactic rules generate. Obviously, however, a full linguistic description must specify this information, since it is evident that speakers know the meanings of the sentences of their language as well as their grammatical structure and pronunciation features.

Although fundamental insights into this question have recently been achieved, this topic is too complex and too new for extended treatment here.[13] The problem for a semantic description is to specify how the speaker who learns the meanings of a finite number of *lexical items,* morphemes, multi-morpheme idioms, plus the rules which characterize the grammatical structure of the sentences which contain these lexical items, determines the meanings of sentences. This can be formulated as a purely formal problem of specifying rules which operate on the grammatical structure (the underlying phrase markers) and the meanings of lexical items, if the notion *meaning of a lexical item* can be formally characterized. This can be done by postulating abstract atomic elements, *semantic markers,* which represent the conceptual content of lexical items. For example, we can postulate a semantic marker (male) which will be associated with the lexical items, *man, boy, father,* or *uncle,* to represent part of the conceptual similarity between these (as opposed for example, to *car, truth, mother, girl*). Besides a dictionary which associates sequences of such semantic markers (*readings*) with lexical items, the semantic component of a linguistic description will also contain a set of *projection rules* which will combine the readings of lexical items in order to obtain derived semantic characterizations for higher order constituents, on up to the constituent sentence itself. These rules will operate on the readings of lexical items plus the grammatical relations which hold between these items, these relations being indicated in the underlying phrase markers in the manner suggested earlier.

The output of the semantic component will be a formal semantic characterization of each constituent of each sentence. These characterizations will provide an explanation of such semantic properties as *ambiguity, paraphrase,*

---

guages," *Handbook of Mathematical Psychology: Volume II,* ed. R. Luce, J. Bush and E. Galanter (New York: Wiley, 1963).

[13] For descriptions of the semantic component cf. Jerrold Katz and J. Fodor, "The Structure of a Semantic Theory," *Language,* XXXIX (1963), 170-211; Jerrold Katz, "Analyticity and Contradiction in Natural Languages," *The Structure of Language: Readings in the Philosophy of Language,* ed. J. Katz and J. Fodor (Englewood Cliffs, N.J.: Prentice-Hall, 1964); Katz and Postal, *op. cit.*

synonymy, or *anomaly.*[14] It should be emphasized that this kind of semantic theory leaves its primary descriptive objects, the semantic markers, uninterpreted. That is, it does not specify the relation of these elements to the non-linguistic world. (This means that such notions as *reference,* and *truth,* are not characterized.) This task is left as a fundamental (and fantastically difficult) psychological problem independent of the problem of formulating linguistic descriptions and the theory underlying them. Interpretation of the system of markers is seen as part of the fundamental problems of concept formation, categorization of experience, etc.

It appears then that the linguistic knowledge whose possession characterizes a speaker of a language has the form of an abstract linguistic object containing three major components of rules. The basic element is a generative syntactic component whose rules generate highly complex structures including a set of phrase markers for each derived string of words. There are then two subsidiary *interpretive* components. The phonological component provides each sentence with a phonetic interpretation and accounts for the speaker's knowledge of the facts of pronunciation. The semantic component provides each sentence with a semantic interpretation in the form of a set of readings and accounts for the speaker's knowledge of the facts of meaning.

It seems that the two interpretative components are each based on a fixed, universal vocabulary of primitive conceptual elements with universally specified relations to the non-linguistic world. In the case of the phonological component, this vocabulary consists of the set of phonetic features with which sentences are described (Voicing, Stress, and Nasality). That is, there is a fixed universal phonetic alphabet which provides all the relevant phonetic information about each sentence. In the case of the semantic component, the vocabulary consists of the set of semantic markers, about which, however, much less is known. The universality of the set of semantic markers is plausible but much work on a wide variety of languages will be needed before it can be verified to anything like the extent to which the universality of the phonetic features has been confirmed. In claiming that the atomic elements of both interpretive components are universal, one is saying that the child who learns a language based on them need not learn these elements or their relations to the non-linguistic world. That is, for example, someone who learns English need not learn what the semantic marker (Male) denotes or what properties of vocal utterances the phonetic feature (Nasal) refers to. He only need determine *if* these elements play a role in English sentences,

[14] These properties are respectively illustrated by:
a. I observed the ball
b. John is a farmer; John is someone who farms
c. not living; dead
d. John married a potato pancake

and if so, how, that is, what rules describe them, what other elements they are related to, etc.

It is unquestionable that the form of the rules in each of the components is a linguistic universal, to be characterized in general linguistic theory. It is also quite likely, I believe, that some of the content of the various components is universal. That is, there are very probably universal rules, and many of the elements which occur in linguistic rules may be universally specified. In particular, there is much hope that the goal of traditional universal grammar, namely, the cross-linguistic characterization of notions like *Noun, Verb, Adjective,* and *Modifier,* can be given in general linguistic theory by limiting the specification to highly abstract underlying phrase markers rather than by attempting to give it in terms of superficial phrase markers wherein all previous attempts have failed.[15]

IMPLICATIONS

In the above sections we have given a quite informal discussion of some of the properties which must be attributed to adequate linguistic descriptions and the theory of language which underlies them. Unfortunately, there has been much confusion about the nature of the subject matter or domain which a linguistic description describes, and the relation between the output of such generative devices and actual speech behavior. This then requires brief discussion.

It must be emphasized that in no sense is a linguistic description an account of actual 'verbal behavior.' Even the grosser aspects of the descriptions of sentences provided by a linguistic description, the phonetic outputs of the phonological component, cannot be identified with real utterances of speakers. Any real utterance will, for example, contain features which provide information about the speaker's age, sex, health, emotional state, etc. And these features have obviously nothing to do with the *language* which the linguistic description characterizes. It is just these 'nonlinguistic' features which differentiate different speakers of the same language and different 'verbal performances' by the same speaker. But it is of course impossible to observe any actual utterances which do not contain such features. It is thus necessary to posit a relation of *representation* which holds between real utterances and the output of linguistic descriptions. The output for any sentence S_1 must be assumed to specify a set of phonetic conditions which any utterance must meet if it is to be an *instance* of S_1.

However, the relation between actual speech behavior and the output of linguistic descriptions is by no means exhaustively described in the above way.

[15] For discussion of these matters cf. Chomsky, *Aspects of the Theory of Syntax.*

It is evident that actual verbal performances contain an enormous number of utterances which do not in the strict sense represent any sentences at all. These are nonetheless perfectly adequate for communication and often more appropriate to the occasion than utterances which do represent full sentences. For example, in answer to questions such as (79)–(81):

(79)   where is the car
(80)   is John inside
(81)   who did it

one can hear such answers as: *inside, yes, Bill*. It is evident that these utterances are understandable because in the context of the previous question they are understood as *versions* of the full sentences:

(82)   the car is inside
(83)   yes John is inside
(84)   Bill did it

It is only the full sentences that should be generated by the linguistic description proper which must draw the line between full sentences and fragments which can represent full sentences in particular environments. Part of the differentia of these two classes of utterances, utterances which directly represent full sentences, and those which do not but are still understandable, is that the former have a *fixed* finite set of semantic interpretations independently of all context, and their interpretation in any one context is simply a selection from among this fixed set. For fragments, however, occurrence in isolation permits no interpretation at all. And their interpretation in context is directly determined by, and does not involve an elimination of fixed interpretations inappropriate to, the context. Thus the fragments given above can as well be answers to (85)–(87) as to (79)–(81):

(85)   where did you leave your coat
(86)   can Hitler really be dead
(87)   who was clawed by the tiger

And in these cases the fragments must be understood as versions of:

(88)   I left my coat inside
(89)   yes Hitler really can be dead
(90)   Bill was clawed by the tiger

In short we see that sentence fragments of the type being discussed have no finitely fixed number of interpretations at all and in this way are radically distinct from utterances which directly represent full sentences. The utterances *inside, yes, Bill* have an infinite number of possible interpretations and can hence not be described *as such* by a finite linguistic description. To account for the understanding of fragments and many other kinds of utterances, suitable for communication in various contexts but distinct from full sentences, it is then evident that linguistic theory must provide a means for extending the description of full sentences to a class of *semi-sentences*. We can say little about this here besides noting that (1) it would be surprising if the apparatus for extension to semi-sentences was not an inherent property of human beings, hence cross-linguistic, and (2) it is obviously impossible to carry out research on the topic of semi-sentences independently of extensive knowledge of the properties of full sentences. And it is just this knowledge which the study of linguistic descriptions in the narrow sense is designed to yield. We conclude then that a linguistic description does not describe actual speech behavior but rather an indefinite class of highly structured (in three distinct though interrelated ways, syntactic, semantic, phonological) abstract objects, *sentences,* which define the *language* which in various ways underlies all speech behavior. A linguistic description is, in other words, a partial account of linguistic *competence.* To extend the characterization of this to an account of linguistic *performance* then requires a number of studies of various types of the way in which this underlying knowledge of linguistic rules is put to use.

The distinction between *competence* and *performance* or *language* and *speech* is quite crucial for understanding at least three goals related to linguistic descriptions proper, goals whose pursuit is crucial if a full account of the domain of language study is to be given. First, there is the task of constructing a *model of speech recognition,* that is, a model of the way speakers use their linguistic knowledge (language) to understand noises that they hear.[16] In terms of the above outline of linguistic structure, this task is the task of determining what sentence the noise represents and then determining the underlying structure of that sentence in order to determine its possible range of semantic interpretations.

When the above tasks have been carried out successfully, the context of the utterance must be applied in some way to pick the interpretation which was 'intended.' Almost nothing can be seriously said at the moment about this problem of contextual *disambiguation* of utterances beyond the obvious point that the problem cannot be seriously posed without understanding of the nature of language or linguistic structure. It appears that every piece of possible human knowledge about the world is relevant to the disambiguation of some sentence and thus to its understanding in context.[17] This has rather obvious implications of two sorts. On the one hand it shows that theoretically there can be no *general* theory of the way contexts serve to permit choice of one of several possible interpretations for some sentence, and on the other,

[16] For a discussion of models of speech recognition and speech production cf. Noam Chomsky and G. A. Miller, "Finitary Models of Language Users," *Handbook of Mathematical Psychology: Volume II*, ed. R. Luce, J. Bush, and E. Galanter (New York: Wiley, 1963) and Katz and Postal, *op. cit.*

[17] This is argued in Katz and Fodor, "The Structure of a Semantic Theory."

it shows that practical attempts to utilize linguistic research for the mechanical replacement of human performers (as in so-called 'machine translation') are doomed to failure.

A third goal which is involved in a full linguistic account is the problem of formulating a *model for the speaker*. This must involve specification of how a desired *message* is given as input to the linguistic description to yield as output a phonetic representation which is the input to the speaker's speech apparatus, the output of this being the actual utterances.[18] It appears that the inputs to the linguistic description must be taken to be *semantic objects*, i.e. *readings* in the sense of our earlier brief discussion. But just as linguistic theory as such does not specify the relation of semantic markers to the non-linguistic world, so also it cannot deal with the relations between a speaker's experiences, verbal or otherwise, and the utterances he produces. That is, it cannot deal with the fantastically complicated question of the *causation* of verbal behavior, although this is a task which modern psychology has too prematurely tried to deal with. Too prematurely, because it is obviously impossible to even *formulate* the problem of causation prior to an understanding of the character of speech behavior. And this, as we have seen, requires prior knowledge of the abstract *language* which underlies such behavior. Hence study of the causation of verbal behavior is two steps removed from reasonable possibility if attempted independently of the kind of studies discussed earlier.[19]

It should be obvious at this point that a linguistic description as such which *generates* sentences, i.e. highly abstract triples of syntactic, semantic, and phonological properties, is neither a model of the speaker or of the hearer although it is often confused with these. *Generation* is not *production* or *recognition*. A linguistic description simply characterizes the objects which a model of recognition must recover from verbal noise and which a model of production must encode into such noise. The study of linguistic descriptions per se is hence logically prior to the study of questions of recognition, contextual determination, production, and causation since it defines the objects

---

[18] It is because this output is determined by other factors besides the phonetic representations which are the most superficial aspects of linguistic structure generated by the linguistic description that the latter can not be said to generate any actual utterances. That is, given a fixed phonetic or pronunciation code as input to the speech apparatus, the output is also determined by such factors as the presence or absence of food in the oral cavity, the speaker's age, sex, state of health (cleft palate or not, etc.), degree of wakefulness or intoxication, etc. Facts like these are sufficient in themselves to demonstrate the futility of any view of language which cannot go beyond the gross observations of utterances to the abstract structures which underlie them, i.e., the futility of any view of language which identifies the significant linguistic objects with what can be obtained from tape recorders.

[19] For a fuller discussion of these points cf. Noam Chomsky, "Review of *Verbal Behavior* by B. F. Skinner," *Language*, XXXV (1959), 26-58.

in terms of which the problems with which these latter studies deal must be formulated.

Finally, the kind of conclusions reached above have obvious and important implications for any study of the problem of language learning. If, as we have argued, the structure of the sentences of natural languages involves an extremely complex and highly abstract set of entities related to actual utterances only by an extensive set of highly structured rules, it follows that the problem of language learning must be phrased in quite specific terms. That is, it is necessary to study the question of how an organism, equipped with a quite complex and *highly specific* characterization of the possible nature of a natural language, determines from various kinds of linguistic data, heard sentences, contexts, corrections, the particular manifestation of this abstract theory used in the community into which he was born. Again the primary constraint on the study of language learning is the logically prior knowledge of the character of the linguistic system which must be learned. And the more specific and detailed this knowledge can be made, that is, the more closely one can describe the general theory of linguistic descriptions which amounts to a hypothesis about the innate genetic knowledge which the human child brings to language learning, the greater is the possibility of being able to formulate the techniques or strategies which the child uses to apply this inherent knowledge of possible linguistic structure to induce the details of a particular language from his linguistic experience. From what was said earlier about the abstract character of linguistic structure, underlying phrase markers, and the like, it is clear that enough is already known about the nature of language to show that views of language learning which restrict attention to the gross phonetic properties of utterances, either by adherence to psychological theories which do not countenance concepts more abstract and specific than 'stimulus,' 'generalization,' 'chaining,' 'response,' etc., or linguistic theories which do not countenance more than the kind of linguistic structure representable by final derived phrase markers, cannot teach us very much about the fantastic feat by which a child with almost no direct instruction learns that enormously extensive and complicated system which is a natural language, a system which has thus far defied the efforts of the best students to describe it in anything like a complete or adequate way.

I hope that the too brief and inadequate remarks of this final section will nonetheless have shown that the study of any aspect of language or linguistic behavior cannot hope to progress beyond superficialities if it is not based on firm knowledge of the character of the highly complex, abstract, finitely specifiable though infinite linguistic system which underlies all observable linguistic performances. In short, I hope to have shown that the results of generative linguistics are not an obscure oddity, of interest only to the specialist in linguistics, but rather provide the kind of knowledge which is prerequisite to the understanding of the domains of the entire range of language studies.

ADDITIONAL REFERENCES

Edward Klima, "Negation in English," *The Structure of Language: Readings in the Philosophy of Language,* ed. J. Katz and J. Fodor (Englewood Cliffs, N.J.: Prentice-Hall, 1964).

Robert B. Lees, *The Grammar of English Nominalizations,* supplement to International Journal of American Linguistics (1960).

Robert B. Lees, "Review of *Syntactic Structures* by N. Chomsky," *Language,* XXXIII (1957) 375-408.

G. H. Matthews, *Hidatsa Syntax* (London: Mouton and Co., 1965).

Words, Meanings and Concepts

JOHN B. CARROLL
Harvard University

How children use words to construct a unified conception of the world is one of psychology's oldest theoretical problems. In this essay John Carroll argues that psychological studies of concept formation have been unnecessarily isolated from theoretical developments in semantics. Noting that each field could contribute much to our understanding of concept learning in schools, Carroll proposes that both disciplines be integrated into a curricular model for teaching and learning. Toward that end, the author reviews several studies on concept formation, language acquisition, and vocabulary development, and he concludes by showing how different concepts from mathematics, science, and social studies can be analyzed and taught by inductive and deductive means.

The teaching of words, and of the meanings and concepts they designate or convey, is one of the principal tasks of teachers at all levels of education. It is a concern of textbook writers and programmers of self-instructional materials as well. Students must be taught the meanings of unfamiliar words and idioms; they must be helped in recognizing unfamiliar ways in which familiar words may be used; and they must be made generally aware of the possibility of ambiguity in meaning and the role of context in resolving it. Often the task that presents itself to the teacher is not merely to explain a new word in familiar terms, but to shape an entirely new concept in the mind of the student.

Whether the teaching of words, meanings, and concepts is done by the teacher, the textbook writer, or the programmer, it is generally done in an intuitive, unanalytic way. The purpose of this article is to sketch, at least in a first approximation, a more analytical approach to this task. One would have thought that volumes would have been written on the subject, but apart from such brief treatments as those of Brownell and Hendrickson[1], Serra[2], Levit[3],

---

[1] William A. Brownell and Gordon Hendrickson, "How Children Learn Information, Concepts, and Generalizations" *Forty-Ninth Yearbook, National Society for the Study of Education, Part I*, ed. N. B. Henry (Chicago: University of Chicago Press, 1950), 92-128.

Harvard Educational Review Vol. 34 No. 2 Spring 1964, 178–202

and Vinacke[4], for example, one searches the literature in vain for any comprehensive treatment of concept teaching. One is reassured that there are gaps to be filled.

There is, in the first place, an unfortunate hiatus between the word "meaning" and the very word "concept" itself. *Meaning* and *concept* have usually been treated as quite separate things by different disciplines. *Meaning*, for example, has been considered the province of a somewhat nebulous and insecure branch of linguistics called *semantics*.[5] *Concept* is almost anybody's oyster: it has continually been the concern of the philosopher, but has received generous attention from psychology. While the meanings of these two terms

---

[2] Mary C. Serra, "How to Develop Concepts and Their Verbal Representations," *Elem. Sch. J.,* LIII (1953), 275-285.

[3] Martin Levit, "On the Psychology and Philosophy of Concept Formation," *Educ. Theory,* III (1953), 193-207.

[4] W. Edgar Vinacke, "Concept Formation in Children of School Ages," *Education,* LXXIV (1954), 527-534.

[5] Even if a technical science of "semantics" is a comparatively modern invention,—dating, say, from Bréal's article on the subject published in a classical journal in 1883,—the field might be said to have been thoroughly discussed. The classic work of Ogden and Richards (C. K. Ogden and I. A. Richards, *The Meaning of Meaning* (3rd ed.; New York: Harcourt, Brace, 1930).), the somewhat faddish writings stemming from Korzybski's doctrines of "general semantics" (A. Korzybski, *Science and Sanity; an Introduction to Non-Aristotelian Systems and General Semantics* (8th ed.; Lakeville, Conn.: 1948).), and the recent work in psychology of Osgood *et al.* (Charles E. Osgood, George J. Suci, and Percy Tannenbaum, *The Measurement of Meaning* (Urbana, Illinois: Univ. of Illinois Press, 1957).), Brown (Roger Brown, *Words and Things* (Glencoe, Illinois: The Free Press, 1958).), and Skinner (B. F. Skinner, *Verbal Behavior* (New York: Appleton-Century-Crofts, 1957).) might be said to have disposed of most of the general problems of a science of meaning. On the other hand, Stephen Ullmann's recent book (Stephen Ullmann, *Semantics, an Introduction to the Science of Meaning* (Oxford: Basil Blackwell, 1962).) claims only to be in the nature of a "progress report," pointing to the "revolution" that has taken place in modern linguistics and the "advances in philosophy, psychology, anthropology, communication engineering and other spheres" that have had "important repercussions in the study of meaning."
There has been a rash of papers on the implications of linguistics for the teaching of English, the teaching of reading, the teaching of foreign languages, and so on. In fact, the idea that linguistics has much to contribute to educational problems in the "language arts" has become almost embarrassingly fashionable. One's embarrassment comes from the fact that despite certain very definite and positive contributions that linguistics can make to these endeavors, these contributions are of relatively small extent. Once we accept such fundamental tenets of linguistics as the primacy of speech over writing, the structure of the language code as a patterning of distinctive communicative elements, and the arbitrariness of standards of usage, and work out their implications in detail, we find we are still faced with enormous problems of methodology in the teaching of such subjects as English, reading, and foreign languages. The position is particularly difficult in connection with the study of meaning, because most branches of linguistics have paid little attention to this study; some linguists have seemed to go out of their way to exclude the study of meaning from their concerns as linguists. Although there are recent attempts (Paul Ziff, *Semantic Analysis* (Ithaca, N. Y.: Cornell Univ. Press, 1960) and Jerrold J. Katz and Jerry A. Fodor, "The Structure of a Semantic Theory," *Language,* XXXIX (1963), 170-210.) to systematize semantic studies, these efforts may be less than completely successful if they fail to take account of the fundamentally psychological problem of how individuals attain concepts and how these individually-attained concepts are related to word meanings. The treatment of this problem offered in the present paper is exceedingly sketchy and must be regarded as only a first approximation.

can be usefully distinguished in many contexts, it is also the case that a framework can be made for considering their intimate interconnections.

Second, there is a gap between the findings of psychologists on the conditions under which very simple "concepts" are learned in the psychological laboratory and the experiences of teachers in teaching the "for real" concepts that are contained in the curricula of the schools. It is not self-evident that there is any continuity at all between learning "DAX" as the name of a certain geometrical shape of a certain color and learning the meaning of the word "longitude." Even if such a continuity exists, it is not clear how the relative difficulty or complexity of concepts can be assessed.

Third, a problem related to the second arises when we ask whether there is any continuity, with respect to psychological "processes," between the inductive, non-verbal type of learning studied in the psychological laboratory under the guise of "concept learning" and the usually more deductive, verbal-explanatory type of teaching used in the classroom and in typical text materials. Take, for example, the kind of concept learning that has been explored so fruitfully by Bruner and his associates.[6] The experimental setting they employed is essentially a game between the experimenter and the subject: the experimenter says he is thinking of a concept—and perhaps he shows an example of his "concept," whereupon the subject's task is to make guesses about other possible instances of the concept in such a way that he will eventually be able to recognize the concept as defined by the experimenter. But in every case, one feels that the experimenter could have "taught" the subject the concept by a very simple verbal communication like "three circles" (for a "conjunctive" concept in which two attributes must occur together) or "any card that has either redness or two borders" (for a "disjunctive" concept) or "any card with more figures than borders" (for a "relational" concept). Teaching a concept in school is usually not all that simple.

In an effort to fill these gaps, we will sketch out a framework for conceptualizing problems of Meaning and Concept. For reasons that will eventually become clear, we must start with the notion of Concept.

THE NATURE OF CONCEPTS

In a totally inorganic world there could be no concepts, but with the existence of organisms capable of complex perceptual responses, concepts become possible. In brief, concepts are properties of organismic experience—more particularly, they are the abstracted and often cognitively structured classes of "mental" experience learned by organisms in the course of their life histories.

---

[6] Jerome S. Bruner, Jacqueline J. Goodnow, and George A. Austin, *A Study of Thinking* (New York: Wiley, 1956).

There is evidence that animals other than human beings behave with regard to concepts in this sense, but we shall confine our attention to human organisms. Because of the continuity of the physical, biological, and social environment in which human beings live, their concepts will show a high degree of similarity; and through language learning, many concepts (classes of experience) will acquire names, that is, words or phrases in a particular language, partly because some classes of experience are so salient and obvious that nearly every person acquires them for himself, and partly because language makes possible the diffusion and sharing of concepts as classes of experience. We use the term "experience" in an extremely broad sense—defining it as any internal or perceptual response to stimulation. We can "have experience of" some aspect of the physical, biological, or social environment by either direct or indirect means; we can experience heat, or light, or odor directly, while our experiences of giraffes or atoms, say, may be characterized as being indirect, coming only through verbal descriptions or other patterns of stimuli (pointer readings, etc.) that evoke these concepts.

One necessary condition for the formation of a concept is that the individual must have a series of experiences that are in one or more respects similar; the constellation of "respects" in which they are similar constitutes the "concept" that underlies them. Experiences that embody this concept are "positive instances" of it; experiences that do not embody it may be called "negative instances." A further necessary condition for the formation of a concept is that the series of experiences embodying the concept must be preceded, interspersed, or followed by other experiences that constitute negative instances of the concept. As the complexity of the concepts increases (i.e., as there is an increase in the number of interrelations of the respects in which experiences must be similar in order to be positive instances), there is a greater necessity for an appropriate sequencing of positive and negative instances in order to insure adequate learning of the concept.[7] At least this is true when the concept has to be formed from *non-verbal* experiences only, i.e., from actual exemplars or referents of the concept as contrasted with non-exemplars. But concept learning from verbal explanation, as will be noted below, must, as it were, put the learner through a series of vicarious experiences of positive and negative instances. For example, in telling a child what a lion is, one must indicate the range of positive and negative instances—the range of variations that could be found in real lions and the critical respects in which other animals—tigers, leopards, etc.—differ from lions.

We have been describing what is often called the process of abstraction. We have given a number of *necessary* conditions for the formation of a con-

[7] Earl B. Hunt, *Concept Learning: An Information Processing Problem* (New York: Wiley, 1962).

cept; exactly what conditions are *sufficient* cannot yet be stated, but in all likelihood this will turn out to be a matter of (a) the number, sequencing, or timing of the instances presented to the individual, (b) the reinforcements given to the individual's responses, and (c) the individual's orientation to the task. The evidence suggests that the learner must be oriented to, and attending to, the relevant stimuli in order to form a concept. The public test of the formation of a concept is the ability to respond correctly and reliably to new positive and negative instances of it; we do not wish to imply, however, that a concept has not been formed until it is put to such a test.

The infant acquires "concepts" of many kinds even before he attains anything like language. One kind of concept that is acquired by an infant quite early is the concept embodied in the experience of a particular object—a favorite toy, for example. As the toy is introduced to the infant, it is experienced in different ways—it is seen at different angles, at different distances, and in different illuminations. It is felt in different positions and with different parts of the body, and experienced with still other sense-modalities—taste, smell. But underlying all these experiences are common elements sufficient for the infant to make an identifying response to the particular toy in question—perhaps to the point that he will accept only the particular specimen that he is familiar with and reject another specimen that is in the least bit different. The acceptance or rejection of a specimen is the outward sign of the attainment of a concept—as constituted by the class of experiences associated with that particular specimen. The experiences themselves are sufficiently similar to be their own evidence that they constitute a class—a perceptual invariant, therefore, together with whatever affective elements that may be present to help reinforce the attainment of the concept (pleasure in the sight, taste, smell, and feel of the toy, for example).

Even the concept contained in a particular object represents a certain degree of generality—generality over the separate presentations of the object. But pre-verbal infants also attain concepts which from the standpoint of adult logic have even higher degrees of generality. A further stage of generality is reached when the infant comes to recognize successive samples of something —e.g., a particular kind of food—as equivalent, even though varying slightly in taste, color, temperature, etc. Because the different samples of food are about equally reinforcing, the infant gradually learns to overcome the initial tendency to reject a sample that is experienced as not quite the same as one previously experienced. That is, what seems to be initially a negative instance turns out to be a positive instance because it provides the same reinforcement as the earlier instance—the reinforcement being in this case a "sign" that the new experience is to be taken in the same class as former ones. An even higher stage of generality is achieved when the child will accept and make a common response to any one of a number of rather different stimuli—for example, any one of a number of different foods. In adult terms, he has attained the concept of "food" in some elementary sense. The explanation of this phenomenon may indeed draw upon the usual primary reinforcement theory (the equivalence of different foods in satisfying a hunger drive) but it also depends upon various secondary reinforcements, as when the parent punishes the child for eating something not considered "food," like ants or mud. This is an elementary case in which culture, as represented by parents, provides signs as to what the positive and negative instances of a concept are.

Direct experience, i.e., the recognition of experiences as identical or similar, allows the infant to attain concepts that in adult language have names such as redness, warmth, softness, heaviness, swiftness, sweetness, loudness, pain, etc. In some cases, the infant's concepts of sensory qualities may be rather undifferentiated. For example, because big things are generally experienced as heavy and strong, and small things are generally experienced as lightweight and weak, the infant's concept of size may not be adequately differentiated from his concepts of weight and strength. Without any social reinforcement to guide him, his concept of "redness" may range over a rather wide range of the color spectrum, and if he happens to have been born into a culture which pays little attention to the difference, say, between what we would call "red" and "orange," his concept of "redness" may remain relatively undifferentiated even after he has learned a language—just as it has been demonstrated that different varieties of blue are not well coded in everyday English.[8]

Furthermore, we can infer from various investigations of Piaget[9] that the child's concepts of size, weight, and other physical attributes of objects do not contain the notion of "conservation" that his later experiences will teach him. For all the infant or young child knows of the physical universe, objects can change in size, weight, etc., in quite arbitrary ways. It is only at a later stage, when the child has had an opportunity to form certain concepts about the nature of the physical universe that his concepts of size, weight, and number can incorporate the notion of constancy or conservation that mature thinking requires. Experience with objects that can expand or contract through stretching or shrinking gives the child a concept of size that can properly explain the fact that a balloon can be blown up to various sizes. Indeed, this explanation may involve the concepts of "expansion" and "contraction." At a still later stage, the child may learn enough about the relation of heat to expansion to explain why it is necessary to have seams in concrete roads, or why one

---

[8] Roger W. Brown and Eric H. Lenneberg, "A Study in Language and Cognition," *J. Abnorm. Soc. Psychol.*, XLIX (1954), 454-462.

[9] John H. Flavell, *The Developmental Psychology of Jean Piaget* (Princeton: Van Nostrand, 1963).

allows for expansion in the building of large bridges. And it will be relatively unlikely that even as an adult he will learn enough about the concept of size to understand the concept of relativity—that the size of a body is relative to the speed at which it is traveling and the system in which it is measured.

Thus, concepts can in the course of a person's life become more complex, more loaded with significant aspects. Concepts are, after all, essentially idiosyncratic in the sense that they reside in particular individuals with particular histories of experiences that lead them to classify those experiences in particular ways. My concept of "stone" may not be precisely your concept of "stone" because my experiences with stones may have included work with pieces of a peculiar kind of vitreous rock that you have seldom seen. To a large extent, how I sort out my experiences is my own business and may not lead to the same sortings as yours.

Nevertheless, I can specify the way I sort out my experiences by noting the *critical attributes* that differentiate them. I can specify what sensory qualities and attributes are necessary before I will classify an experience as being an experience of what I call a stone. But it is not even necessary for a person to be able to specify such attributes. A child who has learned a certain concept—who has learned to recognize certain experiences as being similar—may not necessarily be able to verbalize what attributes make them similar; he may not even be aware of the fact that he has attained a certain concept, since it may be the case that only his behavior—the fact that he consistently makes a certain response to a certain class of stimuli—indicates that he has formed a concept. Such would be the case, for example, for the classic instance where the child is afraid of the barber because he wields instruments (scissors) that look like those of the doctor whom he has already learned to fear, and because he wears a similar white smock.

Indeed, this last instance exemplifies the fact that concepts may include affective components. Because concepts are embodied in classes of experiences they include all the elements of experiences that may occur in common—perceptual and cognitive elements as well as motivational and emotional elements. My concept of "stone" may reflect, let us say, my positive delight in collecting new varieties of minerals, whereas your concept may reflect the fact that you had unpleasant experiences with stones—having them thrown at you in a riot, or finding lots of them in your garden. Osgood's "semantic differential,"[10] in which one is asked to rate one's concepts on scales such as good-bad, strong-weak, fast-slow, active-passive, light-heavy, pungent-bland, etc., is a way of indexing certain relatively universal cognitive and affective components of individual experiences as classed in concepts; it would per-

---

[10] Charles E. Osgood, George J. Suci, and Percy H. Tannenbaum, *The Measurement of Meaning* (Urbana, Illinois: Univ. of Illinois Press, 1957).

haps more properly be called an "experiential differential" than a "semantic differential." The fact that fairly consistent results are obtained when concept ratings from different people are compared or averaged implies that people tend to have generally similar kinds of experiences, at least within a given culture.

It has already been suggested earlier that since man lives in an essentially homogeneous physical and biological environment and a partially homogeneous social environment, it is inevitable that a large number of concepts arrived at by individual people should be the same or at least so nearly identical in their essential attributes as to be called the same; these concepts we may call *conceptual invariants.* We can be sure that throughout the world people have much the same concepts of *sun, man, day, animal, flower, walking, falling, softness,* etc. by whatever names they may be called. The fact that they have names is incidental; there are even certain concepts that for one reason or another (a taboo, for example) may remain nameless.

It is probably when we enter into the realms of science and technology and of social phenomena that the concepts attained by different people will differ most. In science and technology concepts vary chiefly because of differences, over the world, in the levels of scientific and technological knowledge reached; and in the social sphere they will differ chiefly because of the truly qualitative differences in the ways cultures are organized. Nevertheless, within a given community there will be a high degree of commonality in the concepts recognized and attained, in the sense that there will be relatively high agreement among people as to the attributes that are criterial for a given concept. For example, even though types of families vary widely over the world, the concept of *family* within a given culture is reasonably homogeneous. At the same time, differences in intellectual and educational levels will account for differences in the sheer number of concepts attained by individuals within a given culture.

WORDS AND THEIR MEANINGS

In the learning of language, words (and other elements in a linguistic system, including phonemes, morphemes, and syntactical patterns) come to be perceived as distinct entities, and in this sense they form one class of perceptual invariants along with the perceptual invariants that represent common objects, feelings, and events. The child must learn to perceive the various instances of a given sound or word as similar, and eventually to differentiate the several contexts in which a given sound or sound pattern is used. (We know of an instance of a very young child who somehow learned to react violently to the word "no," but she would react just as violently to the word "know," even when it was embedded in a sentence. The process of differentiation took a considerable time.)

Many words or higher units of the linguistic system come to stand for, or name, the concepts that have been learned pre-verbally. Certainly this is true for a long list of words that stand for particular things or classes of things, qualities, and events. For the English language, these categories correspond roughly to proper and common nouns; adjectives; and verbs of action, perception, and feeling. It is perhaps less clear that "function words" like prepositions and conjunctions, or grammatical markers like the past tense sign can represent concepts, but a case can be made for this. For example, prepositions like *in, to, above, below, beside, near* correspond to concepts of relative spatial position in a surprisingly complex and subtle way; and conjunctions like *and, but, however, or* correspond to concepts of logical inclusion and exclusion, similarity and difference of propositions, etc.

The processes by which words come to "stand for" or correspond to concepts can best be described in psychological terms. Without going into the details here, we can only say that in every case there is some sort of reinforcing condition that brands a word as being associated with a given concept. This is true whether the word is learned as what Skinner[11] calls a *mand* (as when a child learns the meaning of *water* as a consequence of having water brought whenever he says "water") or as a *tact* (as where the child is praised or otherwise reinforced for saying "water" when he sees or experiences water), because in either case the word is paired contiguously with the concept *as an experience*. The connection between a word and the concept or experience with which it stands in relation must work in either direction: the word must evoke the concept and the concept must evoke the word.

As a physical symbol, a word is a cultural artifact that takes the same, or nearly the same, form throughout a speech community. It is a standardized product on which the speech community exercises a considerable degree of quality control. Not so with concepts, which as we have seen may vary to some extent with the individual, depending on his experiences of the referents of the words. Society does, however, maintain a degree of "quality control" on the referential meaning of words. The conditions under which the use of words is rewarded or not rewarded—either by successful or unsuccessful communication or by direct social approval or disapproval—can be looked upon as constituting the "rules of usage" of a word, and these rules of usage define the *denotative meaning* of a term. Thus, there is a rule of usage such that the noun *mother* can be used only for a certain kind of kinship relation. One thinks of denotative meaning as something that is socially prescribed. Connotative meaning, however, banks heavily on those aspects of concepts

[11] B. F. Skinner, *Verbal Behavior* (New York: Appleton-Century, Crofts, 1957).

that are widely shared yet non-criterial and perhaps affective (emotional) in content. "Mother" as a noun might evoke various emotional feelings depending upon one's experience with mothers.

Perhaps it is useful to think of words, meanings, and concepts as forming *three* somewhat independent series. The words in a language can be thought of as a series of physical entities—either spoken or written. Next, there exists a set of "meanings" which stand in complex relationships to the set of words. These relationships may be described by the rules of usage that have developed by the processes of socialization and communication. A "meaning" can be thought of as a standard of communicative behavior that is shared by those who speak a language. Finally, there exist "concepts"; the classes of experience formed in individuals either independently of language processes or in close dependence on language processes.

The interrelations found among these three series are complex: almost anyone can give instances where a word may have many "meanings," or in which a given "meaning" corresponds to several different words. The relationships between societally-standardized "meanings" and individually-formed "concepts" are likewise complex, but of a somewhat different nature. It is a question of how well each individual has learned these relationships, and at least in the sphere of language and concepts, education is largely a process whereby the individual learns either to attach societally-standardized words and meanings to the concepts he has already formed, or to form new concepts that properly correspond to societally-standardized words and meanings. A "meaning" of a word is, therefore, a societally-standardized concept, and when we say that a word stands for or names a concept it is understood that we are speaking of concepts that are shared among the members of a speech community.

To the extent that individual concepts differ even though they possess shared elements, misunderstandings can arise. My concept of "several" may correspond to the range "approximately three to five," where yours may correspond to "approximately five to fifteen." Speech communities may differ, too, in the exact ranges in which they standardize meanings. The word *infant* seems to include a higher age range in Great Britain (in the phrase "infants' schools") than it does in the United States, and in legal contexts the word may even refer to anyone who has not attained some legal age like twenty-one years.

The fact that words vary in meaning according to context has given rise to one form of a "context theory of meaning" which seems to allege that the meaning of a word is to be found in its context; this is only true, however, in the sense that the context may provide a *clue* as to the particular meaning (or standardized concept) with which a word is intended to be associated. In fact, the clue usually takes the form of an indication of one or more elements of a concept. For example, in the phrase *A light load* the context suggests (though it does not determine absolutely) that *light* is to be taken as the opposite of heavy because loads vary more importantly in weight than in their color, whereas the context in *A light complexion* suggests the element of color because complexions can vary in color but only very improbably in weight. It is not surprising that normal language texts have been found to have redundancy, for the elements of concepts suggested by the words in a sentence are often overlapping.

Frequently context is the key to the fact that a word is being used in an archaic or unusual sense. A student who cannot square the usual meaning of *smug* with its use in the following lines from Shakespeare's *Henry IV (Part I)*:

> "And here the smug and silver Trent shall run
> In a new channel, fair and evenly"

had better resort to a dictionary, where he will find that an earlier meaning of *smug* is *trim, neat.* We cannot dwell here on the interesting ways in which words change in meaning historically, often in response to changes in emphasis given to the various criterial attributes embodied in the concepts corresponding to words. Just as one example, though, consider the historical change of meaning of "meat" from (originally) "any kind of food" to "edible part of animal body, flesh," where the criterial attribute "part of animal body" gradually came to be reinforced alongside the attribute "edible thing."

DEFINITIONS

What, by the way, is the function of a dictionary definition in the light of the system of ideas being presented here? Aside from the few instances where dictionary definitions present pictures or drawings of the items being defined, two main techniques are used in dictionary entries: (1) the use of verbal equivalents, and (2) the use of formal definition by stating *genus et differentia*. The use of verbal equivalents, as where we are told that *smug* can mean "trim, smooth, sleek," has the function of evoking either a (hopefully) previously known concept to which both the defined word and the defining word stand in the same relation, or a series of (hopefully) previously known concepts from whose common elements the reader can derive the concept to which the defined word properly stands in relation. The use of a formal definition, on the other hand, literally "marks off the boundaries of" the concept by first indicating what it has in common with other experiences (*genus*) and then indicating in what respects or attributes (*differentia*) it differs from other experiences. For example, if we are told that *tarn* is a small mountain lake or pool, we know that in many respects it is similar to other lakes or pools —that it is an enclosed, contained body of water, but that it is a special kind of lake of a given size and location. One could, therefore, presumably acquire the concept named *tarn* by learning to make this response only in connection with the criterial attributes defining it. What could be simpler, particularly if one is verbally told what the criterial attributes are? The only kind of intellectual mishap would occur, one would think, when one of the attributes is misunderstood or overlooked. Calling Lake George (in the Adirondacks) a *tarn* would be grossly to neglect or misunderstand the element of small size.

CONCEPT FORMATION RESEARCH

We are now in a position to inquire into the possible relevance of concept formation research to the learning of the meanings and concepts associated with words in a language.

Practically all concept formation research since the days of Hull[12] has been concerned with essentially the following task: the subject is presented with a series of instances which are differentiated in some way; either the task is finding out in what way the several instances match up with one of a small number of names, or (in the simpler case) it is one of discovering why some instances are "positive" (i.e., instances of the "concept" the experimenter has in mind) or "negative" (not instances of the "concept"). Typically the stimulus material consists of simple visual material characterized by a number of clearly salient dimensions—e.g., the color of the figures, the geometrical shape of the figures, the number of figures, the number of borders, the color of the background, etc. Occasionally the critical characteristics of the concept are not clearly in view—as in Hull's experiment where the critical stroke elements of Chinese characters tended to be masked by the rest of the figures, or as in Bouthilet's[13] experiment where the critical feature was the inclusion of letters found in the stimulus word. Sometimes the critical elements are semantic elements of words, as in Freedman and Mednick's experiment[14] in which the task was to find the common semantic element in a series of words such as *gnat, needle, stone,* and *canary.*

Thus, there are two elements to be studied in any concept-formation task: (1) the attributes which are criterial to the concept—their nature and number, the number of values each attribute has and the discriminability of these values, and the salience of the attributes themselves—that is, whether the attributes command attention and are readily perceivable, and (2) the in-

---

[12] C. L. Hull, "Quantitative Aspects of the Evolution of Concepts," *Psychol. Monogr.,* No. 123, (1920).

[13] L. Bouthilet, "The Measurement of Intuitive Thinking" (unpublished Ph.D. Thesis Univ. of Chicago, 1948).

[14] J. L. Freedman and S. A. Mednick, "Ease of Attainment of Concepts as a Function of Response Dominance Variance," *J. Exp. Psychol.,* LV (1958), 463-466.

formation-handling task required of the subject in view of the order in which positive and negative instances are presented and the amount of information concerning the concept that is furnished by each presentation. Most of what we know about this kind of concept attainment task can be summarized in the following statements:

1. Concept attainment becomes more difficult as the number of relevant attributes increases, the number of values of attributes increases, and the salience of the attributes decreases.

2. Concept attainment becomes more difficult as the information load that must be handled by the subject in order to solve the concept increases, and as the information is increasingly carried by negative rather than positive instances.

3. Various strategies for handling the information load are possible, and some are in the long run more successful than others.

Concept Learning in School

I suspect that anyone who has examined the concept formation literature with the hope of finding something of value for the teaching of concepts in school has had cause for some puzzlement and disappointment, because however fascinating this literature may be, as it wends its way through the detailed problems posed by the methodology itself, its relevance to the learning of concepts in the various school subjects is a bit obscure.

Let us look at the major differences between concept learning in school and in the laboratory.

(1) One of the major differences is in the nature of the concepts themselves. A new concept learned in school is usually a genuinely "new" concept rather than an artificial combination of familiar attributes (like the concept "three blue squares" such as might be taught in a psychological experiment).

(2) New concepts learned in school depend on attributes which themselves represent difficult concepts. In more general terms, concepts learned in school often depend upon a network of related or prerequisite concepts. One cannot very well learn the concept of derivative, in the calculus, until one has mastered a rather elaborate structure of prerequisite concepts (e.g., slope, change of slope, algebraic function, etc.). Further, the attributes on which school-learned concepts depend are frequently verbal, depending on elements of meaning that cannot easily be represented in terms of simple sensory qualities as used in concept formation experiments.

(3) Many of the more difficult concepts of school learning are of a relational rather than a conjunctive character; they deal with the relations among attributes rather than their combined presence or absence. Concept forma-

tion experiments have thus far revealed little about the acquisition of relational concepts.

(4) An important element in school learning is the memory problem involved in the proper matching of words and concepts. Thus, the problems of paired-associate memory are added to those of concept learning itself. For example, a student in biology or social studies has to learn not only a large number of new concepts, but also a large number of unfamiliar, strange-looking words to be attached to these concepts. The rate at which new concepts can be introduced is probably limited, just as the rate at which foreign language words can be acquired is limited.

(5) The most critical difference between school concept learning and concept learning in psychological experiments is that the former is for the most part deductive and the latter is generally inductive. It would be relatively rare to find a concept taught in school by the procedure of showing a student a series of positive and negative instances, labeled as such, and asking him to induce the nature of the concept with no further aid. Such instances could be found, of course; perhaps they would exemplify a pure "discovery method," and perhaps there should be more use of this method than is the case. The fact is that a pure discovery method is seldom used, because it is rather slow and inefficient. Even if a teaching procedure incorporates "discovery" elements, it is likely to be combined with deductive elements. The concept to be taught is described verbally—perhaps by a rule or definition—and the student is expected to attain the concept by learning to make correct identification of positive and negative instances. For example, he is told what an "indirect object" is and then is given practice in identifying the indirect objects (positive instances) among other words (negative instances). Many simple concepts can be taught by a wholly deductive procedure. For most students, the dictionary definition of *tarn* will be a sufficient stimulus for attainment of the concept. On the other hand, it is well known that purely deductive, verbal procedures are frequently insufficient to help learners attain concepts. Concept formation experimentation would be more relevant to school learning problems if it could give more attention to examining the role of verbalization and other deductive procedures in concept attainment.

Nevertheless, there are certain similarities between concept attainment in school and concept formation in psychological experiments. These arise chiefly from the fact that not every concept is learned *solely* in a formalized, prearranged school setting. The school environment is in many ways continuous with the out-of-school environment; concepts are learned partly in school, partly out of school. The process whereby the elementary concepts of a language are learned closely parallels that of the psychological concept formation experiment. A child learns the concept "dog" not by having the concept described to him but by learning to restrict his usage of the word *dog* to instances regarded as positive by the speech community. In this process there are many false responses—either false positives (calling a non-dog a dog) or false negatives (believing a dog to be a non-instance), before an appropriate series of reinforcements produces correct concept attainment. Similar phenomena occur with concepts in the school curriculum. A child who has been told that his cousins visiting him from Peoria are "tourists" may not realize that tourists do not need to be relatives, and when he is told that the Germans who have settled in his town are "immigrants," he may believe that all foreigners visiting his town are immigrants. Concept formation experiments yield information as to the range and variety of instances that have to be furnished for efficient and correct concept formation in the absence of formal instruction.

But if the foregoing statement is true, concept formation studies should also yield insights as to what information has to be furnished for *deductive* concept formation, e.g., from a formal definition. Obviously, a formal definition is successful only to the extent that it correctly identifies and describes all the criterial attributes that are likely to be relevant for a concept, and to the extent that it communicates the proper values and relationships of these to the learner. The burden is both on the definition itself and on the learner. A student may fail to learn the concept *tarn* from the definition previously cited either because it omits some essential criterial attribute (e.g., that a tarn must contain *water* rather than, say, *oil* or *lava*), or because the student fails to comprehend the meaning of its elements (for example, how small is "small"?).

What is actually going on in most school learning of concepts is a process that combines in some way deductive and inductive features.

Descriptions and definitions provide the deductive elements of the process. The several parts of a description or definition specify the attributes and relationships that are criterial for the concept. The order in which these specifications are arranged in the description and presented to the student may have something to do with the ease of concept attainment, particularly in the case of complex concepts with many attributes and complex interrelationships (like the case of *tort* discussed below). As yet we have no well-founded generalizations about the order in which the criterial attributes for a concept should be presented.

At the same time, inductive procedures entail the citing of positive and negative instances of the concept. We know from concept attainment research that learning is facilitated more by positive than by negative instances, even though the "information" conveyed by these instances is the same in a given experimental context. But in real-life concept learning, the number of dimensions that may possibly be relevant is less limited; the function of positive instances is as much to show *which* dimensions are relevant as it is to show what values of them are critical. We may speculate that the real value of what we are calling inductive procedures in concept learning is to afford the learner an opportunity to test his understanding of and memory for the elements of verbal descriptions and definitions. This testing may even involve the construction and testing of alternative hypotheses.

For example, consider the following verbal statement of what a "paradigm" (for research on teaching) is:

"Paradigms are models, patterns, or schemata. Paradigms are not theories; they are rather ways of thinking or patterns for research that, when carried out, can lead to the development of theory."[15]

As a verbal statement, this is hardly adequate; fortunately, Gage proceeds to exhibit a number of positive instances of "paradigms" by which his readers can test out their notions of what this concept might be. Many readers will still have difficulty, however, because he fails to exhibit *negative* instances of paradigms.

What is needed, eventually, is a scientific "rhetoric" for the teaching of concepts—assembled not only from the traditional rhetoric of exposition but also from whatever scientific experiments on concept teaching can tell us. We will be better off, however, if concept-attainment studies begin to give attention to the manner in which real-life, non-artificial concepts can be taught most efficiently—presumably by combination of both deductive and inductive procedures.

ILLUSTRATIONS OF CONCEPT TEACHING PROBLEMS

To suggest the kinds of problems that arise in the teaching of concepts or that might be investigated through formal research, I propose to analyze a small number of concepts of various types, at several levels of difficulty.

Tourist vs. *Immigrant*

A fourth grade teacher reported difficulty in getting her pupils to understand and contrast the meanings of the words *tourist* and *immigrant*. Neither word appears in Dale and Eichholz's[16] list of words known by at least sixty-seven percent of children in the fourth grade, although *tour* (as a sight-seeing trip) was known by seventy percent. In the sixth-grade list, *immigrant* was known by seventy percent and *tourist* by seventy-seven percent; the figures are ninety-

---

[15] N. L. Gage, "Paradigms for Research on Teaching." *Handbook of Research on Teaching*, ed. N. L. Gage (Chicago: Rand McNally, 1963), 94-141.
[16] Edgar Dale and Gerhard Eichholz, *Children's Knowledge of Words* (Columbus: Bureau of Educational Research and Service, Ohio State University, 1960).

seven percent (for *immigration*) and ninety-six percent (for *tourist*) in the 8th-grade list.

To an adult, the differentiation between the concepts designated by *tourist* and *immigrant* looks almost trivially simple. Aside from the sheer memory problem in learning and differentiating the words themselves, what are the sources of confusion for the child? In specific cases, a tourist and an immigrant might have many common characteristics: both might be from a foreign country, or at least from some distance away from the local community; both might be of obviously non-native culture because of dress, complexion, speech, and behavior; both might be doing what would appear to be "sight-seeing," though possibly for different purposes. The differences between a tourist and an immigrant might not be very apparent, being primarily differences of motivation. Indeed, a tourist might become an immigrant overnight, just by deciding to be one.

As we have seen, there is a sense in which the concept-attainment experimental literature is relevant to the child's problem in learning the meanings of the words *tourist* and *immigrant*. If the child is presented with various instances of people who are either tourists or immigrants, properly labeled as such, but with no further explanation, it will be the child's task to figure out what attributes or characteristics are relevant to the differentiation of these concepts. This might occur either in school or outside of school. Most likely the instances of tourists and immigrants will be relatively sporadic over time, and the instances may not vary in such a way as to show what attributes are truly relevant. For example, all the tourists may be obviously American whereas all the immigrants may be obviously Mexican, let us say. The tourists may all be well-dressed, the immigrants poorly dressed, and so on. If the natural environment is like a grand concept-formation experiment, it may take the child a long time to attain the concepts *tourist* and *immigrant*; indeed, the environment may not be as informative as the usual experimenter, since the child may not always be informed, or reliably informed, as to the correctness of his guesses. No wonder a child might form the concept that a tourist is any well-dressed person who drives a station-wagon with an out-of-state license plate!

The purpose of teaching is to short-cut this capricious process of concept attainment within the natural environment. Through the use of language, there should be relatively little difficulty in explaining to a child that an immigrant is one who moves from one country or region to another in order to change his permanent residence, while a tourist is one who travels around for pleasure without changing his permanent residence. One can use simple explanations like: "He's going to stay here, have his home here. . ." or "He's just traveling around for the fun of it while he's on vacation, and someday he'll get back home." There should be no difficulty, at any rate, if the child has already mastered certain prerequisite concepts. Among these prerequisite concepts would be: the concept of home or permanent residence and all that it implies; the concept of the division of world territory into different countries and those in turn into regions; and the concept of traveling for pleasure or curiosity. It is very likely that the child who is having trouble understanding the concept of tourist vs. the concept of immigrant has not got clearly in mind these prerequisite notions that constitute, in fact, the criterial attributes upon which the distinction hangs.

Alternatively, a child might be having trouble because he has not dispensed with irrelevant aspects of these concepts: he might think that a tourist has to be always an American, whereas an immigrant must be a foreigner, because he has seen *American* tourists and *foreign* immigrants, no *American* immigrants nor *foreign* tourists. The ingenious teacher will think of the possible misunderstandings that could arise through the influence of irrelevant attributes of tourists and immigrants.

Time

K. C. Friedman[17] pointed out that elementary school children have much trouble with various time concepts. A child sees no incongruity, for example, in saying, "My older brother was born a long time ago." According to Friedman, it was not until Grade VI that all children in his school could state the date or list the months in perfect order. They had difficulty, he reports, in forming a concept of the "time line" and then in recognizing the placement of various historical events on such a time line. It is easy to see why the child would have these difficulties; even as adults it is difficult for us to appreciate the significance of the fantastically long periods implied by geological time. It should be noted that our concept of a time line is essentially a *spatial* concept whereby we translate temporal succession in terms of spatial order and distances. For a child, time does not flow in a straight line nor in any other particular direction, unless it is around the clock, in a circular or spiral dimension! How can the child form a concept of time and its units? Is time a class of experiences? Does it have criterial attributes? The paradigms of concept-formation experiments do not seem to apply here readily. But let us examine the situation more closely. How can the child have experiences of time and generate the concept of a time line? Certainly there can be experiences of intervals of time —watching a second hand of a clock move through the second-markings, or experiencing the succession of night and day, noticing the change of seasons

17 Kopple C. Friedman, "Time Concepts of Elementary-school Children," *Elem. Sch. J.*, XLIV (1944), 337-342.

or waiting for the end of the school year. Moving from one time period to another could be likened to moving from one square of a sidewalk to the next. It should be an easy transition to thinking of the time line as a sidewalk of infinite extent in both directions—toward the past and toward the future. Marking off the days on the calendar and naming the days and months should help to reinforce this cognitive structure. Extrapolation of the time line is like generalizing these time experiences to all possible such experiences.

One of the difficulties comes, presumably, from the fact that the far reaches of the past and the future cannot be immediately experienced, and one immediately has trouble if one attempts to show a time line that includes historical events in the distant past along with a representation of the relationship between today, yesterday, and the day before yesterday. (Incidentally, it is hard to believe Pistor's[18] claim that young children cannot tell the difference between the present and the past, in view of the fact that they can correctly use the present tenses of verbs in simple situations.) Time lines of different scales must be used, and the concept of scale will itself be hard for children to understand unless it is carefully explained—perhaps by showing maps of the immediate environment in different scales. Only after such ideas have been mastered will it be possible for the child to have any appreciation of such concepts as *year, century, 1492* (as a date), *B.C., generation. Generation* and *eon,* by the way, would have to be introduced as somewhat flexible, arbitrary units of time, as contrasted with fixed, measureable units such as *year* and *century.*

Quantitative expressions like "many," "few," "average"

Ernest Horn[19] pointed out that certain quantitative concepts like *many, few,* and *average* are often so difficult that children do not give reasonable interpretations of them. It is very likely that the source of the difficulty is that children tend not to be able to think in relative terms. Children (and perhaps their teachers) would like to be able to assign definite ranges of numbers for such words as *many, few, average, a sizable amount,* etc., when actually they are all relative terms. There has even been a psychological experiment to demonstrate this: Helson, Dworkin, and Michels[20] showed that adult subjects will consistently give different meanings to a word like "few" when it is put in different contexts. For example, "few" meant about twelve percent on the average, in relation to 100 people, whereas it meant four percent, on the average, in relation to 1,728,583 people.

[18] Frederick Pistor, "Measuring the Time Concepts of Children," *J. Educ. Res.,* XXX (1939), 293-300.

[19] Ernest Horn, *Methods of Instruction in Social Studies* (New York: Scribner, 1937).

[20] Harry Helson, Robert S. Dworkin and Walter C. Michels, "Quantitative Denotations of Common Terms as a Function of Background," *Amer. J. Psychol.,* LXIX (1956), 194-208.

In teaching a child these relational concepts the problem would be to ex-hibit or describe numerous instances in which the absolute base varies but in which the actual numbers of quantities meant would at the same time vary sufficiently to give the impression that these words do not indicate anything like exact amounts. It should be pointed out that 100 things might be "many" in some situations and "few" in others. The use of "average" in such a con-text as "There was an average number of people in church today" can be taught by drawing attention to its relation to the probable extremes of the numbers of people that might be in church, generalizing the concept to other situations like "I caught an average number of fish today." This might lead to the introduction of the average as a statistic or number that gives infor-mation about the "central tendency" of some frequency distribution. It may help to use an unfamiliar or unusual context to bring out this concept in sharp relief. For example, I like to illustrate the utility of the statistical mean or arithmetic average by asking students to imagine that the first space men to reach Mars discover human-like creatures there whose average height is— and this is where the mean becomes really informative—3 inches!

The basic concept of the mean arises in the context of experiences in which there is a plurality of objects measured in some common way. As a first ap-proximation, as far as a child is concerned, the average is a number that is roughly halfway between the highest and lowest measurements encountered, and in some way "typical" of these measurements. Only at some later stage does the child need to learn that the mean is a number that can be computed by a formula and that it has certain properties.

Longitude

It is difficult to understand why E. B. Wesley[21] says that concepts related to the sphericity of the earth, like latitude and longitude, are not easily taught to the average child before Grades VI and VII. Wesley was writing before the advent of the space age when every child knows about space capsules trav-eling around the globe. Though it may still be difficult to get a child to see how the flatness of his immediate environment is only apparent and that the immediate environment corresponds to just a small area on the globe, it can certainly be done, well before Grade VI, through suitable demonstrational techniques. Having established the sphericity of the earth, one should be able to teach latitude and longitude as concepts involved in specifying locations on the globe. Their introduction should properly be preceded by simpler cases in which one uses a system of coordinates to specify location—e.g., equally spaced and numbered horizontal and vertical lines drawn on a blackboard

---

[21] E. B. Wesley and Mary A. Adams, *Teaching Social Studies in Elementary Schools* (Rev. ed.: Boston: D. C. Heath, 1952), p. 307.

with a game to locate letters placed at intersection of lines, a map of one's town or city in which marginal coordinates are given to help locate given streets or places of interest, and finally a Mercator projection map of the world with coordinates of latitude and longitude. Children exposed to the "new math" with its number lines and coordinates should have no trouble with this. Then let us show children by easy stages how a Mercator projection corresponds to the surface of the Earth (certainly an actual globe marked off with latitude and longitude should be used), then how it is necessary to select a particular line (that passes through the Greenwich Observatory) as the vertical coordinate from which to measure, and how the circumference of the earth is marked off in degrees—180° West and 180° East from the Greenwich meridian.

The object is to build for the child a vivid experience of the framework or cognitive structure within which the concept of longitude is defined. The further complications introduced by the use of other kinds of world projections or by the use of regional or even local maps could then be explored. Easily-obtained U.S. Geological Survey maps of one's locality would concretize the meanings of further concepts, e.g., the division of degrees into minutes and seconds, and the fact that a degree of longitude will gradually shrink in length as one moves northward from the equator.

Tort

The concept of *tort* is very likely to be unfamiliar or at least vague to the average reader. Even a dictionary definition[22] may not help much in deciding whether arson, breach of contract, malicious prosecution, or libel are positive instances of torts. The case method used in many law schools, whereby students examine many positive and negative instances of torts in order to learn what they are, is somewhat analogous to a concept formation experiment of the purely inductive variety.

A study[23] of the various laws and decisions relating to torts yields the following approximate and tentative characterization of the concept as having both conjunctive and disjunctive aspects:

$$\text{TORT} = (A+B+C+D+E+F+G+H)\ (I+J)\ (K)\ (-L)\ (-M)\ (-N)\ (-O)$$
where A = battery

      B = false imprisonment

      C = malicious prosecution

      D = trespass to land

[22] The *American College Dictionary* defines *tort* as "a civil wrong (other than a breach of contract or trust) such as the law requires compensation for in damages; typically, a willful or negligent injury to a plaintiff's person, property, or reputation."

[23] For helping me in my treatment of the concepts of *tort* and *mass* I am indebted to my student, Mr. Edward A. Dubois.

E = interference to chattels
F = interference with advantageous relations
G = misrepresentation
H = defamation
 I = malicious intent
 J = negligence
K = causal nexus
 L = consent
M = privilege
N = reasonable risk by plaintiff
O = breach of contract

Within a parenthesis, terms joined by the sign + are mutually disjunctive attributes; a minus sign (–) within a parenthesis signifies "absence of"; the full content of each parenthesis is conjunctive with the content of every other parenthesis. Thus, we can read the formula as follows: "A tort is a battery, a false imprisonment, a malicious prosecution, a trespass to land, . . . , or a defamatory act which is done either with malicious intent or negligently, which exhibits a causal nexus with the injury claimed by the plaintiff, *and* which is done without the plaintiff's consent, *or* without privilege on the part of the defendant, *or* without a reasonable risk by the plaintiff, *or* which is not a breach of contract."

Thus, *tort* turns out to be a concept very much on the same order as *tourist* —a collocation of criterial attributes with both conjunctive and disjunctive features. Deciding whether an act is a tort requires that one check each feature of a situation against what can be put in the form of a formula (as done above). Presumably, a person presented with a properly organized series of positive and negative instances of torts could induce the concept, provided he also understood such prerequisite concepts as *battery, misrepresentation,* etc.

Mass vs. weight

One of the more difficult concepts to teach in elementary physics is that of *mass*. What kind of concept is it and how can one learn it and experience it? How can it be distinguished from the concept of weight? Actually, if we ignore certain subtle questions about mass, such as that of whether inertial and gravitational mass are demonstrably identical, the concept of mass is not as difficult as it might seem; the real difficulty is to teach the sense in which it is different from weight. In fact, weight is perhaps the more difficult concept, because the weight of an object can vary to the point that it can become "weightless."

The concept of mass, one would think, ought to develop for the learner (be he a child or an adult) in much the same way that concepts of other properties of the physical world develop—analogously, that is, to concepts of color, number, and volume. For mass is a property of objects that differentiates them in our experience: there are objects with great mass (like the earth, or a large boulder) and there are objects with small mass (like a feather or a pin or the air in a small bottle), and our experiences of objects with respect to mass can differ enormously, particularly in our proprioceptive senses. Further, mass is a property of objects that is *conserved* regardless of whether the object is in motion or at rest; conservation of mass is learned through experience just as conservation of other properties is learned. Even the physical definition of mass as that property of things which accounts for the relative amount of force which has to be applied to produce a certain amount of acceleration is perceived in common-sense terms as the property of objects that determines the amount of force or effort that one would have to exert to move or lift it. The well-known "size-weight" illusion (in which, for example, we exert an undue amount of effort to lift or push some large but relatively light object) illustrates the fact that our perceptions of an object typically include some impression of its mass. The physical operation of measuring mass by determining the ratio of force to acceleration is an operational extension of the kind of behavior we exhibit when we see how much force it will take to move a heavy trunk.

The real trouble comes in the fact that we are too prone to equate mass with weight, mainly because equal masses also have equal weights when compared by means of a balance, or when measured with a spring balance at the same point on the earth's surface (at least, at the same distance from the earth's center). If we were more easily able to experience the fact that the weight of an object of given mass changes as acceleration due to gravity changes—for example by going to the moon and observing the "weight" of objects there, or by experiencing "weightlessness" in an orbital flight around the earth, weight and mass might be just as easy to distinguish as size and mass. Since such experiences would be rather hard to come by, to put it mildly, we have to be content with the imaginal representation of weight as a *variable* property of objects that really depends upon a relation between the gravitational force exerted on an object and its mass (actually, the product of these two). A child might be made to understand how objects of different masses could have equal "weight"–a relatively large object on the moon and a relatively small one on the earth, for example, as measured by a spring balance which is sensitive to the pull of gravity; or how an object of constant mass would have different weights at different distances from the earth (the pull of gravity thus varying). We would have to conclude that weight, properly speaking, is a relational concept that can only be understood when the total framework in which weight can be defined is described. Mass, on the other hand, is a concept that corresponds much more directly to immediate perceptions of reality.

It will be noted that the teaching of mass and weight concepts involves several prerequisite concepts—e.g., the pull of gravity, the relation between the mass of an object like the earth or the moon and the gravitational force it exerts, and the concept of acceleration. The pull exerted by a magnet could be used for illustrating certain aspects of the concept of gravitational force; a large magnet and a small magnet could represent the respective gravitational pulls of earth and moon; the concept of acceleration can be introduced verbally as "how fast something gets started" and later as an accelerating curve of velocity.

Without really meaning to do so, this discussion of mass and weight has turned out to be a consideration of how such concepts might be taught at relatively early stages—say, somewhere in the elementary school. Nevertheless, some of the same teaching techniques might not be amiss even at high school or college levels. At these levels the chief problem is to give meaning to mathematical formulas such as

$$\text{mass} = \frac{\text{force}}{\text{acceleration}}$$

The implication of this formula, that mass is constant for a given object, can be illustrated by showing with actual physical materials that as force is increased, acceleration is increased proportionately. The effect of increasing mass could be shown by demonstrating that acceleration (roughly indicated by distance traveled against friction) under a constant force diminishes. To a large extent, such experiments can be considered as yielding in precise mathematical terms the relationships that are perceived in every-day experience and that lead to our intuitive understanding of such a concept as mass.

Above all, it should be noted that *mass* is a relational concept, a constant property of objects that reveals itself through the relation between the forces applied to the object and the resultant acceleration. Negative instances can only be properties of objects like weight, size, etc., that are not revealed in this way.

SUMMARY

The basic concern of this paper has been with the teaching of concepts and the relevance of psychological and psycholinguistic theory and experimentation in guiding such teaching.

It has been necessary, first, to point out that concepts are essentially non-linguistic (or perhaps better, *a*linguistic) because they are classes of experience which the individual comes to recognize as such, whether or not he is prompted or directed by symbolic language phenomena. Because the experiences of individuals tend to be in many respects similar, their concepts are also similar, and through various processes of learning and socialization these concepts come to be associated with words. The "meanings" of words are the socially-standardized concepts with which they are associated. One of the problems in teaching concepts is that of teaching the associations between words and concepts, and this is analogous to a paired-associate learning task.

At the same time, new concepts can be taught. One procedure can be called inductive: it consists of presenting an individual with an appropriate series of positive and negative instances of a concept, labeled as such, and allowing him to infer the nature of the concept by noticing invariant features or attributes. This is the procedure followed in the usual concept formation experiment: although our present knowledge allows us to specify several *necessary* conditions for the formation of a concept, we still do not know what conditions are *sufficient*.

Another procedure for concept teaching may be called deductive, and it tends to be the favored procedure in school learning (and, in fact, in all expository prose). It is the technique of presenting concepts by verbal definition or description. This technique has received relatively little attention in psychological experimentation, but it seems to parallel inductive concept attainment in the sense that verbal descriptions are specifications of criterial attributes that can enable the individual to shortcut the process of hypothesis, discovery, and testing that typically occurs in the inductive concept-attainment procedure. Nevertheless, it is not known how relevant our knowledge of critical factors in inductive concept formation is for the guidance of deductive teaching procedures.

It is pointed out, however, that the efficient learning of concepts in school probably involves both inductive and deductive procedures. An analysis of typical concepts of the sort taught in school shows that they do indeed follow the models studied in psychological experimentation, but that they are more likely to involve complex relationships among prerequisite concepts. The difficulties that learners have in attaining a concept are likely to be due to their inadequate mastery of prerequisite concepts and to errors made by the teacher in presenting in proper sequence the information intrinsic to the definition of the concept.

Reading, Writing, and Phonology

CAROL CHOMSKY
Radcliffe Institute and
Harvard University

Drawing on current phonological theory, Carol Chomsky discusses the relationship between conventional orthography and the sound structure of the English language. She argues that this relationship is much closer than is ordinarily assumed and points out that many of the irregularities of English spelling are often motivated by logical rather than arbitrary rules. These rules, she contends, are not always apparent to the ear and eye but reflect deeper systems of organization in the language. Chomsky uses this insight to suggest that reading and spelling instruction should help children construct the underlying correspondences between written and spoken language. These correspondences are best explicated by the systematic study of vocabulary.

The inconsistencies of English spelling are often a source of regret to the reading teacher and to those concerned with reading in general. Because English spelling is frequently not phonetic, because of the large number of words which are lacking in grapheme-phoneme correspondence, it is often concluded that the orthography is irregular and a relatively poor system for representing the spoken language. While it is true that English spelling in many instances is deficient as a phonetic transcription of the spoken language, it does not necessarily follow that it is therefore a poor system of representation. This paper discusses a far more positive view of English orthography which has emerged from recent work in phonological theory within the framework of transformational grammar.

In *The Sound Pattern of English*[1] Chomsky and Halle demonstrate a variety of ways in which the relation of conventional English orthography to the sound structure of the language is much closer than is ordinarily assumed. Simply stated, the conventional spelling of words corresponds more closely to an underlying abstract level of representation within the sound system of the language, than it does to the surface phonetic form that the words assume in the spoken language. Phonological theory, as presented in *The Sound Pattern of English*,

---

[1] N. Chomsky and M. Halle, *The Sound Pattern of English* (New York: Harper & Row, 1968).

Harvard Educational Review Vol. 40 No. 2 May 1970, 287–309

incorporates such an abstract level of representation of words and describes the general rules by which these abstract underlying forms are converted into particular phonetic realizations. English spelling corresponds fairly well to these abstract underlying forms rather than to their phonetic realizations. When viewed in its correspondence to this underlying form, English spelling does not appear as arbitrary or irregular as purely phonetic criteria might indicate. Indeed, from this viewpoint, conventional orthography is seen in its essentials as a "near optimal system for representing the spoken language."[2] In this paper I will attempt to clarify this notion of abstract underlying form, to show its place and function within a grammar of English, and to explain its relation to the spoken language. I will also speculate briefly on the possible relevance of this view of the orthography to reading, the teaching of reading, and the teaching of spelling.

The motivation for postulating an abstract form of words which underlies their phonetic form is roughly as follows. One aspect of writing a grammar for a language is deciding how words are to be represented in the grammar's dictionary, or lexicon. This essentially means deciding on a spelling for each word, what I will call "lexical spelling." One way, obviously, would be to proceed according to pronunciation and use a phonetic transcription, or the type of broad phonetic transcription that is often termed a phonemic transcription. (Those who regret the frequent lack of grapheme-phoneme correspondence in English spelling seem to be looking for just this in the orthography.)

At first glance, this phonetic approach would seem to be the simplest and certainly the most direct way of proceeding. However, the attempt to incorporate into the grammar a spelling system so closely tied to the pronunciation of English immediately runs into trouble. There are numerous reasons why. Let me give one example here. In English, words undergo pronunciation shifts when suffixes are added to them: e.g., the [ey]—[æ] alternation in nation-national, nature-natural, sane-sanity. These pairs of words, because of the vowel alternation, would have to receive two spellings each in a "phonemic" lexicon, each member of the pair constituting a separate lexical item. That is, one spelling would be needed with [ey] for the word in isolation: nation, and another with [æ] for the stem to which certain suffixes are added: nation, -al, -ality, -alistic, etc.

Now these [ey]—[æ] alternations, as it happens, are not isolated cases or irregular occurrences. This type of vowel alternation is very common in English and takes place under specifiable conditions of great generality and wide applicability. It is in fact an integral feature of the phonological system of the language which speakers of English have internalized and which they use automatically in producing and understanding utterances. For we find that the same principles which govern the [ey]—[æ] alternation cited govern also other vowel alterna-

---

[2] N. Chomsky, "Phonology and Reading," in *Basic Studies in Reading*, edited by Levin and Williams (New York: Basic Books, 1970).

tions, such as the [ɪy]—[ɛ] alternation in extr*e*me—extr*e*mity, conv*e*ne-conv*e*n-tion, the [ay]—[ɪ] alternation in exped*i*te-exped*i*tious, w*i*de-w*i*dth, and the [o]—[ɑ] alternation in ph*o*ne-ph*o*nic, comp*o*se-comp*o*site.

Word pairs such as these, though phonetically different, are recognized by speakers of the language as variant forms of the same word. It is revealing, there-fore, when designing the grammar's lexicon, to postulate just one lexical spelling for the vowel, and then to state the general principles which apply to this one shared vowel to produce the two different vowels actually present in the pro-nunciations of the words. The lexical spelling thus acquires the character of an abstract representation, from which the actual phonetic realizations are pre-dictable according to general rules of pronunciation.

This dual feature, of abstract spelling and rules for converting to pronuncia-tion, is a highly desirable feature of a grammar. Among other things, it retains in the lexical spelling similarities which are real in the language. *Nation* and *na-tional* are not different words in the sense that *nation* and *notion* are different words. They are different forms of the same word. For the lexical spelling to cap-ture this sameness, in spite of surface phonetic differences, is highly desirable. Of course this sameness is exactly what is captured by conventional English orthog-raphy in the examples above, where the alternations presented are the familiar long-short vowel alternations. From this viewpoint, this divergence of the con-ventional orthography from phonetic transcription appears well motivated. It offers the advantage of expressing an underlying reality of the language which is masked by surface phonetic features.

In order to clarify the role of the lexical spelling of words within a transforma-tional grammar, let me indicate what place this abstract entity occupies in the grammar. I have said that the lexical spelling is the way words are spelled in the grammar's lexicon. The other components of the grammar that concern us here are the syntactic component and the phonological component. The syntactic com-ponent consists of phrase structure rules and transformational rules. Its output is, among other things, a sentence whose syntactic structure is indicated (see dia-gram below), in which the words are represented in their lexical spelling, just as they come from the lexicon. It is this string of words, together with information about their syntactic structure, that serves as input to the phonological com-ponent. The phonological component in its turn is a complex system of phono-logical rules that apply to this string and convert it into a phonetic representa-tion. This sequence may be diagrammed thus:

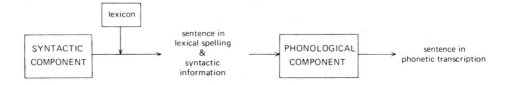

The sentence "We established telegraphic communication," for example, would assume the following forms in the above sequence of operations:

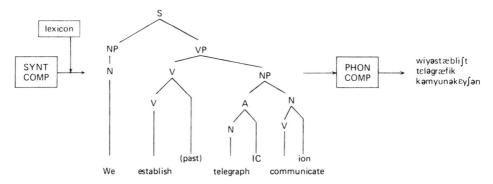

The phonological component contains rules that operate on the lexical spellings, taking into account their syntactic environments, in order to produce a phonetic representation. These are rules that place stress where it belongs, that introduce phonetic effects such as palatalization, velar softening, spirantization, voicing, diphthongization, vowel reduction, vowel shift, laxing and tensing of vowels, and so on. In short, all the rules that make up the phonological system of the language. Their role is to operate on abstract lexical representations within their syntactic context in order to produce the phonetic forms that actually occur in speech.

In producing and interpreting speech, a speaker of the language constantly operates with rules such as these. Certainly he has no conscious knowledge of them any more than he has conscious knowledge of the syntactic rules which enable him to produce and understand sentence structures in his language. In the course of acquiring his language he has internalized the rules of its phonological system, and as a mature speaker he operates in accordance with them both in speaking and in comprehending the spoken language.

Among the interesting decisions that have to be made when designing the grammar is the question of what information properly belongs in the lexical spelling and what should be introduced by the phonological rules. The necessary phonetic output could be achieved with a number of different distributions of information and operations within the grammar. In general, the principle adhered to is that phonetic variation is not indicated in the lexical spelling when it is predictable by general rule. All such predictable phonetic information is left to the phonological rules. As an example, consider the long-short vowel alternations discussed above: nation-national, wide-width, phone-phonic, etc. It is sufficient to use only the long vowel in the lexicon, and to leave it to the phonological rules to shorten this vowel automatically in the presence of certain suffixes. Although the vowel shift could theoretically be introduced either in the lexicon or by the phonological rules, it is preferable to introduce it by phonological rule, as mentioned, for the double reason of expressing the underlying sameness of the vowel, and generality of the feature of vowel shift within the language.

Consider also the common items of words such as *courage/courage-ous,* or *anxi-ous/anxi-ety,* or *photograph/photograph-y/photograph-ic.* Although the phonetic variations are considerable, they are perfectly automatic, and the lexical spellings can ignore them. They will be introduced by the phonological component. Of course, the conventional orthography ignores them as well. These are good examples of cases where the conventional orthography, by corresponding to lexical spelling rather than phonetic representation, permits immediate direct identification of the lexical item in question, without requiring the reader to abstract away from irrelevant phonetic detail. Conventional orthography has itself abstracted away from the phonetic details, and presents the lexical item directly, as it were.

Now it is a feature of English that it has a rich system of phonetic variations which function very much like the vowel alternations discussed. That is, English has many kinds of surface phonetic variations which need not, and preferably ought not, be represented in the lexical spelling of words. They are wholly predictable within the phonological system of the language, and are therefore best introduced within the grammar by means of automatic phonological rules. As with vowel alternation, these other variations obscure an underlying sameness which the lexical spelling is able to capture. And as with vowel alternations, these surface phonetic variations are not reflected in the conventional orthography.

Consider, for example, the extensive system of consonant alternations in English which are surface phonetic variations only. These phonetic variants are expressed neither in the lexical spellings of words in the grammar, nor in the conventional orthography. Such consonant alternations are surprisingly common. Some examples are:

PHONETIC VARIANTS	SAMPLE WORD PAIRS
[k] — [s]	medicate—medicine critical—criticize romantic—romanticize
[g] — [dʒ]	sagacity—sage prodigal—prodigious
[d] — [dʒ]	grade-gradual mode—modular
[t] — [ʃ]	resident—residential expedite—expeditious

[t] — [tʃ]	fac*t*—fac*t*ual
	ques*t*—ques*t*ion
	righ*t*—righ*t*eous
[z] — [ʒ]	revi*s*e—revi*s*ion
[s] — [z]	*s*ign—re*s*ign
	gymna*s*tics—gymna*s*ium

All of these phonetic variations are automatic and predictable within the phonological system of the language. They need not be represented in the lexical spelling of the words, and indeed, underlying similarities which are real in the language would be lost in the grammar if these differences were to be represented on the lexical level. And the same is true of the conventional orthography. By being "unphonetic" in all of these cases, by not exhibiting grapheme-phoneme correspondence, the orthography is able to reflect significant regularities which exist at a deeper level of the sound system of the language, thus making efficient reading easier.

Two other such surface phonetic variations of English, in addition to vowel alternations and consonant alternations, are the interrelated features of stress placement and vowel reduction. Again, these two features are not reflected in the lexical spelling of words because they operate predictably according to rule. The orthography also fails to record them. Surprising as it may seem, the placement of primary stress and the varying degrees of lesser stress in English works largely according to phonological rule, given the lexical spellings of words and information about the syntactic structures in which they appear. Less surprising is the fact that vowel reduction, the pronunciation of certain vowels as a neutral schwa [ə] in unstressed positions, takes place according to rule.

Take, for example, the word *télegraph*. It is stressed on the first syllable. In *telegráphic*, primary stress shifts to the third syllable, and in *telégraphy*, to the second syllable. Since this is a regular variation which many lexical items undergo, and not an unusual feature of this particular word, none of this need be expressed on a lexical level, nor is it expressed in the conventional orthography. It is left to the phonological component of the grammar to introduce these variations.

Consider also the phenomenon of vowel reduction in this same word. The above forms assume the following phonetic shapes in speech:

a)	telegraph	[té lə græf]	
b)	telegraphic	[tɛ lə ǽf]	-ic
c)	telegraphy	[tə lé grəf]	-y

In a) and b) the second vowel is reduced; in c), the first and third vowels. The predictable nature of these variations is discussed by Chomsky and Halle in the following passage from *The Sound Pattern of English*.³

It is quite obvious ... that this phonetic variation (of stress shift and vowel reduction in the three forms of *telegraph*) is not fortuitous—it is not of the same type as the variation between *I* and *we*, which depends on specific assignment of the latter to the category of plurality. Given the grammar of English, if we delete specific reference to the item *we*, there is no way to predict the phonetic form of the plural variant of *I*. On the other hand, the rules for English grammar certainly do suffice to determine the phonetic variation of *telegraph* without specific mention of this lexical item, just as they suffice to predict the regular variation between *cat* and *cats* without specifically mentioning the plural form. It is quite obvious that English grammar is complicated by the fortuitous variation between *I* and *we* but not by the totally predictable variation between *cat* and *cats*. Similarly, the grammar would be more complicated if *telegraph* did *not* undergo precisely the variation in (a)-(c); if, for example, it had one phonetic form in all contexts, or if it had the form (a) in the context -ic, (b) in the context -y, and (c) in isolation.

Once again, surface phonetic variations which are automatic and which obscure similarities in lexical items are not represented at the lexical level (or in the orthography), but are introduced by the phonological component of the grammar.

I have referred several times to the abstract nature of the lexical spellings in the grammar. Now that a number of examples have been given, this abstract character of the lexical level becomes clearer. In the lexical spelling, many predictable phonetic features of the spoken language are suppressed, e.g., vowel alternations, consonant alternations, schwa, stress, and others that I have not gone into. The lexical spelling, and the conventional orthography which corresponds so closely to it, abstract away from these variations in pronunciation and represent deeper similarities that have a semantic function in the language. The lexical items are, after all, the meaning-bearing items in the language. Lexical spellings represent the meaning-bearing items directly, without introducing phonetic detail irrelevant to their identification. Thus on the lexical level and in the orthography, words that *are* the same *look* the same. In phonetic transcription they look different. In reading, one is very likely aided by this feature of the conventional orthography. It permits reading to occur with more efficiency. That is, the spelling system leads the reader directly to the meaning-bearing items that he needs to identify, without requiring that he abstract away from superficial and irrelevant phonetic detail. In speech, on the other hand, one operates on both the abstract and the phonetic levels, with the phonological rules mediating between the two.

³ Chomsky and Halle, *op. cit.*, pp. 11-12.

It seems also that this abstract lexical level is highly resistant to historical change, and remains the same over long periods of time. Pronunciation shifts that occur as a language changes over time appear to be the result of changes in phonological rules rather than changes in the lexical spellings themselves. For this reason a stable orthography remains effective over time in spite of changes in the way a language is pronounced. And it appears that a wide range of dialect differences also stem from adjustments of phonological rules rather than differences in lexical spellings. This would explain why conventional English orthography is a reasonably adequate system of representation for both British and American English, and the vast range of English dialects that exist within each country and around the world.

Given that lexical spellings differ from phonetic representations in the numerous ways just illustrated, the question naturally arises what implications this may have for speakers of the language and their internal organization of its sound system. Are these abstract lexical representations that are postulated by the linguist merely convenient fictions that the linguist manufactures for the purposes of his grammar, or do they have a psychological reality for the language user? In other words, is the claim that the orthography corresponds to something real in the linguistic knowledge of the reader based on anything that the reader can honestly be said to know?

It seems to me that in a very real sense the lexical level of representation and the corresponding aspects of English orthography do have a psychological reality for the language user. I realize that this assertion will be troublesome to many readers, so let me be very specific about what I mean. I spoke above of the "common item" of words such as *anxi-ous/anxi-ety*, and *courage/courage-ous*. Pairs such as *critic-al/critic-ize*, *revis-e/revis-ion*, *illustrat-e/illustrat-ive* also contain common items. There is little question that speakers recognize these words as related. But clearly what is common to these pairs is not their *surface* form, their phonetic representation, for they are pronounced differently:

anxi - ous : $[\acute{æ}\eta k\int]$
anxi - ety : $[æ\eta gz\acute{a}y]$
courage   : $[k\acute{\Lambda}r\partial d\bar{3}]$
courage - ous : $[k\partial r\acute{e}yd\bar{3}]$
critic - al : $[kr\acute{\imath}t\imath k]$
critic - ize : $[kr\acute{\imath}t\imath s]$
revis - e   : $[riv\acute{a}yz]$
revis - ion : $[riv\acute{\imath}\bar{3}]$
illustrat - e   : $[\acute{\imath}l\partial str\varepsilon yt]$
illustrat - ive : $[\imath l\acute{\Lambda}str\partial t]$

What is common to them, as was shown earlier, is their *underlying* form, their lexical spelling, which the orthography corresponds to quite closely. To say that this form has psychological reality is to say only that this common item is recognized by the language user *as a common item,* and that its different phonetic realizations are regular within the sound system of the language. The variations in the pairs listed above are not idiosyncratic within the grammar, as is for example the variation between *woman* and *women,* but take place according to general phonological rule. These variations are automatic and do not complicate the grammar in any way. Indeed they would complicate the grammar if they did *not* occur precisely the way they do.

To look at it another way, one might consider, for example, the status of the [k]-[s] alternation in *kill/sill* as compared to *medicate/medicine.* The difference in status can readily become clear to one who knows the language. In *kill/sill* the phonetic change from [k] to [s] creates a new lexical item. It is both a phonetic and a lexical change. But in *medicate/medicine* it is a phonetic change only. The lexical item remains the same, as does the lexical spelling and the orthography. A speaker who is not aware of this differing status of the two [k]-[s] alternations can have the difference brought to the level of awareness without difficulty, because it reflects a fact about his language that he uses continually, and that is far more general than this one example. In order to become aware of this fact he does not need to be taught it, as a foreigner learning English would, but merely to have it brought to his attention.

The implications of this view of English orthography with regard to reading are several. First, it implies that what the mature reader seeks and recognizes when he reads is not what are commonly called grapheme-phoneme correspondences, but rather the correspondence of written symbol to the abstract lexical spelling of words. Letters represent segments in lexical spelling, not sounds. It is the phonological rule system of the language, which the reader commands, that relates the lexical segments to sounds in a systematic fashion.

Stated somewhat differently, the mature reader does not proceed on the assumption that the orthography is phonetically valid, but rather interprets the written symbols according to lexical spellings. His task is facilitated by the fact that the orthography closely corresponds to this lexical representation. He does not need to abstract away from unnecessary phonetic detail to reconstruct this lexical representation as would be required if the English spelling system were phonetically based. What he needs to identify are the lexical items, the meaning-bearing items, and these are quite readily accessible to him from the lexically based orthography.

It is highly likely that the child, however, in the beginning stages of reading, does assume that the orthography is in some sense "regular" with respect to pronunciation. In order to progress to more complex stages of reading, the child must abandon this early hypothesis, and come eventually to interpret written symbols as corresponding to more abstract lexical spellings. Normally he is able to make this transition unaided as he matures and gains experience both with the sound structure of his language and with reading. It may be, however, that the difficulty encountered by some poor readers is related to the fact that they have not made this crucial transition. This question should be amenable to study. If it appears that this is indeed a factor for some poor readers, then a second related question can be raised, namely how to encourage this progress in children who have not achieved it on their own.

Most methods of teaching reading have little or nothing to offer with respect to this shift in emphasis from a phonetic to a lexical interpretation of the spelling system. Beginning reading instruction that deals analytically with letters and sounds, whether it is based on phonics, the linguistic method, or any other method, tends to treat phonetically accurate spellings as regular in the language, and phonetic inaccuracies as irregular. Children translate spellings into sounds by means of letter-sound correspondences or spelling patterns without ever being expected to apply their knowledge of the phonological system of English to the task. They learn to decode written English much as a foreigner would who knows nothing of English phonology. The child thus gains the impression that spelling is meant to be a direct representation of the pronounced form of words. No provision is made at any point for having him revise this notion in favor of a more realistic view of spelling regularity based on word relationships and underlying lexical similarities. It would seem wise to take this view of regularity into account in dealing with reading beyond the introductory stages. At some point emphasis ought to be shifted away from the phonetic aspects of spelling to a consideration of the underlying lexical properties of the orthographic system. Crucial to this shift in emphasis is the expectation that the child will rely more and more heavily on phonological processing as he learns to decode written English more efficiently.

In practice, this could take the form of discussing "word families" with children, and bringing out the variety of pronunciations associated in a regular way with individual spellings. As soon as the children's vocabulary permits, they could take up words like *major-majority, history-historical-historian, nature-natural,* etc., to see how one and the same root changes its pronunciation as different endings are added to it. They might even profitably be introduced to the idea of the abstractness of spelling by considering that the root alone doesn't really have a specific pronunciation until you know what ending goes with it. For example, *natur-* and *histor-* are recognizable roots, but they need to have endings before you can tell which pronunciation is intended.

In this connection it might be helpful if the teacher of reading were aware that words whose spelling is phonetically accurate do not constitute a distinct and meaningful category in the language. They are not the only systematically spelled words in the language, as is often believed. All words whose conventional spelling is close to their abstract lexical spelling are spelled systematically, and this is the more meaningful category. Within this larger category are words whose spelling is close to pronunciation, and many whose spelling is more distant from pronunciation. The former are phonetically spelled words such as *mat* and *pin,* and the latter are words such as *explanation, courage,* and *resign* which require more extensive phonological processing. The important point is that they are all spelled systematically, given the sound structure of English. Exceptions are words which fall outside the system, i.e., whose conventional spelling displays aspects which bear little relation to their abstract lexical spelling and which appear unmotivated and arbitrary from a phonological point of view. These are words such as *freight, sword, guard,* and the like.

It is of interest to realize that the child, when he learns to read, is not being introduced to a system of representation that is inconsistent with the language that he speaks. It is simply that the orthography bears an *indirect* rather than a direct relation to his pronunciation. The direct correlation is to lexical spelling, a level of linguistic processing that is beneath the surface, related to pronunciation by regular phonological rules that are part of the child's normal linguistic equipment. This correspondence can be diagrammed as follows:

$$\text{LETTERS} = \text{segments in} \underset{\text{lexical spelling}}{\overset{\text{phonological rules}}{\longleftarrow - - - - - - - - - \longrightarrow}} \text{PRONUNCIATION}$$

Letters correspond to segments in lexical spelling, which in turn are related to pronunciation through the medium of the phonological rules. The correspondence is to something real in the child's linguistic system that he is equipped to handle. It is because it is one step removed from his pronunciation that it is not superficially apparent.

To make this point clearer, consider the role that knowing the language plays for an adult in reading English aloud. The written form *photograph,* for example, is convertible into a particular phonetic configuration, with primary stress on the first syllable, lesser stress on the third syllable, second syllable unstressed, reduced second vowel, and full vowel quality expressed by the first and third vowel. The adult speaker of English is able to utilize elementary letter-sound correspondences to recognize the basic morphological components of the word, *foto-græf,* and then to superimpose all the above phonetic information on these components *because he knows the language* and can apply its phonological rule system. Add the written suffix *-y* to this form: *photography,* and the phonetic information which he superimposes is radically different: primary stress on second syllable, first and third syllables unstressed, reduced first and third vowels, full vowel quality of second vowel. He converts to different phonetic configurations in the two cases *because of phonological knowledge which he brings to the reading situation, not because of anything that is explicit in the orthography.* He does not have to be told how to apply stress and change vowel quality in these forms because he already knows.

61

On the other hand, a foreigner who knows no English but has learned the elementary letter-sound correspondences of the English alphabet will be unable to do this. Knowing nothing of the language, such a foreigner finds himself in a very different position when he tries to pronounce these two words. Lacking the necessary information about English phonology, he will read phonetically, and pronounce *photograph* alike in both contexts. What the foreigner lacks is just what the child already possesses, a knowledge of the phonological rules of English that relate underlying representations to sound. To be sure, the child (or adult) has no awareness of this knowledge, and would be hard pressed to bring it to the level of awareness. But of course there is no need to do so. It works automatically and enables English speakers to manage well with an orthography that in a sense tells them what they need to know and leaves the rest to them.

The ability of the child to interpret the orthography directly at the lexical level should increase naturally as his phonological competence increases and as he becomes more familiar with the relations expressed by the spellings of words. The full phonological system of English depends heavily on a learned stratum of vocabulary, including Latinate forms and a network of affixes which account for a large portion of surface phonetic variations. As the maturing child comes to control these forms in the spoken language, he internalizes both their underlying representations and the phonological rules which relate the latter to pronunciations. This process of internalization depends in part on recognizing the relevant similarities in words which are pronounced differently. It is no doubt facilitated in many cases by an awareness of how words are spelled. Thus the underlying system which the child has constructed from evidence provided by the spoken language and which contributes to his ability to interpret the written language may itself be improved by his increased familiarity with the written language.

Another aspect of progress in reading relates to the freedom that the reader has, given the lexical nature of the orthography, to avoid phonological processing as he reads. Earlier I pointed out an advantage of the lexically based orthography: the reader does not have to abstract away from unnecessary phonetic detail to reconstruct the lexical representation of words. It is also true that he does not have to carry out the inverse activity. He does not have to construct phonetic forms from the underlying lexical forms presented by the orthography. Silent reading may take place primarily at the lexical level, without requiring the experienced reader to convert to the surface phonetic level. If he wishes to convert to phonetic representation, as for example in reading aloud, he does so through the automatic application of the phonological rules of the language. But this phonological processing may be minimal in rapid silent reading. Indeed, it may be that part of learning to read rapidly and well is learning to dispense with the application of phonological rules. Experienced readers probably engage in varying degrees of phonological processing depending on the type of material they are reading and the reading speed they employ at any given time. But they have learned how to dispense with a good deal of the phonological processing when they wish to. Less skilled readers may not have acquired this ability. Children probably do pronounce to themselves while they are still inexperienced at reading, and only later begin to be able to relinquish this phonological processing. It is likely that with increasing experience they gradually come to exploit the lexical nature of the orthography more and more effectively. Certainly there would seem to be no need to deal with words at the surface phonetic level, given an orthography that directly represents the underlying form of words. Children's reading, therefore, ought to improve as the amount of phonological processing that they engage in decreases.

From this point of view, reading aloud would seem to be of questionable value in improving silent reading. In the very early stages of reading, when the child reads primarily phonetically, there is probably little difference between the two, and oral reading is useful as a check on what the child is actually doing. But as the child progresses to the point where he begins to interpret lexical representations directly from the orthography, he ought to be encouraged to give up converting these lexical representations to phonetic ones. Phonological processing at this point would be a hindrance rather than a help. Skilled silent reading, as pointed out above, can bypass the phonological rules to some extent or even entirely. By the nature of the orthography it never needs to bring them into play. But reading aloud does require their full application. Reading aloud burdens the experienced reader doubly. It is not only that he has to engage in the motor activity of pronouncing what he has read. In order to pronounce it, he must first engage in the mental activity of determining the full phonetic characteristics of what he has read. That is, instead of performing a minimum of phonological processing as in silent reading, he must perform the maximum when reading aloud. Since phonological processing is essentially extraneous to the mature reading process, it would seem ill-advised to focus children's attention on it when they are finally beginning to read "lexically." The teacher may wish to develop oral reading for its own sake, of course, independent of silent reading. But she should keep in mind the possibility that practice in oral reading may have little positive effect on the child's abilities in silent reading, and may even encourage him to persist in aspects of unskilled silent reading that he ought to be leaving behind.

An interesting and important question which is raised by this view of sound structure and reading concerns the age at which the child achieves a mature command of the phonological structure of his language. It is quite possible, perhaps most likely, that full knowledge of the sound system that corresponds to the orthography is not yet possessed by the child of six or seven, and may indeed be acquired fairly late. Chomsky puts it this way:[4]

[4] Chomsky, N., *op. cit.*

The conventional orthography corresponds closely to a level of representation that seems to be optimal for the sound system of a fairly rich version of ... spoken English. Much of the evidence that determines, for the phonologist, the exact form of this underlying system is based on considerations of learned words and complex derivational patterns. It is by no means obvious that a child of six has mastered this phonological system in full. He may not yet have been presented with the evidence that determines the general structure of this system. . . . It would not be surprising to discover that the child's intuitive organization of the sound system continues to develop and deepen as his vocabulary is enriched and as his use of language extends to wider intellectual domains and more complex functions. Hence the sound system that corresponds to the orthography may itself be a late intellectual product.

A serious possibility, following from these hypotheses, is that one of the important ways to improve reading might be to enrich the child's vocabulary so as to enable him to construct for himself the underlying representations of sound that correspond so closely to the written form. As far-fetched as this possibility may seem at first, it ought to be given serious consideration in light of the close tie that exists between English phonology and English orthography. The orthography assumes a fairly sophisticated degree of internal organization of the sound system of the language. Extending the child's vocabulary to include Latinate forms and polysyllabic derived forms is one of the best ways to provide him with the means of constructing the phonological system of his language more fully as he matures. He ought to become familiar with word groups such as *industry-industrial, major-majority, history-historical-historian, wide-width, sign-signature,* etc., and have their relationships made explicit for him. In general, connections should be brought out among words that he already knows but may not yet have classified together, and new words should be introduced for the purpose of establishing new connections. His awareness of these relationships and the variant phonetic forms that words assume in different contexts will facilitate and accelerate his internalization of the phonology of his language.

Literacy acquisition from this point of view may well extend over a much longer period of time than ordinarily assumed, and be closely interrelated with these other aspects of the child's linguistic development. Although little is known at the present time about the child's acquisition of these deeper aspects of the sound structure of English, it is certainly likely that it continues well into the school years. It would be interesting to try to assess the child's implicit knowledge of this phonological system at various stages of his development. An attempt might also be made to determine the degree to which advances in reading ability form part of this same process of development. It would not be at all surprising, perhaps for adults as well as children, if those who control the sound system of English better also exploit its orthography more effectively.

Spelling is another area of interesting practical application of this view of the orthography. In the case of spelling it seems to me that the major contribution might be to the teacher's own assumptions about the orthography. If she works on the assumption that spelling corresponds to something real, *that it makes sense,* she will encourage the child to recognize and exploit the regularities that do exist. If she is familiar with some of the more obvious regularities it will help, but basically she and the children can work together to characterize regularities, armed primarily with their joint knowledge of the language as native speakers, and the recognition that the conventional spelling system does in fact have a great deal to recommend it.

To start, there are quite specific things that can be pointed out to children who need help, so that they may approach the stage that good spellers seem to reach on their own. Good spellers, children and adults alike, recognize that related words are spelled alike even though they are pronounced differently. They seem to rely on an underlying picture of the word that is independent of its varying pronunciations. And when encountering a troublesome word, they are in the habit of automatically putting to use the idea that related words may vary a good deal in their pronunciation, but that the spelling by and large remains the same. When they are not sure how to spell a particular word, the first thing that they do is bring to mind other related words in the hope of finding one that contains the solution. If it is a reduced vowel that is causing the trouble, a differently stressed variant of the word will often provide the answer. For example, there is no way to guess the second vowel of *industry* from the pronunciation of the word, but thinking of *industrial* solves the problem. And this is often the case with reduced vowels.

After all, how *do* we know that the second vowel of *declaration, inspiration* and *adoration* are written differently, when they are pronounced exactly alike? Obviously because of *declare, inspire,* and *adore.* We do not have to memorize the spellings of *declaration, inspiration,* and *adoration,* but merely be able to make the connection in each case to the related verb. Once the connection is clear, the correct spelling is automatic.

If the child develops the habit of seeking such connections, of thinking of related words that settle his spelling uncertainties for him, he not only spells better, but in the long run he familiarizes himself with the general underlying regularities of the orthography. Instead of memorizing individual words one after the other, he equips himself with the systematic means of dealing with large segments of vocabulary.

The examples which follow suggest several types of "spelling lessons" that can be constructed to bring out a number of these features of the spelling system. These samples are intended primarily to indicate a general approach. In practice, of course, vocabulary would have to be adapted to the abilities of individual classes.

Children could be asked, for example, to fill in the missing reduced vowel in a list such as column (1), and then to justify their choices by thinking of related words which retain vowel quality. They would then produce something like column (2).

(1)	(2)
dem_cratic	democracy
pres_dent	preside
prec_dent	precede
comp_rable	compare, comparison
comp_sition	composer, compose
hist_ry	historical, historian
janit_r	janitorial
manag_r	managerial
maj_r	majority
ill_strate	illustrative
ind_stry	industrial
imm_grate	migrate
cons_lation	console
ab_lition	abolish
comp_tent	compete

Or, simply given column (2), they could be asked to think up other forms of the words, and to characterize the specific ways in which the vowel sounds shift around. Anything that focuses their attention on related words and concomitant pronunciation shifts ought to be good practice for finding specific related words when they need them.

This approach works not only for recovering the full form of reduced vowels, but often for selecting the correct consonant from a choice of two when pronunciation is ambiguous. For example, in column (1), the italicized consonant could, given its pronunciation, be written using either of the letters in parentheses. The related word in column (2) narrows the choice to just one of these.

(1)		(2)
criti*c*ize	(c, s)	critical
medi*c*ine	(c, s)	medical
na*t*ion	(t, sh)	native
gra*d*ual	(d, j)	grade
righ*t*eous	(t, ch)	right
ra*c*ial	(t, c, sh)	race

Another helpful exercise involves consonants which are silent in some words but pronounced in others. For example:

(1)	(2)
mus*c*le	mus*c*ular
si*g*n, (desi*g*n)	si*g*nature, si*g*nal (desi*g*nate)
bom*b*	bom*b*ard
condem*n*	condem*n*ation
mali*g*n	mali*g*nant
sof*t*en	sof*t*

Children could be given column (2) and asked to think of related words in which the underlined consonant becomes silent. Or, conversely, they could be given column (1) and asked to think of related words in which the silent consonant is recovered phonetically. Or they could be given the words in column (1) orally and asked to name the silent consonant. For those who can't do it, the column (2) word can be elicited or, if necessary, pointed out as helpful evidence.

The need for practice in this sort of thinking seems to be quite strong for some children. This was brought home to me recently by a conversation that I had about some of these silent consonants with a seventh-grade girl, a child of average intelligence but a poor speller. The conversation went like this:

What letter is silent in the word "muscle"?
  E.
Ok, you're right. But how about a *consonant* that's silent?
  I don't know. There isn't any.
Well, how do you spell "muscle"?
  M-u-s-l-e
There's something left out. What do you call a man who has a lot of muscles?
  Strong
Yes, but what do you call him that's related to the word "muscle"?
  I don't know.
Did you ever hear the word "muscular"?
  Yeah, I guess so.
Well, how do you spell "muscular"?
  M-u-s-c- . . .
That's all you need. So how do you spell "muscle"?
  M-u-c . . .
Wait. How does "muscular" begin?
  M-u-s-c . . .
Ok. Now "muscle."
  M-u-s-c-l-e . .

It was a struggle, but she got there. The next try showed how little understanding she had of the idea that words are actually connected to each other in meaning and form, even words that she was perfectly familiar with.

How do you spell "sign"?
    S-i-g-h-n
What do you call it when you sign your name?
    Your signature.
How do you spell "signature"?
    S-i-g-n . . .
Ok. So how do you spell "sign"?
    S-i-g-h-n
But you just told me that "signature" begins with *S-I-G-N . . !*
    So what's one got to do with the other?

This is the sort of thing that needs attention if a child is to improve his spelling. Better spelling is not a matter of individual words (S-i-g-h-n on the analogy of *sigh* is actually a pretty good try as an isolated word.), but will come about as an outgrowth of an understanding and awareness of the relationships between words.

Still another type of exercise involves consonant alternations which occur not only in the pronunciation of words, but are reflected in the orthography as well. For example, the letter *t* and *c* alternate in many word pairs:

(1)	(2)
coinciden*t*al	coinciden*c*e
pira*t*e	pira*c*y
presiden*t*	presiden*c*y
presen*t*	presen*c*e
residen*t*	residen*c*e
luna*t*ic	luna*c*y
democra*t*ic	democra*c*y

It helps to recognize the general pattern, for it resolves the question of how to spell the pronounced [s] of column (2). *Presidency* is spelled with *c* and not *s* because it is related to *president, presence* is related to *present,* and so on. The *t-c* alternation is general enough so that being aware of it can be useful.

It is interesting to note that this *t-c* orthographic alternation, which is phonetically a [t]-[s] alternation, is a phonologically predictable alternation. It requires only one underlying lexical spelling, with *t.* I.e., the *t* of the underlying form of *pirate* automatically becomes phonetic [s] in the context *-y,* so that instead of [payrətiy], the phonological rules produce [payrəsiy]. By the same rules *president* + *y* becomes [prɛ zə dən siy], and so on. The orthography chooses to reflect this phonetic change in the case of [t] → [s] whereas it ignores many other such automatic phonetic changes, as we have seen. For example, it does not reflect the phonetic change [k] → [s] as in *medical-medicine*. When the orthography reflects a phonetic change such as [t] → [s] in *pirate-piracy* it corresponds to an internal level of representation which is not as abstract as the lexical level. Some phonological processing has already been applied to the lexical spelling to produce the phonetic variants indicated by the orthography.

Exercises such as these are to be construed as samples of a particular approach which can be extended as the need arises. However, it is perhaps much more to the point for the teacher to develop a way of dealing with spelling errors that the children produce day by day than to equip herself with preselected word lists. Most important is that she transmit to the child the notion that spelling very often is not arbitrary, but rather corresponds to something real that he already knows and can exploit. A good way to handle misspellings that come up in class is to search with the child for a systematic reason why the word should be spelled the way it is, if indeed one can be found. In many cases, such a reason can be found. Often this will mean simply bringing a relation between two familiar words to the child's attention. To use some examples drawn from the spontaneous writing of a group of 3rd and 4th graders, the child who misspells *president* as *presedent* needs to have pointed out that it is related to *preside*. The child who misspells *really* as *relly* needs to think of *reality* to get it right. *Apon* is more likely to be written *upon* if the child realizes that it is a combination of *up* and *on*. *Immagrate* will become *immigrate* if it is connected with *migrate*. *Medisin* will lose the *s* and acquire a *c* if it is connected to *medical*.

Sometimes a related word that could help settle the difficulty for the child is a word that he doesn't know. *Illustrative*, for example, may not be part of the vocabulary of the child who writes *illastrate* for *illustrate*. In such cases, it may make better sense to introduce the new word than to have him memorize a seemingly arbitrary spelling for his familiar word.

Exploiting opportunities that come up naturally in class is certainly one of the most dynamic ways of fitting words into context and developing the idea of word relationships. This can be exciting and can really increase children's language sense if undertaken by a teacher who enjoys etymologies and who is sensitive to language herself. Herbert Kohl's excellent description of just such a beginning and where it can lead in *36 Children*[5] is one of the best examples I have seen recently of how meaningfully this can be done. Starting with one child's use of the word "psyches" as an insult (The children visualized this word as s-i-k-e-s.), he led the class into a discussion of etymologies, Greek myth, word meanings, and word relationships. It caught on. Over a period of time the undertaking was extended to include word origins more generally, the question of how words acquire

[5] Herbert Kohl, *36 Children* (New York: The New American Library, 1967), pp. 23-29.

their meanings, and even a consideration of historical change and the notion of "right" and "wrong" in language in a descriptive vs. prescriptive framework.

The general conclusion to be derived from the view of the orthography presented here is that spelling, far more often than it seems from a purely phonetic standpoint, does make sense. Many spelling errors could be avoided if the writer developed the habit of looking for regularities that underlie related words when in doubt. This is part of the strategy used by good spellers as a matter of course. For the child who spells poorly it is far more productive to learn how to look for these regularities than simply to memorize the spellings of words as isolated examples. Providing him with a strategy based on the realities of the language is clearly the best way to equip him to deal with new examples on his own.

It would be less than realistic to close this discussion of the regularities of English spelling without a glance at the other side of the coin. English spelling does after all have its less consistent aspects. To restore a sense of balance I offer the following passage in conclusion.

Hints on Pronunciation for Foreigners[6]

I take it you already know
Of tough and bough and cough and dough?
Others may stumble but not you,
On hiccough, thorough, laugh and through.
Well done! And now you wish, perhaps,
To learn of less familiar traps?

Beware of heard, a dreadful word
That looks like beard and sounds like bird,
And dead: it's said like bed, not bead—
For goodness' sake don't call it "deed"!
Watch out for meat and great and threat
(They rhyme with suite and straight and debt.)

A moth is not a moth in mother
Nor both in bother, broth in brother,
And here is not a match for there
Nor dear and fear for bear and pear,
And then there's dose and rose and lose—
Just look them up—and goose and choose,
And cork and work and card and ward,
And font and front and word and sword,
And do and go and thwart and cart—

---

[6] From a letter published in the *London Sunday Times* (January 3, 1965), from J. Bland. Cited by Mackay and Thompson, "The Initial Teaching of Reading and Writing," *Programme in Linguistics and English Teaching*, Paper no. 3, University College, London, and Longmans Green and Co., Ltd., London and Harlow, 1968, p. 45.

Come, come, I've hardly made a start!
A dreadful language? Man alive.
I'd mastered it when I was five.

T. S. W.
(only initials of writer known)

Two Functions of Language

CAROL FLEISHER FELDMAN

Elkton, Virginia

For many years scholars have debated the question of the source of meaning in language. In this article Carol Feldman advocates the view that meaning is necessarily dependent upon the communicative function of language and examines the objections, particularly those of Noam Chomsky, to this view. She argues that while Chomsky disagrees with the idea that communication is the essential function of language, he implicitly agrees that it has a function. Feldman discusses in detail Chomsky's examples of noncommunicative functions of language and maintains that each of his examples represents fundamentally communicative uses. Contrary to Chomsky, she concludes that the meaning-determining rules of language can only be understood by reference to the function of communication.

For several decades scholars subscribing to two distinct conceptions of meaning have been engaged in a heated debate. The controversy has been between scholars who claim that meaning can only be understood by reference to communication and those who reject this claim. In his landmark paper "Meaning and Truth," Strawson (1971) refers to the two positions as the "communication-intention" view and the "formal semantics" view. He summarizes the difference between the two positions as follows:

> Where they differ is as to the relations between the meaning-determining rules of the language, on the one hand, and the function of communication, on the other: one party [the communication-intention theorists] insists, and the other [theorists of formal semantics] (apparently) refuses to allow, that the general nature of those rules can be understood only by reference to this function. (p. 176)

One reason for the longevity of the debate may be that the dispute has not been clearly formulated. In particular, it is not yet evident what either side would have to show in order to prove the other side wrong. As a first step toward reformulating the debate, I will outline the positions of the communication-intention theorists and the theorists of formal semantics. Necessarily, these reviews will be both incomplete and abbreviated. Then I will propose that the central claim of the communication-intention theorists—that meaning depends upon communicative function—must be clearly separated into two component claims:

Harvard Educational Review   Vol. 47   No. 3   August 1977, 282–293

that meaning depends on function and that communication is the essential function of language. I will next consider each of these claims separately and evaluate the second one in detail, with special attention to Chomsky's (1975) objections.

It has been fashionable in recent years to talk as if the debate between theorists of formal semantics and theorists of communication-intention was born with the publication of Chomsky's *Syntactic Structures* (1957). Strawson (1971), however, reminds us that the debate has a long history in this century. In the 1930s the philosophers whom he calls theorists of formal semantics held positions on meaning similar to the one Chomsky subsequently took. Indeed, these theorists dominated the philosophy of language in Britain in the period between the two world wars (see, for example, Urmson's interesting discussion [1956]). The communication-intention view of meaning developed in response to the work of earlier formal semanticists. Its main thrust was to overturn the formal semanticists' account of meaning and to replace it with a revolutionary view that had far-reaching consequences in the philosophy of language.

The Position of the Communication-Intention Theorists

The essential insight of the communication-intention theorists was that meaning is a property not of sentences but, rather, of their use. Once a wide variety of sentences was examined, it was seen that certain aspects of meaning, called "emotive" meaning,[1] could not be understood without reference to the speaker. To the communication-intention theorists this observation seemed to reveal a central fact about language, but the theorists of formal semantics saw it as revealing only that there were exceptions to the general rule. The formal semanticists held essentially that: language is used to describe states of affairs; the meaning of a description is exhausted by its truth-value—that is, whether it correctly describes a state of affairs or not; truth-value is an inherent property of sentences, not a property of the use of sentences; and therefore the meaning of sentences does not depend on use.[2]

Against this line of argument, the communication-intention theorists presented many kinds of sentences that were evidently not used to describe states of affairs and whose meaning evidently did not reside in their truth-value, since they

---

1 Jakobson (1972) defines emotive meaning in the following passage:

The so-called EMOTIVE or "expressive" function, focused on the ADDRESSER, [speaker], aims a direct expression of the speaker's attitude toward what he is speaking about. It tends to produce an impression of a certain emotion whether true or feigned; therefore, the term "emotive," launched and advocated by Marty . . . has proved to be preferable to "emotional." (p. 90)

2 Donald Davidson (1970), a contemporary exponent of a version of this view, says:

A theory of the semantics of a natural language aims to give the meaning of every meaningful expression, but it is a question what form a theory should take if it is to accomplish this. . . . I suggest that a theory of truth for a language does, in a minimal but important respect, do what we want, that is, give the meanings of all independently meaningful expressions on the basis of an analysis of their structure. (p. 177)

did not have a truth-value. Among these sentences were questions, commands, and requests. Although the theorists of formal semantics tended to acknowledge that such sentences posed a problem for their theory, they saw these sentences, too, as aberrant. This argument eventually led the communication-intention theorists to turn their attention to the crucial descriptive sentences that best illus-trated the formal semanticists' theory of meaning. The communication-intention theorists sought to show that even the meaning of standard descriptive sentences depends on use. Austin (1962) gave a particularly clear argument for the claim that truth-value itself depends on use:

> Suppose that we confront "France is hexagonal" with the facts, in this case, I suppose, with France, is it true or false? Well, if you like, up to a point; of course I can see what you mean by saying it is true for certain intents and purposes. It is good enough for a top-ranking general, perhaps, but not good enough for a geo-grapher. (p. 143)

Austin's argument, and others like it, showed that even bald descriptions, sen-tences whose meanings were apparently exhausted by their truth-value, are not absolutely true or false. Truth-value is not a property of sentences at all (nor, therefore, of their structure). Rather, truth-value depends on the use to which sentences are put. The communication-intention theorists argued that if this is the case for truth-value, *a fortiori* it must be the case for other aspects of meaning; thus, the meaning of all sentences depends on use.

According to the communication-intention theorists, a speaker may use sen-tences in many different ways, but in every case the speaker has audience-directed intentions. In other words, all uses of sentences serve one or another com-municative purpose. The essential function of language, then, is communication. Since the meaning of a sentence depends on use and all uses are communicative, the meaning-determining rules of language can only be understood with reference to the function of communication. For example, Searle (1972) states: "The purpose of language is communication in much the same sense that the purpose of the heart is to pump blood. In both cases it is possible to study the structure independently of function but pointless and perverse to do so, since structure and function so obviously interact" (p. 16).

The Position of One Theorist of Formal Semantics, Noam Chomsky

Noam Chomsky, a theorist of formal semantics, has attempted to study the structure of language independent of function and meaning independent of use. In general, he has been concerned to describe just those features of language that are invar-iant across uses:

> So far, the study of language has progressed on the basis of a certain abstraction: Namely, we abstract away from conditions of use of language and consider formal structures and the formal operations that relate them. Among these formal struc-tures are those of syntax, namely, deep and surface structures; and also the pho-netic and semantic representations. . . . (1972, p. 11)

The Chomskian "revolution" in linguistics consisted, in part, of the introduction into linguistic theory of certain notions characteristic of the position of the formal-semantics theorists (see, for example, Wittgenstein, 1922). In particular, Chomsky has subscribed to a concept of meaning like that found in formal semantics: namely, that what a sentence means is given in the sentence itself and hence remains the same however the sentence may be used. Although he has not primarily been concerned with developing a theory of sentence meaning, it is nonetheless evident that Chomsky (1975) believes that the meaning of a sentence is independent of its use, as when he says: "Having acquired the system of language, the person can (in principle) choose to use it or not. . . . He cannot choose to have sentences mean other than what they do. . . . " (p. 71). Chomsky refers to the meaning that can be attributed to the sentence itself as its "literal meaning," "strict meaning," and "linguistic meaning." For example, he says (1975): "In [some cases] I, the speaker, have no intention of getting the hearer to know anything or to recognize anything, but what I say has its strict meaning, and I mean what I say" (pp. 63–64).

If meaning is inherent in sentences and, therefore, independent of their use, then meaning must be determined, at least in part, by the structure of sentences. That Chomsky (1957) sees meaning as essentially a matter of structure is evident in the following passage:

> Goodman has argued—to my mind, quite convincingly—that the notion of meaning of words can at least in part be reduced to that of reference of expressions containing these words. . . . Goodman's approach amounts to reformulating a part of the theory of meaning in the much clearer terms of the theory of reference, *just as much of our discussion can be understood as suggesting a reformulation of parts of the theory of meaning that deal with so-called "structural meaning" in terms of the completely nonsemantic theory of grammatical structure.* (p. 103, n. 10, my italics)

Finally, much as Searle believes that structure cannot be studied independent of function, Chomsky (1975) believes that it has to be: "To account for or somehow explain the structure of . . . particular grammars . . . on the basis of functional considerations is a pretty hopeless prospect, I would think. . . ." (p. 58).

As I noted earlier, the central claim of the communication-intention theorists, that meaning depends on the communicative function of language, can be analyzed into two component claims: first, meaning depends on function; and second, communication is the essential function of language.[3] Chomsky rejects both of these claims. If we attempt to evaluate the dispute over the central claim by evaluating the two component claims, we may thus be able to clarify that dispute. Let us now consider Chomsky's objections to the first and second claims in detail.

---

[3] I believe that the central claim can be fully analyzed into these two claims and that they are independent. I do not suppose that these are, in fact, the premises of anyone who asserts the central claim or that anyone who asserts it believes that it is so analyzable or analyzable at all. I also do not want to suggest that Chomsky believes that to defeat the central claim he must defeat the first and second claims or that these are its premises. I have proposed this analysis, and have accepted it *arguendo,* because the dispute over the central claim seems to be clarified by doing so.

Chomsky's Objections to the
Communication-Intention Theorists' View

We have seen that Chomsky considers meaning to be dependent on structure and structure to be independent of function. Thus, Chomsky denies the first claim—meaning depends on function—and holds that the structures that determine meaning are independent of function. On this point, the dispute seems both clear and comprehensible. Ultimately, the resolution of this issue depends on the success of efforts to give a purely structural account of language. If we think that these efforts are successful, we must agree, at least up to a point, that structure is independent of function. If, however, we find that such efforts fail to give a satisfactory account of language, no such concession is warranted. But as long as the structural theory continues to be revised by its proponents to accommodate objections, no verdict on its adequacy can be reached.

What are we to make of Chomsky's rejection of the second claim, that communication is the essential function of language? Chomsky (1975) denies the importance of the communicative function: "communication is only one function of language, and by no means an essential one" (p. 69). He considers other functions more important, indeed, essential: "There is, in fact, a very respectable tradition . . . that regards as a vulgar distortion the 'instrumental view' of language as 'essentially' a means of communication. . . . Language, it is argued, is 'essentially' a system for expression of thought. I basically agree with this view" (pp. 56–57). Thus, in place of the communicative function of language, Chomsky offers an alternative function—the expression of thought. The very claim that this function is essential would seem to support the communication-intention theorists' first claim, that function must be taken into account if we are to understand meaning. Therefore, it would seem that, in spite of his explicit denial of the first claim, Chomsky may be taken to agree with the communication-intention theorists that meaning cannot be understood without reference to function and to merely disagree with them about which function is the essential one. That is, it may be that for Chomsky structure is independent of function, if by function we mean communication, but dependent on function if by function we mean expression of thought. If this is the case, then all the disagreement over the central claim is over the second claim: whether the essential function of language is communication or the expression of thought. As we shall see, Chomsky's statements about the function of language as expression of thought leave it far from clear just what he has in mind. Our problem, then, is to understand what he means by "expression of thought."

One aspect of the meaning of "expression of thought" is clear: this function is noncommunicative. If we can understand what Chomsky thinks communication is, then we shall perhaps have a clearer notion of what it is not and hence a clearer notion of the noncommunicative function, "expression of thought." We need to discover, then, what Chomsky considers to be communicative, and therefore inessential, uses of language and whether these are the same uses that the communication-intention theorists consider communicative and therefore essential. Chomsky's (1975) definition of communication is implicit in the following passage:

> I can be using language in the strictest sense with no intention of communicating. ... As a graduate student, I spent two years writing a lengthy manuscript, assuming throughout that it would never be published or read by anyone. I meant everything I wrote, intending nothing as to what anyone would . . . [understand], in fact taking it for granted that there would be no audience. (p. 61)

After presenting some other cases of noncommunicative uses of language, Chomsky (1975) says: "Note that all of these are cases in which the 'utterer' assumes that there is no audience" (p. 236, n. 36). Since an intended audience is central to both Chomsky's and the communication-intention theorists' conception of communication, it would seem that he and they apply the same criterion for identifying the communicative function of language: whether the speaker has audience-directed intentions. Therefore, it would appear that Chomsky denies the importance of the same function of language that the communication-intention theorists consider essential.

On its face, Chomsky's position is problematic. The claim that "communication is only one function of language, and by no means an essential one" seems to do violence to common sense, but perhaps common sense misleads us here. Therefore, let us consider in detail some of the allegedly noncommunicative uses of language that Chomsky (1975) mentions: "casual conversation" (p. 68); "contemplation, inquiry, normal social interchange, planning and guiding one's own actions, creative writing" (p. 69); "the need ... to impress others and advance his career, to do himself in, or to maintain certain social relations in a group" (p. 71); "clarification of thought" (p. 67); "expression of thought . . . communication with oneself ... [and] thinking in words" (p. 57).

Now, many of these will not do as noncommunicative uses of language. Casual conversation, normal social interchange, impressing others, doing oneself in, and maintaining social relations in a group are manifestly social goals; thus, speech used for these purposes is manifestly communicative. I, at least, cannot visualize any way to carry on these activities while "taking it for granted that there is no audience," much less while believing that "there definitely is no audience" (Chomsky, 1975, p. 236, n. 36).

Continuing our search, we come to creative writing. Is it not true that creative writing is creative by virtue of an imagined effect that it is intended to have on an audience? The unintentionally "creative" patterns produced by a schizophrenic when writing are not considered creative for just the reason that their effect on the audience was unintended. Thus, nothing that we would want to call creative writing is produced without a hypothetical audience in mind, in the absence of audience-directed intentions.

A crucial item on Chomsky's list is "communication with oneself." Although Chomsky apparently agrees with the communication-intention theorists on the definition of *communication*, he disagrees about what it applies to. In particular, he excludes the speaker himself as a possible audience. Thus, he assigns a narrower scope of application to *communication* by virtue of assigning a narrower scope of application to *audience*.

Communication-intention theorists consider talking to oneself (at least certain cases) communicative. For example, Strawson (1971) takes writing oneself a list to be an instance of communication: "in an attenuated form . . . the earlier man communicates with his later self" (p. 187). Searle (1972), too, specifically includes these cases: "We communicate primarily with other people, but also with ourselves, as when we talk or think in words to ourselves" (p. 16). These cases are thought to be instances of communication because they involve the intention that some audience shall (subsequently) understand the speaker.

For Chomsky (1975) a notion of communication that includes the self as a possible audience is "deprived of its essential and interesting character" (p. 57). But, Chomsky offers no systematic, and therefore no acceptable, basis for excluding the self as audience. If it can be shown that the self can function as audience in the same way that others do, then Chomsky's exclusion of these cases cannot be justified. And it is not difficult to see that the self can serve as audience in the same way that others can when we consider cases where the self takes the role of the other. (G. H. Mead [1934] contends that this capacity is essential to human beings.)

We are all able to take roles, that is, to put ourselves in other people's shoes, so to speak. We are then able to participate in dialogues as if we were that person. Also, we can take two roles simultaneously and carry on a dialogue in which we alternate between them (as standup comedians often do in their routines). In such uses of language the self plays two alternate roles, in each of which the self can function both as speaker and as listener, much as in ordinary conversation. Each utterance in the dialogue is communicative because the self, when acting as speaker, has audience-directed intentions toward the self as listener. Moreover, we are able to carry on such essentially dyadic communication "in our minds." This form of dialogue—dialogue between two adopted roles—is manifestly communicative. Thus, it seems that self-communication also fails to supply us with a clear notion of a noncommunicative function of language.

Chomsky and the Ideational Function of Language

Many of Chomsky's examples of noncommunicative uses of language have turned out to be communicative; they are either straightforward instances of communication with others or, as I have argued, essentially communicative self-communication. We are now left with a few items which, because they are not evidently communicative, seem to offer the most promising candidates for a genuinely noncommunicative function of language. The remaining items are: clarification of thought, planning, contemplation, thinking in words, and expression of thought. "Expression of thought" seems to be Chomsky's general term for these noncommunicative uses of language. I shall use this term to label the function which the uses above illustrate.

Although several interpretations of the term are possible, I take the following three as most likely to be correct. First, "expression of thought" might mean the use of sentences to describe states of affairs. Since Chomsky took sentences of this kind to be paradigmatic in his grammatical work (for example, Chomsky, 1965), this may be the correct interpretation; but this is unlikely because it is so obvious that bald descriptions can be used for communication. Second, "expression of thought" might refer to the release function of language best illustrated by expletives. But we can rule out this interpretation, both because this function is evidently too unimportant to be a sensible rival for the communicative function and because it is insufficiently cognitive to work for Chomsky's purposes. A third, and more promising, interpretation for this function is suggested by the work of Vygotsky (1934/1962). Vygotsky, like Chomsky, was concerned with functions of language that are essentially private rather than social. He attributed these functions not to language in general but to a special form of language, "inner speech," that lay at the intersection of language and thought. The functions Vygotsky attributed to inner speech may help us to understand what Chomsky has in mind as a noncommunicative function of language.

Vygotsky (1934/1962) states, "The inner speech of the adult represents his 'thinking for himself' rather than social adaptation.... Out of context, it would be incomprehensible to others because it omits to mention what is obvious to the 'speaker'" (p. 18). Inner speech develops from and has the same functions as the child's egocentric speech; "besides its role of accompaniment to activity and its expressive and release functions, [it] readily assumes a planning function, i.e., turns into thought proper quite naturally and easily" (p. 45). Inner speech, then, evidently has uses that correspond to those which are of interest to Chomsky, e.g., planning. According to Vygotsky (1934/1962), however, inner speech has a peculiar structure. As inner speech emerges, "it shows a tendency toward an altogether specific form of abbreviation: namely, omitting the subject of a sentence and all words connected with it, while preserving the predicate" (p. 139). "The key to this experimentally established fact is the invariable, inevitable presence in inner speech of the factors that facilitate pure predication: we know what we are thinking about—i.e., we always know the subject and the situation" (p. 145). Inner speech, then, is more condensed than ordinary social speech or even speech between close friends.

Inner speech is evidently susceptible of careful definition, and its functions are, I believe, intelligible as psychological processes.[4] Luria (1961) says that the functional systems in which inner speech plays a critical part "enable man to *go far beyond the bounds of his physical capacities* and organize the well-defined forms of active deliberate behavior whose causal explanation has always baffled psychologists" (p. 18). Suppose, for example, that a child is asked to sort a heap of blocks of three colors and two sizes into piles. Without inner speech the young child puts

---

4 Given that inner speech is structurally condensed and tends to be silent, it might be argued that it cannot legitimately be called "language." Some scholars maintain that the silent language of thinking is not language but logic; others contend that the language of ordinary discourse is not language but speech. This kind of argument can get us nowhere. Within limits we have a wide range of choices; we are dealing with a complex phenomenon and can legitimately use the word language to refer to different well-defined portions of it.

those blocks that are identical together; however, he or she cannot put all of the blocks of one size but different colors together because they look so different. The child who has inner speech, on the other hand, is able to label the two dimensions of variation that provide potential categories for sorting and to sort on the basis of those labeled categories. As Luria says, "Inner speech provides a kind of *verbal orientation to our surroundings*, as it were, reflecting the surrounding objects and checking the possibilities of using them to find a way out" (p. 33).[5]

The functions of inner speech provide a possible reading for Chomsky's notion of a noncommunicative function of language, but there are problems with this interpretation. First, Vygotsky attributes such functions only to a specially abbreviated form of speech and not to language in general. Second, Vygotsky claims that inner speech develops from social speech, whereas Chomsky denies that the aspects of language which he studies have a social origin. Nonetheless, the basic function that Vygotsky ascribes to inner speech, unadorned, may supply a noncommunicative function of language for Chomsky.

The function of inner speech is to serve as a symbolic medium for representing one's ideas in order to hold those ideas clearly in mind. We can call this important and well-studied function the "ideational" function of language. The fact that the language of ideation, inner speech, is a form of thought supplies a compelling reason to believe that the ideational function is the language function that Chomsky considers essential.

Chomsky (1972) thinks that the study of language is a "branch of cognitive psychology" (p. 1). He believes that "if we are ever to understand how language is used or acquired, then we must abstract for separate and independent study a cognitive system, a system of knowledge and belief, that develops in early childhood" (p. 4). Chomsky's claim, then, is that a theory of language is necessarily a theory of mind. If his particular interest in the study of language is in the ideational function, this claim ceases to be controversial and becomes instead a definition of his particular focus. So, let us assume, for the moment, that the ideational function is the essential, noncommunicative function of language that Chomsky has in mind.

Is Ideation an Essentially Noncommunicative Function of Language?

If we closely examine the ideational function, we will see that ideation does not provide us with a noncommunicative function of language. Ideation is an essentially communicative function. When we represent the objects of our thought in language, we intend to make use of these representations at a later time. In other

5 Luria focused largely on the role that language plays in the reasoning of young children. In Piaget's discussion of the reasoning of adolescents, we can see a similar role for verbalization. At its most abstract, reasoning applies to objects of thought that are themselves essentially abstractions; for example, relations between blocks rather than blocks themselves. Such abstract objects of thought are most easily held firmly in mind when encoded symbolically, say, in natural language or in symbolic logic.

words, we create these representations in the role of speaker, intending that we ourselves, in the role of listener, shall later reason about them. Thus, when one uses language for ideation, one is engaged in communciation with oneself.

To see exactly the extent to which Chomsky's noncommunicative uses of language are communicative, let us return to them now. When a speaker uses language to clarify thought, the clarification occurs because, once having expressed those thoughts in language, the speaker can assume the role of the listener and examine those ideas from a detached perspective. This is why putting formerly unverbalized thoughts into language is felt to provide essential clarification. If a person verbalizes an idea without intending to consider it subsequently, and never does so, the thought has not been clarified (or would not seem so to him) but has merely been put into words.

Contemplation, too, is evidently a sequential process composed of a succession of statements, when it is verbal at all. In contemplation, a person says something, then considers it, then responds, then considers that response, and so on. Were it not for the speaker's ability to take the roles of speaker and listener alternately, there would be no connected sequence, for the sequence would reach a dead end at the first step.

It is still easier to see the essentially dyadic communication process at work in "planning one's activities." When language is used to plan or guide action, the speaker-self must have audience-directed intentions toward a listener-self. The speaker's utterances count as instances of planning by virtue of his intention that he himself will take them to heart, in his role as listener, at some later time.

Our analysis has now led us to the following conclusion: the counterexamples that Chomsky offers in an attempt to defeat the second claim—that communication is the essential function of language—are not counterexamples after all; that is, he has failed to provide us with a noncommunicative function of language. If this is so, then no claim that he makes about the noncommunicative function is intelligible. Therefore, he has not shown us that the noncommunicative function is the essential function of language; and his objections to the second claim turn out to be without force.

The ideational function—which, all things considered, seems the best candidate for Chomsky's noncommunicative function—is essentially communicative by virtue of the fact that language used for this purpose depends for its meaning on a speaker's intentions toward a listener. Since the ideational function of language retains the essential features of communication, it cannot be adequately accounted for by an analysis of structure abstracted from use, i.e., an analysis that does not take the speaker's audience-directed intentions into account. However, in ideational self-communication, there is a great deal of similarity between speaker and listener since speaker and listener differ only in their communicative role. In ideation the speaker does not adopt the roles of two entirely different people but rather adopts roles of a self at an earlier versus a later time. The communicative function is not itself attenuated in any form of self-communication; but, to the extent that the two roles adopted are similar, communicative intent can be correctly inferred and thus, to that extent, its overt expression can be reduced.[6] When we analyze the sentences produced in the service of ideation without making reference to the speaker's use of language, we give an account of language far less inadequate than if we were to analyze the sentences used for other communicative purposes in this way. This may explain why a structural account of language has seemed to Chomsky to tell so much more complete a story than it has to the theorists of communication-intention. A structural theory gives a relatively more complete account of language used ideationally than of language used for other communicative purposes, and a relatively complete account at that.

Conclusion

I began by adopting Strawson's helpful summary of two conflicting conceptions of meaning. Strawson focused attention on an essential difference between the two positions: namely, that one position insists and the other denies that the meaning-determining rules of language can only be understood by reference to the function of communication. I then attempted to evaluate the claim, referred to here as the "central claim," that meaning can only be understood by reference to communication. The central claim was analyzed into two component claims. The first claim, that meaning depends on function, is explicitly denied by Chomsky. On the other hand, by asserting that a particular function is essential, Chomsky seems to imply that he has no quarrel with the first claim. This confusion with regard to the first claim appears to shift the burden of the debate over the central claim onto the second claim, that communication is the essential function of language. Chomsky also rejects this second claim and contends that the essential function of language is the noncommunicative function, "expression of thought." I attempted to show that sense can be made of "expression of thought" as a function of language if this phrase is understood to refer to the ideational function that has been elaborated and validated by such psychologists as Vygotsky and Luria. However, as is true of all ideational uses of language, Chomsky's examples, upon examination, turn out to be essentially communicative because they all involve intentions toward an audience, i.e., the self. Chomsky has offered no systematic basis for excluding the self as audience, nor is he likely to be able to do so, because the self functions as audience in much the same way that others do. Since no essentially noncommunicative function could be found, it was concluded that Chomsky's objection to the second claim was without force.

If Strawson has correctly characterized the dispute about the nature of meaning, if the present analysis of the central claim into two component claims is sound, and if we may justifiably discount, for the reasons given above, Chomsky's objections to both claims, then we may fairly conclude that Chomsky has given us no acceptable grounds for rejecting the central claim. Until such grounds appear,

---

[6] For an interesting example of how intimacy between speaker and listener can permit the use of condensed forms of expression, see Vygotsky (1934/1962, p. 140); and for an interesting discussion of related matters, see Rommetveit (1974). Also see Feldman (1974).

the well-supported claim that the meaning-determining rules of language can only be understood by reference to the function of communication must be accepted. From this it would follow that efforts to understand language abstracted from the speaker's use of it are always misleading—more so for language used socially, less so for language used ideationally—and, therefore, that any specific claims made in the context of such efforts are, at best, of limited application.

References

Austin, J. L. *How to do things with words.* New York: Oxford University Press, 1962.

Chomsky, N. *Syntactic structures.* The Hague: Mouton, 1957.

Chomsky, N. *Aspects of the theory of syntax.* Cambridge, Mass.: M.I.T. Press, 1965.

Chomsky, N. *Language and mind* (enlarged ed.). New York: Harcourt Brace Jovanovich, 1972.

Chomsky, N. *Reflections on language.* New York: Random House, 1975.

Davidson, D. Semantics for natural languages. In G. Harman (Ed.), *On Noam Chomsky: Critical Essays.* Garden City, N.Y.: Anchor Books, 1974.

Feldman, C. F. Pragmatic features of natural language. In M. W. LaGaly, R. A. Fox, & A. Bruck (Eds.), *Papers from the tenth regional meeting, Chicago Linguistic Society.* Chicago: Chicago Linguistic Society, 1974.

Jakobson, R. Linguistics and poetics. In R. T. DeGeorge & F. M. DeGeorge (Eds.), *The structuralists: From Marx to Lévi-Strauss.* Garden City, N.Y.: Doubleday, 1972.

Luria, A. R. *The role of speech in the regulation of normal and abnormal behavior.* (J. Tizard, Ed.). New York: Liveright, 1961.

Mead, G. H. *Mind. self and society.* (C. Morris, Ed.). Chicago: University of Chicago Press, 1934.

Rommetveit, R. *On message structure: A framework for the study of language and communication.* London: John Wiley, 1974.

Searle, J. R. What is a speech act? In J. R. Searle (Ed.), *The philosophy of language.* London: Oxford University Press, 1971.

Searle, J. R. Chomsky's revolution in linguistics. In G. Harman (Ed.), *On Noam Chomsky: Critical Essays.* Garden City, N.Y.: Anchor Books, 1974.

Strawson, P. F. Meaning and truth. In P. F. Strawson, *Logicolinguistic papers.* London: Methuen, 1971.

Urmson, J .O. *Philosophical analysis: Its development between the two world wars.* Oxford: Clarendon Press, 1956.

Vygotsky, L. S. [*Thought and language.*] (E. Hanfmann & G. Vakar, Eds. and trans.). Cambridge, Mass.: M.I.T. Press, 1962. (Originally published, 1934.)

Wittgenstein, L. *Tractatus logico-philosophicus.* London: Routledge & Kegan Paul, 1922.

From Utterance to Text: The Bias of Language in Speech and Writing

DAVID R. OLSON
Ontario Institute for Studies in Education

In this far-ranging essay David Olson attempts to reframe current controversies over several aspects of language, including meaning, comprehension, acquisition, reading, and reasoning. Olson argues that in all these cases the conflicts are rooted in differing assumptions about the relation of meaning to language: whether meaning is extrinsic to language—a relation Olson designates as "utterance"—or intrinsic—a relation he calls "text." On both the individual and cultural levels there has been development, Olson suggests, from language as utterance to language as text. He traces the history and impact of conventionalized, explicit language from the invention of the Greek alphabet through the rise of the British essayist technique. Olson concludes with a discussion of the resulting conception of language and the implications for the linguistic, psychological, and logical issues raised initially.

The faculty of language stands at the center of our conception of mankind; speech makes us human and literacy makes us civilized. It is therefore both interesting and important to consider what, if anything, is distinctive about written language and to consider the consequences of literacy for the bias it may impart both to our culture and to people's psychological processes.

The framework for examining the consequences of literacy has already been laid out. Using cultural and historical evidence, Havelock (1973), Parry (1971), Goody and Watt (1968), Innis (1951), and McLuhan (1964) have argued that the invention of the alphabetic writing system altered the nature of the knowledge which is

An early version of this paper was presented to the Epistemics meeting at Vanderbilt University, Nashville, Tenn., in February 1974 and will be published in R. Diez-Guerrero & H. Fisher (Eds.), *Logic and Language in Personality and Society*. New York: Academic Press, 1978.

I am extremely grateful to the Canada Council, the Spencer Foundation, and the Van Leer Jerusalem Foundation for their support at various stages of completing this paper. I am also indebted to the many colleagues who commented on the earlier draft, including Roy Pea, Nancy Nickerson, Angela Hildyard, Bob Bracewell, Edmund Sullivan, and Frank Smith. I would also like to thank Mary Macri who assisted with the clerical aspects of the manuscript and Isobel Gibb, Reference Librarian at OISE, who assisted with the reference editing.

Harvard Educational Review Vol. 47 No. 3 August 1977, 257–281

stored for reuse, the organization of that knowledge, and the cognitive processes of the people who use that written language. Some of the cognitive consequences of schooling and literacy in contemporary societies have been specified through anthropological and cross-cultural psychological research by Cole, Gay, Glick, and Sharp (1971), Scribner and Cole (1973), Greenfield (1972), Greenfield and Bruner (1969), Goodnow (1976), and others.

However, the more general consequences of the invention of writing systems for the structure of language, the concept of meaning, and the patterns of comprehension and reasoning processes remain largely unknown. The purpose of this paper is to examine the consequences of literacy, particularly those consequences associated with mastery of the "schooled" language of written texts.

In the course of the discussion, I shall repeatedly contrast explicit, written prose statements, which I shall call "texts," with more informal oral-language statements, which I shall call "utterances." Utterances and texts may be contrasted at any one of several levels: the linguistic modes themselves—written language versus oral language; their usual usages—conversation, story-telling, verse, and song for the oral mode versus statements, arguments, and essays for the written mode; their summarizing forms—proverbs and aphorisms for the oral mode versus premises for the written mode; and finally, the cultural traditions built around these modes—an oral tradition versus a literate tradition. My argument will be that there is a transition from utterance to text both culturally and developmentally and that this transition can be described as one of increasing explicitness, with language increasingly able to stand as an unambiguous or autonomous representation of meaning.

This essay (a word I use here in its Old French sense: *essai*—to try) begins by showing that theoretical and empirical debates on various aspects of language—ranging from linguistic theories of meaning to the psychological theories of comprehension, reading, and reasoning—have remained unduly puzzling and polemical primarily because of different assumptions about the locus of meaning. One assumption is that meaning is in the shared intentions of the speaker and the hearer, while the opposite one is that meaning is conventionalized in a sentence itself, that "the meaning is in the text." This essay continues by tracing the assumption that the meaning is in the text from the invention of the alphabetic writing system to the rapid spread of literacy with the invention of printing. The consequences of that assumption, particularly of the attempts to make it true, are examined in terms of the development and exploitation of the "essayist technique." The essay then proceeds to re-examine the linguistic, logical, and psychological issues mentioned at the outset; it demonstrates that the controversies surrounding these issues stem largely from a failure to appreciate the differences between utterances and texts and to understand that the assumptions appropriate for one are not appropriate for the other.

The Locus of Meaning

The problem at hand is as well raised by a quotation from Martin Luther as by any more contemporary statement: scripture is *sui ipsius interpres*—scripture is its own interpreter (cited in Gadamer, 1975, p. 154). For Luther, then, the meaning of Scripture depended, not upon the dogmas of the church, but upon a deeper reading of the text. That is, the meaning of the text is in the text *itself*.[1] But is that claim true; is the meaning in the text? As we shall see, the answer offered to that question changed substantially about the time of Luther in regard not only to Scripture but also to philosophical and scientific statements. More important, the answers given to the question lie at the root of several contemporary linguistic and psychological controversies. Let us consider five of these.

In linguistic theory, an important controversy surrounds the status of invariant structures—structures suitable for linguistic, philosophical, and psychological analyses of language. Are these structures to be found in the deep syntactic structure of the sentence itself or in the interaction between the sentence and its user, in what may be called the understanding or interpretation? This argument may be focused in terms of the criterion for judging the well-formedness of a sentence. For Chomsky (1957, 1965) the well-formedness of a sentence—roughly, the judgment that the sentence is a permissible sentence of the language—is determined solely by the base syntactic structure of the sentence. Considerations of comprehensibility and effectiveness, like those of purpose and context, are irrelevant to the judgment. Similarly, the rules for operating upon well-formed base strings are purely formal. For Chomsky the meaning, or semantics, of a sentence is also specified in the base grammatical structure. Each unambiguous or well-formed sentence has one and only one base structure, and this base structure specifies the meaning or semantic structure of that sentence. Hence the meaning of a sentence relies on no private referential or contextual knowledge; nothing is added by the listener. One is justified, therefore, in concluding that, for Chomsky, the meaning is in the sentence per se.[2]

The radical alternative to this view is associated with the general semanticists led by Korzybski (1933), Chase (1954), and Hayakawa (1952). They claim that sentences do not have fixed meanings but depend in every case on the context and purpose for which they were uttered. Chafe (1970) offers a more modest alternative to Chomsky's syntactic bias, asserting that the criterion for the well-formedness of a sentence is determined by the semantic structure: a sentence is well-formed if it is understandable to a listener. This semantic structure is necessarily a part of language users' "knowledge of the world," and language can serve its functions precisely because such knowledge tends to be shared by speakers. Thus comprehension of a sentence involves, to some degree, the use of prior knowledge, contextual cues, and nonlinguistic cues.

In his philosophical discussion of meaning, Grice (1957) makes a distinction that mirrors the difference between the views of Chomsky and Chafe. Grice points out that one may analyze either "sentence meaning" or "speaker's meaning." The

---

[1] I am indebted to Frank Smith for pointing out that I use the phrase "the meaning is in the text" as a metaphor for describing language in which the meaning is fully conventionalized.

[2] The hypothesis of autonomous meaning of sentences, that is, the assumption that the meaning is in the text, may simply reflect the presupposition that linguistics, as a discipline, is autonomous.

sentence per se may mean something other than what a speaker means by the sentence. For example, the speaker's meaning of "You're standing on my toe" may be "Move your foot." In these terms Chomsky provides a theory of sentence meaning in which the meaning of the sentence is independent of its function or context. Chafe, in contrast, offers a theory of intended meaning that encompasses both the intentions of the speaker and the interpretations the hearer constructs on the bases of the sentence, its perceived context, and its assumed function.

But these theories differ not only in the scope of the problems they attempt to solve. My suggestion is that these linguistic theories specify their central problems differently because of differing implicit assumptions about language; Chomsky's assumption is that language is best represented by written texts; Chafe's is that language is best represented by oral conversational utterances.

Psychological theories of language comprehension reflect these divergent linguistic assumptions. Psycholinguistic models of comprehension such as that of Clark (1974) follow Chomsky in the assumption that one's mental representation of a sentence depends on the recovery of the unique base syntactic structure underlying the sentence. Hence, a sentence is given the same underlying representation regardless of the context or purposes it is ultimately to serve. Similarly, Fodor, Bever, and Garrett (1974) have claimed that the semantic properties of a sentence are determined exclusively and automatically by the specification of the syntactic properties and the lexical items of the sentence. The assumption, once again, is that the meaning, at least the meaning worth psychological study, is in the text.

Conversely, a number of researchers (Anderson & Ortony, 1975; Barclay, 1973; Bransford, Barclay, & Franks, 1972; Bransford & Johnson, 1973; Paris & Carter, 1973) have demonstrated that sentence comprehension depends in large part on the context and on the prior knowledge of the listeners. In one now famous example, the sentence, "The notes were sour because the seams were split," becomes comprehensible only when the listener knows that the topic being discussed is bagpipes. Bransford and Johnson (1973) conclude, "What is understood and remembered about an input depends on the knowledge structures to which it is related" (p. 429).

Differing assumptions as to whether or not the meaning is in the text may also be found in studies of logical reasoning. Logical reasoning is concerned with the formulation and testing of the relations that hold between propositions. Such studies are based on models of formal reasoning in which it is assumed that the rules of inference apply to explicit premises to yield valid inferences. Subjects can be tested on their ability to consistently apply these formal rules to various semantic contents, and development can be charted in terms of the ability to apply the rules consistently to the meaning in the text (Neimark & Slotnick, 1970; Piaget, 1972; Suppes & Feldman, 1971).

Studies have shown, however, that formal propositional logic is a poor model for ordinary reasoning from linguistic propositions. Some researchers (Taplin & Staudenmayer, 1973) have suggested that logic and reasoning are discontinuous because "the interpreted meaning of a sentence is usually not entirely given by the denotative meaning in the linguistic structure of the sentence" (Staudenmayer, 1975, p. 56); factors such as prior knowledge and contextual presuppositions are also important. Analyzing the protocols of graduate students solving syllogisms, Henle (1962) found that errors resulted more often from an omission of a premise, a modification of a premise, or an importation of new evidence than from a violation of the rules of inference. If logic is considered to be the ability to draw valid conclusions from explicit premises—to operate upon the information in the text—then these students were reasoning somewhat illogically. However, if logic is considered to be the ability to operate on premises as they have been personally interpreted, then these students were completely logical in their operations. The critical issue, again, is whether or not the meaning is assumed to be fully explicit in the text.

Theories of language acquisition also reflect either the assumption that language is autonomous—that the meaning is in the text—or that it is dependent on non-linguistic knowledge. Assuming that language is autonomous and independent of use or context, Chomsky (1965) and McNeill (1970) have argued that an innate, richly structured language-acquistion device must be postulated to account for the child's remarkable mastery of language. Hypothesized to be innate are structures that define the basic linguistic units (Chomsky, 1972) and the rules for transforming these units. Independent of a particular speaker or hearer, these transformations provide the interpretation given to linguistic forms. For example, at the grammatical level, "John hit Mary" is equivalent to "Mary was hit by John," and at the lexical level, "John" must be animate, human, male, and so on. These conclusions seem plausible, indeed inescapable, as long as it is assumed that language is autonomous and the meanings are in the sentences themselves.

Most recent research on language acquisition has proceeded from the alternative assumption that an utterance is but a fragmentary representation of the intention that lies behind it. Thus the meaning of the utterance comes from shared intentions based upon prior knowledge, the context of the utterance, and habitual patterns of interaction. The contextual dependence of child language was emphasized by de Laguna (1927/1970) and Buhler (1934). De Laguna (1927/1970) claimed, "Just because the terms of the child's language are in themselves so indefinite, it is left to the particular context to determine the specific meaning for each occasion. In order to understand what the baby is saying, you must see what the baby is doing" (pp. 90–91).

Recent studies extend this view. Bloom (1970) has shown, for example, that a young child may use the same surface structure, "Mommy sock," in two quite different contexts to represent quite different deep structures or meanings: in one case, the mother is putting the sock on the child; in the other, the child is picking up the mother's sock. The utterance, therefore, specifies only part of the meaning, the remainder being specified by the perceived context, accompanying gestures, and the like. Moreover, having established these nonlinguistic meanings, the child can use them as the basis for discovering the structure of language (Brown, 1973; Bruner, 1973; Macnamara, 1972; Nelson, 1974). In other words, linguistic structures are not autonomous but arise out of nonlinguistic structures. There is no need, then, to attribute their origins to innate structures. Language development is primarily a matter of mastering the conventions both for putting more and more of the meaning into the verbal utterance and for reconstructing the intended meaning of the sentence per se. In de Laguna's terms, "The evolution of language is characterized by a progressive freeing of speech from dependence upon the perceived conditions under which it is uttered and heard, and from the behavior that accompanies it. The extreme limit of this freedom is reached in language which is written (or printed) and read" (1927, 1970, p. 107). Thus the predominant view among language-acquisition theorists is that while the meaning initially is not in the language itself, it tends to become so with development.

Finally, theories of reading and learning to read can be seen as expressions of the rival assumptions about the locus of meaning. In one view the meaning is in the text and the student's problem is to find out how to decode that meaning (Carroll & Chall, 1975; Chall, 1967; Gibson & Levin, 1975). In fact, the majority of reading programs are based upon the gradual mastery of subskills such as letter recognition, sound blending, word recognition, and ultimately deciphering meaning. The alternative view is that readers bring the meaning to the text, which merely confirms or disconfirms their expectations (Goodman, 1967; Smith, 1975). Thus if children fail to recognize a particular word or sentence in a context, their expectations generate substitutions that are often semantically appropriate. Again, the basic assumption is that the meaning is—or is not—in the text.

To summarize, the controversial aspects of five issues—the structure of language, the nature of comprehension, the nature of logical reasoning, and the problems of learning to speak and learning to read—can be traced to differing assumptions regarding the autonomy of texts. Further, the distinction between utterances and texts, I suggest, reflects the different assumptions that meaning is or is not in the sentence per se.

The Beginnings of a Literate Technology

Let us consider the origin of the assumption that the meaning is in the text and the implications of that assumption for language use. The assumption regarding the autonomy of texts is relatively recent and the language conforming to it is relatively specialized. Utterance, language that does not conform to this assumption, is best represented by children's early language, oral conversation, memorable oral sayings, and the like. Text, language that does conform to that assumption, is best represented by formal, written, expository prose statements. My central claim is that the evolution both culturally and developmentally is from utterance to text. While utterance is universal, text appears to have originated with Greek literacy and to have reached a most visible form with the British essayists. My argument, which rests heavily on the seminal works of Havelock (1963), McLuhan (1962), and Goody and Watt (1968), is that the invention of the alphabetic writing system gave to Western culture many of its predominant features, including an altered conception of language and an altered conception of rational man. These effects came about, in part, from the creation of explicit, autonomous statements—statements dependent upon an explicit writing system, the alphabet, and an explicit form of argument, the essay. In a word, these effects resulted from putting the meaning into the text.

Meaning in an Oral Language Tradition

Luther's statement, that the meaning of Scripture depended not upon the dogmas of the church, but upon a deeper reading of the text, seems a simple claim. It indicates, however, the profound change that occurred early in the sixteenth century in regard to the presumed autonomy of texts. Prior to the time of Luther, who in this argument represents one turning point in a roughly continuous change in orientation, it was generally assumed that meaning could not be stated explicitly. Statements required interpretation by either scribes or clerics. Luther's claim and the assumption that guided it cut both ways: they were a milestone in the developing awareness that text could explicitly state its meaning—that it did not depend on dogma or interpretive context; more importantly, they also indicated a milestone in the attempt to shape language to more explicitly represent its meanings. This shift in orientation, which I shall elaborate later in terms of the "essayist technique," was one of the high points in the long history of the attempt to make meaning completely explicit. Yet it was, relatively speaking, a mere refinement of the process that had begun with the Greek invention of the alphabet.

Although the Greek alphabet and the growth of Greek literacy may be at the base of Western science and philosophy, it is not to be assumed that preliterate people were primitive in any sense. Modern anthropology has provided many examples of theoretical, mythical, and technological systems of impressive sophistication and appropriateness. It has been established that a complex and extensive literature could exist in the absence of a writing system. In 1928, Milman Parry (1971) demonstrated that the *Iliad* and the *Odyssey*, usually attributed to a literate Homer, were in fact examples of oral composition composed over centuries by preliterate bards for audiences who did not read. In turn, it was recognized that large sections of the Bible possessed a similar oral structure. The books of Moses and the Prophets, for example, are recorded versions of statements that were shaped through oral methods as part of an oral culture.

To preserve verbal statements in the absence of a writing system, such statements would have to be biased both in form and content towards oral mnemonic devices such as "formalized patterns of speech, recital under ritual conditions, the use of drums and other musical instruments, and the employment of professional remembrances" (Goody & Watt, 1968, p. 31). Language is thus shaped or biased to fit the requirements of oral communication and auditory memory (see, for example, Havelock, 1973, and Frye, 1971). A variety of oral statements such as proverbs, adages, aphorisms, riddles, and verse are distinctive not only in that they preserve important cultural information but also in that they are memorable. They tend, however, *not* to be explicit or to say exactly what they mean; they require context and prior knowledge and wisdom for their interpretation. Solomon, for example, introduced the *Book of Proverbs* by saying: "To understand a proverb and the interpretations; the words of the wise and their dark sayings" (Chapter I:6). Maimonides, the twelfth-century rabbi, pointed out in his *Guide of the Perplexed* that when one interprets parables "according to their external meanings, he too is overtaken by great perplexity!" (1963, p. 6).

The invention of writing did not end the oral tradition. Some aspects of that tradition merely coexist with the more dominant literate traditions. Lord (1960) in his *Singer of Tales* showed that a remnant of such an oral culture persists in Yugoslavia. Even in a predominantly literate culture, aspects of the oral tradition remain. Gray (1973) suggested that Bob Dylan represents the creative end of such an oral tradition in Anglo-American culture; the less creative aspects of that tradition show up in the stock phrases and proverbial sayings that play so large a part in everyday conversational language.

With the introduction of writing, important parts of the oral tradition were written down and preserved in the available literate forms. The important cultural information, the information worth writing down, consisted in large part of statements shaped to fit the requirements of oral memory such as the epics, verse, song, orations, and since readers already knew, through the oral tradition, much of the content, writing served primarily for the storage and retrieval of information that had already been committed to memory, not for the expression of original ideas.

Scripture, at the time of Luther, had just such a status. It consisted in part of statements shaped to the requirements of oral comprehension and oral memory. Scripture had authority, but since the written statements were shorn of their oral contexts, they were assumed to require interpretation. The dogma of the Church, the orally transmitted tradition, had the authority to say what the Scripture meant. In this context Luther's statement can be seen as profoundly radical. Luther claimed that the text supplied sufficient context internally to determine the meaning of the passage; the meaning was in the text. What would have led Luther to make such a radical claim? My suggestion is that his claim reflected a technological change—the invention of printing—one in a series of developments in the increasing explicitness of language, which we shall now examine.

Alphabetic Writing—Making Meanings Explicit

Significant oral-language statements, to be memorable, must be cast into some oral, poetic form. Consequently, as we have seen, these statements do not directly say what they mean. With the invention of writing, the limitations of oral memory became less critical. The written statement, constituting a more or less permanent artifact, no longer depended on its "poetized" form for its preservation.

However, whether or not a writing system can preserve the meanings of statements depends upon the characteristics of the system. An elliptical or nonexplicit writing system, like nonexplicit statements, tends to rely on prior knowledge and expectancies. An explicit writing system unambiguously represents meanings—the meaning is in the text. It has a minimum of homophones (seen/scene) and homographs (lead/lead) at the phonemic and graphemic levels, few ambiguities at the grammatical level, and few permissible interpretations at the semantic level.

The Greek alphabet was the first to approach such a degree of explicitness and yet to be simple enough to provide a base for mass literacy. Gelb (1952) differentiated four main stages in the development of writing systems. The first stage, which goes back to prehistory, involves the expression of ideas through pictures and pictographic writing. Such writing systems have been called ideographic in that they represent and communicate ideas directly without appeal to the structure of spoken language. While the signs are easily learned and recognized, there are problems associated with their use: any full system requires some four or five thousand characters for ordinary usage; their concreteness makes the representation of abstract terms difficult; they are difficult to arrange so as to produce statements (Gombrich, 1974); and they tend to limit the number of things that can be expressed.

The next stage was the invention of the principle of phonetization, the attempt to make writing reflect the sound structure of speech. In an attempt to capture the properties of speech, early phonetic systems—Sumerian, Egyptian, Hittite, and Chinese—all contained signs of three different types: word signs or logogens, syllabic signs, and auxiliary signs.

The third stage was the development of syllabaries which did away both with word signs and with signs representing sounds having more than one consonant. Whereas earlier syllabaries had separate signs for such syllables as *ta* and *tam*, the West Semitic syllabaries reduced the syllable to a single consonant-vowel sequence, thereby reducing the number of signs. However, since these Semitic syllabaries did not have explicit representations for vowels, the script frequently resulted in ambiguities in pronunciation, particularly in cases of writing proper names and other words which could not be retrieved from context. Semitic writing systems thus introduced phonetic indicators called Matres Lectionis (literally: "mothers of reading") to differentiate the vowel sounds (Gelb, 1952, p. 166).

The final stage in the invention of the alphabet, a step taken only by the Greeks, was the invention of a phonemic alphabet (Gelb, 1952; Goody & Watt, 1963). The Greeks did so, Gelb suggests, by using consistently the Matres Lectionis which the Semites had used sporadically. They discovered that these indicators were not syllables but rather vowels. Consequently the sign that preceded the indicator also must not be a syllable but rather a consonant. Havelock (1973) comments: "At a stroke, by this analysis, the Greeks provided a table of elements of linguistic sound not only manageable because of its economy, but for the first time in the history of *homo sapiens,* also accurate" (p. 11).

The faithful transcription of the sound patterns of speech by a fully developed alphabet has freed writing from some of the ambiguities of oral language. Many sentences that are ambiguous when spoken are unambiguous when written—for example, "il vient toujours a sept heures" ("he always comes at seven o'clock") versus "il vient toujours a cette heure" ("he always comes at this hour") (Lyons, 1969, p. 41). However, a fully developed alphabet does not exhaust the possibilities for explicitness of a writing system. According to Bloomfield (1939) and Kneale and Kneale (1962), the remaining lack of explicitness necessitated the invention of the formal languages of logic and mathematics.

To summarize, we have considered the extent to which meaning is explicitly represented in a statement. Oral language statements must be poetized to be remembered, but in the process they lose some of their explicitness; they require interpretation by a wise man, scribe, or cleric. Written statements bypass the limitations of memory, but the extent to which a writing system can explicitly represent meaning depends upon the nature of the system. Systems such as syllabaries that represent several meanings with the same visual sign are somewhat ambiguous or nonexplicit. As a consequence, they again require interpretation by some authority. Statements can become relatively free from judgment or interpretation only with a highly explicit writing system such as the alphabet. The Greek alphabet, through its ability to record exactly what is said, provided a tool for the formulation and criticism of explicit meanings and was therefore critical to the evolution of Greek literacy and Greek culture.

Written Text as an Exploratory Device

Writing systems with a relatively lower degree of explicitness, such as the syllabaries, tended to serve a somewhat limited purpose, primarily that of providing an aid to memory. Havelock (1973) states:

> When it came to transcribing discursive speech, difficulties of interpretation would discourage the practice of using the script for novel or freely-invented discourse. The practice that would be encouraged would be to use the system as a reminder of something already familiar, so that recollection of its familiarity would aid the reader in getting the right interpretation. ... It would in short tend to be something—tale, proverb, parable, fable and the like—which already existed in oral form and had been composed according to oral rules. The syllabic system in short provided techniques for recall of what was already familiar, not instruments for formulating novel statements which could further the exploration of new experience. (p. 238)

The alphabet had no such limits of interpretation. The decrease in ambiguity of symbols—for example, the decrease in the number of homographs—would permit a reader to assign the appropriate interpretation to a written statement even without highly tuned expectations as to what the text was likely to say. The decreased reliance upon prior knowledge or expectancies was therefore a significant step towards making meaning explicit in the conventionalized linguistic system. The technology was sufficiently explicit to permit one to analyze the sentence meaning apart from the speaker's meaning. Simultaneously, written language became an instrument for the formulation and preservation of original statements that could violate readers' expectancies and commonsense knowledge. Written language had come free from its base in the mother tongue; it had begun the transformation from utterance to text.

The availability of an explicit writing system, however, does not assure that the statements recorded in that language will be semantically explicit. As previously mentioned, the first statements written down tended to be those that had already been shaped to the requirements of oral production and oral memory, the Greek epics being a case in point. Over time, however, the Greeks came to fully exploit the powers of their alphabetic writing system. In fact, Havelock (1973) has argued that the Greeks' use of this invention was responsible for the development of the intellectual qualities found in classical Greece:

> And so, as the fifth century passes into the fourth, the full effect upon Greece of the alphabetic revolution begins to assert itself. The governing word ceases to be a vi-

bration heard by the ear and nourished in the memory. It becomes a visible artifact. Storage of information for reuse, as a formula designed to explain the dynamics of western culture, ceases to be a metaphor. The documented statement persisting through time unchanged is to release the human brain from certain formidable burdens of memorization while increasing the energies available for conceptual thought. The results as they are to be observed in the intellectual history of
Greece and Europe were profound. (p. 60)

Some of the effects of the Greeks' utilization of the alphabetic writing system
are worth reviewing. First, as Goody and Watt (1968) and a number of other scholars have shown, it permitted a differentiation of myth and history with a new regard
for literal truth. When the Homeric epics were written down, they could be subjected to critical analysis and their inconsistencies became apparent. Indeed,
Hecataeus, faced with writing a history of Greece, said: "What I write is the account
I believe to be true. For the stories the Greeks tell are many and in my opinion
ridiculous" (cited in Goody & Watt, 1968, p. 45). Second, the use of the alphabetic
system altered the relative regard for poetry and for prose. Prose statements were
neither subtle nor devious; they tended to mean what they said. Havelock (1963)
has demonstrated that Plato's *Republic* diverged from the tradition of the oral
Homeric poets and represented a growing reliance on prose statements.

Third, the emphasis on written prose, as in Aristotle's *Analytics* (see Goody &
Watt, 1968, pp. 52–54), permitted the abstraction of logical procedures that could
serve as the rules for thinking. Syllogisms could operate on prose premises but not
on oral statements such as proverbs. Further, the use of written prose led to the
development of abstract categories, the genus/species taxonomies so important not
only to Greek science but also to the formation and division of various subject-
matter areas. Much of Greek thought was concerned with satisfactorily explaining
the meaning of terms. And formulating a definition is essentially a literate enterprise outside of the context of ongoing speech—an attempt to provide the explicit
meaning of a word in terms of the other words in the system (see, for example,
Bruner & Olson, in press; Goody & Watt, 1968; and Havelock, 1976).

The Greeks, thinking that they had discovered a method for determining objective truth, were in fact doing little more than detecting the properties implicit in
their native tongue. Their rules for mind were not rules for thinking but rather
rules for using language consistently; the abstract properties of their category system were not true or unbiased descriptions of reality but rather invariants in the
structure of their language. Writing became an instrument for making explicit the
knowledge that was already implicit in their habits of speech and, in the process,
tidying up and ordering that knowledge. This important but clearly biased effort
was the first dramatic impact of writing on knowledge.

The Greeks' concern with literacy was not without critics. Written statements
could not be interrogated if a misunderstanding occurred, and they could not be
altered to suit the requirements of listeners. Thus Socrates concluded in *Phaedrus:*
"Anyone who leaves behind him a written manual, and likewise anyone who takes
it over from him, on the supposition that such writing will provide something reliable and permanent, must be exceedingly simple minded" (*Phaedrus,* 277c, cited

in Goody & Watt, 1968, p. 51). In the *Seventh Letter,* Plato says: "No intelligent man will ever be so bold as to put into language those things which his reason has contemplated, especially not into a form that is unalterable—which must be the case with what is expressed in written symbols" (*Seventh Letter,* 341 c-d, cited in Bluck, 1949, p. 176).

The Essayist Technique

Although the Greeks exploited the resources of written language, the invention of printing allowed an expanded and heterogeneous reading public to use those resources in a much more systematic way. The invention of printing prompted an intellectual revolution of similar magnitude to that of the Greek period (see McLuhan, 1962, and Ong, 1971, for fascinating accounts). However, the rise of print literacy did not merely preserve the analytic uses of writing developed by the Greeks; it involved as well, I suggest, further evolution in the explicitness of writing at the semantic level. That is, the increased explicitness of language was not so much a result of minimizing the ambiguity of words at the graphemic level but rather a result of minimizing the possible interpretations of statements. A sentence was written to have only one meaning. In addition, there was a further test of the adequacy of a statement's representation of presumed intention: the ability of that statement to stand up to analysis of its implications. To illustrate, if one assumes that statement X is true, then the implication Y should also be true. However, suppose that on further reflection Y is found to be indefensible. Then presumably statement X was not intended in the first place and would have to be revised.

This approach to texts as autonomous representations of meaning was reflected in the way texts were both read and written. A reader's task was to determine exactly what each sentence was asserting and to determine the presuppositions and implications of that statement. If one could assume that an author had actually intended what was written and that the statements were true, then the statements would stand up under scrutiny. Luther made just this assumption about Scripture early in the sixteenth century, shortly after the invention and wide utilization of printing. One of the more dramatic misapplications of the same assumption was Bishop Usher's inference from biblical genealogies that the world was created in 4004 B.C.

The more fundamental effect of this approach to text was on the writer, whose task now was to create autonomous text—to write in such a manner that the sentence was an adequate, explicit representation of the meaning, relying on no implicit premises or personal interpretations. Moreover, the sentence had to withstand analysis of its presuppositons and implications. This fostered the use of prose as a form of extended statements from which a series of necessary implications could be drawn.

The British essayists were among the first to exploit writing for the purpose of formulating original theoretical knowledge. John Locke's *An Essay Concerning Human Understanding* (1690/1961) well represents the intellectual bias that originated at that time and, to a large extent, characterizes our present use of language.

95

Knowledge was taken to be the product of an extended logical essay—the output of the repeated application in a single coherent text of the technique of examining an assertion to determine all of its implications. It is interesting to note that when Locke began his criticism of human understanding he thought that he could write it on a sheet of paper in an evening. By the time he had exhausted the possibilities of both the subject and the new technology, the essay had taken twenty years and two volumes.

Locke's essayist technique differed notably from the predominant writing style of the time. Ellul (1964) says, "An uninitiated reader who opens a scientific treatise on law, economy, medicine or history published between the sixteenth and eighteenth centuries is struck most forcibly by the complete absence of logical order" (p. 39); and he notes, "It was more a question of personal exchange than of taking an objective position" (p. 41). In his introduction to *Some Thoughts Concerning Education* (Locke, 1880), Quick reports that Locke himself made similar criticisms of the essays of Montaigne. For Locke and others writing as he did, the essay came to serve as an exploratory device for examining problems and in the course of that examination producing new knowledge. The essay could serve these functions, at least for the purposes of science and philosophy, only by adopting the language of explicit, written, logically connected prose.

This specialized form of language was adopted by the Royal Society of London which, according to its historian Sprat (1667/1966), was concerned "with the advancement of science and with the improvement of the English language as a medium of prose" (p. 56). The society demanded a mathematical plainness of language and rejected all amplifications, digressions, and swellings of style. This use of language made writing a powerful intellectual tool, I have suggested, by rendering the logical implications of statements more detectable and by altering the statements themselves to make their implications both clear and true.

The process of formulating statements, deriving their implications, testing the truth of those implications, and using the results to revise or generalize from the original statement characterized not only empiricist philosophy but also the development of deductive empirical science. The result was the same, namely the formulation of a small set of connected statements of great generality that may occur as topic sentences of paragraphs or as premises of extended scientific or philosophical treatise. Such statements were notable not only in their novelty and abstractness but also in that they related to prior knowledge in an entirely new way. No longer did general premises necessarily rest on the data of common experience, that is, on commonsense intuition. Rather, as Bertrand Russell (1940) claimed for mathematics, a premise is believed because true implications follow from it, not because it is intuitively plausible. In fact, it is just this mode of using language—the deduction of counterintuitive models of reality—which distinguishes modern from ancient science (see Ong, 1958).

Moreover, not only did the language change, the picture of reality sustained by language changed as well; language and reality were reordered. Inhelder and Piaget (1958) describe this altered relationship between language and reality as a stage of mental development:

> The most distinctive property of formal thought is this reversal of direction be-
> tween reality and possibility; instead of deriving a rudimentary theory from the
> empirical data as is done in concrete inferences, formal thought begins with a theo-
> retical synthesis implying that certain relations are necessary and thus proceeds in
> the opposite direction. (p. 251)

The ability to make this "theoretical synthesis," I suggest, is tied to the analysis of
the implications of the explicit theoretical statements permitted by writing.

Others have made the same point. Ricoeur (1973) has argued that language is
not simply a reflection of reality but rather a means of investigating and enlarging
reality. Hence, the text does not merely reflect readers' expectations; instead, the
explicitness of text gives them a basis for constructing a meaning and then evaluating their own experiences in terms of it. Thus text *can* serve to realign language and reality. N. Goodman (1968), too, claims that "the world is as many
ways as it can be truly described" (p. 6).

This property of language, according to Popper (1972), opens up the possibility of "objective knowledge." Popper claims that the acquisition of theoretical
knowledge proceeds by offering an explicit theory (a statement), deriving and
testing implications of the theory, and revising it in such a way that its implications are both productive and defensible. The result is a picture of the world derived from the repeated application of a particular literary technique: "science
is a branch of literature" (Popper, 1972, p. 185).

Thus far I have summarized two of the major stages or steps in the creation of
explicit, autonomous meanings. The first step toward making language explicit
was at the graphemic level with the invention of an alphabetic writing system.
Because it had a distinctive sign for each of the represented sounds and thereby
reduced the ambiguity of the signs, an alphabetic system relied much less on
readers' prior knowledge and expectancies than other writing systems. This explicitness permitted the preservation of meaning across space and time and the
recovery of meaning by the more or less uninitiated. Even original ideas could be
formulated in language and recovered by readers without recourse to some intermediary stage.

The second step involved the further development of explicitness at the semantic level by allowing a given sentence to have only one interpretation. Proverbial
and poetic statements, for example, were not permissible because they admitted
more than one interpretation, the appropriate one determined by the context of
utterance. The attempt was to construct sentences for which the meaning was
dictated by the lexical and syntactic features of the sentence itself. To this end, the
meaning of terms had to be conventionalized by means of definitions, and the
rules of implication had to be articulated and systematically applied.

The Greeks perfected the alphabetic system and began developing the writing
style that, encouraged by the invention of printing and the form of extended texts
it permitted, culminated in the essayist technique. The result was not an ordinary
language, not a mother tongue, but rather a form of language specialized to serve
the requirements of autonomous, written, formalized text. Indeed, children are
progressively inducted into the use of this language during the school years. Thus

formal schooling, in the process of teaching children to deal with prose texts, fosters the ability to "speak a written language" (Greenfield, 1972, p. 169).

The Effects of Considerations of Literacy on Issues of Language

Let us return to the linguistic and psychological issues with which we began and reconsider them in the light of the cultural inventions that have served to make language explicit, to put the meaning into the text.

Linguistic Theory

The differences between oral language and written text may help to explain the current controversy between the syntactic approach represented by Chomsky and the semantic approach represented by Chafe. Several aspects of Chomsky's theory of grammar require attention in this regard. For Chomsky, the meaning of language is not tied to the speaker's knowledge of the world but is determined by the sentence or text itself. The meaning of a sentence is assigned formally or mechanically on the basis of the syntactic and lexical properties of the sentence per se and not on the basis of the expectancies or preferred interpretations of the listener (Chomsky, 1972, p. 24). Chomsky's theory is fundamentally designed to preserve the truth conditions of the sentence, and permissible transformations are ones that preserve truth. To illustrate, an active sentence can be related to a passive sentence by means of a set of transformations because they are assumed to share a common base or underlying structure. The equivalence between active and passive sentences is logical meaning: one sentence is true if and only if the other is true (see Harman, 1972; Lakoff, 1972).

My conjecture is that Chomsky's theory applies to a particular specialization of language, namely, the explicit written prose that serves as the primary tool of science and philosophy. It can serve as a theory of speech only when the sentence meaning is a fully adequate representation of the speaker's meaning. In ordinary conversational language this is rarely the case. The empirical studies mentioned earlier have provided strong evidence that experimental subjects rarely confine their interpretations to the information conventionalized in text. Rather, they treat a sentence as a cue to a more elaborate meaning.

As we have seen, other linguistic theories treat language as a means of representing and recovering the intentions of the speaker. The general semanticists and, to a lesser extent, Chafe, have argued that the linguistic system is not autonomous. The meaning of a sentence is not determined exclusively by the lexical and syntactic properties of the sentence itself; rather, the sentence is an indication of the speaker's meaning. While this assumption seems appropriate to the vast range of ordinary oral language, it overlooks the case in which the intended meaning is exactly represented by the sentence meaning as is ideally the case in explicit essayist prose.

We may conclude, then, that the controversy between the syntacticists and the semanticists is reducible to the alternative assumptions that language is appropriately represented in terms of sentence meanings or in terms of speaker's meanings. The latter assumption is entirely appropriate, I suggest, for the description of the ordinary oral conversational language, for what I have called utterances. On the other hand, I propose that Chomsky's theory is not a theory of language generally but a theory of a particular specialized form of language assumed by Luther, exploited by the British essayists, and formalized by the logical positivists. It is a model for the structure of autonomous written prose, for what I have called text.

On Comprehension

The comprehension of sentences involves several different processes. Ordinary conversational speech, especially children's speech, relies for its comprehension on a wide range of information beyond that explicitly marked in the language. To permit communication at all, there must be wide agreement among users of a language as to phonological, syntactic, and semantic conventions. A small set of language forms, however, maps onto an exceedingly wide range of referential events; hence, ambiguity is always possible if not inevitable. Speakers in face-to-face situations circumvent this ambiguity by means of such prosodic and paralinguistic cues as gestures, intonation, stress, quizzical looks, and restatement. Sentences in conversational contexts, then, are interpreted in terms of the following: agreed-upon lexical and syntactic conventions; a shared knowledge of events and a preferred way of interpreting them; a shared perceptual context; and agreed-upon prosodic features and paralinguistic conventions.

Written languages can have no recourse to shared context, prosodic features, or paralinguistic conventions since the preserved sentences have to be understood in contexts other than those in which they were written. The comprehension of such texts requires agreed-upon linguistic conventions, a shared knowledge of the world, and a preferred way of interpreting events. But Luther denied the dependence of text on a presupposed, commonsensical knowledge of the world, and I have tried to show that the linguistic style of the essayist has systematically attempted to minimize if not eliminate this dependence. This attempt has proceeded by assigning the information carried implicitly by nonlinguistic means into an enlarged set of explicit linguistic conventions. In this way written textual language can be richer and more explicit than its oral language counterpart. Within this genre of literature, if unconventionalized or nonlinguistic knowledge is permitted to intrude, we charge the writer with reasoning via unspecified inferences and assumptions or the reader with misreading the text.

Comprehension, therefore, may be represented by a set of procedures that involves selectively applying one's personal experiences or knowledge of the world to the surface structure of sentences to yield a meaning. In so doing, one elaborates, assimilates, or perhaps "imagines" the sentence. And these elaborative procedures are perfectly appropriate to the comprehension of ordinary conversational utterances. In turn, the sentence becomes more comprehensible and dramatically more memorable, as Anderson and Ortony (1975), Bransford and Johnson (1973), and Bransford, Barclay, and Franks (1972) have shown.

The price to be paid for such elaboration and assimilation is that the listener's or reader's meaning deviates to some degree from the meaning actually represented in the sentence. Such interpretation may alter the truth conditions specified by the statement. To illustrate, using Anderson and Ortony's sentence, if the statement "the apples are in the container" is interpreted as "the apples are in the basket," the interpretation specifies a different set of truth conditions than did the original statement. We could legitimately say that the statement had been misinterpreted. Yet that is what normally occurs in the process of understanding and remembering sentences; moreover, as we have shown in our laboratory, it is what preschool children regularly do (Olson & Nickerson, 1977; Pike & Olson, 1977; Hildyard & Olson, Note 1). If young children are given the statements, "John hit Mary" or "John has more than Mary," unlike adults, they are incapable of determining the direct logical implications that "Mary was hit by John" or "Mary has less than John." If the sentence is given out of context, they may inquire, "Who is Mary?" Given an appropriate story or pictorial context, children can assimilate the first statement to that context and then give a new description of what they now know. If the sentence cannot be assimilated to their knowledge base, they are helpless to arrive at its implications; children are unable to apply interpretive procedures to the sentence meaning, the meaning in the text. They can, however, use sentences as a cue to speaker's meaning if these sentences occur in an appropriate context. Literate adults are quite capable of treating sentences in either way. What they do presumably depends on whether the sentence is too long to be remembered verbatim, whether it is written and remains available for repeated consultation, or, perhaps, whether the sentence is regarded as utterance or text.

On Reasoning

Extending the argument to reasoning tasks, it is clear that solutions may be reached in either of two quite different ways. Relying on the processes usually involved in the comprehension of spoken language, one may interpret a premise in terms of previous knowledge of the world, operate on that resulting knowledge, and produce an answer other than that expected on a purely formal logical basis. Such reasoning, based on an intrusion of unspecified knowledge, is not a logical argument but an enthymeme. Nevertheless, it is the most common form of ordinary reasoning (Cole, Gay, Glick, & Sharp, 1971; Wason & Johnson-Laird, 1972).

Logical reasoning, on the other hand, is the procedure of using conventionalized rules of language to draw necessary implications from statements treated as text. For such reasoning, the implications may run counter to expectancies or may be demonstrably false in their extension; however, it matters only that the conclusion follows directly from the sentence meaning, the conventionalized aspects of the statement itself. The fact that most people have difficulty with such operations indicates simply their inability or lack of experience in suspending prior knowledge and expectancies in order to honor the sentence meaning of statements. In fact, Henle (1962) has noted that in reasoning tasks subjects often have difficulty in distinguishing between a conclusion that is logically true, one that is factually true, and one with which they agree. According to the analysis offered here, in the first case the conclusion logically follows from the text—the meaning is restricted to that explicitly represented or conventionalized in the text and to the implications that necessarily follow; in the second case the conclusion follows from unstated but shared knowledge of the world; in the third case the conclusion follows from unspecified and unshared personal knowledge. I would argue that in neither of the latter cases are we justified in calling the reasoning logical.

Logical reasoning as defined here assumes that fully explicit, unambiguous statements can be created to serve as premises. This is a goal that consistently evades ordinary language use. It is extremely difficult if not impossible to create statements that specify all and only the necessary and sufficient information for drawing logical inferences.[3] Hence, formal reasoning has led to a reliance, where possible, on the use of symbols related by a logical calculus. To illustrate the difficulties, I will use three studies from our laboratory. Bracewell (Note 2) has shown that the simple propositional statement employed by Wason and Johnson-Laird (1970), "If p is on one side, then q is on the other," is ambiguous in at least two ways: "one side" may be interpreted as referring to "the showing side" or to "either the showing side or the hidden side"; "if . . . then" may be interpreted as a conditional relation or as a biconditional relation. Differences in subjects' performance can be traced to different interpretations of the proposition. In a similar vein, Hidi (Note 3) has shown that if a simple proposition such as "if you go to Ottawa, you must travel by car" is understood as describing a temporal event, subjects draw quite different inferences than if it is treated purely as a logical statement. In a developmental study, Ford (1976) has shown that, given a disjunctive statement, children (and adults in natural language contexts) treat "or" as posing a simple choice between mutually exclusive, disjoint alternatives (for example, "Do you want an apple *or* an orange?" "An apple."). When children of five or six years of age are presented with "or" commands involving disjoint events as well as overlapping and inclusive events—the latter being involved in Piaget's famous task "Are there more rabbits *or* animals?"—Ford found that children's logical competence breaks down only when the known structure of events runs counter to the presuppositions of the language. Rather than revise their conception of events— rabbits and animals are not disjoint classes—children misinterpret or reject the sentence. They say, for example, "There are more rabbits because there are only two ducks!"

There are, then, at least two aspects to the study of logical reasoning. The first stems from the fact that statements are often ambiguous, especially when they occur out of context. Thus failures in reasoning may reflect merely the assignment of an interpretation that, although it is consistent with the sentence meaning explicit in the text, is different from the one intended by the experimenter. Second, logical development in a literate culture involves learning to apply logical operations to the sentence meaning rather than to the assimilated or interpreted or assumed speaker's meaning. Development consists of learning to confine interpre-

---

[3] This question touches upon the important epistemological issue of the formal adequacy of the methods of science. The most common argument is that almost any important theory can be shown to be formally inadequate (see Gellner, 1975).

tation to the meaning explicitly represented in the text and to draw inferences exclusively from that formal but restricted interpretation.

Whether or not all meaning can be made explicit in the text is perhaps less critical than the belief that it can and that making it so is a valid scientific enterprise. This was clearly the assumption of the essayists, and it continues in our use of language for science and philosophy. Explicitness of meaning, in other words, may be better thought of as a goal rather than an achievement. But it is a goal appropriate only for the particular, specialized use of language that I have called text.

On Learning a Language

The contrast between language as an autonomous system for representing meaning and language as a system dependent in every case upon nonlinguistic and paralinguistic cues for the sharing of intentions—the contrast between text and utterance—applies with equal force to the problem of language acquisition. A formal theory of sentence meaning, such as Chomsky's, provides a less appropriate description of early language than would a theory of intended meanings that admitted a variety of means for realizing those intentions. Such means include a shared view of reality, a shared perceptual context, and accompanying gestures, in addition to the speech signal. At early stages of language acquisition the meaning may be specified nonlinguistically, and this meaning may then be used to break the linguistic code (Macnamara, 1972; Nelson, 1974). Language acquisition, then, is primarily a matter of learning to conventionalize more and more of the meaning in the speech signal. This is not a sudden achievement. If an utterance specifies something different from what the child is entertaining, the sentence will often be misinterpreted (Clark, 1973; Donaldson & Lloyd, 1974). But language development is not simply a matter of progressively elaborating the oral mother tongue as a means of sharing intentions. The developmental hypothesis offered here is that the ability to assign a meaning to the sentence per se, independent of its nonlinguistic interpretive context, is achieved only well into the school years. It is a complex achievement to differentiate and operate upon either what is actually said, the sentence meaning, or what is meant, the speaker's meaning. Children are relatively quick to grasp a speaker's intentions but relatively slow, I suggest, to grasp the literal meaning of what is, in fact, said.

Several studies lend plausibility to these arguments. For example, Olson and Nickerson (1977) examined the role of story or pictorial context on the detection of sentence implications. Five-year-old children were given a statement and asked if a second statement, logically related to the first, was true. For instance, they were told, "John was hit by Mary," then asked, "Did Mary hit John?" The ability of these five-year-olds to answer such a question depended on how much they knew about the characters and context mentioned in the sentences. If they did not know who John and Mary were or why the experimenter was asking the question, they could not assign a full semantic interpretation to the sentence. This and other studies suggest that children, unlike adults, assign a speaker's meaning to a simple sentence if that sentence is contextually appropriate and directly assimilable to their prior knowledge, but they have difficulty assigning a meaning to the statement alone (Carpenter & Just, 1975; Clark, 1974; Olson & Filby, 1972; Hildyard & Olson, Note 1). But by late childhood, at least among schooled children, meanings are assigned quite readily to the sentence per se. Children come to see that sentences have implications that are necessary by virtue of sentence meaning itself. They become progressively more able to exist in a purely linguistically speci- fied, hypothetical world for both purposes of extracting logical implications of statements and of living in those worlds that, as Ricoeur (1973) notes, are opened up by texts. This, however, is the end point of development in a literate culture and not a description of how original meanings are acquired in early language learning.

On Reading

The relations between utterances and texts become acute when children are first confronted with printed books. As I have pointed out, children are familiar with using the spoken utterance as one cue among others. Children come to school with a level of oral competence in their mother-tongue only to be confronted with an exemplar of written text, the reader, which is an autonomous representation of meaning. Ideally, the printed reader depends on no cues other than linguistic cues; it represents no intentions other than those represented in the text; it is ad- dressed to no one in particular; its author is essentially anonymous; and its mean- ing is precisely that represented by the sentence meaning. As a result, when chil- dren are taught to read, they are learning both to read and to treat language as text. Children familiar with the use of textlike language through hearing printed stories obviously confront less of a hurdle than those for whom both reading and that form of language are novel.

The decoding approach to reading exploits both the explicit nature of the al- phabet and the explicit nature of written prose text. Ideally, since the meaning is in the text, the programmatic analysis of letters, sounds, words, and grammar would specify sentence meaning. But, as I have indicated, it is precisely with sentence meaning that children have the most difficulty. Hence, the decoding of sentence meaning should be treated as the end point of development, not as the means of access to print as several writers have maintained (Reid, 1966; Richards, 1971).

On Language and Meaning: Summary and Conclusions

Clearly some aspects of meaning must be sufficiently conventionalized in the lan- guage to permit children and adults to use it as an all-purpose instrument. Thus, children must learn grammatical rules and lexical structure to use language in different contexts for different purposes. However, the degree to which this lin- guistic knowledge is conventionalized and formalized need not be very great in oral contexts since the listener has access to a wide range of information with which to recover the speaker's intentions. Generally, nonlinguistic cues appear to predominate in that if the speaker is elliptical or even chooses the wrong word or grammatical form, we can successfully recover the speaker's intention.

To serve the requirements of written language, however, all of the information relevant to the communication of intention must be present in the text. Further, if the text is to permit or sustain certain conclusions, as in the essayist technique, then it must become an autonomous representation of meaning. But for this purpose the meanings of the terms and the logical relations holding between them must be brought to a much higher degree of conventionalization. Words must be defined in terms of other words in the linguistic system, and rules of grammar must be specialized to make them suitable indications of the text's underlying logical structure. Once this degee of conventionalization is achieved, children or adults have sufficient basis for constructing the meaning explicitly represented by the text. Written text, I am suggesting, is largely responsible for permitting people to entertain sentence meaning per se rather than merely using the sentence as a cue to the meaning entertained by the speaker.

The differences between utterances and texts may be summarized in terms of three underlying principles: the first pertains to meaning, the second to truth, and the third to function. First, in regard to meaning, utterance and text relate in different ways to background knowledge and to the criteria for successful performance. Conventional utterances appeal for their meaning to shared experiences and interpretations, that is, to a common intuition based on shared commonsense knowledge (Lonergan, 1957; Schutz & Luckmann, 1973). Utterances take for content, to use Pope's words, "What oft was tho't but ne'er so well expressed" (cited in Ong, 1971, p. 256). In most speech, as in poetry and literature, the usual reaction is assent—"How true." Statements match, in an often tantalizing way, the expectancies and experiences of the listener. Because of this appeal to expectancies, the criterion for a successful utterance is understanding on the part of the listener. The sentence is not appropriate if the listener does not comprehend. A well-formed sentence fits the requirements of the listener and, as long as this criterion is met, it does not really matter what the speaker says—"A wink is as good as a nod."

Prose text, on the other hand, appeals to premises and rules of logic for deriving implications. Whether or not the premise corresponds to common sense is irrelevant. All that is critical is that the premises are explicit and the inferences correctly drawn. The appeal is formal rather than intuitive. As a consequence, the criterion for the success of a statement in explicit prose text is its formal structure; if the text is formally adequate and the reader fails to understand, that is the reader's problem. The meaning is in the text.

Second, utterance and text appeal to different conceptions of truth. Frye (1971) has termed these underlying assumptions "truth as wisdom" and "truth as correspondence." Truth in oral utterance has to do with truth as wisdom. A statement is true if it is reasonable, plausible, and, as we have seen, congruent with dogma or the wisdom of elders; truth is assimilability to common sense. Truth in prose text, however, has to do with the correspondence between statements and observations. Truth drops its ties to wisdom and to values, becoming the product of the disinterested search of the scientist. True statements in text may be counter to intuition, common sense, or authority. A statement is taken to be true not because the premises from which it follows are in agreement with common sense but rather because true implications follow from it, as Russell (1940) pointed out in regard to mathematics.

Third, conversational utterance and prose text involve different alignments of the functions of language. As Austin (1962) and Halliday (1970) argue, any utterance serves at least two functions simultaneously—the rhetorical or interpersonal function and the logical or ideational function. In oral speech, the interpersonal function is primary; if a sentence is inappropriate to a particular listener, the utterance is a failure. In written text, the logical or ideational functions become primary, presumably because of the indirect relation between writer and reader. The emphasis, therefore, can shift from simple communication to truth, to "getting it right" (Olson, 1977). It may be this realignment of functions in written language that brings about the greater demand for explicitness and the higher degree of conventionalization.

The bias of written language toward providing definitions, making all assumptions and premises explicit, and observing the formal rules of logic produces an instrument of considerable power for building an abstract and coherent theory of reality. The development of this explicit, formal system accounts, I have argued, for the predominant features of Western culture and for our distinctive ways of using language and our distinctive modes of thought. Yet the general theories of science and philosophy that are tied to the formal uses of text provide a poor fit to daily, ordinary, practical, and personally significant experience. Oral language with its depth of resources and its multitude of paths to the same goal, while an instrument of limited power for exploring abstract ideas, is a universal means of sharing our understanding of concrete situations and practical actions. Moreover, it is the language children bring to school. Schooling, particularly learning to read, is the critical process in the transformation of children's language from utterance to text.

Reference Notes

1. Hildyard, A., & Olson, D. R. *On the mental representation and matching operation of action and passive sentences by children and adults,* in preparation.
2. Bracewell, R. J. *Interpretation factors in the four-card selection task.* Paper presented to the Selection Task Conference, Trento, Italy, April 1974.
3. Hidi, S. *Effects of temporal considerations in conditional reasoning.* Paper presented at the Selection Task Conference, Trento, Italy, April 1974.

References

Anderson, R. C., & Ortony, A. On putting apples into bottles: A problem of polysemy. *Cognitive Psychology,* 1975, 7, 167–180.
Austin, J. L. *How to do things with words.* (J. O. Urmson, Ed.). New York: Oxford University Press, 1962.

Barclay, J. R. The role of comprehension in remembering sentences. *Cognitive Psychology,* 1973, **4,** 229–254.

Bloom, L. *Language development: Form and function in emerging grammars.* Cambridge, Mass.: M.I.T. Press, 1970

Bloomfield, L. *Linguistic aspects of science.* Chicago: University of Chicago Press, 1939.

Bluck, R. S. *Plato's life and thought.* London: Routledge & Kegan Paul, 1949.

Bransford, J. D., Barclay, J. R., & Franks, J. J. Sentence memory: A constructive versus interpretive approach. *Cognitive Psychology,* 1972, **3,** 193–209.

Bransford, J. D., & Johnson, M. K. Consideration of some problems of comprehension. In W. Chase (Ed.), *Visual information processing.* New York: Academic Press, 1973.

Brown, R. *A first language: The early stages.* Cambridge, Mass.: Harvard University Press, 1973.

Bruner, J. S. From communication to language: A psychological perspective. *Cognition,* 1973, **3,** 255–287.

Bruner, J. S., & Olson, D. R. Symbols and texts as the tools of intellect. In *The Psychology of the 20th Century, Vol. VII: Piaget's developmental and cognitive psychology within an extended context.* Zurich: Kindler, in press.

Buhler, K. *Sprachtheorie.* Jena, Germany: Gustav Fischer Verlag, 1934.

Carpenter, P., & Just, M. Sentence comprehension: A psycholinguistic processing model of verification. *Psychological Review,* 1975, **82,** 45–73.

Carroll, J. B., & Chall, J. S. (Eds.). *Toward a literate society.* New York: McGraw-Hill, 1975.

Chafe, W. *Meaning and the structure of language.* Chicago: University of Chicago Press, 1970.

Chall, J. S. *Learning to read: The great debate.* New York: McGraw-Hill, 1967.

Chase, S. *The power of words.* New York: Harcourt, Brace, 1954.

Chomsky, N. *Syntactic structures.* The Hague: Mouton, 1957.

Chomsky, N. *Aspects of a theory of syntax.* Cambridge, Mass.: M.I.T. Press, 1965.

Chomsky, N. *Problems of knowledge and freedom.* London: Fontana, 1972.

Clark, E. Non-linguistic strategies and the acquisition of word meanings. *Cognition,* 1973, **2,** 161–182.

Clark, H. H. Semantics and comprehension. In T. A. Sebeok (Ed.), *Current trends in linguistics, Vol. 12: Linguistic and adjacent arts and sciences.* The Hague: Mouton, 1974.

Cole, M., Gay, J., Glick, J., & Sharp, D. *The cultural context of learning and thinking.* New York: Basic Books, 1971.

de Laguna, G. *Speech: Its function and development.* College Park, Md.: McGrath, 1970. (Originally published, 1927.)

Donaldson, M., & Lloyd, P. Sentences and situations: Children's judgments of match and mismatch. In F. Bresson (Ed.), *Current problems in psycholinguistics.* Paris: Editions du Centre National de la Recherche Scientifique, 1974.

Ellul, J. *The technological society.* New York: Vintage Books, 1964.

Fodor, J. A., Bever, T. G., & Garrett, M. F. *The psychology of language.* Toronto: McGraw-Hill, 1974.

Ford, W. G. *The language of disjunction.* Unpublished doctoral dissertation, University of Toronto, 1976.

Frye, N. *The critical path.* Bloomington: Indiana University Press, 1971.

Gadamer, H. G. *Truth and method.* New York: Seabury Press, 1975.

Gelb, I. J. *A study of writing.* Toronto: University of Toronto Press, 1952.

Gellner, E. Book review of *Against Method* by P. Feyerabend. *British Journal for the Philosophy of Science,* 1975, **26,** 331–342.

Gibson, E. J., & Levin, H. *The psychology of reading.* Cambridge, Mass.: M.I.T. Press, 1975.

Gombrich, E. The visual image. In D. R. Olson (Ed.), *Media and symbols: The forms of expression, communication and education.* (The 73rd Yearbook of the National Society for the Study of Education). Chicago: University of Chicago Press, 1974.

Goodman, K. S. Reading: A psycholinguistic guessing game. *Journal of the Reading Specialist*, 1967, **6**, 126–135.

Goodman, N. *Languages of art: An approach to a theory of symbols.* Indianapolis: Bobbs-Merrill, 1968.

Goodnow, J. The nature of intelligent behavior: Questions raised by cross-cultural studies. In L. Resnick (Ed.), *New approaches to intelligence.* Potomac, Md.: Erlbaum and Associates, 1976.

Goody, J., & Watt, I. The consequences of literacy. In J. Goody (Ed.), *Literacy in traditional societies.* Cambridge, Eng.: Cambridge University Press, 1968.

Gray, M. *Song and dance man: The art of Bob Dylan.* London: Abacus, 1973.

Greenfield, P. Oral and written language: The consequences for cognitive development in Africa, the United States, and England. *Language and Speech,* 1972, **15**, 169–178.

Greenfield, P., & Bruner, J. S. Culture and cognitive growth. In D. A. Goslin (Ed.), *Handbook of socialization: Theory and research.* Chicago: Rand-McNally, 1969.

Grice, H. P. Meaning. *Philosophical Review,* 1957, **66**, 377–388.

Halliday, M. A. K. Language structure and language function. In J. Lyons (Ed.), *New horizons in linguistics.* New York: Penguin Books, 1970.

Harman, G. Deep structure as logical form. In D. Davidson & G. Harman (Eds.), *Semantics of natural language.* Dordrecht, Holland: Reidel, 1972.

Havelock, E. *Preface to Plato.* Cambridge, Mass.: Harvard University Press, 1963.

Havelock, E. Prologue to Greek literacy. *Lectures in memory of Louise Tatt Semple, second series, 1966–1971.* Cincinnati: University of Oklahoma Press for the University of Cincinnati Press, 1973.

Havelock, E. *Origins of western literacy.* Toronto: Ontario Institute for Studies in Education, 1976.

Hayakawa, S. I. *Language in thought and action.* London: Allen and Unwin, 1952.

Henle, M. On the relation between logic and thinking. *Psychological Review,* 1962, **63**, 366–378.

Inhelder, B., & Piaget, J. *The growth of logical thinking.* New York: Basic Books, 1958.

Innis, H. *The bias of communication.* Toronto: University of Toronto Press, 1951.

Korzybski, A. *Science and sanity: An introduction to non-Aristotelian systems and general semantics.* Lancaster, Pa.: Science Press, 1933.

Kneale, W., & Kneale, M. *The development of logic.* Oxford: Clarendon Press, 1962.

Lakoff, G. Linguistics and natural logic. In D. Davidson & G. Harman (Eds.), *Semantics of natural language.* Dordrecht, Holland: Reidel, 1972.

Locke, J. *An essay concerning human understanding.* (J. W. Yolton, Ed.). London: Dent, 1961. (Originally published, 1690.)

Locke, J. *Some thoughts concerning education.* (Introduction and Notes by R. H. Quick). Cambridge, Eng.: Cambridge University Press, 1880.

Lonergan, B. J. F. *Insight: A study of human understanding.* New York: Philosophical Library, 1957.

Lord, A. B. *The singer of tales* (Harvard Studies in Comparative Literature, 24). Cambridge, Mass.: Harvard University Press, 1960.

Lyons, J. *Introduction to theoretical linguistics.* Cambridge, Eng.: Cambridge University Press, 1969.

Macnamara, J. The cognitive basis of language learning in infants. *Psychological Review,* 1972, **79**, 1–13.

Maimonides, M. [*Guide of the perplexed*] (S. Pines, trans.). Chicago: University of Chicago Press, 1963.

McLuhan, M. *The Gutenberg galaxy.* Toronto: University of Toronto Press, 1962.

McLuhan, M. *Understanding media: The extensions of man.* Toronto: McGraw-Hill, 1964.

McNeill, D. *The acquisition of language.* New York: Harper & Row, 1970.

Neimark, E. D., & Slotnick, N. S. Development of the understanding of logical connectives. *Journal of Educational Psychology,* 1970, **61**, 451–460.

Nelson, K. Concept, word, and sentence: Interrelations in acquisition and development. *Psychological Review,* 1974, **81,** 267–285.

Olson, D. R. The languages of instruction. In R. Spiro (Ed.), *Schooling and the acquisition of knowledge.* Potomac, Md.: Erlbaum and Associates, 1977.

Olson, D. R., & Filby, N. On the comprehension of active and passive sentences. *Cognitive Psychology,* 1972, **3,** 361–381.

Olson, D. R., & Nickerson, N. The contexts of comprehension: Children's inability to draw implications from active and passive sentences. *Journal of Experimental Child Psychology,* 1977, **23,** 402–414.

Ong, W. J. *Ramus, method and the decay of dialogue.* Cambridge, Mass.: Harvard University Press, 1958. (Reprinted by Octagon Books, 1974.)

Ong, W. J. *Rhetoric, romance and technology: Studies in the interaction of expression and culture.* Ithaca: Cornell University Press, 1971.

Paris, S. G., & Carter, A. Y. Semantic and constructive aspects of sentence memory in children. *Developmental Psychology,* 1973, **9,** 109–113.

Parry, M. The making of Homeric verse. In A. Parry (Ed.), *The collected papers of Milman Parry.* Oxford: Clarendon Press, 1971.

Piaget, J. Intellectual evolution from adolescence to adulthood. *Human Development,* 1972, **15,** 1–12.

Pike, R., & Olson, D. R. A question of *more* or *less. Child Development,* 1977, **48,** 579–586.

Popper, K. *Objective knowledge: An evolutionary approach.* Oxford: Clarendon Press, 1972.

Reid, J. F. Learning to think about reading. *Educational Research,* 1966, **9,** 56–62.

Richards, I. A. Instructional engineering. In S. Baker, J. Barzun, & I. A. Richards (Eds.), *The written word.* Rowley, Mass.: Newbury House, 1971.

Ricoeur, P. Creativity in language: Word, polysemy and metaphor. *Philosophy Today,* 1973, **17,** 97–111.

Russell, B. *An inquiry into meaning and truth.* London: Allen and Unwin, 1940.

Scribner, S., & Cole, M. Cognitive consequences of formal and informal education. *Science,* 1973, **182,** 553–559.

Schutz, A., & Luckmann, T. [*The structures of the life world*] (R. Zaner, & H. Engelhardt, trans.) Evanston, Ill.: Northwestern University Press, 1973.

Smith, F. *Comprehension and learning.* Toronto: Holt, Rinehart & Winston, 1975.

Sprat, T. *History of the Royal Society of London for the improving of natural knowledge.* (J. I. Cope and H. W. Jones, Eds.). St. Louis: Washington University Press, 1966. (Originally published, London, 1667.)

Staudenmayer, H. Understanding conditional reasoning with meaningful propositions. In R. J. Falmagne (Ed.), *Reasoning, representation and process.* Hillsdale, N.J.: Erlbaum and Associates, 1975.

Strawson, P. F. *Meaning and truth: An inaugural lecture delivered before the University of Oxford.* Oxford: Clarendon Press, 1970.

Suppes, P., & Feldman, S. Young children's comprehension of logical connectives. *Journal of Experimental Child Psychology,* 1971, **12,** 304–317.

Taplin, J. E., & Staudenmayer, H. Interpretation of abstract conditional sentences in deductive reasoning. *Journal of Verbal Learning and Verbal Behavior,* 1973, **12,** 530–542.

Wason, P. C., & Johnson-Laird, P. N. A conflict between selecting and evaluating information in an inferential task. *British Journal of Psychology,* 1970, **61,** 509–515.

Wason, P. C., & Johnson-Laird, P. N. *The psychology of reasoning.* London: B. T. Batsford, 1972.

Reading Reconsidered

THOMAS WOLF
New England Foundation for the Arts

During the last two centuries reading has come to refer almost exclusively to the interpretation of written material. In this article Thomas Wolf uses the etymology of the word "read" and the results of current psychological research to reveal the narrowness of this definition. Wolf reviews the research that has led to a new formulation of the reading process and emphasizes the remarkable similarities that have been found in processes underlying reading and other cognitive capacities: memory, perception, reasoning, and problem-solving. Wolf argues that by considering the connection between reading and these other processes we enrich our appreciation of reading and allow for the resurrection of the original meaning of reading as a process applicable to a variety of fields. Using the example of developments in woodcut book illustrations, Wolf examines the relations between the process of reading and the history of artistic styles. He concludes that investigators must look beyond the conventional bounds of reading theory—and other theories as well—if serious advances in human knowledge are to occur.

The verb *read* is, superficially, one of the least ambiguous words in the English language. Indeed, if we were to ask someone to define it, it is almost certain that the definition would suggest a process by which meaning is extracted, through a system of symbolic decoding, from something written or printed like a book, a billboard, or a letter. But this idea—that reading is no more than a mental interaction with the written word—is actually rather new; new, that is, when one considers the etymology of the word.

The verb *read* derives from the Teutonic word *rædan*. In its original form the word implied nothing about decoding texts; rather, it could be used in a number of contexts to mean giving counsel, taking charge, or explaining the obscure. The original Teutonic verb spawned a number of descendants in various languages,

Copyright © Thomas Wolf, 1977.

I would like to thank four psychologists who made suggestions on an earlier version of this article—Courtney B. Cazden, Paul A. Kolers, Sheldon H. White, and Dennis P. Wolf. Many of the theoretical ideas were first developed in conversations with members of Harvard's Project Zero. The section on artistic styles was originally presented as a lecture for the Bates College Psychology Club.

Harvard Educational Review   Vol. 47   No. 3   August 1977, 411–429

and in almost every case it is this last meaning—the interpretation of something obscure—that has gained prominence. Only in the English language and only in the last two centuries has the word *read* come to mean almost exclusively the interpretation of written material.

In modern English, vestiges of earlier meanings of *read* abound, although it may be primarily at the level of popular culture that the word retains its original meaning—to advise, to interpret, to explain. Thus, Madame Salina, the "Reader" who hangs her shingle across from Harvard's Widener Library, does a very different kind of reading from that which goes on across the street. She is a fortune teller—both an "advisor" and a "reader" (if one is to believe her sign), and though this may seem rather redundant, we can forgive Madame Salina for catering to modern ignorance. So, too, in contemporary folk culture is the multisensory dimension of the word *read* retained. When, in a Marvel comic book, a character can be seen yelling, "Yes, sir, I read you loud and clear," we are to understand that he hears a message, not that he sees it. By choosing his words in such a fashion, our comic-book hero continues a tradition at least as old as Spenser's *Faerie Queene* (1590)—a tradition that admits to the verb *read* the possibility of interpreting sounds as well as visual stimuli: "Right hard it was for wight which did it heare/ To reade what manner musicke that mote bee."

The etymology of the word *read* has been on the minds of psychologists ever since Huey (1908/1968) conducted his pioneering research into the reading process in the early years of this century. Nor is this interest surprising. Just as early uses of *read* point to a complex process of interpretation, so modern psychological investigations have revealed that reading—particularly skilled reading—is, in fact, a complex form of information gathering, sorting, interpretation, and analysis. This research has produced other payoffs. Remarkable similarities have been demonstrated in the way people read text, the way they view pictures, the way they read music, and the way they study maps. In addition, the study of reading processes has begun to shed light on more basic kinds of human activity —attention, perception, and thinking itself.

In the pages that follow, I will review briefly the events that led to a new formulation of psychological theories of reading. These events have been part of a larger revolution within the field of psychology—a revolution that began in the mid-1950s and that has brought about a fundamental reconceptualization of human thought processes. Following the historical review, I will outline one of the many interesting applications of the new theories of reading to fields formerly thought to be totally unrelated, specifically the relationship between theories of reading and the history of artistic styles.

The Historical Perspective

In 1956 the *Psychological Review* published George A. Miller's "The magical number seven, plus or minus two: Some limits on our capacity for processing information." Now considered a classic, this paper encouraged a decade of energetic experimentation in the realms of short-term (or immediate) memory, attention, perception, and other aspects of human thought processes. Toward the end of that period, psychologists began to apply the new theoretical knowledge to the study of skilled reading.

For anyone attempting to understand the dynamics of skilled reading, Miller's original paper and a number of others that followed posed certain theoretical dilemmas. As long as one regarded the human mind as a kind of great sponge with the ability to soak up myriad amounts of perceptual information, there was no problem in explaining the fantastic speeds of skilled readers going about common, everyday reading tasks. But Miller had proposed that at any moment in time the human mind could process only about seven pieces of random information, such as a string of unrelated letters. Further, Kolers and Katzman (1966) had demonstrated that recognition of a single letter required between a quarter and a third of a second. If one assumed that a skilled reader dealt with text by reading individual letters, then the theory of skilled reading added up to a mathematical paradox. Many readers, in practice, could handle between 300 and 350 words per minute; in theory, however, it would take no less than five minutes to decode the 1,500 or so letters that these words contained. The situation was not unlike the notable case reported by physicists who claimed that according to available theoretical laws a bumble bee should not be able to fly. In the same way psychologists who were fixed on the notion that skilled reading involved letter-by-letter decoding were at a loss to explain the remarkable speeds achieved by adult readers. The maximum theoretical speed was short of the actual speed achieved by many skilled readers by a factor of five!

Most psychologists were willing to grant that a skilled reader did not have to decode each letter individually (though as late as 1972 psychologist Philip Gough was still making such a claim), but they could not explain either the details of processing or how a reader could overcome memory constraints. Miller's paper provided a solution to this dilemma. True, his magic number was seven, but this number referred to information slots in short-term memory. Each slot might be filled with a single bit of information. However, if the bits were not random but were somehow related, then they could be grouped together, or chunked, and still occupy only one slot.

The chunking mechanism proposed by Miller and others had obvious implications for reading theory. It certainly improved the mathematical odds that skilled reading could occur. More importantly, if letters could be grouped and processed as chunks, then certain problems that had frustrated experimenters could be resolved. The first difficulty concerned the rapid recognition of long words, which could not be explained by the letter-by-letter processing model. If a reader had to discriminate each letter of a word in order to recognize it and if only seven letters could be retained in the mind at any given moment, then one can imagine the first letter of a long word falling out of memory as soon as the eighth letter of the same word was reached. However, if letter groups could be processed as single units, then longer words could be read smoothly, coherently, and quickly. A second problem had been posed by the Kolers and Katzman (1966) equation, which showed that identification time for single letters equaled roughly a quarter to a third of a second. If more than one letter was discriminated at a time, then in a quarter of a second a reader could discriminate an interrelated letter cluster and thus read much faster than the equation had seemed to predict.

Since the chunking mechanism offered obvious advantages, it was hardly surprising that psychologists attempted to establish that this process actually occurred in skilled reading. Gibson, Pick, Osser, and Hammond (1962), for example, attempted to demonstrate experimentally that there existed a critical indivisible unit, composed of more than one letter, that readers consistently used. But Miller's magic number left other problems unsolved. There were simply too many of these units in certain long words like "antidisestablishmentarianism." And if the problem of explaining the discrimination of a word like "pneumonoultramicroscopic-silicovolcanoconiosis" seemed troublesome, it was compounded immeasurably by the apparently effortless successes of skilled readers in recognizing word groups and even long phrases, seemingly at a single glance. Nor were these the only unexplainable phenomena. Many readers would read a word correctly even when several letters were incorrect or missing; in the same way, they would correctly insert a word into a phrase—often completely unaware that they had done so. In most cases, the insertions were logical and necessary, as when a printer had inadvertently left a word out of the text. But if it was true that readers always read what they saw, then why should they also read what they did not see?[1]

One more finding was disturbingly inconsistent with a theory of reading that stressed the discrimination of letters or letter-groups. When experimenters analyzed the mistakes in oral reading, a surprising pattern emerged. Many of the errors made in tests of oral reading were mistakes of substitution in which one word was read in place of another. Logically, it was expected that virtually every misreading would center around look-alike forms. Thus, one might expect a reader to say something like "faint" for "saint" or even "grille" for "pellet." In either case, the mistake could be explained as a perceptual error based on the similarity of letter forms in the correct and incorrect words. In a large number of cases, however, the words substituted in oral reading did not resemble visually the correct words printed in the text; rather, the new words were distinguished by their logical relation to either the meaning or the grammar of the sentences in which they occurred. For example, in the sentence: "Chew your food carefully or you may get some chunks caught in your throat," a reader might substitute the word "stuck" for "caught."

Clearly, something was wrong with existing theory. There were simply too many things that did not add up. As Kolers (1970) was to point out, experimenters had consistently underestimated the complexity of reading and had been guilty of trying to find a simple answer for a number of difficult questions:

---

1 Proofreaders complain of a similar problem out of which grows their golden rule: "Read what you see, not what you think you see." The mind seems to correct typographic mistakes in the text even when one is trying consciously to see them. Slow, deliberate reading is the only solution. This is why many proofreaders work in teams with one reading aloud, carefully noting every word and mark of punctuation, while the other checks the reading against the original.

Despite the obvious **complexity** of the reading process, the greater number of investigators have sought relatively simple, strictly causal explanations of it. By strictly causal, I mean such simplistic theses as reading is principally the activating of conditional meanings, reading is principally a matter of discriminating the geometry of letters, and reading is a matter of translating graphemes into sounds. There have been few efforts since Huey's masterpiece in 1908 to deal with the whole phenomenon, to account for the variety of events that go into reading. (p. 90)

While Neisser claimed in his *Cognitive Psychology* (1967) that the practice of skilled reading could not be fully explained by existing information-processing theory, he also presented what would be the germ of a new theory of reading. Neisser developed a full-scale model of perception which he called "analysis-by-synthesis." According to this model, perception was not a passive process in which the brain received a myriad of unorganized and undifferentiated information. This was far too uneconomical given the constraints of short-term memory. Rather, perception was an active process of construction. Given a stimulus, the perceiver would begin by organizing data into significant and related units. Based on past experience with similar stimuli—experience stored in long-term memory—this preliminary process of organization would resemble a matching game in which the perceiver, in a fraction of a second, would ask, "Have I seen, heard, felt, tasted, experienced anything like this before?" After organizing the sensory information into significant clusters, the perceiver would begin to construct a hypothesis about the nature of the stimulus. Neisser called such hypotheses "matches," presumably in honor of the many successes in which hypothesized meanings corresponded with the significant information contained in the original stimulus. Occasionally, synthesized matches would turn out to be inaccurate as additional information from the stimulus became available. However, an original hypothesis could be modified easily and a more accurate match generated.

It was readily apparent that Neisser's perceptual model satisfied the requirements of economy dictated by Miller and his followers. A human perceiver, using Neisser's version of analysis-by-synthesis,[2] had great advantages over a machine whose only perceptual strategy was passive intake of information. With only a fraction of the data in hand, the human perceiver could search through long-term memory and come up with a fairly reliable hypothesis about what the rest of the data contained. In the cases of speech or written material, a few sounds or letters might be sufficient for recognition of a word; a few words, in turn, might allow the perceiver to guess a phrase or a whole sentence.

In everyday experience Neisser's analysis-by-synthesis model cleared up many apparent mysteries. In conversations with people who spoke very slowly, for example, many listeners often desired and occasionally carried out the completion of sentences. How was it possible to complete a speaker's sentence with ac-

---

[2] I have referred to this perceptual model as "Neisser's version of analysis-by-synthesis." In other contexts (most notably in linguistics) the term "analysis-by-synthesis" has a strict technical meaning. Neisser uses the term in a somewhat diluted form to mean something like using one's knowledge to aid in interpreting what one is faced with.

curacy if speech perception involved only listening to sound patterns and combining the spoken sounds into organized meaning? According to the new model, the sentence-completion phenomenon was not difficult to explain. The listener's perceptual apparatus, having generated a likely completion to the sentence long before the speaker had articulated the words, was hungry for new material, not for the confirmation of a hypothesis already known as true.

Analysis-by-synthesis also explained why in rapid reading such a large number of minor misprints went unnoticed by skilled readers, a phenomenon that had been proven experimentally as far back as Pillsbury's experiments in 1897. The earlier perceptual model which characterized reading as a discrimination task involving letters or letter groups was hard put to explain why proof reading, or the finding of minor errors, was such a difficult skill for rapid readers to cultivate. According to the letter-discrimination model of reading, misprints should interfere with accurate word recognition; one would therefore expect that they would be both distracting and noticeable. For those common cases in which skilled readers either corrected or inserted words without being distracted, the letter-discrimination model could offer no reasonable explanations.

Analysis-by-synthesis, however, explained these occurrences easily and sensibly. According to this model, skilled readers searched only for enough clues to allow them to make reasonable hypotheses about the probable meanings of words, phrases, and sentences. In attempting to guess the meaning of a word, for example, readers might use such clues as the initial letter, the terminal letter, letters with ascenders or descenders, or the whole word's length and shape. If the hypothesis about a particular word made sense grammatically and conveyed a meaning which seemed to fit the context, it would not be necessary to search for more clues; instead, the reader could move on to the next word or group of words. This explained the difficulty of finding incorrect letters within words: if a hypothesis had been formed about a word's meaning without making use of the delinquent letters, and if the reader's eyes moved on to the next word after that hypothesis had been formed, what strategy existed to discover that the word was actually misspelled?

The odds against finding minor misprints were further increased by the fact that in rapid reading words were not always processed individually. Once the reader had enough clues to suggest the meaning of a phrase, there was no reason to verify each component word within the phrase. Given the tendency to scan word clusters, the reader's apparent difficulty in noticing incorrect letters within words was hardly a mystery, nor was the reader's propensity for correcting or inserting words without any awareness of having done so. The meaning of the phrase or sentence subsumed the meanings of individual letters and words and often controlled what the reader thought he or she saw. In rare cases, it is true, the predicted meanings did not make sense contextually, and in such cases the reader might be forced to reread the phrase word-by-word. Usually, however, as Neisser (1967) remarks, "In rapid reading, we attain a meaning without identifying individual words" (p. 136).

Although admitting an embarrassing ignorance concerning many of the details of skilled reading, Neisser came to characterize it as "a kind of analysis-by-synthesis"; in so doing, he was quick to draw the connection between the reading process and thought itself:

> Where rapid reading is concerned . . . the end product of cognitive activity is not a bit of verbal behavior but a deep cognitive structure; not a verbalized name but a continuing silent stream of thought. Reading for meaning seems to be a kind of analysis-by-synthesis, a construction which builds a non-sensory structure just as "lower levels" of cognition synthesize visual figures or spoken words. Reading is externally guided thinking. (p. 136)

Here at last was a formulation that could provide the groundwork for a new theory of skilled reading—a theory that de-emphasized decoding and stressed instead information integration, interpretation, and generation. Although other cognitive psychologists were to work out the actual model of reading as a process of construction, Neisser's foundations for information-processing theory were to aid them greatly.

Perhaps most important, the new theory implied that the practice of skilled reading was completely analogous to other tasks in which the perceiver actively organized the symbolic units of a display in order to interpret it. It implied, according to Kolers (1970), "that the understanding of the mechanisms of reading can illuminate the means by which any symbolic information (instrument dials, road signs, musical scores, circuit diagrams, paintings) is interpreted and used" (p. 118). Thus formulated, the theory left open the opportunity to characterize reading quite broadly as the ability to interpret diverse sorts of information. In concrete terms, the new formulation suggested that there were many similarities between the skilled reading of text on the one hand and the reading of music (Wolf, 1976) or pictures (Kolers, 1973) on the other; and it also implied that the process of "reading" clouds, maps, the images on film, or even artistic styles was, in information-gathering terms, not unlike the process of reading pages of print.

The significance of these discoveries was immediately obvious: fields of inquiry once thought to be distinct now appeared to be related through reading theory. Equally important was the implication for research: if these fields could be related, then the study of one could lead to important discoveries in another. In fact, the new theories of reading had themselves been brought to light by psychologists such as Miller, Neisser, and Kolers who had begun by studying other problems. But now reading theory, in turn, was to shed light on other disciplines having their own orthodoxies and well-established methods of study. It is to one of these other disciplines that we shall turn in the following section.

Reading Theory and the History of Artistic Styles[3]

> A style, like a culture or climate of opinion, sets up a horizon of expectation, a mental set, which registers deviations and modifications with exaggerated sensitivity. In noticing relationships the mind registers tendencies. The history of

[3] The term "artistic styles" in this section refers to styles in all art forms, not merely in the visual arts.

art is full of reactions that can only be understood in this way. (Gombrich, 1960, p. 60)

When educated perceivers stand before a painting, listen to a piece of music, or read a poem or a novel, they actively engage in a process of interpretation. If they immediately recognize the work in question by placing it in a period, they have responded to certain tendencies within the work that reveal a great deal about it. Though we may marvel at the achievement, the immediate recognition of a work of art is not much more than a simple parlor trick if the perceiver is properly trained. For educated viewers or listeners have certain mental structures that they can match to a work; they have, as Gombrich has called it, "a horizon of expectation" or a "mental set" which allows them to recognize works immediately even though they have not seen or heard them before.

The act of aesthetic perception can logically be characterized as a form of skilled reading. The reader—whether of a printed page, a painting, or a musical work—is faced with a myriad of sensory information, much of it highly symbolic. If we remind ourselves of Miller's magic number, which sets certain constraints on the human perceptual apparatus, it is immediately apparent that readers cannot extract meaning from the vast array of sensory data until they have found significant and revealing relationships within the material. These relationships allow them to chunk the diverse bits of information into a very few telling perceptual clues. According to Neisser, the reader, whether of text or of artistic styles, must analyze the meaning of the symbolic material by synthesizing the relationships within it. According to Kolers, the reader must construct these relationships. Whatever terms are used, it is clear that skilled reading—either of an unadorned page of print or of a lavish work of art—involves a good deal of perceptual condensation, reorganization, and interpretation.

For the reader of a printed page, the interpretive process is made possible by certain symbolic clues intrinsic to the communication medium—letters and words. The more familiar the reader is with the alphabet, certain letter combinations, phonic rules, and familiar words and phrases, the more rapidly he or she will be able to construct the meanings that the letters and words contain. For the aesthetic perceiver, clues to meaning are to be found in certain stylistic conventions—use of perspective, brush stroke, harmonic sequences, sentence structure. These, like letters and words for the reader of text, offer the means by which significant information can be extracted, sorted, evaluated, and interpreted.

There is at least one fundamental difference between the conventions of written communication and the conventions of artistic styles. Language conventions are relatively stable, changing slowly over a period of generations, sometimes centuries. Stylistic conventions, by way of contrast, are highly volatile and subject to rapid and revolutionary change. One generation of artists rarely adopts the conventions of its predecessors without major alterations in technique and subject matter. In periods of relatively tranquil stylistic development we see what Ackerman (1962) has called "the clearest indication of a recurrent pattern in art—the development of techniques from a stage of crudity and exploration to a stage of refinement" (p. 233). At the time of more revolutionary style shifts, one can observe the virtual replacement of one set of conventions with another, often in the space of a decade or two. Compare Albrecht Dürer's use of line with that of his predecessors, or Haydn's use of sonata form with the earlier convention of baroque *fortspinnung;* contrast James Joyce's version of interior monologue with that of Henry James. In each example, selected from different centuries and different media, we see the rapidity with which one set of stylistic conventions can replace another.

Rapid style shifts have an interesting and predictable effect on aesthetic perceivers (or readers). Familiarity with the conventions of the older style causes the new to seem difficult, strange, virtually unreadable. Remember that familiarity with a style implies an ability to reduce the myriad of sensory information to a small number of clues about meaning. Indeed, the chunking process, which countless psychologists have referred to since the appearance of the Miller paper, requires a fundamental understanding of the relationships among parts, an ability to isolate the important from the peripheral, a strategy for identifying what is figure and what is ground. When new stylistic conventions take over, the relationships between clues and meanings shift. Different bits of information take on significance; others become less important. Specific clusters no longer are to be related. Aesthetic readers often become confused and angry as they find their strategies for processing the old conventions—strategies which have become second nature—not counting for much.

Consider, for example, the adverse reaction to Schoenberg's music in the early decades of this century. Listeners reared on the symphonies of Brahms and the operas of Wagner could no longer expect the implied tension and relaxation contained in the familiar concords and discords. The relationships between pitches upon which the entire tonal system was built were no longer germane. Intervals, chords, the entire harmonic system no longer worked the way it was supposed to. Nor were Faulkner's unchronological accounts, particularly in works like *The Sound and the Fury,* understandable to a generation of readers raised on the novels of Dickens. Faced with this new approach to storytelling, a reader's obligation was to think about the novel (and particularly the telling of it), "in its disorder, as Faulkner placed it before us" (Edel, 1962, p. 164). But this was hardly easy for a reader who had come to expect chronological accuracy as a given of the narrative style.

There exists, then, an important relationship between changes in stylistic conventions and the process of aesthetic perception. Predictable crises in reading can be expected when style shifts occur rapidly. But beyond this, we can also see another relationship between style shifts and the reader, one which has even more far-reaching effects on the history of style. What we can observe is a causal relationship between the perceptual constraints of the reader and the revolutionary shifts in style which signal the virtual replacement of one set of conventions with another.

If we look at the history of almost any artistic medium and analyze what happens to stylistic development in any given period, we can observe two basic kinds of changes, one gradual, the other rapid. Once a new style has become accepted, it goes through a period of gradual development from a stage of simplicity and exploration toward one of increased refinement. Compare, for example, Giotto's paintings with those of Leonardo, either for expressivity, the sculptural quality of the figures, or the use of three-dimensional perspective. Even for the untrained observer, Leonardo's paintings show the evidence of sophisticated stylistic development. Generally, along with this increased refinement, later stages of development reveal increased complexity of stylistic conventions. Compare Wagner's use of the tonal system with Mozart's or even Beethoven's. In Wagner's music, a single chord can be so complex as to spawn vigorous debate over its precise function and meaning.[4]

The development of a style toward increased refinement and complexity does not go on indefinitely, however. Indeed, once it reaches a certain point the whole stylistic system seems to become overburdened, to flounder, and to fail. Very rapidly the existing style is replaced with a totally new set of stylistic conventions. The new style, though often difficult to accept at first, generally reflects a simplification, an unburdening and separation from a complex, rule-governed system. Compare James Joyce's sentence structure with that of Henry James. Joyce's sentences, by and large, are either short and simple or divided into discrete phrases; by contrast, James's sentences are complex, often thrice-embedded monsters that can each take up half a page of print. An important change in style is clearly reflected in Joyce's simpler approach to sentence construction.

Why do styles seem to change in this way? Why is there the gradual development toward complexity and refinement and why, most particularly, do revolutionary style shifts occur? There are two traditional answers to these questions. First, style shifts are the products of artists; styles develop gradually until such time as creative geniuses change the course of history by developing new ones. Second, style shifts are the products of changing cultural, economic, political, and social conditions. As long as these conditions are relatively stable, style development is gradual. However, when cataclysmic changes occur in the society, revolutionary changes in artistic style inevitably follow.

While there is a good deal of truth in both of these traditional explanations of style changes, neither focuses attention on the aesthetic perceiver. This is a serious flaw since perceivers (or readers) are often at the very center of the process of stylistic development and change. As consumers, aesthetic readers play important roles. As long as they enjoy, buy, attend—in a word, reinforce—the dominant style, it flourishes. When they withdrew their support, the style comes under heavy pressure and must change.

And there is a psychological explanation for why aesthetic perceivers withdraw their support for a set of sylistic conventions when they become overly complex. Remember the constraints under which all of us operate. There is a limit to the complexity of material that the human mind can absorb—a limit indicated by

---

[4] The justly famous "Tristan chord" at the opening of Wagner's *Tristan and Isolde* serves as an ideal example. It has been extensively analyzed by scholars and composers (Mitchell, 1967; Piston, 1941) and admits many possible interpretations.

Miller's magic number and the chunking strategies that perceivers have at their disposal when they look at a painting, listen to music, or read a book. Beyond this complexity endpoint a style cannot develop without leaving the great majority of its audience mystified, frustrated, or unsatisfied.

It is interesting to speculate, in this connection, why young people so often resist the appreciation of great works of art just when a style seems to have reached its fullest flowering. Perhaps it is because extremely refined styles generally carry with them a complex system of conventions. For the older generation, raised in a milieu in which these conventions are well understood, the perceptual effort to decipher may be challenging and enjoyable. Not so for the young. They respond more positively to newer, simpler styles that speak more directly and eloquently to them; and in time it is their predilections and tastes that will determine the course of stylistic development.

If it is true that style shifts are determined by both great artists and historical forces, it also can be argued that they are determined by the perceptual constraints of aesthetic perceivers. Stylistic development does not go on indefinitely but is bounded by what we have called complexity endpoints, points at which psychological factors become critical. These psychological factors, in turn, are based on perceptual limitations imposed by the processing capacity of the human brain. As we have seen, about seven clusters of information can be processed at a single moment of time. When works of art become so complex that they push this limit, the pressure for stylistic change becomes very great.

Style Shifts: The Case of the Woodcut Book Illustration

The history of art provides useful examples of stylistic development and change. Let us examine one very simple and striking change in style—the use of the contour outline in fifteenth-century woodcut illustrations. In this example it is possible to trace the development of a style toward increased refinement and complexity, to a complexity endpoint, and to observe a rapid style shift that brought with it a simplification of the earlier system. At the same time, the example will reveal the close correlation between reading theory and the history of artistic styles.

By the mid-fifteenth century, when Johann Gutenberg was printing his famous Bible—widely believed to be the first book printed from moveable type—the practice of cutting pictures on blocks of wood and printing the material from the uneven, cut surface was already several centuries old. The Chinese craft of woodblock printing was introduced to Europe during the Middle Ages, and from the twelfth century onward block printing was used extensively in the West for the printing of textiles. At the end of the fourteenth century woodblocks were also used to print playing cards (Bland, 1969). Thus, by the time the first illustrated printed books began appearing in the 1460s, the style and technique of the woodcut printer's art were highly developed.

The first book printed from moveable type which also contained woodcuts was produced in the print shop of the Bamberg printer Albrecht Pfister in 1460 or 1461. Within a decade, books illustrated with woodcuts were appearing in most of the printing towns throughout Germany. The woodcuts reflected certain stylistic assumptions closely tied to the technical requirements of fifteenth-century printing. Such printing as a means of pictorial mass production was essentially a one-color technique. While it was possible to produce multicolored prints, the various techniques for doing so were time-consuming and costly. The fifteenth-century printer found it convenient to adopt the style then popular for fabric printing, producing designs that consisted of simple black lines. Instead of printing colors, the printer hired an illustrator or illuminator to fill in the colors by hand; the woodcut itself contained only the pictorial outlines (see Figure 1). As Bland (1969) has remarked: "Nearly all these cuts were in simple outline and seem to have been conceived simply as a basis for color" (p. 104).

It was not long before printers realized that it was unnecessary to resort to expensive hand coloring. Increasingly, books were produced and sold with uncolored woodcuts. Artists responded by occasionally filling up the enclosed white spaces with primitive suggestions of shading. French artists in particular used parallel lines or curved lines that followed contours to suggest shadows or depths. But by the end of the fifteenth century it was clear that the existing style would not do. The subject matter of illustrations was becoming increasingly complex. Without a means of rendering tones or hues, it was more difficult for the artist to suggest depth or to draw the reader's attention to the important elements within a picture. The artist could employ certain traditional devices to indicate an important character in a crowded woodcut, such as moving the character to center stage and rendering the figure very large. But such devices had obvious disadvantages. If the figure was in the center, the entire scene had to be designed around it—not the happiest arrangement in certain renderings of battle scenes; when the main character was excessively large, the entire picture was thrown out of proportion.

As the desire for complicated subject matter in illustrations became more common, the inadequacy of the dominant woodcut style with its simple outlining became more noticeable. Many artists began to show their dissatisfaction by experimenting with the new medium of copper engraving, which was to become dominant in book illustrations a century later. But this technique created problems for the printer since engravings required a different type of press and, as a result, had to be printed separately from the text. Because of this technical difficulty, most illustrators remained faithful to the woodcut medium and simply allowed their pictures to become more complex. But while this increasing complexity may have solved certain technical problems for artists, it created perceptual problems for readers. By increasing the number of lines and choosing to include more pictorial material in the prints, artists were forcing readers to spend more time and effort in deciphering the meaning of an illustration. The earlier contour-outline prints had been much clearer, with their simple subject matter and the broad expanses of contrasting colors applied by the illuminator. But by the end of the fifteenth century, many of the prints being produced posed severe challenges to readers.

Let us review in strictly psychological terms the nature of the new intelligibility problem. A reader given a woodcut print had, as always, to create meaning by

FIGURE 1

The Ploughman Meets Death, a characteristic woodcut of the earliest period of printed book illustrations. Note contour outlines and lack of internal shading. This print was probably destined for the hand of an illuminator who was to fill the white spaces with color before the book was sold. The woodcut is taken from *Der Ackerman aus Böhmen*, printed by Albrecht Pfister in Bamberg between 1460 and 1462. It is quite possible that this book was the first printed from moveable types which also contained woodcut illustrations.

reducing the sensory data and chunking it into familiar pattern clues. Since short-term memory placed severe constraints on the number of information chunks that could be processed simultaneously, the reader had to reduce the many lines of the print into a very few meaningful pattern clues. Figure 2 provides an interesting example of this dilemma.

In terms of visual information processing, this work represents irreducible complexity regardless of the chunking strategies employed. There is much detail and, more important, the detail does not encourage organization into clear units of visual information. No figure really stands out, and everything seems equally significant; as a result the reader is forced to process the visual information piecemeal. This, then, is what we mean when we speak of a complexity endpoint in stylistic development. The dominant woodcut style had developed beyond the point where the perceptual/reading process was simple and straightforward.

According to our theory, a complexity endpoint is followed by the organization of new styles, and indeed at the end of the century certain artists, most notably Albrecht Dürer, were using the lines of the woodcut in a novel way. A new style was in a critical stage of development—a style that assimilated to woodcut art the possibility of sophisticated internal shading. Few would dispute the fact that Dürer's woodcuts represent a completely new approach to the medium. (See Figure 3.) The new use of line signaled a massive style shift in book illustration; and Dürer's woodcuts made the reading of complex pictorial subject matter much simpler.

The new use of line de-emphasized the outline contour; in its place, artists attempted to model figures through intricate internal line work that suggested shadows and highlights. This internal shading made possible the same three-dimensional layering that Renaissance painters had achieved by using different shades and hues of color. Essentially, it permitted the woodcut artist to apply the principles of Renaissance perspective to pictorial subject matter, indicating, by the selective use of different kinds of line, things that were close and things that were far away. As a result, the clarity of subject matter was increased by the differentiation of important elements from mere background. The new use of line brought with it a richness in tonal values that went well beyond the simple contrast of black and white achieved in the earlier style. In perceptual terms, the greater range of tones facilitated the reading of spatial relationships and tended to unify the component parts of the picture. A reader could once again reduce and organize the multiplicity of linear elements into a few meaningful subject clues. The noted art critic Heinrich Wölfflin (1905/1971) calls attention to this characteristic of Dürer's work by citing specific examples: "His scale of light and dark was very much richer and he replaced the archaic, even light effects of the earlier woodcuts with powerful tonal contrasts. For example, clouds stand brightly in front of a dark background, a dark sky hangs above a light landscape. These are painterly effects" (p. 48).

According to our theory, the coming of a new style, though engendered by one kind of perceptual crisis, inevitably spawns its own "crisis in reading." Perceivers, accustomed to certain conventions, are confused when the relationships be-

FIGURE 2

Battle Scene, a French woodcut produced for the Parisian publisher-printer, Antoine Verard, probably near the turn of the century (circa: 1498). The existing contour outline style does not facilitate visual processing in works of this kind where the subject matter is complex. Illumination in contrasting colors makes these prints readable, but few woodcuts were illuminated after the turn of the century and the practice was already on the decline in the 1490s. (For bibliographic information on this woodcut, cf. Rothschild [1893], pp. 457-458.)

FIGURE 3

Christ Taken Captive. Albrecht Dürer, who executed this print, is principally responsible for the new style in woodcut book illustration. Here the contour outline has given way to line work and modeling. The various kinds of lines are used to suggest highlights and shadows, depth, and color. Although the subject matter of the print is complex, the relationship between elements is clear and there is an increase in readability over similar scenes executed in the earlier style. This woodcut is taken from *The Great Passion*, published in 1510.

tween clues and meanings have been radically shifted. The perceptual upheaval connected with massive style shifts has been noted and described by Wöfflin in his biography of Dürer: "New styles have always a disintegrating effect at first; they are understood only partially, interest is concentrated on details and the sense of the whole becomes weaker" (pp. 75–76). Wölfflin is quite specific about the nature of this so-called "disintegrating effect" in the case of Dürer's woodcuts. Perceivers, accustomed to the clear, bold outlines of the previous style, were disturbed that Dürer's figures did not stand out. Though earlier perceptual strategies always began with attention to the individual figure, this was an ineffective processing scheme to apply to Dürer's prints. It was the linear and tonal coherence of the whole that was the essential characteristic of his style, not the single motif.

Indeed, this is precisely the crux of Dürer's genius. The new style that he pioneered made possible the internal coherence and consistency of a complex picture rendered in only one color—black. Though the engravers of the seventeenth century would perfect the style to a point that would make Dürer's woodcuts appear less refined and certainly less readable, Dürer's initiative hastened the coming of a style that made the processing of visual information much less complex.

In the space of less than fifty years, then, the dominant woodcut style underwent a radical change. As we analyze this fifty-year development, it is clear that there are many ways to explain the style shift. Dürer's genius is certainly one factor. So is the economy of book production, particularly when one considers that copper engravers had put increased pressure on woodcut artists to produce convincing, painterly illustrations. But at the same time we must consider carefully the psychological explanation for this radical shift in style. The perceptual constraints of readers determined to a large extent the direction of the shift toward visual simplification and readability. Indeed, Dürer's options were limited by what readers could process easily and comfortably. And, as one looks at other revolutionary style shifts in the history of art, it is striking just how often the same observation can be made.

Conclusion

For at least the last hundred years, the subject of reading has been connected quite directly to the concept of literacy; both reading and literacy, in turn, have been linked with the written word. Learning to read has meant learning to read words, and research into reading has, until recently, been directed toward finding out how people can learn to read words more quickly and effectively. But, as the title of this article suggests, reading has gradually come under closer scrutiny. Recent research has shown that the reading of words is but a subset of a much more general human activity which includes symbol decoding, information intergration and organization, and the use of various short- and long-term memory systems. Indeed, reading—in the most general sense—can be thought of as a form of perceptual activity. The reading of words is one manifestation of this activity; but there are many others—the reading of pictures, maps, circuit diagrams, music, or less conventionalized systems found in the natural world (the reading of clouds in the sky or wind patterns on water, for example).

In the last decade, research into reading has gone beyond text, beyond classrooms, beyond schoolchildren and focused on the most basic of mental structures—storage systems in the brain, systems of attention and memory. As a result, we not only understand more about fundamental human thought processes, but we also understand more about literacy and learning to read words. Many researchers now believe, for example, that they should look beyond a child's ability to recognize the shapes of letters and should analyze the child's capacity for processing information of various kinds. Perhaps this is what "reading readiness" is all about. It may have less to do with alphabets and books than with a child's processing speed and capacity.

At the same time that we have learned about reading in the most conventional sense, researchers have made discoveries about other forms of reading. One of these was discussed in the section on artistic styles. It is both exciting and significant that psychologists have found such a rich harvest in investigations that look beyond the conventional bounds of reading theory. For it suggests that only when reading—or any other subject—is considered from the broadest possible perspective can serious advances in human knowledge and understanding occur.

References

Ackerman, J. S. A theory of style. *Journal of Aesthetics and Art Criticism,* 1962, **20**, 227–239.

Bland, D. *A history of book illustration.* Berkeley: University of California Press, 1969.

de Rothschild, J. *Catalogue des livres de M. le Baron . . .* (Vol. 3). Paris: Damascene Morgand, 1893.

Edel, L. *The modern psychological novel.* New York: Grosset & Dunlap, 1964.

Gibson, E. J., Pick, A., Osser, H., & Hammond, M. The role of grapheme-phoneme correspondence in the perception of words. *American Journal of Psychology,* 1962, **75**, 554–570.

Gombrich, E. H. *Art and illusion.* Princeton, N.J.: Princeton University Press, 1960.

Gough, P. B. One second of reading. In J. F. Kavanagh & I. G. Mattingly (Eds.), *Language by ear and by eye.* Cambridge, Mass.: M.I.T. Press, 1972.

Huey, E. B. *The psychology and pedagogy of reading.* Cambridge, Mass.: M.I.T. Press, 1968. (Originally published, 1908.)

Kolers, P. A. Three stages of reading. In H. Levin & J. P. Williams (Eds.), *Basic studies on reading.* New York: Basic Books, 1970.

Kolers, P. A. Some modes of representation. In P. Pliner, L. Krames, & T. Alloway (Eds.), *Communication and affect: Language and thought.* New York: Academic Press, 1973.

Kolers, P. A., & Katzman, M. T. Naming sequentially presented letters and words. *Language and Speech,* 1966, **9**, 84–95.

Miller, G. A. The magical number seven, plus or minus two: Some limits on our capacity for processing information. *Psychological Review,* 1956, **63**, 81–97.

Mitchell, W. J. The Tristan prelude: Techniques and structure. In W. J. Mitchell & F. Salzer (Eds.), *The music forum* (Vol. I). New York: Columbia University Press, 1967.

Neisser, U. *Cognitive psychology.* New York: Appleton-Century-Crofts, 1967.

Pillsbury, W. B. The reading of words: A study in apperception. *American Journal of Psychology,* 1897, **8**, 315–393.

Piston, W. *Harmony*. New York: W. W. Norton, 1941.

Spenser, E. *Faerie Queene* (P. C. Bayley, Ed.). New York: Oxford University Press, 1965. (Originally published, 1590.)

Wolf, T. A cognitive model of musical sight-reading. *Journal of Psycholinguistic Research,* 1976, 5, 143–171.

Wölfflin, H. [*The art of Albrecht Dürer*] (A. Grieve & H. Grieve, trans.). London: Phaidon Press, 1971. (Originally published, 1905.)

CHAPTER 2

Experimental Studies
in Language
& Reading

Three Processes in the Child's Acquisition of Syntax

ROGER BROWN
URSULA BELLUGI
Harvard University

In this pathbreaking study, Roger Brown and Ursula Bellugi identify three processes underlying children's acquisition of syntax. The authors observe that children acquiring language frequently imitate and then reduce parents' speech into telegraphic utterances, preserving both sentence order and major content words; while parents often expand these utterances to adhere more closely to the grammatical regularities of adult speech. Noting the complementary and cyclic nature of these strategies, Brown and Bellugi suggest that the pattern of imitation, reduction, and expansion may lead children to induce the latent structure of their language. As one alternative to this hypothesis, the authors also suggest that children's innate ability to formulate hypotheses about the rules underlying language may overshadow the importance of environmental or parental interactions.

Some time in the second six months of life most children say a first intelligible word. A few months later most children are saying many words and some children go about the house all day long naming things (*table, doggie, ball,* etc.) and actions (*play, see, drop,* etc.) and an occasional quality (*blue, broke, bad,* etc.). At about eighteen months children are likely to begin constructing two-word utterances; such a one, for instance, as *Push car.*

A construction such as *Push car* is not just two single-word utterances spoken in a certain order. As single word utterances (they are sometimes called holophrases) both *push* and *car* would have primary stresses and terminal intonation contours. When they are two words programmed as a single utterance the primary stress would fall on *car* and so would the highest level of pitch. *Push* would be subordinated to *car* by a lesser stress and a lower pitch;

This investigation was supported in whole by Public Health Service Research Grant MH7088 from the National Institute of Mental Health.

Harvard Educational Review Vol. 34 No. 2 Spring 1964, 133–151

the unity of the whole would appear in the absence of a terminal contour between words and the presence of such a contour at the end of the full sequence.

By the age of thirty-six months some children are so advanced in the construction process as to produce all of the major varieties of English simple sentences up to a length of ten or eleven words. For several years we have been studying the development of English syntax, of the sentence-constructing process, in children between eighteen and thirty-six months of age. Most recently we have made a longitudinal study of a boy and girl whom we shall call Adam and Eve. We began work with Adam and Eve in October of 1962 when Adam was twenty-seven months old and Eve eighteen months old. The two children were selected from some thirty whom we considered. They were selected primarily because their speech was exceptionally intelligible and because they talked a lot. We wanted to make it as easy as possible to transcribe accurately large quantities of child speech. Adam and Eve are the children of highly-educated parents; the fathers were graduate students at Harvard and the mothers are both college graduates. Both Adam and Eve were single children when we began the study. These facts must be remembered in generalizing the outcomes of the research.

While Adam is nine months older than Eve, his speech was only a little more advanced in October of 1962. The best single index of the level of speech development is the average length of utterance and in October, 1962, Adam's average was 1.84 morphemes and Eve's was 1.40 morphemes. The two children stayed fairly close together in the year that followed; in the records for the thirty-eighth week Adam's average was 3.55 and Eve's, 3.27. The processes we shall describe appeared in both children.

Every second week we visited each child for at least two hours and made a tape recording of everything said by the child as well as of everything said to the child. The mother was always present and most of the speech to the child is hers. Both mother and child became very accustomed to our presence and learned to continue their usual routine with us as the observers.

One of us always made a written transcription, on the scene, of the speech of mother and child with notes about important actions and objects of attention. From this transcription and the tape a final transcription was made and these transcriptions constitute the primary data of the study. For many purposes we require a "distributional analysis" of the speech of the child. To this end the child's utterances in a given transcription were cross-classified and relisted under such headings as: "*A* + noun"; "Noun + verb"; "Verbs in the past"; "Utterances containing the pronoun *it*," etc. The categorized utterances expose the syntactic regularities of the child's speech.

Each week we met as a research seminar, with students of the psychology of language,[1] to discuss the state of the construction process in one of the two children as of that date. In these discussions small experiments were often suggested, experiments that had to be done within a few days if they were to be informative. At one time, for instance, we were uncertain whether Adam understood the semantic difference between putting a noun in subject position and putting it in object position. Consequently one of us paid an extra visit to Adam equipped with some toys. "Adam," we said, "show us the duck pushing the boat." And, when he had done so: "Now show us the boat pushing the duck."

Another week we noticed that Adam would sometimes pluralize nouns when they should have been pluralized and sometimes would not. We wondered if he could make grammatical judgments about the plural, if he could distinguish a correct form from an incorrect form. "Adam," we asked, "which is right, 'two shoes' or 'two shoe'?" His answer on that occasion, produced with explosive enthusiasm, was "Pop goes the weasel!" The two-year-old child does not make a perfectly docile experimental subject.

The dialogue between mother and child does not read like a transcribed dialogue between two adults. Table 1 offers a sample section from an early

TABLE 1

A Section from Adam's First Record

Adam	Mother
See truck, Mommy.	
See truck.	
	Did you see the truck?
No I see truck.	
	No, you didn't see it?
	There goes one.
There go one.	
	Yes, there goes one.
See a truck.	
See truck, Mommy.	
See truck.	
Truck.	
Put truck, Mommy.	
	Put the truck where?
Put truck window.	
	I think that one's too large to go in the window.

[1] We are grateful for intellectual stimulation and lighthearted companionship to Dr. Jean Berko Gleason, Mr. Samuel Anderson, Mr. Colin Fraser, Dr. David McNeill, and Dr. Daniel Slobin.

transcribed record. It has some interesting properties. The conversation is, in the first place, very much in the here and now. From the child there is no speech of the sort that Bloomfield called "displaced," speech about other times and other places. Adam's utterances in the early months were largely a coding of contemporaneous events and impulses. The mother's speech differs from the speech that adults use to one another in many ways. Her sentences are short and simple; for the most part they are the kinds of sentences that Adam will produce a year later.

Perhaps because they are short, the sentences of the mother are perfectly grammatical. The sentences adults use to one another, perhaps because they are longer and more complex, are very often not grammatical, not well formed. Here for instance is a rather representative example produced at a conference of psychologists and linguists: "As far as I know, no one yet has done the in a way obvious now and interesting problem of doing a in a sense a structural frequency study of the alternative syntactical in a given language, say, like English, the alternative possible structures, and how what their hierarchical probability of occurrence structure is."[2] It seems unlikely that a child could learn the patterns of English syntax from such speech. His introduction to English ordinarily comes in the form of a simplified, repetitive, and idealized dialect. It may be that such an introduction is necessary for the acquisition of syntax to be possible but we do not know that.

In the course of the brief interchange of Table 1 Adam imitates his mother in saying: "There go one" immediately after she says "There goes one." The imitation is not perfect; Adam omits the inflection on the verb. His imitation is a reduction in that it omits something from the original. This kind of imitation with reduction is extremely common in the records of Adam and Eve and it is the first process we shall discuss.

IMITATION AND REDUCTION

Table 2 presents some model sentences spoken by the mothers and the imitations produced by Adam and Eve. These were selected from hundreds in the records in order to illustrate some general propositions. The first thing to notice is that the imitations preserve the word order of the model sentences. To be sure, words in the model are often missing from the imitation but the words preserved are in the order of the original. This is a fact that is so familiar and somehow reasonable that we did not at once recognize it as an empirical outcome rather than as a natural necessity. But of course it is not a necessity, the outcome could have been otherwise. For example, words could

[2] H. Maclay and C. E. Osgood, "Hesitation phenomena in spontaneous English speech," *Word*, XV (1959), 19-44.

TABLE 2

Some Imitations Produced by Adam and Eve

Model Utterance	Child's Imitation
Tank car	*Tank car*
Wait a minute	*Wait a minute*
Daddy's brief case	*Daddy brief case*
Fraser will be unhappy	*Fraser unhappy*
He's going out	*He go out*
That's an old time train	*Old time train*
It's not the same dog as Pepper	*Dog Pepper*
No, you can't write on Mr. Cromer's shoe	*Write Cromer shoe*

have been said back in the reverse of their original order, the most recent first. The preservation of order suggests that the model sentence is processed by the child as a total construction rather than as a list of words.

In English the order of words in a sentence is an important grammatical signal. Order is used to distinguish among subject, direct object, and indirect object and it is one of the marks of imperative and interrogative constructions. The fact that the child's first sentences preserve the word order of their models partially accounts for the ability of an adult to "understand" these sentences and so to feel that he is in communication with the child. It is conceivable that the child "intends" the meanings coded by his word orders and that, when he preserves the order of an adult sentence, he does so because he wants to say what the order says. It is also possible that he preserves word order just because his brain works that way and that he has no comprehension of the semantic contrasts involved. In some languages word order is not an important grammatical signal. In Latin, for instance, "Agricola amat puellam" has the same meaning as "Puellam amat agricola" and subject-object relations are signalled by case endings. We would be interested to know whether children who are exposed to languages that do not utilize word order as a major syntactic signal, preserve order as reliably as do children exposed to English.

The second thing to notice in Table 2 is the fact that when the models increase in length there is not a corresponding increase in the imitation. The imitations stay in the range of two to four morphemes which was the range characteristic of the children at this time. The children were operating under some constraint of length or span. This is not a limitation of vocabulary; the children knew hundreds of words. Neither is it a constraint of immediate memory. We infer this from the fact that the average length of utterances produced spontaneously, where immediate memory is not involved, is about the same as the average length of utterances produced as immediate imitations. The constraint is a limitation on the length of utterance the children are able to program or plan.[3] This kind of narrow span limitation in children is characteristic of most or all of their intellectual operations. The limitation grows less restrictive with age as a consequence, probably, of both neurological growth and of practice, but of course it is never lifted altogether.

A constraint on length compels the imitating child to omit some words or morphemes from the mother's longer sentences. Which forms are retained and which omitted? The selection is not random but highly systematic. Forms retained in the examples of Table 2 include: *Daddy, Fraser, Pepper,* and *Cromer; tank car, minute, briefcase, train, dog,* and *shoe; wait, go,* and *write; unhappy* and *old time.* For the most part they are nouns, verbs, and adjectives, though there are exceptions, as witness the initial pronoun *He* and the preposition *out* and the indefinite article *a.* Forms omitted in the samples of Table 2 include: the possessive inflection *-s,* the modal auxiliary *will,* the contraction of the auxiliary verb *is,* the progressive inflection *-ing,* the preposition *on,* the articles *the* and *an,* and the modal auxiliary *can.* It is possible to make a general characterization of the forms likely to be retained that distinguishes them as a total class from the forms likely to be omitted.

Forms likely to be retained are nouns and verbs and, less often, adjectives, and these are the three large and "open" parts-of-speech in English. The number of forms in any one of these parts-of-speech is extremely large and always growing. Words belonging to these classes are sometimes called "contentives" because they have semantic content. Forms likely to be omitted are inflections, auxiliary verbs, articles, prepositions, and conjunctions. These forms belong to syntactic classes that are small and closed. Any one class has few members and new members are not readily added. The omitted forms are the ones that linguists sometimes call "functors," their grammatical *functions* being more obvious than their semantic content.

Why should young children omit functors and retain contentives? There is more than one plausible answer. Nouns, verbs, and adjectives are words that make reference. One can conceive of teaching the meanings of these words by speaking them, one at a time, and pointing at things or actions or qualities. And of course parents do exactly that. These are the kinds of words that children have been encouraged to practice speaking one at a time. The child arrives at the age of sentence construction with a stock of well-practiced nouns, verbs, and adjectives. Is it not likely then that this prior practice causes him to retain the contentives from model sentences too long to be reproduced in full, that the child imitates those forms in the speech he hears which are

---

[3] Additional evidence of the constraint on sentence length may be found in R. Brown and C. Fraser. "The acquisition of syntax," C. N. Cofer and Barbara Musgrave, eds., *Verbal Behavior and Learning* (New York: McGraw Hill, 1963).

already well developed in him as individual habits? There is probably some truth in this explanation but it is not the only determinant since children will often select for retention contentives that are relatively unfamiliar to them.

We adults sometimes operate under a constraint on length and the curious fact is that the English we produce in these circumstances bears a formal resemblance to the English produced by two-year-old children. When words cost money there is a premium on brevity or to put it otherwise, a constraint on length. The result is "telegraphic" English and telegraphic English is an English of nouns, verbs, and adjectives. One does not send a cable reading: "My car has broken down and I have lost my wallet; send money to me at the American Express in Paris" but rather "Car broken down; wallet lost; send money American Express Paris." The telegram omits: *my, has, and, I, have, my, to, me, at, the, in*. All of these are functors. We make the same kind of telegraphic reduction when time or fatigue constrains us to be brief, as witness any set of notes taken at a fast-moving lecture.

A telegraphic transformation of English generally communicates very well. It does so because it retains the high-information words and drops the low-information words. We are here using "information" in the sense of the mathematical theory of communication. The information carried by a word is inversely related to the chances of guessing it from context. From a given string of content words, missing functors can often be guessed but the message "my has and I have my to me at the in" will not serve to get money to Paris. Perhaps children are able to make a communication analysis of adult speech and so adapt in an optimal way to their limitation of span. There is, however, another way in which the adaptive outcome might be achieved.

If you say aloud the model sentences of Table 2 you will find that you place the heavier stresses, the primary and secondary stresses in the sentences, on contentives rather than on functors. In fact the heavier stresses fall, for the most part, on the words the child retains. We first realized that this was the case when we found that in transcribing tapes, the words of the mother that we could hear most clearly were usually the words that the child reproduced. We had trouble hearing the weakly stressed functors and, of course, the child usually failed to reproduce them. Differential stress may then be the cause of the child's differential retention. The outcome is a maximally informative reduction but the cause of this outcome need not be the making of an information analysis. The outcome may be an incidental consequence of the fact that English is a well-designed language that places its heavier stresses where they are needed, on contentives that cannot easily be guessed from context.

We are fairly sure that differential stress is one of the determinants of the child's telegraphic productions. For one thing, stress will also account for the way in which children reproduce polysyllabic words when the total is too much for them. Adam, for instance, gave us *'pression* for *expression* and Eve gave us *'raff* for *giraffe*; the more heavily-stressed syllables were the ones retained. In addition we have tried the effect of placing heavy stresses on functors which do not ordinarily receive such stresses. To Adam we said: "You say what I say" and then, speaking in a normal way at first: "The doggie will bite." Adam gave back: "Doggie bite." Then we stressed the auxiliary: "The doggie *will* bite" and, after a few trials, Adam made attempts at reproducing that auxiliary. A science fiction experiment comes to mind. If there were parents who stressed functors rather than contentives would they have children whose speech was a kind of "reciprocal telegraphic" made up of articles, prepositions, conjunctions, auxiliaries, and the like? Such children would be out of touch with the community as real children are not.

It may be that all the factors we have mentioned play some part in determining the child's selective imitations; the reference-making function of contentives, the fact that they are practiced as single words, the fact that they cannot be guessed from context, and the heavy stresses they receive. There are also other possible factors: for example, the left-to-right, earlier-to-later position of words in a sentence, but these make too long a story to tell here.[4] Whatever the causes, the first utterances produced as imitations of adult sentences are highly systematic reductions of their models. Furthermore, the telegraphic properties of these imitations appear also in the child's spontaneously produced utterances. When his speech is not modeled on an immediately prior adult sentence, it observes the same limitation on length and the same predilection for contentives as when it is modeled on an immediately prior sentence.

IMITATION WITH EXPANSION

In the course of the brief conversation set down in Table 1, Adam's mother at one point imitates Adam. The boy says: "There go one" and mother responds: "Yes, there goes one." She does not exactly reproduce the model sentence of the child but instead adds something to it or expands it. What she adds is a functor, the inflection for third-person on the verb, the very form that Adam had omitted when he imitated his mother.

One of the first things we noticed when we began to study child speech several years ago was the frequency with which adults imitated children. Indeed they seemed to imitate more often than did the children themselves. We later came to realize that adult imitations are seldom exact reproductions; they are usually expansions. The mothers of Adam and Eve responded to the

[4] Brown and Fraser, *ibid.*

speech of their children with expansions about thirty per cent of the time. We did it ourselves when we talked with the children. Indeed we found it very difficult to withhold expansions. A reduced or incomplete English sentence seems to constrain the English-speaking adult to expand it into the nearest properly formed complete sentence. Table 3 lists a few sample expansions from the hundreds in the records.

The first thing worthy of attention in the expansions of Table 3 is the fact that the words spoken by the mother preserve the order of the words in the child's sentences. To be sure, words and inflections are added but they are fitted in—before, and after and between the words the child used; they are not generally permitted to disturb the order of the child's words. It is as if these latter were taken as constants by the mother, constants to which some sentence had to be fitted. She acts as if she were assuming that the child means everything he says, all the words and also their order, but as if he might also mean more than he says. From the mother's point of view an expansion is a kind of communication check; it says in effect: "Is this what you mean?"

The second thing to notice about Table 3 is the character of the forms added to the child's utterances. They include the auxiliaries *is* and *will;* the prepositions *in, on, to,* and *up;* the verb forms *is, have, had,* and *having;* the articles *a* and *the;* the pronouns *her, he,* and *it.* For the most part, the words added are functors, and functors are of course the words that the child omits in his reductions.

The interaction between mother and child is, much of the time, a cycle of reductions and expansions. There are two transformations involved. The reduction transformation has an almost completely specifiable and so mechanical character. One could program a machine to do it with the following instructions: "Retain contentives (or stressed forms) in the order given up to some limit of length." The expansion accomplished by Adam's mother when she added the third-person inflection to the verb and said "There goes one"

TABLE 3

Expansions of Child Speech Produced by Mothers

Child	Mother
Baby highchair	*Baby is in the highchair*
Mommy eggnog	*Mommy had her eggnog*
Eve lunch	*Eve is having lunch*
Mommy sandwich	*Mommy'll have a sandwich*
Sat wall	*He sat on the wall*
Throw Daddy	*Throw it to Daddy*
Pick glove	*Pick the glove up*

is also a completely specifiable transformation. The instructions would read: "Retain the forms given in the order given and supply obligatory grammatical forms." To be sure, this mother-machine would have to be supplied with the obligatory rules of English grammar but that could be done. However, the sentence "There goes one" is atypical in that it only adds a compulsory and redundant inflection. The expansions of Table 3 all add forms that are not grammatically compulsory or redundant and these expansions cannot be mechanically generated by grammatical rules alone.

In Table 3 the topmost four utterances produced by the child are all of the same grammatical type; all four consist of a proper noun followed by a common noun. However, the four are expanded in quite different ways. In particular the form of the verb changes: it is in the first case in the simple present tense; in the second case the simple past; in the third case the present progressive; in the last case the simple future. All of these are perfectly grammatical but they are different. The second set of child utterances is formally uniform in that each one consists of a verb followed by a noun. The expansions are again all grammatical but quite unlike, especially with regard to the preposition supplied. In general, then, there are radical changes in the mother's expansions when there are no changes in the formal character of the utterances expanded. It follows that the expansions cannot be produced simply by making grammatically compulsory additions to the child's utterances.

How does a mother decide on the correct expansion of one of her child's utterances? Consider the utterance "Eve lunch." So far as grammar is concerned this utterance could be appropriately expanded in any of a number of ways: "Eve is having lunch"; "Eve had lunch"; "Eve will have lunch"; Eve's lunch," etc. On the occasion when Eve produced the utterance, however, one expansion seemed more appropriate than any other. It was then the noon hour, Eve was sitting at the table with a plate of food before her, and her spoon and fingers were busy. In these circumstances "Eve lunch" had to mean "Eve is having lunch." A little later when the plate had been stacked in the sink and Eve was getting down from her chair the utterance "Eve lunch" would have suggested the expansion "Eve has had her lunch." Most expansions are not only responsive to the child's words but also to the circumstances attending their utterance.

What kind of instructions will generate the mother's expansions? The following are approximately correct: "Retain the words given in the order given and add those functors that will result in a well-formed simple sentence that is appropriate to the circumstances." These are not instructions that any machine could follow. A machine could act on the instructions only if it were provided with detailed specifications for judging appropriateness and no such specifications can, at present, be written. They exist, however, in implicit form in the brains of mothers and in the brains of all English-speaking adults and so judgments of appropriateness can be made by such adults.

The expansion encodes aspects of reality that are not coded by the child's telegraphic utterance. Functors have meaning but it is meaning that accrues to them in context rather than in isolation. The meanings that are added by functors seem to be nothing less than the basic terms in which we construe reality: the time of an action, whether it is ongoing or completed, whether it is presently relevant or not; the concept of possession and such relational concepts as are coded by *in, on, up, down,* and the like; the difference between a particular instance of a class ("Has anybody seen *the* paper?") and any instance of a class ("Has anybody seen *a* paper?") ; the difference between extended substances given shape and size by an "accidental" container (*sand, water, syrup,* etc.) and countable "things" having a characteristic fixed shape and size (*a cup, a man, a tree,* etc.) . It seems to us that a mother in expanding speech may be teaching more than grammar; she may be teaching something like a world-view.

As yet it has not been demonstrated that expansions are *necessary* for learning either grammar or a construction of reality. It has not even been demonstrated that expansions contribute to such learning. All we know is that some parents do expand and their children do learn. It is perfectly possible, however, that children can and do learn simply from hearing their parents or others make well-formed sentences in connection with various nonverbal circumstances. It may not be necessary or even helpful for these sentences to be expansions of utterances of the child. Only experiments contrasting expansion training with simple exposure to English will settle the matter. We hope to do such experiments.

There are, of course, reasons for expecting the expansion transformation to be an effective tutorial technique. By adding something to the words the child has just produced one confirms his response insofar as it is appropriate. In addition one takes him somewhat beyond that response but not greatly beyond it. One encodes additional meanings at a moment when he is most likely to be attending to the cues that can teach that meaning.

INDUCTION OF THE LATENT STRUCTURE

Adam, in the course of the conversation with his mother set down in Table 1, produced one utterance for which no adult is likely ever to have provided an exact model: "No I see truck." His mother elects to expand it as "No, you didn't see it" and this expansion suggests that the child might have created the utterance by reducing an adult model containing the form *didn't.* However, the mother's expansion in this case does some violence to Adam's original version. He did not say *no* as his mother said it, with primary stress and final contour; Adam's *no* had secondary stress and no final contour. It is not easy to imagine an adult model for this utterance. It seems more likely that the utterance was created by Adam as part of a continuing effort to discover the general rules for constructing English negatives.

In Table 4 we have listed some utterances produced by Adam or Eve for which it is difficult to imagine any adult model. It is unlikely that any adult said any of these to Adam or Eve since they are very simple utterances and yet definitely ungrammatical. In addition it is difficult, by adding functors alone, to build any of them up to simple grammatical sentences. Consequently it does not seem likely that these utterances are reductions of adult originals. It is more likely that they are mistakes which externalize the child's search for the regularities of English syntax.

We have long realized that the occurrence of certain kinds of errors on the level of morphology (or word construction) reveals the child's effort to induce regularities from speech. So long as a child speaks correctly, or at any rate so long as he speaks as correctly as the adults he hears, there is no way to tell whether he is simply repeating what he has heard or whether he is actually constructing. However, when he says something like "I digged a hole" we can often be sure that he is constructing. We can be sure because it is unlikely that he would have heard *digged* from anyone and because we can see how, in processing words he has heard, he might have come by *digged*. It looks like an overgeneralization of the regular past inflection. The inductive operations of the child's mind are externalized in such a creation. Overgeneralizations on the level of syntax (or sentence construction) are more difficult to identify because there are so many ways of adding functors so as to build up conceivable models. But this is difficult to do for the examples of Table 4 and for several hundred other utterances in our records.

The processes of imitation and expansion are not sufficient to account for the degree of linguistic competence that children regularly acquire. These processes alone cannot teach more than the sum total of sentences that speak-

TABLE 4

Utterances Not Likely to be Imitations

My Cromer suitcase	*You naughty are*
Two foot	*Why it can't turn off?*
A bags	*Put on it*
A scissor	*Cowboy did fighting me*
A this truck	*Put a gas in*

ers of English have either modeled for a child to imitate or built up from a child's reductions. However, a child's linguistic competence extends far beyond this sum total of sentences. All children are able to understand and construct sentences they have never heard but which are nevertheless well-formed, well-formed in terms of general rules that are implicit in the sentences the child has heard. Somehow, then, every child processes the speech to which he is exposed so as to induce from it a latent structure. This latent rule structure is so general that a child can spin out its implications all his life long. It is both semantic and syntactic. The discovery of latent structure is the greatest of the processes involved in language acquisition and the most difficult to understand. We will provide an example of how the analysis can proceed by discussing the evolution in child speech of noun phrases.

A noun phrase in adult English includes a noun but also more than a noun. One variety consists of a noun with assorted modifiers: *The girl*; *The pretty girl*; *That pretty girl*; *My girl*, etc. All of these are constructions which have the same syntactic privileges as do nouns alone. One can use a noun phrase in isolation to name or request something; one can use it in sentences, in subject position or in object position or in predicate nominative position. All of these are slots that nouns alone can also fill. A larger construction having the same syntactic privileges as its "head" word is called in linguistics an "endocentric" construction, and noun phrases are endocentric constructions.

For both Adam and Eve, in the early records, noun phrases usually occur as total independent utterances rather than as components of sentences. Table 5 presents an assortment of such utterances at Time 1. They consist in each

TABLE 5

Noun Phrases in Isolation
and Rule for Generating Noun Phrases at Time 1

A coat	*More coffee*
*A celery**	*More nut**
*A Becky**	*Two sock**
*A hands**	*Two shoes*
The top	*two tinker-toy**
My Mommy	*Big boot*
That Adam	*Poor man*
My stool	*Little top*
That knee	*Dirty knee*

$$NP \rightarrow M + N$$

M $\rightarrow$ *a, big, dirty, little, more, my, poor, that, the, two.*
N $\rightarrow$ *Adam, Becky, boot, coat, coffee, knee, man, Mommy, nut, sock, stool, tinker-toy, top,* and very many others.

* Ungrammatical for an adult.

143

case of some sort of modifier, just one, preceding a noun. The modifiers, or as they are sometimes called the "pivot" words, are a much smaller class than the noun class. Three students of child speech have independently discovered that this kind of construction is extremely common when children first begin to combine words. [5, 6, 7]

It is possible to generalize the cases of Table 5 into a simple implicit rule. The rule symbolized in Table 5 reads: "In order to form a noun phrase of this type, select first one word from the small class of modifiers and select, second, one word from the large class of nouns." This is a "generative" rule by which we mean it is a program that would actually serve to build constructions of the type in question. It is offered as a model of the mental mechanism by which Adam and Eve generated such utterances. Furthermore, judging from our work with other children and from the reports of Braine and of Miller and Ervin, the model describes a mechanism present in many children when their average utterance is approximately two morphemes long.

We have found that even in our earliest records the M + N construction is sometimes used as a component of larger constructions. For instance, Eve said: "Fix a Lassie" and "Turn the page" and "A horsie stuck" and Adam even said: "Adam wear a shirt." There are, at first, only a handful of these larger constructions but there are very many constructions in which single nouns occur in subject or in object position.

Let us look again at the utterances of Table 5 and the rule generalizing them. The class M does not correspond with any syntactic class of adult English. In the class M are articles, a possessive pronoun, a cardinal number, a demonstrative adjective or pronoun, a quantifier, and some descriptive adjectives—a mixed bag indeed. For adult English these words cannot belong to the same syntactic class because they have very different privileges of occurrence in sentences. For the children the words do seem to function as one class having the common privilege of occurrence before nouns.

If the initial words of the utterances in Table 5 are treated as one class M then many utterances are generated which an adult speaker would judge to be ungrammatical. Consider the indefinite article *a*. Adults use it only to modify common count nouns in the singular such as *coat, dog, cup*, etc. We would not say *a celery*, or *a cereal*, or *a dirt; celery, cereal*, and *dirt* are mass nouns. We would not say *a Becky* or *a Jimmy; Becky* and *Jimmy* are proper nouns. We would not say *a hands* or *a shoes; hands* and *shoes* are plural nouns. Adam and Eve, at first, did form ungrammatical combinations such as these.

[5] M. D. S. Braine, "The ontogeny of English phrase structure: the first phrase," *Language*, XXXIX (1963), 1-13.

[6] W. Miller and Susan Ervin, "The development of grammar in child language," Ursula Bellugi and R. Brown, eds., *The Acquisition of Language, Child Developm. Monogr.* (1964).

[7] Brown and Fraser, "The acquisition of syntax."

The numeral *two* we use only with count nouns in the plural. We would not say *two sock* since *sock* is singular, nor *two water* since *water* is a mass noun. The word *more* we use before count nouns in the plural (*more nuts*) or mass nouns in the singular (*more coffee*). Adam and Eve made a number of combinations involving *two* or *more* that we would not make.

Given the initial very undiscriminating use of words in the class M it follows that one dimension of development must be a progressive differentiation of privileges, which means the division of M into smaller classes. There must also be subdivision of the noun class (N) for the reason that the privileges of occurrence of various kinds of modifiers must be described in terms of such sub-varieties of N as the common noun and proper noun, the count noun and mass noun. There must eventually emerge a distinction between nouns singular and nouns plural since this distinction figures in the privileges of occurrence of the several sorts of modifiers.

Sixteen weeks after our first records from Adam and Eve (Time 2), the differentiation process had begun. By this time there were distributional reasons for separating out articles (*a, the*) from demonstrative pronouns (*this, that*) and both of these from the residual class of modifiers. Some of the evidence for this conclusion appears in Table 6. In general one syntactic class is distinguished from another when the members of one class have combinational privileges not enjoyed by the members of the other. Consider, for example, the reasons for distinguishing articles (Art) from modifiers in general (M). Both articles and modifiers appeared in front of nouns in two-word utterances. However, in three-word utterances that were made up from the total pool of words and that had a noun in final position, the privileges of *a* and *the* were

TABLE 6

Subdivision of the Modifier Class

A) PRIVILEGES PECULIAR TO ARTICLES

Obtained	Not Obtained
A blue flower	*Blue a flower*
A nice nap	*Nice a nap*
A your car	*Your a car*
A my pencil	*My a pencil*

B) PRIVILEGES PECULIAR TO DEMONSTRATIVE PRONOUNS

Obtained	Not Obtained
That my cup	*My that cup*
That a horse	*A that horse*
That a blue flower	*A that blue flower*
	Blue a that flower

---

different from the privileges of all other modifiers. The articles occurred in initial position followed by a member of class M other than an article. No other modifier occurred in this first position; notice the "Not obtained" examples of Table 6A. If the children had produced utterances like those (for example, *blue a flower, your a car*) there would have been no difference in the privileges of occurrence of articles and modifiers and therefore no reason to separate out articles.

The record of Adam is especially instructive. He created such notably ungrammatical combinations as "a your car" and "a my pencil." It is very unlikely that adults provided models for these. They argue strongly that Adam regarded all the words in the residual M class as syntactic equivalents and so generated these very odd utterances in which possessive pronouns appear where descriptive adjectives would be more acceptable.

Table 6 also presents some of the evidence for distinguishing demonstrative pronouns (Dem) from articles and modifiers. (Table 6B). The pronouns occurred first and ahead of articles in three-and-four-word utterances—a position that neither articles nor modifiers ever filled. The sentences with demonstrative pronouns are recognizable as reductions which omit the copular verb *is*. Such sentences are not noun phrases in adult English and ultimately they will not function as noun phrases in the speech of the children, but for the present they are not distinguishable distributionally from noun phrases.

Recall now the generative formula of Table 5 which constructs noun phrases by simply placing a modifier (M) before a noun (N). The differentiation of privileges illustrated in Table 6, and the syntactic classes this evidence motivates us to create, complicate the formula for generating noun phrases. In Table 7 we have written a single general formula for producing all noun phrases at Time 2 [NP $\rightarrow$ (Dem) + (Art) + (M) + N] and also the numerous more specific rules which are summarized by the general formula.

By the time of the thirteenth transcription, twenty-six weeks after we began our study, privileges of occurrence were much more finely differentiated

TABLE 7

Rules for Generating Noun Phrases at Time 2

$NP_1 \rightarrow$ Dem + Art + M + N	$NP \rightarrow$ (Dem) + (Art) + (M) + N
$NP_2 \rightarrow$ Art + M + N	
$NP_3 \rightarrow$ Dem + M + N	
$NP_4 \rightarrow$ Art + N	( ) means class within
$NP_5 \rightarrow$ M + N	parentheses is optional
$NP_6 \rightarrow$ Dem + N	
$NP_7 \rightarrow$ Dem + Art + N	

and syntactic classes were consequently more numerous. From the distributional evidence we judged that Adam had made five classes of his original class M: articles, descriptive adjectives, possessive pronouns, demonstrative pronouns, and a residual class of modifiers. The generative rules of Table 7 had become inadequate; there were no longer, for instance, any combinations like "A your car." Eve had the same set except that she used two residual classes of modifiers. In addition nouns had begun to subdivide for both children. The usage of proper nouns had become clearly distinct from the usage of count nouns. For Eve the evidence justified separating count nouns from mass nouns, but for Adam it still did not. Both children by this time were frequently pluralizing nouns but as yet their syntactic control of the singular-plural distinction was imperfect.

In summary, one major aspect of the development of general structure in child speech is a progressive differentiation in the usage of words and therefore a progressive differentiation of syntactic classes. At the same time, however, there is an integrative process at work. From the first, an occasional noun phrase occurred as a component of some larger construction. At first these noun phrases were just two words long and the range of positions in which they could occur was small. With time the noun phrases grew longer, were more frequently used, and were used in a greater range of positions. The noun phrase structure as a whole, in all the permissible combinations of modifiers and nouns, was assuming the combinational privileges enjoyed by nouns in isolation.

In Table 8 we have set down some of the sentence positions in which both nouns and noun phrases occurred in the speech of Adam and Eve. It is the close match between the positions of nouns alone and of nouns with modifiers in the speech of Adam and Eve that justifies us in calling the longer constructions noun phrases. These longer constructions are, as they should be, endocentric; the head word alone has the same syntactic privileges as the head word with its modifiers. The continuing failure to find in noun phrase positions whole constructions of the type "That a blue flower" signals the fact

TABLE 8

Some Privileges of the Noun Phrase

Noun Positions	Noun Phrase Positions
That (flower)	*That (a blue flower)*
Where (ball) go?	*Where (the puzzle) go?*
Adam write (penguin)	*Doggie eat (the breakfast)*
(Horsie) stop	*(A horsie) crying*
Put (hat) on	*Put (the red hat) on*

that these constructions are telegraphic versions of predicate nominative sentences omitting the verb form *is*. Examples of the kind of construction not obtained are: "That (that a blue flower)"; "Where (that a blue flower)?"

For adults the noun phrase is a subwhole of the sentence, what linguists call an "immediate constituent." The noun phrase has a kind of psychological unity. There are signs that the noun phrase was also an immediate constituent for Adam and Eve. Consider the sentence using the separable verb *put on*. The noun phrase in "Put the red hat on" is, as a whole, fitted in between the verb and the particle even as is the noun alone in "Put hat on." What is more, however, the location of pauses in the longer sentence, on several occasions, suggested the psychological organization: "Put . . . the red hat . . . on" rather than "Put the red . . . hat on" or "Put the . . . red hat on." In addition to this evidence the use of pronouns suggests that the noun phrase is a psychological unit.

The unity of noun phrases in adult English is evidenced, in the first place, by the syntactic equivalence between such phrases and nouns alone. It is evidenced, in the second place, by the fact that pronouns are able to substitute for total noun phrases. In our immediately preceding sentence the pronoun "It" stands for the rather involved construction from the first sentence of this paragraph: "The unity of noun phrases in adult English." The words called "pronouns" in English would more aptly be called "pro-noun-phrases" since it is the phrase rather than the noun which they usually replace. One does not replace "unity" with "it" and say "The *it* of noun phrases in adult English." In the speech of Adam and Eve, too, the pronoun came to function as a replacement for the noun phrase. Some of the clearer cases appear in Table 9.

Adam characteristically externalizes more of his learning than does Eve

TABLE 9

Pronouns Replacing Nouns or Noun Phrases and Pronouns Produced Together with Nouns or Noun Phrases

Noun Phrases Replaced by Pronouns	Pronouns and Noun Phrases in Same Utterances
Hit ball	*Mommy get it ladder*
Get it	*Mommy get it my ladder*
Ball go?	*Saw it ball*
Go get it	*Miss it garage*
Made it	*I miss it cowboy boot*
Made a ship	*I Adam drive that*
Fix a tricycle	*I Adam drive*
Fix it	*I Adam don't*

and his record is especially instructive in connection with the learning of pronouns. In his first eight records, the first sixteen weeks of the study, Adam quite often produced sentences containing both the pronoun and the noun or noun phrase that the pronoun should have replaced. One can here see the equivalence in the process of establishment. First the substitute is produced and then, as if in explication, the form or forms that will eventually be replaced by the substitute. Adam spoke out his pronoun antecedents as chronological consequents. This is additional evidence of the unity of the noun phrase since the noun phrases *my ladder* and *cowboy boot* are linked with *it* in Adam's speech in just the same way as the nouns *ladder* and *ball*.

We have described three processes involved in the child's acquisition of syntax. It is clear that the last of these, the induction of latent structure, is by far the most complex. It looks as if this last process will put a serious strain on any learning theory thus far conceived by psychology. The very intricate simultaneous differentiation and integration that constitutes the evolution of the noun phrase is more reminiscent of the biological development of an embryo than it is of the acquisition of a conditional reflex.

Pre-School Children's Knowledge of English Phonology

CHARLES READ
University of Wisconsin

In this article Charles Read suggests that some pre-school children have an uncon-scious knowledge of aspects of the sound system of English. He argues that these children tacitly organize phonetic segments into categories defined by articulatory features; and that these children base their judgments of phonological relationships on certain specifiable features.

The term *phonology* refers to the sound system of our language, a system of reg-ular processes that determine the pronunciation of English. Part of what we acquire in learning a language is a mastery of these processes, so that when we encounter a new or unfamiliar word, we automatically (and for the most part, unconsciously) know some aspects of its pronunciation. In *telemorphic*, for in-stance, we know (without necessarily knowing what the word might mean) that stress falls on the third syllable and that the first and second vowels are not pro-nounced alike, despite the spelling. Linguists have shown that the processes de-termining these and many other details of English pronunciation are not simple "analogies" to familiar words (such as *telegraphic* in this case); they are a system of intricate but general rules of the language.[1] Exactly how and when we acquire our unconscious mastery of these rules remains largely a mystery; it is clear that we do not memorize individual pronunciations (since the rules extend to new words and sentences) and that we do not learn them directly from a study of English spelling.

In fact, a child must bring some knowledge of English phonology to his first encounter with reading and writing. Part of what he must have learned is that certain sounds are to be regarded as the same, despite differences in their pro-

---

[1] Noam Chomsky and Morris Halle, *The Sound Pattern of English* (New York: Harper & Row, 1968). The phonological analysis assumed in this article is largely that of this work.

Harvard Educational Review Vol. 41 No. 1 February 1971, 1–34

nunciation. For instance, the third segments ([n]) of *ten* and *tenth* are functionally the same in English, even though they are articulated differently; in another language, they might be as distinct as *tin* and *Tim* are to us. Variations in pronunciation take many forms; an example of a different sort is the contrast in timbre, pitch, and other qualities between the speech of a child and that of his father, even though they may be "saying the same thing." Such a contrast appears in all languages, of course, and perhaps need not be learned specifically for English; others must be learned as part of the particular language. For instance, in some languages the difference in aspiration between the [p] of *pit* and the [p] of *spit* would make them distinct sounds, while the difference in voicing between the first segments of *tin* and *din* might be entirely irrelevant; these would be two instances of the same word. As part of his knowledge of his language, a child must learn to attend to certain phonetic differences and to abstract from others in a specific and systematic way. Evidently, children possess some phonological knowledge of this sort in their pre-school years. Otherwise, they could not judge that two different speakers were saying the same thing; they could not understand a speaker of another dialect, however slightly different; ultimately, they could not understand English at all, for speech sounds can and do vary in a multitude of ways, many of which we must systematically disregard in understanding English.

Beyond the general observation that a pre-school child's conception of English phonology is sufficiently abstract to permit him to understand and be understood under normal circumstances, however, we know few details of when and how this conception develops. Evidence about the nature of the development must come from children's judgments of phonetic similarities and differences, and these have proven elusive indeed. This article will present some evidence of such judgments, specifically about how children in their pre-school and kindergarten years tacitly categorize the sounds of English. Which phonetic differences do they treat as important in relating one sound to another, which less important, and which ones do they regularly abstract away from? The evidence here suggests that the children's phonology is (necessarily) highly abstract, and that it differs in specific ways from that of adult speakers of English, including of course the children's parents and teachers.

In addition to its relation to the general question of how children learn a language, this evidence bears on a potentially more practical issue, namely, how a child's phonology compares to the abstract representation of speech that he learns in school—the standard English spelling system. It is obvious that any spelling system is highly abstract (again, necessarily so); in English, for example, all direct representation of pitch, stress, and intonation is entirely excluded. Further, as is well known, the standard alphabet does not provide enough characters to represent distinctly the forty-three or so autonomous "phonemes" that distinguish one word from another, and these phonemes are themselves classes of phonetically different sounds, as in the examples given for /p/ and /n/. A recent article in this journal[2] discussed and justified a class of still further abstractions, in which our spelling does not represent predictable phonetic variations in lexically related forms, as in the non-italicized vowels of *extreme/extremity*, even though we have the alphabetic means to do so. We can compare such an analysis of the abstractions inherent in our spelling system with what we learn about the abstractness of the child's conception of English phonology. Differences between the two systems may define a large and central part of what a child must learn in order to read and write. In making this comparison, I will be assuming that what the child learns in mastering the spelling system is a representation related in complex, but generally systematic, ways to the phonology of English. The contrary assumption—that the child memorizes a long list of generally unpredictable spellings—fails to account for the abilities of mature readers and writers.

The evidence of phonological knowledge comes from pre-school children who invented their own spelling system for English, influenced relatively little by the standard system. In each case, the child first learned the conventional names of the letters of the alphabet; then with blocks or some other movable-alphabet toy, began to spell words; and finally produced written messages of all kinds, including stories, letters, and poems. The writing began as early as age three and one half, usually before the child was able to read, and certain parts of the spelling system persisted well into the first grade, where they gradually gave way to standard spellings under the influence of formal instruction in reading and writing.

Such spontaneous spelling is relatively rare. Apparently, it depends on the coincidence of the child's interests and abilities with various other factors, such as the attitudes of the parents, particularly their tolerance for what appears to be bad spelling. In fact, the invented spellings sometimes look so little like English that parents and teachers may be unable to read them and may disregard or even suppress them. Hence, it is difficult to assess the actual (or potential) frequency of such early invented spelling. This report is based on twenty selected clear cases, together with some marginal ones.

What is significant, even from so few cases, is that each child arrived at roughly the same system, using certain spellings that seem implausible to his parents and teachers, but which can be explained in terms of hypotheses about the children's implicit organization of English sounds.

The structure of the argument, then, is this: to propose an explanation for the invented spellings by showing that they follow from certain assertions about English phonology, independently justified, together with certain hypotheses about

[2] Carol Chomsky, "Reading, Writing, and Phonology," *Harvard Educational Review*, XL (Spring 1970), 287-309. This includes a helpful discussion of the lexicon. See also Noam Chomsky, "Phonology and Reading," *Basic Studies on Reading*, ed. H. Levin and J. Williams (New York: Basic Books, 1970); Chomsky and Halle, 54-55 *et passim*; Wayne O'Neil, "The Spelling and Pronunciation of English," *The American Heritage Dictionary of the English Language*, ed. Wm. Morris (Boston: Houghton Mifflin, 1969), xxxv-xxxvii.

how the children perceive and organize the spoken forms; that is, what they know about English phonology. "Knowledge" and "organization" in this context refer to unconscious beliefs about English sounds and their structure, in the sense in which a reader or listener has notions of sound-structure that enable him to judge two sequences as similar, as in the recognition of rhyme, without his necessarily being aware of either the beliefs or the rhyme itself. This sense of "knowledge" has been explicated more fully and defended elsewhere.[3]

Even for one who accepts, at least tentatively, this line of argument from observed language behavior (performance) to hypothesized judgments and knowledge that underlie it (competence), each step of the argument is open to various questions. Although the statements about English phonology have independent linguistic justification, they are hardly so well established as to be beyond question. For certain fine phonetic details, one can even ask whether the accepted description is based on a physical or perceptual reality that is stable and independent of the linguistic beliefs of the perceiver. There are also questions about the spellings, of course. Children's printing frequently includes marks that are difficult to interpret. Children, like adults, commit apparently non-systematic errors (even compared to the child's own spelling system), false starts, and inexplicable omissions. Sometimes conventional spellings occur; these may not reveal anything about the child's judgments, since one usually cannot know (certainly not from the written record alone) whether they are learned or created; they may have been copied or taken from dictation. Accordingly, I have usually left them out of this account.[4] It is also difficult to know about the children's language experience before they began to spell; none of the parents kept a systematic record of what their child heard or said, nor would such a record guarantee the accuracy of inferences from it about what the child knew. Some assumptions about the bases for the original spelling come from information provided by the parents, other investigations of children's language development, and the evidence of the early spellings themselves.

Consider the problem confronting the pre-school child who wants to spell English messages. He knows the pronunciation of the words; that is, he recognizes the words when someone else says them, and he may pronounce them more or less as an adult does.[5] Without being aware of it, he knows certain syntactic and

---

[3] Noam Chomsky, *Aspects of the Theory of Syntax* (Cambridge, Mass.: M.I.T. Press, 1965), ch. 1; Jerry A. Fodor, *Psychological Explanation* (New York: Random House, 1968).

[4] I do not intend the term "conventional" to suggest that English spelling is conventional in the sense of "arbitrary." The references of footnote 2 discuss some bases of standard spelling.

[5] Idiosyncrasies of a child's pronunciation do not always affect his spelling. Some of these children had well-known non-standard articulations of sibilants, interdentals, and liquids; in some cases, they nevertheless spelled these sounds in the same way as other children. Nor was the parents' speech necessarily a model for spelling, in the case of parents with dialects different from their children's, especially a few non-native speakers of English. The evidence is too limited for any confidence, but it may be that children can abstract away from any one pronunciation in creating their spellings, at least for certain features.

semantic relations among words, such as that *-er* is an agentive ending in a pair like *ride/rider* or that *eat-* is a verb stem in *eating*. He may have mastered certain regular phonetic alternations, such as the [s]—[z] forms for plurals. He recognizes the letters of the alphabet and knows their conventional names, or most of them.

The letter-names provide only partial help to such a child. Assume for the moment that he wishes to represent English consonants at roughly an autonomous phonemic level of detail, and that he considers just those letters whose names contain consonantal segments, therefore leaving aside *a,e,i,o,u,* and *y,* whose names contain only vowels and glides. He has fairly direct clues to the representation of [p,t,k,b,d,f,v,s,z,ǰ,m,n,r, and l] in the corresponding letter-names, and [č] (as in *chin*) is the consonant in the name of *h*.[6] The names of *c,g,q,x,* and *w* provide no additional information, since they contain only consonants already accounted for. This leaves the child with no direct suggestion for representing [θ,ð,š,ž,g,ŋ and h].[7] The various English vowels are much less well provided for, but the children devise rather ingenious spellings for them, as we will see. Notice that to use even this information, the child must analyze the letter-names into their component segments and respect the consonantal or vocalic nature of each. There are indications in the invented spellings that the children can and do perform just such an analysis.

In addition, the children got information from their parents, but ordinarily only when they asked for specific help. Most of them apparently learned from adults the digraphic spellings of [θ], [ð], and [č], as in *thin, then,* and *church.* Certain common words, such as *the, day, Mommy, Daddy,* and the child's own name and those of his family were sometimes copied or dictated, but the evidence also includes invented spellings for each. In general, these pre-school writers are remarkably independent; they create most of their own spellings by trying to represent the sounds as they relate them to the letter-names they know. Occasionally these efforts lead to a standard spelling, but most of the results are non-standard, often extremely so, and they reveal aspects of the child's phonological system.

Vowels

The children's representation of front[8] vowels presents a fairly clear system. The names of the letters *a,e,* and *i* correspond quite directly to the tense vowels in *bait, beet,* and *bite.* In the spontaneous spelling system these letters represent their

---

[6] (Broad) phonetic transcriptions will appear in square brackets; phonological representations, in slashes. The invented spellings will be entirely upper-case; standard spellings and individual letters will be italicized. Ages will be stated as, for example, 5.3 (five years, three months).

[7] As in italicized positions in *thin, then, ship, measure, go, sing,* and *have.*

[8] Vowels are described in terms of the position of the tongue during articulation—front or back, high, mid or low. Tenseness and laxness of vowels refer to a complex of articulatory properties. The vowel of *bite* is back, but unrounded.

own names in such words, usually without the standard devices, such as doubling or final "silent" *e*, to show the tenseness of the vowel. So we have:

D*A*	(day)	L*A*DE	(lady)	T*I*GR	(tiger)
K*A*M	(came)	E*G*LE	(eagle)	L*I*K	(like)
T*A*BIL	(table)	F*E*L	(feel)	M*I*	(my)

More interesting is the spelling of the lax vowels, as in *bit, bet, bat,* and *pot.* Altogether the children must extend the five vowel letters (or others, conceivably) to at least eight lax vowels, as well as some other tense ones. They choose a systematic phonological basis for making this extension.

Standard spelling accomplishes part of what is required by using the same letter to spell the distinct vowels italicized in the following pairs:

div*i*ne—div*i*nity   extr*e*me—extr*e*mity   ph*o*ne—ph*o*nic

These pairs of vowels are related not only historically but lexically; that is, in the lexicon of an optimal grammar of English, the vowel segments of each pair will be represented in the same way. It is generally the case that standard spelling represents these lexical relationships; note that the relationships in meaning are thus embodied in spelling.[9]

Two general processes affect the actual pronunciation of the tense forms in contemporary English, however. The first combines them with a following [y]- or [w]-glide, converting them to diphthongs. The second, known as Vowel Shift, raises their place of articulation from that of the lax forms to the next highest position, lowering the highest to a low position. Other rules further modify their quality. Because all these rules affect only tense vowels, and because there was no corresponding change in spelling when Vowel Shift entered the language, the vocalic portion of a tense diphthong now differs phonetically in height and other qualities from the lax vowel that is usually spelled with the same letter. The phonetic correspondence is as follows:

	tense	lax	tense	lax	tense	lax
Symbol	[īy]	[i]	[ēy]	[e]	[āy]	[a]
Spelling	serene—divinity		came—extremity		line—phonic	

With these correspondences in mind, consider the following typical invented spellings:

F*E*S	(fish)	F*A*LL	(fell)	SC*I*CHTAP	(Scotch tape)
*E*GLIOW	(igloo)	L*A*FFT	(left)	G*I*T	(got)
FL*E*PR	(Flipper)	*A*LRVATA	(elevator)	CL*I*K	(clock)

Such examples could be multiplied many times, for among the children under

---

[9] See the references of footnote 2 for a further discussion of this issue.

5 years, these representations of the lax vowels are extremely regular. The [i] of *fish* and *igloo* is represented as *E*, the [e] of *fell* as *A*, the [a] of *Scotch* as *I*. In other words, the children pair lax vowels with tense vowels on the basis of phonetic relationships. The resulting spellings seem odd to most adults, just because adults have long since learned that spelling represents the lexical level at which the first vowel of *penalty* is related to that of *penal*. To adults this relation has become a perceptual fact, and not always an easy one for beginning students of phonetics to displace.

What is surprising is that the children are able to recognize the phonetic relationships they represent in spelling. The children do not pair lax with tense vowels as if these were unanalyzable segments, as they seem to most adults, but rather on the basis of similarity in place of articulation, abstracting from differences in tenseness, diphthongization, and possibly length. The children organize the vowels according to an analysis of their phonetic features.

Further evidence that the children are employing such a tacit analysis appears much later in their careers as original spellers. After they have learned the standard spellings for the lax vowels, many of the children make a rather systematic mistake. They occasionally spell a high or mid tense vowel with the letter they have recently learned to use for the phonetically corresponding lax form.

SIKE	(seek)	CEME	(came)
AIRFILD	(airfield)	PLEY	(play)
FRONTIR	(frontier)	TEBL	(table)

It is as if, having learned that the spelling of lax vowels is not based on what they can hear in the letter-names, the children attempt to save the phonetic correspondence between lax and tense forms, even at the expense of ignoring the obvious congruence between letter-names and tense vowels that they began with. This error, as they are on the verge of learning the standard system, actually carries them away from it momentarily, overthrowing the best-practiced vowel spellings of all. This seems a plausible error only if general notions of phonetic correspondence, not memorized sequences, underlie the spellings. It suggests that the children's knowledge of such relationships may be a more important basis for their spelling than the establishment of "habits" through practice.

Note that the children analyze the articulation of the three tense diphthongs considered so far in the same way, despite the considerable differences among them. For example, the vowel and glide of [iy] are sufficiently close that the segment is not considered diphthongal by many linguists (e.g., Jespersen, Jones); they consider the vowel of *beet* to be a tense, slightly higher and more fronted version of the vowel of *bit*. On the other hand, [ay] combines a low back vowel with a high front glide. Not surprisingly, the latter spelling is the first to disappear as a child's analysis develops. Children who at first have all three of the above tense-lax relationships later may have only [e]—[ey] and [i]—[iy], employing a new spelling for [a]—not *I*, but *O* or *A*. Some preliminary counting suggests that a common reflection of this early system among the "errors" of first-graders who have, for the most part, learned the official spellings, is *A* for [e] as in KRAPT (crept).

Finally, in their analysis of front vowels all of the children seem to assume that the vowel of *bat* is to be spelled with an *A*—even at the same time that they are writing the "incorrect" forms just discussed. The vowel of *bat* is not a part of any letter-name, nor of any tense vowel in most northern U.S. dialects of English. Unless they learn the spelling of [æ] by asking their parents—and they clearly do not learn the spelling of any other lax vowel in that way—the children presumably choose the letter whose name is closest, in some sense, to it. In place of articulation, *A* [ēy] and *I* [āy] are the two possibilities. That the children always choose *A* may suggest that for them two vowels differing only in height of articulation ([æ—e]) are phonologically closer than two differing only in backness ([æ—a]); therefore they collapse the former pair in spelling. If the most fundamental phonological dimensions for the children are those along which contrasts are most likely to be preserved in spelling, this result contrasts with the suggestion of Jakobson, that height is the primary dimension for vowels.[10] On the same assumption, it is consistent with the hierarchy suggested by Chomsky and Halle, in which backness is the major dimension.[11] The entire discussion is highly tentative. At any rate, in the central and back vowels there is other evidence that backness is a more important determinant of the children's spelling than is height.

One result of the spelling of front vowels is that *bait, bet,* and *bat* all have the same spelling—BAT. Some homography is required by the lack of symbols, but the particular choices appear to reflect the children's own sense of phonological relations. The spellings are phonetic in the sense that they represent relations at a (broad) phonetic level of detail; they are abstract in that distinct segments are represented by a single symbol. The children evidently find this result acceptable enough that they do not introduce invented symbols, unlike those critics who reject standard English spelling for its lack of distinct representations for functionally distinct sounds.[12]

I will not discuss the invented spellings of back vowels in detail here. The phonetic relations are intricate, but the symbols available to the children from the standard alphabet are limited, so their spellings are highly abstract and reveal little internal structure. Also, there is a lack of clear evidence for some of the less frequent vowels. In general, the back rounded vowels of *boot, boat,* and

---

[10] Roman Jakobson, *Child Language, Aphasia, and Phonological Universals* (The Hague: Mouton & Co., 1968), p. 75. First published in 1941, this is the seminal work in this field.

[11] Chomsky and Halle, p. 410.

[12] In principle, the Initial Teaching Alphabet (i.t.a.) is based on this criticism. See ch. 5 of my *Children's Perceptions of the Sounds of English* (unpublished Ph.D. dissertation, Harvard University, 1970).

bought are all spelled *O*. In this, the children disregard differences in height and tenseness, again choosing backness as the dimension to be represented. Typical examples at an early stage of development are:

SOWN	(soon)	GOWT	(goat)	OL	(all)
EGLIOW	(igloo)	POWLEOW	(polio)	COLD	(called)
SOWTKAC	(suitcase)	WENDOWS	(windows)	SMOLR	(smaller)

As these suggest, vowels with back glides, [w] as in *boot* [ūw] and *boat* [ōw], are often spelled *OW*. This remarkably accurate representation provides further evidence that the children can distinguish a vocalic segment from a glide, a distinction that is particularly notable for the vowel of *boat,* where *O* alone might have sufficed, had the children treated the letter-name as an unanalyzed whole.[13]

Further evidence that the children **represent** similarities in backness comes from their spelling of the lax, back, unrounded vowel [Λ], the vowel of *hut.* The younger children (from three and a half to about four and a half years) spell this vowel *I,* indicating a relation to the other back, unrounded vowels [a] and [āy], not to [i].

LIV	(love)	BRITHR	(brother)
DIZ	(does)	SINDAS	(Sundays)
WIS	(was)	WINTS	(once)

Again the difference that the children abstract from is one of height and possibly tenseness. This fact, together with the treatment of back rounded vowels, is consistent with the system applied to front vowels.

The spelling of the "neutral" form to which unstressed lax vowels reduce is of some interest, because it illustrates both what the children know and what they do not yet know. Phonetically, this vowel is central, high or mid, and unrounded; the children pair it, accurately enough, with the vowel of *bit,* which they spell *E* at an early stage for the reasons mentioned above. **This spelling appears in the italicized positions of:**

PLEM*E*TH	(Plymouth)	SEP*E*KOL	(Cepacol)
AN*E*MEL	(animal)	RAJ*E*LASNS	([cong]ratulations)
B*E*NAN*E*	(banana)	PANS*E*L	(pencil)

Later, when the spelling of the vowel of *bit* develops to *I,* the reduced vowel also becomes *I*:

SIG*I*RAT	(cigarette)	KRISM*I*S	(Christmas)
OV*I*N	(oven)	CER*I*T	(carrot)
ROC*I*T	(rocket)	SRK*I*S	(circus)

[13] Further evidence that the children can analyze the letter-names occurs in the front vowels, not only for lax forms, but also in spellings like PLEYS (please), where the glide has been made explicit.

In this detail again we see a system that abstracts from certain phonetic differences to relate one segment to another. Especially notable in this case is that the children give a consistent spelling to a segment that may be represented by various vowel letters in conventional spelling. Again, the reason is that standard spelling represents a lexical form which takes account of derivational relations like the one between *cigarette* and *cigar*, where the second vowel is not reduced. Pre-school children have little or no knowledge of these relations and the lexical forms that preserve them, of course; in fact, it is just such information that they must eventually learn.

Vowel alternations

As noted above, certain pairs of vowels alternate regularly in derivationally related forms in English. The following examples illustrate the major pairs:

	Vowel Alternation	*Spelling*
1.	[āy—i]	div*i*ne—div*i*nity l*i*ne—l*i*near
2.	[īy—e]	pl*ea*se—pl*ea*sant ser*e*ne—ser*e*nity
3.	[ēy—æ]	n*a*tion—n*a*tional prof*a*ne—prof*a*nity
4.	[ōw—a]	t*o*ne—t*o*nic verb*o*se—verb*o*sity
5.	[āw—ʌ]	prof*ou*nd—prof*u*ndity ab*ou*nd—ab*u*ndant
6.	[ūw—ʌ]	red*u*ce—red*u*ction ind*u*ce—ind*u*ction

Chomsky and Halle have shown that these phonetic alternations can be derived from lexical forms in which both members of a pair have essentially the same vowel. The phonological rules that predict the difference in pronunciation are each independently required in the grammar of English. As a result, the fact that English spelling uses the same letter for both members of each pair (except for dropping the *o* in case 5) becomes simply another instance of the general practice in the language, of representing lexical forms in spelling.[14]

The question of how to relate such forms in spelling surely does not arise for children of the age we are discussing. As the examples suggest, the derivational

[14] See Chomsky and Halle, pp. 178-87, for a discussion of the rules relating these pairs. See Carol Chomsky, "Reading, Writing, and Phonology," for a less technical discussion of the alternations and their spelling.

processes involved are typical of the learnéd vocabulary that includes many poly-syllabic forms of Romance origin. One suspects that within young children's vocab-ularies there is little generality to such relationships as these. As a result, if a pre-school child had occasion to write *pleasant,* he would probably not try to display its relation to *please.* The following table contrasts the standard spellings for such pairs with the results of the children's own phonological system:

Phonetic Pair	Examples	Adult Spelling[15]	Child Spelling
1. [āy—i]	divine—divinity	I	Different: I—E
2. [īy—e]	serene—serenity	E	Different: E—A
3. [ēy—æ]	nation—national	A	Same: A
4. [ōw—a]	tone—tonic	O	Different: O(W)—I
5. [āw—Λ]	abound—abundant	(O)U	Different: O(W)—I
			O—U later
6. [ūw—Λ]	reduce—reduction	U	Different: OW—I
			O—U later

In general, the children spell differently the pairs that are the same in standard spelling. On this basis one can suggest some empirical hypotheses: for example, that children find it easier to learn the relationship and the first vowel spelling of *nation/national* and similar forms than that of the derived forms in 1 and 2, and that the spelling of derived forms in 5 and 6 is easier to learn than that of their roots.

There are important questions yet to be answered, of course. We do not know what further development children's phonology may undergo before they begin to learn such words as these, nor do we know the exact role that the derivational relations play in the learning of spelling. Although these relations allow for a systematic account of English phonology and spelling, they may play little or no immediate role in learning. Furthermore, we do not know what individual dif-ferences there may be in pre-schoolers' conceptions of English phonology.

Nevertheless, one general insight seems clear: the children's created spellings, no less than the standard ones, are the results of a systematic categorization of English vowels according to certain articulatory properties. That children may tacitly recognize such phonological relationships spontaneously, even before their first formal encounter with reading and writing in the standard system, sug-gests that they need not approach the latter as a set of arbitrary sound-symbol cor-respondences—that is, as a long list of words to be memorized. Rather, the child's

[15] The adult spelling includes a final "silent" *e* in some of the tense cases. This is not simply a discontinuous digraphic spelling but has an independent function in lexical representations. Chomsky and Halle, pp. 147-50.

task is to master new principles that extend and deepen the already abstract conception of the sound system of English that he brings to school.

Affrication

Turning now to consonants, we find other evidence of the pre-schoolers' phonological judgments embodied in their spelling. Consider the following:

AS CHRAY	(ash tray)	CWNCHRE	(country)
CHRIBLS	(troubles)	JRADL	(dreidel)
CHRIE	(try)	JRAGIN	(dragon)

The invented spelling of [t] and [d] before [r] is *CH* and *J*, respectively.

Again, these representations have a phonetic basis; the first segments of a pair like *truck* and *tuck* are not identical, in fact. Before [r] in English, [t] and [d] are affricated, i.e., released slowly with a resulting "shh" sound. They are articulated in the same place as the stops that we spell *t* and *d*, but in the manner of the palatal affricates [č] and [ǰ] that standard spelling represents as *ch* and *j* respectively. In that respect, they constitute a third possibility intermediate between the two phonological pairs that have distinct standard spellings. Because the affrication before [r] is predictable, standard spelling ignores it, using the lexical representations *tr* and *dr*. Evidently, the children perceive the affrication. Not knowing the lexical representations, they must choose between the known spellings *T/D* or *CH/J* for these intermediate cases. They consistently choose on the basis of affrication, abstracting from the difference in place-of-articulation. They always match affricate [t] and [d] with the affricates that correspond in voicing—[č] and [ǰ], respectively.

Sometimes this preference appears among first-graders, even those who have done no original pre-school spelling. A six-year-old, making average progress in reading and writing in first grade, wrote the following words for me when I asked what words begin with the same sound as *train*. (Note that *R* is usually omitted and *CH* is reversed):

HCEAN	(train)	HCRAK	(track)
HCEK	(check)	HCICN	(chicken)
HCIKMANCK	(chipmunk)	HCITO	(cheetah)
HCRP	(trip)	HCAFE	(traffic)

This boy's spelling is clearly different from that of the pre-schoolers—in the vowels, for instance—but he had no doubt that these words begin with the same sound. Similarly for [dr] sequences:

GIBOLL	(dribble)	(the word I asked about)
GIP	(Jeep)	

```
GIN        (Gene)
GY         (draw)          (I attribute the Y to the [w] in the
                            name of that letter.)
```

Another first-grade boy independently produced very similar answers; *cheat, traps,* and *chap* were all words with the same first sound as *train*. He spelled that sound *H*—remember that the name of the letter includes [č]. He suggested *drink* and *Jim* as having the same first sound as *dribble*. For these boys, [t] and [d] before a vowel were clearly another matter; after they had given me the above answers, I asked each about *toy, table, Dick*, and *dog*. Those are *t* and *d*, they told me, and they wrote them out with those letters.

I have conducted an experimental investigation with 135 children who had done no original spelling, seeking to determine their judgments of these affricates. The details of the test and its results are beyond the scope of this article,[16] but the general outcome provides some support for the inferences drawn from the invented spelling. For example, the children were asked to indicate which words in a set of examples like *train, turkey,* and *chicken* begin with the same sound as *truck*. The children supplied the words themselves, by naming pictures, so that I, as tester, rarely had to give my own pronunciation. There were at least 11 words in a set, so that the consistency of a child's judgment could be measured. Of the 80 kindergarten children, many could not make consistent judgments, but of those who could do so, fully half chose words like *train* and *chicken*, rejecting *turkey, tie*, and the like. The 28 nursery-school children had even more difficulty making the required judgment consistently, a fact which suggests, not surprisingly, that the children who spelled spontaneously were better than most at becoming conscious of their phonological judgments. But again, most of the consistent nursery-school children chose the affricates and rejected the stops.

In a class of 27 first-graders who had encountered *tr*-words in their early reading, most made the adult judgment. However, there were children even in this group who insisted on the similarity between [tr] and [č]. Furthermore, there were four who easily demonstrated their ability to read a set of words like *train, teddy bear*, and *chair*, and who asserted with equal confidence that it is the first and last that begin with the same sound, even while they looked at the printed forms. These children obviously distinguished standard spelling from their own phonetic judgments. Such results as these indicate at least that the spontaneous spellers are not unique in their phonological judgments, although they may be somewhat unusual in their ability to make them explicit, and that the affrication of stops before [r] in English may be an important phonetic fact for young children.

Just as there is no unaffricated [tr] cluster, there is no [čr] cluster within a

---

[16] See chapter 2 of the dissertation referred to in footnote 12.

syllable in English,[17] so, given the standard alphabet, either *tray* or *chray* would represent the word unambiguously. In a strictly taxonomic phonemic analysis, there is no relevant evidence for deciding whether the first segment of *tray* is to be classed with that of *toy* or that of *chin*. As usual, the standard spelling corresponds to the lexical representation from which the actual pronunciation is predictable by a general rule. That the children do not know this lexical representation is simply another instance of the general conclusion that it is such representations that they must learn in mastering standard spelling.

Perhaps the more remarkable fact is that knowing the usual uses of *T* and *CH*, the children are able to choose a consistent representation for this intermediate segment. They abstract from a difference in palatalization (so called because the tongue strikes the palate in the articulation of *chin*) in classifying the first segment of *tray* with that of *chin*, and they do so without parental guidance, obviously. Evidently affrication is for them a phonologically more influential feature than is palatalization, despite the otherwise general importance of place-of-articulation in their system. The children may represent palatalization if they have the alphabetic means to do so, as in SE (see) versus SHE, but they are capable of a more abstract spelling where it is needed, as in the [tr] and [dr] cases. In this, they are spontaneously employing one of the basic devices of spelling systems, namely consistent abstraction from phonetic variations.

The nature of this accomplishment is theoretically more important than the fact that they choose the wrong dimension, from the adult point of view. To learn standard (lexical) spelling, a child must acquire both the principle that spelling does not represent regular phonetic variation and a knowledge of just what is regular—affrication, in this case. The fact that children's spontaneous spelling is already systematically abstract suggests that it is chiefly the facts of English, rather than the principle of spelling, that they have yet to learn. We will examine other cases in which the original spelling is, or rapidly becomes, abstract in this sense. Teachers of primary reading and spelling should be aware of both the principle and the specific instances of it in English. In responding to children's first spelling, we should probably regard efforts that abstract in the wrong direction as misapplications of the right idea.

Flaps

Another case that provides some information about the child's capacity for abstract representation is that of alveolar flaps, as in the following words:

LADR	(letter)	PREDE	(pretty)
WOODR	(water)	BEDR	(better)

[17] As there would be if words like *Christmas*, *chrome*, and *chronic* were pronounced with a first segment like that of *chop*, for instance.

Once again, the *D* in these words represents a phonetically correct perception. There is no contrast between [t] and [d] when they occur between vowels in English; both become a tap of the tongue against the alveolar ridge behind the upper teeth. Because this sound is voiced, it is closer to [d]. The same variation takes place across word boundaries, and the children do not fail to represent it:

AODOV   (out of)   GAD I CHANS   (get a chance)

In this case, the children represent a phonetic variation that the standard system does not. Presumably they have no basis for knowing that there is a lexical /t/ in such words. For the word-internal cases, they cannot receive any direct phonetic evidence, since [t] never occurs there.

Nevertheless, this is one of the earliest invented spellings to disappear. The child who wrote LADR and PREDE at age three and a half or four wrote LATR, SESTR (sister), and PRETE at age five. As these examples themselves show, other invented spellings, such as that of the lax vowels and the unigraphic representation of syllabic /r/ (see below), persisted longer, until age six in this case. Even children who at age six and later maintained some of the original spellings, such as CHR for [tr], stopped representing the flap even in internal positions, as in LETL (little).

How the children learn about the lexical /t/ in such words is not the issue. Most of these children were at least beginning to read at age five, and their parents say that they usually told their children the spelling of any word they asked about. Furthermore, at a boundary [t] alternates with the voiced flap, according to whether the following segment is a vowel, so that either may occur in the same word:

[gɨD ə čæns]   [gɨt sɔm]
get a chance   get some

More important than the source of evidence is the fact that the children learned to abstract away from this particular phonetic variation regularly. The relatively rapid development of this abstraction suggests that voicing contrasts may be less major determinants than others. Another section will present further evidence for this conclusion.

The extension of this abstract spelling to all appropriate instances despite deficient phonetic evidence supports the view that spelling is "rule-governed" behavior—that is, that spellings need not be learned one-by-one, but rather that what is learned is a principle. An important difference is that a principle extends to new instances. One cannot be sure what constitute "new instances" in children's writing, but the word-internal tongue flaps would seem to qualify, for phonetically they are always voiced, and the evidence that they are lexically (therefore graphically) /t/ is quite indirect. Yet once *T* appears in such a position, it appears consistently from then on, displacing *D* in words that the children

164

have written previously. Accordingly, I suggest that the phonological relation between the voiced flap and the corresponding voiceless stop became a part of these children's knowledge of the language, and that they adopted the abstract form in their spelling as a result.

Nasals

Another interesting feature of the children's spelling is the treatment of the nasals [m], [n], and [ŋ], as in *bumpy, end,* and *sing,* respectively. Initially within a syllable, only the first two occur in English, and in this position, the children spell them in the usual way:

    MARED   (married)   NIT   (night)

These two nasals in final position also receive standard spelling:

    POM   (palm)   WAN   (when)

But when any of the nasals occurs before a consonant, the children almost always omit it from spelling:

BOPY	(bumpy)	AD	(and)	WOTET	(want it)
NUBRS	(numbers)	ED	(end)	DOT	(don't)
THOPY	(thumpy)	MOSTR	(monster)	PLAT	(plant)

Velar nasals before phonetic consonants are slightly less common, but examples are:

HACC	(Hanks)	
THEKCE	(think(s?))	
AGRE	(angry)	
SIC	(sink)	written three times in my presence, along with a monologue on its nominal, transitive, and intransitive meanings.
FAC	(Frank)	the [r] is also omitted
NOOIGLID	(New England)	

This treatment of preconsonantal nasals is quite general and consistent; it is the usual (almost without exception) spelling for all the children up to about age five. Then most of them begin to represent the nasal, but still frequently omit it. In fact, on an informal spelling dictation given to 49 first-graders, this spelling accounted for 15 of the 23 erroneous spellings of *went* and *sent.* Unfortunately, these examples are ill-chosen, since *wet* and *set* also happen to be English words, and on that account may be more likely errors. Some first-grade teachers have indicated, however, that the omission of preconsonantal nasals is extraordinarily common.

What appears at first to be another and extremely common instance of this spelling is the use of *EG* and *IG* for *-ing* endings, the former being used by those children who write *E* for [i].

FEHEG	(fishing)	SKEEIG	(skiing)
SOWEMEG	(swimming)	CUMIG	(coming)
GOWEG	(going)	PLAYIG	(playing)
COLAKTGE	(collecting)	FILG	(feeling)

One can not consider these as representing the *g* of conventional spelling and omitting the nasal, however, because the [g] is not realized phonetically in these forms in most dialects. The nasal is the final sound, and it seems plausible that the pre-school spellings represent it, just as they do the other final nasals, but with *g*, since the alphabet provides no separate letter for [ŋ]. The stop [g] that the children otherwise spell *G* as in GEVS (gives) and EGLIOW (igloo) corresponds to [ŋ] in being velar. This suggests that place of articulation is a stronger determinant of the choice of symbol than is nasality, as indeed one would expect from the relative generality of these features in English. So when a nasal precedes a consonant (phonetically) it is not represented in the original spellings, but it is spelled (*M,N,* or *G*) when it does not precede a consonant. In the special case of the velar nasal, these rules give the same spelling for [ŋg] and [ŋ]: *G*. Words which include [ŋg] phonetically, such as *finger, longer,* or *linger,* the children spell FEGR, LOGR, etc., where the *G* evidently represents [g], and the nasal has been omitted.

When a nasal precedes a consonant in English, it must be articulated in the same place as the consonant; that is, within a syllable, only [m] precedes [p] and [b], only [n] precedes [d] and [t], and only [ŋ] precedes [g] and [k]. Thus, in the *-ing* of standard spelling, even when the *g* is not pronounced, we can regard it as corresponding to a lexical form, giving information as to where the nasal is articulated. In their original spellings the children are using *G* for a similar reason, apparently; when they learn standard spelling, they may find it natural in this respect.

The children do not often cooperate with direct requests to write particular words, but occasionally they provide some evidence that they distinguish the velar nasal and omit it before a consonant. One boy wrote FINGR for *finger* but then crossed it out, saying that that would spell [fiŋgr]. He thought for a while, and then with a shrug, wrote FINGR anyway. He was older (6.2) and had begun to spell nasals before consonants in general. Another boy, who did not generally do so, wrote FIGR, sounding it out as [f-iŋ-g-r].

We could explain the children's treatment of nasals by assuming that they follow a strict segmentation principle under which a segment homorganic with and phonetically overlapping an adjacent one is not represented as a separate segment. There is no tongue-movement at all between a nasal and a following consonant, in fact. There is also support for the view that the children omit nasals on the basis of a systematic phonological abstraction.[18] Malécot has shown with spectographic and kymographic evidence that preconsonantal nasals have the effect of nasalizing preceding lax vowels. In fact, the nasals constitute distinct phonetic segments only before voiced consonants, as in *amble, candor,* and *anger.* Before voiceless consonants, as in *ample, cantor,* and *anchor,* the nasal is phonetically realized (and perceptually recognized) through vowel nasalization alone.[19] This result holds in most dialects of English for [ʌ], [i], and [æ], especially the last. Given these phonetic facts, any uniform representation of preconsonantal nasals is an abstraction. We could regard the children as generalizing in the direction of nasalized vowels, contrary to standard spelling, and then abstracting from that nasalization in their spelling.

Finally, the children's judgments may be abstract in a slightly different sense. Nasals are partially redundant in English in just the position in which the children omit them from spelling—preconsonantally. "Partially" in this case means that, given that a nasal occurs before a known consonant, one can predict all its other features, notably its place of articulation. For this reason, English spelling would carry the same information if a single symbol, say *n*, represented any nasal before a consonant. *Bump* would be spelled *bunp; bunt* and *bunk* would be spelled just as they are, and no ambiguity would be introduced. The children's spelling ignores just this one piece of information, albeit a crucial one. In this respect, it is an over-abstraction.

Treating a partially redundant segment as wholly so is not unprecedented. In Old English, and Germanic languages in general, alliteration depends on the second segment of a word if and only if the first is an [s] and the second is a true consonant. That is, [sp] must alliterate with [sp], not with [st] or [sk]. In such a cluster [s] was (and is) partially redundant in almost the same sense as preconsonantal nasals are: given that a consonant occurs initially before a true consonant, it must be [s]. Similarly, in folk-rhymes generally and Faroese Kuæði rhyme particularly, imperfect rhymes are tolerated where rhyming words differ by only one phonetic feature.[20] At the lexical level, *wet* and *went* differ by a segment specified by just one feature.

These three proposed explanations are alike in that they involve abstraction— from articulatory overlap, vowel nasalization, or partial redundancy. They all imply that nasality is a relatively minor, and place of articulation a relatively major, feature in the children's phonological system. The problem is to show how

---

[18] There is no question, incidentally, that the children perceive the nasality that they do not represent—that they hear a distinctive difference between *wet* and *went,* for instance. An independent test with such pairs confirmed this point. The question is where they think the difference lies.

[19] A. Malécot, "Vowel Nasality as a Distinctive Feature in American English," *Language,* XXXVI (1960), 222-29.

[20] I am indebted to Wayne O'Neil for these observations about OE alliteration and folk-rhyme. They are reported in his paper, "The Reality of Grammars: Some Literary Evidence" (unpublished).

these proposals are empirically different and to obtain evidence that distinguishes among them. Confirmation for any of them would raise the problem of explaining how the children acquired the relevant principle. What is clear from the present evidence is that the original spellings are abstracted from a perceived phonetic contrast, even in a case in which the spellers have the appropriate letters available and indeed use them in other contexts.

Syllabic Segments

When [r], [l], [m], or [n] occur in an English word between two consonants or at the end of a word after a consonant, they become syllabic—that is, the segment constitutes a sonority peak (in effect, a loudness maximum) and is perceived as a separate syllable. Because they know that the peak of most syllables is a vowel, and possibly influenced by the conventional spelling, adults perceive a vowel before the liquid or nasal. This perceived vowel is usually spelled *e* and may be represented either before or after the syllabic segment. The children virtually never represent such a vowel.

TIGR	(tiger)	DIKTR	(doctor)
SOGR	(sugar)	OVR	(over)
AFTR	(after)	SMOLR	(smaller)
LITL	(little)	CANDL	(candle)
WAGN	(wagon)	OPN	(open)

This spelling applies to medial syllabic consonants as well:

GRL	(girl)	BRD	(bird)	HRD	(heard)
FRST	(first)	SRKIS	(circus)	SODNLY	(suddenly)
ALRVATA	(elevator, pronounced [elərvēytə], in a dialect common in the Boston area)				

This spelling is particularly persistent; it frequently appears even in words for which a child has otherwise learned aspects of the conventional spelling, such as the two T's in LITTL or the LY in SODNLY. On a spelling-dictation exercise, out of 47 first-graders, 21 (plus some who were inconsistent) produced:

BRATHR (brother)   TABL (table)   FETHR (feather)

These same first-graders produced other spellings consistent with the invented ones (e.g., the nasals discussed above), but none so frequently as this one. Among the spontaneous spellers, this representation persists even in common kinship terms that the children might have occasion to learn the spellings of, to the extent that they learn any spellings.

FOT(H)R (father)   MUTHR (mother)   SESTR (sister)

These spellings appear to be particularly independent of adult influence, and they occur quite consistently in every child's writing. Ultimately, we would like to explain both the occurrence of the spellings and their durability.

To adults these spellings seem to represent inadmissible consonant sequences —even whole words without a vowel—and on that account to violate an apparent principle of English, that each syllable contains a vowel. This principle is true, if at all, only of surface forms, however. A lexical representation that omits predictable detail need not specify the syllabicity—the apparent vocalic quality—of these liquid and nasal segments; it is an automatic effect of the rules of English phonology.[21]

The children's treatment of syllabic segments contrasts with that of syllables consisting of a reduced vowel and an obstruent (a non-nasal true consonant, restricted by definition from being syllabic). Where liquids and nasals are not involved, their general practice is to represent a vowel in each syllable, as in CERIT (carrot), the second syllable of SRKIS, and many other examples. It would be hard to argue that there is any consistent phonetic basis for this distinction, that is, a difference in vowel quality between the syllabic segments and [əC] syllables (where C represents any obstruent). Rather, the basis appears to be that the vowel is redundant in the former cases but not in the latter, generally. In other words, the children represent only lexical (unpredictable) vowels in their spelling.

The explanation must involve one of two assumptions—that the children's knowledge of English phonology is sufficiently abstract to eliminate predictable vowels, or that at some level of the tacit phonological analysis reflected in spelling, syllabics (liquids and nasals) are distinguished from other consonants.[22]

The latter appears to be more nearly correct, for after about age five, when the children begin to represent the (predictable) reduced vowel in past tense endings after [d] or [t], as in STARTID and WONTID, they still do not do so with syllabics.[23] As in other cases, there is phonetic justification for distinguishing liquids and nasals from other consonants. The fact that the former can become syllabic is related to their similarity to vowels, namely that in their articulation there is a less radical obstruction of the flow of breath than in true consonants. This explanation suggests once again that an abstract classification of English segments may be part of the knowledge of the language that a child brings to school. Again the conclusion may apply both to spontaneous spellers and to first-graders who have done no pre-school writing.

[21] See Chomsky and Halle, pp. 85-89, for a discussion of such a rule and an independent justification of a lexical representation that omits syllabicity.

[22] See Chomsky and Halle, pp. 353-55, for a discussion of a classificatory framework that makes this distinction in terms of a feature called *syllabic*.

[23] Furthermore, there is little evidence that the children distinguish between lexical and predictable vowels in syllabic positions. There are, however, the spellings MANTIN (mountain) and ANEMEL (animal) where the vowels explicitly represented must be lexical because they remain in non-syllabic positions, as in *mountainous* and *animality*.

The children's spellings would be the conventional ones if the rules of English spelling were to change so that syllabicity was not represented. Although it would be an over-generalization, such a change would be appropriate to the lexical character of English spelling, since the syllabics are generally single segments at the lexical level. Perhaps it is just this property of these spellings that accounts for their slowness to change. In learning conventional spelling, the child is learning to represent his phonetic perceptions in a way that eliminates redundant variation. These representations of syllabic consonants are already of this sort, generally. In this case, as for preconsonantal nasals and certain others, all quite persistent, the child must learn to mark a phonetic detail.

An interesting footnote concerns the use of a letter to spell the syllable that is its name, as in

STRT   (start)   GRDIN   (garden)

This phenomenon is not limited to liquids and nasals; occasionally the children use this rebus-device in other contexts. It is not typical of invented spelling, and in cases where I have been able to observe the writing first-hand, the child has been quite conscious of using it and somewhat amused at it. Frank, age five, wrote

STṚT   (start)

When I asked him what the dot meant, he replied that it showed that the letter was spelling its own name. He applied this notation fairly regularly for a few months, but only where the syllable was exactly the letter-name, as in

U̦   (you)   OVR̦   (over)
R̦   (are)   ME̦   (me)

This evidence suggests what I believe to be the general case: that the children distinguish the letter-names from the sounds that the letters represent. From the beginning of writing, they use a letter to spell only a certain segment of its name[24]; after some time, they may become conscious of this distinction and exploit it in rebus-fashion, but at no stage do they appear to be confused by the letter-names, as some have suggested in connection with proposals for teaching reading. This distinction is itself no trivial analytic accomplishment, especially for the vowels.

Alternations

One effect of not representing predictable phonetic variation in English spelling is that the alternant forms of certain lexical items are spelled uniformly. The

---

[24] The children apply this principle even in the use of H [ēyč] to spell [č], as in the first-grader's spelling of the initial sound of *try, train*, etc. A parallel example is the use of Y [wāy] to spell [w], as in YUTS (once). This came from a child, 4.6, whose parents often urged her to use the letter that seemed closest when she asked about spelling.

170

past tense ending is *ed*, whether it occurs in its voiceless variant as in *hopped* [hapt], voiced as in *hogged* [hɔgd], or with a vowel as in *wanted* [wantəd]. Exceptional spellings occur where some aspect of pronunciation is not predictable; for past tense, there are two main cases: (1) truly exceptional verb alternations, such as *go/went*, where presumably nothing in the past form is predictable, and (2) a tense-lax alternation in medial vowels, a subregularity of the language restricted to certain verbs and indicated by a final consonant cluster, as in *creep/crept*.

The same general principle carries over in part to the spellings of plurals, where the contrasts among the phonetic realizations [s], [z], and [əz] are completely predictable. [əz] occurs after coronal stridents as in *dishes*, [s] after voiceless consonants as in *cups*, and [z] everywhere else as in *bags*. English spelling marks the first as *-es*, noting its syllabicity, but uses *-s* for both of the others. For both inflections, the spelling system abstracts away from voiced/voiceless alternation. In general, only lexical contrasts are preserved in spelling.

With these facts in mind, we now consider how the children represent predictable contrasts. There are really two questions, although only rather indirect evidence could allow us to separate them: do the children recognize the various occurrences of past tense or plural as belonging to the same morphological item, and is there any evidence from their spelling that they perceive the predictability of the variation? Do they assign phonetic or morphophonemic spellings, and do they treat exceptional items in an exceptional manner?

The answer is that generally they assign phonetic spellings at age three or four, but that a dramatic change occurs around age five or six. For the younger children, the following are typical examples:

MARED (married)
LAFFT (left)
HALPT (helped)

all written at age four. The same child at age five, however, used *-d* fairly uniformly, as in

WALKD (walked)   ARIVD (arrived)
HAPPIND (happened)   STARTID (started)

But he treated irregular verbs differently, often with standard forms, as in *felt* and *slept*, but also:

KUT (cut)   CGOT (caught)
FOTE (fought)

There are no exceptions to this general developmental sequence among the children for whom I have examples. For one child, Edith, there is a revealing month-by-month sequence from 5.10 to 6.3, during which time this change appears to have taken place. At 5.10 she began to mark past tense endings:

171

HOP-T   (hopped)
STOP-T   (stopped)

But she was unable to apply this diacritic orthography to past tense consistently:

HOPPED-T   (hopped, apparently with adult coaching for HOPPED, since
           the double consonant and -ed do not otherwise occur)
CAT-T   (cat)
WAT   (went)
WOCT   (walked)

The following month (5.11) showed more of the same; she had revised her notation slightly, and she treated an exceptional form as if it were regular.

THA'T   (that)
JUS'T   (just)
WAN'T   (went)

At 6.0 (really almost two months later) we have the first uniform treatment of regular past forms. The diacritics disappeared, along with any apparent confusion between verbal inflections and the inherent segments of other words.

PEKD   (peeked)
FILLD   (filled)

The -D of PEKD was the only morphophonemic spelling in this month; it was also the only phonetic [-t] as an inflection. Otherwise, [t] was spelled phonetically.

Two months later (6.2) there was more evidence that Edith could spell past tense endings uniformly; she had also, however, begun to learn that exceptions may be spelled more phonetically, an insight that she applies correctly in one case, fails to apply in another, and over-generalizes in a third.

LAFT   (left)
WAND   (went)
WISPRT   (whispered)
RASTD   (rested)

Beginning the following month, and ever since, Edith treated regular and irregular forms correctly, except for the non-occurrence of the e in -ed endings.

WALKD   (walked)
SLAPT   (slept)

This girl's development in this detail is only a more fully illustrated and more explicit (with her diacritic innovation) version of what the other young spellers appear to have done.[25] Nevertheless, it would be hasty to base deep principles on

[25] She was not the only child who marked inflections. Another girl, Pammie, went from LOOK, T (also NURS, T; CALL, D; NAME, D; etc.) at age seven to LOOK'D, etc. at age eight.

so few cases. What does seem clear is that the invented spellings are phonetic in this detail until late in the pre-school period. Then rather suddenly the children begin to abstract from the phonetic contrast toward a uniform spelling of past tense inflections. At the same time, they rapidly develop a correct distinction of regular and irregular cases, even when the irregularity involves a rather limited class like *wept—slept—crept*.

It would be incorrect, I think, to attribute all of this development to adult teaching. The girl who wrote the last class of examples attended a Montessori school, even in her sixth year, where the practice was to accept all the children's writing with a minimum of correction. Her mother, who had gone to a Montessori school herself, followed much the same practice at home; she told her children spellings only when they asked, and she rarely corrected what they offered. In fact, almost all of these children got correction from their parents only when they asked; that seems to have been a necessary condition for the spontaneous spelling to occur at all. Of course the child has used information from adults—by age six, most children have acquired information from reading as well as oral instruction—but this information apparently has been "filtered" through the child's own notions, which exert a powerful influence on what he writes.

Notice, furthermore, that almost all the spellings deviate from the standard, if not in the ending, then in the vowel, and they do so in regular ways. A uniform -D may appear for both [d] and [t] in regular past forms long before the standard -ed. These spellings are certainly not copied from adults in any simple sense. The development from phonetic to morphophonemic is not a direct move from phonetic to adult spelling; rather, there is a dramatic change in the type of (non-adult) spelling the child creates.

The treatment of plurals appears to be a special case of the general conclusion; from the first writings on, the children spell plurals -s, marking no distinction between the voiced and unvoiced variants. They do (sometimes) mark the vowel of the syllabic ending [əz], as adult spelling does. The following examples are typical:

WENDOWS	(windows)	RASIS	(races)
WANSAS	(Wednesdays)	CIDEJCHES	(sandwiches)
LADYS	(ladies [age five])	HOUESS	(houses)

The same children use -s for voiceless endings, too, of course.

SOKS	(socks)	RABITS	(rabbits)
STMPS	(stamps)		

In fact, s stands for phonetic [z] and [s] in inherent segments as well as in inflections.

CLOWSD	(closed)	BEECOS	(because)	SESTR	(sister)
WUS	(was)	KUS	('cause)	SAND	(send)

173

In general, z occurs rarely and only in positions such as initial pre-vocalic segments, where the occurrence of voicing is not predictable, as in ZIP.

The phonetic difference between [s] and [z] is not as great in final position, at least for some speakers, as in other positions.[26] It may be important, then, to ask whether the children represent the difference medially, where the phonetic contrast is greater and where voicing is also sometimes predictable.[27] (Leaving aside many details, voicing is assimilative, so that [s] occurs in voiceless consonant clusters, but [z] occurs elsewhere.) Evidence is less plentiful, but what there is clearly supports the conclusion that the children ignore the phonetic contrast. Compare, for instance,

RASIS	(races)	SUSE	(Susie)
SESTR	(sister)	CLOWSD	(closed)
PANSEL	(pencil)	PRESINS	(presents)

That the children do not distinguish [s] and [z] in their spelling can be explained in three quite different ways. First, the children may not generally perceive the two sounds as distinct. This result would be a clear counter-instance to the general conclusion that the children perceive fine phonetic differences, including other voicing contrasts, as in the [t]-[d]-[D] alterations, for instance. However, children of even three and a half years can usually answer questions involving pairs that differ only in voicing, such as *sip/zip, racer/razor,* and *bus/ buzz*.[28] Accordingly, I believe that this explanation is untenable.

Second, considering the reversals of letters in children's writing, it is conceivable that the visual distinction between *s* and *ƶ* is too difficult for the children to make consistently; so they settle on one, the more common *s*, as the representation for both. This hypothesis does not deny that the children can make the phonetic discrimination. I am inclined to reject this view for a number of reasons: first, on this supposition one would expect the spelling distinction to reappear among children who make a very angular *z* but a curved *s*, or among children of European background who write a barred *ƶ*, or among children who learn to typewrite (as three of those discussed here did), and who therefore can rely on a positional as well as a shape difference. As far as I can judge, none of these expectations is correct. Furthermore, these children had no serious difficulty with other pairs of letters that are mirror-images or inversions, such as *b/d, w/m,* and *u/n*. There are occasional reversed letters, as in all children's printing, but not nearly enough to cause any of these other distinctions to collapse, nor is the reversal entirely in one direction.

[26] This was pointed out to me by Emmon Bach. Where it applies, it is perhaps a minor reflection in English of a general tendency toward de-voicing of final obstruents, as is the rule in German, for instance.

[27] Some problems remain in the exact formulation. See Chomsky and Halle, pp. 228-29 and 232-33.

[28] See chapter 3 of the dissertation referred to in footnote 12.

A third interpretation is that the children distinguish [s] and [z] quite early and, perhaps even before beginning to write, conclude that their occurrence is predictable, so that spelling can be abstract from this difference without loss of information. This conclusion would be another over-generalization, but not for plurals, the most common examples. If this hypothesis is correct, we have another, and much earlier example of a typical process: the child has fairly narrow phonetic perceptions, but abstracts from these in systematic ways in spelling. In this case the abstraction is from a voicing contrast, just as in the case of the past-tense inflections and the rapid development of *T* for intervocalic flaps. Under this interpretation, the problem is to explain why this treatment of [s] and [z] emerges much earlier than these similar spellings for stops.

Adopting this view, we find evidence about a question raised by Berko in her classic study of children's acquisition of morphology. Having shown that preschool children can form the appropriate [s] or [z] plural of even nonsense forms, and thus that they have acquired knowledge of a rule that extends to new instances, Berko questions whether the rule is morphological or phonological in nature, and notes, "It would be interesting to find out what the child thinks he is saying—if we could in some way ask him the general question, 'How do you make the plural?' "[29] We might look upon the invented spellings as embodying an answer to this general question, namely that the children regard these plural alternants as a single form at the level relevant to spelling—just as adults do, in fact.

Accordingly, a pedagogical orthography, such as i.t.a., that employs distinct symbols for the voiced and voiceless plurals may be introducing phonetic detail that a pre-school child can readily, even spontaneously, learn to abstract away from. Considering the abstract nature of children's invented spellings, we find that phonemic accuracy in pedagogical spellings may be an inappropriate goal. The question is really deeper: which phonetic facts are relevant in the child's own phonological system as he begins to read and write?

Conclusion

We have seen evidence that children tacitly recognize certain phonetic contrasts and similarities, in that they represent these in their original spelling. For systematic reasons, standard English spelling does not reflect these same relationships. The contrasts, such as that between the first segments of *tuck* and *truck,* are predictable in context and therefore irrelevant to meaning and its representation in spelling. The similarities, such as that between tense and lax vowels, are not represented directly in standard spelling because of its abstract lexical character. Perhaps as a result of knowledge of this system, most adults do not recognize these

[29] Jean Berko, "The Child's Learning of English Morphology," in *Psycholinguistics,* ed. Sol Saporta (New York: Holt, Rinehart and Winston, 1961), p. 373.

phonetic relations; they have to learn, or re-learn, them in order to understand the children's judgments. What the children do not know is the set of lexical representations and the system of phonological rules that account for much of standard spelling; what they do know is a system of phonetic relationships that they have not been taught by their parents and teachers.

We have seen that the children choose representations in terms of phonetic properties, such as nasality, syllabicity, backness, height, and affrication. These are some of the terms in which the rules of English phonology must be stated. The contrary result would have been entirely possible; the children might have recognized no relation between the "flap" in *water* and the [d] of *waddle*, or between the vowels of *bite* and *pot*, although these share the properties of voicing and backness, respectively. In fact, the children might not have judged the segmentation of English words as they did; for example, that DIKTR (doctor) has five segments that need to be represented.

Finally, we have seen that children treat certain relationships as more basic than others in their spelling. Backness is preserved in place of tenseness and height for the vowels; affrication and place-of-articulation predominate over nasality and voicing for the consonants. On these bases, the children's spelling is systematically abstract from perceived phonetic detail. This characteristic is particularly notable in the abstraction from nasality, syllabicity, and voicing in certain contexts. These choices are not required by any lack of symbols, since in other contexts the children use letters (M,N,G,E,D, and Z) that represent these qualities. Evidently the children abstract on the basis of their tacit analysis of phonological features (as in distinguishing [r,l,m, and n] from other consonants in syllabic contexts) and possibly the predictability of certain details of pronunciation (such as the voicing of [t] between vowels). In general, the children treat sounds, not as unanalyzed wholes, but as items related by their constituent properties, and modified in regular, hence irrelevant, ways by their contexts. This result conflicts with the assumption that children are necessarily limited to matching spellings with phonemes defined on superficial taxonomic grounds. The children who created their own spellings arrived at a deeper analysis of English phonology a year or more before beginning school.

It would be easy but, I believe, incorrect to disregard the evidence presented here as having been produced by exceptional children. In that they began to spell and, often, to read early, these children were exceptional. Some, but not all, appeared to be independent and creative beyond the average, but their creativity was sometimes a result of their spelling accomplishments. Most of them came from relatively privileged middle-class families, with professional and academic parents, but this fact may have been a result of the informal procedure by which I located young spellers. Within this limitation, the families were quite diverse in beliefs and backgrounds. The one characteristic that all the parents had in common was a willingness to accept the child's own spelling efforts, to provide simple materials (first blocks and other elementary alphabet toys, then paper and pencil), and to answer questions. A cluster of unfortunate attitudes prevalent in our society may suppress this willingness in many parents: a fear that the child's own efforts will lead to "bad habits," a belief that English spelling is bizarre, and a corresponding reliance on the expertise of professional teachers or on some-times complex educational devices that bear the stamp of expert approval. All of the parents provided just the information that any inexpert literate adult could provide: the names of the letters and answers to such questions as, "How do you spell 'chuh'?" They did not coax or expect their children to spell; most were surprised, in fact. There were no unusual educational devices relevant to spelling in any of the homes, and although the parents may have had inner qualms about "bad habits," their manner was relaxed and non-didactic. All of the children now in the primary grades and above have readily mastered standard spelling, with none of the laborious re-training that the notion of "habits" implies. Learning to spell need not be a process of acquiring habits, apparently.

In any case, to attribute the children's accomplishment *a priori* to exceptional general intelligence or an exceptional environment merely begs the important question. The children had tacitly acquired a knowledge of phonological rela-tions of which their parents were themselves unaware. What the children had learned was not related in any obvious way to what they had heard or seen. The important theoretical question is how pre-school children can learn abstract rela-tions of this sort. Until we have serious evidence bearing on this question, we can not assume that general intelligence must be the major factor in acquiring the knowledge that makes spelling possible. Even if it were true that all young spellers are exceptionally intelligent, the statistical observation by itself would not ac-count for the occurrence of the spelling, nor, more important, for the specific and uniform character of what they all learned. Whatever variations there may be in individual development, the crucial conclusion remains that children can (and to some degree, must) make abstract inferences about the sound system of their language before they learn to read and write.

The educational importance of this conclusion seems clear enough, at least in general. We can no longer assume that a child must approach reading and writing as an untrained animal approaches a maze—with no discernible prior conception of its structure. We can not assume, in the essentially digestive meta-phor that Paulo Freire rightly ridicules,[30] that the child is an empty vessel, men-tally inert although physically so dynamic, waiting to be filled with adult spell-ings. Evidently, a child may come to school with a knowledge of some phono-logical categories and relations; without conscious awareness, he may seek to re-late English spelling to these in some generally systematic way. If this inference

[30] Paulo Freire, "The Adult Literacy Process as Cultural Action for Freedom," *Harvard Edu-cational Review*, XL (Spring 1970), 208.

is correct, some long-neglected questions turn out to be crucial for understanding and facilitating the process of learning to read: what levels of phonological analysis do individual children tacitly control at various stages of development; how do these analyses relate to the lexical representations that generally correspond to standard spelling; and how can reading instruction build on this relationship, while encouraging children to extend and deepen their notion of the sound system of the language? Detailed answers to these questions are not at all obvious; in fact, it is difficult to devise means of acquiring some answers, since children's phonological judgments are rarely explicit, as they are in the invented spellings. So far, we have evidence that at least some children do not attend to statistical associations between spellings and autonomous phonemes, which have been the subject of much research in reading. Rather, the children pair spellings with segments abstractly categorized in terms of a hierarchy of articulatory features.

In the classroom, an informed teacher should expect that seemingly bizarre spellings may represent a system of abstract phonological relations of which adults are quite unaware. Until we understand this system better, we can at least respect it and attempt to work with it, if only intuitively. A child who wants to spell *truck* with a *ch-* will not be enlightened by being told that *ch-* spells "chuh," as in *chicken*. He already knows that; in fact, the relation between the first segments of *truck* and *chicken* is exactly what he wants to represent. Nor will exaggerated (or exasperated) pronunciation of *truck* help much, for monolingual adult speakers of English are usually limited to pronouncing the two possibilities that our phonology allows. We will either insert a false vowel after the [t], which does away with the affrication at the cost of distorting the word, or we will exaggerate that very quality which the child wishes to represent. Drill and memorization of words with *tr-* and *dr-* may help the child to learn such cases, but these techniques suggest that spelling is arbitrarily related to speech and can only be memorized. This suggestion is not true of either standard spelling or the child's own invention. Better, it would seem, to say something like, "Yes, *truck* sounds like *chicken* at the beginning, but it is also like the first sound of *toy*, and that's what we show by using a *t*." Similarly for the child who spells *pen* with an *a* (or *dent* without an *n*, *brother* without an *e*, *liked* with a *t*, or *butter* with a *d*). Such a child needs to be told, in effect, that his phonological judgments are not wrong (though they may seem so to most adults), and that it is reasonable, indeed necessary, to categorize abstractly what he hears.

However, he must also learn that standard spelling reflects a system somewhat different from his own. He will have acquired the basis for this adult system only when he has tacitly learned rules such as affrication and vowel shift that make the standard spellings systematically accurate.[31] Then he can learn to read and

---

[31] See Carol Chomsky, "Reading, Writing, and Phonology," for some suggestions as to how this process may be facilitated.

spell on the principle that the written form corresponds to an abstract (lexical) form, not directly to what he hears. He is on his way when he begins to abstract from phonetic variations, as the spontaneous spellers did in their pre-school development. It may be particularly important to recognize when his own efforts are too abstract, or abstract in the wrong direction, and to suggest, at least implicitly, that he is using the right principle, even if in the wrong place. We cannot teach him this principle if we ourselves continue to believe that to learn to spell is to get in the "habit" of associating sounds with letters, or phonemes with graphemes. For at least some children, to learn standard spelling is to learn to broaden and deepen their pre-school phonological analysis, which may already be abstract enough that phoneme-grapheme correspondences are indirect outcomes of an intricate system.

Our understanding of children's phonology is still shallow and fragmentary at best. The reasonable conclusion to be drawn from this work at this time is not that old dogmas should be replaced with new, but that we now have good reason to look more carefully at children's judgments of English phonology and spelling. In the meantime, we must assume that learning to read and write are matters of knowledge rather than habit, to use the terms of an old but honorable distinction.

New Directions in Theories of Language Acquisition

MARILYN H. EDMONDS
Creighton University

Nativistic explanations, which posit innate rather than environmental influences on development, characterize many theories of language acquisition. Marilyn H. Edmonds offers some reasons for this bias and discusses the deficiencies of nativism as an explanatory principle. She reviews and critiques existing theories of syntax and highlights the trend toward a semantic description of linguistic development. Combining this semantic emphasis with a Piagetian framework, Edmonds argues that a satisfactory account of language acquisition will not emerge until this process is viewed within a larger developmental perspective.

Deese (1970) relates an old story about James VI of Scotland, who wanted to find out what language Adam and Eve spoke—the first language. According to the legend, James proposed placing two infants on an uninhabited island in the care of a deaf-mute nursemaid. The infants, isolated from any other language, would then grow up spontaneously speaking the "natural" language of mankind. Scholars have since rejected such simplistic, nativistic ideas about how children acquire language. However, more sophisticated nativistic hypotheses once again prevail in the thinking of many who study the acquisition of language. This article explores some of the reasons for the more contemporary emphases on nativism and then suggests some possible alternatives.

First, I explore three grammatical models of language acquisition, their presumed relationships to the nativistic position, and the problems raised by each model. Next, I argue that analyzing not only syntax (how words are joined together to make sentences) but also other aspects of language organization, in conjunction with the child's developing cognitive abilities, avoids the problems of pure nativism. Finally, I propose that Piagetian theory can organize these aspects of development, and conclude with a brief discussion of the possible role of the social environment in the development of the child's communication system.

Harvard Educational Review   Vol. 46   No. 2   May 1976, 175–198

Conceptions of Language and Psychological Explanations

Although interest in child language dates back at least to the fifth century B.C., systematic research into child language did not begin until the middle of the nineteenth century (Bar-Adon and Leopold, 1971). Since that time a voluminous literature has described many aspects of child language, notably its grammar. Most research on child language since 1900 has assumed, explicitly or implicitly, that children speak an imperfect version of adult language, that they share a grammar although "child language [is] adult language filtered through a great deal of cognitive noise and impoverished of vocabulary" (McNeill, 1966, p. 16). Thus research has often focused on case histories of gradual elimination of errors (Gregoire, 1971; Leopold, 1971), surveys of vocabulary (Smith, 1926), and surveys of frequency of syntactic classes (McCarthy, 1930). Researchers perceived child language as gradually approximating the adult syntactic model.

These early descriptions of child language were an outgrowth of linguistic attempts to construct grammars as models of language, i.e., as theories of how language is organized. A complete grammar describes at least semantics (the organization of meaning in language), syntax (how word classes join together to form phrases and sentences), and phonetics (how sounds join together to form words) of a language. In addition, such a grammar must specify how these semantics, syntax, and phonetics interrelate in constructing sentences. As Sinclair-de-Zwart has remarked, "to understand *how* something is acquired, we first have to know *what* is acquired" (1969, p. 326). Thus we need to understand a grammar before we can explain how it is acquired; our conceptions of how language is organized will constrain and direct the nature of the explanations given to account for how children acquire language.

Recent developments in linguistic theory have challenged older conceptions of the grammatical organization of language. In particular, Chomsky's (1957) highly influential *Syntactic Structures* posed a major challenge to extant theories of language organization and, by implication, to theories of language acquisition. The early syntactic models which described adult language were finite-state grammars, which assumed that any given word in a sentence determined the word that followed it. The alternative to the finite-state grammar was based upon constituent analysis, which examined how word classes (e.g., nouns, modifiers) joined together to form phrases and sentences. When explanations were given to account for changes in child language, they were typically some version of stimulus-response (S-R) or operant theories based on conditioning principles derived from experimental psychology (Skinner, 1957; Mowrer, 1960; Jenkins and Palermo, 1964; Palermo, 1971; Staats, 1971). In contrast, Chomsky emphasized the creative aspect of language: that mature language users can understand and produce an infinite set of sentences, even ones they have never before heard or uttered. He defined the linguist's task "to be that of producing a device of some sort (called a grammar) for generating all and only the sentences of a language" (Chomsky, 1957, p. 85).

In his monograph Chomsky explored the capabilities of three types of grammar for generating all and only the sentences of a language. He assessed their ability to do this and proposed models which could account for the organization of *any* language, rather than that of a specific language. First, Chomsky discussed the finite-state grammar, which defined a sentence as a sequence of left-to-right dependencies with each successive word determining the word or class of words following it. He demonstrated the inadequacies of this grammar by showing that it could not account for some syntactically correct sentences. He (Chomsky, 1965) argued that finite-state grammar is the linguistic manifestation of an S-R response chain (a series of stimulus-response units linked together in a sequence of left-to-right dependencies). The same inadequacies found in finite-state grammar make S-R chains likewise insufficient in their descriptions of the way people organize sentences. Psycholinguistic research (Miller, 1962) supports the view that an S-R chain is an inadequate description of either sentence production or comprehension. Furthermore, Fodor (1971) argues convincingly that extensions of S-R theories of language, such as mediation theory—a more elaborate version of S-R chain models (Mowrer, 1960; Jenkins and Palermo, 1964; Palermo, 1971; Staats, 1971) reduce, in principle, to simple S-R chains. Such psychological models assume that sentences are unilinear chains of word associations with varying probabilities describing the strength of the links between the words or word classes. It appears that language dependencies are not temporally sequential, a problem discussed by Lashley (1951), but until recently largely ignored by American psychologists. Thus empiricism, as realized in S-R theory, no longer seems a tenable approach to the study of language acquisition; some theorists have repudiated their own prior claims (Palermo, 1970).

Phrase-structure grammar is the second model Chomsky discussed. Phrase-structure grammars differ basically from finite-state grammars in that they specify rules for constructing sentences from syntactic classes rather than from probabilities of word associations. A phrase-structure grammar starts with a basic axiom and rewrites the axiom using grammatical rules until a sentence is derived. Much research in language acquisition has typically counted the frequency with which children use different syntactic classes. Linguistic descriptions of this type require at the minimum constituent analysis, i.e., the parsing of sentences. Chomsky argues that constituent analysis presupposes at least a phrase-structure grammar. While some researchers used constituent analysis models of language and postulated S-R mediation theory to explain language acquisition, they erroneously assumed syntactic classes were joined together via chaining processes (Jenkins and Palermo, 1964).

While phrase-structure grammars are more powerful than finite-state grammars in that they can account for left-to-right discontinuities in sentences, they do have

182

certain inadequacies. Chomsky argued that the most powerful linguistic theory will represent the native speaker's knowledge about his or her language, reveal fundamental regularities within the language, and require the fewest rules to represent linguistic knowledge. Phrase-structure grammars fail to meet any of these criteria. For example, they do not reveal relationships between sentences that seem to be related at an underlying level, such as the connection between a declarative sentence and the interrogative derived from it.

Chomsky proposed a third model, transformational grammar, to overcome some of the difficulties associated with phrase-structure grammar. This model (Chomsky, 1957, 1965, 1971) specifies that sentences are represented on two levels—a deep structure which contains the semantic meaning and a surface structure which represents this meaning in sound patterns. Deep structure is generated by phrase-structure rules. Transformational rules then operate upon different parts of the entire deep structure to produce the surface structure. Transformational grammar permits reducing the number of rules necessary to write a complete grammar by specifying context and taking account of the entire phrase-structure derivation. This simplifies the grammar and at the same time reveals the fundamental regularities of language. Psycholinguistic research has provided experimental support for the basic validity of some transformational model of grammar (Miller, 1962; Savin and Perchonock, 1965). Brown (1973a), Fodor and Garrett (1966) provide a valuable critique of much of this work.

Chomsky's arguments have stimulated a renewed interest in child language. Researchers now believe that child language might be productive in the same sense that adult language is productive, i.e., that children possess a finite set of rules capable of generating an infinite set of sentences. Operating on this assumption, linguists (Menyuk, 1963) and psychologists (Braine, 1963; Brown and Bellugi, 1964; Miller and Ervin, 1964) have set out to specify children's production rules and have used transformational grammars to describe young children's syntax and concurrent developmental changes. The basic technique is to tape-record the child's spontaneous speech and then write a grammar that could generate the utterances observed.

Researchers studying unrelated children in a variety of language communities report both similar rule systems and similar developmental sequences (McNeill, 1970a, 1970b). At the onset of sentence production, children seem to speak directly in deep structure, joining together basic grammatical categories (e.g., noun, verb) into the basic grammatical relations (e.g., subject of a sentence) of phrase-structure grammar. Thus, they seem to be inferring these underlying latent structures (Brown and Bellugi, 1964) and operating with deep-structure rule systems. Transformations and more adult-like surface structures appear only later. Children do not seem to be speaking fragments of adult surface structure but rather a language of their own with its own grammatical rules. They do not seem to acquire a collection of sentences they have heard others produce (as proponents of finite-state grammar and S-R theory suggest), but rather to build rule systems enabling them to create an infinite set of sentences.

In an examination of possible explanations for the child's grammar system, Chomsky, as well as other researchers, states that learning theory principles are clearly inappropriate descriptions of language development (Chomsky, 1965; Brown and Bellugi, 1964; Fodor, 1971; Palermo, 1970). Imitation in the strict sense also fails to give a satisfactory explanation. Children produce a great many utterances consistent with the proposed deep-structure and transformational rules, but many of their utterances have no plausible adult model (McNeill, 1966). Furthermore, child imitations of adult sentences are not typically grammatically progressive. That is, while the child sometimes imitates adult sentences, his or her imitations seldom incorporate new grammatical forms; rather, they appear to be reduced versions of the adult model, filtered through the child's grammatical system (Ervin, 1964; Kuczaj and Maratsos, 1975). Changes in the child's rule system often seem to appear first in spontaneous constructions and then in imitations of adult sentences. Faced with these complexities, some researchers (Brown and Bellugi, 1964) have given up attempts at explanation and have limited themselves to description, while others (McNeill, 1970a, 1970b) have turned to a nativistic explanation.

The Nativistic Hypothesis

Following Chomsky's (1965) lead, McNeill (1970a, 1970b) boldly asserted that fundamental, linguistic concepts are innate to the human species, and that children come to the task of language acquisition already knowing the basic form their language must take. Before language acquisition begins, he stated, the child possesses some knowledge both of basic grammatical categories and relations and the fact that sentences are represented on two levels—deep and surface structure. This knowledge is provided by the language acquisition device (LAD). McNeill's theoretical stance has dominated the language-acquisition and child-development literature of the 1960s (Bruner, Olver, & Greenfield, 1966; Deese, 1970; Lenneberg, 1960, 1967). McNeill (1970a) claimed that the basic grammatical relations emerge sequentially during the period of one-word utterances. He argued that from the first moment of speech children are able to communicate grammatical relations in a manner understandable to adults.

The nativistic hypothesis, however, may present more problems than it answers (Riegel, 1970). First, if all that is necessary for LAD to operate is exposure to language, why then doesn't language make an appearance earlier in the child's life? Most children begin to produce their first words around twelve months, while comprehension of others' language appears slightly earlier (McCarthy, 1954). Does LAD require some sort of maturational process before the child can begin to produce or understand language? Milner (1967) suggests that during the second six months of life, development of the motor-speech areas of the brain and the continued myelinization of crucial neural connections between speech areas and temporal-occipital-parietal association areas are crucial for speech development. Nonetheless, the translation from neural development to language acquisition has yet to be explicated.

Second, nativistic theories provide little guidance for intervention. LAD has little to offer the speech therapist working with "language delayed" children. Third, there are scattered accounts of children who produce little linguistically for several years, yet appear "normal" if not "superior" in other respects, and "blossom" later into normal speech (Rigg, 1938). Finally and most important, a nativistic explanation fails to account for LAD's origins; rather, it shifts that burden to some other discipline. In essence, the nativistic hypothesis reduces early language to a set of preformed, static relationships which still require explanation (Piaget, 1970). It appears that the nativism of the 1960s was the product of both an exclusive concern with syntax as *the* aspect of child language and a disenchantment with empiricism as embodied in S-R chains and operant theories.

Reconceptualization of the Problem

One approach to the dilemma raised by nativistic concepts in language acquisition is temporarily to suspend attempts at explanation and reconceptualize the field. Is there more to grammar than syntax? Is there more to language than grammar? Would the systematic use of knowledge about children's development facilitate our understanding of the language-development process? In essence, the question becomes: what might be the prerequisite skills—sensory, motor, conceptual, or social—that together make language or language development possible?

Such a question dictates careful analysis of detailed longitudinal data. Longitudinal studies permit valid inferences about the precursors for language acquisition and about the sequence of language development, while cross-sectional studies can only supply hypotheses about developmental sequences. Moreover, statements based upon summary statistics for groups are often misleading and present a description valid for only a small part of the group (Hunt and Sullivan, 1974; Hovland, 1937). Since the investigator working in a new area is not sure which of the many potentially important variables will pay off, he or she typically studies intensively a very limited number of children (Piaget, 1952, 1954, 1962). Hoping to find an invariant developmental sequence, the investigator may instead discover only idiosyncratic developmental patterns. As Bruner (1974/1975) points out, research of this nature is particularly difficult because the investigator must make decisions about speech and nonspeech influences on language development.

Whatever the findings, the developmental sequences an investigator describes need to be tested with other children; it is entirely possible that there are different developmental routes to the same end point (DeCarie, 1969; Nelson, 1973; White, 1967). Ultimately what is needed, then, is to untangle which particular variables produce which routes and how common outcomes are attained.

Semantic Grammars and Language Development

What, then, of aspects of grammar other than syntax? In the 1960s, researchers interested in transformational grammar at first studied child language only after children had begun to join words to form sentences. Researchers perceived semantics as a separate component of grammar, connected with deep-structure syntax by some form of mapping rules which even now are only sketchily known (Katz and Fodor, 1964). However, a number of students of child language began to emphasize that the meaning of children's speech might be as important to understanding language acquisition as its syntax (Bloom, 1970, 1973; Brown, 1970, 1973a, 1973b; Gleitman, Gleitman, & Shipley, 1972; Schlesinger, 1971). Dissatisfied with a grammar which was semantically empty, some linguists began to develop a model which merged semantics and syntax in a grammar while still preserving the power of the transformational model (Lakoff, 1971).

For example, Lois Bloom (1970) used the transformational grammar model to describe the syntactic development of three young children. However, she also recorded systematic information about the contexts with which her children spoke, and she used that information to decide what meanings young children intend to communicate. As she discovered, the same utterance can have different meanings within different contexts. For example, depending upon the particular events that were taking place as the child spoke, "Mommy sock" might mean that Mommy was putting a sock on the child, or it might mean that the sock that the child had just found belonged to Mommy. Thus Bloom's work demonstrated that even children's very early sentences seemed to intend certain relational meanings—e.g., actor/object acted upon, possessor/possessed—rather than simple listings of various aspects of situations (Brown, 1973b).

From a different semantic perspective Fillmore's (1968) case-grammar system was particularly appealing to psychologists concerned with a more adequate characterization of child language. He postulated a deep structure made up of semantic concepts and related to surface structure in the adult language by transformation rules. In Fillmore's view, deep structure specifies such matters as tense (past, present, future), mood (imperative, indicative, etc.), and proposition. The proposition, a set of relationships between nouns and verbs which is defined by semantic cases, represents "certain types of judgments human beings are able to make about events that are going on around them, judgments about such matters as who did it, who it happened to, and what got changed" (Fillmore, 1968, p. 24). Thus Fillmore's semantic cases represent basic concepts about events and relationships in the world.

In like manner, Greenfield, Smith, and Laufer (1972) utilized a modification of the Fillmore system to characterize the pre-syntactic speech of two children during the single-word phase of language development. In order to describe their children's speech more adequately, the Greenfield et al. system used thirteen semantic cases, deleting some of the Fillmore cases and adding new ones.[1] For example, Fillmore posited an Instrumental Case which he defines as "the case of the inanimate force or object involved in the action or state identified by the verb" (Fillmore, 1968, p. 24). Greenfield et al. (1972) found too few examples of this semantic relation in their sample and thus could not justify including it as a stable semantic case. On the other hand, they found it necessary to postulate a Naming Case to describe the many situations in which their children pointed at or looked at an object and named it, but did not seem to be asserting anything.

Greenfield et al. concluded that even during the one-word period child language is "productive": a limited set of semantic concepts combines with situational elements in a rule-bounded way (only particular semantic relationships are expressed) to express an infinite set of messages (within the limits of the defined types). All of the Greenfield et al. semantic cases which emerge sequentially during the one-word period have counterparts in later two-word utterances (Bowerman, 1973). Using both transformational and case grammar, Bowerman (1973) analyzed the same samples of early child speech, concluding that transformational grammar

> forces us to posit a form of linguistic knowledge that we have not yet demonstrated that children possess. There is in fact a certain amount of evidence (admittedly as yet slight) that the structural components of the rules underlying children's earliest two- and three-word utterances may be semantic concepts like "agent," "action," and "object acted upon" rather than grammatical concepts like "subject," "predicate," and "direct object." (Bowerman, 1973, p. 14)

Thus the semantic approach used both by Greenfield et al. and by Bowerman suggests that the grammar of early patterned speech does not emerge *ex nihilo* but can be traced to a set of relationships from an earlier period of language development.

In my own longitudinal research (Edmonds, 1975), I have used the Greenfield et al. system to characterize the language development of two other subjects during the one-word speech phase. Although I was able to identify all of the Greenfield et al. semantic cases in the speech of my children, I believe that some

---

[1] The thirteen cases which comprise the Greenfield et al. system are: Naming—calling attention to objects; Vocative—using a person's name to get his or her attention; Object of Demand—naming an object the child wants; Negative and Affirmative—rejecting/accepting objects and actions, denying/affirming statements, and expressing the absence/presence of particular objects in that context; Action—naming acts which are voluntary or intentional; Inanimate Object of Action—naming inanimate objects receiving actions causing a change in the object's state, position, etc.; State or Action of an Inanimate Object—expressing object attributes or the result of actions on objects; Association, Possession, and Habitual Location—expressing the state of belonging to a person, thing, or particular position; Locative—expressing position in space or direction of action; Experiencer—naming the animate being affected by a state or action; Agent—naming the initiator of the action; Modification of Event—encoding the direction, time, or manner of an entire event; and Conjunction—listing things alike in some way.

modifications of the Greenfield et al. system would more adequately characterize my data. While other researchers' semantic categories have not been identical, they have found an overlapping set of meanings in child utterances during the one-word and early multiple-word periods (Bloom, 1970, 1973; Bloom, Lightbown, and Hood, 1975; Bowerman, 1973; Brown, 1973a, 1973b; Greenfield et al., 1972; Schlesinger, 1971; Starr, 1975). As Brown (1973a) points out, these differences in detail highlight the fact that such semantic analysis systems are formalisms constructed by the researchers. In any area of study, theories directing research efforts determine, to some degree, both results and the processes invoked to explain them. One must be extremely cautious about attributing to the child the taxonomy system the researcher has used to characterize his or her data (Bowerman, 1975). Nevertheless, adults do perceive that child speech expresses a limited set of meanings which seem to emerge slowly in a rather similar sequence in children during the period of one-word speech. Children later combine these word classes to form what researchers have called "early sentences." While we cannot be sure in just what form children represent (encode and store as concepts) these meanings, since they do express them, it is reasonable to search for the source of these concepts.

The Cognitive Hypothesis

In an attempt to pinpoint the origin of meanings, Cromer (1974) argues that humans "are able to understand and productively to use particular linguistic structures only when [their] cognitive abilities enable [them] to do so" (p. 246). In their attempts to identify these cognitive abilities many researchers turn to Piaget for descriptions of child thought at the onset of speech. Most researchers have *not* measured child thinking. Rather, they have based their analyses on the coincidence between the ages at which their subjects exhibit certain language behaviors and the ages Piagetian norms give for the appearance of particular organizations of child thought. Many theorists discuss the relationship between the appearance and/or use of certain semantic concepts in child language and the transition from the Piagetian sensori-motor period to the Piagetian preconceptual period (Bloom, 1973; Brown, 1973a; Edwards, 1973; Ingram, 1971). Using Piagetian measures and the Greenfield et al. case-grammar system, I traced both the development of child thought and the emergence of child speech in two children from age one month to age two years.

Piaget distinguishes between intelligence and thought. In his view, intelligence is an adaptation to the social and physical environment and precedes thought. Thinking is one form of intelligence, but not the only form. Piaget (1952, 1954, 1962) argues that there is nothing in the period of infancy that permits one to infer thought—the ability to represent and act mentally upon absent objects and events. Rather, thinking ability is slowly constructed during the sensori-motor period through infants' perceptions of and actions on their environment. According to Piaget, infants begin as beings who can act only on the here and now, who do not distinguish between their sensory impressions of and actions on objects. Through gradual organization, children become able to represent to themselves absent objects and events, using symbols which are distinct from their referents (Piaget and Inhelder, 1969). Thought then becomes increasingly free of the immediate concrete and can operate on objects and events distant in time and space. The first indications of thinking in this sense appear in Piagetian Stage VI of the sensori-motor period at approximately eighteen months.

During the Piagetian sensori-motor period infants not only construct initial instruments of thought, they also construct certain basic concepts about the world: space, time, causality, and object permanence (Piaget, 1954). For example, infants initially behave as if objects exist only while they are acting upon them. Piaget (1954) argues that infants begin life at a reflex level of complete self-world undifferentiation: their world is a universe without objects in which concepts of space and time are limited to their actions at any given moment. Gradually, the child learns to distinguish between objects and actions. Finally, by Stage VI the infant constructs the concept of object permanence—the awareness that an object has a separate, independent existence apart from the child, while existing and moving in a space common to both it and the child.

In my own studies I found that neither one of my subjects produced even a single word before sensori-motor Stage VI, as indexed by object-concept measures. One of them did demonstrate a very limited understanding of the speech of others at Stage V Stage VI, however, is most probably not a strict precondition for word production. While my two subjects attained Stage VI earlier than usual, they were no younger at the time of their first words than other children reported in the literature (Greenfield et al., 1972; Bloom 1973). Furthermore, Piaget's (1954) protocols of his children at Stage V include verbalizations, clearly indicating that word production can begin by Stage V for some children. My findings can be considered from two perspectives: the meanings of early child speech and their relation to the development of sensori-motor intelligence; and the symbolic status of early child speech.

According to Piaget, sensori-motor intelligence is completed at Stage V for the immediate, practical realm. For example, in terms of object permanence this means that the child can watch an object being hidden in one place and find it there, repeat the sequence for the same hiding place, and then find the same object when it is observed being hidden in an entirely new place. Thus infants have some conception of the object's independence of their own actions. What they cannot do is solve invisible-displacement problems: they cannot observe an object hidden in an adult's hand, watch the same hand pass under several hiding places while leaving the object under one of them (without the child being able to see this transfer), and then find the object. Typically the child searches only in the adult's hand—the concept of the object is still practical and not yet representational. Children seem to lack any "image" of the vanished object to guide them in their search and help them deduce that the object, once in the adult's hand, *must* now be in one of the observed hiding places. In relating these Piagetian constructs to my subjects' language development, I found that their earliest words expressed an extremely limited set of semantic concepts, such as Action or Inanimate Object of Action. My subjects named their own actions as they performed them; for example, saying "do" as they placed a toy car in a toy garage, or "going" as they walked out of the room. In addition, they named the objects they acted upon. Recall that by Stage V objects exist independently of the child's actions. The Action and Inanimate Object of Action Cases seem to be a verbal expression of this sensori-motor separation of object and actions upon the object. Thus, the language behaviors exhibited by my subjects exemplify the semantic concepts implicit in Stages V and VI. I was able to relate eight of the thirteen Greenfield et al. semantic cases to meanings implicit in Stages V and VI. I also found that these same eight basic cases were the ones used most frequently and flexibly in the early patterned speech of my one subject studied to that point.

I should mention my inability to relate five of the Greenfield et al. cases to meanings implicit in sensori-motor intelligence. This problem may say little about the relationships between sensori-motor intelligence and language acquisition; however, the difficulty may be traced to two sources: (1) the problem of finding the most useful system for analyzing early child speech; and (2) the fact that Piaget did not set out to study all the meanings languages express or even all the meanings implicit in developing sensori-motor intelligence (Brown, 1973a). Thus, this particular failure to demonstrate an isomorphic relationship between the growth of language and the attainment of particular Piagetian stages may say little about the presence or absence of such a relationship and more about the difficulties in constructing analytic systems which adequately reflect the phenomenon of concern.

The Symbolic Function and Language Development

Piagetian theory would appear to provide a useful approach to the difficult problem of explaining *how* the child moves from sensori-motor intelligence to expressing such concepts linguistically. As Piaget's colleague Sinclair-de-Zwart (1969) has pointed out, language is a social symbolic system through which the knowing person expresses his or her knowledge. For the adult, words are symbols that are distinct: they are not the same as their meanings. Mature speakers join words together according to some system (grammar) shared by a speech community. This is done in such a way that speakers are able to communicate their ideas to the listener, even though they may be communicating ideas about objects and events that are absent or imaginary. Sinclair-de-Zwart calls this the knower/symbolization/ known-relationship. When adults act upon or think about some aspect of the world, they typically do so indirectly—through the differentiated knower/symbolization/known-relationship (Sinclair-de-Zwart, 1969). This is true whether or not the adult is aware of these differentiations (Koestler, 1964). While adult language may serve the function of symbolizing in the knower/symbolization/known-relationship, it is not at all clear that child language operates this way. Furthermore, there is some doubt that words function initially as symbols for the child in the sense that they can be used to stand for or evoke meanings. Russian research suggests that words at first function as a "signal," triggering behavior but not directing or regulating it. For example, "no" often seems to stimulate the very behavior a two-year-old's parent is trying to prohibit. Only when children are about four years old do they seem able to use their own language to organize and regulate their behavior before acting (Luria, 1971).

In terms of language acquisition, it now seems clear that children at first acquire words that have a limited set of meanings, seemingly the meanings implicit in sensori-motor intelligence. My own subjects seemed first to acquire words that related in specific ways to their own actions or to events in which they were active participants. Greenfield et al. (1972) and Bloom (1973) reported a similar finding. Furthermore, once my subjects had acquired those words, they typically seemed to produce them when they were in that context or performing those actions. They talked about what they were doing and perceiving while they were doing and perceiving it. For example, they named the objects they were acting on, saying "ball" as they struggled to remove a ball from a shoe; they named where they placed objects, saying "bed" as they put their dolls to bed; they named their own actions, saying "fall" when they fell; they asserted possession, saying "mine" as they recovered objects appropriated by siblings; they denied the actions of their toys, yelling "no" when a toy cow fell over; and so forth. Greenfield et al, reported similar findings for their subjects. My subjects appeared to assimilate words to sensori-motor organizations. (Piaget defines assimilation as the process by which objects and events are fit into the individual's existing behavioral or conceptual organizations.) It then seemed the assimilated word became part of the organization into which it had been assimilated and that the child, in that same context, *had* to produce the word. For example, one child at eighty-eight weeks said "car" forty-one times during thirty minutes as he acted on a toy car. Bloom's (1973) protocols also documented this feature of early child speech.

These data are not systematic, but highly suggestive. Of course, children's words do not remain forever fused with sensori-motor organizations; sooner or later words begin to function more like symbols, and children talk about absent objects and events as well as about what they are presently perceiving and doing. Piaget's conceptualization of the symbolic function seems to provide some help in thinking about this aspect of children's language and how it changes.

Piaget and Inhelder define the symbolic function as "the ability to represent something (a signified something: object, event, conceptual scheme, etc.) by means of a 'signifier' which is differentiated and which serves only a representative purpose" (1969, p. 51). Thus the symbolic function is the ability to represent meanings through intermediaries—symbols that are distinct from what they stand for and that can be used to evoke meanings. Representation, then, is the union of a differentiated symbol, which allows for recall, with the meaning, which is supplied by thought. Piaget notes that at sensori-motor Stage VI a number of new "behavior patterns" emerge that are qualitatively different from behavior patterns of the preceding stages: symbolic play (e.g., a child playing with a spool of thread and a matchbox, pretending they are Mommy and Daddy), deferred imitation (e.g., a child scolding a doll as he or she was scolded), dreams, mental imagery, and language (Piaget and Inhelder, 1969). All are examples of the symbolic function in that all represent meanings and are qualitatively different from preceding behavior—they go "beyond the present, extending the field of adaptation both in time and space" (Piaget, 1962, p. 273).

According to Piaget, the emergence of representation rests upon a sensori-motor equilibrium—a dynamic balance—between the twin processes of assimilation and accommodation. Assimilation is the process by which the child integrates objects and events into already established behavioral or conceptual organizations; accommodation is the alteration of these established organizations to incorporate more adequately aspects of the environment which are assimilated. Assimilation and accommodation begin by being almost totally undifferentiated. For example, when hungry, infants suck efficiently on the nipple; when satiated and alone in their cribs, they may make the same sucking movements although there is nothing to suck and their movements are essentially empty, i.e., applied to nothing. Similarly, infants may respond to a painful stimulus with reflexive crying or may "imitate" the cries of others in the absence of pain. Gradually, as the child's pre-organized behavior patterns contact the environment and are exercised, new aspects of the environment are assimilated. This forces new accommodations and, by Stage V, assimilation and accommodation reach a sensori-motor equilibrium. Thus, the accommodations necessary to assimilate the environment already exist in the child's sensori-motor organization. This adaptation can be seen in the children's performance on object-permanence tasks, e.g., their ability to recover objects that they watch hidden successively in a series of hiding places.

During this same period of infancy, assimilation and accommodation become increasingly distinct from each other and from adapted, equilibrated behavior patterns as well. Thus, when the child behaves in ways that primarily assimilate the environment, he or she makes only limited attempts to accommodate to it. For example, at Stage V, children may quickly turn new adaptations into play rituals. They may start out seriously studying the different effects of throwing actions on a ball. However, they quickly get caught up in the joyous action of throwing and chasing the ball, and pay little attention to the relationship between how the ball is thrown and where it goes. Similarly, when children behave in ways that primarily accommodate to the environment, they make little attempt at assimilating new behaviors to what they already know. For example, at Stage V they become

192

much more precise in their ability to adjust behavior patterns to those exhibited by a model. They may observe the mother touching her own eyebrows and nose and then attempt to imitate her behavior by trying to find and touch their own eyebrows and nose.

The transition to representational intelligence is made when assimilation and accommodation take place *mentally* as well as in action. This entails a double co-ordination of assimilation and accommodation. The signifier, a product of past accommodations, persists into the present as the symbol; functioning organizations must also accommodate to the data of present experience. The signified, a prod-uct of past assimilation, persists into the present as meaning. There is also the assimilation of the present data of experience into the functioning organization. All four aspects must inter-coordinate. Equilibrium here describes the situation where the double accommodation and assimilation are balanced; past and present fit together. Equilibrium can be seen in the Stage VI child's well-adapted proce-dures for recovering objects which go through a series of hidden displacements. For example, the child can now fully observe his or her father hide an object in his hand, pass his hand under a number of different dishtowels and leave the object under one (without the child being able to see the transfer). The child, presum-ably using an image to direct his or her search, seems to be able to deduce that the object, since it is no longer in the adult's hand, must be in one of the places where the adult's hand has been.

If equilibrium is not achieved, then either accommodation or assimilation pre-dominates, and the child is either imitative or else engages in symbolic play. For example, one of my own subjects displayed representational imitation when, having many times watched her mother apply make-up, she went into her mother's room and reappeared sometime later, appropriately lipsticked, rouged, and pow-dered. Presumably, she had some representation of her mother's behavior which allowed her to reproduce it in her mother's absence. When assimilation predomi-nates at this level, on the other hand, the children can be seen at play involving pretense. They treat inadequate stimuli as if they were adequate, as if they were symbols of something else, and mentally alter the environment to fit in with their activities. For example, one of my own subjects picked up a small, plastic Easter-eggshell, lifted it to his lips, and slurped noisily, as if he were drinking from it.

Piaget traces the development of both the symbol and its meaning from the earliest stages of sensori-motor intelligence. According to him, accommodation is the source of the symbol, assimilation the source of its meaning. Accommo-dation, by adjusting organizations more adequately to reality, re-presents in the most basic sense, while assimilation, by fitting reality into existing organizations, supplies reality with meaning. Assimilation and accommodation, then, are part of all behavior from simple sensori-motor activity to highly abstract thinking. How-ever, the relationships between these two processes vary according to the nature of the particular organization in use at that moment. The development of both processes, their gradual differentiation, and their eventual coordination can be seen in the development of imitation (where accommodation predominates), play (where assimilation predominates), and adapted intelligence during the sensori-motor period.

In my own research I replicated Piaget's description of the development of the symbolic function, as indexed by the growth of play and imitation. I also found that the ability to represent did not emerge all at once, but rather it appeared in different cognitive domains over an extended period of time. For example, my subjects were able to represent absent people before they could represent absent objects. After attaining object permanence, they exhibited representational imitation before symbolic play. Only after representation was achieved in these other areas were the children able either to understand or to use language in a way that might indicate that it was beginning to function as a symbol system. For example, after they were observed at symbolic play, they began to use words in the absence of their referents and respond correctly to instructions requiring them to put familiar behaviors together in unfamiliar sequences. Piaget suggests that any stage entails both a phase of attainment and a phase of consolidation. The children in my study seemed to require the level of representation as evidenced by symbolic play before they could begin to differentiate words from the sensori-motor organizations with which they were presumably fused. Bloom (1973) found that her subject's words initially lacked stability—that is, they disappeared from use after a time. She suggested that representational intelligence (sensori-motor Stage VI) may be a precondition for a stable vocabulary. While Bloom made no systematic measures of her subject's Piagetian stage level, her suggestion complements my own findings. Perhaps the beginning of the symbol-referent separation in language requires a consolidating Stage VI representational ability. That is, children cannot discover words as symbols until they have constructed other symbols and practiced using them.

My own research used three criteria to decide whether a Greenfield et al. semantic case was productive: (1) the child uses the case more than two or three times in an observation session; (2) the child uses more than one specific word to express a given case; and (3) the child uses the same word to express more than one specific case in a given observation session. If a case met any two of these criteria, I termed it productive. Neither child achieved productivity for any case until after symbolic play was observed. In an unpublished paper Santmire (1975) suggested that the separation of the word from the referent takes place because the child attaches the same word to a number of different organizations (e.g., "Rover" is used to refer to all dogs on the block) and links a number of different words to the same organization (e.g., "Rover" is also called "dog" and "bow-wow"). Perhaps the case-productivity criteria were also tapping the word-referent differentiation process: the child's use of the same word to express more than one semantic concept may be similar to attaching the same word to a number of different organizations.

Furthermore, using more than one word to express a given semantic case may be similar to attaching a number of different words to the same organization. This might explain why the representational level of symbolic play was necessary before cases could become productive.

According to my own criteria, one would expect symbolic play to occur before semantic cases become productive if 1) children cannot construct words as symbols until they have themselves constructed other symbols and practiced using them; 2) symbolic play is an index that the processes have been taking place; and 3) my case-productivity criteria indeed tap the word-referent differentiation process. The use of words as symbols seems also to be related to whether or not the semantic cases those words expressed have reached productivity criteria. With two exceptions for the eight cases that relate to object permanence, my subjects did not use words in the absence of their physical referents in a semantic case relation until that semantic case had reached productivity criteria.

My data also suggest that the initial symbol-meaning differentiation, as measured by language comprehension, use indices, and case-productivity criteria, may be a precondition for the flexible combination of words into initial multiple-word utterances. Santmire (1975) suggested that it is the processes of the same word functioning as an element of several organizations, and vice versa, that bring the child to the Piagetian preoperational symbol-behavior contradiction (e.g., "What do I name this object?"). This contradiction is supposedly resolved by putting words in the context of other words, that is, by forming multiple-word utterances which identify context and thereby make meaning more precise. My data suggest that this resolution is not possible until the word begins to function as a symbol. Initially, children seem to combine words with their own actions and with events in which they are involved. Only when words are not so intimately fused with their corresponding organizations are children able to combine them with other words as well as with objects and events. The sequence for this particular aspect of language development appears to be: (1) attain a minimum of sensori-motor Stage V; (2) assimilate words to sensori-motor organizations; (3) develop and consolidate representational ability; (4) begin to separate the word from the sensori-motor organization; and (5) join words together for a more precise specification of meaning.

Once children begin to construct the word as a verbal symbol, they are able to acquire language as a system of symbols and to begin acquiring syntax. It is important to recognize that the child still has far to go before his or her words attain the more abstract symbol-meaning relationship that characterizes adult speech. For example, young children believe for a long time that the name of an object somehow inheres in the object (Papandropoulou and Sinclair, 1974). Piaget asserts that the symbol-meaning differentiation and progression toward abstraction are incomplete until the period characterizing mature adult thought, formal operations.

Language Development and Social Perspectives

Language involves more than just a grammar or a symbolic system. Focusing on only one aspect of language can give a distorted picture of the acquisition process. Another aspect of language worth consideration is its use for communication purposes. Language develops into a communication system *par excellence* with social rules for when, where, and how to use it appropriately. An intriguing literature is developing with regard to children's understanding of this aspect of language (Byers and Byers, 1972; Hymes, 1971; Mishler, 1972). A number of theorists suggest that the acquisition of language as a communication system is only to be understood within the child-caretaker matrix (Werner and Kaplan, 1963). Bell and Ainsworth (1972) suggest that infants whose mothers have been sensitive and responsive to their prelinguistic cries develop other modes of communication more rapidly. Bruner (1974/1975) argues that a realistic account of language acquisition must systematically describe the way the child passes from prespeech communication to the use of language proper; how he or she "masters the task of communicating to others his [or her] needs, wishes, and objectives in order to assure either assistance or joint action" (p. 276). Bruner analyzes the development of a number of presumed speech precursors, such as the mother's mode of interpreting the infant's communication intent, the development of joint referential devices that presumably will eventually become the demonstrative pronouns of grammar, and such topic-comment organizations as eye movements and the deployment of attention. Other researchers (Bates, Camaioni, and Volterra, 1975) have traced the prelinguistic development of such aspects of speech acts as performatives, the conventional social acts of ordering, urging, advising, and others.

These emerging perspectives appear to have tremendous potential for enhancing our understanding of the language acquisition process. Naturally, future research must explicate how the various facets of child language interrelate with each other. For example, my research on the development of child thought and the symbolic function is closely related to research tracing the development of communication competence. The child needs basic ways of organizing the world (sensori-motor intelligence) and the ability to express these ways linguistically as semantic concepts in order to develop competence in communication. In addition, he or she needs the general ability to use symbols in order to communicate things distant in time and space. It may be that the sequence of language acquisition, although in some sense universal and invariant, emerges in ways which reflect the particular individual/environment dyad (Rogdon, Jankowski, & Alenskas, 1975). Thus, some children might be relatively advanced in their communication competence but relatively delayed in the range of semantic concepts, while the opposite might be true for others. If we were to view different child strategies for learning language as specific attempts to adapt to specific environments, we might gain a greater understanding of various language outcomes as well as general adaptation processes.

The picture that is emerging is one of continuity and complexity. As language is analyzed more carefully, it may be possible to trace its development to precursors that are largely nonlinguistic; each new skill or piece of linguistic knowledge appears to rest upon some previous skill or piece of knowledge which has its own developmental history.

Conclusion

We are still far from a complete understanding either of language or of language acquisition. The acquisition process, which seems to continue further into childhood than once thought (Chomsky, 1969), is neither sudden nor rapid. While nativistic linguistic explanations appear to be both inappropriate and premature, it also seems that nativism in some form is still a relevant hypothesis. Due to the unique physiological structure of the human species, a predisposition to acquire language seems highly probable. If communication systems and sensori-motor intelligence were sufficient prerequisites, we would have talking cats as well as talking children. Evidence is accumulating that infants are "pre-tuned" to be sensitive to aspects of human speech (Trehub, 1973); neonates move in "precise and sustained synchronous organizations of change of movement with the articulated structure of adult speech" (Condon and Sander, 1974, p. 456). Findings of this nature provide new challenges and provoke new questions about why these abilities exist, how they come into being, and precisely how they relate to the process of acquiring language. A multidiscipline approach which makes use of perspectives such as cognitive theory and developing mother-child interaction patterns—as well as of linguistic theory—should help provide a more satisfactory account of how the child acquires language.

References

Bar-Adon, A., & Leopold, W. (Eds.). *Child language*. Englewood Cliffs, N. J.: Prentice-Hall, 1971.

Bates, E., Camaioni, L., & Volterra, V. The acquisition of performatives prior to speech. *Merrill-Palmer Quarterly*, 1975, 21, 205–226.

Bell, S., & Ainsworth, M. Infant crying and maternal responsiveness. *Child Development*, 1972, 43, 1171–1190.

Bloom, L. *Language development: Form and function in emerging grammars*. Cambridge, Mass.: MIT Press, 1970.

Bloom, L. *One word at a time*. The Hague: Mouton, 1973.

Bloom, L., Lightbown, P., & Hood, L. Structure and variation in child language. *Monographs of the Society for Research in Child Development*, 1975, 40, 1–79.

Bowerman, M. *Early syntactic development*. London: Cambridge University Press, 1973.

Bowerman, M. Commentary by Melissa Bowerman. *Monographs of the Society for Research in Child Development*, 1975, 42, 80–90.

Braine, M. D. S. The ontogeny of English phrase structure: The first phase. *Language,* 1963, **39**, 1–13.

Brown, R. The first sentences of child and chimpanzee. In R. Brown (Ed.), *Psycholinguistics.* New York: The Free Press, 1970.

Brown, R. *A first language.* Cambridge, Mass.: Harvard University Press, 1973. (a)

Brown, R. Development of the first language in the human species. *American Psychologist,* 1973, **28**, 97–107. (b)

Brown, R., & Bellugi, U. Three processes in the acquisition of syntax. *Harvard Educational Review,* 1964, **34**, 133–151.

Bruner, J. From communication to language—A psychological perspective. *Cognition,* 1974/75, **3**, 255–287.

Bruner, J., Olver, R., & Greenfield, P. *Studies in cognitive growth.* New York: Wiley, 1966.

Byers, P., & Byers, H. Nonverbal communication and the education of children. In C. Cazden, V. John, & D. Hymes (Eds.), *Functions of language in the classroom.* New York: Teachers College Press, 1972.

Chomsky, C. *The acquisition of syntax in children from 5 to 10.* Cambridge, Mass.: MIT Press, 1969.

Chomsky, N. *Syntactic structures.* The Hague: Mouton, 1957.

Chomsky, N. *Aspects of a theory of syntax.* Cambridge, Mass.: MIT Press, 1965.

Chomsky, N. Deep structure, surface structure, and semantic interpretation. In D. Steinberg & L. Jakobovits (Eds.), *Semantics.* London: Cambridge University Press, 1971.

Condon, W. S., & Sander, L. W. Synchrony demonstrated between movements of the neonate and adult speech. *Child Development,* 1974, **45**, 456–462.

Cromer, R. F. The development of language and cognition: The cognition hypothesis. In B. Foss (Ed.), *New perspectives in child development.* London: Penguin Education Series, 1974.

DeCarie, T. A study of the mental and emotional development of the thalidomide child. In B. F. Foss (Ed.), *Determinants of infant behavior IV.* London: Methuen & Co., 1969.

Deese, J. *Psycholinguistics.* Boston: Allyn & Bacon, 1970.

Edmonds, M. H. Language acquisition and sensori-motor development: A longitudinal analysis of the evolution of language and its relation to the evolution of cognition. Unpublished doctoral dissertation, University of Nebraska-Lincoln, 1975.

Edwards, D. Sensory-motor intelligence and semantic relations in early child grammar. *Cognition,* 1973, **2**, 395–434.

Ervin, S. Imitation and structural change in children's language. In E. H. Lenneberg (Ed.), *New directions in the study of language.* Cambridge, Mass.: MIT Press, 1964.

Fillmore, C. The case for case. In E. Bach & R. Harms (Eds.), *Universals in linguistic theory.* New York: Holt, Rinehart, & Winston, 1968.

Fodor, J. Could meaning be an r_m? In D. Steinberg & L. Jakobovits (Eds.), *Semantics.* London: Cambridge University Press, 1971.

Fodor, J., & Garrett, M. Some reflections on competence and performance. In J. Lyons & R. J. Wales (Eds.), *Psycholinguistics papers.* Edinburgh: University of Edinburgh Press, 1966.

Gleitman, L., Gleitman, H., & Shipley, E. The emergence of the child as grammarian. *Cognition,* 1972, **1**, 137–163.

Greenfield, P., Smith, J., & Laufer, B. Communication and the beginnings of language. Unpublished working draft, Harvard University, 1972.

Gregoire, A., L'apprentissage du langage. In A. Bar-Adon & W. Leopold (Eds.), *Child Language.* Englewood Cliffs, N. J.: Prentice-Hall, 1971.

Hovland, C. I. The generalization of conditioned responses. I. The sensory generalization of conditioned responses with varying frequencies of tone. *Journal of General Psychology*, 1937, **17**, 125–248.

Hunt, D., & Sullivan, E. *Between psychology and education*. Hinsdale, Ill.: Dryden Press, 1974.

Hymes, D. Competence and performance in linguistic theory. In R. Huxley & E. Ingram (Eds.), *Language acquisition: Models and methods*. London: Academic Press, 1971.

Ingram, D. Transitivity in child language. *Language*, 1971, **47**, 888–910.

Jenkins, J., & Palermo, D. Mediation processes and the acquisition of linguistic structure. In U. Bellugi & R. Brown (Eds.), The acquisition of language. *Monographs of the Society for Research in Child Development*, 1964, **29**, 141–169.

Katz, J., & Fodor, J. The structure of a semantic theory. In J. Fodor & J. Katz (Eds.), *The structure of language*. Englewood Cliffs, N. J.: Prentice-Hall, 1964.

Koestler, A. *The act of creation*. New York: Dell Publishing Co., 1964.

Kuczaj, S., & Maratsos, M. What children can say before they will. *Merrill-Palmer Quarterly*, 1975, **21**, 89–111.

Lakoff, G. On generative semantics. In D. Steinberg & L. Jakobovits (Eds.), *Semantics*. London: Cambridge University Press, 1971.

Lashley, K. S. The problem of serial order in behavior. In L. A. Jeffress (Ed.), *Cerebral mechanisms in behavior*. New York: Wiley, 1951.

Lenneberg, E. H. Language, evolution, and purposive behavior. In S. Diamond (Ed.), *Essays in honor of Paul Radin*. New York: Columbia University Press, 1960.

Lenneberg, E. H. *The biological foundations of language*. New York: Wiley, 1967.

Leopold, W. Patterning in children's language learning. In A. Bar-Adon & W. Leopold (Eds.), *Child language*. Englewood Cliffs, N. J.: Prentice-Hall, 1971.

Luria, A. The role of speech in the regulation of normal and abnormal behavior. In A. Bar-Adon & W. Leopold (Eds.), *Child language*. Englewood Cliffs, N. J.: Prentice-Hall, 1971.

McCarthy, D. The language development of the preschool child. *Institute of Child Welfare Monograph Series* (No. 4). Minneapolis: University of Minnesota Press, 1930.

McCarthy, D. Language development in children. In L. Carmichael (Ed.), *Manual of child psychology* (2nd ed.). New York: Wiley, 1954.

McNeill, D. Developmental psycholinguistics. In F. Smith & G. A. Miller (Eds.), *The genesis of language*. Cambridge, Mass.: MIT Press, 1966.

McNeill, D. *The acquisition of language*. New York: Harper & Row, 1970. (a)

McNeill, D. The development of language. In P. H. Mussen (Ed.), *Carmichael's manual of child psychology* (3rd ed.), Vol. 1. New York: Wiley, 1970. (b).

Menyuk, P. Syntactic structures in the language of children. *Child Development*, 1963, **34**, 407–422.

Miller, G. Some psychological studies of grammar. *American Psychologist*, 1962, **17**, 74, 8–762.

Miller, W. & Ervin, S. The development of grammar in child language. In U. Bellugi & R. Brown (Eds.), The acquisition of language. *Monographs of the Society for Research in Child Development*, 1964, **29**, 9–34.

Milner, E. *Human neural and behavioral development*. Springfield, Ill.: Charles Thomas, 1967.

Mishler, E. G. Implications of teacher strategies for language and cognition: Observations in first-grade classrooms. In C. Cazden, V. John, & D. Hymes (Eds.), *Functions of language in the classroom*. New York: Teachers College Press, 1972.

Mowrer, O. H. *Learning theory and the symbolic processes*. New York: Wiley, 1960.

Nelson, K. Structure and strategy in learning to talk. *Monographs of the Society for Research in Child Development*, 1973, **38**, 1–135.

Palermo, D. Research on language acquisition: Do we know where we are going? In L. R. Goulet & P. B. Baltes (Eds.), *Life-span developmental psychology*. New York: Academic Press, 1970.

Palermo, D. On learning to talk: Are principles derived from the learning laboratory applicable? In D. Slobin (Ed.), *The ontogenesis of grammar*. New York: Academic Press, 1971.

Papandropoulou, I., & Sinclair, H. What is a word? *Human Development*, 1974, **17**, 241–258.

Piaget, J. *The origins of intelligence*. New York: W. W. Norton, 1952.

Piaget, J. *The construction of reality in the child*. New York: Basic Books, 1954.

Piaget, J. *Play, dreams, and imitation in childhood*. New York: W. W. Norton, 1962.

Piaget, J. *Structuralism*. New York: Basic Books, 1970.

Piaget, J., & Inhelder, B. *The psychology of the child*. New York: Basic Books, 1969.

Riegel, K. The language acquisition process: A reinterpretation of selected research findings. In L. R. Goulet & P. B. Baltes (Eds.), *Life-span developmental psychology*. New York: Academic Press, 1970.

Rigg, M. G. A superior child who would not talk. *Child Development*, 1938, **9**, 361–362.

Rogdon, M., Jankowski, W., & Alenskas, L. A multi-functional approach to single-word usage. Unpublished paper, University of Illinois at Chicago Circle, 1975.

Santmire, T. Symbols and behavior. Unpublished paper, Department of Educational Psychology and Measurements, University of Nebraska-Lincoln, September 1975.

Savin, H. B., & Perchonock, E. Grammatical structure and the immediate recall of English sentences. *Journal of Verbal Learning and Verbal Behavior*, 1965, 4, 348–353.

Schlesinger, I. M. Production of utterances and language acquisition. In D. Slobin (Ed.), *The ontogenesis of grammar*. New York: Academic Press, 1971.

Sinclair-de-Zwart, H. Developmental psycholinguistics. In D. Elkind & J. H. Flavell (Eds.), *Studies in cognitive development*. New York: Oxford University Press, 1969.

Skinner, B. F. *Verbal behavior*. New York: Appleton-Century-Crofts, 1957.

Smith, M. E. An investigation of the development of the sentence and the extent of vocabulary in young children. University of Iowa Studies of Child Welfare, 1926, **3** (5).

Staats, A. Linguistic-mentalistic theory versus an explanatory S-R learning theory of language development. In D. Slobin (Ed.), *The ontogenesis of grammar*. New York: Academic Press, 1971.

Starr, S. The relationship of single words to two-word sentences. *Child Development*, 1975, **46**, 701–708.

Trehub, S. Infants' sensitivity to vowel and tonal contrasts. *Developmental Psychology*, 1973, **9**, 91–96.

Werner, H., & Kaplan, B. *Symbol formation*. New York: Wiley, 1963.

White, B. An experimental approach to the effects of experience on early human behavior. In J. P. Hill (Ed.), *Minnesota symposia on child psychology* (Vol. 1). Minneapolis: University of Minnesota Press, 1967.

Stages in Language Development and Reading Exposure

CAROL CHOMSKY
Harvard University

This study of language acquisition investigates selected aspects of children's linguistic competence. Thirty-six children were tested for knowledge of nine complex syntactic structures, five of which were acquired in sequence, revealing five stages in the development of syntax. The nature of specific disparities between adult grammar and child grammar and the wide variation in rate of acquisition in different children are discussed. The author concludes by examining the relationship between children's exposure to written language and their rate of linguistic development. She finds a strong correlation between a number of the reading exposure measures and language development.

This article summarizes a study of linguistic development in elementary school children. We investigated children's knowledge of specific aspects of the syntax of English by testing their comprehension of a number of complex structures. Thirty-six children between the ages of six and ten were in the experiment.

Because the study deals with only a few structures, it does not attempt a general description of children's grammar within the age group. Rather it traces the acquisition of specific structures, revealing interesting aspects of the children's construction of implicit grammatical rules. In addition, the results demonstrate a common order of acquisition of syntactic structures among the different children though there is considerable variation in age of acquisition. This shared order of acquisition of structures defines a developmental sequence of linguistic stages through which all of the children apparently pass. The ages at which different children reach the stages vary, but the sequence of stages appears to be the same for all.

The work reported on here was performed under Office of Education Grant No. OEG-1-9-090055-0114 (010), Project No. 9-A-055, while the investigator was a Scholar at the Radcliffe Institute. This article was prepared from the final report to the Office of Education. The full report, "Linguistic Development in Children from 6 to 10," is available through the Educational Resources Information Center (ERIC) Document Reproduction Service.

Harvard Educational Review Vol. 42 No. 1 February 1972, 1–33

A second aspect of the study investigated the children's exposure to the written language through independent reading and through listening to books read aloud. We examined the relation between rate of linguistic development and exposure to written materials as a source of complex language inputs. Our results show a strong correlation between a number of the reading exposure measures and language development. A description of the reading study is presented in the second half of this paper, along with a discussion of the relations between language development, the reading measures, IQ, and socioeconomic status (SES).

This article is a brief and fairly condensed description of a detailed study of several years' duration, and it attempts to present only the highlights of the methods employed and the experimental results.

Framework for the Linguistic Study

The approach and methods of the linguistic study, described in detail in an earlier work,[1] demonstrate the feasibility of dealing with the learning of complex syntactic structures in children beyond age five through psycholinguistic experimentation. This is the period of life when a major portion of the task of language acquisition has already been accomplished. The child of six exhibits competence with his* native language that appears to approach adult competence. Discrepancies between his grammar and adult grammar are rarely revealed in spontaneous speech.

Our purpose is to explore areas in which the six-year-old's knowledge of his language falls short of adult knowledge, and to gain information about the course of the acquisition of this knowledge as the child matures. In order to deal with these questions, we must first characterize what we mean by knowing one's language. In effect, we must answer the question, "What is the nature of the information that is acquired by the child?"

Clearly, speakers of a language do not draw from a memorized list of all possible sentences in their language each time they wish to say something. Rather, they can understand and produce sentences they have never before heard. Indeed, a major portion of language usage consists of sentences that have never been spoken or written before, for example, this sentence or the closing sentence of any article in today's *New York Times*.

Given any sequence of words we care to devise, speakers can recognize whether or not the sequence constitutes a sentence in their language. This creative

---

[1] C. Chomsky, *The Acquisition of Syntax in Children from 5 to 10* (Cambridge, Mass.: M.I.T. Press, 1969).

* The masculine form of pronoun is used here for convenience; children of both sexes were included in the study. [Ed.]

aspect of language use rests on the fact that we have learned the system of rules for making sentences. This system is called the grammar of the language.

Our knowledge of these rules is implicit. We are not taught them, and we would be hard put to state even the smallest fraction of them. Yet they govern our speech.

Because these rules are implicit, they cannot be observed directly. While the linguist is interested in the speaker's *competence* (the underlying system of rules), he has access only to a speaker's *performance* (the way he uses the rules). Thus, various aspects of performance are used to reveal the nature of underlying competence.

What the child learns, then, as he acquires his language is a complex system of rules that enables him to understand and produce the sentences of his language. He internalizes these rules from what he hears by a process of active construction as yet little understood. His earliest utterances, even at the stage when he begins to put two words together to make sentences, are innovative and rule-governed. The evidence shows he is not just repeating fragments of sentences he has heard, but is creating his own sentences according to grammatical rules that he continually constructs and revises. The acquisition of syntax, then, means developing the rule system, restructuring it with increasing maturity as new evidence is added, and eventually producing an internalized grammar which accords with the facts of the language.

How do we employ this framework in studying knowledge of syntax in children between six and ten? The problem is that by age six, a child's grammar, as revealed in his spontaneous speech, does not appreciably differ from adult grammar. In order to identify areas in which child and adult grammar are different, we must actively probe the child's linguistic performance. We can do this by selecting complex grammatical structures—structures that we consider difficult and, therefore, likely to be acquired relatively late. Children's comprehension and interpretation of these complex structures yield evidence of the syntactic rules employed and the way in which these rules diverge from adult grammar. As we gain information about these child/adult discrepancies, we may contribute to existing notions about language complexity.

On the basis of current linguistic work we are able to select a variety of complex structures that appear to be likely candidates for late acquisition. Potential structures would include those "which deviate from a widely established pattern in the language, or whose surface structure is relatively inexplicit with respect to grammatical relationships, or even simply those which the linguist finds particularly difficult to incorporate into a thorough description." . . .[2] Some candidate structures turn out to be difficult for the children; some do not.

In order to be useful in this study, a structure must also lend itself to testing

[2] Chomsky, p. 4.

with young children. We must be able to devise an operational test of comprehension that even six-year-olds can handle. This requirement sharply limits the selection. The structures and tests finally decided upon are the result of much planning and revision, a good bit of pilot testing, and many discards.

Altogether, we tested nine structures with the children. Of these, only the five that turned out to be relevant to an overall developmental sequence will be discussed here. The other four were either too easy (all the children knew them), too hard (known by only one or two of the children), or they elicited scattered responses not relevant to the sequence. Almost twice as many structures were tested as turned out to be relevant to the developmental sequence. Thus, we proceeded by collecting a range of structures, testing them all, and leaving it up to the experimental results to reveal a sequence, if any.

We did have some theoretical and practical guidelines to aid in selecting structures. For example, the relation between two structures, *promise* and *ask,* is such that a given order of acquisition is implied on theoretical grounds. *Promise* is simpler than *ask* along a particular scale of complexity, and ought therefore to be acquired first. And, in fact, evidence of this predicted order was found in an earlier experiment with *promise* and *ask*.[3] These two structures, then, were useful to include because of their strong potential for yielding developmental data. Another construction, *easy to see,* is recognized as a good indicator of grammatical development from the work of several different researchers[4] although no experimental work has yet suggested a relationship to other constructions in terms of order of acquisition. This construction was included because of its stability as a measure. Use of the measure led to identical conclusions in three separate experiments. Beyond considerations of this sort, there was little to go on. In fact all of the constructions tested with children for the first time here resulted from a fortuitous intersection of complex structures and experimental techniques that could measure them.

Our experimental procedure elicited information from the children by direct interview. By age six, the children are willing to be questioned, play games, carry out tasks, manipulate toys, identify pictures, and engage in conversation. The interview was carried out informally and, for the children, was interesting play.

Our test group ranged in age from five years old, when many of the children gave evidence of not yet knowing the constructions, up to ten years old, when a number of the children exhibited an adult command of the structures. For some structures there was considerable variation in age of acquisition in differ-

[3] Chomsky, 6.
[4] R. F. Cromer, " 'Children are nice to understand':Surface Structure Clues for the Recovery of a Deep Structure." *British Journal of Psychology,* 61, 1970, pp. 397-408; F. S. Kessel, "The Role of Syntax in Children's Comprehension from Ages Six to Twelve," *Monographs of the Society for Research in Child Development,* Ser. no. 139, 35, (September, 1970); C. Chomsky, 1969.

ent children. Of particular interest is that this variation in *age* of acquisition does not seem to affect *order* of acquisition of different structures. For the structures reported here, the evidence is that linguistic development, whether it occurs earlier or later, nevertheless proceeds along similar paths. This has been a basic and repeated finding of longitudinal studies with younger children at earlier stages of language development. It is encouraging that the same principle is demonstrable on the basis of cross-sectional studies with older children at much later stages of linguistic development.

We drew children from an elementary school in Cambridge, Massachusetts, which is predominantly middle-class, but has nevertheless some range in the socioeconomic background of the children. Thirty-six children from kindergarten through fourth grade were selected to ensure a representative sample in terms of age and reading level. The children were interviewed individually at school by the author and an assistant over a period of several months in the fall of 1969, with each interview lasting about a half hour.

The Test Constructions

1. The construction *Easy to See* in the sentence *"The doll is easy to see"*

In this interview we tested the child's ability to determine the grammatical relations which hold among the words in sentences of the form *The doll is easy to see*.

The complexity of this construction derives from the fact that the grammatical relations among its words are not expressed directly in its surface structure. Of the two constructions

    (a) The doll is eager to see.
    (b) The doll is easy to see.

which look alike on the surface, only (a) retains in its surface structure the relations of subject and verb which are implicit in the meaning of the sentence; i.e., not only is *doll* the subject of sentence (a), but it is also the implicit subject of the complement verb *see*. The surface structure of (a) expresses this by normal word order of subject precedes verb. In (b), however, the word order is misleading. *Doll* is actually the implicit *object* of the complement verb *see*, for in (b) it is easy for someone else to see the doll. The implicit subject of *see* is omitted in (b)'s surface structure, and the listener must fill it in for himself as "someone else." The child who has not yet learned to recognize the underlying difference in structure of these two superficially similar sentences will interpret them both according to surface structure, and report that in (b), as well as (a), it is the doll who is doing the seeing. Such a child would interpret (b) incorrectly to mean "It is easy for the doll to see," instead of "It is easy for someone else to see the doll."

The interview was opened by placing a doll, with eyes that close, lying down with eyes closed on a table in front of the child. The child was then asked to say whether the doll was easy to see or hard to see. After responding, he was asked the question "why?" Then he was asked to make the doll either easy to see or hard to see, depending on his response to the first question.

The child who interprets the sentence correctly will answer that the doll is easy to see and support this interpretation when asked by answering that the doll is right there in front of him. When asked to make the doll hard to see he will hide the doll under the table or cover his own eyes or make a similar meaningful response.

The child who misinterprets the sentence and answers that the doll is hard to see will support this interpretation by indicating that her eyes are closed so she can't see and when asked to make her easy to see will open the doll's eyes.

This construction was fairly easy for the children. Everyone over age 7.1[5] succeeded with it, and below this age there was mixed success and failure. Five of the children below 7.1 failed, approximately half of this age group. Our sample did not include children young enough for us to observe onset of acquisition. Below we will see that lack of competence in this construction constitutes Stage 1 in our developmental sequence.

2. The construction *Promise* as in
   "*Bozo promises Donald to stand on the book.*"

Here we examined the child's knowledge of a particular syntactic structure associated with the word *promise*. His ability to identify the missing subject of a complement verb following *promise* was tested, a task which is relatively complex for the following reasons. Consider the sentences

(a) Bozo promised Donald to stand on the book.
(b) Bozo told Donald to stand on the book.

In these sentences the subject of the verb *stand* is not expressed, but must be filled in by the listener. Although the two sentences are superficially alike, differing only in their main verbs *promise* and *tell*, in (a) it is Bozo who is to stand on the book, and in (b) it is Donald who is to stand on the book. Since this information is not given anywhere in the surface structure of these sentences, the listener must, in order to interpret them differently, draw on his underlying knowledge of the verbs *promise* and *tell* and the structures associated with them.

Sentence (b) is a very common structure in English. The missing subject of a complement verb is almost always the first noun phrase preceding it. If Bozo tells Donald to stand on the book, it is Donald who is to do the standing. This is true for almost all verbs in English that can substitute for *tell* in this sentence,

[5] 7.1 is used to indicate 7 years, 1 month.

for example, *persuades, urges, expects, wants, orders, hires, likes,* etc. We learn this rule early and we learn it well. *Promise,* however, is an exception. With *promise* the missing subject is not the closest noun phrase, but a noun phrase farther away. This is a rare construction in English found with only a very few verbs. In order to interpret sentence (a) correctly, we must have learned in dealing with *promise* to discard the general rule and to substitute the special rule for *promise.*

Our expectation was that children who have not yet learned this exceptional feature of the verb *promise* will use their well-learned general principle and interpret sentence (a) according to the structure of (b). They will report that in (a) it is Donald who is to stand on the book; Bozo promises Donald that he, Donald, can stand on the book. In a previous experiment carried out by this writer, this was found to be the case; some children still misinterpreted the construction up to the age of eight and one-half, and uniform success was achieved only above this age.[6]

To test knowledge of this construction we had the child manipulate two toy figures to illustrate the action of a series of test sentences. The figures used were Bozo the Clown and Donald Duck, and a book was provided for them to stand on.

First it was determined that the child knew the meaning of the word *promise* by asking questions such as: Can you tell me what you would say to your friend if you promise him that you'll call him up this afternoon? What do you mean when you make somebody a promise? What's special about a promise?

Then the child was asked to name the two figures. Practice sentences were given to familiarize the child with the actions and with the "intentional" nature of the test sentences. The child has to illustrate how the stated intention of the sentence is carried out because in "Bozo promises Donald to stand on the book," the child shows who stands on the book. The practice sentences introduce this notion: Bozo wants to do a somersault—Make him do it. Bozo wants Donald to do a somersault—Have him do it. Donald decides to stand on the book—Make him do it.

This was followed by five test sentences of the form "Donald promises Bozo to hop up and down—Make him hop."

In general the children easily understood what they were to do, and appeared to enjoy the task. The sentences were repeated freely for those children who required repetitions or who seemed to hesitate.

The children who interpreted the sentences correctly selected the more distant noun phrase as subject of *stand.* For "Bozo promised Donald to stand on the book—Make him do it," they picked up Bozo and placed him on the book. The children who misinterpreted the construction selected the closest noun phrase

---

[6] Chomsky.

as subject of *stand*. In response to this same sentence, they picked up Donald and placed him on the book.

We found the children to be highly consistent in their responses. The most common response was to assign the missing subject the same way in all five sentences, whether correct or incorrect, and to do so rapidly and with assurance. Only a very few children varied their responses, and generally these were the ones who hesitated and appeared confused.

Our results indicate that this construction was relatively easy for the children. Criterion for success was four correct out of five. Two thirds of the thirty-six children succeeded with the construction. The failers, with one exception, were all under eight years old, with failure being the rule for the five-year-olds, as likely as success for the six-year-olds, and the exception for the seven-year-olds. Lack of competence in this construction with the verb *promise* distinguishes children in Stage 2 in our developmental sequence from those in Stage 3.

3. The construction *Ask* as in
   "*The girl asked the boy what to paint.*"

This interview examined the child's knowledge of a particular syntactic structure associated with the verb *ask*. This construction, or the child's handling of the verb *ask* in general, proves to be a particularly good indicator of syntactic development. The child must identify the missing subject of a verb following *ask* in a complement clause, introduced by a question word such as *when* or *what*, for example, the subject of *paint* in

The girl asked the boy what to paint.

The verb *ask* breaks a general structural rule of English as does *promise*. The nature of the complexity of this construction has been treated at length elsewhere,[7] and will be reviewed only briefly here.

Consider the sentences

(a) The girl asked the boy what to paint.
(b) The girl told the boy what to paint.

The missing subject of *paint* in (a) is *the girl*. The correct paraphrase of (a) is *The girl asked the boy what she should paint.* In (b), as in most other sentences of this form in English, the missing subject is *the boy*, that is *the girl told the boy what he should paint.* Since the weight of evidence in the language as a whole favors the (b) interpretation, children who have not yet learned this exceptional feature of the verb *ask* will interpret sentence (a) according to the structure of (b). They will report that in (a) the girl is asking the boy what he is going to paint. This interpretation persists in some children until age ten or later.

[7] Chomsky.

The actual interview consisted of a conversational portion and a picture identification test. In the conversational portion, two children who knew each other well carried out a number of tasks according to instructions. Only one child was being tested, the second child serving as a conversational partner. The two children were seated at a table on which were placed toy food, and figures of Donald Duck, Pluto Pup, and Bozo. We explained to the child that he was going to play some games with the things on the table; he would feed the dog, for example, and so on.

The instructions themselves were then given. *Ask* instructions were interspersed with *tell* instructions, but the opening instruction was always *ask*. The interview proceeded as follows:

Interviewer: Ask Bruce what to feed the dog.
Child: THE HAMBURGER.
Interviewer: Tell Bruce what food to put back in the box.
Child: THE HOT DOG.
etc.

The interview was carried out in an informal conversational manner, with repetitions, extra instructions at the child's point of difficulty, discussion of confusions and inconsistencies, and with special attempts to draw the child's attention to his "errors." Maximum help was given the child to express what he knew.

Errors were of two kinds. Some children told their partner what to do in response to an *ask* instruction, rather than asking him. *The hamburger* above would be a correct response if the instruction had been "Tell Bruce what to feed the dog." Children who respond in this manner have failed to interpret *ask* as requiring a question response, and respond as if instructed to tell. This response error indicated the least competence with the verb *ask*.

When making the other error, children asked their partner a question, but assigned the wrong missing subject to the key verb, responding to "Ask Bruce what to feed the dog" with "What are you going to feed the dog?" The child who answers in this manner understands that he is to ask a question, but has not yet learned that *ask* signals an exception to his well-learned general rule of English for picking missing subjects. He picks his missing subject incorrectly, according to the general rule, which says to choose your partner rather than yourself. He may ask a variety of questions, all with the subject *you* following *ask;* for example,

What do you want to feed the dog? or
What are you going to feed the dog?

This response indicates greater competence with *ask* than the preceding

1a. Correct interpretation   *1b. Incorrect interpretation*

Test Pictures 1a. and 1b.
Test sentence: The girl asks the boy what to paint.

Subject is shown both pictures simultaneously and asked

1. Which picture shows the girl asking the boy what to paint?
2. What is she saying to him?

FIGURE 1

response, but still reveals lack of knowledge of *ask* as signalling an exceptional structure.[8]

Only one third of the children were able to give the correct response, asking a question and assigning the correct subject to the key verb, responding to "Ask Bruce what to feed the dog," with the question "What should I feed the dog?" This response indicates mastery of the construction, and was the only one accepted as correct for our purposes. Criterion for success was correct response to at least four-fifths of the instructions given.[9]

After the conversational portion of the interview was concluded, the partner left, and the subject was shown two pairs of pictures (Figs. 1 and 2). For Pair 1 he was asked: "Which picture shows the girl asking the boy what to paint?" and "What is she saying to him?"; for Pair 2 he was asked: "Which picture shows the boy asking the girl what shoes to wear?" and "What is he saying to her?" The child was instructed to look at both pictures of a pair before deciding on an answer. In each case, the correct choice is Picture a. For Picture 1a, the girl should be quoted as saying, "What should I paint?" and for Picture 2a, the boy should be quoted as saying, "What shoes should I wear?"

Here again, we find the same two kinds of error as with the conversational

[8] The children's performance with *ask* in general reveals a number of levels of competence, which the present discussion only touches on. Since the various degrees of competence short of total mastery do not contribute to our developmental sequence, they are referred to only peripherally here.

[9] The actual number of instructions given varied from child to child because of the informal nature of the interview.

210

2a. Correct interpretation   *2b. Incorrect interpretation*

Test Pictures 2a. and 2b.
Test sentence: The boy asks the girl which shoes to wear.

  Subject is shown both pictures simultaneously and asked

  1. Which picture shows the boy asking the girl which shoes to wear?
  2. What is he saying to her?

FIGURE 2

test of *ask*. Some children choose the wrong picture (b), giving a quote in which one child *tells* the other what to do, e.g., "Wear those shoes." This would be a correct response if the cue had been "Which picture shows the girl telling the boy what shoes to wear?" As before, children who respond in this manner have failed to interpret *ask* as requiring a question response. They respond as if instructed to tell. This response indicates the least competence with the verb *ask*.

The second error is to choose the wrong picture, quote the picture child as asking a question, but the wrong question: "What are you going to paint?"; "What shoes are you going to wear?" Again, the child who answers in this manner understands that he is to ask a question, but has not yet learned the exceptional nature of *ask*. He picks his missing subject incorrectly and proceeds to choose a picture and question consistent with his hypothesis. As before, this response indicates greater competence with *ask* than the preceding response, but falls short of total mastery.

In each of the above errors the picture choice and quoted command or question are consistent with each other. Given the way the child interprets the cue sentence, his response is logical and "correct." He is not confused nor is he guessing. This was true also for the conversational test, where the child's actions supported his words in almost all cases. He is operating successfully according to rule; it is just that his rule differs from the standard. This is a common observation in this type of linguistic testing, where children are often confident when operating with well-entrenched, though inappropriate, rules. Indeed, confusion or hesitation, or recognition that a construction is problematic, may signal progress on the child's part, usually indicating that he has begun the process of restructuring his rule system.

An interesting feature of the results is that the picture test for *ask* was easier for some children than the conversational test. Five children succeeded with the pictures and failed the conversational test, and only one child reversed this pattern. Criterion for success with the *ask* construction as a whole was success with both the pictures and the conversation test.[10]

An analysis of our results showed that this construction was considerably more difficult for the children than our preceding ones, and exhibited strong variability in age of acquisition. Only one third of the children, ranging in age from 7.2 years to 10.0, succeeded at both the conversational interview and the picture test. The ages of those who failed ranged from 5.9 to 9.9. No child under 7.2 succeeded. From 7.2 up, we find the children fairly evenly divided among passers and failers. The mean age of the failers was six months under that of the passers, 8.2 as compared to 8.8.

The striking feature of these results is the high variability in age of acquisition of the structure, and the persistence of lack of knowledge right up to the top age in our sample. Clearly after age seven, individual rate of development is a stronger factor than is age in acquisition of the *ask* construction. Below we will see that knowledge of this construction distinguishes Stage 3 from Stage 4 in our developmental sequence.

It is interesting that the ability to assign a missing subject correctly following *ask* appears later in the child than the ability to carry out what appears to be the same task with the verb *promise*. Both verbs require that a general rule of subject assignment be broken and replaced with a rule specific to these two words. If the specific rule is the same for both *ask* and *promise*, why then does the child consistently learn to apply it first with *promise*?

The answer appears to lie in the greater simplicity of the verb *promise* as compared to *ask*. *Promise* is a consistent verb, whereas *ask* evidences inconsistency when used in two different senses as follows. Consider (a) Seymour asked Gloria to leave, (b) Seymour asked Gloria when to leave. In (a) Gloria is to leave; *ask* behaves as the majority of verbs in English. In (b) Seymour is to leave; *ask* behaves according to the special rule. The child must learn conflicting rules for these two structures with *ask*, whereas no such problem exists with *promise*. *Promise* always requires the special rule—there is no structure such as (a) to complicate matters.

---

[10] This scoring procedure simplifies the stages of our developmental sequence, and was adopted for this reason. Separating the children who passed only the picture test would add one stage to the sequence, which might be useful for some purposes but seemed superfluous here.

4. Constructions following *And* and *Although*

Here we tested the children's ability to identify a missing verb differently in two sentences which differ only in the use of *and* and *although* as clause introducers. Consider the sentences:

(a) Mother scolded Gloria for answering the phone, and I would have done the same.

(b) Mother scolded Gloria for answering the phone, although I would have done the same.

These sentences do not say what I would have done; the listener must fill it in for himself. There are two candidate verbs preceding *done the same* which might serve as referent: *scolded* and *answered*. Following *and,* the referent is *scolded;* following *although,* the referent is *answered;* in (a) I would have scolded Gloria, and in (b) I would have answered the phone.[11]

No careful experimental technique was devised for testing these constructions. We simply read the sentences to the children and asked for each one: "What does this sentence say I would have done?" There was some question in our minds about the effectiveness of this direct approach, but it appears to have been adequate in this case. The results show interesting developmental patterns, and they fit in very well with the rest of our data.

The examples mentioned above were used as well as the sentences: "The cowboy scolded the horse for running away, and I would have done the same—What would I have done?" "The cowboy scolded the horse for running away, although I would have done the same—

What would I have done?"

These sentences were usually read several times to the children, particularly the younger children, before they were able to formulate an answer. Those who could read were given the sentences typed on cards to follow as we read aloud.

We determined in an earlier portion of the interview that all of the children could correctly interpret the shorter sentence, "The cowboy scolded the horse for running away—Who ran away?" None of the children had any trouble assigning *horse* as subject of *running away.*

We also determined earlier in the interview session which children were competent in the use of *although* in simpler sentences where no deletions were involved. All but eight of the children performed successfully on an oral sentence-completion task with sentences such as "Although my favorite TV program was on, I . . ." and "I wore a heavy jacket although. . . ." Those who failed were under seven years of age, and not among the passers of our *and* and *although* test.

This experiment turned out to be more interesting than anticipated. During

---

[11] This interesting and rather unusual aspect of the word *although* was brought to the author's attention by Adrian Akmajian.

the planning stage we considered the *although* sentences to be the difficult ones, and had included *and* sentences only for contrast. As it turned out, not only was the *although* construction very difficult for the children (only four children succeeded with it), but the *and* sentence, surprisingly enough, proved to be interesting in its own right. Unexpectedly, twenty-three children failed the *and* sentence. Whereas we had set out to test *although*, *and* itself proved to be a useful test construction as discussed below.

Scoring was as follows. In the *although* sentences the child had to choose the referent of *done the same* from two candidate verbs preceding it in the sentence: *scolded*, the far candidate, and *answering*, the near candidate. The correct choice is the near candidate, *answering*. Scoring, however, requires caution, for some children will choose the near candidate from lack of knowledge. As we have seen in the constructions of *promise* and *ask*, the child tends to always choose the *near* candidate to fill in a deletion when he works from general principles of English. In our test sentence the near candidate (*answering*) is the correct one, the one the child would choose also from specific knowledge of the *although* construction. Since both general principles and specific knowledge of *although* yield the same answer, how can we determine on what basis the child is choosing? Fortunately, our *and* sentence provides the means for distinguishing. It presents what appears to be the same construction differing only in the replacement of *although* by *and,* and requires the *far* candidate, *scolded,* as referent of *done the same.*

By correctly choosing the far candidate (*scolded*) for *and,* the child shows that he has learned to discard general principles in dealing with this surface structure. When this child then chooses the near candidate for *although* we can assume that he does so not from general principles but because he recognizes the different function of *although* in the sentence.

And indeed we find a pattern of development which supports this hypothesis. The younger children selected the near candidate for both *and* and *although;* apparently they worked from general principles for both words. As age increases children began to select the far candidate for both words; they have learned the exceptional nature of the surface structure, but not the specific *although* rule. In the most advanced stage, children have also learned the specific *although* rule and distinguish the two cases.

The criterion for success with *although,* then, was choosing the near candidate verb as referent of *done the same,* while at the same time choosing the far candidate verb for *and.* Children were scored correct only if all four test sentences were judged correctly. Only four children, ages 7.6, 8.3, 8.11, and 9.9. achieved this success. Clearly age is a poor predictor of success with this construction, and knowledge of it is strongly dependent on individual rate of development.

The relation between our simple use of *although* in the sentence completion task and its more complex use with verb deleted shows the expected course of development. There are children who know neither construction, children who know both, and many intermediate children who know the simple construction but not the complex one. No children reverse this order, and know the complex construction without knowing the simple one.

In summary, all children seven and older succeeded with *although* in its simple construction. The more complex *although* construction was very difficult for the children and only four succeeded at it. Knowledge of the simple construction precedes knowledge of the complex one.

This *although* construction was the most difficult of the constructions reported here, and we will see below that success at it constitutes the highest stage in our developmental sequence.

Considered separately, the *and* construction yielded interesting results. Above we pointed out that the youngest children dealt with *and* according to general principles of English and selected the near candidate to fill in the missing verb.

The parallel of these *and* results with our results for *ask* is remarkably close. Their main feature is the high variability in age of acquisition of the structure, and the fact that we find children up to the oldest failing. After age seven, age is less of a factor in acquisition of the construction than individual rate of development. We will see below that, with only minor exceptions, the same children succeeded with both *ask* and *and*. Accordingly, joint knowledge of *ask* and *and* serves to distinguish Stage 3 from 4 in our developmental sequence.

Overall Developmental Sequence

By measuring children's competence in dealing with individual grammatical constructions, we gain information about patterns of acquisition characteristic of the different constructions. If we are fortunate this information may shed some light on the nature of the constructions themselves. It is far more interesting, however, to deal with a number of related structures. With a variety of structures, we hope to observe developmental sequences in the acquisition of the different constructions.

Thus, for a set of related constructions, with the verb *ask*, for example, we find that an individual child's successes and failures on test questions always assume the same pattern. Consider for the moment two separate *ask* constructions, the one discussed earlier and another, simpler one: (a) Ask Harry what time it is; (b) Ask Harry what to feed the dog.

Sentence *a* is simpler than *b* in that there is no missing subject in the clause —all information is given and nothing has to be filled in by the listener. To interpret (a) or (b) correctly, the child must recognize that *ask* signals a ques-

TABLE 1

Stages in Acquisition of Ask Constructions

	Task 1	Task 2	Task 3
Stage A	—	—	—
Stage B	+	—	—
Stage C	+	+	—
Stage D	+	+	⊤

+ Success
— Failure

tion. To interpret (b) correctly, the child must, in addition, select the missing subject correctly. In effect, the child must carry out the following three tasks:

1. Recognize that *ask* signals a question before the simple construction (a);
2. Recognize that *ask* signals a question before the complex construction (b);
3. Assign a correct missing subject in the complex construction (b).

Now when we test children on these two structures, we find the pattern of successes and failures shown in Figure 3.

Task (3) implies (2), which in turn implies (1).[12]

Given this pattern, we conclude that the children attain competence on these tasks in the order listed. The grammatical development is observed to take place in an orderly fashion, from simple to complex, according to an invariant sequence.

That we can find such sequences when testing closely related structures is not very surprising. Sometimes, however, we find a stage we did not expect (such as the first two lines of Table 1 above). This is more interesting because we have learned something about how individual syntactic rules are adjusted in children's grammatical systems as their linguistic competence increases and they approach the adult linguistic system. This is the heart of the matter in linguistic work of this sort, for in this way we find out what the rules look like, how they change, what steps the child has to go through, what progress actually looks like step by step, what is hard and what is easy.

It is most interesting of all, of course, when structures that are related to each

---

[12] Children who can do Task 3 can always do 2 and 1, and children who can do 2 can always do 1. There are no children who break this pattern, who can do 3, for example, and not 2 and 1; or who can do 2 without being able to do 1; or 1 and 3 without 2. On the other hand we do find children who can do 1 but not 2 or 3; and children who can do 1 and 2, but not 3. When our data are of this sort, when the operations can be arranged into a Guttman scale such that 3 presupposes 2 which in turn presupposes 1, then we have information about order of acquisition. Although we have not observed children over time as they progress from 1 to 2 to 3, we can nevertheless conclude that this is the order of acquisition and that we have an invariant developmental sequence.

TABLE 2

Developmental Stages in Children's Acquisition of Five Test Structures

		easy to see	promise	ask	and	although
STAGE 1:	age 5.9-7.1 n=4	—	—	—	—	—
STAGE 2:	age 5.9-9.5 n=9	+	—	—	—	—
STAGE 3:	age 6.1-9.9 n=12	+	+	—	—	—
STAGE 4:	age 7.2-10. n=7	+	+	+	+	—
STAGE 5:	age 7.6-9.9 n=4	+	+	+	+	+

+ Success
— Failure

other only loosely reveal this same orderly developmental sequence. The five structures discussed exhibit this sequential relationship, in the order presented: *easy to see, promise, ask, and,* and *although.*

These structures appear to be quite divergent, and one would not ordinarily group them together as candidates for a developmental sequence, nor predict a specific order of acquisition. Yet our results show that they are acquired in the order listed. The children's performance on these constructions divides them into five stages as shown in Table 2.

Children who fail all five constructions are at Stage 1; Stage 2 children pass *easy to see* and fail the others; Stage 3 children pass *easy to see* and *promise* and fail the others; Stage 4 children pass all but *although;* Stage 5 children pass all five constructions.

What is interesting in the data is the uniformity of the results. The amount of divergence from this sequence of acquisition is extremely small, the children's individual responses deviating from the observed pattern at the rate of 4 responses per 100.[13]

How do we account for this striking orderliness in the children's acquisition of these seemingly diverse structures? A closer look at the structures themselves reveals that they do have one feature in common. They all require the listener to fill in a missing item in order to understand the sentence. The surface form of these sentences lacks either a noun phrase or a verb phrase which is crucial

---

[13] When the stages are considered as a Guttman scale, the coefficient of reproducibility is .96.

to its understanding, and the listener must know how to fill it in if he is to understand the sentence correctly. In each case it has to be filled in in a manner at variance with the general tendency of the language, which accounts for the difficulty. More technically, the listener, given only the surface structure of the sentence, must recreate its underlying form. To do this he has to know, among other things, the rules governing deletions from underlying to surface structure. If a child has not yet mastered the rules for these constructions, he will make mistakes in filling in the missing items, and end up with wrong interpretations.

The general rule in English for filling in deletions such as in the above constructions is to choose the nearest preceding candidate item in the sentence. The child has learned this as a general principle of the language very early on. These five constructions, though very different from each other, all require that this principle be abandoned. They require instead the rather unusual principle: don't choose the nearest preceding candidate item in the sentence, keep looking. In a sense the child has to be freed from a deeply entrenched constraint in order to interpret each one of these constructions. He has specifically to learn in each of the above cases that his general principle does not apply. Evidently the relative complexities of these five structures are such that children tend to master them in the order listed, with surprisingly little variation.

Table 3 summarizes our test constructions. It illustrates the five structures,

TABLE 3

Correct and Incorrect Interpretations of 5 Test Structures

	to be filled in	*near candidate incorrect*	*other candidate correct*
EASY TO SEE	subject of *see*	doll	somebody else
PROMISE	subject of *lie down*	Donald	Bozo
ASK	subject of *paint*	boy	girl
AND	referent of *done the same*	answered the phone	scolded
ALTHOUGH	referent of *done the same*	scolded*	answered the phone

* likely candidate by analogy with AND sentence, once learned

STRUCTURES:
EASY TO SEE: The doll is easy to see.
PROMISE : Bozo promises Donald to lie down.
ASK : The girl asks the boy what to paint
AND : Mother scolded Gloria for answering the phone, and I would have done the same.
ALTHOUGH : Mother scolded Gloria for answering the phone, although I would have done the same.

218

with the correct and incorrect interpretations given. Children who do not know a construction respond with the incorrect interpretation (near candidate); those who know the construction respond with the "other" candidate.

Several interesting observations may be noted in connection with the sequence of acquisition outlined here.

First, *easy to see,* which was tested along with *promise* and *ask* by the author in an earlier experiment[14] did not precede *promise* in that experiment as it does in this one. The reason for this may be faulty experimental technique in the first experiment, which introduced extraneous cues and made the construction too difficult for the children. The current experiment, with improved technique, may reflect the children's competence more accurately.

Second, *promise* precedes *ask* in this experiment as in the 1969 experiment, confirming the earlier results. Only the final stage in the acquisition of *ask* (Table 1, Stage D) is relevant to this overall developmental sequence.

And finally, *and* and *ask* appear to "come in" together if *ask* is scored from both the conversational portion of the interview and the picture test. Apparently the child learns the *and* construction at about the time he masters *ask*; if this result is borne out by future experimentation, it would suggest that the two constructions are of approximately the same degree of complexity.

In summary, the five constructions tested in this study can be ordered in a Guttman scale, indicating a developmental sequence in children's acquisition of these structures. The five structures, though quite diverse, all require that the child apply a specific principle of sentence analysis that is uncommon in English. Apparently, the child's ability to apply this principle progresses in a regular fashion from simple structures to more complex ones.

Reading

A second portion of this study surveyed the children's reading background and current reading activity. We wished to consider the relation of the amount and complexity of what children read to rate of linguistic development, along with other factors such as IQ and SES. To do this we used the five linguistic stages outlined above as the measure of rate of linguistic development and a variety of information on reading and listening.

Reading information was gathered through questionnaires to both children and parents, and through daily records kept at home of all reading (and listening to books read aloud) engaged in by the child over a one-week period. We calculated amount and complexity of independent reading (and listening), background in children's literature, and recall and recognition of books read and heard. In order to judge the extent of the children's reading at different

[14] Chomsky.

complexity levels, we applied our own formula for measuring syntactic complexity to the books and magazines reported by the children in their week's record of day-to-day reading.

Our records thus contain a variety of measures of each child's reading exposure which together yielded a general picture of some interest. We have information on books read over a week's time, books that the child named in the course of a half-hour interview, parent reports of reading aloud, and so on. By assessing how much and what is read to him, and how much and what he reads on his own, we attempted to characterize each child's independent reading and get a picture of how reading functions in his background and current life. As mentioned above, both the amount read and the complexity of the material were taken into consideration.

Our concern is not so much with the child's level of reading ability as it is with the reading that he actually engages in. That is, the mechanical skill that he has acquired is of interest for our purposes primarily in the way he puts it to use. The written language is potentially of a more complex nature than speech, both in vocabulary and syntax. The child who reads (or listens to) a variety of rich and complex materials benefits from a range of linguistic inputs that is unavailable to the non-literary child. It is this exposure that we wish to examine for its relation to rate of linguistic development.[15]

In the following section we present some of our reading results and discuss their relation to linguistic development.

Relations of Reading Measures to Linguistic Stages

One excellent measure used in our reading survey was Huck's *Taking Inventory of Chidren's Literary Background*.[16] This multiple-choice quiz tests a child's knowledge of the content of sixty widely-read books, poems, and stories from children's literature. Scores on the Huck inventory are positively related to linguistic stage. In other words, the higher the Huck score is, the higher, in general, is the child's linguistic stage in our data.

This can be seen from Table 4, line 1. Each of the Huck scores is the *average* for all children in the stage listed at the head of the column in Table 4.[17]

Other reading measures, developed by the author, also show a positive relation with linguistic stage. Like the Huck score, they appear as within-stage aver-

[15] From the point of view of exposure to the written language, it may matter little whether the child has the book read to him, as would be the case with the younger children in our study, or reads it himself, as do the older children. It is possible, perhaps even likely, that in both situations the contents, style, and language usage of the book are made available to the child with little difference in effectiveness.

[16] Charlotte S. Huck, *Taking Inventory of Children's Literary Background* (Glenview, Ill.: Scott, Foresman, 1966).

[17] For example, 23 is the average Huck score for all children in Stage 1. The notation "n = 4" at the foot of the first column, tells you that four children are at Stage 1.

TABLE 4

Average Scores at Each Linguistic Stage on a Variety of Reading and Other Measures

	Stage 1	Stage 2	Stage 3	Stage 4	Stage 5
Measures good at all stages					
1. Huck *Inventory of Literary Background*	23	31	38	39	43
2. Numerical scores from Child Interview	37	50	55	56	59
3. Numerical scores from Parent Interview	45	55	58	61	64
4. Weighted total books named—Parent Interview	21	30	42	47	49
5. Average level books named—Parent Interview	1.4	2.1	2.4	2.9	3.0
6. Master Book List—top level count	2.3	3.9	4.9	5.0	6.3
7. IQ (WPPSI, WISC) full scale	105	118	123	129	138
8. IQ—verbal	105	119	122	129	141
9. IQ—performance	104	114	120	123	129
	n = 4	n = 9	n = 13	n = 6	n = 4

ages in Table 4. The data from which these measures were derived came from three sources:

1. *Master Book List.* This list contained the titles of some 400 children's books and was left in the home for the child and parent to complete jointly by checking off the titles of books with which the child was familiar. The number of books checked off that were at the top level of syntactic complexity was one positive measure and is presented in Table 4, line 6. The *total* number of books checked off on the Master Book List was also a good measure, though not quite as good as the top level count.

2. *Parent Interview.* One of the child's parents—in all but one case, the mother—was interviewed at home. Questions in the interview centered around the child's reading habits, library trips, reading aloud to the child, favorite books, time spent in independent reading, etc. Special attention was given to eliciting from the parent as many titles as possible of books and magazines that the child had encountered over the years.

Three measures from this interview were found to relate positively to linguistic stage as shown in Table 4: a) average complexity level of books named by the parent (line 5); b) the total number of books named, weighted by complexity levels of the individual books (the raw total was not a distinguishing measure) (line 4); and c) the total numerical score from the interview, calculated from questions with numerical answers such as time spent reading to the child during the early years, the amount of time the child spends reading now, frequency of public library visits, average number of books borrowed from the library each visit, and so on (line 3).

3. *Child Interview.* An interview was held with each child at school. Rough-

ly the same information was sought as in the parent interview. The measure which correlated positively with linguistic stage from this interview was, as in the parent interview, numerical score. This score reflected the child's answers to questions concerning library trips (What books do you have out this week? How many of the books that you take out do you generally read?), favorite books and authors, books reread many times, time spent reading daily or weekly, TV watching (credit given inversely to amount of time spent watching TV), number of people at home who read to you, now or formerly, and so on. This numerical score measure for the child interview appears in Table 4 (line 2).

In addition to demonstrating a positive relation with linguistic stages displayed in Table 4, the five reading measures all relate positively to the Huck score. Four of the correlations were significant beyond the .001 level: Master Book List top level book count, average complexity level and weighted total of books from the parent interview, and the numerical score from the child interview. The Pearson product-moment correlations were .564, .577, .392, and .631 respectively. The numerical score from the parent interview was also positively correlated with the Huck score ($r = .462$, $p = .003$). With a sample of only thirty-six, these correlations indicate a high degree of association.

Given the positive relation of these five measures with linguistic stages in Table 4 (evidenced also by positive Kendall rank order correlations significant at least at the .013 level)[18] and the positive and significant Pearson correlations of these five measures with the Huck score, we conclude that the relation between reading exposure and linguistic stage is not due to a peculiarity of one of the reading measures. To assume otherwise, since the measures are largely non-overlapping, would lead us to claim that each measure has some unique peculiarity that causes it to produce a positive relation with linguistic stage that in fact has little or nothing to do with the child's reading exposure. Experience tells us that concentrating on six such unique measures is unlikely. Therefore, we conclude that a valid relation between reading exposure and linguistic stages exists.

It is worth noting that the Huck Inventory, a direct and easily obtainable measure, apparently functions as an excellent single measure of reading exposure to which linguistic stages are related. We may speculate that the Inventory refines the notion of exposure to written materials by incorporating not just the amount read but internalization and retention of the material as well.

---

[18] Kendall rank-order correlations for these measures are:

Master Book List—top level count	.328	(.002)
Average Level books named—parent	.409	(.001)
Weighted total books named—parent	.274	(.009)
Numerical score—parent	.258	(.013)
Numerical score—child	.327	(.002)

Relationship of Other Measures to Linguistic Stages

One other measure, IQ, is positively related to linguistic development across all stages.

The Wechsler Preschool and Primary Scale of Intelligence (WPPSI) test was given to the six children in the study who were under 6.2 years of age at testing time. The remaining thirty children (ages 6.5 and over) were given the Wechsler Intelligence Scale for Children (WISC) test. IQ's ranged from 98 to 142 and the average scores within each linguistic stage are presented in Table 4, lines 7-9. Not only do the full scale IQ scores increase with linguistic stage but so do the verbal and performance subtests of the test.

The Kendall rank order correlations of linguistic stage with IQ, with each of the IQ subtests, with age, and with grade were all significant at the .001 level while the Pearson correlation of linguistic stage with the Census Bureau measure of SES, whose range is 01-99, was significant at the .02 level.

It is not surprising that SES was highly correlated with IQ but not with age or grade. However, the correlations of SES with reading vocabulary and with reading comprehension grade level scores from standardized tests were also nonsignificant while the correlation of SES with IQ was significant at the .001 level. Moreover, the Pearson correlations of SES with all measures of books from the parent interview, child interview and Master Book List were significant at the .001 level.

What inferences can be drawn from this correlational information? First, if our five stages reflect an underlying developmental sequence, we would expect variables like age, grade, reading grade level scores, and IQ to be positively and significantly correlated with linguistic stage. They are.

Second, it is reasonable to speculate that the various IQ and reading exposure measures are not mere substitutes for the age measure; the exposure measures play an independent role in influencing linguistic stage. This follows because the IQ score and its components are age corrected[19] and are therefore uncorrelated with age. Also, the sample was stratified by age (young, medium, old) and by reading grade level score (low, medium, high). This stratification would lead at most to a negligible correlation between age and reading grade level score.

Third, given the pattern of significant and nonsignificant correlation of SES with various measures, *if* SES acts upon linguistic stage placement through any of the measures included in this study it is through general ability or the reading environment of the child. Statistical techniques for studying this question exist, but a new and larger sample should be drawn.

---

[19] $IQ = \dfrac{\text{Mental Age}}{\text{Chronological Age}} \times 100$

Relationship of Listening Measures to Linguistic Stages

A calculation was made of the amount of time spent reading aloud to the children and the complexity of the books read to them at home during a one-week period. As might be expected, listening to books read aloud decreases sharply after first grade as the children's own reading begins to replace their listening. Even in the first grade independent reading is beginning to predominate for the more able readers.

Among the pre-readers, listening to books read aloud is positively related to linguistic stage. As the next section will show, those pre-readers in higher linguistic stages are read to by more people and hear more books per week, at higher complexity levels than children at lower linguistic stages.

In summary, the measures which discriminate the whole linguistic range of stages include IQ, memory of content of books read (Huck), book counts weighted by complexity level, and questionnaire replies. In addition, certain measures work well at lower linguistic stages, and others at higher linguistic stages. Several of the book counts (number of books recalled and recognized) appear to discriminate best at the lower linguistic stages, and word counts (number of words read during the recorded week) discriminate best at the higher stages. Reading complex materials quite strikingly characterizes the top linguistic stage.

Mini-Comparisons: Uniform Age and IQ,
Different Linguistic Stages

A natural question, given the type of data collected here is: What factors differentiate children in different linguistic stages, who are of roughly the same age and IQ? If we control for age and IQ, do any of the various measures that we used serve to distinguish children in lower linguistic stages from those in higher stages?

The small number of children tested precludes a statistical answer to this question. At most we can compare individual children who meet the requirement of same age and IQ and different linguistic stage. The results are not uninteresting, however. We were able to select three such sets of children, one from among the youngest in the sample, one from the mid-age group, and one from the oldest. In each group there were three children of comparable age and IQ, who were nevertheless at different linguistic stages.

Such a procedure of "mini-comparisons" clearly has its limitations, but we are able in each age group to note a number of factors that vary as does linguistic stage. The overall picture shows that at each age, reading or hearing books read is a strong factor, with many different individual measures of reading exposure contributing to this trend. Interestingly enough, SES appears as a factor most strongly in the youngest group (5.9-6.1), where many of the reading measures vary directly with SES. It is hardly news that higher SES parents read to their

TABLE 5

Mini-comparison 1 Measures that Vary as Linguistic Stage in Three Young Children of Uniform Age and IQ

	Ling. stage 1	Ling. stage 2	Ling. stage 3
age of child	5.9	5.9	6.1
grade in school	K	K	K
IQ (WISC)	118	120	118
SES (Census Bureau scale 01-99)	63	89	93
father's occupation score (Census Bureau scale 01-99)	80	80	99
father's years of education	12	16	20
WISC comprehension subtest	13	14	18
books named on parent and child questionnaires, weighted total	14	40	111
books named on parent and child questionnaires, average level	1	1	3
reading to child in experimental week, total number words read	0	6,700	17,500
reading to child in experimental week, number words read multiplied by complexity factor	0	17,700	62,500
Reported on parent questionnaire:			
books named by parent, weighted total	12	40	62
numerical score on parent's questionnaire	27	37	60
number of people at home who read to child	1	2	2
amount of time child is read to per week at home	1/2 hr.	1/2 hr.	>2 hrs.
average level of books cited by parent as reread to child many times	1	1	2
does child visit public library?	no	no	yes
average number public libarary books taken out each visit	—	—	3
subscriptions to children's magazines	0	0	1
years nursery school attendance	0	0	1
number books from mother's own childhood cited as read to child	0	2	1

young children more; what is interesting is that SES is less of a differentiating factor among the older children. In the middle and oldest group, the children share a relatively high SES. For these children (particularly the oldest group where SES varies least), it is their own activity, not SES differences, that varies with linguistic stage. This suggests the following speculation, which might be interesting to test further: given a high SES, once a child can read, he's on his own. His linguistic progress at this age may well turn out to reflect what he does with his time.

The tables which follow (Mini-comparisons 1, 2, 3) present the individual differentiating measures in each mini-comparison. Only the significant measures are included at each age, although all questions were asked of all children.

Notice that three items appear in all three age groups: the number of books

TABLE 6

Mini-comparison 2 Measures that Vary as Linguistic Stage in Three Mid-age Children of Uniform Age and IQ

	Ling. stage 2	Ling. stage 4	Ling. stage 5
age of child	7.10	8.6	8.3
grade in school	2	3	2
Reading grade score (school record)	voc: 5.2	voc: 7.1	voc: 4.8
	compr: 5.1	compr: 7.0	compr: 5.4
IQ (WISC)	138	136	136
SES (Census Bureau scale 01-99)	81	93	91
father's occupation score (Census Bureau Scale 01-99)	68	94	92
child's reading in experimental week, total number words read	22,100	114,400	322,000
child's reading in experimental week, number words read multiplied by complexity factor	46,700	626,600	2,826,300
Reported on child's questionnaire:			
books named by child, weighted total	23	25	40
average number public library books taken out each visit	1	2	3
recent books read, number named	1	1	5
average level of books cited as recently read	2	2	5
average time TV watched per day	> 1 hr.	1 hr.	< 1/2 hr.
Reported on parent questionnaire			
reads long books to child (now or formerly), continued from day to day	no	yes	yes
average level of long books named	—	3	4
rereads favorite books many times to child (now or formerly)	no	yes	yes
average level favorite books reread	—	3	4
frequency of child's visits to public library	irreg.	biweekly	> weekly
average number public library books taken out each visit	1	2	4
years nursery school attendance	1	2	2
number books from mother's own childhood cited as read to child	0	2	7

named by the child in the course of his interview (child and parent in the youngest group), the average number of books taken out on regular visits to the public library, and, interestingly, the number of books that the mother cited from her own childhood that she has enjoyed reading to the child. This third item, though somewhat of a surprise at first, makes sense once its implications are considered. The mother who recalls certain books with pleasure from her own childhood may well transmit this enjoyment to her child very early on when she reads to him. We may speculate that this child learns to assign a special role to reading, for what his mother enjoys doing with him, he quite naturally comes to enjoy and recognize as a valued activity.

TABLE 7

Mini-comparison 3 Measures that Vary as Linguistic Stage in Three Older Children of Uniform Age and IQ

	Ling. stage 3	Ling. stage 4	Ling. stage 5
age of child	9.4	10.0	9.9
grade in school	4	4	4
reading grade score (school record)	voc: 6.8	voc: 6.7	voc. 5.6
	compr: 6.6	compr: 6.5	compr: 6.3
IQ (WISC)	135	129	136
SES (Census Bureau scale 01-99)	93	96	96
father's occupation score (Census Bureau scale 01-99)	88	96	96
father's years education	16	16	20
Reported on child's questionnaire:			
books named by child, total number	6	10	14
books named by child, weighted total	14	32	39
numerical score on child's questionnaire	50	56	69
average number public library books taken out each visit	—	—	6
number library books out now	0	0	4
number favorite books named	1	2	3
are you in the middle of a book now?	no	yes	yes
child named last book read	no	yes	yes
level of last book read	—	2	3
do you ever read when you get home from school?	no	no	yes
average time spent reading	twice/ wk.	daily < 1/2 hr.	daily > 1/2 hr.
average number books read per week	—	2	3
Reported on parent questionnaire:			
average time child was read to when small	1 hr./ wk.	daily > 15 min	daily > 15 min.
average time child spends reading now	1 hr./ wk.	15 min./ day	> 15 min./ day
number books named by parent as read recently by child	1	1	7
average level of books recently read by child	2	2	3
number books from mother's own childhood cited as read to child	2	2	3

Conclusions

What status can we ascribe to the five linguistic stages observable in our data on the basis of the constructions tested? Given the small sample size and the fact that most of these relationships were observed for the first time here, they clearly should be considered as only suggestive. Further testing with larger groups of children, or at least replication with small groups, would be necessary if one wished to substantiate the order of emergence of the structures. My guess is that the distinction between Stages 3 and 4 would hold up under additional testing, since it has a good theoretical base and was observed here for the second time. The other stages may or may not be borne out by future experimentation. This has been only a first trial, in no sense definitive. It is important to stress that the interest of results such as these lies not so much in the particular structures dealt with as in the confirmation of the continuing and orderly course of language acquisition among older children. The structures are more interesting as means to this end than in themselves.

In this vein, I would like to caution against considering these constructions relevant for practical purposes such as diagnostic procedures or for teaching to children. In interpreting results such as these it is important to recognize that the choice of structures is highly arbitrary as far as children are concerned. The selection reflects more the state of knowledge in the field of linguistics than the field of language acquisition, for knowledge of child grammar is as yet far too rudimentary to guide such a choice. Further, our particular experimental requirements impose certain constraints. Thus our findings with regard to complexity of structure should not be interpreted to mean that because a child of eight does not know a particular construction, therefore we should attempt to teach it to him. All in all, our constructions may have little to do with what is important in children's knowledge and may tell virtually nothing about gaps that might be worth trying to fill in terms of enhancing development. Very likely they do reflect the extent of children's knowledge, but attempting to introduce these arbitrary structures artificially cannot be expected to have much effect on the total range of that knowledge.

What then are the practical implications of work of this sort, and what potential educational significance does it have? It seems to me that its relevance may lie in the continuing language acquisition that it reveals in school age children, and in the connections noted between this language development and reading. These results may have implications with regard to language programs in the elementary schools, and the philosophy underlying curriculum design and selection of materials.

We know very little about the actual processes by which children learn language, but there has been an increasing awareness over the past few years of just how much the child brings to the task by way of his own internal organization and innate human characteristics. He certainly is not "taught" language in any formal sense, but acquires it naturally, so to speak, in the course of maturing and developing in an environment where he is adequately exposed to it. Interestingly enough, we now see that this natural process of acquisition continues actively into the early school years, and perhaps beyond. The variety of linguistic material that the child is still learning on his own during the elementary school years must certainly be extensive, if our few, rather arbitrarily chosen examples (arbitrary from the point of view of language acquisition) uncovered this continuing acquisition so readily.

What results of this sort indicate is that the child enters the classroom equipped to learn language and able to do so by methods of his own. This suggests that perhaps the best thing that we might do for him in terms of encouraging this learning would be to make more of it possible, by exposing him to a rich variety of language inputs in interesting, stimulating situations. The question is how.

Our reading results indicate that exposure to the more complex language available from reading does seem to go hand in hand with increased knowledge of the language. This would imply that perhaps wider reading should find a place in the curriculum. The child could be read to, stimulated to read on his own, not restricted to material deemed "at his level" but permitted access to books well "above his level" to get out of them whatever he may. Perhaps he should be encouraged to skim when he reads, to skip uninteresting portions and get to the "good parts" instead of concentrating at length on controlled texts. In general it may be that the effort should be towards providing more and richer language exposure, rather than limiting the child with restrictive and carefully programmed materials. In this way the child would be permitted to derive what is accessible to him from a wide range of inputs, and put it to use in his own way. This approach would seem to be more closely in accord with the nature of language acquisition as we are coming to understand it.

These remarks are, of course, speculative. Their purpose is to emphasize that the potential relevance of work of this sort to language curricula will lie in its suggestiveness for effective use of classroom time, rather than in its relation to the specifics of grammar teaching.

Trends in Second-Language-Acquisition Research

KENJI HAKUTA
HERLINDA CANCINO
Harvard University

Recent concern with bilingual education has led to an increased interest in under-standing the process of second-language acquisition. In this article Kenji Hakuta and Herlinda Cancino present a critical, historical overview of research on second-language acquisition. In this account the authors outline four analytical ap-proaches—contrastive, error, performance, and discourse analysis—trace the shifts among these approaches, and demonstrate the advantages and disadvantages of each. They also show how the different approaches reflect changing conceptions of language and the nature of learners. The authors give special emphasis to the influence of first-language-acquisition research on studies of second-language ac-quisition, and they speculate on future research trends.

Language provides one of the most readily accessible windows into the nature of the human mind. How children acquire this complex system with such ap-parent ease continues to fascinate the student of human language. The last quarter of a century in particular has witnessed a qualitative leap in our knowledge of the language-acquisition process in young children. In recent years researchers have begun extending their scope of inquiry into the problem of second-language acqui-sition. The motivation underlying this new endeavor is two-fold: first, it provides an added perspective on human language, and second, interest in second-language teaching and bilingual education has resulted in a greater need to understand the mechanisms underlying second-language acquisition. The focus of analysis has undergone distinct shifts in perspective as a function of our changing conceptual-izations of what language is and also what the learner brings to the learning situation.

To anticipate the various approaches to be reviewed in this paper, let us enter-

We would like to thank Helen Tager Flusberg, Bella DePaula, Steven Pinker, and Ellen Winner for helpful comments on this paper. We especially thank Roger Brown and Bruce Fraser for ex-tensive written comments. Preparation of this manuscript was supported in part by Grant BNS 73-09150 from the National Science Foundation to Dr. Roger Brown.

Harvard Educational Review   Vol. 47   No. 3   August 1977, 294–316

tain some ways in which one might proceed in analyzing the process of second-language acquisition. Assume that we had in our possession a year-long record of all the conversations of a second-language learner since initial exposure to the target language. One way to analyze the data, if we knew the grammars of both the native and the target languages, would be through a *contrastive* analysis of the two language structures. Where the two languages differ we would expect errors, and our predictions could be tested against the acquisition data. Another way to proceed in the analysis would be to catalogue all the systematic deviations—the *errors*—in the learner's speech from the target-language norm. These deviations, or errors, could be classified into whatever categories our theory might dictate. If we want more specific information than that provided by error data, we could examine *performance* on particular linguistic structures (such as negatives and interrogatives) and look for both the distributional characteristics of errors and correct usage of those structures. Or, we could look not just at linguistic structure but at *discourse* structure as well. For example, we could ask how linguistic forms might be derived from the way in which they are used in conversation.

Over the past thirty years second-language-acquisition research has passed through the four phases outlined above: *contrastive analysis, error analysis, performance analysis,* and *discourse analysis.* (For a review of earlier studies in this area see McLaughlin, 1977.) In this article, we summarize and critically review each of these research traditions. In addition, we discuss reasons for the transition from one form of analysis to the next, particularly that due to the influence of first-language-acquisition research.

Contrastive Analysis

From the early 1940s to the 1960s, teachers of foreign languages were optimistic that the problems of language teaching could be approached scientifically, with the use of methods derived from structural linguistics. Essentially, the goal of structural linguistics was to characterize the syntactic structure of sentences in terms of their grammatical categories and surface arrangements. Fries (1945/1972) was explicit about the implications of this approach for foreign language teaching. He claimed that "the most effective materials are those that are based upon a scientific description of the language to be learned, carefully compared with a parallel description of the native language of the learner" (p. 9).

Claims like Fries's were reinforced by informal observations of learners' systematic errors, which seemed to reflect the structure of their native language. Although many of the errors were phonological in nature, as illustrated by the native speaker of Japanese who consistently fails to distinguish between /r/ and /l/, others clearly originated at the syntactic and morphological levels. Consider a native speaker of Spanish who says "Is the house of my mother." The Spanish equivalent would be "Es la casa de mi madre." The English utterance contains two errors, whose sources can be clearly traced back to Spanish. Spanish allows subject pronouns to be deleted. When this rule is transferred to English, "This is" or "It is" simply becomes "Is." Also, Spanish uses the possessed-possessor order; thus we have "the house of my mother" ("la casa de mi madre"). It appeared, then,

231

that the foreign-language learner's difficulties could be predicted from the differences in the structures of the two languages. Contrastive analysis was the label given to this comparative approach.

Principles such as imitation, positive and negative transfer, reinforcement, and habit strength were borrowed from the academic psychology of learning and incorporated into the contrastive analysis view of second-language acquisition. Presupposing that language development consisted of the acquisition of a set of habits, errors in the second language were seen as the result of the first-language habits interfering with the acquisition of the habits of the second. In classroom practice the principles of habit formation and interference led to the use of pattern drills in the audio-lingual method of second-language learning. On the basis of contrastive analysis, difficult patterns were predicted and consequently emphasized in the drills. For the interested reader the assumptions underlying the audio-lingual method are carefully examined and evaluated in an important book by Rivers (1964).

The comparison of the structures of languages continues to be a respectable activity within contrastive linguistics (Alatis, 1968) and has come to be conducted within the framework of transformational generative grammar. Its status as a psychological approach to the investigation of the second-language-acquisition process, however, fell into disrepute for several reasons. One reason was the unfortunate association of contrastive analysis with the behaviorist view of language acquisition, an account whose theoretical adequacy came to be seriously questioned, most notably by Chomsky (1959). In our view a more devastating reason was that contrastive analysis fared quite poorly once researchers, instead of relying on anecdotal impressions from the classroom, began collecting data in more systematic ways (Oller & Richards, 1973). From these data, analyses of learners' errors soon showed that a large proportion were not predictable on the basis of contrastive analysis. In fact, many of these errors, such as rule simplification (as in "Mommy eat tapioca") and over-generalization (as in "He writed me a letter") exhibited a striking resemblance to those made by children acquiring a first language. Moreover, learners did not in fact make all the errors predicted by contrastive analysis (Nickel, 1971; Stockwell, Bowen, & Martin, 1965). When the inadequacy of contrastive analysis as a predictive model became apparent, Wardhaugh (1970) drew the useful distinction between strong and weak versions of the approach. The strong version claimed to predict errors, while the weak version simply accounted for errors that occurred. Contrastive analysis survives only in its weak form with an obvious shortcoming; it gives an incomplete representation of the second-language-acquisition process since it can account only for some, not all, of the errors. Recently it has been incorporated into the more general approach of error analysis (Schumann & Stenson, 1975), which analyzes all systematic deviations of the learner's language from the target-language norms.

Error Analysis

Chomsky's (1957) formulation of language as a powerful set of transformational rules was received with enthusiasm by many psychologists, and its impact on the study of language acquisition was almost immediate. By the early 1960s researchers began reporting the regularities in the speech of young children and showed that these regularities could be characterized by a set of rules, a grammar (Brown & Bellugi, 1964b). What motivated much of this research was the assumption that the end state of the developmental process is a transformational grammar. Strictly speaking, however, the grammars that were written to describe children's speech were not transformational. Nevertheless, the system of rules reflected in children's utterances was most impressive, particularly some rules for which no adult model seemed to exist. Many of the regularities were morphological in nature, such as "wented" and "hisself," but others were syntactic, for example, "Where he can go?" Although such utterances are errors from the viewpoint of adult grammar, their systematic occurrence in protocols from children gave convincing support to the notion that they were part of each child's developing grammar or linguistic system. The child's errors, rather than being considered products of imperfect learning, came to be regarded as inevitable results of an underlying, rule-governed system which evolved toward the full adult grammar. From this new perspective the child, in the eyes of researchers, gained the status of an active participant in the acquisition of language.

The influence of early first-language-acquisition research on second-language-acquisition research can be found in the error-analysis approach, best represented in collections by Oller and Richards (1973), Schumann and Stenson (1975), and Svartvik (1973). Many investigators noted similarities between the types of errors reported in the first-language-acquisition literature and the errors made by second-language learners. These errors could not be accounted for within the contrastive analysis framework. On the basis of this similarity, researchers speculated that the processes of first- and second-language acquisition are essentially the same (Corder, 1967; Dulay & Burt, 1972; Richards, 1973). Like children learning their first language, second-language learners were characterized as proceeding through a series of intermediate grammars (Corder, 1971; Nemser, 1971; Selinker, 1972). At any given time the learner was credited with having an "interlanguage," a genuine language in the sense that it consists of a set of systematic rules that can be described in a grammar. An interlanguage incorporates characteristics of both the native and the target language of the learner. Today, the goals of error analysis are twofold: to describe, through the evidence contained in errors, the nature of the interlanguage in its developmental stages and to infer from these descriptions the process of second-language acquisition.

The majority of studies in error analysis attempt to classify the errors made by learners. Generally, errors are divided into two categories: interference (or *inter*lingual) errors and *intra*lingual errors. Interference errors, those errors whose sources can be traced back to the native language of the learner, are the ones that contrastive analysis addressed. An important difference, however, is that within the framework of error analysis these errors are not interpreted as products of the first-language habit interfering with the second-language habit. Since the language-acquisition process is seen as active hypothesis testing on the part of the learner, interference errors are interpreted as a manifestation of the learner's hypothesis that the new language is just like the native language (Corder, 1967). Unlike interference errors, intralingual errors arise from properties of the target language and can be found among children learning it as their first language. Their errors include errors of simplification as well as overgeneralization.

Several researchers have investigated the extent to which learners make errors of each type. In two widely cited papers Dulay and Burt (1973, 1974b) report a study in which they considered two competing hypotheses about the nature of second-language acquisition. The first was that second-language acquisition was essentially the same as first-language acquisition. The alternative hypothesis was the one embodied in contrastive analysis, which viewed second-language acquisition as the acquisition of habits (Lado, 1957). Dulay and Burt's implicit assumptions were that intralingual errors constituted evidence for the first hypothesis, while interference errors were evidence for the alternative hypothesis. Notice that their interpretation of interference errors differed from other workers in error analysis. Using an elicitation device called the Bilingual Syntax Measure (BSM), Dulay and Burt collected speech samples from 179 Spanish-speaking children learning English with varying amounts of English-as-Second-Language instruction in three different areas in the United States. They tallied errors that could be "unambiguously" classified as being either interference, intralingual (defined as similar to those reported in the first-language literature), or unique (neither of the two). The results were dramatic and straightforward: of the 513 unambiguous errors, only about 5 percent were interference, while 87 percent were intralingual, and the remainder were classified as unique. Dulay and Burt interpreted this finding as evidence that "children do not use their 'first language habits' in the process of learning the syntax of their new language" (1974b, p. 134).

Dulay and Burt's results can be interpreted in at least two ways. If we accept their assumption that interference errors constitute evidence for a habit-formation hypothesis, their data make an overwhelming argument against this explanation of second-language acquisition. On the other hand, if we take the viewpoint that interference errors are not products of habit formation but rather a form of active hypothesis testing and language transfer (Corder, 1967), a different conclusion emerges. Dulay and Burt's data might be interpreted as evidence that very little language transfer occurs—that is, the learning of the first language has very little influence on the learning of the second.

Whatever theoretical perspective one might take, however, two underlying assumptions in the study make both of the above interpretations questionable: 1) that an error is an appropriate unit of analysis, and 2) that equal weighting should be given to interference and intralingual errors. These assumptions are seriously called into question when one considers that all omissions of grammatical morphemes—including noun and verb inflections and other high-frequency morphemes such as the verb be—were classified as intralingual errors. Although Dulay and Burt do not provide the exact figures, there were many instances of these kinds of errors. Since interference errors generally involve either larger constituents or changes in word order, the two types of errors appear to originate from sources whose relative opportunities for occurrence are significantly different. Furthermore, interference errors may appear in the speech of learners only at specific points in development, and a cross-sectional sample might not capture learners at critical developmental levels.

Other studies in error analysis attempt to compare the proportions of interference and intralingual errors in adult learners. Corder (1975), citing Duskova (1969), reports that there is a larger proportion of interference errors for adults than Dulay and Burt (1973, 1974b) found for children. Duskova (1969) analyzed errors made in English composition by adult Czechoslovakians and reported that roughly 30 percent of the 1,007 errors collected were interference and the remainder intralingual. A closer look at the breakdown of her data, however, reveals that many interference errors were omissions of articles, a part of speech for which Czech does not have an equivalent. In the Dulay and Burt analysis, omissions of articles were considered intralingual errors, since children learning English as their first language also omit articles. When one tallies the interference errors according to Dulay and Burt's criteria, the proportion in Duskova's study is reduced to 5 percent. Despite differences both in the ages of the subjects and in the data collection instruments (speech versus composition), this figure is comparable to the Dulay and Burt results.

However, our earlier qualification still holds for the interpretation of the results of these studies of adult learners. The theoretical significance attached to interlingual and intralingual processes should not be considered proportionate to the number of the respective error types found in the learner's speech. An analogy with studies of first-language learners serves to illustrate this point. Children overgeneralize rules as in "I go*ed* home," and they simplify their speech into telegraphic form as in "Fraser come Tuesday" (Brown & Bellugi, 1964a). In total speech output there is probably a far greater proportion of oversimplification errors. Yet, no one would argue on this basis that simplification is the more important of the two processes in language acquisition. In fact the errors of overgeneralization in first-language learning are fine examples of the child's rule-governed behavior. Similarly, interference errors in second-language learning are fine examples of language transfer and should be regarded as such in their own right. Such errors strongly point to areas of dynamic interplay between the two languages.

Other studies of errors are taxonomic, generally classifying errors as interference, overgeneralization, and simplification. Such studies include Politzer and Ramirez's (1973) and Cohen's (1975) analyses of the speech of Mexican-American children learning English and a fine paper by Selinker, Swain, and Dumas (1975) analyzing errors in French made by English-speaking children in a language-immersion program (see Swain, 1974). A similar approach in adult studies was used by Jain (1974), Richards (1973), and Taylor (1975).

To summarize thus far, research in error analysis has revealed evidence for three general taxonomic categories of errors: interference, overgeneralization, and simplification. Of these error types, interference errors do not appear with strikingly high frequency. Second-language learners make a large number of overgeneralization and simplification errors; they bear a striking resemblance to errors made by first-language learners. And finally, there appear to be errors which are unique to second-language learners. These findings are of interest because they suggest the reality of distinct processes resulting in the respective types of errors. It is difficult, however, to see how the extent to which these error types occur would be of any empirical value until they are weighted according to their relative opportunities for occurrence. Such attempts, and also attempts at classifying errors with respect to their gravity (James, 1974), should prove informative.

All of the studies cited above used cross-sectional samples; very few studies have followed Corder's (1967) suggestion that errors should be studied longitudinally. Such analyses are needed to tell us whether specific types of errors might be prevalent at specific points in the course of development and whether errors in a learner's speech disappear abruptly or gradually. One of the few studies examining the pattern of interference errors over time was carried out by Cancino (Note 1). Her subject, Marta, a five-year-old Puerto Rican girl, was acquiring English through natural exposure to the speech of English-speaking peers. The data consisted of biweekly, spontaneous speech samples of two hours each, obtained over a period of eight months. In her analysis Cancino classified all instances of possessives (excluding possessive pronouns and adjectives) as being one of the following five types:

1) possessor-possessed order, with 's supplied, e.g., "Freddie's frog,"
2) possessor-possessed with 's omitted, e.g., "Freddie frog,"
3) possessed-possessor order, with preposition of supplied, e.g., "Frog of Freddie,"
4) same as (3) except with of omitted, e.g., "Frog Freddie," or
5) possessed-possessor order, with Spanish preposition de supplied, e.g., "Frog de Freddie."

The distribution for each category, displayed in Table 1, reveals a clear pattern of development.

TABLE 1

Distribution of Possessives used by Marta. Samples are Bi-weekly.

Sample	's supplied	's omitted	of supplied	of omitted	de
1					7
2		3			8
3		1			1
4		1			
5		5			
6		7	3		
7		2	6		1
8	2	1			
9	5	1			
10	7				
11	9				
12	8	1	1		
13	7		1		
14	5		1		1
15	5	1			

Source: Cancino (Note I).

236

First, the Spanish word *de* is used in producing English utterances (Type 5). Next, word order indicates the appearance of obligatory contexts for the English form *'s* —that is, contexts in which adult norms clearly require the form (Type 2). After that, *of* replaces *de* (Type 3) and finally *'s* is gradually supplied in obligatory contexts (Type 1). As far as we are aware, this is one of the clearest empirical illustrations of an interplay between the native language and the target language. Two points should be made here. Interference errors, at least for the possessive form, appear primarily in the earliest stages of acquisition. If, for example, Marta's speech had been sampled at a later point in development as part of a cross-sectional study, interference errors might not have been found. In addition, errors do not seem to disappear abruptly. On the contrary, use of the correct forms appears to be quite variable, and development is gradual.

The pattern of gradual acquisition can be illustrated graphically. Figure 1 plots curves for several grammatical forms acquired by Uguisu, a five-year-old Japanese girl learning English in a natural setting, who was observed over a fifteen-month period (Hakuta, 1976). The graph plots over time the percentage of instances

FIGURE 1

Acquisition curves for the three allomorphs of be *(am, is, are) as the auxiliary to the verb* gonna *(e.g., I'm gonna eat this one) in Uguisu, plotted as percentage supplied in obligatory contexts over time. Each sample represents a two-week interval. (Hakuta, 1975)*

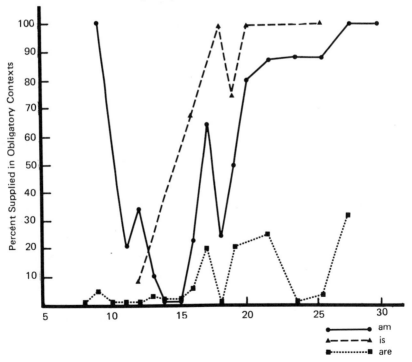

Source: Hakuta, 1975.

when a given form was supplied in obligatory contexts. In terms of errors, each curve represents the complement of errors of omission for a given morpheme. It is clear in this case that for each linguistic item errors disappear slowly and gradually. This pattern, which is characteristic of first-language acquisition (Brown, 1973), may very well hold for second-language learners' acquisition of any sort of linguistic item (Cazden, Cancino, Rosansky, & Schumann, 1975; Hakuta, 1975). Such variability in the usage of linguistic forms, even for a single learner at a given point in development, makes it difficult, if not impossible, to write grammars for corpora of utterances.

The above studies examined errors in production, but it is possible that learners might simply avoid certain linguistic structures on which they would be likely to make errors. Perhaps learners avoid particular structures due to differences between their native language and the target language. Error analysis cannot detect this type of language transfer. Schachter (1974) has provided some convincing evidence of such avoidance by looking at relative-clause constructions in the English compositions of adult learners. Using contrastive analysis, Schachter predicted positive transfer of such construction interference for one group and negative transfer for the other. Surprisingly, the negative-transfer group made fewer errors than the positive-transfer group, which suggests that there was no interference. This counter-intuitive result, however, can be accounted for by the simple fact that the group for which positive transfer was predicted produced twice as many relative-clause constructions as the group for which negative transfer was predicted. The negative-transfer group made fewer errors because they were avoiding such constructions, a fact that the traditional method of error analysis would have obscured. Recently, Kleinmann (1976) found that groups of adult Arabic and Spanish speakers learning English avoided producing a variety of constructions (passives, infinitival complements, direct-object pronouns, and present progressives) for which contrastive analysis predicted difficulties. Hakuta (1976) compared relative-clause constructions in the spontaneous speech of his subject, Uguisu, with those of Cancino's subject, Marta, and found that, as predicted by contrastive analysis, Marta produced more relative clauses. Other writers have also suggested that avoidance may account for some of their data at both the syntactic (Swain, Note 2) and the lexical levels (Tarone, Frauenfelder, & Selinker, 1976).

Contrastive analysis was, in effect, consumed by error analysis because the evidence of interference errors it used failed to account for the learner's non-interference errors. Along similar lines, error analysis does not appear to provide a methodology with adequate sensitivity to detect phenomena such as structural avoidance. With increasing sophistication in the methods available to infer knowledge from performance, error analysis is currently in the process of being incorporated within an attempt to describe the learner's overall performance, not necessarily restricting the scope of analysis to errors alone. This line of work, *performance analysis* (Svartvik, 1973), once again bears the marks of work in first-language acquisition.

Performance Analysis

At the time that researchers of second-language acquisition were focusing on error analysis, first-language-acquisition researchers were beginning to provide rather elegant descriptions of the development of linguistic structures in children. Two studies in particular have had a profound influence in shaping the direction of second-language-acquisition research: **Klima** and Bellugi's (1966) study on the acquisition of negation and Brown's (1973) study on the acquisition order of grammatical morphemes. Both studies based their analyses of performance on longitudinal spontaneous-speech samples from three children—Adam, Eve, and Sarah—learning English as their first language. The studies were important in that they were longitudinal, and documented regularities across children in the acquisition of grammatical morphemes and negation. For the first-language-acquisition researcher these findings were appealing because they hinted at universal aspects in first-language-acquisition processes. For the second-language-acquisition researcher the studies provided norms against which to compare the acquisition of the same structures in second-language learners of English. The research also provided the motivation and methodology to search for universal orders of acquisition of structures across second-language learners. This method was a novel way of testing for the role of language transfer.

Within the framework of performance analysis there has been considerable research on the acquisition of negation and grammatical morphemes in second-language learners of English. We restrict our review to these two types of structures. Less studied, but equally interesting for analysis are *prefabricated utterances,* utterances that are learned as wholes without knowledge of internal structure but that have high functional value in communication. We will end our discussion of performance analysis with a consideration of such prefabricated utterances.

Negation

Klima and Bellugi (1966) described characteristics of three stages in the development of English negation among first-language learners. In Stage I children's negation consists of a negative particle—generally, "no"—placed outside the sentence nucleus to produce such utterances as "No Mommy go" and "no eat." In Stage II the negative element moves into the sentence nucleus and takes forms such as "can't," "not," and "don't" (as in "Mommy don't like tapioca"). However, these negative elements are not full auxiliary verbs, since they lack inflection and flexibility. In Stage III the full form with inflection for tense and number is used.

Among studies of the development of negation in second-language learners, Milon's (1974) report on Ken, a five-year-old Japanese boy learning English in Hawaii, has attracted considerable attention in the literature. Milon claimed that it was possible to apply Klima and Bellugi's (1966) stages for the development of negation in first-language learners in order to summarize Ken's development. He therefore concluded that Ken acquired the English negation system in the same way as first-language learners. Milon's application of Klima and Bellugi's stages to his data involved dividing the protocols into three periods roughly corresponding to the first-language stages. In his tables he reports the percentage of utterances within each of these periods that are accountable by the rules for each of the first-language stages.

In order for Milon's claim to be justified, there must be a majority of utterances within each of Ken's periods to be accounted for by the rules of the corresponding first-language stage. Even a cursory examination of Milon's published tables, however, indicates that this is not the case. The Stage I rule, which involves placing the negative particle outside the sentence nucleus, accounts for well over half the utterances not only for Ken's period I, but also for periods II and III as well. In addition, only 9 percent of the utterances within Ken's Stage III are accounted for by Klima and Bellugi's Stage III rules.

Cazden et al. (1975) conducted a rigorous descriptive study of negation in the acquisition of English by six native speakers of Spanish: two adults, two adolescents, and two children. For each sample they calculated the proportion of occurrence for each of four utterance types and their relative frequency over time. Each of these utterances "peaked" in usage at a certain point in acquisition. Although some subjects never attained the more advanced forms, the order in which the forms emerged was the same for all subjects. In the first form of negation to appear, "no" preceded the verb, such as in "Carolina no go to play." Notice that this form corresponds to Klima and Bellugi's Stage II rule in that the negative element is internal to the sentence (*no + verb*). There was no evidence that these second-language learners went through anything resembling Klima and Bellugi's Stage I, where the negative element is external to the sentence nucleus. The next acquired form was characterized by utterances in which "don't" preceded the verb, such as "He don't like it." The third form, *aux-neg*, included all negative auxiliaries, such as "can't" and "won't," but not the inflected forms of "don't." The final form, which Cazden and colleagues called *analyzed don't*, was essentially the full adult system. For illustrative purposes we include the graph of one of their subjects, Marta, in Figure 2.

Cazden et al. (1975) argue on the basis of their data that the *no + verb* forms represent "the Spanish speakers' first hypothesis . . . that negation in English is like negation in Spanish, hence the learners place *no* in front of the verb" (p. 32). This finding would easily have been obscured had the researchers simply classified learners' utterances according to Klima and Bellugi's stages, since *no + verb, don't + verb,* and *aux-neg* all correspond to their Stage II, and *analyzed don't* occurs in Stage III. This might have forced the conclusion that there was no transfer from Spanish. Other studies have also noted *no + verb* utterances in Spanish speakers learning English (Adams, 1974; Butterworth, 1972; Wong-Fillmore, 1976).

There is an alternative explanation for the *no + verb* construction other than as the product of transfer from Spanish. Klima and Bellugi (1966), Bloom (1970), and Lord (1974) have all reported such forms in the speech of first-language learners. Perhaps it is not necessary to invoke transfer from Spanish to explain these utterances. Data from Gillis and Weber's (1976) two Japanese children and from Uguisu (Hakuta, 1976), however, suggest the transfer interpretation to be the correct one. None of the three children produced the *no + verb* construction, thus making this form likely to be unique to speakers of Spanish. Milon (1974) reports the construction of his Japanese subject, Ken, but there is a simple explanation: Ken was exposed to Hawaiian Creole English, which has this form of negation.

FIGURE 2

*Development of negation in Marta showing proportion of each negating device to total
negatives in each sample.*

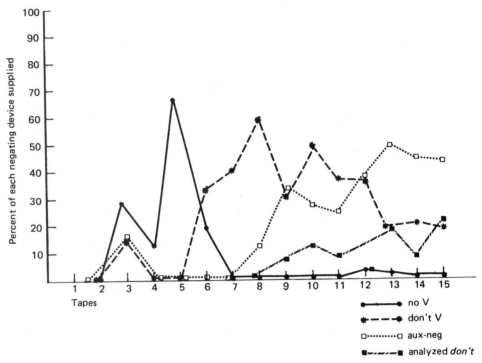

Source: Cazden et al., 1975.

Where does this leave us with respect to the development of negation? We now feel confident that *no + verb,* due to language transfer, is a common developmental step in Spanish speakers learning English. It is worth emphasizing once again that if Cazden et al. (1975) had simply tried to categorize their data into Klima and Bellugi's stages for first-language learners, this finding would not have been revealed. Their conclusion would have been that the learners went through Klima and Bellugi's Stages II and III. Indeed, this conclusion appears to be consistent with all the studies reported above, but it is too general to be of any value. All it tells us is that at first the auxiliary verb (e.g., "don't," "isn't") is unmarked for person or tense, and later that it becomes fully marked. There is no evidence for Stage I, which is theoretically the most interesting stage.

Before closing this section on negation, it should be pointed out that the universality of Klima and Bellugi's stages has been questioned even in first-language learners. Bloom (1970) and Lord (1974), for example, failed to find evidence for Stage I in their subjects. It is easy to overlook the fact that research in first-language acquisition is also still in its infancy. Owing to the tentative nature of the first-language findings, the second-language researcher needs to approach the task of comparing the two processes with extreme caution.

Grammatical Morphemes

With the exception of work by Cazden et al. (1975) the first- and second-language studies mentioned above were distributional, but not in a rigorously quantitative sense. If we are to obtain more accurate descriptions of learner performance, quantitative studies are particularly important. Grammatical morphemes, which include the articles (*a, the*), the copula and auxiliary *be*, and the noun and verb inflections, lend themselves to quantitative analyses. They afford a particular advantage to the researcher because of their high frequency, which is generally independent of the topic of discourse. Furthermore, contexts where they are obligatory (i.e., clearly required according to adult standards) are easily identifiable. For example, "two book" clearly requires the plural morpheme-*s*.

Brown (1973) analyzed fourteen morphemes in data collected longitudinally from three unacquainted native speakers, Adam, Eve, and Sarah. Defining acquisition as the point at which a given morpheme occurred in more than 90 percent of obligatory contexts for three consecutive samples, he found that they were acquired in a roughly invariant order. De Villiers and de Villiers (1973) substantiated this finding in a larger, cross-sectional first-language sample. When Brown (1973) analyzed these morphemes according to semantic complexity and transformational cumulative complexity, he found that both factors predicted the obtained order but that they could not be separated.

Since the findings on first-language learners were so dramatic and the method was easily applicable to second-language speech samples, a plethora of performance studies on second-language learners has been carried out in the last three years. Some have been longitudinal (Hakuta, 1974a, 1976; Gillis, 1975; Rosansky, 1976; Cancino, Note 1; Mulford, Note 3) and others cross-sectional (Bailey, Madden, & Krashen, 1974; Dulay & Burt, 1973, 1974a, 1974c; Larsen-Freeman, Note 4). Longitudinal second-language studies generally have determined the order of acquisition of grammatical morphemes according to Brown's 90 percent criterion described above. In the cross-sectional research the standard procedure is to rank-order the morphemes according to the performance of the entire group. The latter procedure, of course, assumes that all individuals in the sample exhibit the same acquisition order. After obtaining a rank order in either longitudinal or cross-sectional studies, a comparison can be made across learners with different native languages.

Dulay and Burt (1974a) compared the order of acquisition of eleven morphemes for a group of Chinese and Spanish children learning English. They found the order of acquisition to be nearly identical between the two groups, although it was quite different from that established for children learning English as a first language (Brown, 1973; de Villiers & de Villiers, 1973). This similarity in the orders is a striking result in light of the differences between Chinese and Spanish. For example, Chinese, unlike Spanish, has no linguistic marking equivalent to English articles, but both groups performed equally well in supplying these morphemes. A more astonishing result has been obtained from adults receiving formal instruction in English as a second language. The order obtained was again approximately the same as the order found by Dulay and Burt, despite the fact that these adults spoke various native languages (Bailey, Madden, & Krashen, 1974; Larsen-Freeman, Note 4).

Complicating the results in the above studies is the fact that the speech samples were not spontaneous but were elicited with a device called the Bilingual Syntax Measure (BSM) (Burt, Dulay, & Hernandez-Chavez, 1973). One BSM procedure involves asking the subject in the pretest to point to each object in a set of cartoon pictures with the request, "Show me the ——." Perhaps the reason why articles are easy in this task is that they are modeled for the subjects. Thus, the test itself may have influenced the outcome. A pilot investigation by Porter (Note 5) of children learning English as their first language buttresses this idea. Porter administered the BSM with these children and found their order resembled the second-language-learner's order more than it did the order found by Brown!

Rosansky (1976) questioned whether results obtained from a cross-sectional study would correlate well with a longitudinally derived acquisition order. Using longitudinal data from Jorge, a native Spanish-speaking adolescent, she compared the order of acquisition of the morphemes (longitudinal) with the relative accuracy of the use of the morphemes at a given point in development (cross-sectional). Rosansky found that Jorge's longitudinal order did not correlate with his cross-sectional order, and thus she concluded that cross-sectional orders could not be assumed to be the same as longitudinal orders.

However, there are two problems with Rosansky's results. First, she was able to compare the order of only six morphemes, since Jorge did not attain the 90 percent criterion longitudinally for the other morphemes studied. Second, Jorge was supplying all six morphemes in well over 90 percent of their obligatory contexts by the time of the cross-sectional sample. Since grammatical morphemes in general tend to fluctuate within the range between 90 and 100 percent once they attain the 90 percent criterion, Rosansky's failure to find a correlation with the longitudinal order could have been the result of this random fluctuation.

If we compare the order of acquisition of grammatical morphemes for Rosansky's subject, Jorge, with the order obtained in the Dulay and Burt study, the Spearman rank-order correlation coefficient (rho) is +.91. Cancino (Note 1) found that the longitudinal order for Marta compared favorably with Jorge's (rho = +.88) and correlates highly with that of Dulay and Burt's subjects as well (rho = +.93). Another piece of evidence comes from Mulford (Note 3), who studied the longitudinal-acquisition order for Steinar, an Icelandic boy. The correlation coefficients of Steinar's order with the orders of Jorge, Marta, and Dulay and Burt's subjects respectively are +.90, +.85, and +.82. Thus it might seem that there exists a universal order for acquisition of these morphemes.

The existence of a universal order, however, is not supported by analyses of Uguisu's longitudinal order (Hakuta, 1974a, 1976). Resembling none of the above orders, Uguisu's development indicates some interference from Japanese which does not have articles and plurals. A comparison of Uguisu's order with those of two Japanese children studied longitudinally by Gillis (1975) reveals that the three children's orders all differ and that none of them correlates with Dulay and Burt's subjects' order either. One reason for this lack of similarity may be that

Gillis (1975) only reports on the verb-related morphemes and excludes some morphemes such as articles and plurals. Nevertheless, if there indeed is a universal order, the results should not vary according to the particular items chosen for investigation.

We can probably conclude, though, that among all second-language learners of English there may be a tendency to acquire morphemes in a certain order, determined by factors such as their frequency of occurrence (Larsen-Freeman, 1976) and their perceptual salience or distinctiveness (Wagner-Gough & Hatch, 1976). For example, the progressive -ing may be acquired early because of its high salience and high frequency, while the regular third-person indicative -s (as in "she comes") with its low frequency and low salience is acquired relatively late.

Another factor influencing acquisition, semantic complexity of the morphemes (Brown, 1973), may vary depending on the learner's native language. For example, the English articles a and the ("a book" versus "the book"), require rather sophisticated semantic discriminations for their proper use (Brown, 1973; Maratsos, 1971). If a native language makes those contrasts, as Spanish and French do, the learner may already possess the semantic discriminations necessary for using English articles. On the other hand, a native speaker of Japanese or Chinese does not make those discriminations and must learn them in order to make the definite/indefinite contrast. That articles in English have the highest frequency of all grammatical morphemes and appear in a highly predictable position, before nouns, also affects their acquisition. Thus articles may appear early even in Japanese or Chinese learners but with confusions along the definite/indefinite dimension.

Although articles appeared early in her speech, Uguisu had great difficulty with the definite/indefinite contrast, as evidenced by many errors (Hakuta, 1976). Marta and Jorge, on the other hand, acquired articles early and had little difficulty with the definite/indefinite distinction. Their greatest problem appeared to be within the indefinite category, where they initially used one rather than a, reflecting transfer from the Spanish indefinite articles un or una. Frauenfelder (1974), who studied the acquistion of gender marking among English-speaking children in a French immersion program, found that although the children made many errors in gender on articles, they never confused the definite/indefinite contrast. That Dulay and Burt found their Chinese learners acquiring articles so early might be attributed to the scoring method: they did not differentiate between a and the. Finally Fathman (Note 6), who administered an oral-production task (SLOPE) to Korean- and Spanish-speaking children, found a generally similar ordering on various grammatical forms for these two groups. A close look at her data, however, shows a very large discrepancy in the children's performance on articles: the Korean children, whose language has no article equivalents, performed poorly.

Thus, we conceive the order of acquisition of English grammatical morphemes as resulting from an interplay of at least two factors. One factor, consisting of variables such as frequency and salience, seems to direct the order of acquisition toward a universal order. But a second factor, transfer from the native language, modulates the order so as to produce differences between learners of different language backgrounds.

Routine Formulas and Prefabricated Utterances

Since grammatical rules operate on units or constituents within a sentence, it was only natural for researchers interested in grammatical structure to focus on those utterances that indicated the learner's knowledge of individual constituents. In so doing, they excluded from their analysis utterances that seemed to be routine formulas (such as "What's this?" and "I don't know") learned as wholes through imitation. Huang (1971) related a delightful anecdote about the use of such a routine formula. Paul, a Taiwanese boy, used his first English utterance, "Get out of here," as a formula in roughly appropriate situations for warding off unwanted company. Another example is one of Uguisu's first utterances, "Not in particular!" which was used for the purpose of turning down offers of food. Variants of routine formulas are prefabricated patterns (Hakuta, 1974b), sentences such as "This is ——," where nouns can be inserted into the slots. Most investigators have reported in passing the existence of either routines or prefabricated patterns (Adams, 1974; Butterworth, 1972; Cazden et al., 1975). These patterns have not received close attention, because the central focus of study has been on grammatical structure. This lack of emphasis on prefabricated forms was reinforced by the apparent failure of the process of imitation to account for language acquisition (Chomsky, 1959; Ervin-Tripp, 1964; but see Bloom, Hood, & Lightbown, 1974).

If language were to be viewed from the perspective of communication, however, prefabricated utterances take on an added theoretical significance (Hakuta, 1976). Huang (1971) found a considerable amount of prefabricated utterances in Paul's speech. This led him to postulate imitation as an important process, although it was considered to be less important than, and independent of, the process of rule-formation. Uguisu's speech, particularly in the early stages, also contained many prefabricated patterns (Hakuta, 1974b). Such patterns may have value in sustaining second-language learners' motivation by enabling them early on to express a variety of meanings. Since the "breakdown" of these forms is gradual and similar to the acquisition of grammatical rules, the use of prefabricated patterns may motivate the learner to search for internal structure (Hakuta, 1976).

In a recent dissertation on English acquisition by five Spanish-speaking children, Wong-Fillmore (1976) found that over half of the children's utterances contained prefabricated forms. She argued that through the gradual analysis of such forms, later linguistic structure developed: "All of the constituents of the formula become freed from the original construction, [and] what the learner has left is an abstract structure consisting of a pattern or rule by which he can construct like utterances" (p. 645). For example, Wong-Fillmore's subject Nora learned the question, "How do you do dese?" early in development and used only this form. During the next period she attached a noun or prepositional phrase to this form, and created such questions as "How do you do dese flower power?" and "How do you do dese in English?" Later she learned to slot other verbs into the pattern "How do you

———?" and produced such forms as "How do you like to be a cookie cutter?" Nora then began alternating "How do you ———" with "How did you ———." In the last period of observation, she was constructing utterances like "How you make it?" and "How will take and paste?" Although Fillmore's examples are provocative, the principles used by the learner to analyze the prefabricated forms need to be specified; the traditional problem of the emergence of syntax remains to be solved.

Discourse Analysis

The focus of research in both first- and second-language acquisition has shifted only recently to language in the social context. It would be somewhat unfair, however, to claim that earlier researchers did not pay attention to the role of discourse in the language acquisition. Brown (1968), for example, succinctly stated:

> It may be as difficult to derive a grammar from unconnected sentences as it would be to derive the invariance of quantity and number from the simple look of liquids in containers and objects in space. The changes produced by pouring back and forth, by gathering together and spreading apart are the data that most strongly suggest the conservation of quantity and number. The changes produced in sentences as they move between persons in discourse may be the richest data for the discovery of grammar. (p. 288)

Current work on discourse analysis can be roughly divided into two approaches (de Villiers & de Villiers, in press). Researchers employing the first approach (Garvey, 1975; Keenan, 1975) investigate rules of discourse, such as turn taking in dialogue. Discourse rules are considered to be another aspect of language that the child must master more or less independently of syntax. The second approach (Antinucci & Parisi, 1975; Bates, 1976) assumes fundamentally that all language is pragmatic, obeying "rules governing the use of language in context" (Bates, 1976, p. 420). Researchers operating in this vein have investigated the emergence of various pragmatic functions, such as declaratives and imperatives, in very young children. They claim that syntax and semantics can ultimately be seen as derivatives of pragmatics, although it is difficult at this point to envision the specific process of derivation.

In the case of the second-language learner, we certainly would not expect to be able to study the emergence of the various pragmatic functions, since they are by definition universal and, presumably, acquired at a very early age. An interesting approach, however, would be to analyze a given pragmatic function over time. Tracing the development of the linguistic forms that the learner uses for the expression of a function might well reveal orderly and lawful patterns. In addition, such an analysis might reveal interesting differences across native speakers whose languages differ in the linguistic forms chosen for the same pragmatic act. In a sense, this approach would be a contrastive analysis of the way different languages map pragmatic functions onto linguistic forms. We believe this would be an extremely fruitful line of investigation, but it has not been pursued. What is sorely lacking before any such inquiry is an explicitly spelled out theory of pragmatics (Fraser, Note 7). The few studies on discourse reported in the literature have made only preliminary attempts at outlining the structure of discourse and the mechanisms underlying its regulation.

Hatch (1978) found that Huang's (1971) subject Paul initiated discourse by first identifying the topic, waiting for the other person to attend or speak, and then making some further comment. Repetition of the other speaker's previous utterance, (Hatch, 1978; Keller-Cohen, 1978) have received some attention. We suspect that this is the major way in which prefabricated forms (Hakuta, 1974b; Wong-Fillmore, 1976) enter the learner's speech repertoire. A variant on the process of repetition is incorporation (Wagner-Gough, 1975; Wagner-Gough & Hatch, 1976), as illustrated in the following dialogue with Homer, an Iranian child:

> Adult: Where are you going?
> Homer: Where are you going is house.
> (Wagner-Gough & Hatch, 1976, p. 304)

Hatch (1978) has noted that a topic is broken into parts dictated by the constraints of conversation. The following example taken from a Japanese child, Takahiro, shows the learner taking apart and reassembling these various parts in the course of dialogue (Hatch, 1978).

> Takahiro: this
> broken
>
> Adult: broken
>
> Takahiro: broken
> This /iz/ broken.
> broken
>
> Adult: Upside down.
>
> Takahiro: upside down
> this broken
> upside down
> broken

Based on such examples, Hatch speculates that "one learns how to do conversation, one learns how to interact verbally, and out of this interaction syntactic structures are developed." This is essentially the same argument made by Wong-Fillmore (1976) for the emergence of syntax, and it is subject to the same criticism: the ultimate question of how exactly this happens has not been addressed. Furthermore, accounting for interference errors remains problematic, since such errors are aspects of the internal organization of language.

Implicit in studies of discourse is the importance of input. Unfortunately, rigorous empirical studies of the characteristics of input to the learner are nowhere to be seen in the second-language literature. The pedagogical implications of such studies would be powerful, since classroom instruction is essentially the manipulation of input variables. Although first-language-learning research has greatly influenced second-language research, the numerous studies on mother-to-child speech in first-language acquisition (DePaulo & Bonvillian, in press; Snow & Ferguson, in press) have not generated similar studies in second-language acquisition. In an exploratory second-language-learning study, Hatch, Shapira, and Wagner-Gough (Note 8), reinforce the need for future input studies. Anecdotally comparing the input for children with that for adults, they found that the speech addressed to children by native speakers resembled mother-to-child speech reported in the first-language literature: it was simple, short, grammatical, and restricted to here-and-now topics. The speech to adults, on the other hand, possessed many of the characteristics of "foreigner talk": the omission of inflections, an abundance of pauses, and many complex sentence forms (Ferguson, 1977). Furthermore, the topic of conversation often referred to something neither immediate nor present. Whatever the determining sociolinguistic factors, these observations by Hatch and his coworkers should encourage further research in this area. Such investigations may ultimately help explain the difficulty that adults have in acquiring a second language.

The Future

Each of the four trends covered in this paper can be seen as successive attempts by researchers to create an adequate representation of the second-language-acquisition process. We began by describing contrastive analysis, which required only a comparison of the linguistic structures of the two languages. We end with the most recent trend, discourse analysis, in which the learner's status as a social being occupies center stage. Although it may take years of hard work before we develop a rigorous and sophisticated methodology for discourse analysis, the rewards will be great. For the results would create a solid link between the observed acquisition of the linguistic structures of the second language and the yet-to-be-determined variables involved in discourse.

Schumann (1975, 1976) has recently argued that there is a correlation between social factors and the degree to which one acquires a second language. These social variables rest at the heart of second-language acquisition; they determine the circumstances requiring people to acquire a second language. Along similar lines, Gardner and his colleagues (Gardner & Lambert, 1972; Gardner, 1973) have extensively explored the relationships of attitudes and motivation to degree of proficiency in a second language. While it may be difficult to see a direct relationship between these social factors and their supposed effects on the second-language-acquisition process, it is not difficult to imagine social factors influencing the types of discourse in which learners engage. This relationship is rigorously definable. Thus, we see discourse analysis as an empirical bridge to our next potential level of analysis, which might be called *sociolinguistic analysis*. Analysis at this level, we believe, would give greater acknowledgment to the complexity of the second-language-acquisition process.

248

Reference Notes

1. Cancino, H. *Grammatical morphemes in second language acquistion—Marta.* Unpublished manuscript, 1976. (Available from Harvard University, Graduate School of Education, Cambridge, Mass.).
2. Swain, M. *Changes in error: Random or systematic?* Paper presented at the Fourth International Congress of Applied Linguistics, Stuttgart, August 1975.
3. Mulford, R. Personal Communication, December 15, 1976.
4. Larsen-Freeman. D. *The acquistion of grammatical morphemes by adult ESL students.* Paper presented at the Ninth Annual TESOL Convention, Los Angeles, April 1975.
5. Porter, J. *A cross-sectional study of morpheme acquisition in first language learners.* Unpublished manuscript, 1975. (Available from Department of Psychology and Social Relations, Harvard University, Cambridge, Mass.).
6. Fathman, A. *Language background, age, and the order of English structures.* Paper presented at the Ninth Annual TESOL Convention, Los Angeles, April 1975.
7. Fraser, E. *On requesting: An essay in pragmatics.* Book in preparation, 1977.
8. Hatch, E., Shapira, R., & Gough, J. *Foreigner-talk discourse.* Unpublished paper, 1975. (Available from English Department, University of California at Los Angeles, Los Angeles, Calif.).

References

Adams, M. *Second language acquistion in children: A study in experimental methods: Observations of spontaneous speech and controlled production tests.* Unpublished master's thesis, University of California at Los Angeles, 1974.

Alatis, J. *Nineteenth annual round table meeting on linguistics and language studies: Contrastive linguistics and its pedagogical implications.* Washington, D.C.: Georgetown University Press, 1968.

Antinucci, F., & Parisi, D. Early semantic development in child language. In E. H. Lenneberg & E. Lenneberg (Eds.), *Foundations of language development: A multidisciplinary approach* (Vol. 1). New York: Academic Press, 1975.

Bailey, N., Madden, C., & Krashen, S. Is there a "natural sequence" in adult second language learning? *Language Learning*, 1974, 24, 233–243.

Bates, E. Pragmatics and sociolinguistics in child language. In D. Morehead & A. Morehead (Eds.), *Normal and deficient child language.* Baltimore, Md.: University Park Press, 1976.

Bloom, L. *Language development: Form and function in emerging grammars.* Cambridge, Mass.: M.I.T. Press, 1970.

Bloom, L., Hood, L., & Lightbown, P. Imitation in language development: If, when and why? *Cognitive Psychology*, 1974, 6, 380–420.

Brown, R. The development of Wh questions in child speech. *Journal of Verbal Learning and Verbal Behavior*, 1968, 7, 279–290.

Brown, R. *A first language: The early stages.* Cambridge, Mass.: Harvard University Press, 1973.

Brown, R., & Bellugi, U. Three processes in the acquisition of syntax. *Harvard Educational Review*, 1964, 34, 133–151. (a)

Brown, R., & Bellugi, U. The acquisition of language. *Monographs of the Society for Research in Child Development*, 1964, 29 (No. 1). (b)

Burt, M. K., Dulay, H. C., & Hernandez-Chavez, E. *Bilingual syntax measure.* New York: Harcourt Brace Jovanovich, 1973.

Butterworth, G. *A Spanish-speaking adolescent's acquisition of English syntax.* Unpublished master's thesis, University of California at Los Angeles, 1972.

Cazden, C., Cancino, H., Rosansky, E., & Schumann, J. *Second language acquisition sequences in children, adolescents, and adults.* Cambridge, Mass.: Harvard University, Graduate School of Education, 1975. (ERIC Document Reproduction Service No. ED 123 873).

Chomsky, N. *Syntactic structures.* The Hague: Mouton, 1957.

Chomsky, N. A review of *Verbal Behavior* by B. F. Skinner. *Language,* 1959, **35**, 26–59.

Cohen, A. D. *A sociolinguistic approach to bilingual education: Experiments in the American Southwest.* Rowley, Mass.: Newbury House, 1975.

Corder, S. P. The significance of learners' errors. *International Review of Applied Linguistics,* 1967, **5**, 161–170.

Corder, S. P. Idiosyncratic dialects and error analysis. *International Review of Applied Linguistics,* 1971, **9**, 147–160.

Corder, S. P. Error analysis, interlanguage, and second language acquistion. *Language Teaching and Linguistics,* 1975, **14**, 201–218.

DePaulo, B., & Bonvillian, J. The effect on language development of the special characterization of speech addressed to children. *Journal of Psycholinguistic Research,* in press.

de Villiers, J., & de Villiers, P. A cross-sectional study of the acquisition of grammatical morphemes in child speech. *Journal of Psycholinguistic Research,* 1973, **2**, 267–278.

de Villiers, J., & de Villiers, P. Syntax and semantics in the first two years: The output of form and function and the form and function of the input. In L. L. Lloyd & F. Minifie (Eds.), *Communicative & cognitive abilities: Early behavioral Assessment* (NICHD Mental Retardation Research Series). Baltimore: University Park Press, 1978.

Dulay, H., & Burt, M. Goofing: An indicator of children's second language learning strategies. *Language Learning,* 1972, **22**, 235–252.

Dulay, H., & Burt, M. Should we teach children syntax? *Language Learning,* 1973, **23**, 245–258.

Dulay, H., & Burt, M. Natural sequences in child second language acquisition. *Language Learning,* 1974, **24**, 37–53. (a)

Dulay, H., & Burt, M. Errors and strategies in child second language acquisition. *TESOL Quarterly,* 1974, **8**, 129–136. (b)

Dulay, H., & Burt, M. A new perspective on the creative construction process in child second language acquisition. *Language Learning,* 1974, **24**, 253–278. (c)

Duskova, L. On sources of errors in foreign languages. *International Review of Applied Linguistics,* 1969, **7**, 11–36.

Ervin-Tripp, S. Imitation and structural change in children's language. In E. Lenneberg (Ed.), *New directions in the study of language.* Cambridge, Mass.: M.I.T. Press, 1964.

Ferguson, C. A. Toward a characterization of English foreigner talk. In C. E. Snow & C. A. Ferguson (Eds.), *Talking to children: Language input and acquisition.* Cambridge, Eng.: Cambridge University Press, 1977.

Frauenfelder, U. *The acquisition of French gender in Toronto French immersion school children.* Unpublished senior honors thesis, University of Washington, 1974.

Fries, C. *Teaching and learning English as a foreign language.* Ann Arbor: University of Michigan Press, 1972. (Originally published, 1945)

Gardner, R. C. Attitudes and motivation: Their role in second language acquisition. In J. Oller & J. Richards, *Focus on the learner: Pragmatic perspectives for the language teacher.* Rowley, Mass.: Newbury House, 1973.

Gardner, R. C., & Lambert, W. *Attitudes and motivation in second language learning.* Rowley, Mass.: Newbury House, 1972.

Garvey, C. Requests and responses in children's speech. *Journal of Child Language,* 1975, **2**, 41–63.

Gillis, M. *The acquisition of the English verbal system by two Japanese children in a natural setting.* Unpublished master's thesis, McGill University, 1975.

Gillis, M., & Weber, R. The emergence of sentence modalities in the English of Japanese-speaking children. *Language Learning,* 1976, **26**, 77–94.

Hakuta, K. A preliminary report on the development of grammatical morphemes in a Japanese girl learning English as a second language. *Working Papers on Bilingualism,* 1974, **3**, 18–43. (a)

Hakuta, K. Prefabricated patterns and the emergence of structure in second language acquisition. *Language Learning,* 1974, **24**, 287–297. (b)

Hakuta, K. Learning to speak a second language: What exactly does the child learn? In D. P. Dato (Ed.), *Developmental psycholinguistics: Theory and application.* Washington, D. C.: Georgetown University Press, 1975.

Hakuta, K. Becoming bilingual: A case study of a Japanese child learning English. *Language Learning,* 1976, **26**, 321–351.

Hatch, E. Discourse analysis. In E. Hatch (Ed.), *Studies in second language acquisition: A book of readings.* Rowley, Mass.: Newbury House, 1978.

Huang, J. *A Chinese child's acquisition of English syntax.* Unpublished master's thesis, University of California at Los Angeles, 1971.

Jain, M. Error analysis: Source, cause and significance. In J. Richards (Ed.), *Error analysis: Perspectives on second language acquisition.* London: Longman, 1974.

James, C. Linguistic measures for error gravity. *AVLA Journal,* 1974, **12**, 3–9.

Keenan, E. Conversational competence in children. *Journal of Child Language,* 1975, **2**, 163–183.

Keller-Cohen, D. Repetition in the non-native discourse: Its relation to text unification and conversational structure. In O. Freedle (Ed.), *Discourse processing: A multidisciplinary approach.* Hillsdale, N. J.: Ablex Publishing Co., 1978.

Kleinmann, H. *Avoidance behavior in adult second language acquisition.* Unpublished doctoral dissertation. University of Pittsburgh, 1976.

Klima, E., & Bellugi, U. Syntactic regularities in the speech of children. In J. Lyons & R. Wales (Eds.), *Psycholinguistic papers.* Edinburgh: Edinburgh University Press, 1966.

Krashen, S., Madden, C., & Bailey, N. Theoretical aspects of grammatical sequencing. In M. Burt & H. Dulay (Eds.), *New directions in second language learning, teaching and bilingual education.* Washington, D. C.: TESOL, 1975.

Lado, R. *Linguistics across cultures.* Ann Arbor, Mich.: University of Michigan Press, 1957.

Larsen-Freeman, D. An explanation for the morpheme acquisition order of second language learners. *Language Learning,* 1976, **26**, 125–134.

Lord, C. Variations in the acquisition of negation. *Papers and Reports on Child Language Development,* 1974, **8**, 78–86.

Maratsos, M. *The use of definite and indefinite reference in young children.* Unpublished doctoral dissertation, Harvard University, 1971.

McLaughlin, B. Second-language learning in children. *Psychological Bulletin,* 1977, **84**, 438–459.

Milon, J. The development of negation in English by a second language learner. *TESOL Quarterly,* 1974, **8**, 137–143.

Nemser, W. Approximative systems of foreign language learners. *International Review of Applied Linguistics,* 1971, **9**, 115–123.

Nickel, G. Problems of learners' difficulties in foreign language acquisition. *International Review of Applied Linguistics,* 1971, **9**, 219–227.

Olivier, D. *Stochastic grammars and language acquisition devices.* Unpublished doctoral dissertation, Harvard University, 1968.

Oller, J., & Richards, J. (Eds.). *Focus on the learner: Pragmatic perspectives for the language teacher.* Rowley, Mass.: Newbury House, 1973.

Politzer, R., & Ramirez, A. An error analysis of the spoken English of Mexican-American pupils in a bilingual school and a monolingual school. *Language Learning,* 1973, **23**, 39–61.

Richards, J. A non-contrastive approach to error analysis. In J. Oller & J. Richards (Eds.), *Focus on the learner: Pragmatic perspectives for the language teacher.* Rowley, Mass.: Newbury House, 1973.

Rivers, W. *The psychologist and the foreign language teacher*. Chicago: University of Chicago Press, 1964.

Rosansky, E. *Second language acquisition research: A question of methods*. Unpublished doctoral dissertation, Harvard University, Graduate School of Education, 1976.

Schachter, J. An error in error analysis. *Language Learning*, 1974, 24, 205–214.

Schumann, J. Affective factors and the problem of age in second language acquisition. *Language Learning*, 1975, **25**, 209–235.

Schumann, J. Social distance as a factor in second language acquisition. *Language Learning*, 1976, **26**, 135–143.

Schumann, J., & Stenson, N. (Eds.). *New frontiers in second language learning*. Rowley, Mass.: Newbury House, 1975.

Selinker, L. Interlanguage. *International Review of Applied Linguistics*, 1972, **10**, 219–231.

Selinker, L., Swain, M., & Dumas, G. The interlanguage hypothesis extended to children. *Language Learning*, 1975, 25, 139–152.

Snow, C. E., & Ferguson, C. A. (Eds.). *Talking to children: Language input and acquisition*. Cambridge, Eng.: Cambridge University Press, 1977.

Stockwell, R., Bowen, J., & Martin, J. *The grammatical structures of English and Spanish*. Chicago: University of Chicago Press, 1965.

Svartvik, J. *Errata: Papers in error analysis*. Lund, Sweden: Gleerup, 1973.

Swain, M. French immersion programs across Canada. *Canadian Modern Language Review*, 1974, **31**, 117–130.

Tarone, E. Some influences on interlanguage phonology. *Working Papers on Bilingualism*, 1976, **8**, 87–111.

Tarone, E., Frauenfelder, U., & Selinker, L., Systematicity/variability and stability/instability in interlanguage systems: More data from Toronto French immersion. In H. Brown (Ed.), *Papers in second language acquisition*. Ann Arbor, Mich.: *Language Learning*, 1976.

Taylor, B. The use of overgeneralization and transfer strategies by elementary and intermediate university students learning ESL. In M. Burt & H. Dulay (Eds.), *New directions in second language learning, teaching and bilingual education*. Washington, D. C.: TESOL, 1975.

Wagner-Gough, J. Comparative studies in second language learning. *CAL-ERIC/CLL Series on Languages and Linguistics*, 26. Arlington, Va.: Center for Applied Linguistics, 1975.

Wagner-Gough, J., & Hatch, E. The importance of input data in second language acquisition studies. *Language Learning*, 1976, **25**, 297–308.

Wardhaugh, R. The contrastive analysis hypothesis. *TESOL Quarterly*, 1970, 4, 123–130.

Whitehurst, G., Ironsmith, E., & Goldfein, M. Selective imitation of the passive construction through modelling. *Journal of Experimental Child Psychology*, 1974, **17**, 288–302.

Williams, L. *Speech perception and production as a function of exposure to a second language*. Unpublished doctoral dissertation, Harvard University, 1974.

Wong-Fillmore, L. *The second time around: Cognitive and social strategies in second language acquisition*. Unpublished doctoral dissertation, Stanford University, 1976.

Learning about Psycholinguistic Processes by Analyzing Oral Reading

KENNETH S. GOODMAN
YETTA M. GOODMAN
University of Arizona

Kenneth and Yetta Goodman argue that reading, like speaking and writing, is an active language process in which readers display their sophistication as functional psycholinguists. The authors note, however, that it is difficult to gain access to and understand these active, underlying processes. To make such processes accessible, the authors advocate the use of oral reading as a data base. The Goodmans maintain that when oral readers depart from the written text—when miscues occur— the underlying processes of reading begin to be revealed. Using examples from children and adults, the authors present a typology of miscues and demonstrate how miscues provide a window on reading and other language processes. Throughout the article the Goodmans note the implications of miscue analysis for research and teaching.

Over the past dozen years we have studied the reading process by analyzing the miscues (or unexpected responses) of subjects reading written texts. We prefer to use the word *miscue* because the term *error* has a negative connotation and history in education. Our analysis of oral reading miscues began with the foundational assumption that reading is a language process. Everything we have observed among readers from beginners to those with great proficiency supports the validity of this assumption. This analysis of miscues has been in turn the base for our development of a theory and model of the reading process.

In this paper we will argue that the analysis of oral reading offers unique opportunities for the study of linguistic and psycholinguistic processes and phenomena. We will support this contention by citing some concepts and principles that have grown out of our research.

We believe that reading is as much a language process as listening is. In a literate society there are four language processes: two are oral (speaking and listen-

Harvard Educational Review   Vol. 47   No. 3   August 1977, 317–333

ing), and two are written (writing and reading). Two are productive and two receptive. In the study and observation of productive language, we may analyze what subjects say or write; however, except for an occasional slip of the tongue, typographical error, or regression to rephrase, speech and writing offer no direct insight into the underlying process of what the speaker or writer intended to say. The study of receptive language—listening and reading—is even more difficult. Either we analyze postlistening or postreading performance, or we contrive controlled-language tasks to elicit reactions for analysis.

Reading aloud, on the other hand, involves the oral response of the reader, which can be compared to the written text. Oral readers are engaged in comprehending written language while they produce oral responses. Because an oral response is generated while meaning is being constructed, it not only is a form of linguistic performance but also provides a powerful means of examining process and underlying competence.

Consider how Peggy, a nine-year-old from Toronto, reads aloud. Peggy was chosen by her teacher as an example of a pupil reading substantially below grade level. The story she read was considered to be beyond her current instructional level. Peggy read the story hesitantly, although in places she read with appropriate expression. Below are the first fourteen sentences (S1–S14) from "The Man Who Kept House" (1964, pp. 282–283). In this and other excerpts from the story the printed text is on the left; on the right is the transcript of Peggy's oral reading.

text	*transcript*
(S1a) Once upon a time there was a woodman who thought that no one worked as hard as he did.	(S1b) Once upon a time there was a woodman. He threw . . . who thought that no one worked as hard as he did.
(S2a) One evening when he came home from work, he said to his wife, "What do you do all day while I am away cutting wood?"	(S2b) One evening when he . . . when he came home from work, he said to his wife, "I want you do all day . . . what do you do all day when I am always cutting wood?"
(S3a) "I keep house," replied the wife, "and keeping house is hard work."	(S3b) "I keep . . . I keep house," replied the wife, "and keeping . . . and keeping . . . and keeping house is and work."
(S4a) "Hard work!" said the husband.	(S4b) "Hard work!" said the husband.
(S5a) "You don't know what hard work is!	(S5b) "You don't know what hard work is!
(S6a) You should try cutting wood!"	(S6b) You should try cutting wood!"
(S7a) "I'd be glad to," said the wife.	(S7b) "I'll be glad to," said the wife.
(S8a) "Why don't you do my work some day?	(S8b) "Why don't you . . . Why don't you do my work so . . . some day?
(S9a) I'll stay home and keep house," said the woodman.	(S9b) I'll start house and keeping house," said the woodman.

(S10a) "If you stay home to do my work, you'll have to make butter, carry water from the well, wash the clothes, clean the house, and look after the baby," said the wife.

(S10b) "If you start house . . . If you start home to do my work, well you'll have to make bread, carry . . . carry water from the well, wash the clothes, clean the house, and look after the baby," said the wife.

(S11a) "I can do all that," replied the husband.

(S11b) "I can do that . . . I can do all that," replied the husband.

(S12a) "We'll do it tomorrow!"

(S12b) "Well you do it tomorrow!"

(S13a) So the next morning the wife went off to the forest.

(S13b) So the next day the wife went off to the forest.

(S14a) The husband stayed home and began to do his wife's work.

(S14b) The husband stayed home and began to do his wife's job.

Peggy's performance allows us to see a language user as a functional psycholinguist. Peggy's example is not unusual; what she does is also done by other readers. She processes graphic information: many of her miscues show a graphic relationship between the expected and observed response. She processes syntactic information: she substitutes noun for noun, verb for verb, noun phrase for noun phrase, verb phrase for verb phrase. She transforms: she omits an intensifier, changes a dependent clause to an independent clause, shifts a "wh-" question sentence to a declarative sentence. She draws on her conceptual background and struggles toward meaning, repeating, correcting, and reprocessing as necessary. She predicts grammar and meaning and monitors her own success. She builds and uses psycholinguistic strategies as she reads. In short, her miscues are far from random.

From such data one can build and test theories of syntax, semantics, cognition, comprehension, memory, language development, linguistic competence, and linguistic performance. In oral reading all the phenomena of other language processes are present or have their counterparts, but in oral reading they are accessible. The data are not controlled and clean in the experimental sense. Even young readers are not always very considerate. They do complex things for which we may be unprepared; and, not having studied the latest theories, they do not always produce confirming evidence. But they are language users in action.

Miscues and Comprehension

If we understand that the brain is the organ of human information processing, that the brain is not a prisoner of the senses but that it controls the sensory organs and selectively uses their input, then we should not be surprised that what the mouth reports in oral reading is not what the eye has seen but what the brain has generated for the mouth to report. The text is what the brain responds to; the oral output reflects the underlying competence and the psycholinguistic processes that have generated it. When expected and observed responses match, we get little insight into this process. When they do not match and a miscue results, the researcher has a window on the reading process.

Just as psycholinguists have been able to learn about the development of oral-language competence by observing the errors of young children, so we can gain insights into the development of reading competence and the control of the underlying psycholinguistic processes by studying reading miscues. We assume that both expected and unexpected oral responses to printed texts are produced through the same process. Thus, just as a three-year-old reveals the use of a rule for generating past tense by producing "throwed" for "threw" (Brown, 1973), so Peggy reveals her control of the reading process through her miscues.

We use two measures of readers' proficiency: *comprehending,* which shows the readers' concern for meaning as expressed through their miscues, and *retelling,* which shows the readers' retention of meaning. Proficient readers can usually retell a great deal of a story, and they produce miscues that do not interfere with gaining meaning. Except for S3, S8, and S9, all of Peggy's miscues produced fully acceptable sentences or were self-corrected. This suggests that Peggy's usual concern was to make sense as she read. In contrast, many nonproficient readers produce miscues that interfere with getting meaning from the story. In a real sense, then, a goal of reading instruction is not to eliminate miscues but to help readers produce the kind of miscues that characterize proficient reading.

Miscues reflect the degree to which a reader is understanding and seeking meaning. Insight can be gained into the reader's development of meaning and the reading process as a whole if miscues are examined and researchers ask: "Why did the reader make this miscue and to what extent is it like the language of the author?"

Miscue analysis requires several conditions. The written material must be new to the readers and complete with a beginning, middle, and end. The text needs to be long and difficult enough to produce a sufficient number of miscues. In addition, readers must receive no help, probe, or intrusion from the researcher. At most, if readers hesitate for more than thirty seconds, they are urged to guess, and only if hesitation continues are they told to keep reading even if it means skipping a word or phrase. Miscue analysis, in short, requires as natural a reading situation as possible.

Depending on the purpose of the research, subjects often have been provided with more than one reading task. Various fiction and nonfiction reading materials have been used, including stories and articles from basal readers, textbooks, trade books, and magazines. Subjects have been drawn from various levels in elementary, secondary, and adult populations and from a wide range of racial, linguistic, and national backgrounds. Studies have been concluded in languages other than English: Yiddish (Hodes, 1976), Polish (Romatowski, 1972), and American Sign Language (Ewoldt, 1977). Studies in German and Spanish are in progress.

The open-ended retellings used in miscue analysis are an index of comprehension. They also provide an opportunity for the researcher or teacher to gain insight into how concepts and language are actively used and developed in reading. Rather than asking direct questions that would give cues to the reader about what is significant in the story, we ask for unaided retelling. Information on the readers' understanding of the text emerges from the organization they use in retelling the story, from whether they use the author's language or their own, and from the conceptions or misconceptions they reveal. Here is the first segment of Peggy's retelling:

> um ... it was about this woodman and um ... when he ... he thought that he um ... he had harder work to do than his wife. So he went home and he told his wife, "What have you been doing all day." And then his wife told him. And then, um ... and then, he thought that it was easy work. And so ... so ... so his wife, so his wife, so she um ... so the wife said, "well so you have to keep," no ... the husband says that you have to go to the woods and cut ... and have to go out in the forest and cut wood and I'll stay home. And the next day they did that.

By comparing the story with Peggy's retelling and her miscues, researchers may interpret how much learning occurs as Peggy and the author interact. For example, although the story frequently uses "woodman" and "to cut wood," the noun used to refer to setting, "forest," is used just twice. Not only did Peggy provide evidence in her retelling that she knew that "woods" and "forest" are synonymous, but she also indicated that she knew the author's choice was "forest." The maze she worked through until she came to the author's term suggests that she was searching for the author's language. Although in much of the work on oral-language analysis mazes are not analyzed, their careful study may provide insight into oral self-correction and the speaker's intention.

There is more evidence of Peggy's awareness of the author's language. In the story the woodman is referred to as "woodman" and "husband" eight times each and as "man" four times; the wife is referred to only as "wife." Otherwise pronouns are used to refer to the husband and wife. In the retelling Peggy used "husband" and "woodman" six times and "man" only once; she called the wife only "wife." Peggy always used appropriate pronouns in referring to the husband and wife. However, when cow was the antecedent, she substituted "he" for "she" twice. (What does Peggy know about the sex of cattle?)

Comparing Peggy's miscues with her retelling gives us more information about her language processes. In reading, Peggy indicated twice that "said" suggested to her that a declarative statement should follow: One such miscue was presented above (see S2); the other occurred at the end of the story and is recorded below.

text	*transcript*
(S66a) Never again did the woodman say to his wife, "What did you do all day?"	(S66b) *Never again did the woodman say to his wife, "That he ... what did you do all day?"*

In both instances she corrected the miscues. In the retelling she indicated that after "said" she could produce a question: "And then, from then on, the husband did ... did the cutting and he never said, 'What have you been doing all day?'" Even though she had difficulty with the "wh-" question structure in her reading, she was able to develop the language knowledge necessary to produce such a structure in her retelling.

It has puzzled teachers for a long time how a reader can know something in one context but not know it in another context. Such confusion comes from the belief that reading is word recognition; on the contrary, words in different syntactic and semantic contexts become different entities for readers, and Peggy's response to "keep house" suggests this. In S3, where the clauses "I keep house" and later "and keeping house" occur for the first time, Peggy produced the appropriate responses but repeated each several times. In S9 she produced "stay home and keep house" as "start house and keeping house," and she read the first phrase in S10 as "If you start home to do my work." The phrase "keep house" is a complex one. First, to a nine-year-old "keep" is a verb that means being able to hold on to or take care of something small. Although "keeping pets" is still used to mean taking care of, "keeping house" is no longer a common idiom in American or Canadian English. When "stay home" is added to the phrase "keep house," additional complexities arise. Used with different verbs and different function words, "home" and "house" are sometimes synonyms and sometimes not. The transitive and intransitive nature of the verbs as well as the infinitive structure, which is not in the surface of a sentence, add to the complexity of the verb phrases.

Peggy, in her search for meaning and her interaction with the print, continued to develop strategies to handle these complex problems. In S14 she produced "stayed home"; however, in S35 she encountered difficulty with "keeping house" once again and read: "perhaps keeping house . . . home and . . . is . . . hard work." She was still not happy with "keeping house." She read the phrase as written and then abandoned her correct response. Throughout the story "home" appears seven times and "house" appears ten times. Peggy read them correctly in every context except in the patterns "staying home" and "keeping house." Yet she continued to work on these phrases through her interaction with the text until she could finally handle the structure and could either self-correct successfully or produce a semantically acceptable sentence. Thus Peggy's miscues and retelling reveal the dynamic interaction between a reader and written language.

Oral and Written Language

The differences between oral and written language result from differences of function rather than from any differences in intrinsic characteristics. While any meaning that can be expressed in speech can also be expressed in writing and vice versa, we tend to use oral language for face-to-face communication and written language to communicate over time and space. Oral language is likely to be strongly supported by the context in which it is used; written language is more likely to be abstracted from the situations with which it deals. Written language must include more referents and create its own context minimally supplemented by illustrations. Written language can be polished and perfected before it is read; therefore, it tends to be more formal, deliberate, and constrained than oral language.

For most people, oral-language competence develops earlier than written-language competence because it is needed sooner. But children growing up in literate societies begin to respond to print as language almost as early as they begin to talk.

Traffic signs and commercial logos, the most functional and situationally embedded written language in the environment, are learned easily and early (Goodman & Goodman, in press). Despite their differences and history of acquisition, oral- and written-language processes become parallel for those who become literate; language users can choose the process that better suits their purposes. Readers may go from print to meaning in a manner parallel to the way they go from speech to meaning.

Since the deep structure and rules for generating the surface structure are the same for both language modes, people learning to read may draw on their control of the rules and syntax of oral language to facilitate developing proficiency in written language. This is not a matter of translating or recoding print to sound and then treating it as a listening task. Rather, it is a matter of readers using their knowledge of language and their conceptualizations to get meaning from print, to develop the sampling, predicting, confirming, and correcting strategies parallel to those they use in listening. Gibson and Levin (1975) seem to agree with us that recoding print to sound is not necessary for adults, and Rader (1975) finds that it is not even necessary for children.

We are convinced that oral and written language differ much more in how they are taught than in how they are learned. Although most oral-language development is expected to take place outside of school, the expectation is that literacy development will take place in school programs under teachers' control. Attempts to teach oral language in school are not noted for being as successful as what children achieve outside school. Similarly, literacy instruction is not totally successful. Furthermore, capable readers and writers demonstrate the use and integration of strategies not included in the structured literacy curriculum. Although this paper is primarily concerned with the study of the reading process and not with reading instruction, we are convinced that a major error in many instructional programs has been to ignore or underestimate the linguistic competence and language-learning capabilities of children learning to read.

Reading and Listening: Active Receptive Processes

A producer of language can influence the success of communication by making it as complete and unambiguous as possible. The productive process must carry through from thought to underlying structures to graphic or oral production. Written production, particularly, is often revised and edited to correct significant miscues and even to modify the meaning. The receptive process, however, has a very different set of constraints. Listeners and readers must go through the reverse sequence from aural or graphic representation to underlying structure to meaning. Receptive language users are, above all, intent on comprehending—constructing meaning.

Readers and listeners are *effective* when they succeed in constructing meaning and are *efficient* when they use the minimal effort necessary. Thus, through strategies of predicting, sampling, and confirming, receptive language users can leap toward meaning with partial processing of input, partial creation of surface and deep structures, and continuous monitoring of subsequent input and meaning for confirmation and consistency. Many miscues reflect readers' abilities to liberate themselves from detailed attention to print as they leap toward meaning. Consequently, they reverse, substitute, insert, omit, rearrange, paraphrase, and transform. They do this not just with letters and single words, but with two-word sequences, phrases, clauses, and sentences. Their own experiences, values, conceptual structures, expectations, dialects, and life styles are integral to the process. The meanings they construct can never simply reconstruct the author's conceptual structures. That every written text contains a precise meaning, which readers passively receive, is a common misconception detrimental to research on comprehension.

We have argued above that reading is an active, receptive process parallel to listening. Oral-reading miscues also have direct parallels in listening. Although listening miscues are less accessible, since listeners can only report those they are aware of, still these must be quite similar to reading miscues. Anyone who has ever tried to leave an oral message knows that listening miscues are surely not uncommon. In both reading and listening, prediction is at least as important as perception. What we think we have heard or read is only partly the result of sensory data; it is more the result of our expectations

A major difference between reading and listening is that the reader normally can regress visually and reprocess when a miscue has led to a loss of meaning or structure. The listener, on the other hand, must reprocess mentally, await clarification, or ask a speaker to explain. Furthermore, the speaker may continue speaking, unaware of the listener's problem. Readers are in control of the text they process; listeners are dependent upon the speaker.

The receptive activity during the reading process is especially evident in two different types of miscues—those that are semantically acceptable with regard to the whole text and those that are semantically acceptable only with the prior portion of the text. A miscue may change the author's meaning; but, if it fits the story line, it can be considered semantically acceptable. For example, in S2 of the story Peggy read "when I am always cutting wood?" for "while I am away cutting wood?" These two miscues produced a sentence that fitted in with the meaning of the rest of the story. The more proficient a reader is, the greater the proportion of semantically acceptable miscues. The proportion and variety of high-quality miscues suggest that good readers constantly integrate their backgrounds with that of the author as if they are putting the author's ideas into their own language. This ability is often seen in oral language as a mark of understanding. "Tell me in your own words" is a common request from teachers to discover whether a student has understood something.

Semantically acceptable miscues may be more complex than word-for-word substitutions. Many readers produce reversals in phrase structures such as "said Mother" for "Mother said" or other types of restructuring like the one Peggy produced in S12: "Well, you do it tomorrow" instead of "We'll do it tomorrow." Although it seems that Peggy merely substituted "well" for "we'll" and inserted "you," the miscue is more complex at phrase and clause levels. Peggy inserted an interjection prior to the subject "you" to substitute for the noun phrase. There was also a substitution of the verb phrase because the verb marker "will," indicated by the contraction of "we'll," was omitted, and the verb "do" has been substituted for "will do." In addition, Peggy shifted intonation so that the wife rather than the husband says the sentence. Apparently Peggy thought the wife was going to speak, and her shifted intonation reflected changes in the grammatical pattern and meaning, although the sentence retained its acceptability within the story.

A reader's predicting strategies are also evident in those miscues that are acceptable with the prior portion of the text but that do not produce fully acceptable sentences. Such miscues often occur at pivotal points in sentences such as junctures between clauses or phrases. At such points the author may select from a variety of linguistic structures; the reader may have the same options but choose a different structure. Consider these examples from Peggy's reading:

text	*transcript*
(S38a) "I'll light a fire in the fireplace and the porridge will be ready in a few minutes."	(S38b) "I'll light a fire in the fireplace and I'll . . . and the porridge will be ready in a flash . . . a few minutes."
(S48a) Then he was afraid that she would fall off.	(S48b) Then he was afraid that the . . . that she would fall off.

Peggy's use of "I'll" for "the" in the second clause of the first example is highly predictable. Since "and" generally connects two parallel items, it is logical that the second clause would begin with the subject of the first clause. The substitution of "the" for "she" in the second example occurs frequently in young readers' miscues. Whenever an author uses a pronoun to refer to a previously stated noun phrase, a reader may revert to the original noun phrase. The reverse phenomenon also occurs. When the author chooses a noun phrase for which the referent has been established earlier, the reader may use that pronoun. In the second example, Peggy was probably predicting "the cow" which "she" refers to. These miscues clearly show that Peggy is an active language user as she reads.

Readers' monitoring of their predictions is observed through their self-correction strategies. Clay's (1967) research and our own (Goodman & Burke, 1973) support the idea that a miscue semantically acceptable to the story line is less likely to be corrected than one that is not acceptable or is acceptable only with the immediately preceding text. For example, of the ten semantically acceptable miscues that Peggy produced in the first excerpt, she only corrected one ("all" in S11). However, of the six miscues that were acceptable only with the prior portion of the text, she corrected four. Such correction strategies tend to occur when the readers believe they are most needed: when a prediction has been disconfirmed by subsequent language cues.

Sentences that are fully unacceptable are corrected less than sentences with miscues acceptable with the prior portion of the sentence. Perhaps it is harder for readers to assign underlying structure to sentences in which fully unacceptable miscues occur. Without such a structure, they have difficulty unpacking the grammatical or conceptual complexity of a sentence and so are less able to self-correct. We believe that the two most important factors that make reading difficult are hard-to-predict grammatical structures and high conceptual load (Smith & Lindberg, 1973). What any particular reader finds hard to predict and difficult depends on the reader's background and experience.

The linguistic and conceptual background a reader brings to reading not only shows in miscues but is implicit in the developing concepts or misconceptions revealed through the reader's retelling. Peggy added to her conceptual base and built her control of language as she read this story, but her ability to do both was limited by what she brought to the task. In the story, the husband has to make butter in a churn. Peggy made miscues whenever buttermaking was mentioned. For example, in S10 she substituted "bread" for "butter." The next time "butter" appears, in S15, she read it as expected. However, in S18, "Soon the cream will turn into butter," Peggy read "buttermilk" for "butter." Other references to buttermaking include the words "churn" or "cream." Peggy read "cream" correctly each time it appears in the text but had trouble reading "churn." She paused about ten seconds before the first appearance of "churn" and finally said it. However, the next two times churn appears, Peggy read "cream."

text	transcript
(S25a) . . . he saw a big pig inside, with its nose in the churn.	(S25b) . . . he saw a big pig inside, with its nose in the cream.
(S28a) It bumped into the churn, knocking it over.	(S28b) It jumped . . . it bumped into the cream, knocking it over.
(S29a) The cream splashed all over the room.	(S29b) The cream shado . . . splashed all over the room.

In the retelling Peggy provided evidence that her miscues were conceptually based and not mere confusions:

> And the husband was sitting down and he poured some buttermilk and um . . . in a jar. And, and, he was making buttermilk, and then, he um . . . heard the baby crying. So, he looked all around in the room and um, . . . And then he saw a big, a big, um . . . pig. Um . . . He saw a big pig inside the house. So, he told him to get out and he, the pig, started racing around and um . . . he di . . . he um . . . bumped into the buttermilk and then the buttermilk fell down and then the pig, um . . . went out.

Peggy, who is growing up in a metropolis, knows little about how butter is made in churns. Although she knows that there is a relationship between cream and butter, she does not know the details of that relationship. According to her teacher, she has also taken part in a traditional primary-school activity in which sweet cream is poured into a jar, closed up tightly, and shaken until butter and buttermilk are produced. Although Peggy's miscues and retelling suggest that she had little knowledge about buttermaking, the concept is peripheral to comprehending the story. All that she needed to know was that buttermaking is one of the wife's many chores that can cause the woodman trouble.

Reading is not simply knowing sounds, words, sentences, and the abstract parts of language that can be studied by linguists. Reading, like listening, consists of processing language and constructing meanings. The reader brings a great deal of information to this complex and active process. Whenever readers are asked to read something for which they do not have enough relevant experience they have difficulty. That is why even proficient adult readers use such excuses as "It's too technical" and "He just writes for those inside the group." For this reason, proficient readers go to pharmacists or lawyers, for example, to read certain texts for them.

Oral and Silent Reading

The basic mode of reading is silent. Oral reading is special since it requires production of an oral representation concurrently with comprehending. The functions of oral reading are limited. It has become a kind of performing art used chiefly by teachers and television and radio announcers. We have already explained why we use oral reading in miscue analysis. But a basic question remains: are oral and silent reading similar enough to justify generalizing from studies of oral-reading miscues to theories and models of silent reading?

In our view a single process underlies all reading. The cycles, phases, and strategies of oral and silent reading are essentially the same. The miscues we find in oral reading occur in silent reading as well. Current unpublished studies of nonidentical fillers of cloze blanks (responses that do not match the deleted words) show remarkable correspondence to oral-reading miscues and indicate that the processes of oral and silent reading are much the same (Lindberg, 1977; Rousch, Note 1).

Still, there are some dissimilarities between oral and silent reading that produce at least superficial differences in process. First, oral reading is limited to the speed at which speech can be produced. It need not, therefore, be as efficient as rapid silent reading. Next, superficial misarticulations such as "cimmanon" for "cinnamon" occur in oral reading but are not part of silent reading. Also, oral readers, conscious of their audience, may read passages differently than if they read them silently. Examples are production of nonword substitutions, persistence with several attempts at problem spots, overt regression to correct miscues already mentally corrected, and deliberate adjustments in ensuing text to cover miscues so that listeners will not notice them. Furthermore, oral readers may take fewer risks than silent readers. This can be seen in the deliberate omission of unfamiliar words, reluctance to attempt correction even though meaning is disrupted, and avoidance of overtly making corrections that have taken place silently to avoid calling attention to miscues. Finally, relatively proficient readers, particularly adults, may become so concerned with superficial fluency that they short-circuit the basic concern for meaning. Professional oral readers, newscasters for example, seem to suffer from this malady.

The Reader: An Intuitive Grammarian

Recently, linguists have equated or blurred the distinction between deep structure and meaning. We, however, find this distinction useful to explain a common phenomenon in our subjects' reading. Moderately proficient readers are able to cope with texts that they do not understand by manipulating language down to a deep structure level. Their miscues demonstrate this. Readers may also correctly answer a question they do not understand by transforming it into a statement and then finding the sentence in the text with the appropriate structure. Thus, when confronted by an article entitled, "Downhole Heave Compensator" (Kirk, 1974), most readers claim little comprehension. But they can answer the question, "What were the two things destroying the underreamers?" by finding the statement in the text that reads, "We were trying to keep drillships and semi-submersibles from wiping out our underreamers" (p. 88). Thus it is dangerous for researchers and teachers to equate comprehension with correct answers obtained by manipulating and transforming grammatical structures. Our research may not prove the psycholinguistic reality of the deep structure construct as distinct from meaning, but it demonstrates its utility. In our research we judge syntactic acceptability of sentences separately from semantic acceptability, since readers often produce sentences that are syntactically, but not semantically, acceptable. In S10 Peggy read "If you stay home to do my work" as a sentence which she finally resolved as "If you start home to do my work." This is syntactically acceptable in the story but unacceptable semantically since it is important to the story line that the woodman "stay home."

The first evidence used to separate syntactic from semantic acceptability came from research on the phenomenon of nonwords. Such nonsense words help give us insight into readers' grammatical awareness because sentences with nonwords often retain the grammatical features of English although they lose English meaning. Use of appropriate intonation frequently provides evidence for the grammatical similarity between the nonword and the text word. Nonwords most often retain similarities not only in number of syllables, word length, and spelling but also in bound morphemes—the smallest units that carry meaning or grammatical information within a word but cannot stand alone, for example, the *ed* in carri*ed*. The following responses by second, fourth, and sixth graders represent nonwords that retain the grammatical function of the text (Goodman & Burke, 1973). A different subject produced each response. Notice that "surprise" and "circus" are singular nouns and that, in producing the nonwords, the subjects did not produce *s* or *z* sounds at the ends of the words as they would with plural nouns.

expected response	*nonword substitutions*
Second graders:	
The *surprise* is in my box.	*supra, suppa*
Then they will know the *circus* is coming.	*ception, chavit*
"Penny why are you so *excited?*" she asked.	*excedled, encited*
Fourth graders:	
He saw a little *fawn.*	*frawn, foon, faunt*
What queer *experiment* was it?	*espressment, explerm, explainment*

Sixth graders:
Clearly and *distinctly* Andrew said "philo-
sophical." *distikily, distintly, definely*
A *distinct* quiver in his voice. *dristic, distinc, distet*

There is other evidence in miscues of readers' strong awareness of bound morphemic rules. Our data on readers' word-for-word substitutions, whether nonwords
or real words, show that, on the average, 80 percent of the observed responses retain the morphemic markings of the text. For example, if the text word is a non-
inflected form of a verb, the reader will tend to substitute that form. If the word
has a prefix, the reader's substitution will tend to include a prefix. Derivational
suffixes will be replaced by derivational suffixes, contractional suffixes by contractional suffixes.

Miscue analysis provides additional data regarding the phenomenon of gram-
matical-function similarity. Every one of Peggy's substitution miscues in the portion of the text provided earlier had the same grammatical function as the text
word. Table 1 (Goodman & Burke, 1973) indicates the percentage of miscues made
by a sample of fourth and sixth graders that had the same grammatical function.
These substitutions were coded prior to any attempt to correct the miscues.

Our research suggests that nouns, noun modifiers, and function words are substituted for each other to a much greater degree than they are for verbs. Out of
501 substitution miscues produced by fourth graders, only three times was a noun
substituted for a verb modifier, and sixth graders made such a substitution only
once out of 424 miscues.

Evidence from miscues occurring at the beginning of sentences also adds insight
into readers' awareness of the grammatical constraints of language. Generally, in
prose for children, few sentences begin with prepositions, intensifiers, adjectives,
or singular common nouns without a preceding determiner. When readers produced miscues on the beginning words of sentences that did not retain the grammatical function of the text, we could not find one miscue that represented any
of these unexpected grammatical forms. (One day we will do an article called
"Miscues Readers Don't Make." Some of the strongest evidence comes from all the
things readers could do that they do not.)

TABLE 1
Percent of Miscues with Grammatical Function Similarity

Identical Grammatical Function	4th Graders	6th Graders
Nouns	76%	74%
Verbs	76%	73%
Noun Modifiers	61%	57%
Function Words	67%	67%

Source: K.S. Goodman and C.L. Burke, *Theoretically based studies of patterns of miscues in oral
reading performance, final report.* Detroit: Wayne State University, 1973 (ERIC Document Reproduction Service No. ED 079 708), p. 136.

Readers' miscues that cross sentence boundaries also provide insight into the readers' grammatical sophistication. It is not uncommon to hear teachers complain that readers often read past periods. Closer examination of this phenomenon suggests that when readers do this they are usually making a logical prediction that is based on a linguistic alternative. Peggy did this with the sentence (S35): "Perhaps keeping house is harder than I thought." As previously noted, Peggy had problems with the "keeping house" structure. She resolved the beginning of this sentence after a number of different attempts by finally reading "perhaps keeping home is hard work." Since she has rendered that clause as an independent unit, she has nothing to which she can attach "than I thought." She transformed this phrase into an independent clause and read it as "Then I thought."

Another example of crossing sentence boundaries occurs frequently in part of a story (Moore, 1965) we have used with fourth graders: "He still thought it more fun to pretend to be a great scientist, mixing the strange and the unknown" (p. 62). Many readers predict that "strange" and "unknown" are adjectives and intone the sentence accordingly. This means that when they come to "unknown" the voice is left anticipating a noun. More proficient readers tend to regress at this point and correct the stress patterns.

Parts and Wholes

We believe that too much research on language and language learning has dealt with isolated sounds, letters, word parts, words, and even sentences. Such fragmentation, although it simplifies research design and the complexity of the phenomena under study, seriously distorts processes, tasks, cue values, interactions, and realities. Fortunately, there is now a strong trend toward use of full, natural linguistic text in psycholinguistic research. Kintsch (1974) notes:

> Psycholinguistics is changing its character. . . . The 1950's were still dominated by the nonsense syllables . . . the 1960's were characterized by the use of word lists, while the present decade is witnessing a shift to even more complex learning materials. At present, we have reached the point where lists of sentences are being substituted for word lists in studies of recall recognition. Hopefully, this will not be the end-point of this development, and we shall soon see psychologists handle effectively the problems posed by the analysis of connected texts. (p. 2)

Through miscue analysis we have learned an important lesson: other things being equal, short language sequences are harder to comprehend than long ones. Sentences are easier than words, paragraphs easier than sentences, pages easier than paragraphs, and stories easier than pages. We see two reasons for this. First, it takes some familiarity with the style and general semantic thrust of a text's language for the reader to make successful predictions. Style is largely a matter of an author's syntactic preferences; the semantic context develops over the entire text. Short texts provide limited cues for readers to build a sense of either style or meaning. Second, the disruptive effect of particular miscues on meaning is much greater in short texts. Longer texts offer redundant opportunities to recover and self-correct. This suggests why findings from studies of words, sentences, and short passages produce different results from those that involve whole texts. It also raises a major issue about research using standardized tests, which utilize words, phrases, sentences, and very short texts to assess reading proficiency.

We believe that reading involves the interrelationship of all the language systems. All readers use graphic information to various degrees. Our research demonstrates that low readers in the sixth, eighth, and tenth grades use graphic information more than high readers. Readers also produce substitution miscues similar to the phonemic patterns of text words. Although such phonemic miscues occur less frequently than graphic miscues, they show a similar pattern. This suggests that readers call on their knowledge of the graphophonic systems (symbol-sound relationships). Yet the use of these systems cannot explain why Peggy would produce a substitution such as "day" for "morning" or "job" for "work" (S13). She is clearly showing her use of the syntactic system and her ability to retain the grammatical function and morphemic constraints of the expected response. But the graphophonic and syntactic systems alone cannot explain why Peggy could seemingly understand words such as "house," "home," "ground," and "cream" in certain contexts in her reading but in other settings seemed to have difficulty. To understand these aspects of reading, one must examine the semantic system.

Miscue analysis shows that readers like Peggy use the interrelationships among the grammatical, graphophonic, and semantic systems. All three systems are used in an integrated fashion in order for reading to take place. Miscue analysis provides evidence that readers integrate cue systems from the earlier stages of reading. Readers sample and make judgments about which cues from each system will provide the most useful information in making predictions that will get them to meaning. S2 in Peggy's excerpt provides insight into this phenomenon. Peggy read the sentence as follows: "One evening when h . . . he came home from work he said to his wife I want you [two second pause] do . . . all day [twelve second pause]." After the second pause, Peggy regressed to the beginning of the direct quote and read, "What do you do all day when I am always cutting wood?" Peggy's pauses and regression indicate that she was saying to herself: "This doesn't sound like language" (syntactically unacceptable); "this doesn't make sense" (semantically unacceptable). She continued slowly and hesitatingly, finally stopping altogether. She was disconfirming her prediction and rejecting it. Since it did not make sense, she decided that she must regress and pick up new cues from which to make new predictions.

In producing the unacceptable language segment "I want you do all day," Peggy was using graphic cues from "what" to predict "want." She was picking up the syntactic cues from "he said," which suggested that the woodman would use a declarative statement to start his conversation. From the situational context and her awareness of role relationships, she might have believed that, since the husband was returning home from working hard all day, he would be initially demanding to his wife. When this segment did not make sense to Peggy, she corrected herself. She read the last part of the sentence, "when I am always cutting wood," confidently and without hesitation. She was probably unaware that "when" and "always" are her own encodings of the meaning. She had made use of all three of the cue systems; her words fit well into the developing meaning of the story; there-

267

fore, she did not need to correct her miscues. We believe that both children and adults are constantly involved in this process during their silent reading but are unaware that it is taking place.

There are many times when the developing meaning of a story is so strong that it is inefficient to focus on the distinctive graphic cues of each letter or each word. As long as the phrase and clause structure are kept intact and meaning is being constructed, the reader has little reason to be overly concerned with graphic cues. Peggy read "day" for "morning" in S13 and "job" for "work" in S14. These miscues have a highly synonymous relationship to the text sentence, but they are based on minimal or no graphic cues. In S38 Peggy indicated to an even greater extent her ability to use minimal graphic cues. Her prediction was strong enough; and she was developing such a clear meaning of the situation that "in a flash" was an acceptable alternative to "in a few minutes," although she caught her miscue and corrected it.

Another phenomenon that exemplifies the interrelationships among the cueing systems is the associations readers develop between pairs of words. Any reader, regardless of age or ability, may substitute "the" for "a." Many readers also substitute "then" for "when," "that" for "what," and "was" for "saw" in certain contexts. What causes these associations is not simply the words' look-alike quality. Most of these miscues occur with words of similar grammatical function in positions where the resulting sentence is syntactically acceptable. Differences in proficiency are reflected in the ways readers react to these miscues: the more proficient reader corrects when necessary; the less proficient reader, being less concerned with making sense or less able to do so, allows an unacceptable sentence to go uncorrected. This process can only be understood if researchers focus on how readers employ all the cues available to them. For too long the research emphasis on discrete parts of language has kept us from appreciating how readers interrelate all aspects of language as they read.

Sooner or later all attempts to understand language—its development and its function as the medium of human communication—must confront linguistic reality. Theories, models, grammars, and research paradigms must predict and explain what people do when they use language and what makes it possible for them to do so. Researchers have contrived ingenious ways to make a small bit of linguistic or psycholinguistic reality available for examination. But then what they see is often out of focus, distorted by the design. Our approach makes fully available the reality of the miscues readers produce as they orally read whole, natural, and meaningful texts.

Huey (1908/1968) once said:

> And so to completely analyze what we do when we read would almost be the acme of a psychologist's achievements, for it would be to describe very many of the most intricate workings of the human mind, as well as to unravel the tangled story of the most remarkable specific performance that civilization has learned in all its history. (p. 6)

To this we add: oral reading miscues are the windows on the reading process at work.

Reference Notes

1. Rousch, P. *Miscues of special groups of Australian readers.* Paper presented at the meeting of the International Reading Association, Miami, May 1977.

References

Brown, R. *A first language: The early stages.* Cambridge, Mass.: Harvard University Press, 1973.

Clay, M. M. The reading behaviour of five year old children: A research report. *New Zealand Journal of Educational Studies,* 1967, **2,** 11–31.

Ewoldt, C. *Psycholinguistic research in the reading of deaf children.* Unpublished doctoral dissertation, Wayne State University, 1977.

Gibson, E., & Levin, H. *The psychology of reading.* Cambridge, Mass.: M.I.T. Press, 1975.

Goodman, K. S., & Burke, C. L. *Theoretically based studies of patterns of miscues in oral reading performance, Final Report.* Detroit: Wayne State University, 1973. (ERIC Document Reproduction Service No. ED 079 708)

Goodman, K. S., & Goodman, Y. Learning to read is natural. In L. B. Resnick & P. Weaver (Eds.), *Theory and practice of early reading* (Vol. 1). Hillsdale, N.J.: Erlbaum Associates, in press.

Hodes, P. *A psycholinguistic study of reading miscues of Yiddish-English bilingual children.* Unpublished doctoral dissertation, Wayne State University, 1976.

Huey, E. B. *The psychology and pedagogy of reading.* Cambridge, Mass.: M.I.T. Press, 1968. (Originally published, 1908).

Kintsch, W. *The representation of meaning in memory.* Hillsdale, N.J.: Erlbaum Associates, 1974.

Kirk, S. Downhole heave compensator: A tool designed by hindsight. *Drilling-DCW,* June 1974.

Lindberg, M. A. *A description of the relationship between selected pre-linguistic, linguistic, and psycholinguistic measures of readability.* Unpublished doctoral dissertation, Wayne State University, 1977.

The man who kept house. In J. McInnes, M. Gerrard, & J. Ryckman (Eds.), *Magic and make believe.* Don Mills, Ontario: Thomas Nelson, 1964.

Moore, L. Freddie Miller: Scientist. In E. A. Betts & C. M. Welch (Eds.), *Adventures here and there* (Book V-3). New York: American Book Co., 1965.

Rader, N. L. *From written words to meaning: A developmental study.* Unpublished doctoral dissertation, Cornell University, 1975.

Romatowski, J. *A psycholinguistic description of miscues generated by selected bilingual subjects during the oral reading of instructional reading material as presented in Polish readers and in English basal readers.* Unpublished doctoral dissertation, Wayne State University, 1972.

Smith, L. A., & Lindberg, M. A. Building instructional materials. In K. S. Goodman (Ed.), *Miscue analysis: Application to reading instruction.* Urbana, Ill.: ERIC Clearinghouse on Reading and Comprehension Skills and National Council of Teachers of English, 1973.

CHAPTER 3

The Language Arts

Mencken Revisited

RAVEN I. McDAVID, JR.
University of Chicago

Long remembered for his satires of the booboisie, H. L. Mencken is too seldom recognized for his contribution to the study of language. In this article Raven I. McDavid, Jr. argues persuasively that we not overlook Mencken's importance as a scholar and historian of the American language. Stressing the depth and range of Mencken's work, McDavid suggests that modern linguists should consider Mencken's eclecticism as a meaningful alternative to the technical, sometimes narrow, approaches they now use to study language.

Forty-five years after the first edition of H. L. Mencken's *The American Language* (1919), the state of American linguistics is a prosperous one. School people at all levels are interested in what linguists promise to accomplish. If we can believe some of the more eloquent tub-thumpers, linguistics can solve any of the vexing problems of American education, from elementary reading to international understanding.

Beginning with World War II, linguists have been drawn into programs for teaching foreign languages—not only the "exotic languages" like Chinese, Malay, Hindi and Russian, but such more conventional academic languages (if less widely spoken ones) as German, French and Italian. Even languages spoken by relatively few people are of national concern if their habitat lies in an impoverished friendly nation or along the frontier of a potential foe: Korean, Azerbaijani, Pashto and Cambodian begin to appear in American graduate programs, and the Foreign Service Institute of the State Department is prepared to offer training in almost any language to foreign service officers who may need it. In addition, it is now in the national interest to develop programs and textbooks for teaching English to speakers of a wide range of languages, from Arabic to Vietnamese. Almost every university of consequence has such a program, and linguists who are conversant with such languages and interested in overseas programs for training teachers of English can almost name their working conditions.

Linguistics has appeared, not only in the teaching of foreign languages

Harvard Educational Review Vol. 34 No. 2 Spring 1964, 211–225

but in other parts of the curriculum as well. In such orthodox situations as the teaching of English composition and literature, some linguists have been very active, both in asking the basic questions and in offering tentative answers. In the elementary school the cooperation of linguists is being sought for improving the teaching of reading, and experimental programs involving linguists are already under way. Moving beyond conventional academic programs, some linguists have been very active in developing the theory of machine translation, in the hope that computers can be trained to cope with the exponentially growing mass of information printed in other languages. They are encouraged both by the Federal Government and by private industry, for the supply of scientifically and technically competent bilinguals shows no signs of increasing as fast as the amount of technical knowledge.

Not only the practical demands for their services but the professional activities of linguists have greatly increased during the last few decades. The membership of the Linguistic Society of America is several times what it was in the early 1930's. In addition, there are several active local organizations, like the Linguistic Circle of New York (now renamed the International Linguistic Association) and the Georgetown Linguistic Round Table, that issue their own journals and monographs; and several linguistic publications attached to universities, such as *General Linguistics* (Kentucky) and *Anthropological Linguistics* (Indiana). Linguistic articles and reviews are not uncommon in the various journals of the National Council of Teachers of English, and even in local publications like the *Chicago Schools Journal.*

Competing Traditions

Despite snide comments, there is no rigid party line in American linguistics. The American anthropological tradition in linguistic studies, so firmly established by Franz Boas, Edward Sapir and Leonard Bloomfield, has had to compete not only with the older and still developing theories of the comparative grammarians, but with the insights of such European groups as the Prague School of Trubetzkoy and Jakobson; the Copenhagen Circle of Hjelmslev; the London group around J. R. Firth; and most recently the linguists of the Soviet Union. Out of this interchange have come the new grammatical theories of Kenneth Pike; of George L. Trager and Henry Lee Smith, Jr.; of Zellig Harris and Noam Chomsky, to mention only a few. Where a few years ago the followers of Trager and Smith were excoriating Pike and Fries for mixing levels of analysis, the less temperate disciples of Chomsky are now consigning to the ashcan all linguistic theory developed before 1956, only themselves to come under the guns of the mathematical linguists at Illinois Tech and elsewhere. It is not a time for timid souls to dabble with the science of language, but one of exciting intellectual debate, out of which may come a new theory of the rôle of language in human affairs.[1]

Reactions against Linguistics

But this excitement and the current popularity of linguists are not without their disadvantages. One can detect a strong current of anti-linguisticism among the public at large, among the writers in the public press and among the academicians in other disciplines. The hue-and-cry over the Merriam Company's *Webster Third New International Dictionary* (1961) is only a single, if most spectacular, example of this attitude. Editorials and reviews in such publications as *The New York Times, The New Yorker* and the *Saturday Review* have opened fire not only on the imaginary or real defects of the Third (and there are some real defects, which have largely escaped notice so far), but on the entire body of principles from which structural linguistics has grown in the last generation.[2] The National Council of Teachers of English, whose minions once afflicted the American schoolroom with prescriptive grammar and Better Speech Week, is now assailed by the Radical Right for seeking to destroy the purity of the national tongue. The long debate over principles of usage, which seemed settled with the publication of C. C. Fries's *American English Grammar* (1940), has been renewed, and the unlaid ghosts of Lindley Murray and Richard Grant White return to haunt the American teacher.

If the linguists have become straw-men for the neoconservatives to clobber, it is easy for the linguists in turn to stuff their own straw-men and blame them for this reaction. It is true that the liveliness of linguistics, and the insistence of linguists on precise quasi-mathematical formulations, are abhorrent to the genteel tradition of conventional humanism, whose characteristic spokesmen too often have sought the ivory tower as a respectable address in which they would be safe from the rigors of exact knowledge and the dust and soot of everyday life. It is true, also, that some of the most active antilinguists are eloquent popular writers on language, who have deliberately perverted their academic knowledge for the blessings of a fast buck, and who gripe because serious linguists not only reject them but expose their pretensions. Yet neither

---

[1] The most promising theoretical approach is that of Kenneth L. Pike, *Language in Relation to a Unified Theory of Human Behavior* (Prelim. ed., Glendale, Calif., 1954-60).

[2] The *American Heritage Dictionary* (1969) has so blatantly tried to capitalize on resentment against the *Third*—and the structuralists—that it has been humorously called the *Joe McCarthy Dictionary*. As a part of his own campaign against the structuralists, Noam Chomsky, *Reichsführer* of the transformationalists, has told English teachers that transformational grammar is just like the school grammar they are accustomed to teaching. This incredible statement is probably best interpreted in terms of Chomsky's recent proclamation that he is more interested in politics than in linguistics.

prissiness nor spite is enough to explain the reaction. A large part of the fault lies at the doors of the linguists themselves.

The Style of Linguistic Writing

Granted that there can be no rational justification for the anti-scientific attitude of the literary lamas, this attitude has not been helped by either the style or the content of much recent linguistic writing. From the chaotic algebra of Zellig Harris's *Methods in Structural Linguistics* (1951) through the latest tortured exegesis on the transformational revolution, too many linguists have used their claim to scientific precision as an excuse for being incomprehensible to all save the trebly-baptized of their private cliques.[3] Furthermore, too many of the younger linguists—perhaps pardonably biased by the specific directions of their work—deny the flux, the competing forms and styles, the endless possibilities for innovation that a language must possess if it is to be alive. Codified formulas and computerized rules are all very well in their place, and necessary for constructing models of language; and models in turn provide stimulating insights into the act of communication. But, as the Russian linguist Andreyev (1962) reminds us, people speak in languages and not in their models.[4]

The Literary Stance

This emphasis on rigorous models, this denial of variety within language, aggravates rather than reduces the conflict between the linguists and the literary mandarins. As any serious linguist discovers from being brigaded with literary historians and critics, the professional student of literature fights shy of the speechways of the common man and has little use for them save when they are embalmed in the dialogue of long-dead writers such as Shakespeare, and hence subject to the veneration due literary monuments. The typical teacher of English, at whatever level, has withdrawn from the dust and heat of active life, in search of a dignified occupation, and finds the slightest interest in everyday mores a threat to his hard-won respectability.

This position makes it easy for the literary scholar to misinterpret what linguists say. The casual statement of the linguist that any variety of a language is worthy of serious study is *ipso facto* a threat to the humanistic stance: if *it's me* is acceptable and the rules for *shall* and *will* are nonsense, what is to

---

[3] For example, Zellig Harris, *Methods in Structural Linguistics* (Chicago, Ill.: University of Chicago Press, 1951); v. "This book is, regrettably, not easy to read." Among the transformationalists there is an exasperating practice of publishing only revealed dogma, and referring the readers, for evidence, to inaccessible seminar papers.

[4] N. A. Andreyev, "Models as a Tool in the Development of Linguistic Theory," *Word*, XVIII (1962), 197.

set off the poor English teacher from her cousins in the dime stores and on sharecropper farms? In the same way, the insistence of the linguist on strict scientific statement denies the rationale of the usual inspirational teacher of literature, who either is incapable of making exact scientific statements or has rejected the ardors of scientific discipline as destructive of the good and the beautiful.

For this reason, the linguist has difficulty enough talking with his literary colleagues even when he stays in the center of the culture and insists on deriving his statements from living speech and actual documents; but at least he can communicate with the historian, the anthropologist or the social psychologist. When he discards real speechways for formulas and rules, he denies culture and destroys the basis for communication with social scientists as well as with humanists. Lacking such communication, he invites the assaults on his discipline that we have seen in the past two years.

The contest is acerbated by the ironical fact that (leaving aside the sympathy for exact knowledge) the same personality types seem to be drawn to conventional literary study and to quasi-mathematical linguistics. Both disciplines are filled with refugees from the complications of the real world—on the one hand the advocates of clean hands and perfumed sensitivities; on the other, the shattered personalities who trust machines more than human beings—in search of dignity and security. Both tend to foster line-integration:[5]

[5] *Line integrator* and *point integrator*, as personality types, were first used by Edward T. Hall, Henry Lee Smith, Jr., and George L. Trager, in the working seminars of the Foreign Service Institute, Department of State, c. 1950. The most detailed exposition is to be found in Trager and Hall, *The Analysis of Culture* (Washington, D.C.: 1953), 43-44: "It is well at this point to repeat what our analysis indicated: A: there are two ways in which experience is integrated or learned, or two ways in which the organism is modified; also, as in the case of sex, these do not exist in their pure state, *i.e.*, each has characteristics of the other in varying degrees and there are inter-grades. B: these two things exist in complementary relationship to each other and are both necessary; also, as in the case of the sexes, different cultures may enhance or value or emphasize one more than the other. C: within each there will be a hierarchy; just as some men are more masculine than others and some women more feminine, there is also a hierarchy within the two types of integration.

"In order to avoid invidious distinctions, we have termed these two POINT and LINE integration. Both can be either high or low order in their own class, or they can fall between the extremes. They are characterized as follows:

"The LINE INTEGRATOR works within a given system or systems. His function is to make systems go, and his intellectual eyes are turned inward, as it were, towards improving and working within, or manipulating his own frame of reference. When he is a high order line integrator, he learns very rapidly and with great ease, as long as what is given him is integrated into some type of system. Memory work is not arduous to him. By and large he ignores contradictions between the internal logic of his own systems and events which are outside his systems. It must not be assumed that line integrators are not scientists; one can say that some of the best scientific work is done by persons of this type. This is because, given a system, they then go to work and build the solid foundation which gives the system substance. . . .

"The point integrator has to make each point his very own, and consequently may learn more slowly than a line integrator. He is likely to question his teachers and professors about the 'principles' involved in a given scheme. He is deeply disturbed by contradictions, either working out, in a single dimension, an extrapolation of a routine statement in terms of a rigid program. In one instance a work of literature is macerated according to the dogmas of a particular school of criticism (and whether that school is New, Aristottering or Freudulent seems to make little difference) ; in another, the grammatical evidence from a language is racked to fit the preconceptions of a linguistic theory. The usual products of either climate are likely to be zombies rather than critical scholars; both climates are hostile to the point-integrator who takes a problem and insists on working simultaneously in as many dimensions as necessary to achieve a solution and on drawing on whatever disciplines may provide fruitful insights. With more years in Academe than I care to remember, I find that the point-integrator is the far more stimulating teacher, however ill he may fit into preconceived programs. From Allan Gilbert in my incarnation as a Miltonist,[6] from Edward Sapir at my first Linguistic Institute, from Hans Kurath in a quarter-century of association on the Linguistic Atlas, I have received dazzling epiphanies that have enriched all my later work.

The Complexity of Language

Nothing short of highly developed point integration, braced by thorough professional discipline, can produce an adequate view of language. The dimensions of relationships in any linguistic system—regardless of the size of the speech community in which it is used—are many, and to deny any of these dimensions prevents a full understanding, however powerful a restricted view may be for restricted ends. This multi-dimensional language is implicit in the better-known definitions, such as that by Herskovits out of Sapir and Sturtevant:

> A language is a system of arbitrary vocal signals by which members of a social group cooperate and interact, and by means of which the learning process is effectuated and a given way of life achieves both continuity and change.[7]

---

within a given frame of reference or between that frame of reference and what is outside. There are times when he has difficulty with line integrators who do not get his points. His function in regard to society is to create new systems as conditions change; he is, however, restless in a static situation and tends to suffer if he isn't permitted to integrate his points. Having discovered the points, however, he is likely to lose interest and move on, leaving line integrators to fill in the picture, so that in the realm of science he is often accused of being 'unscientific' or lacking proof for his points. Professor Einstein would be an example of a point integrator of the highest order, Napier of a line integrator. No one can deny the contribution of either."

[6] It was typical of Gilbert to make himself an expert horseman in his late forties, to verify the story of a similar feat by an Italian Renaissance figure. During the nearly three decades since I received my doctorate he has never expressed a regret that I deserted Milton for linguistics; rather, he points to what success I have achieved as evidence in support of his theory of education—that an adequately trained scholar can find his own field, regardless of the discipline in which he was trained.

[7] Melville J. Herskovits, Man and His Works (New York: Alfred A. Knopf, 1948), p. 440.

An exegesis of this definition will show the ramifications of linguistics. The *systematic* nature of language relates its study to all science; the formulaic way in which the system can be stated relates linguistics particularly to mathematics, and through mathematics to philosophy. The means by which language communication typically and primarily takes place—the *vocal signals* —ties linguistics to human biology and to acoustics. The function of language in the *social group* links it to all the social and behavioral sciences, and its use as the vehicle of *cultural transmission* (including the appreciation of literature and the other arts and the attempts to understand the unknown) relates it inexorably not only to the social and behavioral sciences but to the theological sciences and the humanities as well. Any theory of linguistics that excludes any of these relationships is narrow, emasculated and self-defeating —whether it be the humanistic approach that gags at precise statement or involvement in the social sciences, or the mathematical one that brushes aside the details of human relationships.

The Place of Mencken

Viewed in this way, Mencken's *The American Language* is still a most important work, without any competition in the English-speaking world. As a work concerned with all the interrelationships of the mode of communication in a speech community, it respects exact knowledge, recognizes the biological and physical aspects of language, understands how a variety of language is intimately associated with the cultural matrix in which it is used, and comments sagely on the tension between the habitual mode of speaking and the linguistic practices of approved authors. Further, the history of *The American Language* reveals the many ways in which Mencken prodded academic scholars into supplying the necessary basic works on the national way of speech. As he often said, one of his important rôles was that of a bird dog: to point out the quarry steadfastly until the hunters got around to bagging it.

Linguistics in 1919

In 1919, linguistics as a science was hardly recognized at all. Where the serious study of language existed, it was simply attached to traditional academic departments: English, Germanic, Romance or Classical Languages and Literature, and occasionally to anthropology. It was heavily biased toward historical grammar, for obvious reasons. The antiquarian interests of the Renaissance and Reformation (including the examination of Old English records by common lawyers seeking in precedent a bridle for arrogant kings) had drawn scholars toward historical problems; the discovery of Sanskrit by Sir William Jones (1786) and the subsequent formulation of Indo-European comparisons by Rask and Grimm and Bopp had introduced the exciting possibilities of historical reconstruction; the publication of Darwin's *Origin of Species* (1859) only confirmed the existing historical and evolutionary bias of linguistics and the human sciences in general, and further diverted them from the task of rigorous taxonomic description.[8]

Not till the end of the nineteenth century did modern descriptive linguistics get under way, principally directed toward the aboriginal tongues of Asia, Africa and the Americas—partly as an aid to colonial administrators, partly as a tool to enable anthropologists to understand disappearing cultures. Not till the 1930's were these rigorous descriptive methods applied to the culture-bearing languages of Europe, and then often to draw the resentment of literary scholars trained in the older tradition.[9]

Language Attitudes in the Schools

If serious interest in language study for its own sake was barely tolerated in the universities of 1919, it had almost no status in the public schools. Our educational system was heavily biased toward the genteel tradition and the cult of respectability. Languages were valued chiefly as cultural ornaments; in the orgy of super-patriotism that engulfed the United States during World War I, the study of German was eradicated from most of the public schools, and departments of German were even abolished in some prominent universities. Higher education was openly designed for the favored few; it was accepted as a fact of life that less than one percent of fourth-grade students would obtain a college degree. Yet no dropout problem existed; it was assumed that those who lacked academic interest would be held back, term after term, until they disappeared from the schools into the world of practical affairs— perhaps to succeed financially, but certainly to repay the condescension of the more fortunate with bitter scorn toward book-learning.[10]

Humanism and Education

Even worse, in language, as in other fields, there was little communication

8 This was pointed out repeatedly by A. L. Kroeber, in the University of Chicago seminar before the Darwin Centennial Celebration of 1959.

9 It is a common argument, among the foes of scientific linguistics, that the descriptivists attempt to apply to the vehicles of great civilizations the same techniques used (as they would put it) to analyze the gibberish of a few dozen half-naked savages. The linguist would reply that the method is valid, whatever the language, though the statements may be more complicated where the speech-community is larger and the records extend over longer periods of time. Working anthropologists have often discovered complicated stylistic variations in aboriginal languages, just as in those of the dominant Western cultures.

10 From my personal experience: in 1919, when I entered the second grade, there was a student in my room a head taller than I was and wearing long pants—at that time a badge of manhood never assumed before the age of 16. He disappeared before the end of the year, and I never saw him again.

between those who professed learning and those who practiced public education. Liberal arts colleges, by and large, neglected teacher training, and despised the institutions devoted to it—an attitude still too common among the humanists.[11] In turn, the English teacher, cut off from the main intellectual currents, forced her charges toward a parroted perversion of Eighteenth Century normative grammar, and viewed departures from that norm (even the tolerated quaintness of backwoods dialects) as badges of intellectual, social and moral obloquy. Students of my era learned little about the organization of the language, but much about the stigma of using non-standard forms; and even in Baptist communities afflicted with a high degree of Victorian prudery, *ain't* was the most horrendous of the four-letter words. Even those who acquired some taint of higher education rarely recovered from this repressive attitude; needless to say, both the illuminati and the lower ranks of pedagogues casually assumed that American English was inferior to the British variety.

Professional Isolation

Finally, in 1919 the few professional linguists had no organization in which persons affiliated with various disciplines could talk with each other. They were scattered among a half-dozen societies: the Modern Language Association, the Philological Association, the Anthropological Association, the Oriental Society, the National Council of Teachers of English, and the Dialect Society. This last, the sole American organization concerned essentially with American English or any other variety of language, was largely manned by amateurs, antiquarian-oriented, as the membership had been at its foundation a generation earlier. Its aim (still unfulfilled in 1964)[12] was to produce an American Dialect Dictionary, analogous to the English Dialect Dictionary and Grammar of Joseph Wright (1898-1905). Conversation among the students of language was possible only informally, in local groups. Even with our historical perspective, and the aid of A. G. Kennedy's *Bibliography of Writings in the English Language,* we find it difficult to know what was happening at that time. The scholars of 1919 must have often been frustrated, though such giants as C. H. Grandgent and G. O. Curme produced memorable work. Certainly, no professional scholar of the time would have dreamed of pre-

11 As an exception to the prevalent pattern of the time, I cite James L. Mann, local superintendent of schools (Greenville, S.C.) in my boyhood, a Ph.D. from the University of Berlin and a man of deep appreciation of serious learning. In one of our last conversations, just before I entered graduate school, he urged me to take Old English right away, and Gothic whenever I had a chance. He was the first person to direct me toward courses in linguistics.

12 In 1965 Frederic G. Cassidy of the University of Wisconsin, a former dialect fieldworker in the North-Central States and one of the editors of the *Dictionary of Jamaican English* (1967), began assembling evidence toward a Dictionary of American Regional English (DARE) with the help of a grant from the U.S. Office of Education; it is now nearing completion.

senting a discussion of the totality of American English. It took a layman, energetic and fearless and delighted in the American scene, to rush in where the academic angels feared to tread.

To resume our mathematical metaphor, Mencken was the epitome of point integration. His lack of formal training in linguistics (he had no more than a high school diploma, though it might be suggested that the Baltimore Polytechnic of the 1890's provided more nourishing intellectual fare than many American colleges of the 1960's) was an advantage, for he didn't know how impossible was the task that he had set himself. Bilingual in English and German, he knew intuitively the differences between linguistic systems. He read voraciously, both for sheer pleasure and as a part of his duties as a newspaperman. On his beats he had observed the rich dialectal diversity of Baltimore—a city astraddle one of the major dialect boundaries in the United States,[13] once dominated by branches of the Virginia aristocracy but now rapidly industrializing, culturally enriched by Germans of the 1848 migrations, a market town for the Pennsylvania German settlements, a rendezvous for oystermen, fishermen, crab-catchers and tobacco-farmers, a magnet for miscellaneous proletarian whites, and a way-station for Negroes on the move from the South to New York. He had read the fascicles of *Dialect Notes* and what was currently available about the study of language, notably the works of A. H. Sayce and William Dwight Whitney. His daily practice as a reporter had not only taught him a vigorous, natural style but had encouraged his amusement at the antics of *homo boobensis Americanus* and his delight at stirring up the animals. Finally, his muzzling by Attorney-General J. Mitchel Palmer's Dogberrys during the heresy hunts of World War I[14] provided him with leisure in which he could draw together his observations on American English, some of which had appeared in the *Baltimore Sun* as early as 1910.

The First Edition

The claims Mencken made in the first edition were modest enough:

It is anything but an exhaustive treatise upon the subject; it is not even an exhaustive examination of the materials. All it pretends to do is to articulate some of those materials—to get some approach to order and coherence to them, and so pave

[13] For the position of Baltimore see Hans Kurath, *A Word Geography of the Eastern United States* (Ann Arbor, Mich.: The University of Michigan Press, 1949) and Hans Kurath and Raven I. McDavid, *The Pronunciation of English in the Atlantic States* (Ann Arbor, Mich.: The University of Michigan Press, 1962).

[14] The venom of these heresy hunts was more virulent than that of the age of McCarthy. One of my noblest friends, John P. Grace, publisher of the Charleston (S.C.) *Mercury*, twice mayor of his city, and a fearless crusader for human rights (among other things, he broke the peonage system on the Sea Islands), was similarly forbidden to write in his own paper because, being of Irish descent, he could not swallow the notion that the English were emblems of unalloyed moral rectitude.

the way for a better work by some more competent man. That work calls for the equipment of a first-rate philologist, which I surely am not. All I have done here is to stake out the field, sometimes borrowing suggestions from other inquirers, and sometimes, as in the case of American grammar, attempting to run the lines myself.

But Mencken's delight in stirring up the animals led him to a calculated statement that the growing divergence of English and American would lead to mutually unintelligible languages. When this was added to his insistence that the American Vulgate was worthy of serious scholarship and his indication of wide areas which American academicians have left uninvestigated, many of the self-appointed guardians of the language took the work as a personal and professional insult. Some of the reviewers, like Bright of the Johns Hopkins (*Modern Language Notes*) and Hulbert of Chicago (*Modern Philology*), sought to draw the teeth from Mencken's arguments by pointing out his lack of formal linguistic training (freely conceded), or to excuse their failure to make a systematic study of the national idiom on the grounds that historical dictionaries and linguistic atlases had not been made. This last excuse, of course, only reinforced Mencken's argument; in his preface he had indicated:

I soon found that no such work [i.e., a study of the differences between British and American linguistic practices] existed, either in England or in America—that the whole literature of the subject was astonishingly meagre and unsatisfactory. . . . On the large and important subject of American pronunciation . . . I could find nothing save a few casual essays. On American spelling, with its wide and considerable divergences from English usages, there was little more. On American grammar there was nothing whatever. Worse, an important part of the poor literature that I unearthed was devoted to absurd efforts to prove that no such thing as an American variety of English existed. . . .

Temperate reviewers, like Brander Matthews of Columbia (*The New York Times*) and Curme (*Journal of English and Germanic Philology*),[15] acknowledged the corn and conceded that Mencken had a sounder understanding of the roots of American speechways than any academic philologist currently in practice. For four decades the debate over *The American Language* has continued along the lines established by its earliest version: its appreciation varies directly with the depth of the reviewer's understanding of language as a manifestation and a vehicle of culture.[16]

[15] Curme published two volumes of a projected *Grammar of the English Language—Accidence* (1935) and *Syntax* (1931)—the largest-scale work of its kind ever undertaken by an American.
[16] The latest version of *The American Language*—the Fourth Edition and the Two Supplements, abridged, with annotations and new material, by Raven I. McDavid, Jr., with the assistance of David W. Maurer—appeared in November, 1963. The paperback edition was published in 1977.

For once Alfred A. Knopf underestimated the appeal of a book by Mencken: only 1500 copies of the first edition were printed, and the type was distributed, so that a reprint was impossible. But the demand was such that Mencken brought out an expanded second edition in 1921 and a still fatter third in 1923. These expansions showed not only the public interest in the work, as evidenced by voluminous correspondence, but Mencken's generosity in acknowledging corrections and his willingness to consult sources he had neglected. With the Third Edition he laid the work aside, to become *diaboli advocatus* during the saturnalia of optimistic hokum that led from Harding to Coolidge to Hoover. The era, and Mencken's role as moral theologian, ended with the *suave qui peut* which converted the overpublicized Hoover Prosperity into the Great Depression.

But Mencken had won his point as an observer of American English. Whether it was simply that the times were ripe, or that the entrance of the United States into world affairs had made its scholars (if not its politicians) aware of the importance of languages, a tremendous growth took place in American linguistics between the first edition of *The American Language* in 1919 and the fourth in 1936. In 1921 appeared Sapir's *Language,* still the best written and most provocative work of its kind; in 1924, the Linguistic Society of America was founded, and J. S. Kenyon issued the first edition of his *American Pronunciation;* in 1925, George Philip Krapp brought out *The English Language in America* (with particular emphasis on historical phonology), Sir William Craigie started editing the *Dictionary of American English* at Chicago, and a group of scholars, egged on by Mencken, launched the journal *American Speech;*[17] in 1929, Sapir and Edgar Sturtevant made the first moves toward the Linguistic Atlas of the United States and Canada; in 1933, Leonard Bloomfield issued his *Language,* still the basic work for the systematic linguist, and began his work toward improving the teaching of reading.

In 1936, Fries, then working toward the *American English Grammar,* established the Linguistic Institute on a permanent basis by bringing it to Michigan for five consecutive summers as a regular feature of the summer school.[18] Since that time, there has always been at least one distinguished summer program in linguistics at some American university, providing not only a wider variety of courses than any single instituton could normally offer, but a forum in which established scholars could test their theories

[17] See "American Speech 1925-1945: the founders look back (comments by Mencken, Louise Pound, Kemp Malone and A. G. Kennedy)," *American Speech,* XX (1945), 241-6.
[18] Previous Linguistic Institutes had been offered by Yale and by the City College of New York, but they carried no credit and there had been no continuing tradition. A history of Linguistic Institutes, by A. A. Hill, is included in the final announcements of the 1964 Institute, held at Bloomington, Indiana, under the auspices of Indiana University.

against the arguments and evidence of their peers and at which beginners could observe the depth and complexity of their discipline. During the same period, Benjamin L. Whorf was advancing his stimulating hypothesis of the interrelationships of language and culture, and a few pioneering institutions, such as Michigan, were establishing courses in American English—naturally centered around Mencken's work.

The Fourth Edition

Most literate Americans are aware that Mencken's impact as a social satirist declined after 1930. This was not an unmixed bane, however, for he was now able to return to *The American Language* and incorporate new evidence, both from his own observations and from the scholarship of others in the preceding decade. With a new organization of his material—an organization virtually unchanged since[19]— and a somewhat less belligerent tone (in recognition of the fact that American academicians had at last begun to fulfil their responsibilities to the language), he introduced a new thesis: instead of diverging, the branches of the English-speaking community were drawing closer together, but the increasing American influence in world affairs was likely to make English, in the future, a sort of dialect of American. Fortunately Mencken did not discard all that he had written: many of his happier statements, such as his capsule history of English noun inflection, have been retained even to the present version. The two Supplements of 1945 and 1948, enjoyable reading as they are, essentially amplify previous statements or revise them in the light of new evidence. The 1963 abridgment is the first weaving together of all of Mencken's observations.

Linguistics Since World War II

The most important change in the climate of opinion since 1936 has been the discovery during World War II that professional students of language, like atomic physicists, could be used to implement military and diplomatic policy. As older linguists found their enrollments increasing and younger ones found themselves readily employable,[20] new outlets for publication and new forums for discussion were established. Reflecting the new order in international politics, the Germans and Japanese, already interested in American English,

---

[19] For the few changes in the current version, see the Editor's Introduction, pp. xi-xiv.

[20] Ironically, since most universities follow the economic rule of buying talent as cheaply as possible, some of the best linguists have had greater difficulty getting properly placed than have raw Ph.D.'s. At least one brilliant theoretician, who made his mark in the profession before 1940, did not achieve academic tenure till 1962; and several others have gravitated to unglamorous if sound institutions.

have begun to study it more systematically,[21] and their American seminars have been emulated not only by our official allies but by our coexisting competitors. This increased interest, at home and elsewhere, has led to a bibliographical explosion comparable to that in the physical sciences, so that the teacher (always more important in linguistics than in most of the humanities) has acquired an added responsibility for providing breadth and depth, and for developing students who can form their own conclusions and not merely parrot someone else.

Mencken's Place Today

In this new situation, Mencken's work has still much to commend it to a generation of technically directed linguists. In fact, these new developments make his work more relevant than ever. He provides a historical orientation to the American way of speech that can be found nowhere else—a profound appreciation of the intricately intermingling influences that have made American English. In addition, he has shown how historical developments—the opening of the West in the early Nineteenth Century, the rise of cities after the Civil War—have been reflected in the changing fashions in linguistic processes and in modes of expression, and in changing attitudes toward both the American variety of English as a whole and toward specific words, pronunciations and grammatical constructions. With the historical orientation he mingles a strong cultural orientation, a concern that extends far beyond the section of Chapter II so designated. Not satisfied with the technical definitions, from John Witherspoon to Mitford Mathews, he repeatedly asks what are the common characteristics of the linguistic features that we will generally recognize as Americanisms, and why such linguistic features have arisen in English-speaking North America. Unanswerable questions? Perhaps. But few fundamental questions are ever answered completely.

There are many specific virtues. It is a beautifully written book, where every page proclaims the author a professional writer who enjoys the work of writing. The range of information, eclectically garnered, is immense. The style ranges from the delicate to the grotesque, from serious scholarship to outrageous buffoonery. It is a work whose bulk requires the reader to put it down, but whose vitality leads him to pick it up again. It can be dipped into for five minutes or studied seriously all afternoon. One finds delight in controversy, generous acknowledgment of the help others have given—especially the beginners in the field. The effect of this generosity cannot be exaggerated: in my own specific case, Mencken's generous acknowledgment and Leonard

---

[21] Noteworthy is Hans Galinsky, of the American Seminar at the Johannes Gutenberg Universität, Mainz. The *Deutsche Gesellschaft für Amerika studium* has also been interested in American English.

Bloomfield's encouragement combined to make me a linguist, against formidable odds.

The chief weakness of the book, as many observers have indicated, is Mencken's failure to understand formulaic structural statements, of whatever school. Part of this, to be sure, comes from the fact that Mencken left mathematics at the Baltimore Polytechnic and never returned. But this is not the whole truth, since Mencken always appreciated exact scientific statements. The rest comes from his suspicion, not without foundation, that many of the younger linguists use their mathematical designs and their gnarled, infelicitous style to conceal their muddled thinking. We must recognize that the public writing of most linguists is pretty bad, far worse than that of physicists or social anthropologists and sometimes approaching the obscurantism of literary critics. Too many linguists deliberately write for their own coteries and never present the evidence on which their argument depends. As a professional linguist attempting to keep up with developments in my field, I cannot deplore too warmly this apparent contempt for the reader, nor resent Mencken's impatience with the brethren guilty of such faults.

IMPLICATIONS OF *The American Language*

Mencken's work thus provides the younger linguist with perspective that their academic training does not give. It also provides a unifying theme to the somewhat diffuse discipline of American studies, since it relates language to the total complex of social and cultural developments in the United States. On a larger scene, it should stimulate the students of language-in-culture, as a model for relating linguistic phenomena to the totality of human behavior. Whatever language one is interested in (and the resources of English are far from exhausted), it suggests how one may take the best linguistic evidence and interpret it against the ground of all the associated aspects of human activity, as studied in sociology, anthropology, psychology, folklore and literature. Here is challenge enough for an army of the intellectually adventurous.

LESSONS FOR LINGUISTS

I pointed out earlier the caution of Andreyev: that people speak in actual languages, and not in their models. To this may be added Mencken's observation that his principal purpose was to convince the academic brethren that the study of American English, in all its complexities, can be interesting—and more than interesting, important. The linguist who shrinks not from designing his model, but remembers that it is only a model, and that new and unpredictable combinations of linguistic forms can be expected from a speech community of 250,000,000 people, "many of them amusing, and some of them wise," is on his way to establishing his discipline in its place as the unifying force among the humanities and social sciences.

CHRONOLOGY

1880	H. L. Mencken born.
1910	First articles on American English, *Baltimore Sun.*
1919	*American Language,* first edition.
1921	*American Language,* second edition.
1923	*American Language,* third edition.
1936	*American Language,* fourth edition.
1945	*American Language,* Supplement One.
1948	*American Language,* Supplement Two; Mencken's writing career terminated by first of a series of strokes.
1956	(February) Death of Mencken.
1963	Raven I. McDavid, Jr. edition.
1977	Paperbank cf 1963 ed.
1980	Mencken Centennial Celebrations Planned: Baltimore, Maryland; Newberry Library, Chicago, Illinois; International Association of University Professors of English, Aberdeen, Scotland.

Toward a Modern Theory of of Rhetoric: A Tagmemic Contribution

RICHARD E. YOUNG
University of Michigan

ALTON L. BECKER
University of Michigan

In this article Richard Young and Alton Becker define the subject matter of rhetoric as it has been traditionally understood since antiquity. Noting serious weaknesses in classical rhetoric the authors then illustrate how aspects of one linguistic theory, tagmemics, can form the basis for a new approach to such problems as invention, arrangement, and style.

Our discussion will be adequate if it has as much clearness as the subject-matter admits of, for precision is not to be sought for alike in all discussions. . . . We must be content . . . in speaking of such subjects and with such premises to indicate the truth roughly and in outline, and in speaking about things which are only for the most part true and with premises of the same kind to reach conclusions that are no better. In the same spirit, therefore, should each type of statement be *received;* for it is the mark of an educated man to look for precision in each class of things just so far as the nature of the subject admits; it is evidently equally foolish to accept probable reasoning from a mathematician and to demand from a rhetorician scientific proofs.

ARISTOTLE, *Nichomachean Ethics* i.3.1094b 12-28.
TRANS. W. D. ROSS

I

Years ago, the heart of a liberal education was the trivium of grammar, logic, and rhetoric. Modern linguistics has come to encompass more and more of

This article was in part supported by the Center for Research on Language and Language Behavior, University of Michigan, under Contract OE 5-14036, U. S. Office of Education.

Harvard Educational Review Vol. 35 No. 4 Fall 1965, 450–468

this trivium, and has in the process become transformed. Traditional grammar is no longer anathema to the linguist, and linguistic description has adopted many of the techniques of logical analysis. Furthermore, linguistics is becoming increasingly interested in the analysis and description of verbal structures beyond the sentence, traditionally a rhetorical concern. It seems fitting, therefore, to explore the relationships of linguistics and rhetoric—discovering, hopefully, just what contributions a theory of language can make to a modern theory of rhetoric.

As Aristotle states in the quotation given above, the nature of the subject matter imposes some constraints on the statements we make about it. It is our intention, therefore, to define the subject matter of rhetoric as it has been understood traditionally, and then to illustrate how aspects of one modern linguistic theory—tagmemics—can form the basis for a new approach to rhetorical problems. The field is broad and there are many points of contact between linguistics and rhetoric which will be passed over here. Nor can we hope to consider all linguistic points of view, each with important contributions to make. We will limit ourselves to a description of three traditional stages in the rhetorical process—invention, arrangement, and style—and then approach the problems of each stage via tagmemic theory.

There are four rhetorical traditions which, taken together, constitute the history of rhetoric. There is sophistic rhetoric, which has as its goal the effective manipulation of language without regard to truth and logic. This tradition continues in modern propaganda and in advertising techniques. There is Platonic anti-rhetoric, which stresses not the art of writing but the quality of the writer in his adherence to truth and virtue: a good writer is a good man writing. There is the rhetoric of literary criticism, which applies the categories and techniques of rhetoric to the analysis and evaluation of poetry, drama, and narration. And finally, there is Aristotelian rhetoric, which had its origins in the law courts of early Greece and which was expanded, systematized, and given a philosophic foundation by Aristotle. After being brought to perfection by Cicero and Quintilian, it constituted a basic, and at times *the* basic, discipline in Western education for fifteen hundred years. It survives today, but with greatly diminished influence. Because this is still the most complete rhetoric ever developed and because it best defines what traditionally has been the scope of rhetoric, we shall focus our attention almost exclusively on the Aristotelian tradition.

For Aristotle, rhetoric was "the faculty of observing in any given case the available means of persuasion."[1] Its immediate end was to persuade a popular audience of what is true and just; its ultimate end was to secure the cooperation necessary for a civilized society. The classical art of rhetoric consisted

---

[1] Aristotle, *Rhetoric*, i.2.1355b 26-27, trans. W. D. Ross, in *The Basic Works of Aristotle*, ed. Richard McKeon (New York: Random House, 1941), p. 1329.

of five separate arts which together embraced the entire process of developing and presenting a persuasive discourse: invention, arrangement, style, memory, and delivery. As the last two concern speaking rather than writing (which has become the principal concern of modern rhetoric), we shall consider only the first three: invention, arrangement, and style.

"Invention," wrote Cicero, "is the discovery of valid or seemingly valid arguments to render one's cause plausible."[2] Rhetoricians distinguished two kinds of arguments: extrinsic arguments, which came ready-made to the writer (e.g., eyewitness testimony, documents, confessions), and intrinsic arguments. The latter were of special interest to rhetoricians because they were subject to discovery by means of a system of topics. These topics were a kind of checklist of mental acts one could use when investigating and collecting arguments on a subject (e.g., definition by genus and differentia, comparison and contrast, cause and effect). Certain of these topics—the "common" topics—were appropriate to all types of speech; others—the "special" topics—were appropriate to only one of the three types of speech studied in the classical system: forensic, political, or ceremonial.

Use of the topics presupposed wide learning since they were primarily a method for putting the writer in contact with knowledge which already existed. Edward Corbett has remarked that Mortimer Adler's *Syntopicon* of Great Ideas of the Western World would have been an ideal reference work for the ancient rhetorician.[3] It was the art of invention which made rhetoric the core of humanistic education until the late Renaissance.

During the Renaissance, under the influence of Bacon and Descartes, logic increasingly came to be seen not as the art of learned discourse, as it had been since Greek times, but as an instrument of inquiry. Rhetoric gradually enlarged its boundaries to include the arts of both learned and popular discourse. The process was finally completed in the nineteenth century in the work of John Stuart Mill; commenting on the proper domains of logic and rhetoric, Mill remarked that

the sole object of Logic is the guidance of one's own thoughts: the communication of those thoughts to others falls under the consideration of Rhetoric, in the large sense in which that art was conceived by the ancients. . . .[4]

This spirit of modern science which was modifying the nature of logic and the scope of rhetoric also had its effect on the art of invention. Since the

[2] Quoted in Wilbur S. Howell, *Logic and Rhetoric in England, 1500-1700* (Princeton, N.J.: Princeton University Press, 1956), p. 66.
[3] Edward P. J. Corbett, *Classical Rhetoric for the Modern Student* (New York: Oxford University Press, 1965), p. 171.
[4] Quoted in Howell, p. 350.

seventeenth century, we have increasingly regarded facts and experimental evidence as the basis for sound argument, rather than relying—as did our ancestors—on the wisdom of the past. That is, we have increasingly put our faith in extrinsic arguments. We have become much more interested in techniques for discovering what is unknown than in techniques for bringing old beliefs to bear on new problems. Thus the classical art of invention has diminished in importance while the modern art of experimental inquiry has expanded immensely. But this art of inquiry is no longer a part of modern rhetoric—each academic discipline having developed its own discovery procedures. The strength and worth of rhetoric seem, however, to be tied to the art of invention; rhetoric tends to become a superficial and marginal concern when it is separated from systematic methods of inquiry and problems of content.

The second art in classical rhetoric was that of arrangement. Rhetoricians developed persuasive patterns for organizing their materials—flexible systems of slots into which appropriate categories of subject matter were fitted. One common arrangement, the Ciceronian, had six slots: the exordium; the narrative, or exposition of the problem's history; the proposition; the demonstration; the refutation of alternative propositions; and the peroration. The functions and structures of each of these slots were systematically developed and described. Arrangement was the art of distributing within this pattern the subject matter gathered in the process of invention; arrangement also involved modifying the pattern by expanding, omitting, or reorganizing the various steps to meet the needs of the audience, speaker, and subject matter. The pattern was employed in all three types of speech: forensic, political, and ceremonial.

Since rhetoric was the art of persuasion, patterns for other modes of discourse (e.g., description, exposition) were given little attention. In the seventeenth century, however, developments in science led to an increasing interest in expository prose, a movement which parallels the shift from intrinsic to extrinsic argument. Other developments, such as the decline in the power of the aristocracy and the growing importance of evangelical religion, led to a rejection of elaborate patterning and the development of simpler, more manageable rhetorical forms, though none was described in the same detail as were the classical patterns.

Implicit in classical theory was a dualistic conception of discourse. Form was treated as independent of both the subject matter and the writer. Since the Renaissance, there has been a tendency to see form as the product of a particular mind or as discoverable within the subject matter itself. In the latter case, the form of a discourse is not separable from the content—the discourse is seen as having an organic unity. In either case, the form of a work is not predictable. If form is a personal matter, or is implicit in the subject matter, the rhetorician can make fewer generalizations about arrangement. Classical rhetoric was a rhetoric of precept; in modern times it has become, for the most part, a rhetoric of practice.

Style, the third of the rhetorical arts in classical rhetoric, was largely the technique of framing effective sentences. Its function was to give clarity, force, and beauty to ideas. Although grammar was its foundation, style was clearly a separate art, concerned with the effective use of language rather than simply with the correct use. Both, however, were concerned with language at the sentence level.

Aristotle justified the study of style on practical grounds. Ideally, rational argument alone should be sufficient to persuade. Since experience suggests that this is often not sufficient, the art of style must be employed if wisdom is to be persuasive. The art of style tended, however, to become an end in itself, at times preempting the entire field of rhetoric, possibly—as in the classical conception of arrangement—because of a dualistic view in which content and style were separable.

In the classical tradition, good style was a deliberate departure from the speech of everyday life. Renaissance classicists ingeniously isolated and systematized figures of speech. Henry Peacham's *Garden of Eloquence* (1577), for example, lists 184 schemes and tropes—artistic departures from ordinary syntax and word meanings. Clarity and appropriateness became less frequent constraints than elegance and ingenuity. As a result, "rhetoric" gained its pejorative connotation of elegant but empty verbosity.

As with the other rhetorical arts, there was a reaction against this concept of style; rhetoricians now sought a norm closer to the speech of everyday life. In the eighteenth century, the dualistic conception of style and content began to compete with monistic conceptions. Style came to mean either the characteristic expression of a particular personality (*Le style c'est l'homme même*) or the mode of expression organically a part of the subject matter itself.

Since the eighteenth century, the analysis of style has become almost exclusively the concern of literary criticism. In rhetoric courses today, style is still seen by and large as the art of framing effective sentences; but the art is much simpler, less systematic, and considerably more intuitive than it was in classical rhetoric.

The classical art of rhetoric has a number of weaknesses which make it inadequate for our time. Without involving ourselves directly in a criticism of the philosophical assumptions upon which classical rhetoric is based, we can note, in general, four major problems. First, the classical art of invention stresses authoritative confirmation of present beliefs, while modern modes of inquiry stress imaginative discovery of new facts and relationships. Second, the art of arrangement includes only patterns of persuasion, and neglects considerations of form in other important rhetorical modes such as description, narration, and exposition. Third, both the art of arrangement and the art of style divorce form from content, failing to consider the importance of the act of discovery in the shaping of form. And finally, the art of style is concerned primarily with embellishing, clarifying, and giving point to sentences, an approach which neglects both the deeper personal roots of style and the ways in which style is manifested in patterns beyond the sentences.

In recent years, numerous rhetoricians have been seeking a new rhetoric which would be as effective on a practical level and as stimulating and coherent on a theoretical level as is classical rhetoric. As Daniel Fogarty puts it, there are numerous "roots for a new rhetoric."[5] While other members of the trivium have changed greatly from their earlier forms (witness the revolution in Mill's *System of Logic*, the later changes in symbolic logic, and the recent revolution in grammatical theory), there has as yet been no comparable change in rhetoric. That is, there has been no change which includes both a complete theory and an explicit practical method. Rhetoric is still in the midst of a chaotic transition period. I. A. Richards is right, unfortunately, when he describes the general state of rhetoric today as

the dreariest and least profitable part of the waste that the unfortunate travel through in Freshman English! So low has Rhetoric sunk that we would do better just to dismiss it to Limbo than to trouble ourselves with it—unless we can find reason for believing that it can become a study that will minister successfully to important needs.[6]

II

The tagmemic approach to language analysis and description, developed primarily by Kenneth L. Pike and his associates in the Summer Institute of Linguistics,[7] has for many years been concerned with problems which have traditionally been within the scope of rhetoric. This concern results, in part, from the strong motivation which such a model gives for moving beyond the

[5] Daniel Fogarty, *Roots for a New Rhetoric* (New York: Bureau of Publications, Teachers College, Columbia University, 1959).

[6] I. A. Richards, *The Philosophy of Rhetoric* (New York: Oxford University Press, 1936), p. 3. Kenneth Burke and S. I. Hayakawa have both developed extremely interesting theories of rhetoric and must be mentioned, along with Richards, as having made notable contributions to the development of a new rhetoric.

[7] The basic source of tagmemic theory is Kenneth L. Pike, *Language in Relation to a Unified Theory of the Structure of Human Behavior* (The Hague: Mouton, 1967). Pike applies tagmemic theory to problems of rhetoric in "Beyond the Sentence," *College Composition and Communication*, XV, No. 3 (October, 1964), and "Discourse Analysis and Tagmeme Matrices," *Oceanic Linguistics* (April, 1965).

specification of well-made sentences. In tagmemic theory, any linguistic unit is assumed to be well defined only when three aspects of the unit are specified: its contrastive features, its range of variation, and its distribution in sequence and ordered classes. This constraint on grammatical description (defined as a description necessary and sufficient to include all relevant aspects of any linguistic unit) has meant that a complete description of sentences, for example, should include a specification of their distribution in paragraphs and other larger units of discourse.

This concern with problems which traditionally have been a part of rhetoric also results from the desire of many who use the tagmemic model to provide a means for producing extended discourse, primarily biblical translation. Translators frequently encounter instances of grammatical constraints extending beyond the sentence. In some Philippine languages, for example, there is a system of focus somewhat like active and passive voice in English though vastly more complex. To produce understandable discourse in these languages apparently requires a marked correlation between situational roles (actor, goal, instrument, setting, etc.) and grammatical roles (subject, predicate, object, locative, etc.) in a sequence of sentences.[8]

As the linguist moves beyond the sentence, he finds himself asking questions which have long concerned rhetoricians. The description of the structure of a sentence and the description of the structure of an expository paragraph, extended argument, or novel are not sharply different kinds of activity, for all involve selecting and ordering language in a significant way. The traditional separation of grammar, logic, rhetoric, and poetics begins to break down.

Selecting and ordering language, however, has two aspects. One sort of inquiry into the selection and ordering of language leads us deeply into the mental activity of the writer and into questions which are difficult, perhaps impossible, to answer except intuitively. Can we specify in detail why a writer chooses to write "John loves Mary" rather than "John is in love with Mary"? Probably not; we can only describe the choices he does make, the characteristic features of his style. Another sort of inquiry, however, leads us to the conventions which constrain the writer. We can specify the reasons why "Love John is Mary in" does not make sense to us except in rather far-fetched ways. In the same way, we believe we can specify why the following sequence of sentences does not make sense:

The trees are budding. Coal is a form of carbon. He has been singing for three hours now. The world used to be round. It seems enough.

[8] Kenneth L. Pike, "A Syntactic Paradigm," *Language*, *XXXIX* (April-June, 1963), 216-30. See also "Discourse Analysis and Tagmeme Matrices," footnote 7.

If we were to prod the reader, insisting that the above "sentence" and "paragraph" do have meaning, he could probably find some sense in them, as many have in Chomsky's "Colorless green ideas sleep furiously." In each case one "discovers" meaning by imposing conventional formal patterns on the deviant sequences.

Both the process of imposing pattern on (or discovering pattern in) apparently meaningless utterances and the process of describing the conventions of language are important to the linguist. In the former process, he uses some sort of discovery procedure; in the latter, he employs a descriptive model which specifies the structures of conventional utterances. Although the act of discovery is in part intuitive, the model does provide both a method for finding significant linguistic patterns and a taxonomy of the sort of patterns the analyst is likely to find—the still tentative universals of language. Discovery procedures are not mechanical; there is as yet no completely systematic way of analyzing a language, just as there is no algorithm for planning an effective literary composition. But there are important guides to the processes: one can learn to analyze a language and he can learn a great deal about how to write an essay or a novel.

We believe that the procedures the linguist uses in analyzing and describing a language are in some important ways like the procedures a writer uses in planning and writing a composition, and hence that tagmemic theory can provide the basis for a new approach to rhetoric. Tagmemic discovery procedures can provide a heuristic comparable to the Aristotelian system of invention; the tagmemic descriptive model can give us a vehicle for describing conventional rhetorical patterns. If our beliefs are sound, this approach will provide a bridge between the traditionally separate disciplines of grammar and rhetoric.

A heuristic is a method of solving problems, a series of steps or questions which are likely to lead an intelligent analyst to a reasonable solution of a problem. There are two different (though related) kinds of heuristic: a taxonomy of the sorts of solutions that have been found in the past; and an epistemological heuristic, a method of inquiry based on assumptions about how we come to know something. Bacon's statement of the distinction is worth quoting:

The invention of speech or argument is not properly an invention: for to invent is to discover that we know not, and not to recover or resummon that which we already know; and the use of this invention is no other but *out of the knowledge whereof our mind is already possessed, to draw forth or call before us that which may be pertinent to the purpose which we take into our consideration.* So as, to speak truly, it is no *Invention,* but a *Remembrance* or *Suggestion,* with an application; which is the cause why the schools do place it after judgment, as subsequent and not precedent. Nevertheless, because we do account it a Chase as well of deer in an inclosed park as in a forest at large, and that it hath already obtained the name, let it be called invention: so as it be perceived and discerned, that the scope and end of this invention is readiness and present use of our knowledge, and not addition or amplification thereof.[9]

Aristotelian rhetoric provides a taxonomy of effective rhetorical arguments which a speaker can use to attain specific ends with specific audiences. Tagmemic theory, on the other hand, provides an epistemological heuristic.

Tagmemic epistemology is based largely on two principles, though other principles are necessary for a complete statement of the theory. These two principles emphasize the active role of the observer in discovering pattern, and hence meaning, in the world around him. The first principle contrasts external and internal views of human behavior—in tagmemic jargon, *etic* and *emic* views. This distinction can be seen in the differences between phonetic and phonemic contrasts in linguistic phonology. A phonetic inventory provides a systematic statement of the overt phonological distinctions which occur in various human languages, while a phonemic description provides a systematic statement of the *significant* phonological distinctions in a particular language. A distinction is judged significant, and hence phonemic, if it signals a difference in the lexical meaning of linguistic units. Though there is much controversy about how phonological signals are to be described, the basic distinction remains valid: the contrast, for example, between aspirated and unaspirated consonants is lexically significant for a native speaker of Hindi or Burmese but not for a native speaker of English, who has difficulty in learning to hear this contrast.

The distinction is especially important when two emic systems come in contact, as when the speaker of English is learning to speak Hindi and is forced to recognize that his native distinctions are emic and not necessarily universal. Likewise, one who finds himself in a different culture must learn to distinguish universals of human behavior from particular customs and mores which taken together comprise the emic distinctions of a culture. The ways of treating time and space, for example, vary throughout the world, and one must learn these ways if he wishes to communicate and cooperate outside his own culture.

Though it is interesting to envision a universal etics of rhetoric—an orderly classification of the rhetorical forms found throughout the world—our present concern must be with the writer of English who is writing for readers of English. Even with this restriction one confronts frequent clashes of emic systems, for if a writer has anything new to say, his image of the world must

[9] Quoted in Howell, p. 367.

be in some way different from that of his reader. It is at this point of difference that his message lies. He may seek to expand or clarify some feature of the reader's image, thus making it more nearly like his own, or he may seek to replace some feature of the reader's image. In the first instance he would be informing; in the second, persuading.

Before developing this discussion of rhetorical intention further, we must introduce the second major principle in tagmemic epistemology. This principle asserts that a complete analysis of a problem necessitates a trimodal perspective. After the trimodal principle had been worked out in tagmemic theory and the so-called *feature, manifestation,* and *distribution* modes had been defined, Pike noted a striking similarity between these modes and the triple perspectives of modern physics—the complementary views of physical phenomena as involving particles, waves, and fields; as a consequence, Pike decided to adopt this second set of terms for his behavioral model.[10]

Language phenomena—and presumably all human behavior—can be viewed in terms of particles (discrete contrastive bits), waves (unsegmentable physical continua), or fields (orderly systems of relationships). For example, a sentence can be viewed as a sequence of separate words or morphemes; as a physical continuum consisting of acoustic waveforms; or as a system of interrelationships manifesting the grammatical, lexical, and phonological rules of English. Tagmemic theory asserts that only by this complementarity of perspectives is a complete analysis of language structure possible.

The principle of trimodalism gives the analyst both a procedure for approaching new problems and a safeguard against a too limited view of the data. Only when he has described his data from all three perspectives can he be reasonably sure that his analysis is complete. The writer, likewise, can use the principle as an aid in discovering a wide range of features in his topic. Though a writer often emphasizes one mode in a particular work, he should be aware of the other possibilities, particularly if his readers customarily emphasize a different mode. Let us consider a simple example. A particle description of a flower emphasizes those features which make it distinctive from other flowers. A wave description emphasizes the flower as a moment in a process from seed to final decay (even this is only a peak in a larger wave) or as merging into a scene. A field description may partition a flower into its functional parts or classify it in a taxonomical system. The flower may also be seen metaphorically or symbolically, in which case it is conceived as part of a new conceptual field (religious, say, or geometric), where certain of its features (its beauty or its shape) are hypostatized, allowing it to manifest

[10] Kenneth L. Pike, "Language as Particle, Wave, and Field," *The Texas Quarterly,* II (Summer, 1959), pp. 37-54.

a category in a new field. One can view any topic trimodally and soon discover a wide range of significant perspectives.[11] The process is broad, flexible, and intuitive, though the intuition is guided by what has proved to be a very fruitful principle. It is especially useful since it is not limited to a particular subject matter. In this sense, it is similar to the "common" topics of classical rhetoric. A generally applicable approach helps to free us from the built-in limitations of a conventional, specialized approach. Thus the discovery procedure has a corrective function also.

This heuristic procedure—based on the emic-etic distinction and trimodal perspective—both helps the writer explore his topic and generates a set of questions which he can use to analyze his reader's preconceptions, that is, his reader's emic system:

1) What are the distinctive features of the reader's conception of the topic? What characteristics does it have that lead him to contrast it with similar things? (Particle view)

2) How are the reader's views on this topic part of a mental process, a phase in the continual development of his system of values and assumptions? (Wave view)

3) How does the reader partition the topic? What are its functional elements for him? How does he classify it? (Field view)
The answers to these questions provide criteria for selecting and ordering the writer's subject matter as he develops his discourse.

The missionary linguist in the field seeks to translate his message into the language and cultural conventions of the people, not to teach them English and his own emic conventions. He does not seek to replace their emic system with his own, but to modify their image after finding within it their motivations for receiving his message.[12] For he realizes that change is most effective and enduring when it occurs within the emic system of those he is trying to convince. Unlike traditional rhetoric which sought to persuade people by confirming authoritative attitudes, modern rhetoric, we believe, must seek identification. That is, the writer must seek to have his readers identify his message with their emic system.

Because it seeks identification rather than persuasion, and because this assumption often leads the writer to modify his own position, modern rhetoric—still in the process of development—is characterized by Kenneth Burke and others as "discussion rhetoric." The basis for a rhetoric of this sort has

---

[11] For further illustrations of the use of tagmemic discovery procedures in rhetorical invention, see Hubert English, "Linguistics as an Aid to Invention," *College Composition and Communication*, XV, No. 3 (October, 1964).

[12] Our conception of the image here is drawn in large part from Kenneth Boulding, *The Image* (Ann Arbor: University of Michigan Press, 1956), and from William Angus Sinclair, *Conditions of Knowing* (London: Routledge & Kegan Paul, 1951).

been developed by Anatol Rapaport in his book *Fights, Games, and Debates,* where it is called Rogerian debate—its assumptions having been derived from the methods of the psychotherapist Carl Rogers.[13] This principle of identification of the writer with his audience points toward a rhetoric not of opposition but of mutual respect.

A comparison of emic systems—different systems of selecting and grouping followed by writer and reader—leads the writer to find what he shares with his reader in his conception of the topic and what he does not share. One of the assumptions of tagmemics is that change can occur only over the bridge of a shared element. There can be no action at a distance. The key to understanding language change, for example, is the identification of the shared features of the initial state and the subsequent altered state. The writer's message is an unshared item in the comparison, while the shared items, insofar as they are relevant to the message, provide the means by which the reader can identify—and identify with—the message. Shared items are the potential bridges over which change can take place. These bridges may be broad cultural conventions or more specific things such as common social roles, problems, or philosophical assumptions. Among the most important of these shared items is a common language—a common set of patterns and rules governing selection and grouping of words or morphemes within a sentence, and of sentences and paragraphs within still larger units of discourse. It is here that the linguist can make his unique contribution to a new theory of rhetoric, especially as he broadens his focus to include units larger than the sentence.

So far we have dealt chiefly with what might be called prewriting problems, problems of discovery. We believe, as did Aristotle and Cicero, that a complete theory of rhetoric must include the entire sequence of acts which result in the finished discourse, beginning with the initial act of mental exploration. We have offered two principles of tagmemic heuristic as an indication, hardly an exhaustive one, of how linguistics can contribute to this aspect of rhetorical theory. We now turn to a description of rhetorical patterns beyond the sentence, extending techniques which have been used in the past in the description of lower-level patterns.

Early tagmemics was essentially, but not entirely, a slot-and-substitution grammar, describing linguistic patterns as sequences of functional slots which are filled, or manifested, by a class of fillers. These slots are seen as functional parts of a pattern and may be stated in a formula such as the following simplified formula for an English transitive sentence:

[13] Anatol Rapaport, *Fights, Games, and Debates* (Ann Arbor: University of Michigan Press, 1961).

$$+ \text{Subject} + \text{Verb} + \text{Object} \pm \text{Manner} \pm \text{Locative} \pm \text{Temporal}$$

(He walked the dog slowly around the block yesterday.) Some of these slots are obligatory (+), some optional (±). Each may be manifested by one of a set of filler constructions; thus the subject slot can be filled by a noun phrase, a pronoun, an adjective phrase, a verbal phrase, a clause, etc. More fully represented, the subject slot in the formula above would be:

$$+ \text{Subject:} \quad \text{np,p,ap,vp,} \ldots \text{c}$$

Tagmemics assumes that language is composed of interlocking lexical, phonological, and grammatical hierarchies. Here, the internal surface structure of the fillers of the subject slot of the sentence are described at the clause, phrase, word, and morpheme levels of the grammatical hierarchy.

In at least two important ways, however, recent tagmemic grammar goes beyond the surface-level descriptions of other slot-and-substitution grammars.[14] First, tagmemic grammars go on to represent the filler class of a functional slot as a multidimensionally ordered set, or, in tagmemic jargon, a matrix. The categories of these ordered sets indicate relationships of concord between one tagmeme and another; thus, the filler class of the subject tagmeme is ordered into categories such as singular-plural and human-nonhuman in concord with these same categories in the predicate, so that, for example, a singular, nonhuman subject specifies the selection of a singular, nonhuman verb, preventing such collocations as "the tree jump fences."

Second, and more important for our present discussion, tagmemic grammars specify in addition to the surface structure of patterns an ordered set of operations to be carried out on the patterns. These include ordered reading rules by which all possible readings of a formula are generated. Then each reading is reordered according to permutation rules. Finally, in each reading and its permuted variants, the tagmeme symbols are replaced by each of the possible filler constructions according to a set of exponence rules. These operations are carried out repeatedly until only morphemes or symbols for morpheme classes manifest the formulas, which are then terminal grammatical strings, not yet sentences until phonological and lexical specifications have been met.

Though a description of English will not specify sentences such as the one mentioned earlier, "Love John is Mary in," it so far contains no constraints to prevent it from accepting a sequence of sentences of this type:

[14] A full description of tagmemic grammatical theory can be found in Robert Longacre, *Grammar Discovery Procedures* (The Hague: Mouton, 1964). Tagmemics is contrasted with transformational and other models in Longacre, "Some Fundamental Insights of Tagmemics," *Language*, XLI, No. 1 (January-March, 1965), pp. 65-76.

The trees are budding. Coal is a form of carbon. He has been singing for three hours now. The world used to be round. It seems enough.

This is not a paragraph because there is no formal connection between the sentences. We can discern no conventional pattern relating them, as we can, for example, in this pair of sentences:

> What is John doing?
> He's washing his face.

This second sequence manifests a conventional rhetorical pattern—Question-Answer. The question is marked by three formal features: the word order, the question word *what,* and (in writing) the punctuation. The second sentence is recognized as an answer to the question by: the pronoun reference (*he* has to be a substitute for *John* here); the parallel grammatical structure, in which the functional slots of the question words in the first sentence (What . . . doing) are filled in the second (washing his face); the parallelism of verb form (is —ing); the fact that *washing* is a possible lexical equivalent for *doing;* and (in writing) the period. Question-Answer is a formal pattern illustrating a number of formal constraints which extend beyond the sentence.

The relationship of these two sentences can be described in numerous ways (probably most simply by seeing the first as a permutation of the second), but the sentences can only be described as a *sequence* by positing the larger Question-Answer pattern, and by specifying the formal ways in which the two functional slots in this larger pattern are related, just as we specify the relationship between subject and predicate in a sentence. A number of these relatively simple two-part patterns can be described, including greetings, cause and result (hypothesis), topic and illustration, topic and partition, disjunction, and so forth. These patterns can be manifested by a single sentence or by two or more sentences. A large number of higher-level units of discourse can be described as chains of these simple two-part patterns.

As we move on to larger rhetorical patterns, the complexity increases. Formal signals become redundant: for example, we can identify the Answer in the Question-Answer pattern above by five of its contrastive features. Further, lexical and semantic features become increasingly important in recognizing patterns: in the example above we recognize *washing* as a lexical equivalent of *doing.* Lexical equivalence chains are probably the most important markers of higher-level patterns.[15] We can illustrate some of this complexity by attempting to describe the paragraph as a formal structure, limiting ourselves here to only one rather simple pattern.

---

[15] The concept of lexical equivalence chains is derived in large part from Zellig S. Harris, *Discourse Analysis Reprints* (The Hague: Mouton, 1963), pp. 7-10.

We believe that written paragraphs are emically definable units—not just groups of sentences isolated by rather arbitrary indentations—and that this fact can be demonstrated. We are presently carrying out controlled testing of the recognition of these units in collaboration with psychologists at the Center for Research on Language and Language Behavior, University of Michigan. Informal investigation has shown that readers, given a text in which all paragraph indentations have been removed, can successfully mark paragraph breaks, with only limited indeterminancy at predictable points. In addition, the readers are able to recognize a number of recurring paragraph patterns and to partition these patterns in predictable ways.

One of the most common of these patterns is the one we have labelled TRI (topic-restriction-illustration) or more formally,

$$+ T^2 \pm R + I^n.$$

(The raised numbers indicate that in reading the formula, T may be read twice; R, once; and I, n number of times recursively.) This is the Topic-Illustration pattern with an optional intermediary slot in which the topic is restricted in some way (e.g., by definition, classification, or partition). The following paragraph illustrates this pattern:

(T) The English Constitution—that indescribable entity—is a living thing, growing with the growth of men, and assuming ever-varying forms in accordance with the subtle and complex laws of human character. (R) It is the child of wisdom and chance. (I) The wise men of 1688 moulded it into the shape we know, but the chance that George I could not speak English gave it one of its essential peculiarities—the system of a Cabinet independent of the Crown and subordinate to the Prime Minister. The wisdom of Lord Grey saved it from petrification and set it upon the path of democracy. Then chance intervened once more. A female sovereign happened to marry an able and pertinacious man, and it seemed likely that an element which had been quiescent within it for years—the element of irresponsible administrative power—was about to become its predominant characteristic and change completely the direction of its growth. But what chance gave, chance took away. The Consort perished in his prime, and the English Constitution, dropping the dead limb with hardly a tremor, continued its mysterious life as if he had never been.[16]

The slots in this tripartite pattern are marked by lexical equivalence classes, two of which have extended domains: 1) English Constitution, indescribable entity, living thing, It, child, . . . English Constitution; 2) men, human character, wise men of 1688, George I, Lord Grey, . . . Consort. Note that the domain of the first chain is the entire paragraph, while that of the second chain is the I slot. Chains can thereby be ranked as head and attribute chains, each paragraph including a head chain and one or more attribute chains.

[16] Lytton Strachey, *Queen Victoria* (New York: Harcourt, Brace, 1921), pp. 300-301.

The slots are also marked by: grammatical parallelism (first and second sentences, third and fourth sentences); tense shift (shift to past in the I slot); pronoun domains; determiners; and transitional function words (then, but).

The TRI pattern has a number of variant forms which can be specified by the reading, permutation, and exponence rules. Only a few of these variants will be illustrated. Since R is optional, the pattern can be read as: + T + I. For example, a paragraph by Marchette Chute:

(T) The only safe way to study contemporary testimony is to bear constantly in mind this possibility of prejudice and to put almost as much attention on the writer himself as on what he has written. (I) For instance, Sir Anthony Weldon's description of the Court of King James is lively enough and often used as source material; but a note from the publisher admits that the pamphlet was issued as a warning to anyone who wished to "side with this bloody house" of Stuart. The publisher, at any rate, did not consider Weldon an impartial witness. At about the same time Arthur Wilson published his history of Great Britain, which contained an irresistibly vivid account of the agonized death of the Countess of Somerset. Wilson sounds reasonably impartial; but his patron was the Earl of Essex, who had good reason to hate that particular countess, and there is evidence that he invented the whole scene to gratify his patron.[17]

If I is read a number of times, the pattern may be broken by indentation into more than one paragraph, although it remains a single emic unit. Indentation, like line ends in poetry, can either correspond to formal junctures or, for various reasons, can interrupt the structure in a way somewhat similar to poetic enjambment.

The TRI pattern can be permuted to IRT, producing the so-called funnel effect or inductive structure. This is comparable to such permutations at the sentence level as "Home is the sailor" from "The sailor is home." Another illustration by Marchette Chute:

(I) The reason Alice had so much trouble with her flamingo is that the average flamingo does not wish to be used as a croquet mallet. It has other purposes in view. The same thing is true of a fact, which can be just as self-willed as a flamingo and has its own kind of stubborn integrity. (R) To try to force a series of facts into a previously desired arrangement is a form of misuse to which no self-respecting fact will willingly submit itself. (T) The best and only way to treat it is to leave it alone and be willing to follow where it leads, rather than to press your own wishes upon it.[18]

This permutation is frequently used to begin or end discourse, probably because it imparts a greater sense of closure than the more open-ended TRI order.

[17] Marchette Chute, "Getting at the Truth," *The Saturday Review*, Sept. 19, 1953, p. 12.
[18] *Ibid.*, p. 44.

Other permutations include TIRI, ITR, and TRIT, to list only the most common. Following exponence rules, slots in paragraph patterns may be filled by other rhetorical patterns. In the following example by Bernard Iddings Bell, the Answer slot in the Question-Answer pattern which we discussed earlier is filled by a TRI pattern, producing a compound paragraph structure:

(Q) Is the United States a nation composed chiefly of people who have not grown up, who think and act with the impulsiveness of adolescents? (A-T) Many shrewd observers of the American scene, both abroad and here at home, are saying that this is indeed the case. (R) They intentionally disturb our patriotic complacency. (I) They bid us view with alarm cultural immaturity revealed by current trends in journalism, by the radio, by the motion picture, by magazines and best-selling books, by mass response to emotionalized propaganda—political and otherwise; by a patent decay of good manners, by the spread of divorce and by other manifestations of parental irresponsibility; by all the various aspects of behavior which indicate to a student of human affairs the health or sickness of a civilization.[19]

Tagmemic matrix theory provides further insight into another traditional problem of rhetoric. We said earlier that form and idea are seen by many as organically unified, a view that we share. The literary statement contains within itself its own dimensions of development. It constitutes a semantic field which is clearly perceived when we try to extend it. The relevant categories of the English Constitution paragraph discussed above can be displayed in the rows and columns of an emic paragraph matrix (see Table 1).

If we were to extend the paragraph, we would be obliged to supply a still more recent illustration of the effect of wisdom on the Constitution. It should be possible from a study of a large number of paragraph matrices to generalize further about various types of paragraph development. The investigation of paragraphs as semantic fields is as yet only beginning.

A writer's style, we believe, is the characteristic route he takes through all the choices presented in both the writing and prewriting stages. It is the manifestation of his conception of the topic, modified by his audience, situation, and intention—what we might call his "universe of discourse." These variables directly affect selecting and grouping in all three linguistic hierarchies: grammatical, phonological, and lexical. An analysis and description of style involves the specification of the writer's characteristic choices at all points in the writing process, although usually only the final choices are directly accessible to the analyst.

The classical conception of style has a number of limitations. To see style

[19] Bernard Iddings Bell, "We Are Indicted for 'Immaturity'," *New York Times Magazine*, July 20, 1947, p. 8.

TABLE 1

Forces shaping the English Constitution / historical manifestations	wisdom	chance
(1688)	The wise men . . . molded it into the shape we know	
(1714)		George I . . . gave it . . . the system of a Cabinet independent of the Crown and subordinate to the Prime Minister.
(1832)	Lord Grey saved it from petrification and set it upon the path of democracy.	
(1840)		[Victoria's marriage made it seem likely that a quiescent element] was about to become its predominant characteristic and change . . . the direction of its growth.
(1861)		[With the death of the Consort] the English Constitution . . . continued its mysterious life as if he had never been.
( )		

as an addition to the message, an affective layer imposed on conventional language, ignores the close connection between language and idea. Seeing it as essentially a matter of sentences ignores stylistic patterns beyond the sentence. In addition, the theory grew out of a very specialized sort of practice—formal public speaking in the courts and legislatures and at ceremonial gatherings. As a result it has a limited range of applicability. Seventeenth-century critics were right in saying that its generalizations were inappropriate to a wide range of important topics, audiences, and situations. Finally, the highly normative approach of classical rhetoric tends to ignore the individuality of the writer, describing *a style* rather than *style* itself.

To consider style, however, (as do some modern rhetoricians) to be the expression of a particular personality lays too much stress on one variable in the universe of discourse and too little on the others. Some stylistic features of a work inevitably remain unexplained if one commits himself to this definition strictly. To see style as a vision of the topic also has limitations; it ignores the influence of situation and audience on choice. It assumes that the act of writing is essentially expressive, not communicative. Both of these views inhibit systematic theorizing about style; when style is seen as something highly personal, generalization becomes difficult.

To see style in the way many linguists do today—as deviation from conventional language—leads to the difficulty of defining conventional language. Somehow, the deviations must be separated from the corpus, perhaps by measuring the frequencies of patterns. However it is done, it leaves conventional language as a styleless language. This view, like the classical view, tends to conceive of style as an embellishment, an added affective layer. Though very unconventional styles can be identified as linguistic deviations, there are "conventional" styles which this approach does not explain. These include the different styles we all use in various situations, with various audiences, and in writing with various intents on various topics.

It seems to us that a full discussion of style must include the prewriting process if it is to interpret the formal manifestations on the written page— the purely linguistic choices that the writer has made. Without the context of a linguistic unit—the universe of discourse—we are able to describe stylistic features only in a fairly trivial way. With the context provided, there is the possibility of explaining the writer's choices. In a complete theory, then, a particular style is a characteristic series of choices throughout the entire process of writing, including both discovery (invention) and linguistic selection and grouping (arrangement).

We have presented what we believe to be the traditional problems of rhetoric and have suggested how a linguistic model which includes both a discovery procedure and a descriptive technique may provide the base for a new approach to rhetoric, a bridge between the humanities and the sciences. A tagmemic rhetoric stands somewhere between the rigorous theories of science and the almost purely intuitive theories of the humanities. We see no reason to reject the insights of either the former or the latter, believing that all new knowledge—like the process of writing itself—involves both intuitive analogy and formal precision.

On the Role of Linguistics in the Teaching of English

PETER S. ROSENBAUM
Thomas J. Watson Research Center
IBM Corporation

The author finds transformational grammar preferable to structural linguistics even though the former approach entails some problems for classroom teaching. He then provides examples showing how transformational grammar might clarify questions concerning the assumptions which underlie curricula in composition.

The growing enthusiasm on the part of many teachers of English for giving careful attention to linguistic matters is noteworthy for several reasons. It speaks well for the teacher since it suggests the birth of a scholarly concern for developments in the field of language study and a professional attitude toward linguistic insights which have potential educational value. Furthermore, this enthusiasm vindicates the many linguists who have held that linguistic science could be of importance in the teaching of English. But discussions of the relevance of linguistics to the teaching of English have been in progress for a considerable time now, and even the most cursory glance at the literature indicates a disappointing lack of progress. Few familiar with this debate and its meager results will disagree that one of the problems has been a continuing inability to answer satisfactorily the obviously central question, namely, "which linguistic description?"

The last thirty years has seen the development of a variety of descriptions

This work was written while the author was a member of the Research Laboratory of Electronics at MIT and was supported in part by the Joint Services Electronics Program under Contract DA36-039-AMC-03200 (E); in part by the National Science Foundation (Grant GP-2495), the National Institutes of Health (Grant MH-04737-05), the National Aeronautics and Space Administration (Grant NsG-496), and the U. S. Air Force (ESD Contract AF 19 (628)-2487). The author wishes to express his gratitude to Professors Noam Chomsky and Paul Postal of MIT and to Professor Israel Scheffler of Harvard University who read earlier versions of this article and provided much helpful criticism.

Harvard Educational Review Vol. 35 No. 3 Summer 1965, 332–348

of the structure of English. Among the more frequently mentioned proposals are the conceptions of Fries; the immediate constituent approach of Bloch, Wells, and Hockett; the phonological syntax of Trager and Smith, and Hill; Harris' morpheme to utterance procedures; and the two distinct transformational notions of Harris on the one hand and Chomsky on the other. The question of which, if any, of these linguistic descriptions might justifiably be employed in the classroom is, of course, many-sided. But one of the more frequently alluded to criteria is entirely linguistic in nature and is bound up in a general concern for the validity or correctness of linguistic descriptions.[1] The historical emphasis on validity or correctness seems entirely appropriate even though it does no homage to the popular pre-occupation with behavioral goals and outcomes as the basis for the evaluation of curricula. The issue is not whether the information contained in a given linguistic description can be taught and learned successfully, for surely there is no description which is so difficult that it cannot be taught and learned in some form,[2] but precisely one of the status of the information itself. One might hope to diminish the centrality of the content, thereby making it unnecessary, perhaps, to choose among the various linguistic descriptions, by demonstrating the utility of one or the other description in the teaching of literate skills, e.g., composition. But this hope should not be taken too seriously since the most recent account of empirical research in this area indicates the inconclusiveness of all such demonstrations.

Reviews of educational research, however, have continually emphasized that instruction in grammar has little effect upon the written language skills of pupils. The interpretation and curricular applications of this general conclusion have ranged from the view that grammar and usage should not be taught in isolation from written **composition to the position that formal grammar merits little or no place in the language arts curriculum.**[3]

[1] See for instance, Summer Ives, "Linguistics in the Classroom," *College English,* 17, 165-172; Donald J. Lloyd, "The Uses of Structure and the Structure of Usage," *The English Record,* 6, 41-46 and "A Linguistic Approach to English Composition," *Language Learning,* 3, 109-116; James Sledd, "Coordination (Faulty) and Subordination (Upside-Down)," in *Readings in Applied English Linguistics,* (henceforth *RAEL*), ed. H. B. Allen, New York, 1958; Robert J. Geist, "Structural Grammar and the Sixth Grade," *American Speech,* 31, 5-12; Archibald A. Hill, "Prescriptivism and Linguistics in English Teaching," *College English,* 15, 395-399; Robert C. Pooley, "New Approaches to Grammar," in *Perspectives on Language,* eds. J. A. Rycenga and J. Schwartz, New York, 1963; Henry Lee Smith, Jr., "The Teacher and the World of Language," *College English,* 20, 172-178; Owen Thomas, "Generative Grammar: Toward Unification and Simplification," *The English Journal,* 51, 94-99; and Charles C. Fries, "Advances in Linguistics," *College English,* 25, 30-37.

[2] This is a special case of J. S. Bruner's hypothesis that "any subject can be taught effectively in some intellectually honest form to any child at any stage of development" as proposed in his *The Process of Education,* Cambridge, 1961, p. 33.

[3] H. C. Meckel, "Research on Teaching Composition and Literature," in *Handbook of Research on Teaching,* ed. N. L. Gage, Chicago, 1963, p. 974.

Thus, the validity of proposed linguistic descriptions remains the most pertinent consideration.

The major approaches to syntactic description can be collapsed under two rubrics. The first, which is known popularly as the *structural-descriptive* approach to linguistic analysis includes the work of Fries, Bloch, Wells, Hockett, Trager, Smith, Hill, and others.[4] The second, the *transformational* version of generative grammar, is represented, for example, by the work of Chomsky, Halle, Lees, Klima, Matthews, and Postal.[5] If the question of the validity of linguistic descriptions is to be spoken to in any serious way, it is necessary to consider two aspects of evaluation. The first pertains to the evaluation of a particular description within a given theoretical framework. For instance, which of two transformational descriptions of the relative clause structure in English is better? The second aspect of evaluation deals with the comparison of various forms of linguistic description. Is it possible, for example, to compare the structural approach to linguistic inquiry with the transformational approach in any meaningful way? In view of the well-documented interest in the validity of linguistic descriptions on the part of those involved in the educational implementation of these descriptions, it may be fruitful to examine the major approaches to linguistic inquiry in terms of evaluation in somewhat greater detail.

Underlying the structural view of language is a set of assumptions about the goals of behavioral studies and scientific inquiry which limit the range of relevant phenomena to a corpus of observed utterances. This limitation suggests a curious contradiction since, quite invariably, representatives of the structural tradition speak of language as a set of behavioral patterns common to members of a given community involving a set of verbal interchanges between two or more people.[6] There is no non-arbitrary upper bound on the

[4] Charles C. Fries, *The Structure of English*, New York, 1952; Bernard Bloch, "Studies in Colloquial Japanese," *Readings in Linguistics*, (henceforth *RIL*), ed. Martin Joos, Chicago, 1951; Rulon Wells, "Immediate Constituents," *RIL*; Charles Hockett, "Two Models of Grammatical Description," *RIL*; Zellig S. Harris, "From Morpheme to Utterance," *RIL* and *Structural Linguistics*, Chicago, 1961; W. Nelson Francis, *The Structure of American English*, New York, 1958; Archibald A. Hill, *Introduction to Linguistic Structures*, New York, 1958; and George L. Trager and Henry Lee Smith, Jr., *An Outline of English Structure*, (Fifth Printing), Washington, 1957.

[5] Noam Chomsky, *Syntactic Structures*, The Hague, 1957; Chomsky, "On the Notion 'Rule of Grammar'," *Proceedings of the Twelfth Symposium in Applied Mathematics*, (henceforth *PAM*), 6-24 and *Aspects of the Theory of Syntax*, Cambridge, 1965; Morris Halle, "On the Role of Simplicity in Linguistic Descriptions," *PAM*, 89-94; Halle, "On the Bases of Phonology" and "Phonology in Generative Grammar," in *The Structure of Language*, (henceforth *SL*), eds. Jerry A. Fodor and Jerrold J. Katz, Englewood Cliffs, 1964; Robert B. Lees, *The Grammar of English Nominalizations*, Bloomington, 1960 and "A Multiply Ambiguous Adjectival Construction in English," *Language*, XXXVI, (1960), 207-221; Jerrold J. Katz and Paul M. Postal, *An Integrated Theory of Linguistic Descriptions*, Cambridge, 1964; Edward S. Klima, "Negation in English," *SL*.

[6] W. Nelson Francis, "Revolution in Grammar," *Quarterly Journal of Speech*, 40, 299-312, especially Section 2.

number of acceptable utterances which could comprise the speech behavior of a given community. Thus the linguists of the structural school seem, at least implicitly, to be thinking of language as a potentially infinite set of utterances. But this position is completely contradicted by the properties of a structural linguistic description. All structural analysis is ultimately based upon observable data, i.e., data recorded by simple listening or by various instruments such as oscillographs, sound-spectrographs, and so on.[7] If this methodological requirement is taken literally, then the result of a structural analysis, the linguistic description of a language, is actually a description of only a finite corpus of events. There is clearly an equivocation on the term "language" here which leads to two equally damaging conclusions. If an arbitrary natural language is taken to consist of an infinite set of sentences, then the results of a structural investigation do not constitute a description of language at all, but of something else. On the other hand, should a language be construed as nothing more than the corpus stored in a set of tape recordings, then the task of saying anything of scientific interest about the psychological and linguistic properties of the endless repertoire of sentences which not only define the language of a speech community but which are the personal property of every normal member of this community belongs to a branch of science other than linguistics.

The extreme pre-occupation with observable data in linguistic analysis probably stems from Leonard Bloomfield's particular version of scientific inquiry, a version which most structural linguists have accepted at face value. In Bloomfield's view, science dealt exclusively with accessible events and the task of scientists was the induction of general laws from these events.[8] Thus, the central object of investigation in a linguistic science as conceived by Bloomfield was necessarily actual speech. For Bloomfield, the only information of scientific interest was that provided by physical phonetics and the context in which phonetic data were observed.[9] This view is implicit in all structural work and one never finds a popularization of structural linguistics which does not give prominence to assertions about the centrality of speech.[10] For our purposes, the effects of Bloomfield's views on the goals of linguistic inquiry are more important than the causes. By restricting the domain of linguistic investigation to phonetic and contextual data, Bloomfield excluded a vast range of perhaps even more accessible data as linguistically and scientifically useless; these data being the extraordinarily rich body of knowledge which a human speaker has about his language. We will return to this neglected aspect of linguistic information later.

[7] Francis, *The Structure of American English*, pp. 15-16.
[8] Leonard Bloomfield, *Linguistic Aspects of Science*, Chicago, 1955.
[9] Bloomfield, *op. cit.*, p. 21 and *Language*, New York, 1933, especially Ch. 2.
[10] For instance, George P. Faust, "Terms in Phonemics," *College Composition and Communication*, 5, (February, 1954), p. 30.

The goal of linguistic science, to determine inductively the laws governing the behavior of observable linguistic data, was unfortunately one step removed from the problem immediately confronting those linguists who were anxious to adopt the Bloomfieldian point of view. The induction of general laws from a body of data presupposes a prior classification of the data. For structural linguistic inquiry, this meant that a requirement for further research was the precise specification of the relevant facts. It was necessary to decide on the linguistic importance of the various aspects of the continuous flow of sound coming from the recording device or from the speaker directly. Thus, in a certain sense, the task before the structural linguist was "pre-scientific": To provide materials upon which a science of language could operate productively. Central to the search for the facts of language was also a concern for the general efficiency with which these facts could be stated.[11] The overall problem, therefore, consisted in providing a methodology which would yield the facts of language in terms of a consistent and optimally efficient classificational scheme.

The structural methodology for discovering the facts of language is now quite well known. In its most general formulation, the method involves a set of putative discovery procedures which are supposed to isolate automatically a set of linguistic units in a hierarchical arrangement and to present an inventory of the speech data which are found to represent these units. Quoting from what is probably the most widely known structural analysis of English:

> The presentation of the structure of a language should begin, in theory, with a complete statement of the pertinent linguistic data. This should be followed by an account of the observed phonetic behavior, and then should come the analysis of the phonetic behavior into the phonemic structure, completing the phonology. The next step is to present the recurring entities—composed of one or more phonemes— that constitute the morpheme list, and go on to their analysis into the morphemic structure. In that process the division into morphology and syntax is made. After the syntax, one may go on from the microlinguistic (linguistics proper—phonology and morphemics) to metalinguistic analyses.[12]

Structural linguists have been more successful in proposing and employing discovery procedures which fairly effectively produce an analysis and classification of sound sequences than they have in determining the measure or measures to be used in evaluating the adequacy of these classifications in terms of efficiency. An important issue is involved in the failure of the structural linguists to come to grips with the problem of evaluation. The question of which measure of efficiency will most appropriately evaluate alternative

[11] For discussion see Charles Hockett, "A System of Descriptive Phonology," *RIL*, p. 101, or Archibald A. Hill, *Introduction to Linguistic Structures*, especially Ch. 4, Sec. 1, on the classification of sounds.
[12] Trager and Smith, *op. cit.*, p.8.

structural descriptions has no obvious answer. How do we know what the right measure is? Is efficiency to be defined in terms of the number of discrete symbols or entities in a description? Is it going to have anything to do with the type of symbols which the description utilizes? These questions cannot be answered without proposing a set of conditions which the measure of efficiency must meet. Suppose I am working for a grocer and he tells me to unpack a crate of oranges and to construct the most efficient display of oranges in the front window. Unless the grocer tells me the conditions that the optimally efficient arrangement must meet, my task is an impossible one. Similarly, unless a set of conditions on the measure of efficiency for linguistic descriptions is established, there is no reason to choose one measure of efficiency over another. Such conditions cannot be an aspect of the subject matter in a science of language, as conceived by Bloomfield, since they would constitute a level of abstraction which has no observable basis whatever. If, on the other hand, such conditions are taken to be theoretical constructs, laws governing the form that a linguistic description may take, then the whole business becomes circular since such laws can be inferred only from a classified set of data in the first place. Since there is no non-arbitrary measure of efficiency which can be employed in the evaluation of alternative structural descriptions of a set of observed data, it is impossible to compare and rank these descriptions.

Furthermore, the taxonomic framework provides no basis for choosing between structural and non-structural descriptions. The fundamental problem here is that a structural linguistic description is a taxonomic classification. No such classification, whether it be of books in the library, fish in the sea, or sounds of speech, can be right or wrong, valid or invalid, true or false. Such a classification is inevitably nothing more than an arrangement of the data which makes no claims whatever about the nature of the data. A linguistic theory which is capable of evaluating the form of a linguistic description must presuppose an explicit statement of the facts which any adequate description must represent and characterize. Given such a statement it is not only possible to develop a theory which will decide on the adequacy of linguistic descriptions in terms of their ability to characterize the facts; it is absolutely necessary to develop such a theory. Without it, there is no possibility of determining the success of any type of linguistic description claiming to account for these facts.

The most readily accessible body of facts about language is the information which is available to any speaker concerning his native language. There are several aspects of a speaker's linguistic competence on which considerable consensus is found in the literature.[13] A speaker can understand sentences

[13] The various linguistic abilities possessed by native speakers of a language are discussed in much of the transformational literature. In the educational literature, see Lees, "Trans-

which he has never heard before. Similarly, he can produce new sentences on the appropriate occasion. Second, a speaker knows implicitly that certain sentences in his language are ambiguous while others are not. Still other sentences are synonymous. Third, he is capable of detecting differences in the relations which words have to one another in sentences even though these relations are not explicitly specified in the phonetic representations of sentences. Many other similar abilities could be cited.

Bloomfield and his followers have rejected such linguistic data with the assertion that introspective evidence involves a spurious mentalism which fails on the grounds of non-objectivity.[14] On this view, one's intuitions about language exist only in the private domain, in one's mind, and are thus not fit materials for a science of language. Essentially, the argument is that the mind is inaccessible to scientific investigation because the attributes of the mind, such as linguistic intuition, are not subject to objective study. Intuitions are not physical events which can be monitored and recorded. Thus the study of linguistic data dealing with the speaker's knowledge of his language necessarily belongs to some field other than linguistic science. This view has been severely criticized in the recent linguistic and philosophical literature[15] and little new can be added to the discussion. If it is the case that any significant linguistic theory must provide evaluation criteria for linguistic descriptions, then the consistency of the introspective data brought forth in support of such a theory is clearly a major consideration. The consistency of introspective evidence is not, however, non-empirical, i.e., incapable of being verified. Suppose one asks, for instance, how to test the judgment that the implicit subject of the complement verb "leave," in the sentence "the boy promised his mother to leave the party early," is the same as the explicit subject of the whole sentence, "the boy," and that the implicit subject of the same verb in the sentence "the boy told his mother to leave the party early" is the same as the object of the verb "tell," i.e., "his mother." This is not only an empirical question, but one with an obvious answer. This supposedly non-objective fact will be attested to by every normal native speaker of English who understands the question. Objectivity, therefore, is not a property which a theory of the speaker's linguistic knowledge necessarily lacks and it is probably pointless to devote further consideration to such objections.

Adopting the view that an adequate linguistic description must account for the speaker's linguistic capacities, we can think of a linguistic theory as

formation Grammars and the Fries Framework," in *RAEL*, pp. 137-146, and Paul M. Postal, "Underlying and Superficial Linguistic Structures," *Harvard Educational Review*, 34, 246-266.

[14] See, in particular, Bloomfield, *Linguistic Aspects of Science*, pp. 12-13, and Archibald A. Hill, "Linguistics since Bloomfield," *Quarterly Journal of Speech*, 41, 253-260.

[15] The most extensive remarks on this subject are found in Jerrold J. Katz, "Mentalism in Linguistics," *Language*, XXXX, 124-137.

being, at least in part, a set of constraints on the form of any description which can attain this end. The constraints specify, in other words, the way in which the goals of the linguistic inquiry can be attained. The linguistic theory acquires, therefore, the capacity to evaluate possible linguistic descriptions in terms of their ability to characterize the speaker's knowledge of his language. Such a theory is said to explain the speaker's knowledge because the form of the linguistic description which most adequately accounts for the facts is a logical consequence of the constraints comprising the linguistic theory.[16]

In this view of linguistic inquiry, the object of research is two-fold: First, to determine precisely the constraints, or laws if you will, which govern the form of the constructs employed in the linguistic descriptions which best characterize the varied instances of human linguistic ability; second, to determine the particular instances of the descriptive constructs within an arbitrary language. The latter constitutes the actual construction of a linguistic description. Recent work on the transformational version of generative linguistics represents the first modern attempt to develop a linguistic theory and a descriptive apparatus which have as a goal the explanation of the speaker's linguistic knowledge. The literature contains a substantial amount of material on both aspects of linguistic inquiry and no reiteration is called for here.[17] The virtue of a transformation approach to linguistic research from the standpoint of the issue of validity is that if a particular version of linguistic description fails to satisfy the constraints imposed by the linguistic theory, then it can be said with justification that the description is wrong. Similarly, if the constraints on the form of the linguistic description do not result in a set of descriptive constructs which satisfactorily account for the facts, then this version of the theory is wrong. Measures for determining the validity of a particular description of a given language as well as a general form of linguistic description are consequently provided.

The discussion of evaluation procedures for contemporary versions of linguistic research provides one fruitful avenue for confronting the issue of the validity of linguistic descriptions. The basic result of this discussion is the finding that the structural approach to linguistic inquiry fails to provide a principled basis for choosing among particular linguistic descriptions and forms of linguistic description. (The fact that taxonomic linguistic descriptions can be evaluated in terms of internal consistency is irrelevant since any linguistic description can be judged in this way.) It would not seem unreason-

---

[16] See Chomsky, "Three Models for the Description of Language," *I. R. E. Transactions on Information Theory*, Vol. IT-2, (1956) and "Explanatory Models in Linguistics," *Logic, Methodology, and Philosophy of Science*, eds. E. Nagel, P. Suppes, and A. Tarski, Stanford, 1962, 528-550. An exceptionally lucid presentation of the more important issues relating to explanation in science is found in Israel Scheffler, *The Anatomy of Inquiry*, New York, 1963.

[17] See the transformational literature referred to earlier.

able, therefore, to exclude structural linguistics from further consideration and to pass over to the deeper and ultimately more important question concerning the pedagogical implementation of a verifiable linguistic theory and description of the structure of English. It is natural to inquire, at this point, into the purely linguistic bases for a program designed to incorporate the valid results of linguistic research into the curriculum. Such an inquiry may prove of little value, however, since certain considerations deriving from what is already known about the nature of the constructs employed in a transformational description of language indicate that the constructs themselves do not and cannot automatically provide any new educational insights. Rather, the ultimate value of valid linguistic descriptions in the teaching of English seems to depend entirely on the ingenuity and imagination of linguists, teachers, and educators competent in both areas.

A transformational grammar characterizing linguistic competence is a finite specification of the infinite set of pairs of phonetic signals and semantic interpretations comprising the sentences in a natural language. This specification is abstract in the sense that it is not detectable on the basis of the physical data alone. It must be inferred from the knowledge which people have about sentences in their language. The specification is, in effect, an abstract representation of this knowledge offered in terms of hypothetical syntactic structure upon which semantic interpretations and phonological realizations are defined. The necessity of positing such abstract sentence structures and the form that these structures must have is a topic to which much attention has been devoted.[18] The formal apparatus employed in the explanation of the speaker's ability to deal with the infinite set of sentences in his language consists of a set of ordered rules which recursively enumerate the sentences of this language. The structures underlying sentences, often represented by tree diagrams, are not objects of substance having material existence in the real world; rather they merely constitute a record of the application of a particular set of rules.

The rules in a transformational grammar are quite different from the rules countenanced by prescriptive linguistic descriptions and from the instructions for sentence building found in so many textbooks. The rules postulated in the syntactic component of a transformational grammar are either those which specify a set of abstract underlying structures, upon which a semantic interpretation for the sentence is based, or those which derive *superficial*, alternatively *surface*, structures, which receive a phonetic interpretation, as a

---

[18] For discussion of the formal aspects of transformational grammars see Chomsky, "Three Models for the Description of Language," (Cf. note 16); also "On the Notion 'Rule of Grammar'," (Cf. note 5) and "Formal Properties of Grammars," in *Handbook of Mathematical Psychology*, (henceforth *HMP*), eds. R. D. Luce, R. R. Bush, and E. Galanter, New York, 1963; Chomsky and George Miller, "Finitary Models of Language Users," and "Introduction to the Formal Analysis of Natural Language," in *HMP*.

function of the underlying structure.[19] These claims about the nature of the rules employed in an adequate description of syntax suggest that recent educational popularizations of transformational grammar have grossly misunderstood the results of transformational research. To quote from one textbook published very recently.

> This chapter is a study of *transformational* grammar. *Transform* means "to change;" thus, you will see how basic sentences are changed, or transformed, to produce other sentences that are interesting and varied.[20]

Ongoing work in transformational grammar shows that it is incorrect to think of two sentences as being related by a transformational rule or set of rules which somehow convert one sentence into another. Rather, when various considerations force the conclusion that two or more sentences are syntactically related, this relation is reflected in those aspects of underlying structure which both sentences share. Thus the burden of representing a common source for two or more sentences falls not on the transformational rules of the grammar which generate surface structures, but on the rules which generate underlying structures.[21]

The abstract constructs offered in a transformational description are designed solely for purposes of description and explanation. Neither the transformational theory nor the transformational description of the syntax of English contains any implicit pedagogical recommendation. From neither does it follow that a transformational description of English should be taught in the classroom. From neither does it follow that instruction in transformational grammar will improve performance in the literate skills. With respect to the latter assertion, consider an analogy from physical education, in particular the pedagogy of the forward pass. Any instance of the physical event identified as a forward pass has certain mechanical properties which are characterized by the Newtonian theory of mechanics. The descriptive apparatus of this theory, consisting of such constructs as mass, acceleration, velocity, time, distance, and so forth, is a consequence of the theoretical constraints imposed upon a description seeking to account for the mechanics of physical events. To teach a potential quarterback the mechanics of the forward pass is to teach him how this type of event works. It is not to teach him how to make it work. The Newtonian theory itself gives us no reason to believe that instruction in the mechanics of the forward pass will affect the quarterback's

---

[19] See Chomsky, *Aspects of the Theory of Syntax,* and Postal, "Underlying and Superficial Linguistic Structures."

[20] Mellie John and Paulene M. Yates, *Building Better English,* (Fourth Edition), New York, 1965, p. 463.

[21] Several illustrations of common underlying structure for related sentences are given in Peter S. Rosenbaum, *The Grammar of English Predicate Complement Constructions,* MIT Doctoral Dissertation, (1965), passim.

becoming a good passer one way or the other. Similarly, to study and practice the constructs of a transformational grammar may result in an understanding of how the student's language works, but not necessarily in an understanding of how to make it work.

But the mere fact that the answers to various educational problems do not spring forth full blown from the linguistic research on transformational grammars does not imply that the results of this research will fail to provide a new and valuable dimension in which to consider traditional problems in the teaching of English. This fact simply asserts that a linguistic description does not enumerate educational benefits. It remains not with the linguistic theory or description, but with the informed educator, whether he is a teacher, linguist, or specialist informed in both areas, to determine the applicability of valid linguistic results to the teaching of English. It may prove informative to devote the remaining pages to a brief illustration of some of the ways in which a transformational approach to language study can make significant contributions to the field of English teaching. The purpose of the following discussion is not to provide a complete manual of applications, but merely to indicate the wide range of educational situations in which the results of transformational research might be utilized. The three cases to be presented concern 1) the content of the English curriculum in general, 2) the evaluation of certain traditional criteria employed in the evaluation of composition, and 3) a possible explanation for the continuing lack of correlation between instruction in grammar and improved performance in the literate skills.

The desirability of including a description of the structure of English in the English curriculum, whether this description be traditional, structural, or transformational, is ultimately a matter of judgment; it is a matter of belief. But the decision is no easier to make for all that it precludes the frustrations often accompanying empirical evaluations. On the contrary, the resolution of this issue demands recourse to a set of principled reasons which provide support for the opinion that there is virtue in instruction in linguistic descriptions. The establishment of such a set of reasons, not to mention their subsequent assessment, is a matter of great complexity. This assertion assumes some importance in view of the fact that the single generally accepted reason for teaching linguistic descriptions turns out to be no reason at all. Reference is being made here to the contention that so called "normative values" in the use of language should be taught and are best taught by means of a suitable linguistic description. Since the object of such instruction is a prescribed performance of spoken and written English, normative considerations do not defend instruction in linguistic descriptions on the grounds of any value which inheres in the subject matter independent of behavioral goals. Rather, they provide a reason for using linguistic descriptions pedagogically in order to achieve certain performance effects in the use of language. There may indeed be merit in achieving these effects, but it is of importance to recall that a belief in the power of instruction in grammar to accomplish this task flies in the face of overwhelming empirical evidence that there is no connection between instruction in linguistic descriptions and the performance of literate skills.

It is a particularly curious fact that normative considerations have often been construed as a reason for ranking a traditional grammar over both structural and transformational grammars. The basis of this argument resides in the assumption that normative values are maintained in a traditional grammar while they are neglected totally in other forms of linguistic description. This argument becomes vacuous when we observe that normative values pertain not to a linguistic description, but to a particular language, in this case a special dialect of English, described by a linguistic description. Any form of description which takes as its subject matter this special dialect of English can be said to be normative. Thus, normative considerations not only fail to offer a good reason for incorporating an arbitrary linguistic description into the English curriculum, they also fail to provide a reason for introducing a specific linguistic description into the curriculum.

Implicit in the goals of a transformational theory of language and the grammars which follow from this theory are several new considerations. A transformational grammar is a system which reveals and expresses the regularities which underlie a given natural language as completely as possible. In providing the most general account of linguistic structure, the transformational approach to linguistic inquiry yields new insights into human intellectual capacity, namely, those innate properties of the human mind which allow for the acquisition and use of language. In pursuing this capacity through the linguistic mechanisms which underlie competence in language, the student is involving himself in a study which has had intrinsic intellectual appeal for centuries, the study of those abilities which make human beings human. The fact that linguists working on syntax have, as yet, treated only the broad outlines of an adequate grammar suggests that this study is a living field, one whose issues provide significance both for studying the results thus far attained and for following the stated aims further. There seems good justification, therefore, for the inclusion of the results of the transformational approach to linguistic inquiry in the English curriculum. The educational implementation of a transformational description of the structure of English not only introduces the student to the live tradition of scholarship in language study, but, perhaps even more important, to the results of the one form of inquiry which has begun to achieve some success in providing an explicit account of one aspect of an extremely complex human competence. It would seem fitting to support the educational implementation of any linguistic description which can justifiably claim success in this area. In any case, it is a non-trivial virtue of the transformational approach to language study that it provides a rationale with which it is at least possible to disagree. This in itself is an event of some importance in the history of classroom applications of linguistic descriptions.

The second illustration is concerned with the fact that the design of curricula for the teaching of composition is conditioned by a variety of factors which take the form of accepted canons for good writing. These canons invariably include such items as clarity (meaning non-ambiguity), grammaticality, logical structure, and so forth. On one level of analysis, these constraints, as well as many others, are entirely reasonable since they set necessary conditions for successful written communication. This fact, however, does not imply that these canons may not, in certain ways, be contradictory. For instance, might it not be the case that to satisfy the condition of clarity it would be necessary to break a rule of grammar, and conversely? A conclusive exploration of this possibility will necessarily depend upon the use of a theoretical framework for language analysis in which considerations of both clarity and grammaticality play a role.

Exploiting a transformational analysis of English, one can prove that the canons for good writing are quite often in conflict. In a typical example, the rule of clarity is incompatible with the grammatical rule disallowing the infamous "split infinitive" construction. It can be shown, furthermore, that emphasis on the former must actually reinforce the use of the latter. By way of illustration, consider the following ambiguous sentence:

(1) Joshua commanded the children to shout forcefully

This sentence is at least two ways ambiguous. The adverb "forcefully" could modify either the main verb "command" or the verb in the complement sentence "shout." In other words, either the "command" could have been "forceful" or the "shout" could have been "forceful." Seeking to conform to the canon of clarity, a student writer must convert this sentence into some nonambiguous form. One mechanism of disambiguation which English allows is the application of an extremely general transformational rule which places an adverb, originating at the end of a verb phrase (i.e., that constituent containing the verb and, optionally, a verbal object), immediately before the verb. For instance,

(2) John swept the floor vigorously
(3) John vigorously swept the floor

In this fashion, sentence (1) can be disambiguated to specify the interpretation of the sentence in which the adverb "forcefully" modifies the main verb "command," as in sentence (4).

(4) Joshua forcefully commanded the children to shout

The adverb placement transformation has the peculiar property that it usually can apply only if a verb is, in fact, the first element in the verb phrase. Thus, in infinitival verb phrases like "to shout," the adverb placement transformation cannot apply since the "to" and not the verb "shout" is the first element.[22] If the adverb placement transformation is forced to apply, that is, if the rule is broken, then split infinitive constructions necessarily result, as in sentence (5).

(5) Joshua commanded the children to forcefully shout

The student writer is caught, therefore, on both horns of the dilemma. If he wishes to disambiguate sentence (1) in such a way as to specify the interpretation of this sentence in which the adverb "forcefully" modifies the complement verb "shout," he must break the adverb placement rule thereby producing a split infinitive construction. If, on the other hand, the preservation of grammaticality is the student's primary concern, then sentence (1) must remain ambiguous.

This logical bind is not the fault of the teacher, who is concerned with compositional excellence defined at least in part in terms of clarity. Nor is it the fault of the student, who is simply incapable of meeting this demand without restructuring his language. Nonetheless, the logical dilemma exists and it becomes clear that, short of ruling all infinitival constructions out of English, a poor compromise, either the canon of clarity must be weakened or the split infinitive must be accepted into the domain of fully grammatical constructions.

This demonstration is presented as evidence that the problem of the split infinitive is not the normative-moral dilemma that it has been conceived to be for such a long time.[23] Similar evidence could be presented for a variety of cases. The transformational perspective provides a tool for examining the consequences of whatever decision is made or, for that matter, of making no decision at all. Deliberation without reasons leads nowhere. The history of the split infinitive is a case in point. It is true, to be sure, that a transformational grammar will not provide the principles for assessing the reasons which bear on the issue of the split infinitive and similar constructions. But this approach to the study of language will provide the raw material for the exercise of judgment; it will provide coherent reasons, and this can only be viewed as a major contribution to the solution of a traditionally muddy set of problems.

The third illustration deals with the outlines of a possible explanation for

---

[22] A defense of this analysis is provided in Rosenbaum, *ibid.*

[23] For an interesting discussion and sufficiently complete bibliography see R. C. Pooley, *Teaching English Usage*, New York, 1946, especially pp. 100-106.

the continuing failure to find successful classroom techniques for changing linguistic performance in speech and composition. The general premise of this explanation is that certain aspects of this problem are the consequence of gravely underestimating the complexity of dialect differences and the problems involved in altering dialects on the syntactic level. It does not take a linguist to determine that there is considerable dialect variation in the United States on the phonological level and on the lexical level, that is, the levels of sound and meaning. But only very recently has it been shown that dialect differences on the syntactic level are far more systematic than has heretofore been recognized.[24] It will prove informative to explore this finding in slightly greater detail.

It is difficult to find a textbook on grammar which does not point out the alternation of the word "for" in the following sentences.

(6) a. Mary would hate for the boys to arrive early
    b. Mary would hate the boys to arrive early

Similarly, such textbooks usually describe the alternation of " 's " in the following sentences.

(7) a. does your mother dislike your brother's coming home late
    b. does your mother dislike your brother coming home late

Simply looking at the linear sequence of words in these pairs of sentences, one finds little reason to suspect that the deletion of "for" in (6b) has anything whatever to do with the deletion of " 's " in (7b). The "for," for instance, precedes the subject of the complement sentence, "the boys;" the " 's " on the other hand, follows the subject of the complement sentence, "your brother."

Considerations brought to bear in the development of a general theory of complement structures, of which (6) and (7) are instances, indicate that the initial impression, based solely upon examination of the linear sequence of words, is incorrect.[25] In the most general description of such complement constructions both the "for" and the " 's " are shown to share exactly the same position in the underlying structure of these sentences. Furthermore, both the "for" and the " 's " are optionally deleted by exactly the same transformational rule. In other words, (6a) is provably related to (6b) in precisely the same way as (7a) is related to (7b), that is, by the transformational rule which deletes "for" in (6) and " 's " in (7).

Implicit in this description is the claim that judgments about these pairs of sentences made by native speakers of English will conform to the linguistic

[24] Rosenbaum, "A Transformational Approach to a Syntactic Dialectology," a paper delivered to the December, 1964, meeting of the Linguistic Society of America in New York City.
[25] Rosenbaum, *The Grammar of English Predicate Complement Constructions*, p. 25.

description. In other words, the grammar predicts that the speaker of the dialect of English in which sentence (6a) is preferred over sentence (6b) will also prefer sentence (7a) over sentence (7b). If the deletion of both "for" and " 's " is correctly characterized in terms of a single rule, then the speaker who does not allow the deletion of "for" also will not allow the deletion of " 's. " On the other hand, the speaker whose grammar contains this single rule will delete both "for" and " 's." Preliminary empirical investigations, which are being reported elsewhere in much greater detail,[26] seem to confirm this prediction.

If it is true, as the above considerations suggest, that superficially diverse linguistic forms are psychologically related, then the task of affecting changes in the linguistic system of a speaker becomes immeasurably more complex. Consider, for instance, the plight of the teacher of composition who is anxious to preserve the grammatical dictum common to many textbooks that the " 's " as in (7a), should not be deleted. It will not be sufficient merely to reinforce the gerundive constructions with the " 's," for every performance of sentences like (6b) to which the student attends may reinforce exactly the opposite usage from that which the teacher desires to elicit. Three other factors make this problem even more complex. First, it may well be that the teacher will consider the syntactically related linguistic forms to be fully grammatical, in which case the probability of producing contradictory behaviors is quite high. In other words, "for" may be deleted in every infinitival complement construction which the teacher utters. Second, it is folly to assume that the linguistic environment outside of the classroom could be appropriately controlled to any significant degree. Finally, and perhaps most problematical, it is not impossible that other rules in the speaker's grammar which are requisite to the production and comprehension of sentences whose grammaticality is beyond question will reinforce the rule which deletes "for" and " 's."[27] In this eventuality, the only way out is an absurdity; to eliminate the reinforcing transformations by somehow ruling the grammatical sentences requiring these rules out of English.

The intent of the third illustration is to argue that the failure of current teaching techniques based on instruction in grammar to implement significant changes in linguistic performance is predictable from the fact that the tasks which these techniques must perform are virtually unknown. To effect a permanent change in linguistic behavior is to effect a change in grammar, the set of rules underlying linguistic competence, with all that such a change might entail. Certain requirements on alterations of this sort were men-

[26] Thomas G. Bever, Peter S. Rosenbaum, "The Psychological Verification of Linguistic Rules," (forthcoming).

[27] A case having just these properties is described in Rosenbaum, *The Grammar of English Predicate Complement Constructions*, pp. 104-119.

tioned above, but those were merely suggestive. It would be wildly presumptuous to speculate on the possibility of improving teaching techniques at the present time. The issue of an improved pedagogy can be addressed seriously only at such time as an explicit account of the linguistic rules which characterize linguistic behavior becomes available. Perhaps our vision of the ultimate task as one of changing linguistic behavior will prove completely misguided. Economy, if nothing else, dictates that it is better to find out what the problem is before trying to solve it. To the extent that transformational grammar continues provide insights of increasing depth into the structures underlying linguistic ability, it would seem only good sense to exploit this form of inquiry to its fullest capacity.

If the preceding arguments are sound, then not only can the transformational approach to linguistic inquiry claim priority in further discussion of the role of linguistics in the teaching of English, but the structurally oriented suggestions for the teaching of English which have actually found use in certain classrooms must be reconsidered. This conclusion should be taken as positive evidence that a new stage in the development of linguistic science is upon us and that the educator may begin to profit from giving his attention to the results of the ongoing linguistic debate. It has taken American linguistics some time to devise theories which can offer valid results for educational purposes, but the time has come. It is now up to all of those persons who are in any way concerned with the teaching of English to respond to this provocative and important new challenge.

A Structural Curriculum in English

JAMES MOFFETT

Harvard University

An emphasis on "structure" is one of the key elements in recent curriculum development. In this article James Moffett explores a structural approach to the teaching of English as a symbol system and as a set of rhetorical and conceptual skills. In contrast to traditional emphases on the linguistic and literary content of most English curricula, the author contends, a structural curriculum would stress the commonalities among all forms of spoken and written discourse.

... the curriculum of a subject should be determined by the most fundamental understanding that can be achieved of the underlying principles that give structure to that subject.

> *The Process of Education*
> JEROME BRUNER

The structure of a thing is the way it is put together. Anything that has structure, then, must have parts, properties or aspects which are somehow related to each other. In every structure we may distinguish the *relation* or *relations*, and the items *related*.

> *An Introduction to Symbolic Logic*
> SUZANNE LANGER

Structure

To do full justice to Professor Bruner's proposal, we must understand "structure" in the formal sense that a logician such as Suzanne Langer would hold it to, for the value of the concept lies in its emphasis on relations rather than things. The distinction is difficult to maintain, however; in the act of talking about structure we reify it into substance. The form of one man's short story is the content of another man's critical essay. We begin by envisioning lines of force that magnetize a whole field and point the pedagogical way; then the first thing we know, we are beholding a mere "main idea" or "principle,"

Harvard Educational Review Vol. 36 No. 1 Winter 1966, 17–28 which, even if it is new, is still a something like any other old piece of content and thus risks being treated the same old way. Any English teacher could drum up a grandiose thesis (such as, "Great literature reflects man's tragic conflict with himself"), illustrate it with selections from literature, and say that he had created a structural curriculum. I have four objections to this: it is old hat; it encourages a pre-digested, moralizing approach; it reveals more the structure of psychology and sociology than of literature; and even the structure of literature is not the structure of English. How, then, *do* we arrest the subtle transformation of structure into substance?

Anything is a structure. If we presuppose that some things are structures and other things are substantive elements which go into structures, we have trapped ourselves at the outset. Everything is both, which is to say that things and relations are matters of conceptual option. To understand the option one is playing one must be aware of where one has mentally placed himself. A tree is an element of a landscape, a thing, until we choose to isolate the tree, at which time it becomes a structure (if we talk about it at all) or set of relations among trunk, limbs, and branches. By calling something a structure, we mean that we are preferring to strip it of context, in fact to make it itself the context for some smaller structures. A molecule is a structure of atoms, which are structures of smaller "things," etc. A word is an element in a sentence, which is an element in a paragraph, which is an element in a composition. The physicist must consider his atom, the grammarian his sentence, as a structure, even though he knows perfectly well that in the next biggest context it is only a particle. In this "infinite regress of contexts," as Gregory Bateson has called it, elements stake out the field of vision, and relations among the elements rope it off; one does not see beyond, because "beyond" is where one is looking from.

Now, it is not hard to find *a* structure in English. All the particles—word, sentence, paragraph, compositional whole, literary "form"—offer us structures, a regress of increasingly larger contexts. But what are they *sub*-structures of? For the regress is only theoretically infinite; our conception is always finite. Some ultimate context or super-structure is exactly what English as a school subject has always lacked.

English

Untidy and amorphous as it is, "English" seems like a very unattractive candidate for a structural curriculum, which undoubtedly is a main reason for its being the caboose on the train of educational renovation. Sometimes it is defined as contents—literature, language, and composition (a non-parallel series if I ever saw one, since composition *ought* to be an activity). At other times it is defined as "arts" or skills—reading, writing, listening, speaking. (I think we should add thinking to this list.) Right away we confront the main dilemma, parallel to the dichotomy of substance and structure. How much is teaching English a matter of covering content, and how much a matter of developing skills, which are independent of any particular matter? Frequently the dilemma has been resolved by claiming that certain contents are essential to learning the skills. That is—to write one must know, as information, certain linguistic codifications and facts of composition; to read literature, one must be told about prosody and "form." But learning "form" this way is really learning content, and the result is quite different than if the student *practices* form or feels it invisibly magnetize the whole curriculum. *Learning* and *learning how to* result in very different kinds of knowledge. (Compare the psychiatrist's telling the patient, "You have an Oedipus complex," with the deep liberating reorganization that takes place gradually through the transference process.)

But, partly because it is easier to tell somebody than it is truly to lead him, partly because we assimilate English, by false analogy, to such subjects as history and science, we have misconstrued it and mistaught it. Although it is certainly the business of the English teacher to know as information the history and science of language and literature, it does not follow at all that he should teach these as contents to his primary and secondary students. If he does teach, say, the history of literature or the science of language, organized as a corpus, he must justify doing so either on grounds that they improve certain skills or that they have value in their own right. Although some filling-in of historical context may be a reasonable adjunct to the reading of some works of literature, that is very different from organizing the whole literature course in historical-survey fashion or from assigning books of literary history. As for the science of language, the evidence from research[1] indicates that teaching grammar, old-fashioned or new-fangled, has no effect on the skills. When I taught French I found that students did fine with *qui* and *que* until we got to the chapter that explained the difference, after which they constantly confused them. Certainly, on the other hand, we wouldn't deny that literary history and linguistics have value in themselves. But in this case a critical problem of priority arises. Why should physics be an elective and literary history required? Why offer linguistics in high school rather than psychology or anthropology, which might be deemed equally "basic"? The same problem exists for the science of literature and the history of language. I don't see how we can justify giving priority to the content specialties of English over those of other subjects, or teaching these specialties before students have thor-

---

[1] *Research in Written Composition* (National Council of Teachers of English, 1963). This study does not cover transformational grammar, but the compositional utility of even a superior grammar will always be kept trivial by the simple fact that linguistics never rises above the level of syntax.

oughly mastered the large English skills (there is a discouraging amount of evidence that this often doesn't occur even by the time of college). If one does believe that skills pre-empt contents in English, then a structural curriculum is already in sight, for teaching functionally, teaching *how to,* keeps the operating relations of the field from becoming things.

Today the approach is far too substantive. Take up practically any textbook on language or composition and you will find it organized in this way: categories, and therefore units of study, are derived by analytically decomposing language into the "elements." This is what I call the particle approach —sound, perhaps, for research, but not for teaching. Although this approach pays lip service to the interrelations of elements, it cannot escape its own format. To cash in on current slogans like "sequential development," publishers often arrange these particles in an order of smaller to larger—from the word to the sentence to the paragraph to the whole composition. I do not know what development this corresponds to—certainly not to the functioning of either the language or the student. For one thing, only in the largest context —the whole composition—can meaning, style, logic, or rhetoric be usefully contemplated. Secondly, little particle to big particle is not even an order of simple to complex, since each sub-structure is as complex as the next largest. What *does* count is that, as context for the next smallest, each of these structures governs everything of significance in the one below. For the same reasons, units on style, logic, and rhetoric can teach little more than abstract information if they are not kept as functions of each other, and they can be kept so only in the ultimate context of somebody-talking-to-somebody-else-about-something.

To the extent the English teacher has an obligation to familiarize the student with what has been written in the past, he rightly has a problem of content-coverage. But any approach that entailed plenty of reading could accomplish this. We no longer agree very much on what every gentleman ought to have read, and the survey of literature seems to have placed us more in the role of historian than we thought appropriate. Virtually any curriculum could sample the range of literature. Genre divisions satisfy a passion for taxonomy. Though perhaps the best classification of literature so far, genres are too cavalierly equated with form and structure. Actually, the structure of a novel or play is at least as much unique to itself as it is shared by other novels and plays. And some stories are poems, some poems stories, some plays essays, and some essays are stories or poems. Perhaps more than anything else, genres are marketing directives. As such, they provide convenient rhetorical bins. Pedagogically, they constitute a hazard by making both teachers and students feel that they have to "define" what a short story or a poem is, i.e., find something similar in all the examples. Even if this were not futile, one would be left with only a definition, another substantive reduction that does not help one to read or write, or even appreciate. Since a definition would have to be of the form, not content, the very difficulty of definition suggests that we exaggerate greatly the formal similarities among members of the same genre.

At the risk of disparaging what a lot of English teachers, including myself, have relied on as curriculum guides, I have emphasized the ways we have unnecessarily deformed our subject to make it into a content like other subjects. But English, mathematics, and foreign languages are not *about* anything in the same sense that history, biology, physics, and other primarily empirical subjects are about something. English, French, and mathematics are *symbol systems*, into which the phenomenal data of empirical subjects are cast and by means of which we think about them. Symbol systems are not primarily about themselves; they are about other subjects. When a student "learns" one of these systems, he *learns how to* operate it. The main point is to think and talk about other things by means of this system.

In insisting on a major division between symbol systems and what is symbolized in the systems, I am attempting to break up the bland surface of our traditional curriculum, whereby the Carthaginian Wars, the theorems of Euclid, irregular German verbs, the behavior of amoebas, and the subordination of clauses all come dead-level across the board as if they were the same kind of knowledge. The failure to distinguish *kinds* and *orders* of knowledge amounts to a crippling epistemological error built into the very heart of the overall curriculum. The classification by "subject matters" into English, history, math, science, French, etc., implies that they are all merely contents that differ only in what they are about. The hidden assumptions of this classification have taught students to be naïve about both symbols and the nature of information; even very bright students are apt to leave high school not understanding the difference between empirical truth and logical validity. Furthermore, we have fooled ourselves.

Fortunately, the curriculum builders of mathematics and foreign languages have made some progress in overcoming this confusion. They have done so by reconceiving their subjects in terms of relations and skills. The most natural assumption about teaching any symbol system should be that the student employ his time using that system in every realistic way that it can be used, not that he analyze it or study it as an object. (In this respect an English curriculum would not differ basically from any other first-language curriculum; what I have to say in this essay applies as well to French for the French or Russian for the Russians.) If such an approach seems to slight literature and language, I can only say that this is a mistake of the substantive view. A student writing in all the same forms as the authors he reads can know literature from the inside in a way that few students ever do today. If the student has to work with language constantly in the functional way the professional does, he will come to know it in the professional's intimate way. Through reading, writing, and discussing whole, authentic discourses—and using no textbooks —students can learn better everything that we consider of value in language and literature than they can by the current substantive and particle approach.

As it is now, I see us turning out glib Advanced Placement students who know all the critical jargon and can talk about writing endlessly, but who do not write well and are not truly sensitive to style, rhetoric, and logic. In many of our writing assignments, I see us feverishly searching for subjects for students to write about that are *appropriate for English;* so we send them to the libraries to paraphrase encyclopedias, or they re-tell the plots of books, or they write canned themes on moral or literary topics for which no honest student has any motivation. Although asking students to write about real life as they know it is gaining ground, still many teachers feel such assignments are vaguely "permissive" and not as relevant as they ought to be. Once we acknowledge that "English" is not properly about itself, then a lot of phoney assignments and much of the teacher's confusion can go out the window. Speaking as one of many university professors who have to stop and teach their graduate students to write, Wendell Johnson has relieved his exasperation in this way:

The second, and more grave, reason for their [English teachers'] failure is that they appear to place the emphasis on "writing," rather than on writing-about-something-for-someone. You cannot write writing.

Johnson catches here just my point about teachers feeling that they have to do "English" about English. Clearly distinguishing symbolizing subjects from symbolized subjects would eliminate such nonsense.

Having said this, however, I must now enter a great paradox: in trying to separate symbol from symbolized, one discovers their inseparability. Ultimately, we cannot free data from the symbols into which they have been abstracted, the message from the code. All knowledge is some codification by man of his phenomenal world. This is precisely what many incoming college freshmen and even graduate students have never learned. The fact is that languages *are* about themselves, in a greater measure than we usually suspect; but this is a wholly different matter from the English teacher's fear that if he does not keep English self-contained it will slip through his fingers and become as big as all outdoors. The ambiguity I am after is that while we speak in English about non-English things, we are using invisible syntactic relations as well as words like "although" and "because" that are not about the phenomenal world—at least not the external one. Every code or language says something about itself while delivering its message. "Codification is the substitution of one set of events for another" (Gregory Bateson). The set of events which we substitute for outer phenomena when we talk about them is an inner set of neural events—activities we learn when we learn the language and about which we are normally unaware. The purpose, I take it, of teaching linguistics and semantics is to make the student aware of how much people's words are about people and words and how much they truly recapitulate outer phenomena. But this is best done by letting students *try* to symbolize raw phenomena of all kinds at all levels of abstraction, and then by discussing these efforts under the guidance of a teacher who is linguistically and semantically sophisticated. I think it will be found that what we might tell the student or have him read about concerning the reflexiveness of language will be much better learned through his own writing and discussion. By this method, teachers may more readily learn what kind of understanding of language the student can take at different ages and in what form they can take it.

Yes, language is about itself, but, in accordance with something like Russell's theory of types, higher abstractions are about lower abstractions, never about themselves. That is, some English words refer to the outer world, other words (like relative pronouns) refer to these first words, and all syntax is about tacit rules for putting together the concrete words. Some notion of a hierarchy of abstraction, defined as greater and greater processing of phenomena by the human mind, is indispensable. Thus, the more abstract language is, the more it is meta-language, culminating in mathematics as the ultimate language about language. So we imagine a symbolic hierarchy going from the codification of our world that most nearly reflects the structure of that world to codification that more and more resembles the structure of the mind. Basically this is what abstraction is all about. To enable the student to learn about this process, we must first separate in the curriculum, and hence in the student's mind, symbolic systems from empirical subjects, and then help him discover both the dependence and independence of one and the other.

I hope it is clear at this point that I am construing English as all discourse in our native language—any verbalizing of any phenomena, whether thought, spoken, or written; whether literary or non-literary. Seen as packets of heterogeneous content, on the one hand, and as skills on the other, English does indeed seem unwieldy and resistant to structure. But if we smelt back down to the simplest relations of discourse all substantive categories, we may be able to re-cast the curriculum so as to accommodate all that we agree is important.

The Structure of Discourse

The elements of discourse are a first person, a second person, and a third person; a speaker, listener, and subject; informer, informed, and information; narrator, auditor, and story; transmitter, receiver, and message. The structure of discourse, and therefore the super-structure of English, is this set of relations among the three persons. But in order to exploit this venerable trinity, we must get beyond its innocent look.

Within the relation of the speaker to his listener lie all the issues by which we have recently enlarged the meaning of "rhetoric"—what A wishes to do by speaking of such and such a subject to B. Within the relation of the speaker to his subject lie all the issues of the abstractive process—how the speaker has symbolically processed certain raw phenomena. But of course these two relations are in turn related: *what* and *what for* are factors of each other. As with all trinities, the relations of persons is a unity—somebody-talking-to somebody-about something. And, lastly, within the relation of the listener to the subject lie all the issues which we call comprehension and interpretation.

In proposing this structure, I am thinking that the student would learn the skills of operating our symbol system by role-playing first and second persons in all the possible relations that might exist between the student and a subject, and between him and a speaker or listener. For the set of relations is of course not static, and, as the ultimate context, this structure governs the variations in style, logic, and rhetoric of all the sub-structures beneath it— the word, the sentence, the paragraph, and the compositional or literary "form." This amounts to proposing that curriculum units and sequence be founded on different kinds of discourse, a "discourse" being defined as any piece of verbalization complete for its original purpose. What creates different kinds of discourse are shifts in the relations among persons—increasing rhetorical distance between speaker and listener, and increasing abstractive altitude between the raw matter of some subject and the speaker's symbolization of it.

There is one thing that no grammar book will ever tell us about the trinity of discourse: first and second persons are of a different order of reality from third person. Whereas *I* and *you* are existential, unabstracted persons, *he* or *it* has merely referential or symbolic reality. That is, *I* and *you* inhabit some space-time, but, in a given communication situation, *he* or *it* inhabits only the timeless realm of abstraction. Thus if Tom and Dick want to exclude Harry, even if he is standing right before them, all they have to do is *refer to him*. This says clearly, "You do not exist in the same way we do." When the servant addresses His Highness, he uses the third person to deny the actual *I-you* relation and thereby maintain the discontinuity of their realities. Perhaps—in a somewhat simplified sense—Martin Buber's distinction between an *I-it* relation and an *I-thou* relation best expresses the two different orders of reality. That is, when something or somebody is an *it* for me, I am manipulating the idea of them I have in my head, which is to say that I am relating only to myself; whereas when something or somebody is a *thou* for me, I am meeting directly their unabstracted, existential reality, which is independent of me and equal to me. Buber rightly associates the *I-it* relation with verbal, discursive, scientific knowing, and the *I-thou* relation with non-symbolic meeting or action. This corresponds in the structure of discourse to the abstractive relation between first and third persons and the rhetorical relation between first and second persons.

My reason for establishing this difference in kind of reality is that it helps us clarify the innocent opaqueness of the conceptual scheme of "persons" so that we can better discriminate between the action relation of human-to-human and the symbolic relation of human-to-referent. *I* and *you* pre-empt the communication process, just as transmitter and receiver exist before message, although they are defined as such only by virtue of sending and receiving messages. The starting point, then, of teaching discourse is "drama": inter-action between the communicants, who are equal and whose relation is reversible. (Within a given communication situation, *I* and *it* cannot reverse roles.) One failure of English teaching has been to consider only messages, or consider them before or without placing them in the whole context of the communication frame wherein the student can see the operation of all relations.

Viewing the student for a moment as an *I* asked to write something, let's think about *what* and *what for*. His *what* does not usually entail his abstracting raw phenomena from the ground up, and as for his *what for*—his motivation for writing the theme, his audience, and how he wishes to act on that audience—we find slim pickings indeed. He is writing always to the same old person, the English teacher, to whom he has nothing to say but who has given him a *what for* by demanding the assignment and by holding the power of grades and disciplinary authority over him. No wonder that what he learns most is to dope out the idiosyncrasies of the teacher and give him what he wants—a fine lesson in rhetoric which Harold Martin once called somewhere the "nice-Nelly" school of writing. While acknowledging that artificiality cannot be eliminated completely from the classroom situation, somehow we must create more realistic communication "dramas" in which the student can practice being a first and second person with better motivation and in a way more resembling how he will have to read, write, speak, and listen in the "afterlife." I recommend training the student to write for the class group, which is the nearest thing to a contemporary world-at-large; accustoming him to having his themes read and discussed workshop fashion; and asking him to write about raw material from his own experience which he is motivated to write about and to invent an appropriate rhetoric for. It is amazing how much so-called writing problems clear up when the student really cares, when he is realistically put into the drama of somebody with something to say to somebody else.

I have suggested structuring English curriculum according to the relations of speaker-listener-subject as the ultimate context within which all our other concerns may be handled functionally and holistically, moving the student in his writing and reading from one kind of actual discourse to the next in a sequence which permits him to learn style, logic, semantics, rhetoric, and literary form continuously through practice as first or second person. Ideally this sequence would correspond both to his own intellectual and emotional growth and to some significant progression in "symbolic transformation," as Suzanne Langer has called the human processing of the world. The structure of the subject must be meshed with the structure of the student. A major failure of education has been to consider the logic of the one almost to the exclusion of the psychologic of the other. Atomizing a subject into analytical categories, inherent only in the subject, necessarily slights the internal processes of the student or language-user, who in any given instance of an authentic discourse is employing all the sub-structures, working in all the categories, at once. We must re-conceive the subject in such a way that we can talk simultaneously about both the operations of the field and the operations of the learner. The title of a paper by Warren McCulloch expresses splendidly this transactional approach: "What Is A Number, That A Man May Know It, and A Man, That He May Know A Number?" We should ask the same question regarding our native language. What assures me that a correspondence is possible between phases of discourse and stages of growth is that all man's artifacts reflect him, and discourse is man-made. I think that in exploring all the shifts that can occur in the rhetorical relation of *I-you* and the abstractive relation of *I-it*, we will find sequences of activities that can be embodied in a curriculum doing justice to both learned and learner. But it is only in the largest context—any instance of a whole, authentic discourse—that the nature of the two can meet. The concept that seems most likely to enable us to think simultaneously about discourse and the learning of discourse is that of abstraction, redefined so as to apply to whole discourses and the rhetorical process behind them. But this is the subject of another paper, in which I hope to identify types of discourse produced by the shifting relations of the trinity, and to array these into a curriculum sequence illustrated with specific assignments.

Summary

This paper is a plea to bring the methods of teaching English as nearly in line as possible with the goals—thinking, speaking, listening, reading, and writing. This is best done, I claim, not by imitating empirical subjects and asking students to read about writing and write about reading, but by asking them to practice the skills themselves with actual raw materials and audiences, continuously but variously, at all ranges of the symbolic spectrum and in all relations that might obtain between speaker, spoken-to, and spoken-about.

The basic structure of English is this set of relations among the three persons—the structure of discourse itself. Rather than decompose discourse into substantive fragments, the teacher should keep all work framed within some kind of a whole discourse, so that the sub-structures of vocabulary, syntax, logic, rhetoric, and compositional form may keep their meaning and be more readily applied in practicing the skills.

The connection between structure and skills is that (1) both are independent of particular matter, and (2) skills keep structure in action, invisible, so that it does not become mere data. Thus I associate a structural curriculum with a functional approach.

The English teacher does not need to prepare bodies of information and advice on style, rhetoric, language usage, and form, for these can be better taught and remembered when they come up as issues in the students' own productions and in documents and literature. At a certain (advanced) age, if his intuitions have been properly developed, the student will probably profit from a joint math-English course combining the latest that is known in linguistics, syntactics, semantics, and mathematical logic.

What the English teacher can and should prepare in advance is a sequence of readings from both literary and everyday discourse that correlates with a sequence of writing tasks. These reading and writing assignments are whole discourses. The teacher assigns the rhetorical distance and the abstraction level of the writing, not the subject matter. Fundamental is the idea that the student should be asked to symbolize raw phenomena from the ground up; that only by generating abstractions of all levels can he handle well those of the highest levels.

Most of the undertakings to improve the teaching of English, such as the Commission on English and the NDEA institutes, have stressed teacher education. I think that a correctly conceived curriculum might well be the best medium for educating teachers already on the job. Functional structure has that virtue, I believe, that it reorganizes the teacher's past education as he teaches by it. Furthermore, working all the time with the real discursive productions of young people, their efforts to abstract raw experience with nothing but their native neural apparatus, teaches the teacher an enormous amount he could not learn from books and courses, especially in the way he needs to know it for teaching. In other words, we should consider solving the problem of teacher education through a teacher-teaching curriculum as well as through courses and summer institutes.

Another remedy prescribed by agencies of English teaching is more and more research. Some research tries to find out what happens in the learning processes of the child at different ages; some is specialty research which investigates what happens in linguistic and communication processes; and some notes what happens when you use such-and-such a practice in an English class. The fact is that the three areas of research overlap; learning psychology, the nature of symbolization, and the proper pedagogy of English may be, at least in some respects, simply different names for essentially the same thing. At present, researchers in all three fields examine the discursive productions of children and adolescents. If these productions were responses to tasks assigned in a functional, structural curriculum, the English classroom might itself become the richest laboratory of all.

Conference Report:
The Dartmouth Seminar

In the summer of 1966, a month-long conference was held at Dartmouth College to analyze the teaching of the English language. Leading educators from England, Canada, and the United States were invited to discuss and debate such questions as:

> What is the nature of English?
>
> How does English relate to the structure of academic disciplines?
>
> What are the effects of testing and tracking on the English curriculum?
>
> How can sequence and continuity be built into English?

The central controversy arose not over the quality of the answers but over the relevance of the questions themselves. The debate followed national boundaries, with the American hosts, in a reaction against Dewey, taking a subject-matter position in contrast to the British, who emphasized the value of a psychologically grounded, child-centered curriculum. Although this may somewhat overstate the differences, it is no exaggeration to say that the presence of the British delegation caused the first major re-evaluation of curriculum development in America since the Woods Hole Conference in 1960.

The principle that emerged from that 1960 conference, as stated by Bruner in *The Process of Education*, was that "the foundations of any subject may be taught to anybody at any age in some form."[1] It followed from this principle that 1) the school curriculum structure ought to mirror the division of professional studies in the university; 2) outstanding thinkers in each field ought to be consulted about the way their subject should be taught to elementary and secondary students; and 3) the school should motivate students to study the structures of knowledge rather than modify the structures of knowledge to the interests of the students.

Most of the recent American curriculum development in mathematics, physics and chemistry, and the social sciences has been strongly influenced by this principle and its corollaries. The academic and financial success of these projects has

---

[1] Jerome Bruner, *The Process of Education*. New York: Vintage Books, 1960, p. 33.

Harvard Educational Review   Vol. 39   No. 2   Spring 1969, 357–372

encouraged leaders in English education to consider the relevance of Bruner's principle for the teaching of language and literature. For the past few years, linguists have been asked to speak, to consult on curriculum development, and even to write texts which convey the structure of linguistics to students; the critical methods of Professors Cleanth Brooks and Robert Penn Warren have become the theoretical standards with which literature teachers have been measured. This influence can clearly be seen in the sequential curriculums that are starting to appear from the federally financed Project English Centers.

The docket of questions posed to the Dartmouth seminarians was intended to enrich and provide theoretical support for Bruner's structural principle. As the proceedings of the Conference become available, however, it is clear that this principle and its corollaries were themselves called into question—mainly by members of the British delegation.[2]

Thus, 1) John Dixon suggests that curriculum be organized not around the divisions found in the university, but rather around the experiences that students bring to the classroom; 2) David Holbrook argues for the consultation of child psychiatrists and group specialists rather than that of subject matter specialists; and 3) James Britton and John Dixon argue for building the literature and language programs around the central concerns of the students. The contrast between the assumptions of American and British representatives caused both delegations to question first principles.

The *Review* has asked two members of the Dartmouth Seminar, one American and one Englishman, to reflect on the experience and to assess the value that this month of discussion has had, and may have on the course of curriculum change in the two countries. We are sure that factors beyond the place of residence have contributed to the extreme differences between these two reflections of the same conference. Perhaps the issues raised in this Report will stimulate readers to become more familiar with the Dartmouth Conference material and to reflect on its implications for curriculum development. Relevant responses to this Report will be published, at the editors' discretion, in future issues of the *Review*.

---

[2] See John Dixon, *Growth Through English*. Reading, England: National Association for the Teaching of English, 1967; Herbert J. Muller, *The Uses of English*. New York: Holt, Rinehart and Winston, 1967; and six monographs on specific topics, published by NCTE, Champaign, 1968: *Creativity in English*, Geoffrey Summerfield, ed.; *Drama in the English Classroom*, Douglas Barnes, ed.; *The Uses of Myth*, Paul Olsen, ed.; *Sequence in Continuity*, Arthur Eastman, ed;. *Language and Language Learning*, Albert Marckwardt, ed.; *Response to Literature*, James R. Squire, ed.

WAYNE A. O'NEIL

Massachusetts Institute of Technology and *Harvard University*

" 'Great noise and little wool!' the devil said as he was shearing a pig": James
Sledd being Irish on the Dartmouth Seminar.

The place was all wrong: that's what first comes to mind a month of months later
as I sit trying to reflect on that month in Hanover, New Hampshire, at Dartmouth when four dozen people plus a couple of dozen short-timers were somehow convinced that they should hang about mulling over English with nothing
particular in mind and nowhere to go. [Nowhere to go: perhaps that's what they
had in mind: 'If our seminarians have nowhere to go they will mull really hard
over English and really answer the Questions.']

I had just spent a summer talking writing reading speaking driving
camping hiking climbing: from Boston in early June to Montreal; straight
across Ontario to Michigan's Upper Peninsula, along Wisconsin's Lake Michigan's
shore, diagonally across Illinois, across a corner of Missouri, through Oklahoma,
through the Texas Panhandle, to the ancient, white, desolate cities of New Mexico
and Arizona; through the present squalor that the American Indian has been
forced to, quickly across Nevada to L.A. and linguists, up the coast of San Francisco,
to Oregon; back to L.A. and linguists, out of California again, through Nevada,
Utah, Colorado and its great Indian ruins, downhill through Kansas, Missouri,
Illinois, Indiana—running now, into Michigan, Ontario, New York, Vermont to
peaceful Dartmouth late in August. 16,000 miles.

I had visited, climbed about, wondered at, gotten to know, the great ancient
cliff cities of Bandelier, Chaco Canyon, Canyon de Chelly, Mesa Verde, deserted
now, empty. I had spoken to English teachers in Chicago in early July just after
the Puerto Ricans had rioted (and it was learnt that there was not a Spanish-
speaking teacher anywhere to be had in the elementary schools of Chicago) and
just before three Blacks were shot down on a hot summer's day for cooling themselves in the public waters of Mayor Daly's fire hydrants; I had spoken to English teachers in Fresno, deep in the Valley that wouldn't pay agricultural workers
and that would help elect Reagan in the fall; and while cops were shooting
Blacks in Chicago, I spoke to English teachers in Houston at Texas Southern
University, where ten months later the cops would shell and then invade. [Sixteen
thousand miles to peaceful Dartmouth. Perhaps that's what they had in mind;
perhaps they had realized that the cities would explode in the summer of 1966:
in response to Watts 1965, in preparation for 1967. 'We can't have that ([fear of]
the world) in the way of the Questions. Contemplate English in the country, in
a quaint New England town, in a Gothic library, in an ancient (well, ancient for
America at least), almost British (perhaps *that's* what they had in mind), Eastern Establishment, Ivy school.']

Everywhere I had spoken about the inefficacy of my discipline (linguistics) to help at all with any of the practical jobs traditionally given over to grammar, about the dangers present in the attempts of highly commercial publishers and publicly-financed curriculum production centers to cram-jam linguistics into the classroom as early and for as long as possible, about the racism inherent in attempting to make black dialect over into Middle Class American, about the frustration of teaching the Middle Class belief in the power of the word to a dis-possessed child whose whole life and existence is evidence that words get noth-ing, whose only hope for escape is through action, about reorganizing schools around ways of knowing and the accessibility of data.

Then I retreated to Dartmouth and its Gothic library and its elitism and its quiet. They had their reasons for packing us out there, into the sleeping country, away from the waking city. For they had this plan, see, and they didn't want anything to go wrong with it. They had worked long and hard on it, organizing it, programming it, role-playing and scenarioing it: they had made up this set of a dozen or so unanswerable questions (like *What is English?*) and it was their plan to randomly assign one seminarian to each question and to have him write an essay in which he soberly pretended to answer the question. It was further their plan to assign (randomly again—though non-random to the extent that the respondent had to be of the other nationality than the original answerer and could not be drawn from the set of original answerers) another seminarian the task of writing out his quibble (and formally presenting it) with the original answer. Each of these answer-quibble pairs was to be presented in order to the seminar group which had then to join in a grand melee over the answer and the quibble. It was further their plan to gather up question, answer, quibble, and the recorded melee and pack these all off together with a sub-group of seminarians who by default or in some other way evidenced interest in the Question, that group's task then being to write an even longer compromised answer (in several hands and sections) to the original Question. *They* were to move about from sub-group to sub-group to make sure that everyone was pulling his own weight.

Things started off well: we were each given half our month's stipend immedi-ately. This created so much good will and jolliness that we all tacitly agreed not to notice that the first unanswerable question hadn't even gotten unanswered: What is English? For the logical consequences of that would have been to return the $500, forego the next $500, give up our comfortable quarters, our month's paid-up meals, board our planes and go home. So we held on and followed the plan for another twenty-six days, and we drank, and we had two good old Ameri-can cookouts high above the Connecticut River, out in the open to be sure but decently: on tables spread with linens and servants doing it all, and we bought liquor cheap in Vermont, and we found the Coolidge Hotel and its Swiss cuisine.

But the key part of the plan never came off. For they, the dichotomizers and compromisers, hadn't reckoned on one thing: the inability of humanists once parted ever to get together again. And it soon became clear that there really were two of us, that there were the Sensitive People: mostly British and Leavis-trained (though neither of these exclusively), pretty much turned off by coherent and rational discussion, turned on by feelings and Lawrence but not yet much with visual and audial things; and there were the Heavies: all-American (if any Englishmen of this temperament exist they wouldn't have been allowed to come, for the British ran a tight ship whose officers and crew had been drawn carefully and narrowly), organized and packaged curriculum people who had smelt New Math, Physics, Bruner and Government Money.

Consequently, though the seminar moved along according to schedule (a week on the Questions, regroup into sub-groups, dash together for a McLuhan second stringer, a minor Skinnerian, two sociolinguists, a brace of real teachers, etc.) with all its smaller details in order, the grand compromise never happened, leaving the two designated reporters with quite a problem on their hands—fortunately these men knew from the beginning that they had each to write a book about the seminar, though it certainly would have been much more entertaining had that task been assigned by lot at the final meeting of the seminar. [Another piece of the plan: one of us (an English English teacher) will write a book for the profession; one of them (an American History teacher) will write a book for the educated public. It is in one (perhaps in both) of these curious books that there is reference to the 'findings' of the Dartmouth Seminar—a strange word to be associated with something so vacuous, so incapable of conclusiveness, so pleasant and cordial as our gatherings, a word that makes it sound as if we were somehow members of a National Advisory Commission on English Disorders instead of well-meaning men on a country holiday. I don't like that word 'findings' at all: we found nothing but friends and pleasant places in the sun.] But since they were prepared, our authors covered it all up pretty well, so well that some now think we are launched on New Era English, that a blueprint has been made. To be sure something has been launched: there is a fairly free flow of Dartmouth seminarians from shore to shore, a small set of Americans now say Maths instead of Math and just feel a hell of a lot better than they used to.

So even without the compromise, we got to the end of the seminar and the summer, caught our planes (richer for our pains) and got home. But there were really three of us: Sensitive People, Heavies, and Terribly Confused People. The Terribly Confused People were some of them American, some British, students generally of the mental disciplines, given to drinking Scotch and to rational, coherent, substantial talk, thus quite unused to seeking answers to nonquestions, to hanging in on a problem long after it had become clear that either (i) there was no problem or (ii) further discussion was fruitless because there was no knowledge to bring to bear on the problem; thus terribly confused by the whole Dartmouth method, one which pretended to operate within the usual rules of rational discourse except that in the general way of literary scholarship the agreed upon meanings of such concepts as "proof," "evidence," "theory," etc. were suspended so that it was possible finally to speak of "findings." Yet it must be clearly understood that the words had really nothing to do with the concepts with which they are generally associated in rational talk, that in fact they were used metaphorically for such notions as "(passionately held) belief," "(arbitrary) decision," "prejudice," etc.

Terribly confused, most of all, by procedures designed to cover up the fact that there was really nothing to talk about after all, by procedures that led them away from what there was to talk about, by procedures that perpetuated English as talk about nothing in particular and therefore freed it of the burden of having to be substantial. New Era English was to be a forever Dartmouth Seminar for the Anglo-American countries. Finding that it had nothing of its own that it valued, English made a grab for the whole universe of talk, the general properties of talk, or at least the Sensitive People did. The Heavies were willing to make a go of it with Language, Literature, and Composition done pure. They feared the universe of talk because it couldn't be packaged into discovery units, and the Sensitive People feared coherence around substance and reaching for certainty because they suspected dwelling on these things led to the death of creativity and to the loss of freedom. They mistook the romanticism and passion of scientific inquiry for the death grip of technology's quest for certainty, James B. Watson for Herman Kahn. The dichotomy hardened into New Curriculum Makers and Free Spirits for whom English was everywhere and everything, her substance to airy thinness beat. Everyone missed a chance to pick up after *What is English?* went unanswered, a chance to pull the plan down, to come to grips with fundamental issues: What is an education about and for?

II

The Dartmouth Seminar did not square off with the issues. Rather it retreated from them. It did, in fact, exactly what school educators are doing in general: in the past schools have been so badly put together that it has been possible to mistake in them teachers filling empty vessels for teachers teaching and rote learning of fact for important learning; this mistake having been uncovered, educators have either (i) sought new ways of obfuscating vessel filling and rote learning so that their not being important teaching and learning is the more difficult to detect, or (ii) they have thrown the notion 'learning' out altogether, substituting for it freedom, love, and all the good words.

These are not, however, the only choices; there's more that we can do than simply disguise a bad job or abandon the goals. There are goals. It is a clear goal and the prime goal of education that children learn how to come to systematic understanding of data, how to seek out explanations for complex sets of quite disparate-looking facts; that they gain an understanding of how to formulate questions and seek tentative answers, hypotheses in explanation of data, to understand the conditions under which generalizations do and do *not* hold, and how much of the relevant data generalizations cover, etc. Children must internalize notions of theory construction and rational discussion: i.e., there must be talk, the development of reasonable argument and coherent talk. This can only take place when in fact there is something manageable and substantial to talk about.

There are of course those who would climb all the trees at once, those who always reach first for the answers to the great cosmic questions, and who always fail because they will not constrain their talk to any clearly formulable question where there can be some measure of answer such that what is answered and what is unanswered emerge as clearly as possible. We can climb all over 'the origins of language' forever and never come close to saying anything that is either right or wrong, reasonable or unreasonable, consonant or disconsonant with the data, for there are no data and thus there can be no theory, no hypothesis, and, finally, no real question.

An education ought to deal with formulating important questions out of a rich acquaintance with data, with formulating hypotheses, and seeking confirmation and disconfirmation of them, with recognizing when in fact there are no questions and no answers because of the inaccessibility of the facts, the difficulty of the task.

To find the center of education in such things can not be easy. For it asks not only that teachers be sensitive guides but it also asks that they know something and know it hard. It also asks that children encounter a range of questions, questions that vary along at least two dimensions: accessibility of data to be explained and extent of coverage of the relevant data by existing theories. These two dimensions are not of course independent one of the other, for in a general sense it is clear that the more accessible the data to the layman the less adequate the theories; the more accessible the data to extended human perception, the more adequate the theories; the more unsure about what in fact constitutes the data, the poorer (unto ludicrous) the theories, the less viable speaking of theories is.

For example, consider astronomy, language, and literature. To find the position of the planets in the sky is a difficult task: instruments are needed, extensive observation is necessary, but the data are magnificently explained by the theory of planetary motion and in fact have been well explained for over three hundred years. In linguistics the data are readily available to us all: the sentences of our native language and our native speaker's intuitions about the structure of sentences and the relationships among them. But the theories, although they handle significant amounts of data, do not come near exhausting them, nor is all that must be dealt with in linguistics well-formulated. Moreover there exist *theories*, different in quite basic ways, as different in kind as older competing theories of planetary motion. For literature the data are uncertain. Are they in fact simply analogous to the data of linguistics: the works of literature, and the general intuition that members of a culture have of the structure of these works and their relationships? Are the psychological responses (whatever these may be) that the reader or beholder make the stuff for literary theory? In any case what constitutes the data of literature is unclear and there are thus no theories of literature worthy of the designation 'theory.'

Schools in their talk ought to be organized around such areas of knowledge and along the dimensions of knowledge sketched in above. Beginning early where data are readily accessible a movement toward informal, common sense explanations is possible; then on to more formal explanations of accessible data and to data available only to the senses artifically extended or to careful laboratory procedures; and then also to areas where there are no strong generalizations, and many competing theories, for example, from language to physics on the one hand, and to history on the other. Proceeding in this way students will come to general ways of accounting for data, to rational explanations of human differences (say language differences, e.g. dialect differences), to an understanding of the limits of rational explanation, to an appreciation of and skill in rational, coherent argument, to an avoidance of irrational, unthinking prejudice.

There is of course no reason to believe that basing an education in rational talk will destroy creativity, harness freedom. But there is reason to believe that intellect could be destroyed by empty talk, talk about nothing firm, about nothing of substance. Other things being equal, I fear more the teacher talking in a vacuum than I do a teacher sure in her knowledge of something worth knowing and aware of the limits of that knowledge and its place in what is known and unknown.

III

The Dartmouth Seminar could have aimed high, it could have tried to offer a blueprint for education in the Anglo-American countries. Instead it narrowed itself to talk about nothing. In so proceeding, it misconceived what it is that needs doing and along the way wasted a good deal of public (Carnegie) money. Its 'findings' should be ignored.

JOHN DIXON

Bretton Hall College of Education

The 1960s have seen steady pressure and at times violent demands for curriculum change—in the United States, in Britain, in France and elsewhere. Looking back, we can see that many of our schools were generally ill-equipped to initiate and carry forward such changes; whether the colleges and universities are well enough equipped is still being tested. Thus, as the pressure has grown, special institutions have been set up on both sides of the Atlantic to undertake or enable curriculum change. The differences in their roles are rather crucial. On the one hand, institutions external to the schools may support and extend what is already going on there among pioneering teachers, offering a new sense of direction, perhaps, by a closer scrutiny of the work and by greater theoretical clarity. On the other hand, the external institution can seek to develop a kind of model curriculum which the schools try out and modify. These are the poles, as it were, and I have interpreted each favourably. It is unfortunately true that external intervention, whatever its expected role, can be casual, unselective and undemanding, or—more likely—paternalistic, dogmatic and limiting. As far as English curriculum is concerned there are already sharp national differences in the form of institution favoured. In part at least these differences represent different answers to possible questions about curriculum development work: for example, is it a "once for all," scheduled roughly every twenty years, or is it to be a continuing process? In part they reflect the pattern of power and influence between schools, colleges, universities, and the central and local government. And in part, they depend on general views of education.

When the U.S. and U.K. delegations met at Dartmouth College in 1966 to discuss "the teaching and learning of English," these differences in the strategy of curriculum development were matched by our mutual surprise at the kind of model curriculum ("syllabus" in England) that each country favoured. Throughout the early sixties there had been a sudden flourishing of new work in secondary departments scattered up and down England. The more traditional started from literature, others from writing, some from drama, but all tended to treat the English lesson as an opportunity for "an intimate study of the complexities, potentialities, and essential conditions of human nature" and human society.[1] A grand claim, it may seem, for the stumbling efforts of 12 year-olds of varying attainment. Nevertheless, this was the direction for spoken and written work that had been developed in England—without the help of a single curriculum project. And when these scattered groups came together in the newly formed National Association for the Teaching of English in 1963, they helped to give it

[1] F. R. Leavis, "Literature and Society," in *The Common Pursuit* (London: Chatto & Windus, 1952).

unusual coherence and vigour. There was sharp criticism in the N.A.T.E. Executive of the failure fully to represent such work (and its Primary School origins) in the delegation sent to Dartmouth. However, seven of the twenty British delegates had been directly involved in the early phase of this quiet revolution in secondary school English; one was the editor of its sole journal till 1963 (*The Use of English*), and two others were among its mentors at the Ministry of Education and the London Institute of Education.

The existence of such a wave of new work in English inevitably affects national planning of curriculum development. The stronger the work in the schools, the likelier it is that external agencies will see their main role as the encouragement, coordination, extension, and clarification of work by groups of teachers up and down the country. And this was a major role accepted in 1965 by the English Committee set up by the Schools Council (the national agency for curriculum development work in England and Wales). But the Dartmouth Seminar was organized with a different model in mind—thus the protests about what the British delegation represented.

Although one or two American teachers from a similar school tradition were present at the Seminar, the U.S. delegation was predominantly drawn from the universities. This reflected, one assumes, the decision of the government-funded Project English Centers to involve university scholars in literature, linguistics and composition in setting up curriculum study centers. From England, where only a fifth of the age group go on to higher education at 18+, this decision seemed to offer nothing but danger; in our schools specialist preparation for university or college entrance begins at 16 and the opportunities for curriculum change immediately narrow or even disappear. But in a country expecting half its students to go on to college, cooperative work on curriculum between schools and colleges is essential, even if it has its growing pains. The first of these will be a tendency for the university professor to dominate the work of the schools, and certainly, as regards representation, this was true at Dartmouth. But where there is any strength in the school tradition of English teaching, that tendency can be overcome. A more lasting influence will be the set or direction given to curriculum change. This proved the cause of the most important unacknowledged or hidden debate that took place at Dartmouth.

The characteristic American strategy to which I refer was well summed up by Professor Kitzhaber of the Oregon Center: the aim was "to redefine the particular subject in the light of the best knowledge available, to identify its central and organizing principles, to select and arrange applications and illustrations of those principles in an orderly sequence appropriate to the capacity of children of various ages, and finally to write radically new textbooks embodying these concepts." Like the aim of the British teachers, it may sound rather grand, but a direction of work is clearly indicated. What to do in the schools has yet to be defined: curriculum starts, as it were, from a tabula rasa in the classroom, and in the process of definition the scholar looks at the "subject" in abstraction from the pupils who will be using and operating in it. Necessarily the work of the scholar comes first; only when his "definition" is complete can schoolteachers begin to "select and arrange applications."

I have deliberately set up a polarity here between two positions on curriculum development. Some members saw this as *the* polarity between U.K. and U.S. It was a choice between blind enthusiasts in the classroom and academic rationalists in the study. But if we learn anything from studying English it is that such simple oppositions apply to language and not to people. (For that matter, the best example of the "English" style of teaching came from Ben DeMott of Amherst, when we discussed how we might take a poem of Hardy's in class. His contribution is available in the N.C.T.E. Dartmouth Seminar Paper: *Response to Literature.*) A polarity of this kind, then, is only useful in suggesting a conceptual framework, and if we stop short at this dichotomy, as some did, we evade the very thing that international exchanges have to offer—a challenge to our hidden and parochial assumptions. Looking back at the Dartmouth Seminar, with all the advantages of hindsight, one sees a strong group of British teachers, confident in their sense of new achievements in the classroom but sealed off from one of the major American problems by a set pattern of specialist education (for the few) at 16+. The initial question of the Seminar—What is English?—was interpreted by this group as an invitation not to "define the subject" but to describe in general terms "what at our best we are doing and hoping to do." This tended to leave the scholars on the sidelines, particularly as the model on which the seminar had been drawn up made no provision for detailed descriptions of classroom work to be available. Rather it started from the other pole—that of subject definition. Thus the major questions for discussion ran:

> What is English?
> What is "continuity" in English?
> One road or many? (tracking, etc.)
> Knowledge and proficiency in English.
> Standards and attitudes.

Clearly the assumption was that, starting from a definition, one would then be able to "select . . . and arrange in an orderly sequence," to decide at what points particular knowledge and proficiency could be expected, and so forth. But in effect this procedure took little or no account of the experience the British had to offer, and, as the Seminar went on, a different kind of model emerged. On the five major questions I doubt that the conflict was ever made explicit or resolved. Thus for those who took the "subject definition" point of view, the Seminar and its reports must have been disappointing failures. But besides the major questions a dozen "minor" topics had been set aside for study groups and it was here that the most productive work was done, especially on the contribution of drama, creative uses of English, ways of building on pre-school language experiences, response to literature, and examinations. With such topics it was possible to start from detailed experience in the classroom and to build up generalizations that would organize and illuminate what was going on; equally it was possible to assume common experiences and to analyze the kinds of process involved.

Before suggesting the limitations of this empirical approach from the point of view of curriculum development, I would like to indicate its strengths. First, as compared with the subject definition approach, it does not separate what is learned from the way it is learned and the uses to which it is put. In some schools, the natural way ahead in curriculum has been to face the schools' particular problems—the drop-outs or young school leavers, for instance. Maybe for these kids (and others who don't so much drop out as hang on) the first changes teachers want to discuss are in ways of working. Thirty or forty desks facing the front? The teacher holding forth at the blackboard? A predetermined "lesson" in the textbook? A sequence of questions you get right or wrong—never an open one, a matter of opinion, say? The set assignment with the mark-out-of-ten at the bottom? Repeated every 45 minute session? This is the hidden curriculum that makes every subject the same. The demand at Dartmouth to talk about concrete experience—what, at our best, are we doing?—led to a discussion of team teaching, group work, the varying roles of the teacher, the flexibility of his lesson plans. In the context of such discussion it is natural, on hearing that a class has read *Silas Marner,* to ask for evidence of the kind of process that was going on in individual readers.

Second, by not assuming an exclusive interest in the subject, one realizes that continuities in learning are of two kinds: within subject boundaries and across them. A strong response to *Macbeth* is not incompatible with a desire to understand more about murder, crime and guilt. I put it delicately, for it is easy to oversimplify the relationship between literature and human experience. Nevertheless, when we consider the daily current of literature, fictional and documentary, that students and teachers hear or read (records, television, film, newspapers and magazines included), the need to spend time in school on themes that draw on more than one subject discipline seems overwhelming.

A third advantage of this approach is that it leads us to discuss, tentatively no doubt, how in his everyday living a student comes to use what he has learned. This is less of a Benthamite question than it looks. If it had been raised earlier it might have driven some of the "new" grammar books off the market. It is, of course, the question least likely to be raised by the scholar, whose life's work is, after all, with the subject.

However, whatever its advantages, an approach which is exclusively empirical is bound to have limitations. The teacher as well as the scholar should feel pressure to reconsider the subject in the light of the best knowledge available. Let us turn therefore to the procedure for curriculum development in what I have called the "subject definition" model.

Remembering the headstart given to curriculum development in the sciences, one can interpret the notion of "identifying central and organizing principles," selecting "applications," etc., as an attempt to assimilate curriculum development in English to some of the very successful work in Mathematics. Since the work that led to *Principia Mathematica,* it has been possible to conceive of a meta-language in which mathematical discourse can be represented and discussed in highly general terms. This, I take it, is a consequence of the exclusion from mathematical discourse of all but logical relationships. However that may be, I cannot conceive of a meta-language in which, let us say, the whole of literature can be similarly represented and discussed in general terms.

There is also a temptation, owing to the extended sense of the word "grammar" now current in philosophy, to ask ourselves whether linguistics in general and modern grammars in particular will not account for language as symbolic logic has done for mathematics. But the central function of language is representation, and such grammars as I know consider language largely in abstraction from its representational function. Taken in this sense, then, the aim of *defining* English and identifying its organizing *principles* seems mistaken. The relevance of new work in literary criticism and linguistics to curriculum development will take a different form.

In Britain we have had a group of teachers for some years attached to the Communications Research Centre under the direction of Professor Halliday. This work in linguistics, initially financed by the Nuffield Foundation, is now continuing with Schools Council support. It has taken four years, and a good deal of uncertain and difficult work, for these selected teachers to reach the point where they can confidently prepare materials for discussion, trial and amendment by a voluntary group of colleagues in the schools. Small wonder, then, that in the month at Dartmouth the linguistic scholars felt unable to agree even in general terms on the exact relevance of their subject to the school curriculum. I think it is significant, however, that two of the areas that emerged as most relevant at Dartmouth were also chosen by this British team: first, the initial teaching of reading and writing, and second, ways of looking at language as it is used in everyday life (designed for grade 10 and above). Moreover, it is the teachers in the unit, and not the linguists, who have finally taken responsibility for these projects and thus for selecting from current linguistic theory what is relevant to their colleagues and to pupils in school. The work is still tentative and there will be a period of interaction between the unit and collaborating schools before publication is considered.

While I have assumed that neither literary criticism nor the linguistic sciences are capable of offering a general theory of English studies, I am not without hope of such a theory being developed in the long run. As a start we need a systematic analysis of the purposes and uses of language as a symbolic system. Work in one segment of this enormous field is now going on in a research project for Schools Council: a Writing Research Unit directed by James Britton is studying the writing across all school subjects of a sample of students aged 11 to 18 and looking for dimensions on which they can map the varieties of written language, possibly including varieties that develop within this age range. Adapting a model of Jacobsen's they have considered shifts of focus from audience to message to language. The sense of audience has been differentiated in some detail. Following suggestions by Sapir and Austin, an attempt is being made to differentiate a writer's sense of his task into one of a group of expressive functions. With the research still in its middle stage it is too early as yet to talk of theoretical results, but what can be said is that the unit and the group of teachers associated with it have achieved unusual insight into writing as a process. Already their work challenges the current choice of writing tasks (across the school subjects) and demonstrates the need for a coherent school policy on written work. It seems likely that there will be several equally fundamental consequences for the specialist teaching of English.

So far it has not been possible to set up parallel researches into varieties of oral English and varieties of dramatic language. But without these, what is best in the current practice of the schools cannot be explained and coordinated, and the patterns of development remain a matter for speculation. While this is the case, the demand for sequence in the English curriculum can only be answered by intuitive observation of successful practice—and I for one hope we shall see more recording, description, and elementary analysis of such practice, pending the emergence of an adequate theory.

The latent weakness of rationalism, I suppose, is to refuse to admit its limitations. I can sympathize with the desire for an over-arching theory, and I hope to see one in my lifetime, but in our present ignorance the best we can do seems to be, first, to extend to the full range of language in ordinary life that disciplined attention we learn in the study of literature, and, second, to gather from all who spent their lives in the study of language—philosophers, linguists, literary men—some tentative analyses of language in operation.

PART II

Language & Reading

CHAPTER 4

The Nature of Literacy

The Politics of Reading

NEIL POSTMAN
New York University

Neil Postman challenges the common assumptions that the literacy process is politically neutral and is the only, or even the best, avenue to jobs and aesthetic riches. He sees a predominantly literacy-based curriculum as obsolete and reactionary in the context of recent advances in electronic communications technology, and recommends broadening the base of school curricula to include "multimedia literacy."

In his *Seventh Letter,* Plato wrote, "No man of intelligence will venture to express his philosophical views in language, especially not in language that is unchangeable, which is true of that which is set down in written characters." As in so many things, Plato knew what he was talking about. A piece of writing is a time-machine which is apt to create an illusion of permanence, so that if you wish to change your ideas, you find it most inconvenient, even embarrassing. The point is that I have changed my ideas, and the essay reproduced here does not reflect how I now view these matters. I am allowing the essay to stand as it was written since it is unseemly to tamper with the facts of one's past. Besides, when originally published, the essay stimulated some worthwhile discussion about the politics of communication media, and may still be capable of doing so. But I beg the reader to bear in mind that I am now in possession of some of the best arguments that would refute what is written here.

NEIL POSTMAN, 1979

Teachers of reading comprise a most sinister political group, whose continued presence and strength are more a cause for alarm than celebration. I offer this thought as a defensible proposition, all the more worthy of consideration because so few people will take it seriously.

My argument rests on a fundamental and, I think, unassailable assumption about education: namely, that all educational practices are profoundly political in the sense that they are designed to produce one sort of human being rather than another—which is to say, an educational system always proceeds from some

An earlier version of this article was presented as the keynote address at the Lehigh University Reading Conference, Bethelem, Pa., 1970.

Harvard Educational Review   Vol. 40   No. 2   May 1970, 244–252

model of what a human being *ought* to be like. In the broadest sense, a political ideology is a conglomerate of systems for promoting certain modes of thinking and behavior. And there is no system I can think of that more directly tries to do this than the schools. There is not one thing that is done to, for, with, or against a student in school that is not rooted in a political bias, ideology, or notion. This includes everything from the arrangement of seats in a classroom, to the rituals practiced in the auditorium, to the textbooks used in lessons, to the dress required of both teachers and students, to the tests given, to the subjects that are taught, and most emphatically, to the intellectual skills that are promoted. And what is called reading, it seems to me, just about heads the list. For to teach reading, or even to promote vigorously the teaching of reading, is to take a definite political position on how people should behave and on what they ought to value. Now, teachers, I have found, respond in one of three ways to such an assertion. Some of them deny it. Some of them concede it but without guilt or defensiveness of any kind. And some of them don't know what it means. I want to address myself to the latter, because in responding to them I can include all the arguments I would use in dealing with the others.

In asserting that the teaching of reading is essentially a political enterprise, the most obvious question I am asking is, "What is reading good for?" When I ask this question of reading teachers, I am supplied with a wide range of answers. Those who take the low ground will usually say that skill in reading is necessary in order for a youngster to do well in school. The elementary teacher is preparing the youngster for the junior high teacher, who prepares him for the senior high teacher, who, in turn, prepares him for the college teacher, and so on. Now, this answer is true but hardly satisfactory. In fact, it amounts to a description of the *rules* of the school game but says nothing about the purpose of these rules. So, when teachers are pushed a little further, they sometimes answer that the school system, at all levels, makes reading skill a precondition to success because unless one can read well, he is denied access to gainful and interesting employment as an adult. This answer raises at least a half-dozen political questions, the most interesting of which is whether or not one's childhood education ought to be concerned with one's future employment. I am aware that most people take it as axiomatic that the schooling process should prepare youth for a tranquil entry into our economy, but this is a political view that I think deserves some challenge. For instance, when one considers that the second most common cause of death among adolescents in the U.S. is suicide, or that more people are hospitalized for mental illness than all other illnesses combined, or that one out of every 22 murders in the United States is committed by a parent against his own child, or that more than half of all high school students have already taken habit-forming, hallucinogenic, or potentially addictive narcotics, or that by the end of this year, there will be more than one million school drop-outs around, one can easily prepare a case which insists that the schooling process be designed for purposes other than vocational training. If it is legitimate at all for schools to claim a concern for the adult life of students, then why not pervasive and compulsory programs in mental health, sex, or marriage and the family? Besides, the number of jobs that require reading skill much beyond what teachers call a "fifth-grade level" is probably quite small and scarcely justifies the massive, compulsory, unrelenting reading programs that characterize most schools.

But most reading teachers would probably deny that their major purpose is to prepare students to satisfy far-off vocational requirements. Instead, they would take the high ground and insist that the basic purpose of reading instruction is to open the student's mind to the wonders and riches of the written word, to give him access to great fiction and poetry, to permit him to function as an informed citizen, to have him experience the sheer pleasure of reading. Now, this is a satisfactory answer indeed but, in my opinion, it is almost totally untrue.

And to the extent that it is true, it is true in a way quite different from anything one might expect. For instance, it is probably true that in a highly complex society, one cannot be governed unless he can read forms, regulations, notices, catalogues, road signs, and the like. Thus, some minimal reading skill is necessary if you are to be a "good citizen," but "good citizen" here means one who can follow the instructions of those who govern him. If you cannot read, you cannot be an obedient citizen. You are also a good citizen if you are an enthusiastic consumer. And so, some minimal reading competence is required if you are going to develop a keen interest in all the products that it is necessary for you to buy. If you do not read, you will be a relatively poor market. In order to be a good and loyal citizen, it is also necessary for you to believe in the myths and superstitions of your society. Therefore, a certain minimal reading skill is needed so that you can learn what these are, or have them reinforced. Imagine what would happen in a school if a Social Studies text were introduced that described the growth of American civilization as being characterized by four major developments: 1) insurrection against a legally constituted government, in order to achieve a political identity; 2) genocide against the indigenous population, in order to get land; 3) keeping human beings as slaves, in order to achieve an economic base; and 4) the importation of "coolie" labor, in order to build the railroads. Whether this view of American history is true or not is beside the point. It is at least as true or false as the conventional view *and* it would scarcely be allowed to appear unchallenged in a school-book intended for youth. What I am saying here is that an important function of the teaching of reading is to make students accessible to political and historical myth. It is entirely possible that the main reason middle-class whites are so concerned to get lower-class blacks to read is that blacks will remain relatively inaccessible to standard-brand beliefs unless and until they are minimally literate. It just may be too dangerous, politically, for any substantial minority of our population *not* to believe that our flags are sacred, our history is noble, our government is representative, our laws are just, and our institutions are viable. A reading public is a responsible public, by which is meant that it believes most or all of these superstitions, and which is probably why we still have literacy tests for voting.

One of the standard beliefs about the reading process is that it is more or less neutral. Reading, the argument goes, is just a skill. What people read is their own business, and the reading teacher merely helps to increase a student's options. If one wants to read about America, one may read DeToqueville or *The Daily News;* if one wants to read literature, one may go to Melville or Jacqueline Susann. In theory, this argument is compelling. In practice, it is pure romantic nonsense. The *New York Daily News* is the most widely read newspaper in America. Most of our students will go to the grave not having read, of their own choosing, a paragraph of DeToqueville or Thoreau or John Stuart Mill or, if you exclude the Gettysburg Address, even Abraham Lincoln. As between Jacqueline Susann and Herman Melville—well, the less said, the better. To put it bluntly, among every 100 students who learn to read, my guess is that no more than one will employ the process toward any of the lofty goals which are customarily held before us. The rest will use the process to increase their knowledge of trivia, to maintain themselves at a relatively low level of emotional maturity, and to keep themselves simplistically uninformed about the social and political turmoil around them.

Now, there are teachers who feel that, even if what I say is true, the point is nonetheless irrelevant. After all, they say, the world is not perfect. If people do not have enough time to read deeply, if people do not have sensibilities refined enough to read great literature, if people do not have interests broad enough to be stimulated by the unfamiliar, the fault is not in our symbols, but in ourselves. But there is a point of view that proposes that the "fault," in fact, *does* lie in our symbols. Marshall McLuhan is saying that each medium of comunication contains a unique metaphysic—that each medium makes special kinds of claims on our senses, and therefore, on our behavior. McLuhan himself tells us that he is by no means the first person to have noticed this. Socrates took a very dim view of the written word, on the grounds that it diminishes man's capacity to memorize, and that it forces one to follow an argument rather than to participate in it. He also objected to the fact that once something has been written down, it may easily come to the attention of persons for whom it was not intended. One can well imagine what Socrates would think about wire-tapping and other electronic bugging devices. St. Ambrose, a prolific book writer and reader, once complained to St. Jerome, another prolific writer and reader, that whatever else its virtues, reading was the most anti-social behavior yet devised by man. Other people have made observations about the effects of communications media on the psychology of a culture, but it is quite remarkable how little has been said about this subject. Most criticism of print, or any other medium, has dealt with the content of the medium; and it is only in recent years that we have begun to understand that each medium, *by its very structure,* makes us do things with our bodies, our senses, and our minds that in the long run are probably more important than any other messages communicated by the medium.

Now that it is coming to an end, we are just beginning to wonder about the powerful biases forced upon us by the Age of the Printed Word. McLuhan is telling us that print is a "hot" medium, by which he means that it induces passivity and anesthetizes almost all our senses except the visual. He is also telling us that electronic media, like the LP record and television, are reordering our entire sensorium, restoring some of our sleeping senses, and, in the process, making all of us seek more active participation in life. I think McLuhan is wrong in connecting the *causes* of passivity and activity so directly to the structure of media. I find it sufficient to say that whenever a new medium—a new communications technology—enters a culture, *no matter what its structure,* it gives us a new way of experiencing the world, and consequently, releases tremendous energies and causes people to seek new ways of organizing their institutions. When Gutenberg announced that he could manufacture books, as he put it, "without the help of reed, stylus, or pen but by wondrous agreement, proportion, and harmony of punches and types," he could scarcely imagine that he was about to become the most important political and social revolutionary of the Second Millennium. And yet, that is what happened. Four hundred and fifty years ago, the printed word, far from being a medium that induced passivity, generated cataclysmic change. From the time Martin Luther posted his theses in 1517, the printing press disseminated the most controversial, inflammatory, and wrenching ideas imaginable. The Protestant Reformation would probably not have occurred if not for the printing press. The development of both capitalism and nationalism were obviously linked to the printing press. So were new literary forms, such as the novel and the essay. So were new conceptions of education, such as written examinations. And, of course, so was the concept of scientific methodology, whose ground rules were established by Descartes in his *Discourse on Reason.* Even today in recently illiterate cultures, such as Cuba, print is a medium capable of generating intense involvement, radicalism, artistic innovation, and institutional upheaval. But in those countries where the printed word has been pre-eminent for over 400 years, print retains very few of these capabilities. Print is not dead, it's just old—and old technologies do not generate new patterns of behavior. For us, print is the technology of convention. We have accommodated our senses to it. We have routinized and even ritualized our responses to it. We have devoted our institutions, which are now venerable, to its service. By maintaining the printed word as the keystone of education, we are therefore opting for political and social stasis.

It is 126 years since Professor Morse transmitted a message electronically for the first time in the history of the planet. Surely it is not too soon for educators to give serious thought to the message he sent: "What hath God wrought?" We are very far from knowing the answers to that question, but we do know that electronic media have released unprecedented energies. It's worth saying that the gurus of the peace movement—Bob Dylan, Pete Seeger, Joan Baez, Phil Ochs, for instance—were known to their constituency mostly as voices on LP records. It's worth saying that Vietnam, being our first television war, is also the most unpopular war in our history. It's worth saying that Lyndon Johnson was the first president ever to have resigned because of a "credibility gap." It's worth saying that it is now commonplace for post-TV college sophomores to usurp the authority of college presidents and for young parish priests to instruct their bishops in the ways of *both* man and God. And it's also worth saying that black people, after 350 years of bondage, want their freedom—now. Post-television blacks are, indeed, our true *now* generation.

Electronic media are predictably working to unloose disruptive social and political ideas, along with new forms of sensibility and expression. Whether this is being achieved by the structure of the media, or by their content, or by some combination of both, we cannot be sure. But like Gutenberg's infernal machine of 450 years ago, the electric plug is causing all hell to break loose. Meanwhile, the schools are still pushing the old technology; and, in fact, pushing it with almost hysterical vigor. Everyone's going to learn to read, even if we have to kill them to do it. It is as if the schools were the last bastion of the old culture, and if it has to go, why let's take as many down with us as we can.

For instance, the schools are still the principal source of the idea that literacy is equated with intelligence. Why, the schools even promote the idea that *spelling* is related to intelligence! Of course, if any of this were true, reading teachers would be the smartest people around. One doesn't mean to be unkind, but if that indeed is the case, no one has noticed it. In any event, it is an outrage that children who do not read well, or at all, are treated as if they are stupid. It is also masochistic, since the number of non-readers will obviously continue to increase and, thereby, the schools will condemn themselves, by their own definition of intelligence, to an increasing number of stupid children. In this way, we will soon have remedial reading-readiness classes, along with remedial classes for those not yet ready for their remedial reading-readiness class.

The schools are also still promoting the idea that literacy is the richest source of aesthetic experience. This, in the face of the fact that kids are spending a billion dollars a year to buy LP records and see films. The schools are still promoting the idea that the main source of wisdom is to be found in libraries, from which most schools, incidentally, carefully exclude the most interesting books. The schools are still promoting the idea that the non-literate person is somehow not fully human, an idea that will surely endear us to the non-literate peoples of the world. (It is similar to the idea that salvation is obtainable only through Christianity—which is to say, it is untrue, bigoted, reactionary, and based on untenable premises, to boot.)

Worst of all, the schools are using these ideas to keep non-conforming youth—blacks, the politically disaffected, and the economically disadvantaged, among others—in their place. By taking this tack, the schools have become a major force for political conservatism at a time when everything else in the culture screams for rapid reorientation and change.

What would happen if our schools took the drastic political step of trying to make the new technology the keystone of education? The thought will seem less romantic if you remember that the start of the Third Millennium is only 31 years away. No one knows, of course, what would happen, but I'd like to make a few guesses. In the first place, the physical environment would be entirely different from what it is now. The school would look something like an electric circus— arranged to accommodate TV cameras and monitors, film projectors, computers, audio and video tape machines, radio, and photographic and stereophonic equipment. As he is now provided with textbooks, each student would be provided with his own still-camera, 8 mm. camera, and tape casette. The school library would contain books, of course, but at least as many films, records, videotapes, audio-tapes, and computer programs. The major effort of the school would be to assist students in achieving what has been called "multi-media literacy." Therefore, speaking, film-making, picture-taking, televising, computer-programming, listening, perhaps even music playing, drawing, and dancing would be completely acceptable means of expressing intellectual interest and competence. They would certainly be given weight at least equal to reading and writing.

Since intelligence would be defined in a new way, a student's ability to create an idea would be at least as important as his ability to classify and remember the ideas of others. New evaluation procedures would come into being, and standardized tests—the final, desperate refuge of the print-bound bureaucrat—would disappear. Entirely new methods of instruction would evolve. In fact, schools might abandon the notion of teacher instruction altogether. Whatever disciplines lent themselves to packaged, lineal, and segmented presentation would be offered through a computerized and individualized program. And students could choose from a wide variety of such programs whatever they wished to learn about. This means, among other things, that teachers would have to stop acting like teachers and find something useful to do, like, for instance, helping young people to resolve some of their more wrenching emotional problems.

In fact, a school that put electric circuitry at its center would have to be prepared for some serious damage to all of its bureaucratic and hierarchical arrangements. Keep in mind that hierarchies derive their authority from the notion of unequal access to information. Those at the top have access to more information than those at the bottom. That is in fact why they are at the top and the others, at the bottom. But today those who are at the bottom of the school hierarchy, namely, the students, have access to at least as much information about most subjects as those at the top. At present, the only way those at the top can maintain control over them is by carefully discriminating against what the students know—that is, by labelling what the students know as unimportant. But suppose cinematography was made a "major" subject instead of English literature? Suppose chemotherapy was made a "major" subject? or space technology? or ecology? or mass communication? or popular music? or photography? or race relations? or urban life? Even an elementary school might then find itself in a situation where the faculty were at the bottom and its students at the top. Certainly, it would be hard to know who are the teachers and who the learners.

And then perhaps a school would become a place where *everybody,* including the adults, is trying to learn something. Such a school would obviously be problem-centered, *and* future-centered, *and* change-centered; and, as such, would be an instrument of cultural and political radicalism. In the process we might find that our youth would also learn to read without pain and with a degree of success and economy not presently known.

I want to close on this thought: teachers of reading represent an important political pressure group. They may not agree with me that they are a sinister political group. But I should think that they would want to ask at least a few questions *before* turning to consider the *techniques* of teaching reading. These questions would be: What is reading good for? What is it better or worse than? What are my motives in promoting it? And the ultimate political question of all, "Whose side am I on?"

The Adult Literacy Process as Cultural Action for Freedom

PAULO FREIRE
Center for the Study of Development and Social Change
Cambridge, Massachusetts

Paulo Freire writes from a Third World perspective, but with obvious implications for education in general. He rejects mechanistic conceptions of the adult literacy process, advocating instead a theory and practice based upon authentic dialogue between teachers and learners. Such dialogue, in Freire's approach, centers upon codified representations of the learners' existential situations and leads not only to their acquisition of literacy skills, but more importantly to their awareness of their right and capacity as human beings to transform reality. Becoming literate, then, means far more than learning to decode the written representation of a sound system. It is truly an act of knowing, through which a person is able to look critically at the culture which has shaped him, and to move toward reflection and positive action upon his world.

Every Educational Practice Implies a Concept of Man and the World

Experience teaches us not to assume that the obvious is clearly understood. So it is with the truism with which we begin: All educational practice implies a theoretical stance on the educator's part. This stance in turn implies—sometimes more, sometimes less explicitly—an interpretation of man and the world. It could not be otherwise. The process of men's orientation in the world involves not just the association of sense images, as for animals. It involves, above all, thought-language; that is, the possibility of the act of knowing through his praxis, by which man transforms reality. For man, this process of orientation in the world can be

This article is part of a longer essay by Paulo Freire, *Cultural Action for Freedom*, Harvard Educational Review Monograph Series, No. 1 (Cambridge, Mass.: Harvard Educational Review, 1970). Copyright © 1970 by Paulo Freire.

The author gratefully acknowledges the contributions of Loretta Slover, who translated this essay, and João da Veiga Coutinho and Robert Riordan, who assisted in the preparation of the manuscript.

Harvard Educational Review   Vol. 40   No. 2   May 1970, 205–225

understood neither as a purely subjective event, nor as an objective or mechanistic one, but only as an event in which subjectivity and objectivity are united. Orientation in the world, so understood, places the question of the purposes of action at the level of critical perception of reality.

If, for animals, orientation in the world means adaptation to the world, for man it means humanizing the world by transforming it. For animals there is no historical sense, no options or values in their orientation in the world; for man there is both an historical and a value dimension. Men have the sense of "project," in contrast to the instinctive routines of animals.

The action of men without objectives, whether the objectives are right or wrong, mythical or demythologized, naive or critical, is not praxis, though it may be orientation in the world. And not being praxis, it is action ignorant both of its own process and of its aim. The interrelation of the awareness of aim and of process is the basis for planning action, which implies methods, objectives, and value options.

Teaching adults to read and write must be seen, analyzed, and understood in this way. The critical analyst will discover in the methods and texts used by educators and students practical value options which betray a philosophy of man, well or poorly outlined, coherent or incoherent. Only someone with a mechanistic mentality, which Marx would call "grossly materialistic," could reduce adult literacy learning to a purely technical action. Such a naive approach would be incapable of perceiving that technique itself as an instrument of men in their orientation in the world is not neutral.

We shall try, however, to prove by analysis the self-evidence of our statement. Let us consider the case of primers used as the basic texts for teaching adults to read and write. Let us further propose two distinct types: a poorly done primer and a good one, according to the genre's own criteria. Let us even suppose that the author of the good primer based the selection of its generative words[1] on a prior knowledge of which words have the greatest resonance for the learner (a practice not commonly found, though it does exist).

Doubtlessly, such an author is already far beyond the colleague who composes his primer with words he himself chooses in his own library. Both authors, however, are identical in a fundamental way. In each case they themselves decompose the given generative words and from the syllables create new words. With these words, in turn, the authors form simple sentences and, little by little, small stories, the so-called reading lessons.

---

[1] In languages like Portuguese or Spanish, words are composed syllabically. Thus, every non-monosyllabic word is, technically, *generative*, in the sense that other words can be constructed from its de-composed syllables. For a word to be authentically generative, however, certain conditions must be present which will be discussed in a later section of this essay. [At the phonetic level the term *generative word* is properly applicable only with regard to a sound-syllabic reading methodology, while the thematic application is universal. See Sylvia Ashton-Warner's *Teacher* for a different treatment of the concept of generative words at the thematic level.—Editor]

Let us say that the author of the second primer, going one step further, suggests that the teachers who use it initiate discussions about one or another word, sentence, or text with their students.

Considering either of these hypothetical cases we may legitimately conclude that there is an implicit concept of man in the primer's method and content, whether it is recognized by the authors or not. This concept can be reconstructed from various angles. We begin with the fact, inherent in the idea and use of the primer, that it is the teacher who chooses the words and proposes them to the learner. Insofar as the primer is the mediating object between the teacher and students, and the students are to be "filled" with words the teachers have chosen, one can easily detect a first important dimension of the image of man which here begins to emerge. It is the profile of a man whose consciousness is "spatialized," and must be "filled" or "fed" in order to know. This same conception led Sartre, criticizing the notion that "to know is to eat," to exclaim: *O philosophie alimentaire!*"[2]

This "digestive" concept of knowledge, so common in current educational practice, is found very clearly in the primer.[3] Illiterates are considered "undernourished," not in the literal sense in which many of them really are, but because they lack the "bread of the spirit." Consistent with the concept of knowledge as food, illiteracy is conceived of as a "poison herb," intoxicating and debilitating persons who cannot read or write. Thus, much is said about the "eradication" of illiteracy to cure the disease.[4] In this way, deprived of their character as linguistic signs constitutive of man's thought-language, words are transformed into mere "deposits of vocabulary"—the bread of the spirit which the illiterates are to "eat" and "digest."

This "nutritionist" view of knowledge perhaps also explains the humanitarian character of certain Latin American adult literacy campaigns. If millions of men are illiterate, "starving for letters," "thirsty for words," the word must be *brought* to them to save them from "hunger" and "thirst." The word, according to the naturalistic concept of consciousness implicit in the primer, must be "deposited," not born of the creative effort of the learners. As understood in this concept, man is a passive being, the object of the process of learning to read and write, and not its subject. As object his task is to "study" the so-called reading lessons, which in fact are almost completely alienating and alienated, having so little, if anything, to do with the student's socio-cultural reality.[5]

[2] Jean Paul Sartre, *Situations I* (Paris: Librairie Gallimard, 1947), p. 31.

[3] The digestive concept of knowledge is suggested by "controlled readings," by classes which consist only in lectures; by the use of memorized dialogues in language learning; by bibliographical notes which indicate not only which chapter, but which lines and words are to be read; by the methods of evaluating the students' progress in learning.

[4] See Paulo Freire, "La alfabetizacion de adultos, critica de su vision ingenua; compreension de su vision critica," in *Introducción a la Acción Cultural* (Santiago: ICIRA, 1969).

[5] There are two noteworthy exceptions among these primers: (1) in Brazil, *Viver e Lutar*, developed by a team of specialists of the Basic Education Movement, sponsored by the National

It would be a truly interesting study to analyze the reading texts being used in private or official adult literacy campaigns in rural and urban Latin America. It would not be unusual to find among such texts sentences and readings like the following random samples:[6]

> *A asa é da ave*—"The wing is of the bird."
> *Eva viu a uva*—"Eva saw the grape."
> *O galo canta*—"The cock crows."
> *O cachorro ladra*—"The dog barks."
> *Maria gosta dos animais*—"Mary likes animals."
> *João cuida das arvores*—"John takes care of the trees."

O pai de Carlinhos se chama Antonio. Carlinhos é um bom menino, bem comportado e estudioso—"Charles's father's name is Antonio. Charles is a good, well-behaved, and studious boy."

Ada deu o dedo ao urubu? Duvido, Ada deu o dedo a arara. . . .[7]

Se você trabalha com martelo e prego, tenha cuidado para nao furar o dedo.—"If you hammer a nail, be careful not to smash your finger."[8]

* * * *

"Peter did not know how to read. Peter was ashamed. One day, Peter went to school and registered for a night course. Peter's teacher was very good. Peter knows how to read now. Look at Peter's face. [These lessons are generally illustrated.] Peter is smiling. He is a happy man. He already has a good job. Everyone ought to follow his example."

In saying that Peter is smiling because he knows how to read, that he is happy because he now has a good job, and that he is an example for all to follow, the authors establish a relationship between knowing how to read and getting good jobs which, in fact, cannot be borne out. This naiveté reveals, at least, a failure to perceive the structure not only of illiteracy, but of social phenomena in general. Such an approach may admit that these phenomena exist, but it cannot perceive their relationship to the structure of the society in which they are found. It is as if these phenomena were mythical, above and beyond concrete situations, or the results of the intrinsic inferiority of a certain class of men. Unable to grasp

Conference of Bishops. (This reader became the object of controversy after it was banned as subversive by the then governor of Guanabara, Mr. Carlos Lacerda, in 1963.) (2) in Chile, the ESPIGA collection, despite some small defects. The collection was organized by Jefatura de Planes Extraordinarios de Educación de Adultos, of the Public Education Ministry.

[6] Since at the time this essay was written the writer did not have access to the primers, and was, therefore, vulnerable to recording phrases imprecisely or to confusing the author of one or another primer, it was thought best not to identify the authors or the titles of the books.

[7] The English here would be nonsensical, as is the Portuguese, the point being the emphasis on the consonant *d*.—Editor

[8] The author may even have added here, ". . . If, however, this should happen, apply a little mercurochrome."

contemporary illiteracy as a typical manifestation of the "culture of silence," directly related to underdeveloped structures, this approach cannot offer an objective, critical response to the challenge of illiteracy. Merely teaching men to read and write does not work miracles; if there are not enough jobs for men able to work, teaching more men to read and write will not create them.

One of these readers presents among its lessons the following two texts on consecutive pages without relating them. The first is about May 1st, the Labor Day holiday, on which workers commemorate their struggles. It does not say how or where these are commemorated, or what the nature of the historical conflict was. The main theme of the second lesson is *holidays*. It says that "on these days people ought to go to the beach to swim and sunbathe..." Therefore, if May 1st is a holiday, and if on holidays people should go to the beach, the conclusion is that the workers should go swimming on Labor Day, instead of meeting with their unions in the public squares to discuss their problems.

Analysis of these texts reveals, then, a simplistic vision of men, of their world, of the relationship between the two, and of the literacy process which unfolds in that world.

A asa é da ave, Eva viu a uva, o galo canta, and *o cachorro late,* are linguistic contexts which, when mechanically memorized and repeated, are deprived of their authentic dimension as thought-language in dynamic interplay with reality. Thus impoverished, they are not authentic expressions of the world.

Their authors do not recognize in the poor classes the ability to know and even create the texts which would express their own thought-language at the level of their perception of the world. The authors repeat with the texts what they do with the words, i.e., they introduce them into the learners' consciousness as if it were empty space—once more, the "digestive" concept of knowledge.

Still more, the a-structural perception of illiteracy revealed in these texts exposes the other false view of illiterates as marginal men.[9] Those who consider them marginal must, nevertheless, recognize the existence of a reality to which they are marginal—not only physical space, but historical, social, cultural, and economic realities—i.e., the structural dimension of reality. In this way, illiterates have to be recognized as beings "outside of," "marginal to" something, since it is impossible to be marginal to nothing. But being "outside of" or "marginal to" necessarily implies a movement of the one said to be marginal from the center, where he was, to the periphery. This movement, which is an action, presupposes in turn not only an agent but also his reasons. Admitting the existence of men "outside of" or "marginal to" structural reality, it seems legitimate to ask: Who is the author of this movement from the center of the structure to its margin? Do so-called marginal men, among them the illiterates, make the decision to move

[9] [The Portuguese word here translated as *marginal man* is *marginado*. This has a passive sense: he who has been made marginal, or sent outside society; as well as the sense of a state of existence on the fringe of society.—Translator.]

out to the periphery of society? If so, marginality is an option with all that it involves: hunger, sickness, rickets, pain, mental deficiencies, living death, crime, promiscuity, despair, the impossibility of being. In fact, however, it is difficult to accept that 40% of Brazil's population, almost 90% of Haiti's, 60% of Bolivia's, about 40% of Peru's, more than 30% of Mexico's and Venezuela's, and about 70% of Guatemala's would have made the tragic *choice* of their own marginality as illiterates.[10] If, then, marginality is not by choice, marginal man has been expelled from and kept outside of the social system and is therefore the object of violence.

In fact, however, the social structure as a whole does not "expel," nor is marginal man a "being outside of." He is, on the contrary, a "being inside of," within the social structure, and in a dependent relationship to those whom we call falsely autonomous beings, inauthentic beings-for-themselves.

A less rigorous approach, one more simplistic, less critical, more technicist, would say that it was unnecessary to reflect about what it would consider unimportant questions such as illiteracy and teaching adults to read and write. Such an approach might even add that the discussion of the concept of marginality is an unnecessary academic exercise. In fact, however, it is not so. In accepting the illiterate as a person who exists on the fringe of society, we are led to envision him as a sort of "sick man," for whom literacy would be the "medicine" to cure him, enabling him to "return" to the "healthy" structure from which he has become separated. Educators would be benevolent counsellors, scouring the outskirts of the city for the stubborn illiterates, runaways from the good life, to restore them to the forsaken bosom of happiness by giving them the gift of the word.

In the light of such a concept—unfortunately, all too widespread—literacy programs can never be efforts toward freedom; they will never question the very reality which deprives men of the right to speak up—not only illiterates, but all those who are treated as objects in a dependent relationship. These men, illiterate or not, are, in fact, not marginal. What we said before bears repeating: They are not "beings outside of"; they are "beings for another." Therefore the solution to their problem is not to become "beings inside of," but men freeing themselves; for, in reality, they are not marginal to the structure, but oppressed men within it. Alienated men, they cannot overcome their dependency by "incorporation" into the very structure responsible for their dependency. There is no other road to humanization—theirs as well as everyone else's—but authentic transformation of the dehumanizing structure.

From this last point of view, the illiterate is no longer a person living on the fringe of society, a marginal man, but rather a representative of the dominated strata of society, in conscious or unconscious opposition to those who, in the same structure, treat him as a thing. Thus, also, teaching men to read and write is no

---

[10] UNESCO: La situación educativa en América Latina, Cuadro no. 20, page 263 (Paris, 1960).

longer an inconsequential matter of *ba, be, bi, bo, bu,* of memorizing an alienated word, but a difficult apprenticeship in naming the world.

In the first hypothesis, interpreting illiterates as men marginal to society, the literacy process reinforces the mythification of reality by keeping it opaque and by dulling the "empty consciousness" of the learner with innumerable alienating words and phrases. By contrast, in the second hypothesis—interpreting illiterates as men oppressed within the system—the literacy process, as cultural action for freedom, is an act of knowing in which the learner assumes the role of knowing subject in dialogue with the educator. For this very reason, it is a courageous endeavor to demythologize reality, a process through which men who had previously been submerged in reality begin to emerge in order to re-insert themselves into it with critical awareness.

Therefore the educator must strive for an ever greater clarity as to what, at times without his conscious knowledge, illumines the path of his action. Only in this way will he truly be able to assume the role of one of the subjects of this action and remain consistent in the process.

The Adult Literacy Process as an Act of Knowing

To be an act of knowing the adult literacy process demands among teachers and students a relationship of authentic dialogue. True dialogue unites subjects together in the cognition of a knowable object which mediates between them.

If learning to read and write is to constitute an act of knowing, the learners must assume from the beginning the role of creative subjects. It is not a matter of memorizing and repeating given syllables, words, and phrases, but rather of reflecting critically on the process of reading and writing itself, and on the profound significance of language.

Insofar as language is impossible without thought, and language and thought are impossible without the world to which they refer, the human word is more than mere vocabulary—it is word-and-action. The cognitive dimensions of the literacy process must include the relationships of men with their world. These relationships are the source of the dialectic between the products men achieve in transforming the world and the conditioning which these products in turn exercise on men.

Learning to read and write ought to be an opportunity for men to know what *speaking the word* really means: a human act implying reflection and action. As such it is a primordial human right and not the privilege of a few.[11] Speaking the word is not a true act if it is not at the same time associated with the right of self-expression and world-expression, of creating and re-creating, of deciding and choosing and ultimately participating in society's historical process.

[11] Paulo Freire, "La alfabetizacion de adultos."

In the culture of silence the masses are "mute," that is, they are prohibited from creatively taking part in the transformations of their society and therefore prohibited from being. Even if they can occasionally read and write because they were "taught" in humanitarian—but not humanist—literacy campaigns, they are nevertheless alienated from the power responsible for their silence.

Illiterates know they are concrete men. They know that they do things. What they do not know in the culture of silence—in which they are ambiguous, dual beings—is that men's actions as such are transforming, creative, and re-creative. Overcome by the myths of this culture, including the myth of their own "natural inferiority," they do not know that *their* action upon the world is also transforming. Prevented from having a "structural perception" of the facts involving them, they do not know that they cannot "have a voice," i.e., that they cannot exercise the right to participate consciously in the socio-historical transformation of their society, because their work does not belong to them.

It could be said (and we would agree) that it is not possible to recognize all this apart from praxis, that is, apart from reflection and action, and that to attempt it would be pure idealism. But it is also true that action upon an object must be critically analyzed in order to understand both the object itself and the understanding one has of it. The act of knowing involves a dialectical movement which goes from action to reflection and from reflection upon action to a new action. For the learner to know what he did not know before, he must engage in an authentic process of abstraction by means of which he can reflect on the action-object whole, or, more generally, on forms of orientation in the world. In this process of abstraction, situations representative of how the learner orients himself in the world are proposed to him as the objects of his critique.

As an event calling forth the critical reflection of both the learners and educators, the literacy process must relate *speaking the word* to *transforming reality*, and to man's role in this transformation. Perceiving the significance of that relationship is indispensible for those learning to read and write if we are really committed to liberation. Such a perception will lead the learners to recognize a much greater right than that of being literate. They will ultimately recognize that, as men, they have the right to have a voice.

On the other hand, as an act of knowing, learning to read and write presupposes not only a theory of knowing but a method which corresponds to the theory.

We recognize the indisputable unity between subjectivity and objectivity in the act of knowing. Reality is never just simply the objective datum, the concrete fact, but is also men's perception of it. Once again, this is not a subjectivistic or idealistic affirmation, as it might seem. On the contrary, subjectivism and idealism come into play when the subjective-objective unity is broken.[12]

---

[12] There are two ways to fall into idealism: The one consists of dissolving the real in subjectivity; the other in denying all real subjectivity in the interests of objectivity." Jean Paul Sartre, *Search for a Method*, trans. Hazel E. Barnes (New York: Vintage Books, 1968), p. 33.

The adult literacy process as an act of knowing implies the existence of two interrelated contexts. One is the context of authentic dialogue between learners and educators as equally knowing subjects. This is what schools should be—the theoretical context of dialogue. The second is the real, concrete context of facts, the social reality in which men exist.[13]

In the theoretical context of dialogue, the facts presented by the real or concrete context are critically analyzed. This analysis involves the exercise of abstraction, through which, by means of representations of concrete reality, we seek knowledge of that reality. The instrument for this abstraction in our methodology is codification,[14] or representation of the existential situations of the learners.

Codification, on the one hand, mediates between the concrete and theoretical contexts (of reality). On the other hand, as knowable object, it mediates between the knowing subjects, educators and learners, who seek in dialogue to unveil the "action-object wholes."

This type of linguistic discourse must be "read" by anyone who tries to interpret it, even when purely pictorial. As such, it presents what Chomsky calls "surface structure" and "deep structure."

The "surface structure" of codification makes the "action-object whole" explicit in a purely taxonomic form. The first stage of decodification[15]—or reading—is descriptive. At this stage, the "readers"—or decodifiers—focus on the relationship between the categories constituting the codification. This preliminary focus on the surface structure is followed by problematizing the codified situation. This leads the learner to the second and fundamental stage of decodification, the comprehension of the codification's "deep structure." By understanding the codification's "deep structure" the learner can then understand the dialectic which exists between the categories presented in the "surface structure," as well as the unity between the "surface" and "deep" structures.

In our method, the codification initially takes the form of a photograph or sketch which represents a real existent, or an existent constructed by the learners. When this representation is projected as a slide, the learners effect an operation basic to the act of knowing: they gain distance from the knowable object. This experience of distance is undergone as well by the educators, so that educators and learners together can reflect critically on the knowable object which mediates between them. The aim of decodification is to arrive at the critical level of knowing, beginning with the learner's experience of the situation in the "real context."

[13] See Karel Kosik, *Dialectica de lo Concreto* (Mexico: Grijalbo, 1967).

[14] [*Codification* refers alternatively to the imaging, or the image itself, of some significant aspect of the learner's concrete reality (of a slum dwelling, for example). As such, it becomes both the object of the teacher-learner dialogue and the context for the introduction of the generative word.—Editor]

[15] [Decodification refers to a process of description and interpretation, whether of printed words, pictures, or other "codifications." As such, decodification and decodifying are distinct from the process of decoding, or word-recognition.—Editor.]

Whereas the codified representation is the knowable object mediating between knowing subjects, decodification—dissolving the codification into its constituent elements—is the operation by which the knowing subjects perceive relationships between the codification's elements and other facts presented by the real context —relationships which were formerly unperceived. Codification represents a given dimension of reality as individuals live it, and this dimension is proposed for their analysis in a context other than that in which they live it. Codification thus transforms what was a way of life in the real context into "objectum" in the theoretical context. The learners, rather than receive information about this or that fact, analyze aspects of their own existential experience represented in the codification.

Existential experience is a whole. In illuminating one of its angles and per- ceiving the inter-relation of that angle with others, the learners tend to replace a fragmented vision of reality with a total vision. From the point of view of a theory of knowledge, this means that the dynamic between codification of ex- istential situations and decodification involves the learners in a constant re-con- struction of their former "ad-miration" of reality.

We do not use the concept "ad-miration" here in the usual way, or in its ethical or esthetic sense, but with a special philosophical connotation.

To "ad-mire" is to objectify the "not-I." It is a dialectical operation which char- acterizes man as man, differentiating him from the animal. It is directly associated with the creative dimension of his language. To "ad-mire" implies that man stands over against his "not-I" in order to understand it. For this reason, there is no act of knowing without "ad-miration" of the object to be known. If the act of knowing is a dynamic act—and no knowledge is ever complete—then in order to know, man not only "ad-mires" the object, but must always be "re-ad-miring" his former "ad-miration." When we "re-ad-mire" our former "ad-miration" (always an "ad-miration of") we are simultaneously "ad-miring" the act of "ad-miring" and the object "ad-mired," so that we can overcome the errors we made in our former "ad-miration." This "re-ad-miration" leads us to a perception of an an- terior perception.

In the process of decodifying representations of their existential situations and perceiving former perceptions, the learners gradually, hesitatingly, and timorously place in doubt the opinion they held of reality and replace it with a more and more critical knowledge thereof.

Let us suppose that we were to present to groups from among the dominated classes codifications which portray their imitation of the dominators' cultural models—a natural tendency of the oppressed consciousness at a given moment.[16] The dominated persons would perhaps, in self-defense, deny the truth of the

[16] Re the oppressed consciousness, see: Frantz Fanon, *The Wretched of the Earth* (New York: Grove Press, 1968); Albert Memmi, *Colonizer and the Colonized* (New York: Orion Press, 1965); and Paulo Freire, *Pedagogy of the Oppressed* (New York: Seabury Press, 1970).

codification. As they deepened their analysis, however, they would begin to perceive that their apparent imitation of the dominators' models is a result of their interiorization of these models and, above all, of the myths of the "superiority" of the dominant classes which cause the dominated to feel inferior. What in fact is pure interiorization appears in a naive analysis to be imitation. At bottom, when the dominated classes reproduce the dominators' style of life, it is because the dominators live "within" the dominated. The dominated can eject the dominators only by getting distance from them and objectifying them. Only then can they recognize them as their antithesis.[17]

To the extent, however, that interiorization of the dominators' values is not only an individual phenomenon, but a social and cultural one, ejection must be achieved by a type of cultural action in which culture negates culture. That is, culture, as an interiorized product which in turn conditions men's subsequent acts, must become the object of men's knowledge so that they can perceive its conditioning power. Cultural action occurs at the level of superstructure. It can only be understood by what Althusser calls "the dialectic of overdetermination."[18] This analytic tool prevents us from falling into mechanistic explanations or, what is worse, mechanistic action. An understanding of it precludes surprise that cultural myths remain after the infrastructure is transformed, even by revolution.

When the creation of a new culture is appropriate but impeded by interiorized cultural "residue," this residue, these myths, must be expelled by means of culture. Cultural action and cultural revolution, at different stages, constitute the modes of this expulsion.

The learners must discover the reasons behind many of their attitudes toward cultural reality and thus confront cultural reality in a new way. "Re-ad-miration" of their former "ad-miration" is necessary in order to bring this about. The learners' capacity for critical knowing—well beyond mere opinion—is established in the process of unveiling their relationships with the historical-cultural world *in* and *with* which they exist.

We do not mean to suggest that critical knowledge of man-world relationships arises as a verbal knowledge outside of praxis. Praxis is involved in the concrete situations which are codified for critical analysis. To analyze the codification in its "deep structure" is, for this very reason, to reconstruct the former praxis and to become capable of a new and different praxis. The relationship between the *theoretical context,* in which codified representations of objective facts are analyzed, and the *concrete context,* where these facts occur, has to be made real.

Such education must have the character of commitment. It implies a movement

---

[17] See Fanon, *The Wretched;* Freire, *Pedagogy.*

[18] See Louis Althusser, *Pour Marx* (Paris: Librairie François Maspero, 1965); and Paulo Freire, *Annual Report: Activities for 1968, Agrarian Reform, Training and Research Institute ICIRA, Chile,* trans. John Dewitt, Center for the Study of Development and Social Change, Cambridge, Mass., 1969 (mimeographed).

from the *concrete context* which provides objective facts, to the *theoretical context* where these facts are analyzed in depth, and back to the *concrete context* where men experiment with new forms of praxis.

It might seem as if some of our statements defend the principle that, whatever the level of the learners, they ought to reconstruct the process of human knowing in absolute terms. In fact, when we consider adult literacy learning or education in general as an act of knowing, we are advocating a synthesis between the educator's maximally systematized knowing and the learners' minimally systematized knowing—a synthesis achieved in dialogue. The educator's role is to propose problems about the codified existential situations in order to help the learners arrive at a more and more critical view of their reality. The educator's responsibility as conceived by this philosophy is thus greater in every way than that of his colleague whose duty is to transmit information which the learners memorize. Such an educator can simply repeat what he has read, and often misunderstood, since education for him does not mean an act of knowing.

The first type of educator, on the contrary, is a knowing subject, face to face with other knowing subjects. He can never be a mere memorizer, but a person constantly readjusting his knowledge, who calls forth knowledge from his students. For him, education is a pedagogy of knowing. The educator whose approach is mere memorization is anti-dialogic; his act of transmitting knowledge is inalterable. For the educator who experiences the act of knowing together with his students, in contrast, dialogue is the seal of the act of knowing. He is aware, however, that not all dialogue is in itself the mark of a relationship of true knowledge.

Socratic intellectualism—which mistook the definition of the concept for knowledge of the thing defined and this knowledge as virtue—did not constitute a true pedagogy of knowing, even though it was dialogic. Plato's theory of dialogue failed to go beyond the Socratic theory of the definition as knowledge, even though for Plato one of the necessary conditions for knowing was that man be capable of a *"prise de conscience,"* and though the passage from *doxa* to *logos* was indispensable for man to achieve truth. For Plato, the *"prise de conscience"* did not refer to what man knew or did not know or knew badly about his dialectical relationship with the world; it was concerned rather with what man once knew and forgot at birth. To know was to remember or recollect forgotten knowledge. The apprehension of both *doxa* and *logos,* and the overcoming of *doxa* by *logos* occurred not in the man-world relationship, but in the effort to remember or rediscover a forgotten *logos.*

For dialogue to be a method of true knowledge, the knowing subjects must approach reality scientifically in order to seek the dialectical connections which explain the form of reality. Thus, to know is not to remember something previously known and now forgotten. Nor can *doxa* be overcome by *logos* apart from the dialectical relationship of man with his world, apart from men's reflective action upon the world.

To be an act of knowing, then, the adult literacy process must engage the learners in the constant problematizing of their existential situations. This problematizing employs "generative words" chosen by specialized educators in a preliminary investigation of what we call the "minimal linguistic universe" of the future learners. The words are chosen (a) for their pragmatic value, *i.e.,* as linguistic signs which command a common understanding in a region or area of the same city or country (in the United States, for instance, the word *soul* has a special significance in black areas which it does not have among whites), and (b) for their phonetic difficulties which will gradually be presented to those learning to read and write. Finally, it is important that the first generative word be tri-syllabic. When it is divided into its syllables, each one constituting a syllabic family, the learners can experiment with various syllabic combinations even at first sight of the word.

Having chosen seventeen generative words,[19] the next step is to codify seventeen existential situations familiar to the learners. The generative words are then worked into the situations one by one in the order of their increasing phonetic difficulty. As we have already emphasized, these codifications are knowable objects which mediate between the knowing subjects, educator-learners, learner-educators. Their act of knowing is elaborated in the *circulo de cultura* (cultural discussion group) which functions as the theoretical context.

In Brazil, before analyzing the learners' existential situations and the generative words contained in them, we proposed the codified theme of man-world relationships in general.[20] In Chile, at the suggestion of Chilean educaors, this important dimension was discussed concurrently with learning to read and write. What is important is that the person learning words be concomitantly engaged in a critical analysis of the social framework in which men exist. For example, the word *favela* in Rio de Janeiro, Brazil, and the word *callampa* in Chile, represent, each with its own nuances, the same social, economic, and cultural reality of the vast numbers of slum dwellers in those countries. If *favela* and *callampa* are used as generative words for the people of Brazilian and Chilean slums, the codifications will have to represent slum situations.

There are many people who consider slum dwellers marginal, intrinsically wicked and inferior. To such people we recommend the profitable experience of discussing the slum situation with slum dwellers themselves. As some of these

---

[19] We observed in Brazil and Spanish America, especially Chile, that no more than seventeen words were necessary for teaching adults to read and write syllabic languages like Portuguese and Spanish.

[20] See Paulo Freire, *Educacao como Pratica da Liberdade* (Rio de Janeiro: Paz e Terra, 1967). Chilean Edition (Santiago: ICIRA, 1969).

critics are often simply mistaken, it is possible that they may rectify their mythical clichés and assume a more scientific attitude. They may avoid saying that the illiteracy, alcoholism, and crime of the slums, that its sickness, infant mortality, learning deficiencies, and poor hygiene reveal the "inferior nature" of its inhabitants. They may even end up realizing that if intrinsic evil exists it is part of the structures, and that it is the structures which need to be transformed.

It should be pointed out that the Third World as a whole, and more in some parts than in others, suffers from the same misunderstanding from certain sectors of the so-called metropolitan societies. They see the Third World as the incarnation of evil, the primitive, the devil, sin and sloth—in sum, as historically unviable without the director societies. Such a manichean attitude is at the source of the impulse to "save" the "demon-possessed" Third World, "educating it" and "correcting its thinking" according to the director societies' own criteria.

The expansionist interests of the director societies are implicit in such notions. These societies can never relate to the Third World as partners, since partnership presupposes equals, no matter how different the equal parties may be, and can never be established between parties antagonistic to each other.

Thus, "salvation" of the Third World by the director societies can only mean its domination, whereas in its legitimate aspiration to independence lies its utopian vision: to save the director societies in the very act of freeing itself.

In this sense the pedagogy which we defend, conceived in a significant area of the Third World, is itself a utopian pedagogy. By this very fact it is full of hope, for to be utopian is not to be merely idealistic or impractical but rather to engage in denunciation and annunciation. Our pedagogy cannot do without a vision of man and of the world. It formulates a scientific humanist conception which finds its expression in a dialogical praxis in which the teachers and learners together, in the act of analyzing a dehumanizing reality, denounce it while announcing its transformation in the name of the liberation of man.

For this very reason, denunciation and annunciation in this utopian pedagogy are not meant to be empty words, but an historic commitment. Denunciation of a dehumanizing situation today increasingly demands precise scientific understanding of that situation. Likewise, the annunciation of its transformation increasingly requires a theory of transforming action. However, neither act by itself implies the transformation of the denounced reality or the establishment of that which is announced. Rather, as a moment in an historical process, the announced reality is already present in the act of denunciation and annunciation.[21]

That is why the utopian character of our educational theory and practice is as permanent as education itself which, for us, is cultural action. Its thrust toward denunciation and annunciation cannot be exhausted when the reality denounced today cedes its place tomorrow to the reality previously announced in the de-

[21] Re the utopian dimension of denunciation and proclamation, see Leszek Kolakowski, *Toward a Marxist Humanism* (New York: Grove Press, 1969).

nunciation. When education is no longer utopian, *i.e.,* when it no longer embodies the dramatic unity of denunciation and annunciation, it is either because the future has no more meaning for men, or because men are afraid to risk living the future as creative overcoming of the present, which has become old.

The more likely explanation is generally the latter. That is why some people today study all the possibilities which the future contains, in order to "domesticate" it and keep it in line with the present, which is what they intend to maintain. If there is any anguish in director societies hidden beneath the cover of their cold technology, it springs from their desperate determination that their metropolitan status be preserved in the future. Among the things which the Third World may learn from the metropolitan societies there is this that is fundamental: not to replicate those societies when its current utopia becomes actual fact.

When we defend such a conception of education—realistic precisely to the extent that it is utopian—that is, to the extent that it denounces what in fact is, and finds therefore between denunciation and its realization the time of its praxis —we are attempting to formulate a type of education which corresponds to the specifically human mode of being, which is historical.

There is no annunciation without denunciation, just as every denunciation generates annunciation. Without the latter, hope is impossible. In an authentic utopian vision, however, hoping does not mean folding one's arms and waiting. Waiting is only possible when one, filled with hope, seeks through reflective action to achieve that announced future which is being born within the denunciation.

That is why there is no genuine hope in those who intend to make the future repeat their present, nor in those who see the future as something predetermined. Both have a "domesticated" notion of history: the former because they want to stop time; the latter because they are certain about a future they already "know." Utopian hope, on the contrary, is engagement full of risk. That is why the dominators, who merely denounce those who denounce them, and who have nothing to announce but the preservation of the status quo, can never be utopian nor, for that matter, prophetic.[22]

A utopian pedagogy of denunciation and annunciation such as ours will have to be an act of knowing the denounced reality at the level of alphabetization and post-alphabetization, which are in each case cultural action. That is why there is such emphasis on the continual problematization of the learners' existential situations as represented in the codified images. The longer the problematization proceeds, and the more the subjects enter into the "essence" of the problematized object, the more they are able to unveil this "essence." The more they

---

[22] "The right, as a conservative force, needs no utopia; its essence is the affirmation of existing conditions—a fact and not a utopia—or else the desire to revert to a state which was once an accomplished fact. The Right strives to idealize actual conditions, not to change them. What it needs is fraud not utopia." Kolakowski, *Toward a Marxist Humanism,* pp. 71-72.

unveil it, the more their awakening consciousness deepens, thus leading to the "conscientization" of the situation by the poor classes. Their critical self-insertion into reality, *i.e.,* their conscientization, makes the transformation of their state of apathy into the utopian state of *denunciation* and *annunciation* a viable project.

One must not think, however, that learning to read and write precedes "conscientization," or vice-versa. Conscientization occurs simultaneously with the literacy or post-literacy process. It must be so. In our educational method, the word is not something static or disconnected from men's existential experience, but a dimension of their thought-language about the world. That is why, when they participate critically in analyzing the first generative words linked with their existential experience; when they focus on the syllabic families which result from that analysis; when they perceive the mechanism of the syllabic combinations of their language, the learners finally discover, in the various possibilities of combination, their own words. Little by little, as these possibilities multiply, the learners, through mastery of new generative words, expand both their vocabulary and their capacity for expression by the development of their creative imagination.[23]

In some areas in Chile undergoing agrarian reform, the peasants participating in the literacy programs wrote words with their tools on the dirt roads where they were working. They composed the words from the syllabic combinations they were learning. "These men are sowers of the word," said Maria Edi Ferreira, a sociologist from the Santiago team working in the Institute of Training and Research in Agrarian Reform. Indeed, they were not only sowing words, but discussing ideas, and coming to understand their role in the world better and better.

We asked one of these "sowers of words," finishing the first level of literacy classes, why he hadn't learned to read and write before the agrarian reform.

"Before the agrarian reform, my friend," he said, "I didn't even think. Neither did my friends."

"Why?" we asked.

"Because it wasn't possible. We lived under orders. We only had to carry out orders. We had nothing to say," he replied emphatically.

The simple answer of this peasant is a very clear analysis of "the culture of silence." In "the culture of silence," to exist is only to live. The body carries out orders from above. Thinking is difficult, speaking the word, forbidden.

"When all this land belonged to one *latifundio,*" said another man in the same conversation, "there was no reason to read and write. We weren't responsible for anything. The boss gave the orders and we obeyed. Why read and write? Now it's a different story. Take me, for example. In the *asentamiento,*[24] I am respon-

---

[23] "We have observed that the study of the creative aspect of language use develops the assumption that linguistic and mental process are virtually identical, language providing the primary means for free expansion of thought and feeling, as well as for the functioning of creative imagination." Noam Chomsky, *Cartesian Linguistics* (New York: Harper & Row, 1966), p. 31.

[24] After the disappropriation of lands in the agrarian reform in Chile, the peasants who were salaried workers on the large latifundia become "settlers" (*asentados*) during a three-year period

sible not only for my work like all the other men, but also for tool repairs. When I started I couldn't read, but I soon realized that I needed to read and write. You can't imagine what it was like to go to Santiago to buy parts. I couldn't get orientated. I was afraid of everything—afraid of the big city, of buying the wrong thing, of being cheated. Now it's all different."

Observe how precisely this peasant described his former experience as an illiterate: his mistrust, his magical (though logical) fear of the world; his timidity. And observe the sense of security with which he repeats, "Now it's all different."

"What did you feel, my friend," we asked another "sower of words" on a different occasion, "when you were able to write and read your first word?"

"I was happy because I discovered I could make words speak," he replied.

Dario Salas reports,[25] "In our conversations with peasants we were struck by the images they used to express their interest and satisfaction about becoming literate. For example, 'Before we were blind, now the veil has fallen from our eyes'; 'I came only to learn how to sign my name. I never believed I would be able to read, too, at my age'; 'Before, letters seemed like little puppets. Today they say something to me, and I can make them talk.'

"It is touching," continues Salas, "to observe the delight of the peasants as the world of words opens to them. Sometimes they would say, 'We're so tired our heads ache, but we don't want to leave here without learning to read and write.' "[26]

The following words were taped during research on "generative themes."[27] They are an illiterate's decodification of a codified existential situation.

"You see a house there, sad, as if it were abandoned. When you see a house with a child in it, it seems happier. It gives more joy and peace to people passing by. The father of the family arrives home from work exhausted, worried, bitter, and his little boy comes to meet him with a big hug, because a little boy is not stiff like a big person. The father already begins to be happier just from seeing his children. Then he really enjoys himself. He is moved by his son's wanting to please him. The father becomes more peaceful, and forgets his problems."

Note once again the simplicity of expression, both profound and elegant, in

---

in which they receive varied assistance from the government through the Agrarian Reform Corporation. This period of "settlement" (*asentamiento*) precedes that of assigning lands to the peasants. This policy is now changing. The phase of "settlement" of the lands is being abolished, in favor of an immediate distribution of lands to the peasants. The Agrarian Reform Corporation will continue, nevertheless, to aid the peasants.

[25] Dario Salas, "Algumas experiencias vividas na Supervisao de Educacao basica," in *A alfabetizacao funcional no Chile.* Report to UNESCO, November, 1968. Introduction: Paulo Freire.

[26] Dario Salas refers here to one of the best adult education programs organized by the Agrarian Reform Corporation in Chile, in strict collaboration with the Ministry of Education and ICIRA. Fifty peasants receive boarding and instruction scholarships for a month. The courses center on discussions of the local, regional, and national situations.

[27] An analysis of the objectives and methodology of the investigation of generative themes lies outside the scope of this essay, but is dealt with in the author's work, *Pedagogy of the Oppressed.*

the peasant's language. These are the people considered absolutely ignorant by the proponents of the "digestive" concept of literacy.

In 1968, an Uruguayan team published a small book, *You Live as You Can* (*Se Vive como se Puede*), whose contents are taken from the tape recordings of literacy classes for urban dwellers. Its first edition of three thousand copies was sold out in Montevideo in fifteen days, as was the second edition. The following is an excerpt from this book.

THE COLOR OF WATER

Water? Water? What is water used for?

"Yes, yes, we saw it (in the picture)."

"Oh, my native village, so far away. . . ."

"Do you remember that village?"

"The stream where I grew up, called Dead Friar . . . you know, I grew up there, a childhood moving from one place to another . . . the color of the water brings back good memories, beautiful memories."

"What is the water used for?"

"It is used for washing. We used it to wash clothes, and the animals in the fields used to go there to drink, and we washed ourselves there, too."

"Did you also use the water for drinking?"

"Yes, when we were at the stream and had no other water to drink, we drank from the stream. I remember once in 1945 a plague of locusts came from somewhere, and we had to fish them out of the water . . . I was small, but I remember taking out the locusts like this, with my two hands—and I had no others. And I remember how hot the water was when there was a drought and the stream was almost dry . . . the water was dirty, muddy, and hot, with all kinds of things in it. But we had to drink it or die of thirst."

The whole book is like this, pleasant in style, with great strength of expression of the world of its authors, those anonymous people, "sowers of words," seeking to emerge from "the culture of silence."

Yes, these ought to be the reading texts for people learning to read and write, and not "Eva saw the grape," "The bird's wing," "If you hammer a nail, be careful not to hit your fingers." Intellectualist prejudices and above all class prejudices are responsible for the naive and unfounded notions that the people cannot write their own texts, or that a tape of their conversations is valueless since their conversations are impoverished of meaning. Comparing what the "sowers of words" said in the above references with what is generally written by specialist authors of reading lessons, we are convinced that only someone with very pronounced lack of taste or a lamentable scientific incompetency would choose the specialists' texts.

Imagine a book written entirely in this simple, poetic, free, language of the people, a book on which inter-disciplinary teams would collaborate in the spirit of true dialogue. The role of the teams would be to elaborate specialized sections of the book in problematic terms. For example, a section on linguistics would deal simply, though not simplistically, with questions fundamental to the learners' critical understanding of language. Let me emphasize again that since one of the important aspects of adult literacy work is the development of the capacity for expression, the section on linguistics would present themes for the learners to discuss, ranging from the increase of vocabulary to questions about communication—including the study of synonyms and antonyms, with its analysis of words in the linguistic context, and the use of metaphor, of which the people are such masters. Another section might provide the tools for a sociological analysis of the content of the texts.

These texts would not, of course, be used for mere mechanical reading, which leaves the readers without any understanding of what is real. Consistent with the nature of this pedagogy, they would become the object of analysis in reading seminars.

Add to all this the great stimulus it would be for those learning to read and write, as well as for students on more advanced levels, to know that they were reading and discussing the work of their own companions. . . .

To undertake such a work, it is necessary to have faith in the people, solidarity with them. It is necessary to be utopian, in the sense in which we have used the word.

Literacy without Schooling: Testing for Intellectual Effects

SYLVIA SCRIBNER
MICHAEL COLE
The Rockefeller University

A variety of claims has been made about the relationship between literacy and intellectual development. Many developmental psychologists hold that skills in reading and writing lead inevitably to major transformations in cognitive capacities. Drawing from their observations of unschooled but literate adults, Sylvia Scribner and Michael Cole have questioned some of the generalizations made about the consequences of literacy. Their research among the Vai of Liberia, a people who have invented a syllabic writing system to represent their own language, provides a unique opportunity to investigate the effects of becoming literate separately from the effects of attending school.

In most discussions of schooling and literacy, the two are so closely intertwined that they are virtually indistinguishable. Yet intellectual consequences have been claimed for each as though they were clearly independent of one another. For several years we have been studying the relation between schooling and literacy, particularly the psychological consequences of each and the extent to which they substitute for each other. Our research among the Vai, a West African people for whom schooling and the acquisition of literacy are separate activities, has led us to reconsider the nature of literacy and its intellectual effects.

Over the centuries and across disciplines, there has been remarkable agreement that the written word has its own peculiar psychological properties. Its relationship to memory and thinking is claimed to be different from that of the spoken word, but conceptions of this relationship are as diverse as the perspectives brought to bear on the question.

Plato considered the issue within the context of basic educational goals and values, suggesting that the relationship of writing to intellect be considered prob-

The preparation of this paper was made possible by support from the Ford Foundation.

Harvard Educational Review   Vol. 48   No. 4   November 1978, 448–461

lematic, rather than taken at face value. To the claim that letters would give men better memories and make them wise, Socrates replied that, on the contrary, letters would create forgetfulness. Learners would not use their memories but rely instead on external aids for "reminiscence." Disciples of the written word would "have the show of wisdom without the reality" (Plato, p. 323). Plato, on the other hand, was suspicious of education that relied solely on the oral mode of the Homeric tradition. Oral thinking in this context was considered the enemy of logic (Havelock, 1963).

The view that the relationship between writing and mental abilities is problematic has given way to the dominant belief that literacy leads inevitably to higher forms of thought. Oral and literate thought are often contrasted in a modern version of the old dichotomy of primitive and civilized thought. Increasingly, literacy instruction is justified not only as a means to material advancement for the individual and society but also as a means of transforming minds. The UNESCO Secretary-General has recently urged the acceleration of worldwide literacy programs to overcome the deep psychological differences between oral and literate thought (UNESCO, 1965). Similar arguments are made in pedagogical discussions here in the United States (Farrell, 1977).

Debates about the cognitive consequences of literacy play a role in determining priorities for national investments in education and in defining the desired outcomes of schooling. Moreover, the claims for consequences themselves have consequences. If, for example, we believe that literacy is a precondition for abstract thinking, how do we evaluate the intellectual skills of nonliterate people? Do we consider them incapable of participating in modern society because they are limited to the particularistic and concrete? If we believe that writing and logical thinking are always mutually dependent, what do we conclude about the reasoning abilities of a college student who writes an incoherent essay? Is this an automatic sign of defective logic? Answers to these questions have implications for social and educational policies that are at least as profound as those questions that concerned Plato.

To examine some of these implications, we will consider recent work in experimental psychology that brings an empirical perspective to these questions. We will analyze how different investigators specify the relationships between literacy and intellectual skills. Oversimplifying, we will contrast two perspectives: one represented by the metaphor of literacy as development, and the other, by literacy as practice. The developmental framework is an established theoretical tradition. Its presuppositions implicitly or explicitly inform the great majority of literacy and instructional writing programs. The framework of practice, or function, is our own attempt at systematizing the knowledge we gained while investigating literacy without schooling among the Vai. Although the two perspectives start from similar questions, we will intentionally sharpen their contrasting features to bring out their different implications for research and educational policy. The differences lie both in the nature of the evidence considered crucial for developing hypotheses about literacy and in the procedures for relating evidence to theory. Our purpose is not to pose them as entirely antagonistic or to argue for the one best model. Rather we advocate an approach to literacy that moves beyond generalities to a consideration of the organization and use of literacy in different social contexts.

Literacy as Development

In the 1960s Greenfield and Bruner (1966) put forward the thesis that writing promotes cognitive development. This was derived largely from Greenfield's (1966) studies in Senegal, comparing the performance of schooled and unschooled Wolof children on experimental cognitive tasks. In one task, children were required to sort pictures or objects into groups of things that belonged together and to explain the basis of their sorting. The items could be exhaustively grouped by form, function, or color. Three aspects of performance were considered especially indicative of levels of abstract thinking. First, school children more often shifted the basis of their grouping from one attribute to another over trials. For example, if they sorted by color on the first trial, on the second trial they might sort by function or form. Second, when asked to explain the basis of their sorting, school children tended to state their reasons in sentences with predication, saying, for example, "these *are* red," instead of using a label "red" or a phrase, *"this red,"* such as unschooled children tended to do. Finally, school children could easily answer questions about why they thought items were alike whereas unschooled children had difficulty doing this. Greenfield interpreted these performance characteristics as measures of a general ability for context-independent, abstract thinking that only school children displayed.

Greenfield (1972) suggested that oral language relies on context for the communication of messages and is, therefore, a context-dependent language. In contrast, written language requires that meaning be made clear, independent of the immediate reference. If one assumes that context-dependent speech is linked with context-dependent thought, and context-dependent thought is the opposite of abstract thought, it follows that abstract thought fails to develop in an oral culture. Put the other way around, societies with written language provide the means for decontextualized abstract thinking; and since schooling relies primarily on written language, those attending school get a greater push toward abstract thought than those not going to school (Bruner, Olver, Greenfield, Hornsby, Kemey, Maccoby, Modiano, Mosher, Olson, Potter, Reisch, & Sonstroem, 1966, p. 318).

Bruner has presented the most general form of this argument—namely that technologies available in a given culture determine the level and range of abilities in its members. Environments with such symbolic technologies as a written language "push cognitive growth better, earlier and longer than others" (Greenfield & Bruner, 1966, p. 654).

Olson also believes that literacy and education push cognitive growth. In recent essays (1975, 1977, 1977) he contends that a unique form of logical competency is linked to literacy. This competency involves the mastery of the logical functions of language apart from its interpersonal functions. According to Olson, literate individuals come to regard meaning as residing in the text. An example is the ability to derive from the sentence "John hit Mary" the logical implication that "Mary was hit by John." Another is drawing logical conclusions from propositions solely from their linguistic evidence and without considering their factual status. Such logical abilities are not universal, Olson (1977) maintains, but are the endpoint of development in literate cultures. To secure evidence for literacy-related logical processes, Olson and his colleagues (for example, Olson & Filby, 1972) have conducted experimental studies of sentence comprehension and reasoning, comparing the performance of preliterate, preschool youngsters with school children of varying ages and with educated literate adults. Olson's speculations about how literacy develops these abilities come from historical analyses of the cultural changes accompanying the invention of the alphabet and the printing press. Both these inventions, Olson says, increase the explicitness of language, biasing cultures toward the development of explicit formal systems and accounting for distinctive modes of thought in Western societies.

This brief summary fails to do justice to the full argument of these psychologists but it does permit us to focus on what we conceive to be certain limitations and difficulties of the developmental perspective. This work is important and innovative, but we wish to caution against the notion that this evidence of the effects of literacy can provide a foundation for educational programs and that it offers a model strategy for future research.

A defining characteristic of the developmental perspective is that it specifies literacy's effects as the emergence of general mental capacities—abstract thinking, for example, or logical operations—rather than specific skills. These abilities are presumed to characterize the individual's intellectual functioning across a wide range of tasks. Thus, based on a limited sample of performance in experimental contexts, the conclusion has been drawn that there is a great divide between the intellectual competencies of people living in oral cultures and those in literate cultures.

From this perspective the capacities generated by literacy are seen not merely as different, but as higher-order capacities because they resemble the abilities that psychological theories attribute to later stages in development. For decades, developmental inquiry has been organized around the notion that children's thinking progresses from the concrete to the abstract. Olson specifically links literacy-related logical operations to Piaget's final stage of formal operational thought. It is within this framework that statements are made about arrested mental growth in cultures without literacy. Since this research compares children of different ages as well as children and adults, a developmental interpretation seems to have some validity. Can it be extrapolated, without further evidence, to characterize changes in the intellectual operations of adolescents and adults? Whether or not these changes are developmental, in a transformational sense, should at the very least be considered an open question.

Perhaps the most serious problem with this work is its vagueness about the mechanisms by which literacy promotes new intellectual capacities. Both Greenfield and Olson present plausible hypotheses about how literacy achieves its effects, but they offer a multitude of possibilities and no systematic theory for selecting the most fruitful for further exploration. Greenfield (1972) variously attributes the effects of literacy to the structure of the written language, to the school-based uses of language, or to growing up in a literate culture and speaking a written language. Olson (1977) stresses the effects on mental skills of the properties of an alphabetic script, of the exposure to the school language of written text, or of the acquisition of bodies of written knowledge. The ways in which these alleged antecedents exert their effects, however, are neither specified nor linked to the observed behaviors. Piaget (1976) has recently pointed out the limitations of this perspective: "To explain a psychological reaction or a cognitive mechanism . . . is not simply to describe it, but to comprehend the process by which it is formed. Failing that, one can but note results without grasping their meaning" (p. vi).

These empirical studies do not clarify the specific contribution of any of these experiences. None tested literacy as such. In all research, literacy was confounded with schooling; yet students are engaged in many learning experiences in school besides learning how to read and write. And we are all aware today that some children spend many years in school without learning how to read and write. There is little guidance here for educational policies and programs. To set educational goals and to plan curricula, research is needed that relates particular kinds of experiences with written language to the development of particular skills.

A final observation is that the developmental perspective supports an "inevitability" interpretation of literacy. It assumes that various components of literacy— say, an alphabetic script or an essayist text—are likely to have the same psychological consequences in all cultures irrespective of the contexts of use or of the social institutions in which literacy is embedded. In reality, however, the developmental model has been elaborated in terms of institutions and technologies specific to our own society. It has been restricted to literacy as practiced in the schools. In addition, confusion stems from failure to differentiate the consequences of literacy over the course of human history from its consequences for the individual in present-day societies. It is a big jump from intellectual and cultural history to a theory of ontogenetic development in any present-day society.

A Functional Approach to Schooling and Literacy

We have long been interested in cultural influences on the development of thought, particularly the influence of literacy (Scribner, Note 1) and formal schooling (Scribner & Cole, 1973); however, we have been skeptical about the usefulness of applying current developmental theory to these problems. Some of our doubts arose from the observation of unschooled nonliterate adults in other societies, some from experiments comparing schooled and unschooled individuals on cognitive tasks. We concluded from these data that the tendency of schooled populations to generalize across a wide range of problems occurred because schooling provides people with a great deal of practice in treating individual learning problems as instances of general classes of problems. Moreover, we did not assume that the skills promoted by schooling would necessarily be applied in contexts unrelated to school experience. This orientation led us to concentrate on the actual practices of literacy that hypothetically produced behavioral changes, looking for likely causal mechanisms. We needed a way to examine the consequences of literacy apart from schooling under conditions that made literate practices most accessible to observation.

The Vai are a traditional society on the northwest coast of Liberia who are well known in that area for their invention of a syllabic writing system to represent their own language. Preliminary reports (for example, Stewart, 1967) and our own observations indicated that between 20 and 25 percent of Vai men could read and write using their own script, which was invented approximately 150 years ago and transmitted from one generation to another without schooling or professional teachers. The mere existence of an indigenous writing system was enough to arouse our curiosity, but we were interested in the Vai for two additional reasons. First, except that they are predominantly Muslim, the Vai, according to ethnographies of Liberia, are virtually indistinguishable from their neighbors in terms of ecology, social organization, economic activities, and material culture. Second, their writing and reading are not activities separate from other daily pursuits, nor does learning to read and write require a person to master a large body of knowledge that is unavailable from oral sources. These two characteristics of Vai literacy provided an extremely interesting, if not unique, opportunity to investigate the effects of becoming literate separately from the effects of attending school or becoming educated, an inquiry that had heretofore eluded social science.

A detailed description of this work is beyond the scope of this article; however, we will briefly describe its major phases to explain what we mean by a functional approach to the study of literacy and thinking. To begin with, we gave questionnaires and tests to more than 700 Vai adults. Our survey included a variety of tasks based on previous research showing the effects of formal schooling among tribal Liberians. These tasks were included to determine if cognitive performance that was improved by schooling was similarly influenced by indigenous Vai literacy. The test battery also contained sorting and verbal reasoning tasks similar to those used by Greenfield and Olson as the basis for speculations about literacy effects. Results were clearcut. As in previous research, improved performance was associated with years of formal schooling, but literacy in the Vai script did not substitute for schooling. Vai literates were not significantly different from nonliterates on any of these cognitive measures, including the sorting and reasoning tasks that had been suggested as especially sensitive to experience with a written language.[1]

In the next phase of our work we moved down one level of generality in the kinds of hypotheses we tested. Instead of looking for improvements in general cognitive performance associated with literacy, we concentrated on the hypothesis that literacy promotes metalinguistic skills—the idea that in acquiring literacy skills an individual acquires the ability to analyze language (Goody, 1977). One task tested nominal realism, the identification of name and object; other items

---

[1] Any effects reported as significant refer to regression analyses in which the variable in question entered the equation at the .05 level of significance or better.

tested the ability to specify the nature of grammatical rules, to reason from evidence provided by a syllogism, and to define words.

This series of studies showed that Vai literacy was associated with small increments in performance for some of the tasks (for example, increased ability to specify the nature of a grammatical error in spoken Vai) but there was no across-the-board evidence of enhanced performance associated with this unschooled literacy. Furthermore, and most damaging to the metalinguistic hypothesis, our results showed virtually no correlations among performances on the various probes of metalinguistic ability.

At the end of our first year of fieldwork, we had not made much progress in illuminating literacy skills among the Vai by administering standard laboratory tasks whose theoretical status with respect to literacy was uncertain. We decided to take a different approach. Instead of working down from developmental theories, we began to work up from actual observations of how literacy was socially organized and used by the Vai. We decided to base our experimental activities on our ethnographic observations—to let our fieldwork generate specific hypotheses and suggest appropriate tasks.

Reading and writing are not prominent activities in the villages; still, the knowledge and use of the script by Vai literates are manifest in many ways. For one thing, the arrival of a taxi often brings letters, written in Vai, from relatives and business associates in other areas of Vai country and other parts of Liberia. We found that Vai literates write and receive between one and forty letters a month, depending upon a number of factors, including the kinds of economic enterprises in which they are involved and the location of the town in which they live. Funerals are a ubiquitous feature of life in a Vai village, where the infant mortality rate exceeds 50 percent and life expectancy is low. Funerals attract relatives and acquaintances from many parts of the country, each of whom is obligated to bring gifts in money or kind that must be reciprocated. Consequently, recording the names of donors and their gifts at funerals, as well as a variety of other administrative activities such as listing political contributions, are features of Vai life in which literacy plays a central and visible role. Some religious and fraternal organizations maintain records in Vai script, and we have documented at least one case in which a Muslim association was governed by a constitution and by-laws written in Vai script (Goody, Cole, & Scribner, 1977). Farmers and craftsmen use the script for business ledgers and technical plans. A few who might qualify as Vai scholars write family and clan histories, keep diaries, and record maxims and traditional tales in copybooks.

Despite test results, we know that Vai literacy functions in the society and that Vai people seem to feel that it functions well since literates are accorded high status. We began to look carefully at the specific skills these literacy activities seemed to involve: what did it require to write a letter, record contributions to a funeral feast, or list contributions to a religious society? We made functional analyses of the skills involved in these activities. Then, on the basis of these analyses, we designed tasks with different content but hypothetically similar skills to determine if prior practice in learning and use of the script enhanced performance.

388

Since letter-writing is the most common use of the Vai script, we closely studied the cognitive consequences of letter-writing. In the psychological literature, written communication is said to impose cognitive demands not encountered in face-to-face oral communication. In writing, meaning is supposed to be carried entirely by the text; thus, effective written communication requires sensitivity to the informational needs of the reader and skill in the use of elaborative linguistic techniques. We speculated that Vai literates' experience in writing and reading letters would contribute to the development of these skills, especially because the ability to communicate in writing with people from different places signifies successful completion of the study of the script.

To test this proposition, we adapted a communication task used in previous research (Flavell, Botkin, Fry, Wright, & Jarvis, 1968). Individuals were taught to play a simple board game with little verbal explanation; they were then asked to explain the game, without the materials of the game present, to a listener unfamiliar with it. In addition, we asked subjects to dictate a letter explaining the game to someone far away who had never seen it before.

The game involves two players taking turns racing their counters on a board of eight colored stripes. A counter's movements are governed by the color of the chip selected from a cup on each turn (Flavell et al., 1968). Board games are familiar to the Vai, who play a game called "ludo," which has a similar racing format.

We coded the transcribed protocols for the amount of game-related information they contained and for the presence of statements describing the materials of the game. On both of these measures of quality of communication, we found that men literate in the Vai script were far superior to nonliterates, and that this pattern was apparent in both the face-to-face explanation and the dictated letter. We also analyzed the protocols to see whether they reflected characteristics of Vai literates' style of communication in their day-to-day letter-writing practices.

Over the years, Vai letters have evolved certain stylized formats. Here is a sample:

> 17/7/1964
> Vaitown
>
> This letter belongs to Pa Lamii in Vonzuan. My greeting to you, and my greeting to Mother.
>
> This is your information. I am asking you to do me a favor. The people I called to saw my timber charged me $160.00. I paid them $120.00 and $40.00 still needed, but business is hard this time. I am therefore sending your child to you to please credit me amount of $40.00 to pay these people. Please do not let me down.
>
> I stopped so far.
>
> I am Moley Doma
> Vaitown

The statements "This is your information. I am asking you to do me a favor." are examples of what we call the contextualization of the communication. They tell the recipient what the communication is all about and what information to expect. This aspect of an effective communication was well understood by Vai literates and clearly explained to us in some of our interviews. In one discussion on what makes a good letter, a middle-aged farmer told us, "You must first make the person to understand that you are informing him through words. Then he will give his attention there. It is the correct way of writing the Vai script." When we examined game instructions for this characteristic we found that Vai literates almost always contextualized their communication by giving some general characterization of the game—for example, "This is a game I am coming to tell you about where two people take a race and one of them wins."

A second set of studies tested for the transfer of skills needed to read Vai text. Our observations of Vai literates deciphering letters from friends and coping with mundane reading indicated that decoding the script is extraordinarily difficult because of special properties of the Vai writing system. Vai script characters map the consonant-vowel syllabic structure of the language in a systematic manner; however, this does not produce a direct one-to-one correspondence between the visual symbols and the units of sound. Vowel tone, a phonological feature that is semantically crucial in the spoken language, is not marked in the script. In addition, because the script is not standardized, the representation of vowel length, another semantically distinctive feature of the language, varies considerably from one script-writer to another. Finally, the script is written without division into words or other language units; a string of syllabic characters runs across the page without spacing or segmentation. Each character, depending on its semantic function, may represent a single-syllable word, one of several such words differentiated by tone, or a component unit of a polysyllabic word.

How does a literate Vai resolve these ambiguities? From observations of men reading letters we found that a common technique is what we have called experimentation in pronunciation—saying strings of syllables aloud recursively, varying vowel tones and lengths until they click into meaningful units. Readers must keep separate syllables in mind until they can be integrated into words or phrases. We supposed that this experience might foster skills in language analysis and integration and that these skills might apply in language contexts that did not involve the script. To test this idea we devised a listening task. Each person listened to tape recordings in which a native speaker of Vai slowly read meaningful Vai sentences. Sentences were segmented either into word units or syllable units. The listener was simply asked to repeat the sentence and answer a comprehension question about it. On sentences containing word units, there was no superiority for individuals with experience in Vai script; but, on sentences composed of syllable units, Vai literates with advanced reading skills outdistanced all others, including those with fewer years of practice in reading.

These two tasks, and the remainder of our research, demonstrate that skills involved in literacy behaviors are indeed transferable to behaviors unrelated to literacy. The effects reported—analyzing oral speech and giving clearer instructions —are neither self-evident nor trivial. Speech perception and instruction have real utility. These studies provide the first direct evidence that what an individual does with text, or with pencil and paper, can promote specific skills that are avail-

390

able to support other behaviors. In terms of the concerns with which the research began, we believe it important that these skills are associated with literacy, not with schooling—they are not byproducts of general learning experiences in the classroom. Although our demonstration of literacy-related skills is limited by the range of literacy practices in Vai society, it stands as the first clear-cut evidence in a present-day society that personal engagement in reading and writing does have psychological consequences. These consequences, however, are all highly specific to activities with the Vai script.

The metaphor of literacy as a practice will help us put the Vai research in a more general framework. By combining several dictionary definitions, we can state what we mean by "a practice." A practice may be considered to be the carrying out of a goal-directed sequence of activities, using particular technologies and applying particular systems of knowledge. It is a usual mode or method of doing something—playing the piano, sewing trousers, writing letters. This definition shares certain features with the notion of practice in educational psychology—repeated performance of an act in order to acquire proficiency or skill. How does this apply to literacy? Consider a goal-directed sequence of activities such as letter-writing. This involves a technology—a particular script and particular writing materials. It also requires knowledge of how to represent oral language in script and of the conventional rules of representation. One must know the form and style suitable for writing personal letters as well as what the intended reader knows about the subject of the message and how the new information will fit into the old. A variety of skills at different levels is required to perform this complex act. As one writes more letters, these skills should become more efficiently organized, less dependent on content, and more transferable to new contents and contexts. We did indeed find transfer of these skills in our game-instruction task but the range of transfer was narrow. In summary, our results show that certain literacy practices among the Vai produced intellectual outcomes closely tied to those practices.

Our negative findings are an equally important part of the story. We did not find that literacy in the Vai script was associated in any way with generalized competencies such as abstraction, verbal reasoning, or metalinguistic skills. The tasks used in North American research as alternative measures of these capacities simply did not show consistency of performance in any group except the schooled group. Furthermore, we did not find that either literacy or schooling had an all-or-none effect; on all experimental tasks, including those showing the strongest effects of Vai literacy, some nonliterates achieved high scores and displayed the same skills as literates.

The results of our research among the Vai present us with two apparently contrasting conclusions about the effects of literacy. The literacy as development view would have us believe that literacy, in combination with schooling, produces generalized changes in the way people think. Our functional perspective suggests that the effects of literacy, and perhaps schooling as well, are restricted—perhaps to the practice actually engaged in or generalized only to closely related practices. These extreme alternatives echo an educational debate that began at the turn of the century. Thorndike and Woodworth (1901) suggested that learning is specific and transfer from one task to another will occur only when both tasks shared identical elements. Their antagonists believed that education, through mental discipline, strengthens the mind in general. (For a summary of the arguments at that time, see Thorndike, 1969, p. 357.) However, no theory guided the search for identical elements and no theory gave substance to the mental discipline position. After seventy-five years of debate and data accumulation, the issue of the effects of practice has not been resolved. We have no illusions that our skimpy data with respect to literacy will resolve the discrepancies between these two viewpoints, but our framework may help us think about literacy and its effects in a way that does not get us lost in unsupported generalities or insignificant particulars.

The specific outcomes that we observed in our studies of Vai literacy confirm earlier observations that certain cognitive skills show little generalizability across experimental tasks among traditional adults. The situation with respect to Vai writing and reading is similar to that of other skilled practices—such as weaving (Childs & Greenfield, in press) or pottery-making (Bunzel, 1953)—in nontechnological societies, in which highly organized, complex skills are applied to a limited set of problems. Previously, we argued that generalized skills might not arise when common operations are applied to a limited set of tasks (Scribner & Cole, 1973). If the uses of writing are few and limited, skills should be applied to each use in a more or less original way. As the repertoire of functions expands, the operations necessary for each may be applied across a range of tasks and contexts. For example, an individual might write a letter to distribute proceeds from a funeral feast—two functions that are usually separate. This example represents the upper limit of typical Vai writing practices because each individual's practices are restricted.

As the technology of any society becomes more complex, the number and variety of tasks to which literacy skills must be applied increases as well. A task might include some mix of a common core of skills like decoding, for example, with new skills or more complicated versions of old skills, as when Vai tradesmen begin to write to people they have never met before because business practice makes this necessary. If our argument that specific uses promote specific skills is valid, we might expect to find the outcomes that Olson or others predict, but only under conditions evoking these skills. Carrying out critical analyses of text, for example, might promote certain analytic operations with language, whereas rote learning from the same text, or reading it for some other purpose, is not likely to do so. Writing poetry is likely to have different consequences for language skills than preparing a letter to a department store requesting a refund for damaged goods.

As practice in any activity continues, we would expect that skills would extend to a wide range of tasks and materials and when the skill systems involved in literacy are many, varied, complex, and widely applicable, the functional and general ability perspectives will converge in their predictions of intellectual outcomes. Whether we choose to interpret these acquired functional skill systems developmentally is a matter of theoretical predilection, the discussion of which lies outside the argument of this article.

Although we do not advocate a single approach to the complex issues of the psychology of literacy, we believe that the strategy of functional analysis emerging from the Vai research may have particularly useful implications for educational research in our own society. It suggests that different literacy activities need to be analyzed independently. If, as we have demonstrated, particular skills are promoted by particular kinds of literacy practices, we need to know a great deal more about just how literacy is practiced. Studies of the range of reading and writing activities carried out in school, including those outside the official curriculum, would be a useful extension of work such as that done by Martin, D'Arcy, Newton, and Parker (1976). We have far fewer precedents, however, for an equally important research task: finding out what people in various communities and walks of life do with literacy—how they use their knowledge of reading and writing, to what tasks they apply it, and how they accomplish these tasks. Such analyses should help us understand the differences between school-based literacy practices and literacy practices unrelated to schooling as well as their possibly different implications for intellectual outcomes. Although attempts to arrive at some overall measures of literacy competencies may be useful for certain comparative purposes, the conceptualization of literacy as a fixed inventory of skills that can be assessed outside of the contexts of application has little utility for educational policies.

We need to acknowledge, however, that we are a long way from having the methods, techniques, and theories required to make a systematic analysis of the component skills involved in reading and writing. Considerable progress has been made in identifying components in decoding activities and, more recently, in the higher-level intellectual skills involved in controlled reading tasks under laboratory-like or highly constrained classroom conditions. (See especially the reports of The Center for the Study of Reading, Note 2). Sticht, Fox, Hauke, and Zapf (1977) have used the skills-analysis approach to reading activities outside the classroom and have distinguished between reading-to-do and reading-to-learn activities. The long-range objective is to devise methods for an adequate description and analysis of skills in out-of-school literacy practices that can be coordinated with the micro-level analyses of laboratory studies.

Both educational practice and research might benefit from a recognition of the complex interrelationships between mental skills and literacy activities. Terms that refer to oral and literate modes of thought, although historically significant, are not useful characterizations of the mental abilities of nonliterate and literate adults in American society; in fact, most research with adults in traditional societies confirms their inappropriateness for any contemporaneous culture. Thus research does not support designing adult literacy programs on the assumption that nonliterates do not think abstractly, do not reason logically, or lack other basic mental processes. In each case, the skills available for learning how to read and write or for improving rudimentary literacy abilities need to be assessed with respect to the accomplishments nonliterates display in other activities—for example, disputation, hypothetical reasoning, or oral narrative. To the question posed at the beginning of this paper—"Is a college student's incoherent essay symptomatic of faulty reasoning?"—our answer would be, "No, it is not a symptom; it is a sign to be evaluated."

If different literacy activities are linked to different intellectual outcomes, a second implication of our research is that reading and writing activities need to be tailored to desired achievements. These outcomes can be defined in terms of the literacy competencies required for participation in our highly technological society, but they need not be defined in narrowly pragmatic terms, reflecting merely the current demand for job security or advance. A skills approach might make it possible to identify a common core of skills that will enable an individual to master more intellectually demanding reading and writing tasks after completing the school curriculum or literacy program. If the educational objective is to foster analytic logical reasoning, that objective should guide the choice of instructional program. It should not be assumed that these skills will follow inevitably from practice in writing essays. Writing essays may be helpful, as may oral practices. This is undoubtedly the common wisdom of the classroom and the educational planner. But it would be helpful to ally this wisdom with the psychological literature on literacy so that the broad conceptual framework informs teaching practice and practice informs the theory.

We realize that the kind of program implied by our discussion may seem difficult to attain. The comments of the Soviet psychologist Vygotsky (1934/1978) some fifty years ago on the status of the specific-skill versus mental-development argument of his day offer useful guidance for our research choices today: "Such a matter cannot be dealt with by a single formula of some kind, but rather suggests how great is the scope for extensive and varied experimental research" (p. 34).

Reference Notes

1. Scribner, S. *The cognitive consequences of literacy.* Unpublished manuscript, Albert Einstein College of Medicine, 1968.
2. Center for the Study of Reading. *Technical reports 1–102.* University of Illinois at Champaign-Urbana, 1975–1978.

References

Bruner, J., Olver, R., Greenfield, P., Hornsby, J., Kemey, H., Maccoby, M., Modiano, N., Mosher, F., Olson, D., Potter, M., Reisch, L., & Sonstroem, A. *Studies in cognitive growth.* New York: Wiley, 1966.
Bunzel, R. Psychology of the Pueblo potter. In M. Mead & N. Calas (Eds.)., *Primitive heritage.* New York: Random House, 1953.
Childs, C., & Greenfield, P. Informal modes of learning and teaching: The case of Zinacanteco weaving. In N. Warren (Ed.), *Advances in cross-cultural psychology,* vol. 2. London: Academic Press, in press.
Farrell, T. Literacy, the basics, and all that jazz, *College English,* 1977, 38, 443–459.

Flavell, J., Botkin, P., Fry, C., Wright, J., & Jarvis, P. *The development of role-taking and communication skills in children.* New York: Wiley, 1968.

Goody, J. *The domestication of the savage mind.* Cambridge, Eng.: Cambridge University Press, 1977.

Goody, J., Cole, M., & Scribner, S. Writing and formal operations: A case study among the Vai. *Africa*, 1977, **47**, 289–304.

Greene, W. The spoken and the written word. *Harvard Studies in Classical Philology*, 1951, **60**, 23–59.

Greenfield, P. On culture and equivalence. In J. Bruner, et al. (Eds.), *Studies in cognitive growth.* New York: Wiley, 1966.

Greenfield, P. Oral or written language: The consequences for cognitive development in Africa, the United States and England. *Language and Speech*, 1972, **15**, 169–178.

Greenfield, P., & Bruner, J. Culture and cognitive growth. *International Journal of Psychology*, 1966, **1**, 89–107.

Havelock, E. *Preface to Plato.* Cambridge, Mass.: Harvard University Press, 1963.,

Martin, N., D'Arcy, P., Newton, B., & Parker, R. *Writing and learning across the curriculum 11–16.* London: Ward Lock Educational, 1966.

Olson, D. Review of *Toward a literate society*, ed. J. Carroll & J. Chall. In *Proceedings of the National Academy of Education*, 1975, **2**, 109–178.

Olson, D. From utterance to text: The bias of language in speech and writing. *Harvard Educational Review*, 1977, **47**, 257–281.

Olson, D. The language of instruction. In R. Anderson, R. Spiro, & W. Montague (Eds.). *Schooling and the acquisition of knowledge.* Hillsdale, N. J.: Erlbaum and Associates, 1977.

Olson, D., & Filby, N. On the comprehension of active and passive sentences. *Cognitive Psychology*, 1972, **3**, 361–381.

Piaget, J. Foreword. In J. Piaget, B. Inhelder, & H. Chipman (Eds.), *Piaget and his school.* New York: Springer-Verlag, 1976.

Plato. Phaedrus. In I. Edman (Ed.), *The works of Plato.* New York: Modern Library, 1928.

Scribner, S., & Cole, M. Cognitive consequences of formal and informal education. *Science*, 1973, **182**, 553–559.

Stewart, G. Notes on the present-day usage of the Vai script in Liberia. *African Language Review*, 1976, **6**, 71–74.

Sticht, T., Fox, L., Hauke, R., & Zapf, D. *The role of reading in the navy* (NPRDC TR 77–40). San Diego, Calif.: Navy Personnel Research and Training Center, 1977.

Thorndike, E. *Educational Psychology*, vol. 2. New York: Arno Press, 1969.

Thorndike, E., & Woodworth, R. The influence of improvement in one mental function upon the efficiency of other functions. *Psychological Review*, 1901, **8**, 247–261.

UNESCO: World Congress of Ministers of Education on the Eradication of Illiteracy, Teheran, 8–19, September 1965. Inaugural speeches, messages, closing speeches. Paris: Author, 1965.

Vygotsky, L. Learning and mental development at school age. In B. Simon, & T. Simon (Eds.), *Educational Psychology in the USSR.* London: Routledge & Kegan Paul, 1963. See also L. Vygotsky, Learning and development. In M. Cole, V. John-Steiner, S. Scribner, & E. Souberman (Eds.), *Mind in society: The development of higher psychological processes.* Cambridge, Mass.: Harvard University Press, 1978.

The Nature of Literacy:
An Historical Exploration

DANIEL P. RESNICK
Carnegie–Mellon University

LAUREN B. RESNICK
University of Pittsburgh

In this article Daniel and Lauren Resnick bring an historical perspective to the present debate over reading achievement. From an historical examination of selected European and American models of literacy, they conclude that reading instruction has been aimed at attaining either a low level of literacy for a large number of people or a high level for an elite. Thus, the contemporary expectation —high levels of literacy for the entire population—represents a relatively recent development. From this stance the Resnicks argue that, contrary to the thrust of the "back to basics" movement, pedagogical practices from the past offer little remedy for reading problems as currently defined.

Reports of low literacy achievement and widespread reading difficulties have lent strength to a still inchoate "back to basics" movement in education. The apparent suggestion is that methods of instruction that succeeded in the past can remedy many of our present problems. Looking backward for solutions, however, can succeed only when social conditions and educational goals remain relatively stable. Only by a serious examination of our history can we determine the extent to which older educational practices are likely to succeed in today's environment, for to-day's purposes. This paper begins such an examination by exploring selected European and American historical models of literacy standards and training in order to assess the degree to which the goals and practices of earlier times are relevant to our present needs.

Our research suggests that there has been a sharp shift over time in expectations concerning literacy. With changed standards come changed estimates of the

This paper was written during our stay at the Center for Advanced Study in the Behavioral Sciences at Stanford University. Lauren Resnick was supported there by a fellowship from the Spencer Foundation. The work was also supported in part by Contract #400-75-0049 of the National Institute of Education with the Learning Research and Development Center, University of Pittsburgh.

Harvard Educational Review Vol. 47 No. 3 August 1977, 370–385

adequacy of a population's literacy. To illustrate, if writing one's name were what was meant by literacy, we would not be worried that illiteracy was a national problem. Yet the signature was not always a demand easy to satisfy. Until well into the nineteenth century, the capacity to form the letters of one's signature was not a skill shared by the majority of the population, even in the more developed nations of Europe.[1] Even a somewhat more stringent literacy criterion would not force recognition of a major problem. If the ability to read aloud a simple and well-known passage were the measure, America would have a few "illiterates" but hardly a crisis. If we expected people to demonstrate after reading this simple passage, that they had registered its content at some low level, perhaps by saying who a story was about or what a named character did, we would probably find a low percentage of illiterates in our adult population.

But the number would start to rise, perhaps quite sharply, if unfamiliar texts were to be read and new information gleaned from them. And, if inferential rather than directly stated information were to be drawn from the text, we would probably announce a true crisis in literacy. If we used as a literacy criterion the ability to read a complex text with literary allusions and metaphoric expression and not only to interpret this text but to relate it sensibly to other texts, many would claim that only a tiny fraction of our population is "truly literate," a charge not infrequently made in discussions about standards of literacy at the university level.

We think that this nation perceives itself as having an unacceptable literacy level because it is applying a criterion that requires, at a minimum, the reading of new material and the gleaning of new information from that material. We shall argue in this paper that this high literacy standard is a relatively recent one as applied to the population at large and that much of our present difficulty in meeting the literacy standard we are setting for ourselves can be attributed to the relatively rapid extension to large populations of educational criteria that were once applied to only a limited elite. The result of this rapid extension is that instructional methods suitable to large and diverse populations rather than small and selected ones have not yet been fully developed or applied. Further, not all segments of our population have come to demand literacy skills of the kind that educators, members of Congress, and other government officials think necessary.

Our argument is that the standards currently applied to mass literacy have been with us for at most three generations. To examine the proposition that the current definition of literacy is a relatively new one, we have undertaken a selective review of published material on standards of literacy in various historical settings and on the social and political conditions under which these standards were applied. Some of the less commonly cited historical models seem especially instructive be-

---

[1] For the use of signatures in public oaths and as a source on literacy in seventeenth- and eighteenth-century England, see Roger S. Schofield, "The Measurement of Literacy in Pre-Industrial England," in *Literacy in Traditional Societies*, ed. Jack R. Goody (Cambridge, Eng.: Cambridge Univ. Press, 1968), pp. 311–25; and Richard T. Vann, "Literacy in Seventeenth-Century England: Some Hearth-Tax Evidence," *Journal of Interdisciplinary History*, 5 (1974), 287–93. The uses of signatures for retrospective literacy assessment in France are discussed in François Furet and Vladimir Sachs, 'La Croissance de l'alphabétisation en France (XVIIIe-XIXe siècles)," *Annales: Économies, Sociétés, Civilisations*, 29 (1974), 714–37.

cause of either the large size of the literate population, the high standards of literacy, or the democratic ideology. We will elaborate three major historical models for literacy development before the twentieth century: the Protestant-religious, the elite-technical, and the civic-national. To illustrate these models, we will describe literacy training and examinations in seventeenth-century Sweden, elite scientific and technical education in France since the eighteenth century, and schooling among the French peasants during the last century. In so doing, we shall try to relate particular kinds of literacy standards and instructional approaches to changing social needs and conditions. Finally, we will trace the changes in literacy standards that occurred in the first part of this century in the United States.

Having examined these historical cases, we will be in a position to consider the degree of fit between certain persisting traditions of education and present-day literacy standards. We shall also note a remarkable match between our conclusions and certain current theories of reading development that are based on observation of the stages through which individuals pass as they gain competence with the written word. In concluding we will consider various implications of our historical and theoretical analysis for current educational policy.

Models from the Historical Experience

Protestant-Religious Education

Historians have come to view the efforts of Protestant communities to bring their members into personal contact with biblical history and the Christian message as very important for the growth of literacy.[2] These efforts have also been recognized as significant in affecting social and economic development.[3] With respect to American development, Bernard Bailyn and Lawrence Cremin have described colonial literacy as so profoundly transforming that its development constituted a break with traditional attitudes.[4]

More recently, the connection between literacy and socioeconomic shifts has been called into question. Kenneth Lockridge has argued that literacy was of little significance for the shaping of modern social values in Protestant colonial New England.[5] The absence of such a relationship between schooling and economic

[2] Lawrence Stone, "Literacy and Education in England, 1640–1900," *Past and Present*, No. 42 (1969), esp. pp. 77–83, examines the relationship of Protestantism to the development of literacy.

[3] For samples of current work exploring the effect of education on economic growth in different contexts, see Roger S. Schofield, "Dimensions of Illiteracy, 1750–1850," *Explorations in Economic History*, 10 (1973), 437–54; and David McClelland, "Does Education Accelerate Economic Growth?" *Economic Development and Cultural Change*, 14 (1966), 257–78. For the effect of education on personality change, see Howard Schuman, Alex Inkeles, and David Smith, "Some Social and Psychological Effects and Non-Effects of Literacy in a New Nation," *Economic Development and Cultural Change*, 16 (1967), 1–14.

[4] See Bernard Bailyn, *Education in the Forming of American Society: Needs and Opportunities for Study* (Chapel Hill: Univ. of North Carolina Press, 1960), esp. pp. 48–49; and Lawrence Cremin, *American Education: The Colonial Experience, 1607–1783* (New York: Harper & Row, 1970), pp. 545–70. The counterargument by Kenneth Lockridge, *Literacy in Colonial New England: An Inquiry into the Social Context of Literacy in the Early Modern West* (New York: Norton, 1974), pp. 28–29 and nn., overstates Cremin's position but not the thrust of his argument.

[5] On the failure of colonial wills to offer evidence of nontraditional social behavior, see Lockridge, pp. 33–35.

development in Lancashire before the mid-nineteenth century has been one of the themes in the revisionist work of Michael Sanderson.[6] However, even for those who have been skeptical about its causal relationship to attitudes, the early modern Protestant experience with literacy has been seen as a watershed because of the great numbers of people who shared in that experience. In colonial New England, Lockridge estimates that male literacy, which was well above 60 percent for the generation born around 1700, became nearly universal by the end of the century;[7] in Scotland, Lawrence Stone found that the rate of literacy among adult males went from 33 percent around 1675 to almost 90 percent by 1800;[8] and in Sweden, Egil Johansson found that the number of males "able to read" in the parishes of Skelleftea went from half the population to 98 percent in the period from 1645 to 1714.[9]

The question of what kinds of knowledge defined literacy in these Protestant experiments has not been directly addressed by historians concerned with the relationship of literacy to economic and social development. We are able to respond to the question by considering the Swedish case, which represents the first instance of systematic record keeping relative to reading. To cite one example, the oldest extant registers of Möklinta parish in central Sweden, for the years from 1656 to 1669, offer columns to note whether or not minimum competency had been met in each of five areas.[10] The first involved the actual words to the text of the *Little Catechism;* the second, Luther's explanations of the words of the text; the third, the Confession of Sin; the fourth, morning and evening prayers; the fifth, prayers said at the table.[11] Questions on Lutheran creed and practice were apparently posed by the pastor on each of these topics. The examination assumed the availability of a printed catechism and prayer book in every home and prior discussion of these materials at catechetical meetings, attendance at which was to be checked off in a final column of the register.

No formal column for the capacity to read, as such, is to be found in this register (although one would be introduced in its successor), but all the questions assume the capacity to read, review, memorize, and recall familiar material.

---

[6] See Michael Sanderson, "Literacy and Social Mobility in the Industrial Revolution in England," *Past and Present,* No. 56 (1972), esp. pp. 89–95, and the later exchange with Thomas Laqueur in "Debate," *Past and Present,* No. 64 (1974), pp. 96–112.

[7] Lockridge, *Literacy in Colonial New England,* pp. 13, 87–88.

[8] For Scotland, see Stone, "Literacy and Education in England," pp. 79–80, 82–83, 123–24, 126–27, 135–36.

[9] Egil Johansson, "Literacy Studies in Sweden: Some Examples," in *Literacy and Society in a Historical Perspective: A Conference Report,* ed. E. Johansson, Educational Reports Umeå (Umeå, Sweden: Umeå Univ. and School of Education, 1973), p. 49. We would like to thank Professor Kjell Härnqvist for his assistance in pursuing this investigation.

[10] This discussion is based on Johansson, "Literacy Studies in Sweden," pp. 41–50, which includes reproductions of two pages from the registers.

[11] The Little Catechism of Luther, translated into Swedish, with officially published "Explanations," functioned as did the Bible in Cromwellian England as a source of religious authority. One of the reasons for this was the failure of various projects to translate the Bible in its entirety into Swedish. The era of cheap Bibles opened in Sweden only at the beginning of the nineteenth century. See Michael Roberts, "The Swedish Church," in *Sweden's Age of Greatness,* ed. M. Roberts (New York: St. Martin's Press, 1973), pp. 138–40. Those who had not learned the Little Catechism were forbidden by law in 1686 to marry. See Claude Nordmann, *Grandeur et liberté de la Suède (1660–1792)* (Paris and Louvain: Béatrice-Nauwelaerts, 1971), p. 118.

A second register, used during the period from 1686 to 1705, includes a corroborating column for "literacy," which was understood as the ability to read to the satisfaction of the examiner. An analysis of this material indicates that, while only one-fourth of the parish residents born in the early part of the seventeenth century were described as literate, the percentage grew to three-fourths for those born at the end of the century.

From the standpoint of current expectations, the literacy criterion that yielded these figures is a limited one. No unfamiliar material was given to the examinee. No writing was expected. No application of knowledge to new contexts was demanded. And no digressions from the text of the catechism and prayers were expected or permitted. The result was an exercise in the reading and memorizing of familiar material, to be recalled upon demand. Nevertheless, the Swedish experience, like the less controlled systems of early Protestant education in Scotland and the American colonies, represents more than simply a baseline of low literacy expectation. Instead, subsequent pedagogic efforts in literacy were heavily influenced by early religious activities.

The Elite-Technical Schools

A quite different tradition of literacy, one aimed at an elite, is represented by the growth of higher technical education in France. This system had its beginnings in the *collèges* and private academies of the Old Regime. The schools were run by such religious orders as the **Oratorians** and Jesuits, largely for sons of the aristocracy and bourgeoisie, although a few extremely able sons of the poor were accepted. Boys could enter at age seven and could stay until age seventeen or eighteen for an extended period of formal schooling. From these schools young men could enter a variety of state technical and professional schools that prepared their graduates for careers in civil and military public service.

By the eighteenth century, mathematics had become established as the touchstone of elite education. At all levels mathematics was stressed as the key to effective reasoning. For La Chalotais, in his *Plan d'éducation nationale* of 1763, it was "very possible and very common to reason badly in theology, or in politics; it is impossible in arithmetic and in geometry; if accuracy of mind is lacking, the rules will supply accuracy and intelligence for those who follow them." For Diderot, geometry was "the best and simplest of all logics, and it is the most suitable for fortifying the judgment and the reason."[12] But mathematics was deemed more than a better way to reason; it was central to the curriculum not only because of its alleged utility for developing young minds, but also because of its per-

---

[12] See François de la Fontainerie, ed. and trans., *French Liberalism and Education in the Eighteenth Century: The Writings of La Chalotais, Turgot, Diderot and Condorcet on National Education* (New York and London: McGraw-Hill, 1932), pp. 95, 230, quoted in Frederick B. Artz, *The Development of Technical Education in France, 1500–1850* (Cambridge, Mass.: M.I.T. Press, 1966), pp. 68, 71. The centrality of mathematics is also discussed in Roger Hahn, *The Anatomy of a Scientific Institution: The Paris Academy of Sciences, 1666–1803* (Berkeley: Univ. of California Press, 1971), esp. pp. 95–97. For efforts to apply mathematics to social questions, see Keith Michael Baker, *Condorcet: From Natural Philosophy to Social Mathematics* (Chicago: Univ. of Chicago Press, 1975), esp. pp. 332–42.

ceived usefulness to the state. It was essential for military purposes, civil engineering, and the monarchy's "civilizing" action in architecture, surveying, standard measures, and public finance.

In this context, literacy necessarily meant the acquisition of theoretical knowledge and the development of problem-solving capacities. But this criterion was thought to be applicable not to the whole population but only to a small elite. Competitive examinations restricted entry to the best state schools from the time of their establishment during the Old Regime; and the École Polytechnique, created during the Revolution, maintained the same standards of competitive entry.

The Revolution in no way challenged the definition or state support of this elite training at either the secondary or the graduate level. Established in 1795, the *écoles centrales* continued at the secondary level the scientific tradition of the *collèges* and academies of the Old Regime. The *écoles centrales* were succeeded by the *lycées,* which came to place greater emphasis on Latin than on mathematics. Despite this change in subject matter, a strong and visible place was maintained within secondary education for students who were preparing for the *grandes écoles*.[13]

Higher technical training was enshrined in the educational program of France and thus became—and continues to be—the distinguishing mark of the French graduate elite. Strong on theory and arrogant about their ability to apply knowledge to a variety of situations, these graduates have only recently found a world of technical literacy in which they feel comfortable despite the limits of their training. As Charles Kindleberger has argued, "Excessively deductive, Cartesian, geometric, mathematical, theoretical by nineteenth century standards, the system is coming into its own in a world of scientific sophistication."[14]

Civic-National Schooling

While elites continued to attend specialized academies, responsibility for mass education gradually shifted from religious communities to public bodies. We again consider France as an example. The French system of primary education has been credited with breaking new ground in secularizing education, universalizing schools, and fostering patriotism. From 1789 to 1914, this system of primary education increased the number of people with basic literacy from less than half to more than 90 percent of the French population.[15]

Primary education became a public commitment during the French Revolution. When the Revolutionary government introduced the first plan for national education in France in 1795, its major interest was military: the preservation of schools and training routes for those entering technical and military careers was

13 For the struggle between humanist classicists and scientists for direction of the secondary-school program, see Antoine Prost, *Histoire de l'enseignement en France, 1800–1967* (Paris: A. Colin, 1968), pp. 55–58.

14 Charles Kindleberger, "Technical Education and the French Entrepreneur," in *Enterprise and Entrepreneurs in Nineteenth- and Twentieth-Century France,* ed. Edward C. Carter, II, Robert Forster, and Joseph N. Moody (Baltimore: Johns Hopkins Press, 1976), pp. 26–27.

15 For eighteenth-century growth rates in literacy, as estimated by marriage-contract signatures, see Furet and Sachs, "La Croissance de l'alphabétisation," 726–27.

considered essential. (Similarly, Napoleon's system of secondary education, the *lycée*, was focused on providing personnel for the nation's military and technical needs.) The 1795 plan contained only the outlines of a system for primary education. It neither provided funding for primary schools nor created a sufficient number to serve the predominantly rural public.[16]

Before legislation abolished the religious orders' endowments and their right to receive public and private contribution, these orders had played a major role in providing basic education. The restrictive measures of the Revolution, in combination with wartime activity, drove many of the clergy underground or abroad. This effectively dismantled the church system of primary education that had functioned at the village level.

However, even in those areas where public primary schools were established, it was difficult to separate primary education from religious instruction. The attempt to do so initially generated much hostility in conservative areas. For this and other reasons the separation between religion and public education was far from complete. Without public funding for school textbooks, religious materials continued to serve as beginning reading matter for children. The personnel of the old church primary schools also tended to reappear in the new secular ones.

Literacy levels appear to have remained fairly stable across the Revolutionary divide, despite the undermining of the church-run primary schools. There was no important growth in literacy, as measured by signatures on marriage contracts, in any department during the thirty years after the opening of the Revolution. Only one-quarter of the French departments had growth rates of more than one percent, in the male capacity to sign, and almost all of that growth was in the range of one to two percent. Twelve departments showed declines in the male capacity to sign during this period, but all were of less than one percent.[17]

The literacy expectations in the primary schools that did function before the 1830s remained modest. This is hardly surprising since primary education was largely a catch-as-catch-can affair for the first two post-Revolutionary generations in rural France. Children usually attended school for only the winter months, since the demands of family and farm had priority, and even then they did so irregularly. Those who attended generally left between the ages of ten and twelve after confirmation in the Church. Communions were held rather early, to coincide roughly with the end of the primary-school course.[18]

[16] For primary and secondary schooling during the Revolutionary and Napoleonic years, see Maurice Gontar, *L'Enseignement primaire en France de la Révolution à la loi Guizot (1789–1833)* (Paris: Belles Lettres, 1959); Louis Liard, *L'Enseignement supérieur en France, 1789–1893*, 2 vols. (Paris: A. Colin, 1888–94); and Robert R. Palmer, ed. and trans., *The School of the French Revolution: A Documentary History of the Collège Louis-le-Grand . . . 1762–1814* (Princeton, N.J.: Princeton Univ. Press, 1975).

[17] Furet and Sachs in "La Croissance de l'alphabétisation," 722–37, argue that the Revolution accelerated trends in progress. The South continued to "catch up," the difference between male and female literacy rates narrowed, and the rate of literacy progress, within a narrow band, slowly moved forward. This argument will be developed further by them in a forthcoming volume. Evidence of some newly appreciated continuities in secondary education over the period from 1780 to 1836 are analyzed in the revisionist work of Dominique Julia and Paul Pressly, "La Population scolaire en 1789," *Annales: Économies, Sociétés, Civilisations*, 30 (1975), 1516–61.

[18] See Eugen Weber, *Peasants into Frenchmen: The Modernization of Rural France, 1870–1914*

In addition to irregular school attendance, poorly prepared teachers may also have contributed to low levels of literacy. Teachers were not professionally trained before the 1830s, even though efforts to impose professional standards for their certification were first made in 1816.[19] The minimum standard was a demonstrated ability to read, write, and use simple figures, yet even this standard was not always met. For example, even after 1830, teachers who hired themselves out by the season at fairs in eastern France reportedly placed one, two, or three feathers in their caps to indicate what subject or subjects they knew how to teach: the first stood for reading, the second for arithmetic, and the third for Latin. In arithmetic, moreover, those who could only add and subtract far outnumbered those who could multiply and divide as well. One teacher, Sister Gandilhon, who ran a school at Selins (Cantal) in the 1840s, taught "prayers, the catechism and the first two rules of arithmetic." According to a contemporary, "she had heard of a third but never learned it."[20] The teaching of arithmetic was further complicated by the use of regional units for weights and measures, like the *pouce* and the *toise,* which had no relationship to the metric system introduced by the Revolution.[21]

The methods of reading instruction were equally primitive. Before the 1840s, the teaching of reading was characterized by instruction in the names of the letters ("ah, bay, say, day . . . ."), independent of any relationship to other vowels and consonants. From the pronunciation of letters, students moved directly to the pronunciation of words.[22] A study of a village in western France noted that one teacher, much respected, read aloud sentences from the children's readers and then had children repeat the sentences. According to a resident of the village:

> The children were not required to make any effort to understand the words or to attempt to associate the shapes with sounds and meanings. They merely repeated what had been said to them and gradually discovered . . . by the place on the page or the approximate shape of what they were being given to read the sounds they were required to emit to avoid being beaten.[23]

It is hardly surprising, given these methods, that many pupils did not learn how to read at all. Further, those who did manage to read generally worked only on religious books and simple readers.

Mastery may also have been rare because the language of instruction did not always match the vernacular of the region. Most of France was a nation of *patois,* and in many regions Provençal, German, Italian, or Catalan was the major language. Since the language of instruction during most of the nineteenth century was almost universally French, the result was predictable. Even when stu-

---

(Stanford, Calif.: Stanford Univ. Press, 1976), p. 319, for an example of this relationship as late as the 1860s.

19 For a discussion of these standards in the context of the 1816 rulings, see Gontard, *L'énseignement primaire,* pp. 300–306.

20 For the contemporary sources, see Weber, *Peasants into Frenchmen,* pp. 305–6.

21 On the metric system, made the only legal measure in 1840, see Weber, pp. 30–35.

22 On the nineteenth-century pedagogy, see the observations of Prost, *Histoire de l'enseignement,* pp. 119–24, 276–82.

23 Roger Thabault, *Education and Change in a Village Community: Mazières-en-Gâtine 1848–1914* (New York: Schocken Books, 1971), p. 61.

dents were able to read the written language fluently, inspectors in Brittanny noted, "No child can give account of what he has read or translate it into Breton; hence there is no proof that anything is understood."[24]

Persisting Limits of the Civic-National Model

School attendance rose sharply throughout France as a result of two major reforms of the primary system of public education, the first in 1833 and the second in 1881–82.[25] Steps were taken under Ministers of Education Guizot and Ferry to democratize the system by increasing the number of primary schools, by reducing school fees, and by increasing the number of training colleges for teachers. These measures, in varying degrees, increased school attendance and contributed to the professionalization of teachers. However, despite these efforts toward democratization, primary schooling remained clearly distinct from the elite-secondary program.

Public schooling, moreover, did not for some time abandon its preoccupation with religious principles. Although in the field of education a civic religion of nationalism ultimately replaced traditional Catholic beliefs, schoolmasters remained dependent on local religious authorities for the nearly fifty years between the two reforms.[26] In 1833 the education minister attempted to make peace with the parish religious authorities in order to convince parents of the value of public primary schooling. "It is on the preponderant and united action of Church and State that I rely to establish primary instruction," Guizot told the legislature.[27] In practice this meant the responsibilities of the primary teacher included encouraging attendance at Mass, teaching prayers and biblical lore, and assisting the priest as needed. Reports from the 1840s and 1850s cite many examples of schools in which an alphabet book in Latin or a fifteenth-century *Life of Christ* served as the reading text.[28]

This educational alliance with the Church was broken by the Ferry reforms of 1881–82. The catechism was eliminated from the school reading program. Every *commune* was required to support a schoolmaster and a public school for girls as well as boys. A policy of free tuition, though not one of free books, replaced the earlier program of limited scholarships. For the first time school attendance was made compulsory, and the primary program was extended to age fourteen.[29] Finally, the national education ministry began a massive program of school construction.

[24] Cited in Weber, *Peasants into Frenchmen*, p. 306.

[25] A table of legislation affecting French education at all levels, 1794–1967, may be found in Prost, *Histoire de L'Enseignement*, pp. 501–11.

[26] For the preprofessional dependence of the French primary school teacher on local religious authority during the early nineteenth century, see Peter V. Meyers, "Professionalization and Societal Change: Rural Teachers in Nineteenth-Century France," *Journal of Social History*, 9 (1976), 542–46.

[27] F. Guizot, *Mémoires*, III, 69–70, cited in Gontard, *L'Enseignement primaire*, pp. 495–96.

[28] See Weber, *Peasants into Frenchmen*, pp. 305–6 and nn. In arguing the laicization of French education by the mid-nineteenth century, Michalina Clifford-Vaughn and Margaret Archer, *Social Conflict and Educational Change in England and France, 1789–1848* (Cambridge, Eng.: Cambridge Univ. Press, 1971), p. 202, have not presented a convincing argument.

[29] Prost, *Histoire de L'Enseignement*, pp. 192–203. Legislation in 1886 was designed to eliminate the religious from a teaching role in public schools.

Instruction was not designed to enlarge the skills of the literate or to encourage critical approaches to reading; rather, it was meant to cultivate a love of the familiar. History and geography texts were introduced to promote love of country.[30] The purpose of history instruction, for example, was unabashedly identified as patriotic. When questioned about the role of history in education, nearly 80 percent of the candidates for a *baccalauréat* in 1897 answered with statements about the "need to exalt patriotism." [31] Thus, despite the new curriculum, many of the criteria for literacy embedded in seventeenth- and eighteenth-century religious instruction were allowed to persist.

By the time of World War I, the successes of public primary schooling were clearly visible. Almost every child in the nation had relatively easy access to schools, and nearly all fourteen-year-olds by then had attended schools for seven years. Teachers were generally graduates of special training colleges located in each *département*. Attendance was increasingly regular for those enrolled in the schools, and students did not leave with the passing of winter. Inability to pay did not directly bar students' access to school. French was clearly the national language, and the metric system had triumphed over local measures. Statistics compiled by the Ministry of Education on years of schooling as well as the dramatic rise in the proportion of military recruits capable of signing their own names[32] are further evidence of these successes.

However, these facts do not inform us about the quality of education or the growth of individual capacity, and on these issues the evidence is mixed. Thabault observed that, while fewer than one-fifth of the inhabitants of his village knew how to form the letters of their names in 1833, more than half were able to do so thirty years later. Nevertheless, "the amount of knowledge that most of them had acquired did not make them very different from the completely illiterate."[33] By the eve of World War I, there had been considerable improvement in the knowledge of history, geography, and the French language. The inculcation of this knowledge took the form of a civic education, a new catechism based on patriotic devotion and civic duty. Eugen Weber has argued that this system, along with the army and improved transportation in the years from 1876 to 1914, contributed to the modernization of the attitudes and behavior of the French peasantry. But acculturation and adaptation do not necessarily produce generalized understanding, transferable learning, or reasoning skills.

[30] For an excellent discussion of the role of Ernest Lavisse in creating the "civic" and "national" history texts, see William R. Keylor, *Academy and Community: The Foundation of the French Historical Profession* (Cambridge, Mass.: Harvard Univ. Press, 1975), pp. 92–100.

[31] From Charles-Victor Langlois and Charles Seignobos, *Introduction aux études historiques* (Paris: Hachette et Compagnie, 1898), pp. 288–89, cited in Keylor, p. 99, and Weber, *Peasants into Frenchmen*, p. 333. On the relationship of this kind of instruction to nation-building, see Karl Deutsch, *Nationalism and Social Communication: An Inquiry into the Foundations of Nationality* (Cambridge, Mass.: M.I.T. Press; and New York: Wiley, 1953), pp. 92–99, 155.

[32] A graph showing the rise in literacy measured by the capacity to sign in the years from 1830 to 1910 is offered in Prost, *Histoire de l'enseignement*, p. 96. Also given (p. 98) is a graph showing the number and distribution of students in primary schooling from 1810 to 1890.

[33] Thabault, *Education and Change*, p. 64. The relationship between capacity to sign and capacity to read is discussed by Schofield, "The Measurement of Literacy in Pre-Industrial England," p. 324; Furet and Sachs, "La Croissance de l'alphabétisation," esp. 715–16, 720–21; and Stone, "Literacy and Education in England," pp. 98–99.

Teaching Methods and Literacy Criteria in America

American methods of teaching reading were influenced initially by approaches developed in Europe. The classic method, as we have seen in the French system, was alphabetic. Children were first drilled on the letter names and then on syllables. No attempt was made to select meaningful syllables or to emphasize comprehension; rather, accurate and fluent pronunciation was emphasized. The following description of reading instruction in the Sessional School in Edinburgh, Scotland, was reported to American educators in 1831. This account suggests the dominant goal of literacy instruction in the United States as well as in Scotland:

> English reading, according to the prevailing notion, consists of nothing more than the power of giving utterance to certain sounds, on the perception of certain figures; and the measure of progress and excellence is the facility and continuous fluency with which those sounds succeed each other from the mouth of the learner. If the child gather any knowledge from the book before him, beyond that of color, form and position of the letters, it is to his own sagacity he is indebted for it, and not to his teacher.[34]

Pedagogical reforms that had been introduced in Britain, Germany, and France during the eighteenth and nineteenth centuries later influenced instructional practice in the United States. The Prussian educator Friedrich Gedike[35] had introduced a "word method" of reading instruction which used words as the starting point for teaching the alphabet and spelling. Other reformers substituted the use of sounds, or "powers," of the letters for their names in the initial teaching of the alphabet. Although these reforms improved the teaching of fluent oral reading, they did not imply any new or greater concern for students' ability to understand what was read.

In the United States many forward-looking educators recognized that a greater emphasis on meaning would enliven instruction and make it more palatable to children. Putnam, in 1836, stressed the need for comprehension while criticizing the dominant instructional practice:

> A leading object of this work is to enable the scholar, while learning to *read*, to *understand*, at the same time, the *meaning* of the words he is reading. . . . if, for example, when the pupil is taught to read, he is enabled, at the same time, to discover the *meaning* of the words he repeats, he will readily make use of the proper inflections, and place the emphasis where the sense demands it. The monotonous sing-song mode of reading, which is common in schools and which is often retained in after life, is acquired from the exercise of reading what is not understood.[36]

Nearly fifty years later, Farnham voiced similar concern when proposing his sentence method of reading instruction:

---

[34] From Mitford Mathews, *Teaching to Read: Historically Considered* (Chicago: Univ. of Chicago Press, 1966), p. 55.

[35] For an assessment of Gedike's work, see Mathews, pp. 37–43.

[36] Samuel Putnam, *The Analytical Reader* (Portland, Maine: Wm. Hyde, 1836), cited in Charles C. Fries, *Linguistics and Reading* (New York: Holt, Rinehart & Winston, 1963), p. 10.

> It is important that this two-fold function of reading should be fully recognized. The first, or silent reading, is the fundamental process. . . . The second, oral reading, or "reading aloud," is entirely subordinate to silent reading. While oral expression is subject to laws of its own, its excellence depends upon the success of the reader in comprehending the thought of the author.[37]

Although these educators laid the groundwork for new methods and standards in literacy, their ideas did not become common educational practice until much later. Fundamental change in the standards applied to reading instruction came early in the twentieth century with the advent of child-centered theories of pedagogy, which stressed the importance of intrinsic interest and meaningfulness in learning, and the introduction of standardized group testing during World War I.

The American entry into the war highlighted a national literacy problem. Under the leadership of Robert Yerkes, then president of the American Psychological Association, a group of psychologists prepared and validated group-administered forms of a general intelligence test.[38] This test had two forms—Army Alpha for literate recruits and Army Beta for recruits unable to take the Alpha form. The tests were administered in 1918 to 1.7 million men, and it was noted with dismay that nearly 30 percent could not understand the Alpha form because they could not read well enough. This discovery evoked the following comment by an American educator, May Ayres Burgess:

> . . . if those [men] examined were fairly representative of all, there must have been over one million of our soldiers and sailors who were not able to write a simple letter or read a newspaper with ease.
>
> . . . although one-fourth of the men could not read well enough to take tests based on reading, this deficiency was not caused by their never having learned to read. The fact is that an overwhelming majority of these soldiers had entered school, attended the primary grades where reading is taught, and had been taught to read. Yet, when as adults they were examined, they were unable to read readily such simple material as that of a daily newspaper.[39]

After army intelligence tests had alerted people to defects in reading instruction, the growth in the 1920s of graded and standardized achievement testing gave educators tools for evaluating their efforts. The development of testing was stimulated in part by the successes of the army testing program and by the growing receptivity of school administrators to what they regarded as scientific tools of management.[40] The army program had demonstrated the practicality and

---

[37] George Farnham, *The Sentence Method* (Syracuse, N.Y.: C. W. Bardeen, 1881), cited in Fries, p. 11.

[38] Clarence S. Yoakum and Robert M. Yerkes, *Army Mental Tests* (New York: Henry Holt, 1920), p. 2; and Lewis M. Terman, "Methods of Examining: History, Development and Preliminary Results," in *Psychological Examining in the United States Army*, ed. Robert M. Yerkes, Memoirs of the National Academy of Sciences, Vol. 15, Part 2 (Washington, D.C.: Government Printing Office, 1921), 299–546.

[39] May Ayres Burgess, *The Measurement of Silent Reading* (New York: Russell Sage Foundation, 1921), pp. 11–12.

[40] See Raymond E. Callahan, *Education and the Cult of Efficiency* (Chicago: Univ. of Chicago

validity of group-administered psychological tests. Because group-administered reading tests required silent reading rather than oral, the ability to answer questions or follow directions based upon a simple text became the most typical test of reading competence. This focus on deriving the meaning of a text fit well with what the most forward-looking educators had already been advocating. The ability to understand an unfamiliar text, rather than simply declaim a familiar one, became the accepted goal of reading instruction and the new standard of literacy.

This newer standard, previously applied only to the programs of elite institutions, required the ability to gain information from reading and use that information in new contexts. The 1920s marked the first time in history that such a rigorous standard had been applied in the United States. This emphasis on deriving meaning from text bolstered the cause of those educators advocating changes in reading instruction. With this change in the criterion of literacy, national aspirations also rose for the portion of the population expected to meet this new standard.

Patterns of school attendance in this century best illustrate these radical changes. Reviewing data from several American cities, Leonard Ayres reported in 1909 that of one hundred children who were in school at age seven, ninety would still be there at age thirteen, fifty at age fourteen, and only thirteen of the original one hundred would remain in school at age sixteen.[41] Equally important were the large numbers of students not promoted; attendance at school for six or seven years by no means assured passage into the sixth or seventh grade. In general, Ayres found that, from any given grade level, 20 percent would not be promoted—if they returned to school at all.[42] Ayres's statistics clearly demonstrate that only a limited percentage of the population completed elementary school in the early part of this century. Whatever the eighth-grade level of reading competence may have been, only half of those attending school ever completed that grade. The literacy level that came closer to being universal was the fifth-grade level, which was comparable to that attained at the completion of primary schooling in nineteenth-century France. Although we cannot estimate exactly the functioning level of literacy at the beginning of the century, it seems fair to conclude that it did not approach present standards.

The Growth of Literacy Expectations

This article documents changes in literacy standards and teaching methods in the United States and some European countries, chiefly France, during the past several centuries. Our evidence suggests a rough progression in literacy expectation and performance. Expectations for popular literacy appeared after a long period in

Press, 1962); and David B. Tyack, *The One Best System: A History of American Education* (Cambridge, Mass.: Harvard Univ. Press, 1974), pp. 198–216.

[41] Leonard P. Ayres, *Laggards in Our Schools: A Study of Elimination and Retardation in City School Systems* (New York: Russell Sage Foundation, 1909). This book was prompted by concern with the large number of schoolchildren who were older than they should have been for their assigned grade level.

[42] Ayres, pp. 20, 38, 66.

which the general population could not read. The earliest mass-literacy effort, Protestant-religious instruction, was intended to develop not a generalized capacity to read but only the mastery of a very limited set of prescribed texts. Although civic-national public schooling introduced a slightly broadened set of texts, students were not expected to use their reading skills to acquire new information but only to become fluent oral readers. Nonetheless, some individuals did learn to read for information and even to engage in critical and inferential reading similar to that demanded by elite schools.

It is only during the present century that the goal of reading for the purpose of gaining information has been applied in ordinary elementary schools to the entire population of students. Today, the term "functional literacy" has come to mean the ability to read common texts such as newspapers and manuals and to use the information gained, usually to secure employment.[43] The objectives of functional literacy may seem limited, yet this mass-literacy criterion is stronger than that of any earlier period of history. Achieving universal literacy as it is now defined poses a challenge not previously faced. We estimate that literacy standards in the United States in the 1990s will be both more demanding and more widely applied than any previous standard. The accompanying Figure 1, permits a schematic comparison between the aspirations which we have projected for the United States and standards met by earlier literacy movements. Depending on how the figure is read we are either attempting to increase by a significant degree the quality of literacy competence in our population, or to increase, also very significantly, the portion of our population to which an already established criterion is to apply.

The historical development of ever more demanding criteria for literacy mirrors to some extent a model for individual development of reading competence that has recently been proposed by Jeanne Chall.[44] In this sense, social phylogeny seems to reflect ontogeny. Chall points out that at successive stages in reading development, "the reader is doing essentially 'different' things in relation to printed matter, although the term reading is used to describe each of these stages." Further, "the successive stages are characterized by growth in the ability to read language of greater complexity, rarity, technicality, and abstractness, and with a change in how such materials are viewed and used."

Chall proposes five stages of reading. After a prereading period the first stage is initial reading or decoding. The essential aspect here "is the learning of the arbitrary set of letters and associating these with the corresponding parts of spoken words. . . . " The second stage is confirmation and fluency: "Essentially reading

43 On functional illiteracy, see David Harman, "Illiteracy: An Overview," *Harvard Educational Review*, 40 (1970), 226–30. The United States Census Bureau, however, uses the completion of six years of schooling as the standard for literacy. For a review of the relationship of six years of schooling to selected measures of reading ability, see John R. Bormuth, "Reading Literacy: Its Definition and Assessment," in *Toward a Literate Society: The Report of the Committee on Reading of the National Academy of Education*, ed. John B. Carroll and Jeanne S. Chall (New York: McGraw-Hill, 1975), pp. 62–63.

44 Jeanne S. Chall, "The Great Debate: Ten Years Later, with a Modest Proposal for Reading Stages," in *Theory and Practice of Early Reading*, I, ed. Lauren B. Resnick and Phyllis Weaver (Hillsdale, N.J.: Erlbaum Associates, 1979).

FIGURE 1

Schematic Representation of Shifts in Literacy Standards

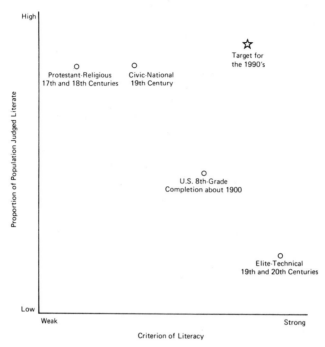

at this stage is a consolidation. . . . By reading familiar stories, smoothness and fluency are gained." Chall points out that at one time the Bible and religious tracts were familiar texts. The congruence between Chall's earlier stages and the literacy standards of the religious and civic-national periods is striking. During these periods reading instruction centered on mastering print, associating letters with words, and reading aloud. Chall's stage of confirmation and fluency seems parallel to the practice, highly valued in the nineteenth century, of public reading of texts. Chall's third stage, "reading for learning the new," is the first point at which mastering the ideas conveyed comes to be the dominant goal. For a long time, reading for new information was not expected of many, and it is only now becoming a nearly universal standard.

Implications for Policy

Our review of the Protestant-religious, civic-national, and elite-technical educational efforts has been very selective, but it nonetheless suggests the novelty of our present situation. Educational leaders often argue as if "real literacy" is compromised by an acceptance of functional-literacy standards tied to very practical demands of work and citizenship such as filing tax returns and reading technical manuals. On the contrary, our findings suggest that the serious application to the entire

410

population of the contemporary standard of functional literacy would represent a real and important increase in literacy. This is not to deny the ultimate possibility and desirability of seeking a still higher literacy criterion, but forms of pedagogy will almost surely have to change to accommodate the changes in both the literacy criterion and target population.

This discussion of changes in literacy standards has implications for the growing "back to basics" movement. Although the claim is frequently made that a return to basics would improve our educational system, the consequences of such a program are not clear. Presumably, proponents of basic education want schools to stress skills of literacy and mathematics more than certain recent additions to the curriculum. This much is reasonable. But, unless we intend to relinquish the criterion of comprehension as the goal of reading instruction, there is little to go *back* to in terms of pedagogical method, curriculum, or school organization. The old tried and true approaches, which nostalgia prompts us to believe might solve current problems, were designed neither to achieve the literacy standard sought today nor to assure successful literacy for everyone. Whatever the rhetoric of the common school, early dropping out and selective promotion were in fact used to escape problems that must now be addressed through a pedagogy adequate to today's aspirations. While we may be able to borrow important ideas and practices from earlier periods, there is no simple past to which we can return.

CHAPTER 5

Language & Reading Instruction

Making Sense of Reading— And of Reading Instruction

FRANK SMITH
Ontario Institute for Studies in Education

For many years researchers and educators have sought to specify the prerequisites for learning to read. Physical, intellectual, and perceptual factors are often cited as the necessary precursors. Frank Smith has often argued that reading is not a matter of decoding but consists of bringing meaning to print. In this essay Smith claims that the essential antecedents of reading consist of two cognitive insights: that written language is meaningful and that written language is different from spoken language. Smith discusses the importance of each of these insights and explains how children typically learn them. He argues that current instructional practices may thwart the learning of these insights and suggests ways in which parents and teachers may help children to understand that reading makes sense.

Children must have two fundamental insights before they can learn to read. These two insights are rarely discussed in the research literature on reading and are generally ignored in reading instruction, which may even suppress the insights in children who have already managed to acquire them. Without these insights reading instruction will remain incomprehensible to children and have the adverse effect of making nonsense of reading.

The two fundamental insights are (1) that print is meaningful and (2) that written language is different from speech. I shall discuss each of the two insights in turn, considering first why the insight is essential for learning to read, then how it is normally acquired, and finally how it may be overlooked or even impeded in reading instruction.

Insight I: Print Is Meaningful

Children are often immersed in spoken language—at home, at play, and even while watching television. But they would make little progress in learning to produce and understand speech unless they could bring meaning to it,[1] and this

---

[1] John Macnamara, "Cognitive Basis of Language Learning in Infants," *Psychological Review*, 79 (1972), 1-13.

Harvard Educational Review   Vol. 47   No. 3   August 1977, 386–395

would be impossible without the fundamental insight that the sounds of speech are not unrelated to other events but in fact make things happen in the world. Children learn language by making sense of the differences that language makes. By "making sense" I mean that children are able to relate the sounds of the language they hear to understandings they already have. Language makes sense—it is meaningful—when meaning can be brought to it. In fact, I would define "meaning" as the relevance that can be imposed on an utterance.[2]

It is not clear how or when infants acquire the insight that different sequences of language sounds are related to different meanings, that one sequence of sounds cannot be substituted arbitrarily for another sequence. This insight is unlikely to be explicit; I do not see how adults can explain the meaningfulness of language to children, nor how children might formulate the insight in words for themselves. Rather, I regard the insight as an implicit decision that certain events warrant attention because they are related to situations and intentions that the child can make sense of and is interested in. I suspect that the key lies in Halliday's observation that children do not learn language independently of its functions.[3] Language to a child always has a use, and the various uses could provide the child a clue to the purposes underlying differences among utterances. A child soon ignores sounds that do not seem to make a difference. There is, in fact, a powerful mechanism in all children preventing them from wasting time on sounds that they cannot make sense of, that do not appear to have a purpose; that mechanism is boredom. Even if the strangeness of the sounds initially stimulates their interest, children will not continue to pay attention to sounds that do not make meaningful differences. That is why they grow up speaking language and not imitating the noise of the air conditioner.

A similar insight—that differences on a printed page have a function, that they are meaningful—must also be the basis for learning written language. As long as children see print as purposeless or nonsensical, they will find attention to print aversive and will be bored. Children will not learn by trying to relate letters to sounds, partly because the task does not make sense to them and partly because written language does not work that way. In my view reading is not a matter of decoding letters to sound but of bringing meaning to print.[4] Orthography only indirectly relates print to spoken language.[5] Phonic generalizations are both cumbersome and unreliable; over two hundred rules with hundreds of exceptions apply to the most common words in our language. Relatively few words can be "blended" from the sounds of their spelling. To overcome this problem, instruction usually tries to limit alternatives by placing severe restrictions on the words a child will

2 Frank Smith, *Comprehension and Learning* (New York: Holt, Rinehart & Winston, 1975).

3 Michael A. K. Halliday, *Explorations in the Functions of Language* (London: Edward Arnold, 1973).

4 Frank Smith, *Understanding Reading* (New York: Holt, Rinehart & Winston, 1971); *Psycholinguistics and Reading* (New York: Holt, Rinehart & Winston, 1973).

5 Noam Chomsky and Morris Halle, *The Sound Pattern of English* (New York: Harper & Row, 1968); Carol Chomsky, "Reading, Writing and Phonology," *Harvard Educational Review*, 40 (1970), 287–309.

meet. In normal reading, unlikely alternatives are more efficiently eliminated through the sense of the context. Phonics will never enable a child to decode the words *horse, mule,* or *donkey* in isolation. There are at least ten different ways of pronouncing *ho* at the beginning of a word, and /horse/ contains one of the uncommon ones; but if context indicates that a word is either *horse, mule,* or *donkey,* then phonics will indeed work. My view on this controversial issue is that teachers often give phonics too much credit because of the limited objectives to which phonics are usually directed, and children contribute to the myth because the best readers are always good at phonics. It is, however, the sense of the text, if the text has any sense, that enables readers to use spelling-to-sound correspondences effectively.

Prediction through meaningfulness is the basis of language comprehension.[6] By prediction I do not mean reckless guessing but rather the elimination of unlikely alternatives on the basis of prior knowledge. The child predicts that a limited range of relationships is likely to occur between language and its setting or within the language itself. Meaning then is the relationships the child finds. If there is no meaning to be found, there can be no prediction, no comprehension, and no learning. But, to repeat, before meaning can assist a child in learning to read, there must be the insight that print is meaningful.

Acquiring the Insight

Research to date has little to offer in the way of relevant data, but it seems a reasonable hypothesis that the majority of children are as much immersed in written language as in speech. I refer to the wealth of print to be found on every product in the bathroom, on every jar and package in the kitchen, in the television guide and television commercials, in comics, catalogs, advertising fliers, street signs, store fronts, billboards, supermarkets, and department stores. All of this print is meaningful; it makes a difference. We do not expect cornflakes in a package labeled *detergent.*

The question is whether children who cannot yet read pay very much attention to all this print.[7] I have reported on a three-and-a-half-year-old boy who obviously could not read the words *luggage* and *footwear* on signs in a department store but who nevertheless asserted that the first sign said "cases" and the second said "shoes."[8] Here was one child who could bring meaning to print long before he could read the actual words—who had acquired the insight that differences in print are meaningful.

I can think of only one way in which such an insight might be achieved, and that is when a child is being read to or observes print being responded to. At this point I am not referring to the reading of books or stories but to the occasions when a child hears "That sign says 'Stop,' " "That word is 'Boy,' " or "There's the bus

---

[6] Frank Smith, "The Role of Prediction in Reading," *Elementary English,* 52 (1975), 305–11.

[7] The only researchers I know who are working in this area are Yetta Goodman at the University of Arizona, Martha Evans at the University of Maryland, and Ingrid Ylisto at Eastern Michigan University.

[8] Frank Smith, "Learning to Read by Reading: A Brief Case Study," *Language Arts,* 53 (1976), 297–99, 322.

for downtown." Television commercials may do the same for a child. They not only announce the product's name, desirability, and uniqueness in spoken and written language, but they even demonstrate the product at work. The point in all of these cases is that no substitution could be made; the print is directly related to the setting in which it occurs, just as is the spoken language of the home. Once the fundamental insight about the meaningfulness of written language is attained, I see no reason why children should not go on spontaneously elaborating upon it as they do with speech. Children can test hypotheses about the meaning of the printed word *toys* not because anyone reads it to them but because it indicates the location of the toy department.

The Relevance of Instruction

I must reiterate that to make sense of any aspect of language a child must perceive a purpose for it. In school, I believe, this need implies that children must understand not only the content of the instruction—the materials they are expected to read—but also the purpose of the instruction. However, this often does not occur, and in the next few paragraphs I describe what I consider to be some aspects of reading instruction which are fundamentally incomprehensible.

One such aspect is the decomposition of spoken words to sounds. The spoken word "cat" makes sense in some contexts, but the sounds /kuh/, /a/, /tuh/ do not. It should not be surprising that children find it difficult to detect these units in speech (until and unless they catch on to the highly conventionalized game that is being taught) because such units do not in fact exist in spoken language, where individual sounds and even words are slurred together. Speech is certainly not understood through an analysis and subsequent synthesis of its parts.[9] Auditory acuity is not essential for reading, although it may be a prerequisite for reading instruction.

Another incomprehensible exercise is the decomposition of written words to letters. The printed word *cat* can make sense in some contexts, since it refers to an object in the real world with which children can meaningfully interact. But the letters *c, a,* and *t* do not have that status. They refer to specialized visual symbols that have nothing to do with anything else in the child's life. Until children have had substantial experience reading, they must find it profoundly unsettling to be confronted with the information that *cat* begins with /see/ or that *bat* and *ball* both start with the same letter. Children who know the alphabet tend to be good readers, but teaching letter names will not turn a poor reader into a good one.[10] Rather, it would seem, fluency with the alphabet comes with being a competent reader.

A third problematic aspect of instruction is the relating of letters to sounds. For a child who has no conception of reading to be told that some peculiar shapes

[9] Alvin M. Liberman, "The Grammar of Speech and Language," *Cognitive Psychology*, 1 (1970), 301–23.

[10] S. Jay Samuels, "The Effect of Letter-Name Knowledge on Learning to Read," *American Educational Research Journal*, 9 (1972), 65–74.

called letters (which have no apparent relevance in the real world) are related in any way to some improbable sounds (that have no existence in the real world) must be the purest Jabberwocky. Of course, with a certain amount of good will and diligence a child might succeed in learning to recite a few of these correspondences. At best, however, such correspondences will not make sense until the child is able to read; at worst, they may persuade the child that reading is a matter of trying to produce meaningless sounds at an impossibly high speed.

The use of metalinguistic terms poses yet other problems. Many of the words that children are expected to understand in order to benefit from reading instruction, in fact, make sense only when one is able to read. The word *letter* is a case in point and so is the word *word*. The status of a word in spoken language is extremely dubious; words cannot be segregated by any mechanical or electronic device from the continuous flow of normal speech,[11] and linguists prefer not to use the term at all. The usual definitions of a word—letters surrounded by white space or a separate item in a dictionary—obviously apply only to written language. It should not be surprising that many novice readers cannot make sense of this and other metalinguistic terms, such as *sentence, paragraph, capital letter,* or even *space,* since only more skilled readers have experienced them meaningfully. Teaching children the definitions of such terms will not make them readers[12] because until they can read, the terms will remain entirely senseless to them.

Finally, many drills and exercises are meaningless. It does not matter how much a teacher might believe or hope that certain exercises have a point; anything that is opaque to a child can contribute nothing positive to reading. Children frequently learn to achieve high scores on boring, repetitive, and nonsensical tasks (especially, once more, those children who happen to be competent readers), but such a specialized skill will not make children into readers. Low scores, on the other hand, can certainly interfere with reading development and not simply because children risk being stigmatized as potential poor readers, but because they may begin to regard rote, meaningless, and difficult activities as a model for what reading is all about.

The content of the material which children are expected to begin reading may also be incomprehensible. As a general rule, isolated words—which are the basis of much initial reading instruction—make no more sense than isolated letters. However, words in a meaningful context—if a child is encouraged to use context—promote prediction, comprehension, and learning. But some elaboration is required. Words that appear by themselves are not necessarily meaningless. In the world outside school, individual words—for example, *gas, exit, burgers*—make a lot of sense. But these single words are not in fact devoid of context; they are given meaning and function by the settings in which they are found. This is not the case when individual words are isolated from any apparent function and are printed alone in lists, on chalkboards, in exercise books, and even under some

11 Colin Cherry, *On Human Communication: A Review, a Survey and a Criticism,* 2nd ed. (Cambridge, Mass.: M.I.T. Press, 1966).

12 John Downing and Peter Oliver, "The Child's Conception of 'A Word,'" *Reading Research Quarterly,* 4 (1974), 568–82.

pictures. Many of the words that are likely to appear in isolation in school have a multiplicity of meanings and grammatical functions. Words like *shoe, house,* and *chalk* can be nouns or verbs, and *open* and *empty* can be adjectives or verbs. To ask children to identify such words is simply to ask them to put a name to them, not a meaning. Conversely, the fact that a word is embedded in a grammatical sentence does not make it meaningful. Sentences can be just as devoid of purpose and meaning as isolated words—*Sam the fat cat sat on the flat mat*—and so can whole paragraphs and "stories" made up of such sentences.

A consequence of all this potential meaninglessness in reading instruction may be to confound children who are striving to learn through making sense of what they are doing. More seriously, the ultimate danger is that children who have not got the insight that written language should make sense will never achieve it, while children who have got it may be persuaded that they are wrong. Unfortunately, a good deal of reading instruction seems to be based on the premise that sense should be the last, not the first, concern of readers.

Such instruction may not be ineffectual. Many students identified as having reading problems in high school struggle to get every word right, drawing on all their resources of phonics, and in this way they may succeed. But they show no apparent concern for meaning and no evident expectation that sense has any bearing on what they are trying to do. As a cure for their obvious disability, they may often be removed entirely from any possibility of reading meaningful text and returned to a meaningless form of beginning reading. Such meaningless materials and activities are occasionally supposed to exemplify "getting back to basics."

Insight II: Print Is Different from Speech

Obviously, spoken language and written language are not the same. It is not difficult to detect when a speaker is reading from a prepared text, especially one written for publication, or when a speaker is reading the unedited transcript of a spontaneous talk. Speech and print are not different languages; they share a common vocabulary and the same grammatical forms. But they are likely to contain different distributions of each. It is not surprising that differences exist between spoken and written language, since each is frequently used for quite different purposes and audiences. Spoken language itself varies radically depending on the purpose for which it is used and the relationships among the people using it. Although it is difficult to specify exactly how or why written and spoken language differ, I believe this difference has a simple and distinct basis: spoken language has adapted itself to being heard while written language is more appropriately read.

To understand how such specialized adaptation might have come about, it is necessary to examine the different demands that the two language forms make upon their recipients. For example, consider the obvious fact that spoken language is ephemeral. The word dies the moment it is uttered and can be recaptured only if it is held in one's fallible memory or if one asks the speaker to go to the trouble of recapitulating. In contrast to the facile way in which we can move back and forth through written text, even tape recording does little to mitigate the essential transience of speech. Writing, unlike speech, is largely independent of the constraints of time. Put in another way—and this is still an untested hypothesis— spoken language often makes a considerable short-term demand on memory while written language does not. The reader can not only attend to several words at a time but can also select what those words will be, the order in which they will be dealt with, and the amount of time that will be spent on them.

There is, however, another demand that written language places upon the reader, related not to memory but to the far more fundamental question of how we make sense of language in the first place. The question concerns how language is verified—how we confirm that the information we are receiving is true, that it makes sense, or, indeed, that we understand the message correctly. For everyday spoken language, the matter of verification is simple: look around. An utterance is usually related to the situation in which it occurs. But, if we do not understand or believe what we read, the ultimate recourse can only be back to the text itself. With written language, difficult and possibly unique skills are required in order to verify, disambiguate, and avoid error. Specifically, the skills involve following an argument, looking for internal consistencies, and thinking abstractly.

These requirements of written language have so impressed some theorists that they have argued that writing has introduced a whole new mode to our repertoire of intellectual skills.[13] It might be objected that spoken language is often as abstract, argumentative, and unrelated to the circumstances in which it is comprehended as a scientific paper. But Olson claims that our ability to produce and understand such spoken language is simply a by-product of our being literate.[14] Only because of our experience in reading can we make sense of abstract speech, which in its form is more like writing than everyday spoken language.

The Need for the Insight

Children who expect to read in the way they make sense of spoken language are likely to have difficulty in comprehending print and thus in learning to read. Their predictions will be all wrong. It does not matter that we cannot define exactly the differences between spoken and written language. We cannot say what the rules of spoken language are; yet children learn to make sense of speech. Nor is there convincing evidence that children need to have the conventions of written language explained to them, provided they can make sense of print. The general requirements of immersion in the problem, of making sense, and of getting feedback to test hypotheses would seem to be just as easily met with written language as with speech. In fact, since a number of alternative tests can be conducted on the same material, written language might seem to have advantages as far as hypothesis testing is concerned. By virtue of its internal consistency, the text itself can provide feedback about the correctness of hypotheses, just as the surrounding situ-

[13] Eric Havelock, *Origins of Western Civilization* (Toronto: Ontario Institute for Studies in Education, 1976); Jack Goody and Ian Watt, "The Consequences of Literacy." In *Literacy in Traditional Societies,* ed. Jack Goody (Cambridge, Eng.: Cambridge Univ. Press, 1968); and David R. Olson, "Utterance to Text: The Bias of Language," *Harvard Educational Review,* 47 (1977), pp. 257-81.

[14] Olson.

ation may provide feedback that is relevant to speech. When reading something you comprehend, you can usually tell if you make a mistake that makes a difference—for the very reason that it *makes* a difference—and you can probably go back to find out why. However, none of this will be of any value to children learning to read if the language from which they are expected to learn is not in fact written language or if they do not have the fundamental insight that written language and speech are not the same.

Acquiring the Insight

How might children acquire and develop the insight that speech and written language are not the same? There can be only one answer: by hearing written language read aloud. When a child's predictions about written language fail because they are based on prior knowledge of spoken language, then an occasion exists for gaining the insight that spoken and written language are different. As written language is heard and comprehended, hypothesis testing will also help children develop an implicit understanding of the particular characteristics of written language. And children can considerably augment this understanding as they become able to do more and more of their own reading.

I suspect it is the higher probability of hearing written language that accounts for the finding that children tend to become proficient readers if they come from homes where a good deal of reading occurs. (Sartre has related his experience of learning to read in this way.[15]) Children are unlikely to learn to read by osmosis (by the mere fact that books are around them), from direct parental instruction, or because they see the value of reading by watching adults perform what initially must seem a pretty meaningless, silent activity. Rather, I would be inclined to credit the simple possibility that such children are merely more likely than other children to hear written language being read.

Actual stories are the kind of reading that I think most familiarizes children with written language. These can range from the contemporary material found in newspapers and magazines, elaborating perhaps upon something already experienced, to the traditional content of fairy tales and adventure stories, to history and myth. These traditional stories fascinate children—possibly fulfilling some of their deepest needs[16]—without pandering to an alleged inability to handle complex language or ideas. All of these story types are truly written language, produced for a purpose in a conventional medium. There is no evidence that children find it harder to understand such complex texts (when they are read to them) than it is for them to understand complex adult speech. In both cases it usually does not matter if large parts of the language are incomprehensible, provided the general theme and interest carry the reader or listener along. Indeed, it is through exposure to such meaningful complexity that children are able to develop and test their hypotheses about the nature of spoken or written language.

[15] Jean-Paul Sartre, *The Words* (New York: Braziller, 1964).
[16] Bruno Bettelheim, *The Uses of Enchantment: The Meaning and Importance of Fairy Tales* (New York: Knopf, 1976).

Most of the material which interests children at school—and from which they would be likely to learn—tends to be too difficult for them to read by themselves. This poses a problem for teachers. One solution would be to help children read or listen to such material. But the alternative often selected is to seek or produce less complex material—pseudoforms—in the expectation that children will find them simpler. And if this specially tailored material also confounds beginners, the assumption may be made that the fault lies with the children or with their language development.

Indeed, the language of school texts is probably unfamiliar to most children. But this situation need not have its roots in the particular kind of spoken language with which a child is familiar nor even in the child's possibly limited experience with print. The source is more likely to be the artificial language of school books, whether of the truncated "cat on the mat" variety or the more florid "Down the hill hand in hand skipped Susie and her friend." This language is so different from any other spoken or written form that it is probably most appropriate to put it into an exclusive category, "school language."

Of course, such language tends to be quite unpredictable for many children, who may then have enormous difficulty understanding and learning to read from it. Ironically, it is often concluded that written language is intrinsically difficult for children who would be better off learning from "spoken language written down." The source for such a hybrid is either someone's intuition of what constitutes spoken language or, worse still, a dialect of that language or even "children's language," the description of any of which confounds professional linguists. The result may be something that is quite unlike written language yet has none of the advantages of everyday speech, since it has to be comprehended out of its setting. Children may learn to recite such print, but I have seen no evidence that it makes them readers. And any insight they might have in advance about the nature of written language is likely to be undermined. Worse, children may be persuaded that the print they first experience in school is a model for all the written language that will confront them throughout their lives—a conviction that would be as discouraging as it is misleading.

Conclusions

I have argued that children need two basic insights to begin to learn to read. Also, I have implied that with these insights children can solve all the other problems associated with print by themselves provided that no extraneous confusion or hindrance is put in their way. They must be able to predict and make sense of language in the first place, and they can do this only by bringing meaning to it. This is certainly the way that all children learn spoken language and is probably the reason that many of them succeed in learning to read despite the instructional method used.

As I have argued elsewhere, the implications for instruction are that a child learns to read by reading and that the teacher's role is to make reading easy. I do not mean that reading is made easy by the use of simple material, which can indeed be difficult because of its probable irrelevance and unpredictability. Rather, I suggest helping children to understand any written material that interests them— whether the help is provided by the teacher, an aide, another child, or a tape recording—or simply by permitting children to make errors and omissions without penalty and without the disruption of unwanted correction. Children seek help when they need it and ignore it when they do not.

There are, of course, many factors that can contribute to failure in reading, including lack of motivation, low expectations, fear of failure, and hostility to the school or to the teacher. But failure also implies that a child sees no sense in what is involved in learning to read. A child's commitment to learn reflects an economic decision made on the basis of perceived cost and return. The problem for the teacher is not just to make reading comprehensible (which may be hard enough) but also to make sure that the instruction makes sense and is relevant to all of the child's concerns. Children who can make sense of instruction should learn to read; children confronted by nonsense are bound to fail. The issue is as simple—and as complicated—as that.

Teaching Reading and Language to the Disadvantaged— What We Have Learned from Field Research

WESLEY C. BECKER
University of Oregon

In late 1967 Project Follow Through was reorganized to select, test, and evaluate promising but different educational programs for disadvantaged youngsters in the first three grades. Now, nearly ten years later, the completed evaluations of Follow Through suggest that one of these programs, the University of Oregon's Direct Instruction Model, has produced significant gains in measures of positive affect, basic skills, and conceptual reasoning. In this article Wesley Becker discusses the distinctive features of this model—its underlying assumptions and basic teaching components. He then explores the implications of teaching reading and language skills to economically disadvantaged children and advocates that immediate steps be taken to teach vocabulary systematically throughout the school years. Viewing this goal as essential for compensatory education, he concludes with an analysis of how vocabulary instruction might best be implemented.

The teaching of reading and language competencies is at the heart of the educational phase of the War on Poverty begun in 1964. A basic assumption of this unprecedented social-action program was that the American dream of equal opportunity could be made a reality. Until recently, the evidence to support this assumption has been noticeably lacking. As early as 1968, Daniel P. Moynihan appeared before the House Subcommittee on Education to summarize the 1967 Title I evaluation by the TEMPO Division of the General Electric Company:

> We had thought [as legislation such as Title I was passed] we knew all that really needed to be known about education in terms of public support, or at the very least, that we knew enough to legislate and appropriate with a high degree of confidence. . . . We knew what we wanted to do in education, and we were enormously

Harvard Educational Review Vol. 47 No. 4 November 1977, 518–543

confident that what we wanted to do could work. That confidence . . . has eroded.
. . . . We have learned that things are far more complicated than we thought. The
rather simple input-output relations which naively, no doubt, but honestly, we had
assumed to obtain in education simply, on examination, did not hold up. They are
not there. (Cited in McLaughlin, 1975, p. 49)

The results of subsequent Title I evaluations (see, for example, Gamel, Tallmadge, Wood, & Blinkley, 1975; Glass, 1970; U.S. Office of Education, 1969, 1976)
did little to challenge the view Moynihan expressed. In some measure Title I did
succeed in equalizing educational opportunity by improving financial and educational resources. Nonetheless, the general failure of its programs to show consistent,
replicable improvements in basic and cognitive skills left educational reformers in
a quandary. To show any positive effects, projects had to be selectively chosen and
then superficially examined the next year (Hawkridge, Chalupsky, & Roberts,
1968).

Field-based experiments can fail for many reasons, as some have suggested.
Senator Robert Kennedy suspected, for example, that the early failures of Title I
were due to the disinterest if not malfeasance of local school administrators (Mc-
Laughlin, 1975). Alice Rivlin thought it was due to the technical inexperience of
local evaluators (McLaughlin, 1975). From our present perspective, several reasons
can be suggested why such projects seem to fail: some programs are not well-
designed initially (Engelmann, 1975); the self-protective bureaucratic structure of
school systems resists change (McLaughlin, 1975); the instruments used to measure
outcomes reveal changes caused by maturation rather than school instruction
(Becker & Engelmann, 1976); some control groups simply make use of children
left over after the disadvantaged are placed in special programs and, in doing so,
fail to randomly select and assign students (Haney, Note 1). The lesson is clear:
when field programs fail, especially if program installation and operation are not
monitored, we have only a heyday for speculation. We learn little of value about
those details needed to design better schools.

By late 1967, the consistent failure of outcome research to find any positive program effects was already evident, leading members of the Office of Education to
take a more analytic approach in designing Project Follow Through. Efforts were
first made to initiate Follow Through as a program designed to extend Head Start
into the elementary grades, but in the wake of a major funding cutback, from 120
million to 15 million dollars, Follow Through shifted its aim from service
to research. With this shift in focus, Follow Through was deliberately organized
to select, test, and evaluate promising, but different, educational programs for
disadvantaged youngsters in the first three grades. This approach was later to be
called a planned variation design. The individual programs were installed and
monitored by their originators or sponsors. Communities electing to participate in
Follow Through made choices among the different models and then worked with
the developers to implement specific programs. Contractual arrangements were
established to encourage community implementation, and independent evaluators were given contracts to monitor the programs and evaluate the outcomes
(Rivlin & Timpane, 1975). In 1968 John Hughes, then director of the Division of

Compensatory Education, felt this decision marked a significant departure from earlier practices:

> The decision to use the very limited funds available for Follow Through . . . to initiate a program which will permit examination in depth of the consequence of different program approaches holds promise of inaugurating what could be literally a new era in governmental support for educational and social ventures, i.e., an era in which the knowledge and technical expertise of the educational specialist, the systems engineer, and the behavioral scientist are brought into harmony with the pluralistic value structure of our society. (Cited by Richard Elmore in Rivlin & Timpane, 1975, p. 23)

The first director of Follow Through, Robert Egbert (Note 2), later remarked:

> With such limited funds it seemed sensible to change Follow Through's primary purpose from "service to children" to "finding out what works". . . . Follow Through now focused its attention on developing, examining and refining alternative approaches to the education and development of young disadvantaged children. (pp. 4–5)

Follow Through eventually came to involve 180 communities, 75,000 children a year, twenty-two sponsors, and an annual budget of fifty-nine million dollars. Garry McDaniels (1975), who designed the final Follow Through evaluation plan, called the program the largest and most expensive social experiment ever launched. He described the sponsors in these words:

> The sponsors represented a range of opinion, theory and rhetoric. Bank Street College in New York City came with a long history of child development philosophy, theory, and practice. Siegfried Engelmann came with his learning theory and experience in highly engineered materials and teacher behaviors. Ira Gordon came with his commitments to parent training as the major vehicle for assisting children. Leonard Sealey brought "open education"; David Weikart brought a cognitively oriented curriculum. (p. 5)

Now, nine years later, the completed evaluations of Follow Through indicate that some educational programs can make a difference in teaching reading, math, and language skills. One of the models, the University of Oregon Direct Instruction Model, shows significant program gains in measures of basic skills, cognitive skills, and positive affect (Abt Associates, 1976, 1977). Given these outcomes, we can now identify more positively the problems that have been hindering Title I and other programs for the economically disadvantaged. As stated previously, when programs fail, we usually learn little about the details that can make a difference; however, with success in specific areas using certain methods, we should be able to make more precise inferences about the critical features of effective programs. The rest of this paper, therefore, will explore the implications of the Direct Instruction Model for teaching reading and language skills to economically disadvantaged children. We will first describe the model briefly.

427

The Direct Instruction Model[1]

The major goal of the Direct Instruction Model is to improve the basic education of children from economically disadvantaged backgrounds and thus increase their life options. Developed by Engelmann and Becker, the model had its roots in Bereiter and Engelmann's experimental preschool and in Becker's behavioral research on classroom management. The model emphasizes small-group, face-to-face instruction by a teacher using carefully sequenced, daily lessons in reading, arithmetic, and language.[2] These lessons utilize modern learning principles and advanced programming strategies (Becker, Engelmann, & Thomas, 1975a, 1975b). Each set of lessons has been meticulously field-tested to determine that low-performing children will achieve the program objectives under carefully monitored conditions.

Four assumptions underlie the model. First, all children can be taught, regardless of their developmental readiness or background. Teaching failure is not excused. Second, learning the basic skills, including logical procedures, is central to intelligent behavior and should be essential to any compensatory education program. Third, disadvantaged youngsters tend to be behind other students in skills needed to succeed in school as they are now structured. Fourth, in order to "catch up," the disadvantaged must be taught more in the time available than advantaged children. The second and third assumptions appear to support a deficit view of poor children. Relative to an educational system established and controlled by the middle class, this view appears to be true; if it were not, there would have been no need for Follow Through. It should be strongly asserted, however, that children from economically disadvantaged backgrounds have a host of functional skills that are adaptive for the settings in which they live and that they are very teachable children. As environmentalists, we recognize the relativistic aspects of culture and realize that what is reinforced and functional in one culture or subculture may not be in another. We view Follow Through as an educational intervention for three or four years that can have the effect, on the average, of increasing the achievement of the economically disadvantaged and thus increasing their life options as well.[3]

The model contains seven essential teaching components. First, the teaching of general cases is emphasized so that children can generalize to all members of a set after being introduced to only a few members of that set. Second, since people are the primary instruments of instruction, the number of classroom instructors is increased. By adding teaching aides, more instruction can be given, especially to

---

[1] This summary is adapted from Becker & Engelmann (Note 3).

[2] The programs are published by Science Research Associates, Chicago, under the trade name DISTAR® and were designed by Siegfried Engelmann.

[3] We do not assume that all minority children have poor language skills. We do assume that there is a higher probability of weaker language skills in children from lower socioeconomic settings (and some of the data presented later support the assumption). In our Follow Through data, this weakness is found least in the big cities of the Northeast (see Havighurst, 1967), but even there compensatory language programs have been considered needed and helpful.

non-readers. Third, the daily program is carefully structured; when time is allocated according to teaching priorities, everyone knows what to do and when to do it. Fourth, rapid-paced, teacher-directed, small-group instruction is employed as an efficient way to individualize instruction for the non-reader. Fifth, positive approaches are used to secure and maintain student attention, reinforce correct responses, and identify mistakes. Sixth, teaching staffs are carefully trained and supervised to ensure that appropriate skills have been provided and are maintained. Seventh, student progress is monitored by means of biweekly criterion-referenced tests and reports-of-lesson-taught, both of which help to detect problems while there is time to correct them.

Nine curricular strands make up the DISTAR model. Collectively they specify the teaching objectives for students in reading, arithmetic, and language. In Reading I and II, reading is taught directly with the emphasis first on decoding skills and then comprehension. In Reading III, the children are taught how to learn from reading and to extract and use new information in stories that primarily have a scientific orientation. These stories make rules available that can be used to solve problems in such areas as astronomy, muscle function, and measurement. The student completing Reading III is prepared to learn from upper-level textbooks as long as the new vocabulary and concepts in those texts are taught in some reasonable way.

Arithmetic I teaches basic addition and subtraction first through a problem-solving approach; next, to prepare for more elaborate problems, children speed up adding and subtracting by memorizing number facts. In Arithmetic II, the students are introduced to multiplication and fractions; addition and subtraction skills are extended, and a variety of measurement concepts involving time, money, length, and weight are taught. The students are also taught how to work story problems, and how to derive unknown facts from those already known. In Arithmetic III, the students are taught algebra, factoring, and division in addition to traditional computation.

Language I and II teach names, classes, properties, and relational terms. Children are taught to make complete statements, to ask questions in order to explore unknown subjects, and to logically describe the world around them. These language programs emphasize comprehension and language production, and students are taught such elements of logic as conditionality, causality, multiple attributes, definitions, deductions, synonyms, and opposites. Language III expands the logical use of language and teaches basic grammatical rules. In addition, many activities in Reading and Language are also geared to building writing and spelling skills.

In developing the model, concern was expressed that children learn arts, crafts, social skills, and values in ways designed to suit local conditions. It was further stressed that instructional methods lead to a sense of personal competence and a positive attitude toward self. A positive self-concept was viewed as a by-product of good teaching rather than as a goal that could be achieved in the abstract. The National Evaluation data support this assumption (Abt Associates, 1977).

Some Distinctive Features of the Model

Many of the distinctive features of the Direct Instruction Model have been openly criticized. Thus, in addition to reviewing some of these features, this section will examine common criticisms of the model and explore appropriate counter-arguments. These issues have, however, been discussed in more depth elsewhere (Engelmann & Becker, Note 3).

Scripted Presentation of Lessons

The use of explicitly detailed lessons—scripts—has been criticized as restricting teachers' initiative. This may be a valid criticism, but one should consider the potential advantages of scripts in providing quality control in a delivery system. The scripts permit the selection and testing of sequences of examples that produce efficient learning if followed. Most teachers simply do not have time to find appropriate words and examples or to sequence skill hierarchies in the most efficient possible manner. When teachers phrase their own questions, they may choose terms unknown to lower-performing children or may include unnecessary verbiage. In choosing examples, moreover, they may teach incorrect rules because the positive examples have some irrelevant feature in common. In sequencing, it is easy to omit those skills critical for later, more complex tasks.

Another advantage of scripts is their potential for teaching teachers about effective classroom instruction. Teachers can learn effective presentation strategies through repeated examples, and it is not uncommon to find teachers using direct-instruction techniques in subjects where scripts are not available. A most critical advantage, moreover, emerges during training and supervision. The precise skills needed to teach particular kinds of lessons can be specified when designing training programs. A supervisor entering a classroom can quickly determine what is happening and compare this with what should be occurring. The supervisor, therefore, is better equipped to provide direct, practical demonstrations or suggestions to the teacher or aide. By standardizing the teaching program in this way, it is also easier to monitor the progress of the children with criterion-referenced tests that children should pass if they have completed lessons at a specified level.

Small-Group Instruction

The use of rapid-paced, teacher-directed, small-group instruction has often been criticized as pushing or placing too much on young children. The data on affective outcomes, however, do not support this conclusion (Abt Associates, 1977). The use of small groups has many advantages. It is more efficient than one-to-one instruction and provides better teacher-direction, supervision, and individualization than large-group instruction. It also emphasizes oral communication skills, which children from non-English and economically disadvantaged backgrounds often need. Finally, small-group instruction provides a setting in which the repetitious practice necessary for some important skills is made more fun by transforming drill into a challenging game. Children enjoy the rapid pacing when circumstances allow them to be successful.

Signals

Prepared scripts direct teachers how and when to use signals to cue a group to respond together. For example, in sounding out a word, a finger is used to point to the letter being sounded out. The children say the sound as long as the teacher touches it. The teacher moves his or her finger from sound to sound as they are to be said and lifts the finger away at the end of the word. To coordinate counting-to-a-number, a foot tap or finger snap might be used as the signal. Often the signal simply involves dropping the hand which was raised to alert the children to "get ready" when a question was asked. Much training is required to learn how to use signals in a natural and clear manner.

The use of signals and choral response, however, has been criticized for fostering an authoritarian role for the teacher. The logic of this interpretation is questionable: carried to a proper conclusion, it would further imply that using signals to direct such groups as choirs or orchestras also promotes submissiveness or authoritarian models. An examination of children's behavior in our classrooms does not support this interpretation. Rather, the evidence tends to suggest that without signals some children merely imitate a "leader" rather than learn the task directly. The use of signals obviates this problem.

The use of signals, finally, has also been criticized as fostering rote learning. The persons drawing such conclusions, however, often overlook the long-term benefits of carefully sequenced teaching examples. The data on cognitive outcomes do not support the criticism of rote learning (Abt Associates, 1977).

Reinforcement

Some educators believe that children should learn for intrinsic rewards. When this does not happen, however, teachers need to know how to use methods that will lead to learning for its own sake. The model encourages the use of positive reinforcement as a means of strengthening motivation and making learning a positive activity in its own right. When children do not respond to games, praise, attention, or success, stronger reinforcers may be necessary. Point systems leading to special rewards are sometimes needed early in a program and are faded out when no longer needed. Principles and procedures which have been the basis for teacher training in this area are now published (Becker, Engelmann, & Thomas, 1971, 1975a).

Training and Supervision

A primary focus of training in this model, therefore, is developing the skills required to teach small groups. To get the most out of each child, teachers also learn procedures for grouping the children and for changing groups. A one-week preservice workshop and continuing inservice training for one or two hours a week is usually adequate for beginners. Manuals to be followed by trainers and participants "program" the training, just as the scripts help to "program" classroom instruction (Becker, Note 4). The most common training procedure follows three steps: *model, lead,* and *test.* Teachers are first shown how a particular task is taught; next, they teach the task with the trainer; and, finally, they practice the task on their own in pairs, each member taking turns being student and teacher. Skilled teachers provide classroom supervision of apprentice teachers and emphasize positive reinforcement.

Biweekly Reports

Attendance information is provided biweekly, as well as results on continuous progress tests on lessons covered in reading, language, and arithmetic. These reports help teachers detect problems they themselves may have in some skill areas, or problems individual children may have. Copies of biweekly reports are further used by teachers, supervisors, and project directors to make changes in student groupings and to plan inservice training. Copies also go to the sponsor for use in monitoring site progress and for process research studies. These reports gauge the quantity and quality of the children's progress.

The Direct Instruction Model: Evaluation Results

The twenty communities which have used the Direct Instruction Model include a cross section of lower socioeconomic groups: rural and inner-city Blacks, rural whites, Mexican-Americans, Spanish-Americans, Native Americans, and students from a variety of ethnically mixed communities. At any given time approximately 8,000 low-income students were in the program. Test results from students who entered the program in thirteen sites from kindergartens in 1969, 1970, and 1971 are given in Table 1. Students were included in the analysis if they met Office of Education poverty guidelines, if they started the program at its earliest grade level, and if tests were available at more than one point in time.[4]

The Tests

Three tests were used. The first, the Wide Range Achievement Test (WRAT), measures reading, arithmetic, and spelling achievement. The reading test is quite reliable and has been demonstrated to reflect instruction that teaches decoding skills. The arithmetic test has questionable reliability and validity for some levels but provides a gross measure of computational skills. The spelling test has reasonable reliability and validity. The second test, the Metropolitan Achievement Test (MAT), assesses reading comprehension, word knowledge, math computation, math concepts, math problem solving, spelling, and language (usage, punctuation,

---

4 This data base provides the largest sample size for measurement of program impact. To check for biases in the outcomes because of attrition, we have also analyzed year-to-year gains and pre-to-post gains (K to 3 or 1 to 3) on the same students. These additional analyses do not materially change any conclusions except to make the actual gains somewhat greater than those reported here. When the percent of the children who did not meet OEO poverty guidelines are added to the analysis, there is another slight increment in the level of performance. Children who enter the program late perform a year lower on the average. This would be expected if the program is effective. (For more details on sponsor data see Becker & Engelmann, Note 5).

and sentence-type). The Metropolitan Achievement Tests have excellent reliability and adequate validity, and provide measures of some of our program's goals. The third test, the Slosson Intelligence Test (SIT), is a short, individually administered test that aims to measure aptitudes similar to those measured by Stanford-Binet. We included it to measure attainment of some of the more general program goals such as language use and reasoning ability. The WRAT and the SIT have been given to nearly all students from the end of the first project year. The MAT was added in the spring of 1972 and was used each year at the end of the first, second, and third grades.

The Results

A major goal of the Direct Instruction Model has been to teach skills that would place Follow Through students above or competitive with national norms by the end of third grade. Table 1 shows the extent to which low-income students who started the program in kindergarten achieved this goal. This table displays what is called a "norm-referenced comparison" (Horst, Tallmadge & Wood, 1975). The intervention group is compared to the test constructor's norm group at pretest and posttest. This procedure assumes that, without the intervention program, relative positions would remain the same, on the average, and that posttest scores could be predicted from pretest scores. We assume, further, that a gain in percentiles then shows that the program is working better for the intervention group than the hypothesized average program used for similar-performing students in the normative sample.

Note that we have scaled the graph in one-fourth standard deviation units but have used percentiles to describe the scale points. This provides the reader unfamiliar with standard deviations a ready reference to percentiles but at the same time shows the magnitude of the gain in statistically more relevant units. In the National Evaluation of Follow Through, Abt Associates (1976, 1977) adopted a convention of judging an effect *educationally important* if the intervention group exceeded the comparison group by one-fourth standard deviation. At the end of third grade, such an effect would mean an approximate gain of three- to four-tenths of a grade level for most measures of achievement. We have adopted a similar convention in our own analysis because with large samples very small differences can be statistically significant but of no practical value.

For all measures on the WRAT, discernible pretest-to-posttest gains in percentiles are present. Overall in reading, low-income students moved from the 18th percentile on the pretest to the 83rd percentile on the posttest. As a group, low-income students are more than one year above the national norm in grade equivalents on these reading skills by the end of third grade. On the arithmetic portion of the WRAT, the group advanced from the 19th to the 54th percentile. In spelling, we found a gain from the 8th percentile to the 49th percentile. On these last two measures, low-income students have caught up with the national norm. The children who have been in the program only three years instead of four, perform on the average one-quarter standard deviation lower.

We have no pretest for the Metropolitan Achievement Test measures. By using

TABLE 1
Direct Instruction Model Follow Through Students

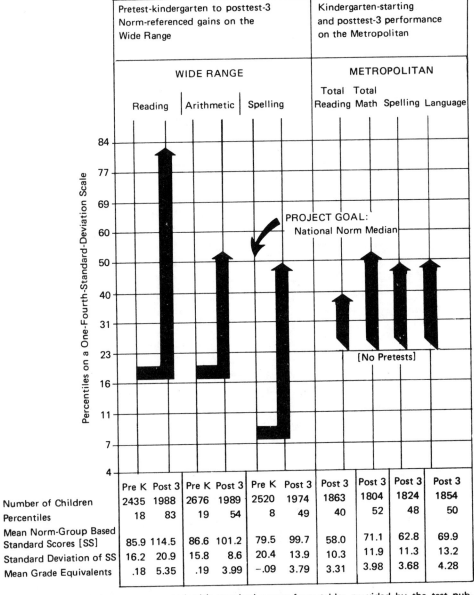

	Pretest-kindergarten to posttest-3 Norm-referenced gains on the Wide Range						Kindergarten-starting and posttest-3 performance on the Metropolitan			

WIDE RANGE — Reading, Arithmetic, Spelling

METROPOLITAN — Total Reading, Total Math, Spelling, Language

Percentiles on a One-Fourth-Standard-Deviation Scale: 84, 77, 69, 60, 50, 40, 31, 23, 16, 11, 7, 4

PROJECT GOAL: National Norm Median

[No Pretests]

	Reading		Arithmetic		Spelling		Total Reading	Total Math	Spelling	Language
	Pre K	Post 3	Pre K	Post 3	Pre K	Post 3	Post 3	Post 3	Post 3	Post 3
Number of Children	2435	1988	2676	1989	2520	1974	1863	1804	1824	1854
Percentiles	18	83	19	54	8	49	40	52	48	50
Mean Norm-Group Based Standard Scores [SS]	85.9	114.5	86.6	101.2	79.5	99.7	58.0	71.1	62.8	69.9
Standard Deviation of SS	16.2	20.9	15.8	8.6	20.4	13.9	10.3	11.9	11.3	13.2
Mean Grade Equivalents	.18	5.35	.19	3.99	−.09	3.79	3.31	3.98	3.68	4.28

Descriptive statistics were computed with standard scores from tables provided by the test publishers. The mean standard scores were then converted to percentiles using the publisher's tables.

the WRAT data, however, and comparable Title I data on low-income students, we have estimated entry-performance levels of our children to average no higher than the twenty-fifth percentile. We have used a slashed-arrow "pretest" point to illustrate this projection in Table 1.[5] At the end of third grade, low-income Direct Instruction students performed at or near the national norm on all measures. On the Metropolitan Total Reading, a test which measures reading comprehension, these students fell 10 percentile points short of the mean.

The data in Table 1 were collected by our research staff at the thirteen sites where children began the program in kindergarten. The National Evaluation of Follow Through by Abt Associates (1976, 1977), based on studies of seven of these sites that started Follow Through in 1970 and 1971, produces nearly identical data on the Metropolitan Achievement Test. When the site medians are averaged, using an equal weighting for each site, the Abt data show Total Reading at the 41st percentile, Total Math at the 48th, Spelling at the 51st, and Language at the 50th (Abt Associates, 1976, 1977; Becker & Engelmann, in press).

The National Evaluation also shows that, when compared to control groups, the Direct Instruction Model produces more statistically and educationally significant differences on tests of basic skills, cognitive-conceptual skills, and affective measures than any other of the eight major models.[6] Thus, in terms of level of achievement and in terms of comparisons with control groups, the Direct Instruction Model was found to be effective. After pointing out that the reading section of the Metropolitan Achievement Test is not as amenable to successful intervention as the math section, the Abt Associates evaluation (1977) concludes:

> Direct Instruction, Behavior Analysis [University of Kansas] and Bank Street models produce predominantly non-negative effects, that is, progress in reading which is either greater than or equal to the progress of comparison children. Only the children associated with the Direct Instruction Model appear to perform above the expectation determined by the progress of the non-Follow Through children. Moreover, the Direct Instruction children are the only group which appears to make more progress in reading, both early and late. In general, most models appear to be more effective during kindergarten and first grade than during second

---

[5] A U.S. Office of Education report (1976) substantiates this approach: "Analyses of all test scores showed that the typical student who received compensatory assistance in reading was at the 20th percentile for grade 2 and the 22nd percentile for grades 4 and 6" (p. 88). Moreover, in a footnote to page 88 this additional information is given: "In conjunction with the Emergency School Aid Act evaluation, children in grades 3, 4, and 5 of a nationally representative sample of minority isolated schools (50% or more non-white) performed at the 23rd, 18th and 19th percentiles, respectively, on reading achievement in the Spring 1973; similar results were obtained for mathematics achievement" (Ozenne, D. G., et al., 1974). The educational requirement for Title I eligibility (one year or more below grade level) is the 20th percentile for Metropolitan Total Reading.

[6] In the National Evaluation report Abt Associates (1977), *Basic Skills* are defined by scores on the Metropolitan subtests for Spelling, Math Computation, Word Knowledge, and Language (grammar). *Cognitive Skills* are defined by scores on MAT Reading, Math Concepts, Math Problem Solving, and Raven's Coloured Progressive Matrices. *Affective Measures* are defined by scores on the Coopersmith Self Esteem Inventory and the Intellectual Achievement Responsibility Scale (IARS). The Coopersmith is designed to assess children's feelings about themselves, about what others think of them, and about school. The IARS measures the extent to which children attribute their success or failures to themselves or to outside forces.

and third grade. The Direct Instruction Model is the only program which consistently produces substantial progress. (pp. 154–155)

To provide a better context for understanding this success, the performance levels of the Direct Instruction Model of the two closest programs and the average of eight major models, excluding Direct Instruction, are shown in Table 2.

TABLE 2

Percentiles for Equally Weighted Site Medians for Major Sponsors Included in the National Evaluation of Follow Through

Metropolitan Test	Direct Instruction	Behavior Analysis	Bank Street	Average of Eight Sponsors (excluding DI)
Total Reading	41	34	30	24
Total Math	48	28	19	16
Spelling	51	49	32	28
Language	50	22	23	20

Data computed by the author from tables for each sponsor on results for cohort II (Abt Associates, 1976) and cohort III (Abt Associates, 1977) for kindergarten-starting sites. When an averaging of raw scores is weighted according to sample size, percentiles differing by a few points are obtained; but there are no remarkable changes in the ordering of outcomes.

These positive findings imply that the Direct Instruction Model has solved some of the problems of delivering effective programs to school systems.

Implications for Improving Schools

These recent data confirm the original assumption of the advocates of the War on Poverty: poor children can succeed in school when better teaching methods are used. The question is, what are the critical elements of these methods? The seven components of the Direct Instruction Model outlined earlier concentrate on changing administrator and supervisor behavior, teacher behavior, and academic programs. We will discuss each of these areas in turn. When considering curricular suggestions, bear in mind that we are talking about teaching elementary school children with a high proportion of low-income parents. The suggestions we make, however, are not restricted to one model or any one way of doing things but focus on strategies that could work with several different methods of implementation.

Administrator and Supervisor Behavior

Tucker (Note 6) designated Behavior Analysis and the Direct Instruction as the two models that were the most successful overall. Each program channeled the actions of supervisors into helping teachers attain specified academic goals. Each program, further, nurtured the concerns of building-level administrators about their children's progress, provided feedback on that progress, and equipped supervisors with the technical skills needed to help teachers foster learning. In view

436

of these findings, product-oriented management and better teacher-support systems appear to be essential for improving the education of the disadvantaged.

Teacher Behavior

Behavior Analysis and the Direct Instruction models carefully detail the components of effective teacher performance and trained teachers in the prescribed procedures. Training manuals were prepared for preservice and inservice use that outlined practices for efficient management of time and specified teaching methods to be used in various situations.

Recent classroom research, relating teacher behavior to student outcomes in reading and math, provides additional support for the use of highly specified behavioral goals in the Direct Instruction Model (Brophy & Evertson, 1974, 1976; Clark, Gage, Marx, Peterson, Stayrook, & Winne, 1976; Soar, 1973; Stallings, 1975; Stallings & Kaskowitz, 1974). These studies show that more is learned in a given subject both when more time is devoted to teaching that subject area *and* when the teaching procedures are effective. Rosenshine (1976) interprets these recent studies as suggesting that a "direct instruction model" is the most effective approach to teaching basic skills (p. 364). Direct instruction, as defined by Rosenshine, involves teacher-directed oral activities in small groups centered on specific teacher questions, a high rate of student response, and adequate teacher feedback to students.

In a subsequent paper, Rosenshine and Berliner (1978) focus on the critical importance of "academic-engaged time" as it affects the relationship between teaching practices and outcome scores in reading and math. Correlations on the order of .50 are found between academic-engaged time and achievement-test results. Rosenshine (Note 7), in reanalyzing data collected by Stallings and Kaskowitz (1974) on six Follow Through models, found a strong relationship between the amount of engaged time a program provided and achievement outcomes. Sponsored programs that did poorly on achievement measures did not allocate as much time to teaching reading and math. Rosenshine also found that only the Oregon and Kansas models showed more academic-engaged time than the non-Follow Through control groups. A simple, logical conclusion follows: the learning of reading and math does not occur unless instructional time is provided, and the students are engaged during that time.

Academic Programs: Teaching the General Case

The Abt IV Report on Follow Through (1977) shows that in terms of grade-level scores and comparison to control groups, the Direct Instruction Model was the only major model effective on measures of academic cognitive skills (MAT Reading, MAT Math Problem Solving, and MAT Math Concepts). The University of Georgia's Mathemagenic Activities Model also did well on these cognitive measures, but since it was used in only three sites it was not considered a major model. The Kansas Behavior Analysis Model was comparable on basic skills (decoding, spelling, math computation) but not on cognitive skills.[7] We believe these findings are

---

[7] This conclusion is based in part on data from the Wide Range Achievement Test used in early grades by the National Evaluation and by sponsors. Decoding, however, is not measured by the tests used for Abt Associates (1977).

a function of the programming strategies used by our group but not by Kansas or the other models.

We believe that principles underlying DISTAR offer an important basis for an improved theory of programmed instruction. These principles were first discussed by Engelmann in *Conceptual Learning* (1969) and considered in more detail in *Teaching 2: Cognitive Learning and Instruction* (Becker, Engelmann, & Thomas, 1975b). In common with other theories of programmed instruction, Engelmann's specifies teaching one thing at a time, providing adequate practice, and designing lessons for a low error rate. Error rate is kept low by analyzing where errors are likely to occur, by using task-design procedures which reduce possible errors, and by pilot testing (Becker et al., 1975b). Engelmann's most salient contributions to programming theory are in specifying procedures needed to teach general cases and to cumulatively build knowledge within sets of related concepts; here errors are more likely to be made because shared properties make discriminations more difficult.

There are three major kinds of general cases: concepts, operations, and problem-solving rules. A general case has been taught when, after learning some members of a set, the student can generalize to all members (cf. Wittgenstein, 1958, paragraph 208).[8] In his analysis of teaching concepts, Engelmann begins with the premise that the programmer must define a concept within a specified universe of concepts: a concept is what is uniquely common to the stimulus properties of a set of instances within a specified universe of concept instances (Engelmann, 1969). Thus, the definition of a concept may change as the universe or set of concepts changes. If the only examples in a universe are *horses* or *boxes,* the learner has many options for choosing which details discriminate *horses* from *boxes.* The concept *horse* in this universe is described by the entire set of differences between *horse* and *box.* When we add *dogs* to the universe, the concept *horse* changes because many of the details that would allow the learner to discriminate between *horse* and *box* will not allow him to discriminate between *horse* and *dog.* The concept *horse* changes again when we add *ponies* to a set that now consists of *horses, boxes, dogs,* and *ponies.*

The notion of a concept that changes as the composition of a universe changes leads to the principle that, in order to make teaching simpler, the programmer must control the universe within which a concept "grows." For example, the student's initial concept of *vehicles* might be "something that can take you places." If instances and noninstances consist only of man-made things, this definition is adequate. When *horses* and *elephants* enter the set, the definition is revised to *"man-made* things that can take you places." Engelmann's definition of a concept makes the programming of instruction largely a logical process, requiring analysis of the distinctive features of finite sets of related concepts.

Given this logical framework, concept learning is viewed as a multiple-discrimination problem rather than a generalization problem: discriminating *between* instances and noninstances on relevant characteristics of each and discriminating *within* instances or noninstances on relevant and irrelevant characteristics. Note that Piaget (1956) refers to relevant characteristics of concepts as invariants and

---

8 Note also that the term "general case" covers the linguist's term "generative." Behavioral procedures have been used to experimentally produce "generative" verbal behavior in a number of studies (see Becker et al., 1975b, 85–86).

irrelevant characteristics as variants. Key programming principles help determine which discriminations are most important to teach and how to sequence examples for teaching them (Becker et al., 1975a, 1975b).

Concepts are the important building blocks for intelligent behavior on the stimulus side. Overt operations—operant responses, or what Piaget calls schemas— are the key building blocks on the response side. Operations are defined by the common effects of a set of responses. For example, no two lifting responses are the same, but there is a common effect produced by lifting responses: an object is moved in an upward direction. Mental operations, we assume, are performed with concepts about overt operations. The mental operation of adding involves refer- ences to possible instances of the overt operation of joining two or more groups to make one. An important step in the analysis of concepts and operations for pro- gramming instruction is the identification of building blocks. Building blocks are identified as the smallest set of stimulus/response (concept/operation) units that can be recombined to provide the largest number of applications. In oral language, a most useful building block is the referent/word unit, and the general case is the sentence or utterance of two or more words with meaning. Grammatical rules enter as a second set of building blocks in constructing the general cases we call sentences. In decoding regular-sound words, a good building block is the symbol/sound unit, and the general case is the orally read word. In writing, a good building block ini- tially is the letter-name/written-letter unit and the general case the written word. With consolidation of learning, the word-name/written-word may become the unit and written sentences the general case.

Problem-solving rules consist of sequences of operations that can be used to solve problems of a particular type. After having been taught some element of the problem set, students should be able to do any element. Assuming, for example, that the concepts *equal* and *plus* have been taught, as well as symbol identification and making lines for numbers, addition problems of the kind shown below can be taught using Rules 1–4.

$$2 + 4 = \square$$

Rule 1. Find the side to start on. (That side cannot have an unknown.)
Rule 2. Make lines for each number of that side.
Rule 3. Count the lines.
Rule 4. Make the sides equal by placing the number counted in the box on the other side.

By teaching one additional skill, counting from-a-number-to-a-number, the stu- dents can also do problems of the form shown in the equation below.

$$2 + \square = 6$$

Rule 1. Find the side to start on.
Rule 2. End up with the same number on the other side by saying the first number "Two" and counting to 6, making a line under the box for each count.

Rule 3. Count the lines under the box and write the number in the box.

Similarly, in teaching decoding in reading, one can teach a set of sounds, blending skills, and rapid pronunciation skills, so that the student can read any regular-sound word composed from the sounds taught (Carnine, 1977). This method of teaching decoding involves a problem-solving rule chain and yields a great saving in teaching time.

These examples display some of the analytic strategies Engelmann uses in building programs to teach the general case. His work represents a fusion of cognitive and behavioral theory. Cognitive theorists will recognize that Engelmann's approach encompasses cognitive processes. The instructional program, however, focuses on the observable behavior with which the teacher and programmer must deal in order to teach children (see Becker et al., 1975a, 1975b; Becker & Engelmann, Note 3; Engelmann & Carnine, Note 8).

Academic Programs: A Problem Linear Set

Probably the most important implication to arise from our nine years of work in teaching more than 25,000 disadvantaged students is that schools are designed to teach middle-class children and need to be redesigned for teaching all students. This observation bears out our initial assumptions. However, in our preoccupation with effective instruction from kindergarten through the third grade, we failed, until now, to explore the broader ramifications of this assumption. In the analysis that follows, we conclude that schools systematically fail to provide instruction in the building blocks crucial to intelligent functioning, namely, words and their referents. Children from homes where there is strong adult support for refining the use of language are more likely to succeed in school than those from homes with less adult-child contact and adults with less education (Coleman, 1975; Freeberg & Payne, 1967; Glass, 1973).

We came to this conclusion when trying to understand our failures and successes. As we have argued, there is little to be learned from programs that fail. When instruction is effective in some areas, however, more precise inferences are possible. Consider the pattern of findings in Table 1. Children in the Direct Instruction Model score at the 83rd percentile on the WRAT Reading; this is a full standard deviation above the national median. But on the MAT Total Reading these same children score at the 40th percentile, a quarter-standard deviation below the national median. In arithmetic, spelling, and language they score at the median. How are these differential findings to be explained?

WRAT Reading is a measure of decoding skills. If decoding is taught by teaching forty sounds and by teaching how to blend sounds rapidly together, a general case can be learned that will permit the reading of any regular-sound English word. A great efficiency in teaching is achieved when a relatively small set of building blocks can be recombined into a large set of applications. The DISTAR method proceeds with these assumptions and is remarkably effective in teaching decoding, especially in comparison to sight-word programs (which were most probably used for a majority of the WRAT norm group).

The levels of achievement in spelling, math, and language can be viewed as products of general cases with smaller ranges of application. The ability to reach the national average in spelling is most likely an outcome of teaching reading-by-sounds. The related process, spell-by-sounds, is an effective procedure for spelling words with regular letter-sound correspondences; the process also assists with irregular words. In our model, arithmetic is taught as several problem-solving skills that operate as general cases. These cases have more limited applications than decoding, however, and thus generate less net gain. The language skills, involving general cases of grammatical rules and word classifications, appear to have about the same level of potency as arithmetic.

The MAT Total Reading is made up of two subtests at the elementary level: Word Knowledge and Reading. The former is a test of vocabulary, the latter a test of comprehension. One is not likely to comprehend texts without knowledge of word meanings. The vocabulary-concept load[9] of the MAT Reading Test (Elementary Level, Form F) is beyond the experience of most disadvantaged third graders. Consider such items as *country* when used to mean nation, *Amazon ant, probably, exterminator, penicillin, disease-causing germs, Egyptians of old, a seated cat.* The test also demands that students make logical inferences and deductions.

In contrast to the general-case learning involved in decoding, arithmetic, grammar, and spelling-by-sounds, the learning of vocabulary and concepts usually involves a "linear-additive set" (Becker & Engelmann, 1976, p. 58). In a linear-additive set, the learning of one element gives little advantage in learning a new element. To be sure, there are families of words that have common root meanings and common meanings of affixes, which permit some limited general cases to be generated. But, by and large, the learning of proper names, new concepts, and the learning of synonyms for concepts already known by another name, involve linear-additive sets in which each new element must be taught. Knowledge of the English language, which is absolutely essential to oral and written comprehension, serves largely to define intelligent behavior (Miner, 1957). Teaching this language involves a task of the first magnitude.

The magnitude of the problem is revealed by the following analysis. Basal reading texts control vocabulary instruction for three years. Chall (1967) indicates that about 1,500 words are covered in this time, although the average student may actually have an oral vocabulary that is two to three times this size. After the third grade, school books shift to an uncontrolled adult vocabulary. Thorndike and Lorge (1944) estimate that the average high-school senior knows about 15,000 words, including proper nouns and derivatives but not inflections. Dupuy (1974) estimates, however, that the average high-school senior knows about 7,000 basic words. Basic words do not include proper nouns, derivatives, inflections, and compounds. On the average, 5,000 of these basic words are learned after third grade. Since schools do not systematically build vocabulary knowledge, students with weak home

---

[9] We use the term "vocabulary-concept load" to make clear that we are referring not just to verbal behavior but also to knowledge of referents.

training in English language skills are often in trouble by fourth grade, if not earlier.

In a recent review of research on socioeconomic factors in intelligence, Terhune (1974) details the correlates of IQ and school achievement (and by implication language comprehension). General language competence is low when: a single parent is in the home; per-capita income is low; education of caretakers is low; birth order of subject is high; and the number of children is large. If we add to this list, "parent's primary language is not English or is not standard English," a set of conditions is described that occurs all too frequently among those called "disadvantaged."

The hypothesis that vocabulary-concept knowledge plays a major role in reading comprehension is supported in the research literature. In his review of research Carroll (Note 9) concludes that

> much of the failure of individuals to understand speech or writing beyond an elementary level is due to deficiency in vocabulary knowledge. It is not merely the knowledge of single words and their meanings that is important, but also the knowledge of the multiple meanings of words and their grammatical functions. (p. 175)

Carroll also argues that vocabulary-concept knowledge is the key area of concern for improving reading comprehension for the economically disadvantaged, but he is quite aware that there is no easy way to make gains in this area.

Chall (1958) noted much earlier that "of the diverse stylistic elements that have been reliably measured and found significantly related to difficulty, only four types can be distinguished: vocabulary load, sentence structure, idea density, and human interest" (p. 157). Of these factors Chall suggests that vocabulary load "is most significantly related to all criteria of difficulty so far used" (p. 157).

Other analyses of our Follow Through data tend to support the view that vocabulary-concept knowledge is not systematically taught by schools. Analysis of the MAT Reading tests indicates a progressive loss on percentiles from end of grade one to end of grade three, which is paralleled by a progressive change in the tests toward an adult vocabulary by the end of third grade. On MAT Total Reading, low-income children in our program are far above the median at the end of first grade (70th percentile), but they drop progressively by the end of second grade (56th percentile) and the end of third grade (40th percentile). This drop is found for all reading subtests—Word Knowledge, Word Analysis,[10] and Reading (Becker & Engelmann, Note 5). Such losses are not found in decoding, math measures, or spelling, in all of which substantial percentile gains occur during kindergarten and first grade and are then maintained.

One might argue that the basis for these differential effects lies in the logical requirements of reading comprehension. This argument, however, does not explain why the effect is also found for Word Knowledge but is not found for Math Prob-

---

[10] This subtest is found only on the first- and second-grade tests.

lem Solving and Math Concepts. From the point of view of programmed instruction, the central problem is the linear-additive set, vocabulary. Logical processes,
such as those involved in some aspects of comprehension and math, are general-
case sets; these can be taught with some efficiency, but vocabulary does not submit
to such methods.

When the children taught by the Direct Instruction method are followed up in
fifth and sixth grades, they maintain superior performance levels on decoding and
spelling but lose about one-half standard deviation against the norm group on
MAT Total Reading and Total Math (Becker & Engelmann, Note 5). The losses
on reading and math are consistent with the hypothesis that fourth-, fifth-, and
sixth-grade teachers are not building on the skills the children had when they left
third grade. However, effective programs in math are available to schools; they
just are not being used or used effectively.

Schools have never had programs in reading that systematically build vocabulary-
concept knowledge. Except for technical vocabularies, this task has been largely
left to parents. Furthermore, since the achievement tests are built by procedures
that measure age changes, and not simply the effects of school instruction, children
from homes with weak support for language development fall progressively behind
on current reading tests. This finding is commonly reported. When student gains
on such instruments are used to evaluate teachers, moreover, those teaching children
with higher socioeconomic status (SES) will appear more competent than those
teaching lower SES children. The tests are not built to be specifically sensitive to
school instruction but to age changes generally (Becker & Engelmann, 1976).

IQ and learning gains of the children in the Direct Instruction Model were analyzed according to IQ blocks (i.e., 71–90, 91–100, 101–110). The data show that
children with high entry IQ's start higher on most achievement measures and stay
higher but do not usually gain proportionately more (Becker & Engelmann, Note
5). Exceptions to this pattern are the first-year gains on WRAT Reading (decoding)
and the gains from the end of second to the end of third grade on MAT Total
Reading (comprehension). In both instances higher IQ groups show proportionally
greater gains than lower IQ groups. This second exception is centrally important.
If we assume that the IQ test is measuring general language competence as developed at home and school, children with greater language competency should excel
on the adult-level vocabulary required by the MAT Reading Test at the elementary
level. Since a more controlled vocabulary is used for the first- and second-grade
tests, language competency, as measured by general IQ, should not provide much
advantage on these tests if there is effective school instruction.

These logical and empirical analyses clearly point to a problem for educators
who strive to teach reading comprehension to all children. The data suggest that
school programs do not systematically build vocabulary-concept knowledge. Current programs are structured to teach middle-class children or children who, to a
large extent, are taught oral-language comprehension at home. We assume that
this form of language learning is then transferred to reading comprehension at
school.

Implications for Curriculum Design

Redesigning curricula to solve the problem of vocabulary-concept learning will not come easily. The first job is to define and analyze a reduced lexicon in a way that will facilitate its teaching. Part of the analytic task is restructuring what has been treated as a linear-additive set into general-case sets. Miller and Johnson-Laird (1976) argue that such restructuring is a difficult but possible task: "We assume that at the heart of the sprawling and ever changing English lexicon some nuclear, widely shared set of words and concepts provides a framework for the development of special vocabularies for special uses" (p. 668). Thus, from the point of view of programming, the task is to specify a minimum, adult-level competency and then systematically build to that goal. The extensive work of Thorndike and Lorge (1944) on word frequencies, the analyses by Ogden (1932) on basic English, the work by Dupuy (1974) on basic words, as well as linguistic research on roots and affixes, all contribute information that could be used to build a system for teaching a basic lexicon or, more simply, a basic vocabulary.

In particular, Dupuy's contribution has been to provide a definition of a basic word which excludes proper nouns, derivatives, inflections, compounds, archaic words, foreign words, and technical terms. Within this framework, he has demonstrated that there must be about 12,300 basic words in English since he found 123 basic words in a 1 percent sample of the 240,000 words in *Webster's Unabridged Dictionary.* He has further shown that the average high-school senior knows about 7,000 of these words (70 words in his initial sample multiplied by 100).

It would, of course, be a major undertaking to repeat Dupuy's analysis 100 times to find these 7,000 basic words. It seems very likely, however, that the basic words known by the average high school senior would be contained in the 30,000 words identified by Thorndike and Lorge (1944) as being most frequent in printed English.[11] Thus, by analyzing the Thorndike-Lorge list for basic words, researchers could considerably short-cut the search. Furthermore, an analysis of this kind would produce a list of high-frequency proper nouns to be included in a vocabulary program and indicate what savings might potentially be made in teaching derivatives, inflections, and compounds. As one indication of how this analysis might proceed, consider this example: The Thorndike-Lorge list contains the words *negate, negative, negation,* and *negatively. Negate* could be treated as a basic word and probably could be taught through carefully presented examples. This decision, however, would depend on what other word-concepts have already been taught. The other words could then be treated as related vocabulary words and taught through general cases dealing with suffixes (*-ive, -ion,* and *-ly*). Of course, such teaching would have to provide adequate practice within diverse contexts.

Given a vocabulary divided into basic and related words, two additional types

---

[11] The Thorndike-Lorge listing gives an overall estimate of word frequencies in written materials, based on averaging frequencies for four samples: (1) the Thorndike general count of 1931, (2) the Lorge magazine count, (3) the Thorndike count of juvenile books, and (4) the Lorge-Thorndike semantic count.

of analyses would be necessary before one could start to engineer a program to efficiently teach vocabulary. First, on the *form side,* the problem would be to identify the morphemes (the smallest units of meaning) contained in the 7,000 basic words. If the basic words could be shown to be made up of only 2,000 to 2,500 morphemes, a potential savings in the analysis and teaching of word *forms* would be possible. Dixon's *Morphographic Spelling Program* (1976) is based on this potential. By teaching 720 morphographs, Dixon has been able to generate spellings for more than 10,000 English words using only five rules for combining morphographs.

Consider, for example, the following sequence, by frequency, of words from the Thorndike-Lorge list: *help, support, insist, September, toil, resist, recognizable, assistance. September* would go into a special list of proper nouns. The others could, in part, be analyzed as shown below.

Basic	Class	Related	Class	Morphemes
help	v,n	helper, etc.	n	help + er
support	v,n	supporter	n	sup + port + er
insist	v	insistence	n	in + sist + ence
toil	v,n	toiler	n	toil + er
resist	v	resistance	n	re + sist + ance
recognize	v	recognizable	nm	re + cogn + ize + able
assist	v	assistance	n	as + sist + ance

(v=verb, n=noun, nm=noun modifier)

Many more related words could be found in the Thorndike-Lorge list that would improve the ratio of basic words to related words, and similarly, other basic words, such as *detract,* could introduce morphemes that would improve the ratio of morphemes to basic words. Further improvements in potential efficiency could result from the analysis of variants or allomorphs, such as *sup-sub, com-con,* and *im-in.* These variations can be accounted for by rules of internal morphology, including devoicing and assimilation. This suggests the possibility of teaching such variations as general cases (Dixon & Becker, Note 10).

The second type of analysis needed to teach vocabulary efficiently would involve the semantic or *concept side* of the word-concept field. The morphographic analysis discussed above could easily provide a basis for determining which words are semantically the sum of their parts and which are not. For example, the components of *compress* quite literally mean "push together"; collectively they provide a direct meaning for compress. The components of *sarcastic,* on the other hand, mean "related to one who is of the flesh" and thus give little clue to the word's meaning.

The analysis of morphographic meaning would assuredly aid in making some program decisions, but a more general approach to the "semantic core" of the lexicon will be clearly needed if the overall task is to become feasible. What is needed is a core vocabulary-concept set that can be initially taught through examples and then used as definitions to teach other word meanings. Ogden's (1932) basic English provides one such core. The system consists of 850 words and guidelines for combining them into meaningful, standard-English sentences. Although Ogden devised the system as a basis for scientific and commercial communication between the nations of the world, it has great potential for use in developing programs to teach English as a primary or secondary language. The translation of *Robinson Crusoe* and the Bible into basic English gives evidence of the system's ability to deal with the conceptual complexities of the language.

It seems reasonable to propose, therefore, that each of Dupuy's estimated 12,300 basic words be defined in Ogden's basic English. For example, *to, give, help* and *work* are considered by Ogden to be basic English words. These may be used to define *assist* as "to give help," or *toil* as "to work." Through computer analysis, groupings of words with related basic definitions could then be identified to provide a basis for developing efficient procedures to teach the semantic side of the language. The vocabulary program envisioned here would first teach the concepts contained in basic English, or test for their knowledge, and then build systematically on this base. The goal, therefore, would be to develop a graded progression of vocabulary words or families of words and their major meanings, where, as much as possible, a word introduced at a given level can be defined in terms of words already introduced. In addition, a systematic plan for introducing inflections, derivatives, compounds, proper nouns, and idioms would have been designed, and cross-checked against other major analyses of reading vocabularies (see, for example, Harris & Jacobson, 1972).

Given Dupuy's findings that the average student at the end of third grade knows about 2,000 basic words, and the average twelfth grader knows about 7,000 basic words, the system would have to teach 550 basic words a year, or twenty-five per school week. The addition of derivatives, compounds, and proper nouns would probably double this requirement but not double the required teaching time. When we recognize that all new learning must be carefully discriminated from prior, related learning, such programs pose no small teaching task. The problem is further complicated by the range of individual differences within any grade between four and twelve. By grade twelve, this range approaches 5,000 basic words (Dupuy, 1974). By the use of carefully structured programs to boost vocabulary competency for low-performing children in the early grades, the number of children in the lower end of this range can be reduced. By structuring school programs to teach basic operations in the various areas of knowledge using basic words, the advanced children would not necessarily be held back.

Given that a basic vocabulary can be defined and graded using empirical and logical criteria, a "free-use" vocabulary could be further defined and used as a guide for preparing texts for upper-grade levels. Free-use words would be those that should be known by at least 80 to 90 percent of the students at a particular grade. Words in a proposed text that are not suitable for a given grade level would be replaced, emphasized in the text, or listed so that the teacher could teach them before beginning a lesson. Now that books can be printed through the use of magnetic tape, a computer program could be used at the level of galley proofs to permit changes or at least provide a supplemental vocabulary listing. The goal would be to furnish text systems that progressively build a knowledge of basic vocabulary throughout the school years. With statements of goals and "free-use rules," all current texts could immediately be analyzed by the author and publisher to provide a vocabulary-building supplement that any teacher could use. Finally, the analysis could be used to produce vocabulary-concept programs by grade levels that could be components in the teaching of reading comprehension. This could be especially important for those children whose language training at home has been insufficient. Such programs, moreover, would also have considerable use in preparing handicapped children for mainstreaming and could take a variety of forms. Perhaps the lower-level programs would resemble the current Direct Instruction programs, whereas middle-level programs would utilize more self-instructional devices such as programmed reading or language masters, and advanced programs would be taught within content areas but coordinated across areas and levels.

Conclusions

A technology exists to achieve the educational goals of the War on Poverty. The Direct Instruction Model has demonstrated that children from low-income homes can be taught at a rate sufficient to bring them up on most achievement measures to national norms by the end of third grade. The model has been most effective in specifying objectives that can be taught as general-case strategies for decoding in reading, solving math problems, and making logical inferences. The model has also been more effective in expanding vocabulary knowledge and other comprehension skills than other models studied by Follow Through. The model, however, did fall somewhat short of its goals to reach national norms in the comprehension area. Our analysis leads to the conclusion that educators have failed to systematically teach words and their referents—among the most important building blocks for intelligent functioning. The DISTAR language and reading programs provide a basis for improvement in this area but do not go far enough. Children coming from home backgrounds that fail to provide adequate training for the continuous growth of vocabulary and concepts are likely to continue to fall behind in public schools. Even after four years of intensive effort, children taught in the Direct Instruction Model are far short of an average high-school senior's vocabulary—a vocabulary that is presumed by most fourth-grade texts. The data on our fifth and sixth graders strongly imply that the schools fail to build skills toward this goal. One might conclude that this is simply more evidence of the failure of compensatory education. When viewed from a different perspective, however, the data point to a failure of school programs to accomplish their assigned roles.

Advocates of compensatory education assumed that all learning problems would be solved by finding the critical stage where some magic could be applied to fertilize cognition. The Follow Through data suggest that a magical solution is unlikely. Massive restructuring of school systems is required. As schools are presently constituted, there is no way that low-performing children can be adequately prepared for the vocabulary they will encounter by the fourth grade. Clearly, the first step toward improving this situation is to recognize that language learning does not end by the third grade. Once this is understood, programs can then be engineered to teach vocabulary-concept knowledge in a systematic way throughout the school years. These programs can also accelerate the learning of logical operations through general-case teaching. Research has shown the job can be done with preschool children, with children in kindergarten through third grade, and with older children in remedial programs. If approached systematically, this job can be done for all.

Reference Notes

1. Haney, W. *Analysis of previous Follow Through national evaluation reports* (Draft Report). Cambridge, Mass.: The Huron Institute, 1976.
2. Egbert, R. *Planned variation in Follow Through.* Paper presented to The Brookings Institution Panel on Social Experimentation, Washington, D.C., April 1973.
3. Engelmann, S., & Becker, W. C. *Forward from basics—the case for direct instruction.* In preparation.
4. Becker, W. C. *Direct instruction implementation manuals* (Follow Through Project). Unpublished manuscript, University of Oregon, 1977.
5. Becker, W. C., & Engelmann, S. *Analysis of achievement data on six cohorts of low income children from 20 school districts in the University of Oregon Direct Instruction Follow Through Model* (Follow Through Project, Technical Report #76–1). Unpublished manuscript, University of Oregon, 1976.
6. Tucker, E. *The Follow Through planned variation experiment.* Paper presented at the meeting of the American Educational Research Association, New York, April 1977.
7. Rosenshine, B. *Academic engaged time, content covered and direct instruction.* Paper presented to the American Educational Research Association, New York, April 1977.
8. Engelmann, S., & Carnine, D. W. *Analysis and psychology of instructional design* (tentative title). In preparation.
9. Carroll, J. B. *Learning from verbal discourse in educational media: A review of the literature.* Princeton, N.J.: Educational Testing Service, 1971. (ETS RM 71–61).
10. Dixon, R., & Becker, W. C. *A proposal for the analysis of a basic vocabulary to facilitate instruction in the language arts.* Unpublished manuscript, University of Oregon, 1977.

References

Abt Associates. *Education as experimentation: A planned variation model* (Vol. III). Cambridge, Mass.: Abt Associates, 1976.

Abt Associates. *Education as experimentation: A planned variation model* (Vol. IV). Cambridge, Mass.: Abt Associates, 1977.

Becker, W. C., & Engelmann, S. The direct instruction model. In R. Rhine (Ed.), *Encouraging change in America's schools: A decade of experimentation.* New York: Academic Press, in press.

Becker, W. C., & Engelmann, S. *Teaching 3: Evaluation of instruction.* Chicago: Science Research Associates, 1976.

Becker, W. C., Engelmann, S., & Thomas, D. R. *Teaching: A course in applied psychology.* Chicago: Science Research Associates, 1971.

Becker, W. C., Engelmann, S., & Thomas, D. R. *Teaching 1: Classroom management.* Chicago: Science Research Associates, 1975. (a)

Becker, W. C., Engelmann, S., & Thomas, D. R. *Teaching 2: Cognitive learning and instruction.* Chicago: Science Research Associates, 1975. (b)

Brophy,, J. E., & Evertson, C. N. *Process-product correlations in the Texas teacher effective-*

ness study. Final report. Austin, Texas: University of Texas, 1974. (ERIC Document Reproduction Service No. ED 013 371)

Brophy, J. E., & Evertson, C. N. *Learning from teaching.* Boston: Allyn & Bacon, 1976.

Carnine, D. W. Phonics versus look-say: transfer to new words. *Reading Teacher,* 1977, **30,** 636–640.

Chall, J. S. Readability: An appraisal of research and application. *Bureau of Educational Research Monographs,* 1958, 34. Columbus, Ohio: Ohio State University.

Chall, J. S. *Learning to read: The great debate.* New York: McGraw-Hill, 1967.

Clark, C. M., Gage, N. L., Marx, R. W., Peterson, P. L., Stayrook, N. G., & Winne, P. H. *A factorially designed experiment on teacher structuring, soliciting, and reacting. Final Report.* Stanford, Calif.: Center for Research and Development in Teaching, 1976. (ERIC Document Reproduction Service No. ED 134 591)

Coleman, J. S. Methods and results in the IEA studies of effects of school on learning. *Review of Educational Research,* 1975, 45, 335–386.

Comptroller General Report to the Congress. *Assessment of reading activities funded under the federal program of aid for educationally deprived children.* Washington, D.C.: U.S. Office of Education, December, 1975.

Dixon, R. *Morphographic Spelling Program.* Eugene, Ore.: E-B Press, 1976.

Dupuy, H. F. *The rationale, development, and standardization of a basic word vocabulary test.* Washington, D.C.: U.S. Government Printing Office, 1974. (DHEW Publication No. [HRA] 74–1334).

Engelmann, S. *Conceptual learning.* San Rafael, Calif.: Dimensions Publishing, 1969.

Engelmann, S. *Your child can succeed.* New York: Simon and Schuster, 1975.

Freeberg, N. E., & Payne, E. Parental influence on cognitive development in early childhood: A review. *Child Development,* 1967, **38,** 65–87.

Gamel, N. N., Tallmadge, G. K., Wood, C. T., & Blinkley, J. L. *State ESEA Title I Reports: Review and analysis of past reports, and development of a model reporting system and format* (Report UR-294). Bethesda, Md.: Research Management Corporation, 1975. (ERIC Document Reproduction Service No. ED 118 684)

Glass, G. V. Problems in implementing the Stull Act. In N. L. Gage (Ed.), *Mandated evaluation of education: A conference on California's Stull Act.* Stanford, Calif.: Stanford Center for Research and Development in Teaching, 1973. (Distributed by Capital Publications, Educational Resources Division, Washington, D.C., 1974)

Glass, G. V., & others. *Data analysis of the 1968–1969 survey of compensatory education (Title I).* Washington, D.C.: U.S. Office of Education, Bureau of Elementary and Secondary Education, August 1970. (ERIC Document Reproduction Service No. ED 057 146)

Harris, A. J., & Jacobson, M. D. *Basic elementary reading vocabularies.* New York: Macmillan, 1972.

Havighurst, R. J. Poverty sub-cultures—The faces of rural poverty. In *Education for the culturally disadvantaged* (Proceedings of the National Conference on educational objectives for the culturally disadvantaged). Hot Springs, Arkansas: South Central Region Educational Laboratory, September 1967. (ERIC Document Reproduction Service No. ED 024 735)

Hawkridge, D. G., Chalupsky, A. B., & Roberts, A. O. H. *A study of selected exemplary programs for the education of disadvantaged children* (Pts. 1 and 2). Palo Alto, Calif.: American Institute for Research in the Behavioral Sciences, September 1968.

Horst, D. P., Tallmadge, G. K., & Wood, C. T. *A practical guide to measuring project impact on student achievement* (Monograph No. 1 on Evaluation in Education). Washington, D.C.: U.S. Government Printing Office, 1975.

McDaniels, G. Follow Through yields new evidence of school effects. *Education Daily,* March 20, 1975, p. 5.

McLaughlin, M. W. *Evaluation and reform.* Cambridge, Mass.: Ballinger, 1975.

Miller, G. A., & Johnson-Laird, P. N. *Language and perception.* Cambridge, Mass.: Belknap Press of Harvard University Press, 1976.

Miner, J. B. *Intelligence in the United States.* New York: Springer, 1957.

Ogden, C. K. *The basic words: A detailed account of uses.* London: Kegan Paul, 1932.

Piaget, J., & Inhelder, B. *The child's conception of space.* London: Routledge & Kegan Paul, 1956.

Rivlin, A. M., & Timpane, P. M. *Planned variation in education.* Washington, D.C.: The Brookings Institution, 1975.

Rosenshine, B. Classroom instruction. In N. L. Gage (Ed.), *The psychology of teaching methods* (75th NSSE Yearbook). Chicago: University of Chicago Press, 1976.

Rosenshine, B. V., & Berliner, D.C. Academic engaged time. *British Journal of Teacher Education,* 1978, 4, 3–16.

Soar, R. S. *Follow Through classroom process measurement and pupil growth (1970–71). Final report.* Gainesville, Fla.: College of Education, University of Florida, 1973. (ERIC Document Reproduction Service No. ED 113 288)

Stallings, J. A. Implementation and child effects of teaching practices in Follow Through classrooms. *Monographs of the Society for Research in Child Development,* 1975, **40,** (7–8, Serial No. 163).

Stallings, J. A., & Kaskowitz, D. H. *Follow Through classroom observation evaluation (1972–73).* Menlo Park, Calif.: Stanford Research Institute, 1974.

Terhune, K. W. A review of the actual and expected consequences of family size (Colspan Report No. DP-5333-G-1, 1974). Washington, D.C.: U.S. Government Printing Office, 1974.

Thorndike, E. L., & Lorge, I. *The teacher's word book of 30,000 words.* New York: Bureau of Publications, Teachers College, Columbia University, 1944.

United States Office of Education. *Education of the disadvantaged: An evaluation report on Title I, Elementary and Secondary Education Act of 1965, Fiscal Year 1968.* Washington, D.C.: U.S. Office of Education, Bureau of Elementary and Secondary Education, 1969.

United States Office of Education. *Annual evaluation report on programs administered by the U.S. Office of Education, FY 1975.* Washington, D.C.: Capital Publications, Educational Resources Division, 1976.

Wittgenstein, L. *Philosophical investigations* (2nd ed.). New York: Macmillan, 1958.

An Interactionist Approach to Advancing Literacy

NAN ELSASSER
VERA P. JOHN-STEINER
The University of New Mexico

In this paper Nan Elsasser and Vera John-Steiner raise the question of how writing and composition skills, often neglected aspects of literacy programs, can best be developed. The authors suggest that instruction in writing must be directed at more than rules of grammar. They maintain that "poor writing" is connected to certain cognitive states and social conditions. Drawing on the work of Paulo Freire and Lev Vygotsky, the authors specify the nature of those states and conditions, the interrelationships between them, and the transformations that must occur if fluent writing is to be achieved. Using examples from a variety of countries, the authors demonstrate the close connection among educational, political, social, and cognitive factors. In the final section the authors illustrate their instructional principles and strategies in a description of an experimental university composition course.

Today millions of people throughout the world who have historically been excluded from institutions which control their lives are claiming their right to an education. Central to their assertion is the recognition that oral communication is inadequate to meet the requirements of the modern world and that written communication is necessary for social and economic well-being. Because of their demands, teachers are now more frequently confronted with students who demonstrate competence in oral communication but who produce written work that is often incoherent. The history of the last decades shows that traditional approaches to teaching writing do not work. As a result educators are being forced to look beyond the age-old debates centered on motor skills and "good" grammar and to raise more significant and pertinent questions concerning literacy. For example, the first issue of *Basic Writing*, a journal devoted to developing theory and strategies to help

We would like to thank Kyle Fiore and Ellen Souberman who provided invaluable editorial assistance; Roberta Benecke who typed the manuscript under the most adverse conditions, and James Sledd, Gil Fernandes, and William Brown for various kinds of critical support and suggestions.

Harvard Educational Review   Vol. 47   No. 3   August 1977, 355–369

students master basic writing skills, addressed itself to these questions: "How do we teach [the student] to judge the degree of common ground he can assume? how far he must go in spelling out his meanings in detail? how many cues of place, sequence and reference he must build in?" (D'Eloia, 1976, p. 11).

Answers to these questions are basic to a theory of written speech, but another set of questions must be answered first—questions regarding the cognitive and social dynamics that produce incoherent writing. In the works of L. S. Vygotsky and Paulo Freire we have found a set of theoretical assumptions from which to develop an analysis of these issues. We believe these works are critical to an understanding of the mental and social processes involved in producing accomplished writing. In addition, they provide the bases of strategies designed to aid learners by expanding their awareness and control of these processes.

Each of these theorists conceived of the use of words both as an historically shaped process and as one which in this century has become increasingly necessary for more and more people. In *Thought and Language* (1934/1962) Vygotsky describes the developmental course of language and the different phases in the interweaving of language and thought. A central theme of his analysis is the concept of internalization: children engaged in the process of acquiring language are viewed as active learners able to unite the diverse strands of their experience to form critical, human consciousnesses. Vygotsky's theory is interactionist in its assumptions and relies upon dialectical concepts as essential tools for analysis of human development. Particularly significant for our theory of the advancement of literacy is Vygotsky's concept of the multiple transformations required to "unfold" inner speech. In the course of their development, young speakers engage in meaningful interactions with members of their community; through this interaction, telegrammatic inner language unfolds to become the basis of competent oral communication.

As we will describe later, a different and more complex set of transformations is necessary to attain competence in written communication. Yet most people have very limited opportunities to develop personally and socially relevant written communication skills. Lacking these opportunities, it is unrealistic to expect that learners will be motivated to perfect their skills beyond the most elementary levels of literacy. However, rapid social changes during the twentieth century, including the rise of technology and an urban style of life, have created a need for more widespread literacy. This combination of social need and lack of individual motivation calls for the development of powerful teaching strategies to advance the rudimentary writing skills of students who spend a limited time in classrooms.

Although many attempts have been made to provide literacy programs for populations previously excluded from their countries' economic and educational institutions, most of these attempts have failed. In our opinion, this lack of success has been due in part to the absence of a meaningful working analysis of the social realities of poverty and rural life.[1] To meet this need, Paulo Freire has developed pro-

---

1 The failure of such programs also stems from their sociohistorical contexts. A student's sense of personal power and control emerges largely as a result of the increasing movement of his or

grams based upon his political understanding of and sensitivity to living conditions that give individuals a profound sense of powerlessness.

In many oppressive societies poor people respond to their feeling of powerlessness through silent forms of resistance (Freire, 1973).[2] One commentator has noted that poor people practice silence "because they have been forced by circumstances to reject as dangerous a 'thrusting' orientation to life" (Greenberg, 1969, p. 79). Children are taught that "silence is safest, so volunteer nothing; that the teacher is the state and tell them only what they want to hear; that the law and learning are white man's law and learning" (Cobb, 1965, p. 106). This silent opposition, the result of their apparent inability to intervene and transform their reality, is often misinterpreted by people who have not been subjected to such oppression. Frustrated, impatient educators who observe this silence often conclude that poor people do not care about the education of their children. Educators and social scientists fail to consider that oppressed peoples have developed their stances toward dominant social groups in response to particular historical experiences.

The silence through which poor people communicate with strangers and officials contrasts sharply with the intensity of daily verbal communication among community people. Labov, in particular, has described this contrast and its educational implication for young black children in urban ghettoes (Labov, 1972, pp. 201–240). These latter exchanges take place within a shared life context that makes certain kinds of verbal elaborations and written explanations unnecessary. Anyone who has ever asked for directions in an isolated rural community has probably experienced bewilderment similar to that of Polly Greenberg, an activist educator working in Mississippi. Greenberg recounts her misadventures in trying for the third time to locate a day-care center of the Child Development Group of Mississippi:

> The directions were "turn right at the puddle"—but it had dried up—"turn left at the dairy farm"—it was a weathered heap of grayboards without visible cows and I didn't know it was a dairy farm—"go a ways"—it was ten miles—"and left at the high embankment where the hogs are"—the whole road was beautiful, high, wild, vine-swarming embankments and the hogs weren't there that day. (Greenberg, 1969, p. 241)

According to Freire's analysis, it is very difficult to sustain dialogues with people who are not members of one's own social and economic community. True communication demands equality between speakers, and this often requires an alteration in current social relationships. Similarly, the increasing urgency with which oppressed peoples are now claiming the right and the need to be taught more complex literacy skills reflects a change in their perception, if not the reality, of their social roles

---

her social group towards self-determination. In the absence of such movement educational intervention is most often futile.

[2] Freire calls this **resistance** "the culture of silence" by which he means the form of passive protest used by the oppressed when confronting individuals of the oppressing classes. Freire's sense of the term is not to be confused with the idea as it is used by verbal deprivationists who believe that oppressed peoples, owing to some inner shortcomings—either cultural or psychological or genetic—do not possess linguistic skills at any but the most minimal level.

and status. Educators genuinely interested in making communication skills available to all members of a society must understand the educational impact of such social transformations.

Turning Thoughts Inside Out

Mastery of written communication requires a difficult but critical shift in the consciousness of the learner, a shift of attention from an immediate audience that shares the learner's experiences and frame of reference to a larger, abstract, and unfamiliar audience. This necessary change in perspective is illustrated in *Letter to a Teacher* by the Schoolboys of Barbiana (1970). The authors decided to footnote all references to people, places, and institutions that might be unfamiliar to readers. However, they did not supply a footnote for Don Borghi, a local priest. When one of the English translators asked the young men why, they replied, "But everyone knows Don Borghi!" (p. 86).

We have found in Vygotsky's theory of thought and language, specifically in his examination of inner speech and its elaboration into written speech, a powerful explanation of why students' writings are often context-bound. He argues that to communicate well in writing a person must unfold and elaborate for an unknown audience an idea which may very well be represented in her or his mind by a single word or short phrase. To write, one must proceed from the "maximally compact inner speech through which experiences are stored to the maximally detailed written speech requiring what might be called deliberate semantics—deliberate structuring of the web of meaning" (Vygotsky, 1934/1962, p. 100). The mastery of such transformations is determined by the internal cognitive processes from which writing derives and the social context in which it is produced.

Vygotsky recognizes written speech as "a separate linguistic function, differing from oral speech in both structure and mode of functioning" (Vygotsky, 1934/1962, p. 98). The key difference between these two forms of communication is the high level of abstraction and elaboration required for minimally comprehensible written speech. The audience for writing most likely does not share the writer's physical or emotional context and, therefore, cannot provide any immediate feedback about the success of the communication effort. The writer lacks the immediate clues of audience response—facial expressions, sounds, pitch, and intonation—all of which are characteristic of oral dialogue. Furthermore, written communication is a system of second-order symbolism: signs replace the sounds of words, which, in turn, are signs for objects and relations present in the real world (Vygotsky, 1978). In oral speech every sentence is prompted by an immediate, obvious motive; in the written monologue "the motives are more abstract, more intellectualized, further removed from immediate needs" (Vygotsky, 1934/1962, p. 99).

For our purpose the most exciting and significant part of Vygotsky's theory of writing is his description of the internal processes that characterize the production of the written word. Vygotsky says that the original mental source of writing is "inner speech," which evolves from a child's egocentric speech and is further abbreviated and personalized. Vygotsky distinguishes four features of inner speech, which is the language of self-direction and intrapersonal communication. One feature is *heavy predication*. Because the speaker always knows the subject of thought, the referent is likely to be either missing completely or vaguely developed. In the following description of a movie, a junior-high-school student has directly transferred inner speech to paper: "He was talking trash. Boy was triing to tell him to get away from her. He said do you want a knuckles sinbwich. He say I am waiting for a chile burger. Then he wint to a liquor store. . . ."[3] *Semantic short cuts* appear because "a single word is so saturated with sense that many words would be required to explain it in external speech" (Vygotsky, 1934/1962, p. 148). Effective written communication requires the transformation of the predicative idiomatic structure of inner speech into syntactically and semantically elaborated forms.[4] When this cognitive act fails to occur, writing may look like the two student samples below:

> The many advantages and disadvantages of inflation and desire to see some of the Northern Colorado, the rush hour, Nursing School at UNM, and tutoring is a big step to want a student to attend UNM or try a smaller college where the population is lower in New Mexico, or a college with more educational advancement.

> Well, I agree with the electricity that people are using more of it. But I think people are overdoing how they should use less energy. They don't think electric is just for fun using it but it's hard to get it.

In *agglutination*, according to Vygotsky, "several words are merged into one word, and the new word not only expresses a rather complex idea but designates all the separate elements contained in that idea." This may be what is occurring when words like *importation, undevplored* (undeveloped and explored) or *bazz* (band and jazz)[5] appear in students' writing. The final feature, *the combination and unity of the senses of different words,* is "a process governed by different laws from those governing combinations of meanings. . . . The senses of different words flow into one another—literally 'influence' one another—so that the earlier ones are contained in, and modify, the later one" (Vygotsky, 1934/1962, p. 147).

In his description of inner speech, Vygotsky recognizes that, as in all aspects of human cognition, an individual changes and develops with age and experience. Language is extraordinarily important in the growing cognitive sophistication of children, as well as in their increasing social affectiveness, because language is the means by which children (and adults) systematize their perceptions. Through words human beings formulate generalizations, abstractions, and other forms of mediated thinking. Yet these words, the fragile bridges upon which our thoughts must travel, are sociohistorically determined and therefore shaped, limited, or expanded through individual and collective experience.

---

[3] Courtesy of Dean Brodkey, Director, English Tutorial Program, University of New Mexico. This example and the two following are from students enrolled in his program.

[4] Throughout this paper we are using the term *elaborated* in Vygotsky's sense as a form of speech (usually written) which is fully deployed and maximally decontextualized because it does not rely on the more usual verbal and visual communicative cues.

[5] These examples are from: The English Tutorial Program, University of New Mexico; D'Eloia, 1976, p. 11; and courtesy of Chris Behling (Note 2), respectively.

For educators the challenge, then, is to develop a teaching methodology that expands this experience, that allows peoples previously excluded to master the written word. As we have shown, Vygotsky and Freire provide a reasonable and fecund explanation of why millions of people have difficulty in learning to write organized prose. But their theories not only provide explanation, they also suggest strategies through which silent speakers can become potent writers. Through Vygotsky's work we can begin to appreciate the nature and complexity of the cognitive changes that are required to expand basic literacy to advanced literacy. And Freire leads us to further understand the dynamics of this intellectual process:

> Knowing, **whatever** its level, is not the act by which a Subject transformed into an object docilely and passively accepts the contents others give or impose on him or her. Knowledge, on the contrary, necessitates the curious presence of Subjects confronted with the world. It requires their transforming action on reality. It demands a constant searching. It implies invention and reinvention. . . . In the learning process the only **person** who really *learns* is s/he who appropriates what is learned, who apprehends and thereby reinvents that learning; s/he who is able to apply the appropriate learning to concrete existential situations. On the other hand, the person who is filled by another with 'content' whose meaning s/he is not aware of, which contradicts his or her way of being in the world, cannot learn because s/he is not challenged. (Freire, 1973, p. 101)

The Historical Basis of Cognitive Change

No one has yet scientifically documented the specific relationship between historical change and the expansion of intellectual and cognitive skills among oppressed peoples. The full analysis of this relationship is a challenge beyond the scope of this paper. However, in the absence of systematic data we have drawn upon the anecdotal accounts of observers in very diverse social settings to examine the historical basis of cognitive change. In addition, we have relied upon Alexander R. Luria's *Cognitive Development: Its Social and Political Implications* (1976), which details some of the psychological changes that took place in the Soviet Union during thirty years of profound social and economic transformation.

Shortly after the Russian Revolution, Vygotsky and his student, Luria, visited remote rural areas of Uzbekistan and Kirghizia. They were impressed by the difference in attitudes between those individuals still personally untouched by the social transformations under way and those who, as a result of experiences on collective farms and in literacy courses, were already becoming "Subjects" in Freire's sense. The people lacking new social and educational experiences were reluctant to enter into dialogue, to participate in discussion as critical beings. When invited to ask the visitors questions about life beyond the village, they responded:

> I can't imagine what to ask about . . . to ask you need knowledge and all we do is hoe weeds in the field.

> I don't know how to obtain knowledge . . . where would I find the questions. For questions you need knowledge. You can ask questions when you have understanding but my head is empty. (Luria, 1976, pp. 137–138)

But the peasants who had participated in the transforming processes of the revolution had many questions about their collective lives:

> How can life be made better? Why is the life of a worker better than that of a peasant? How can I acquire knowledge more readily? Also: Why are city workers more skilled than peasants?

> Well, what could I do to make our kolkhozniks [members of collective farms] better people? ... And then I'm interested in how the world exists, where things come from, how the rich become rich and why the poor are poor. (Luria, 1976, pp. 141–142)

This type of change has been observed in varied contexts where people have begun to transform their sociolinguistic reality—in Chile, Brazil, Guinea-Bissau, Cuba, Mississippi, and the Navajo Nation.[6] When people are convinced that they can shape their social reality and that they are no longer isolated and powerless, they begin to participate in dialogue with a larger world, first orally and then through writing.

This development is not linear; it involves multiple transformations which are complex and dialectical. One transformation brings to individuals a growing sense of control as they change from "objects" into "Subjects." A peasant who had always toiled in the fields expressed the significance of this realization by stating, "I work and in working I transform the world" (Freire, 1973, p. 48). A second transformation reflects the consequences of these altered relationships that are of particular significance in people's cognitive and motivational approaches. Instead of denying their right to engage in dialogue with others as equals, they affirm their responsibility as creators and transformers of their cultures: "Every people has its own culture, and no people has less than others. Our culture is a gift that we bring to you" (Schoolboys of Barbiana, 1970, p. 109). Third, the desire and need for educationally transmitted knowledge become of vital concern as a result of social and personal changes. Although in many instances schools and educational institutions have failed to meet the legitimate aspirations of oppressed groups, parents and students alike recognize that formal education offers skills that they need to transform themselves and their relationships with the dominant society:

> I would like to see the younger Indian people to get a good education so they can compete against the palefaces ... I don't want my kids to go far away to take up a career which won't be of benefit to the Navajos. I prefer that they stay around here ... and become the Indian leaders of tomorrow. (Norris, Note 1, p. 18)

Or, as a young woman replied when asked why she spent her summer vacation attending a "freedom school," "I want to become a part of history also" (Holt, 1965, p. 322).

In spite of the belief, widely held in America, that education in and of itself can transform both people's sense of power and the existing social and economic hier-

---

[6] For information on these programs see: Freire, 1970b and 1973 (Brazil and Chile); Darcy de Oliveira and Darcy de Oliveira, 1976 (Guinea-Bissau); Holt, 1965; Greenberg, 1969 (Mississippi); and Norris, 1970 (Note 1, Ramah, Navajo Nation).

archies, educational intervention without actual social change is, in fact, ineffective. This is particularly true in poor and Third World communities where parents and children have traditionally felt marginal or excluded. Testimonies by a Mississippi subsistence farmer and a Navajo parent illustrate some reactions to such programs:

> They [the school] leaves me out; so I stays out, all the way out. They got no use for me cause they says I ain't got sense. I got no use fer them, neither, cause they ain't got sense enough to treat peoples human. (Greenberg, 1969, p. 100)

> If a student learns in school, then he grows away from what he had learned to value at home. I don't know what parents think about these problems. They're bewildered. (Norris, Note 1, p. 15)

As long as children sense the powerlessness of their community, the impact of educators' best efforts lasts but a short time. Effective education requires the recognition and utilization of the potential in all human beings to participate actively in their own learning. Therefore educational success depends upon a change in the social environment—a break with past alienation and marginality. Thus educational reform is an essential component but not in and of itself a cause of changes in educational engagement.

Although they lived in different times and worked in different hemispheres, Vygotsky and Freire shared approaches that emphasized the crucial intertwining of social and educational change. While Vygotsky focused on the psychological dynamics, Freire concentrated on developing appropriate pedagogical strategies.

The Dialogue in Education

During periods of rapid social change many individuals envision new futures for themselves. However, for people to benefit fully from new possibilities, meaningful educational programs must be created. The ultimate success of these programs depends on two factors. First, mutual respect and understanding must flow between educators and students—between representatives of the larger outside world and the poor with whom they are working. Second, the curriculum must be built upon the "here and now" of the learners (Freire, 1970b). Educational programs that are directed by distant bureaucracies without regard for local interests, resources, or needs produce boredom, frustration, and apathy. In Chile, for example, literacy workers using Freire's methods found that "the peasants became interested in the discussion only when the codification related directly to their felt needs. Any deviation . . . produced silence and indifference" (Freire, 1970b, p. 109).

Freire explains such silence and indifference in this way: "For the act of communication to be successful, there must be accord between the reciprocally communicating Subjects. That is, the verbal expressions of one of the Subjects must be perceptible within a frame of reference that is meaningful to the other Subject" (Freire, 1973, p. 138). This entails more than avoiding or explaining "big" words; often the same word or sign has entirely different meanings to different peoples in different contexts. This type of semantic confusion is illustrated by Greenberg's account, described earlier in this article, of her attempt to locate an isolated day-care center in Mississippi.

Even in classes grounded in the here and now, where there is mutual respect between teachers and students, academic progress is not guaranteed. Chilean educators, for example, found that their adult students were sometimes unable to perceive relationships between their felt needs and the causes of those needs (Freire, 1970b). One explanation for these learning difficulties is found in Luria's work in Uzbekistan and Kirghizia. The tasks Luria and Vygotsky presented included defining abstract concepts—What is the sun? How would you expain it to a blind man? What is freedom?—and generic classification. Nonliterate adults in these communities had great difficulty handling some of these tasks. For example, under the category "tool," peasants often grouped such diverse possessions as a donkey, firewood, an axe, cocoons, and a skull cap. When asked to solve problems requiring logical reasoning skills, individuals had to go beyond the insights gained from practical experience. Decontextualized thought is required to solve such problems and to recognize the connections between felt needs and external conditions. The necessary cognitive operations function within a closed system of logical formulation and are detached from the here and now. But it was just such a mode of cognition with which the peasants Luria studied and many other peoples were unfamiliar.

These kinds of cognitive skills are often both acquired and required in school. From their work in West Africa, Cole and Scribner (1974) have documented the cumulative effects of schooling on the acquisition of logical forms of thought. To interpret their findings, they use Luria's argument that "higher mental functions are complex, organized, *functional* systems" triggered by the task at hand (Luria, 1966, pp. 23ff). As Vygotsky originally described these functional learning systems, both the elements in these systems and their working relationships are formed during the course of an individual's development and are dependent upon the child's social experiences.

Most contemporary education, however, fails to trigger the growth of new functional systems because it follows what Freire has called "the banking concept" which "anesthetizes and inhibits creative power" (Freire, 1970b). The student is only expected to internalize existing knowledge; frequently this means internalizing the objectives of the dominant groups in society. By contrast, meaningful knowledge builds upon the human potential for active learning and is linked to praxis. When teachers and learners are partners in dialogue, a different conception of the processes of knowledge acquisition emerges:

> Insofar as language is impossible without thought and language and thought are impossible without the word to which they refer, the human word is more than vocabulary—it is word-and-action. The cognitive dimensions of the literacy process must include the relationships of men with their world. These relationships are the source of the dialectic between the products men achieve in transforming the words and the conditioning which these products in turn exercise on men. (Freire, 1970a, p. 12)

In no intellectual endeavor are these skills more essential than in the acquisition of mastery of written speech. To move beyond oral speech to writing, students must make an additional leap: they have to acquire a new code which demands further abstraction, semantic expansion, and syntactic elaboration.

Many literacy workers have emphasized the complexities of learning to communicate through an abstract sign system that lacks the cues of oral speech. Freire, however, has demonstrated that literacy can itself be the focal point for transformations of consciousness. When socially significant, "generative" words are employed in literacy programs, they permit learners to reflect on their experience, to critically examine it. In this way teaching adults to read and write is no longer an inconsequential matter of *ba, be, bi, bo, bu* or of memorizing alienated words, but a difficult apprenticeship in "naming the world" (Freire, 1970, p. 11). And such naming is liberating:

> In some areas of Chile undergoing agrarian reform the peasants participating in the literacy programs wrote words with their tools on the dirt roads where they were working. . . . 'These men are sowers of the word' said a sociologist. . . . Indeed, they were not only sowing words, but discussing ideas, and coming to understand their role in the world better and better. (Freire, 1970a, p. 22)

Through this type of education, learners and educators participate together in an ever-widening context; no longer are students limited to their immediate experience. As the circle of communication expands both for teachers and students, the role and structure of the linguistic sign are stretched and transformed. In this process, "it is not merely the content of a word that changes, but the way in which reality is generalized and reflected in a word" (Vygotsky, 1934/1962, pp. 121–122). This transformation, however, does not take place in isolation; as Freire insightfully reminds us: "Just as there is no such thing as an isolated human being there is also no such thing as isolated thinking. Any act of thinking requires a Subject who thinks, an object thought about which mediates the thinking Subjects and the communication between the latter, manifested by linguistic signs" (Freire, 1973, pp. 136–137).

From Literacy to Writing: A Pilot Study

Literacy is valued as a source of other skills and strategies necessary to achieve critical reconstruction of social and personal realities. The aim of the best literacy programs has been, "to challenge the myths of our society, to perceive more clearly its realities and to find alternatives, and, ultimately, new directions for action" (Holt, 1965, p. 103). Basic literacy, however, is not sufficient to achieve these far-reaching ends. People must reach a level of mastery of language skills from which they can critically examine and theoretically elaborate their political and cultural experiences. Simultaneously literacy must be adequately developed so as to provide increasing numbers of women and men with access to technological and vocational skills and information (Darcy de Oliveira & Darcy de Oliveira, 1976).

To date many advanced-literacy programs have lacked the coherence and direction that only a clearly defined and articulated theoretical framework can provide. Some basic-literacy programs, both in the United States and abroad, have been constructed implicitly or explicitly on some of the principles of Vygotsky and Freire. We believe that Freire's methods and Vygotsky's hypotheses concerning the transformation of inner speech to written speech can be not only powerful tools in basic-literacy programs but also a framework for promoting more advanced writing skills.

Using the theories of Freire and Vygotsky, Elsasser, Behling, and others developed a pilot program for advanced literacy within the context of an open-admissions policy at two New Mexico universities.[7] Compared to more usual methods, the results of this approach have been impressive (Behling & Elsasser, Note 2; Elsasser, Note 3). The commonly used anthology-based curricula assume that students' cognitive structures are such that mere exposure to well-formulated literary models is contagious and effective. The behavioristically based curricula, on the other hand, assume that writing skills should be broken down into specialized tasks to be taught individually and sequentially. In contrast to these two approaches, the experimental courses of the Elsasser-Behling pilot study assume an intricate interaction among teachers, learners, and social change which in turn provides a dynamic of continuity and change that enhances the development of written communication. At the beginning of the course teachers explain this interaction to the students in detail. They also discuss Vygotsky's analysis of the elaboration of thoughts to increasingly more decontextualized forms of communication—from intimate verbal speech through more formal verbal communication to fully elaborated written speech. Thus the learners gain an appreciation of both the difficulties and the advantages of expressing their thoughts through the written word. Several specific exercises that built upon the original explanation demonstrate the process of decontextualizing and elaborating one's thoughts. Before students attempt written exposition, Behling and Elsasser's initial exercises offer them an opportunity to become aware of the skills required in writing for an audience that does not share the writer's frame of reference.

The need for one such skill, elaboration, can be illustrated by displaying several pictures that express a similar theme, each with some markedly distinguishable features. The pictures should depict familiar aspects of the learner's environment, such as local landscapes; those used at the University of Albuquerque showed mountains and mesas. Each learner is asked to select one picture and to list a series of words that describe the picture in such a way that other members of the class can easily identify it. In his work Freire observed that simply projecting familiar representations on a board or slide aids learners to "effect an operation basic to the act of knowing: they gain distance from the knowable object . . . the aim of decodification is to arrive at the critical level of knowledge, beginning with the learner's experience of the situation in the 'real' context" (Freire, 1970a, p. 15).

[7] The students involved were predominantly Chicano and Native American. Their communities' powerlessness vis-à-vis the institutions of the larger society is parallel in many ways to the oppression of peasants and workers in other nations.

When learners at the University of Albuquerque shared their lists and attempted to find each other's choices, everyone became more aware of differences among kinds of words. Some words denoting objective, physical attributes (crags, shadows, peaks) were immediately mutually descriptive; other words indicating subjective reactions to the visual stimulus (spacious, inviolate, freedom, proud) were personally descriptive. Through dialogue, especially when different individuals had divergent reactions to the same representation, participants learned what types of further explanation would allow another to comprehend personally descriptive attributes. The need for elaboration in all forms of communication, particularly in writing, thus became apparent.

A second method demonstrates to learners the abbreviated nature of intrapersonal communication and the amount of detail required to flesh it out. This method relies on a common, everyday task like grocery shopping. Each learner is asked to prepare two sets of instructions—one for himself or herself and one for an unknown other person. One's personal set is usually a cryptic, minimal reminder, as these lists from three students demonstrate:

Student A	Student B	Student C
milk	soap	milk
eggs	meat	meat
bread	chips	eggs
soap	beer	potatoes
T.P.	bread	ice cream
		vitamins

The participants discussed what additional kinds of information might be helpful if the task were assigned to someone else: for instance, size, grade, brand, type, price limitations. After the discussion some students immediately prepared elaborated shopping lists which would have been sufficient for any surrogate shopper:

Student A	Student B
Creamland Homogenized Milk, one-half gallon	2 bars of soap
1 dozen grade A large eggs	1 package of hamburger meat
Roman Meal bread—large loaf	1 package of potato chips
Toni soap	2 six-packs of Budweiser
Toilet tissue—individually wrapped Scott	1 loaf of bread

Some simply repeated the lists written for themselves.

In the ensuing conversation students added other hints, including explanations of what foods could be purchased with food stamps and which store was closest to the buyer's home. These comments, in turn, provided the basis for further elaboration suited to an even more removed audience. What if the buyer didn't know about food stamps? Was not familiar with supermarkets? Did not know your neighborhood? In this process students gained a heightened awareness of the need for full description and explanation. Thus an initially simple task stimulated the kind of dialogue that Freire considers crucial to the transformation of the individual's understanding of communicative exchanges. The assignment following this discussion was to write an essay on grocery shopping, incorporating the material discussed.

A third type of exercise used in the program emphasized our everyday reliance in oral speech on verbal and visual cues and aided learners in decontextualizing their explanations. Each member of the class received a geometric design and attempted to give other members of the group verbal instructions for reproducing the design. The instructions had to be sufficiently clear so that, without seeing the original, the listeners could construct reasonable facsimiles of the design. Some students performed facing the class, interacting verbally and visually; others transmitted the instructions with their backs to the group, forfeiting all verbal and visual response. The other students' reproductions immediately indicated the relative adequacy of the explanations. Initially the learners who interacted with their audience performed significantly better than those denied any response, but variations of the task were repeated until every member of the group was cognizant of the audience's needs and what information had to be provided to meet those needs.

This theoretically based program for advanced literacy proceeds sequentially to encourage and guide the unfolding of conceptual knowledge. Through a process of oral discussion in which ideas are continually broadened and fleshed out, constant attention to the types of elaboration required for an unknown other are emphasized. Immediate feedback from both the instructor and the students' peers indicates the success or failure of the written effort. This methodological continuity can lead from the initial tasks to more extended forms of writing traditionally required in composition courses. Among the communicative efforts emphasized within this theoretical framework are definition of an abstract concept, persuasion based on an imagined audience's values, narration of a personal experience, and a letter to an editor. Exercises in written communication can require increasing decontextualization for a removed and impersonal audience. Each assignment can be preceded by a discussion of several topics: what is or is not shared knowledge; the information needs of the intended audience; the particularities of the writer's experience; and the linguistic prejudices of the projected audience. Group discussion of these facts helps learners make their thoughts explicit. It also produces an understanding of the sources of thoughts and the ways in which thoughts change in the process of critical examination and analysis.

Cognitive and Social Dynamics of Writing

The literacy programs we are advocating differ fundamentally from remedial instruction based on behaviorism or nativism. We believe that a more effective approach uses as its basis Vygotsky's interactionist assumption relating the biological substrata of behavior to changing social conditions. He wrote:

> In order to study development in children, one must begin with an understanding of the dialectical unity of two principally different lines (the biological and the

463

cultural); to adequately study this process, then, an experimenter must study both components and the laws which govern their *interlacement* at each stage of a child's development. (Vygotsky, 1978, p. 5)

Vygotsky's "exploration of these interactions is based on a view which regards the human organism as one of great plasticity and the environment as historically and culturally shifting contexts into which children are born and which they, too, eventually will come to change" (John-Steiner & Souberman, 1978, p. 5).

The model we have presented and are committed to developing further evolves from the theories of both Freire and Vygotsky. They argue that language is developed, extended, and modified through the constant interaction of individuals and their social context. Written speech is an act of knowing "the existence of two interrelated contexts. One is the context of authentic dialogue between learners and educators as equally knowing subjects . . . the second is the real, concrete context of facts, the social reality in which men exist" (Freire, 1970a, p. 14). Education designed for active, engaged learners provides an opportunity to understand the nature of the written word, the possibilities for its effective communication, and the difficulties in its production. Above all, such education offers learners a range of strategies which enables them to externalize their thoughts through writing. To develop these strategies we must direct our attention not only to written products but to the cognitive underpinnings of those products. Vygotsky's theory of the structure of language and its transformation into communicatively effective written and oral speech suggests many programmatic possibilities. Short-term improvement in literacy skills can be achieved by motivating students and by reinforcing their written work. But only programs that build upon cognitive processes can help individuals meet the long-term objective of using their literacy as a tool of personal growth and social transformation.

Although most educators now acknowledge the social nature of language, they do not recognize it in their programs. The critical role of dialogue, highlighted by both Freire and Vygotsky, can be put into effect by the conscious and productive reliance upon groups in which learners confront and work through—orally and in writing—issues of significance to their lives.

Reference Notes

1. Norris, R. *A Navajo community develops its own high school curriculum.* Unpublished manuscript, University of New Mexico, Albuquerque, N. M., 1970.
2. Behling, C., & Elsasser, N. *Role taking in writing.* Workshop conducted at the TESOL Convention, New York, March 1976.
3. Elsasser, N. *Turning our thoughts inside out.* Unpublished manuscript, University of New Mexico, Albuquerque, N. M., 1976.

References

Cobb, C. Notes on teaching in Mississippi. In L. Holt (Ed.), *The summer that didn't end.* New York: Morrow, 1965.

Cole, M., & Scribner, S. *Culture and thought.* New York: Wiley, 1974.

Darcy de Oliveira, R., & Darcy de Oliveira, M. *Guinea-Bissau: Reinventing education (Document 11/12).* Geneva: Institute of Cultural Action, 1976.

D'Eloia, S. Teaching standard written English. *Basic Writing,* 1975, 1, 5–14.

Freire, P. *Cultural action for freedom* (Monograph Series No. 1). Cambridge, Mass.: Harvard Educational Review & Center for Study of Development and Social Change, 1970. (a)

Freire, P. *Pedagogy of the oppressed.* New York: Seabury, 1970. (b)

Freire, P. *Education for critical consciousness.* New York: Seabury, 1973.

Greenberg, P. *The devil has slippery shoes.* London: Macmillan, 1969.

Holt, L. (Ed.), *The summer that didn't end.* New York: Morrow, 1965.

John-Steiner, V., & Leacock, L. The structure of failure. In D. Wilkerson (Ed.), *Educating children of the poor.* Westport, Conn.: Mediax, 1979.

John-Steiner, V., & Souberman, E. The dialectic of cognitive growth (Introductory essay). In L. S. Vygotsky [*Mind in society: The development of higher psychological processes*] (M. Cole, V. John-Steiner, S. Scribner, & E. Souberman, Eds.). Cambridge, Mass.: Harvard University Press, 1978.

Labov, W. The logic of nonstandard English. In *Language in the inner city.* Philadelphia: University of Pennsylvania Press, 1972.

Laurence, P. Error's endless train: Why students don't perceive errors. *Basic Writing,* 1975, 1, 23–42.

Luria, A. R. *Cognitive development: Its cultural and social foundations.* Cambridge, Mass.: Harvard University Press, 1976.

Schoolboys of Barbiana. *Letter to a teacher.* New York: Random House, 1970.

Vygotsky, L. S. *Language and thought.* Cambridge, Mass.: M.I.T. Press, 1962. (Originally published, 1934.)

Vygotsky, L. S. [*Mind in society: The development of higher psychological processes*] (M. Cole, V. John-Steiner, S. Scribner, & E. Souberman, Eds.). Cambridge, Mass.: Harvard University Press, 1978.

465

A New Look at the
Literacy Campaign in Cuba

JONATHAN KOZOL
Boston, Massachusetts

In September 1960, Fidel Castro announced to the world that Cuba would, within a year's time, teach more than one million illiterate adult Cubans to read and write. In this article, based on interviews conducted by the author in Cuba and on publications not generally available in the United States, Jonathan Kozol traces the history and documents the success of the Cuban literacy campaign. Outlining the immense logistical and pedagogical challenges of this effort, he describes the recruitment and training of the volunteer teachers and the development of instructional methods that were frankly political in nature and intent. Kozol concludes the article with personal accounts by two young members of the campaign forces that provide a case study of the application of Paulo Friere's educational principles.

My interest in the Cuban literacy struggle began while I was a guest of Ivan Illich at the *Centro Intercultural de Documentación* (CIDOC), outside Cuernavaca, Mexico, in 1969. At that moment, CIDOC was a fascinating crossroads of ideas and people of all possible political positions. Among those who had most recently arrived was the Brazilian scholar, Paulo Freire. Many of Freire's words and recollections—his pedagogic struggles in Brazil, his interest in Chile and in the struggles of poor people in the United States—began to have a tremendous impact on my thinking. One subject, however, Freire's interest in the literacy work that had begun in Cuba during 1961, intrigued me most of all.

Soon after our conversation, I found a document in the library of CIDOC that I had never seen in the United States—its title, "Methods and Means Utilized in Cuba to Eliminate Illiteracy;" its publisher, the Cuban National Commission for UNESCO.[1] I left the center four hours later, convinced that I had discovered the untold education story of our generation.

---

[1] Anna Lorenzetto and Karel Neys, *Methods and Means Utilized in Cuba to Eliminate Illiteracy* (Havana: Cuban National Commission for UNESCO, 1965).

Harvard Educational Review   Vol. 48   No. 3   August 1978, 341–377

After further discussion with Freire, I resolved to visit Cuba, but it was a plan that I was obliged to postpone for seven years. At last, in autumn 1976, after an extensive correspondence with the U.S. State Department and with the Cuban U.N. Mission in New York, I found myself aboard Cubana's Friday evening flight from the Mexico City airport to Havana.

In seeking the story of "the Great Campaign of 1961," I drew, at first, primarily upon the memories of those who had been leaders of that struggle. Soon, however, I was able to discover a number of adults who had been part of the initial teaching force—as well as several people who had learned to read in the course of the campaign and since have followed up with adult-education programs that have led to a university degree. In few cases did the words of the participants conflict with those of government officials. There are a number of reasons for this; one is that the leaders of a genuinely successful and unprecedented struggle of this kind find that it is natural and uncomplex to speak the truth. As David Harman has said:

> There is only one approach that I find credible. It cuts through all the talk of methods, gimmicks, gadgets and the like and gets to the real point. It is very well described in Tolstoy's book, *On Education.* He poses the standard questions and he gives us a good answer: Do we begin with word-sounds or with full-word identifications? The point is: It doesn't matter either way. None of it works, in any case, unless it is allied with something else. That "something else" is what they did in Cuba. It is the promise of a better life for every man and woman in the land—and parallel actions which confirm to the participants that this, indeed, will be the case. This is precisely what UNESCO does not dare to do—and, doubtless, never will. It is the reason why UNESCO's money makes no difference. It is the reason why UNESCO always fails.[2]

On September 26, 1960, Fidel Castro stood before the General Assembly of the United Nations to present his first significant address to an audience which would reach at least five hundred million in almost one-half of the nations of the world.

"In the coming year," said Dr. Castro, in a single paragraph that had been carefully embedded in the high point of his speech, "our people intend to fight the great battle of illiteracy, with the ambitious goal of teaching every single inhabitant of the country to read and write in one year, and with that end in mind, organizations of teachers, students, and workers, that is, the entire people, are [now] preparing themselves, for an intensive campaign. . . . Cuba will be the first country of America which, after a few months, will be able to say it does not have one person who remains illiterate."[3]

Newspapers did not record how various world figures—Adlai Stevenson or Nikita Khrushchev, for example—responded to the words of Dr. Castro, but it is well known that in Cuba, the words of Fidel and, above all, his promise of complete success in less than one year, came as a surprise to many of his coworkers. It is also

---

2 Personal interview with David Harman, Cambridge, Mass., November 1976.

3 For the full text, in translation, of Fidel's four and one-half hour speech to the General Assembly of the United Nations on September 26, 1960, see Martin Kenner and James Petras, eds., *Fidel Castro Speaks* (New York: Grove Press, 1969) pp. 3–36.

true, as a number of leading organizers of the Cuban literacy struggle recollect today, that the promise was generally accepted by a Cuban population which already had been led by Dr. Castro to consider education, along with land reform and health care, as one of the three most serious struggles the revolution had to undertake.

The challenge that faced Cuba was of very great proportions. According to the official (1953) census, 1,032,849 Cuban adults were illiterate in an adult population of slightly more than 4 million. One out of four adults, most of them living in small mountain villages far from town or city, could not read or write.[4] The total teaching force within Cuban classrooms, at the time Batista fled, was 35,000. Moreover, these teachers were in large part obliged to remain in their jobs as teachers of children in the public schools.

The initial question, then, was not one of approach but of manpower. Cuban experts were convinced that no conventional teacher-pupil ratio could bring the reading skills of middle-aged and older *campesinos* ("peasants") even to first- or second-grade level in just eight months. The ideal ratio, they felt, was one to two, although they were prepared to settle for a ratio of one to four at most.[5]

Where could the nation find 250,000 literacy teachers for approximately a million people in the least developed and most isolated sections of Cuba—Las Villas, Oriente, and Piñar Del Rio—provinces where high rates of mass illiteracy together with rugged mountain ranges compounded the task the government then faced? The answer came, as it would many times in the years ahead, from young people. Only by the active intervention of a large proportion of its youth could Cuba possibly achieve its goal. A call went out for student-volunteers. Within a span of sixteen weeks, the call was answered by more than 100,000 boys and girls, almost all between the ages of ten and nineteen.

Exact statistics, compiled by the Literacy Commission at the end of 1961, indicate that 40 percent of all these student-volunteers were ten to fourteen years of age. Forty-seven percent were between fifteen and nineteen and virtually all the rest under thirty. The youngest teacher listed, a child named Elan Menéndez, was eight years old. The oldest student, by way of contrast, was a woman of 106 who had been born and reared as a slave.[6]

In the face of this remarkable response from so many students, the question is frequently asked: why did so many Cuban students answer an appeal for work that could not possibly be easy, safe, or immediately rewarding, but would, on the con-

---

[4] Lorenzetto, *Methods and Means*, p. 15. See later estimate on p. 360 of those who still remained illiterate in January 1961.

[5] Richard Jolly, "The Literacy Campaign and Adult Education," in *Cuba: The Economic and Social Revolution*, ed. Dudley Sears (Westport, Conn.: Greenwood Press, 1964) pp. 194–195 and Lorenzetto, *Methods and Means*, p. 43.

[6] For exact statistics on the ages, provinces of origin, and educational levels of the student-volunteers, see Richard Fagen, *The Transformation of Political Culture in Cuba* (Stanford, Calif.: Stanford University Press, 1969), p. 45. Dr. Lorenzetto calculated a slightly higher percentage of the student-volunteers (52 percent) as being fourteen years old or younger. For her estimate, see *Methods and Means*, p. 45.

trary, require infinite patience and offer only gradual and piecemeal satisfactions? Neither a glib attack nor a romantic slogan will help to clarify such a subtle and complex phenomenon. Only a mindless booster of the Cuban revolution would offer or accept the facile answer: "This is the magic of a socialist revolution!" The answer does unquestionably have to do with revolution—not, however, with a miracle or with guns.

In this article I shall demonstrate some of the most important ways in which the ongoing fact of revolution sparked not just the instigation, but the total sense of ethical exhilaration of the literacy struggle. The question throughout this clarification must remain the same: why, under what political pressure or for what material, ethical, or intellectual reward, did so many people answer the government's appeal? What, if not terror, could have made this program work?

Motivations of the Student-Volunteers

The question cannot be addressed without an awareness of the ongoing military revolution taking place at the same time as the literacy campaign, as well as the fresh memory of the full-scale revolution that had reached its culmination in Havana only twenty-four months before. The manner in which the revolution exercised its impact on the literacy campaign is found not so much in ideological positions as in something that can best be designated "ethical exhilaration," energy exploding like hot anger that had been compressed within a tank for thirty or three hundred years.

During the three decades prior to the revolution, Cuba had stifled under the terror and corruption of Gerado Machado, Grau San Martín, and finally, Fulgencio Batista. The energy that now exploded, at least on the part of those who did not choose the route of exile to the United States, largely transcended ideology at the start. It was, above all else, the sense of freshness, optimism, and bravado that appealed to those who cheered the rebels as they came into Havana hours after General Batista fled the nation in an aircraft loaded with his wealth and jewels.

It was this spirit, first of all, that seems to have been crucial in exciting girls and boys, most of them urban, many middle-class, to share in an adventure which appeared, in certain graphic ways, to carry on the work-and-struggle-in-the-mountains symbolized by Che Guevara and Fidel. I emphasize "exhilaration" as the driving force, rather than a tough, consistent, well-developed Marxist dedication, for two reasons. First, Cuba had not emerged as a Marxist state by the autumn of 1960 or even by the spring of 1961. Honesty, energy, health care for the poor, food for the hungry, and good schools for all were the goals that still remained predominant in public statements and in Fidel's marathon "conversations" with the population of Havana. Second, those who misconceive the driving impulse as Marxist discipline and dogma will not only miss the motivation but will also ignore one of the main results. Socialist conviction was not the major force that prompted so many thousands of young Cubans to spend nearly a year risking their lives, working like fanatics, living on little more than six hours of sleep in the same house and often in the same room as some of the poorest campesinos in the land. Socialism was not the major cause; it was, however, one of the most sweeping consequences.

To forget that Cuba first began its literacy struggle before attempting any consistent ideological consolidation of its population and just prior to the Bay of Pigs attack is to miss the far more serious point that it was the campaign itself which turned 100,000 liberal, altruistic, and utopian kids into a rebel vanguard of committed or, at the very least, incipient socialists. This was true despite the fact that many still were too young to know the full meaning of socialism—and surely too young even to attempt to read the writings of Karl Marx.

There were, to be sure, at least two other factors also working here. One was the charismatic manner of Castro. The theme that "we would not allow Fidel to be embarrassed in the eyes of the whole world" is heard today from many men and women who were only ten or twelve years old in 1961. In addition, a massive organizing effort, led to some degree by Marxists who already formed a close-knit vanguard in the Education Ministry, unquestionably had an impact on the Cuban people's growing consciousness of serious inequities of wealth and poverty. The object of this campaign was to mobilize the kids through "propaganda"—a word used quite openly in Cuba, where it bears none of the connotations that it carries in the United States. It is a term that indicates an open, undisguised, one-sided effort to persuade large numbers of the population to do something which they might not choose to do unless exposed to powerful arguments that attempt to counteract a lifetime of indoctrination from the United States-dominated press, television, and radio. One example of such propaganda was the posters that appeared all over Cuba.

> YOUNG MEN AND WOMEN—
> JOIN THE ARMY OF YOUNG LITERACY WORKERS!
>
> THE HOME OF A FAMILY OF PEASANTS
> WHO CANNOT EITHER READ OR WRITE
> IS WAITING FOR YOU NOW....
> DON'T LET THEM DOWN![7]

What seems, perhaps, the ultimate in the use of propaganda depends upon reiteration of the fact that Cuba had not yet declared itself a socialist society in 1961. Many important United States corporations still had the right to manufacture, sell, and advertise consumer goods. One of these, inevitably, was Coca-Cola. But even here the literacy struggle seems to have been able to make its impact felt. Whether by duress, direct or subtle, or else under an impulse of good will, Coca-Cola ended up by advertising reading skills. Even in the "Year of Education," read the Coca-Cola ad, citizens still need "the pause that refreshes." Use that pause, the

---

[7] Author's on-site visit, the Museum of Literacy, Havana. These and other posters are in the archives of the museum.

advertisement continued, "In Order To Teach A Family How To Read And Write."[8]

It seems quite possible that this is one of the only recent meeting points of capitalist and socialist exhortations conveyed in the same words, presented by the same text, published in the same newspapers, and posted on the same huge signs along the road.

Varadero: The Lantern and the Book

By April 1961 Cuba found itself with more than 100,000 student-volunteers. After exempting those who seemed unable to withstand the rigors of rural life, the final number was 95,777 young men and women. Cuban secondary schools were closed on April 15, elementary schools in early May. The majority of Cuba's 35,000 classroom teachers volunteered to work in the campaign—receiving their ordinary pay for this work. A special program known as "the Attendance Plan" was instituted by the government to offer supervision for the younger children and for those who could not or chose not to participate in the campaign.[9]

Student-volunteers were organized into a military-style brigade, divided into a network of "micro-brigades," named in honor of a Cuban teacher, Conrado Benítez, who was tortured and killed, according to the Cuban Ministry of Education, by counter-revolutionary forces in January 1961, while working in a pilot literacy program. Benítez, a black man, eighteen years old at the time of his death, had been drawn into support of Fidel Castro in the very early years, in the hope that Fidel's revolution represented the first serious chance for abolition of racism in the Caribbean.

According to the Cuban government's display of evidence, Benítez was only one of many volunteers who have been assassinated by anti-Castro forces. In the small Museum of Literacy devoted to commemoration of the origins and progress of the literacy struggle, visitors may study narratives and photographs of several others who encountered the same fate. I know of no other nation where the heroes and heroines of a revolution are so frequently the ones who fought with pen and primer, rather than solely those who fought with guns.[10]

The preparation given to each unit of the youth brigade was concentrated but extremely brief. During the eight- to ten-day training session held at Varadero Beach, an elegant ex-tourist spot about one hour from Havana, *brigadistas* ("stu-

---

[8] Fagen describes the Coca-Cola ad in these words: "With what was undoubtedly unintended irony, an advertisement for the soon-to-disappear Coca-Cola Company showed the lily-white and well-manicured hand of the lady of the household (with a Coke bottle nearby) guiding the darker and rougher hand of a domestic servant through the ABC's." (*Political Culture in Cuba*, p. 57) The version of this story, as well as samples of the posters that were used to mobilize the young, described or shown to me in Cuba, differ a bit from Fagen's versions, but highlight most of the same points.

[9] Fagen, *Political Culture in Cuba*, p. 51; and Lorenzetto, *Method and Means*, p. 39.

[10] For graphic examples of the motivation process, for both learners and teachers, see the following films: Cuban Film Institute (Producer). *Lucia, Part III*, 1969; and *The New School*, 1973. New York: Tricontinental Film Center (Distributor).

dent-volunteers") were given preparation in three basic areas. First, they were given instruction in the use of two essential teaching aids, *Alfabeticemos*, a book of oral readings which would also function as a teacher's manual, and the learner's primer, *Venceremos*. Both are papercover booklets that the government prepared, after extensive research, under the direction of a well-known Cuban educator, Dr. Raúl Gutiérrez.[11] The booklets provided starting points for two to eight months of intensive labor with the adult learners in the villages and farms. One million, five hundred thousand copies of the primer were published, 500,000 of the oral reader.

The second area of preparation had to do with living and working in the distant, largely nonelectrified, and—for almost all the urban kids—entirely unfamiliar setting of the one-room rural farms to which they would be sent to work and live. Each brigadista was assigned two books, a pair of boots, two pairs of socks, an olive-green beret, two pairs of pants, two shirts, a shoulder patch, and a warm blanket. They wore a badge as a reminder of Conrado Benítez, whose tradition they were working to uphold. In many cases, the brigadista wore a chain of beads or of dried seeds similar to those worn by the soldiers of the revolution in the Escambray or the Sierra Maestra.

In addition, each student-volunteer was assigned a hammock, since few host families would be prepared to offer them a bed. They also received a sophisticated, multi-purpose version of a Coleman Lantern. The lantern was essential, not only to provide light by which to travel from house to house on the country roads, but also to provide light by which to carry on the lessons before sunrise, or after sunset, when the farmers and their families had assembled at the kitchen table to learn how to read and write. The traditional lantern, used in Cuba prior to the revolution, was hardly more than a blackened can of kerosene with a small cord extending from a narrow neck. Neither the height nor the intensity of the flame could be adjusted. Apart from its utility, the new lantern was immediately adopted as a symbol of the youth brigades. An anthem was written, and a volume of verse published, both with the title "The Lantern and the Book."

The first brigadistas to arrive at Varadero, approximately 1,000, came on April 15. Two weeks later, there were 7,500 boys and girls in preparation; a few weeks after that, 12,000. When Varadero was in operation at full strength by mid-May, there were nine separate dining rooms, three hundred cooks, and seventy-five large mansions, old estates, and elegant hotels, ready to offer housing to 12,000 pupils at one time. On the day the camp at Varadero was finally closed down, after five months of operation, more than 100,000 pupils had made use of former ballrooms, brothels, cabarets, and gaming tables, in order to gain the skills and to acquire the state of mind to form a virtual "Army of Young Literacy Teachers."[12]

11 *Alfabeticemos: Manual para el alfabetizador* (Havana: National Literacy Commission, Ministry of Education, 1961); and *Venceremos* (Havana: National Literacy Commission, Ministry of Education, 1961). The primer was tested first in photocopy versions during the pilot programs in 1959 and 1960. Its final publication, with a printing of 1,500,000 copies, was completed in the first months of 1961.

12 Fagen, *Political Culture in Cuba*, pp. 43–44.

Heavy emphasis in this period of study, second only to that of the reading preparation itself, was placed on a sensitive process of accommodation to the needs and customs of the poorest people in the land. Special stress was placed upon the brigadista's obligation to share equally in every aspect of the daily work, whether the tasks were those of farmers in the fields or of mothers in the rural homes. The sense of solidarity that was developed by these actions of shared labor in the daytime seems frequently to have become the key to motivation, trust, and perseverance for both the teachers and the learners.

To supplement the rapid-fire preparation given in ten days at Varadero, brigadistas were advised that they would meet in regional sessions, on a weekly basis, with professional educators. On Sunday mornings, as it ultimately worked out, adult teachers met with brigadistas to assist them in the resolution of particularly vexing problems and to help them plan their lessons for the week ahead.

I asked, on several occasions, why there had been so much emphasis—first during the sessions held at Varadero, then in the Sunday morning briefings through the summer and the fall—on the issue of "the-city-and-the-country." Again and again, the point was made that Cuba had been weakened for centuries because of the isolation of the campesinos and the consequent inability of urban students to empathize with the victims of rural poverty and exploitation. One of the explicit objects of the literacy struggle was to build a sense of future solidarity between these two important segments of the Cuban population.

In commenting on this subject, in particular on the need for each half of the nation to discover and to know the other, one of Cuba's oldest educators, Dr. Mier Febles, summarized his feelings to me in the following words:

> The goal of the campaign was always greater than to teach poor people how to read. The dream was to enable those two portions of the population that had been most instrumental in the process of the revolution from the first, to find a common bond, a common spirit, and a common goal. The peasants discovered the word. The students discovered the poor. Together, they all discovered their own *patria*.[13]

Now, as I listen to the tape-recordings of the dialogue in which I frequently engaged with veterans of the year's campaign, I recognize that this campaign, with all its hardships, physical risks, and often very painful loneliness, was nonetheless the seminal moment in their childhood formation as young socialists and active citizens of the newborn nation. No amount of political indoctrination of the kind so often carried out, in tedious and didactic ways, by almost every nation in the modern world, could possibly have generated loyalties, cut off old ties, and forged a consciousness of social justice as did the months these 95,000 Cuban youngsters dedicated to teaching reading to the poorest men and women of the land.

"I could never have known that people lived in such conditions," said one former brigadista, Armando Valdéz, now twenty-nine years old, in the course of conversation in the fall of 1976. "I was the child of an educated, comfortable family. Those months, for me, were like the stories I have heard about conversion to a new

---

[13] Personal interview with Dr. Mier Febles, Havana, September 1976.

religion. It was, for me, the dying of an old life and the start of something absolutely new. I cried, although I had been taught that men must not cry, when I first saw the desperation of those people, people who had so little—*no, they did not have 'so little,' they had nothing!* It was something which at first I could not quite believe.

"I did not need to read of this in Marx, in Lenin, in Martí. I did not need to read of what I saw before my eyes. I wrote my mother and my father. I was only twelve years old. I was excited to be part of something which had never happened in our land before. I wanted so much that we would prove that we could keep the promise that Fidel had made before the world. I did not want it to be said that we would not stand up beside Fidel."[14]

For the participants in the struggle, there remains a note of nostalgia. Others who, for various reasons, were not able to participate in the campaign speak of the fact with deepest disappointment—almost a sense of shame. It is apparent that the campaign was much more than a pedagogic act. It was a moment of political and moral transformation for large numbers of young people who had never before been outside of the small, comfortable circle of their homes.

It is also apparent that there was wide variation in the pedagogic challenges faced by various brigadistas. Some devoted the entire period from May until December to uninterrupted work within one family, often finding it essential to devote four-hour sessions to one person at a time. In other situations, they worked with a mother and grandmother in the morning, proceeded to the fields to help the father and son in their farm labor in the afternoon, and returned again after the sun went down to teach those men to write and read by lantern light. Others were able to complete their work with two or three illiterates in one location in only two or three months, moving on to spend four or five months with another group of people in a town nearby.

Medical services functioned to assist the literacy program on two fronts. Physicians, nurses, and assistants had been mobilized to care for brigadistas in the farthest mountain reaches. This was essential, both to lessen the realistic worries of the parents of young people only ten or twelve years old, and also to alleviate the many physical problems which the brigadistas, unfamiliar with the rural life, inevitably underwent. Doctors also conducted a screening operation to find those in the illiterate population who needed glasses. After the screening process was complete, 177,000 pairs of glasses were distributed and fitted without cost.

In looking back on the passion and the year-long high of the campaign, the present Vice-Minister for Adult Education, Dr. Raúl Ferrer, Vice-Coordinator of the literacy program and the leading personality in adult-education work in Cuba ever since, recalls a conversation with Fidel before the full campaign got under way. "We must do it," said Fidel, "with the whole people—and by a heroic rhythm." Everyone with whom I spoke—in schools, in public buses, in the various bars and little cabarets—expressed the same excitement and the same sense of heroic rhythm that Fidel had first conveyed.

14 Personal interview with Armando Valdez, Havana, September 1976.

Methods and Means: A Search for Active Words

The primer *Venceremos* holds the key to the political approach of Cuban literacy efforts. In the preparation of the primer an organized search was made for "active" words, words associated with emotion, love or longing, ecstasy or rage, among the campesinos and the workers. Using these words as "generative" (charged and connotative) starting points, the technical experts wrote the primer in the form of fifteen lessons, each reiterating basic sounds and themes. Each of the fifteen lessons was presented as a story or discussion of one of the "active" topics and was preceded by a photograph of Cuban life which served to provoke discussion and to clarify the main theme of the chapter.

The photographs included an illustration of an agricultural collective with three farmers briefly resting from their work; two boys waving to a man driving a tractor on his own government-allocated plot of land; children and teenagers planting a young sapling in the midst of an unforested terrain; Cuban fishermen holding up the catch from a day's work for "the cooperative"; a man walking from the doorway of "The People's Store," his arms loaded with heavy bags of food and other produce for his home; a couple standing in the doorway of their own small but attractive house; a mother receiving a child-care lesson from the doctor in a neighborhood prenatal class; a composite photograph of a rifle, farmer's shovel, and the cheerful cover of the primer *Venceremos*—presumably symbolizing victory and solidarity on all three fronts.

In a brief guidebook, *Orientations for the Brigadista,* brigade members were instructed, prior to the lesson itself, to exploit the photographs in order to initiate informal conversation and also to establish the essential sense of equals working in a common cause.[15] "Avoid giving orders!" the teacher was advised. "Say to the pupil 'We are going to work. We are going to study.' Avoid the authoritarian tone. Never forget that the work of learning how to read and write is realized and achieved in common."

Another point, repeatedly emphasized within these guidelines, was stated explicitly during a recent conversation with Raúl Ferrer: "The goal for us was to instruct the brigadista not to try to imitate the condescending manner of the kinds of teachers they had known in public school before the revolution. This was half the job of preparation.

"On the other hand, we did not want a random, affable, but drifting atmosphere to be the substitute for oldtime methods of control. We did not want the kind of aimless atmosphere identified with certain liberal fashions such as Summerhill. We were dealing with poor people, and with people who were not small children but hard-working men and women, thirty, forty, fifty years of age. Then, too, our time was short. We felt that we could not await forever that 'spontaneous moment' of organic curiosity so often elevated to romantic adulation in the literature that we receive from North American and British friends.

"So we were forced to find a new path of our own, firm and clear, but not authori-

---

[15] *Orientaciones para el brigadista* (Havana: Ministry of Education, 1961).

tarian; purposeful, sequential, and well organized for pace but never abusive, never condescending."

In keeping with the point regarding aimlessness and drifting, Dr. Ferrer issued directives for a uniform sequence to be followed in all lessons. "First, reading. Only after that initial step would we ask anyone to write. The goal was, first, to identify each written symbol with the sound it represents. By repetition, and in concord with the teacher, the pupils would master the specific sounds. Then we would ask all pupils to attempt the reading on their own. Once this was done, we would turn to breakdown and analysis of the syllabication.

"The over-all point is that we felt the need to balance the sense of trust and courtesy with strict sequential lessons. If we did not enforce at least this much consistent work, one brigadista could not fill in for another in the case of sudden illness or the like. We also needed to keep track of every learner's progress and attendance: date of the first lesson, date of the last lesson, days when lessons don't take place—and why."[16]

Selections from *The Orientations,* quoted below, carefully provide for each of these points, much as they were laid down by Ferrer:

FIRST STEP: CONVERSATION
Conversation between the brigadista and the pupil in regard to the photograph within the primer . . .
(a) To find out what the pupil knows about the subject of the photo.
(b) To provoke oral expression.
(c) To clarify the concepts.

SECOND STEP: READING
A complete reading of the text (block letters) that appears beside the photo:
(a) First, by the teacher: slowly and clearly.
(b) Second, by the teacher and the pupil at the same time.
(c) Third, by the pupil all alone . . .

THIRD STEP: PRACTICE AND EXERCISE
(a) Sight-recognition of a phrase or sentence that has been selected (Key).
(b) Break-up of that phrase or sentence into syllables.
(c) Examination of each syllable within an exercise.[17]

In addition, brigadistas were advised to keep meticulous diaries of their reactions, emotions, and, particularly, errors, even possible errors, in the course of work in order to share this information with one another.

On the surface, much of this may sound familiar. Teachers at good schools in London, Boston, or New York also are advised to keep a daily journal. The difference lies in the unique respect, almost a sense of awe, which Cuban brigadistas were encouraged to exhibit toward every campesino who showed willingness to learn, as well as in the dialogue which would inevitably result.

In this regard, it is worth observing that the Cuban methods vary drastically, not only from those of the United States, Great Britain, and the West generally, but

16 Personal interview with Dr. Raúl Ferrer, Havana, September 1976.
17 *Orientaciónes,* pp. 2–3.

also from those that have been used in the Soviet Union. Very little in the Cuban style duplicates the stiff approach of Lenin's literacy methods, the North American missionary style and approach devised by Laubach, or the mechanistic methods of UNESCO.[18] The literacy campaign was a Cuban struggle and a Cuban victory in almost all respects.

The primer, as I have said, is divided into fifteen subdivisions. In light of the overt political bias of this method of instruction, the first words and chapters presented to the campesinos are notable. The first word, and also the first chapter title, is a provocative three-letter combination, "O.E.A."—the Spanish-language version of the "O.A.S."—Organization of American States. Since Cuba, by 1961, had already begun to suffer economic isolation as a consequence of actions taken by the O.E.A., farmers who could not obtain replacement parts for antiquated tractors, or other farm equipment, would not react indifferently to these three letters. Cuban educator Abel Prieto, in the course of a conversation with me in 1976, remarked: "It is the only time in history the O.E.A. has ever contributed something of effectiveness to help the poor. They gave us their initials for our primer."[19] The second active word, and second chapter title, is the acronym "INRA,"—the initials of a revolutionary organization, The National Institute of Agrarian Reform, which had just begun the labor of land distribution to the poor.

Subsequent chapters of the primer, each preceded by one of the photographs described above, deal with additional generative themes: "The Cooperatives of the Agrarian Reform," "The Land," "The Cuban Fishermen," "The People's Store." The chapter on "The Land," an early lesson in the book, starts out with three sentences in large print, each standing as a paragraph of its own: "The campesinos now at last are owners of the land. The campesinos cultivate their land. The Cuban land is rich." The lesson on the fishermen begins with similar words: "The fishing cooperative assists the fisherman. The fisherman is not cheated anymore. The fishermen now live a better life."

By the sixth lesson, "The People's Store," sentences are longer and the syntax more complex: "The campesino buys his needs both good and cheap within the people's store. In the people's store there are all kinds of things. The people's store is a cooperative too. We already have more than two thousand people's stores."

Subsequent chapters grow increasingly difficult and also more explicitly political. Chapter Thirteen informs the campesino: "CUBA IS NOT ALONE." It further states: "United we shall overcome aggression. They [that is, the 'foreign interests'] will not be able to stop the revolution." The final chapter of the primer is a verse by Cuban poet Nicolás Guillén. The verse faces a full-page portrait of José Martí. Martí, who died in battle against Spain in 1895, spent much of his life in exile in New York. He produced voluminous works in essay form, polemic, autobiography, and verse. Today in Cuba, he is regarded as the "poet and prophet of the revolution."

---

[18] David Harman discussed the literacy methods of Laubach during our interview, cited above. For a somewhat less acerbic commentary on the work of Laubach, see David Harman, *Community Fundamental Education* (Lexington, Mass.: D. C. Heath, 1974), pp. 48, 65, 67.

[19] Personal interview with Dr. Abel Prieto Morales, Havana, September 1976.

The same themes, words, and syllables also appear once more within the oral reader *Alfabeticemos*. Chapter headings in this book restate the generative themes: "The Land is Ours," "The Right to a Home," "Cuba Had Riches [but] Was Poor," "Workers and Farmers," "War and Peace," "The Abolition of Illiteracy," "The Revolution Converts Barracks Into Schools."

Both of these books appear to have been intricately paced in order to build from single words to basic phrases, then to sentences and simple paragraphs, all continuing to rest on the recognition of initial active words and generative themes. Writing and reading in themselves become the end results, whether the starting themes remain predominant in the learner's mind or not. It is difficult to believe, however, that in the face of so much verbal learning in coordination with so many powerful political beliefs, that many campesinos would be likely, later on, to separate the knowledge of these words from their political and, in this instance, revolutionary implications.

Certain examples offered in the passages above may suggest an approach to literacy that is already identified with the work of Paulo Freire,[20] a Brazilian educator, working from a Christian-Marxist point of view, now in exile in Geneva, but increasingly active in the educational development of several of the newly independent African nations. The Cubans, much like Freire's colleagues in northeast Brazil, not only based their labors on the search for charged and active words, but also insisted upon a dialogical relationship between the teacher and "the one who chooses to be taught." The introduction of a provocative photograph before each lesson also suggests the simple drawings used by Freire's colleagues to initiate the learning process in Brazil.[21]

To the degree that Cuban methods vary from those first used in Brazil, the differences can best be understood by a recognition of the difference in the situations of the two countries. Freire's estimate of forty days of study to achieve a basic literacy skill became almost two hundred days in Cuba. The most obvious reason for the longer period of time required by Cuban educators is that Freire's teachers were adults themselves, not young men and women barely out of grammar school or junior high. It is probably true, as well, that Freire's teachers were much better prepared and were given more continuous supervision. Freire's teachers taught groups that gathered in small villages and towns, whereas the isolated Cuban literacy workers struggled to teach in individual homes using skills gained during their ten-day crash course and from weekly supervision.

Also, the more explicit political nature of the reading matter used in Cuba and the somewhat more directive role assumed by Cuban teachers (for example, the prior selection of a set of active words, rather than their slow discovery, as in Brazil) has to be explained, at least in part, by the embattled posture of the Cuban nation at the same time that the literacy program began. It is no rhetorical exaggeration, in view of the constant attacks by Cuban exiles and the full-scale encoun-

---

20 For the best summary of Paulo Freire's approach to literacy, see his *Pedagogy of the Oppressed* (New York: Seabury Press, 1970).

21 Freire describes in greater detail his methods and practice in Brazil in "Cultural Action for Freedom," *Harvard Educational Review*, 1970, 40, 205–225.

ter at the Bay of Pigs, to say that the Cuban government was literally fighting to survive, while its 95,000 brigadistas headed for the hills to fight another, and perhaps more difficult, battle of their own. It was regarded as essential to the government's defense that isolated campesinos rapidly come to share a common recognition of those undisguised antagonists that Cuba faced. It might perhaps have been left to chance to see how many campesinos struck upon the sound of INRA as an active word. It could not possibly be left to chance, however, to discover if the campesinos would be quick to strike upon an abbreviation like O.E.A.

Thus, although the campesinos in Brazil sooner or later came up with highly political words and phrases wholly on their own, many of which—land, owner, doctor, slum, and hunger—were the same as those that dominate the Cuban texts, Cuba's educators were determined to assume a conscious role in helping to decide which of such words and phrases the campesinos would be likely to learn first. In a state of revolution, as Freire himself has said many times throughout the last ten years, certain things cannot be left to chance.

For all of these apparent differences in both logistics and approach, the similarities between the Cuban struggle and the work of Paulo Freire cannot be ignored. Probably no other nation has applied a method of adult education so similar, in tone and content, to that advocated by Freire and first tested in Brazil. The similarity is no coincidence. Freire and Ferrer are trusted friends. Their views have not been borrowed, each from the other; rather, they have been inspired by a common viewpoint and shared experience. Unlike most other contemporary educators of renown or power, Freire and Ferrer have forged their pedagogic views among the people they set out to teach, close to the soil, living in the villages and homes of the poor, toiling beside the campesinos to win both land and liberation.

War Footing

Many of those who are resolved to find the flaw in Cuba's battle to eradicate illiteracy often draw attention to the military language used by Cuban leaders. Those who point to this aspect of the literacy struggle are not incorrect, although their frequent explanation—future soldiers for bloodthirsty leaders—is absurd in its reduction of a complex syndrome to a single, simplistic goal. The military parallel unquestionably was in many people's minds in 1961. There is also no question but that a certain military fervor, openly avowed by Fidel, helped to fire the passion of the literacy struggle from the start. There were, however, several more tangible reasons for this military tone.

First, as we have seen, the literacy struggle took place amid a formidable military and economic threat from the United States. A seige mentality existed in Cuba from 1959 to 1976. Numerous attacks, many at the cost of human life, made use of staging areas in Florida, Panama, and Nicaragua. The climax came on April 15, 1961, the same day that the literacy campaign officially began, when Cuban exile forces launched an indiscriminate bombing in the region of Havana, resulting in many civilian casualties. Two days later, with the tactical support of United States naval ships and aircraft, piloted by Cubans trained in the United States, 1,200 members of an expeditionary force attempted an invasion at the Bay of Pigs. Although the invasion was almost immediately defeated, the memory—and all that it implied about the intentions of the United States—lingered on.

The murder of young men like Benítez had a similar effect. All of these events had a cumulative impact, manifest in the military style, military uniforms, and military language of the youth brigades. The word "brigade" itself, along with others like "detachment" and "campaign," became standard designations for the literacy struggle. There was an additional reason for the military style. This was the idea of continuity with those who had been members of the revolutionary army from the start; Che, Fidel, and their coworkers in the revolution had dressed in virtually the same clothes as the brigadistas. Each had sought to inculcate in the other the same sense of discipline and self-abnegation. The prevalence of military terms, therefore, was not contrived but was a natural tendency, practical and symbolic at the same time.

The words of Paulo Freire seem particularly appropriate in defining the atmosphere that prevailed from the beginning. "Freedom," Freire has written, "is acquired by conquest, not by gift."[22] The military flavor of the literacy struggle reflects this spirit every bit as much as Che Guevara's military battles of three years before. The students were trained, not to "approach" but to "attack and conquer" both illiteracy and fear among the poor. The mood was militant, not tentative; resolute, not clever; keyed to victory, not keyed to interesting results. The title of the primer was not written in subjunctive or conditional supposition. It was written with declarative determination: "Venceremos" ["We Shall Overcome"]. They did not say "We hope to win" or "We rather think that, with sufficient funds, we might." Instead, they said "We shall." And finally, after very real dangers of defeat, they did.

In mid-summer of 1961 a grave uneasiness swept over the organizers of the literacy struggle. Statistics indicated that the progress that the organizers had expected by this date was nowhere within reach. Although 500,000 Cuban adults were reported to be studying with the brigadistas by the final weeks of June, figures for late August showed that only 119,000 could be listed by their teachers as having successfully completed the requirements of the course. The whole timetable and all expectations of the power even of 95,000 highly motivated volunteers seemed virtually to fall apart.[23]

Government leaders did not take long to respond. The troubling statistics immediately provoked a series of four drastic measures. First, a call went out to factory workers to create a new brigade, *Patria o Muerte*, with the hope of mobilizing 30,000 workers within three days to augment the teaching staff. The workers would receive their ordinary pay while teaching reading to the people in the mountains and on the farms. Nonetheless, a number of factors—reluctance to leave families, unfamiliarity with rural life, the dangers of the countryside, and so forth—proved to be much greater obstacles than the government expected. Twenty-

22 Freire, *Pedagogy*, p. 31.
23 Fagen, *Political Culture in Cuba*, p. 50.

one thousand workers, according to UNESCO, answered the call—less than were needed, less than were requested, but 21,000 more than had been in the teaching force before.[24]

Second, a coalition of revolutionary organizations, chief among them The Federation of Cuban Women and The Committees for the Defense of the Revolution, carried out, at government request, a massive effort at recruitment to convince recalcitrant housewives not to feel ashamed of their illiterate status but to join the learning force. The same groups that carried out recruitment also formed ad hoc brigades of literacy workers. The concept of "The People's Teachers," neighbors teaching neighbors, first enunciated earlier in the year, at last came to fruition.

The vast majority of those who taught as People's Teachers were women. Their students too were predominantly women, since large numbers of illiterate men had been identified in the earlier stages of the screening process, at their place of work or at the agricultural collectives. At this time, women in Cuba were not yet a significant element of the work force. Although a number of Cuban women had played outstanding roles in the urban underground throughout the revolution, the majority remained reluctant, or were forbidden by their husbands, to depart the inner sanctum of the home. Today, after seventeen years of exhortation by Fidel, and many passionate efforts at recruitment by mass and vanguard organizations, women constitute one-third of the entire work force. In education, more than in any other field, women have risen rapidly to high administrative posts. Much of the credit for this change must be attributed to the all-out efforts in the early autumn of 1961.

In a third step, taken by the government in August 1961, the literacy campaign directed all Municipal Education Councils (local school boards) across the nation to assume a power they had not held before—to oversee not only community efforts in every section of their cities, villages, and towns, but also to assume the supervision of all literacy workers, including all the brigadistas, in their jurisdiction.[25] The first step on the part of these highly responsive councils was to break down every local literacy unit into smaller units ("unidades"). Closer observation and more helpful reinforcement became routine.

Finally, in response to the statistics of late August, the government called a national congress to determine whether these measures could turn the tide. With fewer than 120,000 former illiterates having been taught to read, with 800,000 still untaught, and nearly three-fourths of the year already gone, there seemed no option but to reach for still more sweeping tactics. Although not stated in these terms, a highly accelerated plan of operation was agreed upon at the Havana conference.

---

[24] The figure of 21,000 is disputed in the UNESCO text, with the impression given in at least one passage that a realistic figure for the worker-volunteers was closer to 13,000 because of attrition or inaccurate figures at the start. Whichever number we accept, the figures appear to represent a clearcut disappointment from the point of view of those in Cuba who had been accustomed to unqualified and exuberant responses to government appeals. According to Ferrer in September 1976, the figures are not so disturbing as they first appear. Thousands of workers, although they did not leave their homes, nonetheless increased the numbers of the "People's Teachers."

[25] Fagen, *Political Culture in Cuba*, pp. 48–49.

A sense of operating on a "war footing" now became explicit in all areas of the campaign.

First, beginning on September 18, what had once been voluntary service for all classroom teachers ceased to be a matter of choice. A teachers' draft began that day, bringing into the teaching force all those teachers who had not yet volunteered.[26] One direct result was to postpone the start of school at every level from early September until the beginning of January. The government's willingness to take this drastic step not only shows evidence of its single-minded concentration on the literacy goal, but also demonstrates that, even in the midst of sabotage and lack of total solidarity within the Left itself in Cuba's government at that time, organizers felt sufficient popular support to launch a policy that might well have infuriated thousands of mothers and fathers of young children.[27]

Second, a new idea, "Acceleration Camps," was put into operation in all parts of the nation. Wherever a large number of people had fallen behind in their study of the primer, a team of expert educators, brigadistas, and experienced People's Teachers would group together to operate a camp in which all of their students—workers, farmers, older neighbors, men and women—would spend whole days in academic labor. Community organizers, neighbors, or friends would take the students' places on the farm, or, if they were urban workers, in their place of work. The Acceleration Camps, the first of which was set up in Havana Province, operated on a full-day basis, with several teachers working with a single group of pupils at the same time. Throughout the nation, groups of organized workers, Municipal Education Councils, Committees for Defense of the Revolution, set up similar camps on a crash basis.

Third, using car pools or bus service, thousands of the People's Teachers, once they had taught their urban neighbors how to read and write, then went out into nearby rural areas in order to recruit and instruct large numbers of recalcitrant campesinos whom the brigadistas had not yet been able to identify, motivate, and teach.

Finally, one of the most effective of all step-up tactics was put into operation: "Study Coaches," a new brand of pedagogic personnel, suddenly appeared. There were no more than several hundred; but their expertise, inventive energy, and intensive training rendered them dynamic catalysts wherever they appeared. The government sent them where they were most desperately needed, to isolated regions where the brigadistas had encountered resistance from pupils or where their

---

[26] According to my conversation with Ferrer in September 1976, there were 45,000 certified teachers in Cuba at the time Batista fell, of whom 10,000 had no class assignments. If this figure (one Jolly uses as well) is relied upon, then the apparent goal of the September "teachers' draft" was to bring into the literacy struggle those 10,000 "missing teachers" who had not been part of the first wave of 35,000 volunteers. (The remaining 10,000 were not, of course, identical with those 10,000 teachers who did not have jobs. Indeed, many of those teachers who had been without jobs prior to the revolution proved, as a consequence, to be more sympathetic to the revolution and were frequently the first to answer the government appeals.)

[27] The residual conflicts in Cuba's post-revolutionary Left are discussed by Fagen, *Political Culture in Cuba*, pp. 104–106.

own inadequacies as teen-age teachers created problems which the Study Coaches frequently were able to resolve.[28]

By late October, virtually the entire nation had been mobilized. Even on fishing ships at sea, the heightened rhythm of the literacy battle was reflected in the presence of young teachers to provide instruction after the day's work had been done. A slogan, seen on posters everywhere, sums up the same theme: "Those who know, teach. Those who don't, learn." Television and radio exhortations hammered home the theme: "Every Cuban a teacher, every house a school."

From the beginning of the literacy struggle, instructors were required to begin each session with a new pupil by filling out a questionnaire which explored the working career (present job, place of work, hours of work) of the new learner. Specific details about the learner's years of formal education and level of reading ability were sought. "Why couldn't you learn before?" the questionnaire inquired. The instructor was also asked to record the pupil's progress by administering "Initial," "Intermediate," and "Final" tests. The tests and questionnaires performed a dual function. First they gave all needed "catch-up" information to late-arriving brigadistas who came to take the place of ones who had become ill or, for some other reason, had been forced to leave the job undone; and second, they provided Ferrer and his coworkers some early guidelines for revision of their teaching plans. This information was used to lay the groundwork for the energetic Follow-Up programs that Ferrer and others, with great care and with a shrewd sophistication virtually unprecedented in all previous programs of this kind, had already started to conceive.[29]

More important to the government than the series of three tests, and certainly a good deal more poetic, was one final bit of evidence that every person who had learned to read and write was given opportunity to offer. This final evidence was a letter, written by the newly literate person to Fidel Castro in order to offer him the visible results of those many nights and days of work. In the Museum of Literacy, 700,000 "letters to Fidel" have been preserved. The letters provide a record of success which no statistical evidence could ever quite convey.

Finca el Naranjal
November 12, 1961
Year of Education

Dr. Fidel Castro Ruz

Dear Comrade:

I write this to let you know that now I know how to read and write thanks to our Socialist and democratic Revolution. That's why I'm writing to you, so that you can see with your own eyes. I take leave with a firm Revolutionary and democratic salute.

---

[28] Lorenzetto, *Methods and Means*, pp. 47–48.

[29] These documents of the literacy struggle can be found in Lorenzetto, *Methods and Means*, pp. 47–48.

I used to be illiterate.
Patria o Muerte
Teaching, we shall triumph.

Felicia Carpio Barcelo
(My literacy worker is Wilfreydo Neyra R.)[30]

November 14, 1961
Year of Education

Comrade Fidel Castro:
I am very thankful because I know how to write and read. I would like you to send me the Follow-Up books to improve my knowledge more in the reading and in the writing. To be an educated people is to be free.

Your comrade,
Domingo Franco Mesa
Venceremos![31]

By late autumn, these step-up efforts finally began to show results. Whereas the completion figure for final examinations had been not quite 120,000 by late August, the figure for November 1 was 354,000. After an additional six weeks, the total of those who had completed the exam was more than 700,000.[32] Once the last illiterate member of a family had passed the third and last examination and had completed his or her handwritten letter to Fidel, a flag went up above the doorway of that house: *Territorio Libre de Analfabetismo* ("Territory Free from Illiteracy"). The flag, often made of paper, was almost entirely red, with a small book open to the letter "A" in the upper left-hand corner. When the last house in a town, village, or neighborhood within a major city had raised that flag above the door, then the town or neighborhood itself could fly the flag. A friendly sense of competition soon evolved among the provinces of Cuba, in order to know which one could claim the credit for having the first town, city, or neighborhood without a single illiterate man or woman.

The first Cuban town to win the right to fly the flag was a village in Havana Province called Melena del Sur. The village was declared Territorio Libre de Analfabetismo at noon, November 5, 1961. Seven weeks later, on December 22, Cuba itself—a nation dotted now by several hundred thousand paper flags of literate men and women—was declared by Fidel Castro to be Territory Free from Illiteracy.[33] The claim does not exceed the reasonable limits of poetic license. Statistical conclusions, those of the Cuban leaders being virtually the same as those reported by UNESCO, indicate a pedagogic victory unparalleled in the modern world.

30 Fagen, *Political Culture in Cuba*, p. 58. (Fagen's translation is rendered more idiomatic here, with the help of a Cuban translator, Martha Agasta.)
31 This and other letters of the literacy struggle are found in the archives of the Museum of Literacy, Havana.
32 Fagen, *Political Culture in Cuba*, p. 50.
33 Lorenzetto, *Methods and Means*, pp. 48–49.

Doubts and Denunciations

The most authoritative record of the literacy struggle, and the only report compiled within a short period after the campaign, was the UNESCO bulletin, researched during 1964 and published a year later. The report renders the final compilation in the following terms. According to the last census taken prior to the Cuban revolution, 23.6 percent of all Cuban adults were illiterate. This, however, was 1953. The number of illiterates diminished somewhat during the advance of the revolutionary army through the villages of Oriente and Las Villas during 1956, 1957, and 1958. A more substantial decrease in the number of illiterates, possibly as many as 50,000, may be attributed to experimental programs held during 1959 and 1960. By 1961 these factors, together with the vast improvement and redoubled enrollment of the schools, showed their results in a substantial diminution in the numbers of illiterate adults. My own estimate suggests that the illiteracy rate, by early 1961, had been reduced to less than 20 percent.

TABLE 1
Adult Illiteracy in Cuba 1953–1977

Year	Cuban Population	Percent Illiterate
1953	5,885,600	23.6
January 1961	6,938,700	20.0
December 1961	7,000,000	4.0
1977	9,600,000	2.0

Sources: The 1953 figures come from UNESCO, *Methods and Means* (which in turn made estimates from a Cuban government census report) and from Ferrer, *Educación de Adultos en Cuba*. The January 1961 figures are the author's estimates; the December 1961 numbers were taken from UNESCO, *Methods and Means*; and the 1977 data were obtained from the author's interviews with Ferrer and Fernandez.

By 1961, the Education Ministry was able to establish 979,207 as a working figure for illiterate adults in Cuba. Of this number, 707,212 were taught to read in less than nine months; nearly 272,000 partial illiterates remained, within an adult population which, in 1962, was close to 5.5 million. This means that less than 5 percent of Cuba's adult population remained illiterate.[34] No other Latin American nation had yet brought the figure for nonreaders to a point as low as 8 percent. The Latin American median as of 1960 was 32.5 percent.[35] An exact figure for illiteracy in the United States, then or now, is difficult to pin down. UNESCO placed it in 1973 at 6.6 percent,[36] while the *New York Times* has pegged it three times higher

[34] For these statistics, see Lorenzetto, *Methods and Means,* p. 27; also see Jolly, "The Literacy Campaign," pp. 194, 204. The final figure of 4 percent illiterate is based upon my interview with Dr. Raúl Ferrer. Jolly raises the possibility that the figure might have been slightly higher than Ferrer insists, but this difference is not significant (p. 204). The 1953 census figures are found in Raúl Ferrer, *Educación de adultos en Cuba* (Havana: Ministry of Education, 1976), p. 12.

[35] Leo Huberman and Paul Sweezey, *Socialism in Cuba* (New York: Monthly Review Press, 1969), p. 28; and *Statistical Yearbook* (Paris: UNESCO, 1971).

[36] *Statistical Yearbook* (Paris: UNESCO, 1973).

with an estimate of "one in five," or roughly 20 percent. Several scholars, such as Carman St. John Hunter, place it considerably higher than the figure estimated by the *Times*.[37]

Subsequent programs in Cuba have not only kept pace with the population but have reduced that residue of illiterate adults to less than 3 percent.[38] Most of the people represented by this figure are the sick, the aged, and those Cubans whose sole language is a variation of the Haitian tongue.[39]

Of the two individuals assigned by UNESCO to do the on-site study of the Cuban campaign, the better known and more articulate was the Italian scholar, Anna Lorenzetto. Dr. Lorenzetto's study of the Cuban struggle, published first in 1965, involved extensive interviews with several of the men and women whom I met in 1976.

Printed in French, English, and Spanish, the study was a strong, enthusiastic comment on the Cuban struggle, unevasive in its recognition of the inescapable political ingredient, the ideological bias of the primer, and the militant preparation of the brigadistas. The propaganda efforts of the government were reported in straightforward terms, as were the mobilization of manpower and what Dr. Lorenzetto called the aspect of "war footing." Dr. Lorenzetto handled this military parallel not just with openness, but with a note of positive endorsement. She did not suffer from the anti-Cuban inclination to condemn the Cuban people for responding to a state of siege with siege mentality and siege precautions.

"When an illiterate adult starts on a course to learn how to read and write," she noted, "society itself [begins to] go to school. . . . The school opens its door to life experiences, work problems, the tragedy of poverty. Society goes to school and learns to read and write; this process can release unknown forces." Some of them, she stated, prove to be "dangerous." This, she continued, is the only possible explanation for that strange state of affairs by which the adult-education programs fostered by UNESCO prove, every time, to be restricted to those areas of content and concern that never really count—issues that do not stir the heart and cannot motivate the soul.[40]

The words and views quoted or paraphrased above are taken from an essay published by Dr. Lorenzetto in 1968. In 1965, however, in the original report that had been written for UNESCO, Dr. Lorenzetto expressed the same view in even sharper terms:

If the [present] evaluation of this Campaign, which was a great event in the edu-

---

[37] Carman St. John Hunter, in collaboration with David Harman, "Illiteracy in the United States." Unpublished paper prepared for the Ford Foundation, 1978, p. i.

[38] Author's second personal interview with Dr. Raúl Ferrer, Havana, September 1977.

[39] For other studies of the literacy struggles, see Fagen, *Political Culture in Cuba*, pp. 33–68; Raúl Ferrer, "La Campaña No Fué un Milagro," *Bohemia*, 1976, **68**, No. 52, 4–8; Arthur Gillette, *Youth and Literacy* (Paris: UNESCO, 1972); Jolly, "The Literacy Campaign," pp. 190–219; Huberman and Sweezey, *Socialism in Cuba*, pp. 22–52; and Cuban Film Institute (Producer), *Lucia, Part III* (1969); and *El Brigadista* (1978). New York: Transcontinental Film Center (Distributor).

[40] Lorenzetto, "The Experimental Projects Sponsored by UNESCO and the Revolutionary Element in Literacy," *Convergence*, September 1968, 1, 31–36.

cational field, cannot be set apart from a political evaluation, this is due to the fact that the Campaign was, in itself, a political event. The very results of the Literacy Campaign, which were unquestionably positive, cannot be perfectly understood without taking into consideration the social and cultural objectives. . . .

People's participation and a consciousness of the social and economic realities continue to be the basic postulates of all work to abolish illiteracy. . . .[41]

Dr. Lorenzetto ended her commentary on a note of optimism. She mentioned first that cautious elements in Cuba, and many of those watching from the outside, suggested at the start, a three-year rather than a one-year program. "It is possible," she said, "that the illiterate could wait three years. . . . The revolution could not. . . . It is possible that, in three years, the . . . campesino could have learned how to read and write by means of . . . radio, television, and technical . . . procedures." But, she continued, he would not have gained a political consciousness. Thanks to the efforts of the youth brigades, the campesino learned not only to read and write, but also to become a revolutionary. "As we have already pointed out," she wrote,

the post-literacy work will begin shortly. . . . It is a problem as important for Cuba, in the present day, as the struggle against illiteracy was in 1961, a problem whose solution, through the plans of Worker-Farmer Education, should [soon] provide the entire population with a Sixth Grade educational level.[42]

Dr. Lorenzetto's confidence in Cuba's capacity and will to carry out a powerful Follow-Up proved to be in no respect naive. It is one of several points at which she demonstrated a sense of confidence in Cuban claims and resolutions, which have been forcefully confirmed by those who have been visiting and observing the adult-education programs in Cuba during the past two years. My own on-site observations in 1976 and 1977 convince me that the various stages of the Follow-Up have been consistent and effective in achieving their stated goals. Most impressive are the figures that provide the breakdown of each of the three phases of the Follow-Up that started in 1962 and continue to the present time—programs that took up the task of "lifetime education" which the literacy struggle, by necessity, had left undone. Of 707,212 people taught to read during the course of 1961, 500,000 pursued their studies further during the next seven years, first in a program called *Seguimiento* ("Follow-Up"), then in a program called "The Battle for the Sixth Grade." One-half million previously illiterate adults passed the sixth-grade qualification by the end of 1968.

In September 1976, when I talked with the directors of the various adult programs, the Battle for the Sixth Grade had been made more consistent and more systematic under a new name, "EOC"—Worker-Farmer Education. At that time, there were 300,000 men and women in the program. I visited a number of classes of the EOC and was impressed by the intensive curriculum. Several students, many as old as fifty-five or sixty, were reading Mark Twain and Jack London in translation. Others, who had started to learn English, were already reading passages from Charles Dickens.

[41] Lorenzetto, *Methods and Means*, p. 72.
[42] Lorenzetto, *Methods and Means*, pp. 72–73.

I also visited classrooms of the adult secondary-level program, known as "FOC"—Worker-Farmer Faculty—a close equivalent to Cuban junior high school. The pupils were studying algebra, physics, geometry, Spanish composition, and biology. Many had also gained considerable fluency in English. The classes were rigorous and lasted for three hours, four days every week, with one month off a year. In 1976, the combined enrollment of the EOC, the FOC, and several smaller specialized adult programs was more than 600,000.[43] This figure, however, does not include adults who have moved on to the university level.

The exact number of Cuban men and women who have now progressed through these preliminary programs to pre-university proficiency cannot be known for sure, but one good index of numerical success is the present ratio of workers to nonworking pupils in the student populations of the various universities. Out of a total of 120,000 pupils at all six universities in 1976, 48 percent were active workers. These workers were enrolled in either regular programs, extension courses, or night classes.[44]

Today in Cuba, in a population of 9.6 million men, women, and children, 3.3 million people are enrolled in formal education programs at one level or another.[45] In the words of a recent UNESCO publication, the Cuban struggle to eradicate illiteracy and to bring all students and adults to an effective, functional level, has proven itself not just a one-time tour de force but rather "a success story that has no end."[46]

The enthusiasm of UNESCO has to be balanced against the heavy criticism which the Cuban literacy struggle has received in recent years from certain North American and European observers. It is a form of criticism that attacks the Cubans for those very points most fascinating to this author and UNESCO's commentators: the undisguised political coloration of the education process, on the one hand, and the bravado and unqualified extravagance of both the claims and actions of the Cuban leaders, on the other.

First, with respect to the point about politics and ideology, the charge is made that Cuba did not set out in impartial fashion to present a pure, unbiased, and mechanical technique, but instead sought to intermix the use of words with national self-interest. (This criticism comes most frequently from those who have had no experience in the self-repeating failures of the "nonpolitical" and "value-free" approach.) For this reason, the achievement must be viewed primarily as political, not pedagogical. Credit, if credit is to be given, belongs to the Cuban organizers and activists, not to Ferrer, not to the reading teachers, nor even to the kids themselves.

The answers to this type of criticism would seem by now to be self-evident. Very few informed people are likely to deny that education which is financed, governed,

<hr/>

43 Jolly, "The Literacy Campaign," pp. 211–218.

44 Author's interview with Cuban Minister of Education, José Ramón Fernández, Havana, September 1976.

45 Population figures for 1978 are based on projections by Minister Fernández in a second interview, Havana, September 1977.

46 Arthur Gillette, *Youth and Literacy*, p. 55.

and directed by the state will logically seek to propagate the values of that state. In state-financed education, as in almost every other area of public life, the one who pays the piper calls the tune. In the United States methods of ideological and nationalistic bias in the public schools are no less persistent than in any other country. The methods we employ are unquestionably more subtle and more irresistible than those that almost any other nation could conceivably afford. One other major difference between the uses of indoctrination in the United States and those of relatively small and less affluent nations is that in the United States—and in China and the Soviet Union, as well—the consequences of a nationalistic bias threaten not just "discomfort" for pupils in our public schools but imminent disaster for all life on this earth.

If critics, then, are seriously concerned with dangers of indoctrination in the Cuban struggles of a decade past, logic compels us to demand that they address themselves with equal fervor to the far more ominous dangers of world-wide nuclear destruction which cannot help but be the consequence of political indoctrination taking place at every pedagogic level in the United States. This point by no means settles the ethical question of political bias in another nation's schools. It is intended, however, to place that bias in a rational perspective. A large body of material exists by now, much of it written by well-known and respected authors (Samuel Bowles and Herbert Gintis, Ivan Illich, Michael Katz, and Joel Spring, to name just a few),[47] which emphasizes, from very different points of view, that there is neither "neutral education" nor, in the Cuban situation, "neutral literacy." All learning is ideological in one way or another.

My point is not that critics do not have the right to disagree with this increasing body of well-documented work, but rather that they persistently ignore it altogether. Frequently one has the impression that it is not the fact of ideological coloration in a particular educational process that they honestly oppose; rather it is the particular brand of ideology that they detest. All education, unless it is hopelessly boring and irrelevant, is political. People are taught to read so that they will vote by uniform stimuli, read orders, and buy in predictable patterns in response to calculated methods of appeal; or else they learn to read and write in order to strive, in one way or another, for an ethical, idealistic, or emancipating goal. Education is either for domestication or for liberation.

According to Freire, "those who defend the neutrality of adult literacy programmes are right in accusing us of political acts when we try to clarify reality. . . . But they falsify the truth by denying their own efforts to mask reality."[48] All the innovative tricks on earth will not suffice to get around this point.

The second body of criticism against the Cuban literacy program is far more serious. This comes not in the guise of an apolitical defense of the value-free ideals of

---

[47] For additional readings on the ideological bias of education, see Paulo Freire, *Pedagogy of the Oppressed;* Samuel Bowles and Herbert Gintis, *Schooling in Capitalist America* (New York: Basic Books, 1977); Ivan Illich, *Deschooling Society* (New York: Harper & Row, 1971); Michael Katz, *The Irony of Early School Reform* (Cambridge: Harvard University Press, 1968); and Joel Spring, *Education and the Rise of the Corporate State* (Boston: Beacon Press, 1973).

[48] Paulo Freire, "Literacy and the Possible Dream," *Prospects*, 1976, 6, 71.

North American or European interests, but rather from a number of highly knowledgeable friends or former friends of Cuba within the European Left.

The most conspicuous representative of this body of opinion is René Dumont, a French agronomist with a thorough knowledge of the Cuban economic situation. Although viewed by many as an honorable but iconoclastic ally of the Cuban revolution, he is often labeled by others as a venomous and immensely complicated adversary of the Cuban state, writing under the unassailable protection of "a painfully honest critic on the Left." Whether he is, as Cuban leaders now believe, the agent of an anti-Castro organization or simply the abrasive analyst of what he honestly believes to be Castro's Achilles' heel, Dumont makes the only criticism of the Cuban modus operandi that appears to warrant real debate. His point, reduced to few words, is that Dr. Castro spends too much time meddling with specific details—educational, agricultural, and political trivia—of the Cuban state, failing to delegate as much work as he should to those such as Ferrer whom he has already appointed to undertake important tasks. Closely associated with this criticism is Dumont's secondary charge that Fidel's inclination to bravura gestures and extravagant intentions has had the negative consequence of leading Cuba into enterprises it cannot possibly complete.

The first point, as far as education is concerned, is most sensibly discussed by Fidel's own appointed literacy expert, Raúl Ferrer. While fully conceding Fidel's active intervention in the literacy struggle—his personal involvement, for example, in the final preparation of the oral reader *Alfabeticemos,* even to the point of revising specific sentences—Ferrer insists that intervention of this kind in no way undermined his own and his coworkers' sense of dedication to the task at hand. Rather, Ferrer and the other members of his team were assured that what they were doing was of consummate importance to Fidel and would therefore command the absolute backing of the chief of state once it was under way. Certainly, "meddling" is not the word that comes to mind in hearing Ferrer's amusing, but consistently respectful, recollections of the pedagogic contributions of Fidel.

As for the larger point regarding the bravura gestures and extravagant intentions of the Cuban head of state, I know of no final answer other than the simple fact that Fidel's promises and dreams in the case of the literacy campaign proved both realistic and successful. Whether or not Dumont is right about other aspects of Cuban life I have no way of knowing. In the field of education, for all his strident criticism of the ideological coloration of the literacy work, Dumont concedes that the campaign of 1961 was nothing less than a "magnificent" event.[49]

---

[49] René Dumont, while questioning the political nature of Cuban education, nonetheless refers to the literacy struggle with extravagant praise. Another critical observer of the Cuban revolution, K. S. Karol, also takes special pains to praise the literacy campaign, giving the Cubans credit for an even larger reduction in illiteracy in the course of nine months than the facts will justify. (Like many others, he uncritically accepts the 1953 illiteracy figure of 23.6 percent as the proper mathematical starting point for 1961.) In later passages, he continues his high praise of the campaign calling it "remarkable work" (p. 33). See René Dumont, *Is Cuba Socialist?* (London: Andre Deutsch, 1970), p. 27; and K. S. Karol, *Guerrillas in Power: The Course of the Cuban Revolution* (New York: Hill and Wang, 1970), pp. 33, 37–38.

One of the most intelligent and explicit answers to the criticism that I have described, namely, the charge of "lack of prudence" on the part of Cuba's chief of state, is found in a thoughtful and well-researched document by Arthur Gillette, who visited Cuba in 1971. Commenting on this aspect of the literacy campaign, he writes:

> Some critics, notably the French agronomist René Dumont, claim that the revolution could have avoided certain mistakes by being prudent. Whether more prudence would have produced more cows and coffee I do not know; but I do formulate an opposite hypothesis in the sphere of education. Success there, I believe, has been directly proportional to the amount of daring the revolution has displayed. Where daring has given way to prudence (for instance, in retaining exams and marks), the educational revolution has been least successful.[50]

In the wake of this dispute, it seems appropriate to grant the final word to one observer who has no perceptible axe to grind for either Cuba, Dumont, or UNESCO. I have in mind a recent visiting lecturer at Harvard, Dr. David Harman, who was active in the adult-education programs of Israel. Though clearly anti-Communist in his perspective, Harman is a fair-minded, discerning man:

> Everywhere else but Cuba, literacy campaigns of every kind have almost always failed. Even in Mexico, where an independent and ambitious national literacy campaign was undertaken during the 1940s and 1950s, fifteen years of effort ended up with more illiterates than when the program was begun. The final statistics indicate that half the adult population was illiterate.
>
> During those campaigns financed by UNESCO, the evidence of failure was predictable in every case. Eighty percent of those who came dropped out before the program was complete. Of those who stuck it out, 50 percent would lose what they had learned within a single year. At best, if we are kind and optimistic, we can say that 10 percent of those involved might have held on to something they had learned.
>
> For all of these reasons, Cuba, which has turned its back upon the safe and mechanistic methods of UNESCO, must be given credit for a triumph which is totally unique.
>
> Cuba, in few words, has created a new culture and—I hope this doesn't sound too fancy—has been able to accelerate the pace of ethical evolution. . . . No honorable scholar, in the face of all that Cuba has achieved, can claim the right to denigrate its scope, its sweeping energy, and ultimate worth to all the rest of us who have tried so hard but have repeatedly come up with so much less.[51]

A Conversation with Raúl Ferrer

"The campaign," wrote the UNESCO commission, "was not a miracle, but rather a difficult conquest obtained through work, technique, and organization."[52] A vivid sense of some of these details is gained in conversation with Raúl Ferrer. He,

---

[50] Arthur Gillette, *Cuba's Educational Revolution* (London: Fabian Society, 1972), p. 36.
[51] Personal interview with David Harman, Cambridge, Mass., November 1976.
[52] Lorenzetto, *Methods and Means*, p. 72.

more than any other person, helped to shape the tactics of a struggle that involved, at one point, more than 250,000 teachers instructing 900,000 pupils.

In the course of an eight-hour conversation with Ferrer and his associate, Abel Prieto Morales, former Minister of Elementary Education, I questioned Ferrer on aspects of the literacy campaign that seemed of greatest relevance to these struggles taking place today in several other nations. My first questions dealt with ideology and politics, as they influenced the course of the campaign.

Ferrer discussed the routine failure of those multiple campaigns to "end illiteracy forever" which UNESCO has repeatedly begun with considerable fanfare and then quietly put to rest. He pointed to UNESCO projects in Algeria, Tanzania, India, and Iran, and to others in Sudan, Mali, Madagascar.[53] "Why do they fail?" he asked. "They have the money. They have UNESCO. They have the expertise. They have the international promotion. How is it possible, then, that they do not succeed? It is because their starting point is antihuman. . . . They do not dare to use the words we use. They do not dare to speak of land reform, to speak about the sick and poor . . . the international corporations and the banks. . . . They do not dare to put these words into the hands of the poor people. And, because they do not dare, therefore they fail—and they will always fail until they do!"

He stormed at me in pouring out these words. Ferrer's colleague, sitting at his side, said to me, in perfect English: "Do not be afraid. It is his helpless loss of self-control. Raúl is growing old."

I asked Ferrer, in view of his last words, if politics must, in every case, be tied to education for a program of this kind to work. He answered by speaking of the almost physical relationship between the campesino and "the word." A person, he said, "in order to feel that he can be the owner of the word, must sense that he can also be the owner of real things. I mean, the owner of his own existence, of his toil, of the fruit of his own work. In order to sense that it can be within his power to possess the *word*, he must believe that he can thereby gain the power to transform the *world* . . . to shape the world . . . to make it a more noble and more humane place to be. . . . There is no way to do this which is not political."

He then made reference to a phrase current in the United States, "the crisis in the schools." "Ever since the student upheavals in Paris, during May of 1968, hundreds of people have been traveling the world, in order to attempt to isolate the crisis of our pupils from the moral struggles of our times. It is a gross diversion. We deny that there is 'a crisis in the schools.' We believe the so-called crisis in the schools emerges from the struggle of young people to remake society. It is not a crisis in the classroom. It is a crisis in the social order."

Without attempting to pursue a logical sequence, Ferrer went on to speak of several different and wide-ranging issues. "The literacy campaign," he said, "was not a dry event. Therefore, it must not be talked about as if it were. . . . The statistics

[53] For UNESCO's official report on the world-wide literacy programs, see *The Experimental World Literacy Programme: A Critical Assessment* (Paris: UNESCO, 1976). A more critical and insightful evaluation of UNESCO's projects can be found in David Harman, *Community Fundamental Education*. For another report on adult-literacy projects, see H. S. Bhola, *Literacy Teachers for Adults* (Tanzania: UNESCO/UNDP, 1970).

of the end results are very good. Yet this was not at any time our chief concern. This fact was a by-product of a deeper goal. The great heart of the literacy struggle was the revolution; its chief result, a farmer-worker-student coalition. Above all else, as you have seen, the students in the cities learned the greatest lesson of their lives: reading that 'book of life' not from a printed text but from the campesinos whom they were assigned to teach. There is, perhaps, a kind of poetry in this. If so, it is a poetry that is not mine. The poetry is there already in the history of the campaign.

"Fidel said to us once during that year that we had made a revolution bigger than ourselves. He was correct; yet very few people in the world have knowledge of the things that we achieved. Why is this so?

"One reason, of course, is that we all have worked so hard; we did not have the time, at first, to sit down and to publish our results. Then, too, there was the embargo from outside. The real blockade was not the one that planted United States naval craft around our shores. The great embargo was to silence the results of our campaign. People assumed: 'All other struggles in the field of literacy fail. Then so must this one too.' "

Prieto interrupted to explain to me the references which, at that time, I did not understand. "In 1964, UNESCO sent an excellent scholar, Anna Lorenzetto, to report on our campaign. Lorenzetto, it seems, became a great deal too enthusiastic. UNESCO refused to publish her report unless she would agree to censor certain passages and phrases.

"We told UNESCO, 'You have permission to edit a document that you can publish, but you must not cut away materials that will subvert the passion and enthusiasm.' The book, in the final event, was never published by UNESCO. We had to publish it ourselves."

Prieto told me then of the first international conference on adult illiteracy, sponsored by UNESCO and held in Teheran in 1965. UNESCO already had managed effectively to suppress the report simply by keeping a limited number of copies of the study on its bookshelves in New York and Paris. Moreover, according to Prieto, UNESCO went still further by rejecting a request from Cuba that the document be made available to scholars at the worldwide convocation. "You will have heard perhaps of the subsequent confrontation in Iran. Rául Ferrer stood by the door. He held in his hands 500 copies, printed in English, French, and Spanish, and passed them out. It is as if he were a newsboy in New York. In seven minutes, every copy that he had was gone."

The smile vanished from his eyes, as he remarked: "I would like to ask you to imagine the indignity at stake in this . . . not so much to my good friend beside me here as to the Cuban people as a whole. How do you think a nation—no matter how small, or poor, or powerless—would feel?"

At the time I had no background information on the confrontation in Iran. Troubled by what Prieto had reported, I did what I could to get a thoughtful statement from UNESCO. I wrote to the Deputy Director-General John Fobes. Mr. Fobes apparently had no intimate knowledge of the matters that Prieto had described. On the contrary, he spoke with open admiration of the literacy work that has been carried on in Cuba, praised Cuba for the courage it has shown, and indicated that many other nations undoubtedly wish that they could have come up with comparable results.[54]

It is apparent then that UNESCO's present attitude towards the literacy work in Cuba bears little relation to its evasive posture of a decade earlier. From the point of view of Cuban leaders, attitudes have also greatly changed; there is no sense of animosity remaining from the "intellectual embargo" of the past. Ferrer's feelings toward UNESCO are today enthusiastic. He speaks of Fobes with obvious admiration and regards UNESCO as a progressive force. "Times change. . . . We need to speak the truth, and I have done so for this reason. Then we need to set aside the past. UNESCO is a different organization now from what it was before."

Ferrer then took off in an entirely new direction. "Illiteracy, of course, is not an absolute idea. It is forever relative; our approach, therefore, must change as need demands. In 1961, our definition of a literate man or woman was a person who could understand some plain and simple words. . . . In the beginning, as you know, the campesinos studied words like 'INRA' and 'tierra,' 'analfabetismo,' 'O.E.A.' Today, in the Follow-Up, after sixteen years of work, we are making use of an entirely different set of words."

I asked him whether there was nothing he would change other than the words themselves if he were starting back again in 1961. "No theoretical change would seem appropriate," he said. "Organizational patterns would be watched with greater care. Challenges that we did not face before the end of the summer would be dealt with earlier in the year. No reversal of philosophic goals, however, would take place. Social motivation would not change.

"The active words, the generative themes, these are the things that we would alter with the years. We would not speak today of INRA and of O.E.A. They are no longer vitalizing words. We would speak, instead, of mechanized ways of bringing in the crop, of fibers, coffee production, polyclinics, or hydraulic systems. We would speak perhaps about Che's final letter to Fidel, the children of Vietnam, or the struggle of the Cuban women for their equal rights.

"In each generation, new words are 'released,' and old words fade away. We still speak Spanish in Cuba, but we speak new words. Today we speak of irrigation, popular power, citrus groves, and the tobacco crop. Sometimes I listen to a man I knew before the revolution. He speaks now of the nickel export, schools-in-the-country, or the citrus crop. I listen and I find it isn't the same man! Why would a peasant need to speak of citrus crops before the revolution? We did not *have* a citrus crop in Cuba!"

Ferrer paused, to give his patient friend a chance to talk. "My son," said Prieto, "who is only five years old, hears me speaking of a time when blacks and whites were not allowed to dance together. He asks me why; but, when I tell him that it is because of 'racist' views, he does not know that word. He says it is 'ridiculous'—not racist. The whole idea does not make sense. He does not understand that there was once a time when 'racist' was a necessary word. . . . We needed it in order to des-

---

[54] Letter of John Fobes to the author, May 4, 1977.

cribe a real phenomenon—one that does not exist, except in isolated situations, any more."[55]

Ferrer abruptly shifted subjects once again: "In regard to the so-called silence of the poor—you have heard us speak of this before, but there is one more thing I need to say. The vegetable Indian in some small town of Mexico or Guatemala . . . he is a silent man. He does not speak. . . . But put into his hands a revolution—he will begin to talk! He *is* a 'vegetable.' I said it, yes! It is the perfect word, because he has been rooted in that soil for so long!"

Ferrer went on to speak of his idea of "vegetable silence" and the sudden redis-covery, by a person who has been oppressed, of his own voice. "Those who op-pressed us, those who denied us, those who took away our voice of protest—when they were finished, they had married us to the lie. So long as we were not free men, we were compelled to live in company with the lie. The world crumbles when a people choose to live no longer with a lie. . . . When do we free ourselves from the power of that lie? We free ourselves, not when we announce that we are free, but when we bring about events that make us free. A man no longer lives with the lie when he will no longer agree to live in a subjected role."

Ferrer continued: "I want to speak of something else which I have not defined explicitly up to this time. Perhaps you wonder what our ultimate objectives pos-sibly could be—perhaps you don't! Whether you do or not, I want to speak of this a final time. The original goal was for political awareness—plus minimal compe-tence for productive needs. Today, our goal is not just minimal competence. . . . It is the richness and the resonance of culture, solidarity with people in other social-ist lands, a heightened capability to deal with high technology and middle-level expertise. We could not even dream of goals like these before."

Ferrer spoke for a while after that about the adult-education programs in the years since 1961—in particular, of the motivations that would compel a worker to assume the burden of a rigorous evening program, in addition to the obligations of his daily work. Everything that he discussed appeared political at first. At last, however, he began to laugh and, while I waited for the explanation of his laugh-ter, he began to recollect the story of a man who had no serious ideological direc-tion—not the slightest interest in political concerns.

"The man said, 'I want to learn to write.' We asked him why. He said, 'So I can write a letter to the woman I love.' He came into the program and—I'll tell you something—that man learned to read and write extremely fast! When he was done, he wrote a letter to the woman he loved: 'I write one thing that I long to tell you. Inside my body are many fearful things I need to say. Cruel woman, if you do not love me I will die.'

"Many people memorized those words. They were transcribed into a popular

---

[55] My own impression confirms Prieto's claim, but it seems important to remind the reader that I was in Cuba in 1976 for only six weeks, then again in 1977 for an even shorter time. Elizabeth Suth-erland, who was living in Cuba during 1968, assesses the racial situation in interesting detail in *The Youngest Revolution* (New York: Dial Press, 1968), pp. 138–168.

verse, and later set to music by a good song-writer. The trouble is—she didn't love him! But he didn't die! He met another woman he liked better! Still, it is a good poem, even better as a song."

Ferrer began to laugh. "And so you see that everything we do is not political! Most things are; but writing motivation takes a thousand forms. Who would have thought of setting up a primer to enable campesinos to write letters to the man or woman that they love?"

Despite my fascination with Ferrer's conversation and his affable manner, I suddenly realized that the hour was quite late. There was one question that I needed very much to pose before the interview was done. I gathered my courage and took advantage of a pause in his momentum to say, very briskly, that there was one further point I wished to raise.

Ferrer was sitting straight up in his chair: "I am ready to listen. Ask me anything you want."

My question seemed so dry, by now, I hardly had the nerve to speak the words. The question had to do with "budget, costs, and fiscal trade-off." Although I had some sense of the kind of answer I would get, I told Ferrer I had been asked by an editor in the United States to find out what the literacy program had cost, in terms of hard investment, cash, and diversion of resources to a single goal.

"In Cuba," he replied, without apparent indignation, but as calmly as before, "there can be no balance sheet for justice. We know, of course, the nation spent so many million pesos to produce the primer and the manual. Then Fidel issued severe instruction in regard to health and safety of the brigadistas, and in reference to their means of transportation to the places they were sent to work. Some went by bus. Some went by special train. We know the cost was great. It is a cost, moreover, that was shared by local villages and towns. I do not think that we could ever make a proper compilation of that cost.

"Speaking still of money, not humanity, the largest cost was what each family paid whenever a child had gone off to work in one of the brigades. I mean the dual expense, both to support some of the child's costs while living in the mountains and the farms, and also to go out to visit now and then—and to bring food—because the family in the country was so poor.

"I can give no figure. But I can tell you that millions of pesos were expended in the early phase of the campaign. One hundred seventy-seven thousand pairs of glasses had to be produced and fitted, as you know already, to each person who had need for glasses. It was not just the cost to buy the glasses; technicians also had to move into the villages to fit the glasses. Then, too, doctors had to go into the country, as you know, to offer health care to the brigadistas. Do you see how many different kinds of costs we had to face? It was not just the teaching of reading, as a technical idea. It was a concert written by the forces of a total people.

"The salaries of the professional teachers represented another cost as well. From May to December, thirty-five thousand teachers were given their conventional pay to work as guides and as advisers to the brigadistas. Ninety-five thousand lanterns, uniforms, knapsacks, hammocks had to be obtained.

"Then you must recall that we had not declared ourselves a socialist nation at the time that the campaign began. We did so during the campaign; but, in the interim, we still had private enterprise in Cuba so that made it doubly hard.

"What, then, is the total? We can quantify the salaries of teachers. We can add up the production loss, caused by workers who joined the brigadistas during September when it seemed that we might fall behind our goal. But we cannot quantify the salaries of those, the People's Teachers—the ordinary men and women of the land—who gave up two or three hours every day, in order to share their reading skills with neighbors. How can you quantify this kind of cost?"

There was a pause. We had been talking now for almost an entire day. Ferrer leaned forward, placed his hand over my wrist, and then went on. "We must disappoint your editor," he said, "but we will send that man an answer, all the same. It is precisely this, that you North Americans must always count up everything in numbers, and must forever calculate the cost in dollars, that you do not succeed, and never *will* succeed, in struggles of this kind.

"The treasure of the Third World is the treasure of our people, not their cash. We do not deny the necessity of money; but, in these kinds of struggles, the real price is something which cannot be put in numbers."

I watched the energy and passion of this man whom Paulo Freire had described to me, three months before in Canada, as "a great tree of life." Prieto, silent now, almost austere, ascetic in his silence, did not smile any longer but looked with admiration at his long-time friend.

A few minutes later, Prieto—who had suffered from a serious heart attack only a month before—accompanied me along the corridor, pressed my hand warmly, waited with me for the elevator, and then wished me a good journey back to my home in the United States.

Social Relations as Contexts for Learning in School

R. P. McDERMOTT
Rockefeller University

Questions concerning what works in classrooms have been asked many times. The answers so far have not resulted in any substantial educational changes, and our school systems continue to be in considerable disarray. In this article, R. P. Mc-Dermott emphasizes the importance of understanding the way relations between teachers and children affect the development of learning environments and examines how classroom interaction may promote or retard learning. He describes how teaching styles depend on cultural contexts and examines successful and unsuccessful classrooms with examples from a variety of school systems, including Amish and inner-city American. McDermott suggests that the ethnographic study of classrooms will allow us to look carefully at learning in terms of how teachers and students "make sense" of each other and hold each other accountable, given the resources and limits of their community.

Accounts of what is wrong with our schools are legion. But what is it that works in classrooms? Rather than suggesting certain teaching techniques, this paper will examine the importance of the social relations between teachers and children in the development of learning environments in classrooms. Successful learning environments provide children with the possibility of discovering clearly defined tasks and the time to work on them until mastery is achieved (Bloom, 1974). Unsuccessful learning environments are marked by children spending years struggling to get organized and to pay attention rather than learning.

Although the data are anecdotal and the generalizations not powerfully war-

A few pages in the sections of this article on the ethnography of relations and teacher-student relations were adapted from "Ethnography of Speaking and Reading" by R. P. McDermott, in Roger Shuy (Ed.), *Linguistic theory: What can it say about reading?* Newark, Del.: International Reading Association, 1977. Permission to publish these pages has been granted by the author and the publisher. Writing time for the most recent version of this article was supported by grants from the Carnegie Corporation to Michael Cole and the Laboratory of Comparative Human Cognition at The Rockefeller University. Cole and some diligent companions at the Laboratory, John Dore, Ken Gospodinoff, Lois Hood, and Kenneth Traupmann, found the time to criticize the paper and to help it into its current shape. The problems which remain are of my own hand.

Harvard Educational Review Vol. 47 No. 2 May 1977, 198–213

ranted, this article will perform a dual service by reporting some methods for studying the relational foundations of successful pedagogy and by citing some important cases which can alter our sense of "problem" children and the kinds of theories we need to understand such children.

The claim of this paper is that the relations between children and teachers underlie the organizational work necessary for learning tasks to be presented and worked on by children. By the relations between teachers and children, I mean "working agreements" or "consensuses" (Goffman, 1959, 1976; Kendon, in press) about who they are and what is going on between them, agreements which they formulate, act upon, and use together to make sense of each other. In particular, I am interested in what I call "trusting relations," a crucial subset of the working agreements people use to make sense of each other. In the classroom, these issues translate into how the teacher and children can understand each other's behavior as directed to the best interests of what they are trying to do together and how they can hold each other accountable for any breach of the formulated consensus.

It is important that the reader not take "trusting relations" in the ordinary sense, which implies that trust is a property of a person's personality. The developmental literature is filled with references to a child's acquisition of "basic trust" as if it becomes a property of the child to be used in all situations. However, I am talking about trust as a quality of the relations among people, as a product of the work they do to achieve a shared focus. Trust is achieved and managed through interaction (Garfinkel, 1963; McDermott & Church, 1976). It takes constant effort for two or more people to achieve trusting relations, and the slightest lag in that work can demand extensive remedial efforts.

Although I am claiming a central role for trusting relations in the organization of a successful classroom, I am not suggesting that some children or teachers are more trusting than others and thus they learn better in school. Trust is not a property of persons but a product of the work people do to achieve trusting relations, given particular institutional contexts. What I am suggesting is that in contexts that offer teachers and children enough resources to work together to establish a trusting environment, children will have sufficient time and energy to devote themselves to the intellectual tasks set before them. In other words, trusting relations are framed by the contexts in which people are asked to relate, and where trusting relations occur, learning is a possibility. Where trusting relations are not possible, learning can only result from solitary effort.

Behavior modifiers who work in the classroom can point to some excellent short-term results. They can construct environments in which children and their teachers know what to expect of each other. For the duration of the specially prepared environments, both trusting relations and learning can evolve (O'Leary, in press). Their results can seldom be generalized, however, because the larger community does not usually supply the same kind of consistent environment. Still, in the world beyond the reach of most behavior therapists, many communities naturally produce successful learning environments. These positive examples are marked by trusting relational environments which allow the children time on learning tasks. We are just beginning to discover how cultural and institutional resources are crucial to an understanding of the differences between successful and unsuccessful classrooms.

Observers have noted that in the average elementary school about 50 percent of class time is spent in getting organized (Gump, 1975). Success in getting organized for learning depends on how well the participants communicate to each other the importance of the learning tasks. Moreover, the problem of organization operates at all levels of school activity. Even the organizationally efficient teacher who divides a class into small tracked groups will have groups that differ in the amount of time spent on learning tasks even while the teacher is with them. In order to understand why some children spend more time on learning tasks than others do, it is necessary to examine both how children establish relations with their teachers and the contexts in which they are asked to do so.

The first section of this paper will claim that there is an order or logic in the ways people relate to each other. They use this order to organize their behavior with each other, demonstrating the particulars of this in their activities. Sensitive approaches to describing the work people do to organize and maintain the order of their relations have been developed in several branches of social science. Their thrust will be summarized in a discussion of *ethnography* as a tool for the study of relations between people. Generally, this term is used by anthropologists to describe their efforts to record the cultures of different peoples around the world. I will use "ethnography" more specifically to refer to any rigorous attempt to account for people's behavior in terms of their relations with those around them in differing situations.

In the second section, I will examine how an ethnography of classroom relations can offer us a different vision of what children and teachers do there and what might be successful or unsuccessful classroom talk. In particular, I will consider two ways of attempting to gain children's attention in classrooms: an authoritarian method in which a child's every moment in the classroom is organized by the teacher's directives; and a guidance-based method in which the child is encouraged to explore an environment for what is most interesting and most useful for the life of the group. Both methods are forms of coercion that are successful depending upon the relational foundations for communicating in the classroom.

In the last section of this paper, I will apply some of the principles developed in the first two sections to an analysis of how children become organized for learning to read. Although almost no ethnographic research has been done on how children learn to read in schools, we have information indicating that relational contexts are crucial.

The Ethnography of Relations

At its best, an ethnography should account for the behavior of people by describing what enables them to behave sensibly with others in their community.[1] All

---

[1] This use of the term ethnography is consistent with its use in mainstream anthropology. Although rooted in cognitive anthropology (Conklin, 1964; Frake, 1964, 1974) and ethnomethodology

people, especially those from different cultures, appear to behave differently, and we all attempt haphazard ethnographies when we struggle to decipher the logic of the behavior of different peoples. We acknowledge this in everyday talk by saying that successful social relations depend on knowing "where a person is coming from" or "where a person's head is at." Successful psychiatry certainly demands this level of understanding (Sapir, 1932), and so does successful teaching. The first principle of good pedagogy, namely, beginning at a student's present skill level, calls for good ethnography. Too often, however, teachers, psychiatrists, and the rest of us proceed intuitively. Professional ethnographers differ from us only in that they are more disciplined and self-conscious in gathering information about how people relate to the world around them. Rather than assuming "where a person's head is at," they struggle to define rigorously the practices a person displays in interpreting and generating behavior in particular situations.

Consider the following illustrations of what an ethnography attempts to describe. When a scientist publishes a report, the scientific community has procedures for holding her or him accountable for the findings. Was the experiment performed under the proper conditions? Were the proper statistical analyses performed? Were the interpretations of the data consistent with methods previously used for interpreting similar data? These and other questions act as legitimate ways to hold a scientist accountable. This is called a methodology, and it constitutes a canon in terms of which scientists make sense of each other. Such a canon is explicit; ideally scientists should be aware of the assumptions underlying their methodology and its implications. The point of this illustration is that people in everyday life also have methods for holding each other accountable (Garfinkel, 1968). An ethnography is an attempt to describe a group's methodology, that is, an attempt to describe the procedures group members use to relate to each other in culturally sensible ways (Cicourel, 1974; Frake, 1974; Garfinkel, 1967). Unfortunately, the procedures used in everyday life are never very explicit. For example, how many of us can list in detail the procedures we use in greeting another person or walking down a street? Greetings involve a head toss, a presentation of the palm of the hand, a brief motion of the eyebrows, and a flash of the teeth in a smile (Kendon & Ferber, 1973). Walking down a street involves computing complex trajectories for people moving in different directions and discerning who is with whom in order to avoid collisions (Goffman, 1971; Wolf, 1973). We all greet people and navigate the streets, but few of us can be explicit about how we do it.

In science and in everyday life, methodologies and procedures differ and lead to varied consequences. A behaviorist studies different problems and reaches quite different conclusions than a psychologist following a psychoanalytic canon. Similarly, the procedures we use in our daily activities have consequences for us and for all those around us. A successful ethnography should help us to become aware of

(Cicourel, 1974; Garfinkel, 1967; Mehan & Wood, 1975), the kind of ethnography called for here is consistent with the goals of such diverse schools of social science as the ethological (Beck, 1976a, 1976b), the interactionist (Arensberg & Kimball, 1940), the linguistic (Hymes, 1974), and the communicative (Birdwhistell, 1970; Kendon, in press; Scheflen, 1973). Newcomers to the field may want to start with a delightful introduction by Spradley and McCurdy (1972).

our actions and their consequences. If we all walked down the street or greeted each other in the same way without regard for the circumstances, then an ethnography of our street behavior would be uninteresting. We are, however, quite selective in our interaction with others. Some people attract us and others do not, most often for reasons which we ourselves do not understand. Much of what happens to us in everyday life results from the limited and unarticulated methods we use to handle the world and to hold each other accountable. How many of us are aware, for example, that when passing through the neighborhood of a different ethnic group we generally display "the posture of territorial behavior"? We lower our heads, curl our shoulders so that our chests do not protrude, bring our hands close to or in front of our bodies, and keep our eyes down (Scheflen, 1976). Such behavior may make us a little less noticeable, but it also curtails our communication with people in that neighborhood. In other words, such behavior helps to maintain the very boundaries which prevent interethnic communication.

People develop elaborate procedures for relating to each other in different situations. These procedures are rarely obvious to the participants but offer them a quick and easy way of achieving working agreements. We are all embedded in our own procedures, which make us both very smart in one situation and blind and stupid in the next. Any change in these procedures, either cultural or personal, can reveal unimagined consequences of the ways we choose to relate to each other. This is illustrated by the clinical account of a family disrupted by the husband's extreme dependence upon his wife (Watzlawick, Beavin, & Jackson, 1967). According to all involved, the problem was that the man was illiterate and showed little promise of upward mobility. After extensive therapy and instruction, the man acquired enough reading competence to become more independent. Soon after, the wife filed for divorce. Prior to the husband's treatment, the couple apparently had developed a rather special way of dealing with each other which unfortunately left the man dependent upon his wife. When the husband became literate, however, the dependent nature of their relationship was undermined and the marriage dissolved. Apparently neither partner knew what they were each contributing to and gaining from the dependency relationship. Is it possible that the logic of many of our relationships is equally well hidden?

Turning now to education, we hope that the ethnographic study of classrooms will allow us to look carefully at how we as teachers make sense and hold students accountable to our way of making sense. The problem with common sense, of course, is that sense must be made in common with other people within institutional contexts which place different demands on each of the participants. Accordingly, sustained common sense is a rare achievement, and teachers and children often work out mutually regressive relations in their classrooms for reasons generally unrecognized by both groups. All teachers lose some students in every class. Talented teachers and intelligent children sometimes find themselves on opposite sides of the fence. Pain and failure often result for all involved, and no one quite knows why. In the early years some students do not even learn to read, and in later years many suffer from alienation and crippling anxieties. Some analysts blame the children, their genes, their families, or television, while others blame the teachers for being lazy, insensitive, prejudiced, or badly trained. In most cases, neither the children nor their teachers are to be blamed; communication breakdowns always have two sides. The question is not who is at fault, but rather what it is about the way teachers and children relate that enables them to make sense of each other as coparticipants in the educational process, on the one hand, or as enemies, on the other.

Consider the case of Rosa, a failing student in a first-grade classroom that I have been analyzing. She is in the bottom of one of three reading-skill groups in the class where she constantly struggles to get a turn to read. Yet, day after day, she is passed by. Why is Rosa so consistently ignored? How will she ever learn to read if she spends all her time in the classroom trying to get a turn? After analyzing a film I made of the reading group, I began to understand the teacher's position. Rosa is one of the least skilled readers in the group. Although her English is adequate for everyday affairs, her native tongue is Spanish, and she apparently had little training in learning how to read either language before coming to school. There is no reason to think that Rosa's handicap is permanent; not learning how to read by age six says little about what a child can do by age seven or eight if given the proper learning environment (Downing, 1973; Rohwer, 1971; Singer, in press; Wanat, 1976). Bilingualism should offer no serious handicap to a child learning to read, again provided a proper learning environment is available (Diebold, 1968; Modiano, 1973). The teacher's behavior in this particular classroom is sensible; she is simply giving Rosa time to develop enough competence to read without embarrassing her in front of her peers.

Will Rosa ever get the opportunity to master reading in school? I will only outline the answer to the question in order to point to how an ethnographer might proceed and to the interesting results to be had from an ethnographic approach. I proceed by examining repeatedly the film of the reading group in order to isolate the working agreements which Rosa and the teacher use to make sense of each other. Only those agreements which the participants themselves identify in their behavior are accepted as adequately described relational contexts.[2]

What are the relations between Rosa and the teacher? The teacher says of Rosa, "I just can't reach her," and Rosa offers only a blushing silence when asked about her relationship to the teacher. On the surface, their relationship does not sound workable, but an underlying logic can be seen in their interactions. A careful look at Rosa's behavior reveals that she in fact conspires with the teacher in not getting a turn to read. Although she often requests a turn to read, she does so in unusual ways: she checks to see what page the other children are reading, turns to a different page, and then calls for a turn; she waits for the teacher to start to call on another child and then quickly calls for a turn; or she calls for a turn while looking away from the teacher. The teacher often attends to these signals before calling on

---

[2] The procedures and criteria for producing an ethnographically adequate account of activities and their contexts are elaborated in McDermott (1976). For similar procedures and results, see Scheflen (1973); an extensive report by Mehan, Cazden, Coles, Fisher, and Maroules (1976), and a summary statement by Erickson and Schultz (1977).

another child. The teacher organizes the turn taking in the group randomly, so that Rosa never has to be asked to read as she would if the teacher called on children in order around the reading table. Accordingly, too much of the group's time at the table is spent in organizing who is to read next. During these times, outsiders enter the group to ask the teacher questions and group members complain that everyone is not being treated fairly. The result is that the bottom reading group spends only a third as much time on reading tasks as the top group, although they spend an equal amount of time at the reading table. Rosa spends her time avoiding a turn to read.

Rosa's actions make sense when one considers her beginning reading skills, the competitive pressures of the classroom, and the teacher's organizational methods. The teacher's behavior makes sense given her task—teaching a child to read while keeping a whole roomful of children busy at other tasks. Together, they behave sensibly in relation to each other and appear to be doing their best. But together they do not achieve trusting relations. Rosa and the teacher do not understand each other's behavior as directed to the best interest of what they are trying to do together, namely, to get Rosa organized for learning how to read. Their failure to achieve trusting relations has its consequences. Rosa spends little time trying to read in the classroom; she either will learn to read at home or suffer school failure. In fact, at the end of the second grade, Rosa was sent to a special school for slow learners.

Such relational problems run deep in our competitive culture, where school systems are designed to sort out the capable from the incapable (Henry, 1963; Spindler, 1959). Solutions will require more than simple changes in pedagogical style (Cazden, 1976; Church, 1976). To illustrate this point, I will consider two ways of organizing classrooms, the success of both of which depends on the relational work of teachers and children in getting organized for learning tasks. Why some communities have the resources for doing this work while others do not remains an unanswered question.

Teacher-Student Relations

Teaching is invariably a form of coercion. While some teachers handle coercion directly, others are less direct and more guidance-oriented. In the contemporary idiom, the difference is referred to in terms of closed and open classrooms. Although the constraints can be framed differently and with quite different consequences for the organization of the social structure (Bernstein, 1975), coercion is always present in classrooms. All teachers, regardless of their orientation, are faced with the task of getting and directing the children's attention, directing it to a problem, and leading them to some way of handling it (Mishler, 1972).

Generally, teachers use speech to direct children to learning tasks. The specific verbal strategies teachers use are not so important as whether or not the strategies make good sense to the children. A teacher must establish working agreements wherein the children can trust the teacher's coercion to be in their best interests.

504

Successful Authoritarian Classroom Communication

The Old Order Amish schools of Pennsylvania provide an example of a peda-gogically successful, authoritarian strategy for handling classroom activities (Hos-tetler, 1974, 1975; Hostetler & Huntington, 1971). Amish children did not do well academically when forced by local authorities into public schools, and there was little reason to think that they would perform better in their own schools. Amish teachers seldom have more than eight years of academic training; they must teach children raised speaking a Germanic language to read English; and their class-rooms prohibit competition, which many consider to be a key element of group learning in our culture. Finally, the Amish teachers' communicative style, on the surface at least, is contrary to much of the educational ideology in America. The teachers dominate their classrooms, and an analysis of classroom interactions has shown a heavy use of commands and a high degree of direct instruction (Payne, 1971). Nevertheless, Amish community schools are quite successful, not only by Amish standards, but by those of other American schools as well. Amish children score above the norms in standardized reading and arithmetic tests (Hostetler, 1975; Hostetler & Huntington, 1971). What then is the relation between teaching style and these pupils' successes in academic subjects?

To answer this question, we must look to the kinds of social relations which make sense to children raised in the Amish culture. Socialization patterns among the Amish are quite different from those found elsewhere in America. Indeed, many aspects of Amish identity in America have been forged in opposition to and in defense against other ways of being human in a modern technological society. Such a defensive strategy, common among minority cultures, is marked by the merging of individual identities into a group life that is organized around unifying symbols transmitted by a small number of authoritarian leaders (Siegel, 1970). The Amish educational system fits this model nicely. Its symbols are religious and are used to establish trusting relations. The teacher is in total control of the chil-dren's development, telling them what to do and when and how to do it. In terms of learning to read and enhancing an Amish identity, this system is highly suc-cessful. Children and their teachers live in a closed community with highly specific routines, where everyone is accountable to everyone else. Amish community members use a specific code to achieve common sense and mutual trust. In this context, instructions are not blind commands but, rather, sensible suggestions about what to do next to further common goals. There is a warm relational fabric that underlies the instructions and transforms them from orders into sensible ways of organizing everyday life. What appears to many to be an authoritarian and oppressive system for organizing a classroom may in fact make great sense to the children. Outsiders simply miss the cues which ground teacher-student activities in trust and accountability.

Unsuccessful Authoritarian Classroom Communication

No matter how successful authoritarian speech behavior is within small communi-ties, there is much evidence that the authoritarian teacher is encountering difficul-ties in contemporary America. Apparently the trust which makes direct commands possible in the Amish classroom is not present in more open communities. Even in less conservative Amish communities, in fact, teachers use much less direct forms of control (Payne, 1971).

The failure of attempts to teach with direct methods in the absence of a foundation of trusting relations is well documented. In such situations, children simply "don't listen," and the teacher expends most of the class time controlling "behavior problems" or, to borrow a phrase from a past principal of mine, "keeping the lid on." Too often teachers fall back on a formal definition of their role as teachers and expect children to conduct themsleves as if this role placed an exact set of rules on the children's behavior. In such situations, the teacher relies on institutional rewards and punishments, saying, "Do this, because, if you don't, the principal will deal with you," rather than, "Do this, because it's a sensible thing to do."

Teachers' efforts to define roles in the classrooms create some strange forms of behavior. For example, a teacher who fails to motivate a class may camouflage this failure with a lesson directed to a nonexistent audience. Examples of this phenomenon are unfortunately common in ethnographic studies of urban schools (Robert, 1970; Rosenfeld, 1971). Rist (1973) offers an example of what he calls a "phantom performance":

> She asks the children to repeat the poem, and no child makes a sound. She asks the children to repeat the poem line by line after her, first with the words and then a second time through simply saying "lu, lu, lu" in place of the words. The children are completely baffled and say nothing. At the end of the second repetition she comments, "Okay, that was good. We will have to do that again next week." (p. 107)

The relational ground underlying a phantom performance is not fertile soil for building trusting relations. The children's definition of the teacher's role comes to include not attending to the class, and they begin to dismiss teaching as an essentially insensitive task; the teacher is expected to be "mean."

In addition to intensive role definition, direct control over a class can be built on insult and status degradation. Interpersonal warfare, rather than trust and accountability, is the result. Much of what were described to me as teaching and classroom-control techniques by a teacher trainer in the New York City schools amounted to insults that could bind a child into silence. Even when the authoritarian approach to classroom management keeps children under control, if it is not founded on a mutual understanding extending beyond threats of detention or suspension, little learning will take place. Defensive blackboard boredom is no more academically productive than the overt misbehavior of the less controlled blackboard jungle (Robert, 1970; Rosenfeld, 1971). It is in the context of an authoritarian classroom without a grounding in trust and accountability that it is possible to talk of children achieving school failure (McDermott, 1974). In response to the teacher's authority, children develop their own classroom organization, in which not working and disrupting the teacher's procedures become goals.

Unsuccessful Guidance Classroom Communication

Less direct forms of coercing children into attending to classroom tasks are not uniformly better or worse than the authoritarian approach.[3] If there is no proper

506

relational foundation, a child is no more likely to follow a gentle suggestion than a direct order.

Guidance approaches to teaching make much use of question-commands rather than direct orders. A teacher can say, "Close the door" or "Why don't you close the door?" In either case the door must be closed by the student. The child is neither expected nor permitted to answer with a statement such as "I am not closing the door because I don't feel like it." The question is not meant to be a question but rather a command. Linguists have recently been studying such phenomena and have given them the delightful name of "whimperatives" (Green, 1973; Sadock, 1969). A whimperative stands for a command stated in a question form with a "wh–" word. But if "whim" or "whimper" is taken as the root, a whimperative can mean something quite different. So it is with "wh–" commands in everyday conversation; they can be interpreted in many ways, depending on the context in which they are used.[4]

The kind of response elicited by a whimperative depends upon how it is understood, which in turn depends on how the conversationalists define their relations at a particular time. Imagine the difficulty of telling a child what to do when there is no working consensus that the child should do what he or she is told. Now imagine trying to hide from the child that he or she is in fact being told what to do. In this way, a command framed as a question becomes a whimper. In question form, the command to close a door only suggests an expectation that the door be closed and hides the fact that there is likely to be a system of constraints behind the teacher's request. This problem does not arise when a trusting relation underlies the teacher's command; the child interprets the teacher as acting in the best interest of what they are trying to do together in the classroom and simply does what the teacher suggests. Without this relationship, the whimpering nature of the command is more apparent to the child. In such a context, learning tasks seldom receive the attention required for the child to make progress.

Successful Guidance Classroom Communication

Guidance approaches to communication in the classroom need not result in such relational disasters between teachers and children. In a trusting environment, such approaches can be most powerful, particularly when attention is directed

[3] By claiming that guidance approaches to classroom organization are uniformly no better or worse than authoritarian approaches, I am not trying to deny that a particular style of pedagogy has systematic ties to the social structure and value networks in which it is immersed (Bernstein, 1975; J. McDermott, 1976). In fact, my point is quite the opposite. No one pedagogical style is inherently better than any other. If children and teachers can understand the style well enough to construct working agreements and trusting relations, then it will work.

[4] For the most part, linguists are concerned with whimperatives because they represent interesting uses of syntactic form for conveying a variety of linguistic functions. Their concern stems from an effort to account for all the allowable sentences in our language with a finite set of grammatical rules. There is serious question, however, whether this is the most useful goal for linguistic description (Hymes, 1974, particularly chap. 9; Volosinov, 1973). More interesting approaches to requestive systems in actual speech, of which whimperatives are but a subgrouping, and the ways they interface with the social world of people doing relational work with each other are now available in Dore (1978) and Ervin-Tripp (1977).

to the individual needs of the children. Indeed, in many of our urban schools, where children come from diverse communities, a guidance approach may be the best alternative. Without the possibility of drawing on shared images and life experiences, many teachers face the task of creating a system of trusting relations with only the resources of the classroom at hand (Spindler, 1974). In such cases, a guidance approach affords the children an opportunity to explore their environments and to discover learning tasks for themselves. This may be the only way for the teacher to hold the interest of the children long enough to establish a working consensus. Once such working relationships are established, the teacher will have to use them wisely in order to sustain their effectiveness.

Teacher-Student Relations and Learning to Read

I have tried to show that teachers and children use a system of relations to make sense of each other and that this system underlies the sustained attention of children to learning tasks. To understand these relational systems adequately, better ethnographic accounts of life in the classroom are necessary. Even in the absence of such accounts, however, anecdotal reports of children learning to read suggest that the successful acquisition of literacy, like the successful use of a pedagogical style, depends on the achievement of trusting relations. If this hypothesis is correct, we may gain a new perspective on why some children do not learn to read in our schools. Rather than pointing to inadequacies in either the children or their teachers, perhaps we should examine the rational adaptations made by teachers and children within the institutional contexts we offer them.

Consider how the Hanunoo learn to read. The Hanunoo, a small group of farmers isolated in the rugged mountains of the island of Mindoro in the Philippines, achieve a 60-percent literacy rate with a rare Indic-derived script imported centuries ago and virtually unknown to surrounding groups. The Hanunoo receive no formal training in reading and writing and, in fact, are not concerned about literacy until early puberty. They appear, however, to have the ultimate organizational device for learning to read. Literacy is used almost exclusively in courtship among the Hanunoo, and at the time of puberty the children work diligently at learning the script until they can carve songs onto bamboo cylinders in order to support an active love life. They achieve literacy within only months (Conklin, 1949, 1960).

There are numerous examples of similar achievements of people having to master very rapidly an orthography for social and religious purposes in a nonschool environment (Basso & Anderson, 1973; Ferguson, 1972; Goody, Cole, & Scribner, in press; Meggitt, 1967; Walker, 1972). Although none of these accounts specifies the relational contexts which guide the people to learn and become literate, they all raise an important question. If it is the case that people can learn to read quickly and under such diverse conditions, why do so many of our children fail to learn how to read despite so many years in school?

I suspect that many of our children spend most of their time in relational battles rather than on learning tasks. This is especially the case for minority children who enter the schools with an uncertain status in the eyes of teachers. Some have held that minority-group members do badly in schools because they have a different language, dialect, and rules for taking turns in conversation. When minority students and their teachers are unable to understand each other, however, I believe they have a choice of turning their misunderstanding into a social barrier or of working with each other until they can repair their misunderstanding (Erickson, 1975; McDermott & Gospodinoff, 1976). The alternatives chosen depend on the relational contexts in which the misunderstanding arises.

Although equivalent examples of other kinds of communicative-code interference in the classroom are available, the following example from the study of dialect interference in learning how to read seems particularly relevant. Most of the children in the first-grade classrooms studied by Piestrup (1973) in Oakland, California, schools spoke a Black English vernacular. To the extent that their teachers tried to stop them from using dialect in the classroom, the children were unable to get to the task of learning to read. These children's use of dialect either remained the same or increased depending on how often the teachers corrected their speech. For children whose use of dialect was often corrected, reading scores tended to be low. In classrooms where the children were allowed to talk and read in dialect, vernacular use did not increase and reading scores were higher, with many children scoring above national norms. When the dialect was not treated as a barrier to communication, the children and the teacher were able to spend time on reading tasks. However, when dialect was treated as a problem in the relations between the teacher and children, it interfered with their formulating trusting agreements about what they were trying to do with each other. Thus, they spent more time doing relational work and less time learning to read. In this way, the use of dialect and the children's participation in learning tasks become politicized. The logical result is seen in older Black children for whom there are significant correlations among dialect use, school failure, and participation in peer-group gangs (Labov & Robins, 1969).

The problem for many minority-group children in mainstream schools is in establishing trusting relations with the teacher. Even if many of these children come to school different from their peers—lagging behind in the development of certain school skills (phonics, for example), with divergent communicative skills, or with completely different expectations about what a classroom is—they can still learn to read. If, however, these children become engaged in an endless battle to relate to the teacher, they will never have the time to catch up with their peers. Our school system is harsh to those who fall behind; it sorts these children out, labels them, and finally pushes them aside. Certain minorities have bypassed this system by teaching their children how to read outside the public schools, either in private schools or at home. But most minority groups that have relied on the public schools have paid a price; identity struggles replace learning tasks, and children often leave school knowing little more about reading than when they entered.

These examples suggest the primacy of social relations in determining children's success or failure in school. If social relations are, in fact, important, then we may have to reconsider our notions of who are "problem children" and how to best understand and help them. In particular, we may have to question our own role in the failures of these children and examine how we help create such destructive environments.

Conclusion

An awareness of the primacy of trusting relations in the organization of successful classrooms and of the usefulness of ethnography as a tool with which to study the nature of classroom relations leads to questions that may help us to reformulate our theory and practice in teaching children who do not learn in school. Evidence indicates that the efficacy of varying pedagogical styles and ways of learning to read depends on the social relations established with different children in different classrooms.

Since the relations between teachers and children are central to the organization of time in the classroom, we teachers must ask how our ways of relating result in some children spending more time getting organized than being on task. There appears to be an order or logic to our ways of relating, even when they are not successful. We must ask just what our contribution is to this order. The specifics of these difficult questions are probably different across classrooms and children. Two facts, however, may help us understand what we may be doing wrong. First, we often do not see the underlying order in the children's behavior when they engage us in relational struggles. Second, we blame them for their regressive behavior, although they could not act regressively without us.

These facts raise the most crucial question of all: *how do we create environments which allow children to act sensibly, but which also allow us to remain blind to the good sense of their behavior?* In the future, ethnographic studies of the classroom might be addressed to answering this question in empirical terms. In the meantime, simply knowing that the question is important is a major step forward. By asking this question, we alter our perspective on problem children by acknowledging that they are acting sensibly within the environments we have afforded them; any labeling of children as inadequate without a corresponding account of how their behavior makes sense is necessarily unfair. By asking this question, we also require that our theories of problem children account for the uneven distribution of resources available to different children and their teachers for making sense of each other and achieving trusting relations in institutional contexts; any description of problem children is necessarily political. Finally, until we can gain more control over the institutional contexts we share with children, we can reduce our expectation that schools can function as a mechanism for massive social change; until we can control the particulars of our own institutional lives, it is foolish to think that we can easily direct the institutional lives of our children.

Once we start asking this type of question, we will not be able to lay the blame for school failure solely at the children's feet. They simply act much too sensibly for that, and their ways of relating are as much a function of our expectations as theirs. Unidirectional solutions cannot cure relational problems. To reorder our relations with problem children, we must first deal with the relations that have already been established. Efforts to build trusting relations and develop successful learning environments must start with an adequate ethnographic sense of what we are really trying to do with children and of the nature of institutional contexts within which we are making these attempts.

References

Arensberg, C., & Kimball, S. *Family and community in Ireland*. Cambridge, Mass.: Harvard University Press, 1940.

Basso, K., & Anderson, N. The Western Apache writing system. *Science*, 1973, **180**, 1013–1021.

Beck, H. Attentional struggles and silencing strategies in a human political conflict: The case of the Vietnam moratoria. In M. Chance and R. Larson (Eds.), *The social structure of attention*. New York: Wiley, 1976. (a)

Beck, H. Neuropsychological servosystems, consciousness, and the problem of embodiment. *Behavioral Science*, 1976, **21**, 139–160. (b)

Bernstein, B. Class and pedagogies: Visible and invisible. *Educational Studies*, 1975, **1**, 23–41.

Birdwhistell, R. *Kinesics and context*. Philadelphia: University of Pennsylvania Press, 1970.

Bloom, B. Time and learning. *American Psychologist*, 1974, **29**, 682–688.

Cazden, C. How knowledge about language helps the classroom teacher—or does it. Paper presented at the American Educational Research Association Meetings, San Francisco, April 1976.

Church, J. Psychology and the social order. *Annals of the New York Academy of Sciences*, 1976, **270**, 141–151.

Cicourel, A. *Cognitive sociology*. New York: Free Press, 1974.

Conklin, H. Bamboo literacy on Mindoro. *Pacific Discovery*, 1949, **2**, 4–11.

Conklin, H. Maling, a Hanunoo girl from the Philippines. In J. Casagrande (Ed.), *In the company of man*. New York: Harper, 1960.

Conklin, H. Ethnogeneological method. In W. Goodenough (Ed.), *Explorations in cultural anthropology*. New York: McGraw-Hill, 1964.

Diebold, A. R. The consequences of early bilingualism in cognitive development and personality formation. In E. Norbeck, D. Price-Williams, & W. McCord (Eds.), *The study of personality*. New York: Holt, Rinehart & Winston, 1968.

Dore, J. The structure of nursery school conversation. In K. Nelson (Ed.), *Children's language*. New York: Halsted Press, 1978.

Downing, J. *Comparative reading*. New York: Macmillan, 1973.

Erickson, F. Gatekeeping and the melting pot. *Harvard Educational Review*, 1975, **45**, 44–70.

Erickson, F., & Shultz, J. When is a context? Some issues and methods in the analysis of social competence. *Quarterly Newsletter of the Institute for Comparative Human Development*, 1977, 1 (2), 5–10.

Ervin-Tripp, S. "Wait for me, roller-skate!" In C. Mitchell-Kernan & S. Ervin-Tripp (Eds.), *Child discourse*. New York: Academic Press, 1977.

Ferguson, C. Contrasting patterns of literacy acquisition in a multilingual nation. In W. Whitely (Ed.), *Language use and social change*. London: International African Institute, 1972.

Frake, C. A structural description of Subanun "religious behavior." In W. Goodenough (Ed.), *Explorations in cultural anthropology*. New York: McGraw-Hill, 1964.

Frake, C. Plying frames can be dangerous. An assessment of methodology in cognitive anthropology. Paper presented at the Conference on Methods in Cognitive Anthropology, Durham, N.C., April 1974.

Garfinkel, H. A conception of and experiments with "trust" as a condition of stable con- certed actions. In O. J. Harvey (Ed.), *Motivation and social interaction.* New York: Roland Press, 1963.

Garfinkel, H. *Studies in ethnomethodology.* Englewood Cliffs, N.J.: Prentice-Hall, 1967.

Garfinkel, H. Comments. In R. Hill & K. Crittenden (Eds.), *Proceedings of the Purdue symposium on ethnomethodology.* Purdue, Ind.: Purdue Research Foundation, 1968.

Goffman, E. *The presentation of self in everyday life.* New York: Anchor, 1959.

Goffman, E. *Relations in public.* New York: Harper Colophon, 1971.

Goffman, E. Replies and responses. *Language in society,* 1976, 5, 257–313.

Goody, J. Cole, M., & Scribner, S. Writing and formal operations: A case study among the Vai. *Africa,* in press.

Green, G. How to get people to do things with words. In R. Shuy (Ed.), *Some new direc- tions in linguistics.* Washington, D.C.: Georgetown University Press, 1973.

Gump, P. Education as an environmental enterprise. In R. Weinberg & F. Wood (Eds.), *Observation of pupils and teachers in mainstream and special education.* Reston, Va.: Council for Exceptional Children, 1975.

Henry, J. *Culture against man.* New York: Vintage, 1963.

Hostetler, J. Education in communitarian societies. In G. Spindler (Ed.), *Education and cultural process.* New York: Holt, Rinehart & Winston, 1974.

Hostetler, J. The cultural context of the Wisconsin case. In A. Keim (Ed.), *Compulsory education and the Amish.* Boston: Beacon Press, 1975.

Hostetler, J., & Huntington, G. *Children in Amish society.* New York: Holt, Rinehart & Winston, 1971.

Hymes, D. *Foundations in sociolinguistics: An ethnographic approach.* Philadelphia: Uni- versity of Pennsylvania Press, 1974.

Kendon, A. *Studies in the behavior of social interaction.* New York: Humanities, 1977.

Kendon, A., & Ferber, A. A description of some human greetings. In R. Michael & J. Crook (Eds.), *Comparative ecology and behaviour of primates.* New York: Academic Press, 1973.

Labov, W., & Robins, C. A note on the relation of reading failure to peer-group status in urban ghettos. *Florida FL Reporter,* 1969, 7, 54–57, 167.

McDermott, J. *The culture of experience.* New York: New York University Press, 1976.

McDermott, R. P. Achieving school failure. In G. D. Spindler (Ed.), *Education and cul- tural process.* New York: Holt, Rinehart & Winston, 1974.

McDermott, R. P. *Kids make sense: An ethnographic account of the interactional manage- ment of success and failure in one first-grade classroom.* Unpublished doctoral dis- sertation, Stanford University, 1976.

McDermott, R. P., & Church, J. Making sense and feeling good: The ethnography of com- munication and identity work. *Communication,* 1976, 2, 121–142.

McDermott, R. P., & Gospodinoff, K. Social contexts for ethnic borders and school failure. Paper presented at the International Conference on Nonverbal Behavior, Ontario In- stitute for Studies in Education, Toronto, Canada, 1976.

Meggitt, M. Uses of literacy in New Guinea and Melanesia. *Bijdragen Tot de Taal, Land-en Volkenkinde,* 1967, 73, 71–82.

Mehan, H., Cazden, C., Coles, L., Fisher, S., & Maroules, N. *Social organization of classroom lessons* (Report No. 67–68). San Diego: University of California, Center for Human Information Processing Reports, 1976.

Mehan, H., & Wood, H. *The reality of ethnomethodology.* New York: Wiley Interscience, 1975.

Mishler, E. Implications of teacher strategies for language and cognition. In C. Cazden, V. John, & D. Hymes (Eds.), *Functions of language in the classroom.* New York: Teachers College Press, 1972.

Modiano, N. *Indian education in the Chiapas highlands.* New York: Holt, Rinehart & Winston, 1973.

O'Leary, K. D. Token reinforcement in the classroom. In T. Brigham & C. Catania (Eds.), *The analysis of behavior.* New York: Wiley, in press.

Payne, J. Analysis of teacher-student classroom interaction in Amish and non-Amish schools. *Social Problems,* 1971, **19,** 79–90.

Piestrup, A. Black dialect interference and accommodation of reading instruction in first grade. Berkeley: University of California, *Monographs of the Language-Behavior Research Laboratory,* 4, 1973.

Rist, R. *The urban school.* Cambridge, Mass.: MIT Press, 1973.

Robert, J. *Scene of the battle: Group behavior in the classrooms.* New York: Doubleday, 1970.

Rohwer, W. Prime time for education. *Harvard Educational Review,* 1971, **41,** 316–341.

Rosenfeld, G. *"Shut those thick lips": A study in slum school failure.* New York: Holt, Rinehart & Winston, 1971.

Sadock, J. Whimperatives. In J. Sadock & A. Vanek (Eds.), *Studies presented to Robert B. Lees by his students.* Edmonton: Linguistic Research, 1969.

Sapir, E. Cultural anthropology and psychiatry. In D. Mandlebaum (Ed.), *Selected writings of Edward Sapir.* Berkeley: University of California Press, 1949. (Originally published, 1932).

Scheflen, A. *Communicational structure.* Bloomington, Ind.: Indiana University Press, 1973.

Scheflen, A. *Human territories.* Englewood Cliffs, N.J.: Prentice-Hall, 1976.

Siegel, B. Defensive structuring and environmental stress. *American Journal of Sociology,* 1970, **76,** 11–32.

Singer, H. IQ is and is not related to reading. In S. Wanat (Ed.), *Testing reading proficiency.* Arlington, Va.: Center for Applied Linguistics, in press.

Spindler, G. D. *The transmission of American culture.* Cambridge, Mass.: Harvard University Press, 1959.

Spindler, G. D. Schooling in Schonhausen. In G. Spindler (Ed.), *Education and cultural process.* New York: Holt, Rinehart & Winston, 1974.

Spradley, J., & McCurdy, J. (Eds.), *The cultural experience: Ethnography in complex society.* Palo Alto, Calif.: Science Research Associates, 1972.

Volosinov, V. N. *Marxism and the philosophy of language.* New York: Seminar Press, 1973.

Walker, W. Notes on native systems and the design of native literacy programs. *Anthropological Linguistics,* 1972, **11,** 148–166.

Wanat, S. Reading readiness. *Visible Language,* 1976, **10,** 101–127.

Watzlawick, P., Beavin, J., & Jackson, D. *Pragmatics of human communication.* New York: Mouton, 1967.

Wolf, M. Notes on the behavior of pedestrians. In A. Birenbaum & E. Sagarin (Eds.), *People in places.* New York: Praeger, 1973.

CHAPTER 6

Disorders of Language
& Reading

Language Disorders in Childhood

ERIC H. LENNEBERG
Children's Hospital Medical Center
Boston, Massachusetts

From a combined medical and psychological perspective, Eric Lenneberg examines the major categories of speech and language disorders. Finding considerable overlap in the existing distinctions, Lenneberg proposes that each major disorder be characterized by a succinct, usable definition, a developmental and medical history, a list of symptomatology, and a suggested prognosis. Toward that end, Lenneberg reviews several speech and language disorders in children and offers a differential diagnosis for each. Emphasizing children's innate faculty for language, he concludes by suggesting that parents not be overanxious to "teach" their children to speak.

The differential diagnosis of speech and language disorders in children is a practical pediatric problem with direct consequences on plans for treatment and general management. There is a wide-spread preference among practicing physicians and educators to refer the child to others (speech correctionists, social workers, or otolaryngologists) who may or may not have experience in all of the areas that have a direct bearing on the development of speech and language.

Major diagnostic categories are not well defined: there is an unnecessary overlap of terminology and a random collection of criteria for setting up classification. This difficulty is peculiar to the literature on the subject, and *can* be corrected. The following article presents material under the headings of the major causes for these abnormalities and is intended as a guide for individuals concerned with language disorders.

Prepared while the author was USPHS Career Investigator in Mental Health. Grateful acknowledgement is also made for support through grants M-5268 and M-2921 from the National Institute of Mental Health. Dr. Randolph K. Byers and Dr. George E. Gardner have read the manuscript and I am indebted to them for constructive criticism and valuable suggestions.

Harvard Educational Review   Vol. 34   No. 2   Spring 1964, 152–177

DEAFNESS

Definition

It is customary to differentiate between peripheral and central deafness. The terms seem to imply an anatomic criterion whereas the distinction is, in fact, made on symptomatic grounds. Peripheral deafness is assumed when a lowering of pure-tone acuity beyond some arbitrary level (say seventy decibel loss relative to normal threshold) can be demonstrated by audiogram. Central deafness is postulated when pure tone threshold is near normal yet the patient acts in a manner reminiscent of the bona fide deaf. The significance of this latter condition is not well understood and will only be dealt with marginally at the end of the article.

Medical History

In seventy-eight percent of all cases either the well-known antecedents for deafness (German measles in the first trimester, erythroblastosis fetalis, meningitis, bilateral ear infections, etc.) or a family history can be elicited.[1] In these instances parents are forewarned and consult a physician in the patient's early infancy. In the remaining cases the condition appears spontaneously and the chief complaint is failure to begin to speak at the customary age. In the absence of preliminary warning, parents frequently are totally unaware of their child's unresponsiveness to acoustic stimuli, probably because infants in general (and perhaps the deaf in particular) react as quickly to visual and tactual stimuli as to acoustic stimuli and in the normal environment purely acoustic stimuli are relatively rare.

Developmental history

Unless an adventitious disease that has led to deafness has left fixed lesions outside of the hearing apparatus, developmental history is within normal limits. It is a remarkable phenomenon that a congenitally deaf child can and ordinarily does also have a perfectly normal development in his vocalizations during the first four to six months of life.[2] The transition from crying-only to cooing and to babbling do occur on the three- and five-month levels respectively and neither impressionistic nor instrumental analysis[3] of these early sounds reveal a qualitative difference between the normally hearing child and that which is later demonstrably deaf (and has presumably been deaf

---

[1] Harry Best, *Deafness and the Deaf in the United States* (New York: Macmillan, 1943).

[2] Eric H. Lenneberg, "Speech as a motor skill with special reference to non-aphasic disorders." In U. Bellugi and R. W. Brown (Eds.), *The Acquisition of Language, Monographs on the Society for Research in Child Development*, 1964, 29 (1, Serial No. 92), 115–127.

[3] Eric H. Lenneberg, "A laboratory for speech research at the Children's Hospital Medical Center," *New England Journal of Medicine*, 266 (February, 1962), 385–392.

since birth). With practice in listening to children's sounds, differences between the deaf and the hearing can be detected by about the sixth month, but for another few months these differences are rather in quantity than in quality. Even here, the total amount of a deaf child's vocalization may not be different from that of a hearing child, but the hearing child at this age will constantly run through a large repertoire of sounds whereas deaf children will be making the same sounds sometimes for weeks on end and then suddenly change to some other set of sounds and "specialize" in these for a while. There is no consistent preference among deaf children for specific sounds. The voice is always of a normal and pleasing nature in these spontaneous utterances, often including something resembling intonation patterns, the abnormally pitched voice making its first appearance only with the advent of programmatic speech-training. This latter phenomenon is of considerable physiological interest. Apparently, when voice mechanisms come under voluntary control, audition is the primary controlling feed-back mechanism; however, when voicing is essentially motivated by emotional states, the motor coordination is sufficiently controlled by proprioceptive relays.

Symptomatology

In cases of simple and pure deafness, the patient displays normal affect, relates well to his family and visiting friends, shows interest in his surroundings, plays well with adequate concentration span and is free from outstanding behavior problems. He is eager to communicate his needs which is effected by clever gesture or pantomine. There are certain mannerisms which are common but not necessary concomitants, such as approaching people and moving lips in imitation of speech movements, particularly vivid facial expressions including arching of the brows, intensive nodding, shrugging the shoulders or thrusting hands and arms forward with palms supinated as if to ask "What now?" The deaf child babbles and makes a variety of sounds, usually while concentrating on play, but he is often judged to be somewhat more quiet than his hearing siblings or contemporaries. Babbling may include something like "mamama," or other repetitions of sounds; but if the patient is profoundly deaf, his repertoire does not have a single recognizable word. Nor do any of his vocalizations have any fixed semantic value. When calling people's attention to himself or to things in his surroundings, he makes no use whatever in early childhood of his vocal apparatus. A deaf child of three or four who has not had any training directed towards purposeful vocalization seems completely unaware of the possibility of making vocal sounds for communication. Instead, he will poke or push or gesture violently to make himself noticeable. A carefully elicited history and patient observation of play activities in the office should make intelligence testing superfluous in most cases.

However, if assessment of intellectual development is desired, the psychologist should receive special instructions to eliminate all tests that require either understanding of verbal instructions or depend on any verbal responses. The Leiter International Performance Scale[4] has been found to be the most useful single test instrument for assessing a congenitally deaf child.

Management

If suspicion of deafness is confirmed by audiogram, an appropriate hearing aid must be provided for the patient. Most audiologists believe at the present time that all hearing-handicapped children profit from such a prosthesis—the profoundly deaf as well as those whose pure tone acuity is only mildly affected and whose main problem is thought to be perceptual and central. While this radical position still leaves some room for questions, the present paper is not the forum to discuss the pros and cons. In addition to the hearing aid, special-ized pre-school training must be instituted, preparing the child for the more formal speech and voice training that is begun in the schools for the deaf a-round the age of five. In areas where parents have a choice between residential and day care of their children, counseling on the advantages and disad-vantages of each of these modalities is needed. Parents' attention should also be directed towards the Tracy Clinic[5] correspondence course for mothers of young deaf children which provides the parents with considerable guidance and support in daily problems and constructive attitude towards their deaf child.

Prognosis

A deaf child should encounter no difficulty in the acquisition of language through the graphic medium: reading and writing are established in due course, though stylistic and grammatical mistakes commonly persist in some measure throughout life. Skill in lip reading and vocal communication varies greatly from individual to individual, the overall success being well correlated with the age at which hearing is lost and the profoundness of the loss. It is in-teresting to note that when the child is about three years of age, an important milestone is passed. The child who has had normal hearing up to the age of three and who has started on its course towards language acquisition and then suddenly becomes deaf (for instance due to meningitis) has a significant head-start in the language arts in comparison with the congenitally deaf. In all cases the voice itself will sound strained and unpleasant during the patient's efforts to "speak" and there seems to be little training available that will help the patient *permanently* to overcome this problem. A deaf child's progress in aca-

[4] *Leiter International Performance Scale* (Washington, D.C.: Psychological Service Center Press, 1952).
[5] John Tracy Clinic, 806 West Adams Boulevard, Los Angeles 7, California.

demic subjects is generally behind that of the hearing child, but it can be said with certainty today that this academic retardation is definitely not due to a slowed mental development because of the prolonged absence of language in early childhood. On strictly cognitive tasks it has been experimentally shown that even pre-school and thus "pre-language" deaf children perform no worse than hearing children.[6, 7, 8, 9]

Deaf children grow into adults who will encounter almost insurmountable difficulties in their adjustment to and integration with the hearing world. Only a few graduates from the schools of the deaf marry hearing partners.[10, 11] The majority find mates within the deaf population or remain single. While they lead happy and socially successful lives they are automatically assigned to a social minority whose communicative isolation is unparalleled by any other social grouping. This situation often engenders a feeling of ostracism among the adolescent and young adult deaf producing a number of psychological problems that deserve considerably more attention in counselling programs for parents and deaf children than is now given. It is probably preferable to make parents aware of the social inequities that are in store for their child and allow them to prepare themselves as well as their child for the future, rather than gloss over these social difficulties and to portray a falsely optimistic picture of the communicative possibilities.

MENTAL RETARDATION

Definition

For the purpose of the present article differentiation of the various diseases subsumed under the general title of Mental Retardation is not necessary. The *sequence* of developmental motor events is hardly ever significantly changed and the rate of development or degree of retardation is indicated by the customary instruments of intellectual measurement. We are concerned here with the severely retarded, the incidence of which is estimated to be two to three per thousand in the general population. [12]

---

[6] D. G. Doehring and J. Rosenstein, "Visual word recognition by deaf and hearing children," *J. Speech and Hearing Research*, III (1960), 320-326.

[7] H. G. Furth, "The influence of language on the development of concept formation in deaf children," *J. Abnor. Soc. Psychol.*, LXIII (1961), 386-389.

[8] H. G. Furth and N. A. Milgran, "Verbal and cognitive processes in classification tasks performed by normal, deaf, and retarded children," *Genet. Psychol. Monogr.* (1965).

[9] Pierre Oléron, *Recherches sur le Développement Mental des Sourds-Muets*, Centre National de la Recherch Scientifique (1957).

[10] Best, *op. cit.*

[11] E. A. Fay, "Marriages of the deaf in America," *Amer. Annals of the Deaf*, XXXXII (1897), 32ff.

[12] R. L. Masland, S. B. Sarason, and T. Gladwin, *Mental Subnormality* (New York: Basic Books, 1958).

Medical History

In roughly seventy-five percent of all cases the medical history and signs and symptoms of present illness establish the diagnosis beyond much doubt. In the remainder, the medical history gives no clear cues that distinguish these patients physically from certain cases with psychiatric disease and occasionally even from congenital deafness. Here the developmental history and/or the symptomatology of the speech disorder itself may furnish diagnostic indices.

Developmental History

Ordinarily we would expect retardation in reaching all milestones but there are notable exceptions. Even in severely retarding conditions, such as mongolism or genetic microcephaly, the patient is often found to sit, stand, and walk as early as the sixth, eighth and twelfth month, respectively, making it difficult for the mother to accept an early diagnosis of mental retardation. In these cases beginnings of language acquisition, including saying *mama* may appear rapidly after the accomplishment of gait but then development seems to level off or slow down, resulting in a very prolonged period during which no or very few further words are acquired. [13] Very gradually it becomes clear that the child is falling behind in language development; and although progress in most cases will continue throughout childhood, the process will be slow and tedious.

This type of developmental sequence may well have bred the idea that a large proportion of mentally retarded start with a comparatively high IQ (or other developmental index number) and then gradually deteriorate.[14] The lower scores with progressing age are not necessarily due to mental deterioration but are probably a consequence of the specific functions measured by psychological tests at different ages. If we assume that IQ's in the standard population are constant in every individual throughout age, and that development is a linear function of a uniform maturational process (all of which are unwarranted assumptions!), it appears as if the retardates were, from the age of three on, getting duller and duller. Thus, when mental age scores are plotted against chronological age, for instance in mongolism, a negatively accelerating exponential function is obtained (chronological age on the abscissa).[15, 16, 17, 18]

[13] E. H. Lenneberg, I. A. Nichols, and E. F. Rosenberger, "Primitive stages of language development in mongolism," Paper presented at the Association of Research in Nervous and Mental Disease Congress (1962).

[14] F. R. Ford, *Diseases of the Nervous System in Infancy, Childhood, and Adolescence* (Springfield: C. C Thomas, 1962).

[15] Sidney Goda and B. C. Griffith, "Spoken language of adolescent retardates and its relation to intelligence, age, and anxiety," *Child Development* XXXIII (1962), 489-498.

[16] Lenneberg, Nichols, and Rosenberger, *op. cit.*

[17] Masland, *op. cit.*

[18] S. R. Pinneau, *Changes in Intelligence Quotients—Infancy to Maturity* (Boston: Houghton Mifflin, 1961).

This artifact results from the way mental age scores are obtained at various age levels. During the first years of life, observations are primarily based on motor-sensory development whereas after the age of three to four the data elicited concern primarily cognitive skills including memory, concept formation, perception, and interference. In the testing situation it seems likely that different developmental histories are being assessed (motor, cognitive, education) each of which bear, in the normal case, a certain and invariant chronological relationship one to another but which are, nevertheless, independent, at least to a degree. Interestingly enough, language development is dependent upon all of these developmental events presupposing the maturation of certain motor skills before it begins to be functional (the inarticulate child cannot be understood), requiring highly specialized and apparently innate cognitive skills that come into play in speech comprehension as well as speech production, particularly the use of syntax, and also reflecting educational attainment evidenced in size and nature of vocabulary. It is because of this all-pervasive nature of language that some aspects of language appear well correlated with motor maturation, and tests that primarily assess this often reveal "normal" beginning of speech. In an individual where the central-nervous-system-correlates of motor behavior mature at a normal rate, i.e., the relatively lower reflex mechanisms for posture and locomotion, but the central-nervous-system-correlates for higher function are handicapped biochemically, structurally, or physiologically; sitting up, standing, and walking appear in rapid succession and are accompanied by normal appearance of cooing, babbling, and first "word." When the tests begin to concentrate on cognitive skills, the IQ drops; language behavior now appears uncorrelated with test scores because the testing instruments are not designed to investigate the specific skills underlying speech and language.

From these and similar considerations it seems fair to assume that language runs an individual course of development, dissimilar from yet dependent upon motor maturation, and also independent from the child's acquisition of knowledge, yet capable of reflecting this process.

Symptomatology

We restrict ourselves to speech and language. Even within these limitations generalizations are difficult because of considerable individual variation, and what follows must be understood as over-all trends rather than an inevitable picture.

In clinical practice the picture of mental retardation is further complicated by the common secondary development of psychological problems caused by the conditions created by the primary disease. For instance, retardation alone should not suppress affect even though its manifestation may be primitive. This may be seen quite clearly in children with mongolism who are generally affectionate and relate well to their family without any sign of autism. Yet many retarded children will also display behavior that is characteristic of varying degrees of psychosis such as rocking for hours on end, quiet sitting and staring, hair-pulling, etc. The differentiating criterion between mental retardation with secondary psychiatric disease as against primary psychiatric disease is the demonstration of a slowly developing intellect characteristic of retardation, as distinct from regression, which is characteristic of psychiatric disease.

The mentally retarded child makes a normal or increased *amount* of sound in comparison to well children, and vocalizations are qualitatively those that are also heard among healthy children, the only difference being a change in age of appearance. The healthy infant should have done with babbling by twenty-eight months and use exclusively words and phrases and during play make some chanting noises representing some primitive form of singing; he may also imitate sounds of vehicles or animals, but all of his vocalizations seem to fall into distinct patterns. The random aspect of the eight-months-old babbler is conspicuously absent in the healthy child of two and a half. The retardate, however, is heard to make the sounds of the normal eight-months-old at a much later age, the exact occurrence depending on the general rate of development of cognitive function. The sequence of cooing, babbling, words, phrases and sentences is preserved but in severe retardation the final stages may never be attained. As in the normal child, understanding of language is always a bit ahead of production and there must be a close correlation between development of understanding and speaking if the diagnosis is to be maintained. Mutism or highly bizarre sound production such as exclusively meowing like a cat or barking like a dog are definitely not characteristic of mental retardation. Nor should there be any marked discrepancies between the development of the various verbal and language skills. Mental retardation should make it impossible for a child to have the ability to learn long passages of discourse by heart and reproduce them with flawless articulation and grammar in the fashion of an actor. Even in retardates where language is perfectly developed, the semantic content of discourse remains simple, and the sophistications of wit, drama, or propaganda are beyond their comprehension.

Mental deficits which are severe enough to prevent education in even the most rudimentary academic and social skills and seem to interfere with abstraction and concept formation as investigated in intelligence tests, do not necessarily interfere with acquisition of speech and language. A complete and total absence of speech and language is only seen in the lowest grades of idiocy. With a mental age (ascertained by non-verbal tests) of thirty to thirty-six months, primitive stages of language development, such as a small vocabulary,

524

are usually demonstrable. With advance in mental age, higher stages of language development are attained and a mental age of five years leaves no effect upon the essential principles of speech production or language comprehension, even though the content of conversation will obviously be restricted.[19]

Management

Since in these patients the proper development of brain mechanisms for language is arrested or severely slowed, there are no measures available for correction of symptoms. One of the physician's aims in counselling the parents with regard to their child's speech and language problems is to keep them from taking the patient from one speech therapist to the next. There is not enough evidence of positive success to encourage parents, *as a matter of routine,* to incur the expense and trouble of instituting speech therapy.

Prognosis

Speech progresses steadily in the mentally retarded, but at a markedly slower pace than normal, until stabilization is reached early in the first half of the second decade of life. Little further improvement of speech habits can be expected beyond the level of achievement reached at age twelve to fourteen.[20] This does not preclude, however, the acquisition of some new words or names. As indicated above, prognostication of final language accomplishments can only be made within very rough limits on the basis of IQ and it must be borne in mind that the IQ figure itself is not stable throughout a retardate's life.

CHILDHOOD PSYCHOSIS
Definition

Under this heading we shall discuss children with severe disorders in communication behavior due to psychiatric disease. The psychiatric origin of the disorder is usually sufficiently documented by concomitant behavioral aberrations.

Incidence figures are not available, but out of 8000 "problem children" referred to the Bellevue Psychiatric Clinic, roughly 25% were schizophrenic —the largest category of children with communication disorder.[21] The condition needs to be differentiated from mental retardation, and aphasia.

Medical History

The medical history is, typically, non-contributory.

---

[19] Lenneberg, Nichols, and Rosenberger, *op. cit.*
[20] Goda, *op. cit.*
[21] Lauretta Bender, "Diagnostic and therapeutic aspects of childhood schizophrenia," in Peter W. Bowman and Hans V. Mautner, *Mental Retardation* (New York: Grune, 1960).

Developmental History

Motor milestones tend to occur at normal age but the patient's reaction to his social environment is often disturbed from early infancy. Characteristically he has shown disinterest in people and their affection; he has preferred solitary play or passive seclusion to active interaction or to being amused; or there may be a history of hyperactivity, destructiveness or a morbid preoccupation with some single mechanical toy or device, particularly spinning of wheels. The acquisition of social skills or factual knowledge follows no general pattern. Some children give signs of outstanding precocity in some tasks, whereas other children give the impression of retardation which can often be demonstrated to be purely on the surface, so to speak. For instance, a child may be totally inactive over a prolonged period of time and be quite unresponsive in the test situation and yet, with change of motivation or social ambient, may suddenly surprise the examiner, or even the parent, that some task, never done before, has "matured subclinically" and was merely waiting to be properly elicited. These sudden outbursts of accomplished development or, more generally, the *absence of a gradual developmental history,* are probably the most important signs for diagnosis. The general appearance of the developmental history in these children, then, is that the underlying maturational processes that are prerequisite for behavioral development progress at the normal rate but that the child "doesn't choose to make use of it," or that he makes a bizarre, highly individualistic use of it; therefore, a change in psychological orientation can produce sudden and dramatic "snapping out."[22]

Symptomatology

The above point is very well illustrated in the psychotic child's communication behavior. A common psychiatric symptom is mutism. The patient fails to address anyone for periods that may extend over years. Yet these children are rarely incapable of saying something. Usually they can be heard to mumble a word or two and sometimes even phrases and sentences, for instance while standing in a corner staring blankly into space or while engaged in their favorite pastime. These utterances may be muttered under their breath; but even so, they can be understood clearly since their phonology and syntax are well developed. If failure to speak is due to motivational factors, as is assumed here, we are not surprised to find evidence that some language has been learned. Proof for this is the ability of these children to understand what is being said to them. It is common experience in psychotherapy that the patient gives frequent behavioral evidence of having understood commands and some-

[22] J. de Ajuriaguerra, R. Diatkine, and S. Leborici, "Les troubles du développement du langage au cours des états psychotiques prècoces," *La Psychiatrie de L'Enfant,* II, Fascic 1 (n. d.).

times even elaborate explanations. In fact, the treatment of choice in this day and age is psychotherapy which is totally predicated on the assumption that the patient understands language. There are reports in the psychiatric literature of children (and psychotic adults, for that matter) who appeared to be completely incapable of talking, and suddenly were found to be speaking with perfect mastery of the language. These occurrences are, admittedly, rare.

Communication disorders in psychosis are by no means restricted to a diminution in verbal activities. Some patients speak as much or markedly more than is normal for a child of their age. In these cases what is being said, how it is said, and to whom or to what it is said is bizarre. For instance, there may be an interminable repetition of a given sentence; or the patient may reproduce meticulously every detail and mannerism of some actor or of a member of the family. Or he may say nothing but the dialogues of radio and TV commercials, again reproduced with an absolutely perplexing accuracy. When such stereotypy occurs it is commonly but falsely assumed that the patient has merely learned to parrot or to act like a tape recorder but that he has actually learned no more language than the bird or the machine. That this is theoretically impossible can easily be shown[23] but need not be proved in this context. With careful observation of the patient's behavior it becomes immediately obvious that he is in excellent command of all rules of syntax, phonology, and semantics and that he is, in fact, only capable of doing such a marvelous reproductive job because he applies the rules of the common natural language, but puts them to a very unusual use. For instance, we can give the patient a new sentence of considerable length and complexity and he will immediately be able to incorporate this sentence into his peculiar behavior without any evidence of laborious practice or learning by heart such as would be necessary if a native speaker of English were suddenly asked to reproduce a ten-word sentence in Japanese, a language which he does not know. Immediate and accurate repetition of sentences requires perfect knowledge of the language.

The two basic variants in symptomatology, marked decrease or marked increase of verbal output, are, essentially, variations of a common and constant theme: limited acquisition of speech and language with *abnormal use* of these skills, interfering with interpersonal communication and apparently going back to abnormal motivational and emotional states.

Management

Since there can be little doubt that the origin of these particular disorders are of a psychological nature, treatment must be concentrated on this aspect of

---

[23] Eric H. Lenneberg, "Understanding language without ability to speak: A case report," *Journal of Abnormal and Soc. Psychol.*, LXV (1962), 419-425.

the disease. Treatment of the symptoms themselves, that is speech training, is of little use since speech and language are potentially or actually present, unless there is organic disease in addition to the functional. Some authorities hold that the psychotic child must be subjected to more intensive stimulation either because at the common level of intensity speech stimuli are not powerful enough to penetrate into the patient's consciousness; or stimulation ought to be increased because the patient has encapsulated himself within a sound-proof shelter thus warding off all disturbing influences from abroad. I object to these formulations because there is abundant evidence that many of these children have acquired much more language than they show; and because heightening of the sound pressure at the eardrum can hardly be relevant to the purely metaphorical "sound-proof chamber" since the acuity of hearing, as demonstrated by audiogram, is not usually impaired in these patients.

Prognosis

The prognosis for language behavior is identical with that of the primary psychiatric disease and it is well known that prognostication in this realm of medicine is unsafe. The only thing one may say with certainty is that there can be no cases in which the primary psychiatric condition is cleared up while the communication deficit persists.

CONGENITAL INARTICULATION

Definition

This condition is a distinct developmental deficit which, however, has not been well recognized as an autonomous disturbance. It is a congenital inability to coordinate the organs of the vocal apparatus for the purpose of speech and to bring the movement of lips, tongue and pharynx under voluntary control for speech. In the writer's experience it has occurred in boys more often than in girls but this may be due to the vicissitudes of a small sample. In one out of four cases there is a family history. So far there is not enough evidence definitely to rule out the possibility that the disorder is inherited as a Mendelian trait though this does appear to be unlikely.[24] The familial occurrence may be due to anatomic or physiologic factors that increase the possibilities of prenatal trauma or due to an inherited malformation of neuronal arrangement in the mid-brain. A detailed description of a typical case may be found elsewhere.[25] The clinical picture is totally different from psychosis or aphasia. The incidence of occurrence is about five in a thousand.[26]

[24] P. S. Moorhead, W. J. Mellman, and C. Wenar, "A familial chromosome, translocation associated with speech and mental retardation," *Am. J. Hum. Genet.*, XIII (1961), 32-46.
[25] Lenneberg, *op. cit.*
[26] Muriel Morley, *The Development and Disorders of Speech in Childhood* (Edinburgh: Williams and Wilkins, 1957).

Medical History

If a case is well documented, which is unfortunately rare, there is usually a hint of cranial nerve abnormality at birth. For instance in one case studied in our clinic the neonatal cry was thought to be "strange;" two years later a mild but unmistakable abnormality in laryngeal mechanism of phonation was demonstrable by sound spectrography (for a description of the technique see Lenneberg[27]) which, however, was not sufficient to render the patient dysphonic. The abnormal neonatal cry may well have been due to a tenth nerve lesion. In another case a mild asymmetry of facial movements was noted shortly after birth which could be followed through the second year but eventually was compensated for. In addition the child had a marked ptosis on the right. In a third case there seemed to be weakness of both eyelids manifested by mild drooping, and internal strabismus. A fourth patient had a mild VI nerve palsy bilaterally. There are usually no full-blown cranial nerve palsies but deficits run the gamut from III to X nerve which would point to some abnormality or malformation in or immediately around the fourth ventricle. Some authorities believe that peri-aqueductal grey matter is peculiarly involved in coordination of vocalization,[28] an opinion which would fit well into the clinical picture that these patients present. However, lesions in this area in the adult patient do not produce the same combination of deficits. I can think of two alternative explanations for this discrepancy. Either the common cranial nerve findings bear no causal relation to the congenital inarticulation and merely indicate that these children have a lesion comparable to those causing cerebral palsy; or neurophysiological processes are sufficiently different in early childhood from those in adult life that the discrepancy can be ascribed to changes due to growth and maturation. I favor the latter view.

Apart from these neurological findings the medical history should be noncontributory.

Developmental History

Milestones are attained at normal age and emotional and social maturation are usually unremarkable. Due to the difficulty in communication, inordinate shyness or even some babyish behavior may be present. The secondary nature of these behavior problems can be demonstrated by brief separation from the mother (say for thirty to sixty minutes) during which the children often undergo dramatic changes revealing a perfectly adequate social attitude.

The development of vocalization is probably abnormal in all cases but

---

[27] Lenneberg, *New England Journal of Medicine*, 266, 385-392.
[28] H. W. Magoun, "Caudal and cephalic influences of brain stem reticular formation," *Physiol. Rev.*, XXX (1950), 459-474.

since a developmental evaluation of pre-language sounds in infants requires considerable experience, this abnormality is difficult to elicit from parents. In all cases the children are able to modulate the voice to produce a variety of intonation patterns, but babbling is deficient. Instead of the child's emitting, between the age of twelve to twenty months, a wide variety of potential speech sounds, there is a marked paucity in consonants and even the vowels bear little or no resemblance to the phonemes of the language that surrounds them.

Symptomatology

The chief complaint is usually failure to speak intelligibly. In extreme cases the patient's noises do not even remotely resemble language. More frequently, however, vocalizations have certain aspects in common with actual (e.g., English) utterances. The intonation pattern is typical of a declarative sentence or a question and the overall rhythm and duration as well as the phrasing indicate that an attempt is being made to say something *in the language of the environment* which, however, cannot be understood because of an articulatory deficit. This is quite different from random babbling of a twenty-months-old late talker. The latter will produce combinations of speech sounds, all of them close to standard speech sounds, but without any indication of word or phrase division (by appropriately rising or falling intonation or short hesitation pauses technically known as *junctures*). The late talker's utterances sound somewhat as if an American child were naively inventing or imitating a foreign language; whereas the child with congenital inarticulation sounds as if someone were trying to speak English with his mouth full of marbles.

The most outstanding and characteristic feature in this disorder is that the patient always has complete understanding of language such as is adequate for his age. In order to make the diagnosis it must be established that the patient has a vocabulary that is proper for his age (to be tested by having him point to details in pictures) and that he has an appreciation of syntax (to be tested by having him nod yes and no answers to questions). The most efficient office procedure is to tell the patient a short story and watch his interest and attention span; he is to be warned beforehand that he will be asked questions about it afterwards.[29]

The distinguishing mark of this condition from psychiatric disease is the patient's eagerness to communicate at least with his parents, his quick reaction to the spoken word, general cheerfulness, and an absence of any dramatic behavior disorders.

[29] For a practical demonstration of the procedure see my film, "The Acquisition of Language by a Speechless Child," distributed by the Psychological Cinema Register, Pennsylvania State University.

Most of these children are of normal or even bright intelligence. But a combination of this disorder with mild dullness is not uncommon. Since perfect speech is acquired by children with markedly lower intelligence, the intellectual slowness in the cases under discussion cannot be thought of as a causative factor. Apparently, the underlying factor is such that it may produce two types of deficits which are, however, functionally independent one from the other.

Management

The most important measures to be taken are directed towards insuring adequate academic instruction. First-grade school teachers are likely to believe that a child whose speech can't be understood also cannot learn to read and write. Once the patient's intellectual capacity has been demonstrated to be adequate (by non-verbal tests), arrangements have to be made with school authorities to admit the child to a regular class. A persuasive argument for the possibility of teaching him to read and write in the absence of intelligible speech is that deaf children learn these skills regularly and without undue difficulty. In my experience I have arranged to have one boy with this difficulty given intensive reading training, four hours per week for ten weeks, with frankly encouraging results. In this case the disorder was extreme and the child's IQ was no higher than eighty (Leiter Performance Scale) at age eight. Teaching to read can be accomplished if the child, instead of having to give verbal proof of his competence, is allowed to point to things or to match individual words and sentences, much the way the comprehension of language is demonstrated in an adult who is prevented from speaking.

The question of speech training is most acute in these cases. As a rule of thumb, speech training can rarely be effective unless the patient is motivated to improve his articulation, and potentially capable of doing so. Motivation is hardly ever sufficiently present until school age and therapy certainly should never begin before the age of four. The question of capability cannot be answered by simply verifying whether the patient can bring his lips together or move his tongue in all directions. The deficit here is never one of limitation of movement but of clumsiness in executing a vast variety of subtle movements at a fast rate. Nor is this adiadochokinesis of oral structures; to make the patient say quickly *papapa* or the like does not test the same process as the "programming" of a sequence of different articulatory positions. The assessment of capability is best tied to the severity of deficit as a whole, or the degree of intelligibility. In cases where the patient has *no* sounds that resemble (say) English phonemes, direct speech work is premature and the habilitation efforts should be primarily directed toward preventive mental health and, most important, towards instruction in the three R's. In cases where the patient's spontaneous utterances are intelligible, say, fifty percent of the time, speech correction is recommended. Whenever possible, the speech training should be daily and should not exceed twenty minutes per session.

Since the essential work in speech rehabilitation is done by the patient and not by the speech correctionist, one must never expect from speech therapy a sudden, complete, and dramatic reversal of conditions; a reasonable expectation is that speech therapy results in better pronunciation of certain mispronounced sounds. In this connection, the question is frequently asked whether speech habilitation ought to include "exercises" to strengthen the tongue, on the assumption that the deficit is due to muscular weakness. This is certainly false and exercises cannot possibly influence the condition. We can speak with such authority on this subject because of the following considerations: first, most of these children have no difficulty in chewing or swallowing either solids or liquids. The mechanical power required for these activities is many times that required for speech. We get tired of chewing after a few minutes but we can speak for hours (at least many a congressman can). Second, children and adults with pathological muscular weakness including tongue and lips can carry on conversations long after the first appearance of symptoms. Speech is only interrupted at the last stages and shortly before a complete palsy sets in.

The situation is analogous to writing skills. Poor hand-writing is not improved by developing the muscles but only by practicing delicately skilled movements.

Prognosis

In all cases some spontaneous improvement may be observed throughout the first decade. Spontaneous articulatory progress is arrested in the early teens but, within the limitations mentioned, speech therapy may bring about further improvements. The articulatory deficit in itself is never responsible for disturbances in concept-formation or thought processes. In a patient of normal intelligence written language is always attainable.

APHASIA

Definition

The term aphasia has acquired a fairly precise meaning in the realm of adult neurological practice. Since the condition labeled *aphasia* in adult life also occurs in childhood[30, 31] it is essential that the term also preserves its tradi-

[30] R. K. Byers and W. T. McLean, "Etiology and course of certain hemiplegias with aphasia in childhood," *Pediatrics*, XXIX (1962), 376-383.
[31] Eric Guttman, "Aphasia in children," *Brain*, LXV (1942) 205-219.

tional meaning in pediatric practice. It should be used only to designate adventitious loss of language. Therefore, by definition, an infant who has never acquired language should not be said to have aphasia. This terminological argument is not merely academic pedantry, but is based on the belief that terminology is the basis of classification and that classification has a deep heuristic value.

It is customary to subdivide acquired aphasia into motor and sensory (or receptive) forms. Even in the adult patient these two forms never occur to the complete exclusion of each other.[32] In childhood where the course of the disturbance is shorter, the onset more global, and the final stage usually ends with total remission, the distinction between motor and sensory forms is difficult (if at all possible) and of little clinical importance. Usually the patient's disturbance in production is comparable in degree to his difficulty in understanding but occasionally a child seems to have greater difficulty in speaking than understanding. The converse of this, good production in the absence of understanding, has in the writer's experience never been seen in children with true (i.e., acquired) aphasia.

The concept of "congenital receptive aphasia" will be discussed further in the next section. But a comment on the notion of "congenital motor aphasia" is in place now. In contrast to inarticulation and dys- or an-arthria, aphasia always involves higher mental processes (such as disorganization of thoughts, difficulty in voluntary initiation of action, or word finding), which we associate with cortical function. There is a wealth of evidence[33, 34, 35, 36, 37] that during the first three years of life the human cortex preserves a large degree of functional equipotentiality, as Lashley called it.[38] Whatever function becomes localized in adult life can become established in early childhood in spite of the presence of fixed cortical and sub-cortical lesions, and it seems immaterial where these lesions are located. The entire left hemisphere may be incapacitated during the first two years and remain so thereafter without interfering with the establishment of language at the usual age. However, a similar lesion

---

[32] H. Schuell and J. J. Jenkins, "The nature of language deficit in aphasia," *Psychol. Rev.*, LXVI (1959), 45-67.

[33] J. de Ajuriaguerra, "Langage et dominance cerebrale," *J. Francais d'Oto-Rhino-Laryng*, VI (1957), 489-499.

[34] J. de Ajuriaguerra and M. Stambak, "L'évolution des syncinesies chez l'enfant," *Presse Medicale* (28 Mai 1955), 817-819.

[35] L. S. Basser, "Hemiplegia of early onset and the faculty of speech with special reference to the effects of hemispherectomy," *Brain*, LXXXV (1962), 427-460.

[36] W. F. Hillier Jr., "Total left cerebral hemispherectomy for malignant glioma," *Neurology*, IV (1954), 718-721.

[37] Grace Woods, "Natural history of hemiplegia," *Hemiplegic Cerebral Palsy in Children and Adults*, Little Club Clinics in Developmental Medicine, no. 4.

[38] K. S. Lashley, *The Neuropsychology of Lashley*, Selected papers edited by F. A. Beach *et al.* (New York: McGraw Hill, 1960).

would result in irreversible language loss if it occurred during or after the middle of the second decade.[39, 40] Neither trauma nor surgical lesions, nor focal infections, nor agenesis (including of the corpus callosum) regardless of cortical locality will prevent acquisition of language as long as the insult occurs at an early enough age, is confined to a single hemisphere, and does not reduce the individual to a state of idiocy. This indicates that failure to *acquire* language must result from an entirely different cause from *adventitious* loss of language in adult life. In the latter, the lesion is structural and can be defined anatomically, but in the former, we cannot even be certain that there is any structural abnormality. Nor are symptoms which we might call motor aphasia in older children or in adults ever seen on a congenital basis (compare symptomatology of congenital inarticulation with that of aphasia!). Thus there is clearly no justification for speaking of congenital motor aphasia.

Medical History

The two most common causes of aphasia in childhood are trauma and vascular accidents. Aphasia may also follow generalized and protracted seizures, or *status epilepticus,* and transient aphasia lasting for an hour or two is sometime a post-ictal symptom. (The latter will not concern us here.) It may, of course, also ensue from any other cerebral lesion that develops rapidly enough or that leaves catastrophic events in its wake. However, a slowly developing, space-occupying lesion may never affect speech at all in childhood if the rate of growth is so gradual as to allow constant compensation and functional readjustment. The process of readjustment hypothesized here must not be confused with another hypothetical process, that of "taking over of function." It has often been claimed that in adults as well as in children various parts of the brain have the capacity to take over some function that had been lodged in a given portion of tissue before that tissue was destroyed by disease. This conception of brain function seems to presuppose some providential will that assigns function to given parts of the brain and when one part is out of commission it commands another to take over. We do not know what *will* is in physiological terms; yet we do know that there is no homunculus beyond the brain that can throw switches or rearrange function. The recovery from aphasia that takes place during the first six post-traumatic months are most likely due to colateralization of blood supply and there is no evidence whatever to show that in the adult any function once disrupted due to disease can be executed vicariously by structures not heretofore involved in it. On the other hand, the brain during infancy seems to be in a physiologically different condition. Necrosis is less likely to occur in childhood due to a singular vas-

[39] Russell Brain, *Speech Disorders* (Washington: Butterworth & Co., 1961).
[40] W. R. Russell, *Traumatic Aphasia* (London: Oxford, 1961).

cular occlusion because colateralization is much more efficient in the early years of life than later. Second, the acquisition of certain functions such as speech and language seem to involve the entire brain during early infancy so that learning is not restricted to a limited cortical area. Thus if parts of the brain cannot function, the learning process, which is general, is not necessarily disrupted by local dysfunction. Admittedly, this explanation is speculative also, but it accounts for the actual phenomena of loss and recovery at various age levels better than the notion of "taking over."

Language disturbances are very rarely if ever the sole harbinger of brain disease, neither in malignancies, nor in degenerative processes, nor in demyelinating diseases. As a rule other symptoms such as projectile vomiting, ataxia, tremor, or gait disturbances precede the disruption of language function. Physiologically this is important. It tells us once more that speech in childhood is not as localized as in adult life and further, that it is far from being such a subtle, delicate process disturbed at the slightest abnormality as is often claimed, and therefore it is not the most sensitive indicator of brain function. To the contrary, it appears to be a robustly established and firmly anchored process that can resist a wide variety of insults before showing evidence of limitations.

Developmental History

Since we are only considering adventitious disease in this section, developmental history should be within normal limits.

Symptomatology

Transient or permanent hemiparesis, of varying degrees of severity, is the most constant concomitant. Otherwise, the clinical picture varies with age at which insult is sustained. Between three and four years of age the patient appears generally unresponsive at the beginning of the disease but within a week gives signs of understanding, which is soon followed by single word utterances. The course of recovery is very rapid with a sequence of events that roughly correspond to a telescoped normal history of speech acquisition. Within weeks the patient is back at the same developmental stage at which he was premorbidly. Between the ages of five and ten or twelve the first phase is also characterized by general unresponsiveness but the symptoms during recovery are more similar to the typical picture of aphasia in the adult than to a simple re-learning of language. On the receptive side the child seems to have difficulty in understanding; on the productive side his utterances are very short, at the start not more than single words, pronounced usually with good articulation but some slowing, or sluggish and belabored pronunciation is frequent. In contrast to dysarthria and congenital disarticulation, there are always some words or phrases that are produced with ease and without any trace of difficulty. Together with the difficulty of language there is usually an aspect of confusion manifested by perseveration, inappropriate answers, difficulty in finding the right word, and sometimes jargon. In some instances the patient seems to be aware of his own difficulties and is disturbed about the lack of control over his vocal output. Symptoms in the young teenager are no different but the recovery runs a markedly slower course.

Management

In no case is there any need to institute speech therapy before the patient has had a chance to recover spontaneously, say within the first six post-morbid months. After that, indication for speech rehabilitation is dependent upon the nature of the deficit. If the child is discouraged about his own progress and gives evidence of lack of confidence in his own ability, a sophisticated speech therapist may often show him how to make best use of those verbal skills least affected and thus restore confidence and generally increase motivation. Articulatory deficits are rare in childhood aphasia. Occasionally they do occur, in which case speech therapy may be helpful.

Children with aphasia may also have learning difficulties, particularly in reading, writing and arithmetic. Again, these difficulties are more often a reflection of the extent of damage than of its particular distribution and thus serve as a guide to the rehabilitative program. A child who has severe and persistent difficulties is likely to have suffered a greater degree of tissue destruction than one with little difficulty. Therefore the intensity of rehabilitation should not be directly but inversely proportional to the multiplicity of his problems. It makes no sense to subject a patient who has a serious memory defect, who cannot concentrate, who cannot find words, who has difficulty in reading and cannot write at all, to a vast program in which all deficits are worked on at once. Since speech and language can never be taught to someone who lacks the organic and physiological prerequisites, but instead one can only improve on some of these skills if they are essentially present, there is usually less urgency for training in this realm than for training in academic subjects. A psychological assessment ought to be made of the child's potentialities and a curriculum ought to be carefully planned, based on the results of the psychological tests. Only after the more immediate problems of schooling have been settled and a routine is established should speech rehabilitation, i.e., articulatory drill, begin.

Prognosis

The prognosis is related to two factors: patient's age and extent of residual symptoms (i.e., about six months after the disease). If the deficits are restricted to verbal skills and motor system, the prognosis is excellent for patients under ten to twelve; the outlook becoming progressively worse with age. Aphasia in the late teens has the same prognosis as that of an adult; little improvement can be expected after the second year of recovery. If intellectual functions besides language are impaired, prognosis is worse in direct correlation with severity of the loss.

OTHER CONDITIONS

Congenital Receptive Disorder

This condition cannot be distinguished from so-called Central Deafness, Congenital Receptive Aphasia, Auditory Symbolic Disorder, or Congenital Word-Deafness. The child afflicted with this developmental defect does not learn to talk at the usual age and seems chronically inattentive to the spoken word. It is thought that this is the result of an innate inability to associate the complex acoustic patterns of words with visual images or concepts, a presupposition that defies empirical tests for the time being.[41, 42, 43] However, just as it is a fact that there are specific reading disabilities in which the patient has an innate difficulty in relating graphic symbols with spoken words,[44] so it is conceivable that an analogous condition exists in the auditory sphere. It is not certain whether there is an anatomic basis for this condition.

If the disorder appeared in its purest form, we would expect a developmental history similar to that of the congenitally deaf. The patient should be educable in the same way the peripherally deaf are. However, such cases are rare. The auditory "imperception of words" is usually associated with a wide variety of unpredictable symptoms such as hyperactivity, or bizarre behavior, or perceptual disorders attributed to "brain damage" by some psychologists. Thus children with this disorder constitute a very heterogeneous group about which it is impossible to make generalizations such as we have attempted for the other groups above.

Dysarthria

Dysarthria is the counterpart to inarticulation as discussed above but while the latter is congenital, dysarthria is acquired. It is usually caused by acute lesions in the diencephalon or mesencephalon (but chronic dysarthria is seen

[41] I. T. Diamond, J. M. Goldberg, and W. D. Neff, "Tonal discrimination after ablation of auditory cortex," *J. Neurophysiol.*, XXV (1962), 223-235.
[42] J. M. Goldberg and W. D. Neff, "Frequency discrimination after bilateral section of the brachium of the inferior colliculus," *J. Comp. Neurol.*, 116 (1961), 265-290.
[43] J. M. Goldberg and W. D. Neff, "Frequency discrimination after bilateral ablation of cortical auditory areas," *J. Neurophysiol.*, XXIV (1961), 119-128.
[44] N. Geschwind, "The anatomy of acquired disorders of reading," *Reading Disability* (Baltimore, Maryland: Johns Hopkins Press, 1962).

in cerebral palsy) rendering speech uniformly unintelligible, leaving the higher language functions intact. It is always accompanied and usually preceded by other neurological signs and symptoms and its treatment and prognosis is that of the underlying disease and therefore need not concern us here.

Structural Abnormalities in the Oropharyngeal Cavity

It is obvious that gross deviations from normal anatomy of lips, teeth, palate, or tongue will interfere with speech. Diagnosis and treatment will be a matter of plastic surgery in most cases. Speech correction when coordinated with medical treatment is usually helpful. There is one point especially that seems worthwhile making: occasionally a short frenulum is blamed for grossly defective speech or even language deficits. The role of the frenulum is surely exaggerated here. In the most extreme cases of tongue-tiedness no greater interference could be produced than a mild lisp, or defective pronunciation of certain speech sounds, none of them severe enough to render speech unintelligible. This assertion is based on the fact that a partially amputated tongue interferes but little with speech and that speech continues to be quite intelligible in the presence of a variety of physical handicaps introduced into the mouth for experimental purposes.

Infantile Speech is in all cases a psychological problem and ought to be treated by psychologists or psychiatrists rather than speech therapists. The question of mental retardation is frequently brought up in this connection but in order for speech to be retarded due to intelligence deficits, the retardation must be so severe as to leave little doubt about its existence. Also, the speech of the mentally retarded is not babyish but has the hallmark of normal speech developmental stages occurring at the wrong chronological age.

Minor Articulatory Deficits are not ordinarily brought to the attention of a pediatrician and are not a medical problem. The school physician may occasionally be struck by one or another speech problem. Sometimes dramatic relief of symptoms is obtained by asking the patient to rid himself of chewing gum. Speech correction is usually indicated in minor disorders at school age.

Summary and Conclusion

Table 1 gives an abridged summary of all points important for differential diagnosis of speech and language disorders. Table 2 is the outline for a checklist which I have found to be useful for diagnostic decisions in the office.[45]

---

[45] Naturally, cases do not always fall neatly into one or the other diagnostic category. Differentiation is more difficult between psychosis and retardation.

A final note on the role of mother's attitude towards her child's speech development or the role of the environment in general is in order. To what extent could delayed speech be due to faulty language training, poor incentive for speech due to an oversolicitous mother, or taciturn parents? Naturally, the environment plays no small part in developmental achievement in general and also leaves its mark on language development. For instance, the nature and perhaps even the extent of the vocabulary of a small child is correlated with his socio-economic background.[46] In a study still in progress I have found hearing children born to congenitally deaf parents to display many of the speech mannerisms of their parents. Yet despite these traces left by the environment upon the early language development, it is much more interesting to note how a presumably normal child can be relatively immune to dramatic environmental abnormalities with respect to its language accomplishments. Children suffering from severe parental neglect, whose mothers may be frank psychopaths, or whose parents are deaf-mute and whose main contact with normal speech comes through television or, indeed, who are raised in orphanages and are not exposed to much talk, still develop language in all of its infinitely abstract characteristics (such as is comprised by syntax or the very act of naming objects and relations) within the first five years of life. By the time they enter school they never need to be "taught" how to speak; at most their vocabulary has to be extended and some of their utterances made to conform to the standards of polite society. Unless a child is literally raised in a closet he will make use of the language stimuli surrounding him, however impoverished these might be in comparison with the so-called normal ambient. Thus, it is not very likely that failure to acquire speech is due to a mother who anticipates all of her child's wishes or who makes it "unnecessary" for the child to speak. From this it also follows that mothers must not be advised to withhold food or desired objects from her speechless child until he has made an effort to use the word for it. These practices will achieve nothing but tension and unhappiness in the home.

[46] Dorothea McCarthy, "Language development in children," Leonard Carmichael, ed., *Manual of Child Psychology* (2nd ed.; New York: John Wiley, 1954).

TABLE 1

Important Points for Differential Diagnosis of Speech and Language Disorders

Diagnosis	Medical History	Developmental History	Symptomatology	Management	Prognosis
Peripheral Deafness	In 2/3 of cases: family history or infectious disease.	Normal milestones; normal vocalization during 1st 6 mo. Abnormal persistence of babble and complete absence of words.	Normal affect; gestures only but eager to communicate; plays constructively and with concentration; no reaction to sounds.	Establish diagnosis by audiogram; hearing aid; special training.	Good for written language. Oral communication usually poor but depends on age of onset and depth of deafness; no intellectual limitations.
Mental Retardation	Signs and symptoms of central-nervous-system disease.	Slow but steady; motor development sometimes better than cognitive.	Comprehension slightly ahead of speech production. Language is consistent with that of a younger child and free from bizarre stereotypes. Understanding, vocabulary, syntax suffer to an equal extent.	No special measures for language habilitation; speech therapy is of little value.	Good if IQ is 50 or above by chronological age seven.
Childhood Psychosis	Typically, non-contributory.	Normal for motor milestones. Progress is irregular with surprise advances or regressions; socialization defective.	Usually mutism with occasional indications that lang. has been acquired but motivation to speak is lacking; sometimes well developed lang. but bizarre use of it; normal communication process interrupted.	Treatment is restricted to psychiatric disease. Amplification of sound is contraindicated. Articulation exercises are irrelevant.	Potentially good for speech and language but subordinate to prognosis of primary psychiatric disease.

TABLE 1 (cont.)

Diagnosis	Medical History	Developmental History	Symptomatology	Management	Prognosis
Congenital Inarticulation	Perinatal stress with cranial nerve signs after birth. Family (paternal) history of similar disorder or dyslexia common.	Normal milestones, except for development of vocalization.	Intelligent or slightly dull child with normal affect and good motivation for communication; certain consonants consistently omitted or distorted; voice and intonation pattern intact. In severe cases no intelligible speech at all but in all cases understanding of lang. is normal.	Pre-school child: prevention or correction of secondary mental health problems in patient and parents. School child: assure proper instruction in reading and writing by enlightenment of teachers. Speech correction in 2nd or 3rd grade.	Depends on severity of defect but some spontaneous improvement in nearly all cases. Except for severest defects, disorder is outgrown by early teens.
(Acquired) Aphasia	Trauma, cerebral vascular accidents, Status epilepticus.	Within normal limits.	Under 4 years: short period of complete loss of language followed by rapid relearning. After 4 years: well-formed words but apraxia, word-finding difficulty, inappropriate utterances, confusion, jargon, telegraphic style.	After first 6 months of spontaneous recovery, speech rehabilitation often helps to encourage patient and restore self-confidence. If learning difficulties are associated with aphasia, academic help ought to precede articulation drill.	Dependent upon age at cerebral insult: recovery is complete in children under 10 with the recovery period lasting 3 months or less in preschoolers and up to a year in older children. In teenagers residua become increasingly likely with advancing age. In the young adult symptoms present a year after injury are usually irreversible.

TABLE 2

Outline for a Diagnostic Checklist

| | *Motor Speech* | *Evidence for Language* | | *Motivation for Communication* |
		Understands	*Reads or Writes*	
Deaf	0	0	+	+
Mentally Retarded	$\frac{+}{-}$	$\frac{+}{-}$	0	+
Psychotic	+	$\frac{+}{-}$	0	0
Disarticulation	0	+	+	+
Aphasia	$\frac{+}{-}$	$\frac{+}{-}$	$\frac{+}{-}$	+

Legend: 0 = absent
+ = present

$\left.\begin{array}{c}+\\-\end{array}\right\}$ = no generalization possible

Reading and Reading Difficulty: A Conceptual Analysis

MORTON WIENER
Clark University

WARD CROMER
Wellesley College

This article by Morton Wiener and Ward Cromer offers one of the first taxonomies of reading failure based on antecedent-consequent models of reading. Through a consideration of various definitions of reading and previous explanations for reading difficulty, the authors confront several of the major issues in reading research and advance what they believe is a more integrated conceptualization of the reading process and its breakdown.

In trying to impose some coordinating conceptual framework upon the phenomena subsumed under reading and reading difficulty, we believe with T. L. Harris (1962) that "the real issues arise from different conceptions of the nature of the reading process itself and of the learning processes, sets and principles to be stressed" (p. 5). In the present paper we will specify and discuss a number of issues which we believe must be considered to develop a more adequate conceptual framework. The issues are derived from an analysis of the diversity of definitions of reading and the variety of explanations offered to account for reading difficulty. Once the issues are clearly defined, a coordinating framework may be possible. We will spell out what we think to be one such conceptualization of reading and reading difficulty.

AN ANALYSIS OF READING DEFINITIONS

Four interrelated issues emerge from an examination of the many definitions

The authors wish to thank Dr. Joachim F. Wohlwill, Dr. James M. Coffee, and the other colleagues and students who read the manuscript in one or more of its revisions and who made helpful suggestions and criticisms. The time to write this paper was made possible in part by Grant M-3860 from the National Institute of Mental Health, United States Public Health Service.

Harvard Educational Review   Vol. 37   No. 4   Fall 1967, 618–643

of reading. Discussion of these issues may help clarify some of the present ambiguity and confusion about reading.

Identification versus Comprehension. The first issue is, what behaviors define reading? Some definitions focus primarily on the identification of the stimulus configurations (letters, letter patterns, words, clauses, sentences) appearing on the printed page, while others emphasize the comprehension of the material. When identification skills are emphasized, the defining attribute of reading is the correct "saying" of the word. Comprehension, on the other hand, implies the derivation of some form of meaning and the relating of this meaning to other experiences or ideas.

The assessment of identification is restricted to some evaluation of what and how words are "said." (How the word is to be pronounced and the variability permitted are both based on some implicit consensus.) Comprehension, on the other hand, is assessed by such criteria as the ability of the reader to paraphrase, to abstract the contents, to answer questions about the material, or to deal critically with the contents. Comprehension can also be inferred partly from the relative quality of identifications, i.e., by the tone, inflection, and phrasing of the identifications. However, the inability to demonstrate comprehension in any of these ways may be a function of restricted language, restricted experience, limited intelligence, or combinations of these three, rather than a function of a reading difficulty. If comprehension is used as the criterial behavior of reading, then these other possible antecedents of noncomprehension must be ruled out before the problem can be called a "reading difficulty."

When both kinds of behaviors are included in definitions of reading, the question arises whether these are solely a matter of emphasis on two parts of one process, or whether different activities are implied? At first glance, it would appear that these differences are matters of emphasis only. For those holding a single process view, identification can be considered a necessary antecedent to comprehension. Closer examination of the relationships between identification and comprehension shows, however, that rather than this one relationship, several are possible.

Although both identification and comprehension require some discrimination process (i.e., to identify or comprehend the reader must be able to distinguish among words), comprehension and identification do not necessarily imply each other. One example of the occurrence of identification without comprehension is the child who may be able to read (i.e., "say") the words printed in a scientific journal with some facility without having any notion of the meaning of the words. Another example is an American or a Frenchman who, with only a limited amount of training, can pronounce most words in Italian (a language which has a high relationship between spelling and sound), without knowing the meanings of the words. Whether these instances are considered reading depends upon the definition. We recognize that there may be differences between the saying aloud of material by individuals who do not comprehend and by those who do. Comprehension can sometimes be inferred from inflections, tone, and pauses, all of which may be derived from the context of the material read rather than from the sentence construction. These differences, when present, are often both subtle and difficult to denote reliably.

The occurrence of comprehension without identification, on the other hand, is less evident and examples are somewhat more difficult to cite. The best single example is given by Geschwind (1962) in his work with aphasics. He finds that some aphasic patients are able to respond appropriately to the meanings of a written communication, but apparently are unable to identify the words, i.e., to say them. As we understand it, some aphasics may be able to follow printed instructions without being able to "say" them aloud. A more subtle example can be found in "speed reading" which appears to exemplify nonidentification in that the very speed required makes identification unlikely. To acquire speed reading the individual must learn to eliminate persisting identification patterns. We hold, first, that the behavior occurring in speed reading is similar to that of more typical fast readers and, second, that in the advanced stages of reading, the presence of certain identification activities may interfere with the speed of reading and may result in less than maximum comprehension. Once reading skills have been acquired, reading may go from the discrimination of stimuli directly to comprehension without concomitant identification. Further, in good readers identification occurs primarily for novel or difficult material where there is an attempt to achieve some auditory or other discriminations which can be the basis for comprehension[1] (e.g., by sounding out an unfamiliar word).

Acquisition versus Accomplished Reading. A second issue emerging from comparisons of definitions of reading is, does reading refer to the behavior occurring during acquisition of skills or to the behavior manifested after these "skills" have been achieved? Investigators who define reading in terms of accomplished reading often imply that certain other skills are present without spelling them out. Those who emphasize the acquisition of reading give definitions which focus on the skills that need to be mastered, often without stating what constitutes the end-product.[2]

---

[1] We will attempt later to make a distinction between visual and auditory comprehension as components in the acquisition of reading.

[2] The research literature on reading difficulties reflects these same differences in emphasis. Some researchers focus on difficulties that can be considered as problems of acquisition, e.g., difficulty with word recognition or phonetics, etc. (Budoff, 1964; Elkind, 1965; Goens, 1958;

Definitions of reading generally associate acquisition with identification behavior on the one hand, and comprehension with accomplished reading on the other. An emphasis on problems associated with the acquisition of skills most often implies a focus on identification skills, while a focus on accomplished reading often implies a stress on comprehension activities.

The failure to distinguish between acquisition and accomplished reading in definitions partially accounts for the confusion about the *relationship* between identification and comprehension. In the acquisition of reading skills, identification may be a necessary *antecedent* to comprehension (as we will discuss in more detail below, word meanings are typically available to the child primarily in auditory form). But identification, which is essential in the acquisition phase for comprehension, may be irrelevant for the skilled reader who already has meaning associated with the visual forms and who may go directly from the written forms to the meaning without identification: that is, without an intermediary "verbal-auditory" transformation. Put another way, although some form of identification (saying a word either aloud or subvocally) may be essential for comprehension during acquisition, its nonoccurrence is not a problem for an experienced reader. Thus, the final product of reading need not include components that went into its acquisition. To draw an analogy, many of the components that go into the acquisition of good driving skill disappear as the driver becomes more proficient. In early learning there is much more cognitive behavior associated with the sensory-motor behavior, while in the later phases operating a car is almost totally sensory-motor.

Relative versus Absolute Criteria. Another source of ambiguity for conceptualizing reading is the different implicit criteria used for designating "good" reading. Sometimes, reading skill (and reading difficulty) is defined in terms of absolute or ideal criteria, but more often in terms of relative criteria. Both approaches present problems. When absolute or ideal criteria are used, a good reader is typically specified as someone able to read a certain number of words at a given rate with some particular level of comprehension. Insofar as ideal criteria are arbitrary, standards can be designated which include differing proportions of the reading population. Using absolute criteria, children during the acquisition of reading skill would not be considered good readers.

A relative definition of reading skill invokes criteria which specify, either implicitly or explicitly, some normative group. The implication of a relative

Robeck, 1963; Goetzinger, 1960; Marchbanks; 1965). Others focus on difficulties that occur after acquisition is relatively complete, e.g., advancement of comprehension skills, critical reading, or enhancement of experiences (Robinson, 1965; Woestehoff, 1960; Chapman, 1965; Emans, 1965; Gray, 1960).

criterion is that the same kind or level of skill may be called "good or bad reading" depending on who is doing what and when. For example, a second-grade child who has difficulties in phonetic skills (such as blending of sounds into words, which may be a necessary precursor of auditory comprehension) is not considered a reading problem when relative criteria are used, while a child in the sixth grade who lacks this skill is labeled as having a reading difficulty. In both instances, the same skill is missing. In this context, a sixth-grader may be defined as a poor reader, yet a third-grader behaving the same way (as far as we can determine) might be considered a good reader. It becomes evident that very little information can be communicated by statements about good or poor readers unless they are accompanied by clear specifications of the normative group's behaviors. Further, unless the relative criteria are made explicit, there can be no basis for comparing two "poor readers" since they might have been defined as such by different criteria.

The most important problem raised by a relative point of view is that very different behaviors may be given the same label. Having been given the same label, these different behaviors may later be treated as if they were the same phenomenon. The reading-research literature gives evidence that this danger is real in that poor reading is used as a generic term, apparently without the recognition that different investigators may be talking about very different forms of behaviors.

Research approaches and inferences are influenced by whether a relative or an absolute point of view is assumed. These different viewpoints implicitly specify the groups to be studied (those who are taken to be poor readers) and, more importantly, what is considered to be the appropriate control group for the study (the normative baseline against which the experimental group is to be compared). If the criteria are not made explicit, inappropriate control groups may often be established. For example, if a third-grader with an IQ of 75 is compared with other third-graders, he may be defined as a poor reader. Yet if he is compared with other children with IQ's of 75 in the third grade, he may be labeled a good reader by some relative criterion. In the former case, what is at issue may be relevant to intelligence, not to reading.

It may be more useful to specify the "ideal" case of reading and what its components or essential behaviors are. Having spelled out the ideal case, different people can be compared in terms of the presence or absence of these specifications, independent of distinctions between a person learning to read and an accomplished reader, and independent of evaluative statements as to how "good" the reading is.

Reading versus Language Skills. Investigators vary in the extent to which they emphasize the role of already present auditory language (i.e., knowledge of word meaning and the availability of grammatical forms) either as a separate skill or as one included in reading. There may be little or no concern with previously acquired auditory language capabilities when reading is considered as identification. When reading is considered as comprehension, some investigators (Fries, 1962; Lefevre, 1964; Bloomfield & Barnhart, 1961) deal explicitly with the role of language in reading. The majority of research is less explicit, even though comprehension implies the utilization of meanings already available in some other (usually auditory) form. In studying reading difficulty, Milner (1951) explicitly notes the differential experience with verbal language skills in children from middle and lower socioeconomic backgrounds and its relationship to reading skill. Bereiter and Engelmann (1966) also consider this issue a major one as evidenced by their attempt to train culturally deprived children in language skills before introducing reading. A failure to be explicit about the relationship between reading and previously acquired auditory language often leads to ambiguities as to whether a particular difficulty is a reading problem, language problem, or both.

Examination of Specific Definitions

Having noted some issues, we can now examine specific definitions[3] of reading in order to demonstrate their varying degrees of emphasis on: (a) discrimination, identification, and comprehension; (b) acquisition versus the final product of accomplished reading; (c) absolute versus relative criteria for good reading; and (d) the relation of language skills to reading skills.

The first definition reveals an emphasis on the acquisition of reading skills without specification of the attributes of an accomplished reader. More particularly, it focuses on the development of identification processes with comprehension skills noted only incidentally:

> There are several ways of characterizing the behavior we call reading. It is receiving communication; it is making discriminative responses to graphic symbols; it is decoding graphic symbols to speech; and it is getting meaning from the printed page. A child in the early stages of acquiring reading skill may not be doing all these things; however, some aspects of reading must be mastered before others and have an essential function in a sequence of development of the final skill. The average child, when he begins learning to read, has already mastered to a marvelous extent the art of communication. He can speak and understand his own language in a fairly complex way, employing units of language organized in a hierarchy and with a grammatical structure. Since a writing system must correspond to the spoken one, and since speech is prior to writing, the framework and unit structure of speech will determine more

[3] The particular definitions offered here are not meant to be exhaustive but were chosen primarily because they appear to exemplify the different emphases with which we are concerned.

548

or less the structure of the writing system, though the rules of correspondence vary for different languages and writing systems. . . .

Once a child begins his progression from spoken language to written language, there are, I think, three phases of learning to be considered. They present three different kinds of learning tasks, and they are roughly sequential, though there must be considerable overlapping. These three phases are: learning to differentiate graphic symbols; learning to decode letters to sounds ("map" the letters into sounds); and using progressively higher-order units of structure. (Gibson, 1965, pp. 1-2)

In that the above definition focuses on acquisition, we can infer that a relative scale would be used for designating individuals who are not progressing adequately. What is most noteworthy is that there is also some ambiguity in this definition as to whether the development of language skills is part of reading or prior to and/or independent of reading.

In contrast to Gibson, Geschwind (1962, p. 116) working with aphasics, offers a definition which focuses only on the accomplished reader and comprehension and which makes no reference to identification behaviors or processes in acquisition of reading:

The word *read* is used in the narrow sense of "ability to comprehend language presented visually" and not at all in the sense of "ability to read aloud."

By this definition, any reading without comprehension would be designated either as non-reading or as a reading problem, though it does not require "saying" for "reading" to occur. The definition makes no reference to the role of discrimination of the printed stimuli, which we assume must occur in order for comprehension to take place. Further, no explicit statement is made about either the relative or the absolute amount of comprehension which must be present for an individual to be designated a good or poor reader.

The following definition is ambiguous about the relationship of identification to comprehension:

. . . reading involves . . . the recognition of printed or written symbols which serve as stimuli for the recall of meanings built up through the reader's past experience. New meanings are derived through manipulation of concepts already in his possession. The organization of these meanings is governed by the clearly defined purposes of the reader. In short, the reading process involves both the acquisition of the meanings intended by the writer and the reader's own contributions in the form of interpretation, evaluation, and reflection about these meanings. (Bond & Tinker, 1957, p. 19)

The word "recognition," as used here can be taken to mean either discrimination or identification; both usages are incidental to the role of comprehension. Further, this definition refers almost exclusively to the activities of the accomplished reader without apparent concern for the activities necessary for acquiring reading skills (other than the acquisition of meaning). By this definition, most children could be designated as having reading difficulties in that they have not yet acquired the "recognitions" nor the "meanings intended by the writer." This definition also makes little distinction between reading and language skills, thereby making it possible to confuse a language deficiency with a reading difficulty.

In contrast, the next definition makes an explicit distinction between language usage and reading.

The first stage in learning the reading process is the "transfer" stage. It is the period during which the child is learning to transfer from the auditory signs for language signals, which he has already learned, to a set of visual signs for the same signals. This process of transfer is not the learning of the language code or a new language code; it is not the learning of a new or different set of language signals. It is not the learning of new "words," or of new grammatical structures, or of new meanings. These are all matters of the language signals which he has on the whole already learned so well that he is not conscious of their use. This first stage is complete when within his narrow linguistic experience the child can respond rapidly and accurately to the visual patterns that represent the language signals in this limited field, as he does to the auditory patterns that they replace.

The second stage covers the period during which the responses to the visual patterns become habits so automatic that the graphic shapes themselves sink below the threshold of attention, and the cumulative comprehension of the meanings signalled enables the reader to supply those portions of the signals which are not in graphic representation themselves.

The third stage begins when the reading process itself is so automatic that the reading is used equally with or even more than live language in the acquiring and developing of experience—when reading stimulates the vivid imaginative realization of vicarious experience. (Fries, 1962, p. 132)

This definition is also more explicit than most in distinguishing between acquisition and the accomplished reader, the relation of identification to comprehension, and the difference between language skills and reading skills. It does not, however, specify the forms of behaviors which would constitute reading difficulty, except those skills necessary for adequate "transfer" to occur.

The next definition focuses on the sequential development of reading from identification to comprehension. It does not make explicit the role identification plays in the skills which develop later. It also exemplifies the relativity of definitions of reading when it states that what constitutes reading skill depends upon the level of the learner as he progresses from acquisition to accomplished reading.

We may define reading as the act of responding appropriately to printed symbols. For the beginner, reading is largely concerned with learning to recognize the symbols which represent spoken words. As proficiency in reading increases, the individual learns to adapt and vary his method of reading in accordance with his purpose for reading and the restrictions imposed by the nature of the material. As the learner achieves skill in the recognition side of reading, the reasoning side of reading becomes increasingly important. The nature of the reading task, therefore, changes as the learner progresses from less mature to more mature levels; reading is not one skill, but a large number of interrelated skills which develop gradually over a period of many years. (Harris, A. J., 1948, p. 9)

These examples should make evident the diversity of emphases, the ambiguity and confusion in definitions of reading. Further, this discussion has shown that investigators, with few exceptions (e.g., Fries), have not made distinctions between reading activities and language activities, or if so, they have been ambiguous as to the independence or interdependence of language and reading. All definitions that focus on meaning or comprehension imply language as an antecedent, but do not necessarily offer a basis for identifying poor reading as a reading difficulty rather than as a language difficulty.

AN ANALYSIS OF READING DIFFICULTY

The issues raised thus far have been related to different usages of the term "reading." Other issues emerge when the term "reading difficulty" is examined. An analysis of the usages of the term "reading difficulty" indicates that four different assumptions are used to account for reading difficulty and its etiology. Each of the four models implies particular kinds of remediation.

The Assumption of Defect. Investigators who hold that reading difficulty is attributable to some malfunction, i.e., something is not operating appropriately in the person so that he *cannot* benefit from his experiences, exemplify what we call a defect model. This approach generally implies that this impairment is considered to be relatively permanent. Defect explanations typically involve sensory-physiological factors. For example, Reitan (1964) discusses "reading impairment . . . and its relationship to damage of the left cerebral hemisphere" (p. 104). Some investigators appear to assume a defect whenever there is a reading difficulty. We hold that while an assumption of defect may be appropriate for some instances (e.g., cases of visual, hearing or other sensory impairment) there is no evidence that an assumption of defect accounts for all reading difficulties. Further, investigators holding a defect view often do not distinguish between the implications of a defect during acquisition of reading skill and after acquisition has taken place (e.g., blindness, brain damage). This type of explanation also implies that for "normal" reading to occur in individuals with a defect, change must occur (e.g., brain surgery) relatively independent of reading, or a different sequence in the acquisition must be utilized (e.g., teaching a blind person to read through the use of the tactual modality).

The Assumption of Deficiency. Other investigators have argued that reading difficulty is attributable to the *absence* of some function, i.e., a particular factor or process is absent and must be *added* before adequate reading can occur. Most attempts at remedial reading instruction are based on this interpretation of reading difficulties. The child must learn something he has not yet learned (e.g., phonetic skills, language skills, etc.) in order to make up his deficiency. In contrast to the defect explanation of reading difficulty, reversibility is almost always assumed.

The Assumption of Disruption. A third type of model used to account for reading difficulty assumes that the difficulty is attributable to something which is *present* but is *interfering* with reading and must be *removed* before reading will occur. For example, if a child is "anxious," "hyperemotional," or has "intrapsychic conflicts," he may be unable to learn to read (cf., Koff, 1961). An assumption of disruption is implicit in investigations of so-called neurotic learning disabilities. It is also implicit in any approach which maintains that using the wrong methods to teach reading will disrupt and interfere with the learning that takes place when the correct teaching method is used. Occasionally the assumption of disruption operates jointly with the deficiency assumption, the notion being that first the interference must be removed and then the missing components must be added.

The Assumption of Difference. Lastly, various researchers assume that reading difficulty is attributable to *differences* or mismatches between the typical mode of responding and that which is more appropriate, and thus has the best payoff in a particular situation. This model assumes that the individual would read adequately if the material were consistent with his behavior patterns; thus, a *change* in either the material or in his patterns of verbalization is a prerequisite for better reading.

Cromer and Wiener (1966) posit that poor readers have evolved different response patterns; i.e., they elaborate "cues" in a manner different from that of good readers. Within their framework, both good and poor readers "scan" and derive partial information from the printed stimuli; the specific difference between the good and poor readers is that poor readers generally elaborate these cues by responding more idiosyncratically than do good readers, either because they have not learned consensual response patterns or because they have learned idiosyncratic patterns too well. In this framework, reading difficulty is expected to occur when there is a mismatch between the material being read and the response patterns of the reader.

An example of a mismatch is when auditorally- and visually-presented languages are discrepant, as might be the case for a lower-class child who speaks a neighborhood "slang." The child may not be able to elaborate the cues in "formal language patterns." He does not read well because he does not draw from the same language experiences as does the middle-class child for whom a typical reading test is written; there is a mismatch between the reading material and his typical pattern of responding. If, however, the material were presented in the same form as his spoken language, we posit that he would then be able to read more adequately. This child would not be considered a reading problem but rather a language problem in that he does not draw from the same language experiences as the middle-class child for whom a typical reading text is written.

Still another example of a mismatch involves the reading of highly technical material. An individual may have difficulty because he (in contrast to an expert in the same area) has sequences which are less likely to match the reading input. A psychologist reading a physics book or a physicist reading a psychology book would be slowed down, would show more errors in his reading, and would have less comprehension than when each reads in his own field. In this instance, there are differences in reading abilities, depending on the material being read. It does not seem meaningful, however, to consider these differences in skill as reading problems. Thus no pathology is posited for a "reading difficulty" stemming from a mismatch.

Associated with each of the assumption models are implicit differences in the kinds of factors—sensory-perceptual (physiological), experiential-learning, and personality-emotional (psychological)—assumed to account for reading difficulty. Pointing to physiological factors generally implies a defect; i.e., something other than the behaviors involved in reading must be changed or in some way dealt with before improved reading can occur. When the focus is on experience or learning, either a deficiency or a difference is implied; i.e., the individual has not learned a particular skill or has learned a different one. On the other hand, explanations that focus on psychological factors imply a disruption and/or a deficiency. In sum, not only are there different assumptions to account for reading difficulty but in addition, each assumption model implies a particular set of operative factors and a particular form of intervention or remediation.

Models for Conceptualizing Reading Difficulty: Antecedent-Consequent Relationships

Another source of confusion in the literature is the form of explanation offered to account for "reading problems." Some investigators refer to single "causes" of reading difficulty while others state that multiple "causes" need to be invoked. Applying a formal or logical analysis to these kinds of explanatory statements reveals additional conceptual problems. This task can be facilitated by reformulating and extending a model developed by Handlon (1960) to spell out possible forms for explaining schizophrenia.[4] We have substituted the term "reading difficulty" where in Handlon's original application the term schizophrenia appears. We will try to "explain" reading difficulties by relating the variables associated with reading (antecedents) to the variables associated with reading difficulties (consequents).

1. *Model One* (in Handlon's form of explanation) states that reading difficulty "is a class with a single member, this member having a single radical cause." In our conditional form, Model One is "If A, then X," where A is a single specific antecedent and X is a class ("reading difficulty") in which each instance of a reading difficulty is considered equivalent.

An example of Model One is Corrigan's (1959) synaptic transmission (chemical) theory of reading disability. She maintains that disabled readers are part of a population of slow learners characterized by atypical production of two chemicals, ACh (acetycholine) and ChE (cholinesterase). Although the balance and concentration level of these chemicals is affected by environmental (anxiety producing) factors, it is the chemical factor itself which is seen to underly reading disability, that is, reading disability is presented also as if it were a single member class. Another example of Model One, Delacato's (1959) theory of "central neurological organization," attributes reading difficulty to a lack of cerebral cortical dominance.

Although logically possible, Model One does not seem very promising. Most investigators reject both the notion that a single antecedent accounts for all reading difficulties, and the notion that reading difficulty is in fact a class with only a single member.

2. *Model Two* states that reading difficulty is "a class with a single member, that member having multiple factors constituting the radical cause."[5] In our conditional form, Model Two is "If A or B or C..., then X," where A, B, etc. are particular and independent[6] antecedents, and, as in Model One, X is a class with a single member called "reading difficulty."

[4] Handlon, in his model called Single-Multiple Causal Factors uses the terms "cause" and "effect"; with our philosophical bias we prefer the terms "antecedent" and "consequent." These terms will be used here in a conditional ("If, then") rather than a causal form. The conditional statement is not meant to imply either a spatial or temporal relationship, but a relationship in a formal-logical sense. We thank Dr. Roger Bibace who brought this article to our attention.

[5] We will consider this statement only in the form "If A or B or C, then X" rather than the form "If A and B and C, then X," since the latter is logically reducible to "If A, then X," where A stands for a conjunctive category.

[6] By using the symbols A, B, C ... and X_1, X_2, X_3, etc., there is a possible implication that these symbols may be treated as an ordinal series, with the later implying the earlier. In each model except for Model Six (see below), these symbols are used only in the sense of a

Rabinovitch (1959) appears to use a Model Two form of explanation. He defines reading retardation as reading achievement two or more years below the mental age obtained on performance tests and then goes on to list three subclasses of antecedents of reading difficulty (exogenous, i.e., cultural and emotional factors; congenital brain damage; and endogenous, i.e., biological or neurological disturbances). Similarly, Roswell and Natchez (1964) in their treatment of reading disability argue for a multi-causal model and describe a series of antecedents that can "cause" reading difficulty (e.g., intellectual, physical, emotional, environmental, educational, and growth factors). Investigators using this model might *consider* reading difficulty as different for the different "causes," but they do not *specify* nor delineate these differences; that is, they seem to treat reading difficulty as if it were a single member class.

Although this form of explanation may also be logically tenable, we are convinced that the assumption that reading difficulty is a class with a single member is unacceptable. Our belief is that reading difficulty is a multiple-member class and that Model Two forms of statements might better be changed to "If A, then X_1"; "If B, then X_2"; "If C, then X_3" where X_1, X_2, X_3 are particular and independent manifestations within the class reading difficulty (Model Five, see below). We maintain that if an investigator looks carefully enough, he will find different members within the class X which might better meet the criteria of a class with a single member associated with a particular antecedent, and that it is incumbent on investigators to explore their "single consequent" in a multiple-antecedent/single-consequent model to determine whether the consequent is in fact a class with only a single member.

3. *Model Three* states that reading difficulty "is a class with several members, all members having the same single ... cause." This statement can be represented in the following form: "If A, then X_1 or X_2 or X_3..." where A is a particular antecedent and X_1, X_2, etc. are particular members of the class called "reading difficulty." To the extent that investigators have not labeled the specific forms of reading difficulty (that is, different members of the class reading difficulty), then they would be unlikely to apply a model using a single antecedent and multiple consequents. In fact, no appropriate examples of Model Three were located in the literature. Those that appeared at first to be examples of Model Three were found to be more appropriately assigned to Model One, which treats the consequent as a single-member class.

4. *Model Four* states that reading difficulty "is a class with several members, each having single or multiple causes that are not necessarily unique

---

nominal scale (Stevens, 1951) and could be written in the form "If alpha, then X_{alpha}; if aleph, then X_{aleph}; etc."

to that member." In other words, there are many antecedent variables and many manifestations of reading difficulty (consequents) and the relationships between these antecedents and consequents are unspecified or unspecifiable. This model can be represented in the form: "If A and/or B and/or C..., then X_1, or X_2, or X_3...."

This form of explanation appears to be most popular in the current literature; for examples one can turn to almost any comprehensive book on the "diagnostic teaching of reading" (e.g., Strang, 1964; Bond and Tinker, 1957; Bryant, 1963). These textbook approaches list all the possible "causes" of reading difficulty and then discuss techniques for remedial instruction. The relationships between the many antecedents and the many consequents are never clearly specified. The problems inherent in this approach are exemplified most clearly in a study reported by Goltz (1966). Working with "individual remedial reading for boys in trouble," he advocates the simultaneous use of five basic approaches to the teaching of reading (sight word, phonics, combination, linguistic, experiential) in the hope that one will work (he draws the analogy of shotgun pellets). The results of this approach were "some astounding successes and remarkable failures." The need for a theoretical rationale for relating possible difficulties and specific types of intervention is obvious. Again, we argue that it is incumbent on investigators to attempt to locate the particular antecedent and its relationship to a particular consequent.

5. *Model Five* appears to be the most acceptable form for explaining the phenomenon called reading difficulty. It states that reading difficulty is "a class with several members, each member having a single, unique cause. This statement can be represented in the form: "If A, then X_1; or if B, then X_2; or if C, then X_3..." where the X's represent different particular patterns of less-than-ideal reading. This model says that there are many antecedent variables and many manifestations under a general rubric "reading difficulty"; and the relationships between the antecedents and the consequents are, at least in theory, specifiable. Both Model Five and Model Four have multiple antecedents and multiple consequents. Model Five, however, associates a different antecedent with a specific consequent. For example, de Hirsch (1963) attempts to distinguish between two groups of adolescents with language disorders by suggesting that the etiology of each is different. Kinsbourne and Warrington (1963) note that two syndromes of developmental cerebral deficit seem to be associated with different forms of reading difficulty.

6. Model Five assumes that each of the manifestations of reading difficulty (i.e., the X's) is a member of the general class called reading difficulty and that each of these forms is independent. It may be, however, more meaningful to conceptualize the manifestations within the class, reading difficulty,

in a model which includes a notion of sequence. This kind of model is not considered by Handlon; we will elaborate it as *Model Six*. This model can be represented in the following form: "If A, then X_1" and "If X_1, then B" and "If B, then X_2," and "If X_2, then C" and "If C, then $X_3 \ldots X_n$." If, for example, C does not occur nor does X_3, then X_n, the particular form of behavior defined as reading, would not be expected to develop (X_n being defined as a class with a single member, a particular form of reading which is the end-product of the sequence and can be considered as an indicator on an absolute scale). Model Six explicitly includes the notion of an ordinal series and implies that if any member of the sequence were missing, further evolution of the sequence would not be expected, or at least not in the acquisition phase of learning to read. If the sequence has already evolved and there is a disruption, then depending on the point in the sequence where disruption occurs, later forms of reading may be present, even though some or all earlier forms are absent. This kind of formulation can account for differences in the kinds of reading difficulties noted when a disruption is present during acquisition or occurs in an accomplished reader (e.g., the reading of brain-damaged adults who were previously good readers versus the reading of brain-damaged children during the acquisition phase). Another implication is that the arbitrarily designated end point of a sequence specifies the antecedents and prior sequences to be included.

A CONCEPTUALIZATION OF READING AND READING DIFFICULTY

We pointed out earlier that some investigators treat reading as identification while others treat it as comprehension and that this difference has implications for what was defined as reading difficulty. In an effort to integrate these seemingly disparate approaches, reading will be conceptualized and discussed as a two-step process involving first identification and then comprehension. During the discussion, the antecedents for identification will be considered first and then comprehension will be considered.

Identification

Identification will be used to mean "word-naming," in the context of a transformation of stimuli.[7] In the discussion that follows, our formulation comes

[7] Identification presupposes a discrimination of one graphic symbol from others, discrimination of auditory symbols from others, and a transformation of these symbols from one form (usually visual) to a second form (usually auditory). The original visual forms and the transformed auditory forms are considered to be equivalent, differing only in that the referents are represented in different modalities. The two symbol forms are considered equivalent in that they contain the same information for members of a communication

from an analysis of visual-to-auditory transformation; similar analyses could be derived for other transformations. We assume a physiological substrate which is adequate for "normal" functioning to occur.

"Discrimination" constitutes one set of antecedents to identification. Prior to discrimination, however, a child must attend to the stimulus to make sensory input possible. Given sensory input, the child must then be able to make form discriminations. By discrimination, we mean the ability to make proper focal adjustments; to distinguish figure-ground, brightness, lines, curves, and angles; and to respond to differences in the amount of white space surrounding the forms (this latter discrimination is involved in the delineation of word units). These forms of discrimination are antecedents of identification.

Given the ability to discriminate, the child can begin to identify by distinguishing on the basis of angles and curves ("man" from "dog") or word length ("dog" from "good"), by responding to variations in relations among letter sequences ("on" vs. "no"), and by responding to spatial orientations of visual stimuli (left/right and up/down). These antecedents not only make possible new identifications but also make earlier forms of identification easier because the reader can respond to more of the available and co-occurring cues. For example, "dog" and "good" can be discriminated on the basis of word length, and the orientation of the first and last letters.

Using discriminations among sequences and general configurations, the child can now learn to identify a relatively large number of words solely by discriminating the first and last letters in an otherwise similar configuration (e.g., length, round vs. angled, internal letters, etc.). Although this discrimination may be adequate in the early stages of reading acquisition, the child must later learn to discriminate other components in the word such as internal letters ("bat" vs. "but" vs. "bet" vs. "bit"), sequence of letters ("there vs. "three"), additions of letters ("smile" vs. "simile"), etc. In these cases, to increase speed, it would appear that the child has to learn to respond to the variety of available cues and the order of their importance as the basis of discrimination of words within his language.

Antecedents for the identification of words in isolation are not sufficient for reading words in a sequence such as a phrase or a sentence; the individual must learn to say the words in the order given, although he does not necessarily have to "look" at them in that order. A knowledge of language and

---

group. Essentially, then, the major critical antecedents of identification are the discriminations among the original symbols, the discriminations among the transformed symbols, and a "knowledge" of the principles of transformation from one form to the other. Implicit in this conceptualization is that the transformed symbols (i.e., words as said aloud) can become an input for another individual. Implied also is that there is some consensual basis to assess the adequacy of the identification, with consensus meaning only that there is agreement within the group using the particular language or dialect.

language sequences will facilitate the discrimination of words in a sequence insofar as the co-occurrences of words can become an additional basis for discrimination, e.g., "the horse's mane" vs. "the horse's mine."

The antecedents discussed thus far are associated with learning to read using the "look-say" approach, which is essentially how one learns to read an ideographic language. Both this approach and languages requiring its use present special difficulties in that the reader must maintain a great many specific forms in his memory. Although he can discriminate new from old words and even among new words, he has no readily available way of identifying ("saying") the new words. If it were possible for a child to have a source of identifying words the first time he encountered them (e.g., via another person reading it or a speaking typewriter), and if he had the ability to store and recover the words as presented and as said, then the "look-say" method would be sufficient for reading. However, if new or novel words occur and there is no external source for initial identification, then a skill for identifying by oneself is required.

There are at least three different ways in which identification of new words occurs. They can be ordered by degree of explicitness for relating visual to sound forms. First, the individual may respond to some similarities among graphic forms, and he may also respond to some of the patterns of similarity among associated auditory forms. For example, the word "mat" looks like "man" and "hat," such that one approximation of the sound of "mat" could be the combination of the first part of "man" and the last part of "hat." The first sound approximated might not have exactly the same form as if it were emitted in the presence of the object. It could be corrected, however, by the reader's recognizing that the word as said sounds like some other word he had said at some other time.

The second way is like the first in that the reader uses similarities among graphic forms to aid his identification. In the first case, however, this response to similarity is incidental; in the second, it is systematic. An example of a systematic approach is the use of what linguists (such as Fries, 1962) call "spelling patterns." The individual is taught to look for similarities among visual and auditory forms by systematic exposure to various types of possible patterns, their variations, and their associated sounds. For example, if the individual learns to identify the words "man," "ban," "hat," and "fat," he will be able to identify the word "mat." Other examples of spelling patterns are mane/bane/hate/fate; and mean/bean/heat/feat. Thus, the possible similarities among visual forms, among auditory forms, and between visual and auditory forms are made somewhat more explicit by example.

In contrast to these two ways where similarity among graphic configurations is the basis for identifying new configurations, the third way requires the reader to know more explicit rules for transforming specific visual configurations into specific sounds, i.e., phonetics, to use Fries' terminology. For example, there is a "rule" that says when there is only one vowel in a word and it comes at the beginning or middle of a word, it is usually short ("hat," "and," "bed," "end"). These rules also include the notion that various locations and combinations of letters are associated with different sounds. One example is the "rule" that a vowel when followed by an "r" is neither long nor short, but is controlled by the "r"; e.g., "fur," "bird," "term."[8] One major difference between the phonetics approach and the other two is that identification of new words does not require previous experience with similar old words. However, the use of phonetics requires one additional ability, that of ordering letters from the beginning through to the end of a word. This skill, called "scanning," involves systematic eye movements from left to right and an organization of the input in that order.

Knowledge of co-occurrence of letters and words within a language will increase the rate of reading. Because not every word can come at a particular point in a sequence, the individual can identify words or groups of words rapidly even from very brief scanning of the material. Thus, "knowledge" of language or word sequences independent of visual input will reduce the amount of information required from scanning for identification to occur. At later stages, the reader may even be able to skip some of the words in a particular sequence, yet respond adequately with this decreased information. We propose that the ability to respond to this partial information, that is, the "elaboration" of these cues, can be based on learned patterns of sequential occurrences or what has been called "previously learned co-occurrence probabilities" (Kempler and Wiener, 1963). Differences among readers in their ability to identify a sequence correctly may be explained by differences in response availabilities rather than by differences in visual inputs. Since response patterns may be differentially available among individuals, given specific reading materials, a reader may "respond" to the same material with differing degrees of adequacy depending upon the availability of appropriate response patterns, even assuming the "same" input.

Comprehension

If comprehension[9] is now included in the definition of reading, additional antecedents must be considered. In our usage, comprehension refers to the addition of some form of meaning associated with the identifications or dis-

---

[8] In this context, ITA (cf., Downing, 1964; Downing, 1965) is seen as a procedure for simplifying acquisition; that is, for decreasing the number of "rules" the child must learn during acquisition of reading.

[9] A concern with the definition of comprehension and meaning would take us too far afield, even if we were competent to deal with this complex problem.

criminations, i.e., the words elicit shared associations, or consensual indicator responses to or about the referent, or a synonymous response. At least during acquisition, comprehension can occur and be examined at any point at which identification can occur; once the visual forms are transformed to auditory forms, there is a possibility of comprehension, given the presence of appropriate language skills. These language skills can be learned either before or along with the acquisition of identification skills. Language can include not only meaning but also those subjects typically dealt with by linguists (patterns, grammar, sequences, meaningful units, and so on). To the extent that these structural components are critical for meaning, these forms must also have been mastered or, alternatively, they must be learned during the acquisition phase.

It has been implied that meaning is available primarily through language as it occurs in the auditory form. We also have assumed implicitly that once there is a transformation from the visual to the auditory form, comprehension would follow. If the reader's auditory transformation (identification) corresponds to his already available auditory language forms, then meaning can be associated with the visual forms. For example, if a child in his identification says the word "ball" in the same way as he has heard it or as he says it in the presence of the referent object, then meaning can be transferred to the visual form. The assumed sequence has been: discriminations among input forms and output forms; transformation; identification; comprehension —all of these being required.

In all of the discussion thus far, individual differences have not been considered. Yet recognition of individual differences may be highly relevant in accounting for differences in forms of discrimination, identification, or comprehension. For example, individuals with low intelligence or with restricted language skills or restricted experiences might better be considered as having "problems" in these particular areas rather than in reading *per se*. Similarly, there are other instances of non-reading which might better be attributed to the conditions under which reading occurs, the content of the material being read, or the "motivation" of the individual reader and his interest in the material. In these instances, a reading problem cannot be assessed until learning has been tried under more "ideal" conditions with materials of more significance to the reader.

We can now note some instances: (a) where auditory transformations may not lead to comprehension although the reader ostensibly uses the same language as is used in the printed material; and (b) where comprehension facilitates or even makes possible identification which would not otherwise occur.

A first instance of an identification without comprehension is when the reader has had either insufficient or no previous experience with the referent so that it is not part of his meaning-vocabulary. For example, a story about children playing with a kite may elicit no referent (and no meaning) in an individual in a subculture where no one plays with kites. A second instance of identification without comprehension can occur in individuals who have had experience with the referent, but in circumstances where these referents are typically communicated in nonverbal forms such as gesture or tone. This problem is likely to occur in individuals who use what is sometimes called "expressive language" or nonverbal rather than verbal language. For example, a child could point and say "ball" in a particular tone as a substitute for saying, "I want this ball!" or "May I please have the ball?" or "Give me the ball" (cf. Bereiter and Engelmann, 1966; Bernstein, 1965; Deutsch, 1962). For comprehension to occur in these instances, the individual must be taught to use verbal language or at least to recognize that the "message" he communicates gesturally can also be communicated through words. A third way identification can occur without comprehension is when the sounds of the words as read are different from the sounds of the words as they occur in the reader's vocabulary. For some rural Southern children "y' all" may be the commonly heard and said form of "you." If a reader identifies (says) the word "you," he may not transfer the sound "you" to the meaning of "y'all." Another example is a child from a lower-class background who may not "say" the words in the same way or in the same sequence as his middle-class teacher; and therefore, if he makes his transformations into the teacher's language, comprehension may not occur. A fourth instance of identification without appropriate comprehension is when there is a lack of correspondence between the reader's auditory language and that of the material being read. For example, note how difficult it is to read and comprehend the following passage, which is a description of Harlem.

On school: "Everyone shouting and screaming and nobody care about what they is going on. But at least it somewhere to stay away from when they make you go." And on the purpose of fighting gangs: "In this bizness you got have a place of your own and a chain of command and all that. Everything go by the book. Then you get a name. And when you get the name maybe you can stay live a while. Thas why most men get in gangs. To stay live. Thas why the gangs form in the first place." (*Time* Magazine, February 24, 1967, p. 96)

In the third and fourth examples, there is a discrepancy between the language of the material being read and the reader's own language. This discrepancy can be resolved either by "correcting" the reader's language so that it matches the written form or by modifying the written material to correspond to his language patterns. As Labov (1967) notes, however, if the teacher is to locate the source of the difficulty and take appropriate remedial steps, he should "know" the child's nonstandard language. Labov spells out in some detail the possible discrepancies between the disadvantaged students and their teachers in their pronunciations and uses of grammar. He also discusses some of the implications of such discrepancies in the teaching of children who speak a nonstandard dialect.

One further way in which identification can occur without comprehension is when the particular meaning of the graphic material is different from the meaning typically elicited in the individual (e.g., slang, idiomatic expressions, and poetry), all of which depend on less consensual meanings. An example is a foreigner trying to read a popular detective story which uses slang and colloquialisms. Another example would be an accomplished reader reading James Joyce, where the words have highly personalized referents.

On the other hand, comprehension can facilitate identification if the reader has highly advanced language skills available, e.g., vocabulary, sequences, appropriate generating grammar (in Chomsky's, 1957, sense). To the extent that each of these skills facilitates identification by decreasing the range of possibilities of what is likely to occur in the written material, less information is necessary from the visual input to elicit the whole sequence. Thus, there are a number of ways in which knowledge of language in terms of both meaning and structure may aid identification and even make possible specific identifications which otherwise would not occur. First, the context and meaning of the material already read may generate and/or limit new forms of identification via the individual's understanding and elaboration of the material being read. For example, all other factors being constant, two scientists will differ in the rate and understanding of specific scientific material if they have a different familiarity with the subject matter. A second way in which language aids identification is through the structure of the language which limits the possible types of words or sequences which can occur at any given point. Further, comprehension may make possible identifications which otherwise might not occur. A beginning reader who has not learned phonics but who has a good vocabulary and uses language as it typically occurs in written form may be able to "guess" a word he has not previously identified. He can identify the word on the basis of his comprehension of the context, or familiarity with the structure of the language, or both. To exemplify how the structure and context contribute to identification, all one needs to do is to remove words randomly from a story (Cloze technique, Taylor, 1953) and note the limited number and types of word insertions which occur. Third, extensive language experience facilitates speed of reading. Having learned (and being familiar with) possible elaborations, the reader requires fewer cues for a particular response to occur; the assumption here is that the requirement of fewer cues is associated with more rapid scanning, e.g., speed reading of familiar material. Fourth, comprehension facilitates the recognition of errors in reading when there is a mismatch between any of the three possible sources of information mentioned above and the identification as "said." For example, when the word elaborated from the cues is not congruent with later elaborations—it does not fit the content, context, or sequences as previously experienced—the reader will experience the possibility of an error and "check" the input for more cues.

Once reading is defined as comprehension (which we hold can occur only after basic identification and language skills have been mastered), then identification becomes secondary and may eventually be eliminated except for identifying new words. As noted earlier, an individual with good language (meaning and structure) skills can, in the case of speed reading, go directly from the discrimination to the meaning without the intermediate step of (auditory) identification. Typically, readers use identification in "reading" (here "reading" is being defined in terms of comprehension) in the following ways: first, to make the words auditorally overt (i.e., saying the words aloud so they can be understood); second, to make the words covertly auditory (i.e., lip moving); then, implicit identification (i.e., the reader experiences the words as if they were said aloud but there is no evidence of overt saying); and, finally, identification is eliminated when the reader goes directly from the visual configurations—without experiencing the words as auditory forms —to their associated meaning, e.g., speed reading. Theoretically, at least, identification (in contrast to discrimination) is not necessary and, in fact, may not occur in the accomplished reader. It is even possible that a method could be devised for teaching reading (i.e., comprehension) without the intermediate step of auditory identification. If, for example, we could evolve principles for understanding how a child learns his original language— which includes the transformation of the experience of objects into words in auditory form—we might begin to understand how a child might learn to go from an original visual form directly to meaning without an intermediate auditory "naming."

We hope this attempt to impose some order on the diversity of phenomena included under reading or reading difficulty will be of heuristic value to other investigators. Recognizing that we have only touched on the complexities of reading behavior, we hope others will bring to bear other coordinating principles to this area of investigation.

REFERENCES

Bereiter, C. & Engelmann, S. *Teaching disadvantaged children in the preschool.* New York: Prentice-Hall, 1966.

Bernstein, B. A socio-linguistic approach to social learning. In J. Gould (Ed.), *Social science survey*. New York: Pelican, 1965.

Bloomfield, L. & Barnhart, C. L. *Let's read*. Detroit: Wayne State Univer. Press, 1961.

Bond, G. & Tinker, M. *Reading difficulties: their diagnosis and correction*. New York: Appleton-Century-Crofts, 1957.

Bryant, N. D. Learning disabilities in reading. Mimeo.

Budoff, M. & Quinlan, D. Reading readiness as related to efficiency of visual and aural learning in the primary grades. *J. educ. Psychol.*, 1964, **55** (5), 247-252.

Corrigan, Patricia. Broader implications of a chemical theory of reading disability. Paper presented at Amer. psychol. Assn. Meeting, 1959.

Chapman, Carita. Meeting current reading needs in adult literacy programs. In H. A. Robinson (Ed.), *Recent developments in reading*. Supplementary educ. Monogr., Univer. of Chicago Press, 1965, No. 95.

Chomsky, N. *Syntactic structures*. The Hague: Mouton & Company, 1957.

Cromer, W. & Wiener, M. Idiosyncratic response patterns among good and poor readers. *J. consult. Psychol.*, 1966, **30** (1), 1-10.

De Hirsch, Katrina. Two categories of learning difficulties in adolescents. *Amer. J. Orthopsychiat.*, 1963, **33**, 87-91.

Delacato, C. H. *The treatment and prevention of reading problems*. Springfield: Charles C Thomas, 1959.

Deutsch, M. The disadvantaged child and the learning process: some social, psychological and developmental considerations. Paper prepared for the Ford Foundation "Work Conference on Curriculum and Teaching in Depressed Urban Areas." New York: Columbia Univer., 1962.

Downing, J. A. *The initial teaching alphabet*. New York: Macmillan, 1964.

Downing. J. A. *The i.t.a. reading experiment*. Chicago: Scott, Foresman, 1965.

Elkind, D., Larson, Margaret, & Van Doorninck, W. Perceptual decentration learning and performance in slow and average readers. *J. educ. Psychol.*, 1965, **56** (1).

Emans, R. Meeting current reading needs in grades four through eight. In H. A. Robinson (Ed.), *Recent developments in reading*. Suppl. educ. Monogr., Univer. of Chicago Press, 1965, No. 95.

Fries, C. C. *Linguistics and reading*. New York: Holt, Rinehart, and Winston, 1962.

Geschwind, N. The anatomy of acquired disorders of reading disability. In J. Money (Ed.), *Progress and research needs in dyslexia*. Baltimore: Johns Hopkins Press, 1962.

Gibson, E. J. Learning to read. *Science*, 1965, **148**, 1066-1072.

Goens, Jean T. *Visual perceptual abilities and early reading progress*. Suppl. educ. Monogr., Univer. of Chicago Press, 1958, No. 87.

Goetzinger, C. P., Dirks, D. D., & Baer, C. J. Auditory discrimination and visual perception in good and poor readers. *Annals of Otology, Rhinology, and Laryngology*, March 1960, 121-136.

Goltz, C. Individual remedial reading for boys in trouble. *Reading Teacher*, 1966, **19** (5).

Gray, W. S. The major aspects of reading. In H. A. Robinson (Ed.), *Recent developments in reading*. Suppl. educ. Monogr., Univer. of Chicago Press, 1965, No. 95.

Handlon, J. A metatheoretical view of assumptions regarding the etiology of schizophrenia. *AMA Archives of gen. Psychiat.*, January 1960, 43-60.

Harris, A. J. *How to increase reading ability*. London: Longmans, Green, 1948.

Harris, T. L. Some issues in beginning reading instruction. *J. educ. Res.,* 1962, **56** (1).

Kempler, B. & Wiener, M. Personality and perception in the recognition threshold paradigm. *Psychol. Rev.,* 1964, **70**, 349-356.

Kinsbourne, M. & Warrington, E. K. Developmental factors in reading and writing backwardness. *Brit. J. Psychol.,* 1963, **54**, 145-156.

Koff, R. H. Panel on: Learning difficulties in childhood. Reported by E. A. Anthony, *J. Amer. Psychiatric Assn.,* 1961, **9**.

Labov, W. Some sources of reading problems for Negro speakers of nonstandard English. In A. Frazier (Ed.), *New directions in elementary English,* Nat. Council of English, 1967.

Lefevre, C. A. *Linguistics and the teaching of reading.* New York: McGraw-Hill, 1964.

Marchbanks, Gabrielle & Levin, H. Cues by which children recognize words. *J. educ. Psychol.,* 1965, **56** (2), 57-61.

Milner, Esther. A study of the relationship between reading readiness in grade-one schoolchildren and patterns of parent-child interaction. *Child Devel.,* 1951, **22** (2), 95-112.

Rabinovitch, R. D. Reading and learning disabilities. In S. Arieti (Ed.), *American handbook of psychiatry.* New York: Basic Books, 1959.

Reitan, R. Relationships between neurological and psychological variables and their implications for reading instruction. In H. A. Robinson (Ed.), *Meeting individual differences in reading.* Suppl. educ. Monogr., Univer. of Chicago Press, 1964, No. 94

Robeck, Mildred. Readers who lacked word analysis skills: a group diagnosis. *J. educ. Res.,* 1963, **56**, 432-434.

Robinson, Helen M. Looking ahead in reading. In H. A. Robinson (Ed.), *Recent developments in reading.* Suppl. educ. Monogr., Univer. of Chicago Press, 1965, No. 95.

Roswell, Florence & Natchez, Gladys. *Reading disability: diagnosis and treatment.* New York: Basic Books, 1964.

Stevens, S. S. (Ed.) *Handbook of experimental psychology.* New York: John Wiley and Sons, 1951.

Strang, Ruth. *Diagnostic teaching of reading.* New York: McGraw-Hill, 1964.

Taylor, W. "Cloze procedure": a new tool for measuring readability. *Journ. Quart.,* 1953, **30**, 415-433.

Woestehoff, E. Methods and materials for teaching comprehension—in corrective and remedial classes. In Helen Robinson (Ed.), *Sequential development of reading abilities.* Suppl. educ. Monogr., Univer. of Chicago Press, 1960, No. 9.

Alternative Conceptualizations of Dyslexia: Evidence in Support of a Verbal-Deficit Hypothesis

FRANK R. VELLUTINO
The University at Albany
and Albany Medical College

The history of our knowledge about specific reading disability—dyslexia—is checkered with different hypotheses and theories. In this overview of the literature Frank Vellutino critically examines the foci of four prevalent explanations for reading failure in children: visual perception, intersensory integration, temporal-order perception, and verbal functioning. Applying findings from his own laboratory investigations and other selected research to each of the four hypotheses, Vellutino argues that the verbal-deficit hypothesis offers the most convincing explanation. Through the use of direct and indirect evidence Vellutino demonstrates the relationship between reading problems and dysfunction in the semantic, syntactic, or phonological aspects of language. Finally, Vellutino pursues the implications of his position and asserts that the linguistic problems of some poor readers necessitate an emphasis on the internal structure of words in learning to read.

The study of the reading process has made it increasingly evident that the various components of language are of cardinal importance in the acquisition of skill in reading (Kavanagh & Mattingly, 1972), but the status accorded to specific linguistic functions varies. For example, some authors emphasize relationships between reading and the grammatical aspects of language (Goodman, 1965, 1968; Kolers, 1970; Smith, 1971, 1973), while others stress the role of speech in learning to read (Downing, 1973; Elkonin, 1973; Liberman & Shankweiler, in press; Mattingly,

The author expresses his gratitude to Melinda Tanzman whose helpful comments assisted greatly in the preparation of this manuscript. Thanks in abundance are also due Veronica Carney, who valiantly typed far too many revisions of the paper.

This paper was supported in part by a research grant (1R01HD0965901) from the National Institute of Child Health and Human Development. The ideas presented appear in an expanded version in *Dyslexia: Theory and Practice,* Cambridge, Mass.: MIT Press, 1979.

Harvard Educational Review Vol. 47 No. 3 August 1977, 334–354

1972; Savin, 1972). Members of the first group conceptualize reading as a "psycho-linguistic" process in the broad sense and highlight the use of semantic and syntactic cue systems (mnemonics, context clues, and so on) in efficient reading. Spoken and written language are viewed as parallel functions, related ultimately by common semantic and syntactic processes.

Those who emphasize speech-reading relationships, on the other hand, generally view reading as a second-order, language-based skill. They consider the ability to decipher printed symbols to be largely dependent upon the learner's success in establishing phonetic or sound representations of those symbols; Mattingly (1972), for example, suggests that reading is "parasitical" on spoken language. Furthermore, he believes that the development of competence in reading requires that the internal structure of one's language be made explicit and has coined the term "linguistic awareness" to refer to the individual's conscious knowledge of the types and levels of linguistic processes which characterize spoken utterances. Liberman and her associates adopt a similar position.

This current emphasis upon language in learning to read is in sharp contrast to more traditional conceptualizations of the reading process, which ascribe to vision the central role in the acquisition of reading (Young & Lindsley, 1971). Such thinking is particularly evident in the literature concerned with developmental dyslexia or specific reading disability.[1] Indeed, the suggestion that reading disability in children is primarily attributable to visual distortions and dysfunction has been the dominant theme since 1896 when Pringle Morgan wrote his classic description of reading disorder in an otherwise normal child.

In recent years, however, an increasing number of studies suggest that dyslexia is causally related to deficiencies in verbal rather than visual processing. Several researchers (Shankweiler & Liberman, 1972; Vellutino, Steger, & Kandel, 1972; Vellutino, Smith, Steger, & Kaman, 1975), in fact, have now found support for the suggestion that the orientation and sequencing errors typically made by poor readers (e.g., b/d, was/saw) can be classified as verbal-response (naming) inaccuracies. Such errors were long thought to be compelling evidence supporting perceptual-deficit theories of reading disability.

Perceptual- and verbal-deficit theories, however, have not been the only explanations of reading disability. A close rival to the perceptual-deficit hypothesis is Birch's (1962) suggestion that dyslexia may be the result of a failure to integrate information from the sensory systems. Another popular hypothesis (Bakker, 1972) suggests that problems in reading accrue because the learner has difficulty

1 The terms "dyslexia" and "specific reading disability" as employed herein refer to children with severe reading problems *not* apparently attributable to below average intelligence, gross neurological disorder, peripheral sensory impairment, severe emotional disorder, inadequate home or school environments, or other extrinsic factors (Rabinovitch, 1959). These rubrics are employed as a convenience, owing to their widespread application to children with severe reading problems. Their use should not be taken as evidence that the author is committed to any particular explanation of reading disability. We apply them only to children with pervasive reading difficulties characterized by extreme decoding problems which result in deficiencies in all other aspects of reading.

in "perceiving" temporal order in verbal stimuli, an anomaly that is said to be distinctly different from verbal deficiency per se.

Nevertheless, my colleagues and I believe that the evidence accumulating in support of a verbal-deficit explanation of reading disability is impressive and are inclined to agree with those who argue that reading is primarily a language-based skill. A careful analysis of all the cognitive functions involved in learning to read reveals that the heaviest demands are made upon one's linguistic abilities. Consider, for example, five types of categorical information contained in the printed word: *graphic* (visual features), *orthographic* (internal structure), *phonologic* (sound components), *semantic* (meaning), and *syntactic* (part of speech). Three of these five categories refer to linguistic processes. Thus, acquisition of skill in reading would appear to be especially vulnerable to abnormalities in one or more of these aspects of verbal functioning.

The alternative theories mentioned earlier have had greater currency as explanations of reading disability than have verbal-deficit hypotheses. It seems appropriate, therefore, to review and evaluate the evidence for each of these conceptualizations of dyslexia. Inasmuch as my associates and I have been actively researching various aspects of these theories, we will refer to much of our own data, integrating our findings with the results of others. Because of space limitations, however, we must be selective in the choice of studies and will, therefore, refer the reader to other reviews where pertinent.

Theories of Dyslexia

Deficiencies in Visual Processing

The perceptual-deficit hypothesis suggests that reading disability is caused by visual-spatial confusion stemming from some kind of neurological deficiency. This theory was first advanced by Orton (1925, 1937), who attached particular significance to the orientation and sequencing problems observed in letter and word identification. Such disturbances were thought to be manifestations of delayed development of lateral dominance; that is, the two hemispheres of the brain were not sufficiently developed to coordinate cognitive and physiological activities. Believing that each hemisphere stored a "mirror image" of visual events, Orton held that dyslexia occurred when the hemispheres failed to suppress these images, thus causing orientation confusions. Several variants of Orton's hypothesis have appeared subsequently, but all have in common the view that dyslexia is primarily the result of visual organization and memory problems (Bender, 1957; Birch, 1962; Hermann, 1959).

Perceptual-deficit theories of reading disability can be questioned on both logical and empirical grounds. If, for example, it were true that dyslexics literally perceive *b* as *d* or *was* as *saw* as a result of visual-spatial confusion, then they might be expected to show signs of this anomaly in various other activities. Reviews of the literature (Benton, 1962, 1975) indicate a lack of convincing evidence for this position. It is our belief that many of the poor readers' difficulties attributed to visual disorder may be related to dysfunctions in verbal learning. The inaccuracies that characterize the poor readers' processing of visual material may be due not to their inability to stabilize *visual-spatial* relationships, but rather to their difficulty in establishing *visual-verbal* relationships.

As support for this hypothesis, let us examine the demands of reading upon the visual system. Given the redundant use of a limited number of (alphabetic) symbols in recurring combinations (such as *qu, the, tion, ing*), the visual demands in reading are ultimately minimal. However, the discovery and utilization of these redundancies are determined by verbal processes—that is, by one's ability to associate the visual aspects of letters and words with their linguistic counterparts. Thus deficiencies in verbal skills can lead to inefficiency in visual processing.

The results of several empirical studies evaluating Orton's theory support the logic of the argument presented above. For example, Liberman, Shankweiler, Orlando, Harris, and Berti (1971) found that sequence reversals (*was/saw*) and orientation errors (*b/d*) accounted for only a small proportion (25 per cent) of the errors in word lists containing words that could be easily confused (e.g., *bad/dad; not/ton*). Moreover, the sequencing and orientation errors recorded for the same group of children were not highly correlated with each other, contrary to what would be predicted by directional-confusion theories like Orton's. The authors concluded from their results that the positional and directional errors commonly observed in poor readers are linguistic intrusion (mislabeling) errors rather than perceptual inaccuracies.

Further empirical support comes from findings from our own laboratory. In two separate investigations (Vellutino, Steger, & Kandel, 1972; Vellutino, Smith, Steger, & Kaman, 1975) involving carefully selected samples of poor and normal readers between the ages of seven and fourteen, it was found that poor readers performed considerably better in the visual reproduction of three-, four-, and five-letter words (presented tachistoscopically) than they did in pronouncing these same words. In addition, their performance was comparable to that of normal readers on the reproduction task, except in the case of the five-letter words. For children, this approaches the upper limits of short-term visual memory (Simon, 1972).[2] Yet the poor readers pronounced and spelled all of the stimulus words less accurately than the average readers.

The results of both these studies suggest that the visual perception of letters and words may be accurate while the verbal encoding (mental "labeling") of those stimuli may be inaccurate.[3] Put more simply, our findings indicate that when dys-

[2] The number of units or "chunks" of information that can be stored in short-term memory has been estimated to be approximately four to seven for children (Simon, 1972) and five to nine for adults (Miller, 1956). Cattell (1885) discovered some time ago that the number of *familiar* words that could be recalled visually was approximately equal to the number of unconnected letters, thereby indicating that the "unit" of recall is relative. Therefore, words that are not readily recognized will tax short-term visual memory more than familiar words, in which case longer length words can be expected to be especially taxing. Thus by extension, poor readers should have more difficulty in recalling the letters of longer words they cannot read than fluent readers who can read those words. This pattern was observed in the above studies.

[3] Also noteworthy is the disparity between second- and sixth-grade poor readers observed in the second study (Vellutino, Smith, Steger, & Kaman, 1975). As expected, the second graders' perform-

lexics call *b* "d" or *was* "saw," it is not because these figures are literally misperceived, but because dyslexic children cannot remember their names.

In contrast to the above findings are the results of several studies noting differences between poor and average readers on measures of visual memory as well as on high-speed, visual-scanning tasks requiring subjects to match identical stimuli under time constraints (Doehring, 1968; Goyen & Lyle, 1971a, 1971b; Katz & Wicklund, 1971, 1972; Lyle, 1968; Lyle & Goyen, 1968a, 1968b, 1975). On closer examination, however, it is evident that these studies have yielded inconsistent results, finding differences between poor and average readers on some measures of visual perception and memory and no differences on other measures assessing the same functions. Furthermore, these studies frequently compared groups on tasks employing printed letters and words (which, by definition, are problematic for poor readers), and they did not typically control for the possible effects of deficiencies in verbal encoding. Many of the tasks involved short-term memory for briefly exposed materials. We infer from this that poor readers did not differ because they were less proficient in rapidly coding visual material for efficient rehearsal (mental "reminding") and recall. In our view, this slower encoding is quite possibly the result of deficiencies in verbal skills.

A clearer picture of differences between groups on measures of visual processing emerges from investigations which controlled for previous experience with letters and words. For example, in two separate studies of comparably selected reader groups from grades two to six (Vellutino, Pruzek, Steger, & Meshoulam, 1973; Vellutino, Steger, Kaman, & DeSetto, 1975) poor readers performed as well as others on tasks requiring immediate visual recall of varying-length words printed in Hebrew, an unfamiliar orthography. However, none of the children in these studies performed as well as average children familiar with Hebrew's orthographic and linguistic characteristics.

Also noteworthy in these studies is the finding that both poor and average readers unfamiliar with Hebrew had identical (left to right) scanning tendencies as measured by the frequency of omission errors at the right (beginning) positions in the Hebrew words. In contrast, children familiar with Hebrew were inclined to make all their omission errors at the left (final) positions of these words; thus, the right-left scanning in this group conformed with their experience with Hebrew script. These results suggest that poor readers are not inherently deficient in their ability to establish a directional set and that erratic or regressive scan-

---

ance on letter reproduction declined as the length of a word increased; however, poor readers in sixth grade both named and copied from memory the letters in all stimulus words as well as average readers. This was particularly impressive in the case of the naming task in that the letters of a given word were often spelled out correctly immediately after mispronouncing that word. These data suggest that the poor readers were sufficiently well acquainted with the orthographic structure of the words to reproduce their letters in correct sequence, in spite of the fact that they did not identify them verbally as whole words. The latter obviously implies intact visual perception and memory. Perhaps as important, it supports the contention of those (e.g., Kolers, 1970; Liberman & Shankweiler, in press; Smith, 1971) who suggest that word identification is not accomplished by serial letter processing.

ning in such children is a consequence rather than a cause of their reading difficulties.

Finally, additional support for the contention that poor and average readers have comparable visual abilities is derived from several other studies that found no differences between reader groups on measures of long-term memory employing novel visual stimuli (Vellutino, Steger, DeSetto, & Phillips, 1975; Vellutino, Harding, Phillips, & Steger, 1975; Vellutino, Steger, Harding, & Phillips, 1975). Coupled with the results of those studies cited previously, these data suggest that poor and average readers at various stages of development should not differ on measures of visual processing. A suggestion of this kind is only appropriate when controls are applied to guard against the confounding effects that may be caused by group disparities in verbal-encoding ability and/or by previous experiences with letters and words. Thus these findings conflict with visual-deficit theories of reading disability and imply that the origin of the problem will be found elsewhere.[4]

Deficiencies in Intersensory Integration

Another prevalent explanation of specific reading disability is the suggestion that the disorder is caused by deficient integration of the sensory systems. This hypothesis was initially proposed by Birch (1962) and was later given research support by Birch and Belmont (1964), as well as by several other studies that appeared subsequently (Beery, 1967; Birch & Belmont, 1965; Muehl & Kremenak, 1966). In each of these investigations, poor readers between kindergarten and sixth grade were found to be less accurate than average readers in matching simple rhythmic patterns with their visual representations. Similar results were obtained in other studies (Senf, 1969; Senf & Feshbach, 1970; Senf & Freundl, 1972) reporting significant differences between poor and average readers (ages eight to fifteen) in the temporal organization of auditory and visual stimuli presented simultaneously. The tasks employed in all of these studies relied heavily upon attention and memory factors. Such results, therefore, are not necessarily indicative of dysfunction in intersensory integration. This is particularly true of findings involving temporal-order recall, a process which places special demands on short-term memory. Consequently, it is difficult to be certain that differences between reader groups are not attributable to encoding and/or rehearsal problems or other factors influencing a subject's short-term memory.

Indeed, Blank and her associates (Blank & Bridger, 1966; Blank, Weider, & Bridger, 1968) found that disabled readers in the first and fourth grades who had difficulty in intersensory-matching and temporal-ordering tasks also had problems using a verbal-coding system to help remember presented stimuli. This was in contrast to other first- and fourth-grade children, who were apparently more effective in utilizing verbal mnemonics to aid recall. The authors suggested that

---

[4] The above conclusion is, by extension, contrary to multifactor theories of reading disability (e.g., Birch, 1962; Boder, 1970; Mattis, French, & Rapin, 1975) which typically postulate that dyslexia is caused by several neurologically based "syndromes," one of which is a visual-perceptual disorder.

reading disability may result from deficiencies in verbal concepts rather than dysfunction in "cross-modal transfer" (matching auditory and visual equivalents). Kastner and Rickards (1974) came to a similar conclusion after finding that poor third-grade readers did not employ verbal-rehearsal strategies as effectively as normally reading children in a temporal-ordering task involving a response delay of fifteen seconds.

The basic paradigm used by Birch and others has been criticized for producing studies that failed to control for reader-group differences in *intra*sensory functioning (Bryant, 1968). Furthermore, in two separate investigations (Vande Voort, Senf, & Benton, 1972; Zigmond, 1966), it was found that average readers were better on matching identical stimuli within as well as between modalities. Also contrary to Birch's theory are the results of several studies that consistently found no differences between poor and average readers on measures of their ability to associate (pair) non-verbal stimuli from different sensory modalities (Steger, Vellutino, & Meshoulam, 1972; Vellutino, Steger, & Pruzek, 1973; Vellutino, Harding, Phillips, & Steger, 1975). It is noteworthy that the cross-modal transfer tasks employed in these investigations involved associative learning (long-term memory) rather than perceptual matching, and thus controlled for the confounding effects of attention and short-term memory.

To summarize, research results that support the intersensory-deficit explanation of dyslexia are, at best, equivocal. While differences between poor and average readers on a variety of intersensory measures seem well established, the reasons for those differences are not clear. The hypothesis is further undermined on theoretical grounds. Friedes (1974), in an extensive review of this literature, provides evidence that Birch's theory of intersensory development (Birch & Lefford, 1963) and, by extension, his theory of reading disability are questionable. In studies evaluating this theory differences observed between reader groups have yet to be explained. Evidence for the suggestion that poor readers are impaired in temporal-order perception will be reviewed in the next section.

Dysfunction in Temporal-Order Perception

Clinicians and educators (Johnson & Myklebust, 1967; Kirk & Kirk, 1971) have long maintained that poor readers may be deficient in temporal sequencing. Yet in spite of the popularity of this argument among practitioners, it is only in recent years that research assessing this hypothesis has appeared in the literature. Bakker (1970) has attempted to interpret the temporal-ordering differences frequently found between dyslexic and average readers and provides one of the few explanations of this disorder. He suggests that the ability to perceive and serialize a sequence of events is determined by specific mechanisms in the central nervous system. The latter suggestion largely follows from the work of Hirsh (1959) and Hirsh and Sherrick (1961) who provided evidence for an absolute interstimulus threshold to detect a succession of tones—that is, they found that twenty milliseconds need to elapse between two stimuli for a subject to perceive both. Coupling these findings with evidence for hemispheric specialization in temporal ordering (Efron, 1963; Milner, 1962, 1967), Bakker (1972) has theorized that temporal-order perception is supported in the left or language-dominant hemisphere. Thus, Bakker holds that reading disability may be caused by difficulties in sequencing *verbal* stimuli as a result of dysfunction in the language-dominant hemisphere. This inference was not, however, applied to the serial recall of nonverbal stimuli.

In our opinion, Bakker's theory is not supported by existing evidence. His hypothesis that poor and average readers may have different general thresholds in perceiving temporal order has not been validated. To our knowledge, no studies directly assess this possibility employing the methodology used by Hirsh (1959) and others (Hirsh & Sherrick, 1961; Warren, 1974). In fact all of the studies reported by Bakker (Bakker, 1972; Groenendaal & Bakker, 1971) have evaluated temporal-order recall on tasks with stimulus exposures and interstimulus intervals of relatively long durations—longer than those used in studies of the threshold values necessary for perception of serial order. In effect, therefore, Bakker has compared temporal-order recall in poor and average readers with tasks that assess short-term memory and not perception. Thus, it may well be that reader-group disparities on such tasks are due to encoding and memory differences rather than to differences in temporal-order perception. We might also point out that the notion of an absolute threshold for the detection of temporal order has itself been disputed (Warren, 1974).

Several other investigators have tentatively suggested that poor readers may be deficient in temporal sequencing (Corkin, 1974; Doehring, 1968; Senf & Freundl, 1972; Zurif & Carson, 1970). Like Bakker these authors have considered the possibility that serial-order recall requires a memory capacity distinct from gross memory or item recall and that poor readers may be deficient in order recall. However, this may be a false assumption, given the possibility that item and order recall are not different processes. Conrad (1964, 1965) has provided some rather convincing evidence that order errors are in fact intrusions determined by the specific content of the items themselves. Ultimate demonstration of the validity of Conrad's suggestion would, of course, obviate temporal-order theories of reading disability (but see Healy, 1974).

It should be apparent from this account that the temporal-order deficit theory is questionable, although not yet resolved. In our opinion, a plausible alternative explanation of reader-group differences in ordered recall is dysfunction in verbal processing, which will be discussed in the next section.

Deficiencies in Verbal Processing

In the foregoing sections we have suggested that the disparities found between poor and average readers, on a variety of measures assessing perceptual and memory functions, may be due to verbal-encoding deficiencies. The inference we have made is that poor readers neither code (label) nor synthesize (chunk) information for effective storage and retrieval as readily as average readers because of problems in one or more aspects of language. A child, for example, who has significant word-finding or phonologic or syntactic problems may have difficulty in rapidly coding a given stimulus. With a slower rate of coding, processing in short-term memory is less efficient, resulting in difficulties in the permanent storage of the stimulus.

In reading, a rich fund of verbal information not only provides the variety of contexts necessary for sentence comprehension but also assists in developing cue systems for effective decoding of single words and their component parts. It is quite probable that children who ultimately learn to discriminate and name letters and words with many overlapping graphic features (e.g., *b/d, was/saw, lion/loin, not/ton*) have learned to use semantic, syntactic, and phonologic cues to read efficiently. Conversely, the child who continues to confuse these "look-alikes" probably lacks information about one of these linguistic constituents; as a result, this child has fewer alternative cues available for making the fine-grained distinctions necessary for accurate decoding.

Clearly, then, linguistic ability is of the utmost significance in developing skill in all aspects of reading. Yet, as we have pointed out, it is only recently that researchers have actively explored the possible relationships between both normal and abnormal reading and language skill. In the following sections we will briefly review a representative sampling of studies which provide both indirect and direct support for a verbal-deficit explanation of specific reading disability.

Indirect Evidence

Rabinovitch (1959, 1968) was one of the first to consider seriously the possibility that dyslexia may be associated with linguistic deficiencies. In clinical studies Rabinovitch observed that poor readers were characterized by difficulties in expressive-language, word-finding, verbal-concept formation, and symbolic learning. He emphasized that poor readers performed consistently below the level of average readers on measures of "verbal intelligence" but were generally comparable on measures of "nonverbal intelligence": that is, on the Wechsler Intelligence Scale for Children (WISC) verbal and performance scales respectively. From such findings he concluded that dyslexia may be associated with specific language disability.

Concordant with Rabinovitch's observations are the results of a large number of laboratory studies comparing dyslexic and average readers on the WISC subtests (Belmont & Birch, 1966; Huelsman, 1970; Lyle & Goyen, 1968b). In most of these investigations poor readers were found to be significantly below their average peers on the verbal subscales of the WISC but, more often than not, were not different on the performance subscales. That these results were not simply the cumulative effect of prolonged reading disability is suggested by the findings of Lyle and Goyen (1968b). These authors found that differences between reader groups at the first-grade level were of the same magnitude as differences in the sixth grade.

To continue, Ingram and his associates (Ingram & Reid, 1956; Ingram, Mason, & Blackburn, 1970) provide suggestive evidence for developmental language problems in the histories of children who were severely impaired in reading. A similar observation was reported by Lyle (1970), who found that a history of language difficulties in poor readers correlated with measures of reversal tendencies in reading, spelling, and memory for designs, as well as with tests of verbal ability. The author inferred from these results that poor readers may be characterized by a "generalized lag in verbal learning" (p. 489).

Attempts to predict the incidence of reading disability have been undertaken by de Hirsch, Jansky, and Langford (1966), Jansky (1973), and Satz and his colleagues (Satz & Friel, 1974; Satz, Friel, & Rudegeair, 1974a, 1974b). Each of these studies reported that children with verbal-skills deficiencies at the pre-first-grade level were found later to have reading difficulties. Because of sampling problems, however, these results can only be considered suggestive of the relationships in question.

Direct Evidence: Semantic Factors

Several studies have compared poor and average readers on measures of semantic encoding and verbal memory. For example, Perfetti and Goldman (1976) hypothesized that poor readers are less effective than average readers in employing a linguistic code (implicit labeling) for processing verbal information in short-term memory. Poor readers, however, were not expected to exhibit differences in short-term memory. These assumptions have been tested in two separate experiments. Subjects were third and fifth graders (twelve in each group), of average or above average intelligence, selected on the basis of reading-comprehension scores. In the first experiment it was found that poor readers performed as well as other readers on memory for single digits directly following probe digits (Waugh & Norman, 1965). In the second experiment, however, the poor readers did not perform as well on memory for single words following a probe word. The original assumptions were thus supported.

Consistent with these findings are the results of a study by Waller (1976). This author employed a sentence-recognition task (Paris & Carter, 1973) designed to assess differential sensitivity to both the meanings and structural characteristics of sentences. An analysis of false-recognition errors indicated that poor readers apprehended meanings as well as others but were inefficient in retaining such verbal details as grammatical markers and specific word strings. Waller suggested that poor readers may have difficulty in employing a "verbal code" to store information and may rely more heavily upon a "visual code."

The possibility that reading disability may be associated with deficiencies in naming and labeling has been the focus of several other investigations which have recently appeared in the literature (Denckla, 1972a, 1972b). In two of the most recent studies, Denckla and Rudel (1976a, 1976b) compared poor and normal readers (ages seven to twelve) on "rapid automatic naming" tasks and found that the groups differed on both accuracy and latency measures. Poor readers generally made more errors and took longer than average readers to generate the names of common objects, colors, letters, words, and numerals, presented visually. This finding was especially interesting because under ordinary circumstances these poor readers had no difficulty naming most of these objects. The authors interpreted their results within an aphasiological context and suggested that dyslexics may be characterized by basic word-retrieval problems.

Similarly, Perfetti and Hogaboam (1975) found that children who were poor in reading comprehension had significantly longer response times than average comprehenders on rapid naming of high- and low-frequency English words, pseudowords, and words with varying meanings. Since the greatest differences between

576

the groups occurred on the pseudowords, the authors concluded that deficient reading comprehension is likely to result from the poor reader's inability to develop automatized decoding skills. Spring (Spring, 1976; Spring & Capps, 1974) and Eakin & Douglas (1971) have obtained similar results. Briefly, in these studies it was found that the mean number of responses made per second on rapid automatic naming tasks was greater for average than for poor readers.

The last body of supporting evidence for a semantic-deficit explanation of reading disability comes from studies contrasting poor and average readers on verbal and nonverbal learning tasks. These research findings have been reviewed earlier by Brewer (1967) and Zigmond (1966). Our own analysis of this research leads us to believe that in most of the studies reading groups were differentiated more on verbal-associative tasks than on nonverbal tasks. Similar results were obtained in studies conducted in our own laboratory (Steger, et al., 1972; Vellutino, Steger, & Pruzek, 1973; Vellutino, Harding, Phillips, & Steger, 1975; Vellutino, Steger, Harding, & Phillips, 1975).

To summarize this section, the above studies provide some evidence that poor readers are deficient in both the storage and retrieval of printed and spoken words. These deficiencies often become apparent in short-term-memory tasks demanding automatized verbal skills. However, the results of some of these studies should not be accepted without some reservation. For example, poor readers included in studies by Perfetti and Goldman (1976) and Perfetti and Hogaboam (1975) were selected only on the basis of silent-reading measures and may not have been representative of poor readers with semantic-encoding problems. The data are nevertheless suggestive and warrant further investigation.

Syntactic Factors

In recent years a few studies have suggested the possibility that some poor readers may be deficient in syntactic development. Fry (1967) and Schulte (1967), for example, contrasted oral-language samples of poor and average second-grade readers and found that average readers were more sophisticated than the poor readers in a variety of linguistic areas: verbal fluency, speaking vocabularies, organizational and integrative skills, abstract usages, grammar, and complexity of sentence structure. In a later summary Fry, Johnson, and Muehl (1970) did not establish strict cause-effect relationships between oral-language patterns and reading disability. They suggested instead that such linguistic deficiencies could impair both word recognition and comprehension by limiting the number and variety of verbal labels available for learning grapheme-phoneme associations and for abstracting meaning from continuous text. They also pointed out that these deficiencies could not be the result of long-standing reading disorders since the subjects in the sample were only in second grade.

Two other studies are of interest here. Wiig, Semel, and Crouse (1973) compared samples of poor and average nine-year-old readers on a test of morphological usage (Berko, 1958) and found that the poor readers gave fewer correct responses. That the poor readers' error patterns were less predictable than those of the controls suggests that they were using fewer grammatical "rules." Also noteworthy in this study is the finding that "high risk" four-year-olds had less knowledge of morphology than did "low risk" children; and further, that the qualitative differences between these two groups were similar to the differences found between the older children. These results were thought suggestive of a possible relationship between early language deficiencies and later reading disability, at least insofar as linguistic development reflects morphological usage.

Finally, Vogel (1974) contrasted average and dyslexic readers (age seven to eight years) on a large battery of tests measuring a variety of syntactic skills and found significant differences between the groups on seven out of nine measures employed. Controls performed better than poor readers on five separate tests: comprehension of syntax, repetition of sentences, morphological usages, oral "cloze" tests, and recognition of melody. Interestingly, those tests which most successfully differentiated the two groups were measures of morphological usage and recognition of melody. The author concluded from this that dyslexia and syntactic deficiencies are intrinsically related but did not elaborate upon the possible nature of such relationships.

The above studies uniformly suggest that severely impaired readers are not as proficient as other readers in their knowledge of words, syntactic facility, and verbal fluency in general. Although we can not yet specify the relationship between syntactic deficiencies and reading disability, the evidence suggests that both difficulties appear at an early age and may have a common source. Continued research in this area is needed.

Phonologic Deficiencies

A popular notion among practitioners is that reading difficulty in some children is the result of deficiencies in the discrimination of speech sounds. Wepman (1960, 1961) has long advocated this view and suggested that "auditory discrimination" problems in many poor readers are most likely the result of "maturation lag." Wepman apparently considered auditory discrimination as a perceptual skill dependent upon but not guaranteed by intact auditory acuity. In initial tests of his theory Wepman (1960, 1961) presented first and second graders with minimally contrasted words (e.g., *pin* and *pen*) and asked them to indicate whether they were the same or different. He found that many of the children who did not do well on this test were also deficient in reading. From these results the author concluded that reading problems in certain children may be due to deficiencies in auditory discrimination.

There is reason, however, to believe that poor readers, barring any real deficiency in auditory acuity, are able to discriminate (hear) the acoustic differences between minimally contrasted words as well as other children. Some authors (Blank, 1968; Shankweiler & Liberman, 1972), for example, have provided evidence that poor readers competently discriminate single words, even though they may not do as well as others when the words are presented in pairs. Reader group differences with paired words could, therefore, be due to conceptual factors or response bias (Vellutino, DeSetto, & Steger, 1972).

The possibility exists that measures which require relative judgments of same and different may yield spurious impressions of auditory discrimination ability in young children. Thus it may be that poor readers have less ability than average readers to explicate phonemic differences in similar sounding words that they implicitly discriminate. In other words, poor readers may be more sensitive to the acoustic (sounds of words as wholes) than to the phonemic (sounds of parts of words) properties of such words. Under these circumstances poor readers would be able to perceive words as syllabic or articulatory units but have little or no awareness of the word's phonetic structure. Yet detecting the location of phonemic differences in minimally contrasted words would require just this kind of sensitivity. This would be especially true in same/different contrasts, which typically tax the limits of short-term memory and require *selective* attention to critical differences. By extension, segmentation of words into their constituent phonemes may be an important prerequisite to relating varying combinations of printed letters to their spoken counterparts.

This latter conceptualization is, of course, consistent with Mattingly's notion of "linguistic awareness" and reflects the views of several authors. Mattingly (1972), Elkonin (1973), and Downing (1973) have recently suggested that the severity of some children's reading problems may be related to deficiencies in their conscious awareness of the phonetic structure of speech. Liberman and her associates provide the most definitive evidence in support of this view. Shankweiler and Liberman (1972) found that poor readers made more errors in reading words than in repeating the same words read to them orally; further, the observed patterns in reading errors were not the same as errors observed in oral repetition. Most of the reading errors were in the medial and final positions and were more often caused by vowels than by consonants. From these findings the authors suggested that poor readers may not have developed a conscious awareness of the distinctive phonemes in spoken and printed words. As a consequence, poor readers may treat all words as syllabic units, which, as the authors point out, impedes the mapping of alphabetic symbols to sound.

Additional support for this interpretation comes from a number of studies which indicate that phonemic segmentation is a complex skill that takes time to develop (Helfgott, 1976; Liberman, Shankweiler, Fischer, & Carter, 1974; Zifcak, 1976; Treiman, Note 1). In a follow-up study one year after her initial investigation, Liberman found that children who had the greatest difficulty in phonemic segmentation at the kindergarten level also had the greatest difficulty in beginning reading (Liberman, Shankweiler, Liberman, Fowler, & Fischer, 1976).

In several other studies Liberman and her colleagues specifically evaluated the hypothesis that poor and normal readers differ in the degree to which they employ phonetic coding in short-term memory. In one study (Liberman & Shankweiler, in press), for example, second-grade poor readers were not different from average readers on visual recognition of recurring novel designs and photographed faces. In contrast, poor readers performed significantly below other readers on recognition of nonsense syllables presented visually.

These authors found evidence for a phonetic-coding deficit in poor readers in two other investigations using a paradigm similar to the one employed by Conrad

(1964, 1965). In the first of these investigations (Liberman, Shankweiler, Liberman, Fowler, & Fischer, 1976), second-grade poor and average readers were given visual presentations of strings of phonetically confusable (rhyming) and nonconfusable (nonrhyming) letters. It was assumed that the average readers would use an auditory code in short-term memory and thus make more errors on confusable sounding letters than on the nonconfusable letters. The magnitude of the differences between these two conditions was expected to be less in poor readers because of their (presumed) inefficiency in phonetically coding visual information. The expectation was confirmed.

In a second study Shankweiler and Liberman (1976) found similar results when the same stimuli were presented auditorily. In still another investigation these authors (Liberman & Shankweiler, in press) found that the magnitude of differences on false-recognition errors was occasioned by rhyming as opposed to nonrhyming words. This magnitude was greater in the normal-reading group than in poor readers.

In summary, there is now considerable evidence which questions earlier suggestions that reading disability may be intrinsically associated with phonologic deficiencies resulting only from dysfunction in auditory discrimination. An alternative possibility is that many children have not become aware of the phonetic structure of both spoken and printed language and are, therefore, unable to make the important connections between these representations. Such difficulties may characterize only a portion of poor readers, whereas others may be subject to deficiencies in semantic and syntactic processing. None of these problems are mutually exclusive.

General Summary and Conclusions

In the previous sections we have systematically reviewed the alternative conceptualizations of specific reading disability prominent in the literature and have presented research findings relating to each. We suggested that the perceptual-deficit theories of reading disability postulated by Orton and others are highly questionable. We suggested further that the orientation and sequencing errors believed to be classic indicators of visual-spatial confusion in poor readers can be more plausibly interpreted as secondary manifestations of verbal-mediation difficulties. The logical extension of this interpretation is that poor readers lack the implicit linguistic cues (syntactic, semantic, and phonologic) that alert them to the critical differences in letters and words. Consequently, they take longer and have more difficulty in stabilizing positional and directional constancy in reading and spelling. Poor readers, therefore, are typically slow and plodding in processing written material; such perceptual inefficiency, however, would seem to be a *consequence* of dysfunction in visual-verbal learning rather than an indication of visual-perceptual deficit in the strict sense.

As we noted earlier, research data relating to the sensory-integration theory of Birch (1962) are conflicting. Still there is persuasive evidence that the deficiencies observed in poor readers on tasks thought to be measuring cross-modal transfer

580

may have been due to difficulties in verbal encoding. A similar suggestion was made to explain reader-group differences on measures of temporal order; it was then hypothesized that poor readers may not sustain a primary deficiency in temporal perception as proposed by Bakker (1972) and others. Both Birch's and Bakker's explanations of reading disability can also be questioned on theoretical grounds, and we have cited evidence that undermines the basic foundations of these arguments.

The conceptualization of reading disability which we view as the most probable is that such disorders may be attributable to dysfunction in one or more aspects of linguistic functioning. Research for this hypothesis is accumulating and highlights the *semantic, syntactic,* and *phonological* components of language as possible areas of difficulty.

There is now convincing evidence that poor readers may differ from average readers on given types of *semantic* processing, specifically on word encoding, visual-verbal association learning, and word-retrieval. The general impression conveyed by research in this area is that poor readers may have difficulty both in linguistic coding of incoming information and in the retrieval of linguistic referents associated with given stimuli. These interdependent processes are, of course, heavily dependent upon the richness of the lexicon (mental "dictionary") as well as the ease with which material stored in that lexicon can be accessed and retrieved. Given the multiform classes of information that must be processed to decode even a single word (Gibson, 1971), it can be seen that the child must "cross-reference" both the semantic components of a given word and other word features necessary for accurate decoding. In view of the previous discussion it would now seem evident that difficulty in such cross-referencing would result in dysfunction in both reading and spoken language.

That poor readers may lack facility in segmenting and coding information phonetically, as suggested by Liberman and her associates, appears to be a very plausible description of the difficulties encountered by some low achievers. Such children would quite likely fail to apprehend and generalize the separate sounds in spoken and printed words and would, therefore, have difficulty in establishing the grapheme-phoneme correspondences necessary for acquiring the alphabetic code. This view is contrary to currently popular notions (Goodman, 1965, 1968; Smith, 1971, 1973) that poor readers are overly attentive to the structural components of words rather than meanings. Evidence is now emerging that some children are *not* intimately acquainted with the internal structure of words and may be impaired in ways suggested by Liberman.

The relationship between syntactic deficiencies and reading problems may seem somewhat tenuous given that the dyslexic is commonly described as having no ostensible abnormalities in language that can be detected in spoken discourse. We should not, however, discount the possibility that more subtle deficiencies in grammatical competence may impede the development of reading skill. This would certainly apply to deciphering connected text, and it might also cause problems in developing efficient word recognition. Indeed, Goodman (1970) and others (Biemiller, 1970; Weber, 1970) have studied the types of decoding errors made by children at various stages of reading development and have found that inaccuracies are typically determined by semantic and syntactic context. Thus children who lag behind their peers in general language ability—for example, those who have difficulty with grammatic transformational rules, who are unable to make morphophonemic generalizations, who cannot perceive the syntactic invariants and redundancies characteristic of all natural languages—can be expected to have difficulty in one or more aspects of reading. The little available research suggests that some poor readers may be of this description and that the study of basic syntactic deficiencies would be a worthwhile pursuit.

Finally, as Greene (1972) has observed, the dissection of the components of language necessary to understand the etiology of reading disability is both hazardous and formidable, given our limited knowledge of their interrelationships. The problem is further compounded by the fact that the influence of linguistic systems is not easily separated either in the chronically impaired or in the fluent reader. The impaired reader may sustain a specific disorder in one or more aspects of language, which leads to problems in reading. In contrast, fluent readers are able to make efficient and selective use of all their linguistic and cognitive skills, and it is difficult to know precisely what devices they employ in deciphering written communication. It is our hope that continued research in this area will improve our conceptualizations, refine measuring instruments, and ultimately foster greater knowledge of the linguistic correlates of the reading process.

Reference Note

1. Treiman, R. A. *Children's ability to segment speech into syllables and phonemes as related to their reading ability.* Unpublished manuscript, Yale University, 1976.

References

Bakker, D. J. Temporal order perception and reading retardation. In D. J. Bakker & P. Satz (Eds.), *Specific reading disability: Advances in theory and method.* Rotterdam: Rotterdam University Press, 1970.

Bakker, D. J. *Temporal order in disturbed reading, developmental and neuropsychological aspects in normal and reading-retarded children.* Rotterdam: Rotterdam University Press, 1972.

Beery, J. Matching of auditory and visual stimuli by average and retarded readers. *Child Development,* 1967, **38**, 827–833.

Belmont, L., & Birch, H. Intellectual profile of retarded readers. *Perceptual and Motor Skills,* 1966, **22**, 787–816.

Bender, L. A. *Psychopathology of children with organic brain disorders.* Springfield, Ill.: Charles C. Thomas, 1956.

Bender, L. A. Specific reading disability as a maturational lag. *Bulletin of the Orton Society,* 1957, **7**, 9–18.

Benton, A. L. Developmental dyslexia: Neurological aspects. In W. J. Friedlander (Ed.), *Advances in neurology* (Vol. 7). New York: Raven Press, 1975.

Benton, A. L. Dyslexia in relation to form perception and directional sense. In J. Money (Ed.), *Reading disability: Progress and research needs in dyslexia.* Baltimore: Johns Hopkins Press, 1962.

Berko, J. The child's learning of English morphology. *Word,* 1958, 14, 150–177.

Biemiller, A. The development of the use of graphic and contextual information as children learn to read. *Reading Research Quarterly,* 1970, 6, 75–96.

Birch, H. G. Dyslexia and maturation of visual function. In J. Money (Ed.), *Reading disability: Progress and research needs in dyslexia.* Baltimore: Johns Hopkins Press, 1962.

Birch, H. G., & Belmont, L. Auditory-visual integration in normal and retarded readers. *American Journal of Orthophychiatry,* 1964, 34, 852–861.

Birch, H. G., & Belmont, L. Auditory-visual integration, intelligence, and reading ability in school children. *Perceptual and Motor Skills,* 1965, 20, 295–305.

Birch, H. G., & Lefford, A. Intersensory development in children. *Monographs of the Society for Research in Child Development,* 1963, 28 (5, Whole No. 89).

Blank, M. Cognitive processes in auditory discrimination in normal and retarded readers. *Child Development,* 1968, 39, 1091–1101.

Blank, M., & Bridger, W. Deficiencies in verbal labeling in retarded readers. *American Journal of Orthopsychiatry,* 1966, 36, 840–847.

Blank, M., Weider, S., & Bridger, W. Verbal deficiencies in abstract thinking in early reading retardation. *American Journal of Orthopsychiatry,* 1968, 38, 823–834.

Boder, E. Developmental dyslexia: A new diagnostic approach based on the identification of three subtypes. *Journal of School Health,* 1970, 40, 289–290.

Brewer, W. F. *Paired-associate learning of dyslexic children.* Unpublished doctoral dissertation, University of Iowa, 1967.

Bryant, P. E. Comments on the design of developmental studies of cross-modal matching and cross-modal transfer. *Cortex,* 1968, 4, 127–128.

Cattell, J. Ueber die Zeit der Erkennung und Benennung von Schriftzeichen, Bildern und Farben. *Philosophische Studien,* 1885, 2, 635–650.

Conrad, R. Acoustic confusions in immediate memory. *British Journal of Psychology,* 1964, 55, 75–84.

Conrad, R. Order error in immediate recall of sequences. *Journal of Verbal Learning and Verbal Behavior,* 1965, 4, 161–169.

Corkin, S. Serial-ordering deficits in inferior readers. *Neuropsychologia,* 1974, 12, 347–354.

Cruickshank, W. M. The problems of delayed recognition and its correction. In A. H. Keeney & V. T. Keeney (Eds.), *Dyslexia: Diagnosis and treatment of reading disorders.* St. Louis: V. C. Mosby, 1968.

de Hirsch, K., Jansky, J., & Langford, W. *Predicting reading failure.* New York: Harper & Row, 1966.

Denckla, M. B. Color-naming defects in dyslexic boys. *Cortex,* 1972, 8, 164–176. (a)

Denckla, M. B. Performance on color tasks in kindergarten children. *Cortex,* 1972, 8, 177–190. (b)

Denckla, M., & Rudel, R. Naming of object drawings by dyslexic and other learning disabled children. *Brain and Language,* 1976, 3, 1–16. (a)

Denckla, M., & Rudel, R. Rapid "automatized" naming (R.A.N.): Dyslexia differentiated from other learning disabilities. *Neuropsychologia,* 1976, 14, 471–479. (b)

Doehring, D. G. *Patterns of impairment in specific reading disability.* Bloomington: Indiana University Press, 1968.

Downing, J. *Comparative reading.* New York: Macmillan, 1973.

Eakin, S., & Douglas, V. I. "Automatization" and oral reading problems in children. *Journal of Learning Disabilities,* 1971, 4, 31–38.

Efron, R. Temporal perception, aphasia, and déjà vu. *Brain,* 1963, 86, 403–424.

Elkonin, D. B. U.S.S.R. In J. Downing (Ed.), *Comparative reading.* New York: Macmillan, 1973.

Friedes, D. Human information processing and sensory modality: Cross-modal functions, information complexity, memory, and deficit. *Psychological Bulletin,* 1974, 81, 284–310.

Fry, M. A. *A transformational analysis of the oral language structure used by two reading groups at the second grade level.* Unpublished doctoral dissertation, University of Iowa, 1967.

Fry, M. A., Johnson, C. S., & Muehl, S. Oral language production in relation to reading achievement among select second graders. In D. J. Bakker & P. Satz (Eds.), *Specific reading disability: Advances in theory and method.* Rotterdam: Rotterdam University Press, 1970.

Gibson, E. J. Perceptual learning and the theory of word perception. *Cognitive Psychology,* 1971, 2, 351–368.

Gibson, E. J., & Levin, H. *The psychology of reading.* Cambridge, Mass.: M.I.T. Press, 1975.

Goodman, K. S. Dialect barriers to reading comprehension. *Elementary English,* 1965, 12, 853–860.

Goodman, K. S. The psycholinguistic nature of the reading process. In K. S. Goodman (Ed.), *The psycholinguistic nature of the reading process.* Detroit: Wayne State University Press, 1968.

Goodman, K. S. Psycholinguistic universals in the reading process. *Journal of Typographic Research,* 1970, 4, 103–110.

Goyen, J. D., & Lyle, J. Effect of incentives and age on the visual recognition of retarded readers. *Journal of Experimental Child Psychology,* 1971, 11, 266–273. (a)

Goyen, J. D., & Lyle, J. Effect of incentives upon retarded and normal readers on a visual-associate learning task. *Journal of Experimental Child Psychology,* 1971, 11, 274–280. (b)

Greene, J. *Psycholinguistics: Chomsky and psychology.* Baltimore: Penguin, 1972.

Groenendaal, H. A., & Bakker, D. J. The part played by mediation processes in the retention of temporal sequences by two reading groups. *Human Development,* 1971, 14, 62–70.

Healy, A. F. Separating item from order information in short-term memory. *Journal of Verbal Learning and Verbal Behavior,* 1974, 13, 644–655.

Helfgott, J. Phomemic segmentation and blending skills of kindergarten children: Implications for beginning reading acquisition. *Contemporary Educational Psychology,* 1976, 1, 157–169.

Hermann, K. *Reading disability.* Copenhagen: Munksgaard, 1959.

Hirsh, I. J. Auditory perception of temporal order. *The Journal of the Acoustical Society of America,* 1959, 31, 759–767.

Hirsh, I. J., & Sherrick, C. E. Perceived order in different sense modalities. *Journal of Experimental Psychology,* 1961, 64, 1–19.

Huelsman, C. B. The WISC subtest syndrome for disabled readers. *Perceptual and Motor Skills,* 1970, 30, 535–550.

Ingram, T. T. S., Mason, A. W., & Blackburn, I. A retrospective study of 82 children with reading disability. *Developmental Medicine and Child Neurology,* 1970, 12, 271–281.

Ingram, T. T. S., & Reid, J. F. Developmental aphasia observed in a department of child psychiatry. *Archives of Disorders of Childhood,* 1956, 31, 161.

Jansky, J. J. Early prediction of reading problems. *Bulletin of the Orton Society,* 1973, 23, 78–89.

Johnson, D., & Myklebust, H. *Learning disabilities: Educational principles and practices.* New York: Grune and Stratton, 1967.

Kastner, S. B., & Rickards, C. Mediated memory with novel and familiar stimuli in good and poor readers. *The Journal of Genetic Psychology,* 1974, 124, 105–113.

Katz, L., & Wicklund, D. Word scanning rates for good and poor readers. *Journal of Educational Psychology,* 1971, 62, 138–140.

Katz, L., & Wicklund, D. Letter scanning rate for good and poor readers in grades two and six. *Journal of Educational Psychology,* 1972, 63, 363–367.

Kavanagh, J. F., & Mattingly, I. G. *Language by ear and by eye: The relationships between speech and reading.* Cambridge, Mass.: M.I.T. Press, 1972.

Kirk, S. A., & Kirk, W. D. *Psycholinguistic learning disabilities: Diagnosis and remediation.* Chicago: University of Illinois Press, 1971.

Kolers, P. A. Three stages of reading. In H. Levin & J. P. Williams (Eds.), *Basic studies in reading.* New York: Basic Books, 1970.

Liberman, I. Y., & Shankweiler, D. Speech, the alphabet, and teaching to read. In L. Resnick & P. Weaver (Eds.), *Theory and practice of early reading.* Hillsdale, N.J.: Erlbaum Associates, in press.

Liberman, I. Y., Shankweiler, D., Fischer, F. W., & Carter, B. Explicit syllable and phoneme segmentation in the young child. *Journal of Experimental Child Psychology,* 1974, **18**, 201–212.

Liberman, I. Y., Shankweiler, D., Liberman, A. M., Fowler, C., & Fischer, F. W. Phonetic segmentation and recoding in the beginning reader. In A. S. Reber & D. Scarborough (Eds.), *Reading: Theory and practice.* Hillsdale, N.J.: Erlbaum Associates, 1976.

Liberman, I. Y., Shankweiler, D., Orlando, C., Harris, K. S., & Berti, F. B. Letter confusion and reversals of sequence in the beginning reader: Implications for Orton's theory of developmental dyslexia. *Cortex,* 1971, **7**, 127–142.

Lyle, J. G. Performance of retarded readers on the memory-for-designs test. *Perceptual and Motor Skills,* 1968, **26**, 851–854.

Lyle, J. G. Certain antenatal, perinatal, and developmental variables and reading retardation in middle class boys. *Child Development,* 1970, **41**, 481–491.

Lyle, J. G., & Goyen, J. Visual recognition, developmental lag, and strephosymbolia in reading retardation. *Journal of Abnormal Psychology,* 1968, **73**, 25–29. (a)

Lyle, J. G., & Goyen, J. Performance of retarded readers on the WISC and educational tests. *Journal of Abnormal Psychology,* 1968, **74**, 105–112. (b)

Lyle, J. G., & Goyen, J. Effect of speed of exposure and difficulty of discrimination on visual recognition of retarded readers. *Journal of Abnormal Psychology,* 1975, **8**, 673–676.

Mattingly, I. G. Reading, the linguistic process, and linguistic awareness. In J. F. Kavanagh & I. G. Mattingly (Eds.), *Language by ear and by eye: The relationships between speech and reading.* Cambridge, Mass.: M.I.T. Press, 1972.

Mattis, S., French, J. H., & Rapin, I. Dyslexia in children and young adults: Three independent neuropsychological syndromes. *Developmental Medicine and Child Neurology,* 1975, **17**, 150–163.

Miller, G. The magical number seven, plus or minus two: Some limits on our capacity for processing information. *Psychological Review,* 1956, **63**, 81–97.

Milner, B. Laterality effects in audition. In V. B. Mountcastle (Ed.), *Interhemispheric relations and cerebral dominance.* Baltimore: Johns Hopkins Press, 1962.

Milner, B. Brain mechanisms suggested by studies of temporal lobes. In C. H. Millikan & F. L. Darley (Eds.), *Brain mechanisms underlying speech and language.* New York: Grune and Stratton, 1967.

Morgan, W. P. A case of congenital word-blindness. *British Medical Journal,* 1896, **11**, 378.

Muehl, S., & Kremenak, S. Ability to match information within and between auditory and visual sense modalities and subsequent reading achievement. *Journal of Educational Psychology,* 1966, **57**, 230–239.

Orton, S. "Word-blindness" in school children. *Archives of Neurology and Psychiatry,* 1925, **14**, 581–615.

Orton, S. *Reading, writing and speech problems in children.* London: Chapman and Hall, 1937.

Paris, S., & Carter, A. Semantic and constructive aspects of sentence memory in children. *Developmental Psychology,* 1973, **9**, 109–113.

Perfetti, C. A., & Goldman, S. R. Discourse memory and reading comprehension skill. *Journal of Verbal Learning and Verbal Behavior,* 1976, **14**, 33–42.

Perfetti, C. A., & Hogaboam, T. The relationship between single word decoding and reading comprehension skill. *Journal of Educational Psychology,* 1975, **67**, 461–469.

Rabinovitch, R. D. Reading and learning disabilities. In S. Arieti (Ed.), *American handbook of psychiatry*. New York: Basic Books, 1959.

Rabinovitch, R. D. Reading problems in children: Definitions and classification. In A. Keeney & V. Keeney (Eds.), *Dyslexia: Diagnosis and treatment of reading disorders*. St. Louis: C. V. Mosby, 1968.

Satz, P., & Friel, J. Some predictive antecedents of specific reading disability: A preliminary two-year follow-up. *Journal of Learning Disabilities*, 1974, **7**, 437–444.

Satz, P., Friel, J., & Rudegeair, F. Differential changes in the acquisition of developmental skills in children who later become dyslexic: A three year follow-up. In D. Stein, J. Rosen, & N. Butters (Eds.), *Plasticity and recovery of function in the central nervous system*. New York: Academic Press, 1974. (a)

Satz, P., Friel, J., & Rudegeair, F. Some predictive antecedents of specific reading disability: A two-, three-, and four-year follow-up. In *The Hyman Blumberg Symposium on Research in Early Childhood Education*. Johns Hopkins Press, 1974. (b)

Savin, H. B. What the child knows about speech when he starts to learn to read. In J. F. Kavanagh & I. G. Mattingly (Eds.), *Language by ear and by eye: The relationships between speech and reading*. Cambridge, Mass.: M.I.T. Press, 1972.

Schulte, C. *A study of the relationship between oral language and reading achievement in second graders*. Unpublished doctoral dissertation, University of Iowa, 1967.

Senf, G. M. Development of immediate memory for bisensory stimuli in normal children with learning disorders. *Developmental Psychology Monograph*, 1969, **1**, 6.

Senf, G. M., & Feshbach, S. Development of bisensory memory in culturally deprived, dyslexic, and normal readers. *Journal of Educational Psychology*, 1970, **61**, 461–470.

Senf, G. M., & Freundl, P. C. Sequential auditory and visual memory in learning disabled children. *Proceedings of the Annual Convention of the American Psychological Association*, 1972, **7**, 511–512.

Shankweiler, D., & Liberman, A. M. Misreading: A search for causes. In J. F. Kavanagh & I. G. Mattingly (Eds.), *Language by ear and by eye: The relationships between speech and reading*. Cambridge, Mass.: M.I.T. Press, 1972.

Shankweiler, D., & Liberman, I. Y. Exploring the relations between reading and speech. In R. M. Knights & D. J. Bakker (Eds.), *Neuropsychology of learning disorders: Theoretical approaches*. Baltimore: University Park Press, 1976.

Simon, H. On the development of the processor. In S. Farnham-Diggory (Ed.), *Information processing in children*. New York: Academic Press, 1972.

Smith, F. *Understanding reading: A psycholinguistic analysis of reading and learning to read*. New York: Holt, Rinehart and Winston, 1971.

Smith, F. *Psycholinguistics and reading*. New York: Holt, Rinehart and Winston, 1973.

Spring, C. Encoding speed and memory span in dyslexic children. *The Journal of Special Education*, 1976, **10**, 35–40.

Spring, C., & Capps, C. Encoding speed, rehearsal, and probed recall of dyslexic boys. *Journal of Educational Psychology*, 1974, **66**, 780–786.

Steger, J. A., Vellutino, F. R., & Meshoulam, U. Visual-tactile and tactile-tactile paired associate learning in normal and poor readers. *Perceptual and Motor Skills*, 1972, **35**, 263–266.

Symmes, J. S., & Rapoport, J. L. Unexpected reading failure. *American Journal of Orthopsychiatry*, 1972, **42**, 82–91.

Vande Voort, L., Senf, G. M., & Benton, A. L. Development of audio-visual integration in normal and retarded readers. *Child Development*, 1972, **44**, 1260–1272.

Vellutino, F. R. *Theory and research in dyslexia*. Cambridge, Mass.: MIT Press, 1978.

Vellutino, F. R., DeSetto, L., & Steger, J. A. Categorical judgment and the Wepman Test of Auditory Discrimination. *Journal of Speech and Hearing Disorders*, 1972, **37**, 252–257.

Vellutino, F. R., Harding, C. J., Phillips, F., & Steger, J. A. Differential transfer in poor and normal readers. *Journal of Genetic Psychology*, 1975, **126**, 3–18.

Vellutino, F. R., Pruzek, R., Steger, J. A., & Meshoulam, U. Immediate visual recall in poor and normal readers as a function of orthographic-linguistic familiarity. *Cortex,* 1973, **9,** 368–384.

Vellutino, F. R., Smith, H., Steger, J. A., & Kaman, M. Reading disability: Age differences and the perceptual deficit hypothesis. *Child Development,* 1975, **46,** 487–493.

Vellutino, F. R., Steger, J. A., DeSetto, L., & Phillips, F. Immediate and delayed recognition of visual stimuli in poor and normal readers. *Journal of Experimental Child Psychology,* 1975, **19,** 223–232.

Vellutino, F. R., Steger, J. A., Harding, C. J., & Phillips, F. Verbal vs non-verbal paired-associates learning in poor and normal readers. *Neuropsychologia,* 1975, **13,** 75–82.

Vellutino, F. R., Steger, J. A., Kaman, M., & DeSetto, L. Visual form perception in deficient and normal readers as a function of age and orthographic linguistic familiarity. *Cortex,* 1975, **11,** 22–30.

Vellutino, F. R., Steger, J. A., & Kandel, G. Reading disability: An investigation of the perceptual deficit hypothesis. *Cortex,* 1972, **8,** 106–118.

Vellutino, F. R., Steger, J. A., & Pruzek, R. Inter- vs intrasensory deficit in paired associate learning in poor and normal readers. *Canadian Journal of Behavioral Science,* 1973, **5,** 111–123.

Vogel, S. A. Syntactic abilities in normal and dyslexic children. *Journal of Learning Disabilities,* 1974, **7,** 103–109.

Waller, T. G. Children's recognition memory for written sentences: A comparison of good and poor readers. *Child Development,* 1976, **47,** 90–95.

Warren, R. M. Auditory temporal discrimination by trained listeners. *Cognitive Psychology,* 1974, **6,** 237–256.

Waugh, N. C., & Norman, D. A. Primary memory. *Psychological Review,* 1965, **72,** 89–104.

Weber, R. M. First graders' use of grammatical context in reading. In H. Levin & J. P. Williams (Eds.), *Basic studies in reading.* New York: Basic Books, 1970.

Wepman, J. M. Auditory discrimination, speech, and reading. *The Elementary School Journal,* 1960, **9,** 325–333.

Wepman, J. M. The interrelationships of hearing, speech, and reading. *The Reading Teacher,* 1961, **14,** 245–247.

Wiig, E. H., Semel, M. S., & Crouse, M. B. The use of English morphology by high-risk and learning disabled children. *Journal of Learning Disabilities,* 1973, **6,** 457–465.

Young, F. A., & Lindsley, D. B. *Early experience and visual information processing in perceptual and reading disorders.* Washington, D. C.: National Academy of Sciences, 1971.

Zifcak, M. *Phonological awareness and reading acquisition in first grade children.* Unpublished doctoral dissertation, University of Connecticut, 1976.

Zigmond, N. *Intrasensory and intersensory processes in normal and dyslexic children.* Unpublished doctoral dissertation, Northwestern University, 1966.

Zurif, E. B., & Carson, G. Dyslexia in relation to cerebral dominance and temporal analysis. *Neuropsychologia,* 1970, **8,** 351–361.

Varieties of Deficiency in the Reading Processes

MAGDALEN D. VERNON

University of Reading, England

Synthesizing a diverse group of studies, M. D. Vernon argues that reading disability is not a unitary phenomenon but can result from deficiencies in different psychological processes. Previous attempts to group poor readers according to deficiencies in these processes, however, have been largely unsuccessful because, Vernon maintains, they failed to take into account the steps required in learning to read. The author asserts that because of varying psychological dysfunctions, breakdowns can occur at specific points in acquiring reading. Based on the points at which an individual's reading breaks down, Vernon presents a fourfold classifications scheme capable of categorizing all poor readers.

Common wisdom has long maintained that a link exists between intellectual potential and an inability to read. It has become clear, however, that many poor readers have average if not better than average intelligence. These children appear to benefit little from their experience in ordinary school classes. Although the reading problems of some of these poor readers can be attributed to environmental deprivation or emotional disorders, sufficient evidence shows that many children's difficulties result from some basic inherent deficiency or deficiencies in the reading processes.

A second incorrect assumption still held by many is that the cause of reading difficulties is unitary; that is, that all reading problems arise from a single inherent deficiency that is the same in all poor readers. However, reading is not learned as a unitary skill; it necessitates the acquisition of several different skills which are finally integrated. These skills depend on the normal functioning of a number of different psychological processes, including visual and auditory perception, memory, linguistic ability, and reasoning. The actual causes of difficulties in learning to read vary considerably: there are various points of breakdown in different readers, and deficiencies in any of the psychological processes on which reading is based can lead to disturbances. Thus children with reading problems have varieties of deficiencies, and no one deficiency appears in all poor readers.

Harvard Educational Review   Vol. 47   No. 3   August 1977, 396–410

How large a group this heterogeneous collection of poor readers may be is the subject of controversy. A prevalent method of determining the distribution of reading disability in the population has been to find children whose reading achievement is below what might be expected from their performance on intelligence tests. Using a regression equation which analyzed the correlation between I.Q. and reading achievement, Yule (1967) predicted what reading-test scores should correspond to different I.Q. scores. Yule, Rutter, Berger, and Thompson (1974) tested in different parts of England over five thousand nine- to eleven-year-old children using this equation. They found that 3 to 6 percent of the children read worse than was predicted from their intelligence. Yule and his colleagues termed this disparity between actual and expected reading achievement "specific reading retardation." This syndrome was contrasted with another syndrome, "reading backwardness", in which children with low reading achievement had correspondingly low intelligence scores. Moreover, when some of the children were followed up at age fourteen, it was found that the "backward" readers had made some gains; those with "specific reading retardation," however, had not made similar progress (Rutter & Yule, 1975). Thus it would appear that children with this syndrome are not helped by ordinary teaching methods.

In light of this, Rutter and Yule (1975) argued that "specific reading retardation" represents the lower end of a continuous distribution of varying reading ability. These authors suggest that in some cases constitutional and even hereditary factors may be involved but that the origin of low reading ability is multifactorial. Environmental and emotional factors may interact with failure in the normal maturation of cognitive processes in the cerebral cortex. Thus, reading failure is not the unitary phenomenon it is sometimes alleged to be.

In this paper we will explore the possible relationship between basic psychological processes and the points of breakdown in learning to read. For example, children who experience initial reading failure may have problems related to such processes as visual and auditory perception and memory. Children who have normal perception and who are able to learn a few simple words may have inadequate skill in associating letter shapes with letter sounds (grapheme-phoneme association). Still other children might be able to recognize single words but cannot proceed to rapid reading because of some other basic problem, for instance in reasoning. It will be argued in this paper that if the actual point of breakdown in learning to read could be ascertained, it might be possible to identify the deficient psychological process or processes. A classification scheme of poor readers will be suggested in which the reader groups correspond to the points of reading breakdown and the inferred deficiencies.

The Variability of Characteristics in Inadequate Reading

One of the notable features of inadequate reading is that severe and prolonged difficulties with reading and spelling are usually accompanied by other deficiencies in perception, memory, language, and thinking. Making sense of these other problems is important to an understanding of reading disorders but is complicated by divergent descriptions and findings in the literature.

At least some of the variability of reported reading deficiencies and the discrepancies between findings by different investigators is due to inadequate methods of investigation. Although they recognize that cases differ, clinicians do not always assess or specify exact failures in reading. On the other hand, experimentalists more often than not treat poor readers as if they constitute a homogeneous group. There is a failure to discriminate between those whose problems are inherent and those whose problems might be environmental. In some studies reading ages are not measured; the degree of reading deficiency, therefore, is unknown. In other studies only one or two deficiencies may be tested for, and these are averaged for the whole group, masking the incidence of individual variations. What is needed is a combination of the experimental and clinical approaches, where each child's unique difficulties are carefully assessed. Because this kind of assessment is not standard across the studies to be reported, the term "dyslexia"—which refers only to cases where severe, inherent disturbances of reading are clearly present—will not be used.

Several investigators who have recognized the variability in reading disabilities have attempted to group poor readers according to the deficiencies they display. Ingram (1960), for example, distinguished three classes of problems among poor readers: visuo-spatial difficulties, auditory-linguistic difficulties, and difficulties in relating visual symbols to their phonemic equivalents. Later investigators have distinguished mainly between those with visuo-spatial deficiencies and those with auditory-linguistic deficiencies (Johnson & Myklebust, 1967; Kinsbourne & Warrington, 1963; Vernon, 1971).

Detailed studies of individual cases have demonstrated, however, that no exact classification of all cases is possible. There is considerable overlap between categories, and poor readers do not fit neatly into any of them. Naidoo (1972), for example, performed a thorough study of the characteristics of ninety-eight boys, aged eight to thirteen years, who were at least two years below grade level in reading or spelling. They were of average intelligence and had neither environmental problems nor gross neurological or emotional disorders. She compared the boys' performance on a variety of tests measuring visual perception, memory, auditory discrimination, and laterality. From a "cluster analysis" of the test data, four groups were proposed, but almost one-third of the children could not be included in any of these. Although one large group could be characterized by linguistic problems and another smaller group by visual perception and memory problems, the considerable variability within all groups makes a simple classification of all poor readers impossible.

Naidoo, however, did not test for individual variations in the *reading processes.* Indeed, it is unfortunate that in most of these studies one rarely encounters any consideration of variations in the way children read. Without this information we might not know the particular difficulties individual readers are experiencing or the point at which their reading breaks down. It seems possible, therefore, that a wrong approach has been adopted in many studies of poor readers.

There are several possible reasons to explain why these children do not exhibit clear problems or patterns in visual or auditory perception, memory, or thinking —all of which operate at every stage of breakdown. For example, they may fail to apply one (or more) of these processes to reading at a critical learning point. Another possibility is that a child may have a minimal problem which becomes greatly exaggerated when applied to certain reading skills. This author contends that it might be profitable to discover both the particular difficulties experienced by different children in learning to read and the points at which further development seems blocked. If these points in reading development were ascertained, one could test for deficiencies in the psychological processes that underlie these reading difficulties.

We know that reading consists of a series of complex skills acquired as a child progresses from the early stages of learning to the final stage of fluent reading. Proceeding from the assumption that individual children experience different problems at varying points in reading development, in the following discussion we will outline the skills which must be acquired successively in learning to read.

Deficiencies in Visual and Auditory Processes in Reading

The first processes necessary in learning to read must be the differentiation and identification of the shapes of single letters. According to Gibson and Levin (1975), differentiation is performed through the perception and remembering of "invariant distinctive features"—the essental identifying characteristics of each letter shape which must be present despite minor sources of variation such as in handwriting and type face. This discrimination must be succeeded by the identification of letter shapes as wholes, a process involving memory for the individual letter shapes. Most children do not seem to experience much difficulty in learning to discriminate and identify letter shapes; however, the reversible letters *b* and *d*, *p* and *q*, are often confused by young children. Although they usually grow out of this, poor readers often show these kinds of identification errors. Shankweiler and Liberman (1972) found that only a very small proportion of identification errors made by third-grade poor readers were actually letter reversals. Unfortunately in this study we do not know how poor these children's reading achievement was. Reversals seem to be cited most often in clinic cases of very low achievement. In such severe cases it is possible that initial identification of letter shapes may be the area of breakdown.

What may be more difficult for young children than identifying single letters is analyzing words into their constituent letters. This notion is supported by findings that indicate that the ability for visual-perceptual analysis develops fairly late (Vernon, 1976). Several investigators (Crosby, 1968; de Hirsch, Jansky, & Langford, 1966; Lachmann, 1960; Smith & Keogh, 1962), using such measures as the Bender test, have found poor reading to be related to inadequate visual analysis of complex structures. Moreover, Smith and Keogh and de Hirsch et al. gave the visual tests before the children began learning to read; thus poor visual analysis was not caused by inadequacy in reading. That poor readers are even more deficient in the analysis of complex forms than in the identification of single letters is further indicated by some of Crosby's (1968) severe reading cases and by Kolers' (1975) study employing graphic patterns. Kolers, for example, found that twelve-year-old poor readers were far less adept than good readers in reading and recognizing sentences printed in reversed type; he hypothesized that this was caused by a deficiency in analyzing and remembering graphic patterns at the cognitive rather than at the perceptual level.

It may also be that memory for word structures may be more deficient in poor readers than perceptual abilities. J. F. Mackworth (1972) postulates that short-term, visual-memory images are generated from perceptions and that these images pass into long-term memory and are stored there. After grapheme-phoneme association has been acquired, the visual images are associated with verbal-memory traces. But the visual memories, containing all the constituent letters of words, persist and are of paramount importance in spelling. According to Mackworth and Mackworth (1974), these images are confused and imprecise in bad spellers.

Several investigators claim that not only spelling but also reading achievement is related to memory for visual shapes. Lunzer, Dolan, and Wilkinson (1976) showed that the short-term visual memory of five-and-one-half- to six-year-old children for shapes and pictures correlated significantly with their performance on word-recognition tests one year later. It has also been found that visual memory for shapes is particularly deficient in poor readers (Naidoo, 1972; Trieschmann, 1968). Recent studies by Audley (Note 1) indicate that poor readers have no impairment in visual memory for single letter shapes. Together these studies suggest that for some disabled readers, the deficiency must be in the imagery of word structures not in that of single letters.

Another initial step in learning to read involves learning the sounds of letters in words. As a prerequisite to grapheme-phoneme association, children must be able to make auditory discriminations between sounds and analyze words into their constituent phonemes. Until children are aware of the individual letter sounds, they cannot know what is to be associated with the printed letters. Auditory discrimination between similar-sounding words is also important in the initial stages of the association process; de Hirsch et al. (1966) showed that children who had discrimination difficulties subsequently failed in learning to read. Children's auditory analysis of words into their constituent phonemes is very important and has been studied by several researchers. Indeed, Elkonin (1973) devised a special method of teaching this analysis to Russian children, although his test of its effectiveness was not satisfactory. Roberts (1975) found word-sound analysis to be particularly difficult for five- and six-year-old children. Liberman and her associates found that many children of this age were unable to segment short words into phonemes or even tap out the number of phonemes; however, half of these children were able to segment longer words into *syllables* (Liberman, Shankweiler, Fischer, & Carter, 1974). In a similar study Savin (1972) found that children who failed to learn to read in the first grade were particularly poor at analyzing word sounds into phonemes.

Deficiencies in Grapheme-Phoneme Association

Among the most frequent beginning reading problems experienced by children are those that arise in learning to associate graphemes (letter forms) and phonemes (letter sounds). Children may have acquired both visual and auditory discrimination skills and still be unable to integrate the two. In addition, there are different levels of problems which occur in children with this difficulty. In this section and the following two subsections will be presented several bodies of theory which investigate the various difficulties children have in grapheme-phoneme association.

At the most general level it has often been argued that this problem is due to an inherent difficulty in cross-modal association between visual and auditory processes in perception and memory. In the last few years, however, theories emphasizing linguistic processing difficulties have gained prominence. Audley (Note 1), for example, found that seven- and eight-year-old poor readers performed less well than average readers in naming letters and pictures and in rhyming their names. Such a deficiency seemed to persist in the naming of digits, colors, and pictures by older, very poor readers (Spring & Capps, 1974). At ten years, learning the trigrams—three letter words—attached as names to pictures of animals was slower in poor readers (Vellutino, Steger, Harding, & Phillips, 1975). Not only was auditory memory for letters inferior to visual memory in poor readers ten to eleven years old, but also poor readers were confused when they were required to shift from visual to auditory-memory tasks (Farnham-Diggory & Gregg, 1975). From this perspective it is hypothesized that poor readers' basic deficiency in grapheme-phoneme association stems from problems in the cross-modal integration of visual and auditory-linguistic processing.

Deficiencies in Learning Invariant Grapheme-Phoneme Associations

There are, however, more specific levels of problems in grapheme-phoneme association, such as the learning of invariant associations. Most children find it relatively easy to learn the regular and invariant grapheme-phoneme associations in words (Venezky, 1973). Given the fact that only certain sequences of letters are ever found in words and that some are more probable than others, it is possible to expect that certain letters will be followed by only a limited variety of other letters (Smith, 1971). Even children in the first grade are reported to read letters more rapidly when presented familiar three-letter words than single letters (Lott & Smith, 1970). But poor readers are often able to read only a few simple, rote words and seem incapable of grasping the individual grapheme-phoneme associations. Still greater difficulties arise for these poor readers when they are forced to learn irregular and variable associations, where the particular phonemes selected for association depend on the word context (e.g., "he read"). Shankweiler and Liberman (1972), for example, found that the most frequent errors made by third-grade poor readers were in reading the vowels within words, because all vowels possess both variable graphemes and phonemes.

How competent readers learn variable grapheme-phoneme associations is the subject of much controversy. Ackerman (1973), for example, has shown that this skill is easier for readers initially taught not to expect only regular and invariant associations. Gibson and Levin (1975) have concluded that acquisition of grapheme-phoneme associations does not occur through the rote learning of single letters, but rather through the development of "rules" based on regularities between the graphic information of the printed text and the phonemic information of spoken words. Thus, beginners should find it easier to learn to read if they are presented not with single letters and their sounds, but with groups of letters in short words, where grapheme-phoneme correspondences are more regular. Indeed, Swenson (1975) has found that in matching consonant-vowel-consonant (CVC) trigrams, first-grade average readers attended more to combined VC letters than to single letters, whereas poor readers tended to employ the first letter only. If children are presented with words that differ by only one letter, they can hear how the word-sound changes as the letter changes. This procedure also eliminates the difficulty experienced by young children in "blending" single phonemes to form the word sound. But the main object of the procedure is to encourage children to develop a mental set towards discovering, abstracting, and learning invariant patterns of grapheme-phoneme correspondence in a variety of contexts.

Frank Smith (1971, 1973) maintains that children cannot learn to read by being taught spelling-to-sound correspondence "rules" since these rules are far too numerous for effective use. Children must form expectations about the probability with which a particular word with its unique shape will occur. Forming expectations about printed words is assisted by the meaning and grammatical structure of sentences; however, Weber (1968, 1970) and Biemiller (1970) have found that in children's early oral reading, guesses are made from sentence context with little regard to the graphic structure (shape of the word).

Thus we can infer that children must learn to integrate both their expectations and a recognition of some grapheme-phoneme correspondences with the meaning of the text. The complexity involved in this two-way process may cause difficulty in both young and old poor readers (Bannatyne, 1971; Ingram, 1960; Mackworth & Mackworth, 1974). This two-way conceptualization process has been the subject of various investigations. Kress (1971) has hypothesized that reading involves first abstracting visual and phonemic similarities from words and subsequently generalizing them to new words. Vellutino, Harding, Phillips, and Steger (1975) state that many poor readers are unable to abstract and generalize the invariant components of words. They consider this difficulty to be caused by a basic dysfunction in the categorical processing of those words which contain common and predictable elements.

Another difficulty with grapheme-phoneme correspondences can be caused by problems of memory: specifically, how children remember the order of letters in words. Bryden (1972) found that poor readers could not perceive and remember word patterns—especially sequential patterns—as well as average readers. It has frequently been found that many poor readers perform badly on the Digit-Span

594

test of the Wechsler Intelligence Scale for Children (WISC) because their memory for order is deficient (Spring, 1976). In addition, Corkin (1974) showed that long-term memory for order was deficient in poor readers, especially with tests requiring delayed responses. Similarly, Bakker (1972) found that poor readers were deficient in remembering the temporal order of events in any kind of sequential pattern —visual, auditory, or haptic. The impact of this deficiency on reading was clear: 30 percent of the errors made in reading by poor readers were temporal-order errors in letter or word sequences (Bakker, 1970). Even in sixth-grade children, order memory was more deficient than item memory in poor readers (Mason, Katz, & Wicklund, 1975).

In reading it is necessary not only to remember the temporal order of phonemes in spoken words, but also to match this to the spatially ordered graphemes of the printed words. This involves both cross-modal matching and the matching of temporal and spatial sequential patterns. Several investigators have demonstrated that poor readers are deficient in matching visual-sequential patterns of dots against auditory-sequential patterns of clicks or taps. Jorgenson and Hyde (1974) found that performance on matching tasks correlated with sight vocabulary in the first and second grade. Vande Voort, Senf, and Benton (1972) showed that poor readers were less proficient in these matching tasks and did not improve with age. Thus it seems possible that difficulties in grapheme-phoneme association are compounded by confusions in sequential memory, auditory-visual pattern integration, and/or temporal-spatial order integration.

Neurophysiological Processes in Auditory-Visual Integration

Some of the most important research in reading disorders in the last years has come from neurophysiology and neuropsychology. Although the literature on this subject is very extensive and cannot be fully discussed here, a few of these studies will be reviewed to illustrate how this work may have bearing on problems in grapheme-phoneme association.

It has been hypothesized that difficulties in cross-modal auditory-visual integration may result from the fact that visual and auditory-linguistic stimuli are processed in different hemispheres in the brain. Numerous experiments have shown that when linguistic stimuli are presented separately to the two hemispheres, processing is more rapid and accurate in the left hemisphere (Seamon & Gazzaniga, 1973), whereas visual processing is better in the right. Other investigators, however, have produced evidence to show that holistic visual processing (that is, perception of visual structures as wholes) is carried out in the right hemisphere and analytic visual processing in the left (Bradshaw, Gates, & Patterson, 1976). The processing of information about order is also thought to occur in the left hemisphere.

Taken together, these findings would suggest that in poor readers inadequate functioning in the left hemisphere was mainly responsible for reading problems. Nevertheless, it has also been supposed that for adequate reading the functioning of both hemispheres must be fully developed, lateralized, and then subsequently integrated. This integration may not have occurred in the usual way in poor readers, thus leading, perhaps, to difficulties in grapheme-phoneme association. Posner, Lewis, and Conrad (1972) hypothesize that in some poor readers there might in early years have been actual hemispheric rivalry, making subsequent coordination between the two hemispheres difficult. It has also been suggested that some poor readers might have too little differentiation between the functions of the two hemispheres (Olson, 1973) or that there has been delayed or incomplete maturation in the lateralization of the speech functions in the left hemisphere (Satz, Rardin, & Ross, 1971; Zurif & Carson, 1970). Several investigators suggest that right hemispheric functions in poor readers dominate over left hemispheric (Bannatyne, 1971; Witelson & Rabinovitch, 1972). Again, the right hemispheric functions are deficient in temporal ordering (Bakker, 1970). Thus, it would appear that whatever parts are played by right hemispheric functions, they must be subordinated to left hemispheric functions in the final integration for reading to occur.

Such a hypothesis is extremely complicated as is well illustrated in the articles in a recently published book, *The Neuropsychology of Learning Disorders,* edited by Knights and Bakker (1976). It is clear that far more investigation is required to determine the part that hemispherical functions play in reading and in the deficiencies that exist in poor readers. In these studies, again, different types of poor readers must be differentiated; in previous experiments this has not been done.

Deficiencies in Grouping Words in Phrases

Some poor readers appear to have acquired some facility in word recognition but seem unable to attain the more advanced processes in fluent reading. LaBerge and Samuels (1974) point out that the earlier processes must become fully efficient and automatized before children are able to proceed further. Good readers from the third and fifth grade have been found to be better than poor readers, not in their knowledge of the meaning of words, but in the automaticity of grapheme-phoneme processing skills (Perfetti & Hogaboam, 1975). Until these skills are adequate, children must process each word separately and hence can read only one word at a time. Processing even of single words is slower in poor than in average readers (N. H. Mackworth, cited by J. F. Mackworth, 1976). Because memory images are short-lived, slow readers tend to forget the previous word before the next one is processed (J. F. Mackworth, 1972). Thus it is difficult for them to grasp the meanings of whole sentences. Quite simply, these readers are unable to make use of contextual syntax and meaning in processing single words. In support of this view, Clay and Imlach (1971) found that seven-and-a-half-years-old poor readers could not group words syntactically. With no contextually based anticipations operating, all syntactic cues were destroyed by slow and inaccurate reading.

By contrast, fluent readers are able to group words in phrases that are meaningfully and syntactically correct. Studies of eye movements in reading have shown that whereas poor readers fixate on almost every word in a sentence, fluent readers may make only a few fixations on a line of print, and, therefore, do not perceive every word individually (Tinker, 1965). Corroborative findings have been obtained in studies of the eye-voice span. Such tests measure the number of words a reader is able to read ahead from the point in the sentence at which the text is covered from sight (Levin & Turner, 1968; Levin & Kaplan, 1970; Rode, 1974). While poor readers could anticipate only a word or so, fluent readers were able to produce whole phrases. Eye-voice span was also related to the grammatical constraints imposed by the particular sentence as well as to the general effects of context. Thus reading speed and the number of words covered at each fixation varied according to the nature of the context. Children of nine and ten years were able to read complex syntactic units, and older children could assimilate whole clauses (Rode, 1974).

In order to read fluently a child must sample the visual display of the print and not focus exclusively on the structure of each single word (Goodman, 1973). The visual structures of single words should require only a minimum of processing into verbalized words; this should normally occur only with difficult and unfamiliar words. Indeed, some investigators have claimed that in fluent reading the reader always passes directly from the visual symbols to the meanings of whole words and phrases. It is doubtful whether this always occurs, and it is likely that there are individual differences in the degree of fluency. But there is no doubt as to the importance of grouping words; LaBerge and Samuels (1974) have recommended that children should begin learning to organize words into phrase units even before grapheme-phoneme associations are fully automatic. Unfortunately it is not clear whether or how they can be taught to do so.

The poor readers who are incapable of this organization are obviously handicapped in their ability not only to read rapidly but also to understand the meaning of what they read. It has been suggested that this deficiency involves a failure to conceptualize the meanings of single words within the meanings of phrases. It seems possible, however, that these children have not learned to sample visual data and process this information directly into phrase meanings. Poor readers may become so confused in their attempts to construct grapheme-phoneme correspondences that they cannot automatize these correspondences so as to pass directly from the sampled visual data to phrase meanings.

It has been suggested that there may be a general problem in conceptual thinking in some poor readers. Even five- and six-year-old children who have learned to read seem to be more competent than nonreaders in performing classic Piagetian conservation tasks (Briggs & Elkind, 1973). Lunzer and his colleagues (1976), however, found that the word recognition of six-and-a-half- to seven-year-old children did not correlate highly with performance on conservation tests but did correlate with other operational tasks. Operativity was defined as the degree to which a child can impose a coherent logical structure on incoming information; this capacity was assessed by tests of seriation, class inclusion, and order. Presumably the concrete operational processes involved in these later tasks are more similar to the conceptual processes in reading than those underlying conservation.

Several investigators have pointed out that conceptual deficiencies may appear more clearly in older poor readers. Satz and Sparrow (1970), for example, hypothesize that these readers are less able to perform right-left-discrimination tasks. Similarly, Van Meel, Vlek, and Bruijel (1970) have shown that these readers per-

597

form poorly in the construction of categories in an object-sorting task. In tasks that required readers to ignore irrelevant dimensions and generalize solutions to similar problems, poor readers of eight and eleven years were less competent than average readers (Wirtenberg & Faw, 1975). This difference did not lessen as age increased. Though evidence is too scanty to determine the exact nature and extent of general conceptual deficiencies, it would seem that inadequate abstraction and generalization may be significant factors in difficulties with grouping words in phrases.

Classification of Poor Readers in Accordance with Types of Reading Deficiency

To summarize the findings in this paper's framework, there appears to be a series of four main deficiencies which may prevent children from learning to read. In the initial learning phases there may be deficiencies in the capacity to *analyze complex, sequential visual and/or auditory-linguistic structures.* These deficiencies prevent the coding of the linguistic structures and their organization in short- and long-term memory. These processes are so closely linked together in the acquisition of information that a deficiency in any one is likely to affect all. In certain severe cases there may be an impairment of visual- and/or auditory-perceptual analysis. Since the spelling of poor readers is often even worse than their reading, it seems that visual imagery may also be deficient.

The second point at which reading difficulty is likely to occur is in the *linking of visual and auditory-linguistic structures.* We noted that this difficulty had been found even in the naming of pictures and that it had been attributed by several investigators to some delay in hemispheric maturation. This difficulty is further compounded by the fact that children must link visual and auditory-linguistic *symbols,* a process that is entirely novel to young children. Children who have failed to surmount either of the first two types of difficulty may not have grasped the fundamental nature of reading and may, therefore, be unable to read at all or may be greatly impeded in learning. Inability to link visual and auditory-linguistic structures would seem to be a more probable cause of reading failure than are deficiencies in visual or auditory analysis.

A third type of failure, the inability to *establish regularities in variable grapheme-phoneme correspondences,* may be the most frequent cause of poor reading. A basic maturational lag or disability in the development of interhemispheric integration might be operative here also. It seems likely, however, that a deficiency in conceptual thinking—specifically, the abstraction and generalization of invariant grapheme-phoneme correspondences—is additionally involved. Other conceptual deficiencies might affect the ability to abstract the temporal order of phonemes and match this to the spatial order of graphemes.

A fourth type of poor reader may recognize words but cannot *group them into meaningful phrases.* Here another form of cognitive deficiency, related to the conceptualization of phrase meanings, may be operating. It was suggested that there might also be failure in sampling visual data, omitting phonemic correspondences, and passing directly to meanings of phrases. These failures may be caused in part by inability to automatize grapheme-phoneme correspondences. The nature of all these processes remains, however, complex and obscure. Much research is needed before we are able to establish the exact areas of deficiencies for this type of reading problem.

However ill-defined our knowledge may be of the basic nature and cause of all four of these deficiencies, it appears fruitful to this author to classify poor readers according to the four types of failure. To be sure, it is likely that certain deficiencies overlap from one type to another. For example, deficiencies in visual and/or auditory-linguistic analysis that do not altogether prevent children from learning to read may nevertheless have a prolonged retarding effect. Similarly, deficiencies in ordering may occur in the second as well as the third type of poor reader, and inadequate grapheme-phoneme processing may affect the fourth type as well as the third.

Nevertheless, classification of the different types of poor readers might be carried out by differentiating individual reading performances. For example, those who cannot read at all should be studied to discover whether they can analyze or memorize word structures visually or auditorily. Some investigation of general linguistic development is desirable here—for instance, a history of delayed speech and language comprehension. Next, those who can read only a few simple words and appear incapable of comprehending phonic teaching should be studied for difficulties in associating visual and auditory symbolic material. As we refine our ways of measuring normal hemispheric functioning and integration, these readers could be tested to see how effectively the two hemispheres process visual and auditory material respectively. Those readers who can read simple regular words but do not understand how to manipulate irregular grapheme-phoneme correspondences should be tested for any deficiencies in a variety of types of conceptual reasoning. Finally, for those readers who can read single words but cannot group words syntactically into phrases, ability in visual sampling might be studied. In addition, conceptual deficiencies should be investigated in these last poor readers.

Conclusions

From the foregoing argument it should be evident that little will be gained if disabled readers are regarded as a homogeneous group. To begin with, children whose poor reading achievement may result from environmental or emotional problems must be clearly distinguished from those who appear to possess physiologically based cognitive deficiency or deficiencies. Members of this latter group, moreover, must be studied individually to determine the precise nature of their reading failure and the exact point at which learning has broken down. Deficiencies in the basic psychological processes associated with particular reading disabilities must then be investigated.

Such a way of looking at children with reading problems could contribute to our understanding of the reading process in two ways: it could influence researchers to include more detailed analyses of children's specific reading performances in all studies, thus bringing more standardization to the field. Secondly, poor readers would have to be assessed and treated as individuals with different problems, necessitating individual solutions.

Reference Note

1. Audley, R. J. *Reading difficulties: The importance of basic research in solving practical problems.* Presidential Address presented at a meeting of the Psychology Section of the British Association for the Advancement of Science, September 1976.

References

Ackerman, M. D. Acquisition and transfer value of initial training with multiple grapheme-phoneme correspondences. *Journal of Educational Psychology*, 1973, **65**, 28–34.

Annett, M., & Turner, A. Laterality and the growth of intellectual abilities. *British Journal of Educational Psychology*, 1974, **44**, 37–46.

Bakker, D. J. Temporal order perception and reading retardation. In D. J. Bakker and P. Satz (Eds.), *Specific reading disability*. Rotterdam: Rotterdam University Press, 1970.

Bakker, D. J. *Temporal order and disturbed reading*. Rotterdam: Rotterdam University Press, 1972.

Bannatyne, A. *Language, reading and learning disabilities*. Springfield, Ill.: Thomas, 1971.

Biemiller, A. The development of the use of graphic contextual information as children learn to read. *Reading Research Quarterly*, 1970, **6**, 75–96.

Bradshaw, J. L., Gates, A., & Patterson, K. Hemispheric differences in processing visual patterns. *Quarterly Journal of Experimental Psychology*, 1976, **28**, 667–681.

Briggs, C., & Elkind, D. Cognitive development in early readers. *Developmental Psychology*, 1973, **9**, 279–280.

Bryden, M. P. Auditory-visual and sequential-spatial matching in relation to reading ability. *Child Development*, 1972, **43**, 824–832.

Chomsky, C. Reading, writing and phonology. *Harvard Educational Review*, 1972, **40**, 287–309.

Clay, M. M., & Imlach, R. H. Juncture, pitch and stress as reading behavior variables. *Journal of Verbal Learning and Verbal Behavior*, 1971, **10**, 133–139.

Corkin, S. Serial-ordering deficits in inferior readers. *Neuropsychologia*, 1974, **12**, 347–354.

Crosby, R. M. N. *Reading and the dyslexic child*. London: Souvenir Press, 1968.

de Hirsch, K., Jansky, J. J., & Langford, W. S. *Predicting reading failure*. New York: Harper & Row, 1966.

Elkonin, D. B. USSR. In J. Downing (Ed.), *Comparative reading*. New York: Macmillan, 1973.

Farnham-Diggory, S., & Gregg, L. W. Short-term memory function in young readers. *Journal of Experimental Child Psychology*, 1975, **19**, 279–298.

Gibson, E. J., & Levin, H. *The psychology of reading*. Cambridge, Mass.: M.I.T. Press, 1975.

Goodman, K. S. Psycholinguistic universals in the reading process. In F. Smith (Ed.), *Psycholinguistics and reading*. New York: Holt, Rinehart & Winston, 1973.

Ingram, T. T. S. Pediatric aspects of specific developmental dysphasia, dyslexia and dysgraphia. *Cerebral Palsy Bulletin*, 1960, **2**, 254–277.

Johnson, D. J., & Myklebust, H. *Learning disabilities*. New York: Grune & Stratton, 1967.

Jorgenson, G. W., & Hyde, E. M. Auditory-visual integration and reading performance in lower-social-class children. *Journal of Educational Psychology*, 1974, **66**, 718–725.

Kinsbourne, M., & Warrington, E. K. Developmental factors in reading and writing backwardness. *British Journal of Psychology*, 1963, **34**, 145–156.

Knights, R. M., & Bakker, D. J. (Eds.). *The neuropsychology of learning disorders*. Baltimore: University Park Press, 1976.

Kolers, P. A. Pattern-analyzing disability in poor readers. *Developmental Psychology*, 1975, **11**, 282–290.

Kress, R. A. Reactions to reading as cognitive functioning. In H. Singer and R. B. Ruddell (Eds.), *Theoretical models and processes in reading*. Newark: International Reading Association, 1971.

LaBerge, D., & Samuels, S. J. Toward a theory of automatic information processing in reading. *Cognitive Psychology*, 1974, **6**, 293–323.

Lachmann, F. M. Perceptual-motor development in children retarded in reading ability. *Journal of Consulting Psychology*, 1960, **24**, 427–431.

Levin, H., & Kaplan, E. L. Grammatical structure and reading. In H. Levin and J. P. Williams (Eds.), *Basic studies in reading*. New York: Basic Books, 1970.

Levin, H., & Turner, A. Sentence structure and the eye-voice span. In H. Levin, E. J. Gibson, and J. J. Gibson (Eds.), *The analysis of reading skill*. Final Report, Project No. 5-1213. Washington, D.C.: U.S. Department of Health, Education and Welfare, 1968.

Liberman, I. Y., Shankweiler, D., Fischer, F. W., & Carter, B. Explicit syllable and phoneme segmentation in the young child. *Journal of Experimental Child Psychology*, 1974, **18**, 201–212.

Lott, D., & Smith, F. Knowledge of intraword redundancy by beginning readers. *Psychonomic Science*, 1970, **19**, 343–344.

Lunzer, E. A., Dolan, T., & Wilkinson, J. E. The effectiveness of measures of operativity, language and short-term memory in the prediction of reading and mathematical understanding. *British Journal of Educational Psychology*, 1976, **46**, 295–305.

Mackworth, J. F. Some models of the reading process; learners and skilled readers. *Reading Research Quarterly*, 1972, **7**, 701–733.

Mackworth, J. F. Development of attention. In V. Hamilton and M. D. Vernon (Eds.), *The development of the cognitive processes*. London: Academic Press, 1976.

Mackworth, J. F., & Mackworth, N. H. Spelling recognition and coding by poor readers. *Bulletin of the Psychonomic Society*, 1974, **3**, 59–65.

Mason, M., Katz, L., & Wicklund, D. A. Immediate spatial order memory and item memory in sixth-grade children as a function of reader ability. *Journal of Educational Psychology*, 1975, **67**, 610–616.

Naidoo, S. *Specific dyslexia*. London: Pitman, 1972.

Olson, M. E. Laterality differences in tachistoscopic word recognition in normal and delayed readers in elementary school. *Neuropsychologia*, 1973, **11**, 343–350.

Perfetti, C. A., & Hogaboam, T. Relationship between single word decoding and reading comprehension skill. *Journal of Educational Psychology*, 1975, **67**, 461–469.

Posner, M. I., Lewis, J. L., & Conrad, C. Component processes in reading: A performance analysis. In J. F. Kavanagh and I. G. Mattingly (Eds.), *Language by ear and eye*. Cambridge, Mass.: M.I.T. Press, 1972.

Roberts, T. Skills of analysis and synthesis in the early stages of reading. *British Journal of Educational Psychology*, 1975, **45**, 3–9.

Rode, S. S. Development of phrase and clause boundary reading in children. *Reading Research Quarterly*, 1974, **10**, 124–142.

Rutter, M., & Yule, W. The concept of specific reading retardation. *Journal of Child Psychology and Psychiatry*, 1975, **16**, 181–197.

Satz, P., Rardin, D., & Ross, J. An evaluation of the theory of specific developmental dyslexia. *Child Development*, 1971, **42**, 2009–2021.

Satz, P., & Sparrow, S. S. Specific developmental dyslexia. In D. J. Bakker and P. Satz (Eds.), *Specific reading disability*. Rotterdam: Rotterdam University Press, 1970.

Savin, H. B. What the child knows about speech when he starts to learn to read. In J. F. Kavanagh and I. G. Mattingly (Eds.), *Language by ear and eye*. Cambridge, Mass.: M.I.T. Press, 1972.

Seamon, J. G., & Gazzaniga, M. S. Coding strategies and cerebral laterality effects. *Cognitive Psychology*, 1973, **5**, 249–256.

Shankweiler, D., & Liberman, I. Y. Misreading: A search for cues. In J. F. Kavanagh and I. G. Mattingly (Eds.), *Language by ear and eye*. Cambridge, Mass.: M.I.T. Press, 1972.

Smith, C. E., & Keogh, B. K. The group Bender-Gestalt as a reading readiness screening instrument. *Perceptual and Motor Skills*, 1962, **15**, 639–645.

Smith, F. *Understanding reading: A psycholinguistic analysis of reading and learning to read*. New York: Holt, Rinehart & Winston, 1971.

Smith, F. *Psycholinguistics and reading*. New York: Holt, Rinehart & Winston, 1973.

Spring, C. Encoding speed and memory span in dyslexic children. *Journal of Special Education*, 1976, **10**, 35–46.

Spring, C., & Capps, C. Encoding speed, rehearsal and probed recall of dyslexic boys. *Journal of Educational Psychology*, 1974, **66**, 780–786.

Swenson, I. Word-recognition cues used in matching verbal stimuli within and between auditory and visual modalities. *Journal of Educational Psychology*, 1975, **67**, 409–415.

Tinker, M. A. *Bases for effective reading*. Minneapolis: University of Minnesota Press, 1965.

Trieschmann, R. B. Undifferentiated handedness and perceptual development in children with reading problems. *Perceptual and Motor Skills*, 1968, **27**, 1123–1134.

Vande Voort, L., Senf, G. M., & Benton, A. L. Development of audiovisual integration in normal and retarded readers. *Child Development*, 1972, **43**, 1260–1272.

Van Meel, J. M., Vlek, C. A. J., & Bruijel, R. M. Some characteristics of visual information-processing in children with learning difficulties. In D. J. Bakker and P. Satz (Eds.), *Specific reading disability*. Rotterdam: Rotterdam University Press, 1970.

Vellutino, F. R., Harding, C. J., Phillips, F., & Steger, J. A. Differential transfer in poor and normal readers. *Journal of Genetic Psychology*, 1975, **126**, 3–18.

Vellutino, F. R., Steger, J. A., Harding, C. J., & Phillips, F. Verbal vs. non-verbal paired-associates learning in poor and normal readers. *Neuropsychologia*, 1975, **13**, 75–82.

Venezky, R. L. Letter-sound generalizations of first-, second- and third-grade Finnish children. *Journal of Educational Psychology*, 1973, **64**, 288–292.

Vernon, M. D. *Reading and its difficulties*. Cambridge, Eng.: Cambridge University Press, 1971.

Vernon, M. D. Development of perception of form. In V. Hamilton and M. D. Vernon (Eds.), *The development of cognitive processes*. London: Academic Press, 1976.

Weber, R. M. First graders' use of grammatical context in reading. In H. Levin, E. J. Gibson, and J. J. Gibson (Eds.), *The analysis of reading skill*. Final Report, Project No. 5-1213. Washington, D.C.: U.S. Department of Health, Education and Welfare, 1968.

Weber, R. M. A linguistic analysis of first-grade reading errors. *Reading Research Quarterly*, 1970, **5**, 427–451.

Wirtenberg, T. J., & Faw, T. T. The development of learning sets in adequate and retarded readers. *Journal of Learning Disorders*, 1975, **8**, 304–307.

Witelson, S. F., & Rabinovitch, M. S. Hemispheric speech lateralization in children with auditory-linguistic defects. *Cortex*, 1972, **8**, 412–426.

Yule, W. Predicting reading ages on Neale's analysis of reading ability. *British Journal of Educational Psychology*, 1967, **37**, 252–255.

Yule, W., Rutter, M., Berger, M., & Thompson, J. Over- and under-achievement in reading: Distribution in the general population. *British Journal of Educational Psychology*, 1974, **44**, 1–12.

Zurif, E. B., & Carson, G. Dyslexia in relation to cerebral dominance and temporal analysis. *Neuropsychologia*, 1970, **8**, 351–361.

Acquired Disorders of Reading

MARTIN L. ALBERT
*Boston University and Boston Veterans
Administration Hospital*

NORMAN GESCHWIND
Harvard University and Beth Israel Hospital

Emphasizing the neurological mechanisms underlying disorders of reading, Martin Albert and Norman Geschwind consider current definitions, classification schemes, and approaches to alexia—the breakdown of reading in adults due to cerebral damage. Where relevant, the authors indicate the relationship between dyslexia—the disorder in children which affects the acquisition and development of the reading process—and alexia. While they assume that knowledge of dysfunctioning mechanisms involved in adult reading disorders will contribute to our understanding of developmental reading disorders, the authors stress that too great an emphasis on possible alexia/dyslexia parallels may impede more creative approaches to the study of dyslexia.

Childhood dyslexia represents a major educational problem. Although it has often been suggested that this disorder has a neurological basis, anatomical studies of the brains of dyslexic children have been rare, since fortunately these children have a low death rate. Drake (1968) claims to have found an abnormality in the brain of a dyslexic child, but the lack of study of brains of normal controls makes his result difficult to interpret. More recently Galaburda and Kemper (1979) found multiple areas of disruption of the normal architecture of the cortex in the left hemisphere (and in particular in the posterior speech area) of a dyslexic child. The significance of this work will, however, become clear only as brains of similar cases are studied.

The sparseness of neuropathological data in childhood leads readily to the temptation to explain childhood dyslexia on the basis of our much greater knowledge of the location of brain damage in cases of the alexias—i.e., the acquired reading disorders of adults. It would be unwarranted to presume that the mechanisms of developmental reading disorders of childhood are identical to those of acquired disorders of reading in adults. Nevertheless, it seems reasonable to assume that knowledge of mechanisms of reading at any age will increase our ability to explain and deal with reading disorders of childhood.

We are grateful to Ms. Susanna Haberman for preparing the figures.

In this article we will consider the alexias and indicate where appropriate the relevance to developmental dyslexia. Emphasizing neurological mechanisms underlying these disorders, our presentation will include: (1) definitions and historical review; (2) proposed classification schemes and descriptions of the clinical syndromes; (3) a survey of data concerning the location of lesions; (4) a review of neuropsychological studies, research with Japanese alexics, and neurolinguistic studies; (5) a brief discussion of treatment and prognosis; and finally, (6) possible relationships to developmental dyslexia in childhood. We will point out that too great an emphasis on the search for parallels may inhibit creative approaches to the study of developmental reading disorders.

Definitions and Historical Review

Alexia may be defined as an inability to comprehend written language which is acquired as a consequence of brain damage. The term acquired dyslexia is used by some authors synonymously with alexia and may be contrasted with developmental dyslexia. Acquired dyslexia, or alexia, refers to the loss of reading ability in a person who has already learned to read in a normal fashion; developmental dyslexia refers to an inability to learn to read normally dating from childhood. In the definition of alexia, emphasis is placed on the impairment of reading comprehension. Inability to read aloud may, as we shall see, form part of an alexic syndrome, but this defect is neither necessary nor sufficient for the diagnosis of alexia. The term "word blindness" is a classical expression for alexia, and is still in use, especially in continental Europe.

The history of studies on alexia extends back at least two thousand years. In the year 30 A.D. Valerimus Maximus reported the case of a man struck on the head by an axe, who lost his memory for letters but showed no other cognitive deficits. Throughout the centuries case reports appeared sporadically of individuals with acquired reading difficulty in relative isolation from other disorders. Not until the late 1800s, however, was any significant step made to elucidate the neurological mechanisms of alexia.

Dejerine made the main contribution to anatomic and clinical understanding of alexia in the 1800s. In separate reports in 1891 and 1892 he described two different varieties of alexia that resulted from brain damage and that interfered with the normal reading process at different stages. One type, which he called "pure word blindness," was associated with the preserved capacity to write. This variety resulted from a very particular pattern of damage to two areas in the brain: a lesion (some kind of injury or damage) in the visual area (occipital cortex) of the language-dominant hemisphere coupled with a lesion in the posterior portion (splenium) of the large bundle of nerve fibers connecting the two cerebral hemispheres (corpus callosum). Another type of alexia was associated with an acquired disorder of writing ability (agraphia). This variety—alexia with agraphia—was shown to result from a lesion in the angular gyrus, a specific part of the posterior portion of the language zone. In subsequent years the existence of these two basic types of alexia has been confirmed repeatedly. (See Figures 1, 2, 3, and 4.)

The illustrations may help clarify the anatomical distinctions being made. Figure 1 presents a general view of the left cerebral hemisphere, which is dominant for language in more than 90 percent of right handers and more than 60 percent of left

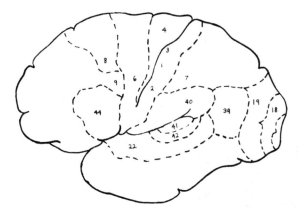

FIGURE 1

Cortical regions of the left hemisphere relevant to language. Numbers refer to Brodmann's classification of cytoarchitectonic areas of the brain:

1, 2, 3	Primary Sensory Cortex
4, 6	Primary Motor Cortex
8	Frontal Eye Field
9	Motor Association Area for Hand
44	Broca's Area (in Frontal Lobe)
7	Somesthetic Association Area (in parietal lobe)
40	Supramarginal Gyrus (mid and posterior part of 40)
39	Angular Gyrus
18, 19	Visual Association Cortex (in occipital lobe)
41, 42	Wernicke's Area (in temporal lobe)
22	Auditory Association Cortex

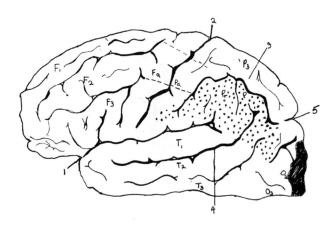

FIGURE 2

Lateral view of left hemisphere of patient with alexia described by Dejerine in 1892. Stippled region represents a recent infarction. Dark region represents an old infarction. (Redrawn from Dejerine, 1892).

605

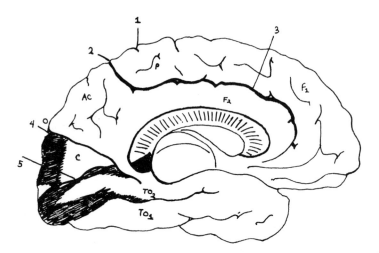

FIGURE 3

Medial view of left hemisphere of brain shown in Figure 2. The corpus callosum is indicated by the radiating lines. The posterior end of the corpus callosum (the splenium) has an area of old infarction. The occipital lobe, which contains the visual cortex, is also shown as having areas of destruction. (Redrawn from Dejerine, 1892).

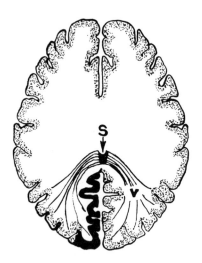

FIGURE 4

Schematic representation of the human brain in horizontal section, illustrating the neurological mechanism proposed to explain alexia without agraphia. S = splenium of corpus callosum; V = visual region. The visual cortex on the left is destroyed (heavy black line). As a result the patient can receive visual information only in the intact right visual region. The splenium of the corpus callosum is destroyed. As a result, written material perceived in the right visual region cannot be transmitted to language areas of the left hemisphere. The patient thus can perceive the form of written words, but cannot comprehend their meaning. (Redrawn from Geschwind, 1970).

handers. Major portions of the left hemisphere thought to be related to language are indicated. Figures 2 and 3 are redrawn from Dejerine's publication of 1892. They demonstrate specific regions of the brain which were damaged in his alexic patient. Figure 4 represents a schematic view of the brain in horizontal section. The connection between the right and left visual areas (that is, the splenium of the corpus callosum) is indicated. Damage to this connection can produce alexia. In a subsequent section of this paper we shall review the anatomical explanations offered for alexia, and shall refer again to these illustrations.

Classification of the Alexias

Classification schemes have differed among various authors depending on the relative emphasis each wished to lay on description or interpretation. One standard practice has been to divide the alexias into clinical types with respect to the major reading deficit: (1) *literal alexia*, the inability to read letters, combined with the relative preservation of ability to read words; (2) *verbal alexia*, the inability to read words combined with the relative preservation of ability to read letters; (3) *global alexia*, the inability to read letters or words. Another approach has been to classify alexias by reference to the presence or absence of writing disorders. Thus we have *alexia without agraphia* (pure alexia, pure word blindness) and *alexia with agraphia* (the loss of writing ability). A third approach has been to consider the reading disorder in terms of the underlying mechanism which may have produced it: for example, *agnosic alexia*, where agnosia refers to the loss of knowledge of the meaning of a perceived item, and *aphasic alexia*, where aphasia refers to the loss of language skills. Each of these disorders results from damage to specific regions of the brain.

Over the years many different labels have been attached to the clinical syndromes of alexia (e.g., cortical alexia, subcortical alexia, parietal alexia, primary vs. secondary alexia, etc.). Despite the different names, virtually all authors agree that there are two principal varieties: *alexia without agraphia* and *alexia with agraphia*. Each of these varieties is clinically distinctive, each has a different anatomical basis, and each has a different theoretical explanation.

Alexia without agraphia (pure alexia, pure word blindness) is manifested clinically as an impaired ability to comprehend written language in the presence of a preserved ability to write. Oral language is normal or nearly normal, although there may be a mild naming deficit where the patient has difficulty finding particular words (anomia). Often one finds, in addition to the alexia, impairment of the abilities to copy and to carry out mathematical operations. Occasionally one finds difficulties in identification of colors and/or objects. A visual field defect for the right half of space (right homonymous hemianopia) is almost always present. Hemiplegia (paralysis of one-half of the body) is rare and, if it occurs at all, usually mild.

Alexia with agraphia may be divided into two types: one form exists in relative isolation from disorders of oral language; the other accompanies certain aphasic syndromes and includes abnormal spoken language. Alexia with agraphia without obvious or significant aphasia is manifested clinically as verbal alexia. Letters can usually be read, and occasionally short commands can be carried out. Long words or long sentences cannot be read with complete understanding. Disorders of writing are severe, and appear in all aspects of writing (spontaneous, to dictation, etc.). Disorders of spoken language are either absent or quite mild, although an anomia is usually found. The ability to spell aloud is always affected. Often, but not always, one may see elements of the Gerstmann Syndrome, i.e., agraphia, acalculia (impaired ability to carry out mathematical operations), right-left spatial disorientation, and impairment in the ability to identify fingers. One of these, acalculia, is almost always found. Hemianopia (blindness in one-half of the visual field) is not necessarily present. Of significance in this variety of alexia is the loss of the perceptual strategies for reading, as defined for normals (Haslerud & Clark, 1957). These strategies tend to be intact in alexia without agraphia.

Syndromes of aphasia in which spoken speech is abnormal frequently have an associated reading disorder. When the reading disorder is a prominent feature of the total aphasic picture, one may speak of *aphasic alexia*. Clinically, the reading disorder may have different characteristics, depending on where the lesion is located. Literal, verbal, or global alexias may be present; writing is always impaired; acalculia is common. *Paralexias* (the substitution of whole words, partial words, or meaningless word sounds for the correct word on a reading task) in oral reading are striking when the alexia accompanies an aphasia with fluently abnormal speech.

To return to an evaluation of *pure alexia* or *alexia without agraphia*, we find that the disorder may demonstrate different subtypes within the main syndrome: literal alexia, verbal alexia, alexia for sentences, and global alexia. In literal alexia the patient is unable to read letters despite a relative preservation of the ability to read words. These patients can usually read some letters some of the time. In fact, in one testing session a subject may be unable to read certain letters and in another testing session be able to read them, but unable to read others. Grammatical function words and nonsense words are more difficult for them to read than words with high semantic content. Visual paralexias, substitutions of words that resemble the correct word in form (e.g., "house" for "mouse"), and semantic paralexias, substitutions of words related in meaning (e.g., "flower" for "daffodil"), are both common. Word length does not seem to be a critical factor. One-step written commands may be carried out, but longer or more complex commands are only partially understood. Reading of numbers and musical notation is usually impaired. In this form, writing is not entirely normal; paragraphias (writing incorrect words or parts of words) are frequent; copying is virtually impossible; and disorders of color recognition are common. Right-visual-field defects are the rule, but exceptions may occur (in contrast to verbal alexias, where right-visual-field defects are almost always present). In this form of alexia without agraphia the subject is unable to read by spelling a word aloud, although some words may be captured globally.

In verbal alexia the subject is unable to read or grasp words globally, but the ability to read and identify letters is preserved. Thus, the subject can spell out the word and come to understand it. Neither the ability to read letters nor the inability to read words is complete. Word length is critical; the longer the word, the more difficult it is to read. Both nonsense words and meaningful words may be read by the spelling-out process. Reading of single digits and short multidigit numbers is preserved. Associated findings are common. Minor spelling mistakes may occur in spontaneous writing. Copying is moderately impaired, but, unlike literal alexia, transposition from block print to cursive writing is possible. Written calculations usually have errors. Oral spelling is intact. A mild anomia is usually present; especially common are problems with color naming. Right homonymous hemianopia is virtually constant.

Hécaen and his co-workers (1977) proposed a separate category which they call "alexia for sentences." The existence of this form of pure alexia has not yet been confirmed in other laboratories. This alexia is characterized mainly by a deficit in reading sentences and paragraphs. The ability to read letters and words is largely preserved, along with the ability to read single- and multidigit numbers. Recognition of nonsense syllables is poor. Paralexias occur in reading individual words due to an incorrect rendering of word endings. Individual words and their meanings may be grasped, but when presented as groups or strings, the words are not easily recognized. Errors increase as the length of a command or sentence becomes longer or as grammatical complexity increases. The nature of the errors implies an incorrect application of the proper syntactic rules for written language. Writing is more impaired in this form of alexia than in the others.

Global alexia refers to a total inability to read letters and words despite the relatively well-preserved ability to read single digits and multidigit numbers and to recognize letters by kinesthetic feedback (i.e., the examiner moves the patient's hand as if writing the letter in space). These subjects can "read" words by actively tracing the letters with their fingers. Writing is normal. Recognition of musical notes is impaired. Acalculia is present. Impaired recognition of objects, pictures, and especially colors is found. Right homonymous hemianopia is the rule.

Anatomical Evidence

The two major clinical syndromes of alexia (with and without agraphia) result from two different sets of underlying lesions. The anatomical evidence comes primarily from clinico-pathological correlations of alexic patients with some kind of cerebral lesion (usually stroke or tumor) and from neurosurgical procedures (e.g., surgical removal of occipital lobes, sections of corpus callosum, etc.) in patients with cerebral pathology (Figures 2, 3, 4).

The Anatomy of Alexia Without Agraphia: A Disconnection Syndrome

According to the disconnection hypothesis — where information from one hemisphere is "disconnected" from the other — two lesions are necessary for the production of pure alexia. One lesion is deep in the occipital lobe of the language-dominant hemisphere; the other is located in the posterior third (the splenium) of the corpus callosum. The lesion in the left occipital lobe — the visual area — prevents stimuli from entering the left hemisphere. Visual stimuli which enter the intact right hemisphere are prevented from reaching the left hemisphere because of destruction of the fibers which cross from the right visual region to the left visual region in the posterior third of the corpus callosum. The intact right visual area is thus disconnected from the intact angular gyrus of the left hemisphere, a necessary way station in the process of reading. Despite arguments which surface periodically against the disconnection hypothesis as an explanation for pure alexia, most researchers agree that some form of disconnection theory can satisfactorily explain most cases of pure alexia. (For the sake of simplicity, we have not introduced the excellent anatomical studies of Greenblatt, 1973, 1976;

Ajax, Schenkenberg, & Kosteljanetz, 1977; or Vincent, Sadowsky, Saunders, & Reeve, 1977, which discuss the anatomical complexities involved in greater detail. Summaries of these are available in Hécaen & Kremin, 1977, and Albert, 1979.)

The Anatomy of Alexia with Agraphia

Less controversy surrounds the anatomical basis of alexia with agraphia. In 1891 Dejerine discussed the anatomy of a syndrome of impaired ability to read and write with minimal disturbances in oral language. He found a cortico-subcortical lesion affecting the left angular gyrus. (See Figure 1.) Since then, most researchers agree that a dominant angular gyrus lesion is the anatomical correlate of this syndrome. In the subtype in which the alexic disturbances occur in relative isolation from aphasic disturbances, the lesion is usually in the dominant angular gyrus. In aphasic alexia the location of the lesion responsible for the syndrome is again the subject of debate. One theory holds that the lesion involves the left superior temporal region with or without involvement of the angular gyrus, a second that the lesion involves the dominant angular gyrus with extension into the superior temporal region.

Neuropsychological Studies

With alexia, as with all aspects of behavioral neurology and neuropsychology, the theoretical bias of the researcher may determine not only the methodology in a given study, but also the interpretation of its results. For the Gestalt theorist, the process of reading does not represent an independent behavioral function. Goldstein (1948) considered pure alexia to be a variety of visual agnosia. According to this theory, the ability to grasp the meaning and significance of simple or complex forms may deteriorate with brain damage; the clinical manifestation of this damage can be any of a variety of syndromes, including the inability to read. The critical feature to be understood is "abstract attitude." Expression of abstract attitude in the normal individual is the ability to discriminate figure from background, and the differentiation of abstract attitude into specific functional abilities. Brain damage causes a loss of abstract attitude, producing an inability to discriminate figures from their backgrounds and a "de-differentiation" of function. According to Gestalt theorists, reading problems are never completely pure but are always associated with other deficits in the "structuration" of forms, i.e., the ability to organize specific figures from a general background. Thus, a cerebral lesion can impair the ability to read by destroying the ability to structure the form (i.e., identify individual letters) or integrate the whole from its parts (i.e., put the letters together to make a word). Within such a paradigm, the notion of particular centers in the brain corresponding to specific higher cortical functions is to be discarded.

We would like to point out, however, that even the Gestaltists accepted both the clinical reality of different types of alexia and the fact that the alexias were more likely to occur with lesions in one hemisphere, and in certain locations within that hemisphere.

A different approach from that of the Gestaltists was presented by other authors, such as Alajouanine (1960) and Hécaen (1967). They base their conclusions on examinations of large groups of brain-damaged patients selected either because of reading difficulties or because of lesion localization. They systematically documented the clusters of clinical features commonly associated with these specific lesion localizations. They observed that reading and writing may function to some extent independently of spoken language, and that despite extensive overlap of anatomical systems for written and spoken language, some degree of anatomical independence may exist. They found that different types of reading disturbances resulted from temporal, parietal, and occipital lesions. With purely temporal lesions, frequency of reading impairment was greater than with parietal or occipital lesions, and the severity of the deficit was directly proportional to task complexity. With occipital lesions, reading of isolated words or short sentences was more impaired than reading of letters or paragraphs.

In a highly schematic and oversimplified manner we might refer to these two theoretical approaches to alexia as the global (or holistic) and the localizationist. A third approach is the associationist. We have already described the anatomical aspects of this approach. While not denying positive aspects of Gestalt theory or cortical localizationism, the disconnection theory emphasizes the critical role of fiber pathways connecting major functional zones of the cortex to provide integration of behavior.

Neuropsychological studies in the 1970s have attempted to dissect with more precision the cognitive deficit associated with alexic syndromes. The detailed case study by Denckla and Bowen (1973) of a thirty-year-old woman with a left occipito-temporal lobectomy is an example. In addition to residual deficits of right homonymous hemianopia, slow color naming, and verbal memory inpairment, the patient also had a variety of acquired alexia which resembled one form of developmental dyslexia. Her psychometric profile on the Wechsler Adult Intelligence Scale was identical to that reported as the most common pattern of children with one of the several syndromes of developmental dyslexia (as tested by the Wechsler Intelligence Scale for children).

In a study of two patients with literal alexia Shallice and Warrington (1977) found that the patients' reading impairment was not specific to letters but rather to stimuli in which more than one item of the same category was simultaneously present in the visual field. They suggested that one form of alexia may be a result of impaired selective attention.[1] Gardner and Zurif (1975) considered oral reading abilities of language-impaired patients and found that the grammatical category of a word and its picturability contribute to the readability of a word, and that words whose referents can be easily manipulated (operative nouns) proved easier to read than words whose referents were difficult to manipulate (figurative).

It is beyond the scope of this paper, which focuses primarily on neurological issues, to consider at length the psychological processing mechanisms disturbed in the various sub-syndromes of alexia. We wish to call the reader's attention, however, to recent experimental issues in the field, which deal with an information-processing analysis of phonemic (deep) dyslexia and semantic (surface) dyslexia (e.g., Marshall & Newcombe, 1973; Warrington & Shallice, 1979); "word-form dyslexia," "visual dyslexia," "central dyslexia," etc. (see *The INS Bulletin*, June 1979).

---

[1] In a subsequent study Warrington and Shallice (1979) briefly review contemporary issues in the neuropsychology of alexia, and discuss at some length the special problem of alexic subsystems, studied experimentally by Saffran and Marin (1977) and others.

Two studies of alexia emphasize *preserved* reading capacities, rather than defective reading. Albert, Yamadori, Gardner, and Howes (1973) described a patient who had alexia with agraphia and mild anomic aphasia, but who had a normal ability to spell words presented to him orally and to recognize words from their letters spelled aloud to him. The patient could neither read aloud nor carry out written commands. By a series of matching and forced choice tests, however, the authors were able to show that the patient could discriminate words on the basis of their meaning, i.e., word perception was intact and semantic understanding was preserved. Caplan and Hedley-Whyte (1974) found that a patient who had alexia without agraphia could respond to written stimuli when a variety of cues was used; they suggested that faulty visual exploration of a written word symbol might explain some alexias. These cases demonstrate the need for clinical neuroscientists to develop instruments that will systematically evaluate preserved capacities in brain-damaged patients and that will be as sensitive and sophisticated as those used for evaluating defects.

Perceptuomotor Problems

Throughout the history of studies on alexia, arguments have been made that one or another form of alexia may result from disorders of visual perception or disorders of oculomotor function or some combination of the two. Right-hemisphere lesions may be associated with reading disorders which form part of the syndrome of unilateral spatial agnosia; these may be called "spatial dyslexia." In such cases the reading difficulty seems to result from an impaired ability to scan the left side of space or from a reduced ability to attend to the left side of space. Since no disorders of oral language are present in these cases, it has been concluded that perceptual factors may contribute to the disorder. In some instances of spatial dyslexia the reading disorder was thought to have been caused by a difficulty in simultaneous visual-form perception or "simultanagnosia." In this condition a person can perceive individual elements of a complex visual array, but cannot integrate the elements sufficiently to grasp the significance of the whole.

In considering the possibility that visual space perception is a relevant variable in alexia, one should take into account those reports in which paralexias (i.e., misreadings) cluster at the ends of words. In many alexics with left-hemispheric lesions, paralexias cluster at the right end of the word. In some patients with spatial dyslexia and right hemispheric lesions, the defect is at the left end of the word. In an Israeli alexic, the impairment was most marked on the left (Sroka, Solsi, & Bornstein, 1973), and in a Japanese patient in the lower part of the word (Sasanuma, 1974, 1975).

Factors that influence normal reading abilities have also been found to influence reading ability in alexics. Howes (1962), for example, found in a patient with pure alexia that higher luminance and longer exposure time facilitated reading and that shorter words were in general easier to read than longer words. In their patient with verbal alexia without agraphia, Woods and Poppel (1974) noted the effects of exposure time and of print size on the recognition of words.

Studies of Japanese Alexics

The Japanese writing system uses ideograms (or logograms, i.e., symbols representing words) called Kanji (derived from Chinese characters) and two types of phonograms (i.e., phonetic symbols, each representing a syllable) called Kana (Kata-Kana and Hiragana). Those who study alexia have had a particular interest in Japanese alexics because of the possibility that cerebral lesions might produce selective impairments in the logographic or phonographic system. It is also of interest that Japanese children seem to have a much lower frequency of developmental reading disabilities than do children in the United States (Makita, 1968).

In a series of studies of Japanese aphasics and alexics, Sasanuma and her colleagues (1971, 1972, 1975) described the independent functioning of the Kana system (phonetic symbols used for syllable sized units) and Kanji system (nonphonetic, logographic, semantic). Their alexic patient had a syndrome of alexia without agraphia accompanied at first by recognition difficulty for pictures, colors, and spatial relations. Copying was impaired equally for Kana and Kanji, but otherwise writing was intact. Reading was severely impaired for words written in Kana, but much less so for words written in Kanji. A variety of tests showed reading performances differed for the two writing systems. Taking her studies together, Sasanuma concluded that selective impairment of Kana and Kanji "represents dysfunction at two different levels of linguistic behavior, i.e., semantic vs. phonologic processing respectively." She ascribed to each of these conditions a different anatomical locus of lesion. Other studies of Japanese alexics (e.g., Yamadori, 1975) support this position.

Western analogues of the Japanese data exist. Patients may be found who are alexic for most written material but who have a preserved capacity to read words which may be perceived as ideographic semantic symbols (e.g., *Coca-Cola, Motel, Bank*).

Studies of Japanese alexics and their Western analogues support the hypothesis of the possible existence of functionally independent visual and auditory-oral language systems. One mechanism underlying alexia may thus be a functional disconnection between these two systems which prevents the alexic from integrating a grapheme with its auditory counterpart.

Neurolinguistic Studies

Systematic attempts to evaluate breakdowns of the reading process in terms of models of normal language and to relate these breakdowns to a neurological substratum have been increasing since the early 1960s. Dubois-Charlier (1972) identified three pairs of contrasting models: in one, written language derived from spoken language is contrasted with written language independent of spoken language (this is seen clinically as aphasic alexia vs. pure alexia); in a second pair, a word formed from a combination of letters is contrasted with the word as an ideogram or semantic unit (this is seen clinically as literal and verbal alexias representing different degrees of severity of the same basic deficit vs. literal and verbal alexia representing different, independent syndromes); in the third pair, reading disorders representing breakdowns in symbolic language function are contrasted with reading disorders resulting from nonlanguage factors (e.g., perceptuomotor problems).

In a series of studies Marshall and Newcombe (1966, 1973) described syntactic and semantic patterns of paralexia in language-impaired patients. Presenting neurological, psychological, and linguistic details, they proposed three types of impairment. "Visual dyslexia" was characterized by paralexias caused by confusions of graphically similar words or letters. The general pattern of visual dyslexia showed striking similarities to patterns of errors seen in normal readers. "Surface dyslexia" described patients whose paralexias were caused by breakdowns in the application of grapheme-phoneme conversion rules. "Deep dyslexia" or "syntactico-semantic dyslexia" was used to describe an instability of the "central language component." The authors used these behavioral patterns of impairment to make tentative steps toward the proposal of a model for word recognition and retrieval.

Shallice and Warrington (1975), using the general approach of Marshall and Newcombe, studied word recognition performance in a patient with "phonemic dyslexia." Reading performance was related to parts of speech, word frequency, and word concreteness; and reading errors were analyzed. The authors concluded that the findings were consistent with a dual encoding model of word recognition. Their patient illustrated that a phonemic route may be impaired, while a direct graphemic-semantic route may be relatively spared.

Hécaen and his collaborators have been studying linguistic aspects of alexia for many years. In 1967, Hécaen summarized his findings and suggested the existence of three clinical types of alexia: pure alexia, caused by an occipital lesion; alexia with agraphia without aphasia, caused by a posterior parietal lesion; and alexia as part of sensory aphasia, caused by a temporal lesion. He distinguished three subtypes of the pure alexias on the basis of the reading disorder and the type of paralexic error: verbal, literal, and global alexia.

Working from Hécaen's classification, Dubois-Charlier (1971, 1972) studied the linguistic performances of alexic patients with a new battery of tests. This battery incorporated tests of naming, discrimination, and comprehension of items at the graphemic, semantic, and syntactic levels. She confirmed the existence of the clinical syndromes described by Hécaen and added a new variety—sentence alexia. On the basis of her analysis she concluded that alexias can result from defective functioning at three different linguistic levels: defects at the graphemic level can produce literal alexia; at the morphologic level, verbal alexia; and at the syntactic level, sentence alexia.

In a broad sense, one might conclude that all neurolinguistic studies support the notion that the alexias can be categorized according to linguistic characteristics into several distinctive syndromes, and that these syndromes, each reflecting a disruption of the reading process at a different linguistic level, are caused by different sets of physiological mechansims.

Treatment and Prognosis

In their review of the alexias, Benson and Geschwind (1969) were pessimistic about treatment and prognosis: "In summary the therapy of alexia must be individualized, demands arduous labor on the part of both the patient and the therapist plus considerable ingenuity on the part of the therapist; and in many cases an end result far below normal levels must be accepted" (1969, p. 436). Little has changed since then. Nevertheless, the contemporary work of behavioral neurologists and neuropsychologists has provided insights into areas where therapeutic ingenuity might be directed.

Alexia is not a single deficit in reading comprehension. There are several alexias, each with its own clinical features and physiological basis. The approach to therapy should take into account qualitative neuropsychological and neurolinguistic differences. If phonemic alexia may be distinguished from semantic alexia, for example, attempts should be made to apply to therapy our knowledge of this fact. The study by Saffran, Schwartz, and Marin (1976) suggests that such attempts are being made; they explored the effects of semantic constraints on the occurrence of paralexic responses in two patients who produced semantic errors when reading aloud. They controlled the patient's tendency to make semantic paralexic errors by limiting the associations evoked by the stimulus word.

A variety of cuing, deblocking, or facilitating devices or techniques have been introduced to aid the alexic. Many authors are studying the usefulness of kinesthetic techniques. Kreindler and Ionasescu (1961) successfully used auditory and visual "unblocking" methods to allow a patient who had apparent pure word blindness to use his preserved reading ability. Stachowiak and Poeck (1976) elaborated this technique in a patient with pure alexia. Using unblocking methods in the tactile, somesthetic, auditory, and visual modalities, they demonstrated preserved reading ability that had previously been hidden. They argued that in the unblocking situation other pathways than the one impaired by the brain lesion are used. With the aid of information other than visually presented graphemes, their patient's visual reading was improved.

In attempting to evaluate new therapy modalities in alexia, we are confronted with the question: what is the natural history of alexia? Geschwind (1965) and Hécaen and Kremin (1977) discuss cases of occipital alexia in which the reading disorder almost completely disappeared even after occipital lobectomy. Others (e.g., Ajax, 1967) describe occipital alexias which cleared minimally, although the major difficulties could be circumvented by extensive retraining. In an interesting and valuable approach to this problem, Newcombe and Marshall (1973) analyzed the stages in recovery from alexia in a patient with a left occipital abscess. They sought to determine if a "lawful" description of stages in recovery could be described. A pattern of recovery did, in fact, emerge during the three-month period of evaluation. They found a parallel between language reacquisition and the initial stages of language acquisition. From this it would appear that further longitudinal studies might clarify the nature of spontaneous recovery patterns in alexia and indicate directions for development of rational therapy programs.

Conclusion

As we indicated at the beginning of this paper, knowledge of the neuroanatomical basis of acquired disorders of reading does not automatically provide insights into the biological nature of developmental dyslexia. Indeed, the search for parallels in the neurology of developmental and acquired reading disorders may even impede a creative experimental approach to the nature of developmental dyslexia. Nevertheless, questions about adult alexia, based on a partial understanding of its neurological basis, may fruitfully be applied to the child with a developmental disorder of reading. Is alexia a disorder of comprehension? of output? or both? What does it mean to be able to read semantically, but not to read phonologically? Is alexia truly a focal disorder of language, or is the problem one of impaired selective attention interacting with certain linguistic skills? Are contributions made by subcortical memory or arousal mechanisms? What is the role played by the right hemisphere in reading? Most important, how can we combine our knowledge of what is *not* lost in the alexic patient with our expectations of what the healthy portions of the brain ought to be able to do, in order to devise a means of helping the patient overcome a reading deficit?

References

Ajax, E. T. Dyslexia without agraphia. *Archives of Neurology*, 1967, **17**, 645-652.

Ajax, E. T., Schenkenberg, T., & Kosteljanetz, M. Alexia without agraphia and the inferior splenium. *Neurology*, 1977, **27**, 685-688.

Alajouanine, T., Lhermitte, F., & Ribancourt-Ducarne, B. Les alexies agnosiques et aphasiques. In T. Alajouanine (Ed.), *Les grandes activities du lobe occipital.* Paris: Masson, 1960.

Albert, M. L. Alexia. In K. Heilman & E. Valenstein (Eds.), *Clinical neuropsychology.* London: Oxford University Press, 1979.

Albert, M. L., Yamadori, A., Gardner, H., & Howes, D. Comprehension in alexia. *Brain*, 1973, **96**, 317-328.

Benson, D. F., & Geschwind, N. The alexias. In P. J. Vinken & G. W. Bruyn (Eds.), *Handbook of clinical neurology: Disorders of speech, perception, and symbolic behavior.* New York: American Elsevier, 1969.

Caplan, L., & Hedley-Whyte, T. Cuing and memory dysfunction in alexia without agraphia: A case report. *Brain*, 1974, **97**, 251-262.

Dejerine, J. Sur un cas de cécité verbal avec agraphie suivi d'autopsie. *Memoires de la Société de Biologie*, 1891, **3**, 197-201.

Dejerine, J. Contribution a l'etude anatomo-pathologique et clinique des differentes varietiés de cécité verbale. *Memoires de la Société de Biologie*, 1892, **4**, 61-90.

Denckla, M., & Bowen, F. Dyslexia after left occipito-temporal lobectomy: A case report. *Cortex*, 1973, **9**, 321-328.

Drake, W. Clinical and pathological findings in a child with developmental learning disability. *Journal of Learning Disabilities*, 1968, **1**, 9-25.

Dubois-Charlier, F. Approche neurolinguistique du problème de l'alexie pure. *Journal de Psychologie Normale et Pathologique*, 1971, **68**, 39-67.

Dubois-Charlier, F. A propos de l'alexie pure. *Langages*, 1972, **25**, 76-94.

Galaburda, A., & Kemper, T. Cytoarchitectonic abnormalities in developmental dyslexia: A case study. *Annals of Neurology*, in press.

Gardner, J., & Zurif, E. Bee but not be: Oral reading of single words in aphasia and alexia. *Neuropsychologia*, 1975, **13**, 181-190.

Geschwind, N. Disconnexion syndromes in animals and man. *Brain*, 1965, **88**, 237-294, 585-644.

Geschwind, N. The organization of language and the brain. *Science*, 1970, **170**, 940-944.

Goldstein, J. *Language and language disturbances.* New York: Grune & Stratton, 1948.

Greenblatt, S. Alexia without agraphia or hemianopia. Anatomical analysis of an autopsied case. *Brain*, 1973, **96**, 307-316.

Greenblatt, S. Subangular alexia without agraphia or hemianopsia. *Brain and Language*, 1976, **3**, 229-245.

Haslerud, G. H., & Clark, R. E. On the reintegrative perception of words. *American Journal of Psychology*, 1957, **70**, 97-101.

Hécaen, H. Aspects des troubles de la lecture (alexie) au cours des lésions cérébrales en foyer. In Homage à Andre Martner. *Word*, 1967, **23**, 265-287.

Hécaen, H., & Kremin, J. Reading disorders resulting from left hemispheric lesions: Aphasic and "pure" alexias. In H. Whitaker and M. Whitaker (Eds.), *Studies in neurolinguistics*, Vol. 2. New York Academic Press, 1977.

Howes, D. An approach to the quantitative analysis of word blindness. In John Money (Ed.), *Reading disability.* Baltimore: Johns Hopkins Press, 1962.

Kreindler, A., & Ionasescu, V. A case of "pure" word blindness. *Journal of Neurology and Neurosurgical Psychiatry*, 1961, **24**, 275-280.

Makita, J. Rarity of reading disability in Japanese children. *American Journal of Orthopsychiatry*, 1968, **38**, 599-614.

Marshall, J. C., & Newcombe, F. Patterns of paralexia: A psycholinguistic approach. *Journal of Psycholinguistic Research*, 1973, **2**, 175-199.

Newcombe, F., & Marshall, J. C. Stages in recovery from dyslexia following a left cerebral abscess. *Cortex*, 1973, **9**, 329-337.

Saffran, E., & Marin, O. Reading without phonology: Evidence from aphasia. *Quarterly Journal of Experimental Psychology*, 1977, **29**, 515-525.

Saffran, E., Schwartz, M. F., & Marin, O. Semantic mechanisms in paralexia. *Cortex*, 1976, **3**, 255-265.

Sasanuma, S. Kanji versus Kana processing in alexia with transient agraphia: A case report. *Cortex*, 1974, **10**, 88-97.

Sasanuma, S. Kana and Kanji processing in Japanese aphasics. *Brain and Language*, 1975, **2**, 369-383.

Sasanuma, S., & Fujimura, O. An analysis of writing errors in Japanese aphasic patients: Kanji vs. Kana words. *Cortex*, 1972, **8**, 265-282.

Sasanuma, S., & Fujimura, O. Selective impairment of phonetic and non-phonetic transcription of words in Japanese aphasic patients: Kana vs. Kanji in visual recognition and writing. *Cortex*, 1972, **8**, 265-282.

Sasanuma, S., & Monoi, H. The syndrome of Gogi (word-meaning) aphasia: Selective impairment of Kanji processing. *Neurology*, 1975, **25**, 627-632.

Shallice, T., & Warrington, E. K. The possible role of selective attention in acquired dyslexia. *Neuropsychologia*, 1977, **15**, 31-42.

Shallice, T., & Warrington, E. K. Word recognition in a phonemic dyslexic patient. *Quarterly Journal of Experimental Psychology*, 1975, **27**, 187-199.

Sroka, H., Solsi, P., & Bornstein, B. Alexia without agraphia with complete recovery. *Confinia Neurologica*, 1973, **35**, 167-176.

Stachowiak, F. J., & Poeck, K. Functional disconnection in pure alexia and color naming deficit demonstrated by facilitation methods. *Brain and Language*, 1976, **3**, 135-143.

Valerius, Maximus. In A. Benton & R. Joynt, Early descriptions of aphasia. *Arhives of Neurology*, 1960, **3**, 205-222.

Vincent, F. J., Sadowsky, C. H., Saunders, R. I., & Reeve, A. G. Alexia without agraphia, hemianopia, or color-naming defect: A disconnection syndrome. *Neurology*, 1977, **27**, 689-691.

Warrington, E., & Shallice, T. Semantic access dyslexia. *Brain*, 1979, **102**, 43-64.

Woods, B. T., & Poppel, E. Effect of print size on reading time in a patient with verbal alexia. *Neuropsychologia*, 1974, **12**, 31-41.

Yamadori, A. Ideogram reading in alexia. *Brain*, 1975, **98**, 231-238.

PART III

Selected Book Reviews

How To Do Things with Words: The William James Lectures, 1955
by John L. Austin. Edited by J. O. Urmson.
Cambridge, Mass.: Harvard University Press, 1962.

The philosophical point of view underlying these lectures on language is pungently suggested by the following observations on philosophy and language made by the late John Austin in the course of an attack on certain contemporary theories of knowledge and perception:

> My general opinion about this doctrine is that it is a typically *scholastic* view, attributable, first, to an obsession with a few particular words, the uses of which are oversimplified, not really understood or carefully studied or correctly described; and second, to an obsession with a few (and nearly always the same) half-studied 'facts'. (I say 'scholastic', but I might just as well have said 'philosophical'; over-simplification, schematization, and constant obsessive repetition of the same small range of jejune 'examples' are not peculiar to this case, but far too common to be dismissed as an occasional weakness of philosophers.) The fact is, as I shall try to make clear, that our ordinary words are much subtler in their uses, and mark many more distinctions, than philosophers have realized. . . It is essential, here as elsewhere, to abandon old habits of *Gleichshaltung*, the deeply ingrained worship of tidy dichotomies.[1]

While it may seem perverse to begin a review of one book with an extended quotation from another, especially when that other book is not (overtly) concerned with the topic of the first book—a general analysis of how we do things with words, the passage does give

us an excellent indication of some of Austin's philosophical motives for undertaking a detailed study of language use as the performance of verbal acts. Austin is interested in looking at the 'facts' of language, and not just a few already overworked ones.

Why this ethologist's approach to language? For one thing, Austin is convinced that lack of proper attention paid to *distinctions in use* which are embedded in ordinary language leads us into philosophical difficulties of our own making. The assumption behind this, which Austin shares with a great many contemporaries, is that such distinctions not only must be accounted for by philosophers (*and* by linguists and psychologists) but also must constitute the point at which any systematic inquiry into the workings of language should begin (p. 122).

Let us follow the ethologist analogy one step further and say that Austin has noticed what he considers to be a *significant* fact about the behavior of words in their natural habitat (the everyday speech of the "plain man" engaged in the *practical* business of life) and that these lectures are an attempt to see whether a general characterization of how language works can be developed out of an examination of the distinction marked (apparently) by this fact.

Two things concerning Austin's strategy should be noted before we follow him on his peregrinations among the uses. First, appeals to the 'facts' of ordinary language have hitherto been made by philosophers whose concern it is to investigate the "logical geography" of individual words and expressions or clusters of them which figure impor-

[1] *Sense and Sensibilia*, ed. G. J. Warnock (New York: Oxford Univ. Press, 1962).

tantly in what have been considered to be fairly well-defined philosophical problems. Austin's approach to ordinary language analysis is certainly within this frame of reference (especially his attention to the *uses* rather than to any formal properties of language as such). However, although he has done his share of direct polemical battle with 'misleading' philosophical positions within the framework of traditional issues,[2] he has done so by shifting the focus of these issues away from the concept in question (as being encrusted with too many 'philosophical' attempts at it) and onto a variety of words and their uses which, when examined in terms of their relations, one to another, enable us to get through to what the real issue is.[3] Thus Austin, like Wittgenstein, is concerned with the reformulation of philosophical problems and the shift of focus which enables clear vision. His ingenuity at doing this is well-known,[4] and it is a major principle of his strategy in these lectures.

The second thing we want to note is that Austin's philosophical convictions lead him to the doing of what some philosophers say is 'grammar' rather than philosophy. Austin accepts the charge, and justifies his strategy on the following interesting grounds: that his doing of 'grammar' is simply "sorting out a bit the way things have already begun to go and are going with increasing momentum in some parts of philos-

ophy," (p. 163) and that perhaps there will prove to be no ultimate boundary between the 'logical grammar' of words and expressions (the concern of many contemporary philosophers) and "a revised and expanded *Grammar*."[5] Thus Austin's shift of focus suggested above may be thought of as a logical extension of the 'linguistic revolution' in philosophy, and as a shift from an analysis of the philosophical implications of the uses of language to a methodologically prior task which I shall call the working out of a 'grammar of use'; that is, an attempt to develop categories which will accord with our intuitions about what we are doing when we use words.

Austin's strategy is, then, not only a philosophical strategy in the sense suggested, but an approach to the *empirical* study of language. As such, it needs to be evaluated not only for its philosophical fruitfulness, but also as to whether it is an effective or even plausible step toward the construction of a systematic theory, or what Austin once called a "true and comprehensive *science of language*."[6]

The 'fact' of language which Austin invites us to consider in the William James Lectures is that there appears to be a class of sentences in English which, although they have the (traditional) grammatical form of statements, are not (usually) either intended as or *count* as statements, but are (usually) intended as and count as the performance of a *conventional* act if they are uttered under *appropriate* conditions. Austin calls such sentences, "performative utterances," and spends the greater part of the lectures investigating the possibility of marking a systematic distinction between such utterances and 'genuine' statements (which he calls "constative utterances") by laying out what

[2] See especially his articles on "Truth," "Other Minds" and "The Meaning of a Word" reprinted in *Philosophical Papers*, ed. J. O. Urmson and G. J. Warnock (New York: Oxford Univ. Press, 1961)

[3] The articles entitled "Ifs and Cans" and "A Plea for Excuses" also in *Philosophical Papers*.

[4] Austin's strategy has been criticized as being beside the philosophical point. See, for example, the article-reviews by A. Ambrose, M. Lazerowitz and W. F. R. Hardie in *Philosophy*, July 1963.

[5] "Ifs and Cans", *op. cit.*, p. 180.

[6] *Ibid.*

appear to be unique features of performatives and seeing whether these features apply to all and only those utterances which we intuitively regard as the performance of kinds of certain acts and which are not regarded as (primarily) statements of fact.

The primary distinction, for Austin, lies in the fact that, unlike statements which are used to make truth claims and can be verified as true or false,[7] performatives do not make truth claims but are judged rather as either 'happy' or 'unhappy,' i.e. either they come off or they do not. For example, consider the case (which appears to be the paradigm on which the distinction is constructed) of sentences beginning with the expression, "I promise." As Austin noted in an earlier article, "If I say 'I promise', I don't say I *say* I promise, I *promise*."[8] Obviously, in saying "I promise. . . .", I am not reporting, describing, or saying anything which can be judged as either true or false. The first job, then, for Austin, is to formulate the conditions which performatives like "I promise" must meet in order to be considered 'happy,' and to determine the ways in which performatives may be 'unhappy.' It should be noted that the distinction proposed is essentially a distinction between ways of *appraising* utterances and between the sorts of criteria we use for such appraisal.

The conditions which performatives must meet are of two types. The first may be called "conventional" conditions which must be met if the utterance is to be considered as part of some *act* it is intended to accomplish. Principal among these is the condition that "There must exist an accepted conven-

tional procedure having a certain conventional effect . . ." (p. 14). This attempts to define the class of performatives as appraisable according to certain specifiable rules of procedure and suggests that the uttering of performatives is a sort of ceremonial act. The second type might be called "sincerity" conditions. Failure to meet these does not *void* the act, but counts as an 'abuse' of the conventions if, for example, the proper thoughts, feelings, and intentions are not present. If, on the other hand, the "conventional" conditions are not met, the act is said to have 'misfired.'

Austin's strategy for distinguishing performatives now takes the form of piecing out the ways in which a purported act including a certain utterance can go wrong. This he calls the doctrine of 'Infelicities,' which constitutes the set of categories in terms of which our intuitions about the performative-constative distinction may be explicated. But now things (which have not been entirely unanticipated) begin to go awry; for it becomes clear that in order for a purported act involving a performative to be designated as 'happy,' *certain statements about the act have to be true,* i.e., statements the truth of which, suggests Austin, is *implied, presupposed,* or *entailed* in some interesting ways. For example, "I promise. . . ." implies "I am promising," presupposes "certain conditions obtain," and entails "I ought. . . ."

Austin here makes ingenious interpretations of these notions usually applied to relations among statements to show not only that performatives are "infected" with questions of truth and falsity, but also that statements may be appraised as either 'happy' or 'unhappy.' For example, "The cat is on the mat" *contextually* implies "I believe the cat is on the mat." If this is not the case (i.e., the implication fails) then it is a case of "insincerity." If there is no mat

[7] Austin seems to accept some verifiability criterion as at least necessary for distinguishing statements from other types of utterance, p. 2.

[8] "Other Minds", in *Philosophical Papers*, op. cit., p. 67.

for the cat to be on, then reference fails, a necessary condition for the statement to *count* as either true or false is not met, and the statement is considered to be *void* in just the same way performatives are. The entailment relation is more complex, but it can be seen that there is a strong 'parallel' between "x is red entails x is colored" and " 'I promise . . .'' entails 'I ought . . .'."

The "appraisal" distinction does not seem to work, since the ways in which we judge performatives and constatives overlap in some crucial ways; and this overlap appears to do great damage to any *functional* distinction between classes of utterance as such. Austin now shifts his focus and attempts to discover a grammatical criterion for the distinction. But this fails as well. If, for example, we note that clear cases of performatives like "I promise . . ." are uttered in the first person, singular, present indicative, we also discover that other clear cases like "You are offside" are not. Moreover, it is impossible to tell, simply by looking at the utterance, whether utterances like "The bull is on the rampage" are to be regarded as performatives or constatives. Austin tries to skirt this problem by suggesting that the act (if it is one) which is being performed when certain utterances are issued can be made *explicit* by appending a 'performative verb' and thereby transforming an implicit or 'primary' performative into an 'explicit' performation, e.g., "I warn you, the bull is on the rampage.[9] But this fails also, since the grammatical criterion admits expressions like "I feel," (which is a re-

[9] Explicit performatives, Austin suggests, are a development in the language from primary performatives. The view that language becomes more explicit in the sense that it enables us to make clear what our verbal acts are is an interesting suggestion.

port and not an act or part of one[10]) and, for that matter, "I state," the telltale mark, for Austin, of the constative.

It becomes apparent that the failure of both the appraisal and the grammatical criteria is due to: 1) an oversimplified notion of what it is to judge a statement as either true or false, 2) an assimilation of statement-making to the *act of saying* something *simpliciter*. (But, clearly, when we say something, we may be doing any one of a number of things besides just saying; we may be *stating* or promising, both of which are performances. As Austin suggests, "When we issue any utterance whatever, are we not 'doing something'?" (p. 91)); 3) in general, a mistaken concentration on utterances as such, when what we really need to do is to concentrate on "the total speech act in the total speech situation," (p. 147) and to consider "the senses in which to say something is to do something" (p. 120).

This time, Austin makes a major shift in focus from the examination of utterances to an examination of *acts;* however, it should be noticed that, while the unit of investigation appears to change, we are back to what is essentially an attempt at a functional distinction—this time among acts. We now are asked to consider saying something as the performance of three sorts of act: 1) saying as a 'locutionary' act—the issuing of an utterance which has meaning (that is, has sense and reference); 2) saying as an 'illocutionary' act—the doing of something *in* the saying of certain words having a certain meaning; and 3) saying as a 'perlocutionary' act —the doing of something *by* the saying of certain words having a certain meaning.

[10] This assumes that reports of feelings are appraisable as either true or false; a matter on which philosophers disagree violently.

Here we have two major distinctions. The first, between performing a locutionary act on the one hand and performing an illocutionary or a perlocutionary act on the other. But, it might be asked whether we *ever* perform a locutionary act *per se* without, at the same time, doing something which has a certain 'force' over and above what we understand the words in any sentence to mean? The second distinction, which is more important to Austin, is that between illocutionary and perlocutionary acts. An illocutionary act has a 'force' or *conventional* significance (in the sense outlined by Austin in his discussion of performatives), while the perlocutionary act is *"the achieving of* certain *effects* by saying something."[11] Compare 'In saying I would shoot him I was threatening him,' and 'By saying I would shoot him I alarmed him.' (p. 121).

Austin suggests further that there are ways by which a judge "should be able to decide, by hearing what was said, what locutionary and illocutionary acts were performed, but not what perlocutionary acts were achieved" (p. 121).[12] This seems an excellent test, for it is true that, generally, if we can understand what a person is saying in a given situation, we can judge what sort of thing he is doing (warning, pleading, asserting, etc.) but we cannot (usually) tell what he has, *in fact*, achieved by doing what he is doing. However, formulating systematically the characteristics of illocutionary acts which we might use to distinguish them from perlocutionary or other types of doings which do not clearly fit any of these categories, requires that we again attempt to discover *grammatical* criteria for the dis-

[11] Ibid. The emphasis is Austin's.

[12] Austin's reliance on legal and other "rule-governed" situations is consistent throughout and is an important feature of his general approach.

tinction. Austin's suggestion that a list of explicit performative verbs (promise, bet, warn, etc.) might, when used, indicate an illocutionary act, runs into very much the same trouble as it had earlier in isolating the performative. Also, the formula, "In saying x, I was doing y," as a grammatical normal form for illocutionary acts, lets in acts which do not fit the intuitive characterization of illocutionary acts as *conventional*. E.g., "In saying 'Iced uck' I was uttering the noises 'I stuck.'" (p. 123)

Austin is forced to conclude that a systematic distinction among acts will not work, and that, perhaps, every 'speech act' (that is, every utterance which we regard as a saying of something) should be examined, *piecemeal*, in terms of the type of situation in which it might occur. Further, and this is the heart of the whole investigation, it is suggested that every utterance (in the above sense) has an *illocutionary force* and therefore may be appraised as either happy or unhappy. Also important is Austin's suggestion that the notion of 'truth' be interpreted as the satisfaction of certain conditions by an utterance in certain circumstances. On this view, all genuine utterances have a truth/falsehood dimension as well as a happiness/unhappiness dimension, and a 'factual' aspect as well as an 'evaluative.' What remains is to classify and examine what turn out to be explicit performative verbs (which Austin now views as the names of illocutionary forces of utterances) in terms of the various dimensions Austin has outlined.

Where has the original proposed distinction gone? It has, in effect, disappeared as a viable linguistic distinction, and has been replaced by a collection of "more general *families* of related and overlapping speech acts" (p. 149), classified according to the types of illocutionary force any given speech act may have according to the types of situation in which it is performed. Once more, and tirelessly, Austin attempts to "divide Gaul." He appears to be moving in just the direction we might predict: toward a finer intuitive perception of complexities and away from any of the simplification of phenomena which is a characteristic of systematic theory.

How shall we assess Austin's labors? Clearly they have uncovered for us some interesting facts about how we do things with words. But for the purpose of understanding the way language works, are they significant facts? It is difficult to believe that Austin's program for the piecemeal analysis of utterances will result in even a set of low-level generalizations about language on which a theory might be developed. Nevertheless, this book is of great value; not only because it exhibits the degree of complexity ordinary language possesses, but also because it demonstrates, I think, the failure of an extended attempt to employ our analytic intuitions about the uses of words and expressions to arrive at any general features of language which these words and expressions might mark. There *is* a sense in which it is of course true that ordinary language embodies a great many philosophically interesting *and* theoretically fruitful distinctions. But it is also true that these distinctions which we make when we use words in certain ways will not be fully accounted for nor explicated without an articulated theory. Austin, it might be said, did not shift the focus quite enough. Given his philosophical commitments, it is doubtful that he could have.

JACK REITZES
Brandeis University

THOUGHT AND LANGUAGE.
by Lev Semenovich Vygotsky; edited and translated by Eugenia Hanfmann and Gertrude Vakar.
Published jointly by MIT Press and John Wiley, 1962.
[With (separately published) *Comments* by Jean Piaget. 14 pp.]

The name of Vygotsky, a Russian psychologist who lived from 1896 to 1934, has been known in the English-speaking world in two ways: first as the author of two singularly perceptive articles, one on language and thought in children, and one on schizophrenic language, which had been translated and published in American medical periodicals, and second, as the originator of the "Vygotsky test," a high-level concept formation test adapted for clinical use in 1937 by Hanfmann and Kasanin. It was known, however, that Vygotsky had left much more to posterity than only these things—the pity was that his writings were in Russian. His major work, *Myshlenie i rech'* (*Thought and Language*) was not published until a few months after his death. We are told that this work was not very well organized; even though Vygotsky had attempted to combine several previously written essays into a coherent whole, it was written in haste and in an involved style, contained much unnecessary polemical discussion, and was unsystematic in its use of references.

The present translation remedies all these defects. What we have is a book written in admirable English, every page of which presents something meaty and striking—whether it be a theoretical discussion, a critique of another's position, or a report of experimental findings. The seven chapters, even though recognizably originating from separate essays, can be read in a continuous sequence, indeed must be read in that way. For this transformation (it is much more than a translation), we have to thank Eugenia Hanfmann and Gertrude Vakar, the former a well-known psychologist of Russian birth who has resided in the U. S. since 1930, and the latter a professional translator.

Why, after twenty-eight years, bring out a translation of a work originally published in 1934? For one thing, a work of the character of Vygotsky's does not become obsolete in twenty-eight years, and perhaps not even in eighty-eight. The Soviet Union saw fit to republish Vygotsky's work in 1956, after long years of suppression or neglect, and Vygotsky's thinking is today a major influence in Soviet psychology. But further, it can be said that Vygotsky's approach to problems of language and thought was far ahead of his time even at the first posthumous publication both in the Soviet Union and in other parts of the Western world. In the United States, psychology was still mightily under the domination of stimulus-response theories (Vygotsky would have called them reflexological), and even the Gestaltist and Freudian positions did not readily admit the kind of cognitive theory espoused by Vygotsky. Only in the last decade has Western psychology turned its attention squarely in the direction of problems of thought and knowing; only in the last five years has the establishment of an organization with a title like the Center for Cognitive Studies not seemed slightly quixotic. The appearance of the Hanfmann-Vakar redaction, therefore, is timely. The book is a challenge to solve

what Vygotsky calls the "focal issue of human psychology" (p. xxi)—the interrelation of thought and language.

Not all of Vygotsky's thought is still novel, of course, for it is not as though nothing had been accomplished in the psychology of thought and language in the intervening years. We hardly need to be supplied with the further "experimental evidence that word meanings undergo evolution during childhood" (p. xx) that Vygotsky offers as one of his major contributions. For whether we mean by "word meaning" the institutionalized correspondence between a symbol and some class of referents, or the "mediational process" that is said by some psychologists to occur in the individual in response to a word, we know rather clearly, at least in principle, the conditions under which word meanings change. In point of fact, Vygotsky does not report in any detail his experimental evidence to the effect that word meanings change. One of the keenly disappointing things about the book is that it offers little information concerning the experiments that Vygotsky and his students did to support their conclusions. The style of writing in Russian psychology, then as now, shows little of the kind of concern with the exact particulars of methodology on which American behavioral science lays so much stress. We must be content, therefore, with the often striking and provocative formulations of Vygotsky, many of which are essentially hypotheses awaiting experimental check.

If I were asked to epitomize Vygotsky's point of view, I think I could hardly do better than to quote the final sentence in the book: "A word is a microcosm of human consciousness." (p. 153) Early in the book, the author had been at pains to indicate that his "unit of analysis" was the *word*—the total constellation embracing both the sound and the meaning. He avoided any breaking down of the word into "elements" such as sounds and aspects of meaning. The meaning of a word or expression, in his view, is not to be equated to a referent or thing to which it refers, because the same referent can be symbolized with different expressions like "the victor at Jena" or "the loser at Waterloo." "There is but one category of words," he writes, "—proper names—whose sole function is that of reference." (p. 73) A major part of his exposition is devoted to an explication of *meaning*; the treatment is almost philosophical in manner. Word meaning is the "internal aspect of the word" (p. 5), and in word meaning, thought and speech unite to form a "verbal thought." The basic problem of language and thought is to describe how thought and speech interact in the verbal thought unit, and to study how these units develop and function.

Thought and speech are viewed by Vygotsky as independent processes, each with its own life and growth. We may accept Vygotsky's demonstration (Chapter IV) that there can be pre-linguistic thought activity (both in animals and in children) and also pre-intellectual speech activity (in children). Thought and speech nevertheless interact; at times, one is ahead of the other in development, while at other times, the positions are reversed. But "at a certain point these lines meet, whereupon thought becomes verbal and speech rational." (p. 44) This statement is not to be taken quite literally, however, for "fusion of thought and speech, in adults as well as in children, is a phenomenon limited to a circumscribed area." (p. 48) It must exclude cases like reciting a poem without thinking of its meaning or speaking "lyrically" under the influence of emotion.

The formal analysis of Vygotsky's exposition runs into a certain difficulty when we try to distinguish between word meaning as a "unit of verbal thought," and the *concept*. Although there are places (e.g., p. 5) where word meaning is spoken of as a "generalization," or where the term *concept* is used in connection with words (p. 7: "children often have difficulty in learning a new word not because of its sound but because of the concept to which the word refers," and p. 120, "The meaning of every word is a generalization or a concept"), the treatment of the term *concept* is carried out independently of the treatment of word meaning. Indeed, whereas Vygotsky supplies numerous definitional statements for the term *meaning*, he gives no formal definition of the term *concept*. We are thus left to infer the meaning of the term from Vygotsky's treatment of it. Such inferences as I have been able to draw are not wholly satisfactory, and thus the somewhat informal organization of Vygotsky's writing becomes at times lamentable. It is more to be regretted because some of the most interesting and provocative materials in this book are those having to do with the development of concepts.

Concept seems to be a developmental term for Vygotsky. In the studies of concept formation carried out by his colleague Sakharov (whose name perhaps ought to be attached to the famous "Vygotsky" block test), "true" concepts were not formed until the period of adolescence—"seldom at first, then with increasing frequency." (p. 79) Earlier, the responses showed primitive syncretic forms of thinking, then "thinking in complexes," followed by the use of "potential" concepts before the "true" concept was attained. To be sure, the Sakharov block test uses "artificial" rather than "real" concepts; that is to say, it uses concepts based on contrived combinations of attributes like "small and tall" or "big and thin." But the same developmental phenomena are said to occur for "real" concepts such as those found in the teaching of "science" (actually, *social* science; Vygotsky's experiments often dealt with whether children could understand concepts like "exploitation").

Vygotsky borrows Piaget's contrast between "spontaneous" and "non-spontaneous" or "scientific" concepts—the former being the concepts formed naturally by the child on the basis of everyday experience, the latter being the concepts which the child is likely to acquire on the basis of specific, directed instruction. Thus, the child may acquire for himself concepts like those represented by the words "brother" and "flower," but he is unlikely to acquire concepts like "Planned economy is possible in the U.S.S.R. because there is no private property . . ." without specific instruction. For Vygotsky, a "concept" is something essentially in the realm of thought, not words: apprehending a concept is apprehending a thought "behind" the word, and not at all identical with it. In this particular example, what he is concerned with is whether the child apprehends the relation indicated by the conjunction "because." He reports that children are often better able to complete sentences ending in *because* when the setting is "scientific" (i.e., social science) than when the setting is non-scientific and deals with "spontaneous" concepts, as "A boy fell and broke his leg because. . . ." In the latter case, the child is likely not to be aware of the concept of "because" and will supply something like "he was sick" or "he went to the hospital." It is on the basis of this kind of evidence that Vygotsky makes the interesting suggestion that practice with "scientific" concepts transfers to "nonscientific" concepts in such a way as to accelerate their development. Thus, conceptualization in the non-spontane-

ous domain tends to run ahead of that in the spontaneous domain.

A hard-nosed reaction to this evidence would be to ask whether the results could not be explained on the basis of the increased verbal practice given in the "scientific" instruction as compared to wholly fortuitous amounts of practice with spontaneous concepts. Vygotsky's experiments deserve to be repeated with more adequate controls.

Like so many other treatments of the problem of language and thought, Vygotsky tends to get bogged down because of the failure to define terms precisely and operationally. If the term "concept" cannot be used consistently to mean the same thing, or if there are insufficient qualifications associated with its use, we cannot derive a series of unequivocal propositions about it. Vygotsky juggles with a number of dimensions—the degree to which a concept is part of a system of thought, the degree to which it is within awareness and under conscious control, the degree to which it is formed as a result of instruction, and the degree to which it conforms to a "mature" or adult form, but he never clearly indicates to what extent "concepts" can be regarded as corresponding to "word meanings," and indeed, there is little consideration of the influence of language in the formation of concepts. This, to be sure, is a topic that has been taken up by a number of later Russian investigators, e.g., Luria, and Liublinskaya, as one may learn by reading Simon's *Psychology in the Soviet Union* (Stanford University Press, 1957) or Luria and Yudovich's *Speech and the Development of Mental Processes in the Child* (London, 1959). As far as his basic views on language and thought are concerned, Vygotsky offers not a fully-formed theory but some interesting components of a theory.

Let us turn, therefore, to some of the

more interesting ideas that can be found in this work.

Although at times Vygotsky seems to espouse the kind of notion put forward by Piaget that there are natural constitutional limits to development, represented perhaps by a series of age-timed steps, he is much more willing than Piaget (both the Piaget of the early 'twenties—the one known by Vygotsky, and the Piaget of today) to allow the possibility of accelerating or at least strengthening the course of the child's conceptual development. What Vygotsky has to say about instruction (and he calls it that unabashedly) will be of interest and use to educators.

> Instruction is one of the principal sources of the schoolchild's concepts and is a powerful force in directing their evolution; it determines the fate of his total mental development. (p. 85)

He reviews, and rejects, three theories of the relation of instruction to development: (1) that instruction must hobble along after development, waiting for certain stages of development to begin or to be completed before it can do its work; (2) that development and instruction are identical, since development is nothing more than the accumulation of conditioned reflexes; and (3) that development has two interdependent aspects, maturation and learning. In connection with the last of these, he feels that Thorndike's critique of formal discipline "did not touch its valuable kernel" because Thorndike ignored qualitative differences between lower and higher functions of the mind. In Vygotsky's view, "the ability to gauge the length of lines may not affect the ability to distinguish between angles, but the study of the native language—with its attendant sharpening of concepts—may still have some bearing on the study of arithmetic." (p. 97) In this year 1963, we do not even yet have sufficient evidence positively to confirm or to deny this view, but it still seems reasonable if transfer takes place through identical elements. Indeed Thorndike's later writings show that he would probably have accepted Vygotsky's opinion.

Vygotsky's own "tentative" theory is stated by him as follows: "The only good kind of instruction is that which marches ahead of development and leads it: it must be aimed not so much at the ripe as at the ripening function." (p. 104) This entirely reasonable idea emerges, we are told, from four series of empirical investigations, described all too briefly, in the teaching of various school subjects. Only one of these series will be mentioned here—the one that examined the levels of development of the "psychic functions" requisite for learning the school subjects—reading and writing, arithmetic, and natural science. This investigation disclosed, for example, that in writing (that is, composing, not merely handwriting) it is the abstract quality of written language that is the main stumbling block—not poor motor coordination or the like. The author also states, without citing evidence, that "our analysis clearly showed the study of grammar to be of paramount importance for the mental development of the child," apparently because it forces the child to become aware of grammatical concepts and to get them under conscious control.

To a few close students of the subject, Vygotsky's critique of Piaget's conception of the function of egocentric speech (in which the child "talks to himself") was already familiar from a brief translated article published in the journal *Psychiatry* in 1939. Vygotsky had suggested that egocentric speech, far from representing a transition from autistic speech to socialized speech, is rather a stage on the way to the interiorization of speech, "inner speech," or "silent speech." The evidence was ingeniously derived. It was shown that at a certain stage of development, egocentric speech normally occurred only when the child was in the presence of other children; in the absence of other children, it could be assumed that whatever thinking processes were occurring were accompanied by interiorized speech. "Egocentric speech" could occur under another condition: a child sitting alone and performing some activity like drawing would normally not speak, but if his task was interrupted, or if some difficulty were interposed, egocentric speech would appear. Again, the interpretation was that in the silent period inner speech was occurring, but that when a difficulty presented itself the child would regress, so to speak, to the use of overt speech.

It is interesting now to find that Piaget himself, having had an opportunity to examine Vygotsky's postulations on egocentric speech, is completely willing to entertain them. His only reservation is that Vygotsky may have failed to recognize the parallel existence of another type of egocentric speech in which the child is truly talking "for himself," or perhaps (to take the suggestion of the French child psychologist Zazzo) "according to himself" (*selon lui*), a stage in which he has not truly learned to take full account of his audience. Piaget has a number of reservations, too, about other parts of Vygotsky's theory, but we shall not consider them here. Like Piaget, we can only close with an affirmation of our genuine respect for the extraordinary grasp of his subject and the penetrating insights exhibited by Vygotsky in this fascinating book.

JOHN B. CARROLL
Harvard University

LEARNING TO READ: THE GREAT DEBATE
by Jeanne S. Chall.
New York: McGraw-Hill, 1967.

Every careful reader of this impressive book will recognize and sympathize with the toil which Dr. Chall's huge task has exacted and will note appreciatively how —with increasing success from chapter to chapter—she has managed to impose an intelligible order upon materials which too often must have seemed unbearably and unnecessarily tiresome. Some of her best pages, indeed, are those describing the shocking state of research literature and its interpretations, the extravagations of the manuals to the Basal-Reading Series, the near strangleholds of "conventional wisdom," and the obstacles both to intelligent innovation and to any adequate appraisal or even notice of anything

that departs sufficiently from received and accredited though often self-conflicting practice. Most of her strictures are so quietly phrased that they may not be given their due weight: "A sense of humor and simple honesty are needed if negative findings are to be reported from, say, a one-half or one-million dollar research project carried out over a five-year period, or even longer" (p. 98). "The consensus on beginning reading instruction in the 1950's and early 1960's was so strong that only a variety of attacks together could challenge it. Except for a few dissenters here and there—looked upon by most people in the field as the lunatic fringe— everyone implicitly assumed that most of

631

what was important . . . had already been discovered . . . . It takes individuals with a great deal of courage, enthusiasm and dedication to take a stand against so strong a consensus" (p. 295). Compare the morals she draws against the hunger—a hunger, she notes, for consensus—not felt in England (pp. 301-2).

Why do "new methods" often produce better results at first than they do later? Novelty? Perhaps; but this she doubts. Her further suggestion—based on observation —is more charmingly cynical: "In all probability when the pure sight approach was proposed as the 'true' and 'natural' way to start, teachers persisted in teaching the children something about the letters and sounds, although this was not part of the sight method" (p. 283). "They got out their old phonics charts, *closed the doors,* and hoped the supervisor or principal would not enter unannounced" (p. 284). May this not happen, in reverse, again? "Should the stronger decoding programs . . . begin to be used widely by teachers who have not the benefit of experience with a different approach, results may be inferior because these teachers will lack the experience necessary to temper the method's excesses" (p. 295).

The above excerpts may in part suggest the author's strong efforts to maintain an impartial viewpoint. Nonetheless, in her conclusions and recommendations (pp. 305-14) she comes out clearly in favor of an increase in "code-emphasis" for *beginning* readers. By this is meant a method "that views beginning reading as essentially different from mature reading and emphasizes learning of the printed code for the spoken language" (p. 307). I shall not comment further on these recommendations. Undoubtedly they will be much discussed; all specialists in the field will have read them with sharp attention, though, no doubt, not without bias. The author is sensible as well as shrewd about the judgments evinced by proponents: "While these people were all anxious that I not come to a hasty conclusion about

their programs, each was quick to do so about competing ones" (p. 269). I can use my space here to better effect, I believe, by concentrating upon some theoretical considerations. Dr. Chall is excellent on this: "We will need, most of all, the few who have the imagination and the insight to create the theories which may then be confirmed or denied by years of careful research" (p. 98). I would only add that we need also to recall and give some attention to those (some not at all recent) who have had such imagination and insight.

I may begin with the big question that, as the author says, "underlies the rest of this book": *"Do children learn better with a beginning method that stresses meaning or with one that stresses learning the code?"* (p. 75). As Dr. Chall observes, "most researchers . . . have settled for an insufficiently rigorous definition of the methods and programs under study" (p. 336). She has herself taken great pains to make her own definitions as precise as the material and time-labor factors allow. Nonetheless she will not be surprised if a number of her readers find them insufficient for the work they are required to do, and notably so with this "big question." In particular, I have three deep troubles with it: I need more help than I can find anywhere in the book on (1) what I should be understanding by 'meaning'; and on (2) what the essentials of 'learning the code' may be. And further (3) I feel that 'stress' with 'emphasis' are words which confuse the problem here rather than clarify it.

To take this third difficulty first: Do not *stress* and *emphasis* too much suggest presence in relative amounts, quantitative proportions among ingredients in a mixture, or forces in a composition and so on? And is not our problem much more one of achieving a valid insight or a testable theory, as to how 'meaning' and 'learning the code' interact, as to how each takes part in the development of the other? I do not doubt that Dr. Chall knows this very well, but I have found little beyond some mentions of "our code-meaning continuum" and a sound remark that "all code programs . . . give practice in reading for meaning and all meaning programs give practice in the code" (p. 103). And an argument from Bloomfield that "meaning comes naturally as the code is broken . . . since the words in the first readers are already part of the child's listening and speaking vocabulary" (p. 29). It is true that Dr. Chall in decribing the Basal-Reading Series is constantly concerned with how, if at all, their phonics ingredient, as offered, helps the child in mastering the code. But these observations do not meet my need—which is for a more precise concept of 'meanings' (as they enter here) and of 'the graphic code' and of their interplay with one another and with oral language.

Here it is fit that we recall how Coleridge, in the midst of celebrating Wordsworth's first excellence ("a perfect appropriateness of the words to the meaning") looks back to "the advantages which language . . . with incomparably greater ease and certainty than any other means, presents to the instructor of impressing modes of intellectual energy so constantly, so imperceptibly, and as it were by such elements and atoms, as to secure in due time the formation of a second nature . . . ." Remembering that, he trusts "we shall learn to value earnestly and with a practical seriousness a mean, already prepared for us by nature and society, of teaching the young mind to think well and wisely by the same unremembered process, and with the same never forgotten results, as those by which it is taught to speak and converse" (*Biographia Literaria*, Ch. XXII). *Modes of intellectual energy*, be it noted, are what the passage to written language can enable us to install.

Coleridge's insight here can be rephrased by pointing out that the acquisition of a first notation (writing)[1] for verbal lan-

[1] Not in the special sense that Nelson Goodman is working upon but in a more general sense in which whenever two *or more*

guage can give the learner a new power of control and check upon what he has been managing hitherto so skillfully with ear and tongue. It can do more than this: it can offer him an instrument with which he can examine at another tempo and in another form and for the first time the miracles he has been accomplishing fleetingly in speech. With written language, and step-by-step through the process by which he learns its use, he can come into a new cognizance of what he has been talking of and hearing about only. He gains, in brief, *means of exploring and comparing* he never had before. Imagine what a third eye or hand could do for us. Learning to read, *if rightly conducted*, can do far more for the child than that. At this point a diagram may, for some, be of service.

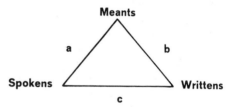

(Where *b* is the interpretation of the meaning of written symbols and *c* is the decoding of symbols into sounds.)

The Great Debate has been almost entirely about whether *b* or *c* should be given some sort of initial or continuing predominance. Relatively little attention has been paid to the fact that the prime service of reading-writing is to the advancement

channels (e.g. ear and eye) are jointly engaged in the perception or management of a situation, each may be regarded as offering a notation for the other (s). Thus, with *writing*, what the hand is doing, what the eye, checking the script, is doing, what the organs of speech may be doing, what auditory imagery and motor imagery of the sentence being written may be doing, etc. etc.: all these, in my usage, are *notations* for one another. Theory of notations, so conceived, may have much relevance to learning theory. See my recent *So Much Nearer* (New York: Harcourt, Brace & World, 1968).

of *a*—the improvement, namely, in how the child is thinking and in how he is managing to utter his thoughts *and* understand *and* check the utterances of others. From this point of view, both sides in the Great Debate can seem often to have been taking absurdly limited views of the endeavor they are concerned about. As a result, we may find they may have been overlooking powerful means of combining —in a radically new approach—the merits of the aims to which they have severally been attached.

Turn now to my second difficulty: 'learning the code.' 'Code', as I have argued at length elsewhere,[2] is a peculiarly treacherous word in linguistics and information theory. No one by mastering the Morse Code gains any further insight into the messages he codes and decodes. But in other senses of 'code', *all* understanding of a verbal utterance may depend upon tactful discernment of how codes are working (*and* failing). To decide just what opportunities a sequence of instruction is offering, to which sorts of children, for advance in their grasp of which aspects of the verbal codes, is an undertaking for future research far beyond anything that linguistics and learning theory can *as yet* attempt. But enough insight into what is involved has accumulated to show that most of the concepts most displayed in The Great Debate have been insufficient —too crude for their job. For example, a "one letter—one sound" predilection should, in general, be suspect. As Levin (1963) found, the observation that *g*, say, is pronounced two ways (as in *go* and in *gem*) "has greater transfer value." Letters with these odd ways can become interesting characters. Thus it is not necessary to cripple composition and make an unintelligible hash of what is put before the children for study by attempting to avoid such things: *This is his——. causes no English-speaking* child any trouble.

Can adequate invitations to explore sound-letter relations for themselves be combined collaboratively with a progressive full use of script in the study of meanings? The answer, I suggest, is 'Yes'— subject to four vital conditions:

(1) A designed sequencing of the utterances offered for study such that the earlier prepare for the later and are, in turn, exercised and confirmed by them. (The currilum principle on a cellular or molecular scale. It is also, of course, a strict form of programing.)

(2) Use in these utterances of, at first, a minimal number of letters, so that the forms and collocations of these letters become highly familiar before further letters are admitted in calculated fashion and at due intervals to the dance.

(3) Use of depictions of a hieroglyphic simplicity—not as *cues* merely to word meanings but as an accompanying pictorial language, pruned of distractive possibilities.

(4) Use in these sequences of fully and immediately verifiable statements. Words in isolation are no more than possible components of sentences. The only full utterances are sentences.

I will discuss these conditions briefly in turn, starting with the fourth which leads us into analysis of 'meanings.'

(4) *'Meanings'*. Dr. Chall has severe things to say about research on beginning reading. How good a job has been done? "The answer is disturbing. Taken as a whole, the research on beginning reading is shockingly inconclusive" (p. 88). She suggests various explanations. It has been under-endowed, trivial, promotional, parochial, fashion-bound, lacking in perspective. She might have added

[2] Cf. "The Future of Poetry," Appendix to *The Screens and Other Poems* (1960) by I. A. Richards (New York: Harcourt, Brace & World, 1960); and "Variant Readings and Misreadings" in *Style in Language*, edited by Thomas A. Sebeok (Cambridge, Mass.: M.I.T. Press, 1960.) Both have been reprinted in *So Much Nearer*.

another. What she rightly says of the research could be said with equal justice of the composition of the materials concocted for the children, of the instructions and the educational theory presented to the teachers and, with rare exceptions, of the linguistics and psychology employed—so far as these have really been used at all. Research on, and through, such hodge-podges could not fairly have been expected to yield much in results. And nothing in all this, in spite of the ubiquitous appeals to 'meaning', has been weaker or more timid or more brash than the handling of this key concept. It should need no saying that an attempt to dispense with a theory of comprehension and of meaning is here disabling. We might as well try to advance dietetics while ignoring biochemistry and physiology.

For the grounds for what follows I must refer the reader elsewhere.[3] Among the components of normal intact meanings, analysis must distinguish straight statement of ostensible fact—which can be verified or refuted—from all others, notably from effective-volitional and fictive functions. Of these plain statements, those that can be *immediately tested* for truth or falsity by means well within the child's capacity, have—for instruction —peculiar importance, above all when what is being learned is the command of a notation. *Nothing is implied in this* against the use, for other educational purposes, of *Cinderella*. By all means, indeed, let the contrast be brought out. But through the initial stages the ad-

---

[3] See "Towards a Theory of Comprehension" in *Speculative Instruments* (New York: Harcourt, Brace & World, Harvest paperback, 1967), and "Meanings Anew" in *So Much Nearer,* where work on these questions develops, I believe, earlier treatments in C. K. Ogden and I. A. Richards, *The Meaning of Meaning* (New York: Harcourt, Brace, 1920) and I. A. Richards, *Practical Criticism* (New York: Harcourt, Brace, 1930), will be found. See also my forthcoming *Design for Escape.*

vantages of the directly verifiable statement are immense. What we can give the child with it is a means by which he can control, *for himself,* the validity of what he is doing.

(3) *Depictions.* Nothing is more clearly and dismayingly brought out by Dr. Chall's book than the ineptitudes of thought about the role of pictures. She is fairly cutting in her discussions of Basal-Reading Series—her interviews with the publishers and their men are full of such comedy—but she is not nearly stern enough about the connivance by all concerned in the circulation of these absurd, distractive diversions of the child from his due task.

What pictures can do for beginning readers is to supply them with a second *notation* by reference to which they can check their developing use of the prime notation of writing. The notion of "clues for intelligent guesses" (p. 14, note 8) needs to be at once discarded. What depictions can and should do here is to enable a hypothesis to validate or invalidate itself from nothing more than careful observation and comparison. We should remember always—though generations of reading-experts seem almost wholly to forget it—that children are learning to read not *just to read,* not even *just to enjoy stories,* not *just to be able to spell and pronounce correctly,* and not *just to get jobs*—but to develop further their distinctive quality as human beings: resourceful, self-corrigible discernment. To this development, the guess—to be O.K.'d or not by the teacher—is a grim danger. Those who have taught literature in seminars know too well what havoc the guessing habit wreaks there, as later everywhere in world affairs. Is it surprising that more reflective teachers so often wonder how much blame for this continuing incapacity may be traceable to the Basal-Reading Series?

(2) *Letter-intake.* It should surely not require much insight or any recondite

theory for us to agree that recognition of configurations will be aided if the components entering into them are initially as *few* and as *distinguishable* as possible. (Incidentally, the I.T.A. innovations seem open to much criticism on this last ground.) By operating at the start with *seven selected letters only*, instead of twice or three times that number, we give the child a more favorable chance of facing up successfully to his first great task as a beginning reader—that of seeing composedly and not with bewilderment what he has to deal with. Endless laboratory and kindergarten experience bears this out. Moreover, in so proceeding, we better help him to discover that analysis and synthesis (taking things to pieces and putting them together again) are useful as well as amusing games to play.

(1) *Strict sequencing.* Its aim is not only to ease the child's progress, but to help him to realize that the answer to what comes next can be found in what he has done already: that it is, in fact, from the start staring him in the face there if he will look for it. We have also the great duty of so arranging things that he can see for himself *why* he is right when he is right, and what he has done when he is wrong.

Dr. Chall has acute things to say both about the use of research by proponents: "If you select judiciously and avoid interpretations, you can make the research 'prove' almost anything you want it to" (p. 87), and about the way in which designs for learning and reports on outcomes have so often "gotten lost in the shuffle" or been simply ignored if they depart from "the educational preferences of the time" (pp. 92-3). She is wise too about the importance, could they be obtained, of follow-up studies of children subjected to new approaches (pp. 80, 92). She notes that "very little of the research evidence tells us about differences in results...at the end of the fourth grade or beyond." One piece of such evidence perhaps appeared too late to attract her attention. An experimental group using the design just described and a carefully matched control group using Scott, Foresman reading materials from 1958 to 1961 were compared in 1964-5 as seventh-grade students in junior high school. There were thirty-three experimentals and thirty-seven controls left of the original 150 pupils who had entered first grade at the beginning of the three-year study. Examination of their seventh-grade record, as reported by Mrs. Doris Flinton and Professor Morris Eson of the State University of New York at Albany, reveals the following:

> Since these groups had been equated on the basis of reading readiness and intelligence and sex, and groups had been heterogeneous in nature, a survey was made of their distribution in the seventh grade groups. In the junior high pupils are assigned to Sections according to ability levels.
>
> Five honor rolls (Dec. 1, 1964-May 7, 1965) were examined for the number of times each pupil was represented there during the year. Honor rolls are made up of all those who received grades of A or B in all subjects during a marking period. All ability levels were represented on the honor roll. The experimental pupils had a chance of placing 33x5, or 165 times. The controls had 37x5, or 185 possibilities. Investigation showed that the experimentals made 46 entries on the honor rolls as compared with 19 entries by the controls.
>
> The results show that the experimental pupils had 27% of their group on the honor roll compared with 10% of the controls. These figures are not biased by the distribution among the various ability levels.
>
> From this long-range study it may be concluded that the pupils of the

experimental group are using their abilities better in their studies than the control group.[4]

The indication would seem to be that children invited from the start to use their minds and *enabled to do so by the design of the invitation,* can really benefit later. It may be mentioned that this was the same design, in essence, as that used by MacKinnon (1959) when he did, as Dr. Chall describes it, "a very rare and worthwhile thing—he observed the day-to-day reading performance of children on different kinds of reading material, in addition to testing at the end of the experiment" (p. 101). It is interesting to note, on the same page, the author's strong remarks on the superiority of earlier research (Buswell, 1922; Gates, 1927 and 1928; Winch, 1925; and Valentine, 1913) to contemporary work. The kinds of psychology inquirers were studying in those days were far more humane and apprised and far more relevant to the investigation of learning, than the promotionally more intent psychologies which captured the field from them.

In her hopes for adequate changes our author is very moderate. She does not doubt the need; what is being done is not good enough. But she is unusually aware of the powers of resistance the vast complex of activities she so well describes can exert. For all her restraint, parts of her account are daunting—to those who can read between the lines. But perhaps the system—like slavery, the horse carriage, and domestic service—can be technologically by-passed. Dr. Chall welcomes, on her last page but one, the

computer storage and retrieval system for reading research soon to be housed at Indiana University. Her book may have been completed too soon for her to have included notice of the mind-stretching possibilities the computer promises for collection and analysis of just such observations as she praises MacKinnon for, as well as for instant-by-instant accommodation of the presented problem to the momentary needs of the learner—thus concentering teaching ability at the point where it can do most for the billions who most need *that.*

Of course computers will be misused and their capacities applied prematurely. We need not be as much encouraged as Dr. Chall seems to be by the taking over of educational publishers by industrial *collossi* (p. 303). As vaster and more competitive concerns enter, why should we suppose that they will be wiser or more regardful of others' interests than their forerunners? Nonetheless, high technologies do have a way of minding their own business successfully. After sad false dawns we may be in sight of means of knowing more than anyone has ever dreamed we ever could about the outcomes of our doings. The technique of teaching reading may conceivably thus be made self-corrigible. And this just in time to meet the desperate need for instruction in reading of about half of the world's population. Dr Chall seems to accept a figure of from 10 to 15 per cent failures in grades above the first (p. 124); and this without marked signs of consternation. What may the figures in some African elementary programs be: just when the failed youth are pouring —in Bruner's vivid phrase—"their familial and tribal boats burned," into cities where no help is to be had? We do well to remind ourselves here—at the close of such a review as this—that if learning to read extends human ability, failure in the attempt to learn can grievously

[4] Christine M. Gibson and I. A. Richards, "Development of Experimental Audiovisual Devices and Materials for Beginning Readers," Cooperative Research Project No. 5, 0642 (U.S. Office of Education), p. 27.

impair: no one yet knows how much. And we have enough evidence of increases of violence and incapacity near home not to let the prospect of failure on a global scale spur us to less than our utmost effort.

I. A. RICHARDS
Harvard University

THE SOUND PATTERN OF ENGLISH
by Noam Chomsky and Morris Halle.
New York: Harper and Row, 1968.

This long-awaited study will be received in the world of linguistics with the kind of intellectual passion reserved for only the most critically important of works. The field of lingusitics is faced today with the kind of challenge which Thomas Kuhn would term a "conceptual revolution." For while the quiet, almost unnoticed appearance in 1957 of Chomsky's *Syntactic Structures*[1] could be said to have been no less epoch-making, *Sound Pattern* differs from the earlier study in two important respects. First, it is much more ambitious in scope, more heavily detailed, and more integrated in design —certainly it is very much longer. And, second, it serves to close a steadily increasing body of empirical work which has hitherto been preoccupied mainly with syntax and semantics. It is now possible, with this exhaustive study in phonology, to obtain a tentative overall picture of how a transformational grammar formally describes the relationship between sounds and meaning in a language. If Karl Popper is correct in observing "that the most lasting contributions to the growth of scientific knowledge that a theory can make are the problems which it raises,"[2] there can be no denying that *The Sound Pattern of English* will make a lasting contribution, for it raises fundamental questions both for linguistic theory and for the application of linguistics to psychology and learning.

Since the articulation of the notion of the phoneme and phonemic level has, historically, been the greatest contribution of neo-Bloomfieldians to linguistic thought, it has been possible to postpone the incipient basic confrontation between the older descriptive theory (often called "structural" or "taxonomic" linguistics) and the phonological theory of the transformationalists. Rumblings of the approaching clash began some years ago[3] when various articles began to raise serious questions about the viability of the whole concept of taxonomical phonemics. These articles, along with Paul Postal's recent study, *Aspects of Phonological Theory*,[4] have raised the following criticisms of the structural theory:

1) There is no convincing evidence for positing a *separate* level of pho-

[1] Noam Chomsky, *Syntactic Structures* (The Hague: Mouton and Co., 1957).

[2] Karl R. Popper, *Conjectures and Refutations* (New York: Basic Books, 1963), p. 222.

[3] See Morris Halle, *The Sound Pattern of Russian* (The Hague: Mouton and Co., 1959), his two articles, "Phonology in a Generative Grammar," and "On the Bases of Phonology," in Jerry A. Fodor and Jerrold J. Katz (eds.), *The Structure of Language: Readings in the Philosophy of Language* (Englewood Cliffs: Prentice-Hall, 1964); Noam Chomsky, *Current Issues in Linguistic Theory* (The Hague: Mouton and Co., 1964); and Noam Chomsky, Morris Halle, and F. Lukoff, "On Accent and Juncture in English," in *For Roman Jakobson* (The Hague: Mouton and Co., 1956).

[4] Paul M. Postal, *Aspects of Phonological Theory* (New York: Harper & Row, 1968).

nemic descriptions in the grammar of a language. The notion of the phoneme, as defined by the distributional principle of minimal contrast (of *meaning* as well as sound),[5] is nothing more than a methodological artifact which contributes little explanatory power when viewed from the point of a full analysis of the sound pattern of a language;

2) the notion of the phoneme as a near "surface" feature *constant* is misconceived. Phonemes must be viewed as abstractions which are potentially subject to phonological transformations, such alterations being the result of environmental conditions which can thus be formalized by phonological rules;

3) taxonomical phonemics is in principle incapable of arriving at an adequate description of the sound pattern of a language because of its insistence on maintaining a strict separation between the level of phonemics and morphology, and because of the critical absence of any notion of the part played by ordered rules in a linguistic formalism.

Phonemicists have replied to some of these criticisms, of course. But most have held in some form or other to the notion of independent level of phonemics on practical if not theoretical grounds, since it could always be argued that final judgment might be postponed until transformational theory could present in some detail its alternative to the older theory. The published appearance of *The Sound Pattern of English* now makes it impossible for taxonomical phonemicists to delay final evaluative judgment.

The detailed phonological sketch of the English sound system presented in the book's first five chapters concentrates on three main areas: 1) the cyclic rules for lexical stress placement, 2) the word-level vowel transformations, and 3) the consonant transformations. For, as the reader who has any familiarity with transformational thought knows by now the fundamental insight, from which much of the theory derives, lies in the distinction drawn between deep and surface levels of linguistic structure.[6] In the case of phonology, this means that certain abstract phones at deep structure may appear altered or transformed at the surface level, such alterations being generated by the application of various ordered rules. If we leave aside the whole issue of how the rules work, how they are ordered and in what manner "ordered," we may observe the basic process by considering certain consonant alternations. In each of the following pairs, the first item recovers the deep level abstract form, and the second item represents the surface transformed phone:

medi*c* ~ medi*c*ine; sagaci*ty* ~ sa*ge* (velar softening)

si*g*n ~ de*s*ign; gymna*s*tic ~ gymna*s*ium (s-voicing)

residen*t* ~ residen*c*e; eva*de* ~ eva*s*ive (spirantization)

par*t* ~ par*t*ial; rela*te* ~ rela*t*ion (spirantization and palatalization)

ac*t* ~ ac*t*ual; gra*d*ate ~ gra*d*ual; sen*se* ~ sen*s*ual; vi*s*ible ~ vi*s*ual (palatalization)

And although the facts about vowel alternations are complicated by the question of stress-placement, they show precisely the same basic process. Consider these alternations between tense and lax vowels (the upper case letters are used

---

[5] Thus, since /pit/ and /pet/ differ "minimally"—i.e., only one sound varies—and since they have different meanings, structuralists would argue that /i/ and /e/ are *phonemes*.

[6] For a concise exposition of this distinction, see Paul M. Postal, "Underlying and Superficial Structure," *Harvard Educational Review*, XXXIV (Spring, 1964), 246-266.

here to represent "long" vowels, but not the so-called diphthongs.)

sIgn ~ signify; serEne ~ serenity; sAne ~ sanity; abound ~ abundant; lose ~ lost; verbOse ~ verbosity (laxing)

manager ~ managErial; harmony ~ harmOnious; manic ~ mAnia (tensing)

The interesting point to note about the examples above is that the "orthography" —the word's representation in the written alphabet—generally captures the deep level abstract form and fails to record the altered form (except for simple "spirantization," and certain of the back vowel alternations). A little reflection will tell us why this orthographic failure is in no way incapacitating for adults. The phonetic alternations of transformed phones need not be recorded by the orthography, since the native speaker of English is able to bring his tacit knowledge of the phonological rules to bear on lexical items which reflect the relevant environmental conditions for the operation of such rules. While learning to read, therefore, a child is engaged in two closely related tasks— 1) "learning" the phonological system of his language from the general speech environment, and 2) learning how to relate such phonological knowledge to the task of reading printed symbols.

Since the orthography plugs in at the more abstract phonological level, the child may first have to disconfirm those expectations that may lead him to assume that orthographies are normally phonetically valid. This early "hypothesis" would be a function of the simple early reading vocabulary in which the match between phones (sounds) and graphemes (letters)[7] is of a simple and untransformed kind. Granting all of these speculations for the moment, it is quite clear that English orthography, and

perhaps most naturally established orthographies,[8] to the extent that they are morphophonemic, are most highly valued for *native adult* speakers of a language. Consider for a moment what would happen if we constructed an orthography based on the principles of taxonomical phonemics. It would be necessary to write alternations such as those above in a way (e.g., medical ~ medisin; native ~ nashon; graduate ~ grajual) which would serve effectively to obliterate nearly all information about derivational relationships. For adults it would appear that orthographies which retain such information are more highly valued than those which have been artificially "regularized" to conform with the principles of taxonomic phonemics. We have unfortunately simplified many other interesting facts which give support to the contention regarding the underlying "regularity" of English orthography. We have failed to remark on the underlying reality of certain types of terminal silent "e" (compare sage ~ sag)[9]; we have not pointed to the effect of geminated consonants reflected by the orthography in preventing vowel tensing (compare pUce~ prussic; mUsic ~ mussle; prUde ~ puddle, etc.). But enough has been shown here to call into question the reasonableness of expecting that any useful natural orthography should be based on the principle of taxonomical phonemics, Fries *et al.* to the contrary.

Two main conclusions seem to emerge. First, in learning to read, a child is essentially learning the rules that relate abstract representations of words to their superficial vocal representations. In other

[7] Or grapheme clusters like "th."

[8] See Sanford A. Schane, *French Phonology and Morphology* (Cambridge: MIT Press, 1968), pp. 16-17.

[9] Consider the very common fact about the recovery of "silent" consonants in pairs like /debt ~ debit/, /bomb ~ bombardment/, /doubt ~ dubiety/, etc. Taxonomical phonemics is *in principle* incapable of explaining such facts.

words, he is learning how to use the sound pattern of his language. If there is any validity to this assertion, then the whole issue is complicated by another highly probable fact. The full articulation of the sound system of English depends upon the introduction of a heavily polysyllabic "learned vocabulary." Such vocabulary is not normally possessed by young children in the early grades of school. Thus two consequences follow. First, reading acquisition might be, from a temporal point of view, a much more protracted process than first realized[10] and it may very well progress through various "stages" of organization. In any case, reading acquisition might be more profitably viewed as a part of a much more general process, that is, the maturational development of the "sound pattern" of English. So conceptualized, the study of how children learn to read has to be construed as a genuine psycholinguistic investigation. Thus, such behavioral notions as habit skill[11] or spelling patterns[12] would fail to provide satisfactory explanations, since the psychological and linguistic models from which such notions derive are inadequate.

The second conclusion is, in any event, not at all speculative. This second point has to do with the whole question of phoneme/grapheme correspondence.[13] Since neither the sound system nor the orthography of English makes any special allowance for, nor in any way reflects the independent existence of a separate level of phonemics, the voluminous research

into the whole question of phoneme/grapheme correspondence is *essentially misconceived*. It is altogether wrong to expect that graphemes in a natural orthography would show any correspondence to an artifact (i.e., phonemic level) which has no particular linguistic or psychological reality. Research of this kind provides us with another classic example of the futility of engaging in research into any aspect of language behavior which is motivated by or modelled on faulty linguistic models. To say that English orthography is in some sense or other 85% "regular"[14] is to say something which is not only uninteresting, but, in fact, altogether misleading. *The Sound Pattern of English,* in disconfirming such statements, presents those interested in reading research and psycholinguistics with challenges which have very real practical implications.

As we look further into the book, we find that the title, "The Sound Pattern of English," fails to indicate the full measure of the sweep and scope of the work. The second half of the text is given over to important questions related to diachronic linguistics[15] and problems of general phonological theory. Chapter 6, for instance, presents evidence for the hypothesis that historical sound change might be interpreted as the addition and reordering of phonological rules in a grammar. As such, it accords with Halle's earlier schematic remarks[16] and provides documentary evidence from English supporting Postal's criticism of the entrenched interpretation of sound changes as a gradual process.[17] Chapter 7 advances a highly cohesive, if somewhat ten-

---

[10] See Jeanne S. Chall, *Learning to Read: The Great Debate* (New York: McGraw-Hill, 1967).

[11] See Arthur W. Staats, *Learning Language and Cognition* (New York: Holt, Rinehart, and Winston, 1968).

[12] See Charles C. Fries, *Linguistics and Reading* (New York: Holt, Rinehart, and Winston, 1962).

[13] See many of the articles in *Project Literacy Reports* (Ithaca, N. Y.: Cornell University Press).

[14] See John B. Carroll, *The Study of Language* (Cambridge: Harvard University Press, 1952).

[15] The study of language as it changes over time.

[16] See Halle, "Phonology in a Generative Grammar."

[17] Compare C. F. Hockett, "Sound Change," *Language,* XLI (1965), 185-204, with Postal, *Aspects of Phonological Theory.*

tative, exposition of the hitherto rather unsystematic aspect of linguistics known as phonetic theory. The insights should be of particular interest to phoneticians and especially British linguists; for taxonomical phonemicists, it raises certain questions regarding their inclination to relegate phonetics to the periphery of legitimate linguistic investigation.[18] Chapter 8 presents many suggestions regarding general aspects of theoretical phonology—particularly relevant to the whole question of rule construction and evaluative measures governing choices between alternative formalisms. The remarks in Chapter 9 on the principle of markedness serve to rehabilitate and formalize the insights first advanced by Jakobson, Trubetskoy and others of the Prague Circle in the 1930's. The theory of markedness attempts to define in an explicit way the intuitive notion of "naturalness" in language sound systems, and raises a powerful challenge to *ad hoc* phonemic descriptions. That the principle of markedness can explain otherwise curious empirical facts can be shown by the following example. In the maturational development of English-speaking children's sound systems, it has long been observed that over a population, certain sounds appear earlier than others.[19] Usually the last sounds to emerge are the afficates [č] and [j] and the dental fricatives [θ] [ð]. The question is why? The stops ([p] [b] [t] [d] etc.) are naturally non-strident and therefore unmarked for stridency; thus *strident* stops, being the less natural "feature" for stops, are "marked" for stridency as [+ strident]. Continuants, on the other hand ([f] [v]

[s] [z] etc.) are naturally strident and therefore unmarked for stridency; thus non-strident continuants (i.e., [θ] [ð]), being the less natural state, must be "marked" for non-stridency. There is much more to the question than this, of course, but the point is raised to demonstrate that linguistic theory, if explicit enough, may contain all manner of explanatory insights for otherwise curious and inexplicable empirical facts. Those interested in language acquisition and developmental phonology (however it is conceptualized), can ill-afford to ignore the explanatory implications provided by Chomsky and Halle's theoretical formulations.

The significance of the last remark cannot be overemphasized. Research in reading and verbal behavior has, in general, worked on the misguided assumption that if exhaustive enough descriptive data were collected, explanations of some reasonable kind would eventually emerge from the mass of empirical facts. The altogether indeterminate results of the most heavily researched area in education today, namely reading,[20] give the lie to such naive and misplaced beliefs. Very clearly, empirical research can be more profitably carried on under the direction and guidance of explicit theoretical formalizations.[21] The message for reading research is clear. To ignore any longer the insights provided by such a theoretical analysis as that found in *The Sound Pattern of English* is tantamount to condemning reading research to the same persistent inconclusiveness which has hitherto proved to be its only outstanding characteristic.

JOHN. W. MACDONALD
University of Toronto

[18] See Henry A. Gleason, *An Introduction to Descriptive Linguistics* (New York: Holt, Rinehart, and Winston, 1961).

[19] See Mildred C. Templin, *Certain Language Skills in Children* (Minneapolis: University of Minnesota Press, 1957) and William Stern, *Psychology of Early Childhood* (New York: Henry Holt, 1930).

[20] See Chall.

[21] Witness the superiority of recent research in first language acquisition by Brown, Bellugi, Cazden, McNeill, *et al.*, over earlier descriptions conducted in the absence of an explanatorily adequate linguistic theory.

LANGUAGE BY EAR AND BY EYE
edited by J. F. Kavanagh and I. G. Mattingly.
Cambridge, Mass.: MIT Press, 1972.

From the nineteenth century beginnings of modern psychology, the processes of reading have intrigued psychologists. E. B. Huey, in his well-known work, *The Psychology and Pedagogy of Reading*, (1908) aptly declared that to completely analyze what we do when we read would be the height of a psychologist's achievements, involving a description of the many intricate workings of the human mind. Since that time an extraordinary volume of research on both the psychology and pedagogy of reading has been amassed.

Along with Huey, among the earliest experimental investigators of reading and related cognitive activities were Cattell (1885), Dearborn (1906), and Pillsbury and Meader (1928). Interest in this area of human psychology declined while behaviorism was in favor among American psychologists. Currently there is a resurgence of interest in language and other mental processes, well-documented in such journals as *Cognitive Psychology* and the *Reading Research Quarterly*. In addition, the proceedings of recent conferences, e.g., Francis and Lindsay (1970), provide valuable summaries of contemporary research.

It is somewhat disappointing to find that despite enormous effort and modern technology, few of the issues raised by Huey and other early researchers have been satisfactorily resolved. There are a number of reasons for this. The foremost is that reading is not a unitary process. Skilled reading is a coordinated set of highly practised activities including controlled eye movements, complex linguistic analyses, and the mysterious projection of exquisitely detailed fantasies upon the stimuli prepared by an author. In addition, the parochialism of contemporary research has made the analysis of this complex activity more difficult. Researchers in psychology departments and education departments typically proceed parallel to one another in ignorance, even within the same university. Psychology itself has become Balkanized into dozens of areas each with its own journals, traditions, and standards. Real problems often remain untouched because they do not fall into one of these areas or into an established paradigm. Although reading has become an increasingly important psychological phenomenon, today it rarely appears in the index of an introductory psychology text. There is, however, no lack of attention to such topics as the antics of apes with so-called linguistic ability.

Language by Ear and by Eye reports a research conference of experimental psychologists and linguists exploring the relationships between speech and learning to read. It has been published as a sequence of conference papers and edited discussions of the papers. It is very much to the credit of sponsors of the conference, the National Institute of Child Health and Human Development (NICHD), that the interdisciplinary nature of reading research is acknowledged and that efforts to increase communication among scientists in various relevant fields have been supported in this and previous conferences (e.g., Smith and Miller, 1966; Kavanagh, 1963). The organizers of the conference recognized that no single participant's work examined the comparisons between reading and speech perception; they did an excellent job of gathering knowledgeable researchers of different backgrounds.

The primary issue addressed by the conference was the difference between reading and listening. Why is it that children who learn to speak and understand their native language with no apparent difficulty or overt instruction frequently have difficulty becoming skilled readers? What problems are unique in learning to read?

The anthology is organized in three parts, each taking up a somewhat different aspect of the relationship between speech perception and reading. Part I considers speech and writing as different vehicles of language. Part II considers the overlap between speech skills and reading skills; Part III explores specific skills required of a reader in addition to those available to him as a listener.

Traditionally there has been agreement that reading skills are based in large part on an individual's previously learned linguistic knowledge. Not surprisingly, many researchers have focused on the visual system and its link to existing linguistic knowledge as the primary factor in the differences between listening and reading. But it is a matter of considerable interest and disagreement how and at what linguistic level the auditory and visual inputs converge.

Linguistic theory describes speech events from a number of perspectives or linguistic levels. Each level has its own descriptive vocabulary and bears a specified relation to certain other levels. Thus an utterance "Stop!" may be described as an acoustic object, a consequence of characteristic articulatory gesture, a string of phones, a string of abstract phonological segments, a string of morphemes, a hierarchically organized syntactic structure, and a semantic object or message. The relatively recent formulization of linguistic theory inspired to a large degree by the work of Noam Chomsky, Morris Halle, and their students has had an important impact on reading research, and this conference in particular. While everyone was certainly aware of some relation between reading and linguistic knowledge, lack of a formal linguistic theory previously had hindered turning those speculations into useful hypotheses. Considerable progress in understanding reading may result from this factor alone.

Various theoretical accounts of reading were presented at the conference. Perhaps the simplest and most common characterization is that reading is the process of transducing the printed record and letters, into an articulatory and finally an acoustic representation which is interpreted in the same fashion as speech. Simply put, reading is listening to oneself talk. Reading and listening converge at the acoustic level, and teaching reading involves teaching methods for converting print to an appropriate sound. Much of the experimental evidence bearing on this general issue is presented in a paper for the conference by Conrad, which incorporates much of his own important research on this subject.

In contrast to this common-sense, traditional view, a number of contributors to the conference considered an alternative theory based on the phonological work of Chomsky and Halle (1968). They maintain that English orthography is at a level of representation more abstract than a phonetic representation. English orthography, in this view, is not a phonetic symbolism but rather an abstract phonological or systematic phonemic symbolism from which phonetic correspondences must be derived in accordance with general phonological (transformational) rules. Klima discusses this proposal from the perspective of several very general principles of orthographic representation, and various aspects of the proposal are further discussed by O'Neil, Gough, Shankweiler and Liberman, and Mattingly.

Issues of awareness, and related ones of consciousness, introspection, and linguistic intuition, all play a significant role in current theories of linguistics and cognitive processes. It is unfortunate that no systematic effort was made at the conference to examine the interrelationship among these topics; they are implicit in nearly every one of the papers in this volume. What, for example, do Piaget's ideas about the emergence of a child's ability to reflect on his or her own mental operations signify for the teaching of reading? Why should a newly developed ability to generalize or introspect reflect the operative causal mechanisms of psychological processes?

Mattingly suggests that an individual's awareness of his phonological system is a prerequisite to becoming a skilled reader. This concern arises in his analysis of the differences in ease of learning to listen and learning to read. Mattingly echoes the introductory remarks of the co-chairpersons of the conference, J. J. Jenkins and A. Liberman, in his contention that the initial acquisition of language—how to talk and listen—is mediated by certain very specialized, innate language-learning mechanisms. Reading, on the other hand, is learned through conscious effort, in which an emergent awareness of linguistic levels plays a necessary role. Listening, therefore, is said to be a more natural skill than reading.

Mattingly's argument (especially pp. 134-138) stresses that auditory coding is more complex than the visual orthographic code. The visual, printed record is essentially an ordered string of segments that correspond in large degree to the elements of abstract phonological representation proposed by Chomsky and Halle (1968). This is in contrast to the acoustic signal, which is *not* an ordered string of sounds. Cooper (p. 29) points out that in a syllable such as "bag" it is not possible to isolate a sequence of separate segments corresponding to the phones [b], [æ], and [g]. In short, the English printed record is a closer approximation to the level of phonological representation than is the acoustic or phonetic level.

I emphasize *English* here because the relationship between script and linguistic level is essentially a historically conditioned one rather than a psychological or linguistic universal. Languages can and do have orthographies that map onto various levels—phonetic, phonemic, syllabic, and morphemic. Several of the papers in addition to Klima's, in particular those of Samuel E. Martin, John B. Carroll, and

John Lotz, evaluate alternative orthographies and their implications. It is commonly argued that an optimal writing system is one where the mapping from script to acoustic or phonetic level is simple and direct, in contrast to that of English where the mapping is quite indirect or Chinese where the phonological system is bypassed almost completely. Lotz (p. 121) points out, however, that perhaps the optimal writing system is one which achieves continuity and secures literacy for a large number of people through a long period of time. In practice this demands a writing system that cannot reflect fluctuations of language within social and regional dialects or too rapidly reflect fluctuations due to historical change. Lotz suggests that there is a trade off between the continuity which an orthography can achieve and the ease with which that orthography can be learned. In effect, the learner pays a high price for entrance into the extensive culture of English or Chinese.

I initially sympathized with Mattingly's basic points. Reading and listening are not simply parallel input channels to the same processing mechanisms. Linguistic awareness is a prerequisite to learning to read; and listening is a more natural language activity than reading, therefore more readily learned. However, Mattingly's arguments are not convincing; they make me suspicious of my own intuitions on these matters. For one thing, the attitude is conveyed not only by Mattingly (e.g., p. 136), but by others at the conference that auditory decoding is complex, while visual decoding is relatively simple. This is far from clear. Arguments concerning the difficulty of devising an automatic speech recognition device and the poor legibility of visible speech, as in a sound spectrogram, are hardly relevant.

In several respects the listener has an advantage over the reader, largely unexplored at the conference. One obvious advantage of the listener is that the acoustic signal must be ordered within certain narrow limits by the nature of the speech production process. The role of the listener is relatively passive; the signal itself is time-ordered and self-decaying. The printed record, on the other hand, is itself a linear sequence of discrete symbols. The reader, however, must *actively* scan the page in order to construct that sequence internally. Thus, the acoustic stimulus has a natural structure while the printed stimulus has a structure imposed by the reader. As an illustration, first try not to listen to someone and then try not to read something.

The articulatory apparatus and the auditory system necessarily must have evolved in concert. All humans speak and listen, but not all humans read. This is certainly consonant with the claim that listening is more natural than reading. What is missing from Mattingly's argument, however, is some suggestion of how the characteristics of the *"faculté de langage"* (cf. Chomsky, 1965, p. 56) are related to those of the articulatory and auditory systems. Is the *faculté* a system for analyzing whatever data comes to it, or does it selectively process articulatory and auditory data? Could the articulatory and auditory systems impose certain universal constraints on the character of human language sufficient to account for the various formal universals that are currently ascribed to the *faculté*? If so, language is truly a particular, rather than a common, sense.

To the beginning reader the printed text must present a bewildering overload of information. Philip Gough, in a valiant attempt to spell out precisely what must occur within one second of reading, points out that each eye fixation takes in all letters within an oval roughly two inches wide and an inch high. This means that on an average page some letters from lines above and below the experienced or focal line are picked up at each fixation, suggesting that our phenomenal experience of reading a line of print does not result from the raw data picked up at each fixation. Somehow it remains for the

mind's eye to construct a focal string of letters or words from the letters in three to six lines of print on the actual page. At this point in the reading process many things can go wrong in interpreting letter orientation and the ordering of letters within a word, as in so-called "strephosymbolia." Next, the saccadic eye movement to the next fixation point must be programmed and executed. We know that little if any information is picked up while the eye is moving ballistically to that position. Finally, the information gathered from contiguous fixations must be integrated.

It is clear that none of these three activities is trivial; each depends to some extent on language-specific knowledge or a convention that must be learned. We still have little understanding of the information processing and control mechanisms involved. Gough's model, as I understand it, does not take into account possible problems, theoretical and practical, created by the first two tasks. I cannot believe that these aspects of visual perception do not contribute greatly to the intrinsic difficulty of learning to read. Conversely, I suspect the seeming naturalness of listening is in large measure due to the lack of active components in auditory perception; there is nothing comparable to the focussing, convergence, coping with involuntary eye movements, and controlling voluntary ones required in visual perception.

Reading differs from listening in at least one other respect. Much of what the listener hears, particularly the beginning listener, concerns objects which are physically present and activities which are immediate. For the reader, on the other hand, the referents of the text are either totally imaginary or bear an extremely indirect relationship to his current situation. Imagination seems to play much more of a role in reading than in listening; indeed, perhaps the development of imagination is a prerequisite for learning how to read. For children and adults alike the major attraction of reading is the vicarious experience it offers. Analyses of reading focusing on its relation to speech predictably neglect the role of imagination.

In this anthology, only George Miller's paper suggests a consideration of cognitive aspects of reading beyond the convergence of visual and auditory information. Fundamental issues of meaning, common to both listening and reading, are inexplicably ignored throughout. Yet there are many indications that reading is more than talking to oneself. McLuhan (1962) has suggested that literacy changes the conscious experience not only of an individual but of an entire society. Shor (1970) suggests that many common reading situations involve the same psychological processes called into play during hypnosis. Recent research into imagery and its function (cf. Sheehan, 1972), and the asymmetrical functioning of the cerebral hemispheres (cf. Gazzaniga, 1970), raises a number of questions regarding prerequisites for literacy. Similarly, one wonders about the effect of literacy on a language itself, with later consequences for the users of that language.

It is not surprising that learning to read is more difficult than learning to listen. Once learned, however, reading does seem to be a more efficient process than listening. There is disagreement on the extent of this increased efficiency. Gough, who argues that reading is a serial processing of individual letters, is very skeptical of claims that individuals read at rates of more than 800 words per minute, i.e., more than three or four times the rate of listening. Mattingly (p. 135) refers to certain readers capable with perfect comprehension of over 2000 words per minute. Whatever the exact figures, there are several reasons for the greater efficiency of reading. These are related, I would guess, to precisely those factors that make reading difficult to learn. They include the fact, as discussed above, that the printed code itself is already partially interpreted.

In addition, the information on the printed page is permanently available. Most important, the greater flexibility of active reading, once it is mastered, stands in contrast to listening, which is necessarily passive. A skilled reader can exercise considerable control over the processing of the printed page.

Skilled readers may adopt quite different reading strategies depending on their purpose. Eleanor Gibson makes this important point. Looking up a word in the dictionary, reading a detective novel, studying a lesson, or reading a poem all may evoke somewhat different modes of reading. At least some of the controversy surrounding reading rates stems from the fact that there are many activities called reading.

The conference as a whole raised many more questions than it answered, several of which stand out as especially important. One concerns the relation between psychological research, including theoretical linguistics, and the teaching of reading. How will a deeper understanding of these processes help us teach children how to read and help reduce functional illiteracy among adults? Psychologists and linguists hope that their research will have a bearing on these problems. But Morris Halle, speaking directly to this point (p. 151), raised another possibility: that the main pedagogical problems include pupil motivation and attitudes of teacher and pupil to subject matter and to each other—issues not under consideration at this conference. O'Neil (p. 156) goes even further, suggesting that perhaps the fault may lie with the American education system and its attempts at cultural assimilation. This conference was not prepared to address the wider social aspects of literacy, but future conferences would do well to do so.

Psychological research surely does have some bearing on reading problems. Many youngsters of middle class background and average mental test scores fail to read well. Why is it, for instance, that males across diverse cultural groups have more than their share of reading difficulties? O'Neil's discussion of Klima's paper, I believe, may have important bearing on this question. If the Halle-Chomsky phonological theory accurately portrays the sound pattern of English, then English orthography is optimally designed for readers with a mature grasp of English. This raises the possibility that the early teaching of reading, before the child's phonological system matures, may be counterproductive. Harris Savin (p. 324) makes a similar point on a slightly different basis. Learning to read is a complex task; this complexity is compounded by a dynamically evolving phonological system. A stable phonological system probably is not established before age 7 or 8, perhaps as late as 11. This kind of "reading readiness" has nothing to do with visual discrimination or overt verbal fluency. Instead it concerns linguistic knowledge and how it is encoded. A child's speech may remain constant, but as the child matures, underlying phonological representations grow increasingly abstract, and listening processes become more efficient. Behavioral differences corresponding to these changes can only be observed in experimental situations; for example, in explorations of verbal transformations (Warren, 1968) or perception of very rapid speech.

If O'Neil is right, the disadvantages stemming from premature reading instruction would probably be magnified for males, who may lag behind females in physical maturation by as much as twelve months. O'Neil suggests two alternatives: modification of the orthography for children to make it more consonant with their phonology, or else delay of formal reading instruction until greater phonological maturity is achieved. The former suggestion has been under investigation for some time, but strikes me as impractical. The other alternative presents a straightforward research question: do reading problems on the average decrease when reading instruction is begun at ages 7 or 8 rather than 5 or 6? This question should be further explored.

Donald Shankweiler and Isabelle Y. Liberman introduce another complex of questions deserving continued attention. They report (p. 298) that problems of learning to read are very much related to the difficulty of synthesizing syllables. If one decodes too slowly, one loses track of the meaning. Harris Savin (p. 235) reiterates this point in his paper proposing that spelling of each syllable be taught without analyzing the spoken syllables into phonemes. He suggests that even proficient readers may want to do this, learning for themselves the syllabic, spelling-to-sound correspondences rather than the letter-to-phoneme correspondences. For example, one learns that *doe* and *dough* may correspond to the same sound. Of course this is entirely an empirical, not a formal, issue. There is no *a priori* reason why the printer's unit—the letter—must be the operative psychological unit in reading. Some configuration of letters might do just as well. Savin's paper indirectly raises a number of related questions about the role of syllables in reading, listening, and talking.

Despite the potential contribution of contemporary linguistics to the study of reading, a word of caution may be necessary about uncritical acceptance of linguistic theory as psychological theory. Constructs of the two kinds of theory are evaluated under differing empirical and theoretical constraints and generally are not isomorphic or interchangeable with one another, even when they concern the same phenomena. Klima's paper (p. 59) illustrates this point; in his analysis of orthography he distinguishes the actual language user from an ideal language knower. Too often the implications of such distinctions have not been carefully considered by psychologists or linguists. One major consequence of *Language by Ear and Eye,* I hope, will be an increasing synthesis of the goals of linguistic and psychological theory.

JOHN LIMBER
University of New Hampshire

References

Cattell, J. McK. On the time required for recognizing and naming letters and words, pictures and colors, 1885. In A.T. Poffenberger (ed.), *James McKeen Cattell: Man of science (Vol. 1 Psychological research).* Lancaster, Pa.: Science Press, 1947, pp. 13-23.

Chomsky, N. *Aspects of the theory of syntax.* Cambridge, Mass.: MIT Press, 1965.

Chomsky, N., & Halle, M. *The sound pattern of English.* New York: Harper & Row, 1968.

Dearborn, W. F. The psychology of reading. *Archives of Philosophy, Psychology, and Scientific methods* (1906), 4.

Gazzaniga, Michael S. *The bisected brain.* New York: Appleton-Century-Crofts, 1970.

Huey, E. B. *The psychology and pedagogy of reading.* New York: Macmillan, 1908. Reprinted Cambridge, Mass.: MIT Press, 1968.

Kavanagh, J. F. (ed.). *Communicating by language: The reading process.* Bethesda, Md.: U.S. Department of Health, Education and Welfare, National Institute of Health, Government Printing Office, 1963.

McLuhan, M. *The Gutenberg galaxy: the making of typographical man.* Toronto: Univ. of Toronto Press, 1962.

Pillsbury, W. B., & Meader, C. L. *The psychology of language.* New York : D. Appleton, 1928.

Sheehan, P. (ed.). *The function and nature of imagery.* New York: Academic Press, 1972.

Shor, R. E. The three factor theory of hypnosis as applied to the book reading fantasy and to the concept of suggestion. *The International Journal of Clinical and Experimental Hypnosis,* 18 (April, 1970), 89-98.

Smith, F., & Miller, G.A. (eds.). *The genesis of language: A psycholinguistic approach.* Cambridge, Mass.: MIT Press, 1966.

Warren, R. W. Verbal transformation effect and auditory perceptual mechanisms. *Psychological Bulletin,* 70 (October, 1968), 261-270.

Young, F. A., & Lindsey, D. B. *Early experience and visual information processing in perceptual and reading disorders.* Washington, D. C.: National Academy of Sciences, 1970.

THE PSYCHOLOGY OF READING
by Eleanor J. Gibson and Harry Levin.
Cambridge, Mass.: MIT Press, 1975.

The Psychology of Reading contributes significantly to the field through its synthesis of research on the nature of the reading process. Gibson and Levin's motivation in developing this extensive work derives from two goals: first, to propose a theory of how individuals learn to read

and, second, to assist in decision-making related to reading instruction. While *The Psychology of Reading* contributes toward both goals, a careful examination of the work reveals that we are still a great distance from achieving either.

In the early chapters of the book, Gibson and Levin set forth a basic psychological theory and discuss linguistic concepts, language development, writing systems, and word perception. In the bulk of the text, the authors present a developmental view of the reading process that extends from prereading skills through skilled reading. The last section of the text is, in effect, a postscript unrelated to the previous chapters of the work, discussing topics ranging from dyslexia to the role of parents in reading instruction.

The theoretical viewpoint posited by the authors stems directly from their theory of perceptual learning. Specifically, they view reading as the process of extracting from the printed page information which includes text, pictures, graphs, and so forth. Central to Gibson and Levin's thesis is the view that "higher-order structures" are basic to perceiving patterns of distinctive features in written language and to comprehending oral- and written-language forms. These structures are viewed as a set of rule systems that describe subordinate relationships among the phonological, syntactic, and semantic components involved in reading. The key processes in developing such rule systems include abstracting relationships, ignoring irrelevant information, locating high-potential information areas, using distinctive features, and obtaining intrinsic reinforcement through the discovery of structure and the reduction of uncertainty.

The argument posed by the authors is convincing on a generalized level; however, the abstract nature of these processes leaves many questions, both theoretical and practical, unanswered. For example, what process leads to the abstraction of relationships? How does the beginning reader decide what information is relevant and ignore what is irrelevant to the decoding process? Even though the authors discuss strategies of organization—such as systematic search and discovery designed to facilitate intra-individual learning—the reader is left with numerous questions

about the nature of these strategies. While Gibson and Levin's principles are helpful in developing a general understanding of the nature of the reading process from a perceptual-learning perspective, one must seriously question to what extent these general principles can be applied by classroom teachers on a day-to-day basis.

Gibson and Levin evaluate attempts to model the reading process and conclude that, due to the complexity of reading, such efforts provide limited insights. Their observations on modeling seem problematic, however. For example, they criticize the Goodman model as being "too vaguely specified to be checked" (p. 481). Yet this criticism can be applied equally to the Gough model, as well as to Gibson and Levin's own general principles. Certainly, reading is a complex process, and most models of the process are attempts to illustrate the complex interaction of various components at a given developmental stage. Models, by specifying decision-making junctures, can explain the reader's alternatives at particular points in the process. Modeling, if it has sufficient specificity, can also be of value in communicating a viewpoint, in formulating testable hypotheses, and in bridging the chasm between theory and practice. That Gibson and Levin, despite their own conclusions, devote a chapter to modeling lends support to its importance.

In addition to these broad theoretical concerns, several specific issues warrant closer examination. In the portion of the text that deals with linguistics, which has proved to be of substantial value to the reading field, the development of concepts is extremely brief, and highly complex issues are given minimal treatment. The discussion of morphophonemics, for example, is very limited. While this field is not completely worked out, as the authors note, it has developed substantially beyond their introduction. Furthermore, this reviewer hoped to find that the authors had gone beyond the sentence unit to discuss connective prose and discourse analysis—a promising new area for the study of language processing. In short, readers who want to obtain a basic understanding of linguistics will need to use the discussion and recommended sources as only a point of departure.

The presentation on language development emphasizes, for the most part, the period from five to seven years. Recent work suggests that language development continues well into the formal school years, and it is unfortunate that at least some of this research was not reviewed. The reader will find, however, that the section dealing with segmentation—specifically with phonemes, syllables, and words—is of great help in understanding the relationship between the perceptual process and reading acquisition.

Teachers will find particularly interesting the description of the Project Literacy Multi-Level Reading Program, a program based on research reported in this text. The authors describe in detail the program of instruction for spelling-sound correspondences, and a brief rationale is provided for the letter-sound correspondences introduced. One disappointment was the authors' failure to delineate the rationale for the way in which their program accounts for motivation and comprehension, areas given high priority in the text. This part of the discussion provided excellent opportunity to clearly illustrate the way in which research can be applied to assist curriculum formulation but failed to do so.

The difficulty of evaluating reading programs is reflected in the authors' conclusion about the effectiveness of their own program:

We are left with the modest claim that children learn to read and that there are a host of methods and materials which teachers may exploit in any way they see fit. For our purposes, we would be most pleased to see teachers be aware of the nature of reading and choose those methods and materials that make sense to them rather than be tyrannized by some prescription about how reading *must* be taught. (pp. 331–332)

In addition to recognizing the evaluation problem, the authors appear to be saying that the teacher's role is to derive principles of instruction from theory and research. Of basic concern here is the ecological validity of laboratory research. Generalization from such research to the instructional setting is difficult even for the advanced researcher; numerous variables that are found in the classroom are not accounted for experimentally. It is extremely important that research efforts and theory-based principles and generalizations be formulated within the context of classroom instructional variables.

Aside from the problems identified, *The Psychology of Reading* will undoubtedly have a substantial impact on the field of reading. The detailed research review and the principles formulated by Gibson and Levin should help reading specialists and researchers better understand the nature of the reading process from a perceptual-learning perspective. The greatest value of the work, however, will reside in providing the basis for generating researchable hypotheses which, through future research, will lead to an improved understanding of the reading process.

ROBERT B. RUDDELL
University of California, Berkeley

MEANING IN CHILD LANGUAGE: ISSUES IN THE STUDY
OF EARLY SEMANTIC DEVELOPMENT
by Laurence B. Leonard.
New York: Grune & Stratton, 1976.

While linguists and students of child language were instrumental in the 1960s in changing the focus of research and of some educational programs from individual words to syntactic structure, the emphasis has now moved toward understanding which sentence meanings children are able to convey. In *Meaning in Child Language* Leonard contributes to this shift by developing a semantic-relationship approach. This method allows for systematic and continuous descriptions of a young child's passage from gestures plus vocalizations through the one-word stage to sentences with more and more complex structures. Such an orientation leads to important applications for teaching language to children who do not acquire it by themselves, as well as for the teaching of reading and writing in the schools. A few details concerning these applications will be presented after the book's content has been reviewed.

The focus of Leonard's book is upon the developing ability of young children to express relevant relations in their environment. Given this emphasis upon the emergence of "semantic notions" (Leonard's term for relational meanings such as agent, action, object, instrument, and location), the study and the ideas presented in this volume represent a movement from the earlier syntactic-semantic work of Bloom (1970) and Brown (1973) toward a nonsyntactic-semantic description of children's first utterances.

The particular focus upon semantic relations distinguishes this book from other recent child-language studies which deal with other aspects of meaning. For example, referential meaning, the meanings of individual words, has been the topic of a number of papers (Clark, 1973; Nelson,

1973). Pragmatics, the use of language in its social context, enters into Leonard's discussion of relational meaning, but its development has been treated more directly by Bates (1976), Bruner (1975), and Dore (1974). With regard to syntax, Braine (1976) and Bloom, Lightbown, and Hood (1974) have investigated the acquisition of particular grammatical structures.

The two major topics of this volume concern the emergence of the semantic notions underlying young children's speech and the way in which these notions interact with children's learning of the linguistic code (grammatical structure). To this end, language protocols collected longitudinally for eight children were analyzed. The small sample size is consistent with traditional child-language investigations, which emphasize detailed descriptions of the speech performance of a few children at several points in time. Here the data are presented primarily as illustrations of the theoretical and methodological framework that is the author's main interest.

Leonard reviews a number of investigations that suggest that semantic notions emerge in a fairly orderly sequence during Stage I speech, when the child's mean length of utterance (MLU) is less than 2.25 morphemes (smallest units of meaning). This sequence seems much more orderly when viewed independently from the syntactic constructions used to code such notions. Some evidence is also reviewed to support the hypothesis that the order of emergence for semantic notions parallels the course of cognitive development. In particular, an attempt is made to relate the emergence of semantic notions to structural developments during the period of sensorimotor intelligence. Despite the fact that Leonard provides an understandable review of literature relevant to this possible relationship and develops some fascinating speculations, he seems to have been somewhat sidetracked in the first chapter from the primary goal of specifying semantic notions and documenting developmental order.

After a discussion about the emergence of semantic notions that appear to be universal—that is, acquired by all children—Leonard proceeds to review the literature concerning individual differences in the linguistic coding of these relational meanings. He discusses the proposal initiated by Bloom (1970) that children with the same mean-utterance-length may be expressing different semantic relations. For example, some children within the two-word stage seem to express predominantly functional relations (where the relational meaning between the words depends upon the meaning of one word, such as "no" or "more"), while other children seem to express many more grammatical relations (where the structural meaning derives from word order, such as "hit doggy" or "boy hit").

Whereas Bloom interpreted these differences in terms of individual children using different strategies of grammatical acquisition, Leonard explores the hypothesis that functional relations predominate at an earlier time for all children and that grammatical relations emerge later. To investigate this hypothesis, Leonard discusses various theories and reinterprets published child-language protocols. Leonard finds no evidence of a difference in semantic development associated with different emphases upon functional versus grammatical relations. At the end of this section, Leonard concludes that cognition and the vocal act are to some degree separable and that the acquiring of semantic relations appears to be more closely linked to cognitive development than to changes in the superficial features of language. The implication of this is that the common procedure of characterizing a child's level of language development in terms of utterance length may not provide an adequate view.

A primary contribution of this volume is Leonard's proposals for grammar writing (identification of the rules generating the sentences produced by children at a particular time in their development). A systematic means is provided for examining the underlying semantic notions of a child's linguistic system during Stage I speech. It attempts to capitalize on the strengths of other semantic approaches and attempts to solve some of the problems associated with each. The summaries of these other approaches, presented in an appendix, will be most useful to both practitioners and students of child language.

Leonard's proposed grammar consists of a hierarchical organization of semantic relations and rewrite rules indicating the allowable combinations. For example, as the child learns to express developing semantic notions, the grammar goes through systematic refinements to incorporate these changes. Leonard presents a detailed comparison of his semantic grammar with the well-known grammars of Brown (1973) and Bowerman (1973). He argues that the proposed approach, because it is the least syntactic, accounts for a greater proportion of Stage I utterances. In particular, once the procedures are sufficiently developed, Leonard's grammar will change the manner of characterizing single-word utterances. This change should permit continuity of description between the one-word and multi-word periods.

The author's use of spontaneous utterances with accompanying contextual information as data seems to lend itself to ascertaining which semantic notions are significant to the child. Leonard provides a view of how semantic notions emerge within the proposed framework. Beginning with the earliest word combinations of Stage I and ending with speech just beyond this stage, he uses the longitudinal data collected from eight children as a basis for developing grammars for three different periods: combined samples with MLU range from 1.10–1.30 morphemes, 1.70–1.90 morphemes, and 2.30–2.50 morphemes. It seems to this reviewer, however, that a grammar developed for several children must inevitably obscure many of the specific details of individual semantic growth. This is especially true in the light of Leonard's own conclusion that utterance length may not be an appropriate index of language level. Despite some unavoidable problems with frequency of occurrence, the observed developmental sequence of semantic notions was consistent with those of other investigators as well as with the course of cognitive development.

Leonard's book has several important applications. His semantic approach could provide for a description of language delay in terms of the semantic relationships that an individual child can express effectively. Remediation based on this approach would emphasize certain semantic relationships and particular combinations of these relationships, the order of which would be derived from developmental norms.

The goal of reading instruction within this view would be to abstract from each printed sentence the semantic relationships. While many recognize that the point of reading is to grasp the author's intended meaning, a formal theory of semantic relationships and their acquisition would provide, I believe, a firmer linguistic base for appropriate instruction than has been available previously. Similarly, effective expression of one's ideas has been the traditional goal of writing instruction, but it is only now that linguists are analyzing the ideas expressed by sentences. For example, two important aspects of written-language development during the school years are the abilities to compress a greater number of ideas into one sentence and to express semantic relations between more and more complex ideas. Increasing mean-sentence-length may reflect such processes, but longer sentences may also result from less mature or less sophisticated techniques, such as juxtaposition of ideas. Extrapolating from Leonard's work with toddlers, one might suggest that cognitive advances during the school years could be indicated by the sophistication of semantic relationships expressed in children's writings and in the accuracy with which they grasp semantic ideas underlying what they read.

In summary, Leonard's work reviews and reinterprets child-language literature and presents an approach to writing Stage I grammars that permits a systematic description of semantic development. A major conclusion should be that the level of language development might best be characterized in terms of semantic notions underlying utterances. Secondly, the relationship between semantic and cognitive development can be expected to be much stronger than the relationship between superficial language features and cognition. An important contribution, *Meaning in Child Language* is a book with significance for individuals interested in both early child language and in language skills acquired during the school years.

ELLEN BOUCHARD RYAN
University of Notre Dame

References

Bates, E. Pragmatics and sociolinguistics in child language. In D. Morehead & A. Morehead (Eds.), *Normal and deficient child language.* Baltimore: University Park Press, 1976.

Bloom, L. *Language development: Form and function in emerging grammars.* Cambridge, Mass.: M.I.T. Press, 1970.

Bloom, L., Lightbown, P., & Hood, L. Structure and variation in child language. *Monographs of the Society for Research in Child Development,* 1975, **40** (2).

Bowerman, M. *Early syntactic development: A cross-linguistic study with special reference to Finnish.* New York: Cambridge University Press, 1973.

Braine, M. Children's first word combinations. *Monographs of the Society for Research in Child Development*, 1976, **41** (1).

Brown, R. *A first language: The early stages.* Cambridge, Mass.: Harvard University Press, 1973.

Bruner, J. The ontogenesis of speech acts. *Journal of Child Language*, 1975, **2**, 1–19.

Clark, E. What's in a word? One child's acquisition of semantics in his first language. In T. Moore (Ed.), *Cognitive development and the acquisition of language.* New York: Academic Press, 1973.

Dore, J. A pragmatic description of early language development. *Journal of Psycholinguistic Research*, 1974, **3**, 343–350.

Nelson, K. Structure and strategy in learning to talk. *Monographs of the Society for Research in Child Development*, 1973, **38** (1).

SPEECH PLAY
edited by Barbara Kirshenblatt-Gimblett.
Philadelphia: University of Pennsylvania Press, 1976. 307 pp. $15.00.

Okka bokka soda crokka
Okka bokka boo;
In comes Uncle Sam
And out goes YOU. (p. 102)

Why are fire engines red?
One and one are two.
Two and two are four.
Three times four is twelve.
There are twelve inches in a ruler.
Queen Mary was a ruler.
Queen Mary rules the sea.
The fish have fins.
The Finns fought the Russians.
The Russians are red.
Fire engines are always rushin'.
That's why fire engines are red. (p. 92)

Why did the dog go out into the sun?
He wanted to be a hot dog. (p. 115)

These are examples of speech play. Play of any kind can be defined as a "framed" world in Gregory Bateson's (1955/1972) sense of an experience set apart for interpretation in a special, nonliteral way. In speech play, features of language, such as sound patterns, word meanings, grammatical structures, or conversational conventions, are the focus of attention. The playful use of language ranges from spontaneous creations, such as puns, which are uniquely appropriate at the moment of utterance, to more traditional speech play, such as rhymes and riddles, which children learn from others.

Speech Play is the first collection of studies of "how various speech communities select and group certain features from their linguistic and social resources in order to produce speech behaviors they define as playful, and of how they use such speech patterns in social life" (p. 2). The book is the sixth in a Conduct and Communication series that includes volumes by Goffman, Birdwhistell, Labov, and Hymes. The editor of this volume, Kirshenblatt-Gimblett, is on the faculties of Folklore and Folklife at the University of Pennsylvania and of Yiddish Studies at Columbia; the fields of the contributors include anthropology, Romance languages, linguistics, and developmental psychology.

The book is organized into four sections. The first, "Speech play as language structure," demonstrates how an analysis of speech play can reveal aspects of the player's language and cognitive structure—as messages encoded in pig latin could reflect the speaker's understanding of word boundaries. This section includes three chapters: J. Sherzer on play languages in Cuna (Panama), French, and Javanese; R. and S. Price on Caribbean Creole play languages; and Bricker on Zinacanteco

(Mexico) joking strategies. In the second section, "Initial and continuing acquisition," Sanches and Kirshenblatt-Gimblett relate children's traditional speech play to processes of language acquisition; Sutton-Smith relates changes in riddle content to Piagetian stages of classification; and Gossen analyzes the verbal dueling of adolescent boys in Chamula (Mexico). The third section, "Creativity: Institutional and individual," has two chapters: Backhouse describes Japanese mnemonics used to remember numbers and historical dates; and D. Sherzer presents a study of gnomic expressions, general sayings like proverbs and aphorisms, in a Beckett novel. Finally, in the last section the editor presents a brief note on needed research, an extensive bibliographic survey, and fifty-seven pages of references.

The rest of this review is organized by topics rather than chapters. It explores what we can learn from these studies about language development, about the role of speech play in children's social life, and, more speculatively, about possible uses of speech play in education. While the introduction indicates that this volume is concerned with all kinds of speech play, discussion of traditional play predominates.[1]

Language Development

Children's speech play, like that of adults, involves an attention to the form as well as the content of utterances. There are, however, differences between the ways children and adults play with language. Sanches and Kirshenblatt-Gimblett analyze how three general aspects of child language may account for some of the features of children's speech play. First, there is a relatively greater salience of sound patterns in child language. Gibberish jump-rope rhymes, such as "Okka bokka soda crokka" above, reflect children's at-

tention to language sounds. Second, qualitative differences in the organization of word meanings may produce chains of associations, as in the riddle about why fire engines are red. Third, quantitative limits on children's speech production can account for stylistic devices such as rhymed couplets, that are structured over short spans, and concatenations of memorized series, such as numbers or the alphabet, that extend overall length.

Sanches and Kirshenblatt-Gimblett also suggest a developmental sequence in the linguistic features that children focus on in play—a sequence in which "the child's concerns shift from phonological to grammatical to semantic and finally to the sociolinguistic level of language" (p. 102). They hypothesize that the developmental sequence may be universal, while the particular poetic devices incorporated in play may vary from language to language. This progression is consistent with the rhymes they collected from five- to fourteen-year old children, but it oversimplifies the general developmental picture of children's speech play. Garvey (1977) has presented examples of all four categories of speech play—phonological, grammatical, semantic, and sociolinguistic—from children under six, and concludes that "from about three and a half virtually all levels of language structure were used as a basis for social play" (p. 66). Moreover, to the extent that it is true that play "reflects an exercise in whatever part of the language structure the child is currently mastering" (p. 96), it can't be true that the focus in play shifts so neatly with age from one level to another. Language is not learned by levels. Sounds seem to be learned first because children's vocalizations are identified as speech only when they conform to recognized sound patterns, but, in fact, meanings begin to be acquired before any words are spoken and continue to be acquired throughout life.

The full story of developmental sequences in children's speech play requires a more fine-grained analysis of both the

---

[1] The chapter on "Play with language" in Garvey (1977) is a complementary presentation of nontraditional play.

linguistic features used and the genres of speech play produced. Fortunately, the chapters by Sutton-Smith and Gossen do just that. Sutton-Smith looks at changes with age in "the specific semantic devices that give the riddler the materials for his exercise of arbitrary power in the rhetorical context" (p. 113). Gossen describes how Chamula boys acquire the ability to improvise dueling sequences that follow strict rules of phonological continuity, using minimal sound shifts, and of semantic continuity, using derogatory or obscene responses.

Social Life

Because traditional speech play has been studied mostly by folklorists and nontraditional play by psychologists, their studies have primarily focused on the development and forms of speech play rather than on its functions in social life. Ethnographic analysis of speech play is one of the important contributions of this collection of articles. J. Sherzer indicates that a common feature of play languages, such as pig latin, is "concealment and a corresponding delineation of social groups and subgroups" (p. 34). Bricker writes that "joking strategies are primarily a male activity in Zinacantecan, where men use word play as an opportunity to prove and reaffirm their masculinity" (p. 55). Sanches and Kirshenblatt-Gimblett quote from Bernstein's (1960) discussion of the psychological and sociological implications of the use of traditional speech play: "[It] continuously signals the normative arrangements of the group rather than the individual experience of its members. . . . language does *not* facilitate the unique verbalization of subjective intent. Its use reinforces solidarity with the group, its functions, roles and aims" (quoted on p. 73). But analysis of play's social functions remains a weaker part of the book than analysis of its formal features.

Sutton-Smith's analysis of historical changes in speech-play preferences illustrates what we still do not know about the social functions of speech play. While grade-school girls in the United States continue to use rhymes for jumping rope and bouncing balls, singing games are evidently now less widely known. Sutton-Smith comments: "One is tempted to say that children today do not, to the same extent, need to have games to structure their social relationships. They are socially so much more mature that many of their relationships can be carried on in conversational terms" (p. 70).

What kind of conversation has replaced singing games on the playground? Is it the need for stylized routines that has changed or only the speech forms that serve that need? Kirshenblatt-Gimblett asks that future research explore "how joking and other forms of speech play [may] be used to create interaction" (p. 177). Stylized routines have particular significance in creating interaction—where they function more to enhance relationships than to convey information. (See, for example, Bruner and Sherwood's [1976] analysis of peekaboo games.) As Bernstein (1960) makes clear, traditional speech play is only one form of "habitual automatic sequences." If it seems to disappear from children's social life, then we need to know whether the function of language has changed or only its form. Does television, for example, supply today's children with a new set of stylized routines?

Separate from questions about the function of speech play in children's social life at the moment of playing is speculation about the role of play as a means of children's enculturation over time. For example, Sutton-Smith speculates about the kinds of societies in which riddles are common. Defining a riddle as a "game of rhetoric or arbitrary power in which victory is achieved by prior access to arcane knowledge" (p. 112), he hypothesizes that:

> riddles would appear cross-culturally in a context in which adults quizzed children orally and in which the children were required to be attentive and re-

sponsive to such quizzing. The under-lying assumption formulated by John M. Roberts and myself was that conflict induced by child training procedures leads to the development of expressive models within which children both re-state the paradox and gain buffered ex-perience in dealing with it. (p. 111)

Roberts confirmed this hypothesis in a search through material on 146 cultures in the Human Relations Area Files: riddles exist in cultures where rote learning and oral interrogation are emphasized.

Several chapters, notably Bricker's and Gossen's, suggest how learning to engage in speech play requires and contributes to the acquisition of culturally important se-mantic categories and interactional struc-tures. Two unpublished papers by Mc-Dowell (Note 1; Note 2) have extended such an analysis to the riddles of five-to eight-year-old Chicano children. Mc-Dowell contrasts "descriptive routines" with true riddles. Descriptive routines ex-press knowledge of cultural categories, for example: *What's round and it gots a lot of jelly? A jelly doughnut.* True riddles, by contrast, violate these categories in some way, as in, *What's black and white and red all over? A skunk with heat rash.* Mc-Dowell comments:

Riddling as an enculturation device al-lows children to work through the dual vectors of language, towards order and towards anti-order, in a stimulating and enjoyable social context. In riddling, at various ages, children learn to formulate culturally acceptable classification; to articulate classifications at variance with cultural conventions; and finally to as-sess language and indeed classification as arbitrary instruments reflecting only partially the continuous texture of ex-perience. (Note 2, p. 12)

Education

In introducing this collection, Kirshen-blatt-Gimblett promises that "the rele-vance of speech play to current issues in folklore, psychology, anthropology, lin-guistics and literature" (p. 3) will be dis-cussed. Since education is not mentioned, the book cannot be criticized for neglect-ing it. Nor can the authors be held respon-sible for my speculations on the relevance of speech play to education. Kirshenblatt-Gimblett's bibliographic survey does men-tion, however, two important studies rele-vant to education: Roskies's (in press) his-torical research on alphabet instruction in the Eastern European *heder,* the primary school of Eastern European Jews prior to World War I, and a formative evaluation of children's comprehension and enjoy-ment of speech play presented on tele-vision (Fowles & Glanz, Note 3).

Let us consider first the relationship be-tween traditional speech play and educa-tion. Readers and other curriculum ma-terials often include traditional lore. For example, the primary level of Interaction materials created by Moffett and pub-lished by Houghton Mifflin includes a booklet of *Jump Rope Jingles and Other Useful Rhymes* as well as activity cards which encourage children to tell and write their own. This booklet was a special fav-orite of the Black girls in my primary class-room in California two years ago. If Bern-stein is right, the special value of such materials is the interaction and group partici-pation that they encourage. Pass It On, a curriculum developed by the Children's Folklore Program at the Southwest Edu-cational Development Laboratory, consists of chants, jump rhymes, riddles, and trad-ing-time activities. Scriven (Note 4) and his team of classroom observers praised the curriculum for its power to engage the at-tention and participation of early elemen-tary-school children, boys as well as girls. Castro (1971) has described how, as a speech-improvement teacher in a Brooklyn school, she collected games and rhymes from her pupils and used them to develop creative dramatics, a school festival, and a guide to help other teachers do the same.

Roskies (in press) studied the alphabetic

basis of children's traditional speech play: "the Hebrew alphabet found its ways into the folklore of heder students in songs, proverbs, counting-out rhymes, secret languages and rhyme verses." The *heder* teachers often used rote learning and mnemonic devices. For example, to aid visual discrimination of letters, the *heder* teachers used alphabet metaphors: letters were given limbs (*shin* has three heads) or compared to familiar objects (*alef* looks like a water carrier). The *heder* teachers do not, however, seem to have incorporated alphabet folklore created by children into their pedagogy. At a later time, "interesting conscious and directive use of alphabet lore was part of the experimentation in the Yiddish secular school movement in Europe and America between the two world wars."

Different questions arise about possible educational values of nontraditional forms of speech play. I have speculated on the possible benefits of such play for literacy (Cazden, 1974). Briefly, my hypothesis is that speech play increases the player's "metalinguistic awareness" by bringing elements of language structure to focal attention, and that such awareness in turn aids learning to read. Ryan (in press) carries further the second part of this argument in her call for needed research.

Finally, what about the value of presenting speech play to children? This question is important, for example, in the design of television programs. Kirshenblatt-Gimblett quotes a comment from Lesser that *Sesame Street* viewers enjoy word play but do not understand puns. In the design of *The Electric Company*, children's comprehension of verbal humor was critical since the goal was to focus children's attention on elements of the written code. For example, would the poor readers for whom the show was designed get the joke when the word *that*, in the animated sentence, *That doesn't swing*, starts to swing wildly to and fro? No, according to Fowles and Glanz's (Note 3) extensive formative

evaluation; the child viewers did not understand the joke although they did attend to the word *that,* the focus of the segment, because it was central to the action.

Educators may not realize the historical antecedents of these literacy-oriented television shows. According to Roskies, "the most elaborate alphabet folklore for children were the spelling dramas of ancient Greece. Actors were costumed, appearing as different letters. They danced in pairs, forming nonsense syllables which the student audience had to identify and chant according to a set meter" (in press). Questions about the role of speech play in education have an old and honorable history.

COURTNEY B. CAZDEN
Harvard University

Reference Notes

1. McDowell, J. H. *Interrogative routines in Mexican-American children's folklore* (Working Papers in Sociolinguistics, No. 20). Austin, Tex.: Southwest Educational Development Laboratory, December 1974.
2. McDowell, J. H. *Riddles and enculturation: A glance at the cerebral child* (Working Papers in Sociolinguistics, No. 36). Austin, Tex.: Southwest Educational Development Laboratory, July 1976.
3. Fowles, B., & Glanz, M. *Comprehension of verbal humor on "The Electric Company."* New York: Children's Television Workshop, February 1976.
4. Scriven, M. *Evaluation of Southwest Education Development Laboratory's Children's Folklore Project: "Pass It On."* Berkeley, Calif.: Educational and Development Group, n.d.

References

Bateson, G. A theory of play and fantasy. In *Steps to an ecology of mind.* New York: Ballantine Books, 1972. (Reprinted from *Psychiatric Research Reports,* 1955, 2.)
Bernstein, B. Review of *The lore and language of schoolchildren* by I. & P. Opie. In *Class, codes and control* (Vol. 1). Beverly Hills, Calif.: Sage Publications, 1971. (Reprinted from *British Journal of Sociology,* 1960, 11.)

Bruner, J. S., & Sherwood, V. Peekaboo and the learning of rule structures. In J. S. Bruner, A. Jolly, & K. Sylva (Eds.), *Play: Its role in development and evolution.* New York: Basic Books, 1976.

Castro, J. Untapped verbal fluency of Black schoolchildren. In E. B. Leacock (Ed.), *The culture of poverty: A critique.* New York: Simon & Schuster, 1971.

Cazden, C. B. Play with language and metalinguistic awareness: One dimension of language experience. *The Urban Review,* 1974, 7, 23–39.

Erikson, E. H. *Toys and reasons: Stages in the ritualization of experience.* New York: Norton, 1977.

Garvey, C. *Play.* Cambridge, Mass.: Harvard University Press, 1977.

Roskies, D. Alphabet instruction in the East European heder. *YIVO Annual of Jewish Social Science,* 17, in press.

Ryan, E. B. Metalinguistic development and reading. In F. Murray (Ed.), *The development of the reading process.* Newark, Del.: International Reading Association, in press.

LITERATURE AS EXPLORATION
by Louise M. Rosenblatt.
New York: Noble and Noble, 1968.

Literature as Exploration first appeared in 1938, under the aegis of the Commission on Human Relations of the Progressive Education Association. Its revision and reappearance today are highly significant from the vantage points of English teaching and the general "crisis in the classroom." Originally written as a challenge to the preoccupation with literary history and/or literary technique then dominating English classrooms, Louise Rosenblatt's book developed an approach focusing upon the *experiences* made possible by works of literature. Addressed to classroom teachers, it proposed ways of involving diverse young people responsibly, meaningfully, and personally with literary art. The commitments of Deweyan philosophy permeate every chapter, the very commitments now being "discovered" throughout American education, as more and more educators become enthusiastic about open classrooms, individualized learning, and the free exploration of subject matters. In addition, Professor Rosenblatt's argument connects provocatively with recent critical talk of "human engagement" with and "participation" in imaginative literature. There is an approach to the difficult question of relevance in her pages which makes current pronouncements on the subject sound strangely tinny to the ear.

One point must be made clear immediately. This is not a book which treats literary art as solely instrumental, a mere adjunct to the development of mental health or moral standards or sociological perspective. Nor does it vulgarize literary masterpieces in order to merge them with the popular culture and thereby render them relevant. The heart of the matter for Dr. Rosenblatt is the need to nurture the fullest, most authentic understanding of literary works—each of which must be imaginatively apprehended and *lived through* in its integrity. But this cannot be accomplished, she says, if such works are treated in isolation from their readers' lived predicaments:

On the one hand, emphasis on abstract verbalization, on intellectual concepts cut off from their roots in concrete sensuous experience, is destructive of responsiveness to literature. On the other hand, image, form, structure, the whole sensuous appeal of literature, can be fully apprehended only within the framework of a complex sense of life. Sensitivity to literary technique should be linked up with sensitivity to the array of human joys and sorrows, aspirations and defeats, fraternizings and conflicts (pp. 50-51).

The literary experience (as the new critics sometimes choose to forget) is a function of a transaction between a live, idiosyncratic human being and the "work itself." When the human being involved is an adolescent who is unacquainted with the wider reaches of life and, at once, insatiably in quest of fulfillments, answers, recognition, and identity, his puzzlements and preoccupations are bound to feed into his interpretations of literature. Dr. Rosenblatt asserts, quite simply, that the teacher ought to be well enough informed to understand something about these preoccupations; not because she is called upon to reduce *Hamlet* or *The Sun Also Rises* or "Richard Cory" to adolescent identity-quests, but because she needs to be aware of the ways in which role confusion, intensity of desire, or simple innocence can distort literary perception. Louise Rosenblatt knows full well there can never be a single "correct" reading of a literary text. She points out, in fact, the importance of acquainting students with the possibility of varying interpretations. But she also knows that the necessary "recreation" of the verbal constructs which are literary texts can be impeded by misunderstanding, unwarranted projection, stereotyping, and dogmatisms.

Works of literature are not insulated from personal and social problems. In many senses, art's formed presentations originate in the stuff of such problems. Until young people reach the relatively advanced stage at which they can perceive a work of art as what Sartre calls an "unreal object" existing (as Wellek and Warren put it) within a "frame of fictionality," it is unreasonable to ignore what they (licitly or illicitly) bring *to* the work. Even if the teacher's primary interest is in communicating the notion of fictionality, she can scarcely avoid talking of the urgent "real-life" concerns which impinge upon the students' consciousness when they encounter particular works. Clearly, she needs sufficient knowledge to talk intelligently. She needs to know how to frame questions, how to stimulate the kinds of interchange which permit individuals to see what others have discovered in a text and thereby to widen their own visions of what is possible.

There is another use, as well, for psychological and sociological insights. When literary experiences are reflected upon, when characters and themes are openly discussed, the teacher's preconceptions with respect to personality and society will (if she is open to her class) come into play. Works of art are not, of course, to be evaluated in terms of social theories or personality theories; fictional characters are not to be treated as case studies, anymore than are the social arrangements depicted in fiction to be judged in political terms. In classrooms, however, statements are constantly being made which refer, directly or indirectly, to beliefs about behavior, morality, patterns of cultural life. This is legitimate, Professor Rosenblatt believes, when such discussion is evoked by actual experiences with literature. She points out "that we are concerned with social and psychological insights as they flower from the actual esthetic experience" and thereby separates herself from those who take a predominantly "social" or "psychological" approach to literary study. It must be remembered that she has not tried to write a *Poetics;* she has not attempted to develop a theory of literature. Her concern throughout is with the teaching of literature, which means enabling people to have significant literary experiences they would not have had without being so taught.

This is why she can move, without becoming guilty of a heresy, to consideration of the uses of studying literary traditions, styles, even biographies. Dr. Rosenblatt talks about "concentric circles of interest focused on the student's sense of a work" and about the ways in which an understanding of context can "clarify personal response." She never claims that an author's biography or social background can account for his created work in every particular; but she does see form and technique as choices made by the author, "intimately related to what he was seeking to convey." Describing a student discussion of *A Doll's House,* she demonstrates how the students themselves can raise the sorts of questions which demand recourse to cultural history. Acknowledging that "the teacher had had pedantic twinges of conscience about the attention paid to subjects that could not be strictly defined as literary," she nevertheless concludes that treatments of changing values, changing views of personality and the like may lead young people "toward a fuller appreciation of the play itself."

The criterion, she stresses, of the usefulness of extra-literary information is to be found in the student's need for it and his ability to assimilate it into his literary experiences. She gives the impression that this sort of assimilation can take place only when the classroom is transformed into a place where critical, probing talk takes place, where students are challenged to defend and test their interpretations. The focus is ostensibly upon deepened understanding of literature; but there are, in many places, indications that the other, perhaps more significant "use" for this kind of discussion is that it will produce increased understanding of self, the world, and the whole process of critical thought.

The question, then, of whether literary study is of instrumental value inevitably arises. Does literary study, for example, help to arm people for the struggle against depersonalization? Does it help

them counter the cold objectivity today associated with the sciences? Does it widen perspective? Does it make individuals more humane? There is a sense in which this book is very much of the early progressive era, the period *before* the vast burgeoning of technology now characterizing our society. Dr. Rosenblatt speaks of "the spirit of the scientific method and its application to human affairs" with an optimism seldom found among humanists today. She distinguishes properly enough between literature and science but sees nothing inherently inimical in their relationship. Speaking of the "framework of ideas concerning what is general and what is unique" which the scientist attempts to discover, she writes that "this framework of knowledge, these guiding principles, offered by the scientist are never irrelevant to the experience derived from either life or art."

Clearly, they are not irrelevant for the teacher concerned, as Louise Rosenblatt is, to clarify faulty assumptions and correct **what Charles Sanders Peirce used to call** "tenacious beliefs" deriving from the past. They are not irrelevant for the teacher intent upon communicating warranted beliefs—about, say, social and cultural conditioning, the effects of learning, the adequacy of particular value systems. Throughout the book there is an implicit preoccupation with the nurture of intelligence, along with a faith in reflective thinking as the most dependable means of coping with a changing, often threatening environment. The author believes that the teacher of literature can help to promote "positive emotional drives" and the safeguarding of human values while fulfilling her esthetic purposes. Because she continually returns to those purposes and to the need for enriched experiences with actual works of literature, she avoids the **trap of didacticism. There is no question,** however, that she *does* view literature as one of several ways of becoming more tolerant, more sensitive, more humane.

Talking of the youth who manages to free himself from archaic attitudes and ideas, she writes: "Literary experiences may help to fasten his emotions upon new and happier types of relationships or upon the images of new and more socially valuable satisfactions to be derived from life. Thus he may acquire the sympathy and insight, the critical attitudes, and the sense of human values needed for his creation of new ideals and new personal goals."

We are not so sanguine, although we would like to be. We recall C. P. Snow's less flattering view of the literary intellectual. We recall George Steiner's reminders that graduates of some of the finest arts faculties in Europe were the accomplices of "political bestiality" of the worst kind (and that many of them found it perfectly possible to read Rilke and Goethe the night before pushing people into gas chambers). Dr. Rosenblatt might say (and with justice) that mere acquaintance with works of literary art does not guarantee humane sensitivity. All depends on how literature is taught, on what transpires in the classroom. She hopes to see "active participation in literature—the reader living through, reflecting on, and criticizing his own responses to the text." This seems to mean that the reflective process is as necessary as the imaginative engagement, if there is to be a full and productive literary experience. It means that literary experience can stimulate emotional and intellectual growth when (perhaps only when) it is nurtured in teaching-learning situations of a special kind: where major premises are continually examined, where students are personally involved, where critical thinking is the rule.

The moral and intellectual responsibility of the English teacher is greater than we ever thought, if the implications of Professor Rosenblatt's argument are followed through. Responding to the implicit challenge, no teacher can be mere clerk or missionary or functionary of some sort. No teacher can simply set forth ready-made knowledge or impose ready-made ideas. No teacher can content herself with making available the purely esthetic values in works hermetically sealed away from life. She must be willing to open herself and her knowledge claims to searching examination, to undertake critical thinking before her class, to act in such a way that her students learn to question intelligently, learn to analyze—learn, indeed, to learn.

There is something tonic about all this, especially at a time when literature is being shunted aside in many places in favor of film, and when many teachers (trying desperately to be "with it") are choosing the productions of mass culture over works of art as means of coming in contact with the young. Dr. Rosenblatt's cause, it happens, has recently received support from an unexpected quarter: Pauline Kael, the greatly talented film critic of *The New Yorker*, has recently expressed her own concern about the current neglect of literature by both young and old.

Writing on January 23, 1971, she said:

> If some people would rather see the movie than read the book, this may be a fact of life that we must allow for, but let's not pretend that people get the same things out of both, or that nothing is lost. The media-hype encourages the sacrifice of literature.
>
> Movies are good at action; they're not good at reflective thought or conceptual thinking. They're good for immediate stimulus, but they're not a good means of involving people in the other arts or in learning about a subject. The film techniques themselves seem to stand in the way of development of curiosity.
>
> Movies don't help you to develop independence of mind. They don't give you much to mull over, and they don't

give you the data you need in order to consider the issues they raise.

Louise Rosenblatt is much interested in giving students "much to mull over," as she is interested in making literary study an occasion for "reflective thought or conceptual thinking." Her method of doing so is to involve people as thinking, feeling, *and* imagining beings; and she has enough confidence in the young to believe that, if the focus is on their concern and their experience, they will choose to involve themselves.

We are left with the wish that *Literature as Exploration* had moved sufficiently into the contemporary moment to confront the unprecedented problems of an entirely new generation, afflicted by unending war, hypocrisy in high places, and a terrible feeling of powerlessness. There remains the problem of young people's distrust of the scientific method and what they call "the myth of objectivity." There remains the demand for spontaneity in the classroom, for private and subjective encounters, for a quest for authenticity which often goes beyond the "reflective" and the "critical," sometimes beyond words. Agreeing with Professor Rosenblatt that students are too often hindered by outmoded notions with respect to human beings and society, we nonetheless want to hold in mind the fact that teachers (strangers to what Margaret Mead calls the emerging prefigurative culture) are themselves too frequently hindered by commitments which strike students as outmoded. There must be, as Dr. Rosenblatt would certainly agree, explorations on both sides. Literature still speaks to old as well as young when it whispers (like Rilke's torso of Apollo) "You must change your life."

MAXINE GREENE
Teachers College
Columbia University

LANGUAGE AND LEARNING
by James Britton.
Coral Gables, Fla.: University of Miami Press, 1971.

Despite the seemingly endless stream of volumes on the teaching of English, the discipline has chronically suffered from the lack of organizing principles—it has never had an adequate psychology. Mired in lifeless notions of what literature is and how language functions, the profession's first response to the new "discoveries" in linguistics, for example, was to ossify in kind. Chomsky was mistakenly transformed into Roberts,[1] and claims were made that at last true knowledge about language was being taught. In the face of such attitudes and practices it is only the rare English teacher who has a dynamic sense of what he is about, who judges the results of his classroom in terms of how his students go on to live their respective lives.

In *Language and Learning*, a synthesis of the most recent findings and observations in the field of language and psychology, James Britton sketches out a clearer picture than we have had to date of how our use of and confrontation with language, both inside and outside of the school, consciously or otherwise, is such a crucial factor in both our mental and personal development. Through his delicate insistence upon the humanizing function

[1] Noam Chomsky's transformational grammar represents a revolution in linguistic thinking, but it continues to be exploratory in nature. Paul Roberts, among others, rigidly poured these "findings" into graded English series which in some cases have been adopted on a state-wide basis.

664

of language, Britton, who has been teaching English in Great Britain since 1930, challenges us to make English education, and all education for that matter, the liberating and on-going process it ought to be.

Britton's chief purpose is to elaborate the conception that we spend much of our lives ordering the confusion that surrounds us, a process that involves creating for ourselves a coherent and workable picture of how the environment impinges upon us:

> . . . by various means of representation, and with the aid of language as an organizing principle, we construct each for himself a world representation: that we modify this representation in the light of further experience in order that our predictions may be better; and that we improvise upon it for a variety of reasons. (p. 31)

This idea for building up successive representations is borrowed from George Kelly, whose work, Britton emphasizes, provides a new way of looking at learning, especially as it might be stimulated in the English classroom. Britton quotes Kelly extensively:

> Man looks at his world through transparent patterns or templates which he creates and then attempts to fit over the realities of which the world is composed. The fit is not always very good. Yet without such patterns the world appears to be such an undifferentiated homogeneity that man is unable to make any sense out of it. Even a poor fit is more helpful to him than nothing at all . . . .
> Experience is made up of the successive construing of events. It is not constituted merely by the succession of events themselves. . . . It is not what happens around him that makes a man's experiences; it is the successive construing and reconstruing of what happens, as it happens, that enriches the experience of life. . . . The constructions one places upon events are working hypotheses which are about to be put to the test of

experience. As one's anticipations or hypotheses are successively revised in the light of the unfolding sequence of events, a construction system undergoes a progressive evolution.[2] (pp. 17-18)

What Kelly is describing is a transactional model of human experience. As our experience accumulates with interactions with the environment, we continue to construct and demolish explanatory constructs. Just as at some point new scientific data require new scientific theories, so, too, as we develop, new experience taxes the thresholds of our old constructs, and this forces us to create new models of the world. Men are always reconsidering events, trying to interpret them and attach meaning to them, but unfortunately for many people the growth process stops and they become locked into patterns which they use over and over again to understand the continual influx of experience. However, from birth until the onset of this rigidity, the individual dynamically orders and reorders his experience as his personality is being formed.

With the idea of templates in mind it is easy to see the crucial importance of language, for language is the stuff out of which we represent experience. Most of Britton's book is centered upon this integral use of language to symbolize what is occurring around us. To operate with some modicum of efficiency, the individual needs to build up some sense of stability and predictability. Language, being one step removed from the actual sensing of experience in the environment, grants us this lead time. It allows us to explore and play with the meanings and possibilities of experience, freed from the realities of onrushing time.

Language, of course, is expressed in many modes and serves countless ends. The distinction Britton expands upon is between participant and spectator language. A "participant" is "participating *in the*

[2] From George A. Kelly, *A Theory of Personality* (New York: W.W. Norton, 1963).

665

world's affairs" (Can you help me find the glue? Top drawer . . . etc.). A "spectator" is "contemplating experiences, enjoying them, vividly reconstructing them perhaps —but experiences *in which he is not taking part*" (Last week when I was in church. . . .) (p. 104). There are many gradations along this continuum, but what is most important to remember is that at times we are in the midst of action while at other times we are enjoying or analyzing the representation of actions, real and imagined, ours and others. To explain these categories more precisely Britton fills his book with numerous examples and transcripts of language being used in its various forms by children and adults. And in presenting this evidence, Britton synthesizes much current research from Piaget to Bruner; but although a framework is sketched out (how children first discover and extend their language, the importance of talk at all stages of development, and so on), Britton, like the thinkers he refers to, is careful to point out that our knowledge in these areas is still rudimentary.

The implications of Kelly's schema for the teaching of English are profound. The conventional conception of education whereby one's experience and knowledge result from the linear accruing of events and data is no longer valid (and to be sure this static conception has already been attacked on many fronts by many of the people whose work Britton cites). Rather, learning is much more a matter of the successive discovery, construction, and modification of symbolic models. To take a specific example of how this would influence current practices, let us consider Britton's approach to reading instruction. Reading is too frequently viewed as a word upon word buildup until some conclusion is reached at the end of a particular piece. In contradistinction to this, Britton tells us reading is the filling in of details for a pattern of focused expectations. "The meaning is an *emergent pattern* of relationships—more like a negative in the de-

veloping dish than it is like a train coming out of a tunnel" (p. 161). As we read at any level our anticipation is either borne out or jarred. If the latter, we must construct a new pattern as we re-read and re-interpret. Consequently any teaching which involves the piecemeal presentation of items simply does not match the dynamic psychological process the student undergoes when he is reading (or learning). Thus Britton predictably comments:

> The notion of 'providing vocabulary' is a limited and misleading one, suggesting an all too static conception of language. Language in use is a flow, a current of activity, and not any sort of reservoir. The words a child can come by in this deliberate fashion at the teacher's providing—in the course of a vocabulary lesson—will tend to be those of limited use, necessary at times but with little power to vitalize the current of speech. Teachers need to care about the flow— about reading 'as though it made sense', and writing and talking—and when they do, the reservoir will look after itself. To put it another way, it is from successive experiences of words in use— words used for some actual profit or pleasure—that a child builds up his resources, and there is little point therefore in our dragging things in by their names. (p. 163)

It is in the area of literature, it seems to me, that Britton is most helpful for the English teacher. For too long we have lived amid a herd of sacred cows, squeezed between the revered classics and the rigid canons of literary criticism. In this tradition literature is an object, something to be collected and classified, and dutifully passed on like the periodic table in chemistry. Britton's view is transactional in nature (something Louise Rosenblatt, among others, has been telling us for years,[3]), *i.e.*,

[3] See Louise Rosenblatt's *Literature as Exploration*, rev. ed. (New York: Noble and Noble, 1968).

literature is an object requiring a subject, and, furthermore, it is the *written form of language in the role of spectator*. Such a notion at first glance debases accepted literary standards, but Britton anticipates such criticism:

> I think it is helpful to have a way of defining literature which refers to the sort of thing *it is* rather than one which brings in the judgment as to how good it is of its kind. It is not that I feel the question 'how good is it?' is not a highly important question, but I think it should come *after* and not instead of the question, 'what is it?'. (Picasso is a better painter than an average child in the Infant School, yet they both *paint*.) If we operate only with a normative definition of literature—one that begins to apply above a certain threshold of excellence —we are left with the difficulty of deciding what a piece of writing is that tries but fails to rise above the threshold. It must be *something*. We have only to think of the kind of writing done every day by thousands of children in school to see that this is not an entirely frivolous objection. (p. 108)

Given that written language in the role of spectator describes the kind of thing literature is, we next see that its use in and out of the classroom ought to be concerned with how human contingencies are presented and subsequently with the refinement of our templates of experience. As David Holbrook,[4] borrowing from the "object-relations" school of psychoanalysis, he argued, the development of a secure and loving identity is a function of the extent to which the individual is able to build a coherent picture of external reality which matches his internal reality (what he sees vs. what he feels). Literature provides much symbolic content which allows for the verification of these psychic

[4] See David Holbrook's *Human Hope and the Death Instinct* (New York: Pergamon Press, 1971).

realities. And it is only when we step back as spectators that we can work on the meanings of and create patterns for the experience that continually confronts us. This is the central purpose of literature (which includes children's writings) and ought to be the goal of English instruction.

Naturally, this notion of literature and English teaching sounds very liberal and free-wheeling—relevance and the child are the thing! Yet Britton easily transcends the merely voguish practices and facile rhetoric of the educational romantics. He is for trusting students, to be sure; still, he is very clear about the teacher having a professional role, one which is neither the "subject-specialist" nor the "pseudo-parent." The relationship between the teacher and student, despite its inevitable closeness, must never be an object in and of itself; rather, it is a means to the end of the student's learning and personal growth. Similarly, Britton is clear about what children or adolescents can and cannot handle emotionally. Relevance is not keeping up with the *avant-garde*, but using material which offers sufficient predictability to the student so as to be accessible and challenging, without being overly threatening. Such a view, for instance, gives us a better perspective on "trash" literature, which teachers have been castigating for years. Many books, although not necessarily noteworthy for their style or message, might be entirely appropriate in terms of the themes and situations they allow the student to contemplate. This is not to say that anything goes, but that some works make more demands upon us as readers (spectators), and that the road to a mature response (not just to literature but to life) is long and circuitous. Again the point is to work on our representations, not to find easy formulas.

With regard to the contemporary propensity to impose a disjunction between cognitive and affective modes of representation, Britton writes:

> Psychologists in general have tradition-

ally concentrated upon cognitive organization and tended to regard emotion as itself disorganized and possessing a disorganizing influence. We need to recognize the value and importance both of the discursive logical organization and at the same time that of the undissociated intuitive processes, the organization represented in its highest form in works of art. (p. 217)

It is this split which causes much harm in English education today. In advocating the "free expression" of the child (the affective revolt against the long reign of cognition) too many romantics forget that to create we need content to work upon, and that the literary process involves more than freedom—it is the exploration of inner modes of representation symbolized in language as they compare to outer forms of reality. The result is so much relativity; yet Britton has illuminated some philosophical boundaries which we can make use of as we attempt to order our language and, one hopes, our lives.

At the end of *Language and Learning*, Britton cautions us against overestimating the role of language in the representation of experience: "There will always be a gap between our total response to what confronts us and any formulation we can make of what was there and what took place." And so he returns to Kelly:

A person is not necessarily articulate [Kelly says], about the constructions he places upon his world. Some of his constructions are not symbolized by words: he can express them only in pantomime. Even the elements which are construed may have no verbal handles by which they can be manipulated and the person finds himself responding to them with speechless impulse. Thus in studying the psychology of man-the-philosopher, we must take into account his subverbal patterns of representation and construction. (p. 277)

And to this end Britton discusses the role of dramatics in English. Still, in expressing both our conscious and unconscious tendencies, language is of central importance. It is the chief means by which we can develop increasingly more valid constructs of our experience. This, it seems to me, is what English teaching should be about—helping children (and adults) to use language and literature to better enjoy and control their lives. And Britton's book helps us to be much more aware of how we might go about this.

GORDON MORRELL PRADL
New York University

TRADITION AND REFORM IN THE TEACHING OF ENGLISH: A HISTORY
by Arthur N. Applebee.
Urbana, Ill.: The National Council of Teachers of English, 1974.

Arthur Applebee has produced the first well-documented study of the teaching of English in American public schools, a comprehensive survey of developments in English curriculum from the *New England Primer* of 1690 to the current debates on accountability and behavioral objectives. His book is intelligible to the lay reader while being thorough enough for the specialist English teacher. In publishing *Tradition and Reform* the National Council of Teachers of English has departed from its usual concern with methodology and curriculum development.

Applebee gives an accurate report of the marches and counter-marches in the struggle to establish and develop English as a subject of study. His study fascinates most when he points out the perplexities and incongruities which accompany the mingling of different traditions and techniques. Despite the paucity of sources for the period 1690–1890, Applebee's review identifies the roots of the ethical, classical, and nonacademic traditions and provides perspective on later developments. The greater part of the book is then devoted to a discussion of events after 1894, when the Report of the Conference of the National Education Association finally established English as a subject of study in the public schools (pp. 22–23, 36, 38).

The ethical tradition in the teaching of English stems from the mid-fifteenth century when the invention of the printing press made the Bible available in the vernacular to a wider populace. By the time of the Reformation, learning to read Scripture was the aim; literacy was considered close if not next to godliness. Often perplexed by the pagan writings of Greece and Rome, Christian teachers over the centuries followed the recommendation of St. Jerome: "In reading the ancient poets we absorb the things of life and beauty, leaving that which is but idolatry, error, or lust, to pass to its natural decay."[1]

As this approach to literature became genteel and pointedly moralistic, selections for school books were written to convey moral messages which were sometimes overwhelmingly simplistic. In the United States, the explicitly moral use of literature was epitomized by the *New England Primer*, which coupled moral aphorisms with each letter of the alphabet. The concern that literature should be morally uplifting ultimately led to the effort to purify

[1] The statement is attributed to St. Jerome by Aneas Sylvius (afterwards Pope Pius II) in "De Liberorum Educatione" in *Vittorino da Feltre and Other Humanist Educators*, ed. William Harrison Woodward (New York: Teachers College Press, Columbia Univ., 1963), p. 150.

it through the rejection of major literary works and the bowdlerization of the survivors. Toward this end, the *New England Journal of Education* in 1893 gave editorial support to students who refused to read an unexpurgated edition of *Hamlet*: "All honor to the modest and sensible youths and maidens of the Oakland High School.... The indelicacies of Shakespeare in the complete edition are brutal" (p. 22).

In contrast, proponents of the classical tradition perceived the study of literature as an occasion for acquaintance with the greatest authors, whom they sought to defend from writers who would cut and trim famous works to suit timid and banal tastes. The most famous exponents of the classical tradition in America were Mortimer J. Adler and Robert M. Hutchins, who urged during the 1930s that the works of the hundred greatest writers from the time of Homer to the present be the basis of a liberal education. Their more comprehensive view of literature included classics of science, history, and philosophy in addition to the traditional literary fare. The essence of the classical approach today continues to lie in its respect for the thought and expression of great writers. Clear evidence of the tradition is found in the frequent appearance of Shakespeare, Milton, Coleridge, Eliot, Lowell, and Macaulay on reading lists for school English classes.

The nonacademic tradition in the teaching of English began with what Applebee calls "the extracurriculum" (pp. 12–13). Benjamin Franklin was among the first to urge the practical value of English literature as a model for writing, declamation, and oral reading. By the early nineteenth century, the study of English in such schools as Boston English High School offered an alternative to the traditional program of Greek and Latin studies, and finishing schools provided practical English courses for students who were not going on to college.

The effort to develop methods for teaching English as a school subject relied heavily upon the rhetorical tradition developed at Edinburgh and transmitted to America mainly through Hugh Blair's *Lectures on Rhetoric and Belles Lettres*.[2] Models of scholarship for the study of English were also taken from the traditions of philological studies at Göttingen, Harvard, and Johns Hopkins. As a consequence, prior to 1900, educators placed much emphasis on close textual analysis and study of the characteristics and history of various literary genres. Such methods easily become pedantic; as the pressure of college entrance requirements grew, schools were increasingly inclined towards the study of a literary canon, and English studies often became bound to a specific content. Perhaps the ultimate expression of this tendency was the reading lists contained in the Uniform Entrance Requirements in English requested by the National Education Association Committee on College Entrance Requirements in 1899.

Progressive educators reacted strongly to this hardening of the curriculum and to the idea of treating school students as miniature scholars. It was John Dewey and his followers in the early 1900s whose arguments for emphasis on the interests and abilities of the pupil presented a direct challenge to such a content-based and rigidly formal study of English.

The debate continues even now between those who would use the study of English as a means for pupils to explore and enrich their own experience and those who would present it to pupils as a distillation of superior experience to be assimilated by them. The post-Sputnik reaction which called for academic rigor in all subjects, including English, has been countered in the last few years by a move towards using English studies for pupils' self-exploration and self-expression. This expressive emphasis has much in common with the earlier progressive tradition but it often goes further to view expressive activities as a kind of therapy. Recent work on the role of language in socialization has encouraged the idea that language teachers can and should help students learn by facilitating their development of self-concepts and relations with other people.[3]

It is when Applebee begins to assess problems in the teaching of English that I must differ with him. His appraisal overlooks a number of vital issues. For example, English teachers have recently been urged to engage in therapy by encouraging students to express themselves while refraining from judging the quality of that expression. The expressive efforts of the pupils then become attempts at self-disclosure, leading, it is hoped, to better understanding and acceptance of oneself. When pursued in a more careless fashion, the practice of English as therapy degenerates into an emphasis on socialization through group experience, reducing the content of English to a loosely organized and self-conscious discussion.

The author's position on the teaching of English is ultimately a fusion of principles from the classical and progressive traditions. From the classical he derives the belief that the inspiration and meaning of literature are not to be dissipated through preoccupation with imparting a set of defined skills. From the progressive he draws the idea of building upon the interest of the student, starting where the student is, and allowing for individual variations. Thus, like the classicist, he believes that insofar as teachers of English emphasize specific knowledge or content they are in conflict with the acknowledged concerns of literature teaching, namely "questions of values and perspective—the kinds of

[2] Hugh Blair, *Lectures on Rhetoric and Belles Lettres* (Dublin: Messrs. Whitestone, etc., 1783).

[3] See, for example, John Dixon, *Growth Through English* (London: Cox and Wyman, 1967); and James Britton, *Language and Learning* (London: Penguin, 1970).

goals usually summed up as those of a 'liberal' or 'humanistic' education" (p. 246). He is disconcertingly vague when he asserts that literature is at odds with the teaching of skills: "More progress might be expected in the teaching of literature if teachers recognized that it involves a response to patterns of experience not necessarily dependent upon reading skills at all" (p. 250). One wonders if Applebee is committed to the classical-humanistic tradition for its own sake, or whether he embraces it as an alternative to the emphasis on teaching skills in English.

In the end, Applebee's objections to a skills emphasis appear to be reactions to behavioral attempts to define all significant parts of teaching English. Although his discussion of behavioral objectives in teaching English is limited to a brief reference to Robert Mager's book, *Preparing Objectives for Programmed Instruction,*[4] and a passing mention of B.F. Skinner (p. 234), Applebee's main objection to behaviorism seems to be the constraints on teachers when they are required to specify educational goals in terms of skills for students to learn. Yet when he urges a wider and richer purpose for the teaching of English, he is evocative rather than informative:

> [T]he teaching of literature is a more tentative enterprise than [the behaviorists' position] implies; we know too little about fostering the kind of development we seem to cherish. The very materials with which we are working are so complex, touching upon such different aspects of the child's linguistic and moral development, that they may *always* resist formulation in the short-term stages that behavioral objectives imply. What we seek to do in English is not to add discrete components of skill or knowledge, but gradually to elaborate the linguistic and intellectual repertoire of our students, a process that is more fluid than linear, more fortuitous than predictable. (pp. 254–55)

I find it difficult to understand why Applebee should make such a point of resisting attempts to define skills which should be taught as part of the teaching of English. Attention to teaching specific skills need not lead to the banalities of vocabulary control and strict adherence to readability formulas. In objecting to these excesses of the Dick-and-Jane graded reading program, he seriously overlooks the possibility that attention to significant skills could greatly improve the quality of instruction.

Although good teachers will surely try to avoid teaching skills in isolation and will eschew the artificiality of studies centered on vocabulary lists, grammatical drills, and other crutches of lame English programs, they need not shrink from defining skills at all. They can be helpful to students precisely insofar as they can identify the points at which pupils' skills are strong or inadequate.

One can use a set of structuring principles—a tradition—without being committed to a set format of skills. In fact, structuring principles, if they mean anything at all, provide grounds both for defining the subject of English teaching and for distinguishing the more important elements from the less important. Applebee refuses to commit himself to any further definition and takes refuge in "literary values," which he implies are pertinent to moral and social development.

In summary, he rejects behavioral definitions, expounds on the moral value of literature, but fails to provide any alternative clarification of what English teaching might involve. To have done so, Applebee would have had to undertake a substantial discussion of methodology of teaching English. To embark upon meth-

[4] Robert F. Mager, *Preparing Objectives for Programmed Instruction* (San Francisco: Fearon, 1961).

odology would have meant the writing of a second book. We may properly excuse him from such a task, but it is still true that some of the important and useful questions raised in *Tradition and Reform*

in the Teaching of English cannot be considered properly without an effective discussion of methodology.

RALPH M. MILLER
University of Calgary, Alberta

CLASS, CODES AND CONTROL. VOLUME 1. THEORETICAL STUDIES TOWARD A
SOCIOLOGY OF LANGUAGE
by Basil Bernstein.
London: Routledge & Kegan Paul, 1972.

Language as a social institution is the powerful theme of Basil Bernstein's work. A precis of that work begins with his distinction between the *universal* "frames of consistency" represented in the syntax and morphology of a language, and the *distinctive* linguistic forms or codes "which induce in their speakers *different* ways of relating to objects and persons" (p. 123). Bernstein focuses particularly on a "restricted" and an "elaborated" code which he associates with lower- or working-class and middle-class speakers of English respectively. His argument is developed almost entirely in the context of England, though it has been much used, and, in Bernstein's view, abused, by Americans.

Most of the syntactical and morphological characteristics of the restricted and elaborated codes, i.e., the regularities of their grammar and vocabulary, seem to have been worked out by Bernstein in his early formulations of a "public" and a "formal" language. The more recent work has added certain subtleties to these characteristics, but has concentrated more on demonstrating their distribution among different social strata and on defining more theoretically their social functions. Thus in one of the earliest essays one finds the following contrasts.

Public Language

(1) Short, grammatically simple, often unfinished sentences, a poor syntac-

tical construction with a verbal form stressing the active mode.

(2) Simple and repetitive use of conjunctions (so, then, and, because).

(3) Frequent use of short commands and questions.

(4) Rigid and limited use of adjectives and adverbs. (See pp. 42-43 for these and the additional features of public language.)

Formal Language

(1) Accurate grammatical order and syntax regulate what is said.

(2) Logical modifications and stress are mediated through a grammatically complex sentence construction, especially through the use of a range of conjunctions and relative clauses.

(3) Frequent use of prepositions which indicate logical relationships as well as prepositions which indicate temporal and spatial contiguity.

(4) Frequent use of impersonal pronouns (it, one).

(5) A discriminative selection from a range of adjectives and adverbs. (See p. 53 for these and additional features of formal language.)

Explication of individual meanings is the basic function of an elaborated code, whereas a restricted code assumes that the speakers share more of their meanings in common. Speakers of any social class make use of restricted code on certain occasions: in reference to experiences they have shared intimately and do not need to elaborate to each other, or in various ritualized situations, in church or, equally, in the opening gambits of a cocktail party. The basic reason Bernstein gives for middle-class speakers alone using elaborated code is that their stratum possesses "access to the major decision-making areas of the society." The elaborated code, existing at a psychological level between assumed deep linguistic structures and speech, orients a listener to the relative significance of different spoken signals, and regulates the listener's selection and organization of words, sequences, and extra-verbal signals for his reply. Middle-class parents socialize their children to the use of this code in anticipation of the decision-making the children will have access to. Working-class parents do not socialize their children for this decision-making, or do not reflect access to it in their own speech. Teachers not only use elaborated code in school, but they demand that children use it. The children respond as a function of their earlier socialization, middle-class children succeeding and working-class children failing to speak in elaborated code. Thus the relative positions of the social classes are maintained.

"For various reasons," Bernstein writes, "in particular the occupation of the mother before marriage and the role differentiation within the family, there will not be a one-to-one correlation between the use of a restricted code and the working class stratum, but the probability is certainly very high" (p. 91). The role differentiation referred to here is explicated elsewhere by Bernstein in terms of positional versus person-oriented families. This distinction is itself associated with the dynamics of restricted versus elaborated code, and a working-class family that happened to regard its members as more individuated persons might develop the open communications system of an elaborated code.

More often than not these days, one has to fight against the misconstruction of "significant" differences between social classes, or the extension of the terms of a difference to virtually every member of the classes compared. A finding that fourteen percent of middle-class parents, in comparison to "only" eleven percent of working-class parents, name creativity as something they value in their children's behavior, is liable to be translated as middle-class parents value creativity, working-class parents do not. Melvin Kohn finds that social class (or, more specifically, education and the conditions of fathers' work) *consistently* predicts what parents value in their children, but at the same time he acknowledges that most of the variance is still not accounted for; yet Kohn then proceeds to associate middle-class parents with autonomy and working-class parents with conformity.[1] This is the sort of overgeneralization that one might expect to be involved in Bernstein's reasoning. But Bernstein's statistical confidence levels are high with relatively low *n*'s, and one comes to appreciate how immediate and all-pervasive the association of a language code with class might be, and what potential this might have for socialization.

Bernstein makes empirical statements only about England, and, indeed, it makes sense that an English scholar would be the first to attend to class, codes, and control. Bernstein seems to have believed at one point that the language of the "negro subculture" in the U.S.A. is a form of restricted code. Today he would surely have no difficulty agreeing with the observation that Black English is a dialect that for many years has included both restricted and elaborated codes.

A more fundamental problem is Bernstein's definition of the function of restricted code. The very term "restricted,"

[1] Melvin L. Kohn, *Class and Conformity: A Study in Values.* (Homewood, Ill.: The Dorsey Press, 1969).

by comparison even with "public," has a deficit connotation. Bernstein's attempt to disown this, in fact to shift the deficit interpretation to others' misreading of his work, falls flat. The following passages are typical of his "Critique of the Concept of Compensatory Education."

Now when we consider the children in school we can see that there is likely to be difficulty. For the school is necessarily concerned with the transmission and development of universalistic orders of meaning. The school is concerned with the making explicit and elaborating through language, principles and operations, as these apply to objects (science subjects) and persons (arts subjects). One child, through his socialization, is already sensitive to the symbolic orders of the school, whereas the second child is much less sensitive to the universalistic orders of the school. The second child is oriented towards particularistic orders of meaning which are context bound, in which principles and operations are implicit, and towards a form of language-use through which such meanings are realized. The school is necessarily trying to develop in the child orders of relevance and relation as these apply to persons and objects, which are not initially the ones he spontaneously moves toward. (p. 196)

Because a code is restricted it does not mean that a child is nonverbal, nor is he in the technical sense linguistically deprived, for he possesses the same tacit understanding of the linguistic rule system as any child. It simply means that there is a restriction on the *contexts* and on the *conditions* which will orient the child to universalistic orders of meaning, and to making those linguistic choices through which such meanings are realized and so made public (p. 197).

In the *applied* discourse of this and other of Bernstein's discussions of educa-

tion, one seeks in vain for a more positive representation of the function of restricted code. Ironically, Bernstein himself defines the positive function of restricted codes in any number of *theoretical* passages. It is communality or unity.

A restricted code is generated by a form of social relationship based upon a range of closely shared identifications self-consciously held by the members. An elaborated code is generated by a form of social relationship which does not necessarily presuppose such shared, self-consciously held identifications with the consequence that much less is taken for granted. (p. 108)

So far as the child is concerned, in positional families he attains a strong sense of social identity at the cost of autonomy; in person-centred families, the child attains a strong sense of autonomy but his social identity may be weak. (p. 185)

Were we to speak of a "communal" code versus an "individuated" code, the ideological issue might be drawn more clearly.

What difference might it make if one asked how a communal code would function in school? We might see the necessity of it for expressions of solidarity, whether in spontaneous language or in the rites and ceremonies of the children's cultures of origin, so grossly neglected at the same time that "mainstream" rites and ceremonies are imposed upon children in school. We might understand better the function of a teacher's, or a parent's,[2] more abbreviated commands, in terms of their producing less social distance between the adult and the child than more elaborately justified requests, whatever the contribution of the latter might be to the children's cognitive facility. Again, we might connect a

[2] Robert D. Hess and Virginia C. Shipman, "Early Experience and the Socialization of Cognitive Modes in Children," *Child Development*, 36 (Dec., 1965), pp. 869-886.

communal code to the sporadic finding that low-SES children have more positive self-concepts than middle-SES children (always a surprise, since we know how much better off the middle-class children are!).[3] Perhaps we could find that children from communal code families cooperated more than children from individuated code families, not in the sense of a highly role-differentiated form of cooperation, but in the sense of simple sharing of property, attention, jobs, and roles.

All this is highly speculative. It is meant to suggest a potential line of research growing out of Bernstein's theory, one that seems to have been neglected because of the ideological bias reflected in the terms "restricted" and "elaborated," especially as these terms have been applied to current emphases in educational practice. Bernstein's special theory, one might say, is couched in the general framework of *Gemeinschaft-Gesellschaft* that has been so productive for sociology, especially Durkheim's formulations of mechanical and organic solidarity.[4] It is because the *Gemeinschaft* concept has been fruitfully applied to other aspects of human activity that one expects it to yield in the study of language functions as well.

Two essays that are very provocative in this connection can be read in the book, *Functions of Language in the Classroom,* edited by Courtney Cazden, Vera John, and Dell Hymes.[5] Both essays, one by Stephen Boggs and the second by Susan Philips, contrast children's positive response to being addressed as members of a collective including themselves and adults, with their negative response to being addressed, by the teacher or the adult observer, as individuals. Both provide clues

that the use of a communal or restricted language code is associated with the children's solidarity with each other and with adults. Only a few days after reading the Boggs and Philips essays, one of us happened to observe an elementary school celebration of Black History Week, and was intrigued by the incongruity between the ritual mode of the different classes' presentations and the show and tell mode of the school principal as m.c. of the affair. Had the principal's language behavior been more oriented to the *communitas* of the occasion, it might not have detracted so from an otherwise profound event. For example, when the principal called upon one child to face the rest of the audience and *"explain* how we should behave," at which point the child "forgot" what he had thought he knew—quite like the children in analogous situations within their classrooms in the Boggs and Philips essays. Is there not as much to learn about creating community in a school as there is about individuating the children? The Cazden, John, and Hymes book testifies to the power of Bernstein's point of view, but at the same time it broadens the scope of the language functions considered.

A separate review could be written alone about the last chapter of *Class, Codes and Control,* "On the Classification and Framing of Educational Knowledge." Bernstein distinguishes between collected and integrated classifications of curricular contents, the first being characterized by strong boundaries insulating the curriculum contents, and the second characterized by weak boundaries reducing this insulation. He distinguishes also between strong and weak framing in the pedagogical relationship between teacher and pupil:

> Frame refers us to the range of options available to teacher and taught in the *control* of what is transmitted and received in the context of the pedagogical relationship. Strong framing entails reduced options; weak framing entails a

[3] Norma Trowbridge, "Self Concept and Socio-Economic Status in Elementary School Children," *American Educational Research Journal,* 9 (Fall, 1972), 525-537.

[4] Emile Durkheim, *The Division of Labour in Society* (Glencoe, Ill.: Free Press, 1933).

[5] New York: Teachers College Press, 1972.

range of options. Thus frame refers to the degree of control teacher and pupil possess over the selection, organization, and pacing of the knowledge transmitted and received in the pedagogical relationship. (pp. 205-206)

Bernstein treats classification and framing as the two formal variables of "knowledge codes." A collection code is characterized by strong content boundaries and a tendency to strong framing; an integrated code has weak content boundaries and a tendency to weak framing. The "tendency" wording is the reviewers', however. Bernstein writes explicitly about significant variations in the strength of the framing associated with one or the other knowledge code, and we have inferred the tendencies from the examples he discusses.

What is at stake here is the knowledge code itself that is transmitted to the learner—the form and the process of knowledge as it is given or constructed in the educational environment. Bernstein observes that there seems to be a long-run trend toward openness in English education, that is, toward more permeable content boundaries and looser or more flexible pedagogical framing. We might connect this with a parallel trend toward more individuated learning, stretching out the matter that is polarized in the contrast of restricted and

elaborated codes, and note that there too Bernstein sees as the crucial issue the code that is made available to the learner. Just as we have argued with respect to language codes, therefore, we would urge that a sociology of knowledge should be alert to the positive functions of collected *and* integrated knowledge codes equally. Paradoxically, because the universality of the elaborated code and the integration of the integrated code are accomplished by *individuals* according to increasingly *internalized* standards, they *can* be associated with the disintegration of those external ties of the individual to the group that have constituted much of the meaning of specific language cultures and knowledge disciplines. A sociology of knowledge may be prone to the bias of favoring rational or rationalized systems over arbitrary or contextual ones. But the construction of the human creature is too complex to allow this. Durkheim saw the problem clearly. Bernstein is painting broad strokes and fine details alike on the canvas Durkheim stretched for us, but the picture that emerges must be full in its proportions.

JOSEPH C. GRANNIS
ALEXANDRA W. GRANNIS

*Teachers College
Columbia University*

TOWARD A LITERATE SOCIETY
edited by John B. Carroll and Jeanne S. Chall.
New York: McGraw-Hill, 1975.

Late in 1969, United States Commissioner of Education James E. Allen, Jr. mounted the Right-to-Read Program, an all-out effort to achieve literacy throughout the country by 1980. At his request the National Academy of Education appointed a blue-ribbon group of academics to make

recommendations, assess national needs, and develop both definitions of literacy and strategies for achieving it. This Committee on Reading met in January, 1970 and commissioned a set of papers on topics covering the questions posed by Dr. Allen. In June of that year, participants in a conference presented the papers, and the committee developed the substance of the final report.

Unfortunately, Dr. Allen was dismissed by President Nixon before the June meeting, and the Right-to-Read effort foundered. Questions arose. What should the committee do? How should it focus its report so that its impact would be maximized? Did anyone still want to read it? The editors of this book tell us only that "changes in the Office of Education, alterations in the form of the federal reading program, and difficulties encountered by the committee in the course of its work have delayed this report" (p. x). The report was indeed delayed. Most of the papers were updated in 1973, and the present volume, consisting of the report and the papers, did not appear until 1975.

The report includes a diagnosis of the national reading problem, followed by a series of recommendations on how to attack the problem. It is a straightforward, sensible, and thorough document. There are no surprises. As perhaps it should be, the report is optimistic, yet cautious, in tone: we *can* make progress, even if we may not reach the ultimate goal of literacy for all. The remainder of the book consists of twelve supporting papers. The quality of the papers is uneven—a few are good, but several are quite disappointing.

What are the accomplishments, problems, and prospects for the future in the field? First, considerable progress has been made in basic research and theory development over the past decade. We have come a long way toward defining a psychology of reading. Eleanor Gibson's chapter is a good summary statement of her own theory, and, while there certainly are other approaches, her work reflects very well the efforts and accomplishments in building such a psychology of reading. But what does all of this work imply for instruction? According to Gibson, and she is not alone in this opinion, the implica-

tions of reading theory for educational practice do not, as yet, go much beyond the usual justification for studying education in general. Thus, states Gibson, if a teacher understands the general principles of the psychology of reading, he or she will have "some wisdom to apply to the individual case" (p. 317).

There is also, today, no dearth of new materials for teaching reading. Helen Popp's chapter presents a thorough and thoughtful analysis of developments in beginning reading instruction since 1967, when Jeanne Chall's landmark book, *Learning to Read: The Great Debate*, was published (Chall, 1967). Chall's basic recommendations prompted the publishers of several of the widely-used basal reader series to incorporate some phonic or code emphasis in their approach. Indeed, most current instructional programs offer a balance between decoding and comprehension skills rather than emphasizing only one of these. Other trends include increased emphasis on literature, writing, and communication skills within the reading program; increased availability of audio and visual aids; and greater diversity of ethnic groups and socioeconomic levels portrayed in basal readers. Attempts to individualize instruction appear more frequently, and there is a strong move toward criterion-referenced testing. These recent developments in instructional materials clearly reflect the eagerness with which innovations are sought and used.

And what is the impact of all the new research and theory on instructional materials and procedures? While it would be unfair to say that there has been no impact, the "contributions" of theory are often of mixed value. Sometimes gimmicky ideas for instruction are based only on small bits of theory or data; fortunately, classroom teachers usually do not accept mere gimmicks. Also of limited value are the trivial contributions—for example, the inclusion of the now-classic

Gibson graphemes in visual perceptual readiness materials even though we now know that there is little benefit from any such visual perceptual practice. The only positive aspect of some of these "contributions" is that they indicate the high regard in which research is currently held.

Technology, on the other hand, has given us something truly valuable—television. The success of *Sesame Street* and *The Electric Company* is real. In their chapter Samuel Gibbon, Edward Palmer, and Barbara Fowles do a good job of describing both the research and the production ideas of the **Children's Television Workshop** (CTW). Television can overcome the restrictions of ordinary print media and thus provide all sorts of strategies (pixillation, animation, "rendering print iconic") to capture and maintain attention and to focus on specific cues. Television's greatest limitation as an instructional medium, however, is its inability to provide feedback, and these authors' descriptions of attempts to overcome this restriction are interesting and informative. Of course, it did not hurt that the CTW projects were funded substantially enough to attract creative and intelligent people who could offer the music, humor, and general professionalism that would enhance the production and ensure its appeal. But even when such enormous capital outlay for production is not available, television offers something unique. It is worth noting that most of the "innovative" and successful aspects of these TV productions are derived not from new advances in a theory of reading, but from technological advances coupled with traditional knowledge about learning and instruction.

Attempts to teach adult illiterates have not fared well. Training programs in the military, in industry, and in penal institutions often die out after the initial eagerness and seed money are exhausted. Adults apparently lack the motivation to acquire reading skills—Rose-Marie Weber suggests that this is because no one has really demonstrated that literacy skills are significant in qualifying adults for wider employment opportunities. Adult literacy training tends to use the same objectives and curricula as children's instruction, but perhaps these approaches are totally inappropriate for adults. In any event, it is clear that adults often feel that beginning reading instruction is an affront to their dignity, and many people want to avoid the exposure of their illiteracy more than they want to read.

There is a great deal of emphasis on motivation and attitude throughout the volume, an emphasis echoed in the report. In their chapter Lauren Resnick and Betty Robinson cover topics such as the use of external reinforcers, expectations of the student and of the teacher, needs for privacy, and the necessity of success experience. They end their chapter with suggestions for motivating the teacher to value students and to have high aspirations for them. But even teachers may question whether literacy is the royal road to job opportunity or other "happiness," and it may not be so easy, after all, to bring their attitudes around.

Will we be able to assess the extent to which we are accomplishing our goals? Can we evaluate how far we really are from those goals right now? Unless we know what we mean by "literacy," and until we have good measures of literacy, the answer to both these questions is *no*. John Bormuth points out that to define a person's literacy we must consider not only that person's reading ability but also the difficulty or readability of the materials that must be read. It might be more useful in some cases to make the task requirements less stringent than to improve reading ability. (Income-tax forms, for example, have been revised, but not well enough.) The more basic question of what minimal level of reading ability to aim for—the old question of "functional literacy"—is often asked but rarely answered.

The last two chapters on the political and economic implications of a national reading effort raise issues that academicians seldom face. Is the political climate one in which a program to eradicate illiteracy can succeed? How, and to whom, do we sell the program, and who will implement it? How does universal literacy compete as a priority with the war on cancer, national defense, or the conquest of space? Natalie Saxe and Richard de Lone believe that illiteracy is not seen as a major problem in this country, and they are pessimistic that a national effort to overcome it would succeed. The report itself, however, is relatively sanguine.

The report's recommendations are varied: massive funding for further research and development and for the training of more qualified personnel, and the upgrading of all services that we now provide, especially remedial services. The committee also recommends the establishment of a powerful, high-level agency within the Department of Health, Education and Welfare to administer federal programs and to encourage state and local initiative. The committee emphasizes the need to work through schools, citing evidence that schools in which achievement levels are higher than expected have eager and enthusiastic administrators who work hard for good results. The majority of the specific recommendations would seem reasonable to most people in the field; the ideas are not new, but they are sensible.

Committee thinking tends to emphasize conventional wisdom and to suppress the serious evaluation of basic assumptions. Thus the worthiness of the ultimate goal of universal literacy receives no real consideration in this book. David Olson, who was commissioned by the National Academy of Education to review the Carroll and Chall volume in its publication,

performs this "challenger" function with gusto (Olson, 1975). He has written a long essay that focuses primarily on the history of language. Written language, he says, is far from simply a code for representing speech; it is actually a way of shaping statements and cognitive processes. Moreover, literacy has deep effects upon a society: a shared writing system is a tool of nationalism, and nationalism gains strengths at the expense of cultural diversity and pluralism. I mention this review not because it successfully squelches the report; it is really rather off the point. And Olson himself admits (rather grudgingly, it appears) that in twentieth-century America, literacy is indeed valuable both to the individual and to the society. I mention this review because it provides an excellent counterpoint to this "Establishment" report. It is full of provocative assertions, and it is fun to read—something that the Carroll and Chall volume, by its very nature, cannot be. But there is something more: although Olson certainly did not intend to do so, he forcefully reminds one that conventional wisdom, however mundane, is often correct —which is why it became conventional.

Whatever the conventional wisdom about teaching reading, the realities of literacy programs are depressing. On February 5, 1976, the *New York Times* reported in a front-page story that "an ambitious UNESCO project to eradicate illiteracy, begun a decade ago, has been a dismal failure, according to the organization's own report" (Freund, 1976). Furthermore, said the *Times*, while there were 735 million illiterates in the world in 1965, there are now 800 million. The UNESCO "experimental world literacy program" reached only a million of these people— and to *reach* is not to *teach*. Our own national effort, Right-to-Read, is not the only "failure."

But there are other more realistic and sensible ways of assessing progress. Although support for research and development is not as strong as it might be, federal funding continues. Many universities have established graduate programs in reading, and many special-education programs are emphasizing reading. Very importantly, teachers at all educational levels are now being offered training in reading instruction. Progress, after all, comes slowly.

JOANNA WILLIAMS
Teachers College, Columbia University

Chall, J. S. *Learning to read: The great debate.* New York: McGraw-Hill, 1967.

Freund, A. Illiteracy rises despite UNESCO effort. *New York Times*, February 5, 1976, pp. 1; 9.

Olson, D. R. Review of *Toward a literate society* by J. Carroll and J. Chall (Eds.). *Proceedings of the National Academy of Education* (Vol. 2). Stanford, Calif.: National Academy of Education, 1975.

PEDAGOGY IN PROCESS: THE LETTERS TO GUINEA–BISSAU
by Paulo Freire. Translated by Carman St. John Hunter.
New York: Seabury Press, 1978.

A new book by Paulo Freire is an important event in education. Since the publication in 1970 of *Pedagogy of the Oppressed*, those concerned with and involved in Third World educational development have come to respect and anticipate Freire's work. His influence on progressive thought in the realms of development and adult literacy education has been significant. *Pedagogy in Process: The Letters to Guinea–Bissau* is, therefore, a volume that will be carefully read by adherents and afficionados of Freirian thought. The book is of particular interest because, unlike his previous volumes, it is a report of an attempt by Freire himself to put his ideas into practice.

Pedagogy in Process contains a lengthy introduction, a series of seventeen letters written by Freire to colleagues in Guinea–Bissau over a period of a year and a half, and a postscript which is essentially a continuation of the introduction. Freire considers this book "the most explicit" of all his works and states that "as the experience described in the book progresses, I will feel obliged to continue to report" (p. 176).

Eleven of the letters are addressed to Mario Cabral, the Commissioner of State for Education and Culture in Guinea–Bissau, and six to members of the team working on the development of the literacy program with which Freire is associated. The letters comprise two essentially different, but related correspondences: the former dealing with more general issues of collaboration and program policy, the latter with details of the program development process.

The letters to Cabral should be read as the "stage props" to the process. They serve to establish and maintain the more official contact as well as to indicate the manner in which literacy work is to be forged as a component of overall educational policy in the country. Freire is careful to keep his correspondent apprised of the progress being made in the actual work. In the earlier letters one finds statements relating to Freire's general approach —statements reflecting his sensitivity to the need to establish mutual trust based upon an appreciation of local realities and desires and upon his own willingness to be helpful but not prescriptive. In a sense, the letters to Cabral relate to the "progress" component of the book's title, indicating the phases in the development of both the program itself and the working relationship.

The letters to the members of the Literacy Commission relate to the "pedagogy" part of the title. One gets the feeling that Freire views his penmates as members of a seminar in which he is expounding his ideas. Each of these letters is an essay corresponding, perhaps, to a seminar session. Against the backdrop of the letters to Cabral, the letters to the team form the play itself.

In moving narrative, Freire relates his feelings and reactions about working in a newly independent society engaged in "revolutionary reconstruction." He states in the Introduction that his encounter with Guinea–Bissau was "a reencounter with myself," in a sense a reliving of his earlier Brazilian experiences during which he first developed and experimented with the educational approach that has become associated with his name. He goes on, however, to admonish that "experiments cannot be transplanted; they must be reinvented," explaining that "one of our most pressing concerns when we were preparing as a team for our first visit to Guinea–Bissau was to guard against the temptation to overestimate the significance of some aspects of an earlier experience, giving it universal validity" (pp. 9–10). It is surprising and somewhat disconcerting, therefore, to find Freire writing in one of the letters that "my intention is always the same, that of inviting the comrades to whom I write to assume a critical posture that could result in recreating, within a specific situation, the situation described by my pen" (p. 128). Indeed, throughout the book one finds evidence of the extent to which Freire is a prisoner of his own experience, political as well as pedagogical. Although careful throughout his correspondence not to give "any prescriptive significance" nor to "bureaucratize" his working relationship with local workers, Freire nonetheless

continuously reverts to his own experiences in Brazil and Chile as guidelines—both theoretical and concrete—for the work in Guinea–Bissau. At one point he even suggests using materials prepared years earlier for Brazilian peasants "with some of your groups of learners . . . to study their reaction" (p. 94). Clearly, this is inimical to an educational philosophy, the basic tenet of which is that "the pedagogy of the oppressed . . . must be forged *with*, not *for* the oppressed" (Freire, 1970, p. 33).

Freire's main contribution to literacy education—to all education, for that matter—has been in his stressing the confluence of two themes: the need to relate content to thematic apperceptions (generative words) prevalent among specific population groups, and the importance of dialogue in the dual processes of learning and instruction. While central to his literacy work, the belief that self-reflection upon praxis will necessarily lead to participatory "revolutionary reconstruction" is inherently political, not pedagogical. "Conscientização," a term preferred by Freire (1970, p. 19) over its English translation of "critical consciousness" because of its broader connotation—"learning to perceive social, political, and economic contradictions, and to take action against the oppressive elements of reality"—is the ultimate aim of the educational process and the starting point of the process of reconstitution. These processes are closely linked, indeed intertwined, in Freirian thought. These points are reiterated in the current volume, both in the introduction and in several of the letters, unfortunately building upon Freire's earlier experience as a model for emulation despite protestations to the contrary.

There is a further difficulty in the choice of content and structure for the book. The reader is made privy to a series of letters written *to* Guinea–Bissau but is not shown any *from* there. Reactions to Freire's letters and reflections upon his discussions can be gleaned only from his own analysis.

Lacking, then, is the very dialogue which is so important to Freire. The essence of the book is in Freire's repeating his beliefs and ideas in letter form, not in an attempt to reconcile them with a new reality. The fact that all the letters were written to Guinea–Bissau almost seems to be incidental.

This may appear to be harsh criticism. It is not intended, however, to denigrate in any way the validity of Freire's pedagogical intuitions and ideas. In a certain respect it may, in fact, be complimentary, for it indicates the extent to which Paulo Freire himself is so deeply imbedded in his own culture and experience. It perhaps shows that what Freire is seeking to do in this book is to explain his experience to others who are trying to create their own rather than to impose his pedagogy upon a culture in which he is alien. The book's title and repeated references to the writings and sayings of Amilcar Cabral, whom Freire considers a "political pedagogue" like "Samora Machel, Fidel, Nakarenko, Freinet, Nyrere" (p. 157), camouflage that intention, if indeed it is the author's objective. As an explanation of Freire, one cannot but agree with Jonathan Kozol, who states in the foreword to the book that "while not his classic work—[it is] unquestionably his most accessible" (p. 4). As a presentation of Freire's ideas, this is an important contribution; as a narrative of how those ideas are put in practice in a new situation, it is a misrepresentation.

Freire's comments regarding literacy, peppered throughout the book, are noteworthy, as they present a notion of reading which constitutes a significant alternative to conventional adult literacy work. Like many others, Freire posits that the act of reading cannot be neutral; that it is of necessity related to concrete acts of praxis, to which it can be applied. UNESCO too arrived at a similar conclusion when it first launched its Experimental World Campaign for Universal Literacy, premised upon functionality and work orientation (UNDP/UNESCO, 1976). Freire continues, however, to suggest that literacy and post-literacy cannot be separated—that is, that the actual learning of reading must be interwoven with its subsequent uses. In this suggestion Freire deviates from conventional thinking. While UNESCO realized, in the conduct of its projects, that functional literacy is the ability to "engage in all those activities in which literacy is required for effective functioning" (UNESCO, 1962), it is difficult for UNESCO to abandon the notion that one must first know how to read and only then apply the newly learned skill to practical matters. Freire argues that the actual act of learning has to be related to subsequent uses, that the literacy instruction phase must convey to learners reality, relevance, and functionality.

The process of identifying generative words and then codifying them as a basis for developing adult literacy curricula is a Freire hallmark. In his letters to the team working in Guinea–Bissau, Freire discusses both the theory behind this approach and the practicalities involved in the identification of the themes. These several discussions constitute the most lucid available explication of the approach by Freire himself and are important for that reason alone. They leave, however, a number of unsolved issues from a methodological point of view. The most serious of these relates to the transition from the generative words to actual instruction. Using the words codified, Freire proposes that they be taught through a "synthetic," or "sound-syllabic" method—recognizing the letters and sounds associated with each and then forming them into different word and syllable combinations. This rather mechanical and highly repetitive approach has been found to be boring to adults and not very effective (Harman, 1974). Learners soon lose sight of the words and their significant meanings and find themselves engaged in activities that cannot have much appeal. Related to this is yet another problem: the teaching of reading in this fashion requires sequencing. A learner who has missed a session or several consecutive sessions, a very normal occurrence in adult literacy programs, may well find that so much has been missed as to make continuation extremely difficult, if not impossible. Precisely this syndrome has been the root cause of high drop-out rates in literacy programs (Harman, 1977). The approach suggested by Freire in this, as in his previous works, neither acknowledges this problem nor seeks its solution.

A further instructional problem encountered in adult literacy work relates to the use of primers. Primers are the basic textbook format found in such programs and typically consist of pamphlet-type, sequentially organized and graduated material. It has often been found that the primer itself is a constraint. Learners often have problems with the first few, relatively simple lessons and are easily discouraged when they see how complex the later texts become. Attrition from programs can and does result. Freire, too, is opposed to the use of traditional primers: "Literacy education as cultural action, as I have said so often, cannot use traditional primers" (p. 168). He goes on, however, to describe the material for the Guinea–Bissau program and, in so doing, describes a very traditional primer, different from the others only in that it is called a "notebook" rather than a primer. Semantic differences, as Freire knows so well and indicates so often, are not real differences.

From a methodological and pedagogical point of view, the book is disappointing because it does not deal effectively with these issues, which Freire has not addressed in his previous work and which thus remain major hurdles for those who seek in this corpus a new and viable approach to the effective conduct of adult literacy programs. One final note: *Pedagogy in Process* is the easiest of Freire's books to read and understand, possibly due to the fine work done in translating and editing the volume. Carman St. John Hunter, the translator, is to be complimented on a task well done.

DAVID HARMAN
*Harvard University and
Hebrew University of Jerusalem*

References

Freire, P. *Pedagogy of the oppressed.* New York: Seabury Press, 1970.

Harman, D. *Community fundamental education.* Lexington, Mass.: Heath, 1974.

Harman, D. "A different approach to the teaching of reading to illiterate adults: An example from Thailand." In T. P. Gorman (Ed.), *Language and literacy: Current issues and research.* Teheran: International Institute for Adult Literacy Methods, 1977.

UNESCO. *International committee of experts on literacy: Report.* Paris: Author, 1962.

UNESCO/UNDP. *The experimental world literacy programme: A critical assessment.* Paris: UNDP Press, 1976.

How Children Fail
by John Holt.
New York: Pitman, 1964.

Here is a book in the genre and the tradition of Rousseau's *Emile*, Pestalozzi's *Evening Hour of a Hermit*, Dewey's *My Pedagogic Creed*, and Neill's *Summerhill*. It is the personal testament of John Holt, based upon his intuitions and observations as a result of teaching, watching others teach, and (most important of all) watching others being taught, in the Colorado Rocky Mountain School, the Lesley-Ellis School, and elsewhere. Because it is personal, intuitive, subjective, and based on faith, it is going to annoy a lot of people—just as have the other books mentioned. It may not succeed in annoying as many people as have these more famous works, because it may not be as widely read. But this, in my opinion, will be a pity. For it is full of insights from which anyone with responsibility for the upbringing of a child can profit, and it is grounded in a faith in the ultimately healthy impulses of children that we sorely need in this era of conservative reaction.

Holt is concerned about the penalties of failure in a success-oriented culture. He is concerned with those who fail in an obvious sense—by dropping out of school or college. He is also concerned with those who fail in fact if not nominally: they pass only because we decide to push them through the grades even though they know nothing. But, above all, he is concerned with another kind of failure, which afflicts almost all children: "they fail to develop more than a tiny part of the tremendous capacity for learning, understanding, and creating with which they were born and of which they made full use during the first two or three years of their lives."

The book is in the form of a number of memos, written in the evening after teaching or observing during the day, over a period of about three years. A small number of these memos have been selected, edited, and rearranged under four topics: Strategy; Fear and Failure; Real Learning; and How Schools Fail.

In the section on Strategy, Holt describes the ways in which children try to meet or dodge the demands that adults make on them in school. He gives some rather horrifying, but convincing, examples of the way children concentrate on safety and avoid risk in the classroom, and of the way teachers reinforce this sad practice. For children, he suggests, the central business of school is not learning but getting their imposed tasks done, or at least out of the way, with a minimum of effort and unpleasantness. They don't particularly care how each task is disposed of: "If they can get it out of the way by doing it, they will do it; if experience has taught them that this does not work very well, they will turn to other means, illegitimate means, that wholly defeat whatever purpose the taskgiver may have had in mind."

Schools and teachers abet this process by focusing predominantly on *right answers*. Holt gives examples that show how teachers are so obsessed with the "right answer" hidden in their minds that they are unable to hear or understand what children are really saying and thinking. Schools give every encouragement to what Holt calls "producers" (students who are interested only in getting right answers and who make uncritical use of rules and formulae to get them) and discourage "thinkers" (students who try to think about the meaning of the problem under examination). Hence, children become not learners but strategists whose aim is to "beat the system." As a result of this miseducation, in which "right answers" are the only ones that pay off, children fail to learn how to learn from mistakes. For example, Holt recounts that, in playing Twenty Questions with them (guessing a number between 1 and 10,000), if they say, "Is the number between 5,000 and 10,000?" and he says "yes," they cheer; if he says "no," they groan, even though they obtain the same amount of information in each case. The more anxious ones will repeatedly ask questions that have already been affirmatively answered, just for the satisfaction of hearing a "yes."

In the second section of his book, Holt deals with the interaction in children of fear and failure and the effect of this on strategy and learning. He found that even in a school that is considered progressive, which does its best not to put pressure on children or make them feel they are in some kind of race, the children are scared: scared of failing, of being kept back, of being called stupid, of feeling themselves stupid. And so, many children paradoxically take sanctuary in incompetence. Not only does demonstrated incompetence reduce what others expect and demand of the child, but it also reduces what he expects from or even hopes for himself. When one sets out to fail he is less liable to be disappointed. As Holt reminds us, you can't fall out of bed when you sleep on the floor.

Children are so afraid of failure, he thinks, because they have been taught to value success too highly and become too dependent upon it. He suggests that we praise children too much for good work. For if we make a child feel "good" when he does good work, might we not unwittingly be making him feel "bad" when he does bad work? A child does not need to be told he has done well when he accomplishes something. In fact, Holt suggests, when we praise him we are "horning in on his accomplishment, stealing a little of his glory, edging our way into the limelight, praising ourselves for having helped to turn out such a smart child."

What children need, he maintains, is the experience of doing something really well—so well that they know, without having to be told, that they have done it well. Instead, we trap them inside a box of failure and fear: we make them afraid, consciously and deliberately, in order more easily to control their behavior and make them docile to our wishes.

In the part on Real Learning, Holt discusses the difference between what children appear to know and what they really know. In distinguishing between the two, he suggests that a child who has really learned something can use it and does use it. "It is connected with reality in his mind, therefore he can make other connections between it and reality when the chance comes." Unreal learning, by contrast, "has no hooks in it; it can't be attached to anything, it is of no use to the learner."

Needless to say, Holt thinks that schools are encouraging unreal or phony learning and inhibiting the acquisition of real learning. His views contain many echoes of Rousseau. For example: "Our teaching is too full of words, and they come too soon. . . . The essential is that this sort of process not be rushed. . . . Our aim must be to build soundly, and if this means that we must build more slowly, so be it." He draws many examples from his teaching of arithmetic, and he insists that knowledge not discovered by the children themselves will almost certainly prove useless and be soon forgotten.

Teachers must stop demanding that students solve problems *the* way or the *best* way, he maintains. Children who are allowed to work through problems in their own way, at their own pace, can work without fear. Moreover, they can devise methods from which they can really learn, because they are their *own* methods. We have to learn to recognize that the primitive, crude discovery of one child is just as important and as worthy of encouragement as the more sophisticated discovery of a more advanced student. In other words, says Holt, "the invention of the wheel was as big a step forward as the invention of the airplane. . . . We teachers will have to learn when our students are, mathematically speaking, inventing wheels and when they are inventing airplanes; and we will have to learn to be as genuinely excited and pleased by wheel inventors as by airplane inventors. *Above all, we will have to avoid the difficult temptation of showing slow students the wheel so that they may more quickly get to work on airplanes."* (my italics)

In the section on How Schools Fail, the author analyzes the ways in which schools foster unfortunate strategies, increase children's fears, and foster learning that is fragmentary, distorted, and short-lived. He takes the opportunity to indict the test-examination-marks business as an enormous hoax, "the purpose of which is to enable students, teachers, and schools to take part in a joint pretense that the students know everything they are supposed to know, when in fact they know only a small part of it—if any at all." The "Tell-'em-and-test-'em" way of teaching, he claims, leaves most students confused, aware that their academic success is based on shaky foundations, and convinced that school is a place where they follow meaningless procedures to obtain meaningless answers to meaningless questions. School, in other words, is a place where children learn to be stupid. Since school is a kind of jail, children escape the relentless pressure of their jailers by withdrawing the most intelligent and creative parts of their minds from the scene: they have other and more important uses for their intelligence.

The other major sin of the school besides the inculcation of fear is the imposition of boredom. Boredom, like fear, makes children stupid. Holt is hesitant (thank goodness) about classifying some children as intelligent and some as unintelligent. He thinks a child is intelligent when the reality before him arouses in him a high degree of attention, interest, concentration, involvement—that is, when he cares deeply about what he is doing. We should therefore try to make school as interesting and exciting as possible, not just so that it will be a pleasant place, but so that students will get into the habit of acting intelligently.

The school, Holt maintains, is a dishonest as well as a frightening and boring place. In our textbooks we present the children with a false and distorted picture of the world. We think it our right and duty to tell them not the truth but whatever will serve our cause —that is, the cause of making them grow up to be the kind of people we want them to be. We lie for the "good" of the children: or sometimes we lie just for our own convenience. We are, moreover, dishonest about our feelings, and we won't let the children be honest with us: they have to think and feel and say the appropriate things.

Instead of all this, instead of forcing phony learning into scared, uninterested children, Holt thinks we should be trying to turn out people who love learning so much and learn so well that they will retain the ability to learn in the future whatever needs to be learned. We are frightened of wasting time. We should have more faith in the autonomous powers of the child. We should have schools and classrooms in which each child in his own way can satisfy his curiosity, develop his talents, pursue his interests, and gain from adults and other children a glimpse of the great variety and richness of life.

I am reluctant to criticize a book like this—although there are many who will, for it will provoke much opposition. It seems to me to have a personal validity that disarms criticism. There are, of course, lots of questions that one could ask Mr. Holt. For example, he says nothing about community: his is a plea for the development of autonomous individuals. And hence it is potenially liable to some of the criticisms that have been made of the individualistic excesses of some manifestations of progressive education. Again, there is the problem that appreciation of education often *follows* education. Hence, there is at least a *prima facie* case to be made for an element of compulsion in education—especially to introduce the richness of the world to those whose home backgrounds would not lead them to suspect it. Thirdly, he does not explicitly recognize the power of an objective element in education to provide a discipline and an authority against which the growing child can toughen and measure himself.

But I have no doubt that the author has thought of these and other difficulties that occur to me. He might argue, for example, in response to my first criticism, that our present educational approach does not appear to be achieving much in the way of developing a spirit of community, either, and that a genuine community can be composed only of autonomous individuals, never by frightened, bored, organization men who are sophisticated in the strategy of getting ahead. This is a short book, and the author seems more concerned to start us thinking than to present a comprehensive treatment.

Specific reservations are not immediately important. What is important is that this personal statement, a distillation of a sensitive person's observation and reflection, has an integrity that allows it to stand as it is. To indulge in carping criticisms would be to commit the very faults the author is indicting. It is a book to be read, reflected upon, and responded to in action.

PAUL NASH
Boston University

HUMAN CHARACTERISTICS AND SCHOOL LEARNING
by Benjamin S. Bloom.
New York: McGraw-Hill, 1976.

ACCENT ON LEARNING
by K. Patricia Cross.
San Francisco: Jossey-Bass, 1976.

These are two of the most challenging yet optimistic books to have appeared in a very long time. Both are concerned with students who fail but are passed on through the elementary grades into high school and, in more recent years, passed on to college. Bloom's concern is with failure at all levels; Cross is concerned mainly with the "New Students" in college—those from the bottom third in high-school achievement, who would not be in college if it were not for open-admissions policies.

Both books offer solutions to this major educational problem through learning and particularly through school learning. They represent a major departure from the studies headed by Coleman[1] in the 1960s and Jencks[2] in the early 1970s

[1] James S. Coleman, Ernest Q. Campbell, Carol J. Hobson, James McPartland, Alexander M. Mood, Frederic D. Weinfeld, and Robert L. York, *Equality of Educational Opportunity* (Washington, D. C.: Government Printing Office, 1966).

[2] Christopher Jencks, Marshall Smith, Henry Acland, Mary Jo Bane, David Cohen, Herbert Gintis, Barbara Heyns, and Stephan Mi-

which consistently found that social, cultural, ethnic, racial, and linguistic factors predict school achievement best and would have to be changed to reduce school failure. Bloom and Cross argue forcefully—from their own work and the research of others—that early school achievement is essential for later school achievement, for entrance into a job, and for success in that job. Although both writers acknowledge the importance of family and social factors in school and later success, each concludes that most student failure can be overcome through adjustments of the learning conditions in school.

Teachers, administrators, and educators should be encouraged by these books, although carrying out the school-based solutions proposed will not be easy. It will, however, not be necessary for educators to turn themselves into political activists or social workers to improve failing pupils' achievement.

Both books are revolutionary but in different ways. Cross calls for many changes in the conditions of learning for the failing "New Students" and for changes in curriculum and in jobs. Bloom is perhaps more revolutionary. Although he leaves decisions on curriculum to those in policy positions, he states in a low-keyed manner the daring thesis that most can learn what only some now learn: "Most students can attain a high level of learning capacity if instruction is approached sensitively and systematically, if students are helped when and where they have learning difficulty, if they are given sufficient time to achieve mastery, and if there is some clear criterion of what constitutes mastery" (p. 4).

Acknowledging the influence of John B. Carroll's school-learning model,[3] Bloom

chelson, *Inequality: A Reassessment of the Effect of Family and Schooling in America* (New York: Basic Books, 1972).

[3] John B. Carroll, "A Model of School Learning," *Teachers College Record*, 64 (1963), 723–33.

presents results from ten years of his work and the work of his students on mastery learning. Together with other microscopic learning experiments and large-scale national and international studies of aptitudes and learning, these studies form the basis of his Theory of School Learning—a theory to predict, explain, and modify individual differences. Bloom's book is, for all purposes, a development of this theory, the aim of which is a system of schooling virtually error-free or at least with a significant reduction in error.

According to Bloom, the theory is value-free and should be judged mainly on its effectiveness for predicting and accounting for individual differences in learning in diverse schools, curricula, and countries. Although the theory is value-free—that is, it can be used in schools that have different values, objectives, and methods—the author states simply and clearly that he is not. On many occasions we are presented with his own values—for example, that smaller individual differences in learning are to be preferred to larger individual differences and that a system of schooling with a minimum of error is to be preferred to one with a maximum of error.

According to Bloom's theory, if individual differences are to be minimal and if most students are to learn what only the current achievers now learn, care must be given to the three independent variables for each individual—entering skills, motivation, and appropriate instruction. With regard to a learner's entering skills, Bloom believes that the experiences in the home and in the larger society must be considered along with the previous school learning. Generally, these variables are more predictive than such static variables as socioeconomic status, education of parents, and ethnicity. Home experiences can be changed, Bloom asserts, if parents are informed of what the more enhancing experiences are. Bloom puts major emphasis, however, on the school even for developing cognitive entering behaviors.

Bloom emphasizes, therefore, that mastery learning or remedial instruction needs to be given at the earliest possible time. In addition, Bloom is mindful that the success from mastery learning, which has been demonstrated in research, is possible only when an entire school makes provision for mastery and individualized learning. Results will not be as great if only a few teachers adopt it.

The crucial importance of previous learning for later learning is brought out most clearly in the case of reading comprehension. Bloom synthesizes the findings from numerous studies that have correlated children's reading achievement in the early grades with their achievement in later grades. The correlations are remarkably high from the first grade on. Indeed, by the sixth grade, reading achievement is highly correlated with most other academic achievement, with high-school grades, and with college matriculation. Bloom concludes that for such "generalized cognitive entry behaviors" as reading comprehension a high level of competence or even overlearning should be sought for all.

Bloom thus brings theoretical and empirical support to the long-held view that reading is the key to most school learning; further, he suggests that, without remedial efforts, a significant and persistent gap in reading achievement forebodes continued academic failure. Bloom's data also confirm, in principle, the compensatory efforts of the 1960s—the emphasis on reading of Title I, Headstart, and Right-to-Read, as well as the concern with dyslexia and adult illiteracy. The data do not support the position of some prominent intellectuals who wrote during the 1960s that reading may be overrated and that, in an age of electronic media, teaching reading to those who find it especially difficult to learn may be an imposition.

That assistance to those who find difficulty in learning to read should start early is emphasized throughout Bloom's book. In one section Bloom describes with great poignancy the frustrations of a first-grader

who fails to learn how to read and the snowballing effects of this experience on later efforts to learn to read, on learning in general, and on the child's feelings. For such children Bloom recommends immediate help. This will not sound revolutionary to those familiar with the practices of good private and public schools. Most private schools offer diagnostic and remedial services either covered by tuition or at extra expense to the family. Good public schools give predictive tests in kindergarten and provide special help as early as kindergarten and first grade. But to provide such services for *all* children would be revolutionary. In taking this position Bloom supports the thrust of the learning-disability movement, which has been proposing early testing and special remedial help for children with extreme learning difficulties.

Many researchers hold that it is counterproductive to call attention to the differences in reading and general academic achievement among students of different socioeconomic status (SES) and ethnic groups. Unfortunately, this attention has too often been misinterpreted to mean that some groups are lacking in general ability. Bloom confronts this issue by taking great care to demonstrate that the differences found are not inherent but can be explained by widely differing amounts of environmental stimulation. Where there is a rich environment, children learn well regardless of class and ethnicity.

Whether the usual SES variables or the more dynamic environmental factors are considered, it is generally the children of the less affluent families who have been less prepared for school. All who stumble and fall will benefit from application of Bloom's theory (the children of the rich are not exempt), but it is the children of the poor who will probably benefit most. If applied widely, Bloom's theory can be a tremendous force for social mobility.

Bloom does not stop with an espousal of a theory but also pursues its implications. For example, if his recommendations are widely implemented and all children succeed in school, enter college, and graduate, what will society do with so many doctors, scientists, poets, and writers? In considering this question, Bloom asserts that all will have to learn for themselves rather than for jobs and status alone.

As a final illustration of Bloom's thought, I present this excerpt from his last chapter:

> If humans are born equal or can become equal with regard to learning, then the home and the school have responsibilities far greater than they have assumed in the past. If equality of learning is possible, then the selective function of schools must be largely abandoned in favor of the developmental functions which schools must increasingly serve. (p. 209)

Although Bloom's proposals for change in the schools remain within the generally accepted goals of school learning, Cross proposes the need for more drastic and immediate changes in goals and curriculum. This is due, perhaps, to her major concern with the college level, whereas Bloom focuses on elementary and secondary levels. In contrast to Bloom, Cross's book is looser and more wide-ranging. This stems partly, I think, from the relative newness of her topic, the "New College Students." In both books, however, one is aware of a passion for hard evidence, a love for learning, and a compassion for those who find it difficult to learn.

Cross opens with a statement of values and purposes: "American higher education has worked hard for the past quarter of a century to achieve educational opportunity for *all*. It looks very much as though we shall spend the remaining years of this century working to achieve 'education for *each*'" (p. 3). According to Cross, in the 1950s and 1960s, we were so obsessed with attaining minimal educational rights for everyone that we gave little attention to maximizing learning for each individual.

While access and remediation are laudable goals, the minimal standards implied by these concepts are not sufficient for higher education. Educational opportunity implies the right to develop one's talents to maximum effectiveness: "The central thesis of this book is that education has the obligation to offer *all students the opportunity for high level achievement*. Attaining this goal requires some improvement of instruction and some reshaping of the curriculum" (p. 4).

Cross synthesizes the relevant literature and recommends changes in the education of the New Student. Most are first-generation college students and Caucasian (mostly sons and daughters of blue-collar workers). About a quarter are Black, and about 15 percent belong to other minorities. Overrepresented among the New Student population are Black Americans, Mexican-Americans, and American Indians. Although New Students tend to come from the low socioeconomic levels, not all are from "disadvantaged homes." About one-fourth of the low-achieving students entering open-door colleges are children of fathers who attended college, but these students' "sense of failure is just as personally destructive as that of their financially disadvantaged peers" (p. 7).

Supporting her position with recent data, Cross argues convincingly for the New Students' interest in, and capacity for, a college education. Conservative and suspicious of "innovative" education, these students want from college what they see others obtaining—better jobs, more money, higher social status.

Among the many proposed solutions for improving the education of these students are special tutoring, mastery learning, and better learning of general entry skills, particularly literacy. In discussing these solutions, Cross draws on her rich experience and knowledge of the various programs designed for the New Student. She points out that the remedial and developmental education programs of the 1960s suffered because no one seemed to know how to compensate for the "disadvantaged" students' lack of adequate education. Remedial courses were made to look as much like "regular school" as possible. Premature claims of success were common. Those who suggested the efforts were *not* successful were likely to be called "racists."

Cross would alter remediation and development programs by radical changes in curriculum and in academic requirements. With regard to remediation, she cautions that there is much that we do not know, including what skills are necessary for academic survival. She emphasizes that research is needed in this area and presents excellent summaries and interpretations of the current research. To change curriculum, Cross would broaden the goals of higher education to include knowledge of people and interpersonal skills and ability to work with objects and materials, as well as the traditional knowledge of ideas. Concerning academic requirements, Cross advocates reducing them for the new student.

While acknowledging that with enough time and money these students may be brought through the regular curriculum, she asks, to what end? Like Bloom, Cross faces the question of what will happen to the demand for college education if high-level jobs are not available. She is optimistic about jobs for the New Student degree holders, since she expects jobs will be more plentiful for those strong in interpersonal skills and practical knowledge. Along with Bloom, however, she asks about the possible devaluation of the college degree when most people have one. Her answer, like his, is that "the emphasis must shift from the value of the credential to the value of the knowledge and skills gained through college" (p. 7).

It seems to me that both Cross and Bloom underplay the effects of such changes. Although learning for the sake of learning may appeal to some, particularly to those from more affluent and more educated families, it is difficult to envision the wide acceptance of this notion of education among groups who are entering higher education for the first time. These groups primarily perceive a college education as a means to better paying and more prestigious jobs. How will they feel and how will they act when the rules change? What will happen when there are not enough professional jobs for all college graduates? Since some professionals will always be needed, who will fill these positions? Will selective criteria still be used, or will the criteria be changed from high aptitude scores and grades to amount of time taken to learn? That is, will professional success come to those who reach the highest levels of achievement irrespective of the amount of mastery learning or remedial instruction needed, or will fine distinctions be made among students according to who completes the work fastest?

In spite of and because of these kinds of questions, both books have much to say to education researchers, theorists, policy makers, and practitioners. Both authors have faith in the ability of schools and colleges to educate those who have heretofore failed or dropped out. This faith sets them apart from many educational reformers, romantics, and prophets of the 1960s. To substantiate their faith, they present hard data and offer procedures that have been **demonstrated** to work. The realistic solutions Bloom and Cross present will not be easy to carry out; yet, if they are widely applied, the nature of learning in schools and colleges will be vastly changed, as will the students and teachers who apply them.

JEANNE S. CHALL
Harvard University

ERRORS AND EXPECTATIONS:
A GUIDE FOR THE TEACHER OF BASIC WRITING
by Mina P. Shaughnessy.
New York: Oxford University Press, 1977.

In 1970 the City University of New York radically modified its traditional criteria for admission. Under an open-admissions policy every City resident with a high-school diploma was guaranteed entrance. As a result, thousands of students who otherwise might not have continued their formal schooling chose to enter college. Although highly motivated by a faith in the benefits of higher education, most of these young adults were far from ready for regular college courses. In fact, writing teachers were stunned by the students' lack of even the most basic writing skills.

The task of preparing these students for traditional college-level courses in three semesters of basic writing classes was a formidable one. No textbooks or guidelines existed for such a student population. After five years of experience with these students, Mina Shaughnessy, Director of the City University's Instructional Resource Center, has written *Errors and Expectations* as a guide for teachers of Basic Writing. Based upon an analysis of over four thousand essays, this book represents a pioneering effort in an area deserving considerable attention. The problems of these Basic Writing students are in many ways simply the problems writ large of most of our youth and adult population.

Errors and Expectations does not provide teachers with a highly structured writing program for widespread application. Rather, it describes, in a profound and moving way, the difficulties with formal written English evidenced by Basic Writing students and the approaches developed by their teachers to help these students write readable expository prose. The book contains six chapters on the writing errors of Basic Writing students: handwriting, punctuation, syntax, usage, spelling, vo-

cabulary, and units of discourse beyond the sentence level.

Shaughnessy gives numerous examples of the various problems that occur in each category, explores the possible causes, and suggests ways in which a teacher might attempt to handle them. Guiding Shaughnessy's analysis is the explicit philosophy that errors are not capricious or "illogical." Instead, they are clues pointing to the inexperienced writer's misunderstanding or ignorance of the requirements and characteristics of the written code. Many reading researchers feel that children's reading miscues reveal the strategies children are misusing or failing to use in reading for meaning. Using similar reasoning, Shaughnessy holds that efforts to determine the causes of written errors yield useful diagnostic information and insights that enable teachers to decide more intelligently upon instructional priorities and strategies. The following writing samples from students will enable the reader to evaluate the cogency of Shaughnessy's reasoning:

> The main point of this topic is that the **Children** and College students aren't learning how to read and write for that they will used later in life. I don't believe society has prepared me for the work I want to do that. is in education speaking, that my main point is being here, If this isn't a essay. of a thousand word's that because I don't have much to say. for it has been four years since I last wrote one, and by the time I am finish here I hope to be able to write a number of essay . (p. 19)

> My parent were both born in a small town in Ireland, which far better or worse was untouch by modurn science. This was not a hinderance to any of the mother at that time. They were all experience with the proper knowledge of

childbirth. One thing that was very influenced to my life occur the man and woman decided to marry. (p. 91)

At this critical point in the academic life of these students, both the kinds and quantity of writing errors appearing in these passages cannot be ignored, nor need they be. Basic Writing students are not children, but sensitive young adults with mature ideas, perceptions, and ways of thinking. They deeply sense the value attached to literacy in a society that depends so strongly upon the written word, and they are keenly aware of their own inadequate skills. Shaughnessy feels that the writing teacher's responsibility is not to ignore student errors but to respect the intellectual and linguistic resources students have by showing them the "logic of their mistakes." Students can be taught to apply the reasoning they bring to bear in other areas of life to the language they are attempting to shape in writing. In this way they can be helped to acquire confidence in their ability to cope with error and bring it under control.

By no means, however, should concern about error interfere with the composing process. Shaughnessy's point is that errors can be dealt with appropriately as long as the correction of error is taught as part of the process of revising and of careful proofreading. She is not suggesting that the proportion of time spent on remedying error in class should equal the vast amount of time teachers devote to the analysis of error outside of class. Most class time is best used in more positive ways—by helping beginning writers generate and discuss ideas and by supervising actual writing practice.

Other reasons for focusing on errors concern their effect on the reader. Intended meaning may emerge through a plethora of errors, but they clearly distract a reader and tend to shift attention from *what* the writer is trying to say to *how* it is said. As Shaughnessy points out, any departure

from the accepted conventions of written language costs a writer something. A few errors may be tolerated, but too many deviations cause a reader to withdraw attention altogether, unless the reader is the student's teacher. Thus, the teacher of Basic Writing students must now, at the eleventh hour of their education, help them see that most writing is a social act and that a primary goal is to enable the intended reader to understand as efficiently and as easily as possible what the writer means.

While research evidence suggests no relationship between grammar teaching and writing *ability,* the most effective tool for helping Basic Writing students understand many of their errors is grammar study. As many of the samples quoted in *Errors and Expectations* indicate, Basic Writing students do not write like elementary school children. They are, nevertheless, unable to use the complex structures of written language to express complex thoughts. Grammar study provides them with a vocabulary for talking about language and a structure for understanding the requirements of the written code. As Shaughnessy observes, "Grammar still symbolizes for some students one last chance to understand what is going on with written language so that they can control it rather than be controlled by it" (p. 11).

It is not very surprising that grammatical instruction looms so large in a writing program for young adults, who, for the most part have little familiarity with the vocabulary and language patterns of formal written English. Thus, learning formal written English is like learning a foreign language. The stress during the sixties and early seventies on the legitimacy of the many vernacular forms of oral speech was psychologically sound in a society which often judges worth and intelligence by degree of adherence to one standardized form of oral language. However, the failure of many educators to point out the differences between the informal patterns of oral speech and the formal patterns and characteristics of written language may have been a great disservice to students who lack familiarity with written language. Much of the difficulty students have with punctuation, syntax, spelling, and vocabulary stems from a failure to differentiate the features and patterns of spoken discourse from those of written discourse, and this is a point Shaughnessy reiterates throughout her book.

One may judge that part of the task of teachers is to help students understand that the acquisition of the conventions of formal written English does not imply a negation of their background or identity and that an attempt to teach these conventions and patterns does not represent the imposition of alien values. Helping students master the written code gives them the most powerful instrument humans have devised for exploring thought. As all experienced writers have learned through the often agonizing process of writing, rewriting, and revising, our thoughts and perceptions become most accessible through the medium of written language.

As one reads the writing samples of the Basic Writing students, a nagging question arises over and over again. How is it possible, after twelve years of formal schooling, for students to produce writing that is barely intelligible—that seems to ignore almost all the conventions of written language? The writer of the first passage quoted above suggests one explanation: too little writing has been demanded in earlier years. While this may certainly be part of the explanation, it does not seem sufficient to account for the glaring deficiencies in the most basic writing skills, such as understanding sentence structure, using the period, or using capital letters.

In recent years, many elementary-school teachers have tended to disregard young children's writing errors and have emphasized, quite appropriately, the positive elements in students' efforts to express themselves in writing. We do not know when the transition toward a more critical attitude, an insistence on proofreading, and the needs of an unseen audience occurs, or if this transition occurs at all. In other classrooms, many teachers have undoubtedly continued to practice a pedagogy focusing more on correctness, form, and product rather than on motivation and process; in doing so, they have inhibited their students' interest and development in writing. Unfortunately, there seem to be no large-scale studies of how writing has actually been taught in the public schools over the past decade. We do not know what has "gone wrong" in the earlier writing classes of Basic Writing students. Although students do graduate from high school still eager to learn, many are confused and resentful about their incompetencies with the language of formal schooling.

What are the expectations for Basic Writing students at the college level? From her experiences, Mina Shaughnessy knows that they do respond to instruction. Despite the many obstacles beyond the teacher's control, Shaughnessy firmly believes that the prospects for improvement are better than most teachers expect and that competency can be achieved, given sufficient time and resources, as well as teachers' patience, understanding, and cooperation.

Although intended for teachers of basic writing courses at the college level, *Errors and Expectations* deserves a far wider audience. Writing should be the concern of teachers at all levels and in all areas of the curriculum, especially the teacher of reading. After reading Mina Shaughnessy's lucid description and analysis of the skills the would-be writer must master, one realizes that the teacher who teaches students how to write is also teaching them how to think and read critically. Writing and reading are essentially inseparable processes. The deliberate nature of the writing, rewriting, and proofreading process can be used by the responsive teacher to stimulate higher levels of thinking and reading. Teachers who would improve their students' reading skills might well consider teaching them writing skills and accomplishing simultaneously both aims of the literacy program. A society that has spent millions of dollars to improve the teaching of reading might secure even richer returns by investing more of its resources to improve the teaching of writing.

SANDRA STOTSKY
Curry College

LANGUAGE DEVELOPMENT AND LANGUAGE DISORDERS
by Lois Bloom and Margaret Lahey.
New York: Wiley, 1978.

This comprehensive new book by Lois Bloom and Margaret Lahey is directed to both students of normal language development and practitioners dealing with language-disordered children. *Language Development and Language Disorders* will be accompanied by two books of readings, one on language development and the other on language disorders. Although it may seem natural for the two topics, normal language development and language disorders, to be treated together, this has not historically been the case. Linguists studying child language typically have not addressed the practical problems of language disturbance; speech pathologists have labored to help children without having an adequate model of language development in normal children. Bloom and Lahey attempt to provide both an ordered account of how children learn language and a plan for using that information to help children with language problems. Thus for both theory and practice this book represents an important advance.

Bloom and Lahey consider the ways children use language in everyday life rather than how they produce it in response to test questions. They are concerned with three aspects of language: with its external *form*, whether sentences are constructed correctly; with its *content*, whether the child is able to express an appropriate variety of meanings; and with its *use*, whether the child can produce language appropriate to a variety of social situations. Their view of language development, one that deals with the whole linguistic child, represents a synthesis of much of the last ten years' thinking about child language, not only by grammarians but also by sociolinguists and cognitive psychologists.

In order to appreciate the breadth of the authors' view, it is useful to consider the decade of child-language research following the publication of Noam Chomsky's *Syntactic Structures* in 1957. Child-language studies initially were dominated by grammatical formalism: researchers studied how children acquire and internalize grammatical forms such as questions, passives, and negatives. Major attempts were made to write content-free grammars of emerging child language. These early grammars were based primarily on the distribution of words within children's utterances and made no reference to what the children might actually mean or what their reasons for speaking might be. Utterances with the same form were treated as equivalent regardless of differences in meaning.

Lois Bloom's doctoral dissertation on the language development of three intensively studied children appeared toward the end of that decade of formalism (see Bloom, 1970). Subtitled "Form and Function in Emerging Grammars," the dissertation was one of the works that led to what psychologist Roger Brown (1973) called the "rich interpretation" of evidence from children's language. Bloom found that it is necessary to study the context in which an utterance is produced in order to understand the meaning the child is trying to express. The child who says "Mommy sock" while pointing at the dirty laundry intends something quite different from when she says "Mommy sock" while her mother helps her dress. An analysis that does not distinguish between the two homonymous but different utterances has less sophistication than the mind of a twenty-one-month-old.

Bloom, along with Brown and a number of other researchers, has shown that children who are in the one- and two-word stage of language development talk about a limited number of things. Children all over the world express the same kinds of thoughts and intentions because of the constraints of the sensorimotor stage of cognitive development. About a dozen kinds of utterances characterize most of what very young children say—naming ("This doggie"), recurrence ("More juice"), location ("Go store"), and non-existence ("All gone cookie"), for instance. In the 1970s, the notion developed that a complete description of what children are doing when they speak includes not only the actual forms produced and their context but also the social use of that speech. Is the utterance a request for information or a comment on the world? Does it take account of the knowledge the hearer shares or does not share with the speaker? Thus the forms, the content or intended meaning, and the social uses of speech have emerged as the tripartite focus of most current child-language study.

Those areas—content, form, and use—make up the framework that holds the two parts of Bloom and Lahey's book together. The first half sets forth clear distinctions for these three areas, deals with definitions

of language, and traces the course of normal language development. Bloom and Lahey also describe their own empirical observations of a small group of children and discuss in detail the methodological and theoretical issues involved in collecting and analyzing samples of children's language. By the end of the first half of the book, the reader has been given a thorough description of children's early linguistic and cognitive development. The remaining part of the book builds upon this foundation.

The final twelve chapters of the book deal with language disorders and remediation. The plan for remediation that Bloom and Lahey suggest is based on what is known about normal development of the three dimensions of language and about their interactions. The authors programmatically describe the developmental sequence of language acquisition through eight phases, from the one-word stage through the production of relative clauses and past tenses. By phase eight, the child not only can produce complete syntax but also has learned social skills, such as how to talk to younger children, and can talk about a great variety of events and relations. For each phase, the authors suggest remediation goals focusing on use, content, and form. For instance, a child who appears to be in most respects at phase one but who never exhibits a typical phase-one utterance, such as denial, would be encouraged through environmental assistance to learn such expressions. The therapist or parent might model these expressions for the child and provide other instructional opportunities. The child might be shown an unusual object, for example, a piece of a clock, and told, "This is a cookie"; ideally, this statement would encourage the child to deny that the object is a cookie.

It is, of course, impossible to plan what a child should learn unless one has assessed his or her current level of functioning. The authors feel that the best way to assess a child's development of language is through the analysis of a sample of the child's naturally occurring speech. The sample should preferably be collected at home; but, if in a clinic, it should be obtained in the least structured atmosphere possible. Interviews with parents or teachers can add information, and the clinician can also answer specific questions by employing elicited imitation or similar techniques. Detailed procedures for collecting, transcribing, coding, and analyzing language samples are set forth, so that the book can be used as a practical manual.

Bloom and Lahey discuss many standardized language-assessment measures. Standardized tests are easy to score, but the evaluation and interpretation of the scores can be problematic. The authors' view is that highly structured assessments are inadequate, in part, because they offer no insight into how children actually use language in everyday life. The analysis of spontaneous speech is far more difficult, but it has been undertaken successfully both by these authors and by many of their students, as well as by some other researchers.

Bloom and Lahey thus present one approach to language assessment and dismiss other methods as essentially not useful; this will be distressing to many professionals interested in language disorders. There are obvious problems associated with analyzing natural-language samples, not the least of which is obtaining an adequate sample that is representative of the full range of a child's abilities. Coding schemes for such language analysis can also be difficult to learn, and there may be problems in obtaining interjudge reliability. Thus, despite Bloom and Lahey's important emphasis on the analysis of spontaneous speech, structured tests will continue to be useful to clinicians in assessing children's language abilities, particularly in cases where the children say little but appear to comprehend well.

Bloom and Lahey believe that lan-

guage intervention should be based on the child's linguistic behavior. They do not consider etiology and the correlates of the linguistic disorder important since children who suffer from deafness, aphasia, mental retardation, autism, and environmental deprivation all suffer language disorders in addition to their other problems, and language is the only target here. The authors also discount the remedial approach that focuses on improving specific abilities thought necessary for language processing. For example, they maintain that research has not yet demonstrated the value of determining whether a language-disordered child is able to distinguish the sounds of her or his language—that is, if words like "pat" and "bat" sound the same. They argue that the value of testing for such abilities or deficits has not been established.

In discounting the value of studying isolated specific abilities, the authors neglect the fact that language problems are sometimes solved by indirection. Because we do not know everything about language development or how best to help language-disordered children, we still have to ask questions, some of which may not provide immediately useful answers. Diagnostic tests are also research tools, and the heuristic value of the information they provide may give us some clues to the way language is represented in the human brain. Furthermore, seemingly unrelated findings may have eventual practical application. At the Boston Veterans' Administration Hospital, for instance, a group of adult aphasics who had not been helped by any conventional therapy are now learning to talk again because it was noted that they retained the specific ability to sing. The new approach, melodic intonation therapy, builds on singing to start these patients speaking. Such examples foster hope that breakthroughs in treatment may develop from findings on nonlinguistic correlates of disorders like autism.

Regardless of one's orientation, *Lan-*

guage Development and Language Disorders contains a great deal of valuable information, but there are problems. The first half of the book is not as interesting or as useful as the second. In addition, the first chapter contains some examples that may be confusing to the reader. In discussing the arbitrariness of the symbols used by a code, for instance, the authors explain that a cookie can be represented by a picture, a map, or a graph: "a graph of the cookie might represent such information as the size of the cookie in relation to the number of bumps on the cookie or the number of bites it takes to eat it." Such a graph would have only one point on it and would be most unusual indeed. Later in the same chapter, the ambiguous sentence "Flying planes can be dangerous" is presented with the explanation that by pausing in the appropriate place, one can make clear whether the intended meaning is that "it is dangerous to fly planes" or that "planes that are flying are dangerous." For most speakers, disambiguation is not facilitated by a pause. Perhaps the book's most serious limitation is that it does not discuss the acquisition of the phonology (sound system) of the language or any suggestions for helping children who have phonological disorders. The authors felt this topic has been adequately treated elsewhere, but it would be helpful to know how the phonologically impaired child fits into their theoretical model.

The second half of the book is out-standing in its presentation of a single cohesive picture of what is known about children's linguistic, cognitive, and sociolinguistic skills at each successive stage of development. This approach to language development and remediation is bound to broaden the perspective of linguists and clinicians alike. Other approaches to these topics are not without merit, but the view presented by Bloom and Lahey is an important one, and this is an important book. In the past, specialists who treated language-disordered children frequently had access only to those fragments of research that could easily be translated into an intervention model. In this book Bloom and Lahey, researchers with clinical skills, have presented both a developmental model of language acquisition and a plan for intervention that proceeds in a logical sequence. The model is invaluable; learning to use the plan may not be easy, but those who take the time to do so will be rewarded with new insights into the language of children.

JEAN BERKO GLEASON
Boston University

References

Bloom, L. *Language development: Form and function in emerging grammars.* Cambridge, Mass.: M.I.T. Press, 1970.

Brown, R. *A first language: The early stages.* Cambridge, Mass.: Harvard University Press, 1973.

Chomsky, N. *Syntactic structures.* The Hague: Mouton, 1957.

THE NEUROPSYCHOLOGY OF LEARNING DISORDERS:
THEORETICAL APPROACHES
edited by Robert M. Knights and Dirk J. Bakker.
Baltimore: University Park Press, 1976.

The term "learning disabilities" encompasses a group of problems characterized by unexplained gaps between academic achievement and measures of intelligence —or, if you prefer, gaps between performance and potential. To work in the field of learning disabilities is to ask oneself and others, "How can a smart person do such a stupid thing?" as well as, "How can an apparently stupid person do such a smart thing?" The difficulties inherent in defining who is and who is not learning disabled are readily apparent to the educator; the measurements involved in the comparison of achievement scores with intelligence scores are neither easily defined nor universally accepted. In fact, the underlying great question that shapes the field of learning disabilities is: what is the nature and structure of normal intelligence?

While the term "learning disabilities" describes a group of problems identified by the test-score differences discussed above, the diagnoses given to children with learning problems—for example, "psychiatrically based learning disability" or "neurologically based learning disability"— are thought to provide some level of explanation for the discrepancy between achievement and intelligence-test scores. Many professionals, however, use the words "learning disabilities" as if a neurological basis were implicit. Thus, there is an expectation in common parlance that physiological or brain factors are to some degree instrumental in the problems subsumed under learning disabilities.

At present, hypotheses about what sort of brain factors may be involved in learning disabilities range all the way from old-fashioned, literal hole-in-the-head brain damage to new-fangled, environmentalist normal-brain-eating-the-wrong-foods brain dysfunction. Of course, no single type of brain factor underlies the problems we call learning disabilities; multiple brain factors are probably involved in many of these problems, to say nothing of the contribution of emotional, social, and cultural factors.

Clearly, then, we have a long way to go before we can answer most questions about learning disabilities at either an anatomical or a chemical level. Nonetheless, in scientific inquiry, clear descriptions of "what" traditionally precede knowledge of "why." For the area of learning disabili-

ties, the discipline of neuropsychology has provided the most sophisticated technical and theoretical tools to describe brain-mind correlates of learning problems.

My reactions to and recommendations concerning *The Neuropsychology of Learning Disorders* are varied. I am forced to begin with the cliché that this book belongs on the shelves of all persons involved in the field, particularly those with a research orientation. However, as in all multi-author volumes that are the products of meetings or symposia, the chapters of *The Neuropsychology of Learning Disorders* cover issues at very different levels and from quite divergent perspectives. Had I been able to take scissors and paste in hand I would have arranged this book very differently, perhaps even in several separate paperback volumes. Conceptually its contents are of four kinds: classic articles that should be read by virtually everyone, whether teacher, clinician, or researcher; theoretical or conceptual outlines of key problems in the field; articles containing interesting pieces of data that have not been published or placed in the frames of reference provided by these articles; and chapters that map out future research needs. Only the first three categories will be discussed in this review.

The classics include Yule and Rutter's chapter on epidemiology, Wender's chapter on the unitary, chemical hypothesis of minimal brain dysfunction,[1] Taylor's model for a classical neurological impairment (temporal-lobe epilepsy) that leads to changes in development, Satz's overview of the cerebral-dominance problem, Shankweiler and Liberman's chapter on the issue of language as the foundation or infrastructure for the reading process and, finally, Douglas's masterful article on the

[1] The unitary, chemical hypothesis of minimal brain dysfunction (MBD) holds that some chemical is missing from the brain and that most, if not all, MBD is caused by this deficiency.

hyperactive syndrome (how happy I am to find it in updated form after years of photocopying the 1972 version). Each of the chapters in this classic "section" is extraordinarily well written, and all of the authors provide a good balance between inference and evidence.

My next group of articles includes those that set forth important technical and conceptual issues in the field of learning disabilities. Into this category falls Sheer's article, "Focussed Arousal and the 40-Hz EEG."[2] This article presents interesting data and at the same time sets out many of the theoretical issues involved in correlating electroencephalograms (EEGs) with behavior. Rourke's discussion of the development-lag or development-deficit problem, a topic discussed later in this review, is another one of those useful conceptual "roadmaps." Witelson's article on developmental dyslexia as abnormal specialization of hemispheric functions and Buffrey's article on sex differences fit together nicely in the way they place learning disabilities in the context of the normal variance of human abilities.

Satz's seminal review of the cerebral-dominance literature outlines a compelling set of conceptual problems regarding the way we study lateral asymmetry.[3] In his discussion of "floor and ceiling effects" he points out that the problem of asymmetry is most marked in the *middle* range of task demand—that is, when the task is neither so hard that the subject cannot cope with it using any eye, ear, or hand, nor so simple that the subject copes easily with either eye, ear, or hand. The importance of such

a mapping of an "accuracy-asymmetry space" in the study of developmental hemisphere (brain-half) specialization is, unfortunately, rarely considered so carefully as in this particular cautionary tale by Satz.

At this point in the review, before proceeding to my third group of articles, let me explore the distinct but intertwined concepts of cerebral dominance and developmental lag. These two concepts are central to any explanation of learning disabilities at the brain-mechanism level. While developmental lag implies a *time* frame of reference, cerebral dominance implies a *space* frame of reference (to date, mostly right and left hemispheres). Developmental lag is inferred from the observation that a child performs a task at the level of a younger child; for example, a ten-year-old child receives a score appropriate for an eight-year-old child. In psychometrics this observation is most familiar as the ratio of mental age to chronological age. There are problems at both an observational and an interpretative level if the quantitative score is the only index or source of inference for developmental lag. If we are either to describe a performance as developmentally subnormal or to infer that some physical brain factor is simply lagging in time, there should be strict qualitative aspects of performance that are just like those of a younger child.

Even strict adherence to the criterion of qualitatively young behavior does not allow us to infer that a part of the brain is normal but simply taking its time. Our experience from mental retardation sadly teaches us that "slow" may be the outward manifestation of permanently, not just transiently, abnormal brain tissue. Retardation bumps its figurative head on a "ceiling effect" for some functions and matures into "deficiency" for others. For example, once you walk, you are walking well enough, but no such ceiling exists for thinking. Between a late start at walking and a late start at thinking, there is a relatively

[2] Forty hz (hertz, a term for frequency now used instead of "cycles per second") is an EEG pattern. Forty repeating waveforms occur within a one-second movement of EEG paper.

[3] Lateral asymmetry of function refers to evidence that one brain-half is more important or necessary to the performance of a certain function than is the other brain-half. Hemispheric specialization is inferred from observable lateral asymmetry on a given task.

long period during which false optimism may be engendered by describing delayed walking as developmental lag. An example from my own experience with the correlates of reading disability will illustrate. Digit span (immediate oral repetition of digits spoken by an examiner), which consistently correlates with acquisition of reading skills, has an effective ceiling age of 12.5 years. Subtly language-impaired children who are spectacularly poor at repeating digits will outgrow this particular developmental lag. Yet, these same children, language-impaired at fourteen no less than at seven, may also be described as showing permanent deficiency in word retrieval, a continuous-growth function. We have at present no evidence that one piece of the brain "grows up" slowly, while a closely related piece of the brain develops abnormally. The nature of two of the functions involved in digit span and word retrieval—repetition and naming—must be better studied both in normal and in overtly brain-damaged individuals before we can use developmental lag as an explanation, rather than as a description, of brain functioning.

The use of cerebral dominance as a descriptive or explanatory term has its own traps as well. Here the issue is one of inferring left- and right-brain contributions to those necessary and sufficient conditions for achievement. What we observe as lateral asymmetry in, for example, motor, visual, auditory, or tactual tasks is the right side or left side "winning." What we then infer is that the right side of the brain is dominant for a particular achievement. Simply stated, the dominant side contributes more than the other but may not be, in and of itself, sufficient or necessary for accomplishing a task. The best-established, extreme case for the necessity of a hemisphere is that of speaking, which in the adult, right-handed person depends upon a healthy left hemisphere. The left hemisphere is then said to be dominant for speech. Note the careful set of conditional

statements about this best-established case of left-hemisphere dominance: for speech, not all language; in adults, not children; and in right-handers, not nonright-handers.

Matters are muddier for conclusions about cerebral dominance in recognition of alphabet letters, frequently studied by briefly flashing sets of letters simultaneously into both the left and right visual fields (right field goes to left brain and vice versa). In this seemingly innocent lateral-asymmetry competition, whether a subject better reports information flashed to the left or right visual field varies with number, spatial organization, meaningfulness, familiarity of the letters, and difficulty of the task, as well as age, sex, and handedness of subjects! A decision to score for speed of response as opposed to accuracy of report may yet again shift the inferred dominance pattern. Clearly, then, psychology is always involved in the course of arriving at anatomical inferences about the right brain and left brain. Since most complex performances involve several subroutines that are, in turn, dependent upon several parts of the brain, there is usually more than one source of difficulty and compensation. Qualitative analysis of the way a complex performance is accomplished may reveal imbalances between or within the systems underlying subroutines; this, then, is the neuropsychological contribution to the future understanding of cerebral dominance. The study of lateral asymmetry as a marker for cerebral dominance will mean the analysis of both what kind of error and what kind of successful strategy are characteristic of what part of the brain—right, left, back, front, up, or down.

Proceeding now to my third category of articles, I would recommend this group to those experienced in the field, for it contains some interesting pieces of data on many technical topics, including cerebral dominance. The article by McBurney and Dunn, for example, brings up the haunting but not well understood problem of "mixed preference" and the possible disadvantages of nonright-handedness. Consideration should also be given to Tallal's description of the issue of rate or speed of processing information. Central to many spoken- and written-language disabilities, processing rate has immediate therapeutic implications whether or not we can translate it into terms of underlying brain mechanisms. The article by Leisman and Schwartz on oculomotor variables is full of provocative bits of data. Frankly, however, I was not able to identify what the authors were trying to convince me was "chicken" and what was "egg" in the relationship between the role of the eyes and the role of focused attention. Like Dr. Spreen, the postconference reviewer, I found myself flipping back and forth between this article and Sheer's article on focused arousal, trying to relate the specific findings and decide whether eyes lead attention or whether attention is manifested in eyes. Finally, intriguing findings are reported throughout Hughes's chapter on physiological-biochemical correlates of learning disabilities; however, many of these findings are, as yet, difficult to string together into a meaningful pattern.

The book's section on drug studies seems to me the most limited in interest, perhaps appealing only to the practicing physician. The most interesting bit of data that emerges from this section is that reported by Sprague and Sleator on the effects of stimulant medication. Their data indicate that, as I have often suspected, optimal social benefits and optimal academic benefits from medication can be quite different in terms of their dose-response curves. I would recommend that this article be read carefully by any pediatrician or neurologist who is going to be involved in prescribing stimulants and in evaluating responses on the basis of parent and teacher questionnaires.

The only negative thing I have to say about this volume is that some of the articles are so theoretical that they left me with no impression whatsoever. Even within the articles too theoretical for my taste, however, nice paragraphs summarize other issues. For example, Friedman provides a lovely summary of the Russian work on the relationships among language, thought, and self-control and a very clear discussion of the field-dependence dimension.

This book, like all multi-author works, will receive mixed reviews depending upon the orientations of the reviewers. Nonetheless, one might also say that, like a smorgasbord, there is something here for everyone. Comparing it to the only other volume of similar orientation, *Child Neurology* (the recently published outcome of the First International Congress of Child Neurology held in Toronto in 1975), I would have to state that I would be unwilling to choose between the two; each has something to offer in consistency of approach and richness of data. Despite some overlap, the two volumes together will bring anyone up to date on both the intriguing clues and the massive unknowns that characterize the field of developmental disorders of learning.

MARTHA BRIDGE DENCKLA
*Children's Hospital Medical Center,
Boston, Massachusetts*

702

THE PSYCHOLOGY AND PEDAGOGY OF READING.
by Edmund Burke Huey. Foreword by John B. Carroll; Introduction by
Paul A. Kolers.
*Cambridge, Mass.: MIT Press, 1968 (paper). First published by
The Macmillan Company, 1908.*

E. B. Huey's *Psychology and pedagogy of reading* stands out as the most significant text in the field of reading research, a field that for practical reasons became specialized as an independent academic discipline shortly after the appearance of Huey's text. It is rare that a discipline of study has one undisputed historical classic. The M.I.T. Press has now made this classic easily available in paperback form. It now also includes prefatory material by two psychologists, Carroll and Kolers, who give historical information about Huey's career and tell of the relevance of his book to modern work. The text constitutes roughly three books in one: the psychology of reading; a history of literacy; and literacy acquisition and advice on reading instruction. The historical information is now perhaps better obtained from Gelb's *A study of writing* (1963) and Mathews's *Teaching to read: historically considered* (1966). However, Huey's text is still strikingly relevant for the present day.

Just prior to the turn of the century, Huey received his training from the most highly regarded group of American pedagogical psychologists, at that time located at Clark University. After completing a doctoral dissertation on the psychology and physiology of reading, he travelled to France and Germany for postdoctoral study where he met and worked with several leading figures in European research on reading. Certainly never in the history of reading research has there been a period of more intense excitement than there was at the turn of the century. Huey's book could be viewed as a product of that period's intensity, and it is thus a window that opens to us a view of a great era of imaginative research and developing theory. The era roughly from 1890 to 1910 was a momentous one for cognitive psychology and for what we now call "psycholinguistics,"[1] and also for educational research.

An acquaintance with Huey's work forces us to examine an important difference between the attitudes of later American psychologists and those of Huey's day. Recently, language skills such as reading have been viewed as so complex and mysterious that psychologists have only lately been able to approach them and that the statistical procedures have but recently been refined enough to permit the investigation of language. In Huey's time the situation was somewhat the reverse of this. The study of language was fundamental for psychology whose task was to characterize principles of cognition in humans. Language was taken as the best mirror of mental processes; therefore the psychologist should become well acquainted with the nature of language and linguistic skills before he approaches psychology. Linguistics was at that time seen as a more advanced science than psychology (a situation that has been rediscovered with much acclaim by psychologists in the 1950's). Thus Wilhelm Wundt, founder of experimental psychology (ca. 1879), wrote more on language than has any other psychologist; and thus William James was always heavily concerned with verbal expression. It may be that the course of modern theoretical psychology

[1] For a further description of this early material see, Arthur L. Blumenthal, *Language and psychology: historical aspects of psycholinguistics* (New York: John Wiley & Sons, 1970).

will again adopt this orientation (see Chomsky's *Language and mind*, 1968).

At the time he wrote, Huey apparently believed that the psychology of reading was the most important and fundamental undertaking anywhere in the study of psychology, and that to succeed here would be "the acme of a psychologist's achievement" (p. 6). The reason for this is that to describe scientifically the skill of reading would be to understand the most uniquely human characteristics of mental processes. Reading is a dramatic special case of the human ability to use language in general. After reading *The psychology and pedagogy of reading,* this reviewer would like to encourage the M.I.T. Press to republish other similar and little known works from that era; there are many.

Although it holds fascination for the reader, Huey's work is troubling when we see that it is quite difficult to discern any advance in our understanding of the reading process since 1908, whereas revolutionary advances had been made in the quarter century prior to Huey's text. It is likely that some of the early work came to be overlooked or forgotten later, and, as Carroll indicates in his *Foreword,* the later books and chapters on reading have failed to measure up to Huey's. One suspects that the reason for this lies not superficially with the reading researchers, but rather more deeply with the psychological framework that has been dominant in American psychology. The situation in twentieth century Europe is easy to understand in view of the wars, the social upheavals, and the decline of great universities. But in the United States the quantity of psychological and educational research has expanded in amazing proportions since early in the century; yet explanatory theory of the reading process has not advanced noticeably.

It is not true that Huey wrote at the very end of a period, for the tradition that he represents continued for perhaps 20 years or at least into the 1920's with men like C. H. Judd, G. Buswell, R. Dodge, and C. T. Gray, to mention a few. (Huey's life was tragically cut short.) Much of the work of these later investigators was published by the University of Chicago Press in its *Supplementary educational monographs* which should be available in most university libraries.

But then, according to most accounts, psychology as a whole changed. Thus, the modern reader may not be fully prepared to grasp the framework of turn of the century psychology. In commenting on Huey's theoretical discussions, Carroll and Kolers do not give enough emphasis to this rather important aspect of the text which today's reader should be made more aware of. Huey wrote within a system and frequently used a terminology that disappeared following upon the behaviorist movement. And the "strange" terms and systems are too easily dismissed today as archaic or even as nonsensical. Therefore, in certain places the reader may not fully appreciate the implications of the discussion. For one example, the term "apperception" had a technical usage that was in vogue around 1900. Today this notion would likely be presented as "focus of attention," but the casual reader of Huey could easily miss that meaning. Such pitfalls, however, are no real weakness in Huey's work which has the value of representing an historical period and, furthermore, the truly interested reader should be able to determine the nature of Huey's discussions.

To be sure, there are passages in the book that are rightly regarded as out of date. But on the other hand, the development of cognitive psychology and psycholinguistics during the past ten years make Huey's work seem much more modern than it might have appeared fifteen years ago. For example, according to Huey the fundamental unit of language is the sentence (compare to Chomsky, *Syntactic structures,* 1957). The processes of perception and comprehension for Huey are ones of internal mental construction based upon imperfect external cues, rather than being responses to appropriate stimuli (compare to Neisser, *Cognitive psychology*, 1967). And further, Huey's recommendations on how reading should be taught resemble the claims of modern educational romantics (for example, John Holt) more than any others.

For the most part, Huey's book is a summary of the investigations of numerous researchers and of the output of various laboratories and institutes that are now forgotten. A considerable amount of that early work was originally reported in German or French journals difficult to obtain, so that Huey's summaries and translated excerpts are of practical importance for students. The material is incomplete, lacking the several significant investigations by the later generation of researchers. Yet no more readable book of such broad coverage on this topic exists. Today one could not be considered an "authority" in the field of reading if he is unfamiliar with this landmark book. Indeed, in 1970 it would still be an excellent selection as a text for a course in the psychology and pedagogy of reading.

ARTHUR L. BLUMENTHAL
Harvard University

Notes on Contributors

MARTIN L. ALBERT, M.D., is Associate Professor of Neurology at Boston University Medical School and Chief of the Clinical Neurology Section of the Boston Veterans Administration Hospital. Co-author of *Human Neuropsychology* (1978) and *The Bilingual Brain* (1978), he is particularly interested in behavioral neurology and neuropsychology.

ALTON L. BECKER is Professor of Linguistics and Anthropology at the University of Michigan. With major interests in ethnolinguistics and Southeast Asian literature, Professor Becker has co-authored *Rhetoric: Discovery and Change* (1970) and *The Imagination of Reality* (1979). He has studied and taught in Burma and Indonesia as a linguistic consultant for the Ford Foundation.

WESLEY C. BECKER is Associate Dean, Division of Developmental Studies and Professor of Educational Psychology and Special Education, University of Oregon. His professional interests are direct instruction technology and the design of systems for teaching language to disadvantaged students. He is author of *Parents Are Teachers* (1971) and co-author of several books on classroom instruction.

URSULA BELLUGI is Director, Laboratory for Language and Cognitive Studies at the Salk Institute for Biological Studies, San Diego. Among her professional interests are the study of sign language, the biological foundations of language, and language acquisition. She has contributed extensively to the literature on sign language and children's speech, and is co-author of *The Signs of Language* (1979).

ARTHUR L. BLUMENTHAL is Lecturer in the Department of Psychology at the University of Massachusetts, Boston. He is the author of *Language and Psychology* (1970) and *The Process of Cognition* (1977).

ROGER BROWN is John Lindsley Professor of Psychology in Memory of William James at Harvard University. Psycholinguistics and social psychology are his chief professional interests. He is author of *Words and Things* (1958), *Social Psychology* (1965), *A First Language* (1973), and co-author of *Psychology* (1975).

HERLINDA CANCINO, a doctoral candidate at Harvard University, has been a consultant to bilingual programs. Her current interests focus on second-language acquisition as well as the influence of language on cognition and self-concept. She is co-author of *Second Language Acquisition Sequences in Children, Adolescents, and Adults* (1975) and of several articles on second-language acquisition.

JOHN B. CARROLL is the William R. Kenan, Jr. Professor of Psychology and Director of the Thurstone Psychometric Laboratory at the University of North Carolina at Chapel Hill. He was formerly the Roy E. Larsen Professor of Educational Psychology at Harvard University. Present professional interests are the psychology of language performance abilities and individual differences in human cognitive abilities. His publications include *The Study of Language* (1963),

Language and Thought (1964), and *The Teaching of French as a Foreign Language in Eight Countries* (1975).

COURTNEY B. CAZDEN is Professor of Education at Harvard University. Interested in the development of children's verbal abilities, she is author of *Child Language and Education* (1972) and is co-editor of *Functions of Language in the Classroom* (1972).

JEANNE S. CHALL, Professor of Education and Director of the Reading Laboratory at Harvard University, has published research on readability, vocabulary, and the psychology and teaching of reading. She authored *Learning to Read: The Great Debate* (1967) and co-edited both *Toward a Literate Society* (1975) and the NSSE Yearbook, *Education and the Brain* (1978).

CAROL CHOMSKY is Lecturer in Education at Harvard University, with special interest in language development, linguistic awareness in children, and tactile aids for speech perception by the deaf. Author of *The Acquisition of Syntax in Children from 5 to 10* (1969), she is currently preparing a textbook on grammar for elementary schoolchildren.

MICHAEL COLE is Professor of Psychology and Coordinator of the Communications Program at the University of California at San Diego and is the editor of *Soviet Psychology*. His interests include the study of the influence of cultural experience on the development of intellectual abilities. He is co-author of *The New Mathematics and an Old Culture* (1967), *The Cultural Context of Learning and Thinking* (1971), and *Culture and Thought* (1974).

WARD CROMER is Chief of the Community Mental Health Unit of Bunker Hill Health Center of the Massachusetts General Hospital and Instructor in Psychology at Harvard Medical School. His special interest is in children's clinical services, including the problems of learning disability.

MARTHA BRIDGE DENCKLA, M.D., is Assistant Professor of Neurology at the Harvard Medical School and Director of the Learning Disabilities Clinic, Children's Hospital Medical Center, Boston. She has written numerous publications on learning disabilities, dyslexia, hyperactivity, language, and motor skills. A summary of her work appears in the NSSE Yearbook, *Education and the Brain* (1978).

JOHN DIXON is returning to Bretton Hall College, Wakefield, England, after four years as Director of Schools Council English 16–19 Project, to set up a regional Language Development Unit. He is co-author of *Patterns of Language* (1973) and author of *Education 16–19: The Role of English and Communication* (1979).

MARILYN H. EDMONDS is Assistant Professor of Educational Psychology and Measurement at the University of Nebraska–Lincoln. Her major professional concerns are in human development and in the educational implications of developmental theory. Her study of "The Symbolic Function, Language Acquisition, and Implications for Development" appears in *Piagetian Theory and its Implications for the Helping Professions* (1978).

NAN ELSASSER is a Fulbright Junior Teaching Fellow at the College of the Bahamas where she is Lecturer in the college preparatory program. She is co-author of the forthcoming book, *Las Mujeres: Conversations with Hispanic Women of the Southwest*, an oral history of Chicana women.

CAROL FLEISHER FELDMAN, formerly on the faculties of the University of Chicago, the University of Houston, and Harvard University, is involved in research in the philosophy of psychology, language and thought, and cognitive development. She is senior author of *The Development of Adaptive Intelligence* (1974).

PAULO FREIRE has served as Fellow of the Center for the Study of Development and Social Change, Visiting Professor at Harvard University, Center for Studies in Education and Development, and General Coordinator of the National Plan of Adult Literacy in Brazil. He is now Special Adviser in Education to the World Council of Churches in Geneva, Switzerland. His work includes *Pedagogy of the Oppressed* (1970), *Education for Critical Consciousness* (1973), and *Pedagogy in Process: Letters to Guinea–Bissau* (1978).

NORMAN GESCHWIND is James Jackson Putnam Professor of Neurology at Harvard University Medical School and Director of the Neurological Unit at Beth Israel Hospital in Boston. The author of the seminal essay, "Disconnexion Syndromes in Animals and Man" (1965), and *Selected Papers on Language and the Brain* (1974), he has done extensive research in aphasia and asymmetries in the brain.

JEAN BERKO GLEASON is Professor of Psychology at Boston University. The author of numerous articles on language and aphasia, she is currently focusing on the language of parents and neurolinguistics.

KENNETH S. GOODMAN is Professor of Education at the University of Arizona. Author of *Miscue Analysis* (1974), Professor Goodman has long been interested in the development of a model of reading that incorporates insights from psycholinguistics and that is useful for instructional purposes. He and Dr. Yetta Goodman are Co-directors of the developing Arizona Institute for Language and Literacy.

YETTA M. GOODMAN is Professor of Education at the University of Arizona and President of the National Council of Teachers of English. Concerned with the application of sociolinguistic and psycholinguistic research to language arts and reading, she is the author of many articles and the co-author of *Reading Miscue Inventory* (1972).

ALEXANDRA W. GRANNIS is Language and Learning Disability Specialist at St. Luke's Child Psychiatric Clinic, New York. Her chief professional interest is in both normal and deficient language development.

JOSEPH C. GRANNIS is Professor in both the Departments of Applied Human Development, and Sociology and Education, Teachers College, Columbia University. Socialization and educational environments are of major professional interest. His study, "Task Engagement and the Distribution of Pedagogical Controls," was published in *Curriculum Inquiry* (1978).

MAXINE GREENE is Professor of Philosophy and Education at Teachers College, Columbia University, where she has taught educational philosophy and literature since 1965. A former editor of the *Teachers College Record*, she is the author of *The Public School and the Private Vision* (1965), *Existential Encounters for Teachers* (1967), *Teacher as Stranger* (1973), and *Landscapes of Learning* (1978), as well as numerous articles on the arts, philosophy, and education.

KENJI HAKUTA is Assistant Professor of Psychology at Yale University. His professional interests are in first- and second-language acquisition and bilingual education. He is the author of numerous articles in both of these fields.

DAVID HARMAN is Senior Lecturer at the Hebrew University of Jerusalem and Associate in Education at Harvard University. Among his professional concerns are parent education, adult illiteracy, and early childhood policies. His publications include *Community Fundamental*

Education (1974), *Early Childhood: A New Look at Policymaking* (1978), and *Adult Literacy in the United States* (1979).

VERA JOHN-STEINER is Professor of Educational Foundations and Linguistics at the University of New Mexico and Director of the Language and Behavior Program, Yeshiva University. Her major professional interests are in psycholinguistics, cognitive psychology, cross-cultural education, and women's studies. She is co-editor of both *Functions of Language in the Classroom* (1972) and the translation of Vygotsky's *Tool and Symbol in Child Development* (1978).

JONATHAN KOZOL, writer and teacher, is Visiting Lecturer at the University of Massachusetts, Amherst. Best known for his book *Death at an Early Age* (1967), he is presently interested in adult literacy, urban studies, and political socialization in the public schools. His most recent book is *Children of the Revolution: A Yankee Teacher in the Cuban Schools* (1978).

ERIC H. LENNEBERG was Professor of Psychology and Neurobiology at Cornell University until his death in 1975. As a Russell Sage Fellow, a Guggenheim Fellow, and as a Member of the Society for Research in Child Development, he was accorded several academic honors in his lifetime and was widely regarded as one of the leading researchers in childhood language disorders. Included among his publications are *The Language of Experience* (1956), *New Directions in the Study of Language* (1965), and *Biological Foundations of Language* (1967).

JOHN LIMBER is Associate Professor in the Department of Psychology, University of New Hampshire at Durham. His work is concerned with cognition and the psychology of language, specifically speech perception, semantics, and language development in primates. He is currently preparing a monograph for publication on the subject of language in primates.

JOHN W. MACDONALD is Professor of English and Chairman of the Department of English at the Faculty of Education, University of Toronto. With a special interest in the educational implications of linguistic theory for first- and second-language learning, he has written a variety of texts for high school, the most recent of which is *Grammar Lives* (1975).

RAVEN I. MCDAVID, JR., Professor Emeritus of English and Linguistics at the University of Chicago, is Editor-in-Chief of *Linguistic Atlases* for the Middle and South Atlantic States, the North Central States, and Oklahoma. He is author of an abridgement of *Mencken* (1963/1977), *Varieties of American English* (1979), and *Dialects in Culture* (1979).

R. P. MCDERMOTT is Assistant Professor of Anthropology in the Laboratory of Comparative Human Cognition at the Rockefeller University. Formerly a grade-school teacher in the New York City schools, he is interested in social organization and ethnographic psychology.

MARK K. MCQUILLAN is Coordinator of English for the Plymouth–Carver Regional School District. A former HER Board Member, he has taught English and reading in the Boston and Newton public schools. He is especially interested in writing research and has just completed a study on writing assessment for the Huron Institute, Cambridge, Massachusetts.

RALPH M. MILLER, Professor of Education, chairs the Department of Educational Curriculum and Instruction at the University of Calgary. His present area of professional interest is philosophy of education, particularly the objectives and function of education in relation to social and individual concerns. He has published several articles on developmental education and curriculum.

709

JAMES MOFFETT, author, educational consultant, and member of the National Humanities Faculty, was formerly Research Associate in Education at Harvard University and Visiting Lecturer at the University of California at Berkeley. He is author of *Teaching the Universe of Discourse* (1968) and co-author of *Student-Centered Language Arts and Reading K–12* (1976).

PAUL NASH, whose professional interest is synergetic theory, is Professor of Education at Boston University and Director of the Division of Humanistic, Developmental, and Organizational Studies. He is author of *Authority and Freedom in Education* (1966).

DAVID R. OLSON is Professor in the Department of Applied Psychology at the Ontario Institute for Studies in Education. His research focuses on language, cognition, and instruction, and he has written widely in these fields. Included among his publications are *Cognitive Development: The Child's Acquisition of Diagonality* (1970) and the NSSE Yearbook, *Media and Symbols: The Forms of Expression, Communication and Education* (1974).

WAYNE O'NEIL is Professor of Humanities and Linguistics, Massachusetts Institute of Technology, and Visiting Professor of Education, Harvard University. The author of *Kernels and Transformations: A Modern Grammar of English* (1965), and "Spelling and Pronunciation of English" in *The American Heritage Dictionary of the English Language* (1969), he has published widely in several areas, including poetics, education and society, and world literacy.

PAUL M. POSTAL is a Research Staff member of the T. J. Watson Research Center of IBM. His principal professional interest is grammatical theory with special emphasis on English and French grammar. He is the author of several books, the most recent of which are *Beginning English Grammar* (1974) and *Some Syntactic Rules in Mohawk* (1979). He is co-author of *Arc Pair Grammar* (in press).

NEIL POSTMAN is Professor of Media Ecology at New York University. He is Editor of *Et Cetera* and author of *Teaching as a Subversive Activity* (1969) and *Teaching as a Conserving Activity* (1979).

GORDON MORRELL PRADL is Associate Professor of English Education at New York University, where he is engaged in sociolinguistic research into the writing (composing) process. He has contributed articles to several professional journals on language arts instruction.

EUGENE RADWIN, a former HER Board Member, was Education Policy Fellow attached to the National Institute of Education, HEW (1978–1979). Co-editor of *Reading, Language, and Learning* (1977), he is primarily interested in literacy and cognition. In previous years he organized adult literacy education programs.

CHARLES READ is Professor of English and Linguistics at the University of Wisconsin, Madison. His major professional interest is in children's language, particularly the beginnings of reading and writing in various languages. He is author of *Children's Categorization of Speech Sounds in English* (1975).

JACK REITZES, an educational consultant, is President of Paidaeia Associates in New York City. Formerly Associate Professor of Contemporary Studies at Brooklyn College, he is now concerned with the design and evaluation of post-secondary education programs.

DANIEL P. RESNICK is Professor of History at Carnegie-Mellon University. He is author of *The White Terror and the Political Reaction after Waterloo* (1966) and co-author of *The Shaping of Western Civilization* (1970). He has written articles on social history, particularly European, and reform movements.

LAUREN B. RESNICK is Professor of Psychology and of Education at the University of Pittsburgh, where she is also Co-Director of the Learning Research and Development Center. She is editor of *The Nature of Intelligence* (1976) and *Practice of Early Reading* (1979), and co-author of *Psychology of Mathematics for Instruction* (1979).

I. A. RICHARDS is University Professor Emeritus of Harvard University and holds an Hon. L. L. D. from Cambridge University and an Hon. Litt. D. from Harvard. With present interests in World English, Professor Richards is the author and co-author of many works, including *The Meaning of Meaning* (1923), *Principles of Literary Criticism* (1924), *Practical Criticism* (1929), *Speculative Instrument* (1955), *World Education Through Modern Media* (1968), and *New and Selected Poems* (1978).

PETER S. ROSENBAUM, whose chief professional interest is computer-based education, is Manager of Courseware Development of the Control Data Education Company. He has written numerous articles on linguistics and is co-author of the Ginn series, *Grammar*, and a senior author of the Holt Basic Reading Series, 1977–1980.

ROBERT B. RUDDELL, Acting Dean and Professor of Education at the University of California, Berkeley, is author of *Reading-Language Instruction: Innovative Practices* (1974), co-editor of *Theoretical Models and Processes of Reading* (1976), and senior author of *Pathfinder: The Allyn and Bacon Reading Program* (1978). His chief professional interests are in-service teacher education and the influence of psycholinguistic and sociolinguistic variables on reading acquisition and development.

ELLEN BOUCHARD RYAN, Associate Professor and Chairman of the Psychology Department of the University of Notre Dame, is a psycholinguist whose research interests are bilingualism and the role of language in reading.

SYLVIA SCRIBNER, formerly Senior Research Associate, The Rockefeller University and Associate Director of the National Institute of Education, is now Senior Scientist at the Center for Applied Linguistics. Her professional interests include cultural influences on cognitive development and the intellectual consequences of literacy. She is co-author with Michael Cole of *Culture and Thought* (1974) and of a forthcoming book on the psychology of literacy.

FRANK SMITH, author of *Understanding Reading* (1971/1978), *Comprehension and Learning* (1975), and *Reading Without Nonsense* (1979), is Professor of Education, Ontario Institute for Studies in Education. Interested in all aspects of language, he is most recently investigating the learning and uses of writing.

SANDRA STOTSKY is Assistant Professor and Coordinator of Elementary Education at Curry College. As chairman of the College Coordinators' Curriculum Committee, she is helping to develop a K-12 writing program for the Boston Public Schools. She is the author of numerous articles on vocabulary and writing instruction and has most recently completed work on Macmillan's forthcoming series, *Grammar and Composition*.

FRANK R. VELLUTINO is Director of the Child Research and Study Center at the University of Albany and Albany Medical College of Union University, and Associate Professor in the Departments of Educational Psychology and Pediatrics. He has published extensively in the area of developmental disabilities in children, particularly on the subject of reading disabilities. He is author of *Dyslexia: Theory and Research* (1978).

711

MAGDALEN D. VERNON is Emeritus Professor of Psychology, University of Reading, England. The psychology of reading, child development, and visual perception are among her professional interests. Her major works include *Backwardness in Reading* (1957), *Perception through Experience* (1970), and *Reading and its Difficulties* (1971).

MORTON WIENER is Professor of Psychology and Director of Clinical Psychology Training at Clark University, where his chief professional interest is in verbal and nonverbal communication.

JOANNA WILIAMS, Professor of Psychology and Education at Columbia University, Teachers College, is primarily concerned with the psychology of reading. She is co-editor of *Basic Studies in Reading* (1970), a past editor of the *Journal of Educational Psychology* (1973-1978), and past president of the Division of Educational Psychology of the American Psychological Association.

MARYANNE WOLF is Assistant Professor of Psychology at Brandeis University. A former HER Board Member, teacher, and co-editor of *Reading, Language and Learning* (1977), she is primarily interested in a neurolinguistic approach to reading and language and reading disorders. Her chapter, "The Word-Retrieval Process and Reading," will appear in the forthcoming series, *Children's Language*.

THOMAS WOLF is Executive Director of the New England Foundation for the Arts. Originally trained as a flutist, he soloed with the Philadelphia Orchestra and toured the United States with the Goldovsky Opera Theatre before taking his doctorate in education at Harvard University. He has written two books on the performing arts and teaches Arts Administration at Radcliffe College.

RICHARD E. YOUNG is Head of the Department of English and Professor of English and Rhetoric at Carnegie-Mellon University. His special interest is rhetorical theory and pedagogy. Formerly Chairman of the Department of Humanities, College of Engineering, University of Michigan, Professor Young is co-author of *Rhetoric: Discovery and Change* (1970).

Index

length of language sequence and, 266; as literacy standard, 406-407, 411, 548; and "making sense" of written language, 416-417, 423-424; vocabulary-concept knowledge and, 441-447; identification vs., 544-545, 546, 548-550, 557, 560-564; deficiency in (dyslexia and), 576-577 (alexia), 604. *See also* Meaning

Church, J., 499, 504

Chute, Marchette, 304

Cicero and Ciceronian rhetoric, 290, 291, 292, 300

Cicourel, A., 501

City University of New York, 692

Clark, C. M., 437

Clark, E., 102, 652

Clark, H. H., 87, 103

Clark, R. E., 608

Class, Codes and Control. Vol. I. (Bernstein): reviewed, 672-676

Clay, M. M., 261, 596

Cobb, C., 453

Codification defined, 330, 371n

Cognitive Development: Its Social and Political Implications (Luria), 456

Cognitive hypothesis, 188-190

Cognitive Psychology (journal), 643

Cognitive Psychology (Neisser), 113, 705

Cohen, A. D., 235

Cole, Michael, 85, 100, 386, 388, 392, 459, 508, 707

Coleman, James S., 440, 687

Coleridge, Samuel Taylor, 633

Coles, L., 503n

Communication: as function, debated, 72-74, 75, 76-78, 80-82; -intention theory, 73-78, 82-83, 88, 104, 135; and noncommunicative/ideational function, 76-82, 105; with self, 77-78, 81, 82; in conversation, 99, 247; and knower/symbolization known-relationship, 190-191; language development and, 196, 452, 548; prefabricated utterances in, 239, 245-246; and discourse analysis, 246-248, 331-334, 371; literacy and, 389-390, 451-464; interethnic (territorial behavior), 502; classroom, 505-508; deafness and, 519, 520-521; nonverbal, 562; and importance of dialogue in learning process, 681-682. *See also* Comprehension; Literacy; Meaning; Speech; Verbalization; Written language

Comprehension: sentence, 86-87, 99-100, 104, 182, 313; and expectation/prediction of meaning in reading and listening, 89, 113-114, 259-262, 266-268, 417, 421, 423, 594, 635; preverbal, 184, 189; test of, in young children,

204, 385; during oral reading, 254, 256, 262, 263, 264, 266; misconception concerning, 260; length of language sequence and, 266; as literacy standard, 406-407, 411, 548; and "making sense'; of written language, 416-417, 423-424; vocabulary-concept knowledge and, 441-447; identification vs., 544-545, 546, 548-550, 557, 560-564; deficiency in (dyslexia and), 576-577 (alexia), 604. *See also* Meaning

Computer technology, 637

Concept(s): formation/attainment of, 19, 26-50, 189-190; vs. "meaning," 27, 35, 50; "conjunctive," "disjunctive," "relational," 28, 38-39; nature of, 28-33; experience in information of, 29, 31; preverbal, 30-31, 34, 189; idiosyncratic, 32, 34, 35; and conceptual invariants, 33; research on formation of, 37-38, 40; learning of (in school), 38-50 (in psychological experiments), 38, 39, 50; "tourist vs. immigrant," 41-43; of time, 43-44; quantitative, 44-45; longitude (and sphericity), 45-46; of tort, 46-47; mass vs. weight, 47-49; and miscues, 262; defined, 438-439; and "vocabulatory-concept load," 441-447; Vygotsky's use of term, 628-629. *See also* Semantics

Conceptual Learning (Englemann), 438

Conditioning (psychological), 181, 630

Condon, W. S., 197

Conjunction Case, 187n

Conklin, H., 500 n, 508

Conrad, C., 596, 644

Conrad, R., 574, 579

Conscientization, 378

Consonant(s): alternation, in pronunciation and spelling, 55-57, 59, 68-69; silent, in spelling, 67; in child's invented spelling, 154, 161-164, 168-169; and preconsonantal nasals, 165-167, 170; non-nasal true (obstruent), 169

Constituent analysis (parsing), *see* Sentence(s)

Constituent structure rules, 12-17

"Contentives," *see* Semantics

Context, 35-36, 97; children's dependence on, 88, 89,100, 186, 258, 267, 419-420, 594, 696; functors in, 141; in oral vs. written language, 258. *See also* Comprehension

Conversation, *see* Communication; Utterance(s)

Corbett, Edward P. J., 291

Corder, S. P., 233, 234, 235, 236

Corkin, S., 574, 595

Corrigan, Patricia, 554

Craigie, Sir William, 284

Cremin, Lawrence, 398

Cromer, R. F., 188

Cromer, Ward, 552, 707

Ellul, J., 96
Elmore, Richard, 427
Elsassar, Nan, 461, 707
Emans, R., 546n
Empiricism, 96, 182, 185, 248, 314, 329; and empirical studies, 237, 247, 309, 622. *See also* Psycholinguistic research
Endocentric construction, *see* Noun Phrase
Engelmann, Siegfried, 426–431 *passim*, 435, 438, 440–443 *passim*, 548, 562
English language: teaching of, 26–28, 276–277, 281, 308–324, 326–336, 342–350, 669–672; orthography, 51–70, 150, 155, 159, 640–641, 644, 645, 648; phonetic variations in, 55–62; American, 58 (attitudes toward), 281, 285–287; foreign students of, 59, 60, 62; Royal Society of London and, 96; word order in, 135; "open" parts-of-speech in, 136; "telegraphic," 137 as second language, 231, 234–247, 273, 442, 446; structural analysis of, 312; structural curriculum in, 325–336; basic, 444–446. *See also* Dialect(s); Language acquisition (second language)
English Language in America, The (Krapp), 284
Enthymeme(s), 100. *See also* Logical reasoning
Erickson, F., 503n, 509
Errors: reading, 112, 114, 254–255, 593, 595; grammatical/syntactic (oversimplification, overgeneralization) of child, 142, 232, 233, 234, 235; spelling, of child, 156–157; syntactic interpretation, of child, 206, 208, 209, 210–212, 214–215, 217; and error analysis in acquisition of second language, 231, 232–238; interference (interlingual), 233–235, 236, 237, 238, 247; intralingual, 233–235; disappearance of (in acquisition of second language), 236, 237, 238; and miscues in oral reading, 253–258, 260–266, 268; and miscues in reading and listening, 260, 264, 265; and nonwords, 264–265; and "miscues readers don't make," 265; analysis of, 438; orientation/sequencing (dyslexic), 569–571, 574–582 *passim;* and error-free schooling, 688; in basic writing skills, 692–695. *See also* Language disorders
Errors and Expectations: A Guide for the Teacher of Basic Writing (Shaughnessy): reviewed, 692–695
Ervin-Tripp, Susan, 144, 183, 184, 245, 507n
Eson, Morris, 636
Essay Concerning Human Understanding, An (Locke), 95
"Essayist technique," 85, 89–90, 95–98, 99, 102 104
Ethnography of classroom relations, 500–504. *See also* Social relations

Evertson, C. N., 437
Ewoldt, C., 256
Expansion, *see* Imitation (in speech development)
Experience, *see* Concept(s)
Experiencer Case, 187n
Expletives, 79
Expression, *see* Thought, expression of

Faerie Queene (Spenser), 110
Farnham, George, 406
Farnham-Diggory, S., 593
Farrell, T., 383
Fathman, A., 244
Faulkner, William, 117
Faw, T. T., 598
Febles, Mier, 473
Feldman, Carol Fleisher, 707
Feldman, S., 87
Ferber, A., 501
Ferguson, C. A., 248, 508
Ferrer, Raúl, 474, 475–476, 479, 483, 488, 490, 491–497
Feshbach, S., 572
Fights, Games, and Debates (Rapaport), 300
Filby, N., 103, 385
Fillmore, C., 186–187
Firth, J. R., 274
Fischer, F. W., 579, 580, 592
Fisher, S., 503n
Flaps (alveolar), in children's spelling, 163–165
Flavell, J., 389
Flinton, Doris, 636
Fobes, John, 493–494
Fodor, Jerry A., 87, 182, 183, 184, 186
Fogarty, Daniel, 294
Folk-rhymes, 167. *See also* Poetry
Follow Through project, 425–448
Ford, W. G., 101
Foreign languages: national interest in, 273. *See also* Language acquisition (second language)
Foreign students of English, *see* English language
Fowler, C., 579, 580
Fowles, Barbara, 658, 659, 678
Fox, L., 393
Frake, C., 500n, 501
France: and French language, 244; literacy in, 400–406, 408
Franklin, Benjamin, 669
Franks, J. J., 87, 99
Fraser, E., 247
Frauenfelder, U., 238, 244
Freeberg, N. E., 440
Freedman, J. L., 37
Freire, Paulo, 177, 452–453, 456–464 *passim*, 466–467, 478–480, 489, 497, 680–683, 708

Korzybski, A., 86
Kosteljanetz, M., 610
Kozol, Jonathan, 682, 709
Krapp, George Philip, 284
Krashen, S., 242, 243
Kreindler, A., 615
Kremenak, S., 572
Kremin, J., 610, 615
Kress, R. A., 594
Kuczaj, S., 184
Kuhn, Thomas, 638
Kurath, Hans, 278

LaBerge, D., 596, 597
Labov, W., 453, 509, 562-563, 655
La Chalotais, Louis Renéde, 400
Lachmann, F. M., 591
LAD (language acquisition device), 184-185. *See also* Language acquisition (by child)
Lado, R., 234
Lahey, Margaret, 695-698
Lakoff, G., 98, 186
Lambert, W., 248
Langer, Suzanne, 325, 334
Langford, W., 576, 591
Language: as set of symbols, 6; written vs. oral representation of, 87; evolution of, 89; -reality relationship, 96-97, 268; "natural," 180; creative aspect of, 181, 202-203; pragmatic, 246-247; defined, 278; "school," 423; "participant" vs. "Spectator," 665-666; "public" and "formal," 672. *See also* Communication; Speech; Symbols; Utterance(s); Written language
Language (Bloomfield), 284
Language (Sapir), 284
Language, foreign, *see* Language acquisition (second language)
Language, receptive, *see* Listening
Language acquisition (by child): text vs. utterance and, 97, 102-103; and Syntax acquisition, 131-149, 195, 203, 233, 247, 256; one-word and clearly multiple-word periods in, 131-132, 187-188, 195, 653, 696; syntactic errors (oversimplification, overgeneralization) in, 142, 232, 233, 234, 235; discovery of latent structure in, 143; new directions in theories of, 180-197, 230; nativistic hypotheses, 180, 184-185, 197; LAD theory, 184-185; cognitive hypothesis, 188-190; symbolic function and, 190-195; and communication, 196, 452, 548; grammatical morphemes in, 242-243; fundamental insights and, 415-424; internalization concept in, 452, 454, 459. *See also* Language disorders; Psycholinguistic research

Language acquisition (second language), 273; research trends, 230-248; contrastive analysis in, 231-232, 233, 238, 248; audio-lingual method of, 232; error analysis in, 232-238; possessives categorized (Spanish-English), 236; performance analysis in, 238-246; grammatical morphemes in, 239, 242-245; negation in, 239-241; discourse analysis in, 246-248; social factors in 297, 299 (and sociolinguistic analysis), 248; and formal written English as "second language," 693-694. *See also* English language
Language and Learning (Britton): reviewed, 664-668
Language and Mind (Chomsky), 704
Language by Ear and by Eye (Kavanagh and Mattingly, eds.): reviewed, 643-649
Language Development and Language Disorders (Bloom and Lahey): reviewed, 695-698
Language disorders, 517-542; deafness, 518-521, 537, 539, 540, 542, 697; mental retardation, 521-525, 538n, 540, 542, 697, 700; childhood psychosis, 525-528, 538n, 540, 542; congenital inarticulation, 528-532, 534, 535, 537, 540, 542; aphasia, 528, 532-537, 540, 542, 545, 549, 576, 608, 612, 697; dysarthria, 535, 537-538; congenital receptive disorder, 537; dyslexia, 567-582, 590, 603-604, 611, 612, 613-614, 615, 650, 689, 700; alexia, 604-616; agraphia, 604, 607-608, 610, 612, 614; anomia, 607, 608, 609, 612; assessment and remediation of, 696-698; autism 697. *See also* Reading difficulties.
Larsen-Freeman, D., 242, 243, 244
Lashley, K. S., 182, 533
Latin and Latinate forms, 62, 64, 135, 401, 669
Laubach, Frank, 477
Laufer, B., 186
Learning: deductive and inductive (in concept formation), 39, 40-41, 50, 193; and induction of latent grammatical structure, 141-149; vs. "learning how to," 327-329; process, dynamics of, 456; ideology and, 489; in school, social relations as contexts for, 498-511. *See also* English Language; Language acquisition (by child); Language acquisition (second language); Learning to read; Teachers and teaching methods
"Learning disabilities," 698-702. *See also* Language disorders; Reading difficulties
Learning to read, 177-179; decoding approach to, 89, 103, 125, 409, 440, 443, 548-550, 559, 568, 577, 648; and expectation/prediction of meaning, 89, 259-262, 266, 267-268, 415-424, 548, 594; as transformation from utterance or

Phonetics: and "phonetically possible morpheme," 17; and phonetic features (voicing, stress, nasality), 19, 174, 175, 176; English orthography and, 51-64, 68-69; and phonetic vs. "lexical" spelling, 60-61, 171-174; early systems of, 92; pre-school children's judgment of, 151, 153-154, 163-164, 168, 174-175, 179; defined, 181; Bloomfield's view of, 311; "Scanning" in, 560. *See also* Articulation; Phonology; Pronunciation; Syllabicity

Phonics, 416-417, 420. *See also* Phonetics; Sound system

Phonology, 312; rules of, and phonetic representation, 17, 19, 53-57, 297; and (English) orthography, 51-70, 150, 155, 159, 169, 644; transformational grammar and, 51-53, 638-642; defined, 150; pre-school children's knowledge of, 150-179; palatalization, 163; alliteration, 167; and phonologic deficiencies, 578-580. *See also* Orthography; Pronounciation

Phrase markers, 8-17, 20

Pharase structure rules, 12-17

Piaget, Jean, 31, 80n, 87, 96, 101, 185, 188-193 *passim,* 385, 386, 438, 439, 630, 631, 666; and Piagetian theory, 180, 190, 194, 195, 597, 629, 644, 656

Pick, A., 112

Piestrup, A., 509

Pike, Kenneth L., 274, 294, 298

Pike, R., 100

Pillsbury, W. B., 114, 643

Piston, Walter, 118n

Pistor, Frederick, 44

"Pivot" words, *see* Modifier(s)

Plato, 94, 95, 290, 355 374, 382-383

Play, *see Speech Play;* Symbols

Poeck, K., 615

Poetry: as mnemonic device, 91, 92; and folk rhymes, 167. *See also* Homer and Homeric epics; Scripture

Polish Language, 256

Politics of reading, 355-362, 489, 492, 495-496

Politzer, R., 235

Pope, Alexander, 104

Popp, Helen, 677

Poppel, E., 612

Popper, Karl, 97

Porter, J., 243

Portuguese language, 364n, 366n, 367n, 375n

Posner, M. I., 596

Postal, Paul M., 310, 638, 641, 710

Postman, Neil, 355, 710

Potter, M., 384

Pradl, Gordon Morrell, 668, 710

Pragmatic functions, 246-247

Prediction of meaning, *see* Comprehension; Context

Preparing Objectives for Programmed Instruction (Mager), 671

Price, R. and S., 655

Prieto Morales, Abela, 477, 492, 493, 494, 497

Primers, *see* Learning to read

Printing: invention of, 85, 91, 95, 97, 359, 669; woodblock, 119-125. *See also* Written language

Process of Education, The (Bruner), 337

"Promise" (test of), *see* Psycholinguistic research

Pronoun(s): reflexive, rules governing use of, 9-12; replacing noun phrase, 11, 148, 149, 261; demonstrative, children's use of, 145-146, 196; possessive, 146, 236

Pronunciation: phrase marker relevance to, 9; phonological components and, 19, 52-57, 150, 159; suffix addition and, 52; vowel alternation and, 52-55, 57, 159; consonant alternation and, 55-56, 57, 59; vowel reduction in, 56-57; stress placement in, 56-57, 61; historical shifts in, 58; and spelling, 60-61; pre-school conception of phonology and 150-151, 153-154; reading ability and, 570. *See also* Phonetics; Phonology; Reading aloud

Prose statements, *see* Text(s); Written language

Pruzek, R., 571, 573, 577

Psychiatry (journal), 630

Psycholinguistic research, 88-89, 181, 194, 196 201-229, 336, 631-638; on sentence interpretation, 102; into reading, 125-126, 202, 219-227; and S-R theory, 182; on sentence structure, 183-184, 186-188; longitudinal, 185, 187, 188, 205, 236, 239, 242, 243, 652-654; cross-sectional, 185, 205, 235, 236, 237, 242, 243; Russian, 191, 274, 456, 592; on constructions "easy to see," "promise," "ask," "and," "although," 205-219; and influence of test on outcome, 243; and miscue analysis, 253-268; shift in, 266, 268; of paragraph patterns, 303; on teaching grammar, 327, 695; on literacy vs. schooling, 382-394; U.S. army intelligence tests, 407-408; on reading failure, 567-582, 591-600, 643-648; on neurolinguistic disorders, 604-616; and Project Literacy Multi-Level Reading Program, 651. *See also* Empiricism; Psychology

Psychological Review, 110

Psychology: and "concepts," 27-28, 38, 39, 50; and psychological reality of orthography, 58-59; of reading, 110-126, 553, 677, 703-705; and psychological unity of noun phrase, 148, 149; and stimulus-response (S-R) theory, 181-182, 183, 185, 627; and psychological conse-

Rogers, Carl, 300
Rohwer, W., 503
Romatoksi, J., 256
Rosansky E. 238, 242, 243
Rosenbaum, Peter S., 711
Rosenblatt, Louise M., 660-664, 666
Rosenfeld, G., 506
Rosenshine, B., 437
Roskies, D. 658, 659
Ross, J., 596
Roswell, Florence, 555
Rousch, P., 263
Rousseau, Jean Jacques, 683, 685
Royal Society of London, 96
Ruddell, Robert B., 651, 711
Rudegeair, F., 576
Rudel, R., 576
Russell, Bertrand, 96, 105, 331
Rutter, M., 589, 699
Ryan, Ellen Bouchard, 654, 659, 711

Sadock, J., 507
Sadowsky, C. H., 610
Saffran, E., 611n, 615
Sakharov block test, 628
Salas, Dario, 379
Samuels, S. J., 596, 597
Sander, L. W., 197
Sanderson, Michael, 399
Santmire, T., 194, 195
Sapir, Edward, 274, 278, 284, 350, 501
Sartre, Jean Paul, 365, 422, 661
Sasanuma, S., 612; et al., 613
Satz, P., 576, 596, 597, 699, 700
Saunders, R. I., 610
Savin, Harris B., 183, 568, 592, 648
Saxe, Natalie, 679
Sayce, A. H., 282
Schachter, J., 238
Scheflen, A., 501n, 502, 503n
Schenkenberg, T., 610
Schlesinger, I. M., 186, 188
Schoolboys of Barbiana, 454, 457
Schulte, C., 577
Schumann, J., 232, 233, 238, 248
Schutz, A., 104
Schwa, 56, 57
Schwartz, M. F., 615
Scotland: literacy in, 399, 406
Scribner, Sylvia, 85, 386, 388, 392, 459, 508, 711
Scripture, 90, 669; Luther's view of meaning of, 86, 90, 91, 95, 99; and Bible in basic English, 446
Scriven, M., 658

Sealey, Leonard, 427
Seamon, J. G., 595
Searle, J. R., 74, 75, 78
Second language, acquisition of, see Language acquisition (second language)
Selinker, L., 233, 235, 238
Semantics: and "meaning," 18, 19, 27; semantic markers/objects (reading), 18-19, 23; as modern "science," 27n; and "semantic differential," 32-33; formal, theory of, 72-74, (Chomsky and) 74-75, 86; and "contentives" in children's speech, 136-138, 139; defined, 181; as separate component of grammar, 186; and miscues, 258, 260-261, 264, 267; and semantic short cuts, 455; and semantic-relationship approach ("semantic notions"), 652. See also Concept(s); Meaning
Semel, M. S., 577
Semitic writing systems, 92
Senf, G. M., 572, 573, 574, 595
Sentence(s): length of 5-6, 132; generation of, 6, 23, 182, 202, 314; syntatic/grammatical structure of, 6-17, 24, 54, 86, 231, 439; bracketing/parsing of, 7-8, 182; imperative, 9, 12-14 (and "whimperatives"), 507; reflexive, 9-13; active-passive, equivalence of, 14-15, 88, 98, 100, 102, 385; fragmentary (semi-), 21-22; truth-value of, 73-74; comprehension of, 86-87, 99-100, 104, 182, 313; declarative-interrogative connection, 102, 183; defined (Chomsky), 182; "early," of children, 188; boundaries, crossing (in reading aloud), 266; tagmemic theory of, 298; as fundamental unit of language, 704
Sentence-completion phenomenon, 114. See also Comprehension
Sentence meaning: semantic component and, 18, 19; Chomsky's theory of, 75, 76, 86, 98-99, 102, 296; vs. "speaker's meaning," 86-87, 93, 98-99, 101, 102, 102-103; explicitness of, 95, 97, 102, 104; lack of, 420
Serra, Mary C., 26
SES, see Socioeconomic status
Sesame Street (TV program), 659, 678
Seventh Letter (Plato), 95, 355
Shakespeare, William, 36, 276
Shallice, T., 611, 614
Shankweiler, Donald, 567, 568, 570, 571n, 578-580 passim, 591-593 passim, 644, 648, 699
Shapira, R., 248
Sharp, D., 85, 100
Shaughnessy, Mina P., 692-695
Sheehan, P., 647
Sherrick, C. E., 573, 574
Sherwood, V., 657

Weikart, David, 427
Wells, Rulon, 309, 310
Wepman, J. M., 578
Werner, H., 196
Wesley, E. B., 45
"'Whimperatives," 507
White, B., 185
White, Richard Grant, 275
Whitney, William Dwight, 282
Whorf, Benjamin L., 285
Wicklund, D., 571, 595
Wiener, Morton, 552, 560, 712
Wiig, E. H., 577
Wilkinson, J. E., 592
Williams, Joanna, 680, 712
Winne, P. H., 437
Wirtenberg, T. J., 598
Witelson, S. F., 596, 700
Witherspoon, John, 286
Wittgenstein, L., 75, 438, 622
Woestehoff, E., 546n
Wolf, Maryanne, 501, 712
Wolf, Thomas, 115, 712
Wölfflin, Heinrich, 122, 125
Women: in Cuban literacy campaign, 481
Wong-Fillmore, L., 240, 245-246, 247
Wood, C. T., 426, 433
Wood, H., 501n
Woodcut illustrations, 119-125
Woods, B. T., 612
Woods Hole Conference (1960), 337
Woodworth, R., 391
"Word blindness", (alexia), see Language disorders
Word(s): as symbols, 6, 8, 190-191, 194-195; order of, in child's speech, 14-15, 135, 205, 653; as entities, 33-36; "function," 34; associated with concepts, 34-36, 191, 194; and word families in teaching spelling, 60; definitions of, 104, 419; assimilated, 191; and non-words, 264-265; "generative," 375, 460, 475, 682; basic vocabulatry, 441-447; identification of ("word-naming") vs. comprehension, 544-

545, 546, 548-550, 557, 560-564; as Vygotsky's "unit of analysis," 627-628. See also Vocabulary
Word pairs: in "lexical" spelling, 53, 55-56, 58-59; associations between (and miscues), 268
Wright, J., 389
Written language: and creative writing as communication, 77; invention of alphabetic system of, 84-85, 89-94, 97, 387; absence of, and oral culture, 90-91, 358, 382-383; explicitness/ambiguity of, 91, 92-93, 95-97, 99, 105; four stages in development of, 91-93; effect of, on knowledge and development, 94-95, 125, 384, 391, 394, 633; conventionalization in, 104, 105; and learning to write, 179, 330, 333-335, 451-452, 460, 461, 464; children's exposure to, 202, 219-229, 417-418, 422; complexity of, 220; comprehension of, while reading aloud, 254; vs. oral, 258-259, 384, 420-423, 454-456; instruction in grammar and, 309; "making sense" of, 416-417, 423-424; units of, 439; defined, 454, 464; agraphia and (writing disorder), 604, 607-608, 610, 612, 614; and basic writing skills, 692-695. See also Ideograms; Learning to read; Literacy; Orthography; Printing; Reading aloud; Style; Text(s)
Wundt, Wilhelm, 703

Yamadori, A., 612, 613
Yerkes, Robert, 407
Yiddish language, 256
Young, F. A., 568
Young, Richard E., 712
Yugoslavia: oral tradition in, 91
Yule, W., 589, 699

Zapf, D., 393
Zazzo (French psychologist), 631
Zifcak, M., 579
Zigmond, N., 573, 577
Zurif, E. B., 574, 596, 611